SPENCER A. RATHUS
NEW YORK UNIVERSITY

JEFFREY S. NEVID
ST. JOHN'S UNIVERSITY

LOIS FICHNER-RATHUS
THE COLLEGE OF NEW JERSEY

EDWARD S. HEROLD
UNIVERSITY OF GUELPH

SUE WICKS McKENZIE
DAWSON COLLEGE

SECOND CANADIAN EDITION

HUMAN SEXUALITY
IN A WORLD OF
DIVERSITY

PEARSON

and

Toronto

Dedicated with love to our children Taylor Lane Rathus and Michael Zev Nevid, who were born at the time the first edition of this book was written.

—S.A.R., L.F.-R., J.S.N.

Dedicated with love to my wife Yvette and my daughter Malia.

—E.S.H.

Library and Archives Canada Cataloguing in Publication

Human sexuality in a world of diversity / Spencer A. Rathus ... [et al.].—2nd Canadian ed.

Includes bibliographical references and index.
ISBN 0-205-46013-5

1. Sex—Textbooks. 2. Sex customs—Canada—Textbooks. I. Rathus, Spencer A.

HQ21.H84 2006   306.7   C2005-907525-2

Vice President, Editorial Director: Michael J. Young
Senior Acquisitions Editor: Ky Pruesse
Sponsoring Editor: Carolin Sweig
Executive Marketing Manager: Judith Allen
Developmental Editor: Michelle Harrington
Supervising Developmental Editor: Suzanne Schaan
Production Editor: Avivah Wargon
Copy Editor: Gilda Mekler
Proofreader: Karen Alliston
Production Manager: Wendy Moran
Composition: Phyllis Seto
Permissions and Photo Research: Sandy Cooke
Art Direction: Mary Opper
Interior Design: Jennifer Stimson
Cover Design: Jennifer Stimson
Cover Image: © IT Stock Int'l/eStock Photo

2 3 4 5   10 09 08 07

Printed and bound in the United States of America.

Brief Contents

Contents

Chapter 12
Sexuality Across the Life Cycle   330

Chapter 13
Sexual Dysfunctions   374

Preface

Living in Canadian society in the twenty-first century means navigating an increasingly complex world full of messages and issues related to human sexuality. The mass media inundate us with ever more graphic depictions of sexuality. Sexuality of many kinds is embraced and exploited by popular culture. Scientific advances in areas such as genetic engineering force us to question fundamental aspects of human life and sexuality. Meanwhile, governments struggle to keep pace by creating new legislation to try to meet the many challenges introduced by these social and scientific changes. Underlying all of this is an astounding diversity, as our sexuality is shaped by both human biology and a richness of sociocultural factors.

Human Sexuality in a World of Diversity, Second Canadian Edition, embraces the richness of this human diversity while recognizing the unique realities of Canadian society. The comparisons made across the regions of Canada not only reflect the ethnic and cultural diversity within Canada, but also help to describe the unique social landscape of our country. This reality is also reflected in and shaped by Canadian laws and government policy, and references to relevant Canadian legislation and social policy are included throughout the text.

Changes to the Second Canadian Edition

The second Canadian edition is more concise than the first—17 chapters plus an epilogue rather than 20 chapters—because we were mindful of the experience of many enthusiastic users who found it too long for their courses. However, it retains a focus on research and offers lots of real-world applications.

The following list provides a brief overview of some of the new content and changes from the first edition.

Chapter 1 emphasizes the diversity of Canadian sexuality and notes how sexual attitudes and behaviours differ across the regions of Canada. In addition, the chapter

- discusses differences between Canada and the United States with respect to key demographic factors and sexual trends
- discusses how recent politics affect sex education and sexual legislation
- presents new research on how immigrants from Iran view Canadian sexuality

Chapter 2 presents recent Canadian research sources of human sexuality data, including the 2002 Canada Youth and AIDS survey and the 2002 Canadian Contraceptive survey, and

- discusses trends in Canadian sexuality research
- provides examples of research issues involving specific sampling groups, including gay and bisexual males, First Nations people, and sex workers

Chapter 3 now covers both female and male sexual anatomy and physiology. This chapter

- presents recent statistics on breast, cervical, and prostate cancer
- discusses research on women who have coitus during menstruation
- highlights controversy over premenstrual dysphoric disorder
- gives current research on the effect of prostate surgery on sexual functioning

Chapter 4 presents new perspectives by leading Canadian experts on sexual arousal and

- gives new research on identical twins and orgasm experience
- discusses the effect of crystal meth on sexual functioning
- discusses disability and sexuality. This section was moved to this chapter to emphasize that most people with disabilities still enjoy sexual activity

Chapter 5 presents new Canadian data on gender differences in health care, university attendance, and attitudes toward the workplace. The chapter also

- discusses the case study of Winnipeg's David Reimer to illustrate the conflict between biological and social perspectives on gender identity
- gives new information on cross-cultural surveys of gender differences in preferred number of sexual partners

Chapters 6 and 7 present a national survey on Canadians' preferences for the ideal spouse. As well, these chapters

- present new research on online dating and attraction among Canadians
- discuss a research study on the use of sexually direct approaches in singles bars

Chapter 8 features information on the sexual behaviours of Canadians. This chapter

- provides new research regarding online masturbation
- includes new research on gay male sexual behaviours
- discusses new research on gender differences in desired foreplay

Chapter 9 details the legislative and court changes that have increased equality for gay males and lesbians and emphasizes that sexual orientation is broader in scope than sexual behaviour. The chapter also

- discusses new research on birth order and sexual orientation
- presents new research on same-sex marriage
- discusses new theories and research on the coming-out process
- outlines key issues in counselling gay males and lesbians

Chapters 10 and 11 examine national data on contraceptive use and abortion in Canada, as well as social and regional variations in breast-feeding. They also

- cover recent Canadian legislation on reproductive technologies
- present research on lesbian mothers and postpartum depression
- discuss new research on the effect of breast-feeding on sexuality
- present the latest recommendations from the World Health Organization on missed oral contraceptive pills, emergency contraception, and the length of the waiting period following a vasectomy

Chapter 12 combines two previous chapters, Sexuality in Childhood and Adolescence and Sexuality in Adulthood, into one chapter, Sexuality across the Life Cycle. This chapter

- outlines new research on factors predictive of sexual experience
- discusses gender differences in response to experiencing sexual intercourse for the first time
- discusses Canadian trends in teenage pregnancy
- reports on older singles who never plan to marry
- discusses issues of aging among gay males and lesbians

Chapter 13 cites national surveys on rates of sexual problems and dysfunctions among Canadians and examines contributing factors. It also

- highlights the debate over whether lack of sexual desire among women should be classified as a dysfunction
- discusses sexual frustration among young women

- gives new research on men's and women's responses to Viagra
- discusses how few helping professionals are given adequate training about sexuality and sexual counselling and therapy

Chapter 14 presents current national data on trends of sexually transmitted infections, HIV and AIDS, and also

- discusses declining condom use among heterosexual females and gay males and reasons for not using condoms
- presents data indicating that youth are less knowledgeable about HIV/AIDS today than in previous years

Chapter 15 highlights controversies regarding how paraphilias are defined. The chapter also

- discusses an increase in female public exhibitionism
- presents new research on the causes and treatment of paraphilias

Chapter 16 presents new Canadian data on sexual violence and sexual harassment, and in addition

- discusses increasing use of drugs to facilitate sexual assault
- discusses Internet luring of underage youth
- discusses child sex tourism
- presents new research on sexual assault against men
- highlights community treatment programs of sex offenders
- highlights gender differences in perceptions of sexual harassment

Chapter 17 highlights controversies regarding the definition of pornography (we use the term *sexually explicit materials* instead). In addition, this chapter

- provides recent research on the use of online sexually explicit materials
- cites research on the possible benefits of sexually explicit materials
- discusses research on customers of prostitutes who attend "john school"
- provides new research on the backgrounds of female street prostitutes

The **Epilogue** discusses the role of sex education in promoting responsible decision-making and presents new research on sex education in Canada.

Themes

Research Before writing this edition, we searched extensively for new Canadian materials. Numerous new Canadian references have been added, including data from several national surveys, such as the 2001 census, the National Longitudinal Survey of Children and Youth, the 2002 Canadian Contraception survey, and the second Canada Youth and AIDS survey.

Theory Various theories used to explain sexual attitudes and behaviours are detailed in the first chapter. These theories are then illustrated in almost every chapter, demonstrating the usefulness of theory in guiding our understanding of diverse aspects of human sexuality.

Canadians and the Internet Throughout the text, we highlight the relationships between sexuality and the technological and societal transformations that are occurring across the country and around the world. For example, many Canadians now use the Internet to find, meet, and date sexual partners. The Internet has also become an excellent resource for reliable sex information and advice aimed at a diverse audience, including teens, adults, parents, educators, and health professionals. Each chapter provides links to valuable Internet resources, such as The Sex Information and Education Council of Canada and Parents and Friends of Lesbians and Gays.

Critical Thinking and the Mass Media One of the main goals of this text is to encourage students to become critical thinkers. Gender- and sex-related attitudes and behaviours are greatly influenced by newspapers, magazines, television programs, and other mass media. Critical thinking requires a willingness to challenge conventional wisdom; it means scrutinizing definitions of terms, evaluating the premises of assumptions that underlie arguments, and examining the logic of arguments. Some of the feature boxes include newspaper and magazine articles that illustrate conflicting values in Canadian society. These pieces raise issues that demand critical thinking, encouraging students to analyze and evaluate their own beliefs and attitudes toward gender roles and sexuality in light of the accumulated scientific evidence.

Feature Boxes and Additional Learning Aids

The second Canadian edition of *Human Sexuality in a World of Diversity* continues to use a variety of features that stimulate student interest and enhance understanding.

Research in Action is a new feature that emphasizes the importance of scientific research, providing in-depth discussion of specific research topics and/or trends. Most of these sections feature Canadian research (as indicated by a maple leaf icon), such as studies on women's response to sexually explicit materials when watching with a partner or friend (p. 516).

Applied Knowledge, another new feature box, assists students in their personal decisions, giving information and advice—for example, "Optimizing the Chances of Conception" (pp. 265–266), "How Do You Find a Qualified Sex Therapist?" (pp. 402–403), and "Preventing STIs" (pp. 435–436).

World of Diversity boxes highlight the rich variety of human sexual customs and practices in Canadian society and around the world. Viewing human sexuality in a multicultural context helps students better understand how cultural beliefs, values, and attitudes can influence the expression of sexuality. New boxes in this edition include a look at gay and transsexual Muslims in Canada (p. 6) and a focus on women who have cosmetic surgery on their vaginas to enhance sexual pleasure for both themselves and their partners (pp. 53–54).

Each chapter begins with an **outline** that organizes the subject matter. **Key terms** are boldfaced in the text and a **running glossary** provides their definitions in the margins close to where they appear. Selected **Web sites** listed in the margins point students to online information about human sexuality and coping with sexually related issues in their own lives.

At the end of each chapter, **Summing Up** organizes and reviews the subject matter according to the heads within the chapter.

Test Yourself provides multiple choice and critical thinking questions, prepared by Sue Wicks McKenzie, which are designed to help students study and to promote class discussion. The **Answer Key** is printed at the end of the book.

Student Supplements

Companion Website (**www.pearsoned.ca/rathus**): The Companion Website, created specifically for this text, provides a variety of study aids, including self-grading quizzes and practice tests, as well as links to relevant online resources.

Study Guide (ISBN 0-205-46526-9): The Study Guide contains chapter summaries, learning objectives, and a variety of exercises to help students learn the key concepts and test their knowledge.

Instructor Supplements

Instructor's Resource CD-ROM (ISBN 0-205-49414-5): This CD-ROM gathers together the following instructor supplements:

Instructor's Resource Manual: This manual includes a variety of resources, including Chapter-at-a-Glance tables (correlating chapter topics and learning objectives with the offered resources), teaching tips, activities, additional lecture material, and recommended readings, videos, and Web sites.

Pearson TestGen: Approximately 2000 test questions are provided in TestGen format. TestGen is a testing software that enables instructors to view and edit the existing questions, add questions, generate tests, and distribute the tests in a variety of formats. Powerful search and sort functions make it easy to locate questions and arrange them in any order desired. TestGen also enables instructors to administer tests on a local area network, have the tests graded electronically, and have the results prepared in electronic or printed reports. TestGen is compatible with Windows and Macintosh operating systems, and can be downloaded from the TestGen Web site located at www.pearsoned.com/testgen. Contact your local sales representative for details and access.

Test Item File: All the test questions offered in the TestGen software are also provided in Microsoft Word format in this Test Item File.

PowerPoints: Chapter-by-chapter presentations highlight the key points from the text, supported by diagrams and visuals.

Some of these instructor supplements are also available for download from a password-protected section of Pearson Education Canada's online catalogue (vig.pearsoned.ca). Navigate to your book's catalogue page to view a list of those supplements that are available. See your local sales representative for details and access.

Videos: A selection of recommended videos from the Films for the Humanities and Social Sciences collection is available for adopters of this text. Titles include *Understanding Sex*, a broad overview of plant, animal, and human sexuality; *Love & Sex*, which covers topics such as love, monogamy, hetero- and homosexuality; *Facts on STDs*, a conversational yet authoritative electronic reference guide for students; *Healthy Lifestyles*, which provides information to make the best decisions for living a healthy lifestyle and feeling good; *Sexually Transmitted Diseases: The Silent Epidemic*, which provides specific information about the prevention, diagnosis, and treatment of the most common non-HIV STDs; and *Unsafe Sex and Its Consequences*, which emphasizes the need and the means for preventing the most common STDs other than HIV. Please contact your Pearson Education Sales Representative for full information about these videos and the qualifying criteria.

Video Workshop Student Learning Guide and Instructor Teaching Guide: A CD-ROM with 14 video clips (50 minutes) of course-specific video footage comes with a workbook that includes 10 questions for each video. The Student Guide with CD may be packaged with this textbook at no extra cost, and an Instructor Guide is available from your Pearson representative. To view clip samples and content, visit www.ablongman.com/html/videoworkshop/disciplines/features.html.

Pearson Advantage: For qualified adopters, Pearson Education is proud to introduce the **Pearson Advantage**. The Pearson Advantage is the first integrated Canadian service program committed to meeting the customization, training, and support needs for your course. Our commitments are made in writing and in consultation with faculty. Your local Pearson Education sales representative can provide you with more details on this service program.

Content Media Specialists: Pearson's Content Media Specialists work with faculty and campus course designers to ensure that Pearson technology products, assessment tools, and online course materials are tailored to meet your specific needs. This highly qualified team is dedicated to helping schools take full advantage of a wide range of educational technology, by assisting in the integration of a variety of instructional materials and media formats.

Acknowledgments

The authors owe a great debt of gratitude to the many researchers and scholars whose contributions to the body of knowledge of human sexuality are represented in these pages. Underscoring the interdisciplinary nature of this area of study, we have drawn upon the work of scholars in such fields as psychology, sociology, medicine, anthropology, theology, and philosophy, to name a few. We are also indebted to the many researchers who have generously allowed us to quote from their work and to reprint tabular material representing their findings.

The authors and publishers wish to thank the many professional colleagues who provide feedback on this text at various stages in its development. Online survey respondents included Jan Cioe, Okanagan University College; Thomas A. Fish, St. Thomas University; Kathryn Jones, Grant MacEwan College; and B. J. Rye, St. Jerome's University at the University of Waterloo. The following people reviewed the previous edition and/or manuscript chapters: Jessica Ayala, University of Calgary; Shaniff Esmail, University of Alberta; Deborah Foster, University of Alberta/Athabasca University; Julie M. Fraser, University of Windsor; Susan Leslie-Berkis, Humber Institute of Technology and Advanced Learning; Jennifer MacKenzie, Seneca College of Applied Arts and Technology; Dawn More, Algonquin College of Applied Arts and Technology; James Ponzetti, University of British Columbia; B J Rye, St Jerome's University at the University of Waterloo; and Karen Tee, Vanier College.

As the Canadian author, I am deeply grateful to all of those Canadian scholars who provided me with copies of their research as well as helpful ideas that enabled me to write this second Canadian edition of *Human Sexuality in a World of Diversity*. I am especially grateful to my University of Windsor colleague, Eleanor Maticka-Tyndale, whose solid theoretical and methodological expertise has greatly contributed to our research on tourism and sexuality.

I am also indebted to colleagues and the administrators at the University of Guelph who have supported my teaching and research in the area of sexuality. I especially acknowledge the role that Richard Barham played in the 1970s in helping to obtain a Family Planning Fellowship that enabled me to expand my own research program, develop human sexuality courses at the graduate level, and initiate the Guelph Sexuality Conference.

I owe considerable thanks to Dayna Fischtein, who had a major research role in the preparation of the first Canadian edition, and to Jaclyn Cattrysse, who was extremely helpful in assisting with this second Canadian edition. Their hard work, enthusiasm, organizational strengths, and many useful ideas are much appreciated.

I am grateful to the many people at Pearson Education Canada for all their valuable assistance with this project. Arlene Mahood, who was a sales representative at the time, initially encouraged me to write the Canadian edition. Carolin Sweig, Sponsoring Editor, played a key role in shaping the new edition, using faculty reviews to develop a detailed revision plan that was extremely helpful. Michelle Harrington, Developmental Editor, was equally helpful and patient. She provided enthusiasm, encouragement, and many good ideas during the writing phases. Avivah Wargon did an excellent job of coordinating production editorial activities, and Gilda Mekler was extremely detailed and thorough in her copy editing. Karen Alliston was a very helpful proofreader. I am also grateful to Sue McKenzie for her detailed development of the quiz questions for each chapter.

Finally, I wish to sincerely thank my wife, Yvette, and daughter, Malia, for their support and patience. For both Canadian editions of this book, Yvette voluntarily provided considerable editorial assistance and I very much appreciate her efforts.

Edward S. Herold, PhD

Chapter 1
What Is Human Sexuality?

We are about to embark on the study of human sexuality. But why, you may wonder, do we need to *study* human sexuality? Isn't sex something to *do* rather than to *talk about?* Isn't sex a natural function? Don't we learn what we need to know from personal experience or from our parents or our friends?

Yes, we can learn how our bodies respond to sexual stimulation—what turns us on and what turns us off—through personal experience. Personal experience teaches us little, however, about the biological processes that bring about sexual response and orgasm. Nor does experience inform us about the variations in sexual behaviour that exist around the world, or in the neighbourhood. Experience does not prepare us to recognize the signs of sexually transmitted infections or to evaluate the risks of pregnancy. Nor does experience help us deal with most sexual problems, or dysfunctions.

There is also something of a myth in our culture that love conquers all—that love is all we need to achieve and sustain satisfying and healthy relationships. Yet how likely are we to establish healthy and mutually satisfying relationships without some formal knowledge of our own and our partner's sexuality? Without some knowledge of the biology of how our bodies function? Without some awareness of the psychological aspects of our sexuality? In a scientific vacuum?

Concerns about AIDS and unwanted teenage pregnancies have focused greater attention today on the importance of sex education. Many children receive some form of sex education as early as elementary school. Courses on human sexuality, which were rarely offered as recently as the 1950s, are now routine on university campuses across Canada and the United States. You may know more about human sexuality than your parents or grandparents did at your age—perhaps more than they do today. But how much do you really know? What, for example, happens inside your body when you are sexually stimulated? What causes erection or vaginal lubrication? Can people who are paralyzed from the neck down become erect or lubricated? What do we know of the factors that determine a person's sexual orientation? What are the causes of sexual dysfunctions? How do our sexual responsiveness and interests change as we age? Can you contract a sexually transmitted disease and not know that you have it until you wind up sterile? Can you infect others without having any symptoms yourself?

These are just a few of the issues we will explore in this book. Before we proceed further, let us define our subject.

What Is Human Sexuality?

What *is* human sexuality? This is not a trick question. Consider the meaning, or rather meanings, of the word *sex.* The word derives from Latin roots that mean "to cut or divide," signifying the division of organisms into male and female genders. One use of the term *sex*, then, refers to our **gender**, or state of being male or female. The word *sex* (or *sexual*) is also used to refer to those anatomic structures, called sex (or sexual) organs, that play a role in reproduction or sexual pleasure. We may also speak of sex when referring to physical activities that involve our sex organs and are engaged in for purposes of reproduction or pleasure: masturbation, hugging, kissing, **coitus**, and so on. Sex also relates to **erotic** feelings, experiences, or desires, such as sexual fantasies and thoughts, sexual urges, or feelings of sexual attraction to another person.

We usually make our usage of the term *sex* clear enough in our everyday speech. When we ask about the sex of a newborn, we are referring to anatomic sex. When we speak of "having sex" (a rather ugly phrase, which seems to imply that we engage in sexual activity much as we "have" a ham sandwich), we generally mean the physical expression of erotic feelings.

The term *sexual behaviour* refers to physical activities that involve the body in the expression of erotic or affectionate feelings. This description of sexual behav-

Gender One's personal, social, and legal status as male or female.

Coitus (co-it-us or co-EET-us). Sexual intercourse.

Erotic Arousing sexual feelings or desires. (From the Greek *eros*, which means "love.")

Research in Action

WHAT IS THIS THING CALLED SEX?

Although in this textbook we have adopted a broad definition of what sex involves, many Canadians focus on intercourse as their definition of sex. In a study of Canadian students on spring break in Florida (one the lead Canadian author of this textbook was involved in), most of the students referred to intimate behaviours other than vaginal intercourse as "fooling around" (Maticka-Tyndale et al., 1998).

New Brunswick researchers Hilary Randall and Sandra Byers (2003) asked university students to indicate which behaviours they would define as "having sex" with someone if they were the ones engaging in those behaviours. The only behaviours that most students considered as sex were penile–vaginal intercourse and penile–anal intercourse. Only about one-fifth considered oral–genital contact as sex and even fewer (10%) considered touching of genitals leading to orgasm as sex. Interestingly, for each of the behaviours there was a slight increase in the percentage of students defining that behaviour as sex if it resulted in orgasm.

However, when the researchers modified the question, far more students indicated that they would define someone as their "sexual partner" if that person were engaging in those behaviours with them. For example, about two-thirds considered anyone with whom they had oral–genital contact to be a sexual partner, and about one-half considered touching of genitals as an indicator.

Next, the researchers asked the students which of the behaviours they would consider as indicators of their partner being "unfaithful." For each behaviour, more than three-fourths considered it a sign of being unfaithful. Actually, 16 of 18 items were considered by more than 90% of the respondents as examples of a partner being unfaithful. The two items that had the lowest percentage agreement involved behaviours occurring at a distance—masturbating to orgasm while in telephone contact with another person (85%) and masturbating to orgasm while in computer contact with another (79%). Clearly, what is considered as being unfaithful or "cheating" is much broader than what is considered as having sex.

iour includes, but is not limited to, behaviour involving reproduction. *Masturbation*, for example, is sexual behaviour that is performed for pleasure, not reproduction. Kissing, hugging, manual manipulation of the genitals, and oral–genital contact are all sexual behaviours that can provide sensual stimulation, even though they do not directly lead to reproduction. They may also be used as forms of **foreplay**, which leads to coitus, which can lead to reproduction.

We can now define **human sexuality** as the ways in which we experience and express ourselves as sexual beings. Our awareness of ourselves as females or males is part of our sexuality, as is the capacity we have for erotic experiences and responses. Our sexuality is an essential part of ourselves, whether or not we ever engage in sexual intercourse or sexual fantasy, and even if we lose sensation in our genitals because of injury.

The Study of Human Sexuality

The study of human sexuality is an interdisciplinary enterprise that draws upon the scientific expertise of anthropologists, biologists, medical researchers, sociologists, and psychologists, to name but a few of the professionals involved in the field. These disciplines all make contributions because sexual behaviour reflects our biological capabilities, our psychological characteristics, and social and cultural influences. Biologists inform us about the physiological mechanisms of sexual arousal and response. Medical science teaches us about sexually transmitted diseases and the biological bases of sexual dysfunctions. Psychologists examine how our sexual behaviour and attitudes are shaped by perception, learning, thought, motivation and emotion, and personality. Sociocultural theorists consider the sociocultural contexts of sexual behaviour. For example, they examine relationships between sexual behaviour and religion, race, and social class. Anthropologists focus on cross-cultural

Foreplay Mutual sexual stimulation that precedes sexual intercourse.

Human sexuality The ways in which we experience and express ourselves as sexual beings.

similarities and differences in sexual behaviour. Scientists from many disciplines explore parallels between the sexual behaviour of humans and that of other animals.

There are a number of organizations promoting sex research and sex education. In Canada, a leading organization is the Sex Information and Education Council of Canada (SIECCAN) which publishes *The Canadian Journal of Human Sexuality*. Two major American organizations are the Society for the Scientific Study of Sexuality (SSSS) which publishes *The Journal of Sex Research* and the American Association of Sex Educators, Counselors and Therapists (AASECT) which provides education and certification for educators, counsellors, and therapists.

Canadian Society and Sexuality

In order to understand the complexity of factors influencing sexual attitudes and behaviours in Canada, it is important to be aware of the diverse nature of Canadians. Of course, prior to the European discovery of North America, Canada was inhabited by First Nations people. The first European explorers to the region of Canada were mainly French or British, and for many years these two ethnic groups have been the dominant ones in Canada. In the latter half of the twentieth century an increasing number of immigrants came from non-European countries. Currently, more than half of immigrants come from Asia and less than one-fifth come from Europe. As a result, Canadians of French or British ancestry today make up only about half of the population.

The most notable change in the Canadian mosaic has been the dramatic increase in the proportion of visible minorities. In the 2001 Canadian Census, 13% of Canadians identified themselves as such. Statistics Canada (2005) projects that by the year 2017 visible minorities will make up 20% of the Canadian population, and more than half the population of Toronto and Vancouver.

The **values** of immigrants often differ from those of the rest of Canadian society. In South Asian communities, for example, arranged marriages are still fairly common. Some immigrants from Muslim countries maintain the practice of female circumcision, a procedure, usually performed on young girls, that involves surgical removal of the clitoris and in some cases parts of the labia. This practice, often referred to as "genital mutilation," is contrary to Canadian values. (The Canadian and U.S. governments have declared performing female circumcisions illegal; however, within some immigrant communities, the procedure is still being done.) Some groups use sex selection techniques, such as abortion, to ensure that they have a boy rather than a girl. And, since sex is a taboo subject in many cultures, parents in these cultures do not provide sex education to their children.

For the most part, the sexual behaviours of immigrants are more conservative than the rest of Canadian society. This is particularly pronounced in relation to the age of first intercourse. Among young people born in Canada who are between the ages of 20 and 24, about three-quarters had their first sexual intercourse before the age of 20, compared with less than half of those not born in Canada (Maticka-Tyndale et al., 2001). Similar patterns are found in comparing Canadians who refer to themselves as "white" with those who refer to themselves as "non-white." To help new Canadian families deal with sexuality issues, the Sexuality Education Resource Centre in Winnipeg has developed an Intergenerational Communication project that trains parents from diverse ethnic communities to act as sexuality educators in their respective communities (SERC, 2001).

Children of immigrant parents often get caught in a culture clash between the traditional values of their parents and the more permissive values of Canadian society. Some parents use severe punishment as a means of controlling the teenager's behaviour, especially that of girls. In Kitimat, British Columbia, a father from the Indo-Canadian community stabbed his 17-year-old daughter to death after he discovered she was having a secret relationship with a boy.

Values The qualities in life that are deemed important or unimportant, right or wrong, desirable or undesirable.

Research in Action

ETHNOCULTURAL COMMUNITIES AND SEXUALITY

Based on its concern over the spread of HIV/AIDS, Health Canada sponsored a study of a diversity of ethnic groups in Canada. The study, entitled *Ethnocultural Communities Facing AIDS*, was conducted in consultation with representatives of each of the ethnic groups involved. Participants came from South Asian, Chinese, South African, Caribbean, Latin American, and Arabic communities. Most of the participants reported that a double standard exists for sexual behaviour, whereby women are expected to be virgins at marriage and monogamous after marriage, while men are allowed to be sexually permissive before and to some extent after marriage. In the South Asian community, girls are not even allowed to date. It is often taken for granted that at least some men will have sex with prostitutes and/or have sex with women from outside their ethnic group. Homosexuality is treated as if it did not exist in their communities, and as a result homosexuals are made to feel ashamed. **Gender roles** are rigidly prescribed, with the man considered to be the "boss" of the family. Women are not expected to have much interest in or knowledge of sex, and they lack the power to ask their husbands to use condoms.

Eleanor Maticka-Tyndale at the University of Windsor and two visiting researchers from Iran, Khosro Rafaie Shirpark and Maryam Chinichian (2005), conducted research with immigrants from Iran. As in the Ethnocultural Communities study, they found maintaining female virginity prior to marriage was considered essential for a girl to maintain a good reputation and the honour of her family. The Iranian adults were fearful of having their children exposed to sexuality from the broader Canadian society and especially from the media. Based on images they saw on Canadian television, the Iranian immigrants believed that most Canadian adolescents begin having sexual intercourse by the age of 13 or 14. They also perceived that Canadians do not seem to care about marital loyalty and having extramarital relationships. Accordingly, the women worried that their husbands would be tempted to engage in affairs because of the sexual freedoms in Canada. The men worried that in Canada it would be too easy for their wives to walk out of a marriage. Respondents also believed that sex education in Canadian schools emphasized the use of condoms rather than abstinence before marriage..

As the children of immigrants become acculturated to the Canadian way of life, they may face increasing conflict with their parents, especially in relation to gender and sexual values. For example, a study of Asian students in British Columbia found that those who had been in Canada longer had more liberal sexual values and more sexual experience than did more recent arrivals (Meston et al., 1998).

TABLE 1.1
Sexual Activity Among Unmarried Youth, Ages 15–19

Country and Year of Study	Percentage of Unmarried Youth Who Have Ever Had Sex	
	Females	Males
Kenya, 1998	37	54
Uganda, 1995	42	64
Philippines, 1998	2	no data
Brazil, 1996	24	63
Jamaica, 1997	37	74
Romania, 1999	11	45
United States, 1995	51	56
Canada, 1996	51	42

Source: Table adapted from Issues in World Health (2001, Fall). Population Reports, XXIX (3), 7.

Gender roles Complex clusters of ways in which males and females are expected to behave within a given culture.

A World of Diversity

SEXUAL ORIENTATION MEANS MANY MUSLIMS SHUNNED

Asad pulls out his scrapbook crammed with pictures of queer Muslims at a recent Pride Week—snapshots of people sharing good times, laughing and mugging for the camera.

They are typical scenes resembling many cultural gatherings in Toronto. Except for one thing.

This is a group shunned by its ethnic community at large because of the sexual orientation of its members. Many Muslims are unwilling even to discuss homosexuality among themselves, let alone reach out for any kind of dialogue.

"When I came out and started having a partner and dating men, I really did move away from a lot of my Muslim community," says Adil, 33, who was born and raised in Toronto. The reason: fear of being rejected.

For queer Muslims, worshipping means attending a mosque but not letting others know they're gay. Or not having a support group to help new arrivals.

When Rabia, a transsexual from Turkey, arrived in Toronto, she was dressed as a man but couldn't go to the Muslim community for shelter. Rabia now attends mosque on Fridays as a woman and hasn't had problems. But she doesn't disclose her personal life.

"They don't know I'm transsexual. We are first, servants of God and I

Muslims like Rabia (left), a transsexual, and Asad (centre), who is gay, have not disclosed their sexuality to the Muslim community at large for fear of rejection. Nergiz (right), a transsexual belly dancer, says that when people find out, "I can tell from their eyes that I am not welcome."

don't need to tell anyone. I'm Rabia. I'm a person. I don't have to tell them I'm transsexual."

Nergiz, another transsexual from Turkey, who teaches and performs belly dancing, also has experienced rejection.

"If people realize you're a transsexual, they won't allow you in," says Nergiz. "They won't tell me to leave, but I can tell from their eyes that I am not welcome."

Adil says he's fortunate his mother knows he's gay and is accepting. But it's not that way with his gay friends.

"I can bring my partner over whenever and there's no problem," he says. "One of my ex-partners wasn't 'out' to his family and he was Arab so I had to go there as a friend and not a boyfriend. As long as I was a friend it's fine. The minute they found out I was a boyfriend it wasn't fine. So it's a lot

harder to be an out gay Muslim person for those people than it is for me."

Mohammed El Masry, president of the Canadian Islamic Congress, representing about 70 percent of Canada's 570,000 Muslims, says Islam teaches that homosexuality is an unnatural act against God's natural law.

Masry says the community here either pretends there is no such thing as a homosexual Muslim or they are shunned altogether.

Nergiz, Adil, Asad and Rabia all belong to a gay Muslim group in Toronto called Salaam (**www.salaamcanada. com**) which has about 80 members and hopes to promote a safe space for queer Muslims and reach out to straight Muslims.

Source: "Finding a Place in Muslim Society," *Peter Krivel,* Toronto Star, *June 19, 2003, p. J3. Reprinted with permission— Torstar Syndication Services.*

COMPARING CANADA WITH OTHER COUNTRIES Tremendous variation in sexual attitudes and behaviour is found among the different countries of the world. Many of these variations will be presented throughout this textbook. For example, Table 1.1 shows how some countries differ with respect to rates of sexual activity for youth. Whereas the percentages for Canadian and American females are higher than in the other countries, fewer Canadian males have experienced sexual intercourse compared with males in the other countries. The fact that in Canada more adolescent females than males are sexually experienced suggests that less of a sexual double standard exists here than in other countries.

COMPARING CANADA AND THE U.S. Although there are many similarities between Canadians and Americans, there are also many differences. For example, a much higher proportion of the U.S. population comes from Spanish or African backgrounds. Consequently, ethnic comparisons in the U.S. are often based on three categories: African Americans, Latin Americans, and European Americans. In Canada, ethnic comparisons are typically between French-speaking people in Quebec and English-speaking Canadians across the country. It is important to be aware of social and demographic differences between the two countries because they account for some major differences in sexual attitudes and behaviours.

The birthrate in Canada is lower than in the United States, especially for women in their 20s. According to Statistics Canada (2002), this is because Canadian women marry later than do American women. As well, the teenage pregnancy rate is much higher in the United States than in Canada. Population growth in Canada is more dependent on immigration from other countries than in the U.S.

The American population (about 10 times as large as Canada's) is widely spread throughout the various regions of the United States, whereas the majority of people in Canada live in large metropolitan areas near the U.S. border. And since most new immigrants choose to live in these areas, they also have the highest rates of population growth. Canada's population is especially concentrated in the areas of Southern Ontario, Montreal, the Vancouver region, and the Calgary–Edmonton corridor (Statistics Canada, 2002). Almost two-thirds of Canada's 30 million people live in the two largest provinces, Ontario and Quebec.

More Americans (39%) than Canadians (33%) attend university shortly after high school. However, in the United States, income plays a larger role in determining if someone attends university, with 63% of Americans from the top income quartile attending university compared with only 15% of those whose family income is in the bottom quartile. In Canada, this income gap is lower, with 45% of those from the top income quartile attending university compared with 24% of those from the bottom income quartile (Statistics Canada, 2005).

Americans go to church more often than do Canadians (Statistics Canada, 2002). According to the 2001 Census, nearly 5 million Canadians—including 40% of those under the age of 25—say they have no religion at all.

Michael Adams, founder of the Canadian polling firm Environics Research, has conducted numerous large-scale surveys in Canada and the U.S. In his 2003 book *Fire and Ice*, he concludes that the Canadian identity is distinct from that of Americans and that the cultural gap between the two countries is increasing. Adams's surveys indicate that Canadians are more liberal and tolerant than Americans. For example, Canadians are less likely than Americans to oppose immigration by visible minorities.

When it comes to sexuality issues, Canadians are somewhat more liberal than are Americans. For example, national surveys find that more Canadians (54%) than Americans (41%) are in favour of same-sex marriages (Associated Press, 2003). In other chapters of this textbook, we will present more comparisons of American and Canadian attitudes and behaviours.

POLITICS AND SEX IN CANADA AND THE U.S. In the U.S., Christian fundamentalists, otherwise known as the "religious right," have a greater presence than in Canada. Consequently, in the U.S. they have had a much stronger voice in persuading governments to take a conservative stance on the regulation of sexual values. For example, the religious right has persuaded the U.S. Congress to spend hundreds of millions of dollars on educational programs that teach abstinence from sex and that do not allow for the teaching of contraceptive methods to adolescents. In contrast, the Canadian approach includes discussion of birth control as well as abstinence.

When George W. Bush won his second presidential term in office in 2004, he received overwhelming support from Christian fundamentalists. In return, he vowed to have the American government be guided by conservative Christian values. Accordingly, his political speeches typically use religious references to support his arguments and he has stated that he wants to appoint to the Supreme Court only judges who would make judicial decisions based on fundamentalist religious principles.

Two major concerns of Christian fundamentalists have been the banning of same-sex marriage and the restriction of abortion rights. Many political analysts believe that Bush's opposition to same-sex marriage played an important role in his re-election.

In contrast, Canadian politicians have largely maintained a separation between religion and the state. The Canadian Charter of Rights and Freedoms has helped to maintain this separation, as the Charter views individual rights as taking precedence over religious values. This has been shown in judicial decisions regarding same-sex marriage. Despite protests from various religious groups, the Canadian courts have consistently decided that not allowing same-sex marriage was a violation of the individual rights of gays and lesbians. Prime Minister Paul Martin adopted a similar position. Although he is a practising Roman Catholic and received intensive pressure from Catholic Church officials to oppose same-sex marriage, Martin stated that his own religious values should not override personal freedoms.

In 2005 Canada became the fourth country in the world to legally allow same-sex marriage. The main political opposition to this legislation came from the federal Conservative party and the Alberta Conservative party. In fact, the leader of the federal Conservatives, Stephen Harper, indicated that if his party were to form the government he would have another vote in the House of Commons to overturn the law. Here Harper was going against public opinion, as a survey conducted by the Strategic Council after the same-sex legislation was passed found that 55% of Canadians wanted the next government to leave the legislation in place and only 39% wanted the law repealed.

It should be noted that the federal Conservative party, after it united with the Alliance party of Canada, hinted at introducing restrictive legislation in other areas of sexuality. In particular, they wished to raise the legal age of consent to 16 from 14. Previously, the federal Conservatives had followed a middle-of-the-road approach. In fact, it was the Conservative government of Brian Mulroney that in 1987 lowered the age of sexual consent from 18 to 14.

Despite the fears of some Canadian religious groups that they would be forced to perform same-sex marriages, Bill C-68 governing same-sex marriage specifically states that the legislation is only binding on city halls and not on religious organizations.

Issues around sexuality have generally had a higher profile in U.S. politics than in Canada. However, in the 2005 British Columbia election, lawyer John Ince formed the Sex Party, which ran three candidates. The party did not expect to win any seats but wanted to make Canadians aware of the role politicians play in deciding what kinds of sexual activities are acceptable or not. The Sex Party called for a sex-positive approach in Canadian schools and other institutions and the repeal of sex-negative laws so that prostitution would be fully legal. Much of the platform of the Sex Party is based on John Ince's book, *The Politics of Lust* (2003), in which he argues that powerful antisexual forces in Canada and the U.S. are causing anxiety, fear, and negativity about sexual pleasure.

A World of Diversity

CANADIANS ON THE INTERNET

About two-thirds of Canadians surf the Internet at least once a month (Léger Marketing, 2003). More than half of Canadian teenagers in a 2003 Strategic Counsel survey said that the Internet is more important than TV. Many Canadians are being exposed to all kinds of sexual issues and behaviours on the Internet that they might not otherwise have seen.

While much has been written about online pornography, many other aspects of the Internet have been less explored. For example, in 2001, 60% of Canadian Internet users sought medical or health-related information online (Canadian Press, 2002). Many sexual health organizations have educational Web sites, several of which are noted in this text. As well, numerous discussion groups may be found online for all kinds of sexuality issues, such as those relating to gays and lesbians. Finally, an increasing number of Canadians are using the Internet to find dating and marriage partners.

Sexuality and Values

Our society is pluralistic. It embraces a wide range of sexual attitudes and values. Some readers may be liberal in their sexual views and behaviour. Others may be conservative or traditional. Some will be staunchly pro-choice on abortion, others adamantly pro-life. Some will approve of premarital sex for couples who are dating casually. Others will hold the line at emotional commitment. Still others will believe that people should wait until marriage.

Because we encourage you, as you study this text, to explore your own values about the issues we discuss, let us reveal two values that guided *our* writing:

1. *Sexual knowledge and critical thinking skills are of value because they allow us to make informed sexual decisions.* We hope that readers will confirm our belief. Having agreed on this much, your authors admit that they hold different values about a number of the issues we discuss. Therefore, we—your authors—do not try to persuade readers to adopt a particular stance concerning issues raised in the textbook. We present opposing points of view on controversial matters such as abortion and the distribution of condoms in schools. We hope that readers will critically consider their preconceptions and that the views they form will be their own.

2. *Students should take an active role in enhancing their health.* In the course of this text, we will urge you, for example, to examine your body for possible abnormalities, to see your physician when you have questions about painful menstruation or other physical complaints, to become sensitive to the signs of sexually transmitted infections, to get good prenatal care, and so forth.

People's sexual attitudes, experiences, and behaviours are shaped to a large extent by their cultural traditions and beliefs. Because our world consists of diverse peoples and cultures, the study of human sexuality is really the study of human sexual*ities*. In this book we highlight the many ways in which people experience their sexuality.

Thinking Critically About Human Sexuality

We are inundated with so much information about sex that it is difficult to separate truth from fiction. Newspapers, TV shows, and popular books and magazines contain one feature after another about sex. Many of these presentations contradict one another, contain half-truths, or draw misleading or unsubstantiated conclusions. A scientific approach to human sexuality encourages people to think critically about claims and findings that are presented as truths.

Sad to say, most of us take certain "truths" for granted. We tend to assume that authority figures such as doctors and government officials provide us with factual information and are qualified to make decisions that affect our lives. When two doctors disagree on the need for a hysterectomy, however, or two officials disagree about whether condoms should be distributed in public schools, we wonder how both can be correct. Critical thinkers never say, "This is true because so-and-so says it is true."

To help students evaluate claims, arguments, and widely held beliefs, most universities encourage *critical thinking*. Critical thinking has several features. One aspect of critical thinking is skepticism—not taking things for granted. It means being skeptical of things that are presented in print, uttered by authority figures or celebrities, or passed along by friends. Another aspect of critical thinking is the thoughtful analysis and probing of claims and arguments. Critical thinking requires willingness to challenge the conventional wisdom and common knowledge that many of us take for granted. It means scrutinizing definitions of terms and evaluating the premises of arguments and their logic. It also means finding *reasons* to support your beliefs, rather than relying on feelings. When people think critically, they maintain open minds. They suspend their beliefs until they have obtained and evaluated the evidence.

Principles of Critical Thinking

Here are some suggestions for critical thinking:

1. *Be skeptical.* Politicians, religious leaders, and other authority figures attempt to convince you of their points of view. Even researchers and authors may hold certain biases. Resolve to adopt the attitude that you will accept nothing as true—including the comments of the authors of this text—until you have personally weighed the evidence.

2. *Examine definitions of terms.* Some statements are true when a term is defined in one way but are not true when it is defined in another. Consider the statement "Love is blind." If love is defined as head-over-heels infatuation, there may be substance to the statement. Infatuated people tend to idealize loved ones and overlook their faults. If, however, love is defined as deep caring and commitment involving a more realistic (if still somewhat slanted) appraisal of the loved one, then love is not so much blind as a bit nearsighted.

3. *Examine the assumptions or premises of arguments.* Consider the statement "Abortion is murder." *Webster's New World Dictionary* defines *murder* as "the unlawful and malicious or premeditated killing of one human being by another." The statement can be true, according to this dictionary, only if the victim is held to be a human being (and if the act is unlawful and either malicious or premeditated). Pro-life advocates argue that embryos and fetuses are human beings. Pro-choice advocates claim that they are not. Hence the argument that abortion is murder would rest in part on the assumption that the embryo or fetus is a human being.

4. *Be cautious in drawing conclusions from evidence.* In Chapter 14 we shall discuss research findings that show that married people who cohabited before marriage are more likely to get divorced eventually than are those who didn't cohabit first. It may seem at first glance that cohabitation is a *cause* of divorce. However, married couples who cohabit before marriage may differ from those who do not in ways other than choosing cohabitation—which brings us to our next suggestion for critical thinking.

5. *Consider alternative interpretations of research evidence.* For example, cohabitors who later get married may be more likely to get divorced eventually because they are more liberal and less traditional than married couples who did not cohabit before marriage. Eventual divorce would then be *connected* with cohabitation but would not be *caused* by cohabitation.

6. *Consider the kinds of evidence on which conclusions are based.* Some conclusions, even seemingly "scientific" conclusions, are based on anecdotes and personal endorsements. They are not founded on sound research.

7. *Do not overgeneralize.* Consider the belief that gay males are effeminate and lesbians are masculine. Yes, some gay males and lesbians fit these stereotypes. However, many do not. Overgeneralizing makes us vulnerable to accepting stereotypes.

The Venus of Willendorf. Anthropologists believe that the Venus is an ancient fertility symbol.

Perspectives on Human Sexuality

Human sexuality is a complex topic. No single theory or perspective can capture all its nuances. In this book we explore human sexuality from many perspectives. In this section we introduce a number of perspectives—historical, biological, evolutionary, cross-species, cross-cultural, psychological, and sociocultural—that we will draw on in subsequent chapters.

The Historical Perspective

History places our sexual behaviour in context. It informs us whether our sexual behaviour reflects trends that have been with us through the millennia or the customs of a particular culture and era.

History shows little evidence of universal sexual trends. Attitudes and behaviours vary extensively from one time and place to another. Contemporary Canadian society may be permissive when compared with the Victorian and postwar eras. Yet it looks staid when compared with the sexual excesses of some ancient societies, most notably the ruling class of ancient Rome.

PREHISTORIC SEXUALITY: FROM FEMALE IDOLS TO PHALLIC WORSHIP

Information about life among our Stone Age ancestors is drawn largely from cave drawings, stone artifacts, and the customs of modern-day preliterate peoples whose existence may have changed little over the millennia.

Art produced in the Stone Age, some 20 000 years ago, suggests the worship of women's ability to bear children and perpetuate the species (Fichner-Rathus, 2004). Primitive statues and cave drawings portray women with large, pendulous breasts, rounded hips, and prominent sex organs. Most theorists regard the figurines as fertility symbols. Emphasis on the female reproductive role may also have signified ignorance of the male's contribution to reproduction.

As the ice sheets of the last ice age retreated (about 11 000 B.C.) and the climate warmed, human societies turned agrarian. Hunters and gatherers became farmers and herders. As people grew aware of the male role in reproduction, **phallic worship** sprang into being. Knowledge of paternity is believed to have developed around 9000 B.C., which is about the time that people shifted from being hunters and gatherers to being farmers and shepherds.

Phallic worship Worship of the penis as a symbol of generative power.

Phallic symbols Images of the penis.

Incest taboo The prohibition against intercourse and reproduction among close blood relatives.

Monogamy The practice of having one spouse. (From the Greek *mono-*, which means single" or "alone.")

Gender roles Complex clusters of ways in which males and females are expected to behave within a given culture.

Bisexual Sexually responsive to either gender. (From the Latin *bi-*, which means "two.")

In any event, the penis was glorified in art as a plough, an axe, or a sword. **Phallic symbols** figured in religious ceremonies in ancient Egypt. Ancient Greek art revered phalluses, rendering them sometimes as rings and sometimes as necklaces. Some phalluses were given wings, suggesting the power ascribed to them. In ancient Rome, a large phallus was carried like a float in a parade honouring Venus, the goddess of love.

The **incest taboo** may have been the first human taboo (Tannahill, 1980). All human societies apparently have some form of incest taboo (Harris & Johnson, 2000; Whitten, 2001). Societies have varied in terms of the strictness of the taboo, however. Brother–sister marriages were permitted among the presumably divine rulers of ancient Egypt and among the royal families of the Incas and of Hawaii, even though they were generally prohibited among commoners.

THE ANCIENT HEBREWS The ancient Hebrews viewed sex, at least sex in marriage, as a fulfilling experience intended to satisfy the divine injunction to "be fruitful and multiply." Male–male and female–female sexual behaviour was strongly condemned, because it was believed to represent a threat to the perpetuation of the family. Adultery, too, was condemned—at least for a woman. Although the Hebrew bible (called the Old Testament in the Christian faith) permitted polygamy, the vast majority of the Hebrews were **monogamous**.

The ancient Hebrews approved of sex within marriage not simply for procreation but also for mutual pleasure and fulfillment. They believed that the expression of sexual needs and desires helped strengthen marital bonds and solidify the family.

What of the feminine **gender role** among the ancient Hebrews? Women were to be good wives and mothers. What *is* a "good wife"? According to the Book of Proverbs, a good wife rises before dawn to tend to her family's needs, brings home the food, instructs the servants, tends the vineyards, makes the clothes, keeps the ledger, helps the needy, and works well into the night. Even so, among the ancient Hebrews, a wife was considered the property of her husband. If she offended him, she could be divorced on a whim (although this almost never happened). A wife could be stoned to death for adultery. She might also have had to share her husband with his secondary wives and concubines. Men who committed adultery by consorting with the wives of other men were considered to have violated the property rights of those men. Although they were subject to harsh penalties for such violation of property rights, they were not put to death.

THE ANCIENT GREEKS The classical or golden age of ancient Greece lasted about 200 years, from about 500 B.C. to 300 B.C. Within this relatively short span lived the philosophers Socrates, Plato, and Aristotle; the playwrights Aristophanes, Aeschylus, and Sophocles; the natural scientist Archimedes; and the lawgiver Solon. Like the Hebrews, the Greeks valued family life. But the Greeks did not cement family ties by limiting sexual interests to marriage—at least not male sexual interests. The Greeks expressed sexual interests openly. They admired the well-developed male body and enjoyed nude wrestling among men in the arena. Erotic encounters and off-colour jokes characterized the works of Aristophanes and other playwrights.

The Greeks viewed their gods—Zeus, god of gods, Apollo, who inspired art and music, Aphrodite, the goddess of carnal love whose name is the basis of the word *aphrodisiac*, and others—as voracious seekers of sexual variety. Not only were they believed to have sexual adventures among themselves, but they were also thought to have seduced mortals.

Three aspects of Greek sexuality are of particular interest to our study of sexual practices in the ancient world: male–male sexual behaviour, pederasty, and prostitution. The Greeks viewed men and women as **bisexual**. One of their heroes, Heracles (Hercules), is said to have ravished 50 virgins in a night. Nevertheless, he also had affairs with men.

Pederasty means love of boys. Greek men might take on an adolescent male as a lover and pupil. Sex between men and prepubescent boys was illegal, however. Families were generally pleased if their adolescent sons attracted socially prominent mentors. Pederasty did not impede the boy's future male–female functioning, because the pederast himself was usually married, and the Greeks believed people equally capable of male–female and male–male sexual activity.

Prostitution flourished at every level of society. Prostitutes ranged from refined **courtesans** to **concubines**, who were usually slaves. Courtesans were similar to the geisha girls of Japan. They could play musical instruments, dance, engage in witty repartee, or discuss the latest political crisis. They were also skilled in the arts of love. No social stigma was attached to visiting a courtesan. Their clients included philosophers, playwrights, politicians, generals, and the very affluent. At the lower rungs of society were streetwalkers and prostitutes who lived in tawdry brothels.

Women in general held low social status. The women of Athens had no more legal or political rights than slaves. They were subject to the authority of their male next-of-kin before marriage and to that of their husbands afterward. They received no formal education and were consigned most of the time to women's quarters in their homes. They were chaperoned when they ventured out-of-doors. A husband could divorce his wife without cause and was obligated to do so if she committed adultery.

THE WORLD OF ANCIENT ROME Much is made of the sexual excesses of the Roman emperors and ruling families. Emperors such as Caligula sponsored orgies at which guests engaged in a wide variety of sexual practices. These sexual excesses were found more often among the upper classes of palace society than among average Romans. Unlike their counterparts in ancient Greece, Romans viewed male–male sexual behaviour as a threat to the integrity of the Roman family and to the position of the Roman woman.

The family was viewed as the source of strength of the Roman Empire. Although Roman women were more likely than their Greek counterparts to share their husbands' social lives, they still were considered the property of their husbands.

THE EARLY CHRISTIANS Christianity emerged within the Roman Empire during the centuries following the death of Christ. Early Christian views on sexuality were largely shaped by Saint Paul and the Church fathers in the first century and by Saint Augustine in the latter part of the fourth century.

In replacing the pagan values of Rome, the early Christians, like the Hebrews, sought to restrict sex to the marriage bed. They saw temptations of the flesh as distractions from spiritual devotion to God. Paul preached that celibacy was closer to the Christian ideal than marriage.

Christians, like Jews before them, demanded virginity of brides. Masturbation and prostitution were condemned as sinful (Allen, 2000). Early Christians taught that men should love their wives with restraint, not passion. The goal of procreation should govern sexual behaviour—the intellect should rule the flesh.

Over subsequent centuries, Christian leaders took an even more negative view of sexuality. Particularly influential were the ideas of Saint Augustine (A.D. 353–430), who associated sexual lust with the original sin of Adam and Eve in the Garden of Eden.

Nonprocreative sexual activity was deemed most sinful. Masturbation, male–male sexual behaviour, female–female sexual behaviour, oral–genital contact, anal intercourse—all were viewed as abominations in the eyes of God. Marital sex was deemed somewhat less sinful when practised for procreation and without passion.

Pederasty Sexual love of boys. (From the Greek *pai-dos*, which means "boy.")

Courtesan A prostitute—especially the mistress of a noble or wealthy man. (From Italian roots meaning "court lady.")

Concubine A secondary wife, usually of inferior legal and social status. (From Latin roots meaning "lying with.")

An Illustration from the Kama Sutra.
The Kama Sutra, *an Indian sex manual believed to have been written sometime between the third and fifth centuries A.D., contained graphic illustrations of sexual techniques and practices.*

SEXUALITY AND THE EASTERN RELIGIONS. Islam, the dominant religion in the Middle East, was founded by the prophet Muhammad. Muhammad was born in Mecca, in what is now Saudi Arabia, in about A.D. 570. The Islamic tradition treasures marriage and sexual fulfillment in marriage. Premarital intercourse invites shame and social condemnation; in some fundamentalist Islamic states, it incurs the death penalty.

The family is the backbone of Islamic society. Celibacy is frowned upon (Ahmed, 1991). Muhammad decreed that marriage represents the only road to virtue (Minai, 1981). Islamic tradition permits a sexual double standard, however. Men may take up to four wives, but women are permitted only one husband. Public social interactions between men and women are severely restricted in Islamic societies. Women in most traditional Islamic societies are expected to keep their heads and faces veiled in public and to avoid all contact with men other than their husbands.

In the cultures of the Far East, sexuality was akin to spirituality. To the Taoist masters of China, who influenced Chinese culture for millennia, sex was anything but sinful. Rather, they taught that sex was a sacred duty. It was a form of worship that was believed to lead toward immortality. Sex was to be performed well and often if one was to achieve harmony with nature.

The Chinese culture was the first to produce a detailed sex manual, which came into use about 200 years before the birth of Jesus. This manual helped educate men and women in the art of lovemaking. The man was expected to extend intercourse as long as possible, thereby absorbing more of his wife's natural essence, or *yin.* Yin would enhance his own masculine essence, or *yang.*

Taoists believed that it was wasteful for a man to "spill his seed." Masturbation, though acceptable for women, was ruled out for men. Sexual practices such as anal intercourse and oral–genital contact (**fellatio** and **cunnilingus**) were permissible, so long as the man did not squander *yang* through wasteful ejaculation. Another parallel to Western cultures was the role accorded women in traditional Chinese society. Here the "good wife," like her Western counterparts, was limited largely to the domestic roles of child rearing and homemaking.

Perhaps no culture has cultivated sexual pleasure as a spiritual ideal to a greater extent than the ancient Hindus of India. From the fifth century onward, temples show sculptures of gods, heavenly nymphs, and ordinary people in erotic poses (Gupta, 1994). Hindu sexual practices were codified in a sex manual, the *Kama Sutra.* The *Kama Sutra* illustrates sexual positions, some of which would challenge a contortionist. This manual remains the most influential sex manual ever produced.

In its graphic representations of sexual positions and practices, the *Kama Sutra* reflected the Hindu belief that sex was a religious duty, not a source of shame or guilt. In the Hindu doctrine of *karma,* actions in one life may determine the course of future lives: sexual fulfillment was regarded as one way to become reincarnated at a higher level of existence.

All in all, early Indian culture viewed sex as virtuous and natural. Indian society, however, grew more restrictive toward sexuality after about A.D. 1000 (Tannahill, 1980).

THE MIDDLE AGES The Middle Ages, sometimes called medieval times, span the millennium of Western history from about A.D. 476 to A.D. 1450. These years are sometimes termed the dark ages because some historians have depicted them as an era of cultural and intellectual decay and stagnation. The Roman Catholic Church

Fellatio A sexual activity involving oral contact with the penis.

Cunnilingus A sexual activity involving oral contact with the female genitals.

continued to grow in influence. Its attitudes toward sexuality remained largely unchanged since the time of Augustine.

Two conflicting concepts of women dominated medieval thought: one, *woman as Eve*, the temptress; the other, *woman as Mary*, virtuous and pure. Contemporary Western images of women still reflect the schism between the good girl and the bad girl—the Madonna and the whore.

THE PROTESTANT REFORMATION During the Reformation, Martin Luther (1483–1546) and other Christian reformers such as John Calvin (1509–1564) split off from the Roman Catholic Church and formed their own sects, which led to the development of the modern Protestant denominations of Western Europe (and later, the New World). Luther disputed many Roman Catholic doctrines on sexuality. He believed that priests should be allowed to marry and rear children. To Luther, marriage was as much a part of human nature as eating or drinking (Tannahill, 1980). Calvin rejected the Roman Catholic Church's position that sex in marriage was permissible only for the purpose of procreation. To Calvin, sexual expression in marriage fulfilled other legitimate roles, such as strengthening the marriage bond and helping to relieve the stresses of everyday life. However, extramarital and premarital sex remained forbidden, and were sternly punished.

THE VICTORIAN ERA The middle and later parts of the nineteenth century are generally called the Victorian period after Queen Victoria of England. Victoria assumed the throne in 1837 and ruled until her death in 1901. Her name has become virtually synonymous with sexual repression. Victorian society in Europe and North America, on the surface at least, was prim and proper. Sex was not discussed in polite society. Many women viewed sex as a marital duty to be performed for procreation or to satisfy their husbands' cravings. Consider the following quotation:

> I am happy now that Charles calls on my bed chamber less frequently than of old. As it is, I now endure but two calls a week and when I hear his steps outside my door I lie down on my bed, close my eyes, open my legs and think of England.
>
> —Attributed to Alice, Lady Hillingdon, wife of the Second Baron Hillingdon

Women were assumed not to experience sexual desires or pleasures. "I would say," observed Dr. William Acton (1814–1875), an influential English physician, in 1857, "that the majority of women (happily for society) are not much troubled with sexual feeling of any kind." Women, thought Acton, were born with a sort of *sexual anesthesia*.

It was widely believed among medical authorities that sex drains the man of his natural vitality. Physicians thus recommended that intercourse be practised infrequently. The Reverend Sylvester Graham (1794–1851) preached that ejaculation deprived men of the "vital fluids" they need to maintain health and vitality. Graham preached against "wasting the seed" by masturbation or frequent marital intercourse. (How frequent was frequent? In Graham's view, intercourse more than once a month could dangerously deplete the man's vital energies.) Graham recommended that young men control their sexual appetites by a diet of simple foods based on whole-grain flours.

It appears, though, that the actual behaviour of Victorians was not as repressed as advertised. Despite the belief in female sexual anesthesia, Victorian women, just like women before and after them, certainly did experience sexual pleasure and orgasm. One piece of evidence was provided by an early sex survey conducted in 1892 by a female physician, Celia Duel Mosher. Although her sample was small and nonrandom, 35 of the 44 women who responded admitted to desiring sexual intercourse. And 34 of them reported experiencing orgasm. Women's diaries of the time also contained accounts of passionate and sexually fulfilling love affairs (Gay, 1984).

Prostitution flourished during the Victorian era. Men apparently thought that they were doing their wives a favour by looking elsewhere.

THE FOUNDATIONS OF THE SCIENTIFIC STUDY OF SEXUALITY It was against this backdrop of sexual repression that scientists and scholars first began to approach sexuality as an area of legitimate scientific study. An important early contributor to the science of human sexuality was the English physician Havelock Ellis (1859–1939). Ellis compiled a veritable encyclopedia of sexuality: a series of volumes published between 1897 and 1910 entitled *Studies in the Psychology of Sex*. Ellis drew information from various sources, including case histories, anthropological findings, and medical knowledge. He challenged the prevailing view by arguing that sexual desires in women were natural and healthful. He promoted the idea that many sexual problems had psychological rather than physical causes. He also promoted acceptance of the view that a gay male or lesbian sexual orientation was a naturally occurring variation within the spectrum of normal sexuality, not an aberration. Presaging some contemporary attitudes, Ellis treated gay male and lesbian sexual orientations as inborn dispositions, not as vices or character flaws.

Another influential **sexologist**, the German psychiatrist Richard von Krafft-Ebing (1840–1902), described more than 200 case histories of individuals with various sexual deviations in his book *Psychopathia Sexualis*. His writings contain vivid descriptions of deviations ranging from sadomasochism (sexual gratification through inflicting or receiving pain) and bestiality (sex with animals) to yet more bizarre and frightening forms, such as necrophilia (intercourse with dead people). Krafft-Ebing viewed sexual deviations as mental diseases that could be studied and perhaps treated by medical science.

At about the same time, a Viennese physician, Sigmund Freud (1856–1939), was developing a theory of personality that has had an enormous influence on modern culture and science. Freud believed that the sex drive was our principal motivating force.

Alfred Kinsey (1894–1956), an Indiana University zoologist, conducted the first large-scale studies of sexual behaviour in the 1930s and 1940s. It was then that sex research became recognized as a field of scientific study in its own right. In 1938 Kinsey had been asked to teach a course on marriage. When researching the course, Kinsey discovered that little was known about sexual practices in American society. He soon embarked on an ambitious research project. Detailed personal interviews with nearly 12 000 people across the United States were conducted. The results of his surveys were published in two volumes, *Sexual Behavior in the Human Male* (1948) and *Sexual Behavior in the Human Female* (1953). These books represent the first scientific attempts to provide a comprehensive picture of sexual behaviour in the United States.

Kinsey's books made for rather dry reading and were filled with statistical tables rather than racy pictures or vignettes. Nevertheless, they became best sellers. They exploded on a public that had not yet learned to discuss sex openly. Their publication—especially that of the book on female sexuality—unleashed the dogs of criticism. Kinsey's work had some methodological flaws, but much of the criticism branded it immoral and obscene. *The New York Times* refused to run advertisements for the 1948 volume on male sexuality. Many newspapers refused to report the results of his survey on female sexuality. A congressional committee in the 1950s went so far as to claim that Kinsey's work undermined the moral fibre of the nation, rendering it more vulnerable to a Communist takeover (Gebhard, 1976).

Kinsey died in 1956. His death may have been hastened by the emotional strain he suffered because of the public's reaction to his work (Gagnon, 1990). Even so, Kinsey and his colleagues made sex research a scientifically respectable field of

Sexologist A person who engages in the scientific study of sexual behaviour.

study. They helped lay the groundwork for greater openness in discussing sexual behaviour.

THE SEXUAL REVOLUTION The period of the mid-1960s to the mid-1970s is often referred to as the *sexual revolution*. Dramatic changes occurred in sexual attitudes and practices during the "Swinging Sixties." When folksinger Bob Dylan sang "the times they are a-changin'," our society was on the threshold of major social upheaval, not only in sexual behaviour, but also in science, politics, fashion, music, art, and cinema. The so-called Woodstock generation, disheartened by commercialism and the Vietnam War, tuned in (to rock music on the radio), turned on (to drugs), and dropped out (of mainstream society). The heat was on between the hippies and the hardhats. Films became sexually explicit. Critics seriously contemplated whether the pornography classic *Deep Throat* had deep social implications. Hard rock music bellowed the message of rebellion and revolution.

No single event marked the onset of the sexual revolution. Social movements often gain momentum from a timely interplay of scientific, social, political, and economic forces. The war (in Vietnam), the bomb (fear of the nuclear bomb), the pill (the introduction of the birth-control pill), and the tube (TV, that is) were four such forces. The pill greatly reduced the risk of unwanted pregnancy for young people. It permitted them to engage in recreational or casual sex, rather than procreative sex (Asbell, 1995). Pop psychology movements, such as the Human Potential Movement of the 1960s and 1970s (the "Me Decade"), spread the message that people should get in touch with and express their genuine feelings, including their sexual feelings. "Do your own thing" became one catchphrase. "If it feels good, do it" became another. The lamp was rubbed. Out popped the sexual genie.

The sexual revolution was tied to social permissiveness and political liberalism. In part reflecting the times, in part acting as catalyst, the media dealt openly with sex. Popular books encouraged people to explore their sexuality. Film scenes of lovemaking became so commonplace that the movie rating system was introduced to alert parents. Protests against the Vietnam War and racial discrimination spilled over into broader protests against conventional morality and hypocrisy. Traditional prohibitions against drugs, casual sex, and even group sex crumbled suddenly.

Two other features of the sexual revolution have become permanent parts of our social fabric: the liberation of female sexuality and a greater willingness to dis-

Today the threat of AIDS hangs over every sexual encounter. Although many young people today are selective in their choice of partners and take precautions to make sex safer, more teenagers are engaging in sexual activity, and are doing so at younger ages, than in previous generations.

Research in Action

THE HISTORY OF DESIRE

Much of the historical analysis of sexual practices over various time periods has focused on the role of religion and cultural traditions. University of Toronto professor Edward Shorter in his book *Written in the Flesh: A History of Desire* (2005) has also analyzed the role of other influences on sexual behaviour. He argues that past constraints suppressed not only the amount of sex that people had but also the variety of sexual behaviours that they experienced.

According to Shorter, features of everyday life such as poor hygiene, inadequate diets, periods of hunger, rampant disease including plagues and sexually transmitted infections, plus lice and scabies infestation put a damper on sexual desire and decreased the sexual attractiveness of one's partners. For most people there was also a lack of privacy, given crowded living conditions with children often sleeping in the same room as parents. Accordingly, sex was often done quickly, in the dark and under the bed covers. Finally, since death in childbirth was common, women's fear made many want to avoid having sex. With religious prohibitions against sex for pleasure added to these constraints, it is not surprising that historically, for most people, sex was not seen as a source of adventure.

cuss sex openly. In 1998, TV networks broadcast during daytime hours U.S. President Bill Clinton's grand jury testimony, which included explicit references to oral sex with White House intern Monica Lewinsky.

What, then, does history tell us about sex? Is there a universal standard for defining sexual values, or are there many standards? All societies have some form of an incest taboo. Most societies have placed a value on procreative sex within the context of an enduring relationship. Other sexual practices—masturbation, promiscuous sex, male–male sexual behaviour, female–female sexual behaviour, prostitution, polygamy, and so on—have been condemned in some societies, tolerated by others, and encouraged by others still.

The Biological Perspective

The biological perspective focuses on the roles of genes, hormones, the nervous system, and other biological factors in human sexuality. Sex, after all, serves the biological function of reproduction. We are biologically endowed with anatomic structures and physiological capabilities that make sexual behaviour possible and, for most people, pleasurable.

Study of the biology of sex acquaints us with the mechanisms of reproduction. It informs us of the physiological mechanisms of sexual arousal and response. By studying the biology of sex, we learn that erection occurs when the penis becomes engorged with blood. We learn that vaginal lubrication is the result of a "sweating" action of the vaginal walls. We learn that orgasm is a spinal reflex as well as a psychological event.

Knowledge of biology has furthered our understanding of sexuality and our ability to overcome sexual problems. To what extent does biology govern sexual behaviour? Is sex controlled by biological instincts? Or are psychosocial factors, such as culture, experience, and decision-making ability, more important? Although the sexuality of other species is largely governed by biological processes, culture and experience play essential roles—and in some cases, the more vital roles—in human sexuality. *Human* sexuality involves a complex interaction of biological and psychosocial factors.

The Evolutionary Perspective

Species vary not only in their physical characteristics but also in their social behaviour, including their mating behaviour. Scientists look to the process of **evolution** to help explain such variability. What is evolution? How might the sexual behaviour of various species, including our own, be influenced by evolutionary forces?

The English naturalist Charles Darwin (1809–1882), the founder of the modern theory of evolution, believed that animal and plant species were not created independently but, rather, evolved from other life forms. The mechanism by which species evolved was **natural selection**, or, in the vernacular, "survival of the fittest."

In each species, some individuals are better adapted to their environment than others. Better-adapted members are more likely to survive to reproduce. Therefore, they are also more likely to transmit their traits to succeeding generations. As the generations pass, a greater proportion of the population of the species comes to carry the traits of the fittest members. Over time, natural selection favours traits that contribute to survival and reproduction. When environmental conditions change, natural selection favours those members of a species who possess traits that help them adapt.

In recent years, some psychologists have suggested that there is a genetic basis to social behaviour, including sexual behaviour, among humans and other animals. This theory, which is called **evolutionary psychology**, proposes that dispositions toward *behaviour patterns* that enhance reproductive success—as well as physical traits that do so—may be genetically transmitted. If so, we may carry behavioural traits that helped our prehistoric ancestors survive and reproduce successfully, even if these traits are no longer adaptive in modern culture. "Modern culture"—dating, say, from classical Greece—is but a moment in the lifetime of our species.

EVOLUTIONARY PERSPECTIVE AND EROTIC PLASTICITY Consider the concept of "erotic plasticity" (Baumeister, 2000), the observation that in response to various social and cultural forces, people show different levels of sex drive and express their sexual desires in a variety of ways. Roy Baumeister (2000) reports evidence that women show greater erotic plasticity than men do. For example, (1) individual women show greater variation than men in sexual behaviour over time, (2) women seem to be more responsive than men to most specific cultural factors, such as cultural permissiveness or restraint, and (3) men's sexual behaviour is more consistent with their sexual attitudes than is that of women. Baumeister concludes that evolutionary, biological forces may be an important factor in the greater female erotic plasticity.

Evolutionary psychologists are interested in sexual behaviour because it is so interwoven with reproductive success. They seek common sexual themes across cultures in the belief that common themes may represent traits that helped our ancestors survive and became part of the human genetic endowment. For example, there is considerable cross-cultural evidence that men are more promiscuous than women and have "spread their seed" widely.

Some evolutionary psychologists argue that men are naturally more promiscuous because they are the genetic heirs of ancestors whose reproductive success was related to the number of women they could impregnate (Bjorklund & Kipp, 1996; Buss, 1994). Women, by contrast, can produce only a few offspring in their lifetimes. Thus, the theory goes, they have to be more selective with respect to their mating partners. Women's reproductive success is enhanced by mating with the fittest males, not with any Tom, Dick, or Harry who happens by. From this perspective, the male's "roving eye" and the female's selectivity are embedded in their genes (Townsend, 1995).

To some evolutionary psychologists, human beings are like marionettes on strings being tugged by invisible puppet masters—their genes. Genes govern the

Evolution The development of a species to its present state, a process that is believed to involve adaptations to its environment.

Natural selection The evolutionary process by which adaptive traits enable members of a species to survive to reproductive age and transmit these traits to future generations.

Evolutionary psychology The theory that dispositions toward behaviour patterns that enhance reproductive success may be genetically transmitted.

biological processes of sexual maturation and the production of sex hormones. Hormones, in turn, are largely responsible for regulating the sexual behaviour of other animal species. Extending evolutionary psychology to human behaviour sparks considerable controversy, however. Critics contend that learning, personal choice, and sociocultural factors may be more important determinants of human behaviour than heredity (Shibley-Hyde & Durik, 2000).

Critics also claim that evolutionary psychology is largely conjectural. No one, for example, has yet discovered genes for promiscuity. There is no direct evidence that either male promiscuity or female selectivity is genetically determined. Critics also point to examples of cultural diversity as evidence that culture and experience, not genetics, play the pivotal role in human behaviour. Nor is cross-cultural similarity in sexual practices necessarily proof of a common genetic factor. Different cultures may adopt similar customs because such customs serve a similar function. For example, marriage exists in some form in every human society. Perhaps marriage serves similar functions in various cultures, such as regulating the availability of sexual partners and furnishing an economic and social arrangement that provides for the care of offspring. All in all, the evidence that human social and sexual behaviours are direct products of our genes is far from clear or compelling.

The Cross-Species Perspective

The study of other animal species places human behaviour in a broader context. A surprising variety of sexual behaviours exist among nonhumans. There are animal examples, or **analogues**, of human male–male sexual behaviour, female–female sexual behaviour, oral–genital contact, and oral–oral behaviour (that is, kissing). Foreplay is also well known in the animal world. Turtles massage their mates' heads with their claws. Male mice nibble at their partners' necks. Most mammals use only a rear-entry position for **copulation**, but some animals, such as apes, use a variety of coital positions.

Cross-species research reveals an interesting pattern. Sexual behaviour among "higher" mammals, such as primates, is less directly controlled by instinct than it is among the "lower" species, such as birds, fish, and lower mammals. Experience and learning play more important roles in sexuality as we travel up the evolutionary ladder.

The Cross-Cultural Perspective

The cross-cultural perspective, like the historical perspective, provides insight into the ways in which cultural beliefs affect sexual behaviour and people's sense of morality. Unlike historians, who are limited in their sources to the eyewitness accounts of others and the shards of information that can be gleaned from fading relics, anthropologists can observe other cultures first-hand. Interest in the cross-cultural perspective on sexuality was spurred by the early twentieth-century work of the anthropologists Margaret Mead (1901–1978) and Bronislaw Malinowski (1884–1942).

In *Sex and Temperament in Three Primitive Societies* (1935), Mead laid the groundwork for recent psychological and sociological research challenging gender-role stereotypes. In most cultures characterized by a gender division of labour, men typically go to business or to the hunt, and—when necessary—to war. In such cultures, men are perceived as strong, active, independent, and logical. Women are viewed as passive, dependent, nurturant, and emotional. Mead concluded that these stereotypes are not inherent in our genetic heritage. Rather, they are acquired through cultural expectations and socialization. That is, men and women learn to behave in ways that are expected of them in their particular culture.

Malinowski lived on the Trobriand island of Boyawa in the South Pacific during World War I. There he gathered data on two societies of the South Pacific, the

Analogue Something that is similar or comparable to something else.

Copulation Sexual intercourse. (From the Latin *copulare*, which means "to unite" or "to couple.")

Trobrianders and the Amphett islanders. The Amphett islanders maintained strict sexual prohibitions, whereas the Trobrianders enjoyed greater freedom. Trobrianders, for example, encouraged their children to masturbate. Boys and girls were expected to begin to engage in intercourse when they were biologically old enough. Adolescents were expected to have multiple sex partners until they married.

Malinowski found the Trobrianders less anxiety-ridden than the Amphett islanders. He attributed the difference to their sexual freedom, thus making an early plea to relax prohibitions in Western societies.

Kissing.
Kissing is a nearly universal way of expressing affection or enhancing sexual arousal in Canada and the United States. But it is unpopular in Japan and unknown in many African and South American cultures.

CROSS-CULTURAL COMMONALITIES AND DIFFERENCES IN SEXUAL BEHAVIOUR In 1951, Clellan Ford, an anthropologist, and Frank Beach, a psychologist, reviewed sexual behaviour in preliterate societies around the world, as well as in other animals. They found great variety in sexual customs and beliefs among the almost 200 societies they studied. They also found some common threads, although there were exceptions to each. Ford and Beach's work is more than half a century old, but it remains a valuable source of information about cross-cultural and cross-species patterns in sexuality (Frayser, 1985).

Ford and Beach reported that kissing was quite common across the cultures they studied, though not universal. The Thonga of Africa were one society that did not practise kissing. Upon witnessing two European visitors kissing each other, members of the tribe commented that they could not understand why Europeans "ate" each other's saliva and dirt. The frequency of sexual intercourse also varies from culture to culture, but intercourse is relatively more frequent among young people everywhere.

Societies differ in their attitudes toward childhood masturbation. Some societies, such as the Hopi Native Americans of the southwest United States, ignore it. Trobrianders encourage children to stimulate themselves. Other societies condemn it.

The cross-cultural perspective illustrates the importance of learning in human sexual behaviour. Societies differ widely in their sexual attitudes, customs, and practices. The members of all human societies share the same anatomic structures and physiological capacities for sexual pleasure, however. The same hormones flow through their arteries. Yet their sexual practices, and the pleasure they reap or fail to attain, may set them apart. Were human sexuality completely or predominantly determined by biology, we would not find such diversity.

Psychological Perspectives

Psychological perspectives focus on the many psychological influences—perception, learning, motivation, emotion, personality, and so on—that affect our sexual behaviour and our experience of ourselves as female or male. Some psychological theorists, such as Sigmund Freud, focus on the motivational role of sex in human personality. Others focus on how our experiences and mental representations of the world affect our sexual behaviour.

SIGMUND FREUD AND PSYCHOANALYTIC THEORY Sigmund Freud, a Viennese physician, formulated a grand theory of personality termed **psychoanalysis**. Freud believed that we are all born with biologically based sex drives. These drives must be channelled through socially approved outlets if family and social life are to carry on without undue conflict. Freud proposed that the mind operates on conscious and unconscious levels. The conscious level corresponds to

Psychoanalysis The theory of personality originated by Sigmund Freud, which proposes that human behaviour represents the outcome of clashing inner forces.

Acquisition of Gender Roles.
According to social-learning theory, children learn gender roles that are considered appropriate in their society via the reinforcement of certain behaviour patterns and by observing the gender-role behaviours of their parents, peers, and other role models in media such as TV, films, and books.

Unconscious mind Those parts or contents of the mind that lie outside of conscious awareness.

Defence mechanisms In psychoanalytic theory, automatic processes that protect the ego from anxiety by disguising or ejecting unacceptable ideas and urges.

Repression The automatic ejection of anxiety-evoking ideas from consciousness.

Erogenous zones Parts of the body, including but not limited to the sex organs, that are responsive to sexual stimulation.

Psychosexual development In psychoanalytic theory, the process by which sexual feelings shift from one erogenous zone to another.

Fixation In psychoanalytic theory, arrested development, which includes attachment to traits and sexual preferences that are characteristic of an earlier stage of psychosexual development.

Oedipus complex In psychoanalytic theory, a conflict of the phallic stage in which the boy wishes to possess his mother sexually and perceives his father as a rival in love. (The analogous conflict for girls is the *Electra complex*.)

our state of present awareness. The **unconscious mind** consists of the darker reaches of the mind that lie outside our direct awareness. The ego shields the conscious mind from awareness of our baser sexual and aggressive urges via **defence mechanisms** such as **repression**, the motivated forgetting of traumatic experiences.

Freud introduced us to new and controversial ideas about ourselves as sexual beings. For example, he originated the concept of **erogenous zones**—the idea that many parts of the body, not just the genitals, are responsive to sexual stimulation.

One of Freud's most controversial beliefs was that children normally harbour erotic interests. He believed that the suckling of the infant in the oral stage was an erotic act. So too was anal bodily experimentation, through which children learn to experience pleasure in the control of their sphincter muscles and the processes of elimination. He theorized that it was normal for children to progress through stages of development in which the erotic interest shifts from one erogenous zone to another, as, for example, from the mouth or oral cavity to the anal cavity. According to his theory of **psychosexual development**, children undergo five stages of development: oral, anal, phallic, latency, and genital, which are named according to the predominant erogenous zones of each stage. Each stage gives rise to certain kinds of conflicts. Moreover, inadequate or excessive gratification in any stage can lead to **fixation** in that stage and to the development of traits and sexual preferences characteristic of that stage.

Freud believed that it was normal for children to develop erotic feelings toward the parent of the other gender during the phallic stage. These incestuous urges lead to conflict with the parent of the same gender. In later chapters we shall see that these developments, which Freud termed the **Oedipus complex**, have profound implications for the assumption of gender roles and sexual orientation.

LEARNING THEORIES To what extent does sexual behaviour reflect experience? Would you hold the same sexual attitudes and do the same things if you had been reared in another culture? We think not. Even within the same society, family and personal experiences can shape unique sexual attitudes and behaviours. Whereas psychoanalytic theory plumbs the depths of the unconscious, learning theorists focus on environmental factors that shape behaviour.

Behaviourists such as John B. Watson (1878–1958) and B. F. Skinner (1904–1990) emphasized the importance of rewards and punishments in the learning process. In psychology, events (such as rewards) that increase the frequency or likelihood of behaviour are termed reinforcements. Children left to explore their bodies without parental condemnation will learn what feels good and tend to repeat it. The Trobriand child who is rewarded for masturbation and premarital coitus through parental praise and encouragement will be more likely to repeat these behaviours (at least openly!) than the child in a more sexually restrictive culture, who is punished for the same behaviour. When sexual behaviour (such as masturbation) feels good but parents connect it with feelings of guilt and shame, the child is placed in conflict and may vacillate between masturbating and swearing it off.

If we as young children are severely punished for sexual exploration, we may come to associate sexual stimulation *in general* with feelings of guilt or anxiety. Such early learning experiences can set the stage for sexual dysfunctions in adulthood.

Social-learning theorists also use the concepts of reward and punishment, but they emphasize the importance of cognitive activity (anticipations, thoughts, plans, and so on) and of learning by observation. Observational learning, or **modelling**, refers to acquiring knowledge and skills by observing others. Observational learning involves more than direct observation of other people. It includes seeing models in films or on television, hearing about them, and reading about them. According to social-learning theory, children acquire the gender roles that are deemed appropriate in a society through reinforcement of gender-appropriate behaviour and by observing the gender-role behaviour of their parents, their peers, and other models on television, in films, and in books.

Psychological theories shed light on the ways in which sexuality is influenced by rewards, punishments, and mental processes such as fantasy, thoughts, attitudes, and expectations. Sigmund Freud helped bring sexuality within the province of scientific investigation. He also helped make it possible for people to recognize and talk about the importance of sexuality in their lives. Critics contend, however, that he may have placed too much emphasis on sexual motivation in determining behaviour and on the role of unconscious processes.

Sociocultural Perspectives

Sexual behaviour is determined not only by biological and psychological factors, but also by social factors. Social factors contribute to the shaping of our sexual attitudes, beliefs, and behaviour. Whereas anthropologists contribute to our understanding of cross-cultural variance in sexuality, sociocultural theorists focus on differences in sexuality among the subgroups of a society, as defined, for example, by differences in religion, race/ethnicity, country of origin, socioeconomic status, marital status, age, educational level, and gender.

SOCIOCULTURAL FACTORS RELATED TO SEXUAL ATTITUDES AND BEHAVIOURS While some national surveys of sexual attitudes and behaviours have been conducted in Canada (see Chapter 2), they have been limited in scope. *Maclean's* magazine, however, has sponsored annual surveys of Canadians about a number of social issues, including sexual attitudes and behaviours. Consider the issue of how frequently people have sex. Figure 1.1 shows the results of a national survey concerning the frequency of sex per month as reported by Canadians in each of the provinces (*Maclean's*/CTV Poll, 1993). The highest frequency for sexual

Behaviourists Learning theorists who argue that a scientific approach to understanding behaviour must refer only to observable and measurable behaviours and who emphasize the importance of rewards and punishments in the learning process.

Social-learning theory A cognitively oriented learning theory in which observational learning, values, and expectations play key roles in determining behaviour.

Modelling Acquiring knowledge and skills by observing others.

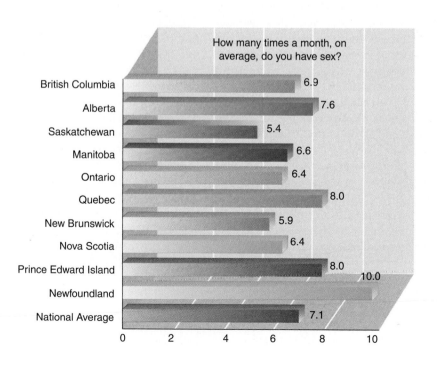

Figure 1.1 Monthly Frequency of Sex for Canadian Adults, by Province.

There are considerable differences in sexual attitudes and behaviours across Canada.

Source: Courtesy of CTV News.

How many times a month, on average, do you have sex?

Province	Times per month
British Columbia	6.9
Alberta	7.6
Saskatchewan	5.4
Manitoba	6.6
Ontario	6.4
Quebec	8.0
New Brunswick	5.9
Nova Scotia	6.4
Prince Edward Island	8.0
Newfoundland	10.0
National Average	7.1

A World of Diversity

CANADIAN ATTITUDES TOWARD WOMEN GOING TOPLESS

In many European countries and Australia, it is commonplace for women to go topless at public beaches. In Canada, however, this has not been the case. In fact, until a few years ago, it was illegal for women to go topless. In 1991, University of Guelph student Gwen Jacobs caused a sensation when, on a hot summer day in downtown Guelph, she removed her shirt, exposing her breasts. She was arrested by the police and convicted of committing an indecent act in a public place. Jacobs brought her case to the Ontario Court of Appeal, arguing that because men had the right to go topless she had a constitutional right to go topless as well. In 1996 the Ontario Court of Appeal overturned the conviction, stating that her act was not degrading or dehumanizing and carried no sexual connotation.

This ruling brought out the central issue in the debate over toplessness: Is it a sexual act or not? In a study of university students in Australia, Herold, Corbesi, and Collins (1994) found that women who had gone topless at the beach believed that this was a "natural" act and not sexual when done at the beach. Conversely, women who had never gone topless argued that it was indeed sexual and a type of exhibitionism. How do you feel about this issue? Do you think a woman going topless on a beach is sexual or not?

Despite the court ruling, few women in Canada are willing to go topless in public, even at the beach. The perception that others would disapprove is an obvious deterrent. And

when a woman does go topless, it can cause a sensation. A Canadian woman was recently reported to the police because she was standing topless in a soccer field next to a major country road outside of Guelph, Ontario. The complainant was concerned that she was distracting motorists, thereby creating a traffic hazard.

Table 1.2 shows the differing responses of major demographic groupings in Canada to the issue of whether it should be legal for women to go topless on public beaches.

Consider gender. Males, according to the survey, are more likely than females to think that it is okay for women to go topless on public beaches. Throughout the text, we will be focusing on gender differences and on why men seem generally more likely than women to have permissive sexual attitudes and behaviours. Why do you think women are less accepting than men of toplessness?

More than half of those under the age of 50 accept topless behaviour at the beach while fewer than half of those over 50 do. Older respondents entered adulthood prior to the sexual revolution and were thus generally exposed to more conservative sexual attitudes. We shall find this sort of age difference, or age gradient, throughout the text as well.

The average age of Canadians has almost doubled over the last century, from 22.7 in 1901 to 37.6 in 2001. The fastest-growing age group are those 80 and over; from 1991 to 2001 their numbers increased by 41% (Statistics Canada, 2002). And as the number of older Canadians increases in the coming years, they can be expected to wield more influence over policy issues.

Level of education is also connected with sexuality. Generally speaking, education appears to provide a liberalizing influence. Therefore, it is not surprising that people who have completed university are likely to have more liberal attitudes toward issues such as going topless, as shown in Table 1.2. This text will present other examples where educational differences have an even more substantial effect.

If education is a liberating influence on sexuality, conservative religious values would appear to be a restraining factor. In sexuality research, one of the strongest predictors of conservative sexual values is attendance at religious services. About one-fifth of Canadians attend church or other religious services on a weekly basis, although older adults are more likely to attend church on a regular basis. Table 1.2 shows that only one-third of Canadians who attend religious services once a week or more approve of topless beaches, while more than half of those who attend less than once a week approve.

When asked for the basis of their moral views, less than one-fifth of Canadians specifically mentioned religion (17% of adults and 16% of teenagers). Rather than using religion as a basis for their moral values, most Canadians believe that morals are a relative issue and based on one's personal opinion (Bibby, 2001). For example, among Canadian Roman Catholics, 91% approve of birth control methods such as condoms and 82% are accepting of sex before marriage (Barrett et al., 2004).

There are many regional differences in sexual attitudes and behaviours. Table 1.2 reveals that people in British

Columbia and Quebec are the most approving of toplessness at the beach, while those in the Atlantic provinces and the Prairies are the least approving. Other studies have shown that French Canadians in Quebec have more liberal sexual attitudes and behaviours than do people in the rest of Canada (Barrett et al., 2004). For example, they are more likely to have sexual intercourse at younger ages and more likely to live in common-law relationships. They are also more likely to admit to having extramarital sex (*Maclean's*/CTV Poll, 1994). These differences are all the more remarkable given that, until the 1960s, the dominance of the Catholic Church in Quebec meant that French

Gwen Jacobs.
Gwen Jacobs (on the left) successfully challenged the legal prohibition against women going topless in Canada.

people in that province were among the most conservative in Canada. However, along with the rise of the political separatism movement in the 1960s, the French in Quebec increasingly challenged Church teachings. Prior to the 1960s Quebec had the highest rate of church attendance in Canada but today it has the lowest, with only about 7% attending church every week (Statistics Canada, 2002). As a result of this trend toward secularization, the Catholic Church now has far less influence over the sexual decision-making of most people in Quebec. The influence of religion has also declined in English Canada, but less dramatically (Barrett et al., 2004).

TABLE 1.2
Sociocultural Influences on Attitude to Toplessness on Public Beaches

Percentage of Canadians Who Think It Should Be Legal for Women to Go Topless on Beaches

Gender			College/technical school	53
Male	63		Some university/college	54
Female	43		High school graduate	45
			Some high school	43
Age			Elementary school	56
20s	55			
30s	54		**Attendance at Religious Services**	
40s	58		Once a week or more	32
50s	45		Less than once a week	57
60+	39			
			Region	
Marital Status			Atlantic	44
Single	57		Quebec	56
Married/cohabiting	49		Ontario	54
			Prairies	44
Education			British Columbia	61
Post-graduate	58			
University graduate	65			

Source: Compas (1998). Modern life survey of the Canadian adult population.

A World of Diversity

THE MEDIA AND SEXUALITY

The media can play a powerful role in influencing sexual attitudes. In recent years, Canadian news and documentary programming have become far more explicit in their presentation of sexual issues. These informative programs typically discuss sexual topics in formats that are both serious and entertaining. For example, the Discovery Channel series *The Sex Files* has been bold in openly dealing with topics, such as masturbation and anal sex, that have been traditionally avoided by the mainstream media. With an audience numbering in the millions, *The Sex Files* is by far the most watched series ever produced by

the Discovery Channel. The series is also shown on the Life Channel, where it has been adapted as *Sexual Secrets*.

One of the most popular shows on the Women's Television Network has been the *Sunday Night Sex Show* hosted by Sue Johanson, who provides frank advice in response to questions from callers. Toronto's CityTV produces *Sextv*, which uses a news-magazine format to present a diverse range of sexuality topics, including erotic art and photography. This series formed the basis for the Sextv digital cable channel, which is focused exclusively on sex. Numerous Canadian documentaries have been produced on such topics as domination and submission (which included scenes of people being tied up

and whipped). Another sexually oriented series is *Sex, Toys and Chocolate* with hosts Robin Milhausen and Michael Cho. This show involves guests discussing personal sexual preference in intimate detail. There is also the series *Kink*, which shows Canadians engaging in varied bondage and sadomasochistic sexual behaviours.

Many comedy and drama series have also presented sexual themes, including the U.S. series *Sex and the City* and *The Sopranos*. And in recent years, the pay-per-view adult videos shown late at night have been moneymakers for the cable industry. Viewer ratings clearly indicate that many Canadians enjoy watching shows that present sexual topics in an open manner.

activity was in Newfoundland, followed by Quebec and P.E.I. The lowest frequency was in Saskatchewan.

For 12 of the 13 years that the poll has been conducted, Newfoundland has shown the highest frequency of sexual activity. Unfortunately, researchers have not probed deeper to determine why people in Newfoundland consistently have the highest levels of sexual activity. Can you think of possible reasons?

One of the most comprehensive surveys of relationships and sexuality in Canada was conducted in 1998 by the Compas polling organization on behalf of the Sun newspaper group. The lead Canadian author of this text was a consultant for that survey and suggested several of the questions that were used. The methodology for this study is described in Chapter 2. Additional sociocultural analyses of this study are presented in several chapters throughout this text, including the feature box on Canadian Attitudes Toward Women Going Topless.

The sociocultural perspective informs us of the relationship between sexuality and one's social group within a society. Sociocultural theorists view sexual behaviour as occurring within a particular sociocultural system. They study the ways in which the values, beliefs, and norms of a group influence the sexual behaviour of its members. To a certain extent, we share attitudes and behaviour patterns with people

The number of gay men and lesbians presented on television has increased significantly. The popular *Will & Grace* features two gay men in principal roles. *Queer as Folk*, another groundbreaking series, features the lives of five gay men and two lesbians. The shows contain a lot of nudity and sexual scenes, including oral sex and group sex. Interestingly, one study found that about half the viewers were heterosexual women, many of whom admitted they were attracted by the male nudity (Bawden, 2002). *The L-Word* is situated in the lesbian community of West Hollywood, and explores relationship and sexual issues among lesbians. This show is highly popular among lesbians in Canada. There is even a Canadian cable channel (formerly Pride Vision, now OUTv) centred on gay and lesbian themes.

The media have been instrumental in bringing topics into the open that only a few years ago would have been considered too controversial. We have come a long way since the 1960s, when one of the most popular radio personalities in Toronto, Larry Solway, was fired because he read over the airwaves some explicit passages from one of the best-selling sex manuals at the time. Today, attempts to push the boundaries of public acceptability include, for example, the promotion of intimate disclosure. A reporter who auditioned with about a thousand other Canadians for the American show *Blind Date* was instructed to be as detailed as possible: "We're not supposed to say, for example, we like sex. We're supposed to say we like it three times a day, especially in the morning, on the kitchen counter" (Eckler, 2000). The Canadian Broadcast Standards Council chastised a radio station in Toronto for broadcasting material that was too sexually explicit during its morning show because children could be listening at that time. In addition to discussing fellatio, the radio station was cited for "explicitly describing the sex lives of the hosts and various celebrities" (Quill, 2002, p. D3). Probably the best explanation for these trends is that the media are following the old adage "Sex sells."

from similar backgrounds—for example, people with the same ethnic identity. Even so, not all members of a given ethnic group act or think alike.

Multiple Perspectives on Human Sexuality

Given the complexity and range of human sexual behaviour, we need to consider multiple perspectives to understand sexuality. Each perspective—historical, biological, cross-species, cross-cultural, psychological, and sociocultural—has something to offer in this enterprise. Let us venture a few conclusions based on our overview of these perspectives. First, human sexuality appears to reflect a combination of biological, social, cultural, sociocultural, and psychological factors that interact in complex ways, perhaps in combinations that are unique for each individual. Second, there are few universal patterns of sexual behaviour, and views on what is right and wrong show great diversity. Third, although our own cultural values and beliefs may be deeply meaningful to us, they may not indicate what is normal, natural, or moral in terms of sexual behaviour. The complexity of human sexuality—complexity that causes it to remain somewhat baffling to scientists—adds to the wonder and richness of our sexual experience.

Summing Up

What Is Human Sexuality?

The term *human sexuality* refers to matters of gender, sexual behaviour, sexual feelings, and the biology of sex. Human sexuality comprises all the ways in which we experience and express ourselves as sexual beings.

The Study of Human Sexuality

The study of human sexuality draws on the expertise of anthropologists, biologists, medical researchers, sociologists, psychologists, and other scientists.

Sexuality and Values

Our pluralistic society embraces a wide range of sexual attitudes and values.

Thinking Critically About Human Sexuality

The text encourages critical thinking to help students evaluate claims, arguments, and widely held beliefs. Critical thinking encourages the thoughtful analysis and probing of arguments, willingness to challenge conventional wisdom and common knowledge, and keeping an open mind.

Principles of Critical Thinking

The text enumerates several features of critical thinking. These include being skeptical, examining definitions of terms, examining the assumptions or premises of arguments, being cautious in drawing conclusions from evidence, considering alternative interpretations of evidence, and avoiding oversimplification and overgeneralization.

Perspectives on Human Sexuality

Human sexuality is a complex field, and no single theory or perspective can capture all its nuances. The text offers diverse perspectives on sexuality:

The Historical Perspective

History places our sexual behaviour in the context of time. History shows little evidence of universal sexual trends. There is evidence of prehistoric worship of generative power in women and men. Jews and Christians have emphasized the role of sex as a means of propagation and have generally restricted sex to the context of family life. The ancient Greeks and Romans lived in male-oriented societies that viewed women as chattel. Some Eastern civilizations have equated sexual pleasure with religious experience and have developed sex manu-

als. Repressive Victorian sexual attitudes gave way to the sexual revolution of the 1960s and 1970s in the West.

The Biological Perspective

The biological perspective focuses on the role of biological processes, such as genetic, hormonal, vascular, and neural factors, in explaining human sexual behaviour. Knowledge of biology helps us understand how our bodies respond to sexual stimulation and enhances aspects of our sexual health.

The Evolutionary Perspective

Darwin's theory of evolution proposes that organisms tend to inherit those traits that enabled their ancestors to reach the age of sexual maturity and reproduce. Evolutionary psychology proposes that dispositions toward behaviour patterns that enhance reproductive success—as well as physical traits that do so—may be genetically transmitted.

The Cross-Species Perspective

The study of other animal species reveals a surprising variety of sexual behaviours among nonhumans. There are, for example, animal analogues of male–male sexual behaviour, female–female sexual behaviour, oral sex, and foreplay. Still, we must be cautious in generalizing from lower animals to humans. We find that experience and learning play more important roles in sexuality as we travel up the evolutionary ladder.

The Cross-Cultural Perspective

This perspective, like the historical perspective, provides insight into the ways in which cultural beliefs affect sexual behaviour and people's sense of morality. Anthropologists observe other cultures first-hand when possible. Cross-cultural evidence challenges the notion of the universality of gender-role stereotypes. All cultures apparently place some limits on sexual freedom (and nearly all cultures place some prohibitions on incestuous relationships), but some cultures are more sexually permissive than others.

Psychological Perspectives

Psychological perspectives focus on the psychological factors of perception, learning, motivation, emotion, personality, and so on that affect gender and sexual behaviour in the individual. Sigmund Freud formulated the theory of psychoanalysis, which proposes that biologically based sex drives come into conflict with social codes. Erogenous zones shift through the process of psychosexual development, and defence mechanisms banish threatening ideas and impulses from conscious awareness. Learning theorists focus on the roles of rewards, punishments, and modelling in sexual behaviour.

Sociocultural Perspectives

Sociocultural theorists focus on differences in sexuality among the groups within a society, as defined, for example, by differences in religion, race, country of origin, socioeconomic status, age, educational level, and gender.

Multiple Perspectives on Human Sexuality

Given the complexity and range of human sexual behaviour, we need to consider multiple perspectives to understand human sexuality.

Test Yourself

Multiple-Choice Questions

1. Most Canadian university students would say that they are "having sex" when the behaviour is
   a. oral–genital contact
   b. penile–vaginal contact
   c. manual stimulation of the genitals
   d. deep kissing

2. Attention has been focused on the need for sex education today primarily because of
   a. Canada-wide standards for sexuality education
   b. the world-wide AIDS epidemic
   c. increased interest in research
   d. increases in the incidence of sexual dysfunctions

3. Thinking critically about human sexuality is important because it helps us to
   a. overcome skepticism
   b. get in touch with our feelings
   c. challenge conventional wisdom
   d. accept "expert" opinions

4. The sexual revolution resulted from
   a. the death of Queen Victoria
   b. tabloids' sensationalizing celebrity lifestyles
   c. laws legalizing same-sex marriages
   d. many economic, social, and political factors

5. Evolutionary psychology suggests that
   a. behaviour patterns that favour reproduction are genetically transmitted
   b. men and women are equally promiscuous
   c. biology has nothing to do with sexuality
   d. women are more promiscuous than men

6. During the Victorian era, physician William Acton wrote that women
   a. experienced little or no pleasure from sex
   b. used their sexuality to control men
   c. were lustful and oversexed
   d. should not indulge in sexual activity for any reason

7. Punishing a child for masturbating, according to a behaviourist,
   a. always results in sexual dysfunction
   b. results in repression
   c. may disrupt psychosexual development
   d. will not always eliminate the behaviour

8. Ford and Beach's research on preliterate societies found
   a. a wide variety of sexual customs and beliefs
   b. that intercourse was more common among older people
   c. that childhood masturbation was universally condemned
   d. kissing in all societies studied

9. Margaret Mead's research laid the groundwork for more recent studies in
   a. sociobiological research into anthropological theory
   b. research challenging gender-role stereotypes
   c. anthropological research on extramarital sex
   d. research on cross-cultural problems in infertility

10. Historically, _____ was most likely the first sexual taboo.
    a. incest
    b. sex before marriage
    c. male homosexuality
    d. masturbation

Answers to the Test Yourself questions in each chapter are found on page 527.

Critical Thinking Questions

1. What are your goals for this course in human sexuality? Do you think that what you learn in this course will help you later on in life? Why or why not?

2. Religions have historically been major factors influencing human sexual behaviour. Do you think this is still true in Canada today? Why or why not?

3. A friend of yours insists that something is true because she found it on the Internet. As a critical thinker, do you accept your friend's argument as proof? If not, what would you do to determine the truth or falsity of your friend's claim?

Visit our Companion Website at www.pearsoned.ca/rathus, where you can use the interactive Study Guide and link to additional resources on topics discussed in this text.

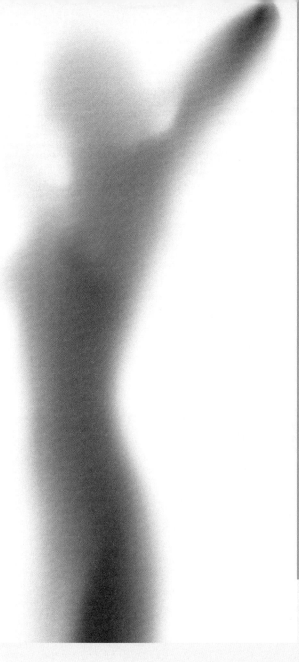

Chapter 2
Research Methods

Empirical Derived from or based on observation and experimentation.

Abstracts from the *Journal of Sex Research* Excellent reference source that includes abstracts from research published in the *Journal of Sex Research*.

www.sexuality.org/l/s ex/jsexrall.html

Have you ever wondered about questions such as these: Are my sexual interests and behaviour patterns unique or shared by many others? Does alcohol stimulate or dampen sexual response? Why do people engage in male–male or female–female sexual behaviour? How do people contract AIDS? Does pornography cause rape?

You may have thought of such questions. You may even have expressed opinions on them. But scientists insist that opinions about behaviour, including sexual behaviour, be supported by evidence. Evidence, in turn, must be based on careful observations in the laboratory or in the field.

A Scientific Approach to Human Sexuality

Scientists and researchers who study human sexuality take an **empirical** approach. That is, they base their knowledge on research evidence, rather than on intuition, faith, or superstition. Scientists' and other people's intuitions or religious beliefs may suggest topics to be studied scientifically, but once the topics are selected, answers are sought on the basis of the scientific method.

Research in Action

THE CANADIAN RESEARCH SCENE

Relatively few Canadian researchers focus exclusively on sexological research, and few Canadian universities have more than one or two sexologists. The Canadian Sex Research Forum (CSRF), the main organization that focuses on sexuality research, holds annual meetings at which Canadian researchers discuss findings from their most recent studies. The proceedings of these meetings are published in *The Canadian Journal of Sexuality*. In Quebec, the main organization for sexologists is l'Association des sexologues du Québec and the primary sexuality journal, published mainly in French, is *Revue Sexologique/Sexological Review*.

Canadian researchers also publish their findings in highly rated international journals such as *The Journal of Sex Research* and *Archives of Sexual Behavior*. They also discuss their studies at international conferences, such as the annual meetings held by the Society for the Scientific Study of Sexuality and the International Academy of Sex Research.

In July 2005, many Canadian researchers gave presentations at the 17th World Congress of Sexology, held in Montreal. Congress meetings are held every two years in a different country under the auspices of the World Association for Sexology (WAS). Researchers from every part of the globe attend these world conferences, with the official conference language being English. The Montreal conference was chaired by Montreal researcher and therapist Dr. Pierre Assalian.

At the Montreal conference, Eleanor Maticka-Tyndale and Catherine Brooke (2005) from the University of Windsor presented an analysis of Canadian sexuality research. They concluded that 85% of the research is focused on three areas—HIV/AIDS, adolescent sexuality, and sexual dysfunctions—with most research funding allocated to HIV/AIDS. Another 10% of Canadian research is on sexual violence and coercion, with the remaining 5% on either sex work or sexual relationships.

To date, only limited funding has been available for sexuality research in Canada. Two key sources of funding are the Social Sciences and Humanities Research Council and the Canadian Institutes of Health Research.

Funding for sexuality research in Canada has been based on societal concern with sexual health issues. In the 1970s, for example, concern over adolescent pregnancy led to federal funding of a number of projects. Since the 1980s the government has funded several projects on sexuality and HIV prevention, although most of the funding has been for studies dealing with the medical aspects of HIV/AIDS. Specific groups of Canadians who had been neglected in the past are now being studied, including gay males, First Nations people, drug users, and street youth. Researchers have also begun studying sexual topics that had been considered taboo, such as oral and anal sex. In this chapter's research feature, we discuss Canadian surveys concerning First Nations people, gay and bisexual men, and sex workers.

Given the disproportionate focus on only a few content areas, it is not surprising that for many topics we have little or no Canadian data. An example of this is the use of sex toys. Despite the large increase in the number of sex stores and Internet sites selling sex toys, we do not know how many Canadians use them or how often.

Only one Canadian university research chair in sexuality has been funded. Eleanor Maticka-Tyndale holds a Canada Research Chair in Social Justice and Sexual Health at the University of Windsor.

There are also limited opportunities at the graduate level in Canadian universities for students who want to specialize in the sexuality area. This will be discussed in more detail in the last chapter.

The Scientific Method

Critical thinking and the scientific approach share the hallmark of skepticism. As skeptics, scientists question prevailing assumptions and theories about sexual behaviour. They are willing to dispute the assertions of authority figures such as political and religious leaders—and even other scientists. Scientists also recognize that they cannot gain perfect knowledge. One era's "truths" may become another era's ancient myths and fallacies. Scientists are involved in the continuous quest for truth, but they do not see themselves as experiencing revelations or defining final truths.

The *scientific method* is a systematic way of gathering scientific evidence and testing assumptions through research. It has a number of elements:

1. *Formulating a research question.* Does alcohol inspire or impair sexual response? Scientists formulate research questions on the basis of their observations of, or theories about, events or behaviour. They then seek answers to such questions by conducting empirical research.

2. *Framing the research question in the form of a hypothesis.* Experiments are usually undertaken with a **hypothesis** in mind—a precise prediction about behaviour that is often derived from theory. A hypothesis is tested through research. For instance, a scientist might theorize that alcohol enhances sexual responsiveness either by directly stimulating sexual response or by reducing feelings of guilt associated with sex. He or she might then hypothesize that an intervention (called, in experimental terms, a treatment), such as drinking alcohol in a laboratory setting, will lead to heightened sexual arousal in the presence of erotic stimuli (such as sexually explicit films).

3. *Testing the hypothesis.* Scientists then test hypotheses through carefully controlled observation and experimentation. A specific hypothesis about alcohol and sexual arousal—that alcohol either increases or decreases sexual responsiveness—might be tested by administering a certain amount of alcohol to one group of people and then comparing their level of sexual arousal following specific types of sexual stimulation (such as exposure to sexually explicit films) to the level of sexual arousal of another group of people who were shown the films but not given any alcohol.

4. *Drawing conclusions.* Scientists then draw conclusions or inferences about the correctness of their hypotheses on the basis of their analyses of the results of their studies. If the results of well-designed research studies fail to bear out certain hypotheses, scientists can revise the theories that served as the frameworks for the hypotheses. Research findings often lead scientists to modify their theories and, in turn, generate new hypotheses that can be tested in further research.

Hypothesis A precise prediction about behaviour that is often derived from theory and is tested through research.

Variables Quantities or qualities that vary or may vary.

Demographic Concerning the vital statistics (density, race, age, etc.) of human populations.

Vasocongestion Congestion resulting from the flow of blood. (From the Latin *vas*, which means "vessel.")

Penile strain gauge A device for measuring sexual arousal in men in terms of changes in the circumference of the penis.

Vaginal photoplethysmograph A tampon-shaped probe that is inserted in the vagina and suggests the level of vasocongestion by measuring the light reflected from the vaginal walls.

GOALS AND METHODS OF THE SCIENCE OF HUMAN SEXUALITY The goals of the science of human sexuality are congruent with those of other sciences: to describe, explain, predict, and control the events (in this case, the sexual behaviours) of interest. Let us discuss some of the general goals of science and how they relate to the study of human sexuality as a science.

Description is a basic objective of science. To understand sexual behaviour, for example, we must first be able to describe it. Therefore, the description of behaviour precedes understanding. Scientists attempt to be clear, unbiased, and precise in their descriptions of events and behaviour. The scientific approach to human sexuality describes sexual behaviour through techniques as varied as the field study, the survey, the individual case study, and the laboratory experiment.

Researchers attempt to relate their observations to other factors, or **variables**, that can help explain them. For example, researchers may attempt to explain variations in the frequency of coitus by relating—or *correlating*—coitus with **demographic** variables such as age, religious or social background, and cultural expectations. The variables that are commonly used to explain sexual behaviour include biological (age, health), psychological (anxieties, skills), and sociological (educational level, socioeconomic status, ethnicity) variables.

Theories provide frameworks within which scientists can explain what they observe and can make predictions. It is not sufficient for theories to help us make sense of events that have already occurred. Theories must also enable us to make predictions. Sex researchers study factors that may predict various types of sexual behaviour. Some researchers, for example, have examined childhood interests and behaviour patterns that may predict the development of a gay male or lesbian sexual orientation. Others have explored factors, such as the age at which dating begins

Research in Action

PHYSIOLOGICAL MEASURES OF SEXUAL AROUSAL

Scientific studies depend on the ability to measure the phenomenon of interest. The phenomena of sexual arousal may be measured by different means, such as self-report and physiological measures. Self-report measures of sexual arousal are considered *subjective*. They ask people to give their impressions of the level of their sexual arousal at a given time, such as by circling their response on a 10-point scale that ranges from zero, "not at all aroused," to 10, "extremely aroused." Physiological devices measure the degree of vasocongestion that builds up in the genitals during sexual arousal. (**Vasocongestion**—that is, congestion with blood—leads to erection in men and to vaginal lubrication in women.) In men, vasocongestion is frequently measured by a **penile strain gauge**. This device is worn under the man's clothing. It is fitted around the penis and measures his erectile response by recording changes in the circumference of the penis. The device is sensitive to small changes in circumference that may

not be noticed (and thus will not be reported) by the man.

Physiological measurement of sexual arousal in women is most often accomplished by means of a **vaginal photoplethysmograph**—is a tampon-shaped probe with a light and a photocell in its tip. It is inserted in the vagina and indicates the level of blood congestion by measuring the amount of light reflected from the vaginal walls. The more light that is absorbed by the vaginal walls, the less that is reflected. Less reflected light indicates greater vasocongestion.

Sex researchers sometimes measure sexual arousal in response to stimuli such as erotic films or audiotaped dramatizations of erotic scenes. What happens when physiological devices give a different impression of sexual arousal than those offered by self-report? Objectively (physiologically) measured sexual arousal does not always agree with subjective feelings of sexual arousal, as measured by self-report. For example, a person may say that he or she is relatively unaroused at a time when the physiological measures suggest otherwise. Which is the *truer* measure of arousal, the person's subjective report or the level shown on the objective instruments?

Discrepancies across measures suggest that people may be sexually aroused (as measured by physiological indicators) but psychologically unprepared to recognize it or unwilling to admit it. In the real world of human relationships, sexual arousal has psychological as well as physiological aspects. The reflexes of erection and vaginal lubrication do not necessarily translate into "Yes."

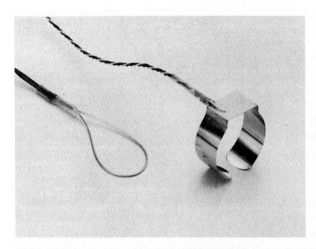 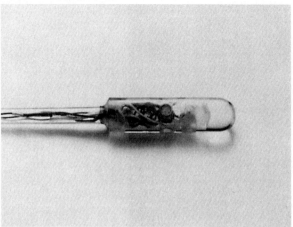

The Penile Strain Gauge and Vaginal Photoplethysmograph.
These devices measure vasocongestion in the genitals of men and women, providing an objective measure of the subjects' level of arousal. Can you think of other aspects of sexual arousal?

and the quality of the relationships between teens and their parents, that may predict the likelihood of sexual intercourse during adolescence.

The science of human sexuality does not tell people how they *ought* to behave. It does not attempt to limit or expand the variety of their sexual activities. Rather, it furnishes information that people may use to help themselves or others make decisions about their own behaviour. For instance, the science of human sexuality provides information that increases the chances that a couple who are having difficulty becoming pregnant will be able to conceive. At the same time, it develops and evaluates means of birth control that can be used to help couples regulate their reproductive choices. The science of human sexuality also seeks to develop techniques that can help people overcome sexual dysfunctions and enhance the gratification they find in sexual relations. "Control" also takes the form of enabling couples to give and receive more sexual pleasure, enhancing fetal health, and preventing and curing sexually transmitted infections.

Operational Definitions

How do we study concepts such as sexual satisfaction or the even broader concept of marital satisfaction? One of the requirements in sex research, as in other types of research, is specifying the definitions of the concepts, or "constructs," of interest. Different investigators may define these concepts in different ways.

What, for example, is sexual arousal? Many studies seek to assess the effects of various stimuli on sexual arousal, but sexual arousal can mean several things. It can mean a subjective feeling. It may refer to direct physiological measures (see the nearby Research in Action box). The **operational definition** of a construct links its meaning to the methods used to measure it. Different studies may use different definitions, and we should recognize that the results of a study are dependent on how the construct is defined.

> **Operational definition**
> A definition of a concept or variable in terms of the methods used to measure it.

Populations and Samples: Representing the World of Diversity

Researchers undertake to learn about populations. **Populations** are complete groups of people, such as the entire Canadian population. Other researchers focus on specific population groups, such as First Nations or gay males. These are termed the *populations of interest*, or *target populations*. These target populations are all sizable. It would be expensive, difficult, and all but impossible to study every individual in them.

Because of the impossibility of studying all members of a population, scientists select individuals from the population and study them. The individuals who participate in research are said to compose a **sample**. However, we cannot truly learn about the population of interest unless the sample *represents* that population. A *representative sample* is a research sample of participants who accurately represent the population of interest.

If our samples do not represent the target populations, we cannot extend, or **generalize**, the results of our research to the populations of interest. If we wished to study the sexual behaviour of Asian Canadians, our population would consist of *all* Asian Canadians. If we used only Asian Canadian college students as our sample, we could not generalize our findings to all Asian Canadians.

Including all people in Canada in a study of sexual behaviour would be impossible. We cannot even *find* all people in Canada when we conduct the census. And incorporating sex research into the census would undoubtedly cause many more people to refuse to participate. Sampling a part of a target population makes research practical and possible—if imperfect.

Sampling Methods

A **random sample** is one in which every member of the target population has an equal chance of participating. Researchers overcome biased sampling by drawing *random* or *stratified random* samples of populations. In a random sample, every member of a population has an equal chance of participating. In a **stratified random sample**, known subgroups of a population are represented in proportion to their numbers in the population. For instance, about 51% of the Canadian population is female. Researchers could therefore decide that 51% of their sample must be female if the sample is to represent all people in Canada. The randomness of the sample would be preserved, because the members of the subgroups would be selected randomly from their particular subgroups.

Another problem is that sexual research is almost invariably conducted with people who volunteer to participate. Volunteers may differ from people who refuse to participate. For example, volunteers tend to be more open about their sexuality than the general population. They may even tend to exaggerate behaviours that others might consider deviant or abnormal.

The problem of **volunteer bias** is a thorny one for sex researchers, because the refusal of people who have been randomly selected to participate in the survey can ruin the representativeness of the sample. It would be unethical to coerce people to participate in a study on sexual behaviour (or in any other type of study), so researchers must use samples of volunteers, rather than true random samples. A low response rate to a voluntary survey is an indication that the responses do not represent the people to whom the survey was distributed.

In some cases, samples are samples of convenience. They consist of individuals who happen to be available to the researcher and who share some characteristics with the target population—perhaps religious background or sexual orientation. Still, they may not truly represent the target group. Convenience samples often

---

Population A complete group of organisms or events.

Sample Part of a population.

Generalize To go from the particular to the general.

Random sample A sample in which every member of a population has an equal chance of participating.

Stratified random sample A random sample in which known subgroups in a population are represented in proportion to their numbers in the population.

Volunteer bias A slanting of research data that is caused by the characteristics of individuals who volunteer to participate, such as willingness to discuss intimate behaviour.

consist of European Canadian, middle-class university students who volunteer for studies conducted at their schools.

Methods of Observation

Once scientists have chosen those whom they will study, they observe them. In this section, we consider several methods of observation: the case-study method, the survey method, naturalistic observation, ethnographic observation, participant observation, and laboratory observation.

The Case-Study Method

A **case study** is a carefully drawn, in-depth biography of an individual or a small group. The focus is on understanding one or several individuals as fully as possible by unravelling the interplay of various factors in their backgrounds. In most case studies, the researcher comes to know the individual or group through interviews or other contacts conducted over a prolonged period of time. The interviewing pattern tends to build upon itself with a good deal of freedom, in contrast to the one-shot, standardized set of questions used in survey questionnaires.

Reports of innovative treatments for sexual dysfunctions usually appear as well-described case studies. A clinician typically reports the background of the client in depth, describes the treatment, reports the apparent outcomes, and suggests factors that might have contributed to the treatment's success or failure. In writing a treatment case study, the therapist tries to provide information that may be helpful to therapists who treat clients with similar problems. Case studies or "multiple case studies" (reports concerning a few individuals) that hold promise may be subjected to controlled investigation—ideally, to experimental studies involving treatment and control groups.

Despite the richness of material that may be derived from the case-study approach, it is not as rigorous a research design as an experiment. People often have gaps in memory, especially concerning childhood events. The potential for observer bias is also a prominent concern. Clinicians and interviewers may unintentionally guide people into saying what they expect to hear. Then, too, researchers may inadvertently colour people's reports when they jot them down—shape them subtly in ways that reflect their own views.

The Survey Method

Surveys typically gather information about behaviour through questionnaires or interviews. Researchers may interview or administer questionnaires to thousands of people from particular population groups to learn about their sexual behaviour and attitudes. Interviews such as those used by Kinsey and his colleagues (1948, 1953) have the advantages of allowing face-to-face contact and giving the interviewer the opportunity to *probe*—that is, to follow up on answers that seem to lead toward useful information. A skilled interviewer may be able to set a respondent at ease and establish a sense of trust or *rapport* that encourages self-disclosure. On the other hand, unskilled interviewing may cause respondents to conceal information.

Questionnaires are less expensive than interviews. The major expenses are printing and distribution. Questionnaires can be administered to many people at once, and respondents can return them unsigned. (Anonymity may encourage respondents to disclose intimate information.) Questionnaires, of course, can be used only by people who can read and record their responses. Interviews can be used even with people who cannot read or write. But interviewers must be trained, sometimes extensively, and then paid for their time.

Most surveys have *something* to offer to our understanding of human sexuality, but some are more methodologically sound than others. None fully represents the

Case study A carefully drawn, in-depth biography of an individual or a small group of individuals that may be obtained through interviews, questionnaires, and historical records.

Survey A detailed study of a sample obtained by means such as interviews and questionnaires.

Alfred Kinsey.
Kinsey and his colleagues con-
ducted the first large-scale scientific
study of sexual behaviour in the
United States.

Reliability The consistency
or accuracy of a measure.

Incidence A measure of
the occurrence or the
degree of occurrence of an
event.

Validity With respect to
tests, the degree to which a
particular test measures the
constructs or traits that it
purports to measure.

Canadian population at large, however. Most people consider their sexuality to be among the most intimate, *private* aspects of their lives. People who willingly agree to be polled about their political preferences may resist participation in surveys concerning their sexual behaviour. As a result, it is difficult, if not impossible, for researchers to recruit a truly representative sample of the population. Bear in mind, then, that survey results provide, at best, an approximation of the sexual attitudes, beliefs, and behaviours of the Canadian population.

Let us review the sampling techniques used in some of the major studies of human sexuality in the United States and Canada. Throughout the book we shall reconsider the findings of these surveys.

THE KINSEY REPORTS   Kinsey and his colleagues (1948, 1953) interviewed 5300 males and 5940 females in the United States between 1938 and 1949. They asked a wide array of questions on various types of sexual experiences, including masturbation, oral sex, and coitus that occurred before, during, and outside of marriage. Kinsey could not use more direct observational methods, such as sending his researchers to peer through bedroom windows. Kinsey chose not to try to obtain a random sample. He believed that a high refusal rate would wreck the chances of accurately representing the general population. Instead, he adopted a *group sampling* approach. He recruited study participants from the organizations and community groups to which they belonged, such as college fraternities and sororities. He contacted representatives of groups in diverse communities and tried to persuade them to secure the cooperation of fellow group members. Even so, he made an attempt to sample as broadly as possible from the groups he solicited. In some cases, he obtained full participation. In other cases, he obtained a large enough proportion of the group membership to help ensure representativeness, at least of the group.

Still, Kinsey's samples did not represent the general population. People of colour, people in rural areas, older people, the poor, and Catholics and Jews were all underrepresented in his samples. Statisticians who have reviewed Kinsey's methods have concluded that there were systematic biases in his sampling methods but that it would have been impossible to obtain a true probability sample from the general population (see, for example, Cochran et al., 1953). There is thus no way of knowing whether Kinsey's results accurately mirrored the U.S. population at the time. His estimate that 37% of the male population had reached orgasm at least once through male–male sexual activity was probably too high. But the *relationships* Kinsey uncovered, such as the positive link between level of education and participation in oral sex, may be more generalizable.

To his credit, Kinsey took measures to encourage candour in the people he interviewed. For instance, study participants were assured of the confidentiality of their records. Kinsey's interviewers were also trained to conduct the interviews in an objective and matter-of-fact style. To reduce the tendency to slant responses in a socially desirable direction, participants were reassured that the interviewers were not passing judgment on them. Interviewers were trained not to show emotional reactions that the people they interviewed could interpret as signs of disapproval (they maintained a "calm and steady eye" and a constant tone of voice).

Kinsey also checked the **reliability** of his data by evaluating the consistency of the responses given by several hundred interviewees who were re-examined after at least 18 months. Their reports of the **incidence** of sexual activities (for example, whether or not they had ever engaged in premarital or extramarital coitus) were highly reliable. That is, participants tended to give the same answers on both occasions. Kinsey recognized, however, that consistency of responses across time—or *retakes*, as he called them—did not guarantee their **validity**. That is, the retakes did not show whether the reported behaviours had some basis in fact. One indirect measure was comparison of the reports of husbands and wives—for example, with respect to the *incidence* of oral–genital sex or the *frequency* of intercourse. There was a remarkable consistency in the reports of 706 pairs of spouses; this lends support to the view that their self-reports were accurate.

The 2004 Hollywood film *Kinsey* gives a realistic portrayal of the interview techniques that Kinsey and his colleagues used in their research. As portrayed in the film, many research participants experienced emotional relief by discussing, for the first time in their lives, intimate behaviours they had felt anxious and guilty about. Most important, Kinsey's interviewers' nonjudgmental response reassured participants that they were normal.

THE NHSLS STUDY The National Health and Social Life Survey of Americans was intended to provide general information about sexual behaviour in the United States and also specific information that might be used to predict and prevent the spread of AIDS. It was conducted by Edward O. Laumann of the University of Chicago and three colleagues—John H. Gagnon, Robert T. Michael, and Stuart Michaels—in the 1990s and published as *The Social Organization of Sexuality: Sexual Practices in the United States* in 1994. A companion volume—authored by Michael, Gagnon, Laumann, and Gina Kolata (a *New York Times* science reporter)—was also published: *Sex in America: A Definitive Survey. Sex in America* is a bit less technical in presentation but offers some interesting data not found in the other version. The NHSLS study was originally to be supported by government funds, but Republican senator Jesse Helms of North Carolina blocked federal financing on the grounds that it was inappropriate for the government to be supporting sex research (Bronner, 1998). The research team therefore obtained private funding but had to cut back the scope of the project.

The sample included 3432 people. Of this number, 3159 were drawn from English-speaking adults living in households (not dormitories, prisons, and so forth), aged 18 to 59. The other 273 were obtained by purposely oversampling African American and Latino and Latina American households, so that more information could be obtained about these ethnic groups.

The researchers identified samples of households in geographic areas—by addresses, not names. They sent a letter to each household, describing the purpose and methods of the study, and an interviewer visited each household a week later. The people targeted were assured that the purposes of the study were important and that the identities of participants would be kept confidential. Incentives of up to $100 were offered for cooperating. A high completion rate of close to 80% was obtained in this way. All in all, the NHSLS study could be the only one since Kinsey's day that offers a reasonably accurate picture of the sexual practices of the general population of the United States.

CANADIAN MEDIA–SPONSORED SURVEYS In 1984, *Maclean's* magazine began using survey organizations to ask Canadians about a diversity of social issues, including sexuality.

The Kinsey Institute
Home page for the Kinsey Institute, which focuses on sexual behaviour and attitudes.
www.indiana.edu/~kinsey

The Canadian Journal of Human Sexuality.
Published by the Sex Information and Education Council of Canada, this is the major journal that focuses on Canadian sexuality research.

The Canadian Journal of Human Sexuality

VOLUME 14 - NUMBER 1-2 2005

PUBLISHED BY SIECCAN
THE SEX INFORMATION & EDUCATION COUNCIL OF CANADA
http://www.sieccan.org

Research in Action

SURVEYING CANADIAN EXPERIENCES

Many of the Canadian studies on sexuality are based on limited samples, such as university or high school students. Statistics Canada does, however, fund some large-scale national surveys that include questions on sexuality and/or fertility, such as the National Longitudinal Study of Children and Youth and the National Population Health Survey. These studies use computer-assisted telephone interviews to collect the data.

Two national Canada Youth and AIDS surveys have focused on the sexual health of adolescents. The first was conducted in 1989 (King et al., 1989). The second was conducted in 2002 by researchers at four Canadian universities: Acadia, Alberta, Laval, and Queen's (Boyce et al., 2003). The main objective was to understand the determinants of adolescent sexuality and sexual health for different age groups. The study involved students in Grades 7, 9, and 11 from all provinces and territories, except for Nunavut. The study was coordinated by Education Ministers from across Canada and funded by Health Canada.

Students needed the consent of a parent/guardian to take part in the study. Fewer sexual questions were asked of the Grade 7 students in order to make the survey more acceptable to parents and school boards.

The original sample size objective was 33 000 students. However, a number of school districts that were approached did not take part in the survey. Because of objections and concerns raised by several school administrators regarding some of the sexual questions, the final sample ended up being 11 074.

Reginald Bibby at the University of Lethbridge in Alberta is one of Canada's foremost experts on adolescents. He has conducted national surveys on a diversity of topics. Bibby's (2001) survey of 3500 Canadian youth aged 15 to 19 is one of the most comprehensive in that it analyzed relationship issues such as dating in addition to sexual attitudes and behaviours.

Four national surveys on contraceptive use were sponsored by the Ortho-Janssen pharmaceutical company beginning in the 1990s. The 2002 study sampled women aged 15 to 44 from across Canada (Fisher, Boroditsky, & Morris, 2004). Of 3345 questionnaires mailed out, 1582 were returned. The surveys studied the contraception awareness, attitudes, and behaviours of a representative sample of Canadian women of childbearing age. The surveys also included some questions on sexual behaviours, such as whether respondents have ever experienced sexual intercourse, have experienced sexual intercourse in the previous six months, and have experienced certain sexual difficulties in the previous year.

Statistics Canada
Statistics Canada offers census documents and statistics.

www.statcan.ca

These were the first national surveys to ask Canadians questions about their sexual behaviours. Decima, the polling organization that conducted the interviews, was apprehensive about asking survey questions about sex over the telephone. Allen Gregg, president of Decima, feared that "people will hang up on us" (Jenish, 1994, p. 26). A key interview strategy, however, was to ask the sexual questions at the end of the interview, after the interviewer had established a rapport with the respondent. Not only did almost all of the respondents answer the questions, but many also volunteered for follow-up interviews.

The *Maclean's* surveys typically involve telephone surveys of about 1600 adult Canadians selected randomly from the 10 provinces. The sample includes a disproportionate number from the smaller provinces in order to allow for adequate statistical analysis of respondents from all provinces. The sample is considered to be a statistically accurate representation of the Canadian population as a whole within 2.8 percentage points, 19 times out of 20. The accuracy is reduced for those questions that have lower response rates (Jenish, 1994).

In 1998 the Compas survey organization, on behalf of the Sun newspaper chain, conducted one of the more comprehensive national surveys about relationships and sexuality (Compas, 1998). There were 1479 respondents in this survey. Their demographic characteristics, such as age and education, were proportionally similar to those of the Canadian population. Questions were asked regarding sexual orientation, age of first intercourse, number of intercourse partners, sexual frequency, oral sex, sexual communication, sexual problems, sex and the workplace, attitudes toward casual sex, and attitudes toward toplessness and prostitution. More than 95% of those who took part in the survey responded to the sexuality questions. The highest nonresponse was for the question on oral sex, with 15% of the females and 5% of the males not responding.

MAGAZINE SURVEYS OF READERS Unlike *Maclean's* magazine, which hires a research organization to conduct national surveys of the Canadian population, most magazines simply ask their readers to complete questionnaires included in the magazine and mail them back. Major readership surveys have been conducted by popular magazines, such as *Psychology Today*, *Redbook*, *Ladies' Home Journal*, *McCall's*, *Cosmopolitan*, and even *Consumer Reports*. Although these surveys all offer some useful information and may be commended for obtaining large samples (ranging from 20 000 to 106 000!), their sampling techniques are inherently unscientific and biased. Each sample represents, at best, the readers of the magazine in which the questionnaire appeared. Moreover, we learn only about readers who volunteered to respond to the questionnaires. These volunteers probably differed in important ways from the majority of readers who failed to respond. Finally, readers of these magazines are more affluent than the public at large, and readers of *Cosmopolitan*, *Psychology Today*, and even *Redbook* tend to be more liberal. The samples may therefore represent only those readers who were willing to complete and mail in the surveys.

RELIABILITY OF THE SURVEY METHOD How do we know whether respondents are telling us the truth when they take part in sex surveys? Reliability can be determined by checking for consistency in responses. In a study of gay males in Toronto, for example, reliability was determined by giving the same interviews to the men 72 hours apart (Coates et al., 1986). The high degree of response consistency between the two interviews indicated that the data were reliable. Also in Toronto, in a study of men with AIDS or an AIDS-related condition and their male partners, Coates et al. (1988) found a high degree of agreement between the men regarding details about their sexual encounters. Reliability of responses was very high for behaviours such as anal intercourse but somewhat less so for less risky behaviours such as anal finger insertion.

McGill University researchers Eric Ochs and Yitzchak Binik (1999) obtained data from 70 heterosexual couples concerning 68 sexual behaviours to determine the degree of consistency in the responses of the partners. On individually completed questionnaires, both partners in a couple gave similar responses, suggesting high reliability. Similarly, among university students in British Columbia, only a few gave responses that were biased in a socially desirable direction (Meston, Heiman, Trapnell, and Paulhus, 1998).

LIMITATIONS OF THE SURVEY METHOD Problems in obtaining reliable estimates may occur when interviewers and respondents are of different genders or racial or socioeconomic backgrounds. Let us consider several weaknesses of the survey method.

Volunteer Bias Many people refuse to participate in surveys. Samples are thus biased by the inclusion of large numbers of volunteers, who are in general willing to take the time to participate. In the case of sex surveys, they also tend to be more sexually permissive and liberal-minded than nonvolunteers. At an Ontario university, for example, students who volunteered for a study on human sexuality were more sexually experienced, more interested in sexual variety, and had more permissive attitudes toward sexuality than those students who did not volunteer (Bogaert, 1996). There were also important personality differences, with the volunteers being higher in sensation seeking and less likely to conform to societal norms and rules. Accordingly, the results of a survey based on a volunteer sample may not accurately reflect the population at large.

Social desirability A response bias to a questionnaire or interview in which the person provides a socially acceptable response.

Many of the Canadian researchers who study sexuality are based in university social science departments, and for the sake of convenience they frequently obtain samples from their own departments. However, since relatively few males are enrolled in many social science courses it is difficult to make adequate gender comparisons. Researchers at an Ontario university found that fewer males than females volunteered to take part in a sexuality study, which of course exacerbated the gender-ratio problem (Senn & Demarais, 2001). Interestingly, more students volunteered to take part in the sexuality study than in a study on memory.

Faulty Estimation Respondents may recall their behaviour inaccurately or may purposely misrepresent it. People may not recall the age at which they first engaged in petting or masturbated to orgasm. People may have difficulty remembering or calculating the frequencies of certain behaviours, such as the weekly frequency of marital intercourse ("Well, let's see. This week I think it was four times, but last week only two times, and I can't remember the week before that"). Kinsey and Hunt speculated that people who desire more frequent sex tend to underestimate the frequency of marital coitus, whereas people who want less frequent sex tend to overestimate it.

Social-Desirability Response Bias Even people who consent to participate in surveys of sexual behaviour may feel pressured to answer questions in the direction of **social desirability**. Some respondents, that is, try to ingratiate themselves with their interviewers by offering what they believe to be socially desirable answers. Although some respondents may readily divulge information concerning the frequency of marital coitus, they may deny experiences involving prohibited activities such as child molestation, voyeurism, or coerced sexual activity. (People who engage in these proscribed activities may also be more likely to decline to participate in sex surveys.)

Some people may not divulge sensitive information for fear of the interviewer's disapproval. Others may fear criminal prosecution. Even though interviewers may insist that they are nonjudgmental and that study participants will remain anonymous, respondents may fear that their identities will be uncovered someday.

Differences in Meanings of Terms In 1998, when the White House sex scandal broke, Bill Clinton asserted that he had never had "sexual relations" with a young intern there. The tabloids feasted on the fact that President Clinton did not consider "sexual relations" to include fellatio.

Research in Action

EXPLAINING GENDER DIFFERENCES IN REPORTING NUMBER OF PARTNERS

One of the big question marks in sex research is the discrepancy in number of sexual partners reported by men and women. Men consistently report having more partners than do women. One possible explanation for this difference is that men exaggerate the number of partners, whereas women report fewer partners than they have actually had so that they do not appear to be promiscuous. Researchers at

the University of Alberta (Brown & Sinclair, 1999) have an alternative explanation; namely, that men and women use different estimation strategies. They found that men are more likely to give rough approximations when trying to estimate the number of partners, and that this tends to result in an overestimation. Women, on the other hand, try to do a precise count of their partners and in doing so may have forgotten some of them. Brown and Sinclair therefore concluded that men and women are not intentionally misrepresenting their sexual histories. What explanations would you give?

Survey respondents can respond only to the questions posed by interviewers or included in questionnaires. A word or phrase may mean different things to different people, however. As a result, responses may differ among those whose behaviour may be the same. For example, the polling agency for the *Maclean's* magazine surveys did not consult with any sexuality researchers regarding the survey questions, and as a result some of the questions were poorly constructed. To respond to the question "Do you consider yourself sexually active?" the interviewees were asked to choose from among the following: Very sexually active, Somewhat sexually active, Not very sexually active, and Not sexually active at all. Of course, the problem with this wording is that "sexually active" can refer to activities other than intercourse, including masturbation. Thus, respondents may have differing interpretations of the meaning of this question. *Maclean's* magazine even gave an example of this ambiguity when it cited an interviewee's request for clarification: "Respondent wanted to know if we mean by himself or with others" (Jenish, 1994, p. 26). The response categories are also very subjective in that one person may define having sex once a week as "very sexually active," whereas another may define it as "not very sexually active."

How questions are worded can strongly bias the responses that are obtained. This is particularly true in measuring attitudes toward such controversial topics as prostitution. When *Maclean's* asked Canadians whether paying for sex is acceptable, only 15% of men and 6% of women said that it was (DeMont, 1999). However, when Compas polling (1998) asked Canadians "Do you think that prostitution should be: Completely against the law, Legal and tightly regulated by health authorities, or Completely legal," most (69% of men and 67% of women) said that it should be legal and regulated. The *Maclean's* wording produced polling results that clearly suggest that Canadians are opposed to prostitution, whereas the Compas wording produced the opposite result. These findings can have significant public policy implications, in that those who seek more restrictive prostitution laws would use the first set of results to bolster their argument, whereas those who seek less restrictive laws would use the second.

The Naturalistic-Observation Method

In **naturalistic observation**, also called the *field study*, scientists directly observe the behaviour of animals and humans where it happens. Anthropologists, for example, have lived among preliterate societies and reported on their social and sexual customs. Other disciplines, too, have adopted methods of naturalistic observation in their research on human sexuality. For example, sociologists have observed the street life of prostitutes, and psychologists have observed patterns of nonverbal communication and body language between couples in dating situations.

The Ethnographic-Observation Method

Anthropologists have lived among societies of people in the four corners of the earth in order to observe and study human diversity. Margaret Mead (1935) reported on the social and sexual customs of various peoples of New Guinea.

Bronislaw Malinowski (1929) studied the Trobriand islanders, among other peoples. Ford and Beach's (1951) account of sexual practices around the world and in nonhuman species remains a classic study of cross-cultural and cross-species comparisons. **Ethnographic** research has provided us with data concerning sexual behaviours and customs that occur widely across cultures and those that are limited to one or few cultures. Ethnographers are trained to be keen observers, but direct observation has its limits in the study of sexual behaviour. Sexual activities are most commonly performed away from the watchful eyes of others, especially from those of visitors from other cultures. Ethnographers may thus have to rely on methods

Naturalistic observation A method in which organisms are observed in their natural environments.

Ethnography The branch of anthropology that deals descriptively with specific cultures, especially preliterate societies.

Participant observation
A method in which observers interact with the people they study as they collect data.

such as personal interviewing to learn more about sexual customs. Alean Al-Krenawi from Israel and John Graham (1999) from the University of Calgary, for example, used ethnographic methods to study the coping strategies used by six women in an Arab village in Israel who were married to the same man.

The Participant-Observation Method

In **participant observation**, the investigators learn about people's behaviour by directly interacting with them. Participant observation has been used in studies of male–male sexual behaviour and mate swapping. In effect, participation has been the "price of admission" for observation.

The Laboratory-Observation Method

In *Human Sexual Response* (1966), William Masters and Virginia Johnson were among the first to report direct laboratory observations of individuals and couples engaged in sexual acts. In all, 694 people (312 men and 382 women) participated in the research. The women ranged from 18 to 78 in age, the men from 21 to 80. There were 276 married couples, 106 single women, and 36 single men. The married couples engaged in intercourse and other forms of mutual stimulation, such as manual and oral stimulation of the genitals. The unmarried people participated in studies that did not require intercourse, such as measurement of female sexual arousal in response to the insertion of a penis-shaped probe, and male ejaculation during masturbation. Masters and Johnson performed similar laboratory observations of sexual response among gay people for their 1979 book *Homosexuality in Perspective.*

Direct laboratory observation of biological processes was not invented by Masters and Johnson. However, they were confronting a society that was still unprepared to speak openly of sex, let alone to observe people engaged in sexual activity in the laboratory. Masters and Johnson were accused of immorality, voyeurism, and an assortment of other evils. Nevertheless, their methods offered the first reliable set of data on what happens to the body during sexual response. Their instruments permitted them to measure directly vasocongestion (blood flow to the genitals), myotonia (muscle tension), and other physiological responses.

Perhaps their most controversial device was a "coition machine." This was a transparent artificial penis outfitted with photographic equipment. It enabled them to study changes in women's internal sexual organs as the women became sexually aroused. From these studies, Masters and Johnson observed that it is useful to divide sexual response into four stages (their "sexual response cycle," discussed in Chapter 4).

Researchers have since developed more sophisticated physiological methods of measuring sexual arousal and response. Researchers at McGill University, for example, have reported that an ultrasound machine measuring blood flow in the clitoris is a reliable way of determining sexual arousal in women (Khalife et al., 2000).

How many of us would assent to performing sexual activities in the laboratory while we were connected to physiological monitoring equipment in full view of researchers? Some of the women observed by Masters and Johnson were patients of Dr. Masters who felt indebted to him and agreed to participate. Many were able to persuade their husbands to participate as well. Some were medical students and graduate students who may have been motivated to earn extra money (participants were paid for their time) as well as by scientific curiosity.

Another methodological concern of the Masters and Johnson approach is that observing people engaged in sexual activities may in itself alter their responses. People may not respond publicly in the same way they would in private. Perhaps sexual response in the laboratory bears little relationship to sexual response in the bedroom. The physiological monitoring equipment may also alter the subjects' nat-

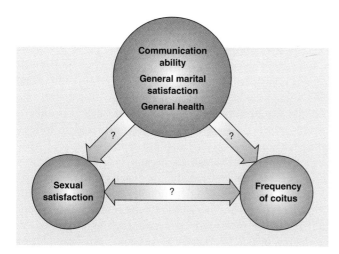

Figure 2.1 What Is the Relationship Between Frequency of Intercourse and Sexual Satisfaction?

Married couples who engage in more frequent sexual relations report higher levels of sexual satisfaction, but why? Because researchers have not manipulated the variables, we cannot conclude that sexual satisfaction causes high coital frequency. Nor can we say that frequent coitus causes greater sexual satisfaction. Perhaps both variables are affected by other factors, such as communication ability, general marital satisfaction, and general health.

ural responses. Given these constraints, it is perhaps remarkable that the people studied by Masters and Johnson were able to become sexually aroused and reach orgasm.

The Correlational Method

What are the relationships between age and frequency of coitus among married couples? What is the connection between socioeconomic status and teenage pregnancy? In each case, two variables are being related to one another: age and frequency of coitus, and socioeconomic status and rate of teenage pregnancy. Correlational research describes the relationship between variables such as these.

A **correlation** is a statistical measure of the relationship between two variables. In correlational studies, two or more variables are related, or linked, to one another by statistical means. The strength and direction (positive or negative) of the relationship between any two variables are expressed with a statistic called a **correlation coefficient**. Correlations may be *positive* or *negative*. Two variables are positively correlated if one increases as the other increases. Frequency of intercourse, for example, has been found to be positively correlated with sexual satisfaction (Blumstein & Schwartz, 1983). That is, married couples who engage in coitus more frequently report higher levels of sexual satisfaction (see Figure 2.1).

Research has shown relationships (correlations) between marital satisfaction and a host of variables: communication skills, shared values, flexibility, frequency of social interactions with friends, and churchgoing, to name a few. Although such research may give us an idea of the factors associated with marital satisfaction, the experimenters have not manipulated the variables of interest. For this reason we cannot say which, if any, of the factors is causally related to marital happiness.

The Experimental Method

The best method (though not always a feasible method) for studying *cause-and-effect* relationships is the **experiment**. Experiments permit scientists to draw conclusions about cause-and-effect relationships because the experimenter is able to control or manipulate the factors or variables of interest directly and to observe their effects.

In an experiment on the effects of alcohol on sexual arousal, for example, a group of participants would receive an intervention, called a **treatment**, such as a dose of alcohol. (In other experiments, the intervention or treatment might involve the administration of a drug, exposure to violent sexual material, or a program of sex education.) They would then be carefully observed to learn whether that treatment made a difference in their behaviour—in this case, their sexual arousal.

Correlation A statistical measure of the relationship between two variables.

Correlation coefficient A statistic that expresses the strength and direction (positive or negative) of the relationship between two variables.

Experiment A scientific method that seeks to confirm cause-and-effect relationships by manipulating independent variables and observing their effects on dependent variables.

Treatment In experiments, an intervention that is administered to participants (such as a test, a drug, or a sex education program) so that its effects can be observed.

Aspects of the Experimental Method

INDEPENDENT AND DEPENDENT VARIABLES In an experiment, the variables (treatments) that are hypothesized to have a causal effect are manipulated or controlled by the researcher. Consider an experiment designed to determine whether alcohol stimulates sexual arousal. The design might involve giving one group of participants a specified amount of alcohol and then measuring its effects. In such an experimental arrangement, the dose of alcohol is considered an **independent variable**, whose presence and quantity are manipulated by the researchers. The measured results are called **dependent variables**, because changes in their values are believed to depend on the independent variable or variables. In this experiment, measures of sexual arousal would be the dependent variables. Dependent variables are outcomes; they are observed and measured by the researchers, but not manipulated. Sexual arousal might be measured by means such as physiological measurement (gauging the degree of penile erection in the male, for example) or self-report (asking participants to rate their sexual arousal on a rating scale).

In a study of the effects of sex education on teenage pregnancy, sex education would be the independent variable. The incidence of teenage pregnancy would be the dependent variable. Researchers would administer the experimental treatment (sex education) and track the participants for a period of time to determine their pregnancy rates. But how would experimenters know whether the treatment had made a difference in the pregnancy rate?

EXPERIMENTAL AND CONTROL GROUPS Well-designed experiments randomly assign people or animal-study participants to experimental and control groups. Participants in **experimental groups** receive the treatment. Participants in **control groups** do not. Every effort is made to hold all other conditions constant for both groups. By using random assignment and holding other conditions constant, researchers can be reasonably confident that the independent variable (treatment), and not extraneous factors (such as the temperature of the room in which the treatment was administered or differences between the participants in the experimental and control groups), brought about the results.

WHY IS RANDOM ASSIGNMENT IMPORTANT? Why do experimenters assign individuals at random to experimental and control groups whenever possible? Consider a study conducted to determine the effects of alcohol on sexual arousal in response to sexually explicit films. If we permitted study participants to choose whether they would drink alcohol, we might not know whether it was the alcohol itself that accounted for the results. Some other factor, called a **selection factor**, might discriminate between people who would and those who would not choose to drink alcohol. Perhaps people who chose to drink might also have more permissive attitudes toward sexually explicit material. Their permissiveness, rather than the alcohol, could affect their sexual responsiveness to these stimuli. If this were the case, experimental outcomes might reflect the effects of the selection factor rather than the alcohol.

Ottawa researchers John Bradford and Anne Pawlak conducted an experiment to determine the effectiveness of cyproterone acetate (CPA), an anti-androgen, in treating men convicted of sex crimes. The 19 men who were studied were randomly assigned to receive either CPA or a placebo for a three-month period. The study was double blind, meaning that neither the men nor the researchers who administered the drugs knew which of the men were receiving CPA and which the placebo. (The double-blind approach controls for the placebo effect that can occur when people take any kind of medication and eliminates the possibility of the researchers' own biases distorting their findings.) As predicted by the researchers, the CPA drug was associated with a significant reduction in aspects of sex behaviour, especially deviant fantasies such as having sex with children (Bradford & Pawlak, 1993).

Independent variable A condition in a scientific study that is manipulated so that its effects can be observed.

Dependent variables The measured results of an experiment, which are believed to be a function of the independent variables.

Experimental group A group of study participants who receive a treatment.

Control group A group of study participants who do not receive the experimental treatment. However, other conditions are held comparable to those of individuals in the experimental group.

Selection factor A bias that may operate in research when people are allowed to determine whether they will receive a treatment.

Research in Action

STUDYING THE SEXUAL BEHAVIOURS OF DIVERSE POPULATIONS

Ontario First Nations

More than 1 million Canadians identify as First Nations people. Rates of sexually transmitted infections (STIs) are much higher among First Nations people than among the general population, yet a notable lack of sex research has been conducted with this ethnic group.

Concern about the spread of AIDS, however, led to the development of the Ontario First Nations AIDS and Healthy Lifestyle Survey by researchers from the University of Toronto and representatives from the First Nations (Myers, Calzavara, Cockerill, & Marshall, 1993). Eleven reserve communities took part in the study, with participants randomly selected from the list of on-reserve members. Almost all (87%) of those selected agreed to be interviewed. Interviews were conducted face to face by trained First Nations interviewers, and an answer booklet was used for questions about sexuality and alcohol use. The interviewer would read the question from the interview schedule and the respondent would check off the answers in his or her answer book and then seal the book in an envelope. At the beginning of the sexual questions, respondents were given the choice between having the sexual acts described using slang terms or technical terms.

Of those who had sex in the previous year, 58% reported only one sexual partner, 30% reported two to four partners, and 12% had five or more partners (Calzavara et al., 1999). Almost all of those who had experienced sex in the previous 12 months had engaged in sexual intercourse, 53% had experienced oral sex, and 13% had experienced anal intercourse. Individuals who engaged in sex with partners from both within and outside of the community were more likely to experience oral and anal sex (Calzavara et al., 1999). Only 9% of those who had engaged in vaginal intercourse reported always using condoms, and only 11% of those who had engaged in anal sex always used condoms. Alcohol use was not related to whether or not a condom was used (Myers et al., 1997).

Gay and Bisexual Men

Until the 1980s only limited research was focused on men who have sex with men. With the advent of the AIDS epidemic, however, the Canadian government targeted millions of dollars for research into the prevention and treatment of AIDS. Because AIDS affected gay males far more than any other group in Canada, several research projects were funded to analyze sexual behaviours and condom use among gay and bisexual men. The first national survey of men who have sex with men was a joint project involving researchers from the University of Toronto, Laval University, and the University of Montreal (Myers, Orr, Locker, & Jackson, 1993). The project was designed by the researchers along with the Canadian AIDS Society and AIDS organizations from across Canada. A sample of 4803 men ranging in age from 16 to 75 was obtained from gay bars, bathhouses, and community dances in 35 Canadian cities. Data were obtained by questionnaires. The response rate was very high, with 86% of those who were approached agreeing to take part in the survey; response rates were higher in bars and at dances than in the bathhouses.

More than half (57%) attended bars at least once a week, but only 7% attended a bathhouse once a week or more.

Respondents were asked if they had engaged in any of the following behaviours in the previous three months: deep tongue kissing, mutual masturbation, receptive and insertive oral–anal sex, receptive and insertive oral sex with and without semen in the mouth, and receptive and insertive anal intercourse with and without a condom. They were also asked whether they had been tested for HIV and whether, to their knowledge, they were HIV-positive. Twenty-three percent of the men reported at least one experience of unprotected anal intercourse in the previous three months. Two-thirds had been tested at least once for HIV, and 12% reported that they knew they were HIV-positive (Myers et al., 1996).

The second major Canadian survey of gay and bisexual men was conducted by University of Toronto researchers in 2002 with a sample of 5080 men in Ontario (Myers et al., 2004). As with the previous national survey, the researchers consulted extensively with AIDS service organizations in developing the research design.

The study recruited a more diverse sample than had the previous national survey. In particular, the researchers purposely recruited a higher proportion of men who were either under the age of 20 or over the age of 50 and those who had lower levels of education. Most importantly, the study recruited the largest number of non-Caucasian gay and bisexual men that had ever been surveyed in Canada. Compared with the previous national survey there was a notable increase in the number of gay men who were meeting partners on the Internet. A key finding was an increase in the number of gay and bisexual men who reported at least one episode of unprotected anal intercourse (Myers et al., 2004).

Sex Workers

Frances Shaver from Concordia University in Montreal is one of Canada's leading experts on sex work and has conducted three major surveys on this topic. In the first study she interviewed male, female, and transgender workers in Montreal and San Francisco. In the second study Shaver compared female and male sex workers with hospital workers in Montreal and Toronto in terms of working conditions, experiences, and stresses. The third study, done in Montreal and Toronto, focused on the different types of sex work (massage, exotic dancing, escort, and domination) (Shaver, 2005).

Shaver (2005) outlines three main challenges in researching groups, such as sex workers, that are stigmatized by the general society. The first difficulty is obtaining a representative sample. Researchers have typically sampled only sex workers on the street because they are the most visible. However, those working on the streets differ in many ways from those working indoors. The second challenge arises because people whose work is illegal or stigmatized are less willing to be interviewed and may be less honest in their responses. The third challenge is the traditional stereotype that sex workers are inherently exploited victims rather than autonomous individuals who freely choose their occupation. Accompanying this stereotype is the belief that sex workers are all basically alike rather than being diverse individuals.

To overcome these challenges, Shaver uses a number of strategies. She asks an advisory group of sex workers for advice on the type of questions to ask and how to obtain research data. It is essential to convince sex workers that the researchers are nonjudgmental and respect them and their privacy. Also, Shaver notes that researchers need to distinguish themselves from other professionals such as police officers or social workers.

One of Shaver's findings that challenges traditional wisdom is that the majority of sex workers do *not* work for pimps. More of her findings will be presented in the chapter on commercial sex.

Ethics in Sex Research

Sex researchers are required to protect the people being studied. This means that people will not be subjected to physical or psychological harm and will participate of their own free will. In colleges, universities, hospitals, and research institutions, ethics review committees help researchers weigh the potential harm of administering the independent variables and review proposed studies in light of ethical guidelines. If the committee finds fault with a proposal, it may advise the researcher how to modify the research design to comply with ethical standards and may withhold approval until the proposal has been modified. Let us consider a number of ethical issues:

- Exposing participants to harm: Individuals may be harmed if they are exposed to pain or placed in stressful situations. For this reason, researchers do not expose children to erotic materials in order to determine the effects. Nor do researchers expose human fetuses to male or female sex hormones to learn whether they create predispositions toward tomboyishness, gay male or lesbian sexual orientations, and other variables of interest.

- Confidentiality: Researchers can do many things to ensure the confidentiality of participants. They can make questionnaires anonymous. Interviewers may not be given the identities of interviewees. In reports of research, enough information about participants' backgrounds can be given to make the studies useful (size of city of origin, region of country, religion, age group, race, educational level, and so on) without divulging their identities. Once the need for follow-up has passed and the results have been fully analyzed, the names and addresses of participants and their records can be destroyed.

- Informed consent: The principle of **informed consent** requires that people freely agree to participate after being given enough information about the procedures and purposes of the research, and its risks and benefits, to make an informed decision. Once the study has begun, participants must be free to withdraw at any time without penalty.

Informed consent
Agreement to participate in research after receiving adequate information about the purposes and nature of the study and about its potential risks and benefits.

■ The use of deception: Ethical conflicts may emerge when experiments require that participants not know all about their purposes and methods. For example, in experiments on the effects of violent pornography on aggression against women, participants may be misled into believing that they are administering electric shocks to women (who are actually confederates of the experimenter), even though no shocks are actually delivered. The experimenter seeks to determine participants' willingness to hurt women following exposure to aggressive erotic films. Such studies could not be carried out if participants knew that no shocks would actually be delivered.

Research is the backbone of human sexuality as a science. This textbook focuses on scientific findings that can illuminate our understanding of sexuality, help enhance sexual experience, prevent and treat sexually transmitted diseases, and build more rewarding relationships.

Confidentiality.
Ethics requires that sex researchers keep the identities and behaviours of research participants confidential. Sometimes records are coded so that someone breaking into them would not be able to decipher the identity of participants. Records are also usually destroyed after all useful information has been gleaned from them.

Summing Up

A Scientific Approach to Human Sexuality

Scientists insist that assumptions about sexual behaviour be supported by evidence. Evidence is based on careful observations in the laboratory or in the field.

The Scientific Method

The scientific method is a systematic way of gathering scientific evidence and testing assumptions through empirical research. It entails formulating a research question, framing a hypothesis, testing the hypothesis, and drawing conclusions about the hypothesis.

Goals and Methods of the Science of Human Sexuality

The goals of the science of human sexuality are to describe, explain, predict, and control sexual behaviours. People often confuse description with inference. Inferences are woven into theories, when possible.

Operational Definitions

The operational definition of a construct is linked to the methods used to measure it, enabling diverse researchers to understand what is being measured.

Populations and Samples: Representing the World of Diversity

Research samples should accurately represent the population of interest. Representative samples are usually obtained through random sampling.

Methods of Observation

The Case-Study Method

Case studies are carefully drawn biographies of individuals or small groups that focus on unravelling the interplay of various factors in individuals' backgrounds.

The Survey Method

Surveys typically gather information about behaviour through interviews or questionnaires administered to large samples of people. The use of volunteers and the tendency of respondents to offer socially desirable responses are sources of bias in surveys.

The Naturalistic-Observation Method

In naturalistic observation, scientists directly observe the behaviour of animals and humans where it happens—in the "field." The scientists remain unobtrusive.

The Ethnographic-Observation Method

Ethnographic research has provided us with data concerning sexual behaviours and customs that occur widely across cultures and those that are limited to one or few cultures.

The Participant-Observation Method

In participant observation, investigators learn about people's behaviour by interacting with them.

The Laboratory-Observation Method

In the laboratory-observation method, people engage in the behaviour under study in the laboratory setting. When methods of observation influence the behaviour under study, that behaviour may be distorted.

The Correlational Method

Correlational studies reveal the strength and direction of the relationships between variables. However, they do not show cause and effect.

The Experimental Method

Experiments allow scientists to draw conclusions about cause-and-effect relationships because the scientists directly control or manipulate the variables of interest and observe their effects. Well-designed experiments randomly assign individuals to experimental and control groups.

Ethics in Sex Research

Ethics concerns the ways in which researchers protect participants in research studies from harm.

Pain and Stress

Ethical standards require that research be conducted only when the expected benefits of the research out-weigh the anticipated risks to participants and when the experimenter attempts to minimize expected risks.

Confidentiality

Sex researchers keep the identities and responses of participants confidential to protect them from embarrassment and other potential sources of harm.

Informed Consent

The principle of informed consent requires that people agree to participate in research only after being given enough information about the purposes, procedures, risks, and benefits to make informed decisions.

The Use of Deception

Some research cannot be conducted without deceiving people as to its purposes and procedures. In such cases, the potential harm and benefits of the proposed research are weighed carefully.

Test Yourself

Multiple-Choice Questions

1. You have decided on an interesting question in human sexuality. Before you can carry out your research, you need to establish _____ of the important variables.
   a. correlation coefficients
   b. operational definitions
   c. new theories
   d. population groups

2. A representative sample
   a. consists of at least 75 males and 75 females
   b. is a group of people who volunteer to participate in the study
   c. is a sample that accurately reflects the composition of the population
   d. is one in which each member of the population has an equal chance of participating in the study

3. A random sample
   a. consists of at least 75 males and 75 females
   b. is a group of people who volunteer to participate in the study
   c. is a sample that accurately reflects the composition of the population
   d. is one in which each member of the population has an equal chance of participating in the study

4. Interviewing people about their sexual behaviour is an example of _____ research.
   a. survey
   b. clinical
   c. experimental
   d. experiential

5. A problem with much of the research on human sexual behaviour is
   a. religious bias
   b. commercial bias
   c. volunteer bias
   d. sexual bias

6. Masters and Johnson's research on sexual response is an example of
   a. participant observation of sexual behaviour
   b. laboratory observation of sexual behaviour
   c. correlational research on sexual behaviour
   d. experimental research on sexual behaviour

7. Correlational studies provide information about
   a. whether a change in one variable is causing a change in another
   b. statistical relationships between two variables
   c. the margin of error due to a variable
   d. the degree of bias in a sample

8. If you wish to answer questions about cause-and-effect relationships, the best research method to use is a(n) _____.
    a. interview
    b. questionnaire
    c. laboratory observation
    d. experiment

9. Concerns about the anonymity and confidentiality of sexual information are examples of _____ issues.
    a. ethical
    b. religious
    c. political
    d. commercial

10. A basic ethical requirement for all research on human sexuality is the provision of
    a. adequate compensation
    b. legal permission
    c. informed consent
    d. parental approval

Critical Thinking Questions

1. Have you ever responded to a survey on sexual behaviour (either in a magazine or on the Internet)? What influenced your decision to participate or not to participate? Did you answer truthfully? Why or why not?

2. Many people question the validity of research on sexual behaviour. Do you think that research in this field contributes to our understanding of behaviour? Why or why not?

3. Is the use of deception as part of a research study ever justified? Why or why not?

Chapter 3
Female and Male Anatomy and Physiology

Female Anatomy and Physiology

The French have a saying, *Vive la différence!* ("Long live the difference!"), which celebrates the differences between men and women. Men have historically exalted their own genitals. Too often, the less visible genitals of women have been deemed inferior. Even today, this cultural heritage may lead women to develop negative attitudes toward their genitals. Consequently, girls are more likely than boys to avoid self-pleasuring and to have negative feelings about oral sex.

This chapter discusses the ins and outs of sexual anatomy and physiology. We will begin with discussing female structures and in the second part of the chapter will focus on males.

Some women are concerned about the appearance of their vaginal lips and, to boost their sexual confidence and pleasure, are asking plastic surgeons to redesign their vaginas. Others believe that a "tighter" vagina would enhance their partner's as well as their own sexual pleasure. This is discussed in the nearby World of Diversity box.

A World of Diversity

DESIGNER VAGINAS: THE LATEST IN SEX AND PLASTIC SURGERY

Women from around the world flock to David Matlock's marble waiting room carrying purses stuffed with porn. The magazines are revealed only in the privacy of his office, where doctor and patient debate the finer points of each glossy photograph.

The enterprising gynecologist sees countless images of naked women, but none are more popular than *Playboy's* fresh-faced playmates. They represent, he says, with a knowing smile, the perceived ideal.

"Some women will say, 'Hey, you take this picture and hang it up in the operating room and refer back to it when you're sculpturing me,'" he said in an interview in his clinic overlooking hazy Los Angeles. "I say 'Okay, all right, fine.'"

Dr. Matlock is a colourful pioneer in a controversial—and growing—frontier of plastic surgery: nipping and tuck-

ing vaginas. Patients from the United States and more than 30 other countries pay thousands of dollars for his "designer vagina," a purely aesthetic procedure that includes shortening or plumping up the labia, or vaginal lips. He attracts even more women for an operation he claims improves sex by tightening or "rejuvenating" the vagina.

"There's a need for this," he said. "Women are driving this. I didn't create the market, the market was there."

While doctors have long known how to enhance women's genitals, demand for vaginal surgery has mushroomed in recent years because physicians—led by Dr. Matlock—market it as enhancing sexual satisfaction. Doctors working in the field, including those in Canada, report higher caseloads and longer waiting lists. And the American Society of Plastic Surgeons says the increase is so great that it expects to soon start tracking volumes.

Plastic surgery's spread to women's nether regions alarms those who see it as a manifestation of society's air-

brushed standards of the female form that exploits women's deep-seated insecurities.

"I think it's appalling and frightening and one more way in which perfectly normal, beautiful women are terrorized by the possibility of being less than a perfect 10," said Joy Davidson, a certified sex therapist and author in Seattle.

However, women who have had their genitals surgically enhanced say it has transformed their lives. While some patients have genuine health problems, such as incontinence, many also ask their doctors to perform additional procedures while they are on the operating table. Others are solely driven by cosmetic or sexual reasons.

For the past 14 years, Julie Gause was troubled by the after-effects of an "extremely awful episiotomy," which is an incision to facilitate childbirth, that she had while delivering her son. But "the No. 1" reason she sought the surgery was to "enhance" her sex life.

"It's definitely going to be worth it for the rest of my life," the bubbly, tanned, 35-year-old Los Angeles resident said in an interview. "It takes you back to before children, for sure. It's an amazing difference. It's unbelievable."

In June, she paid Dr. Matlock $16,000 (U.S.) for what she laughingly called "the full monty": reconstruction of the after-effects of the episiotomy, reduction of her labia and tightening of her vaginal muscles.

Not all procedures are even surgical. On the recommendation of a friend, Katia Neves came to Dr. Matlock for the doctor's so-called G-shot, an $1,800 collagen-based injection in her G-spot that he says amplifies orgasms and lasts for about four months.

"It's a pretty expensive procedure for a short period of time," said the 36-year-old cosmetologist, who was born in Brazil and now lives in L.A. "It does increase your pleasure. It makes a difference, and even if you don't have

problems you can feel the difference."

Calgarian Sally Marshall turned to cosmetic surgery to fix something she first noticed at the age of 5: Her inner labia protruded beyond the outer lips, which made riding a bike and wearing a swimsuit or tight jeans an excruciating experience.

The question of why women seek plastic surgery for an area of their bodies that few people—including themselves—ever really see is hotly debated. Critics note that men benefit when their partners undergo vaginal tightening and say they, along with society at large, intentionally or otherwise steer women's interest in genital enhancement.

Pornography's drift into the mainstream and a growing candour about sexuality often lead to the thorny subject of anatomical comparisons, says Leroy Young, chairman of the American Society of Plastic Surgeons' emerging trends task force.

"[Women] get a comment from their spouse or boyfriend or whoever that, 'Gee you don't look like whoever' and a comment about a sensitive area like that, of course, is a huge emotional blow. So I think a lot of the women who pursue that are concerned about issues like, 'How am I going to be perceived?'"

While Dr. Matlock acknowledges vaginal tightening benefits men, he insists his patients come to him because they want to change.

"They say, 'Look, I want to enjoy this. I want to have the best sexual experience possible. It's for me.' That's what they're doing. If a man was pushing a woman to come in, I'm not going to do it."

Source: Jill Mahoney, Globe and Mail, *August 13, 2005, pp. 1, 8. Reprinted with permission from* The Globe and Mail.

Girls and boys are both sometimes reared to regard their genitals with shame or disgust. Both may be reprimanded for expressing normal curiosity about them. They may be reared with a "hands-off" attitude and warned to keep their "private parts" private, even to themselves. Touching them except for hygienic purposes may be discouraged.

If you have seen the film *Fried Green Tomatoes*, you may recall the scene where a group of women are encouraged to bring mirrors to one of their meetings in order to examine their genitals.

Women readers may wish to try this while following the text and the illustrations in this chapter. You may discover some new anatomic features. You will see that your own genitals can resemble those in the illustrations and yet also be unique.

External Sex Organs

Taken collectively, the external sexual structures of the female are termed the **vulva**. Vulva is a Latin word that means "wrapper" or "covering." The vulva consists of the *mons veneris*, the *labia majora* and *minora* (major and minor lips), the *clitoris*, and the vaginal opening (see Figure 3.1). Figure 3.2 shows variations in the appearance of women's genitals.

The Mons Veneris

The **mons veneris** consists of fatty tissue that covers the joint of the pubic bones in front of the body, below the abdomen and above the clitoris. At puberty the mons becomes covered with pubic hair that is often thick and curly but varies from person to person in waviness, texture, and colour.

Vulva The external sexual structures of the female.

Mons veneris A mound of fatty tissue that covers the joint of the pubic bones in front of the body, below the abdomen and above the clitoris. (The name is a Latin phrase that means "hill or mount of Venus," the Roman goddess of love. Also known as the *mons pubis*, or simply the *mons*.)

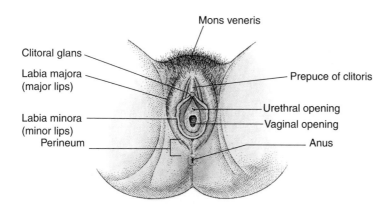

Mons veneris

Clitoral glans

Labia majora
(major lips)

Prepuce of clitoris

Urethral opening

Labia minora
(minor lips)

Vaginal opening

Perineum

Anus

Figure 3.1 External Female Sex Organs.

This figure shows the vulva with the labia opened to reveal the urethral and vaginal openings.

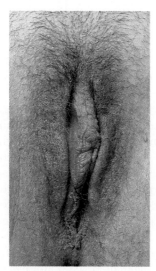
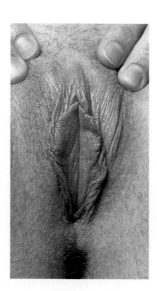

Figure 3.2 Normal Variations in the Vulva.

The features of the vulva show a great deal of variation. A woman's attitude toward her genitals is likely to reflect her general self-concept and early childhood messages rather than the appearance of her vulva per se.

The mons cushions a woman's body during sexual intercourse, protecting her and her partner from the pressure against the pubic bone that stems from thrusting motions. There is an ample supply of nerve endings in the mons, so caresses of the area can produce pleasurable sexual sensations.

The Labia Majora

The **labia majora** are large folds of skin that run downward from the mons along the sides of the vulva. The labia majora of some women are thick and bulging. In other women, they are thinner, flatter, and less noticeable. When close together, they hide the labia minora and the urethral and vaginal openings.

The outer surfaces of the labia majora, by the thighs, are covered with pubic hair and darker skin than that found on the thighs or labia minora. The inner surfaces of the labia majora are hairless and lighter in colour. They are amply supplied with nerve endings that respond to stimulation and can produce sensations of sexual pleasure. The labia majora also shield the inner portion of the female genitals.

Labia majora Large folds of skin that run downward from the mons along the sides of the vulva. (Latin for "large lips" or "major lips.")

The Labia Minora

The **labia minora** are two hairless, light-coloured membranes located between the major lips. They surround the urethral and vaginal openings. The outer surfaces of the labia minora merge with the major lips. At the top they join at the prepuce (hood) of the clitoris.

The labia minora differ markedly in appearance from woman to woman. The labia minora of some women form protruding flower shapes that are valued greatly in some cultures, such as that of the Hottentots of Africa. In fact, Hottentot women purposely elongate their labia minora by tugging at them.

Rich in blood vessels and nerve endings, the labia minora are highly sensitive to sexual stimulation. When stimulated they darken and swell, indicating engorgement with blood.

The Clitoris

The clitoris is the only sex organ whose only known function is the experiencing of pleasure.

Clitoris (Figure 3.1) derives from the Greek word *kleitoris*, which means "hill" or "slope." The clitoris receives its name from the manner in which it slopes upward in the shaft and forms a mound of spongy tissue at the glans. The body of the clitoris, termed the clitoral shaft, is about 2.5 centimetres (1 inch) long and $\frac{1}{2}$ centimetre ($\frac{1}{4}$ inch) wide. The clitoral shaft consists of erectile tissue that contains two spongy masses called **corpora cavernosa** ("cavernous bodies") that fill with blood (become engorged) and become erect in response to sexual stimulation. The stiffening of the clitoris is less apparent than the erection of the penis, because the clitoris does not swing free from the body as the penis does. The **prepuce** (meaning "before a swelling"), or hood, covers the clitoral shaft. It is a sheath of skin formed by the upper part of the labia minora. The clitoral glans is a smooth, round knob or lump of tissue. It resembles a button and is situated above the urethral opening. The clitoral glans may be covered by the clitoral hood but is readily revealed by gently separating the labia minora and retracting the hood. It is highly sensitive to touch because of its rich supply of nerve endings.

The clitoris is the female sex organ that is most sensitive to sexual sensation. The size of the clitoris varies from woman to woman, just as the size of the penis varies among men. There is no known connection between the size of the clitoris and sensitivity to sexual stimulation. The clitoral glans is highly sensitive to touch. Women thus usually prefer to be stroked or stimulated on the mons, or on the clitoral hood, rather than directly on the glans.

In some respects, the clitoris is the female counterpart of the penis. Both organs develop from the same embryonic tissue, which makes them similar in structure, or **homologous**. They are not, however, fully similar in function, or **analogous**. Both organs receive and transmit sexual sensations, but the penis is directly involved in reproduction and excretion by serving as a conduit for sperm and urine, respectively.

It is ironic that many cultures—including Victorian culture—have viewed women as unresponsive to sexual stimulation. Yet women, not men, possess a sex organ that is apparently devoted solely to pleasurable sensations. The clitoris is the woman's most erotically charged organ, which is why women most often masturbate through clitoral stimulation, not vaginal insertion.

Surgical removal of the clitoral hood is common among Muslims in the Middle East and Africa. As we see in the nearby World of Diversity feature, this "rite of passage" to womanhood leaves many scars—physical and emotional.

Labia minora Hairless, light-coloured membranes, located between the labia majora. (Latin for "small lips" or "minor lips.")

Clitoris A female sex organ consisting of a shaft and glans located above the urethral opening. It is extremely sensitive to sexual sensations.

Corpora cavernosa Masses of spongy tissue in the clitoral shaft that become engorged with blood and stiffen in response to sexual stimulation. (Latin for "cavernous bodies.")

Prepuce The fold of skin covering the glans of the clitoris (or penis). (From Latin roots that mean "before a swelling.")

Homologous Similar in structure; developing from the same embryonic tissue.

Analogous Similar in function.

The Vestibule

The word *vestibule*, which means "entranceway," refers to the area within the labia minora that contains the openings to the vagina and the urethra. The vestibule is richly supplied with nerve endings and is very sensitive to tactile or other sexual stimulation.

The Urethral Opening

Urine passes from the female's body through the **urethral opening** (see Figure 3.1), which is connected to the bladder by a short tube called the urethra (see Figure 3.3), where urine collects. The urethral opening lies below the clitoral glans and above the vaginal opening.

The proximity of the urethral opening to the external sex organs may pose some hygienic problems for sexually active women. The urinary tract, which includes the urethra, bladder, and kidneys, may become infected from bacteria that are transmitted from the vagina or rectum. Infectious microscopic organisms may pass from the male's sex organs to the female's urethral opening during sexual intercourse. Manual stimulation of the vulva with dirty hands may also transmit bacteria through the urethral opening to the bladder. Anal intercourse followed by vaginal intercourse may transfer microscopic organisms from the rectum to the bladder and cause infection. For similar reasons, women should wipe first the vulva, then the anus, when using the bathroom.

> **Urethral opening** The opening through which urine passes from the female's body.
>
> **Clitoridectomy** Surgical removal of the clitoris.

A World of Diversity

CLITORIDECTOMY— RITUAL GENITAL MUTILATION

Cultures in some parts of Africa and the Middle East ritually mutilate or remove the clitoris, not just the clitoral hood. Removal of the clitoris, or **clitoridectomy**, is a rite of initiation into womanhood in many of these predominantly Islamic cultures. It is often performed as a puberty ritual in late childhood or early adolescence (not within a few days of birth, like male circumcision).

The clitoris gives rise to feelings of sexual pleasure in women. Its removal or mutilation represents an attempt to ensure the girl's chastity, because it is assumed that uncircumcised girls are consumed with sexual desires. Some groups in rural Egypt and in the northern Sudan, however, perform clitoridectomies primarily because it is a social custom that has been maintained from ancient times by a sort of unspoken consensus (Missailidis & Gebre-Medhin, 2000). It is done by women to women (Nour, 2000). Some perceive it as part of their faith in Islam. However, the Koran—the Islamic bible—does not authorize it (Crossette, 1998; Nour, 2000). The typical young woman in this culture does not see herself as a victim. She assumes that clitoridectomy is part of being female. As one young woman told gynecologist Nawal M. Nour (2000), the clitoridectomy hurt but was a good thing, because now she was a woman.

Clitoridectomies are performed under unsanitary conditions without benefit of anaesthesia. Medical complications are common, including infections, bleeding, tissue scarring, painful menstruation, and obstructed labour. The procedure is psychologically traumatizing. An even more radical form of clitoridectomy, called *infibulation* or Pharaonic circumcision, is practised widely in the Sudan. Pharaonic circumcision involves complete removal of the clitoris along with the labia minora and the inner layers of the labia majora. After removal of the skin tissue, the raw edges of the labia majora are sewn together. Only a tiny opening is left to allow passage of urine and menstrual discharge (Nour, 2000). The sewing together of the vulva is intended to ensure chastity until marriage (Crossette, 1998). Medical complications are common; they include menstrual and urinary problems and even death. After marriage, the opening is enlarged to permit intercourse. Enlargement is a gradual process that is often made difficult by scar tissue from the circumcision. Hemorrhaging and tearing of surrounding tissues are common. It may take three months or longer before the opening is large enough to allow penile penetration.

The Canadian government has outlawed ritual genital mutilation within its borders. Yet calls from Westerners to ban the practice in parts of Africa and the Middle East have sparked controversy on grounds of "cultural condescension"—that people in one culture cannot dictate the cultural traditions of another.

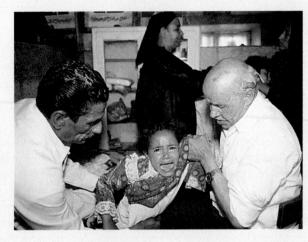

Ritual Genital Mutilation. Some predominantly Islamic cultures in Africa and the Middle East ritually mutilate or remove the clitoris as a rite of initiation into womanhood. Novelist Alice Walker drew attention to the practice in her novel Possessing the Secret of Joy. *She has called for its abolition in her book and film,* Warrior Marks.

Cystitis An inflammation of the urinary bladder. (From the Greek *kystis,* which means "sac.")

Gynecologist A physician who treats women's diseases, especially of the reproductive tract. (From the Greek *gyne,* which means "woman.")

Cystitis is a bladder inflammation that may stem from any of these sources. Its primary symptoms are burning and frequent urination (also called *urinary urgency*). Pus or a bloody discharge is common, and there may be an intermittent or persistent ache just above the pubic bone. These symptoms may disappear after several days, but consultation with a **gynecologist** is recommended, because untreated cystitis can lead to serious kidney infections.

So-called honeymoon cystitis is caused by the tugging on the bladder and urethral wall that occurs during vaginal intercourse. It may occur upon beginning coital activity (though not necessarily on one's honeymoon) or upon resuming coital activity after lengthy abstinence. Figure 3.3 shows the close proximity of the urethra and vagina.

A few precautions may help women prevent serious inflammation of the bladder:

■ Drinking two quarts of water a day to flush the bladder.

■ Drinking orange or cranberry juice to maintain an acid environment that discourages growth of infectious organisms.

Figure 3.3 The Female Reproductive System.

This cross-section shows the location of many of the internal sex organs that compose the female reproductive system. Note that the uterus is normally tipped forward.

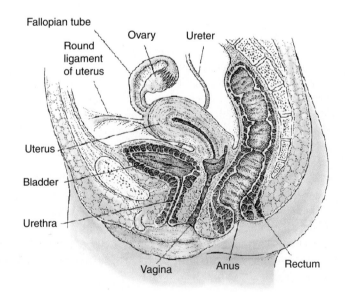

- Decreasing use of alcohol and caffeine (from coffee, tea, or cola drinks), which may irritate the bladder.
- Washing the hands prior to masturbation or self-examination.
- Washing one's partner's and one's own genitals before and after intercourse.
- Preventing objects that have touched the anus (fingers, penis, toilet tissue) from subsequently coming into contact with the vulva.
- Urinating soon after intercourse to help wash away bacteria.

The Vaginal Opening

One does not see the entire vagina, but rather the vaginal opening, or **introitus**, when one parts the labia minora, or minor lips. The introitus lies below, and is larger than, the urethral opening. Its shape resembles that of the **hymen.**

The hymen is a fold of tissue across the vaginal opening that is usually present at birth and may remain at least partly intact until a woman engages in coitus. For this reason the hymen has been called the "maidenhead." Its presence has been taken as proof of virginity, and its absence as evidence of coitus. However, some women are born with incomplete hymens, and other women's hymens are torn accidentally, such as during horseback riding, strenuous exercise, or gymnastics—or even when bicycle riding. A punctured hymen is therefore poor evidence of coital experience. A flexible hymen may also withstand many coital experiences, so its presence does not guarantee virginity.

Figure 3.4 illustrates various vaginal openings. The first three show hymen shapes that are frequently found among women who have not had coitus. The fifth drawing shows a *parous* ("passed through") vaginal opening, typical of a woman who has delivered a baby. Now and then the hymen consists of tough fibrous tissue and is closed, or *imperforate*, as in the fourth drawing. An imperforate hymen may not be discovered until after puberty, when menstrual discharges begin to accumulate in the vagina. In these rare cases, a simple surgical incision will perforate the hymen.

The **perineum** consists of the skin and underlying tissue between the vaginal opening and the anus. The perineum is rich in nerve endings. Stimulation of the area may heighten sexual arousal. During labour, many physicians make a routine perineal incision, called an **episiotomy**, to facilitate childbirth.

Introitus The vaginal opening. (From the Latin for "entrance.")

Hymen A fold of tissue across the vaginal opening that is usually present at birth and remains at least partly intact until a woman engages in coitus. (Greek for "membrane.")

Perineum The skin and underlying tissue that lies between the vaginal opening and the anus. (From Greek roots that mean "around" and "to empty out.")

Episiotomy A surgical incision in the perineum that may be made during childbirth to protect the vagina from tearing. (From the Greek roots *epision*, which means "pubic region," and *tome*, which means "cutting.")

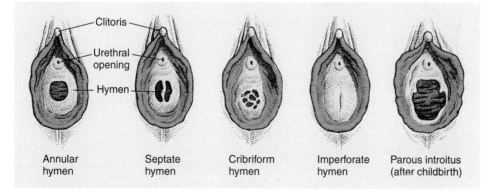

Figure 3.4 Appearance of Various Types of Hymens Before Coitus and the Introitus (at Right) as It Appears Following Delivery of a Baby.

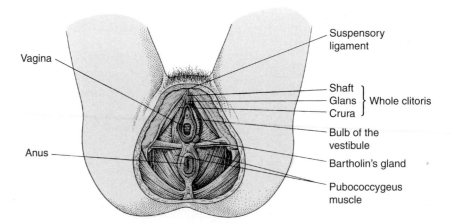

Figure 3.5 Structures That Underlie the Female External Sex Organs.

If we could see beneath the vulva, we would find muscle fibres that constrict the various body openings, plus the crura ("legs") of the clitoris, the vestibular bulbs, and Bartholin's glands.

Structures That Underlie the External Sex Organs

Figure 3.5 shows what lies beneath the skin of the vulva. The vestibular bulbs and Bartholin's glands are active during sexual arousal and are found on both sides (they are shown on the right in Figure 3.5). Muscular rings **(sphincters)** that constrict bodily openings, such as the vaginal and anal openings, are also found on both sides.

The clitoral **crura** are wing-shaped, leglike structures that attach the clitoris to the pubic bone beneath. The crura contain corpora cavernosa, which engorge with blood and stiffen during sexual arousal.

The **vestibular bulbs** are attached to the clitoris at the top and extend downward along the sides of the vaginal opening. Blood congests them during sexual arousal, swelling the vulva and lengthening the vagina. This swelling contributes to coital sensations for both partners.

Bartholin's glands lie just inside the minor lips on each side of the vaginal opening. They secrete a couple of drops of lubrication just before orgasm. This lubrication is not essential for coitus. It was once believed that Bartholin's glands were the source of the vaginal lubrication, or wetness, that women experience during sexual arousal. It is now known that engorgement of vaginal tissues during sexual excitement results in a form of "sweating" by the lining of the vaginal wall. During sexual arousal, the pressure from this engorgement causes moisture from the many small blood vessels that lie in the vaginal wall to be forced out and to pass through the vaginal lining, forming the basis of the lubrication. In less time than it takes to read this sentence (generally within 10 to 30 seconds), beads of vaginal lubrication, or "sweat," appear along the interior lining of the vagina in response to sexual stimulation, in much the same way that rising temperatures cause water to pass through the skin as perspiration.

Pelvic floor muscles permit women to constrict the vaginal and anal openings. They contract automatically, or involuntarily, during orgasm, and their tone may contribute to coital sensations. Gynecologist Arnold Kegel (1952) developed exercises to build pelvic muscle tone in women who had problems controlling urination after childbirth. Kegel found that women who practised his exercises improved their urinary control along with their genital sensations during coitus. He believed that many women could enhance vaginal sensations during coitus by exercising their **pubococcygeus (P-C) muscles** through exercises that are now known as "Kegels."

Sphincters Ring-shaped muscles that surround body openings and open or close them by expanding or contracting. (From the Greek for "that which draws close.")

Crura Anatomic structures resembling legs that attach the clitoris to the pubic bone. (Singular: crus. A Latin word that means "leg" or "shank.")

Vestibular bulbs Cavernous structures that extend downward along the sides of the introitus and swell during sexual arousal.

Bartholin's glands Glands that lie just inside the minor lips and secrete fluid just before orgasm.

Pubococcygeus muscle The muscle that encircles the entrance to the vagina.

Applied Knowledge

KEGELS

Kegel exercises are commonly used to help women heighten their awareness of vaginal sensations. They may also have a psychological benefit, because women who perform Kegel exercises assume a more active role in enhancing their genital sensations. Sex therapist Lonnie Barbach (1975) offers instructions for Kegel exercises:

1. Locate the pubococcygeus (P-C) muscle by purposely stopping the flow of urine. The muscle you squeeze to stop the urine flow is the P-C muscle. (The P-C muscle acts as a sphincter for both the urethral and vaginal openings.)

2. In order to learn to focus consciously on contracting the P-C muscle, insert a finger into the vaginal opening and contract the muscle so that it can be felt to squeeze or contain the finger. (The P-C muscle can contract to contain objects as narrow as a finger.)

3. Remove your finger, squeeze the P-C muscle for three seconds, and then relax. Repeat several times. This part of the exercise may be performed while seated at a class-room or business desk. No one (except the woman herself) will be the wiser. Many women practise a series of Kegel exercises consisting of 10 contractions, 3 times a day.

4. The P-C muscle may also be tensed and relaxed in rapid sequence. Since this exercise may be more fatiguing than the above, women may choose to practise it perhaps 10 to 25 times, once a day.

Internal Sex Organs

The internal sex organs of the female include the innermost parts of the vagina, the cervix, the uterus, and two ovaries, each connected to the uterus by a fallopian tube (see Figures 3.3 and 3.6). These structures comprise the female reproductive system.

The Vagina

The **vagina** extends back and upward from the vaginal opening (see Figure 3.3). It is usually 7.5 to 12.5 centimetres (3 to 5 inches) long at rest. Menstrual flow and babies pass from the uterus to the outer world through the vagina. During coitus, the penis is contained within the vagina.

The vagina is commonly pictured as a canal or barrel, but when at rest, it is like a collapsed muscular tube. Its walls touch like the fingers of an empty glove. The vagina expands in length and width during sexual arousal. It can also expand to allow the insertion of a tampon, as well as the passage of a baby's head and shoulders during childbirth.

> **Vagina** The tubular female sex organ that contains the penis during sexual intercourse and through which a baby is born. (Latin for "sheath.")

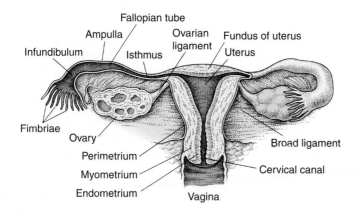

Figure 3.6 Female Internal Reproductive Organs.

This drawing highlights the relationship of the uterus to the fallopian tubes and ovaries. Note the layers of the uterus, the ligaments that attach the ovaries to the uterus, and the relationship of the ovaries to the fimbriae of the fallopian tubes.

The Vagina Monologues.
The Vagina Monologues, *a celebrated American play that presents the diversity of emotions women have about their vaginas, has also been popular with audiences in Canada.*

The vaginal walls have three layers. The inner lining, or *vaginal mucosa*, is made visible by opening the labia minora. It is a mucous membrane similar to the skin that lines the inside of the mouth. It feels fleshy, soft, and corrugated. It may vary from very dry (especially if the female is anxious about something, such as examinations) to very wet, in which case fingers slide against it readily. The middle layer of the vaginal wall is muscular. The outer or deeper layer is a fibrous covering that connects the vagina to other pelvic structures.

The vaginal walls are rich with blood vessels but poorly supplied with nerve endings. Unlike the sensitive outer third of the vaginal barrel, the inner two-thirds are insensitive to touch. The entire vaginal barrel is sensitive to pressure, however, which may be experienced as sexually pleasurable.

The vaginal walls secrete substances that help maintain the vagina's normal acidity (pH 4.0 to 5.0). Normally the secretions taste salty. The odour and taste of these secretions may vary during the menstrual cycle. Although the evidence is not clear, the secretions are thought to contain substances that may act as sexual attractants. Women who frequently **douche** or use feminine deodorant sprays may thus remove or mask substances that may arouse sex partners. Douching or spraying may also alter the natural chemical balance of the vagina, which can increase the risk of vaginal infections. Feminine deodorant sprays can also irritate the vagina and evoke allergic reactions. The normal, healthy vagina cleanses itself through regular chemical secretions that are evidenced by a mild white or yellowish discharge.

The Cervix

The **cervix** is the lower end of the uterus. Its walls, like those of the vagina, produce secretions that contribute to the chemical balance of the vagina. The opening in the middle of the cervix, or **os**, is normally about the width of a straw, although it expands to permit passage of a baby from the uterus to the vagina during childbirth. Sperm pass from the vagina to the uterus through the cervical canal.

A **Pap test** examines a sample of cervical cells that are smeared on a slide to screen for cervical cancer and other abnormalities. The Canadian Cancer Society (2002) recommends that all women have Pap tests once they become sexually active. It also recommends that these tests be done once every one to three years. Most Canadian women do have regular Pap tests. About four-fifths of those who have experienced sexual intercourse report having a Pap test within the previous two years (Fisher et al., 1999).

Douche Application of a jet of liquid to the vagina as a rinse. (From the Italian *doccia,* which means "shower bath.")

Vaginitis Vaginal inflammation.

Cervix The lower end of the uterus. (Latin for "neck.")

Os The opening in the middle of the cervix. (Latin for "mouth.")

Pap test A test of a sample of cervical cells that screens for cervical cancer and other abnormalities. (Named after the originator of the technique, Dr. Papanicolaou.)

Applied Knowledge

PREVENTING VAGINITIS

Vaginitis is any vaginal inflammation, whether it is caused by an infection, an allergic reaction, or chemical irritation. Vaginitis may also stem from use of birth-control pills or antibiotics that alter the natural body chemistry, or from other factors, such as lowered resistance (from fatigue or poor diet). Changes in the natural body chemistry or lowered resistance may permit microscopic organisms normally found in the vagina to multiply to infectious levels. Vaginitis may be recognized by abnormal discharge, itching, burning of the vulva, and urinary urgency. Its

causes and treatments are discussed in Chapter 14.

Women with vaginitis are advised to seek medical attention, but let us note some suggestions that may help prevent vaginitis (Boston Women's Health Book Collective, 1992):

1. Wash your vulva and anus regularly with mild soap. Pat dry (taking care not to touch the vulva after dabbing the anus).

2. Wear cotton panties. Nylon underwear retains heat and moisture that cause harmful bacteria to flourish.

3. Avoid pants that are tight in the crotch.

4. Be certain that sex partners are well washed. Condoms may also reduce the spread of infections from one's sex partner.

5. Use a sterile, water-soluble jelly such as K-Y jelly if artificial lubrication is needed for intercourse. Do *not* use Vaseline. Birth-control jellies can also be used for lubrication.

6. Avoid intercourse that is painful or abrasive to the vagina.

7. Avoid diets high in sugar and refined carbohydrates because they alter the normal acidity of the vagina.

The incidence of cervical cancer has declined dramatically in Canada since the early 1970s, largely because most women have regular Pap tests. In 2002 there were an estimated 1400 cases of cervical cancer and 410 deaths in Canada resulting from this disease (Canadian Cancer Society, 2002). Cervical cancer is more common among women who have had many sex partners, women who became sexually active at a relatively early age, women of lower socioeconomic status, and women who smoke. All women are at risk, however.

Canadian researchers (Franco et al., 2003) have ascertained that the greatest risk factor for cervical cancer is having been infected with the sexually transmitted human papillomavirus (HPV). Indeed, the evidence strongly indicates that HPV infection is necessary for cervical cancer to occur.

Most cases of cervical cancer can be successfully treated by surgery and **radiotherapy** if they are detected early. However, cervical cancer can also be prevented when precancerous changes are detected by a Pap test.

Women who are uncomfortable with the Pap test are less willing to be tested. In a study of older women living in Prince Edward Island, who were not being screened for cervical cancer, many expressed feelings of discomfort and embarrassment about the Pap test (Van Til et al., 2003). Also, many did not feel that disease prevention was an important priority. These women felt that the test was something to be avoided. However, they also felt that being in a relationship of "professional trust" with a doctor could help them to overcome their negative feeling.

The Uterus

The **uterus**, or womb (see Figures 3.3 and 3.6), is the organ in which a fertilized **ovum** implants and develops until birth. The uterus usually slants forward (is *antro-*

Radiotherapy Treatment of a disease by X-rays or by emissions from a radioactive substance.

Uterus The hollow, muscular, pear-shaped organ in which a fertilized ovum implants and develops until birth.

Ova Egg cells. (Singular: ovum.)

Canadian Health Network
Health information and resources sponsored by Health Canada.
www.canadian-health-network.ca
The Canadian Women's Health Network
www.cwhn.ca

Fundus The uppermost part of the uterus. (*Fundus* is a Latin word that means "base.")

Endometrium The innermost layer of the uterus. (From Latin and Greek roots that mean "within the uterus.")

Endometriosis A condition caused by the growth of endometrial tissue in the abdominal cavity, or elsewhere outside the uterus, and characterized by menstrual pain.

Myometrium The middle, well-muscled layer of the uterus. (*Myo-* comes from the Greek *mys*, which means "muscle.")

Perimetrium The outer layer of the uterus. (From roots that mean "around the uterus.")

Hysterectomy Surgical removal of the uterus.

Complete hysterectomy Surgical removal of the ovaries, fallopian tubes, cervix, and uterus.

Fallopian tubes Tubes that extend from the upper uterus toward the ovaries and conduct ova to the uterus. (After the Italian anatomist Gabriel Fallopio, who is credited with their discovery.)

Isthmus The segment of a fallopian tube closest to the uterus. (A Latin word that means "narrow passage.")

Ampulla The wide segment of a fallopian tube near the ovary. (A Latin word that means "bottle.")

Infundibulum The outer, funnel-shaped part of a fallopian tube. (A Latin word that means "funnel.")

verted), although about 10% of women have uteruses that tip backward (are *retroverted*). In most instances a retroverted uterus causes no problems, but some women with retroverted uteruses find coitus in certain positions painful. (They quickly learn more comfortable positions by trial and error.) A retroverted uterus normally tips forward during pregnancy. The uppermost part of the uterus is called the **fundus** (see Figure 3.6). The central region of the uterus is called the body. The narrow lower region is the cervix, which leads downward to the vagina.

LAYERS OF THE UTERUS Like the vagina, the uterus has three layers (also shown in Figure 3.6). The innermost layer, or **endometrium**, is richly supplied with blood vessels and glands. Its structure varies according to a woman's age and the phase of the menstrual cycle. Endometrial tissue is discharged through the cervix and vagina at menstruation. For reasons not entirely understood, in some women endometrial tissue may also grow in the abdominal cavity or elsewhere in the reproductive system. This condition is called **endometriosis**, and the most common symptom is menstrual pain. If left untreated, endometriosis may lead to infertility.

Cancer of the endometrial lining is called endometrial cancer. Risk factors include obesity, a diet high in fats, early menarche or late menopause, history of failure to ovulate, and estrogen-replacement therapy (Grodstein et al., 1997). For women who obtain hormone replacement therapy (HRT), combining estrogen with progestin mitigates the risk of endometrial cancer (Grodstein et al., 1996; Rose, 1996). One of the symptoms of endometrial cancer is abnormal uterine staining or bleeding, especially after menopause. The most common treatment is surgery (Rose, 1996). The five-year survival rate for endometrial cancer is up to 95% if it is discovered early and limited to the endometrium (Rose, 1996). (Endometrial cancer is usually diagnosed early because women tend to report postmenopausal bleeding quickly to their doctors.) The survival rate drops when the cancer invades surrounding tissues or metastasizes.

The second layer of the uterus, the **myometrium**, is well muscled. It endows the uterus with flexibility and strength and creates the powerful contractions that propel a fetus outward during labour. The third or outermost layer, the **perimetrium**, provides an external cover.

HYSTERECTOMY A **hysterectomy** may be performed when women develop cancer of the uterus, ovaries, or cervix or have other diseases that cause pain or excessive uterine bleeding. A hysterectomy may be partial or complete. A **complete hysterectomy** involves surgical removal of the ovaries, fallopian tubes, cervix, and uterus. It is usually performed to reduce the risk of cancer spreading throughout the reproductive system. A partial hysterectomy removes the uterus but not the ovaries and fallopian tubes. Sparing the ovaries allows the woman to continue to ovulate and produce adequate quantities of female sex hormones.

The hysterectomy has become steeped in controversy. It is generally accepted that the operation can relieve symptoms associated with various gynecological disorders and improve the quality of life for many women (Kjerulff et al., 2000). However, many gynecologists believe that hysterectomy is often recommended inappropriately, before necessary diagnostic steps are taken or when less radical medical interventions might successfully treat the problem (Broder et al., 2000). We advise women whose physicians suggest a hysterectomy to seek a second opinion before proceeding.

The Fallopian Tubes

Two uterine tubes, also called **fallopian tubes**, are about 10 centimetres (4 inches) in length and extend from the upper end of the uterus toward the ovaries (see Figure 3.6). The part of each tube nearest the uterus is the **isthmus**, which broadens into the **ampulla** as it approaches the ovary. The outer part, or **infundibulum**, has fringelike projections called **fimbriae** that extend toward, but are not attached to, the ovary.

Ova pass through the fallopian tubes on their way to the uterus. The fallopian tubes are not inert passageways. They help nourish and conduct ova. Because ova must be fertilized within a day or two after they are released from the ovaries, fertilization usually occurs in the infundibulum within a few centimetres of the ovaries. The form of sterilization called tubal ligation ties off the fallopian tubes so that ova cannot pass through them or become fertilized.

In an **ectopic pregnancy**, the fertilized ovum implants outside the uterus, most often in the fallopian tube where fertilization occurred. Ectopic pregnancies can eventually burst fallopian tubes, causing hemorrhaging and death. Ectopic pregnancies are thus terminated before the tube ruptures. They are not easily recognized, however, because their symptoms—missed menstrual period, abdominal pain, and irregular bleeding—suggest many conditions. Experiencing any of these symptoms is an excellent reason for consulting a gynecologist.

The Ovaries

The two **ovaries** are almond-shaped organs each about 4 centimetres ($1\frac{1}{2}$ inches) long. They lie on either side of the uterus, to which they are attached by ovarian ligaments. The ovaries produce ova (egg cells) and the female sex hormones **estrogen** and **progesterone.**

Estrogen is a generic term for several hormones (such as estradiol, estriol, and estrone) that promote the changes of puberty and regulate the menstrual cycle. Estrogen also helps older women maintain cognitive functioning and feelings of psychological well-being (Ross et al., 2000; Sourander, 1994). Progesterone too has multiple functions, including regulating the menstrual cycle and preparing the uterus for pregnancy by stimulating the development of the endometrium (uterine lining). Estrogen and progesterone levels vary with the phases of the menstrual cycle.

The human female is born with all the ova she will ever have (about 2 million), but they are immature in form. About 400 000 of these survive into puberty, each contained in the ovary within a thin capsule, or **follicle**. During a woman's reproductive years, from puberty to menopause, only 400 or so ripened ova, typically 1 per month, will be released by their rupturing follicles for possible fertilization.

In Canada, about 2500 cases of ovarian cancer and 1550 deaths resulting from it are reported each year (Canadian Cancer Society, 2005). Women most at risk are those with blood relatives who had the disease, especially a first-degree relative (mother, sister, or daughter). Other risk factors are also important, because about 9 women in 10 who develop ovarian cancer do not have a family history of it. Researchers have identified several risk factors that increase the chances of developing the disease: never having given birth, prolonged use of talcum powder between the anus and the vagina, infertility, a history of breast cancer, a diet rich in meat and animal fats, and cigarette smoking (Gnagy et al., 2000; Marchbanks et al., 2000).

Early detection is the key to fighting ovarian cancer. When it is detected before it spreads beyond the ovary, 90% of victims survive. Unfortunately, ovarian cancer is often "silent" in the early stages, showing no obvious signs or symptoms. The most common sign is enlargement of the abdomen, which is caused by the accumulation of fluid. Periodic complete pelvic examinations are important. The Pap test, which is useful in detecting cervical cancer, does not reveal ovarian cancer.

Surgery, radiation therapy, and drug therapy are treatment options. Surgery usually includes the removal of one or both ovaries, the uterus, and the fallopian tubes.

Fimbriae Projections from a fallopian tube that extend toward an ovary. (Singular: fimbria. Latin for "fibre" or "fringe.")

Ectopic pregnancy A pregnancy in which the fertilized ovum implants outside the uterus, usually in the fallopian tube. (*Ectopic* derives from Greek roots that mean "out of place.")

Ovaries Almond-shaped organs that produce ova and the hormones estrogen and progesterone.

Estrogen A generic term for female sex hormones (including estradiol, estriol, estrone, and others) or synthetic compounds that promote the development of female sex characteristics and regulate the menstrual cycle. (From roots that mean "generating" [-*gen*] and "estrus.")

Progesterone A steroid hormone secreted by the corpus luteum or prepared synthetically that stimulates proliferation of the endometrium and is involved in regulation of the menstrual cycle. (From the root *pro-*, which means "promoting," and the words *gestation*, *steroid*, and *one*.)

Follicle A capsule within an ovary that contains an ovum. (From a Latin word that means "small bag.")

Figure 3.7 Use of the Speculum and Spatula During a Pelvic Examination.

The speculum holds the vaginal walls apart, while the spatula is used to scrape cells gently from the cervix. The Pap test screens for cervical cancer and other abnormalities.

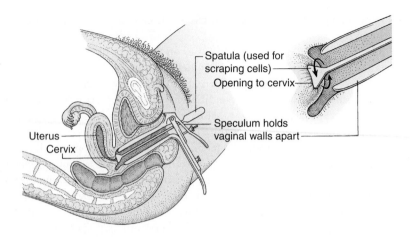

The Pelvic Examination

With the pelvic examination, the physician first examines the woman externally for irritations, swellings, abnormal vaginal discharges, and clitoral adhesions. The physician normally inserts a speculum to help inspect the cervix and vaginal walls for discharges (which can be signs of infection), discoloration, lesions, or growths. This examination is typically followed by a Pap test to detect cervical cancer. A sample of vaginal discharge may also be taken to test for the sexually transmitted disease gonorrhea.

To take a Pap smear, the physician will hold the vaginal walls open with a plastic or (prewarmed!) metal speculum so that a sample of cells (a "smear") may be scraped from the cervix with a wooden spatula (see Figure 3.7). Women should not douche prior to Pap tests or schedule them during menstruation, because douches and blood confound analysis of the smear.

The speculum exam is normally followed by a bimanual vaginal exam in which the index and middle fingers of one hand are inserted into the vagina while the lower part of the abdomen is palpated (touched) by the other hand from the outside. The physician uses this technique to examine the location, shape, size, and movability of the internal sex organs, searching for abnormal growths and symptoms of other problems. Palpation may be somewhat uncomfortable but physical discomfort is usually mild. Severe pain is a sign that something is wrong. A woman should not try to be "brave" and hide such discomfort from the examiner.

It is normal for a woman who has not had one, or who is visiting a new doctor, to be anxious about a pelvic exam. Talking about it with the examiner often relieves psychological discomfort. If the doctor is not reassuring, the woman should feel free to consult another doctor. She should not forgo the pelvic examination itself, however. It is essential for early detection of problems.

The Breasts

The degree of attention which breasts receive, combined with the confusion about what the breast fetishists actually want, makes women unduly anxious about them. They can never be just right; they must always be too small, too big, the wrong shape, too flabby.

—Germaine Greer, *The Female Eunuch*

Some college women recall:

I was very excited about my breast development. It was a big competition to see who was wearing a bra in elementary school. When I began wearing one, I also liked wearing see-through blouses so everyone would know. . . .

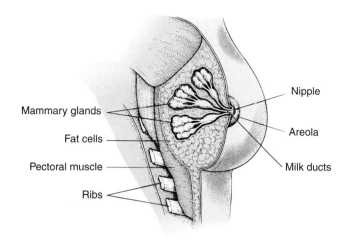

Figure 3.8
A Breast of an Adult Woman.

This drawing reveals the structures underlying the breast, including milk ducts and fat cells.

Mammary glands
Fat cells
Pectoral muscle
Ribs
Nipple
Areola
Milk ducts

My breasts were very late in developing. This brought me a lot of grief from my male peers. I just dreaded situations like going to the beach or showering in the locker room. . . .

All through junior high and high school I felt unhappy about being "overendowed." I felt just too uncomfortable in sweaters—there was so much to reveal and I was always sure that the only reason boys liked me was because of my bustline. . . .

—Morrison et al., 1980, pp. 66–70

In some cultures, the breasts are viewed merely as biological instruments for feeding infants. In our culture, however, breasts have taken on such erotic significance that a woman's self-esteem may become linked to her bustline.

A World of Diversity

THE STRONG BREAST REVOLUTION

In Canadian society, there is a fascination with female breasts. Among the two most viewed episodes of the Canadian Discovery Channel's *Sex Files* series were those on female breasts.

Under the direction of drama professor Kim Renders, University of Guelph female students collectively created a play, largely based on their own experiences, designed to educate and entertain. *The Strong Breast Revolution* explores breast-feeding, breast cancer, breasts and sexuality, and women's anxieties about their breasts, as well as the pleasure they give.

A mainly female audience at the university's conference on sexuality gave the play a standing ovation.

The Strong Breast Revolution. *Actors went topless to show that women should feel proud of their breasts.*

Secondary sex characteristics Traits that distinguish women from men but are not directly involved in reproduction.

Mammary glands Milk-secreting glands. (From the Latin *mamma*, whhic means both "breast" and "mother.")

Areola The dark ring on the breast that encircles the nipple.

The breasts are **secondary sex characteristics**. That is, like the rounding of the hips, they distinguish women from men but are not directly involved in reproduction. Each breast contains 15 to 20 clusters of milk-producing **mammary glands** (see Figure 3.8). Each gland opens at the nipple through its own duct. The mammary glands are separated by soft, fatty tissue. It is the amount of this fatty tissue, not the amount of glandular tissue, that largely determines the size of the breasts. Women vary little in their amount of glandular tissue, so breast size does not determine the quantity of milk that can be produced.

The nipple, which lies in the centre of the **areola**, contains smooth muscle fibres that contract to make the nipple erect. The areola, or area surrounding the nipple, darkens during pregnancy and remains darker after delivery. Oil-producing glands in the areola help lubricate the nipples during breast-feeding. Milk ducts conduct milk from the mammary glands through the nipples. Nipples are richly endowed with nerve endings, so stimulation of the nipples heightens sexual arousal for many women. Male nipples are similar in sensitivity. Gay males often find nipple stimulation pleasurable. Male heterosexuals generally do not, perhaps because they have learned to associate breast stimulation with the female sexual role.

Figure 3.9 shows normal variations in the size and shape of the breasts of adult women. The sensitivity of the breasts to sexual stimulation is unrelated to their size. Small breasts may have as many nerve endings as large breasts, but they will be more densely packed.

Women can prompt their partners to provide breast stimulation by informing them that their breasts are sensitive to stimulation. They can also guide a partner's hands in ways that provide the type of stimulation they desire. The breasts vary in sensitivity with the phases of the menstrual cycle, and some women appear less responsive to breast stimulation than others.

Breast Cancer

One in nine Canadian women is expected to develop breast cancer during her lifetime. For the year 2005, the Canadian Cancer Society estimated that there were 21 600 diagnosed cases of breast cancer among women and 5400 deaths caused by this disease. The incidence of breast cancer increased in Canada until the early 1990s, then decreased since 1993; the five-year survival rate for women diagnosed with breast cancer is now 82% (Canadian Cancer Society, 2005).

Many people are not aware that men can also get breast cancer. The Canadian Cancer Society (2005) estimates that in 2005 there were 150 men diagnosed with breast cancer and 45 deaths caused by this.

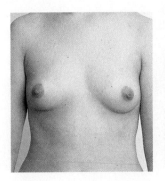 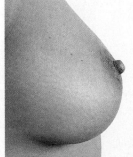 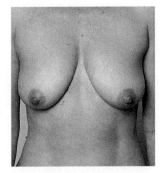

Figure 3.9 Normal Variations in the Size and Shape of the Breasts of Adult Women.

The size and shape of the breasts have little bearing on ability to produce milk or on sensitivity to sexual stimulation. Breasts have become highly eroticized in our culture.

RISK FACTORS Breast cancer is rare in women under age 25. The probability rises with age. Still, the probability of a 60-year-old woman developing breast cancer before the age of 70 is only 3% (Canadian Cancer Society, 2002). Genetic factors are involved in breast cancer (Lichtenstein et al., 2000). The risk of breast cancer is higher among women with a family history of the disease (Armstrong et al., 2000).

A key risk factor in breast cancer is prolonged exposure to estrogen, which stimulates breast development in young women and also the proliferation of breast cancer cells (Brody, 1998b). The following all heighten the risk of breast cancer because they increase the woman's exposure to estrogen: early onset of menstruation (before age 14), late menopause (after age 55), delayed childbearing (after age 30), and never giving birth (Brody, 1998a). Despite the fact that birth-control pills contain estrogen, a review of 54 studies involving more than 150 000 women concluded that, generally speaking, there is no connection between using the pill and breast cancer (Gilbert, 1996). However, other research suggests that the pill may increase the risk of breast cancer in women with a family history of the disorder (Grabrick et al., 2000). Canadian researchers have also discovered that heavy use of alcohol contributes to the risk of breast cancer as well as other cancers (Aronson, 2003). Exercise, by the way, appears to reduce the risk of breast cancer, presumably by decreasing the amount of fatty tissue in the body (Dreyfuss, 1998).

DETECTION AND TREATMENT Women with breast cancer have lumps in the breast, *but most lumps in the breasts are not cancerous.* Most are either **cysts** or **benign** tumours called **fibroadenomas.** Breast cancer involves lumps in the breast that are **malignant.**

Early detection and treatment reduce the risk of mortality. The sooner cancer is detected, the less likely it is to have spread to critical organs. The Ontario Breast Screening Program has shown that women over the age of 50 who have a family history of breast cancer are the most likely group to benefit from regular breast cancer screening (Halapy et al., 2004).

Breast cancer may be detected in various ways, including breast self-examination, physical examination, and mammography. Through mammography, tiny, highly curable cancers can be detected—and treated—before they can be felt by touch (Brody, 1995a). **Mammography** is a kind of X-ray technique that detects cancerous lumps in the breast.

The Canadian Cancer Society (2002) recommends the following screening practices to detect breast cancer:

- Mammography every two years for women between the ages of 50 and 69.
- Clinical breast examination by a trained health professional at least every two years for all women.
- Regular breast self-examination. Women should report any changes to their doctor.

A large-scale Canadian study calls into question whether women with breast cancer that has been detected via mammography have a higher survival rate than women with breast cancer that has been detected by physical examination. This study of nearly 50 000 women followed subjects for several years at a number of health centres (Miller et al., 2000). It was found that mammography is apparently no better than physical examination at reducing mortality from breast cancer (Miller et al., 2000). On the surface, it may appear that a woman can forgo mammography, but several factors give us pause. First, the women in the study all received careful regular physical examinations and self-screening. Moreover, the women receiving mammography in addition to physical examination detected cancerous growths some two years earlier than the women receiving physical examination alone. Therefore, they had a significantly longer period of time in which to undergo cancer treatment. It is true that this particular study did not find that the

Cysts Saclike structures filled with fluid or diseased material.

Benign Doing little or no harm.

Fibroadenoma A benign, fibrous tumour.

Malignant Lethal; causing or likely to cause death.

Mammography A special type of X-ray test that detects cancerous lumps in the breast.

The Canadian Cancer Society
www.cancer.ca

Applied Knowledge

BREAST SELF-EXAMINATION

The Canadian Cancer Society recommends that women conduct a breast self-examination at least once a month, preferably about a week after their period ends (when the breasts are least influenced by hormones), so that any changes can be reported promptly to a physician (see Figure 3.10). However, women are advised to undertake their initial breast self-examinations with a physician in order to determine what degree of "lumpiness" seems normal for them and to learn the proper technique.

1. *In the shower.* Examine your breasts during your bath or shower; hands glide more easily over wet skin. Keep your fingers flat and move gently over every part of each breast. Use the right hand to examine the left breast and the left hand for the right breast. Check for any lump, hard knot, or thickening.

2. *Before a mirror.* Inspect your breasts with your arms at your sides. Next, raise your arms high overhead. Look for any changes in the contour of each breast, a swelling, dimpling of skin, or changes in the nipple. Then rest your palms on your hips and press down firmly to flex your chest muscles. Your left and right breasts will not exactly match. Few women's breasts do. Regular inspection shows what is normal for you and will give you confidence in your examination.

3. *Lying down.* To examine your right breast, put a pillow or folded towel under your right shoulder. Place your right arm behind your head. This position distributes breast tissue more evenly on the chest. With your left hand, fingers flat, press gently with the finger pads (the top thirds of the fingers) of the three middle fingers in small circular motions around an imaginary clock face. Begin at the outermost top of your right breast for 12 o'clock, then move to 1 o'clock, and so on around the circle back to 12. A ridge of firm tissue in the lower curve of each breast is nor-

mal. Then move in a few centimetres, toward the nipple. Keep circling to examine *every part of your breast,* including the nipple. This requires at least three more circles. Now slowly repeat the procedure on your left breast. Put the pillow beneath your left shoulder, place your left arm behind your head, and use the finger pads on your right hand.

After you examine your left breast fully, squeeze the nipple of each breast gently between your thumb and index finger. Any discharge, clear or bloody, should be reported to your doctor immediately.

Research shows that many women who know how to do breast self-examinations do not do them regularly. Why? There are many reasons, including fear of what one will find and doubts about whether self-examination will make a difference (Kash, 1998). But the most frequently mentioned reasons are being too busy and forgetting (Friedman et al., 1994).

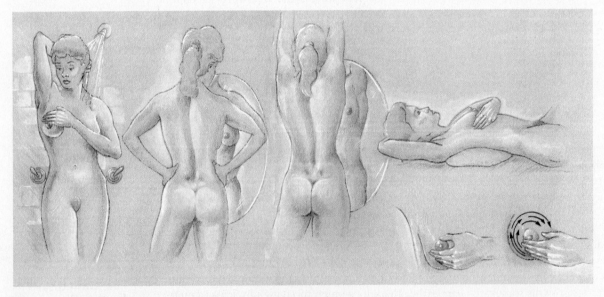

Figure 3.10 A Woman Examines Her Breast for Lumps.

additional time was connected with a higher survival rate. Given that the medical community is divided on the value of mammography, the decision rests with a woman and her doctor. Consult your doctor for the latest research information.

The practice of breast self-examination is also controversial. After reviewing the results of teaching about self-examination, in 2001 the Canadian Task Force on Preventive Health Care concluded that there was no evidence that self-examination benefited women, and that there was even a risk of some harm, such as by causing women needless worry. Based on these recommendations, Cancer Care Ontario, through its Ontario Breast Screening Program, ended its promotion of breast self-examinations (although it still provides instruction to those women who wish to be taught). It is important to note that this new policy is contrary to that of the Canadian Cancer Society, whose screening recommendations were presented above. Given the fact that the medical community is divided on this issue, women, in consultation with their doctor, will have to make their own decision about whether they wish to do breast self-examinations. Only about one-third of Canadian women self-examine their breasts each month, with older women being more likely to do so (Fisher et al., 1999).

Early detection may offer another benefit. Smaller cancerous lumps can often be removed by **lumpectomy,** which spares the breast. More advanced cancers are likely to be treated by **mastectomy.**

Research is also being done on alternative ways of detecting breast cancer. The Canadian company Z-Tech has developed a quick, painless, and relatively inexpensive method (still in clinical trials) using an electrical charge instead of X-rays (Hamilton, 2002).

Many drugs are used to treat breast cancer, and others are in the research pipeline. For example, *tamoxifen* locks into the estrogen receptors of breast cancer cells, thereby blocking the effects of estrogen that would otherwise stimulate the cells to grow and proliferate.

Many women who have had mastectomies have had surgical breast implants to replace the tissue that has been removed. Other women have breast implants to augment their breast size. Articles published in *The New England Journal of Medicine* and *The Journal of the American Medical Association* suggest that breast implants appear to have no effect on the probability of developing breast cancer (Bryant & Brasher, 1995), rheumatoid arthritis (Kolata, 1996), and a number of other health problems (Sanchez-Guerrero et al., 1995), casting doubts on previous studies that had implicated them in the development of these problems. However, this issue remains quite controversial.

The Menstrual Cycle

Menstruation is the cyclical bleeding that stems from the shedding of the uterine lining (endometrium). Menstruation takes place when a reproductive cycle has not led to the fertilization of an ovum. The word *menstruation* derives from the Latin *mensis,* which means "month." The human menstrual cycle averages about 28 days in length.

The menstrual cycle is regulated by the hormones estrogen and progesterone and can be divided into four phases. During the first phase of the cycle, the *proliferative phase,* which follows menstruation, estrogen levels increase, causing the ripening of perhaps 10 to 20 ova (egg cells) within their follicles and the proliferation of endometrial tissue in the uterus. During the second phase of the cycle, estrogen reaches peak blood levels, and **ovulation** occurs. Normally only one ovum reaches maturity and is released by an ovary during ovulation. Then the third phase of the cycle—the *secretory,* or *luteal,* phase—begins right after ovulation and continues through the beginning of the next cycle.

Lumpectomy Surgical removal of a lump from the breast.

Mastectomy Surgical removal of the entire breast.

Menstruation The cyclical bleeding that stems from the shedding of the uterine lining (endometrium).

Ovulation The release of an ovum from an ovary.

The term *luteal phase* is derived from **corpus luteum**, the name given the follicle that releases an ovum. The corpus luteum functions as an **endocrine gland** and produces large amounts of progesterone and estrogen. Progesterone causes the endometrium to thicken, so that it will be able to support an embryo if fertilization occurs. If the ovum goes unfertilized, however, estrogen and progesterone levels plummet. These falloffs trigger the fourth phase, the *menstrual phase*, which leads to the beginning of a new cycle.

Ovulation may not occur in every menstrual cycle. Anovulatory ("without ovulation") cycles are most common in the years just after **menarche**. They may become frequent again in the years prior to menopause, but they may also occur irregularly among women in their 20s and 30s.

Although the menstrual cycle averages about 28 days, variations among women, and in the same woman from month to month, are quite common. Girls' cycles often are irregular for a few years after menarche but later assume reasonably regular patterns. Variations from cycle to cycle tend to occur during the proliferative phase that precedes ovulation. That is, menstruation tends to follow ovulation reliably by about 14 days. Variations of more than 2 days in the postovulation period are rare.

Although hormones regulate the menstrual cycle, psychological factors can influence the secretion of hormones. Stress can delay or halt menstruation. Anxiety that she may be pregnant and thus miss her period may also cause a woman to be late.

Age of menarche is related to a number of health problems. Girls who menstruate at very young ages are at greater risk for such problems as breast and endometrial cancer. Malcolm Koo and colleagues (2002) at the University of Toronto have studied factors related to age of menarche. They found that girls who have a higher intake of dietary fibre or a lower intake of monounsaturated fat begin menstruating later.

Regulation of the Menstrual Cycle

The menstrual cycle involves finely tuned relationships between structures in the brain—the **hypothalamus** and the **pituitary gland**—and the ovaries and uterus. All these structures are parts of the endocrine system, which means that they secrete chemicals directly into the bloodstream. The ovaries and uterus are also reproductive organs. The chemicals secreted by endocrine glands are called **hormones**. (Other bodily secretions, such as milk, saliva, sweat, and tears, arrive at their destinations by passing through narrow, tubular structures in the body called ducts.)

Behavioural and social scientists are especially interested in hormones because of their behavioural effects. Hormones regulate bodily processes such as the metabolic rate, growth of bones and muscle, production of milk, metabolism of sugar, and storage of fats. Several hormones play important roles in sexual and reproductive functions.

The gonads—the **testes** (or testicles) in the male and the ovaries in the female—secrete sex hormones directly into the bloodstream. The female gonads, the ovaries, produce the sex hormones estrogen and progesterone. The male gonads, the testes, produce the male sex hormone **testosterone**. Males and females also produce sex hormones characteristic of the other gender, but in relatively small amounts.

The hypothalamus is a pea-sized structure in the front part of the brain. It weighs about 4 to 5 grams and lies above the pituitary gland and below (hence the prefix *hypo-*, for "under") the thalamus. Despite its small size, it is involved in regulating many states of motivation, including hunger, thirst, aggression, and sex.

The pituitary gland, which is about the size of a pea, lies below the hypothalamus at the base of the brain. Because many pituitary secretions regulate other

Corpus luteum The follicle that has released an ovum and then produces copious amounts of progesterone and estrogen during the luteal phase of a woman's cycle. (From Latin roots that mean "yellow body.")

Endocrine gland A ductless gland that releases its secretions directly into the bloodstream.

Menarche ("men-AR-kee") The first menstrual period.

Hypothalamus A bundle of neural cell bodies near the centre of the brain that are involved in regulating body temperature, motivation, and emotion.

Pituitary gland The gland that secretes growth hormone, prolactin, oxytocin, and others.

Hormone A substance that is secreted by an endocrine gland and regulates various body functions. (From the Greek *horman*, a verb meaning "to impel.")

Testes The male gonads.

Testosterone The male sex hormone that fosters the development of male sex characteristics and is connected with the sex drive.

endocrine glands, the pituitary has also been called the *master gland*. Pituitary hormones regulate bone and muscle growth and urine production. Two pituitary hormones are active during pregnancy and motherhood: **prolactin**, which stimulates production of milk; and **oxytocin**, which stimulates uterine contractions in labour and the ejection of milk during nursing. The pituitary gland also produces **gonadotropins** (literally, "that which feeds the gonads") that stimulate the ovaries: **follicle-stimulating hormone (FSH)** and **luteinizing hormone (LH)**. These hormones play central roles in regulating the menstrual cycle.

The hypothalamus receives information about bodily events through the nervous and circulatory systems. It monitors the blood levels of various hormones, including estrogen and progesterone, and releases a hormone called **gonadotropin-releasing hormone (Gn-RH)**, which stimulates the pituitary to release gonadotropins. Gonadotropins, in turn, regulate the activity of the gonads.

Phases of the Menstrual Cycle

We noted that the menstrual cycle has four stages or phases: the proliferative, ovulatory, secretory, and menstrual stages (see Figure 3.11). It might seem logical that a new cycle begins with the first day of the menstrual flow, this being the most clearly identifiable event of the cycle. Many women also count the days of the menstrual cycle beginning with the onset of menstruation. Biologically speaking, however, menstruation is really the culmination of the cycle. In fact, the cycle begins with the end of menstruation and the initiation of a series of biological events that lead to the maturation of an immature ovum in preparation for ovulation and possible fertilization.

THE PROLIFERATIVE PHASE The first phase, or the **proliferative phase**, begins with the end of menstruation and lasts about 9 or 10 days in an average 28-day cycle (see Figure 3.11). During this phase the endometrium develops, or "proliferates." This phase is also known as the *preovulatory* or *follicular phase*, because certain ovarian follicles mature and the ovaries prepare for ovulation.

Low levels of estrogen and progesterone are circulating in the blood as menstruation draws to an end. When the hypothalamus senses a low level of estrogen in the blood, it increases its secretion of Gn-RH, which in turn triggers the pituitary

Prolactin A pituitary hormone that stimulates production of milk.

Oxytocin A pituitary hormone that stimulates uterine contractions in labour and the ejection of milk during nursing.

Gonadotropins Pituitary hormones that stimulate the gonads. (Literally, "that which feeds the gonads.")

Follicle-stimulating hormone (FSH) A gonadotropin that stimulates the development of follicles in the ovaries.

Luteinizing hormone (LH) A gonadotropin that helps regulate the menstrual cycle by triggering ovulation.

Gonadotropin-releasing hormone (Gn-RH) A hormone that is secreted by the hypothalamus and stimulates the pituitary to release gonadotropins.

Proliferative phase The first phase of the menstrual cycle, which begins with the end of menstruation and lasts about 9 or 10 days. During this phase, the endometrium proliferates.

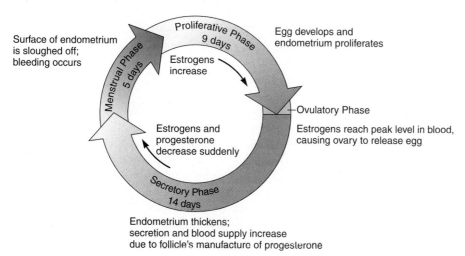

Figure 3.11 The Four Phases of the Menstrual Cycle.

The menstrual cycle consists of the proliferative, ovulatory, secretory (luteal), and menstrual phases.

Figure 3.12 Maturation and Eventual Decomposition of an Ovarian Follicle

Many follicles deveop and produce estrogen during the proliferative phase of the menstrual cycle. Usually only one, the graafian follocle, ruptres and releases an ovvum. The graafian follicle then develops into the corpus luteum, which produces copious quantities of estrogen and progesterone. When fertilization does not occur, the corpus luteum decomposes.

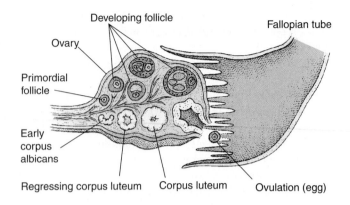

gland to release FSH. When FSH reaches the ovaries, it stimulates some follicles (perhaps 10 to 20) to begin to mature. As the follicles ripen, they all start to produce estrogen. Normally, however, only one of them—called the *graafian follicle*—will reach full maturity in the days just preceding ovulation. As the graafian follicle matures, it moves toward the surface of the ovary, where it will eventually rupture and release a mature egg (see Figure 3.12).

Estrogen causes the endometrium in the uterus to thicken to about $\frac{1}{3}$ centimetre ($\frac{1}{8}$ inch). Glands develop that will eventually nourish the embryo if fertilization occurs. Estrogen also stimulates the appearance of a thin cervical mucus. This mucus is alkaline and provides a hospitable, nutritious medium for sperm. The chances are thus increased that sperm that enter the female reproductive system at the time of ovulation will remain viable.

THE OVULATORY PHASE During ovulation, or the **ovulatory phase**, the graafian follicle ruptures and releases a mature ovum *near* a fallopian tube, not actually *into* a fallopian tube (see Figure 3.12). The other ripening follicles degenerate and are harmlessly reabsorbed by the body. Occasionally, two ova mature and are released during ovulation, and if both are fertilized, fraternal (nonidentical) twins develop. Identical twins develop when one fertilized ovum divides into two separate **zygotes.**

Ovulation is set into motion when estrogen production reaches a critical level. The high level of estrogen is detected by the hypothalamus, which triggers the pituitary to release copious amounts of FSH and LH (see Figure 3.12). The surge of LH triggers ovulation, which usually begins 12 to 24 hours after the level of LH in the body has reached its peak.

The synthetic hormone **clomiphene** is chemically similar to LH and has been used by women who ovulate irregularly to induce reliable ovulation. The induction and accurate prediction of the timing of ovulation increase the chances of conceiving.

A woman's *basal body temperature*, taken by oral or rectal thermometer, dips slightly at ovulation and rises by about 0.5°C (1°F) on the day following ovulation. Many women use this information to help them conceive or avoid conceiving.

Some women have discomfort or cramping during ovulation, a condition termed **mittelschmerz**. Mittelschmerz is sometimes confused with appendicitis. Mittelschmerz, however, may occur on either the right or the left side of the abdomen, depending on which ovary is releasing an ovum. A ruptured appendix always causes pain on the right side.

THE SECRETORY PHASE The phase following ovulation is called the postovulatory or **secretory phase**. Some people refer to it as the *luteal phase*, which reflects the name given the ruptured (graafian) follicle—the *corpus luteum*. Figure 3.12 shows the transformation of the graafian follicle into the corpus luteum.

Ovulatory phase The second stage of the menstrual cycle, during which a follicle ruptures and releases a mature ovum.

Zygote A fertilized ovum (egg cell).

Clomiphene A synthetic hormone that is chemically similar to LH and induces ovulation.

Mittelschmerz Pain that occurs during ovulation. (German for "middle pain," reflecting the fact that the pain occurs midway between menstrual periods.)

Secretory phase The third phase of the menstrual cycle, which follows ovulation. Also referred to as the *luteal phase*, after the *corpus luteum*, which begins to secrete large amounts of progesterone and estrogen following ovulation.

Under the influence of LH, the corpus luteum, which has remained in the ovary, begins to produce large amounts of progesterone and estrogen. Levels of these hormones peak at around the 20th or 21st day of an average cycle. These hormones cause the glands in the endometrium to secrete nutrients to sustain a fertilized ovum that becomes implanted in the uterine wall.

If implantation does not occur, the hypothalamus responds to the peak levels of progesterone in the blood by signalling the pituitary to stop producing LH and FSH. The levels of LH and FSH decline rapidly, leading the corpus luteum to decompose. After its decomposition, levels of estrogen and progesterone fall precipitously.

THE MENSTRUAL PHASE: AN END AND A BEGINNING The **menstrual phase** is the sloughing off of the uterine lining (the endometrium) in the menstrual flow. Menstruation occurs when estrogen and progesterone levels decline to the point where they can no longer sustain the uterine lining. The lining then disintegrates and is discharged from the body along with the menstrual flow. Menstruation itself is the passing of the lining through the cervix and vagina.

The low estrogen levels of the menstrual phase signal the hypothalamus to release Gn-RH, which in turn stimulates the pituitary to secrete FSH. FSH prompts ovarian secretion of estrogen and the onset of another proliferative phase. Thus a new cycle begins. The menstrual phase is a beginning as well as an end.

Menstrual flow contains blood from the endometrium (uterine lining), endometrial tissue, and cervical and vaginal mucus. Although the flow can appear persistent and may last for five days or more, most women lose only a total of 60 to 90 millilitres of blood (4 to 6 tablespoons). Extremely heavy or prolonged (over a week) menstrual bleeding may reflect health problems and should be discussed with a health-care provider.

Prior to 1933, women generally used external sanitary napkins or pads to absorb the menstrual flow. In that year, however, **tampons** were introduced and altered the habits of millions of women. Women who use tampons can swim without concern while menstruating, can wear more revealing or comfortable apparel, and feel generally less burdened.

Tampons are inserted into the vagina and left in place to absorb menstrual fluid. In recent years, questions have arisen about whether or not tampons cause or exacerbate infections. For example, tampon use has been linked to toxic shock syndrome (TSS), an infection that is sometimes fatal. Signs of TSS include fever, headache, sore throat, vomiting, diarrhea, muscle aches, rash, and dizziness. Peeling skin, disorientation, and a plunge in blood pressure may follow.

Many women now use regular rather than superabsorbent tampons to reduce the chance of creating a breeding ground for staph bacteria. Some women alternate tampons with sanitary napkins during each day of menstruation. Some change their tampons three or four times a day. Other women have returned to external sanitary napkins.

Coitus During Menstruation

Many couples continue to engage in coitus during menstruation, but others abstain. One study found that men and women are less likely to initiate sexual activity during menstruation than during any other phase of the woman's cycle (Harvey, 1987). Some people abstain because of religious prohibitions. Others express concern about the "fuss" or the "mess" of the menstrual flow. Despite traditional attitudes that associate menstruation with uncleanliness, there is no evidence that coitus during menstruation is physically harmful to either partner. Ironically, menstrual coitus may be helpful to the woman. The uterine contractions that occur during orgasm may help relieve cramping by dispelling blood congestion. Orgasm achieved through masturbation may have the same effect.

Menstrual phase The fourth phase of the menstrual cycle, during which the endometrium is sloughed off in the menstrual flow.

Tampon A cylindrical plug of cotton that is inserted into the vagina and left in place to absorb menstrual fluid. (A French word meaning a gun barrel "plug.")

Research in Action

MENSTRUAL SEX

Among female students at the University of Waterloo, being comfortable with one's sexuality in general was associated with being comfortable with menstruation. Women who engaged in coital sex during menstruation were more likely to also be aroused by a wide diversity of sexual activities such as group sex and spanking. This indicates that women who engage in menstrual sex are more willing to push the boundaries of what is considered to be conventional sex (Rempel & Baumgartner, 2003).

Women may be sexually aroused at any time during the menstrual cycle. The preponderance of the research evidence, however, points to a peak in sexual desire in women around the time of ovulation (Kresin, 1993).

Human coital patterns during the phases of the menstrual cycle apparently reflect personal decisions, not hormone fluctuations. Some couples may decide to increase their frequency of coitus at ovulation in order to optimize the chances of conceiving; others may abstain during menstruation because of religious beliefs or beliefs linking menses with uncleanliness. Some may also increase their coital activity preceding menstruation to compensate for anticipated abstinence during menses or increase coital activity afterward to make up for deprivation.

Menopause

Menopause, or the "change of life," is the cessation of menstruation. Menopause is a process that most commonly occurs between the ages of 46 and 50 and lasts for about two years. However, it may begin any time between the ages of 35 and 60. There is at least one case of a woman who became pregnant at age 61.

Menopause is a specific event in a long-term process known as the **climacteric** ("critical period"), the gradual decline in the reproductive capacity of the ovaries. The climacteric generally lasts for about 15 years, from ages 45 to 60 or so. After about the age of 35, the menstrual cycles of many women shorten, from an average of 28 days to 25 days at age 40 and to 23 days by the mid-40s. By the end of her 40s, a woman's cycles often become erratic, with some periods close together and others missed.

In menopause, the pituitary gland continues to pour normal levels of FSH and LH into the bloodstream, but for reasons that are not well understood, the ovaries gradually lose their capacity to respond. The ovaries no longer ripen egg cells or produce the sex hormones estrogen and progesterone.

The deficit in estrogen may lead to a number of unpleasant physical sensations, such as night sweats and hot flashes (suddenly feeling hot) and hot flushes (suddenly looking reddened) (Dennerstein et al., 2000). Hot flashes and flushes may alternate with cold sweats, in which a woman feels suddenly cold and clammy. Anyone who has experienced "cold feet" or hands from anxiety or fear will understand how dramatic the shifting patterns of blood flow can be. Hot flashes and flushes stem largely from "waves" of dilation of blood vessels across the face and upper body. All of these sensations reflect *vasomotor instability*. That is, disruptions occur in the body mechanisms that dilate or constrict the blood vessels to maintain an even body temperature. Additional signs of estrogen deficiency include dizziness, headaches, pains in the joints, sensations of tingling in the hands or feet, burning or itchy skin, and heart palpitations. The skin usually becomes drier. There is some loss of breast tissue and decreased vaginal lubrication during sexual arousal. Women may also encounter sleep problems, such as awakening more frequently at night and having difficulty going back to sleep.

Menopause The cessation of menstruation.

Climacteric A long-term process, including menopause, that involves the gradual decline in the reproductive capacity of the ovaries.

A World of Diversity

HISTORICAL AND CROSS-CULTURAL PERSPECTIVES ON MENSTRUATION

One of the more common epithets given menstruation through the course of history is "the curse." It is a common folk belief that menstruating women are contaminated. Men thus avoid contact with menstruating women for fear of their lives. To prevent their contaminating others, menstruating women in tribal societies may be dispatched to special huts on the fringe of the village. In the traditional Navajo Indian culture, for instance, menstruating women were consigned to huts set apart from other living quarters. In many Islamic societies, a menstruating woman is considered polluted and is not permitted either to pray or to enter a mosque.

Throughout the history of Western culture, menstruation has been seen as unclean, contaminating, and even magical. The Old Testament (Leviticus 15:19) warns against any physical contact with a menstruating woman, including, of course, coitus.

Negative societal attitudes toward menstruation can have a profound effect on women. Women who believe the myths about menstruation may see themselves as sources of pollution and may endure anxiety, depression, and low self-esteem.

Long-term estrogen deficiency has been linked to brittleness and porosity of the bones—a condition called **osteoporosis** (Delmas et al., 1997). Bones break more readily, and some women develop so-called dowager's hump. Osteoporosis can be severely handicapping, even life threatening. The increased brittleness of the bones increases the risk of serious fractures, especially of the hip, and many older women never recover from these fractures (Marwick, 2000). Drinking milk, which is high in calcium, increases bone density among girls and is likely to help prevent osteoporosis later in life. Calcium supplements also seem to be helpful in decreasing the number of bone fractures among postmenopausal women (Eastell, 1998).

Estrogen deficiency also has psychological effects. It can impair cognitive functioning and feelings of psychological well-being (Ross et al., 2000; Yaffe et al., 2000).

HORMONE REPLACEMENT THERAPY (HRT) Some women who experience severe physical symptoms have been helped by **hormone replacement therapy (HRT)**, which typically consists of synthetic estrogen and progesterone. These synthetic hormones are used to offset the loss of their naturally occurring counterparts. HRT may help reduce the hot flushes and other symptoms brought about by hormonal deficiencies during menopause (den Tonkelaar & Oddens, 2000). It is especially helpful in preventing the development of osteoporosis (Davidson, 1995; Delmas et al., 1997).

In 2002, major controversy over the use of HRT erupted in Canada and many other countries when researchers conducting the Women's Health Initiative study in the United States ended the project after three years instead of eight because they found a 26% increase in the incidence of breast cancer among women taking HRT (Health After 50, 2002). Specifically, after five years, it was expected that 38 women on HRT would be diagnosed with breast cancer compared with 30 women who were taking a placebo. Because of this increased risk, the Canadian Cancer Society is advising women to avoid the use of HRT. Although this increase is statistically significant, the actual increased risk for an individual woman is still small (less than one-tenth of 1%). Similar increased risks were found for stroke, heart attack, and blood clots. On the other hand, HRT decreased risks for colorectal cancer and hip fractures (Humphries & Gill, 2003).

Osteoporosis A condition caused by estrogen deficiency and characterized by a decline in bone density, such that bones become porous and brittle. (From the Greek *osteon*, which means "bone," and the Latin *porus*, which means "pore.")

Hormone replacement therapy (HRT) Replacement of naturally occurring estrogen or estrogen and progesterone with synthetic equivalents, following menopause.

Because of the overall increased health risks, many women may decide not to use HRT. However, despite the risks, some women use HRT because they feel the quality of their life is better as a consequence of having fewer menopausal symptoms such as hot flashes, night sweats, dry vagina, etc. Accordingly, women are advised to explore the health benefits and risks of HRT with their doctors.

In ending this section, we feel it is important to put the symptoms of menopause into a balanced perspective. Most women cope quite well with menopause and discover ways of minimizing unpleasant symptoms. Many are quite relieved that they no longer have to worry about the possibility of an unplanned pregnancy. Not worrying about contraception can make sexual relationships more enjoyable, and most women continue to have an active and pleasurable sex life.

Menstrual Problems

Although menstruation is a natural biological process, 50 to 75% of women experience some discomfort prior to or during menstruation (Sommerfeld, 2000). About 30% of Canadian women report that they usually experience extremely painful menstrual periods (Fisher et al., 1999). Taking the birth control pill reduces the severity of menstrual periods for many women but does not seem to reduce the incidence of premenstrual syndrome (PMS).

Table 3.1 contains a list of commonly reported symptoms of menstrual problems. The problems we explore in this section include dysmenorrhea, mastalgia, menstrual migraine headaches, amenorrhea, and PMS.

Dysmenorrhea

Pain or discomfort during menstruation, or **dysmenorrhea**, is the most common type of menstrual problem. Most women at some time have at least mild menstrual pain or discomfort. Pelvic cramps are the most common manifestation of dysmenorrhea. They may be accompanied by headache, backache, nausea, or bloated feelings. Women who develop severe cases usually do so within a few years of menarche. **Primary dysmenorrhea** is menstrual pain or discomfort in the absence

Dysmenorrhea Pain or discomfort during menstruation.

Primary dysmenorrhea Menstrual pain or discomfort that occurs in the absence of known organic problems.

TABLE 3.1
Symptoms of Menstrual Problems

Physical Symptoms	Psychological Symptoms
Swelling of the breasts	Depressed mood, sudden tearfulness
Tenderness in the breasts	Loss of interest in usual social or recreational activities
Bloating	
Weight gain	Anxiety, tension (feeling "on edge" or "keyed up")
Food cravings	
Abdominal discomfort	Anger
Cramping	Irritability
Lack of energy	Changes in body image
Sleep disturbance, fatigue	Concern over skipping routine activities, school, or work
Migraine headache	A sense of loss of control
Pains in muscles and joints	A sense of loss of ability to cope
Aggravation of chronic disorders such as asthma and allergies	

of known organic pathology. Women with **secondary dysmenorrhea** have identified organic problems that are believed to cause their menstrual problems. Their pain or discomfort is caused by, or *secondary to*, these problems. Endometriosis, pelvic inflammatory disease, and ovarian cysts are just a few of the organic disorders that can give rise to secondary dysmenorrhea. Yet evidence is accumulating that supposed primary dysmenorrhea is often *secondary* to hormonal changes, although the precise causes have not been delineated. For example, menstrual cramps sometimes decrease dramatically after childbirth, as a result of the massive hormonal changes that occur with pregnancy.

BIOLOGICAL ASPECTS OF DYSMENORRHEA Menstrual cramps appear to result from uterine spasms that may be brought about by copious secretion of hormones called prostaglandins. **Prostaglandins** apparently cause muscle fibres in the uterine wall to contract, as during labour. Most contractions go unnoticed, but powerful, persistent contractions are discomfiting in themselves and may temporarily deprive the uterus of oxygen, another source of distress. Women with more intense menstrual discomfort apparently produce higher quantities of prostaglandins. Prostaglandin-inhibiting drugs, such as ibuprofen, indomethacin, and Aspirin, are thus often helpful. Menstrual pain may also be secondary to endometriosis.

Pelvic pressure and bloating may be traced to pelvic edema (Greek for "swelling")—the congestion of fluid in the pelvic region. Fluid retention can lead to a gain of several pounds, sensations of heaviness, and **mastalgia**—a swelling of the breasts that sometimes causes premenstrual discomfort. Masters and Johnson (1966) noted that orgasm (through coitus or masturbation) can help relieve menstrual discomfort by reducing the pelvic congestion that spawns bloating and pressure. Orgasm may also increase the menstrual flow and shorten this phase of the cycle.

Headaches frequently accompany menstrual discomfort. Most headaches (in both sexes) stem from simple muscle tension, notably in the shoulders, the back of the neck, and the scalp. Pelvic discomfort may cause muscle contractions, thus contributing to the tension that produces headaches. Women who are tense about their menstrual flow are thus candidates for muscle tension headaches. Migraine headaches may arise from changes in the blood flow in the brain, however. Migraines are typically limited to one side of the head and are often accompanied by visual difficulties.

Amenorrhea

Amenorrhea, the absence of menstruation, is a primary sign of infertility. **Primary amenorrhea** is the absence of menstruation in a woman who has not menstruated at all by about the age of 16 or 17. **Secondary amenorrhea** is delayed or absent menstrual periods in women who have had regular periods in the past. Amenorrhea has various causes, including abnormalities in the structures of the reproductive system, hormonal abnormalities, growths such as cysts and tumours, and psychological problems, such as stress. Amenorrhea is normal during pregnancy and following menopause. Amenorrhea is also a symptom of **anorexia nervosa**, an eating disorder characterized by an intense fear of putting on weight and a refusal to eat enough to maintain a normal body weight, which often results in extreme (and sometimes life-threatening) weight loss. Hormonal changes that accompany emaciation are believed to be responsible for the cessation of menstruation. Amenorrhea may also occur in women who exercise strenuously, such as competitive long-distance runners. It is unclear whether the cessation of menstruation in female athletes is due to the effects of strenuous exercise itself, to related physical factors such as low body fat, to the stress of intensive training, or to a combination of factors.

Secondary dysmenorrhea Menstrual pain or discomfort that is caused by identified organic problems.

Prostaglandins Hormones that cause muscle fibres in the uterine wall to contract, as during labour.

Mastalgia A swelling of the breasts that sometimes causes premenstrual discomfort.

Amenorrhea The absence of menstruation.

Primary amenorrhea Lack of menstruation in a woman who has never menstruated.

Secondary amenorrhea Lack of menstruation in a woman who has previously menstruated.

Anorexia nervosa A psychological disorder of eating characterized by intense fear of putting on weight and refusal to eat enough to maintain normal body weight.

Premenstrual Syndrome (PMS)

The term **premenstrual syndrome (PMS)** describes the combination of biological and psychological symptoms that may affect women during the four- to six-day interval that precedes their menses each month. For many women, premenstrual symptoms persist during menstruation. Table 3.2 shows the symptoms of **premenstrual dysphoric disorder (PMDD),** a less common condition more severe than ordinary PMS.

Fifty-eight percent of Canadian women experience premenstrual syndrome (Fisher et al., 1999). The great majority of cases involve mild to moderate levels of discomfort. PMS is not unique to our culture.

The causes of PMS are unclear, but evidence is accumulating for a biological basis. Researchers are looking to possible relationships between menstrual problems, including PMS, and chemical imbalances in the body.

When PMS includes severe changes in mood and impairment of social functioning, it is categorized in the American Psychiatric Association's newest Diagnostic and Statistical Manual as *premenstrual dysphoric disorder (PMDD)*. According to Hamilton medical researchers Lori Ross and Meir Steiner (2003a, 2003b), both biological factors and social factors such as life stress, sexual abuse, and negative social attitudes contribute to PMDD.

However, this diagnostic category has caused considerable controversy. Ottawa researchers Alia Offman and Peggy Kleinplatz argue that the research support for PMDD is weak. They are concerned that pharmaceutical companies have supported research that legitimizes this diagnostic concept in order to promote increased use of drug products (Offman & Kleinplatz, 2004).

Only a generation ago, PMS was seen as something a woman must put up with. No longer. Today there are many treatment options. These include exercise, dietary control (for example, eating several small meals a day rather than two or three large meals, limiting salt and sugar, and taking vitamin supplements), hormone treatments (usually progesterone), and medications that reduce anxiety or increase the amount of serotonin in the nervous system (Mortola, 1998). If you have PMS, get a clear idea which symptoms affect you most by using a PMS calendar or simply paying close attention to what happens. Then check with your physician about the most up-to-date treatment approaches.

TABLE 3.2
Symptoms of Premenstrual Dysphoric Disorder (PMDD)*

1. Feelings of sadness, hopelessness, or worthlessness	6. Difficulty concentrating
2. Tension, anxious, feeling "on edge"	7. Fatigue, lethargy, lack of energy
3. Notable changes in mood, including frequent crying	8. Notable changes in appetite, such as binge eating or craving certain foods.
4. Persistent irritability and anger, often leading to increased interpersonal conflict	9. Hypersomnia (sleeping too much) or insomnia
5. Lessened interest in usual activities, possibly with withdrawal from social relationships	10. Feeling overwhelmed or out of control
	11. Other physical symptoms, for example, tenderness or swelling of the breasts, headaches, joint or muscle pain, feelings of bloating, weight gain

Source: DSM-IV-TR (2000). Washington, DC: American Psychiatric Association.

* In order to diagnose PMDD, the DSM-IV-TR requires that symptoms have been present for most menstrual cycles over a given year. Five or more of the symptoms must be present most of the time during the week before the period and ending within a few days after the period begins. At least one symptom must be one of the first four. The symptoms must notably impair functioning at work or school or in social activities and relationships.

Applied Knowledge

HOW TO HANDLE MENSTRUAL DISCOMFORT

Most women experience some degree of menstrual discomfort. Women with persistent menstrual distress may profit from the suggestions listed below. Researchers are exploring the effectiveness of these techniques in controlled studies. For now, you might consider running a personal experiment. Adopt the techniques that sound right for you—all of them, if you wish.

1. Don't blame yourself! Menstrual problems were once erroneously attributed to women's "hysterical" nature. This is nonsense. Menstrual problems appear, in large part, to reflect hormonal variations or chemical fluctuations in the brain during the menstrual cycle. Researchers have not yet fully identified all the causal elements and patterns, but their lack of knowledge does *not* mean that women who have menstrual problems are hysterical.

2. Keep a menstrual calendar so that you can track your menstrual symptoms systematically and identify patterns.

3. Develop strategies for dealing with days when you experience the greatest distress—strategies that will help enhance your pleasure and minimize the stress affecting you on those days. Activities that distract you from your menstrual discomfort may be helpful. Go see a movie or get into that novel you've been meaning to read.

4. Ask yourself whether you harbour any self-defeating attitudes toward menstruation that might be compounding distress. Do close relatives or friends see menstruation as an illness, a time of "pollution," a "dirty thing"? Have you adopted any of these attitudes—if not verbally, then in ways that affect your behaviour, such as by restricting your social activities during your period?

5. See a doctor about your concerns, especially if you have severe symptoms. Severe menstrual symptoms are often secondary to medical disorders such as endometriosis and pelvic inflammatory disease (PID). Check it out.

6. Develop nutritious eating habits and continue them throughout the entire cycle (that means always). Consider limiting your intake of alcohol, caffeine, fats, salt, and sweets, especially during the days preceding menstruation. Research suggests that a low-fat, vegetarian diet reduces the duration and intensity of menstrual pain and the duration of premenstrual symptoms (Barnard et al., 2000).

7. Eat several smaller meals (or nutritious snacks) throughout the day, rather than a few highly filling meals.

8. Some women find that vigorous exercise—jogging, swimming, bicycling, fast walking, dancing, skating, even jumping rope—helps relieve premenstrual and menstrual discomfort. Evidence suggests that exercise helps to relieve and possibly prevent menstrual discomfort (Choi, 1992). By the way, develop regular exercise habits. Don't become solely a premenstrual athlete.

9. Check with your doctor about vitamin and mineral supplements (such as calcium and magnesium). Vitamin B6 appears to have helped some women.

10. Ibuprofen (brand names: Medipren, Advil, Motrin, etc.) and other medicines available over the counter may be helpful for cramping. Prescription drugs such as anti-anxiety drugs (such as alprazolam) and anti-depressant drugs (serotonin-reuptake inhibitors) may also be of help (Mortola, 1998). "Anti-depressants" affect levels of neurotransmitters in a way that can be helpful for women with PMS. Their benefits do not mean that women with PMS are depressed. Ask your doctor for a recommendation.

11. Remind yourself that menstrual problems are time-limited. Don't worry about getting through life or a career. Just get through the next couple of days.

Male Anatomy and Physiology

Phallic symbols Images of the penis that are usually suggestive of generative power.

Testes The male sex glands, suspended in the scrotum, that produce sperm cells and male sex hormones. Singular: *testis*.

Testicles Testes.

In the first part of this chapter we have explored female sexual anatomy and physiology. We now turn our attention to the male.

From the earliest foundations of Western civilization, male-dominated societies elevated men and exalted male genitalia. The ancient Greeks carried oversized images of fish as **phallic symbols** in their Dionysian processions, which celebrated the wilder and more frenzied aspects of human sexuality. In the murky predawn light of Western civilization, humankind engaged in phallic worship.

Men held their own genitals in such high esteem that it was common courtroom practice for them to swear to tell the truth with their hands on their genitals—as we swear to tell the truth in the name of God or by placing our hands on the Bible. The words **testes** and **testicles** derive from the same Latin word as *testify*. The Latin *testis* means "a witness."

Even today, we see evidence of pride in—indeed veneration of!—the male genitalia. Men with large genitals are accorded respect from their male peers and sometimes adoration from female admirers. Slang describes men with large genitals as "well hung" or "hung like a bull" (or stallion).

Given these cultural attitudes, it is not surprising that young men (and some not-so-young men) belittle themselves if they feel, as many do, that they are little—that is, that their penises do not measure up to some ideal. Some men feel so insecure about the size of their penis that they have operations to lengthen it. In Toronto, plastic surgeon Ken Stubbs has performed penis enlargement operations on hundreds of men since 1993. On average, he lengthens the visible penis by 3 centimetres (1¼ inches) (Nichols, 1999). In examining male sexual anatomy and physiology, we attempt to sort out truth from fiction. We see, for example, that despite his lingering doubts, a man's capabilities as a lover do not depend on the size of his penis (at least within broad limits).

In our exploration of male sexual anatomy and physiology, as in our exploration of female sexual anatomy and physiology, we begin with the external genitalia and then move inward. Once inside, we focus on the route of sperm through the male reproductive system.

External Sex Organs

The external male sex organs include the penis and the scrotum (see Figures 3.13 and 3.14).

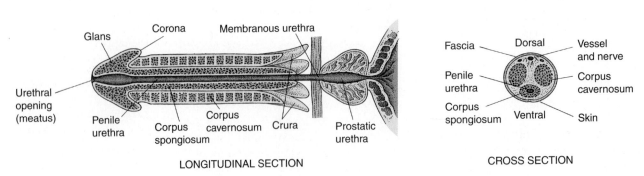

LONGITUDINAL SECTION

CROSS SECTION

Figure 3.13 The Penis.

During sexual arousal, the corpora cavernosa and corpus spongiosum become congested with blood, causing the penis to enlarge and stiffen.

Figure 3.14 The
Male Reproductive
System.

The external male sex
organs include the penis and
the scrotum.

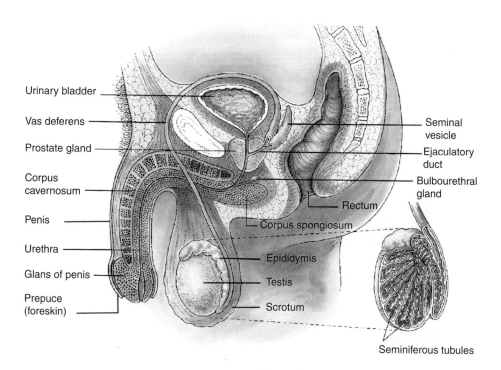

Urinary bladder
Vas deferens
Prostate gland
Corpus cavernosum
Penis
Urethra
Glans of penis
Prepuce (foreskin)

Seminal vesicle
Ejaculatory duct
Bulbourethral gland
Rectum
Corpus spongiosum
Epididymis
Testis
Scrotum

Seminiferous tubules

The Penis

Is that a gun in your pocket, or are you just glad to see me?
—Mae West

At first glance, the **penis** may seem rather simple and obvious in its structures, particularly when compared with women's organs. This apparent simplicity may have contributed to cultural stereotypes that men are straightforward and aggressive, whereas women tend to be complicated and perhaps mysterious. Yet, as Figure 3.13 shows, the apparent simplicity of the penis is misleading. Much goes on below the surface.

The penis, like the vagina, is the sex organ used in sexual intercourse. Unlike the vagina, however, the penis also serves as a conduit for urine. Both semen and urine pass out of the penis through the urethral opening. The opening is called the urethral *meatus* (pronounced me-ATE-us), which means "passage."

Many mammals, including dogs, have penile bones that stiffen the penis to facilitate copulation. Despite the slang term *boner*, the human penis contains no bones. Nor, despite another slang term, *muscle*, does the penis contain muscle tissue. However, muscles at the base of the penis, like the muscles surrounding the vaginal and urethral openings in women, are involved in controlling urination and ejaculation.

Rather than bones or muscles, the penis contains three cylinders of spongy material that run its length. The larger two of these cylinders, the **corpora cavernosa** (see Figure 3.13), lie side by side and function like the cavernous bodies in the clitoris. These cylinders fill up with blood and stiffen during sexual arousal. In addition, a **corpus spongiosum** (spongy body) runs along the bottom, or ventral, surface of the penis. It contains the penile urethra that conducts urine through the penis to the urinary opening (urethral meatus) at the tip. At the tip of the penis, the spongy body enlarges to become the glans, or head, of the penis.

All three cylinders consist of spongy tissue that swells (becomes engorged) with blood during sexual arousal, resulting in erection. The urethra is connected to the

Penis The male organ of sexual intercourse. (From the Latin for "tail.")

Corpora cavernosa Cylinders of spongy tissue in the penis that become congested with blood and stiffen during sexual arousal.

Corpus spongiosum The spongy body that runs along the bottom of the penis, contains the penile urethra, and enlarges at the tip of the penis to form the glans.

Corona The ridge that separates the glans from the body of the penis. (From the Latin for "crown.").

Frenulum The sensitive strip of tissue that connects the underside of the penile glans to the shaft. (From the Latin *frenum*, which means "bridle.")

Root The base of the penis, which extends into the pelvis.

Shaft The body of the penis, which expands as a result of vasocongestion.

Foreskin The loose skin that covers the penile glans. Also referred to as the *prepuce*.

Circumcision Surgical removal of the foreskin of the penis. (From the Latin *circumcidere*, which means "to cut around.")

The Circumcision Resource Center Informs the general public and professionals about circumcision.

www.circumcision.org

bladder, which is unrelated to reproduction, and to those parts of the reproductive system that transport semen.

The glans of the penis, like the clitoral glans, is extremely sensitive to sexual stimulation. Direct, prolonged stimulation can become irritating, even painful. Men generally prefer to masturbate by stroking the shaft of the penis rather than the glans, although some prefer the latter. The **corona**, or coronal ridge, separates the glans from the body of the penis. After the glans, the parts of the penis that men tend to find most sensitive are the corona and an area on the underside of the penis called the frenulum. The **frenulum** is a thin strip of tissue that connects the underside of the glans to the shaft. Most men find the top part of the penis to be the least sensitive part.

The base of the penis, which is called the **root**, extends into the pelvis. It is attached to pelvic bones by leglike structures, called crura, that are like those that anchor the female's clitoris. The body of the penis is called the penile **shaft**. The penile shaft, unlike the clitoral shaft, is free-swinging. Thus, when sexual excitement engorges the penis with blood, the result—erection—is obvious. The skin of the penis is hairless and loose, allowing expansion during erection. It is fixed to the penile shaft just behind the glans. Some of it, however, like the labia minora in the female, folds over to partially cover the glans. This covering is the prepuce, or **foreskin**. It covers part or all of the penile glans just as the clitoral prepuce (hood) covers the clitoral shaft. The prepuce consists of loose skin that freely moves over the glans. However, smegma—a cheeselike, foul-smelling secretion—may accumulate below the prepuce, causing the foreskin to adhere to the glans.

CIRCUMCISION **Circumcision** is the surgical removal of the prepuce (Figure 3.15). Male circumcision has a long history as a religious rite. Jews traditionally carry out male circumcision shortly after a baby is born.

Advocates of circumcision believe that it enhances hygiene because it eliminates a site where smegma might accumulate and disease organisms might flourish. Opponents of circumcision believe that it is unnecessary because regular cleaning is sufficient to reduce the risk of these problems. The number of circumcisions has been declining in Canada; today, about one-quarter of male babies are circumcised. The circumcision rate varies widely across the country—in Ontario, for example, about 50% of male babies are circumcised, compared with 20% in the Maritimes (Keung, 1999).

The Circumcision Information Resource Centre, a Montreal-based lobby group, seeks to ban male circumcision on infants and children in Canada in the same way that female circumcision has been made illegal. In a 1996 report on circumcision, the Canadian Paediatric Society concluded that the procedure is not medically necessary and recommended against circumcisions being performed as a

Figure 3.15
Normal Variations in the Male Genitals.

The penis and scrotum vary a good deal in appearance from one man to another. The penis in the photo to the right is uncircumcised.

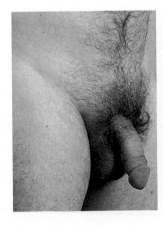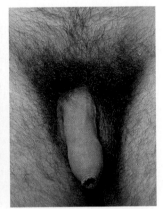

A World of Diversity

ON PENIS SIZE AND SEXUAL PERFORMANCE

The belief that the size of the man's penis determines his sexual prowess is based on the assumption that men with bigger penises are better equipped to satisfy a woman sexually. Zilbergeld (1978) and others point out, however, that women rarely mention penis size as an important element in their sexual satisfaction. Quite regularly they *do* mention ability to communicate with partners, the emotional atmosphere of the relationship, and sensitivity to employing sexual techniques that enhance their partner's pleasure.

The diameter of the penis may have a greater bearing on a partner's sexual sensations than its length, because thicker penises may provide more clitoral stimulation during intercourse. Even though the inner vagina is relatively insensitive to touch, some women find the *pressure* of deeper penetration sexually pleasurable. Others, however, find deeper penetration to be uncomfortable or painful, especially if thrusting is too vigorous.

There has been a notable lack of research into women's preferences regarding penis size. In a 1998 national survey of Canadian women, the Compas polling organization asked "What is the ideal penis size?" Most women preferred either an average (37%) or somewhat larger than average penis (45%). Hardly any preferred either a much larger than average one (3%) or a somewhat smaller than average one (4%), and 12% didn't express an opinion.

routine practice. Still, the Society took the view that parents should have the right to decide whether to have their infants circumcised (Keung, 1999).

Some research suggests that circumcision may reduce the transmission of sexually transmitted infections (STIs). For example, studies show that urinary tract infections are more common among uncircumcised male infants than among circumcised infants (Herzog, 1989). Research in Africa suggests that uncircumcised men are at greater risk than circumcised men of becoming infected by the AIDS virus, at least during male–female sexual relations (Bailey, R., 2000; Halperin & Bailey, 1999; Cohen, 2000).

Physicians once agreed that circumcision was the treatment of choice for **phimosis**, a condition in which it is difficult to retract the foreskin from the glans. But today, only a small minority of males with phimosis are circumcised for that reason (Rickwood et al., 2000).

PENIS SIZE In our culture the size of the penis is sometimes seen as a measure of a man's masculinity and his ability to please his sex partner (see the nearby Closer Look feature).

Masters and Johnson (1966) reported that the penises of the 312 male subjects they studied generally ranged in length from 9 centimetres $3\frac{1}{12}$ inches) to a little more than 10 centimetres (4 inches). The average erect penis ranges from 13 to 18 centimetres (5 to 7 inches) in length (Reinisch, 1990). There appears to be little relationship between the size of a given penis when flaccid and when erect. Penises that are small when flaccid tend to gain more size when they become erect. Larger flaccid penises gain relatively less (Jamison & Gebhard, 1988). Nor is there a relationship between penis size and body weight, height, or build (Money et al., 1984).

Even when flaccid, the same penis can vary in size. Factors such as cold air or water and emotions of fear or anxiety can cause the penis (along with the scrotum and testicles) to draw closer to the body, reducing its size. The flaccid penis may also grow in size in warm water or when the man is relaxed.

Phimosis An abnormal condition in which the foreskin is so tight that it cannot be withdrawn from the glans. (From the Greek *phimos*, which means "muzzle.")

The Scrotum

The **scrotum** is a pouch of loose skin that becomes covered lightly with hair at puberty. The scrotum consists of two compartments that hold the testes. Each testicle is held in place by a **spermatic cord**, a structure that contains the **vas deferens**, blood vessels and nerves, and the cremaster muscle. The **cremaster muscle** raises and lowers the testicle within the scrotum in response to temperature changes and sexual stimulation. (The testes are drawn closer to the body during sexual arousal.)

Sperm production is optimal at a temperature that is slightly cooler than the 37°C (98.6°F) that is desirable for most of the body. Typical scrotal temperature is a few degrees lower than body temperature. The scrotum is loose-hanging and flexible. It permits the testes and nearby structures to escape the higher body heat, especially in warm weather. In the middle layer of the scrotum is the **dartos muscle**, which (like the cremaster) contracts and relaxes reflexively in response to temperature changes. In cold weather, or when a man jumps into a body of cold water, it contracts to bring the testes closer to the body. In warm weather it relaxes, allowing the testes to dangle farther from the body. The dartos muscle also increases or decreases the surface area of the scrotum in response to temperature changes. Smoothing allows greater dissipation of heat in hot weather. Tightening or constricting the skin surface helps retain heat and gives the scrotum a wrinkled appearance in the cold.

The scrotum is developed from the same embryonic tissue that becomes the labia majora of the female. Thus, like the labia majora, it is quite sensitive to sexual stimulation. It is somewhat more sensitive than the top side of the penis but less so than other areas of the penis.

Internal Sex Organs

The male internal sex organs consist of the testes, the organs that manufacture sperm and the male sex hormone testosterone; the system of tubes and ducts that conduct sperm through the male reproductive system; and the organs that help nourish and activate sperm and neutralize some of the acidity that sperm encounter in the vagina.

The Testes

The testes are the male gonads (*gonad* derives from the Greek *gone*, which means "seed"). In slang the testes are frequently referred to as "balls" or "nuts." These terms are considered vulgar, but they are reasonably descriptive. They also make it easier for many people to refer to the testes in informal conversation.

The testes serve two functions analogous to those of the ovaries. They secrete sex hormones and produce mature **germ cells**. In the case of the testes, the germ cells are **sperm** and the sex hormones are **androgens**. The most important androgen is **testosterone.**

Scrotum The pouch of loose skin that contains the testes. (From the same linguistic root as the word *shred*, which means "a long, narrow strip," probably referring to the long furrows on the scrotal sac.)

Spermatic cord The cord that suspends a testicle within the scrotum and contains a vas deferens, blood vessels, nerves, and the cremaster muscle.

Vas deferens A tube that conducts sperm from the testicle to the ejaculatory duct of the penis. (From Latin roots meaning "a vessel" that "carries down.")

Cremaster muscle The muscle that raises and lowers the testicle in response to temperature changes and sexual stimulation.

Dartos muscle The muscle in the middle layer of the scrotum that contracts and relaxes in response to temperature changes.

Germ cell A cell from which a new organism develops. (From the Latin *germen*, which means "bud" or "sprout.")

Sperm The male germ cell. (From a Greek root that means "seed.")

Androgens Male sex hormones. (From the Greek *andros*, which means "man" or "males," and -*gene*, which means "born.")

Testosterone A male steroid sex hormone.

Figure 3.16 Interstitial Cells.

Testosterone is produced by the interstitial cells, which lie between the seminiferous tubules in each testis. Sperm (seen in the middle of the diagram) are produced within the seminiferous tubules.

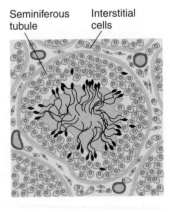

Seminiferous tubule   Interstitial cells

TESTOSTERONE Testosterone is secreted by **interstitial cells**, which are also referred to as **Leydig's cells**. Interstitial cells lie between the seminiferous tubules and release testosterone directly into the bloodstream (see Figure 3.16). Testosterone stimulates the prenatal differentiation of male sex organs, sperm production, and the development of **secondary sex characteristics**, such as the beard, deep voice, and the growth of muscle mass.

In men, several endocrine glands—the hypothalamus, pituitary gland, and testes (see Figure 3.17)—keep blood testosterone levels at a more or less even level. This contrasts with the peaks and valleys in levels of female sex hormones during the phases of the menstrual cycle. Testosterone levels vary slightly with stress, time of day or month, and other factors, but a feedback loop among the endocrine glands keeps them relatively stable.

The testes usually range between 2.5 and 4.5 centimetres (1 and 1¾ inches) in length. They are about half as wide and deep. The left testicle usually hangs lower, because the left spermatic cord tends to be somewhat longer.

SPERM Each testicle is divided into many lobes. The lobes are filled with winding **seminiferous tubules** (see Figure 3.14). Although packed into a tiny space, these tubules, placed end to end, would span the length of several football fields. Through a process called **spermatogenesis**, these threadlike structures produce and store hundreds of billions of sperm through the course of a man's lifetime.

Sperm cells develop through several stages. It takes about 72 days for the testes to manufacture a mature sperm cell (Leary, 1990). In an early stage, sperm cells are called **spermatocytes**. Each one contains 46 chromosomes, including one X and one Y sex chromosome. Each spermatocyte divides into two **spermatids**, each of which has 23 chromosomes. Half the spermatids have X sex chromosomes, and the other half have Y sex chromosomes. Mature sperm cells, called **spermatozoa**, look something like tadpoles when examined under a microscope. Each has a head, a cone-shaped midpiece, and a tail. The head is about 5 microns (.00005 centimetre) long and contains the cell nucleus that houses the 23 chromosomes. The midpiece contains structures that provide the energy the tail needs to lash back and forth in a swimming motion. Each sperm cell is about 50 microns (.0005 centimetre) long, one of the smallest cells in the body (Thompson, 1993).

During fertilization, the 23 chromosomes from the father's sperm cell combine with the 23 chromosomes from the mother's ovum, furnishing the standard ensemble of 46 chromosomes in the offspring. Among the 23 chromosomes borne by sperm cells is one sex chromosome—an X sex chromosome or a Y sex chromosome.

> **Interstitial cells** Cells that lie between the seminiferous tubules and secrete testosterone. (*Interstitial* means "set between.")
>
> **Leydig's cells** Another term for *interstitial cells*.
>
> **Secondary sex characteristics** Traits that distinguish the genders but are not directly involved in reproduction.
>
> **Seminiferous tubules** Tiny, winding, sperm-producing tubes that are located within the lobes of the testes. (From Latin roots that mean "seed bearing.")
>
> **Spermatogenesis** The process by which sperm cells are produced and developed.
>
> **Spermatocyte** An early stage in the development of sperm cells, in which each parent cell has 46 chromosomes, including one X and one Y sex chromosome.
>
> **Spermatids** Cells formed by the division of spermatocytes. Each spermatid has 23 chromosomes.
>
> **Spermatozoa** Mature sperm cells.

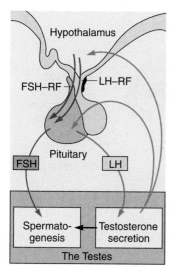

Figure 3.17 Hormonal Control of the Testes.

Several endocrine glands—the hypothalamus, the pituitary gland, and the testes—keep blood testosterone levels at a more or less constant level. Low testosterone levels signal the hypothalamus to secrete LH-releasing hormone (LH-RH). Like dominoes falling in line, LH-RH causes the pituitary gland to secrete LH, which in turn stimulates the testes to release testosterone. Follicle-stimulating-hormone-releasing hormone (FSH-RH) from the hypothalamus causes the pituitary to secrete FSH, which, in turn, causes the testes to produce sperm cells.

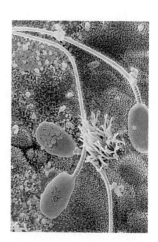

Human Sperm Cells Magnified Many Times.

Epididymis A tube that lies against the back wall of each testicle and serves as a storage facility for sperm. (From Greek roots that mean "upon testicles.")

Seminal vesicles Small glands that lie behind the bladder and secrete fluids that combine with sperm in the ejaculatory ducts.

Ejaculatory duct A duct, formed by the convergence of a vas deferens with a seminal vesicle, through which sperm pass through the prostate gland and into the urethra.

Cilia Hairlike projections from cells which beat rhythmically to produce locomotion or currents.

Ova contain X sex chromosomes only. The union of an X sex chromosome and a Y sex chromosome leads to the development of male offspring. Two X sex chromosomes combine to yield female offspring. Thus, whether the father contributes an X or a Y sex chromosome determines the baby's gender.

The testes are veritable dynamos of manufacturing power, churning out about 1000 sperm per second, or about 30 billion—yes, *billion*—per year. Mathematically speaking, 10 to 20 ejaculations hold enough sperm to populate the earth.

Sperm proceed from the seminiferous tubules through an intricate maze of ducts that converge in a single tube called the **epididymis**. The epididymis lies against the back wall of the testicle and serves as a storage facility for sperm.

The Vas Deferens

Each epididymis empties into a vas deferens (also called *ductus deferens*). The vas is a thin, cylindrical tube about 40 centimetres (16 inches) long that serves as a conduit for mature sperm. In the scrotum, the vas deferens lies near the skin surface within the spermatic cord. Therefore, a **vasectomy**, an operation in which the right and left vas deferens are severed, is a convenient means of sterilization. The tube leaves the scrotum and follows a circuitous path up into the abdominal cavity. Then it loops back along the rear surface of the bladder (see Figure 3.18).

The Seminal Vesicles

The two **seminal vesicles** are small glands, each about 5 centimetres (2 inches) long. They lie behind the bladder and open into the **ejaculatory ducts**, where the fluids they secrete combine with sperm (see Figure 3.18). A vesicle is a small cavity or sac; the seminal vesicles were so named because they were mistakenly believed to be reservoirs for semen, rather than glands.

The fluid produced by the seminal vesicles is rich in fructose, a form of sugar, which nourishes sperm and helps them become active, or motile. Sperm motility is a major factor in male fertility. Before reaching the ejaculatory ducts, sperm are propelled along their journey by contractions of the epididymis and vas deferens and by **cilia** that line the walls of the vas deferens. Once they become motile, they propel themselves by whipping their tails.

At the base of the bladder, each vas deferens joins a seminal vesicle to form a short ejaculatory duct that runs through the middle of the prostate gland (see Figure 3.18). In the prostate, the ejaculatory duct opens into the urethra, which leads to the tip of the penis.

Figure 3.18 Passage of Spermatozoa.

Each testicle is divided into lobes that contain threadlike seminiferous tubules. Through spermatogenesis, the tubules produce and store hundreds of billions of sperm over the course of a man's lifetime. During ejaculation, sperm cells travel through the vas deferens, up and over the bladder, into the ejaculatory duct, and then through the urethra. Secretions from the seminal vesicles and the bulbourethral glands join with sperm to compose semen.

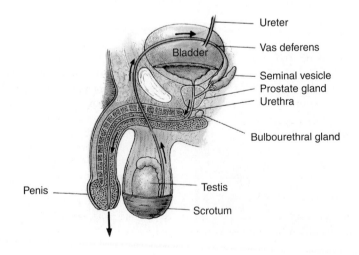

Is There a *Manopause?*

The scientific jury is still out on the existence of the "male menopause." Women encounter relatively sudden age-related declines in sex hormones and fertility during menopause. Men experience a gradual decline in testosterone levels as they age, but nothing like the sharp plunge in estrogen levels that women experience during menopause (Sheehy, 1998). Testosterone levels begin to fall at about age 40 or 50 and may decline to one-third or one-half of their peak levels by age 80 (Brody, 1995c).

The drop in testosterone levels that occurs as men age may be connected to a variety of age-related symptoms, including reduced muscle mass and strength, accumulation of body fat, reduced energy levels, lowered fertility, and reduced erectile ability. However, despite a decline in testosterone levels, most men remain potent throughout their lives. Little is known about the critical levels of testosterone needed to maintain erectile ability. Certain age-related changes, such as reduced muscle mass and strength and increased body fat, may be due not to declining testosterone production but to other factors associated with aging, such as a gradual loss of *human growth hormone*, a hormone that helps maintain muscle strength and that may prevent fat buildup. Some experts believe that testosterone replacement may help avert erectile problems, bone loss, and frailty, in much the same way that estrogen replacement benefits postmenopausal women (Brody, 1995c). Others worry that excessive use of the hormone may increase the risks of prostate cancer and cardiovascular disease.

Is There a Manopause?
The term menopause *is sometimes used to convey the negative, harmful stereotype of the aging person as crotchety and irritable. The scientific jury is still out on whether there is a "male menopause," but men do experience a gradual decline in testosterone levels as they age. The decline in testosterone is connected with age-related symptoms such as reduced muscle strength, accumulation of fat, reduced energy, lowered fertility, and reduced erectile ability. Nevertheless, at least half of men maintain erectile ability throughout their lives.*

The Prostate Gland

The **prostate gland** lies beneath the bladder and is approximately the shape and size of a chestnut (about 2 centimetres [³⁄₄ inch] in diameter). Note the spelling of the name of the gland—pros*tate*, not pros*trate*. (*Prostrate* means lying with one's face on the ground, as in some forms of prayer.) The prostate gland contains muscle fibres and glandular tissue that secrete prostatic fluid. Prostatic fluid is milky and alkaline. It provides the texture and odour characteristic of the seminal fluid. The alkalinity neutralizes some of the acidity of the vaginal tract, prolonging the life span of sperm as seminal fluid spreads through the female reproductive system. The prostate is continually active in mature males, but sexual arousal further stimulates secretions. Secretions are conveyed into the urethra by a sievelike duct system. There the secretions combine with sperm and fluid from the seminal vesicles.

A vasectomy prevents sperm from reaching the urethra but does not cut off fluids from the seminal vesicles or prostate gland. A man who has had a vasectomy thus emits an ejaculate that appears normal but contains no sperm.

Cowper's Glands

The **Cowper's glands** are also known as the **bulbourethral glands**, in recognition of their shape and location. These two structures lie below the prostate and empty their secretions into the urethra. During sexual arousal they secrete a drop or so of clear, slippery fluid that appears at the urethral opening. The functions of this fluid are not entirely understood. It may help buffer the acidity of the male's urethra and lubricate the urethral passageway to ease the passage of seminal fluid. The fluid is not produced in sufficient amounts to play a significant role in lubricating the vagina during intercourse.

Fluid from the Cowper's glands precedes the ejaculate and often contains viable sperm. Thus, coitus may lead to pregnancy even if the penis is withdrawn prior to ejaculation. This is one reason why people who practise the "withdrawal method" of birth control are frequently called "parents."

Prostate gland The gland that lies beneath the bladder and secretes prostatic fluid, which gives semen its characteristic odour and texture.

Cowper's glands Structures that lie below the prostate and empty their secretions into the urethra during sexual arousal.

Bulbourethral glands Another term for *Cowper's glands.*

Semen

Sperm and the fluids contributed by the seminal vesicles, the prostate gland, and the Cowper's glands make up **semen**, the whitish seminal fluid that is expelled through the tip of the penis during ejaculation. The seminal vesicles secrete about 70% of the fluid that constitutes the ejaculate. The remaining 30% of seminal fluid consists of sperm and fluids produced by the prostate gland and the Cowper's glands. Sperm themselves account for only about 1% of the volume of semen. This is why men with vasectomies continue to ejaculate about as much semen as before, although their ejaculates are devoid of sperm.

Semen is the medium that carries sperm through much of the male's reproductive system and the reproductive tract of the female. Semen contains water, mucus, sugar (fructose), acids, and bases. It activates and nourishes sperm, and the bases help shield sperm from vaginal acidity. The typical ejaculate contains between 200 and 400 million sperm and ranges between 3 and 5 millilitres in volume. (Five millilitres is equal to about 1 teaspoon.) The quantity of semen decreases with age and with frequency of ejaculation.

Diseases of the Urogenital System

Because the organs that make up the urinary and reproductive systems are near each other and share some "piping," they are referred to as the urinogenital or urogenital system. A number of diseases affect the urogenital system. The type of physician who specializes in their diagnosis and treatment is a **urologist.**

Urethritis

Men, like women, are subject to bladder and urethral inflammations, which are generally referred to as **urethritis**. The symptoms include frequent urination (urinary frequency), a strong need to urinate (urinary urgency), burning during urination, and a penile discharge. People with symptoms of urinary frequency and urinary urgency feel the pressing need to urinate repeatedly, even though they may have just done so and may have but another drop or two to expel.

Preventive measures for urethritis parallel those suggested for cystitis (bladder infection): drinking more water, drinking cranberry juice (125 millilitres [4 ounces], two or three times a day), and lowering intake of alcohol and caffeine. Cranberry juice is highly acidic, and acid tends to eliminate many of the bacteria that can give rise to urethritis.

Cancer of the Testes

Cancer of the testicles remains a relatively rare form of cancer. In 2004, there were 850 cases of testicular cancer resulting in 30 deaths among Canadian men (Canadian Cancer Society, 2005). It is, however, the most common form of solid-tumour cancer to strike men between the ages of 20 and 34 (Vazi et al., 1989). It accounts for nearly 10% of all deaths from cancer among men in that age group.

There is no evidence that testicular cancer results from sexual overactivity or masturbation. Men who had **cryptorchidism** as children (a condition in which one or both testicles fail to descend from the abdomen into the scrotum) stand about a 40 times greater chance of contracting testicular cancer.

Although testicular cancer was generally fatal in earlier years, the prognosis today is quite favourable, especially for cases that are detected early. Treatments include surgical removal of the diseased testis, radiation, and chemotherapy.

The surgical removal of a testicle may have profound psychological implications. Some men who have lost a testicle feel less "manly." Fears related to sexual

Semen The whitish fluid that constitutes the ejaculate, consisting of sperm and secretions from the seminal vesicles, prostate gland, and Cowper's glands.

Urologist A physician who specializes in the diagnosis and treatment of diseases of the urogenital system.

Urethritis An inflammation of the bladder or urethra.

Cryptorchidism A condition in which one or both testicles fail to descend from the abdomen into the scrotum.

Applied Knowledge

SELF-EXAMINATION OF THE TESTES

Self-examination (see Figure 3.19) is best performed shortly after a warm shower or bath, when the skin of the scrotum is most relaxed. The man should examine the scrotum for evidence of pea-sized lumps. Each testicle can be rolled gently between the thumb and the fingers. Lumps are generally found on the side or front of the testicle. The presence of a lump is not necessarily a sign of cancer, but it should be promptly reported to a physician for further evaluation. Men should watch for these warning signals:

1. A slight enlargement of one of the testicles.
2. A change in the consistency of a testicle.
3. A dull ache in the lower abdomen or groin. (Pain may be absent in cancer of the testes, however.)
4. Sensation of dragging and heaviness in a testicle.

performance can engender sexual dysfunctions. From a physiological standpoint, sexual functioning should remain unimpaired, because adequate quantities of testosterone are produced by the remaining testis.

Because early detection is crucial to survival, men are advised to examine themselves monthly following puberty (Reinisch, 1990) and to have regular medical checkups.

Disorders of the Prostate

The prostate gland is tiny at birth and grows rapidly at puberty. It may shrink during adulthood but usually becomes enlarged past the age of 50.

BENIGN PROSTATIC HYPERPLASIA The prostate gland becomes enlarged in about one-quarter of men past the age of 60 (Walsh, 1996). When enlargement is due to hormonal changes associated with aging rather than to other causes, such as inflammation from sexually transmitted diseases, it is referred to as **benign prostatic hyperplasia**. Because the prostate surrounds the upper part of the urethra (see Figure 3.14), enlargement constricts the urethra. Resultant symptoms include urinary frequency (including increased frequency of nocturnal urination), urinary urgency, and difficulty starting the flow of urine. Several treatments are available to relieve the pressure on the urethra and increase the flow of urine. They include medicines such as finasteride and alpha-adrenergic-agonist drugs ("alpha blockers") and surgical removal of part of the prostate (Wasson, 1998).

CANCER OF THE PROSTATE A more serious and life-threatening problem is prostate cancer, which is the most common form of cancer among Canadian men. One in 7 men will develop prostrate cancer during their lifetime, with most developing it after age 70. About 20 500 Canadian men were diagnosed in 2004 with prostate cancer and an estimated 4300 men died from it (Canadian Cancer Society, 2005). However, recently developed methods of detecting prostate cancer earlier are increasing the survival rate for men who develop the disease (Merrill & Brawley, 2000).

Prostate cancer involves the growth of malignant prostate tumours that can metastasize to bones and lymph nodes if not detected and treated early. Men whose diets are rich in animal fats have a substantially higher chance of developing advanced prostate cancer than do men with a low intake of animal fat. The incidence of prostate cancer also increases with age (Tarone et al., 2000). More than

Benign prostatic hyperplasia Enlargement of the prostate gland due to hormonal changes associated with aging and characterized by symptoms such as urinary frequency, urinary urgency, and difficulty starting the flow of urine.

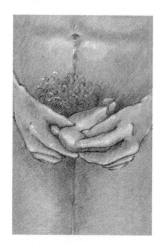

Figure 3.19 Self-Examination of the Testes.

80% of cases of prostate cancer are diagnosed in men aged 65 or above (National Cancer Institute, 2000). Genetic factors are also apparently involved (Lichtenstein et al., 2000). Moreover, testosterone spurs the development of prostate cancer (D'Amico et al., 2000). A study of men in Quebec also indicated that having a vasectomy increased the risk of getting prostate cancer (Emard et al., 2001).

One of the more intriguing factors related to prostate cancer is frequency of ejaculation. Australian researchers found that men who ejaculated frequently when they were between the ages of 20 and 50 were less likely to develop prostate cancer than those men who had a low level of ejaculation frequency (Giles et al., 2003). The researchers speculate that the longer semen is left in the ducts, the greater the chance of it becoming carcinogenic. Frequent ejaculation thus acts as a "flushing" mechanism to clear the body of potentially harmful biological materials.

The early symptoms of cancer of the prostate may mimic those of benign prostate enlargement: urinary frequency and difficulty in urinating. Later symptoms include blood in the urine, pain or burning on urination, and pain in the lower back, pelvis, or upper thighs (National Cancer Institute, 2000). Most cases occur without noticeable symptoms in the early stages.

The Canadian Cancer Society (2002) recommends that men over the age of 50 discuss with their doctor the potential benefits and risks of early detection of prostate cancer. Men at higher risk, especially those who have a family background of prostate cancer or are of African ancestry, should consider being tested at earlier ages. Because the medical community is divided over how often the tests should be performed, the Cancer Society has not provided more specific guidelines regarding the frequency of testing.

Prostate cancer is the second most common cause of death from cancer among Canadian men. Former federal health minister Allan Rock, who had his prostate removed after being diagnosed with prostate cancer, is one of several well-known Canadians who have made their case public in order to encourage men to have regular tests for prostate cancer.

In testing for the possibility of prostate cancer, the physician inserts a finger into the rectum and feels for abnormalities in the prostate gland. Unfortunately, many men are reluctant to undergo a rectal examination. Avoidance of, or ignorance of the need for, regular exams is a major contributor to the death rate from prostate cancer.

When a cancerous growth is suspected on the basis of a rectal examination or a PSA blood test, further testing is usually done via additional blood tests, ultrasound, or biopsy. PSA (prostate-specific antigen) is a protein that helps transform a gel-like substance in the prostate gland into a liquid that transports sperm when it is ejaculated. In the diseased or enlarged prostate, PSA seeps into the blood at higher levels, giving higher test readings. Early detection is important because treatment is most effective before the cancer has spread.

There is controversy over how effective screening for prostate cancer is in the general population. On the one hand, a blood test for PSA can detect evidence of prostate cancer even among men whose prostates feel normal upon physical examination (Tarone et al., 2000). However, the PSA test is only moderately reliable. The Ontario Ministry of Health recommends against use of the PSA test to screen males who do not have symptoms of prostate cancer or a family history of it. Accordingly, the Ministry does not cover the cost of this screening test in its health plan (Prostate Cancer in Ontario, 2003).

The most widely used treatment for prostate cancer is surgical removal of the prostate gland (Klein, E. A., 2000). However, surgical prostate removal may damage surrounding nerves, leading to problems in controlling the flow of urine or in erection or ejaculation (Stanford et al., 2000). Recently introduced surgical techniques tend to spare the surrounding nerves and to reduce, but not eliminate, the risk of complications. Other treatments include radiation, hormone treatment, and anticancer drugs (Klein, E. A., 2000). Hormone treatment in the form of androgen (testosterone) suppression therapy and anticancer drugs may shrink the tumour and relieve pain for long periods of time. One study found that the combination of radiation therapy and androgen suppressive therapy was more effective than radiation therapy alone (D'Amico et al., 2000). Men who have their prostate glands removed are more likely to experience urinary incontinence (loss of control over urination) and sexual dysfunction (trouble attaining erection) than men who use radiation (Potosky et al., 2000). In a large-scale study of men who had prostate surgery in Quebec, 75% experienced erectile dysfunction and 6.6% experienced severe problems with urination (Karakiewicz et al., 2004). Unfortunately, medical treatments such as pills like Viagra are the least likely to be successful with men whose erectile dysfunction is a result of prostate surgery (Schover et al., 2004). After prostate surgery, many men still feel uncomfortable seeking help to deal with sexual problems. Those who have the highest feelings of distress over the loss of erectile function are the most likely to seek medical assistance for this problem (Schover et al., 2004).

But many physicians argue that surgery remains the best choice in terms of survival rates. Among older men with slow-growing prostate cancer, physicians often prefer "watchful waiting" to surgery. The men may die from causes other than cancer.

Several prostate cancer support groups have formed across Canada for men who are either considering treatment options or undergoing treatment. These groups provide a forum where men can share their experiences, fears, and concerns.

PROSTATITIS Many infectious agents can inflame the prostate, causing **prostatitis**. The chief symptoms are painful ejaculation and an ache or pain between the scrotum and the anal opening. In a study of men from Canada and several other countries, 19% of those with urinary tract infections reported pain on ejaculation (Nickel et al., 2005). Men with more severe symptoms of urinary infection were the most likely to experience pain at ejaculation. Also, 72% of those who had painful ejaculation experienced problems with erectile dysfunction.

Prostatitis is usually treated with antibiotics. Although Aspirin and ibuprofen may relieve the pain, men with these symptoms should consult a physician. Painful ejaculation may discourage masturbation or coitus, which is ironic, because regular flushing of the prostate through ejaculation may be helpful in the treatment of prostatitis.

The Canadian Prostate Cancer Network
Plays a key role in creating and maintaining prostate cancer support groups.
www.cpcn.org
The Prostate Research Foundation of Canada
Provides in-depth information about prostate cancer.
www.prostatecancer. on.ca

Prostatitis Inflammation of the prostate gland.

Research in Action

CONCERNS ABOUT PROSTATE SURGERY

For men considering prostate surgery, a major fear is that the surgery will lead to erectile dysfunction. An interview survey in Toronto of men who experienced sexual dysfunction problems after prostate surgery concluded that the "preservation of manhood" was a central concern (Fergus et al., 2002). The researchers uncovered five major issues related to this concern:

1. choosing the type of surgery that would increase the chance of survival while minimizing the extent of sexual dysfunction

2. the belief that sexual dysfunction meant the loss of one's manhood

3. the fear that sexual dysfunction would lead to loss of status, especially among peers

4. feeling pressure to still focus on a high level of giving and receiving sexual pleasure despite loss of erectile functioning.

5. working to overcome the sexual loss, typically by acknowledging the value of being alive as being more important than sexual pleasure. Also, some men refocused their sexual expression away from penile–vaginal intercourse to other kinds of sexual activities and to having a more intimate emotional relationship with their partner.

Male Sexual Functions

The male sexual functions of erection and ejaculation provide the means for sperm to travel from the male's reproductive tract to the female's. There the sperm cell and ovum unite to conceive a new human being. Of course, the natural endowment of reproduction with sensations of pleasure helps ensure that it will take place with or without knowledge of these biological facts.

Erection

Erection is caused by the engorgement of the penis with blood, such that the penis grows in size and stiffens. The erect penis is an efficient conduit, or funnel, for depositing sperm deep within the vagina.

In mechanical terms, erection is a hydraulic event. The spongy, cavernous masses of the penis are equipped to hold blood. Filling them with blood causes them to enlarge, much as a sponge swells when it absorbs water. This simple description belies the fact that erection is a remarkable feat of biological engineering that involves the cooperation of the vascular (blood) system and the nervous system.

In a few moments—as quickly as 10 or 15 seconds—the penis can double in length, become firm, and shift from a funnel for passing urine to one that expels semen. Moreover, the bladder is closed off when the male becomes sexually aroused, decreasing the likelihood that semen and urine will mix.

What accounts for the firmness of an erection? A sponge that fills with water expands but does not grow hard. It happens that the corpora cavernosa are surrounded by a tough, fibrous covering called the *tunica albuginea.* Just as the rubber of a balloon resists the pressure of pumped-in air, this housing resists expansion, causing the penis to become rigid. The corpus spongiosum, which contains the penile urethra, also engorges with blood during erection. It does not become hard, however, because it lacks the fibrous casing. The penile glans, which is formed by the crowning of the spongiosum at the tip of the penis, turns a dark purplish hue as it becomes engorged, but it too does not stiffen.

Erection is reversed when more blood flows out of the erectile tissue than flows in, restoring the pre-erectile circulatory balance and shrinking the erectile tissue or spongy masses. The erectile tissue thus exerts less pressure against the fibrous covering, resulting in a loss of rigidity. Loss of erection occurs when sexual stimulation ceases or when the body returns to a (sexual) resting state following orgasm. Loss of erection can also occur in response to anxiety or perceived threats. Loss of erection in response to threat can be abrupt, as when a man in the throes of passion suddenly hears a suspicious noise in the adjoining room. Yet the "threats" that induce loss of erection are more likely to be psychological than physical. In our culture, men often measure their manhood by their sexual performance. A man who fears that he will be unable to perform successfully may experience **performance anxiety,** which can prevent him from achieving erection or lead to a loss of erection at penetration.

The male capacity for erection quite literally spans the life cycle. Erections are common in babies, even within minutes after birth. Evidence from ultrasound studies shows that male fetuses may even have erections months prior to birth. Men who are well into their 80s and 90s continue to experience erections and to engage in coitus.

Erections are not limited to the conscious state. Men have nocturnal erections every 90 minutes or so as they sleep. These generally occur during REM (rapid eye movement) sleep. REM sleep is associated with dreaming. It is so named because the sleeper's eyes dart about rapidly under the closed eyelids during this stage. Erections occur during most periods of REM sleep.

Erection The enlargement and stiffening of the penis as a consequence of its engorgement with blood.

Performance anxiety Feelings of dread and foreboding experienced in connection with sexual activity (or any other activity that might be judged by another person).

The mechanism of nocturnal erection appears to be physiologically based. That is, erections occur along with dreams that may or may not have erotic content. Morning erections are actually nocturnal erections. They occur when the man is awakened during REM sleep, as by an alarm clock.

Reflex A simple, unlearned response to a stimulus that is mediated by the spine rather than the brain.

Spinal Reflexes and Sexual Response

Men may become sexually aroused by a range of stimuli, including tactile stimulation provided by their partners, visual stimulation (such as from scanning photos of nude models in men's magazines), and even mental stimulation from engaging in sexual fantasies. Regardless of the source of stimulation, the man's sexual responses, erection and ejaculation, occur by **reflex,** as shown in Figure 3.20.

Erection and ejaculation are reflexes: automatic, unlearned responses to sexual stimulation. So too are vaginal lubrication and orgasm in women. We do not control sexual reflexes voluntarily, as we might control the lifting of a finger or an arm. We can set the stage for them to occur by ensuring the proper stimulation, but once the stage is set, the reflexes are governed by automatic processes, not by conscious effort. Efforts to control sexual responses consciously by force of will can backfire and make it more difficult to become aroused (for example, to attain erection or vaginal lubrication). We need not try to become aroused. We need only expose ourselves to effective sexual stimulation and allow our reflexes to do the job for us.

The reflexes governing erection and ejaculation are controlled at the level of the spinal cord. Thus, they are considered spinal reflexes. How does erection occur? Erections may occur in response to different types of stimulation. Some erections occur from direct stimulation of the genitals, as from stroking, licking, or fondling of the penis or scrotum. Erectile responses to such direct stimulation involve a simple spinal reflex that does not require the direct participation of the brain.

Erections can also be initiated by the brain, without the genitals being touched or fondled at all. Such erections may occur when a man has sexual fantasies, when he views erotic materials, or when he catches a glimpse of a woman in a bikini on a beach. In the case of the "no-hands" type of erection, stimulation from the brain travels to the spinal cord, where the erectile reflex is triggered.

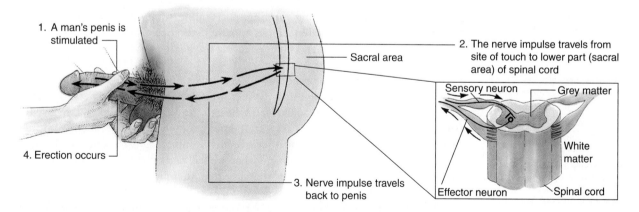

Figure 3.20 Reflexes.

Reflexes involve sensory neurons, effector neurons, and sometimes interneurons that connect the two in the spinal cord. Reflexes need not involve the brain, although messages to the brain may make us aware when reflexes are occurring. Reflexes are the product of "local government" in the spine.

When the nerve pathways between the brain and the upper spinal cord are blocked or severed, men cannot achieve "psychogenic erections"—that is, erections in response to mental stimulation alone.

The brain can also stifle sexual response. A man who is highly anxious about his sexual abilities may be unable to achieve an erection even with the most direct, intense penile stimulation. Or a man who believes that sexual pleasure is sinful or dirty may be filled with anxiety and guilt and hence be unable to achieve erection when he is sexually stimulated by his partner.

In some males, especially adolescents, the erectile reflex is so easily tripped that incidental rubbing of the genitals against their own undergarments, the sight of an attractive passerby, or a fleeting sexual fantasy produces erection. Spontaneous erections may occur under embarrassing circumstances, such as on a public beach, or just before classes change. In an effort to distract himself from erotic fantasies and to allow an erection to subside, many a male adolescent in the classroom has desperately renewed his interest in his algebra or foreign-language textbook before the bell has rung. (A well-placed towel may serve in a pinch on a public beach.)

As men mature, they require more penile stimulation to achieve full erection. Partners of men in their 30s and 40s need not feel that their attractiveness has waned if their lovers no longer have instant "no-hands" erections when they disrobe. It takes men longer to achieve erection as they age, and direct penile stimulation becomes a more critical source of arousal.

THE ROLE OF THE AUTONOMIC NERVOUS SYSTEM Although stimulation that brings about an erection can originate in the brain, this does not mean that erection is a voluntary response, like raising your arm. Whatever the original or dominant source of stimulation—direct penile stimulation or sexual fantasy—erection remains an unlearned, automatic reflex.

Automatic responses, such as erection, involve the division of the nervous system called the **autonomic nervous system** (ANS). *Autonomic* means "automatic." The ANS controls automatic bodily processes such as heartbeat, pupil dilation, respiration, and digestion. In contrast, voluntary movement (such as raising an arm) is under the control of the *somatic* division of the nervous system.

The ANS has two branches, the **sympathetic** and the **parasympathetic**. These branches have largely opposing effects; when they are activated at the same time, their effects become balanced out to some degree. In general, the sympathetic branch is in command during processes that involve a release of bodily energy from stored reserves, such as during running, performing some other athletic task, or being gripped by fear or anxiety. The sympathetic branch also governs the general mobilization of the body, such as by increasing the heart rate and respiration rate in response to threat.

The parasympathetic branch is most active during processes that restore reserves of energy, such as digestion. When we experience fear or anxiety, the sympathetic branch of the ANS quickens the heart rate. When we relax, the parasympathetic branch curbs the heart rate. The parasympathetic branch activates digestive processes, but the sympathetic branch inhibits digestive activity. Because the sympathetic branch is in command when we feel fear or anxiety, such stimuli can inhibit the activity of the parasympathetic system, thereby slowing down the digestive process and possibly causing indigestion.

The divisions of the autonomic nervous system play different roles in sexual arousal and response. The nerves that cause penile arteries to dilate during erection belong to the parasympathetic branch of the autonomic nervous system. It is thus the parasympathetic system that largely governs erection. The nerves governing ejaculation belong to the sympathetic branch, however. One implication of this division of neural responsibility is that intense fear or anxiety, which involves sympathetic nervous system activity, may inhibit erection by counteracting the activity

Autonomic nervous system The division of the nervous system that regulates automatic bodily processes, such as heartbeat, pupil dilation, respiration, and digestion. Abbreviated *ANS*.

Sympathetic The branch of the ANS most active during emotional responses that draw on the body's reserves of energy, such as fear and anxiety. The sympathetic ANS largely controls ejaculation.

Parasympathetic The branch of the ANS most active during processes that restore the body's reserves of energy, such as digestion. The parasympathetic ANS largely controls erection.

of the parasympathetic nervous system. Because sympathetic arousal is involved in triggering the ejaculatory reflex, anxiety or fear may also accelerate ejaculation, causing **premature ejaculation**. Intense emotions such as fear and anxiety can thus lead to problems in achieving or maintaining erection, as well as causing hasty ejaculation.

Because erections seem spontaneous at times, and because they often occur when the man would rather not have them, it may seem to men that the penis has a mind of its own. Despite this common folk belief, however, the penis possesses no guiding intelligence

ERECTILE ABNORMALITIES Some men find that their erect penises are slightly curved or bent. Some degree of curvature is perfectly normal, but men with **Peyronie's disease** have excessive curvature that can make erections painful or make it difficult to enjoy coitus. The condition is caused by a buildup of fibrous tissue in the penile shaft. Although some cases of Peyronie's disease appear to clear up on their own, most require medical attention.

Some men experience erections that persist for hours or days. This condition is called *priapism*, after Priapus of Greek myth, the son of Dionysus and Aphrodite who personified male procreative power. Priapism is often caused by leukemia, sickle-cell anemia, or diseases of the spinal cord, although in some cases the cause remains unknown. Priapism occurs when the mechanisms that drain the blood that makes the penis erect are damaged and so cannot return the blood to the circulatory system. Priapism may become a medical emergency, because erection prolonged beyond six hours can starve penile tissues of oxygen, leading to tissue deterioration. Medical intervention in the form of drugs or surgery may be required to reverse the condition and allow blood to drain from the penis.

Ejaculation

Ejaculation, like erection, is a spinal reflex. It is triggered when sexual stimulation reaches a critical point or threshold. Ejaculation generally occurs together with **orgasm**, the sudden muscle contractions that occur at the peak of sexual excitement and result in abrupt release of the sexual tension that had built up during sexual arousal. Orgasm is accompanied by subjective sensations that are generally intensely pleasurable. Ejaculation, however, is simply the expulsion of semen from the tip of the penis. Orgasm and ejaculation are *not* synonymous, nor do they always occur simultaneously. For example, **paraplegics** can ejaculate if the area of the lower spinal cord that controls ejaculation is intact. They do not experience the subjective aspects of orgasm, however, because the sensations of orgasm do not reach the brain.

Conversely, prepubertal boys may experience orgasms even though they emit no ejaculate. Orgasms without ejaculate are termed "dry orgasms." Boys do not begin to produce seminal fluid (and sperm) until puberty. Mature men, too, can experience dry orgasms. They can take the form of "little orgasms" preceding a larger orgasm, or they can follow "wet orgasms" when sexual stimulation is continued but seminal fluids have not been replenished.

Ejaculation occurs in two stages. The first stage, often called the **emission stage**, involves contractions of the prostate, the seminal vesicles, and the upper part of the vas deferens (the **ampulla**). The force of these contractions propels seminal fluid into the prostatic part of the urethral tract—a small tube called the **urethral bulb**—which balloons out as muscles close at either end, trapping the semen. It is at this point that the man perceives that orgasm is inevitable. Masters and Johnson term this feeling a sense of "ejaculatory inevitability" (Masters & Johnson, 1966). Men might colloquially describe the feeling as being about to "come." The man feels that a point of no return has been passed and that nothing can prevent ejaculation.

Premature ejaculation A sexual dysfunction in which the male persistently ejaculates too early to afford the couple adequate sexual gratification. (Yes, what is on time in one relationship may be considered premature—or late—in another.)

Peyronie's disease An abnormal condition characterized by an excessive curvature of the penis that can make erections painful.

Orgasm The climax of sexual excitement.

Paraplegic A person with sensory and motor paralysis of the lower half of the body.

Emission stage The first phase of ejaculation, which involves contractions of the prostate gland, the seminal vesicles, and the upper part of the vas deferens.

Ampulla A sac or dilated part of a tube or canal.

Urethral bulb The small tube that makes up the prostatic part of the urethral tract and that balloons out as muscles close at either end, trapping semen prior to ejaculation.

Expulsion stage The second stage of ejaculation, during which muscles at the base of the penis and elsewhere contract rhythmically, forcefully expelling semen and providing pleasurable sensations.

Retrograde ejaculation Ejaculation in which the ejaculate empties into the bladder. (From the Latin *retrogradi*, which means "to go backward.")

The second stage, which is often referred to as the **expulsion stage**, involves the propulsion of the seminal fluid through the urethra and out of the urethral opening at the tip of the penis. In this stage, muscles at the base of the penis and elsewhere contract rhythmically, forcefully expelling semen. The second stage is generally accompanied by the highly pleasurable sensations of orgasm.

In ejaculation, the seminal fluid is released from the urethral bulb and expelled by forceful contractions of the pelvic muscles that surround the urethral channel and the crura of the penis. During ejaculation, the bladder is closed off so that urine cannot escape. The first few contractions are most intense and occur at 0.8-second intervals. Subsequent contractions lessen in intensity, and the interval between them gradually increases. Seminal fluid is expelled in spurts during the first few contractions. The contractions are so powerful that seminal fluid may be propelled as far as 30 to 60 centimetres (12 to 24 inches), according to observations made by Masters and Johnson. Some men, however, report that semen travels but a few centimetres or just oozes from the penile opening. The force of the expulsion varies with the condition of the man's prostate, his general health, and his age. There is some correspondence between the force of the expulsion and the pleasure of orgasm. That is, more intense orgasms, psychologically speaking, often accompany more forceful ejaculations.

The amount of time the male is sexually aroused prior to ejaculation influences the amount of ejaculate that is produced. A longer time period of arousal usually results in a great volume of ejaculate and greater sperm concentration (Pound et al., 2002).

Although ejaculation occurs by reflex, a man can delay ejaculation by maintaining the level of sexual stimulation below the critical threshold, or "point of no return." Men who suffer from premature ejaculation have been successfully treated in programs that train them to learn to recognize their "point of no return" and maintain sexual stimulation below it

RETROGRADE EJACULATION Some men experience **retrograde ejaculation**, in which the ejaculate empties into the bladder rather than being expelled from the body. During normal ejaculation an external sphincter opens, allowing seminal fluid to pass out of the body. Another sphincter, this one internal, closes off the opening to the bladder, preventing the seminal fluid from backing up into the bladder. In retrograde ejaculation, the actions of these sphincters are reversed. The external sphincter remains closed, preventing expulsion of the seminal fluid, while the internal sphincter opens, allowing the ejaculate to empty into the bladder. The result is a dry orgasm. No ejaculate is apparent because semen has backed up into the bladder. Retrograde ejaculation may be caused by prostate surgery (much less so now than in former years), by drugs such as tranquillizers, by certain illnesses, and by accidents. Retrograde ejaculation is usually harmless in itself, because the seminal fluid is later discharged with urine. Infertility can result, however, and there may be some changes in the sensations associated with orgasm. Persistent dry orgasms should be medically evaluated; their underlying cause may be a threat to health.

Summing Up

Female Anatomy and Physiology
External Sex Organs
The female external sexual structures are collectively known as the vulva. They consist of the mons veneris, the labia majora and minora, the clitoris, the vestibule, and the vaginal opening.

The Mons Veneris
The mons veneris consists of fatty tissue that covers the joint of the pubic bones in front of the body.

The Labia Majora

The labia majora are large folds of skin that run downward from the mons along the sides of the vulva.

The Labia Minora

The labia minora are hairless, light-coloured membranes that surround the urethral and vaginal openings.

The Clitoris

The clitoris is the female sex organ that is most sensitive to sexual sensation, but it is not directly involved in reproduction.

The Vestibule

The vestibule contains the openings to the vagina and the urethra.

The Urethral Opening

Urine passes from the female's body through the urethral opening.

The Vaginal Opening

The vaginal opening, or introitus, lies below the urethral opening.

The Perineum

The perineum is the area that lies between the vaginal opening and the anus.

Structures That Underlie the External Sex Organs

These structures include the vestibular bulbs, Bartholin's glands, the sphincters, the clitoral crura, and the pubococcygeus (P-C) muscle.

Internal Sex Organs

The internal female sex organs—or female reproductive system—include the innermost parts of the vagina, the cervix, the uterus, the ovaries, and the fallopian tubes.

The Vagina

Menstrual flow and babies pass from the uterus to the outer world through the vagina. During coitus, the vagina contains the penis.

The Cervix

The cervix is the lower end of the uterus.

The Uterus

The uterus or womb is the pear-shaped organ in which a fertilized ovum implants and develops until birth.

The Fallopian Tubes

Two fallopian tubes extend from the upper end of the uterus toward the ovaries. Ova pass through the fallopian tubes on their way to the uterus and are normally fertilized within these tubes.

The Ovaries

The ovaries lie on either side of the uterus and produce ova and the sex hormones estrogen and progesterone.

The Pelvic Examination

Regular pelvic examinations are essential for early detection of problems involving the reproductive tract.

The Breasts

In some cultures the breasts are viewed merely as biological instruments for feeding infants. In our culture, however, they have taken on erotic significance. The breasts are secondary sex characteristics that contain mammary glands.

Breast Cancer

Breast cancer is the second leading cancer killer in women, after lung cancer. Women with breast cancer will have lumps in the breast, but most lumps in the breasts are benign. Breast cancer may be detected in a number of ways, including breast self-examination, medical examinations, and mammography. Early detection yields the greatest chance of survival.

The Menstrual Cycle

Menstruation is the cyclical bleeding that stems from the shedding of the endometrium when a reproductive cycle has not led to the fertilization of an ovum. The menstrual cycle is regulated by estrogen and progesterone.

Regulation of the Menstrual Cycle

The menstrual cycle involves finely tuned relationships among the hypothalamus, the pituitary gland, and the ovaries and uterus. Hormones produced by the hypothalamus regulate the pituitary, which in turn secretes hormones that regulate the secretions of the ovaries and uterus.

Phases of the Menstrual Cycle

The menstrual cycle has four stages or phases: the proliferative, ovulatory, secretory, and menstrual phases. During the first phase of the cycle, which follows menstruation, ova ripen within their follicles and endometrial tissue proliferates. During the second phase, ovulation occurs. During the third phase, the corpus luteum produces copious amounts of progesterone and estrogen that cause the endometrium to thicken. If the ovum goes unfertilized, a plunge in estrogen and progesterone levels triggers the fourth, or menstrual, phase, which leads to the beginning of a new cycle.

Coitus During Menstruation

Couples are apparently less likely to initiate sexual activity during menstruation than during any other phase of the woman's cycle.

Menopause

Menopause, the cessation of menstruation, most commonly occurs between the ages of 46 and 50. Estrogen deficiency in menopause may give rise to night sweats, hot flashes, hot flushes, cold sweats, dry skin, loss of breast tissue, and decreased vaginal lubrication. Long-term estrogen deficiency has been linked to osteoporosis. Hormone replacement therapy can offset the loss of estrogen and progesterone but has been linked to a slightly increased risk of breast and endometrial cancers, though also to a reduction in the risk of osteoporosis. For most women, menopausal problems are mild. Psychological problems can reflect the meaning of menopause to the individual.

Menstrual Problems

Most women experience some discomfort prior to or during menstruation. Common menstrual problems include dysmenorrhea, amenorrhea, and premenstrual syndrome (PMS).

Dysmenorrhea

Dysmenorrhea is the most common menstrual problem, and pelvic cramps are the most common symptom. Dysmenorrhea can be caused by problems such as endometriosis, pelvic inflammatory disease, and ovarian cysts.

Amenorrhea

Amenorrhea can be caused by problems such as abnormalities in the structures of the reproductive system, hormonal abnormalities, cysts, tumours, and stress.

Premenstrual Syndrome (PMS)

As many as three women in four have some form of PMS. The causes of PMS are unclear, but most researchers look to potential links between menstrual problems and hormone levels.

How to Handle Menstrual Distress

Women with persistent menstrual problems may benefit from a number of active coping strategies for handling menstrual distress.

Male Anatomy and Physiology
External Sex Organs

The male external sex organs include the penis and the scrotum.

The Penis

Semen and urine pass out of the penis through the urethral opening. The penis contains cylinders that fill with blood and stiffen during sexual arousal. Circumcision—the surgical removal of the prepuce—has been carried out for religious and hygienic reasons. In our culture, the size of the penis is sometimes seen as a measure of a man's masculinity and his ability to please his sex partners, although there is little if any connection between the size of the penis and sexual performance.

The Scrotum

The scrotum is the pouch of loose skin that contains the testes. Each testicle is held in place by a spermatic cord, which contains the vas deferens and the cremaster muscle.

Internal Sex Organs

The male internal sex organs consist of the testes, a system of tubes and ducts that conduct sperm, and organs that nourish and activate sperm.

The Testes

The testes serve two functions analogous to those of the ovaries. They secrete male sex hormones (androgens) and produce germ cells (sperm). The hypothalamus, pituitary gland, and testes keep blood testosterone at a more or less constant level through a hormonal negative-feedback loop. Testosterone is produced by interstitial cells. Sperm are produced by seminiferous tubules. Sperm are stored and mature in the epididymis.

The Vas Deferens

Each epididymis empties into a vas deferens that conducts sperm over the bladder.

The Seminal Vesicles

The seminal vesicles are glands that open into the ejaculatory ducts, where the fluids they secrete combine with and nourish sperm.

The Prostate Gland

The prostate gland secretes fluid that accounts for the texture and odour characteristic of semen.

Cowper's Glands

During sexual arousal, the Cowper's glands secrete a drop or so of clear, slippery fluid that appears at the urethral opening.

Semen

Sperm and the fluids contributed by the seminal vesicles, the prostate gland, and the Cowper's glands make up semen, the whitish fluid that is expelled through the tip of the penis during ejaculation.

Diseases of the Urogenital System
Urethritis

Men, like women, are subject to bladder and urethral inflammations, which are generally referred to as urethritis.

Cancer of the Testes

This is the most common form of solid-tumour cancer to strike young men between the ages of 20 and 34.

Disorders of the Prostate

The prostate gland generally becomes enlarged in men past the age of 50. Prostate cancer involves the growth of malignant prostate tumours that can metastasize to bones and lymph nodes. The chief symptoms of prostatitis are painful ejaculation and an ache or pain between the scrotum and anal opening.

Male Sexual Functions

Erection

Erection is the process by which the penis becomes engorged with blood, increases in size, and stiffens. Erection occurs in response to sexual stimulation but is also common during REM sleep.

Spinal Reflexes and Sexual Response

Erection and ejaculation occur by reflex. Although erection is a reflex, penile sensations are relayed to the brain, where they generally result in pleasure. Erection and ejaculation also involve the autonomic nervous system (ANS). The parasympathetic branch of the ANS largely governs erection, whereas the sympathetic branch largely controls ejaculation.

Ejaculation

Ejaculation, like erection, is a reflex. It is triggered when sexual stimulation reaches a critical threshold. Ejaculation usually (though not always) occurs with orgasm, but the terms are not synonymous. The emission phase of ejaculation involves contractions of the prostate, the seminal vesicles, and the upper part of the vas deferens. In the expulsion stage, semen is propelled through the urethra and out of the penis. In this stage, muscles at the base of the penis and elsewhere contract rhythmically, forcefully expelling semen. In retrograde ejaculation, the ejaculate empties into the bladder rather than being expelled from the body.

Test Yourself

Multiple-Choice Questions

1. The female external sex organs are called the
   a. uterus
   b. ovaries
   c. vulva
   d. cervix

2. The only organ whose sole function is to provide sexual pleasure is the

   _____.
   a. penis
   b. clitoris
   c. vagina
   d. mons

3. Which of the following is not one of the three layers of the uterus?
   a. the perimetrium
   b. the exometrium
   c. the endometrium
   d. the myometrium

4. The two pituitary hormones involved in the regulation of the menstrual cycle are
   a. GnRH and estrogen
   b. oxytocin and prolactin
   c. FSH and LH
   d. LH and testosterone

5. During menopause, lower levels of _____ may cause "hot flashes" and other physical symptoms.
   a. prolactin
   b. oxytocin
   c. androgen
   d. estrogen

6. Many Canadian men equate _____ with masculinity.
   a. penis size
   b. muscle mass
   c. hair length
   d. testicle size

7. Sperm cells are carried out of the testicle through the
   a. seminiferous tubules
   b. dartos muscle
   c. vas deferens
   d. cremasteric tube

8. Surgical removal of the foreskin is known as
   a. excision
   b. infibulation
   c. incision
   d. circumcision

9. The purpose of testicular self-examination is to detect _____ in its early stages.
   a. AIDS
   b. infertility
   c. cancer
   d. erectile dysfunction

10. _____ is the most common form of cancer among Canadian men.
    a. prostate cancer
    b. testicular cancer
    c. penile cancer
    d. inguinal cancer

Critical Thinking Questions

1. Many people grow up with messages about what menstruating women should or should not do (such as: don't take a shower, don't go swimming, don't get a perm, don't touch babies). What negative messages did you hear as a child or adolescent? From whom did you hear these messages? Were any of them specific to your particular culture or ethnic group?

2. If you are a woman, did growing up with negative messages (if any) about menstruation affect how you feel about your body and its functions? If you are a man, do these messages affect how you might feel about a partner or potential partner's body?

3. Have you ever felt uncomfortable or embarrassed to have a partner see your body? Which parts of it do you not like? Why do you think you feel this way?

4. If you are a man, how does reading a letter to a men's magazine that starts "I may be only 8 inches long, but . . . ." make you feel about your own penis? If you are a woman, would reading such a statement make you feel differently about your partner's penis?

5. Would you have a male child circumcised? Why or why not?

Companion Website

Visit our Companion Website at www.pearsoned.ca/rathus, where you can use the interactive Study Guide and link to additional resources on topics discussed in this text.

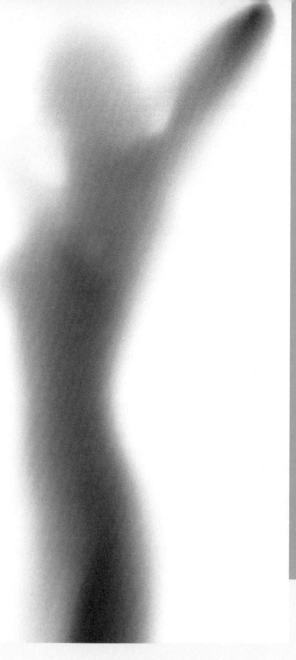

Chapter 4
Sexual Arousal and Response

In this chapter we look at factors that contribute to sexual arousal and the processes related to sexual response. Because our experience of the world is initiated by our senses, we begin the chapter by focusing on the role of the senses in sexual arousal.

Making Sense of Sex: The Role of the Senses in Sexual Arousal

We come to apprehend the world around us through our senses—vision, hearing, smell, taste, and the skin senses, which include that all-important sense of touch. Each of the senses plays a role in our sexual experience, but some senses play larger roles than others.

Vision: The Better to See You With

It was the face of Helen of Troy, not her scent or her melodic voice, that "launched a thousand ships." Men's and women's magazines are filled with pictures of comely members of the other gender. (However, a glance at women's magazines suggests that many women also like looking at pictures of good-looking women.) In measuring the physiological response of males to slides of partially clothed women, researchers at Queen's University found that penile response was greater in reaction to the slides of the more attractive women (Lalumiere & Quinsey, 1998).

Visual cues can be sexual turn-ons. We may be turned on by the sight of a lover in the nude, disrobing, or dressed in evening wear. Lingerie companies hope to convince customers that they will enhance their sex appeal by wearing strategically concealing and revealing nightwear. In Toronto, a store selling erotic products has capitalized on the visual appeal of lingerie by having female models wearing lingerie stand in the store window. This visual display attracted so much attention that it caused "traffic and pedestrian chaos" (Menon, 2002, p. B5). (One cyclist was so distracted by the sight that he nearly crashed into a mailbox.) Some couples find it arousing to observe themselves making love in an overhead mirror or on videotape. Some people find sexually explicit movies arousing. Others are bored or offended by them. Though both genders can be sexually aroused by visual erotica, men are more interested in it.

Sex as a Traffic Stopper.
A lingerie model at the Miss Behav'N adult store on Queen Street West in Toronto checks out passersby—and vice versa. Scantily clad models stop traffic outside the store, which caters to female customers. Clearly, visual cues can be sexual turn-ons!

Smell: Does the Nose Know Best?

Although the sense of smell plays a lesser role in governing sexual arousal in humans than in lower mammals, odours can be sexual turn-ons or turn-offs. Perfume companies, for example, bottle fragrances purported to be sexually arousing. Companies have also successfully persuaded males that using a specific type of deodorant body spray would make them irresistible to women. Unilever captured much of the male market with its "Axe" body spray. Its advertisements unabashedly tell men that using the product will make them successful in attracting women sexually. Gillette has developed "Tag," a competing product.

Most Westerners prefer their lovers to be clean and fresh smelling. People in our society learn to remove or mask odours by using soaps, deodorants, and perfumes or colognes. The ancient Egyptians invented scented bathing to rid themselves of offensive odours (Ramirez, 1990). The ancient Romans had such a passion for perfume that they would bathe in fragrances and even dab their horses and household pets (Ackerman, 1990).

Inclinations to find underarm or genital odours offensive may reflect cultural conditioning rather than biological predispositions. In some societies, genital secretions are considered **aphrodisiacs**.

PHEROMONES For centuries, people have searched for a love potion—a magical formula that could make other people fall in love with or be strongly attracted to the wearer. Some scientists suggest that such potions may already exist in the form of chemical secretions known as **pheromones.**

Only a few years ago, most researchers did not believe that pheromones played a role in human behaviour. Today, however, it appears that people do possess vomeronasal organs (Bartoshuk & Beauchamp, 1994), and this field of research has attracted new interest.

In a typical study, Winnifred Cutler and her colleagues (1998) had heterosexual men wear a suspected male pheromone, whereas a control group wore a placebo. The men using the pheromone increased their frequency of sexual intercourse with their female partners but did not increase their frequency of masturbation. The researchers concluded that the substance increased the sexual attractiveness of the men to their partners, although they did not claim that it directly stimulated sexual behaviour. In fact, it has not been conclusively shown that pheromones—or suspected pheromones—directly affect the behaviour of people (Wysocki & Preti, 1998).

Even so, some other studies are also of interest. Consider a couple of double-blind studies that exposed men and women to certain steroids (androstadienone produced by males and estratetraenol produced by females) suspected of being pheromones. They found that both steroids enhanced the moods of women but not of men; the substances also apparently reduced feelings of nervousness and tension in women, but again, not in men (Grosser et al., 2000; Jacob & McClintock, 2000). The findings about estratetraenol are not terribly surprising. This substance is related to estrogen, and women tend to function best during the time of the month when estrogen levels are highest (Ross et al., 2000; Sourander, 1994). The fact that the women responded positively to the androstadienone is of somewhat greater interest. It suggests that women may generally feel somewhat better when they are around men, even if the chemical substances that may be connected with their moods have not been shown to have direct sexual effects. Of course, being in a good (or better) mood could indirectly contribute to a woman's interest in sexual intercourse.

MENSTRUAL SYNCHRONY Research by several investigators suggests that exposure to other women's sweat can modify a woman's menstrual cycle. In one study, women exposed to underarm secretions from other women, which contained

Aphrodisiac Any drug or other agent that is sexually arousing or increases sexual desire. (From *Aphrodite,* the Greek goddess of love and beauty.)

Pheromones Chemical substances that are secreted externally by certain animals and that convey information to, or produce specific responses in, other members of the same species. (From the Greek *pherein,* which means "to bear [a message]" and *hormone.*)

Erogenous zones Parts of the body that are especially sensitive to tactile sexual stimulation. (*Erogenous* is derived from roots that mean "giving birth to erotic sensations.")

Primary erogenous zones Erogenous zones that are particularly sensitive because they are richly endowed with nerve endings.

Secondary erogenous zones Parts of the body that become erotically sensitized through experience.

steroids that may function as pheromones, showed converging shifts in their menstrual cycles (Bartoshuk & Beauchamp, 1994; Preti et al., 1986). Similar synchronization of menstrual cycles has been observed among women who share dormitory rooms. In another study, 80% of the women who dabbed their upper lips with an extract of perspiration from other women began to menstruate in sync with the cycles of the donors after about three menstrual cycles (Cutler, 1999). A control group, who dabbed their lips with alcohol, showed no changes in their menstrual cycles.

The Skin Senses: Sex as a Touching Experience

The sense of touch has the most direct effects on sexual arousal and response. Any region of that sensitive layer we refer to as skin can become eroticized. The touch of your lover's hand upon your cheek, or your lover's gentle massage of your shoulders or back, can be sexually stimulating.

EROGENOUS ZONES **Erogenous zones** are parts of the body that are especially sensitive to tactile sexual stimulation—to strokes and other caresses. **Primary erogenous zones** are erotically sensitive because they are richly endowed with nerve endings. **Secondary erogenous zones** are parts of the body that become erotically sensitized through experience.

Primary erogenous zones include the genitals; the inner thighs, perineum, buttocks, and anus; the breasts (especially the nipples); the ears (particularly the earlobes); the mouth, lips, and tongue; the neck; the navel; and, yes, the armpits. Preferences vary somewhat from person to person, reflecting possible biological, attitudinal, and experiential differences. Areas that are exquisitely sensitive for some people may produce virtually no reaction, or even discomfort, in others. Many women, for example, report little sensation when their breasts are stroked or kissed. Many men are uncomfortable when their nipples are caressed. On the other hand (or foot), many people find the areas between their toes sensitive to erotic stimulation and enjoy keeping a toehold on their partners during coitus.

Secondary erogenous zones become eroticized through association with sexual stimulation. For example, a woman might become sexually aroused when her lover gently caresses her shoulders, because such caresses have been incorporated as a regular feature of the couple's lovemaking. A few of the women observed by Masters and Johnson (1966) reached orgasm when the smalls of their backs were rubbed.

A Touching Experience.
The sense of touch is intimately connected with sexual experience. The touch of a lover's hand on the cheek or a gentle massage can be sexually stimulating. Certain parts of the body—called erogenous zones—have special sexual significance because of their response to erotic stimulation. People are also highly responsive to images and fantasies. This is why the brain is sometimes referred to as the primary sexual organ or an erogenous zone. Some women report reaching orgasm through fantasy alone (Kinsey et al., 1953). Men regularly experience erection and nocturnal emissions ("wet dreams") without direct stimulation of the genitals.

Taste: On Savoury Sex

Some people are sexually aroused by the taste of genital secretions, such as vaginal secretions or seminal fluid. We do not know, however, whether these secretions are laced with chemicals that have biologically arousing effects or whether arousal reflects the meaning that these secretions have to the individual. That is, we may learn to become aroused by, or to seek out, flavours or odours that have been associated with sexual pleasure. (Others are turned off by the taste or odour of these secretions.)

Hearing: The Better to Hear You With

The sense of hearing also provides an important medium for sexual arousal and response. Like visual and olfactory cues, sounds can be turn-ons or turn-offs. The sounds of one's lover, be they whispers, moans of pleasure, or animated sounds that may attend orgasm, may be arousing during the heat of passion. For some people, key words or vocal intonations may become as arousing as direct stimulation of an erogenous zone. Many people are aroused when their lovers "talk dirty." Spoken vulgarities spur their sexual arousal. Others find vulgar language offensive.

Music itself can contribute to sexual arousal. Music can relax us and put us "in the mood" or evoke powerful associations ("They're playing our song!"). Many couples find background music "atmospheric"—a vital accoutrement of lovemaking.

Aphrodisiacs

An aphrodisiac is a substance that arouses or increases one's capacity for sexual pleasure or response. However, the belief that a substance has sexually stimulating effects may itself inspire sexual excitement. A person who tries a supposed aphrodisiac and feels sexually aroused may well attribute the turn-on to the effects of that substance, even if it had no direct effect on sex drive.

Foods that in some way resemble male genitals have now and then been considered aphrodisiacs. These include oysters, clams, bulls' testicles ("prairie oysters"), tomatoes, and "phallic" items such as celery stalks, bananas, and even ground-up reindeer antlers, elephant tusks, and rhinoceros horns (which is one derivation of the slang term *horny*). Sadly, myths about the sexually arousing properties of substances extracted from rhinoceroses and elephants are contributing to the rapidly diminishing numbers of these animals.

Drugs and psychoactive substances may have certain effects on sexual arousal and response. The drug *yohimbine*, an extract from the African yohimbe tree, does

A World of Diversity

TEACHING THE SKILL OF SEDUCTION

www.seduction.net

The new millennium has seen some changes in Italy. Once upon a time, Latin lovers would never have admitted to needing some help, but nowadays they can pay $192 for a seduction course that purports to teach them the skills of a Casanova.

The two-day course, which can be accessed via **www.seduction.net**, attracts students aged 19 to 60. Most are in their 30s. Lest the course be equated with male chauvinism, impresario Carlo della Torre notes that it is also open to women.

The Age-Old Art of Seduction.
The art of seduction is now being facilitated by Web sites such as **www.seduction.net***, an online magazine (e-zine) that offers advice and advertises courses (you've got to hand over the cash) on the topic.*

Johan's Guide to Aphrodisiacs
Go to this site, not for scientific confirmation but for interesting facts about who believes what.

www.santesson.com/ aphrodis/aphrhome. htm

stimulate blood flow to the genitals (Brody, 1993). However, its effects are limited and unreliable (Morales, 1993). Yohimbine also happens to be toxic (Brody, 1993).

Amyl nitrate (in the form of "snappers" or "poppers") has been used, mostly by gay men but also by some heterosexuals, in the belief that it heightens sensations of arousal and orgasm. Poppers dilate blood vessels in the brain and genitals, producing sensations of warmth in the pelvis and possibly facilitating erection and prolonging orgasm. Amyl nitrate does have some legitimate medical uses, such as helping reduce heart pain (angina) among cardiac patients. It is inhaled from ampoules that "pop" open for rapid use when heart pain occurs. However, poppers can cause dizziness, fainting, and migraine-type headaches. They should be taken only under a doctor's care for a legitimate medical need, not to intensify sexual sensations.

The drug Viagra was originally developed as a treatment for angina (heart pain) because it was thought that it would increase the blood flow to the heart. It does so, modestly. However, it is more effective at dilating blood vessels in the genital organs, thereby facilitating vasocongestion and erection in the male. Viagra is marketed as a treatment for erectile dysfunction (also termed *impotence*). Is Viagra also an aphrodisiac? It is a matter of definition. Although Viagra facilitates erection, it still takes a sexual turn-on for erection to occur (Lewan, 1998). If an aphrodisiac must be directly sexually arousing, Viagra is not an aphrodisiac.

But certain drugs do appear to have aphrodisiac effects, apparently because they act on the brain mechanisms controlling the sex drive. For example, drugs that affect brain receptors for the neurotransmitter dopamine, such as the antidepressant drug bupropion (trade name Wellbutrin) and the drug L-dopa, used in the treatment of Parkinson's disease, can increase the sex drive (Brody, 1993).

The safest and perhaps the most effective method for increasing the sex drive may be not a drug or substance, but exercise. Regular exercise not only enhances general health, but also boosts energy and increases the sex drive in both genders (Brody, 1993). Cindy Meston and Boris Gorzalka (1995) of the University of British Columbia conducted an experiment to see if exercise could affect sexual arousal in women. In one of the sessions, women engaged in 20 minutes of intense exercise prior to viewing an explicit film. While watching the film, the women who had exercised showed a greater increase in measures of physiological sexual arousal than women who had not exercised. However, there was no significant difference in perception of sexual arousal.

Because routine can diminish desire, perhaps the most potent aphrodisiac of all is novelty. In a study of men's physiological responses to slides of a partially nude female, researchers at Queen's University found that repeated exposure resulted in diminishing penile response (Lalumiere & Quinsey, 1998).

Partners can invent new ways of sexually discovering one another. They can make love in novel places, experiment with different techniques, wear provocative clothing, share or enact fantasies, or whatever their imaginations inspire.

Anaphrodisiacs

Some substances, such as potassium nitrate (saltpeter), have been considered inhibitors of sexual response—**anaphrodisiacs**. Saltpeter, however, does not directly dampen sexual response. As a diuretic that can increase the need to urinate, it indirectly diminishes sexual response by making the thought of sex unappealing.

Other chemicals do dampen sexual arousal and response. Tranquillizers and central nervous system depressants, such as barbiturates, can reduce sexual desire and impair sexual performance. These drugs may paradoxically enhance sexual arousal in some people, however, by lessening sexual inhibitions or fear of possible repercussions from sexual activity. Antihypertensive drugs, which are used in the treatment of high blood pressure, may produce erectile and ejaculatory difficulties in men and may reduce sexual desire in both genders. Certain antidepressant drugs, such as fluoxetine (brand name: Prozac), amitriptyline (brand name: Elavil), and

Anaphrodisiacs Drugs or other agents whose effects are antagonistic to sexual arousal or sexual desire.

imipramine (brand name: Tofranil), appear to dampen sex drive (Brody, 1993; Meston & Gorzalka, 1992). Antidepressants may also impair erectile response and delay ejaculation in men and impair orgasmic responsiveness in women (Meston & Gorzalka, 1992). (Because they delay ejaculation, some of these drugs are used to treat premature ejaculation.)

Nicotine, the stimulant in tobacco smoke, constricts the blood vessels. Thus it can impede sexual arousal by reducing the capacity of the genitals to become engorged with blood. Chronic smoking can also reduce the blood levels of testosterone in men, which can in turn lessen sex drive or motivation.

Anti-androgen drugs may have anaphrodisiac effects. However, their effectiveness in modifying deviant behaviour patterns such as sexual violence and sexual interest in children is questionable.

> **Anti-androgen** A substance that decreases the levels of androgens in the bloodstream.

Psychoactive Drugs

Psychoactive drugs, such as alcohol and cocaine, are widely believed to have aphrodisiac effects. Yet their effects may reflect our expectations of them, or their effects on sexual inhibitions, rather than direct stimulation of sexual response.

ALCOHOL Small amounts of alcohol are stimulating, but large amounts curb sexual response. This fact should not be surprising, because alcohol is a depressant. Alcohol reduces central nervous system activity. Large amounts of alcohol can severely impair sexual performance in both men and women.

People who drink moderate amounts of alcohol may feel more sexually aroused because of their expectations about alcohol, not because of its chemical properties (George et al., 2000). That is, people who expect alcohol to enhance sexual responsiveness may act the part. Moreover, men with problems achieving erection may turn to alcohol in hopes of finding a cure (Roehrich & Kinder, 1991). The fact is that alcohol is a depressant and can reduce sexual potency rather than restore it.

Alcohol may also lower sexual inhibitions, because it allows us to ascribe our behaviour to the effects of the alcohol rather than to ourselves (Crowe & George, 1989; Lang, 1985). Alcohol is connected with a liberated social role and thus provides an excuse for dubious behaviour. "It was the alcohol," people can say, "not me." When drinking, people may express their sexual desires and do things that they would not do when sober. For example, a person who feels guilty about sex may become sexually active when drinking because he or she can later blame the alcohol.

Alcohol can also induce feelings of euphoria. Euphoric feelings may enhance sexual arousal and also sweep away qualms about expressing sexual desires. Alcohol also appears to impair the ability to weigh information ("information processing") that might otherwise inhibit sexual impulses (MacDonald et al., 2000; Steele & Josephs, 1990). When people drink, they may be less able to foresee the consequences of misconduct and less likely to ponder their standards of conduct.

What Are the Effects of Alcohol on Sexual Behaviour?
Small doses of alcohol can be stimulating, can induce feelings of euphoria, and can lower inhibitions, all of which could be connected with sexual interest and facilitate social and sexual behaviour. Furthermore, alcohol reduces fear of the consequences of engaging in risky behaviour—sexual and otherwise. Alcohol also provides an excuse for engaging in otherwise unacceptable behaviour, such as sexual intercourse on the first date (or upon casual meeting). Alcohol is expected to be sexually liberating, and people often live up to social and cultural expectations. Yet, as a depressant drug, alcohol in large amounts will biochemically dampen sexual response and may make sexual response impossible.

HALLUCINOGENICS AND MARIJUANA There is no evidence that marijuana or hallucinogenic drugs directly stimulate sexual response. However, fairly to strongly intoxicated marijuana users claim to have more empathy with others, to be more aware of bodily sensations, and to experience time as passing more slowly. These sensations could heighten subjective feelings of sexual response. Some marijuana users report that the drug inhibits their sexual responsiveness, however (Wolman, 1985). The effects of the drug on sexual response may depend on the individual's prior experiences with the drug, on her or his attitudes toward the drug, and on the amount taken.

Other hallucinogenics, such as LSD and mescaline, have also been reported by some users to enhance sexual response. Again, these effects may reflect dosage level and user expectations, experiences, and attitudes toward the drugs, as well as altered perceptions.

STIMULANTS Stimulants such as amphetamines ("speed," "uppers," "bennies," "dexies") have been reputed to heighten arousal and sensations of orgasm. High doses can give rise to irritability, restlessness, hallucinations, paranoid delusions, insomnia, and loss of appetite. These drugs generally activate the central nervous system but are not known to have specific sexual effects. Nevertheless, arousing the nervous system can contribute to sexual arousal (Palace, 1995). The drugs can also elevate the mood, and perhaps sexual pleasure is heightened by general elation.

Cocaine is a natural stimulant that is extracted from the leaves of the coca plant. Cocaine is ingested in various forms, snorted as a powder, smoked in hardened rock form ("crack" cocaine) or in a freebase form, or injected directly into the bloodstream in liquid form. Cocaine produces a euphoric rush, which tends to ebb quickly. Physically, cocaine constricts blood vessels (reducing the oxygen supply to the heart), elevates the blood pressure, and accelerates the heart rate.

Despite the popular belief that cocaine is an aphrodisiac, frequent use can lead to sexual dysfunctions, such as difficulty attaining erection and ejaculating among males, decreased vaginal lubrication in females, and sexual apathy in both men and women (Weiss & Mirin, 1987). Some people do report initial increased sexual pleasure with cocaine use; however, that increase may reflect cocaine's loosening of inhibitions. Over time, though, regular users may become dependent on cocaine for sexual arousal or lose the ability to enjoy sex (Weiss & Mirin, 1987).

More recently, crystal methamphetamine, otherwise known as "crystal meth" or "ice," is being used as an aphrodisiac that boosts sexual arousal and lowers sexual inhibitions. This drug is one of the most addictive street drugs, and the addiction is difficult to treat. Withdrawal typically results in severe pain and depression. It has several negative side effects, including irritability, insomnia, paranoia, and increased aggression. There is concern that it can also damage brain cells, causing memory loss, and can lead to heart attacks and strokes (Ah Shene, 2003). The Canadian AIDS society has warned that use of crystal meth may increase HIV infection because the lowered inhibitions encourage sexual risk-taking.

Sexual Response and the Brain: Cerebral Sex?

The brain may not be an erogenous zone, but it plays a central role in sexual functioning (Fisher, 2000). Direct genital stimulation may trigger spinal reflexes that produce erection in the male and vaginal lubrication in the female without the direct involvement of the brain. The same reflexes may be triggered by sexual stimulation that originates in the brain in the form of erotic memories, fantasies, visual images, and thoughts. The brain may also inhibit sexual responsiveness, as when we experience guilt or anxiety in a sexual situation or when we suddenly realize, well into a sexual encounter, that we have left the car lights turned on.

Figure 4.1 The Limbic System.

The limbic system lies along the inner edge of the cerebrum. When part of a male rat's hypothalamus is electrically stimulated, the rat engages in its courting and mounting routine. Klüver and Bucy (1939) found that destruction of areas of the limbic system triggered continuous sexual behaviour in monkeys. Electrical stimulation of the hippocampus and septal nuclei produces erections in monkeys.

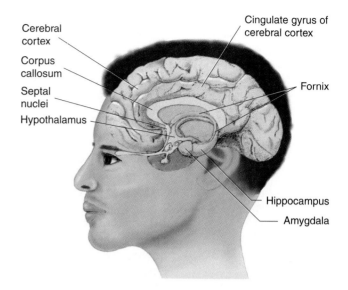

Parts of the brain—in particular the **cerebral cortex** and the **limbic system**—play key roles in sexual functioning. Cells in the cerebral cortex fire (transmit messages) when we experience sexual thoughts, images, wishes, fantasies, and the like. Cells in the cerebral cortex interpret sensory information as sexual turn-ons or turn-offs. The sight of your lover disrobing, the anticipation of a romantic kiss, a passing sexual fantasy, or the viewing of an erotic movie can trigger the firing of cortical cells. These cells, in turn, transmit messages through the spinal cord that send blood rushing to the genitals, causing erection or vaginal lubrication. The cortex also provides the conscious sense of self. The cortex judges sexual behaviour to be proper or improper, moral or immoral, relaxing or anxiety- or guilt-provoking.

Areas of the brain below the cortex, especially the limbic system (see Figure 4.1), also play roles in sexual processes (Everitt, 1990; Kimble, 1992). For example, when the rear part of a male rat's hypothalamus is stimulated by an electrical probe, the animal mechanically runs through its courting and mounting routine. It nibbles at the ears and the back of the neck of a female rat and mounts her when she responds.

> **Cerebral cortex** The wrinkled surface area (grey matter) of the cerebrum.
>
> **Limbic system** A group of structures active in memory, motivation, and emotion; the structures that are part of this system form a fringe along the inner edge of the cerebrum.

Research in Action

MALE AND FEMALE BRAIN RESPONSE

Researchers in Montreal (Karama et al., 2002) used magnetic resonance imaging to analyze gender differences in brain activation in response to viewing erotic films. While viewing the films, both men and women showed increased activation in similar parts of the brain. However, activation in the hypothalamus was significantly greater for the men. And only among men was the magnitude of hypothalamic activity positively related to reported levels of sexual arousal. The researchers suggested that the greater sexual arousal generally experienced by men when viewing erotica may be related to gender differences in activation of the hypothalamus.

Sex Hormones: Do They "Goad" Us into Sex?

In a TV situation comedy, a male adolescent was described as "a hormone with feet." Ask parents why teenagers act the way they do, and you are likely to hear a one-word answer: hormones! **Hormones** are chemical substances that are secreted by the ductless glands of the endocrine system and discharged directly into the bloodstream. The word *hormone* derives from the Greek *horman*, meaning "to stimulate" or "to goad." And we could say that they very much goad us into sexual activity. Hormones also regulate various bodily functions, including growth and resistance to stress as well as sexual functions.

Sex hormones released at puberty also cause the flowering of **secondary sex characteristics**. In males, these include the lengthening of the vocal cords (and consequent lowering of the voice) and the growth of facial and pubic hair. In females, the breasts and hips become rounded with fatty tissue, and pubic hair grows.

Sex Hormones and Sexual Behaviour: Organizing and Activating Influences

Sex hormones have organizing and activating effects on behaviour. That is, they exert an influence on the type of behaviour that is expressed (an *organizing* effect) and on the frequency or intensity of the drive that motivates the behaviour and the ability to perform the behaviour (*activating* effects). For example, sex hormones predispose lower animals and possibly people toward stereotypical masculine or feminine mating behaviours (an organizing effect). They also facilitate sexual response and influence sexual desire (activating effects).

Prenatal sex hormones are known to play a role in the sexual differentiation of the genitalia and of the brain structures, such as the hypothalamus. Their role in patterning sexual behaviour in adulthood remains unknown, however. Researchers have speculated that the brains of **transsexual** individuals may have been prenatally sexually differentiated in one direction while their genitals were being differentiated in the other (Money, 1994). It has been speculated that prenatal sexual differentiation of the brain may also be connected with sexual orientation.

What of the activating effects of sex hormones on human sex drive and behaviour? Although the countless attempts to extract or synthesize aphrodisiacs have failed to produce the real thing, men and women normally produce a genuine aphrodisiac—testosterone. Whatever the early organizing effects of sex hormones in humans, testosterone activates the sex drives of both men and women (Guzick & Hoeger, 2000).

Sex Hormones and Male Sexual Behaviour

Evidence of the role of hormones in sex drive is found among men who have declines in testosterone levels as a result of chemical or surgical castration. Surgical castration (removal of the testes) is sometimes performed as a medical treatment for cancer of the prostate or other diseases of the male reproductive tract, such as genital tuberculosis. And some convicted sex offenders have voluntarily undergone castration as a condition of release.

Regardless of the reason for castration, men who are surgically or chemically castrated usually exhibit a gradual decrease in the incidence of sexual fantasies and of sexual desire (Bradford, 1998; Gijs & Gooren, 1996; Rösler & Witztum, 1998). They also gradually tend to lose the capacities to attain erection and to ejaculate— an indication that testosterone is important in maintaining sexual functioning as

Hormone A substance that is secreted by an endocrine gland and regulates various body functions. (From the Greek *horman*, which means "to stimulate" or "to goad.")

Secondary sex characteristics Physical traits that differentiate males from females but are not directly involved in reproduction.

Transsexual A person with a gender-identity disorder who feels that he or she is really a member of the other gender and is trapped in a body of the wrong gender.

well as drive, at least in males. Castrated men show great variation in their sexual interest and functioning, however. Some continue to experience sexual desires and are able to function sexually for years, even decades. Learning appears to play a large role in determining continued sexual response following castration. Males who were sexually experienced before castration show a more gradual decline in sexual activity. Those who were sexually inexperienced at the time show relatively little or no interest in sex. Male sexual motivation and functioning thus involve an interplay of hormonal influences and experience.

Further evidence of the relationship between hormonal levels and male sexuality is found in studies of men with **hypogonadism**, a condition marked by abnormally low levels of testosterone production. Hypogonadal men generally experience loss of sexual desire and a decline in sexual activity (Carani et al., 1992). Here again, hormones do not tell the whole story. Hypogonadal men are capable of erection, at least for a while, even though their sex drives may wane (Bancroft, 1984). The role of testosterone as an activator of sex drives in men is further supported by evidence of the effects of testosterone replacement in hypogonadal men. When such men obtain testosterone injections, their sex drives, fantasies, and activity are often restored to former levels (Cunningham et al., 1989; Goleman, 1988).

Though minimal levels of androgens are critical to male sexuality, there is no one-to-one correspondence between hormone levels and the sex drive or sexual performance in adults. In men who have ample supplies of testosterone, sexual interest and functioning depend more on learning, fantasies, attitudes, memories, and other psychosocial factors than on hormone levels. At puberty, however, hormonal variations may play a more direct role in stimulating sexual interest and activity in males. Udry and his colleagues (Udry et al., 1985; Udry et al., 1986; Udry & Billy, 1987) found, for example, that testosterone levels among teenage boys predicted sexual interest, masturbation rates, and the likelihood of engaging in sexual intercourse. A positive relationship has also been found between testosterone levels in adult men and frequency of sexual intercourse (Dabbs & Morris, 1990; Knussman et al., 1986). Moreover, drugs that reduce the levels of androgens in the blood system, called *anti-androgens*, lead to reductions in the sex drive and in sexual fantasies (Bradford, 1998).

Sex Hormones and Female Sexual Behaviour

The female sex hormones estrogen and progesterone play prominent roles in promoting the changes that occur during puberty and in regulating the menstrual cycle. Female sex hormones do not, however, appear to play a role in determining sexual motivation or response in human females.

In most mammals, females are sexually receptive only during *estrus* ("in heat")—a brief period of fertility corresponding to ovulation. Estrus occurs once a year in some species; in others, it occurs periodically during the year in so-called sexual or mating seasons. Estrogen peaks at time of ovulation, so there is a close relationship between fertility and sexual receptivity in most female mammals. Women's sexuality, however, is not clearly linked to hormonal fluctuations. Unlike most mammalian females, the human female is sexually responsive during all phases of the reproductive (menstrual) cycle—even during menstruation, when ovarian hormone levels are low—and after menopause.

There is some evidence, however, that sexual responsiveness in women is influenced by the presence of circulating androgens, or male sex hormones, in their bodies. The adrenal glands of women produce small amounts of androgens, just as they do in males (Guzick & Hoeger, 2000). The fact that women normally produce smaller amounts of androgens than men does not mean that they necessarily have weaker sex drives. Rather, women appear to be more sensitive to smaller amounts of androgens. For women, it seems that less is more.

Are Adolescents "Hormones with Feet"?
Research shows that levels of androgens are connected with sexual interest in both male and female adolescents. Hormone levels are more likely to predict sexual behaviour in adolescent males, however, perhaps because society places greater restraints on female sexuality.

Women who receive **ovariectomies**, which are sometimes carried out when a hysterectomy is performed, no longer produce female sex hormones. Nevertheless, they continue to experience sex drives and interest as before. Loss of the ovarian hormone estradiol may cause vaginal dryness and make coitus painful, but it does not reduce sexual desire. (The dryness can be alleviated by a lubricating jelly or by estrogen-replacement therapy.) However, women whose adrenal glands *and* ovaries have been removed (so that they no longer produce androgens) gradually lose sexual desire. An active and enjoyable sexual history seems to ward off this loss, however, providing further evidence of the impact of cognitive and experiential factors on human sexual response.

Research provides further evidence of the links between testosterone levels and women's sex drives (Williams, 1999). In the studies by Udry and his colleagues mentioned earlier, androgen levels were also found to predict sexual interest among teenage girls. In contrast to boys, however, girls' androgen levels were unrelated to the likelihood of coital experience. Androgens apparently affect sexual desire in both genders, but sexual interest may be more likely to be directly translated into sexual activity in men than in women (Bancroft, 1990). This gender difference may be explained by society's imposing greater restraints on adolescent female sexuality.

Other researchers report that women's sexual activity increases at points in the menstrual cycle when levels of androgens in the bloodstream are high (Morris et al., 1987). Another study was conducted with women whose ovaries had been surgically removed ("surgical menopause") as a way of treating disease. The ovaries supply major quantities of estrogen. Following surgery, the women in this study were treated with estrogen-replacement therapy (ERT), with ERT *plus* androgens, or with a placebo (an inert substance made to resemble an active drug) (Sherwin et al., 1985). This was a double-blind study. Neither the women nor their physicians knew which drug the women were receiving. The results showed that the combination of androgens and ERT heightened sexual desire and sexual fantasies more than ERT alone or the placebo. The combination also helps women maintain a sense of psychological well-being (Guzick & Hoeger, 2000).

Androgens thus play a more prominent role than ovarian hormones in activating and maintaining women's sex drives. As with men, however, women's sexuality is too complex to be explained fully by hormone levels.

The Sexual Response Cycle

Although we may be culturally attuned to focus on gender differences rather than similarities, Masters and Johnson (1966) found that the physiological responses of men and women to sexual stimulation (whether from coitus, masturbation, or other sources) are quite alike. The sequence of changes in the body that take place as men and women become progressively more aroused is referred to as the **sexual response cycle**. Masters and Johnson divided the cycle into four phases: *excitement*, *plateau*, *orgasm*, and *resolution*. Figure 4.2 suggests the levels of sexual arousal associated with each phase.

Both males and females experience **vasocongestion** and **myotonia** early in the response cycle. Vasocongestion is the swelling of the genital tissues with blood, which causes erection of the penis and engorgement of the area surrounding the vaginal opening. The testes, nipples, and even earlobes become engorged as blood vessels in these areas dilate. Myotonia is muscle tension. It causes voluntary and involuntary muscle contractions, which produce facial grimaces, spasms in the hands and feet, and eventually, the spasms of orgasm.

Excitement Phase

In younger men, vasocongestion during the **excitement phase** produces penile erection as early as 3 to 8 seconds after stimulation begins. Erection may occur

Ovariectomy Surgical removal of the ovaries.

Sexual response cycle Masters and Johnson's model of sexual response, which consists of four phases.

Vasocongestion The swelling of the genital tissues with blood, which causes erection of the penis and engorgement of the area surrounding the vaginal opening.

Myotonia Muscle tension.

Excitement phase The first phase of the sexual response cycle, which is characterized by erection in the male, by vaginal lubrication in the female, and by muscle tension and increases in heart rate in both males and females.

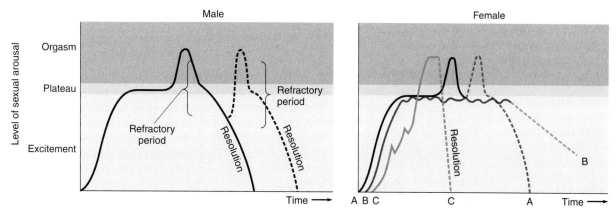

Figure 4.2 Levels of Sexual Arousal During the Phases of the Sexual Response Cycle.

Masters and Johnson divide the sexual response cycle into four phases: excitement, plateau, orgasm, and resolution. During the resolution phase, the level of sexual arousal returns to the prearoused state. For men there is a refractory period following orgasm. As shown by the broken line, however, men can become rearoused to orgasm once the refractory period is past and their levels of sexual arousal have returned to preplateau levels. Pattern A for women shows a typical response cycle; the broken line indicates multiple orgasms, should they occur. Pattern B shows the cycle of a woman who reaches the plateau phase but for whom arousal is "resolved" without her experiencing orgasm. Pattern C shows the possibility of orgasm in a highly aroused woman who passes quickly through the plateau phase.

Research in Action

PHYSICAL VERSUS PSYCHOLOGICAL AROUSAL

Although males and females are similar in terms of their physiological responses, they differ significantly in their subjective perception of arousal. When males are physically aroused, they are almost always subjectively aware of this. However, women vary in the degree to which they are aware of physical arousal. Researchers in British Columbia discovered that older women are more subjectively aware when they are physically aroused than are younger women (Brotto & Gorzalka, 2002). Thus, it seems that for many women it takes time and a learning process to be able to distinguish the physical signs of sexual arousal.

Vancouver therapist Rosemary Basson (2002) discusses how sexual arousal for women is a more complex process than for men. According to Basson, when a woman experiences genital vasocongestion, there can be a range of subjective responses:

1. She may not be aware of the physical arousal.

2. She may be only vaguely aware of arousal.

3. She may be aware of the physical sensations yet not define them as being sexual.

4. She may interpret the arousal as sexual but not experience the sensation as being enjoyable.

Basson analyzes a number of factors that may account for these responses, such as past negative sexual experiences, feelings of inadequacy or guilt, and distractions such as concerns over personal appearance, safety of the situation, and feelings toward one's partner.

more slowly in older men, but the responses are essentially the same. Erection may subside and return as stimulation varies. The scrotal skin thickens, losing its baggy appearance. The testes increase in size. The testes and scrotum become elevated.

Sex flush A reddish rash that appears on the chest or breasts late in the excitement phase of the sexual response cycle.

Plateau phase The second phase of the sexual response cycle, which is characterized by increases in vasocongestion, muscle tension, heart rate, and blood pressure in preparation for orgasm.

Orgasmic platform The thickening of the walls of the outer third of the vagina, due to vasocongestion, that occurs during the plateau phase of the sexual response cycle.

In the female, vaginal lubrication may start 10 to 30 seconds after stimulation begins. Vasocongestion swells the clitoris, flattens the labia majora and spreads them apart, and increases the size of the labia minora. The inner two-thirds of the vagina expand. The vaginal walls thicken and, because of the inflow of blood, turn from their normal pink to a deeper hue. The uterus becomes engorged and elevated. The breasts enlarge, and blood vessels near the surface become more prominent.

Late in this phase, the skin may take on a rosy **sex flush**, which varies with intensity of arousal and is more pronounced in women. The nipples may become erect in both genders, especially in response to direct stimulation. Both men and women show some increase in myotonia, heart rate, and blood pressure.

Plateau Phase

A plateau is a level region, and the level of arousal remains somewhat constant during the **plateau phase** of sexual response. Nevertheless, the plateau phase is an advanced state of arousal that precedes orgasm. Men in this phase show a slight increase in the circumference of the coronal ridge of the penis. The penile glans turns a purplish hue, a sign of vasocongestion. The testes are elevated further into position for ejaculation and may reach one and a half times their unaroused size. The Cowper's glands secrete a few droplets of fluid that are found at the tip of the penis (see Figure 4.3).

In women, vasocongestion swells the tissues of the outer third of the vagina, contracting the vaginal opening (thus preparing it to "grasp" the penis) and building the **orgasmic platform** (see Figure 4.4). The inner part of the vagina expands fully. The uterus becomes fully elevated. The clitoris withdraws beneath the clitoral

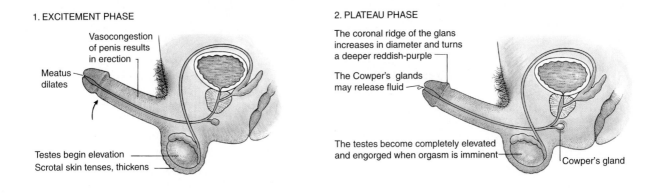

1. EXCITEMENT PHASE

Vasocongestion of penis results in erection

Meatus dilates

Testes begin elevation
Scrotal skin tenses, thickens

2. PLATEAU PHASE

The coronal ridge of the glans increases in diameter and turns a deeper reddish-purple

The Cowper's glands may release fluid

The testes become completely elevated and engorged when orgasm is imminent

Cowper's gland

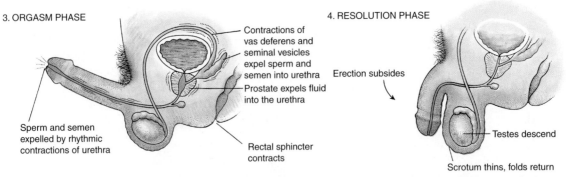

3. ORGASM PHASE

Contractions of vas deferens and seminal vesicles expel sperm and semen into urethra

Prostate expels fluid into the urethra

Sperm and semen expelled by rhythmic contractions of urethra

Rectal sphincter contracts

4. RESOLUTION PHASE

Erection subsides

Testes descend

Scrotum thins, folds return

Figure 4.3 The Male Genitals During the Phases of the Sexual Response Cycle.

1. EXCITEMENT PHASE

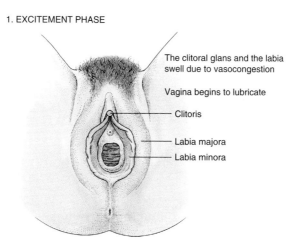

The clitoral glans and the labia swell due to vasocongestion

Vagina begins to lubricate

Clitoris

Labia majora

Labia minora

Figure 4.4 The Female Genitals During the Phases of the Sexual Response Cycle.

2. PLATEAU PHASE

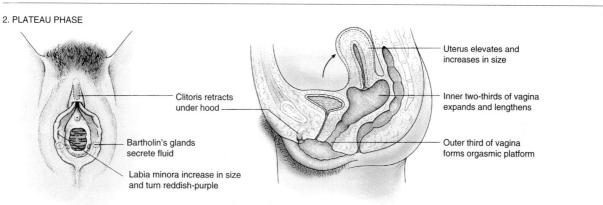

Clitoris retracts under hood

Bartholin's glands secrete fluid

Labia minora increase in size and turn reddish-purple

Uterus elevates and increases in size

Inner two-thirds of vagina expands and lengthens

Outer third of vagina forms orgasmic platform

3. ORGASM PHASE

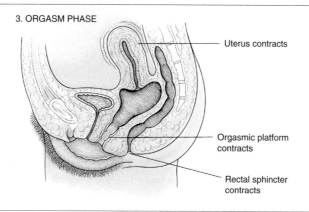

Uterus contracts

Orgasmic platform contracts

Rectal sphincter contracts

4. RESOLUTION PHASE

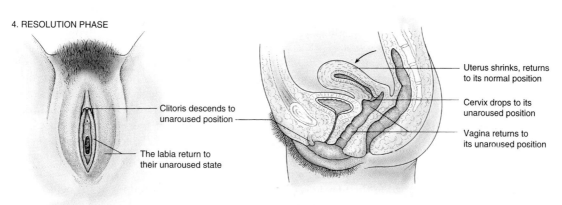

Clitoris descends to unaroused position

The labia return to their unaroused state

Uterus shrinks, returns to its normal position

Cervix drops to its unaroused position

Vagina returns to its unaroused position

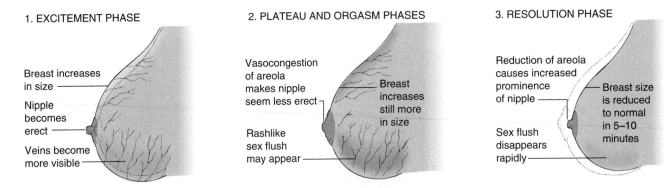

1. EXCITEMENT PHASE

Breast increases in size

Nipple becomes erect

Veins become more visible

2. PLATEAU AND ORGASM PHASES

Vasocongestion of areola makes nipple seem less erect

Breast increases still more in size

Rashlike sex flush may appear

3. RESOLUTION PHASE

Reduction of areola causes increased prominence of nipple

Breast size is reduced to normal in 5–10 minutes

Sex flush disappears rapidly

Figure 4.5 The Breasts During the Phases of the Sexual Response Cycle.

hood and shortens. Thus a woman (or her partner) may feel that the clitoris has become lost. This may be mistaken as a sign that the woman's sexual arousal is waning, when it is actually increasing.

Coloration of the labia minora, referred to as the **sex skin**, appears. The labia minora become a deep wine colour in women who have borne children and bright red in women who have not. Further engorgement of the areolas of the breasts may make it seem that the nipples have lost part of their erection (see Figure 4.5). Bartholin's glands secrete a fluid that resembles mucus.

About one man in four, and about three women in four, show a sex flush, which often does not appear until the plateau phase. Myotonia may cause facial grimaces and spasmodic contractions in the hands and feet. Breathing becomes rapid, like panting, and the heart rate may increase to 100 to 160 beats per minute. Blood pressure continues to rise. The increase in heart rate is usually less dramatic with masturbation than during coitus.

Orgasmic Phase

The orgasmic phase in the male consists of two stages of muscular contractions. In the first stage, contractions of the vas deferens, the seminal vesicles, the ejaculatory duct, and the prostate gland cause seminal fluid to collect in the urethral bulb at the base of the penis (see Figure 4.3). The bulb expands to accommodate the fluid. The internal sphincter of the urinary bladder contracts, preventing seminal fluid from entering the bladder in a backward, retrograde ejaculation. The normal closing off of the bladder also serves to prevent urine from mixing with semen. The collection of semen in the urethral bulb produces feelings of ejaculatory inevitability—the sensation that nothing will stop the ejaculate from "coming." This sensation lasts for about 2 to 3 seconds.

In the second stage, the external sphincter of the bladder relaxes, allowing the passage of semen. Contractions of muscles surrounding the urethra and urethral bulb and the base of the penis propel the ejaculate through the urethra and out of the body. Sensations of pleasure tend to be related to the strength of the contractions and the amount of seminal fluid. The first three to four contractions are generally most intense and occur at 0.8-second intervals (5 contractions every 4 seconds). Another 2 to 4 contractions occur at a somewhat slower pace. Rates and patterns vary somewhat from man to man.

Orgasm in the female is manifested by 3 to 15 contractions of the pelvic muscles that surround the vaginal barrel. The contractions first occur at 0.8-second

Sex skin The reddening of the labia minora that occurs during the plateau phase.

Research in Action

SUBJECTIVE EXPERIENCE OF ORGASM

The sensations of orgasm have challenged the descriptive powers of poets. Words like *rush, warmth, explosion,* and *release* do not adequately capture them. We may assume (rightly or wrongly) that others of our gender experience pretty much what we do, but can we understand the sensations of the other gender?

Studies suggest that the orgasms of both genders may feel quite similar. In one study, Kenneth Mah from Princess Margaret Hospital in Toronto and Yitzchak Binik of McGill University (2002) developed a scale to measure the subjective experiences of orgasm among men and women. They wanted to determine what characteristics were common to human experiences of orgasm. University students were asked to rate adjectives describing their orgasm experiences occurring both in masturbation and sex with a partner. The findings supported a two-dimensional model of the psychological experience of orgasm. The first is the sensory dimension, which has the following components:

- Building sensation
- Flooding sensation
- Flushing sensation
- Shooting sensation
- Throbbing sensation
- General spasms

The second, cognitive-affective dimension of orgasm experience includes the following:

- Pleasurable satisfaction
- Relaxation
- Emotional intimacy
- Ecstasy

Mah and Binik found that, although the intimacy ratings were lower in the masturbation situation, students' ratings for orgasms obtained through masturbation were generally similar to orgasms obtained through sex with a partner. Orgasm ratings were similar for males and females, except that males gave a higher rating for shooting sensations, reflecting the male process of ejaculation.

intervals, producing, as in the male, a release of sexual tension. Another 3 to 6 weaker and slower contractions follow. The spacing of these contractions is generally more variable in women than in men. The uterus and the anal sphincter also contract rhythmically. Uterine contractions occur in waves from the top to the cervix. In both genders, muscles go into spasm throughout the body. Blood pressure and heart rate reach a peak, with the heart beating up to 180 times per minute. Respiration may increase to 40 breaths per minute.

Resolution Phase

The period following orgasm, in which the body returns to its prearoused state, is called the **resolution phase**. Following ejaculation, the man loses his erection in two stages. The first occurs in about a minute. Half the volume of the erection is lost, as blood from the corpora cavernosa empties into the other parts of the body. The second stage occurs over a period of several minutes: The remaining tumescence subsides as the corpus spongiosum empties. The testes and scrotum return to normal size, and the scrotum regains its wrinkled appearance.

In women, orgasm also triggers release of blood from engorged areas. In the absence of continued stimulation, swelling of the areolas decreases, then the nipples return to normal size. The sex flush lightens rapidly. In about 5 to 10 seconds, the

Resolution phase The fourth phase of the sexual response cycle, during which the body gradually returns to its prearoused state.

Refractory period A period of time following a response (e.g., orgasm) during which an individual is no longer responsive to stimulation (e.g., sexual stimulation).

clitoris descends to its normal position. The clitoris, vaginal barrel, uterus, and labia gradually shrink to their prearoused sizes. The labia minora turn lighter (the "sex skin" disappears) in about 10 to 15 seconds.

Most muscle tension (myotonia) tends to dissipate within 5 minutes after orgasm in both men and women. Blood pressure, heart rate, and respiration may also return to their prearousal levels within a few minutes. About 30% to 40% of men and women find their palms, the soles of their feet, or their entire bodies covered with a sheen of perspiration. Both men and women may feel relaxed and satiated. However . . .

Although the processes by which the body returns to its prearousal state are similar in men and women, there is an important gender difference during the resolution phase. Unlike women, men enter a **refractory period** during which they are physiologically incapable of experiencing another orgasm or ejaculation (in much the same way as the flash attachment to a camera cannot be set off again immediately after it is used—it has to be recharged). The refractory period of adolescent males may last only minutes, whereas that of men aged 50 and above may last from several minutes (yes, it could happen) to a day. Women do not undergo a refractory period and so can become quickly rearoused to the point of repeated (multiple) orgasm if they desire and receive continued sexual stimulation (see Figure 4.2).

Myotonia and vasocongestion may take an hour or more to dissipate in people who are aroused who do not reach orgasm. Persistent pelvic vasocongestion may cause "blue balls" in males—the slang term for a throbbing ache. Some men insist that their dates should consent to coitus, on the theory that it is unfair to decline after stimulating them to the point where they have this condition. This ache can be relieved through masturbation as well as coitus, however, or can be allowed to dissipate naturally. Although it may be uncomfortable, it is not dangerous and is no excuse to pressure or coerce another person into any sexual activity. "Blue" sensations are not limited to men. Women, too, may experience unpleasant pelvic throbbing if they have become highly aroused and do not find release. And women, too, can relieve pelvic throbbing through masturbation.

Kaplan's Three Stages of Sexual Response

Helen Singer Kaplan was a prominent sex therapist and author of several professional books (1974, 1979, 1987) on sex therapy. Whereas Masters and Johnson had proposed a four-stage model of sexual response, Kaplan developed a three-stage model consisting of (1) desire, (2) excitement, and (3) orgasm. Kaplan's model is an outgrowth of her clinical experience in working with people with sexual dysfunctions. She believes that their problems can best be classified according to these three phases. Kaplan's model makes it convenient for clinicians to classify sexual dysfunctions involving desire (low or absent desire), excitement (such as problems with erection in the male or lubrication in the female), and orgasm (such as premature ejaculation in the male or orgasmic dysfunction in the female).

Kaplan's model is noteworthy for designating desire as a separate phase of sexual response. Problems in lack of sexual interest or desire are among those most commonly brought to the attention of sex therapists.

Basson's Intimacy Model of Female Sexual Response

Womyns' Ware This Vancouver based sex shop offers sex advice.

www.womynsware. com

Rosemary Basson (2001), a Vancouver therapist, has developed an intimacy-based model of female sexual response that she argues is especially relevant for women in long-term relationships. Her main criticism of previous models is that they do not take into account the factor of intimacy. According to Basson, most women in longer-term relationships are motivated to respond to sexual stimuli if they feel that becoming sexually involved will enhance intimacy with their partner.

Often a woman will begin sexual encounters with a nonsexual or neutral state of mind. Once the woman has begun to become sexually aroused for "intimacy reasons," she will continue the experience for "sexual reasons." At this point she will be responsive to sexual stimulation, such as breast or genital touching, that will increase her arousal. If the woman finds the outcome to be both physically and emotionally satisfying, it will increase her feelings of intimacy with her partner and motivate her to become sexually involved again in the future.

This model allows for the possibility that arousal may precede sexual desire and that arousal may not lead to orgasm. Basson does acknowledge the possibility that spontaneous sexual desire can occur among women outside of the intimacy model, and that this may lead to self-stimulation or casual sex.

Controversies About Orgasm

Are women capable of experiencing multiple orgasms? Are men? Physiologically speaking, is there but one type of orgasm? Or are there different types of orgasms, depending on the site of stimulation? Do women ejaculate during orgasm? If so, what fluid do they emit?

Could there be a biological reason why some women are able to experience orgasm easily while other women have difficulty obtaining an orgasm? A study of female twins in London, England, found that identical twins were more similar in their orgasm experiences than were non-identical twins, suggesting that genetics plays a role in ability to have an orgasm (Dunn, Cherkas, & Spector, 2005).

Few other topics in human sexuality have aroused more controversies over the years than orgasm. We do not have all the answers, but some intriguing research findings have shed light on some of these continuing controversies.

Multiple Orgasms

Kinsey's report (Kinsey et al., 1953) that 14% of his female respondents regularly had **multiple orgasms** sent shock waves through the general community and even surprised his fellow scientists. Many people were aghast that women could have more than one orgasm in succession. There were comments (mostly by men, of course!) that the women in the Kinsey surveys must be "nymphomaniacs" who were incapable of being satisfied with the "normal" complement of one orgasm per occasion. However, only 13 years later, Masters and Johnson (1966) reported that most if not all women are capable of multiple orgasms. Though all women may have a biological capability for multiple orgasm, not all women report them. A recent survey of 720 female nurses showed that only 43% reported experiencing multiple orgasms (Darling et al., 1991).

It is difficult to offer a precise definition of multiple orgasm. (Note that the pattern shown by the broken line for the male in Figure 4.2 does *not* constitute a multiple orgasm, even if it occurs reasonably rapidly after the first orgasm, because he *does* return to a preplateau level of sexual arousal between orgasms.) The lines of demarcation between the excitement and plateau stages of arousal are not obvious, however. Therefore, a person may experience two or more successive orgasms within a short time but not know whether these are, technically speaking, "multiple orgasms." Whether or not the orgasm fits the definition has no effect on the experience, but it does raise the question of whether both men and women are capable of multiple orgasm.

By Masters and Johnson's definition, men are not capable of achieving multiple orgasms because they enter a refractory period following ejaculation during which they are physiologically incapable of achieving another orgasm or ejaculation. Put

> **Multiple orgasms** One or more additional orgasms following the first, which occur within a short period of time and before the body has returned to a preplateau level of arousal.

more simply, men who want more than one orgasm during one session may have to relax for a while and allow their sexual arousal to subside. Yet women can maintain a high level of arousal between multiple orgasms and have them in rapid succession.

Women do not enter a refractory period. Women can continue to have orgasms if they continue to receive effective stimulation (and, of course, are interested in continuing). Some men thus refrain from reaching orgasm until their partners have had the desired number. This differential capacity for multiple orgasms is one of the major gender differences in sexual response.

Some men have two or more orgasms without ejaculation ("dry orgasms") preceding a final ejaculatory orgasm. These men may not enter a refractory period following their initial dry orgasms and may therefore be able to maintain their level of stimulation at near-peak levels.

Masters and Johnson found that some women experienced 20 or more orgasms by masturbating. Still, few women have multiple orgasms during most sexual encounters, and many are satisfied with just one per occasion. Some women who have read or heard about female orgasmic capacity wonder what is "wrong" with them if they are content with just one. Nothing is wrong with them, of course; a biological capacity does not create a behavioural requirement.

How Many Kinds of Orgasms Do Women Have? One, Two, or Three?

Until Masters and Johnson published their laboratory findings, many people believed that there were two types of female orgasms, as proposed by the psychoanalyst Sigmund Freud: the *clitoral orgasm* and the *vaginal orgasm*. Clitoral orgasms were achieved through direct clitoral stimulation, such as by masturbation. Clitoral orgasms were seen by psychoanalysts (mostly male psychoanalysts, naturally) as emblematic of a childhood fixation—a throwback to an erogenous pattern acquired during childhood masturbation.

The term *vaginal orgasm* referred to an orgasm achieved through deep penile thrusting during coitus and was theorized to be a sign of mature sexuality. Freud argued that women achieve sexual maturity when they forsake clitoral stimulation for vaginal stimulation. This view would be little more than an academic footnote except for the fact that some adult women who continue to require direct clitoral stimulation to reach orgasm, even during coitus, have been led by traditional (generally male) psychoanalysts to believe that they are sexually "fixated" at an immature stage or, at least, are sexually inadequate.

Despite Freudian theory, Masters and Johnson (1966) were able to find only one kind of orgasm, physiologically speaking, regardless of the source of stimulation (manual–clitoral or penile–vaginal). By monitoring physiological responses to sexual stimulation, they found that the female orgasm involves the same biological events whether it is reached through masturbation, petting, coitus, or just breast stimulation. All orgasms involve spasmodic contractions of the pelvic muscles surrounding the vaginal barrel, leading to a release of sexual tension. Gertrude Stein wrote, "A rose is a rose is a rose." Biologically speaking, the same principle can be applied to orgasm: An orgasm is an orgasm is an orgasm. In men, it also matters not how orgasm is achieved—through masturbation, petting, oral sex, coitus, or fantasizing about a fellow student in chem lab. Orgasm still involves the same physiological processes: Involuntary contractions of the pelvic muscles at the base of the penis expel semen and release sexual tension. A woman or a man might prefer one source of orgasm to another (she or he might prefer achieving orgasm with a lover rather than by masturbation, or with one person rather than another), but the biological events that define orgasm remain the same.

Although orgasms attained through coitus or masturbation may be physiologically alike, there are certainly key psychological or subjective differences. (Were it not so, there would be fewer sexual relationships.) The coital experience, for example, is often accompanied by feelings of attachment, love, and connectedness to one's partner. Masturbation, by contrast, is more likely to be experienced solely as a sexual release.

The purported distinction between clitoral and vaginal orgasms also rests on an assumption that the clitoris is not stimulated during coitus. Masters and Johnson showed this to be a *false* assumption. Penile coital thrusting draws the clitoral hood back and forth against the clitoris. Vaginal pressure also heightens blood flow in the clitoris, further setting the stage for orgasm (Lavoisier et al., 1995).

One might think that Masters and Johnson's research settled the question of whether there are different types of female orgasm. Other investigators, however, have proposed that there *are* distinct forms of female orgasm, but not those suggested by psychoanalytic theory. For example, Singer and Singer (1972) suggested that there are three types of female orgasm: *vulval, uterine,* and *blended.* According to the Singers, the vulval orgasm represents the type of orgasm described by Masters and Johnson (1966) that involves *vulval* contractions, that is, contractions of the vaginal barrel. Consistent with the findings of Masters and Johnson (1966), they note that the vulval orgasm remains the same regardless of the source of stimulation, clitoral or vaginal.

According to the Singers, the uterine orgasm does not involve vulval contractions. It occurs only in response to deep penile thrusting against the cervix. This thrusting slightly displaces the uterus and stimulates the tissues that cover the abdominal organs. The uterine orgasm is accompanied by a certain pattern of breathing: Gasping or gulping of air is followed by an involuntary holding of the breath as orgasm approaches. When orgasm is reached, the breath is explosively exhaled. The uterine orgasm is accompanied by deep feelings of relaxation and sexual satisfaction.

The third type, or blended orgasm, is described as combining features of the vulval and uterine orgasms. It involves both an involuntary breath-holding response and contractions of the pelvic muscles. The Singers note that the type of orgasm a woman experiences depends on factors such as the parts of the body that are stimulated and the duration of stimulation. Each produces its own kind of satisfaction, and no one type is necessarily better than or preferable to any other.

The Singers' hypothesis of three distinct forms of female orgasm remains controversial. Researchers initially scoffed at the idea that orgasms could arise from vaginal stimulation alone. The vagina, after all, especially the inner two-thirds of the vaginal cavity, is relatively insensitive to stimulation (erotic or otherwise). Proponents of the Singers' model counter that the type of uterine orgasm described by the Singers is induced more by pressure resulting from deep pelvic thrusting than by touch.

The G-Spot

A part of the vagina, notably a bean-shaped area within the anterior wall, may have special erotic significance. This area is believed to lie about 2.5 to 5 centimetres (1 to 2 inches) from the vaginal entrance and to consist of a soft mass of tissue that swells from the size of a dime to that of a half-dollar when stimulated (Davidson et al., 1989). It has been called the **Grafenberg spot**—the "G-spot" for short (see Figure 4.6). This spot can be directly stimulated by the woman's or her partner's fingers or by penile thrusting in the rear-entry and the female-superior positions. Some researchers suggest that stimulation of the spot produces intense erotic sensations, and that with prolonged stimulation a distinct form of orgasm occurs. This orgasm is characterized by intense pleasure and, in some cases, by a biological event

Grafenberg spot A part of the anterior wall of the vagina, whose prolonged stimulation is theorized to cause particularly intense orgasms and a female ejaculation. Abbreviated *G-spot.*

Figure 4.6 The Grafenberg Spot.

It is theorized that the "G-spot" can be stimulated by fingers or by intercourse in the rear-entry or the female-superior positions. Does stimulation of the G-spot produce intense erotic sensations and a distinct form of orgasm?

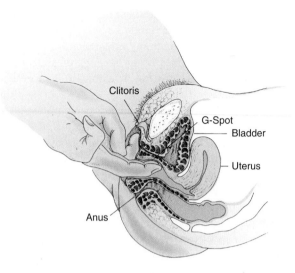

earlier thought to be exclusively male in nature: ejaculation (Perry & Whipple, 1981; Whipple & Komisaruk, 1988). These claims, like other claims of distinct forms of female orgasm, have been steeped in controversy.

The G-spot was named after a gynecologist, Ernest Grafenberg, who first suggested the erotic importance of this area. Grafenberg observed that orgasm in women could be induced by stimulating this area. He also claimed that such orgasms may be accompanied by the discharge of a milky fluid, or "ejaculate," from the urethra. In a laboratory experiment, Zaviacic and his colleagues (1988a, 1988b) found evidence of an ejaculate in 10 of 27 women studied. Some researchers believe that this fluid is urine that some women release involuntarily during orgasm (Alzate, 1985). Other researchers believe that it differs from urine (Zaviacic & Whipple, 1993). The nature of this fluid and its source remain controversial, but Zaviacic and Whipple (1993) suggest that the fluid may be released during sex by a "female prostate," a system of ducts and glands called *Skene's glands,* in much the same way as semen is released by the prostate gland in men. Zaviacic and Whipple suggest that "many women who felt that they may be urinating during sex [may be helped by] the knowledge that the fluid they expel may be different from urine and a normal phenomenon that occurs during sexual response" (1993, p. 149). Some women, however, may actually expel urine during sex, perhaps because of urinary stress incontinence (Zaviacic & Whipple, 1993). Zaviacic and Whipple also note that stimulation of the G-spot may be related to ejaculation in some women but not in others.

Even proponents of the existence of the G-spot recognize that it is difficult to locate, because it is not apparent to the eye (Ladas et al., 1982). Perry and Whipple (1981) suggest that women may try to locate the spot either by self-exploration or with the assistance of a partner. In either case, two fingers should be used to press deeply but gently into the front, or anterior, wall of the vagina to locate the spot, which may feel like a small lump within the anterior wall (see Figure 4.6). When the spot is stimulated by stroking, the woman may initially experience an urge to urinate, perhaps because the sensitive area lies close to the bladder and urethra. A few minutes of continued stimulation lead to strong sensations of sexual pleasure in some women, which is accompanied by vasocongestion that swells the area. More prolonged stimulation may lead to an intense orgasm; however, fear of loss of urinary control leads some women to avoid such prolonged stimulation (Ladas et al., 1982).

The very existence of the G-spot remains debatable. Ladas, Whipple, and Perry (1982) reported locating the G-spot in every one of more than 400 women they examined. Zaviacic and his colleagues (1988a& b) reported finding the spot in each of 27 women they examined. However, other researchers have been unable to find an area of heightened sensitivity corresponding to the G-spot (Alzate & Londono, 1984; Masters et al., 1989). Some researchers (e.g., Hock, 1983) deny the existence of the G-spot as a distinct anatomic structure. They argue that the entire anterior wall of the vagina, not just any one spot or area, is richly supplied with nerve endings and sensitive to erotic stimulation.

Although the existence of the G-spot continues to be debated among researchers, a recent survey of 1289 professional women in the health and counselling professions revealed that a majority believe that the G-spot exists and that they have experienced sexual pleasure when it has been stimulated (Davidson et al., 1989). Still, there was considerable confusion among these women as to the precise location of this sensitive area. About three out of four women reported experiencing an orgasm from stimulation of this area, most frequently from manual stimulation.

More research is needed to determine the scientific basis of the claims for different kinds of orgasms in women and whether there are specific sites in the vagina, such as the G-spot, that may be especially sensitive to erotic stimulation.

Sex and Disability

Like older people, people with disabilities (especially those whose physical disabilities render them dependent on others) are often seen as sexless and childlike (Nosek et al., 1994). Such views are based on misconceptions. Some of these myths and stereotypes may be eroding, however, in part because of the success of the civil and social rights movements of the disabled in the 1970s and the attention focused on the sexuality of people with disabilities in films such as *Coming Home, Born on the Fourth of July,* and *My Left Foot.*

A person may have been born with or acquire a bodily impairment or suffer a loss of function or a disfiguring change in appearance. Although the disability may require the person to make adjustments in order to perform sexually, most people with disabilities have the same sexual needs, feelings, and desires as people without disabilities. Their ability to express their sexual feelings and needs depends on the physical limitations imposed by their disabilities, their adjustment to their disabilities, and the availability of partners. The establishment of mature sexual relationships generally demands some distance from one's parents. Therefore, people with disabilities who are physically dependent on their parents may find it especially difficult to develop sexual relationships (Knight, 1989). Parents who acknowledge their children's sexual development can be helpful by facilitating dating. Far too often, parents become overprotective:

> Adolescent disabled girls have the same ideas, hopes, and dreams about sexuality as able-bodied girls. They will have learned the gender role expectations set for them by the media and others and may experience difficulty if they lack more substantive educational information about sexuality and sex function. In addition their expectations may come in conflict with the family, which may have consistently protected or overindulged the child and not permitted her to "grow up." . . . In many cases the families are intensely concerned about the sexual and emotional vulnerability of the daughter and hope that "nothing bad" will happen to her. They may, therefore, encourage her to wear youthful clothing and to stay a safe little girl. The families can mistakenly assume there may be no sexual life ahead of her and protect her from this perceived bitter reality with youthful cloth-

ing and little-girlish ways. The result can be, of course, that the young emerging woman may become societally handicapped in learning how to conduct herself as a sexual woman. She will be infantilized. (Cole, 1988, pp. 282–283)

In such families, young people with disabilities get the message that sex is not for them. As they mature, they may need counselling to help them recognize the normalcy of their sexual feelings and to help them make responsible choices for exploring their sexuality.

Unfortunately, most health-care professionals are not equipped to provide sexual counselling to the physically disabled. In a study of 226 health-care professionals in Ontario, 95% said that they had not been given adequate knowledge about sexuality and the physically disabled (Molloy & Herold, 1985). While they were highly supportive of the idea that the physically disabled should receive sexual counselling as part of their rehabilitation, relatively few had actually provided such counselling.

To what extent should caregivers assist the physically disabled to experience sexual pleasure? In Denmark, it is accepted for social workers to arrange for clients who do not have a sexual partner to engage in sex with a prostitute. In Barrie, Ontario, a group of health-care attendants sued the local association for the physically disabled over having to assist disabled clients with their sexual needs ("Workers cry foul," 1996). The attendants claimed they were fired after they refused to provide this service, which included helping clients put on condoms and get into bed to have sex as well as helping some clients to masturbate. Whose side would you take in this dispute?

Physical Disabilities

According to Margaret Nosek and her colleagues (1994), sexual wellness, even among the disabled, involves five factors:

- Positive sexual self-concept; seeing oneself as valuable sexually and as a person
- Knowledge about sexuality
- Positive, productive relationships
- Coping with barriers to sexuality (social, environmental, physical, and emotional)
- Maintaining the best possible general and sexual health, given one's limitations

This model applies to all of us, of course. Let us now consider aspects of specific physical disabilities and human sexuality.

CEREBRAL PALSY **Cerebral palsy** does not generally impair sexual interest, capacity for orgasm, or fertility (Reinisch, 1990). Depending on the nature and degree of muscle spasticity or lack of voluntary muscle control, however, afflicted people may be limited to certain types of sexual activities and coital positions.

People with disabilities such as cerebral palsy often suffer social rejection during adolescence and perceive themselves as unfit for or unworthy of intimate sexual relationships, especially with people who are not disabled. They are often socialized into an asexual role. Sensitive counselling can help them understand and accept their sexuality, promote a more positive body image, and provide the social skills to establish intimate relationships (Edmonson, 1988).

SPINAL CORD INJURIES People who suffer physical disabilities as the result of traumatic injuries or physical illness must not only learn to cope with their physical limitations but also adjust to a world designed for nondisabled people (Trieschmann, 1989). The majority of people who suffer disabling spinal cord

Cerebral palsy A muscular disorder that is caused by damage to the central nervous system (usually prior to or during birth) and is characterized by spastic paralysis.

injuries are young, active males. Automobile or pedestrian accidents account for about half of these cases. Other common causes include stabbing or bullet wounds, sports injuries, and falls. Depending on the location of the injury relative to the spinal cord, a loss of voluntary control (paralysis) can occur in either the legs (*paraplegia*) or all four limbs (*quadriplegia*). A loss of sensation may also occur in parts of the body that lie beneath the site of injury. Most people who suffer such injuries have relatively normal life spans, but the quality of their lives is profoundly affected.

The effect of spinal cord injuries on sexual response depends on the site and severity of the injury. Men have two erection centres in the spinal cord: a higher centre in the lumbar region that controls psychogenic erections and a lower one in the sacral region that controls reflexive erections. When damage occurs at or above the level of the lumbar centre, men lose the capacity for psychogenic erections, the kinds of erections that occur in response to mental stimulation alone, such as when viewing erotic films or fantasizing. They may still be able to achieve reflexive erections from direct stimulation of the penis; these erections are controlled by the sacral erection centre located in a lower portion of the spinal cord. However, they cannot feel any genital sensations because the nerve connections to the brain are severed. Men with damage to the sacral erection centre lose the capacity for reflexive erections but can still achieve psychogenic erections so long as their upper spinal cord remains intact (Spark, 1991). Overall, researchers find that about three of four men with spinal cord injuries are able to achieve erections but that only about one in ten continues to ejaculate naturally (Geiger, 1981; Spark, 1991). Others can be helped to ejaculate with the aid of a vibrator (Szasz & Carpenter, 1989). Their brains may help to fill in some of the missing sensations associated with coitus and even orgasm. When direct stimulation does not cause erection, the woman can insert the limp penis into the vagina and gently thrust her hips, taking care not to dislodge the penis.

Although the frequency of sexual activity among men with spinal cord injuries tends to decline following the injury (Alexander et al., 1993), a study of almost 1300 men with these injuries found that about one out of three (35%) continued to engage in sexual intercourse (Spark, 1991). Only about one in five of the men received any kind of sexual counselling to help them adjust sexually to their disability. The men typically reported increased interest in alternative sexual activities, especially those involving areas above the level of the spinal injury, such as the mouth, lips, neck, and ears.

Retention of sexual response in women also depends on the site and severity of the injury (Seftel et al., 1991). Women may lose the ability to experience genital sensations or to lubricate normally during sexual stimulation. However, breast sensations may remain intact, making this area even more erotogenic. Most women with spinal cord injuries can engage in coitus, become impregnated, and deliver vaginally. A survey of 27 women with spinal cord injuries showed that about half were able to experience orgasm (Kettl et al., 1991). Some also report "phantom orgasms" that provide intense psychological pleasure and are accompanied by non-genital sensations that are similar to those experienced by nondisabled women (Perduta-Fulginiti, 1992). Spinal-cord-injured women can heighten their sexual pleasure by learning to use fantasized orgasm, orgasmic imagery, and amplification of their physical sensations (Perduta-Fulginiti, 1992).

Couples facing the challenge of spinal cord injury may expand their sexual repertoire to focus less on genital stimulation (except to attain the reflexes of erection and lubrication) and more on the parts of the body that retain sensation. Stimulation of some areas of the body, such as the ears, the neck, and the breasts (in both men and women), can yield pleasurable erotic sensations (Knight, 1989; Seftel et al., 1991).

SENSORY DISABILITIES Sensory disabilities, such as blindness and deafness, do not directly affect genital responsiveness. Still, sexuality may be affected in many

The Canadian Abilities Foundation Provides information for the disabled on support groups in many cities across the country.

www.enablelink.org

The Wellness and Disability Initiative of the BC Coalition of People with Disabilities Collects and produces material about healthy sexuality and disability

www.bccpd.bc.ca/wdi/ sex&dis.html

ways. A person who has been blind since birth or early childhood may have difficulty understanding a partner's anatomy. Sex education curricula have been designed specifically to enable visually impaired people to learn about sexual anatomy via models. Anatomically correct dolls may be used to simulate positions of intercourse.

Deaf people, too, often lack knowledge about sex. Their ability to comprehend the social cues involved in forming and maintaining intimate relationships may also be impaired. Sex education programs based on sign language are helping many hearing-impaired people become more socially perceptive as well as knowledgeable about the physical aspects of sex. People with visual and hearing impairments often lack self-esteem and self-confidence, problems that make it difficult for them to establish intimate relationships. Counselling may help them become more aware of their sexuality and develop social skills.

OTHER PHYSICAL DISABILITIES AND IMPAIRMENTS Specific disabilities pose particular challenges to, and limitations on, sexual functioning. **Arthritis** may make it difficult or painful for sufferers to bend their arms, knees, and hips during sexual activity. Coital positions that minimize discomfort may be helpful, as may applying moist heat to the joints before sexual relations.

A male amputee may find that he is better balanced in the lateral-entry or female-superior position than in the male-superior position (Knight, 1989). A woman with limited hand function may find it difficult or impossible to insert a diaphragm and may need to request assistance from her partner or switch to another method of contraception (Cole, 1988). Sensitivity to each other's needs is as vital to couples in which one member has a disability as it is to nondisabled couples.

Psychological Disabilities

People with psychological disabilities, such as developmental disabilities, are often stereotyped as incapable of understanding their sexual impulses. People with developmental disabilities are sometimes assumed to maintain childlike innocence through their lives or to be devoid of sexuality. Some stereotype people with developmental disabilities in the opposite direction: as having stronger-than-normal sex drives and being incapable of controlling them (Reinisch, 1990). Some people with developmental disabilities do act inappropriately—by masturbating publicly, for example. The stereotypes are exaggerated, however, and even many people with developmental disabilities who act inappropriately can be trained to follow social rules (Reinisch, 1990).

Parents and caretakers often discourage people with developmental disabilities from learning about their sexuality or teach them to deny or suppress their sexual feelings. Although the physical changes of puberty may be delayed in people with developmental disabilities, most develop normal sexual needs (Edmonson, 1988). Most are capable of learning about their sexuality and can enter into rewarding and responsible intimate relationships.

One of the greatest impediments to sexual fulfillment among people with disabilities is finding a loving and supportive partner. Some people engage in sexual relations with people with disabilities out of sympathy. By and large, however, the partners are other people with disabilities or nondisabled people who have overcome stereotypes that portray disabled people as undesirable. Many partners have had some prior positive relationship, usually during childhood, with a person who had a disability (Knight, 1989). Experience facilitates acceptance of the idea that a disabled person can be desirable. Depending on the nature of the disability, the nondisabled partner may need to be open to assuming a more active sexual role to compensate for the limitations of the partner with the disability. Two partners with disabilities need to be sensitive to each other's needs and physical limitations.

Arthritis A progressive disease characterized by inflammation or pain in the joints.

Applied Knowledge

A COMPREHENSIVE GUIDE TO SEX AND DISABILITY

Toronto educators Miriam Kaufman, Cory Silverberg, and Fran Odette (2003) conducted a survey among people living with disabilities regarding their beliefs, feelings, and unmet needs around sexuality. The survey responses provided the basis for their book, *The Ultimate Guide to Sex and Disability*. This sex guide is aimed at people living with disabilities, chronic pain, and illness and is inclusive of all ages and sexual identities.

The book is intended to improve readers' sexual self-esteem and sex lives, and to help them become sexually independent. Among the topics are

■ where to find partners and how to talk to partners about sex and disability

■ how to discuss sex with health care providers

■ instruction on masturbation, oral sex, vaginal penetration, and anal sex

■ sexual positions to minimize stress and maximize pleasure

■ how to deal with fatigue, pain, and spasms during sex

■ adapting sex toys to make them work for you

The book also provides an extensive list of resources.

People with disabilities and their partners may also need to expand their sexual repertoires to incorporate ways of pleasuring each other that are not fixated on genital stimulation.

The message is simple: Sexuality can enrich the lives of nearly all adults at virtually any age.

Summing Up

Making Sense of Sex: The Rôle of the Senses in Sexual Arousal
Each sense plays a role in sexual experience, but some play more of a role than others.

Vision: The Better to See You With
Visual information plays a major role in human sexual attraction. Visual cues can be sexual turn-ons or turnoffs.

Smell: Does the Nose Know Best?
Although the sense of smell plays a lesser role in governing sexual arousal in humans than in lower mammals, particular odours can be sexual turn-ons or turn-offs. Many organisms are sexually aroused by naturally produced chemicals called pheromones, but their role in human sexual behaviour remains unclear.

The Skin Senses: Sex as a Touching Experience
The sense of touch has the most direct effects on sexual arousal and response. Erogenous zones are especially sensitive to tactile sexual stimulation.

Taste: On Savoury Sex
Taste appears to play only a minor role in sexual arousal and response.

Hearing: The Better to Hear You With
Like visual and olfactory cues, sounds can be turn-ons or turn-offs.

Aphrodisiacs
Alleged aphrodisiacs, such as foods that in some way resemble the genitals, have not been shown to contribute to sexual arousal or response.

Anaphrodisiacs
Some drugs, such as antidepressants, dampen sexual arousal and response.

Psychoactive Drugs
The alleged aphrodisiac effects of psychoactive drugs, such as alcohol and cocaine, may reflect our expectations

of them or their effects on sexual inhibitions rather than their direct stimulation of sexual response. Alcohol is also connected with a liberated social role and thus provides an external excuse for dubious behaviour. Some people report increased sexual pleasure with an initial cocaine use, but frequent use can lead to sexual dysfunctions.

Sexual Response and the Brain: Cerebral Sex?

The brain plays a central role in sexual functioning. The cerebral cortex interprets sensory information as sexual turn-ons or turn-offs. The cortex transmits messages through the spinal cord that cause vasocongestion. Direct stimulation of parts of the limbic system may cause erection and ejaculation in male animals.

Sex Hormones: Do They "Goad" Us into Sex?

Sex hormones have organizing and activating effects on behaviour. Both men and women produce one genuine aphrodisiac: testosterone. Female sex hormones do not appear to play a direct role in determining sexual motivation or response in human females. Yet levels of testosterone in the bloodstream have been associated with sexual interest in women.

The Sexual Response Cycle

Masters and Johnson found that the physiological responses of men and women to sexual stimulation are quite alike. Both experience vasocongestion and myotonia early in the response cycle.

Excitement Phase

Sexual excitement is characterized by erection in the male and vaginal lubrication in the female.

Plateau Phase

The plateau phase is an advanced state of arousal that precedes orgasm.

Orgasmic Phase

The third phase of the sexual response cycle is characterized by orgasmic contractions of the pelvic musculature. Orgasm in the male occurs in two stages of muscular contractions. Orgasm in the female is manifested by contractions of the pelvic muscles that surround the vaginal barrel.

Resolution Phase

During the resolution phase, the body returns to its prearoused state.

Kaplan's Three Stages of Sexual Response

Kaplan developed a three-stage model of sexual response consisting of desire, excitement, and orgasm. Kaplan's model makes it more convenient for clinicians to classify and treat sexual dysfunctions.

Basson's Intimacy Model of Female Sexual Response

Basson argues that for women, intimacy plays a key role in sexual response.

Controversies About Orgasm

Multiple Orgasms

Multiple orgasm is the occurrence of one or more additional orgasms following the first, within a short period of time and before the body has returned to a preplateau level of arousal. Most women, but not most men, are capable of multiple orgasms.

How Many Kinds of Orgasms Do Women Have? One, Two, or Three?

Freud theorized the existence of two types of orgasms in women: clitoral and vaginal. Masters and Johnson found only one kind of orgasm among women. Singer and Singer suggested that there are three types of female orgasms: vulval, uterine, and blended.

The G-Spot

The G-spot—an allegedly distinct area of the vagina within the anterior wall—may have special erotic significance. Some researchers suggest that prolonged stimulation of this spot produces an orgasm that is characterized by intense pleasure and, in some women, by a type of ejaculation. The nature of this ejaculate remains in doubt.

Sex and Disability

People with disabilities may suffer from prejudice that depicts them as sexless or as lacking the means to express their sexual needs or feelings.

Physical Disabilities

Cerebral palsy does not usually impair sexual interest, capacity for orgasm, or fertility, but afflicted people may be limited to certain types of sexual activities and coital positions. People with spinal cord injuries may be paralyzed and lose sensation below the waist. They often respond reflexively to direct genital stimulation. Sensory disabilities do not directly affect sexual response but may impair sexual knowledge and social skills.

Psychological Disabilities

Most people with developmental disabilities can learn the basics of their own sexuality and develop responsible intimate relationships.

Test Yourself

Multiple-Choice Questions

1. There is some evidence that _____ have aphrodisiac effects.
   a. antihypertensives and Prozac
   b. antidepressants and antihistamines
   c. bupropion and L-dopa
   d. amyl nitrate and alcohol

2. Psychoactive drugs such as _____ and _____ are believed by many people to have aphrodisiac effects.
   a. speed; ecstasy
   b. anti-androgens; anti-psychotics
   c. alcohol; cocaine
   d. antidepressants; antihistamines

3. Alcohol may increase feelings of sexual arousal because
   a. it has a stimulating effect on the nervous system
   b. it has a depressant effect on the nervous system
   c. people expect it to have an effect
   d. all of the above

4. Frequent cocaine use can result in
   a. urinary tract infections
   b. sexual dysfunctions
   c. phimosis
   d. damage to the foreskin

5. Parts of the brain involved in sexual arousal and sexual response include the
   a. cerebellum and corpus callosum
   b. cerebral cortex and limbic system
   c. thalamus and auditory bulb
   d. medulla and central sulcus

6. Research suggests that gender differences in sexual arousal to visual stimuli may be related to different levels of activation in the
   a. thalamus
   b. medulla
   c. olfactory bulb
   d. hypothalamus

7. The body's basic physiological responses to sexual stimulation are vasocongestion and _____.
   a. orgasm
   b. resolution
   c. myotonia
   d. sex flush

8. The three stages of Kaplan's model of sexual response are
   a. desire, excitement, and orgasm
   b. plateau, desire, and arousal
   c. desire, resolution, and orgasm
   d. orgasm, plateau, and resolution

9. Basson's model puts more emphasis on _____ than either Masters and Johnson or Kaplan.
   a. desire
   b. affection
   c. intimacy
   d. stimulation

10. A major impediment to sexual fulfillment among people with disabilities is
    a. the severity of the disability
    b. the absence of any sexual feelings or desires
    c. the lack of lubrication or erection
    d. the difficulty of finding a loving and supportive partner

Critical Thinking Questions

1. Compare and contrast Masters and Johnson's, Kaplan's, and Basson's models for sexual response.

2. You are a hearing-impaired student who uses a sign language interpreter in your human sexuality class. The interpreter seemed comfortable earlier in the semester, but now that topics are getting more personal, and the lectures are getting more graphic, the interpreter tells you that he is no longer willing to attend the lectures, and furthermore, that he really doesn't think anyone with a disability should even be thinking about sex. How might you deal with this issue?

3. If you are a woman, consider the following: Although every magazine you read has at least one article per month telling you how great it is to have multiple orgasms, you have difficulty having one, let alone several. How might this make you feel? Do you think that just because some women *can* have multiple orgasms, all women should?

4. If you are a man, consider the following: Although you know that women can have multiple orgasms, your partner sometimes has difficulty having just one. How does this make you feel? Do you think that the knowledge that women can have multiple orgasms puts pressure on males to provide them?

Visit our Companion Website at www.pearsoned.ca/rathus, where you can use the interactive Study Guide and link to additional resources on topics discussed in this text.

Chapter 5
Gender Identity and Gender Roles

Sexual differentiation
The process by which males and females develop distinct reproductive anatomy.

Chromosome One of the rodlike structures, found in the nucleus of every living cell, that carry the genetic code in the form of genes.

Zygote A fertilized ovum (egg cell).

This chapter addresses the biological, psychological, and sociological aspects of gender. First we focus on sexual differentiation—the process by which males and females develop distinct reproductive anatomy. We then turn to gender roles—the complex behaviour patterns that are deemed "masculine" or "feminine" in a particular culture. The chapter examines empirical findings on actual gender differences, which may challenge some of the preconceptions that many of us have about the differences between men and women. We next consider gender typing—the processes by which boys come to behave in line with what is expected of men (most of the time), and girls with what is expected of women (most of the time). We shall also explore the concept of psychological androgyny, which applies to people who display characteristics associated with both genders.

Prenatal Sexual Differentiation

Over the years many ideas have been proposed to account for **sexual differentiation**. Aristotle believed that the anatomical difference between males and females was due to the heat of semen at the time of sexual relations. Hot semen generated males, whereas cold semen made females (National Center for Biotechnology Information, 2000).

When a sperm cell fertilizes an ovum, 23 **chromosomes** from the male parent normally combine with 23 chromosomes from the female parent. The **zygote**, the beginning of a new human being, is only 0.04 centimetres ($1\frac{3}{4}$ of an inch) long. Yet, on this tiny stage, one's stamp as a unique individual has already been ensured whether one will have black or blond hair, grow bald or develop a widow's peak, or become male or female.

The chromosomes from each parent combine to form 23 pairs. The 23rd pair are the sex chromosomes. An ovum carries an X sex chromosome, but a sperm carries either an X or a Y sex chromosome. If a sperm with an X sex chromosome fertilizes the ovum, the newly conceived person will normally develop as a female, with an XX sex chromosomal structure. If the sperm carries a Y sex chromosome, the child will normally develop as a male (XY).

After fertilization, the zygote divides repeatedly. After a few short weeks, one cell has become billions of cells. At about three weeks, a primitive heart begins to

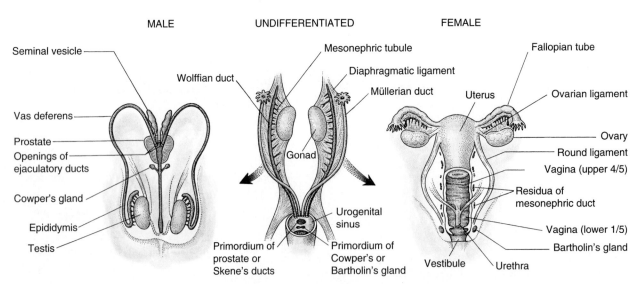

Figure 5.1 Development of the Internal Sex Organs from an Undifferentiated Stage at About Five or Six Weeks Following Conception.

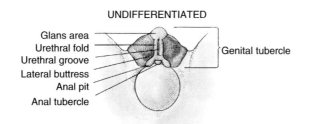

UNDIFFERENTIATED

Glans area
Urethral fold
Urethral groove
Lateral buttress
Anal pit
Anal tubercle

Genital tubercle

Figure 5.2 Development of the External Sex Organs from an Undifferentiated Stage at About five or six Weeks Following Conception.

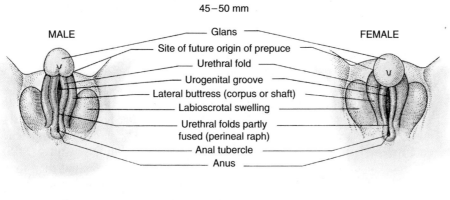

45–50 mm

MALE   FEMALE

Glans
Site of future origin of prepuce
Urethral fold
Urogenital groove
Lateral buttress (corpus or shaft)
Labioscrotal swelling
Urethral folds partly fused (perineal raph)
Anal tubercle
Anus

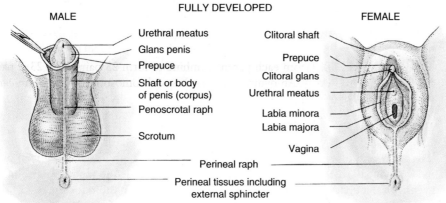

FULLY DEVELOPED

MALE   FEMALE

Urethral meatus
Glans penis
Prepuce
Shaft or body of penis (corpus)
Penoscrotal raph
Scrotum

Clitoral shaft
Prepuce
Clitoral glans
Urethral meatus
Labia minora
Labia majora
Vagina

Perineal raph
Perineal tissues including external sphincter

drive blood through the embryonic bloodstream. At about five to six weeks, when the **embryo** is only $\frac{1}{2}$ to 1 centimetre ($\frac{1}{4}$ to $\frac{1}{2}$ inch) long, primitive gonads, ducts, and external genitals whose gender cannot be distinguished visually have formed (see Figures 5.1, 5.2). Each embryo possesses primitive external genitals, a pair of sexually undifferentiated gonads, and two sets of primitive duct structures, the Müllerian (female) ducts and the Wolffian (male) ducts.

During the first six weeks or so of prenatal development, embryonic structures of both genders develop along similar lines and resemble primitive female structures. At about the seventh week after conception, the genetic code (XX or XY) begins to assert itself, causing changes in the gonads, genital ducts, and external genitals. Genetic activity on the Y sex chromosome causes the testes to begin to differentiate (National Center for Biotechnology Information, 2000). Ovaries begin to differentiate if the Y chromosome is absent. Those rare individuals who have only one X sex chromosome instead of the typical XY or XX arrangement also become females, because they too lack the Y chromosome.

Thus, the basic blueprint of the human embryo is female. The genetic instructions in the Y sex chromosome cause the embryo to deviate from the female developmental course.

Embryo The stage of prenatal development that begins with implantation of a fertilized ovum in the uterus and concludes with development of the major organ systems at about two months after conception.

By about the seventh week of prenatal development, strands of tissue begin to organize into seminiferous tubules. Female gonads begin to develop somewhat later than male gonads. The forerunners of follicles that will bear ova are not found until the fetal stage of development, about 10 weeks after conception. Ovaries begin to form at 11 or 12 weeks.

The Role of Sex Hormones in Sexual Differentiation

Without male sex hormones, or **androgens**, we would all develop into females in terms of anatomic structure (Federman, 1994). Once genes have done their work and testes develop in the embryo, they begin to produce androgens. The most important androgen, **testosterone**, spurs differentiation of the male (Wolffian) duct system (see Figure 5.1). Each Wolffian duct develops into an epididymis, vas deferens, and seminal vesicle. The external genitals, including the penis, begin to take shape at about the eighth week of development under the influence of another androgen, *dihydrotestosterone* (DHT). Yet another testicular hormone, one secreted during the fetal stage, prevents the Müllerian ducts from developing into the female duct system. It is appropriately termed the Müllerian inhibiting substance (MIS).

Small amounts of androgens are produced in female fetuses, but they are not normally sufficient to cause male sexual differentiation. In female fetuses, the relative absence of androgens causes degeneration of the Wolffian ducts and prompts development of female sexual organs. The Mullerian ducts evolve into fallopian tubes, the uterus, and the upper two-thirds of the vagina. These developments occur even in the absence of female sex hormones. Although female sex hormones are crucial in puberty, they are not involved in fetal sexual differentiation. If a fetus with an XY sex chromosomal structure failed to produce testosterone, it would develop female sexual organs.

Descent of the Testes and the Ovaries

The testes and ovaries develop from slender structures high in the abdominal cavity. By about 10 weeks after conception, they have descended so that they are almost even with the upper edge of the pelvis. The ovaries remain there for the rest of the prenatal period. Later they rotate and descend farther to their adult position in the pelvis. About four months after conception, the testes normally descend into the scrotal sac through the **inguinal canal**. After their descent, this passageway is closed.

In a small percentage of males, one or both testes fail to descend. They remain in the abdomen at birth. The condition is termed **cryptorchidism**. In most cases of cryptorchidism, the testes migrate to the scrotum during infancy. In still other cases, the testes descend by puberty. Men with undescended testes are usually treated through surgery or hormonal therapy, because they are at higher risk for cancer of the testes. Sperm production is also impaired because the undescended testes are subjected to a higher-than-optimal body temperature, causing sterility.

Sex-Chromosomal Abnormalities

Abnormalities of the sex chromosomes can have profound effects on sexual characteristics, physical health, and psychological development. **Klinefelter syndrome**, a condition that affects about 1 in 500 males, is caused by an extra X sex chromosome, so the man has an XXY rather than an XY pattern. Men with this pattern fail to develop appropriate secondary sex characteristics. They have enlarged breasts and poor muscular development, and because they fail to produce sperm, they are infertile. They also tend to have mild mental retardation.

Androgens Male sex hormones.

Testosterone The male sex hormone that fosters the development of male sex characteristics and is connected with the sex drive.

Inguinal canal A fetal canal that connects the scrotum and the testes, allowing the latter to descend. (From the Latin *inguinus,* which means "near the groin.")

Cryptorchidism The condition defined by undescended testes. (From roots that mean "hidden testes.")

Klinefelter syndrome A sex-chromosomal disorder caused by an extra X sex chromosome.

Turner syndrome, found only in women, occurs in 1 in 2000 to 5000 girls. It is caused by the loss of some X chromosome material. These girls develop typical external genital organs, but they are short and their ovaries do not develop or function normally.

Prenatal Sexual Differentiation of the Brain

The brain, like the genital organs, undergoes prenatal sexual differentiation. Testosterone causes cells in the hypothalamus of male fetuses to become insensitive to the female sex hormone estrogen. In the absence of testosterone, as in female fetuses, the hypothalamus does develop sensitivity to estrogen.

Sensitivity to estrogen is important in the regulation of the menstrual cycle of women after puberty. The hypothalamus detects low levels of estrogen in the blood at the end of each cycle and initiates a new cycle by stimulating the pituitary gland to secrete FSH. FSH, in turn, stimulates estrogen production by the ovaries and the ripening of an immature follicle in an ovary. Sexual differentiation of the hypothalamus is most likely to occur during the second trimester of fetal development (Pillard & Weinrich, 1986).

Gender Identity

Our awareness of being male or being female—our **gender identity**—is one of the most obvious and important aspects of our self-concepts. Gender identity is not necessarily an automatic extension of our anatomic gender. Gender identity is psychological—a sense of being male or being female. **Gender assignment** reflects the child's anatomic gender and usually occurs at birth. Gender identity is so important to parents that they may want to know "Is it a boy or a girl?" before they begin to count fingers and toes.

Most children first become aware of their anatomic gender by about the age of 18 months. By 36 months, most children have acquired a firm sense of gender identity (Rathus, 2003).

Nature and Nurture in Gender Identity

What determines gender identity? Are our brains biologically programmed along masculine or feminine lines by prenatal sex hormones? Does the environment, in the form of postnatal learning experiences, shape our self-concepts as males or females? Or does gender identity reflect an intermingling of biological and environmental influences?

Gender identity is nearly always consistent with chromosomal gender. Such consistency does not, however, prove that gender identity is biologically determined. We also tend to be reared as males or females, in accordance with our anatomic genders. How, then, can we sort out the roles of nature and nurture, of biology and the environment?

Clues may be found in the experiences of rare individuals, **intersexuals**, who possess the gonads of one gender but external genitalia that are ambiguous or typical of the other gender. Intersexuals are sometimes reared as members of the gender other than their chromosomal gender. Researchers have wondered whether the gender identity of these children reflects their chromosomal and gonadal gender or the gender in accordance with which they were reared. Before going further with this, let us distinguish between hermaphrodites and intersexuals.

Hormonal errors during prenatal development produce various congenital defects. Some individuals are born with both ovarian and testicular tissue. They are called **hermaphrodites**, after the Greek myth of the son of Hermes and Aphrodite, whose body became united with that of a nymph while he was bathing. True her-

Turner syndrome A sex-chromosomal disorder caused by loss of some X chromosome material.

Gender identity The psychological sense of being male or female.

Gender assignment The labelling of a newborn as a male or a female.

Intersexual A person who possesses the gonads of one gender but external genitalia that are ambiguous or typical of the other gender. (Also termed pseudohermaphrodite.)

Hermaphrodites People who possess both ovarian and testicular tissue. (From the names of the male and female Greek gods *Hermes* and *Aphrodite*.)

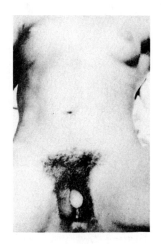

Figure 5.3
A Hermaphrodite.

This genetic (XX) female has one testicle and one ovary and the gender identity of a male.

Congenital adrenal hyperplasia A form of intersexualism in which a genetic female has internal female sexual structures but masculinized external genitals.

Androgen-insensitivity syndrome A form of intersexualism in which a genetic male is prenatally insensitive to androgens. As a result, his genitals do not become normally masculinized.

Dominican Republic syndrome A form of intersexualism in which a genetic enzyme disorder prevents testosterone from masculinizing the external genitalia.

maphrodites may have one gonad of each gender (a testicle and an ovary) or gonads that combine testicular and ovarian tissue.

Regardless of their genetic gender, hermaphrodites usually assume the gender identity and gender role of the gender assigned at birth. Figure 5.3 shows a genetic female (XX) with a right testicle and a left ovary. This person married and became a stepfather with a firm male identity. The roles of biology and environment remain tangled, however, because true hermaphrodites have gonadal tissue of both genders.

True hermaphroditism is extremely rare. More common is intersexualism, which occurs in perhaps 1 infant in 1000. Intersexuals have testes or ovaries, but not both. Unlike hermaphrodites, their gonads (testes or ovaries) match their chromosomal gender. Because of prenatal hormonal errors, however, their external genitals and sometimes their internal reproductive anatomy are ambiguous or resemble those of the other gender.

The most common form of female intersexualism is **congenital adrenal hyperplasia** (CAH), in which a genetic (XX) female has female internal sexual structures (ovaries) but masculinized external genitals (see Figure 5.4). The clitoris is so enlarged that it may resemble a small penis. The syndrome occurs as a result of excessive levels of androgens.

Another type of intersexualism, **androgen-insensitivity syndrome**, describes genetic (XY) males who, as the result of a mutated gene, have lower-than-normal prenatal sensitivity to androgens (Adachi et al., 2000; Hughes, 2000). Consequently, their genitals do not become normally masculinized. At birth their external genitals are feminized, including a small vagina, and their testes are undescended. Because of insensitivity to androgens, the male duct system (epididymis, vas deferens, seminal vesicles, and ejaculatory ducts) fails to develop. Nevertheless, the fetal testes produce Müllerian inhibiting substance, preventing the development of a uterus or fallopian tubes. Genetic males with androgen-insensitivity syndrome usually have no or sparse pubic and axillary (underarm) hair, because the development of hair in these locations is dependent on androgens.

Another type of intersexualism is named **Dominican Republic syndrome** because it was first documented in a group of 18 affected boys in two rural villages in that nation (Imperato-McGinley et al., 1974). Dominican Republic syndrome is a genetic enzyme disorder that prevents testosterone from masculinizing the external genitalia. The boys were born with normal testes and internal male reproductive organs, but their external genitals were malformed. Their penises were stunted and resembled clitorises. Their scrotums were incompletely formed and resembled female labia. They also had partially formed vaginas.

The boys with Dominican Republic syndrome also resembled girls at birth and were reared as females. At puberty, however, their testes swung into normal testosterone production, causing startling changes: The testes descended, their voices deepened, their musculature filled out, and their "clitorises" expanded into penises. Of the 18 boys who were reared as girls, 17 shifted to a male gender identity. Sixteen of the 18 assumed a stereotypical masculine gender role. Of the remaining 2, 1 adopted a male gender identity but continued to maintain a feminine gender role, including wearing dresses. The other maintained a female gender identity and later sought gender-reassignment surgery to "correct" the pubertal masculinization. The nearby box provides an in-depth account of Winnipeger David Reimer's struggle with issues of gender identification.

Many scientists conclude that gender identity is influenced by complex interactions between biological and psychosocial factors. Some place relatively greater emphasis on psychosocial factors (Money & Ehrhardt, 1972). Others emphasize the role of biological factors (Collaer & Hines, 1995; Diamond, 1996; Legato, 2000), even though they allow that nurture plays a role in gender identity. The debate over the relative contributions of nature and nurture is likely to continue.

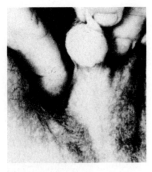

Figure 5.4 Intersexualism.

In congenital adrenal hyperplasia, a genetic (XX) female has female internal sexual structures (ovaries) but masculinized external genitals.

A World of Diversity

A TRAGEDY OF MISGUIDED SCIENCE

David Reimer was the victim of an experiment gone totally awry—an experiment that suggested nurture could trump nature. The 38-year-old Winnipeg man, who was born a boy but raised as a girl after a botched circumcision, took his own life in May 2004. But for some, his death and his life will not be in vain. Thanks to Reimer, many psychiatrists and psychologists have had to rethink their theories on what determines sex, says Ken Zucker, psychologist-in-chief at Toronto's Centre for Addiction and Mental Health and a specialist in gender identity.

After a botched circumcision led to the removal of his penis, Reimer was renamed Brenda and raised as a girl, later receiving female hormones. His parents were following the advice of psychologist Dr. John Money of Johns Hopkins University in Baltimore. Positive reports in medical journals suggested Reimer was adapting successfully to his new gender as a girl. Many, from feminists to learning theorists, embraced the case, using it as an example that gender could indeed be taught.

But nothing was further from the truth in this case, said Dr. Keith Sigmundson, who was a supervising psychiatrist for Reimer from when he was 8 to 20 years old. Reimer didn't adjust well to being a girl at all and began having difficulties at school. "By the time Reimer was 11, the whole experiment was falling apart," said Sigmundson, who was brought into the case by the Winnipeg school system.

David Reimer is shown at his Winnipeg home with his wife, Jane, and son, Anthony, in 2000.

Reimer was eventually told when he was 13 that he had been born a boy. He rebelled and went back to being a boy. "From that point on he sought out all the surgery," said Sigmundson. "He totally changed how he was presenting himself and struggled with a number of operations. He eventually lived his life as a man."

Reimer got a job in a meat-packing plant in Winnipeg. He married and was a stepfather to three children. Up until about a year ago, he was in "top form," said Sigmundson, who remained in contact with him.

But Reimer felt responsible for the suicide of his twin brother two years ago, the psychiatrist said. Then he slumped into even more of a depression after losing his job and separating from his wife. His mother, Janet Reimer, believes her son would still be alive had it not been for the devastating gender study. "I think he felt he had no options. It just kept building up and building up."

"At the time, there was a major controversy in our society over whether an individual's personality and their adaptation of their gender was a result of how they were born versus how they were raised," explained Sigmundson. The only thing that is clear today is that gender is a combination of many factors, including biology and learning, he noted. "There are certain immutable things that happen in your chromosomes and in utero that develop the gonads that have an impact on your brain which set the pattern for the rest of your life," he said. "That's essentially what we know now."

Source: Debra Black. Toronto Star. *Toronto, Ont: May 11, 2004. p. A.03. Copyright © 2004 Toronto Star. All Rights Reserved.*

Research in Action

GENDER IDENTITY DISORDER IN BOYS AND GIRLS

One of Canada's leading researchers on gender identity is Ken Zucker, head of the Child and Adolescent Gender Identity Clinic at the Centre for Addiction and Mental Health in Toronto. According to Zucker (2002), **intersexuality** is now the preferred term to encompass "syndromes characterized by some abnormality or anomaly in physical sex differentiation" (p. 4). This term is broader than the traditional *hermaphroditism*. Zucker's research demonstrates both biological and psychological factors. Biological influences were indicated in one of his studies, in which boys with gender identity disorder were more likely to be left-handed than a control group (Zucker et al., 2001). Social influences were

indicated in another study, which found that boys were more than six times as likely as girls to be referred to a special clinic for gender identity disorder (Zucker et al., 1997). The first cross-cultural study in the field, conducted by Zucker and colleagues (Cohen-Kettenis, et al., 2003) found that far more boys than girls were referred to gender-identity clinics in the Netherlands as well as Canada. Zucker and his colleagues believe that society is less accepting of cross-gender in boys than in girls, so, parents of cross-gender boys are more likely to see the situation as a problem in need of professional remedy. In both countries, boys were more likely to have problems with peers than were girls. This further supports the idea that cross-gender behaviour among girls is better tolerated than among boys.

Transsexualism

Intersexuality All the different types of syndromes characterized by some abnormality or anomaly in physical sex differentiation.

Transsexuals People who strongly desire to be of the other gender and live as a person of the other gender.

Gender dysphoria A sense of incongruity between one's anatomic sex and gender identity.

Homosexual transsexuals Extremely feminine gay males who seek sex reassignment.

Autogynephilic (aw-toe-gone-uh-FEE-lick) Descriptive of transsexuals who are sexually stimulated by fantasies that their own bodies are female. (From roots meaning "self," "woman," and "love" or "desire.")

In 1953 an American ex-GI who journeyed to Denmark for a "sex-change operation" made headlines. She became known as Christine (formerly George) Jorgensen. Since then, thousands of **transsexuals** (also called *transgendered* people) have undergone gender-reassignment surgery.

Gender-reassignment surgery cannot implant the internal reproductive organs of the other gender. Instead, it generates the likeness of external genitals typical of the other gender. This can be done more precisely with male-to-female than with female-to-male transsexuals. After such operations, people can participate in sexual activity and even attain orgasm, but they cannot conceive or bear children.

Transsexuals experience **gender dysphoria**. That is, according to John Money (1994), they have the subjective experience of incongruity between their genital anatomy and their gender identity or role. They have the anatomic sex of one gender but feel that they are members of the other gender. As a result of this discrepancy, they wish to be rid of their own primary sex characteristics (their external genitals and internal sex organs) and to live as members of the other gender. A male transsexual perceives himself to be a female who, through some quirk of fate, was born with the wrong genital equipment. A female transsexual perceives herself as a man trapped in a woman's body.

Ray Blanchard at the Centre for Addiction and Mental Health in Toronto (1988, 1989) and J. Michael Bailey (2003a, 2003b) have another view. Based on their extensive research with transsexuals, they contend that men who seek to become women tend to fall into two categories: either men who are extremely feminine or men who are sexually aroused by the idea of becoming a woman. The first category includes what Blanchard terms **homosexual transsexuals**—men who are extremely feminine gays and not fully satisfied by sexual activity with other males. The second category refers to males who are **autogynephilic,** or sexually stimulated by fantasies of their own bodies as being female.

Transsexuals usually show cross-gender preferences in play and dress in early childhood. Many report that they have felt that they belong to the other gender for as long as they can remember. Only a few were unaware of their transsexual feelings until adolescence. Male transsexuals generally recall that as children, they preferred playing with dolls, enjoyed wearing frilly dresses, and disliked rough-and-tumble play. They were often perceived by their peers as "sissy boys." Female transsexuals usually report that as children they disliked dresses and acted much like "tomboys." They also preferred playing "boys' games" and doing so with boys. Female transsexuals appear to have an easier time adjusting than male transsexuals (Selvin, 1993). "Tomboys" generally find it easier to be accepted by their peers than "sissy boys." Even in adulthood, it may be easier for a female transsexual to don men's clothes and "pass" as a slightly built man than it is for a brawnier man to pass for a tall woman.

THEORETICAL PERSPECTIVES No clear understanding of the nature or causes of transsexualism has emerged (Money, 1994). Views on its origins somewhat parallel those on the origins of a gay male or lesbian sexual orientation, which is surprising, given the key differences that exist between gay people and transsexuals.

Psychoanalytic theorists have focused on early parent–child relationships. Male-to-female transsexuals, in this view, may have had "close-binding mothers" (extremely close mother–son relationships) and "detached-hostile fathers" (fathers who were absent or uninterested) (Stoller, 1969). Such family circumstances may have fostered intense **identification** with the mother, to the point of an inversion of typical gender roles and identity. By the same token, girls with weak, ineffectual mothers and strong, masculine fathers may identify with their fathers, rejecting their own female identities.

There is some evidence that male-to-female transsexuals tend to have had unusually close relationships with their mothers during childhood. Female-to-male transsexuals tend to have identified more with their fathers and to have perceived their mothers as cold and rejecting (Pauly, 1974). Yet one problem with the psychoanalytic view is that the roles of cause and effect may be reversed. It could be that as children, transsexuals gravitate toward the parent of the other gender and reject the efforts of the parent of the same gender to reach out to them and engage them in gender-typed activities. These views also do not account for the many transsexuals whose family backgrounds fail to match the proposed patterns. Moreover, these views lack predictive power. Most children—in fact, the vast majority—who emerge from such family backgrounds do *not* become transsexuals (or gay). The early onset of transsexual feelings suggests that critical early learning experiences, if they occur, do so in the preschool years.

Transsexuals may also be influenced by prenatal hormonal imbalances. The brain is in some ways "masculinized" or "feminized" by sex hormones during prenatal development. Researchers in the Netherlands have discovered that a small region of the hypothalamus is about 50% larger in men than in women, and nearly 60% larger in men than in male-to-female transsexuals (Angier, 1995). It is possible that the brain could be influenced in one direction, even as the genitals are being differentiated in the other.

GENDER REASSIGNMENT Gender reassignment for transsexuals has been controversial since its inception. Yet psychotherapy is not considered a reasonable alternative, because it has been generally unsuccessful in helping transsexuals accept their anatomic genders (Roberto, 1983).

Surgery is one element of gender reassignment. Because the surgery is irreversible, health professionals conduct careful evaluations to determine that people seeking reassignment are competent to make such decisions and have thought through the consequences. They usually require that the transsexual live openly as

Identification In psychoanalytic theory, the process of incorporating within ourselves our perceptions of the behaviours, thoughts, and feelings of others.

a member of the other gender for a trial period of at least a year before surgery. In Canada, gender-reassignment surgery is paid for in the provinces of Newfoundland, Quebec, Manitoba, Saskatchewan, Alberta, and British Columbia. Ontario began paying for sex-change operations in 1969, but stopped doing so in 1998 when, to save money, the Conservative government reduced the types of procedures it would pay for. In 2005, in response to an investigation by the Ontario Human Rights Commission, Ontario premier Dalton McGuinty agreed that the province would reinstate payment for sex-change operations.

Once the decision is reached, a lifetime of hormone treatments is begun. Male-to-female transsexuals receive estrogen, which fosters the development of female secondary sex characteristics. It causes fatty deposits to develop in the breasts and hips, softens the skin, and inhibits growth of the beard. Female-to-male transsexuals receive androgens, which promote male secondary sex characteristics. The voice deepens, hair becomes distributed according to the male pattern, muscles enlarge, and the fatty deposits in the breasts and hips are lost. The clitoris may also grow more prominent. In the case of male-to-female transsexuals, "phonosurgery" can be done to raise the pitch of the voice (Brown et al., 2000).

Gender-reassignment surgery is largely cosmetic. Medical science cannot construct internal genital organs or gonads. Male-to-female surgery is generally more successful. The penis and testicles are first removed. Tissue from the penis is placed in an artificial vagina so that sensitive nerve endings will provide sexual sensations. A penis-shaped form of plastic or balsa wood is used to keep the vagina distended during healing.

In female-to-male transsexuals, the internal sex organs (ovaries, fallopian tubes, and uterus) are removed, along with the remaining fatty tissue in the breasts. The nipples are moved to keep them at the proper height on the torso. Either the urethra is rerouted through the enlarged clitoris, or an artificial penis and scrotum are constructed of tissue from the abdomen, the labia, and the perineum through a series of operations. In either case, the patient can urinate while standing, which appears to provide psychological gratification. Although the artificial penis does not stiffen and become erect naturally, a variety of methods, including implants, can be used to allow the artificial penis to approximate erection.

Some transsexuals hesitate to undertake surgery because they are repulsed by the prospect of such extreme medical intervention. Others forgo surgery so as not to jeopardize high-status careers or family relationships (Kockott & Fahrner, 1987). Such people continue to think of themselves as members of the other gender, however, even without surgery.

OUTCOMES OF GENDER-REASSIGNMENT SURGERY Following the introduction of gender-reassignment surgery in North America in the 1960s, most reports of postoperative adjustment were positive (Pauly & Edgerton, 1986). An influential study conducted in the 1970s at the Gender Identity Clinic at Johns Hopkins University was quite negative, however (Meyer & Reter, 1979). The study included a control group of transsexuals who did not receive gender-reassignment surgery. Psychological adjustment was more positive among transsexuals in the control group than among those who had undergone surgery.

Other reviews report more positive outcomes for gender-reassignment surgery (Kockott & Fahrner, 1987; Lundstrom et al., 1984; Pauly & Edgerton, 1986). One study of 42 postoperative male-to-female transsexuals found that all but one would repeat the surgery and that the great majority found sexual activity more pleasurable as a "woman" (Bentler, 1976).

Reviewers of the international literature reported in 1984 that about 90% of transsexuals who undergo gender-reassignment surgery experience positive results (Lundstrom et al., 1984). In Canada, a follow-up study of 116 transsexuals (female-to-male and male-to-female) at least one year after surgery found that most of them were content with the results and were reasonably well adjusted (Blanchard et al., 1985). Positive results for surgery were also reported in a study of 141 Dutch transsexuals (Kuiper & Cohen-Kettenis, 1988). Nearly 9 out of 10 male-to-female and female-to-male transsexuals in a study of 23 transsexuals reported they were very pleased with the results of their gender-reassignment surgery (Lief & Hubschman, 1993). Still another study (Abramowitz, 1986) reported that about two out of three cases showed at least some postoperative improvement in psychological adjustment. These favourable results do not mean that postoperative transsexuals were ecstatic about their lives. In many cases it meant that they were less unhappy. Most transsexuals are socially maladjusted prior to gender reassignment, and many remain lonely and isolated afterward. Moreover, about half incur postoperative medical complications (Lindermalm et al., 1986).

Male-to-female transsexuals whose surgery permitted them to pass as members of the other gender showed better adjustment than those whose surgery left telltale signs (such as breast scarring and leftover erectile tissue) that they were not "real" women (Ross & Need, 1989). Social and family support also contributed to postsurgical adjustment (Ross & Need, 1989).

Male-to-female transsexuals outnumber female-to-males, but postoperative adjustment is apparently more favourable for female-to-males. Nearly 10% of male-to-female cases, as compared with 4% to 5% of female-to-males, have had disturbing outcomes, such as severe psychological disorders, hospitalization, requests for reversal surgery, and even suicide (Abramowitz, 1986). One reason for the relatively better postoperative adjustment of the female-to-male transsexuals may be society's more accepting attitudes toward women who desire to become men (Abramowitz, 1986). Female-to-male transsexuals tend to be better adjusted socially before surgery as well (Kockott & Fahrner, 1988; Pauly, 1974), so their superior postoperative adjustment may be nothing more than a selection factor.

Aaron Devor, formerly Holly Devor, is dean of Graduate Studies at the University of Victoria. Prior to 2002, he was a self-described "masculine lesbian" (Macqueen, 2003). Devor, who is one of the world's experts on transsexuals, provides a comprehensive analysis of transsexual adjustment phases in the book *FTM: Female-to-Male Transsexuals in Society* (1997). Based on interviews with 45 participants living in the U.S., Canada, and New Zealand, Devor concludes that the development of female-to-male transsexuals progresses through many stages. Table 5.1 provides a summary of these stages.

Aaron Devor, formerly Holly Devor, is dean of Graduate Studies at the University of Victoria.

TABLE 5.1
Identity Development Stages: Female-to-Male Transsexualism

Development Stage	Some Characteristics	Some Actions Taken
Abiding Anxiety	Unfocussed gender and sex discomfort.	Preference for masculine activities and companionship.
Identity Confusion	First doubts about suitability of assigned gender and sex.	Reactive gender and sex conforming activities or preference for masculine activities and companionship.
Identity Comparison	Seeking and weighing alternative female identities.	Adoption of mannish lesbian identity. Secret identity as a man and a male.
Discovery	Learning that female-to-male transsexualism exists.	Accidental contact with information about transsexualism.
Identity Confusion	First doubts about the authenticity of own transsexualism.	Seeking more information about transsexualism.
Identity Comparison	Testing transsexual identity using transsexual reference group.	Start to disidentify as women and females. Start to identify as transsexual.
Identity Tolerance	Identify as probably transsexual.	Increasingly disidentify as women and females.
Delay	Waiting for changed circumstances. Looking for confirmation of transsexual identity.	Seeking more information about transsexualism. Reality testing in intimate relationships and against further information about transsexualism.
Identity Acceptance	Transsexual identity established.	Tell others about transsexual identity.
Delay	Transsexual identity deepens. Final disidentity as women and females. Anticipatory socialization as men.	Learning how to do gender and sex reassignments. Saving money. Organizing support system.
Transition	Changing genders, between sexes.	Gender and sex reassignments.
Identity Acceptance	Identities established as transsexual men.	Successful "passing" as men and as males.
Integration	Transsexuality mostly invisible.	Stigma management.
Identity Pride	Publicly transsexual.	Transsexual advocacy and activism.

Source: H. Devor (1997). FTM: Female-to-Male Transsexuals in Society. Bloomington, IN: Indiana University Press, p. 600.

The Intersex Society of North America
For individuals with ambiguous genitals. The message is that people should feel free to be or remain what they are.
www.isna.org

Researchers have conducted relatively few studies of societal attitudes toward transsexuals. B. J. Rye (2001) of the University of Waterloo found that university students were about evenly divided in liking or disliking transsexuals. The students reported more negative attitudes toward transsexuals than toward homosexuals, however.

Programs exist that help transsexuals come to terms with themselves and adjust to living in a society in which they rarely feel welcome. Gay and lesbian organizations have expanded their services to include formerly excluded groups such as transsexual and trangendered individuals. One such program is Supporting Our Youth in Toronto. This program provides cultural, recreational, and employment training opportunities as well as a mentoring and housing program (Lepischak, 2004). Such programs help create a sense of community for a group of people who feel alienated from the larger society.

Transgendered.
Amanda Taylor organized the Miss Shemale World pageant in Toronto. Shemales are men who live their lives as women and undergo procedures such as breast, cheek, and lip implants and electrolysis to look female, but keep their male genitals. They prefer to be referred to as "she" or "her."

Gender Roles and Stereotypes

"Why can't a woman be more like a man?" You may recall this lyric from the song that Professor Henry Higgins sings in the musical *My Fair Lady*. In the song, the professor laments that women are emotional and fickle, whereas men are logical and dependable. The "emotional woman" is a **stereotype**—a fixed, oversimplified, and sometimes distorted idea about a group of people. The "logical man" is also a stereotype, albeit a more generous one. Even emotions are stereotyped. People assume that women are more likely to experience feelings of fear, sadness, and sympathy, whereas men are more likely to experience anger and pride (Plant et al., 2000). Gender roles are stereotypes in that they evoke fixed, conventional expectations of men and women.

Our gender identities—our identification of ourselves according to our concepts of masculinity and femininity—do not determine the roles or behaviours that are deemed masculine or feminine in our culture. Cultures have broad expectations of men and women that are termed **gender roles.**

Females are generally seen as warm and emotional, males as independent, assertive, and competitive. The times are a-changin'—somewhat. Women, as well as men, now bring home the bacon. Today a majority of Canadian women work outside of the home. In 2001, 71% of Canadian women were in the workforce compared with only 44% in 1971 (Statistics Canada, 2004a). But women are still more often expected to fry it in the pan and bear the primary responsibility for child rearing (Deaux & Lewis, 1983). A survey of 30 countries confirmed that these gender-role stereotypes are widespread (Williams & Best, 1994).

Perhaps because of these differing expectations, men and women take different attitudes to the workplace. A survey of 2500 Canadians found that female university graduates were more likely than male graduates to value respect, communication, and relationships in the work environment. Women were also more concerned than men about the gap between their desire for work–family balance and what their jobs allowed (Perry, 2003).

> **Stereotype** A fixed, oversimplified, conventional idea about a group of people.
>
> **Gender roles** Complex clusters of ways in which males and females are expected to behave.

An Elementary School Teacher.
If you think there is something wrong with this picture, it is because you have fallen prey to traditional gender-role stereotypes. Tradition has prevented many women from seeking jobs in "male" preserves such as construction work, the military, and various professions. Tradition has also prevented many men from obtaining work in "female" domains such as secretarial work, nursing, and teaching at the elementary school level.

Femina
Links to generally responsible sites "for, by, and about women." Issues include gender roles and sexism.

www.femina.cybergrrl. com

Sexism

We have all encountered the effects of **sexism**—the prejudgment that because of gender, a person will possess certain negative traits. These negative traits are assumed to disqualify the person for certain vocations or to prevent him or her from performing adequately in these jobs or in some social situations.

Sexism may even lead us to interpret the same behaviour in different ways, depending on whether it is performed by women or by men. We may see the man as "self-assertive" but the woman as "pushy." We may look upon *him* as flexible but brand *her* fickle and indecisive. *He* may be rational, whereas *she* is cold. *He* is tough when necessary, but *she* is bitchy. When the businesswoman engages in stereotypical masculine behaviours, the sexist reacts negatively by branding her abnormal or unhealthy.

Although more Canadian women today are entering a wider diversity of occupational fields, about 70% are still clustered in the traditional female occupational groups of teaching, nursing, clerical, sales, and service. Less than one-third of men are in these occupations (Drolet, 2002). Men are more likely to work in manufacturing, construction, and transportation, and in the natural sciences and engineering. The fact that there is still such a major gender segregation of occupations suggests the powerful role of gender stereotyping. This seems especially true for men who choose to enter what are considered to be female occupations. In a study of male nurses, Joan Evans at Dalhousie University found that many felt the need to justify their career choice, as they were often subject to ridicule and questioning about their sexuality (Evans, 2001).

The feminist movement in Canada has played a major role in reducing discrimination and helping to achieve greater equality for women. Marlene Mackie (1991) has traced the evolution of Canadian feminism in her book *Gender Relations in Canada*. She argues that feminism is not one homogeneous movement but has three major dimensions—liberal, socialist, and radical. According to Mackie, liberal feminists have worked to achieve gender equality through education and legislation. Socialist feminists have focused on structural inequalities, resulting not only from gender, but also from social class, sexual orientation, and ethnicity. Radical feminists have focused on issues such as sexual assault, harassment, and pornography, and have been instrumental in establishing sexual assault and battered women's shelters as well as in changing Canada's pornography laws.

In the 1990s, an increasing number of Canadian women became openly critical of what they viewed as extremism within the feminist movement. In *The Princess at the Window: A New Gender Morality*, Donna Laframboise (1996) critiqued feminists who appeared to espouse the stereotypes that men were inherently bad and exploitative in their relations with women and that women were morally superior to men. Indeed, because the extremist views of certain radical feminists were so widely publicized in the media, an increasing number of young women refused to identify themselves as feminists even though they upheld the most basic principles of feminism, such as the belief in gender equality. Only 13% of Canadian female respondents to the national Compas survey said they definitely considered themselves to be feminists, and another 28% said they probably did (Compas, 1998).

Gender Differences: *Vive la Différence or Vive la Similitude?*

If the genders were not anatomically different, this book would never have been written. How do the genders differ in cognitive abilities and personality, however?

Sexism The prejudgment that because of gender, a person will possess certain negative traits.

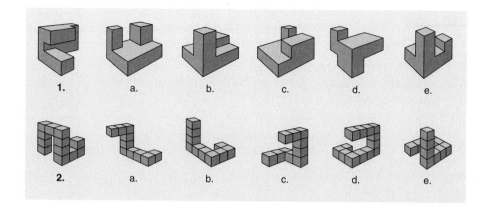

Figure 5.5 Rotating Geometric Figures in Space.

Visual–spatial skills (for example, the ability to rotate geometric figures in space) are considered part of the male gender-role stereotype. But such gender differences are small and can be modified by training.

Differences in Cognitive Abilities

Assessments of intelligence do not show overall gender differences in cognitive abilities (Halpern & LaMay, 2000). However, reviews of the research suggest that girls are somewhat superior to boys in verbal abilities, such as verbal fluency, ability to generate words that are similar in meaning to other words, spelling, knowledge of foreign languages, and pronunciation (Halpern, 1997). Far more boys than girls have reading problems, ranging from reading below grade level to severe disabilities. Among Grade 6 students in Ontario in 2003, 65% of girls compared with 51% of boys met or exceeded the provincial standard for reading. For writing skills, the gender gap was even greater, with 63% of girls and only 45% of boys meeting or exceeding the provincial standard for writing (Hallett, 2004). Similarly, in Alberta, girls have outperformed boys in reading and language skills (Bauer, 2001).

Males generally exceed females in visual–spatial abilities (Grön et al., 2000; Halpern & LaMay, 2000). Visual–spatial skills include the ability to follow a map when travelling to an unfamiliar location, to construct a puzzle or assemble a piece of equipment, and to perceive relationships between figures in space. (See Figure 5.5.)

Studies find that males generally obtain higher scores on math tests than females (Beller & Gafni, 2000). Yet differences in math are small and are narrowing at all ages. In an achievemement test given to 41 000 Canadian students in 2002, 48% of the 16-year-old females compared with 53% of the males achieved the target score level in mathematics. However, in the problem-solving portion of the test, more of the 13-year-old girls (70%) than of the boys (65%) achieved the target score level (Sokoloff, 2003). In the 2003 province-wide testing of elementary school students in Ontario, the girls performed better than the boys on the math test. Among students in Grade 6, 60% of girls compared with 56% of boys scored at the higher levels (Hallett, 2004).

Three factors should caution us not to attach too much importance to these gender differences, however.

Are There Gender Differences in Cognitive Abilities?
The physical differences between females and males are well established—and well celebrated! But are there cognitive differences between the genders? If so, what are they? How large are they? Are they the result of nature (heredity) or nurture (environmental influences such as educational experiences and cultural expectations)?

1. In most cases, the differences are small (Hyde & Plant, 1995). Differences in verbal, mathematical, and spatial abilities are also getting smaller (Hyde et al., 1990; Maccoby, 1990; Voyer et al., 1995).

2. These gender differences are *group* differences. Variation in ability on tests of verbal or math skills is larger *within each gender* than between the genders (Maccoby, 1990).

3. The small differences that may exist may largely reflect environmental influences and cultural expectations. Spatial and math skills are stereotyped in our culture as masculine, whereas reading skills are stereotyped as feminine.

Differences in Personality

There are also many gender differences in personality. According to a meta-analysis of the research literature, females exceed males in extraversion, anxiety, trust, and nurturance (Feingold, 1994). Males exceed females in assertiveness, tough-mindedness, and self-esteem. The assertiveness is connected with aggressiveness, as we see below. The tough-mindedness has unfortunate implications for men's health, as we also see.

Women are, however, more willing than men to disclose their feelings and personal experiences (Dindia & Allen, 1992). The stereotype of the "strong and silent" male may not discourage men from hogging the conversation, but it may inhibit them from expressing their personal feelings.

In most psychological studies on aggression, males have been found to behave more aggressively than females. Nonetheless, females are likely to act aggressively under certain conditions. The rate of aggression among girls seems to have increased in recent years. Although bullying used to be associated with only boys, researchers such as Wendy Craig at Queen's University and Debra Pepler of York University are now also studying bullying among girls. As well, the Earlscourt Child and Family Centre in Toronto has developed a pioneering program targeted specifically for aggressive girls (Teotonio, 2002). University of Western Ontario researchers Anne Cummings and Alan Leschied (2002) have also conducted extensive research on aggression by girls and published their findings in *Research and Treatment for Aggression with Adolescent Girls*. They found that compared with boys, adolescent girls who are aggressive are more likely to experience isolation, powerlessness, and depression. Most of the girls came from broken homes and most had seen violence between their parents.

Today, bullying refers to more than physical aggression; the term has been broadened to include emotional abuse such as humiliating and degrading comments. In one study of schoolyard bullying in Toronto (Craig & Pepler, 1997), boys bullied more than girls and were more likely to bully victims of the same sex, usually by repeatedly targeting the same victim. Girls were as likely to bully boys as they were to bully other girls. There were no gender differences in the type of bullying and the use of aggression.

Two cases that occurred on opposite sides of Canada illustrate these trends. In Halifax, a 14-year-old boy shot himself because he could no longer stand the bullying and threats he received from a gang led by an adolescent girl. In Vancouver, a 14-year-old-girl hanged herself after suffering intense verbal abuse from a group of girls (Schmidt, 2002).

Among both genders, acting as a bully in elementary school is highly predictive of aggression in future dating relationships. An Ontario study found that bullies started dating earlier than non-bullying youth and were more likely to engage in physical and social aggression with their dating partners (Connolly, Pepler, Craig, & Taradash, 2000).

Differences in Health

Men's life expectancies are shorter, on the average, than women's. At the beginning of the twentieth century, women were expected to live 50.1 years, which was 4 years longer than men. By 1981 the gap increased to 7.1 years. The gender gap in life expectancy is narrowing but is still large. In 2002, the life expectancy for Canadian men was 77.2 years compared with 82.1 years for women—a difference of 4.9 years (Statistics Canada, 2004). The increased rate of smoking among women is a major reason why the life expectancy gap is narrowing.

Data on the health of Canadians was obtained from a longitudinal study that began in 1994. The 1998/99 survey was based on 14 619 respondents who were randomly chosen from across Canada (Catlin, 2002). The study's main conclusion was that women lead healthier lifestyles than men. Its key findings include the following:

- Women are more likely to consider health issues when selecting food.
- More men (56%) than women (38%) are overweight.
- More men (26%) than women (7%) engage in binge drinking at least once a month.
- Women are more likely than men to experience stress.
- Women are more resilient in response to illness, partly because they are more likely to have a network of friends who provide emotional support.

Another major gender difference is women's greater willingness to seek health care (Catlin, 2002). Men often let symptoms go until a problem that could have been prevented or readily treated becomes serious or life-threatening. Women, for example, are much more likely to check themselves for breast cancer than men are to check for the symptoms of prostate cancer. In 2003, the Canadian Community Health Survey with a sample of 135 000 individuals found that twice as many men as women had not looked for a regular family doctor. Slightly more men (16%) than women (14%) were considered obese. While rates of obesity have increased in Canada, they are much higher in the United States (Statistics Canada, 2004).

The Canadian Community Health Survey was the first Canadian survey to ask about sexual orientation. Homosexuals and bisexuals were more likely than heterosexuals to report that they had unmet health-care needs and that they felt their lives were stressful.

On Becoming a Man or a Woman: Gender Typing

We have chronicled the biological process of sexual differentiation, and we have explored some gender differences in cognitive abilities and behaviour. In this section, we consider various explanations of **gender typing**.

Biological Perspectives

Biological views on gender typing tend to focus on the roles of genetics and prenatal influences in predisposing men and women to gender-linked behaviour patterns. Biological perspectives have also focused on the possible role of hormones in sculpting the brain during prenatal development.

THE EVOLUTIONARY PERSPECTIVE: IT'S ONLY NATURAL From the evolutionary perspective, the story of the survival of our ancient ancestors is etched in our genes. Those genes that bestow attributes that increase an organism's chances of surviving to produce viable offspring are most likely to be transmitted to future generations. We thus possess the genetic remnants of traits that helped our ancestors

Gender typing The process by which children acquire behaviour that is deemed appropariate to their gender.

survive and reproduce (Bjorklund & Kipp, 1996; Fisher, 2000). This heritage influences our social and sexual behaviour as well as our anatomic features.

According to the evolutionary perspective, men's traditional roles as hunters and warriors, and women's roles as caregivers and gatherers of fruits and vegetables, are bequeathed to us in our genes. Men are better suited to war and to the hunt because of physical attributes passed along since ancestral times. Upper-body strength, for example, would have enabled them to throw spears and overpower adversaries. Men also possess perceptual–cognitive advantages, such as superior visual–motor skills, which would have enabled them to aim spears or bows and arrows. Personality traits like aggressiveness also make for effective hunting.

Women, it is argued, are genetically predisposed to be empathic and nurturant because these traits enabled ancestral women to respond to children's needs and enhance the likelihood that their children would flourish and eventually reproduce, thereby transmitting their own genetic legacy to future generations. Prehistoric women thus tended to stay close to home, care for the children, and gather edible plants, whereas men ventured from home to hunt and raid their neighbours' storehouses.

The evolutionary perspective is steeped in controversy. Although scientists do not dispute the importance of evolution in determining physical attributes, many are reluctant to attribute complex social behaviours, such as aggression and gender roles, to heredity. The evolutionary perspective implies that stereotypical gender roles—men as breadwinners and women as homemakers, for example—reflect the natural order of things. Critics contend that biology is not destiny; that our behaviour is not dictated by our genes.

PRENATAL BRAIN ORGANIZATION   Researchers have sought the origins of gender-typed behaviour in the organization of the brain. Is it possible that the cornerstone of gender-typed behaviour is laid in the brain before the first breath is taken?

The hemispheres of the brain are specialized to carry out certain functions (Levy, 1985). In most people, the right hemisphere ("right brain") appears to be specialized to perform visual–spatial tasks. The "left brain" appears to be more critical to verbal functions, such as speech, in most people.

We know that sex hormones are responsible for prenatal sexual differentiation of the genitals and for the gender-related structural differences in the hypothalamus of the developing prenatal brain. Sexual differentiation of the brain may also partly explain men's (slight!) superiority at spatial-relations tasks, such as interpreting road maps and visualizing objects in space. Testosterone in the brains of male fetuses spurs greater growth of the right hemisphere and slows the rate of growth of the left hemisphere. This difference may be connected with the ability to accomplish spatial-relations tasks.

Might boys' inclinations toward aggression and rough-and-tumble play also be prenatally imprinted in the brain? Some theorists argue that prenatal sex hormones may masculinize or feminize the brain by creating predispositions that are consistent with gender-role stereotypes, such as rough-and-tumble play and aggressive behaviour in males (Collaer & Hines, 1995).

Psychological Perspectives

Children acquire awareness of gender-role stereotypes by the tender ages of 2 to 3 (Etaugh & Rathus, 1995). Both boys and girls generally agree, when asked to describe the differences between the genders, that boys build things, play with transportation toys such as cars and fire trucks, enjoy helping their fathers, and hit other children. Both boys and girls also agree that girls enjoy playing with dolls and helping their mothers cook and clean and that they are talkative, dependent on others for help, and nonviolent. Psychologists have applied psychodynamic, social-learning, and cognitive-developmental theories in an effort to explain how children acquire such knowledge and adopt stereotypical behaviour patterns.

PSYCHODYNAMIC THEORY   Sigmund Freud explained gender typing in terms of identification. Appropriate gender typing, in Freud's view, requires that boys come to identify with their fathers and girls with their mothers. Identification is completed, in Freud's view, as children resolve the **Oedipus complex** (which is sometimes called the Electra complex in girls).

According to Freud, the Oedipus complex occurs during the phallic period of psychosexual development, from the ages of three to five. During this period, the child develops incestuous wishes for the parent of the other gender and comes to perceive the parent of the same gender as a rival. The complex is resolved by the child's forsaking incestuous wishes for the parent of the other gender and identifying with the parent of the same gender. Through identification with the same-gender parent, the child comes to develop gender-typed behaviours that are typically associated with that gender.

SOCIAL-LEARNING THEORY   Social-learning theorists explain the development of gender-typed behaviour in terms of processes such as observational learning, identification, and socialization. Children can learn what is deemed masculine or feminine by observational learning, as suggested by the results of an experiment by Perry and Bussey (1979). In this study, eight- and nine-year-old boys and girls watched adult role models indicate their preferences on each of 16 pairs of items—pairs such as toy cows versus toy horses and oranges versus apples. What the children didn't know was that the expressed preferences were made arbitrarily. The children then were asked to indicate their own preferences for the items represented in the pairs. The boys' choices agreed with the adult men's an average of 14 out of 16 times. Girls chose the pair item selected by the men an average of only 3 out of 16 times.

In social-learning theory, identification is viewed as a continuing and broadly based learning process in which rewards and punishments influence children to imitate adult models of the same gender—especially the parent of the same gender (Storms, 1979). Identification is more than imitation, however. In identification, the child not only imitates the behaviour of the model but also tries to become like the model in broad terms.

Socialization also plays a role in gender typing. Almost from the moment a baby comes into the world, it is treated according to its gender. Parents tend to talk more to baby girls, and fathers especially engage in more roughhousing with boys (Jacklin et al., 1984). When children are old enough to speak, parents and other adults—even other children—begin to instruct children in how they are expected to behave. Parents may reward children for behaviour they consider gender-appropriate and punish (or fail to reinforce) them for behaviour they consider inappropriate for their gender. Girls are encouraged to practise caretaking behaviours, which are intended to prepare them for traditional feminine adult roles. Boys are handed Lego or doctor sets to help prepare them for traditional masculine adult roles.

Fathers generally encourage their sons to develop assertive, instrumental behaviour (that is, behaviour that gets things done or accomplishes something) and their daughters to develop nurturant, cooperative behaviour. Fathers are likely to cuddle their daughters gently. They are likely to carry their sons like footballs or toss them into the air. Fathers also tend to use heartier and harsher language with their sons, such as "How're yuh doin', Tiger?" and "Hey you, get your keester over here" (Jacklin et al., 1984). Being a nontraditionalist, your first author made sure to toss his young daughters into the air, which raised immediate objections from the relatives, who chastised him for being too rough. This, of course, led him to modify his behaviour: He learned to toss his daughters into the air when the relatives were not around.

Oedipus complex A conflict of the phallic stage in which the boy wishes to possess his mother sexually and perceives his father as a rival in love.

Socialization The process of guiding people into socially acceptable behaviour patterns by means of information, rewards, and punishments.

Generally speaking, from an early age, boys are more likely to receive toy cars and guns and athletic equipment and to be encouraged to compete aggressively. Even relatively sophisticated university students are likely to select traditionally masculine toys as gifts for boys and traditionally feminine toys for girls (Fisher-Thompson, 1990). Girls are spoken to more often, whereas boys are handled more frequently and more roughly. Whatever the biological determinants of gender differences in aggressiveness and verbal skills, early socialization experiences clearly contribute to gender typing.

Parental roles in gender typing are apparently changing. With more mothers working outside the home, daughters today are exposed to more women who represent career-minded role models than was the case in earlier generations. More parents today are encouraging their daughters to become career-minded and to engage in strenuous physical activities, such as organized sports. Many boys today are exposed to fathers who take a larger role than men used to in child care and household responsibilities.

Schools are also important socialization influences. Teachers often expect girls to perform better than boys in reading and language arts and have higher expectations of boys in math and science. Special programs in math and science held for girls after school and in the summer have helped bolster the girls' confidence and interest in these subjects.

Educators are becoming increasingly concerned about the fact that boys are failing in school at a much higher rate than girls. In Ontario, the high school drop out rate for boys is four times that of girls (Halley, 2004).

In Canada, more women than men attend university and women account for most of the growth in university enrollment. In 2001, 57% of Canadian university students were women (Statistics Canada, 2003) and today the percentage of women at university is probably even higher.

Only recently have some educators proposed that special efforts need to be made to assist boys in catching up to the higher academic achievements of girls. The Durham District School Board in Whitby, Ontario, is one of the few school boards in the country to have implemented special teaching methods for improving the reading and writing skills of boys (Bauer, 2001).

Ontario Minister of Education Gerard Kennedy has expressed concern that a lack of male teachers in the school system may undermine the school performance of boys who do not have academic male role models. Only 10% of teachers under the age of 30 in Ontario are men ("Lack of," 2004).

COGNITIVE-DEVELOPMENTAL THEORY   Psychologist Lawrence Kohlberg (1966) proposed a cognitive-developmental view of gender typing. From this perspective, gender typing is not the product of environmental influences that mechan-

Gender Typing Through Observational Learning.
According to social-learning theory, people learn about the gender roles that are available to them—and expected of them—at an early age. Gender schema theory adds that once children have learned the expected gender roles (i.e., the gender schema of their culture), they blend these roles with their self-concepts. Their self-esteem comes to be dependent on their adherence to the expected gender roles.

ically "stamp in" gender-appropriate behaviour. Rather, children themselves play an active role. They form concepts, or **schemas**, about gender and then exhibit behaviour that conforms to their gender concepts. These developments occur in stages and are entwined with general cognitive development.

According to Kohlberg, gender typing entails the emergence of three concepts: *gender identity*, *gender stability*, and *gender constancy*. Gender identity is usually acquired by the age of three. By the age of four or five, most children develop a concept of **gender stability**—the recognition that people retain their genders for a lifetime. Prior to this age, boys may think that they will become mommies when they grow up, and girls may think they will be daddies.

The more sophisticated concept of **gender constancy** develops in most children by the age of seven or eight. They recognize that gender does not change even when people alter their dress or behaviour. Hence gender remains constant even when appearances change. A woman who wears her hair short (or shaves it off) remains a woman. A man who dons an apron and cooks dinner remains a man.

According to cognitive-developmental theory, children are motivated to behave in gender-appropriate ways once they have established the concepts of gender stability and gender constancy. They then make an active effort to learn which behaviour patterns are considered "masculine" and which "feminine" (Perry & Bussey, 1979). Once they obtain this information, they imitate the "gender-appropriate" pattern.

GENDER SCHEMA THEORY: AN INFORMATION-PROCESSING APPROACH   Gender schema theory proposes that children develop a **gender schema** as a means of organizing their perceptions of the world (Bem, 1981, 1985; Martin & Halverson, 1981). A gender schema is a cluster of mental representations about male and female physical qualities, behaviours, and personality traits. Gender gains prominence as a schema for organizing experience because of society's emphasis on it. Even young children start to mentally group people of the same gender in accordance with the traits that represent that gender.

Children's gender schemata determine how important gender-typed traits are to them. Consider the dimension of *strength–weakness*. Children may learn that strength is connected with maleness and weakness with femaleness. (Other dimensions, such as *light–dark*, are not gender-typed and thus may fall outside children's gender schemata.) Children also gather that some dimensions, such as strong–weak, are more important to one gender (in this case, male) than to the other.

Once children acquire a gender schema, they begin to judge themselves in accordance with traits considered appropriate to their genders. In doing so, they blend their developing self-concepts with the prominent gender schema of their culture. The gender schema furnishes standards for comparison. Children with self-concepts that are consistent with the prominent gender schema of their culture are likely to develop higher self-esteem than children whose self-concepts are inconsistent. Jack learns that muscle strength is a characteristic associated with "manliness." Thereafter, he is likely to think more highly of himself if he perceives himself as embodying this attribute than if he does not. Barbara is likely to discover that the dimension of kindness–cruelty is more crucial than strength–weakness to the way women are perceived in society.

Gender Roles and Sexual Behaviour

Gender roles have had a profound influence on dating practices and sexual behaviour. Children learn at an early age that men usually make dates and initiate sexual interactions, whereas women usually serve as the "gatekeepers" in romantic relationships (Bailey et al., 2000). In their traditional role as gatekeepers, women are expected to wait to be asked out and to screen suitors. Men are expected to make the first (sexual) move and women to determine how far advances will proceed.

Schema Concept; way of interpreting experience or processing information.

Gender stability The concept that people retain their genders for a lifetime.

Gender constancy The concept that people's genders do not change, even if they alter their dress or behaviour.

Gender schema A cluster of mental representations about male and female physical qualities, behaviours, and personality traits.

Female-superior position
A coital position in which the woman is on top.

Male-superior position
A coital position in which the man is on top.

Because women have the gatekeeper role, most men believe that women have the greater sexual power. When Canadians were asked "Who do you think has more control over whether a couple will have sex?" more men (65%) than women (47%) believed the woman does (Compas, 1998).

Men as Sexually Aggressive, Women as Sexually Passive

The cultural expectation that men are initiators and women are gatekeepers is embedded within the larger stereotype that men are sexually aggressive and women are sexually passive. Men are expected to have a higher number of sex partners than women do (Mikach & Bailey, 1999). Men consistently report having more sexual partners than do women. In comparing data regarding number of partners in Canada, the United States, Great Britain, and Norway, Tom Smith (1992) from the University of Chicago argues that gender differences in reporting (with men over-reporting and women underreporting) seems to be the most likely explanation for the discrepancy.

Men not only initiate sexual encounters; they are also expected to dictate all the "moves" thereafter, just as they are expected to take the lead on the dance floor. The 1998 Compas survey asked Canadians "When a man and a woman decide to have sex, who do you think gets them in the mood first?" Three times as many people (60%) believed that it is the man, with only 20% believing it is the woman, and the rest saying that it is both genders equally.

Moreover, people who adhere to the masculine gender-role stereotype, whether male or female, are more likely to engage in risky (unprotected) sexual behaviour (Belgrave et al., 2000). According to the stereotype, women are supposed to let men determine the choice, timing, and sequence of sexual positions and techniques. Unfortunately, the stereotype favours men's sexual preferences, denying women the opportunity to give and receive their preferred kinds of stimulation. For example, a woman may more easily reach orgasm in the **female-superior position**, but her partner may prefer the **male-superior position**. If the man is calling the shots, she may not have the opportunity to reach orgasm. Even expressing her preferences may be deemed "unladylike."

The stereotypical masculine role also imposes constraints on men. Men are expected to take the lead in bringing their partners to orgasm, but they should not ask their partners what *they* like because men are expected to be natural experts. ("Real men" not only don't eat quiche; they also need not ask women how to make love.)

Fortunately, more flexible attitudes are emerging. Women are becoming more sexually assertive, and men are becoming more receptive to expressing tenderness and gentleness. Still, the roots of traditional gender roles run deep.

A World of Diversity

THE EYE THAT ROVES AROUND THE WORLD?

A study of 10 different areas of the world found that in every culture surveyed, men were more likely than women to desire multiple sex partners. According to the sexual strategies theory, this sex difference reflects human adaptation to environmental forces.

One of the more controversial sex differences in the field of human sexuality is the suggestion that males are naturally polygamous, whereas females are naturally monogamous. If this were

Do Men Around the World Have Roving Eyes? A study of 10 different areas of the world found that in every culture surveyed, men were more likely than women to desire multiple sex partners. According to the sexual strategies theory, this sex difference reflects human adaptation to environmental forces. Does this research finding mean that it is "unnatural" to expect men to remain faithful to their partners?

so, it would place a greater burden on societies in which men are expected to remain loyal to their mates. If the man strayed, after all, he could have the attitude, "Don't blame me. It's in my genes." Women, moreover, might wonder how realistic it is to expect that their partners will remain faithful.

Evolutionary psychologists have hypothesized a so-called *sexual strategies theory*, which holds that men and women differ in their long-term and short-term mating strategies, with men more interested in sexual variety in the short term (Barash & Lipton, 2001; Buss & Schmitt, 1993; Klusmann, 2002). In the long term, both males and females may seek a heavy investment in a relationship, feelings of love, companionship, and a sharing of resources. Even so, men are hypothesized to place more

value on signals of fertility and reproductive value, as found in a woman's youth and physical appearance. Women are hypothesized to place relatively more value on a man's social status, maturity, and resources—cues that are relevant to his ability to provide over the long term. The qualities that men and women seek are believed to help solve adaptive problems that humans have faced over their evolutionary history.

In the short term, men are more interested in one-night stands and relatively brief affairs. According to the theory, this is because men would have a greater chance of contributing their genes to future generations by impregnating as many women as possible. Women, evolutionarily speaking, would have little to gain from such encounters. Impregnation requires a long-term commitment to child-rearing, and evolutionary forces would favor the survival of the children of women who created a long-term nurturing environment.

Because a "universal" form of behavior is more likely to be embedded in people's genes, the evolutionary theory of different sexual strategies would find support if males and females from various cultures showed similar sex differences in short-term mating strategies. In seeking just such evidence, David Schmitt (2003) supervised a survey of 16 288 people across 10 major regions of the world, including North America, South America,

Western Europe, Eastern Europe, Southern Europe, Middle East, Africa, Oceania, South/Southeast Asia, and East Asia. He indeed found that sex differences in the desire for sexual variety were culturally universal.

Table 5.2 and Figure 5.6 reveal some of Schmitt's key findings as to the desire for variety in short-term and long-term relationships. When asked whether they would like to have more than one sex partner in the next month, men from all 10 areas of the world were significantly more likely than women to say that they would. For example, 23.1% of North American men would like more than one partner, as compared with just 2.9% of North American women (Table 5.2). When asked about the mean (average) number of sex partners they would like to have over the next 30 years, men from every area said they would like to have significantly more sex partners than the women (Figure 5.6).

The chances that any sex differences within a given region are due to chance is less than one in 1000 ($p < .001$).

We cannot conclude that these research findings, intriguing as they are, "prove" the validity of the evolutionary approach to understanding sex differences in "sexual strategies." For example, we could point to details such as the fact that Oceanic women reported that they wanted more sex partners in the long term than did African men (Figure 5.6). We can also accept the universality of the finding but consider rival explanations for the data. For example, in a world with common global communication, it might not be surprising that there is worldwide overlap in gender roles. This overlap might affect the ways in which parents and cultural institutions influence children around the world.

The ideal model for demonstrating instinctive (inborn) behavior is to rear an individual in isolation from all other members of its species and then observe whether its behavior parallels or differs from that of other members of its species. For both practical and ethical reasons, this type of experiment has never been carried out with humans and most likely never will be. Therefore, the most we can expect are findings that are consistent with this sort of theorizing in humans, not findings that clearly prove them.

Table 5.2
Sex Differences in the Percentage of Men and Women Who Desire More Than One Sex Partner "in the Next Month" Across 10 World Regions

World Region	Percentage of Men Wanting More Than One Sexual Partner	Percentage of Women Wanting More Than One Sexual Partner
North America	23.1	2.9
South America	35.0	6.1
Western Europe	22.6	5.5
Eastern Europe	31.7	7.1
Southern Europe	31.0	6.0
Middle East	33.1	5.9
Africa	18.2	4.2
Oceania	25.3	5.8
South/Southeast Asia	32.4	6.4
East Asia	17.9	2.6

Source: Table 5. David P. Schmitt (2003). Universal sex differences in the desire for sexual variety: Tests from 52 nations, 6 continents, and 13 islands. Journal of Personality and Social Psychology, 85(1), 85–104.

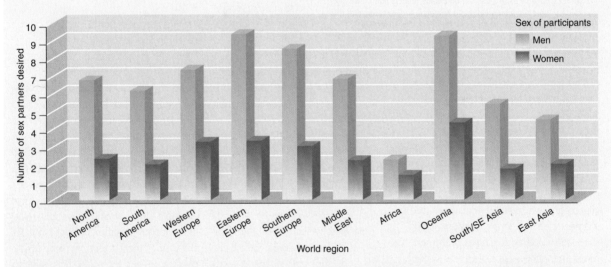

Figure 5.6 Mean Number of Sexual Partners Desired by Men and Women "in the Next 30 Years" Across 10 World Regions.

Source: David P. Schmitt (2003). Universal sex differences in the desire for sexual variety: Tests from 52 nations, 6 continents, and 13 islands. Journal of Personality and Social Psychology, 85(1), 85–104.

Men as Overaroused, Women as Underaroused

According to another stereotype, men become sexually aroused at puberty and remain at the ready throughout adulthood. A study conducted at an Ontario university found that 85% of the women believed that "it's easy for a woman to sexually arouse a man if she really wants to" (Clements-Schreiber & Rempel, 1995).

Women, the stereotype continues, do not share men's natural interest in sex, and a woman discovers her own sexuality only when a man ignites her sexual flame. Men must continue to stir women's sexual embers, lest they die out. This stereotype denies that "normal" women have spontaneous sexual desires or are readily aroused.

It was widely believed in the Victorian period (even by so-called sex experts!) that women were naturally asexual and "unbothered" by sexual desires. The contemporary residues of this stereotype hold that women do not enjoy sex as much as men and that women who openly express their sexual desires are "whores" or "sluts." In the Ontario study, however, only 25% of the women agreed that "in general, women do not really enjoy sex as much as men" (Clements-Schreiber & Rempel, 1995). But when the 1998 Compas survey asked "Who has the greater sexual needs?" far more Canadians (58%) said that men do, with only 9% saying that women do and about one-quarter believing that it is equal. There were no gender differences in the responses. Considerable gender differences were revealed, however, in the acceptability of casual sex. When single Canadians were asked if they would have sexual intercourse with an attractive person the same day they had just met, about two-thirds of the women and only one-fifth of the men said they defisnitely would not (Compas, 1998).

THE DOUBLE STANDARD The stereotype that women are undersexed also supports the traditional double standard: It is natural for men to sow their wild oats, but women who are sexually active outside of committed relationships are sluts or *nymphomaniacs*. In a study by University of Guelph researchers of university students and patrons at a singles bar (Milhausen & Herold, 2001), the majority (79% men and 89% women) believed that women who have many sexual partners are judged more harshly than men who have many partners. In another study by the same researchers, the majority of women also believed that women are more severe in their judgments of women's sexual behaviour than men are (Milhausen & Herold, 1999). (The nearby photo presents a recent case in which a female judge ejected a female lawyer from the courtroom for dressing "too provocatively." Do *you* think the lawyer dressed inappropriately?)

Of the respondents in the Millhausen and Herold 2001 study, twice as many women (67%) as men (35%) believed that men have greater sexual freedom than women. The women thought it was easier for men to have many partners and to engage in casual sex; the men, on the other hand, felt that women have greater freedom because they are the ones who decide whether or not sex will occur. The men typically felt that they were put at a disadvantage because they want sex more than women do.

Although most respondents believed a double standard exists in Canada, the majority personally endorsed a single standard for both women and men. This was determined by measuring attitudes toward such behaviours as watching sexually explicit videos and having many sexual partners. While only a minority of men held a sexual double standard, a minority of women held a reverse double standard whereby they judged the behaviour of men more negatively than that of women.

In another possible indication of a reverse double standard, both genders were more likely to discourage their female friends from dating a man who had many sexual partners than they were to discourage a male friend from dating a highly experienced woman. It appears that people see the man who has many partners as more likely to be exploitative. Indeed, a common term used to describe a man with many

Dressed to Excess?
Lawyer Laura Joy poses in the suit that got her ejected from a courtroom by Justice Micheline Rawlins.

partners was "player," meaning someone who deceives women into having sex. Although the majority of both genders used negative words to describe both men and women who had many partners, none of the respondents used the word "player" for a woman who has many partners. (Table 5.3 presents a summary of the word categories used.) Given the heightened awareness of such issues as sexual harassment and sexual assault, and the fact that most perpetrators are men, it appears that more negative evaluations of male sexuality exist today than was the case a few years ago.

The 2001 study illustrates the complexity of the double standard concept and the need to use a diversity of measures when studying the topic. Certainly, the divergence between the belief that the double standard exists and the fact that most of the respondents did not support it themselves calls for more research. Further research is also needed with a diversity of samples. It may be, for example, that the double standard is still practised among certain ethnic groups and in lower-income groups (Milhausen & Herold, 2001).

CHANGING PERCEPTIONS OF WOMEN'S SEXUALITY Despite the stereotype that women are undersexed, they are no less arousable than men. Nor do they wait for men to discover their sexuality. Long before they have intimate relationships, children of both genders routinely discover that touching their genitals produces pleasurable sensations.

Many women are attempting to change the perception of women as not being interested in sex. Sex therapist Joy Davidson (2004) in her book *Fearless Sex* encourages women to

■ let go of sexual inhibitions and "bad girl" attitudes

■ electrify their libidos

■ liberate their most daring fantasies

■ feel good about their "kinkier" sexual desires and explore them safely

When Canadian singer Alanis Morissette posed nude for her album *Thank U*, she explained that "I need to let girls see that you can just be who you are" (Johnson, 1999, p. 48). In Morissette's album *You Oughta Know*, the lyrics include "Is she perverted like me? Would she go down on you in a theatre?" (p. 50). Similarly, Shania Twain, in singing about the joys of being a woman, presents a highly sexualized image. And in her interviews with women in Canada and the U.S., Canadian author Wendy Dennis (1992) found that some of the women specifically wanted men to be informed that women's sex drive can be just as strong as men's.

TABLE 5.3
Word Categories Used to Describe Men and Women Having Many Sexual Partners

	Descriptions of Men		Descriptions of Women	
	Men	Women	Men	Women
Sexual predator	38%	37%	0%	0%
Promiscuous	40	30	75	66
Psychologically damaged	10	3	7	9
Stud	25	8	0	0
Sexually liberated	11	5	8	16

Source: R. R. Milhausen and E. S. Herold (2001). Reconceptualizing the sexual double standard. Journal of Psychology and Human Sexuality, 13, *63–83.*

In determining the strength of women's sex drive, age is an important factor to consider. Researchers surveyed women from different parts of Canada and the U.S. to determine whether there was any truth to the stereotype that women reach their sexual "peak" in their early 30s (Schmitt et al., 2002). While women in their early 30s did in fact report higher levels of sexual desire than women in any of the other age groups, they did not report having more partners. The findings were similar for both the Canadian and American women. The researchers concluded that women in the 30 to 34 age group were more lustful than the average of all other women, thus supporting the idea of a sexual peak for this age group. Yet the researchers also cautioned that their findings were exploratory and that more research would be needed to confirm their conclusions.

In recent years the media have turned the spotlight on women who have sex with younger men. "Cougars" are women in their 30s and over who seek out younger men solely for sex. In her book *Cougar*, *Toronto Sun* columnist Valerie Gibson (2002) describes dating younger men as liberating, empowering, and fun. A self-proclaimed pioneer cougar, Gibson says cougars want lots of great sex with hot young men.

A trend toward casual sex is also seen among certain groups of lesbians. In Toronto, a group of lesbians rented a gay male bathhouse on a monthly basis to provide a supportive environment for women who wanted to have casual sex with other women. They named this bathhouse the "Pussy Palace." In her book *Good Girls Do: Sex Chronicles of a Shameless Generation*, Simona Chiose (2001) describes her visit to the Pussy Palace. She quotes one of the organizers: "We are socialized to not own our desires. The bathhouse challenges that. We're all here because we're horny" (p. 55). Chiose details the various activities that transpired at the Palace, including striptease dancing, masturbation, group sex, and watching lesbian sex videos. She argues that the women were able to engage in behaviours that they might not have otherwise because they were in an environment where they did not fear being judged: "I think of that night as a walk on the wild side of female sexuality, of what women are capable of and of how open they can be about their desires" (p. 56).

Yet, despite her acceptance of casual sex for others, Chiose notes that she has difficulty in accepting casual sex for herself:

Shania Twain.
In singing about the joys of being a woman, Shania Twain presents a highly sexualized image.

> I have always been envious of friends I've had who have said in passing that they were going to meet a new man for an evening and in response to my question as to whether they thought it might become something, shrugged and said they didn't want it to be. They just wanted to get laid, to have a moment of physical and emotional union with someone they didn't know very well nor did they wish to know them. I can't do it and I'm sorry for that sometimes—for not being able to leave my thinking self behind and simply immerse myself in experience—but I am a product of the world I grew up in and it's pointless for me to try. All I would get is a nervous breakdown. (p. 53)

We end this section with a note of caution. Our society tends to overemphasize gender differences. In many situations these differences may actually be quite small, and there is usually greater variation within each gender than between the genders (Muehlenhard, 2000). Sometimes other variables may account for the gender difference. For example, the Compas survey of Canadians found that the respondent's age dramatically affects findings regarding gender and the reported age of first sexual intercourse. Among older Canadians, men consistently report having had intercourse at much earlier ages than females. However, among Canadians in their 20s, there is hardly any difference (Fischtein & Herold, 2002).

Psychological androgyny
A state characterized by possession of both stereotypical masculine traits and stereotypical feminine traits.

Psychological Androgyny: The More Traits, the Merrier?

Most people think of masculinity and femininity as opposite ends of one continuum. People tend to assume that the more masculine a person is, the less feminine he or she must be, and vice versa. Thus, a man who exhibits stereotypical feminine traits of nurturance, tenderness, and emotionality is often considered less masculine than other men. Women who compete with men in business are perceived not only as more masculine than other women but also as less feminine.

Some behavioural scientists, such as Sandra Bem (1993), argue that masculinity and femininity instead constitute separate personality dimensions. A person who is highly masculine, whether male or female, may also possess feminine traits—and vice versa. People who exhibit "masculine" assertiveness and instrumental skills (skills in the sciences and business, for example) along with "feminine" nurturance and cooperation fit both the masculine and the feminine gender-role stereotypes. They are said to show **psychological androgyny** (see Figure 5.6). People who are high only in assertiveness and instrumental skills fit the masculine stereotype. People who are high only in traits such as nurturance and cooperation fit the feminine stereotype. People low in the stereotypical masculine *and* feminine patterns are considered "undifferentiated" in terms of gender-role stereotypes.

People who are psychologically androgynous may be capable of summoning up a wider range of masculine and feminine traits to meet the demands of various situations and to express their desires and talents. Researchers, for example, have found psychologically androgynous persons of both genders to show "masculine" independence under group pressures to conform and to show "feminine" nurturance in interactions with a kitten or baby (Bem, 1975; Bem et al., 1976).

People who oppose the constraints of traditional gender roles may perceive psychological androgyny as a desirable goal. Some feminist writers, however, criticize the model of psychological androgyny because it is defined in terms of, and thereby perpetuates, concepts of masculine and feminine gender roles (Lott, 1985).

Psychologically androgynous people tend to have higher self-esteem and to be generally better adjusted psychologically than people who are feminine or undifferentiated. Yet it appears that these benefits are more strongly related to the presence of masculine traits than to the combination of masculine and feminine traits (Whitley, 1983; Williams & D'Alessandro, 1994). That is, masculine traits such as assertiveness and independence may be related to psychological well-being, whether or not they are combined with feminine traits such as warmth, nurturance, and cooperation.

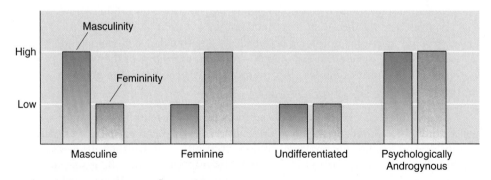

Figure 5.7 A Model of Psychological Androgyny.

Some behavioural scientists argue that masculinity and femininity are independent personality dimensions. People who exhibit "masculine" assertiveness and instrumental skills along with "feminine" nurturance and cooperation are said to be psychologically androgynous.

Some evidence shows psychologically androgynous men and women to be more comfortable with their sexuality than are masculine men and feminine women (Walfish & Mayerson, 1980). Perhaps they can draw upon a broader repertoire of sexual behaviours. They may be comfortable with cuddling and tender holding *and* with initiating and directing sexual interactions. Researchers also find that androgynous women experience orgasm more frequently (Radlove, 1983), and express greater sexual satisfaction (Kimlika et al., 1983), than feminine women do.

In this chapter, we have focused on the biology and psychology of gender. Our gender, both anatomically and psychologically, is a primary aspect of our sexuality. In the next chapter, we begin to explore how we express our sexuality through intimate relationships with others.

Summing Up

Prenatal Sexual Differentiation

During the first six weeks or so of prenatal development, embryonic structures of both genders develop along similar lines and resemble primitive female structures.

Genetic Factors in Sexual Differentiation

At about the seventh week after conception, the genetic code (XX or XY) begins to assert itself, causing changes in the gonads, genital ducts, and external genitals.

The Role of Sex Hormones in Sexual Differentiation

Testosterone spurs differentiation of the male (Wolffian) duct system. In the absence of testosterone, the Wolffian ducts degenerate, and female sex organs develop.

Descent of the Testes and the Ovaries

The testes and ovaries develop in the abdominal cavity. About four months after conception, the testes descend into the scrotal sac.

Sex-Chromosomal Abnormalities

Abnormalities of the sex chromosomes can have profound effects on sexual characteristics, physical health, and psychological development. Examples include Klinefelter syndrome and Turner syndrome.

Prenatal Sexual Differentiation of the Brain

Gender-specific changes occur in the hypothalamus during prenatal development. Testosterone causes cells in the hypothalamus of male fetuses to become insensitive to estrogen.

Gender Identity

One's gender identity is one's sense of being male or of being female.

Nature and Nurture in Gender Identity

Gender identity is nearly always consistent with anatomic gender.

Hermaphroditism

Some individuals—hermaphrodites—are born with both ovarian and testicular tissue. Hermaphrodites usually assume the gender identity and gender role of the gender assigned at birth. Pseudohermaphrodites can acquire the gender identity of the other chromosomal gender when they are reared as members of that gender.

Transsexualism

Transsexuals harbour a deep sense of discomfort about their anatomic gender. Hormone treatments and gender-reassignment surgery provide transsexuals with many of the characteristics of the other gender.

Gender Roles and Stereotypes

Cultures have broad expectations of men and women that are termed *gender roles*. In our culture, the stereotypical female is seen as gentle, dependent, kind, helpful, patient, and submissive. The stereotypical male is tough, competitive, gentlemanly, and protective.

Sexism

Sexism is the prejudgment that because of gender, a person will possess certain negative traits that disqualify him or her for certain vocations or prevent him or her from performing adequately in these jobs or in some social situations. Women have been historically excluded from "male occupations," and stereotypical expectations concerning "men's work" and "women's work" filter down to the primary grades.

Gender Differences: *Vive la Différence* or *Vive la Similitude?*

Differences in Cognitive Abilities

Boys have historically been seen as excelling in math and spatial-relations skills, whereas girls have been viewed as excelling in language skills. Gender differences in these areas are small, however, and cultural expectations play a role in them.

Differences in Personality

Stereotypical gender preferences for toys and play activities are in evidence at an early age. Males are more aggressive than females, but the question is *why?*

Differences in Health

Men's life expectancies are shorter, on average, than women's. Canadian women lead healthier lifestyles than men, and are more willing to seek health care.

On Becoming a Man or a Woman: Gender Typing

Biological Perspectives

Biological views on gender typing focus on the roles of genetics and prenatal influences in predisposing men and women to gender-linked behaviour patterns. Testosterone in the brains of male fetuses spurs greater growth of the right hemisphere, which may be connected with the ability to manage spatial-relations tasks.

Psychological Perspectives

Psychologists have attempted to explain gender typing in terms of psychodynamic, social-learning, and cognitive-developmental theories. Freud explained gender typing in terms of identification with the parent of the same gender through resolution of the Oedipus complex.

Social-learning theorists explain the development of gender-typed behaviour in terms of processes such as observational learning, identification, and socialization.

According to the cognitive-developmental view, children form concepts about gender and then make their behaviour conform to their gender concepts. According to Kohlberg, gender typing entails the emergence of three concepts: gender identity, gender stability, and gender constancy.

Gender schema theory proposes that children develop a gender schema as a means of organizing their perceptions of the world. They then begin to judge themselves in terms of traits considered appropriate to their gender. In doing so, they blend their developing self-concepts with the prominent gender schema of their culture.

Gender Roles and Sexual Behaviour

Stereotypical gender-role expectations affect dating practices and sexual behaviour.

Men as Sexually Aggressive, Women as Sexually Passive

According to this stereotype, men are sexual initiators and women sexual gatekeepers. Men not only initiate sexual encounters; they are also expected to initiate all the "moves."

Men as Overaroused, Women as Underaroused

According to another stereotype, women do not share men's interest in sex and discover their own sexuality only when a man ignites their sexual flame.

Psychological Androgyny: The More Traits, the Merrier?

Masculinity and femininity may be two independent personality dimensions. People who combine stereotypical masculine and feminine behaviour patterns are psychologically androgynous. Masculine and androgynous people of both genders tend to be better psychologically adjusted than people who are feminine or undifferentiated. Psychologically androgynous men and women are more comfortable with their sexuality than masculine men and feminine women.

Test Yourself

Multiple-Choice Questions

1. The process through which males and females develop a distinct sexual anatomy is known as
   a. sexualization
   b. homologous development
   c. sexual differentiation
   d. Müllerian stage

2. The basic blueprint of the human embryo is
   a. male
   b. female
   c. both male and female
   d. neither male nor female

3. Which of the following chromosome patterns would be found in males with Klinefelter syndrome?
a. YYY
b. XXX
c. XYY
d. XXY ✓

4. Turner syndrome results when a fertilized egg has
a. only one chromosome—an X ✓
b. only one chromosome—a Y
c. three X chromosomes
d. three Y chromosomes

5. Research suggests that a part of the brain known as the _____ may be involved in the development of gender identity.
a. amygdala
b. hippocampus
c. frontal cortex
d. hypothalamus ✓

6. Individuals with androgen insensitivity syndrome, congenital adrenal hyperplasia, and Dominican Republic Syndrome are considered to be
a. intersexuals ✓
b. transsexuals
c. homosexuals
d. asexuals

7. Cross-cultural research by Zucker and his colleagues suggests that
a. more girls than boys are treated for gender identity disorder

b. more boys than girls are treated for gender identity disorder ✓
c. equal proportions of boys and girls are treated for gender identity disorder
d. gender identity disorders do not appear until early adulthood

8. Children learn behaviours that are appropriate for their gender by the process of
a. gender reinforcement
b. gender expectation
c. gender typing ✓
d. gender fixation

9. Teasing or belittling a man because he has chosen to study nursing is an example of
a. gender typing
b. sexism ✓
c. gender reassignment
d. homophobia

10. In terms of gender differences in health, which of the following is *not* true?
a. Women are more resilient in dealing with health problems.
b. More women than men are overweight. ✓
c. Women are more likely than men to experience stress.
d. Women are more likely to consider health issues when selecting food.

Critical Thinking Questions

1. What is your ultimate definition of gender? Is it biological? Psychological? A bit of each?

2. When transsexuals undergo gender reassignment surgery to bring their physical appearance more in line with their gender identity, has anything really changed?

3. When you were growing up, what messages about traditional gender roles did you receive from your parents? Did you receive different messages from your friends? How have you reconciled any conflicts?

4. Have you ever experienced sexism? What were the circumstances? What effect (if any) did it have on you?

5. Do you think men have stronger sex drives than women? Why or why not?

Companion Website

Visit our Companion Website at www.pearsoned.ca/rathus, **where you can use the interactive Study Guide and link to additional resources on topics discussed in this text.**

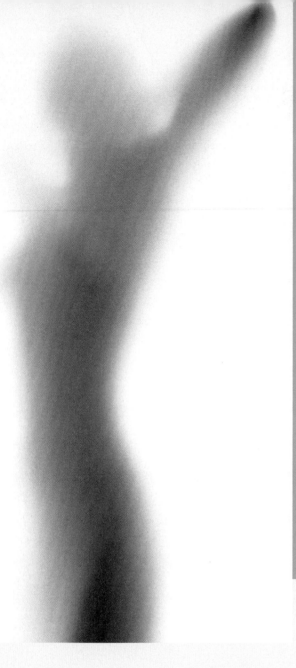

Chapter 6
Attraction and Love

Candy and Stretch. A new technique for controlling weight gain? No, these are the names of a couple who have just met at a camera club that doubles as a meeting place for singles.

Candy and Stretch stand above the crowd—literally. She is almost 6 feet tall, an attractive woman in her early 30s. He is more plain looking, but "wholesome." He is in his late 30s and 6 feet 5 inches tall. Stretch has been in the group for some time. Candy is a new member. Let us follow them as they meet during a coffee break. As you will see, there are some differences between what they say and what they think (Bach and Deutsch 1970).

They Say	(They Think)
STRETCH: Well, you're certainly a welcome addition to our group.	(Can't I ever say something clever?)
CANDY: Thank you. It certainly is friendly and interesting.	(He's cute.)
STRETCH: My friends call me Stretch. It's left over from my basketball days. Silly, but I'm used to it.	(It's safer than saying my name is David Stein.)
CANDY: My name is Candy.	(At least my nickname is. He doesn't have to hear Hortense O'Brien.)
STRETCH: What kind of camera is that?	(Why couldn't a girl named Candy be Jewish? It's only a nickname, isn't it?)
CANDY: Just this old German one of my uncle's. I borrowed it from the office.	(He could be Irish. And that camera looks expensive.)
STRETCH: May I? (He takes her camera, brushing her hand and then tingling with the touch.) Fine lens. You work for your uncle?	(Now I've done it. Brought up work.)
CANDY: Ever since college.	(Okay, so what if I only went for a year?)
It's more than being just a secretary. I get into sales, too.	(If he asks what I sell, I'll tell him anything except underwear.)
STRETCH: Sales? That's funny. I'm in sales, too, but mainly as an executive. I run our department.	(Is there a nice way to say used cars? I'd better change the subject.)
I started using cameras on trips. Last time I was in the Bahamas.	(Great legs! And the way her hips move—)
CANDY: Oh! Do you go to the Bahamas, too? I love those islands.	(So I went just once, and it was for the brassiere manufacturers' convention. At least we're off the subject of jobs.)
STRETCH:	(She's probably been around. Well, at least we're off the subject of jobs.)
I did a little underwater work there last summer. Fantastic colours. So rich in life.	(And lonelier than hell.)

continued

They Say	(They Think)
CANDY:	(Look at that build. He must swim like a fish. I should learn.)
I wish I'd had time when I was there. I love the water.	(Well, I do. At the beach, anyway, where I can wade in and not go too deep.)

So begins a relationship. Candy and Stretch have a drink and talk, talk, talk—sharing their likes and dislikes. Amazingly, they seem to agree on everything, from clothing to cars to politics. The attraction they feel is very strong, and neither of them is willing to turn the other off by disagreeing.

Attraction

Let us explore some of the factors that determine interpersonal attraction.

Physical Attractiveness: How Important Is Looking Good?

We might like to think of ourselves as so sophisticated that physical attractiveness does not move us. We might like to claim that sensitivity, warmth, and intelligence are more important. However, we may never learn about other people's personalities if they do not meet our minimum standards for physical attractiveness. Research shows that physical attractiveness is a major determinant of interpersonal and sexual attraction (Langlois et al., 2000; Sangrador & Yela, 2000; Strassberg & Holty, 2003). In fact, physical appearance is the key factor in consideration of partners for dates, sex, and marriage (Hatfield & Sprecher, 1986).

IS BEAUTY IN THE EYE OF THE BEHOLDER?   What determines physical attractiveness? In certain African tribes, long necks and round, disklike lips are signs of feminine beauty. Women thus stretch their necks and lips to make themselves more appealing. Women of the Nama tribe persistently tug at their labia majora to make them "beautiful"—that is, prominent and elongated (Ford & Beach, 1951).

In our culture, women consider taller men to be more attractive (Pawlowski & Koziel, 2002). Undergraduate women prefer their dates to be about 15 centimetres (6 inches) taller than they are. Undergraduate men, on the average, prefer women who are about 11 centimetres ($4\frac{1}{2}$ inches) shorter (Gillis & Avis, 1980). Tall women are not viewed so positively. Shortness, though, is perceived as a liability for both men and women (Jackson & Ervin, 1992).

Female plumpness is valued in many preliterate societies (Anderson et al., 1992; Frayser, 1985). Wide hips and a broad pelvis are widely recognized as sexually appealing. In our culture, however, slenderness is in style. Some young women suffer from an eating disorder called **anorexia nervosa**, in which they literally starve themselves to conform to the contemporary ideal. Both genders find slenderness (though not anorexic thinness) attractive, especially for females (Fallon & Rozin, 1985; Franzoi & Herzog, 1987; Rozin & Fallon, 1988).

Both genders find obese people unattractive (Goode, 2000), but there are gender differences in impressions of the most pleasing body shape. On average, university men think their present physiques are close to ideal and appealing to women (Fallon & Rozin, 1985). University women generally see themselves as much heavier than the figure that is most alluring to men, and heavier still than the figure they perceive as the ideal feminine form.

Anorexia nervosa
A potentially life-threatening eating disorder characterized by refusal to maintain a healthful body weight, intense fear of being overweight, a distorted body image, and, in females, lack of menstruation (amenorrhea).

Beauty and Culture.
Can you find Mr. or Ms. Right among these people? Are your judgments of physical beauty based on universal standards or on your cultural experiences?

The hourglass figure is popular in Canada and the United States. In one study by researchers at Dalhousie University (Lalonde et al., 2004), female students rated women of average weight with a waist-to-hip ratio of 0.7 as most attractive. Small and medium waists were generally preferred, regardless of body weight. For the moderate and heavy figures, those with large hips received the lowest attractiveness ratings. With larger figures, a more tubular body shape was considered more attractive. The results indicated that in evaluating physical attractiveness, body weight, waist size, and hip size all interact to influence ratings of women's attractiveness.

Cohen and Tannenbaum (2001) conducted an Internet study in which they posted various women's body shapes and asked lesbian and bisexual women to indicate which were most sexually attractive to them. The respondents, like heterosexual men and women, found women with a 0.7 waist-to-hip body ratio to be the most sexually attractive. However, they differed from the heterosexual women and men in that their first choice was for *heavy* women with a 0.7 waist-to-hip body ratio and large breasts. Their second choice was for heavy women with the same waist-to-hip body ratio but with small breasts. The authors suggest that the women in this study were rejecting what they might view as societal emphasis on excessive slenderness.

Do men idealize the *Penthouse* centrefold? What bust size do men prefer? Women's beliefs that men prefer large breasts may be somewhat exaggerated. The belief that men want women to have bursting bustlines leads many women to seek breast implants in the attempt to live up to an ideal that men themselves don't generally hold (Rosenthal, 1992). Researchers in one study showed young men and women (aged 17 to 25 years) a continuum of male and female figures that differed only in the size of the bust for the female figures and in that of the pectorals for the male figures (Thompson & Tantleff, 1992). The participants were asked to indicate the ideal size for their own gender and the size they believed the average man and woman would prefer.

The results show some support for the "big is better" stereotype—for both men and women. Women's conception of ideal bust size was greater than their actual average size. Men preferred women with still larger breasts, but not nearly so large as the breasts women *believed* that men prefer. Men believed that their male peers preferred women with much bustier figures than their peers themselves said they preferred. Ample breasts and chests may be preferred by the other gender, but people seem to have an exaggerated idea of the sizes that the other gender actually prefers. And some women, of course, have too much of a good thing. Some of them go for breast-reduction surgery.

People who are attractive know it. In one study, men and women rated each other for attractiveness and also rated themselves (Marcus & Miller, 2003). By and large, the individuals' self-ratings meshed with those by others, both female and male. Women's judgments were most closely related to how men perceived them, suggesting that they were reflecting men's opinions of them more so than women's.

HOW TRAITS AFFECT PERCEPTIONS OF PHYSICAL ATTRACTIVENESS: ON THE IMPORTANCE OF NOT BEING ERNEST What factors other than physical appearance contribute to attractiveness? Gender-role expectations may affect perceptions of attractiveness. For example, women are more likely to be attracted to socially dominant men than men are to be attracted to socially dominant women (Buunk et al., 2002). Women who viewed videos of prospective dates found men who acted outgoing and self-expressive more appealing than men who were passive (Riggio & Woll, 1984). Another study found that highly feminine women are more likely to be attracted to dominant "macho" men than less feminine women are (Maybach & Gold, 1994). Yet men who viewed videos in the Riggio and Woll (1984) study were put off by outgoing, self-expressive behaviour in women. In yet another study, women rated videos of dominant college men (defined in this study as social control over a troublesome interaction with an instructor) as more appealing than submissive men. Again, male viewers were put off by similarly dominant women (Sadalla et al., 1987). Men are more likely to be jealous of socially dominant men, whereas women are more likely to be jealous of physically attractive women (Dijkstra & Buunk, 2002).

WHAT DO YOU LOOK FOR IN A LONG-TERM, MEANINGFUL RELATIONSHIP? In a survey of university men and women in the early 1980s, physical attractiveness rated high in a partner for a sexual relationship. However, for a meaningful, long-term relationship, both men and women rated psychological characteristics such as warmth, fidelity, honesty, and sensitivity as more important than physical attractiveness (Nevid, 1984). (Nevertheless, physical appeal probably plays a "filtering" role. Unless a prospective date meets minimal physical standards, we might not look beneath the surface for "more meaningful" traits.) For both types of relationships, men placed more emphasis on physical characteristics than did women. Women placed more value on qualities such as warmth, assertiveness, wit, and ambition.

Nevid's results have been replicated in several studies. Women place relatively greater emphasis than men on such traits as vocational status, earning potential, expressiveness, kindness, consideration, dependability, and fondness for children. Men give relatively more consideration to youth, physical attractiveness, cooking ability (can't they switch on the microwave by themselves?), and frugality (Howard et al., 1987; Sprecher et al., 1994). When it comes to mate selection, females in a sample of students from Germany and the Netherlands also emphasized the financial prospects and status of a potential mate, whereas males emphasized the importance of physical attractiveness (de Raad & Doddema-Winsemius, 1992). A study of more than 200 Korean college students found that in mate selection, women placed more emphasis than men on education, jobs, and family of origin (Brown, 1994). Men placed more emphasis on physical attractiveness and affection. (Yes, men were more "romantic" and women more pragmatic.)

A World of Diversity

WIDE-EYED WITH . . . BEAUTY?

Some aspects of beauty seem to be largely cross-cultural. Research suggests that European Americans, African Americans, Asian Americans, and Latino and Latina Americans tend to agree on the facial features that they find to be attractive (Cunningham et al., 1995). They all prefer female faces with large eyes, greater distance between the eyes, small noses, narrower faces with smaller chins, high, expressive eyebrows, larger lower lips, and a well-groomed, full head of hair.

Consider the methodology of a study that compared the facial preferences of people in Japan and England. Perrett (1994) created computer composites of the faces of 60 women. Figure 6.1(a) is a composite of the 15 women who were rated the most attractive. He then used computer enhancement to exaggerate the differences between the composite of the 60—that is, the average face—and the composite of the 15 most attractive women. He found that both Japanese and British men deemed women with large eyes, high cheekbones, and narrow jaws to be the most attractive (Perret, 1994). Computer enhancement resulted in the image shown in Figure 6.1(b). The enhanced composite has even larger eyes, yet higher cheekbones, and a still narrower jaw. Figure 6.1(b) was then rated as the most attractive image. Similar results were

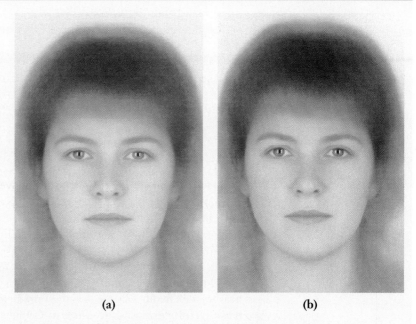

(a)   **(b)**

Figure 6.1 What Features Contribute to Facial Attractiveness?

In both England and Japan, features such as large eyes, high cheekbones, and narrow jaws contribute to perceptions of the attractiveness of women. (a) A computer composite of the faces of 15 women rated as the most attractive of a group of 60. (b) A computer composite that exaggerates the features of these 15 women. That is, they are developed further in the direction that separates them from the average of the full group.

found for the image of a Japanese woman.

Susan Sprecher and her colleagues (1994) surveyed a national probability sample of 13 017 English- or Spanish-speaking people, age 19 or above, living in households in the United States. In one section of their questionnaire, they asked respondents how willing they would be to marry someone who was older, younger, of a different religion, not likely to hold a steady job, not good-looking, and so forth. Each item was followed by a 7-point scale in which 1 meant "not at all willing" and 7 meant "very willing." As shown in Table 6.1, women were more willing than men to marry someone who was not good-looking. On the other hand, women were less willing to marry someone not likely to hold a steady job.

A World of Diversity

GENDER DIFFERENCES IN PREFERENCES IN MATES ACROSS 37 CULTURES

What do men in Nigeria, Japan, Brazil, Canada, and the United States have in common? For one thing, men in these countries report that they prefer mates who are younger than themselves. Buss (1994) reviewed survey evidence on the preferred age difference between oneself and one's mate in 37 cultures (representing 33 countries) in Europe, Africa, Asia, Australia, New Zealand, and North and South America. In every culture, men pre-

ferred younger mates (the range was from 0.38 year to 6.45 years). Women, however, preferred older mates (the range was from 1.82 years to 5.1 years). Gender differences in the preferred age of mates paralleled actual differences in age of men and women at the time of marriage.

Buss finds that in all 37 cultures, men placed greater value on a prospective partner's "good looks" than did women. On the other hand, women in 36 of the 37 cultures placed greater value on "good earning capacity" in prospective mates.

The consistency of Buss's findings lends credence to the notion that

there are widespread gender differences in preferences with respect to age, physical characteristics, and financial status of prospective mates. Generally speaking, men place greater value on the physical attractiveness and relative youth of prospective mates. Women place relatively greater value on the earning capacity of prospective mates. Buss interprets women's preferences for relatively older mates as additional evidence that women appraise future mates on the basis of their ability to provide for a wife and family, because age and income tend to be linked among men.

In 2005 the Compas survey asked a national sample of Canadians what they felt should be the attributes of the ideal spouse. The men valued only one characteristic more than did the women: "good-looking." Women valued such traits as "manages money well," "is financially successful," "is well educated and intelligent," and "shares your religion" more highly than did the men.

There have been relatively few studies of mate preference attributes among ethnic groups in Canada. Researchers at York University (Lalonde et al., 2004) found that among second-generation Southeast Asians the strength of connectedness to one's family was the strongest predictor of traditional mate attribute preference. Despite extensive exposure to Canadian values, most respondents preferred their future spouses to have traditional attributes. Men had more traditional sex-role expectations than did women.

ARE ATTRACTIVENESS PREFERENCES INHERITED? On the surface, gender differences in perceptions of attractiveness seem unbearably sexist, and perhaps they are. Yet some evolutionary psychologists believe that evolutionary forces favour the continuation of gender differences in preferences for mates because certain preferred traits offer reproductive advantages (Bjorklund & Kipp, 1996; Fisher, 2000). Some physical features, such as cleanliness, good complexion, clear eyes, good teeth, good hair, firm muscle tone, and a steady gait are universally appealing to both genders (Ford & Beach, 1951). Perhaps they are markers of reproductive potential (Symons, 1995). Youth and health may be relatively more important to a woman's appeal because these characteristics tend to be associated with her reproductive capacity: the "biological clock" limits her reproductive potential. Physical characteristics associated with a woman's youthfulness, such as smooth skin, firm muscle tone, and lustrous hair, may thus have become more closely linked to a woman's appeal (Buss, 1994). A man's reproductive value, however, may depend more on how well he can provide for his family than on his age or physical appeal. The value of men as reproducers, therefore, is more intertwined with factors that contribute to a stable environment for child rearing, such as economic status and

TABLE 6.1
Gender Differences in Mate Preferences

How willing would you be to marry someone who ...	Men	Women
was not "good-looking"?	3.41	4.42**
was older than you by 5 or more years?	4.15	5.29**
was younger than you by 5 or more years?	4.54	2.80**
was not likely to hold a steady job?	2.73	1.62**
would earn much less than you?	4.60	3.76**
would earn much more than you?	5.19	5.93**
had more education than you?	5.22	5.82**
had less education than you?	4.67	4.08**
had been married before?	3.35	3.44
already had children?	2.84	3.11*
was of a different religion?	4.24	4.31
was of a different race?	3.08	2.84**

*Difference statistically significant at the 0.01 level of confidence.

**Difference statistically significant at the 0.001 level of confidence.

Source: Based on information in Susan Sprecher, Quintin Sullivan, and Elaine Hatfield (1994). "Mate Selection Preferences: Gender Differences Examined in a National Sample." Journal of Personality and Social Psychology, 66(6), 1074–1080. Copyright © 1994 by the American Psychological Association. Reprinted by permission.

reliability. Evolutionary psychologists argue that these gender differences in mate preferences may have been passed down through the generations as part of our genetic heritage (Buss, 1994; Symons, 1995).

Men's interest in younger women occurs in both preliterate and industrialized societies (Buss, 1994). However, it is not only heterosexual men who prefer younger partners.

Research in Action

PARTNER PREFERENCES AND AGE, GENDER, AND ORIENTATION

Researchers at Queen's University in Ontario compared the age-based partner preferences of heterosexual men, heterosexual women, gay men, and lesbians (Silverthorne & Quinsey, 2000). Adults were shown pictures of 15 male and 15 female faces arranged into five age categories ranging from 18 to 60 years. The lesbians rated female faces aged 42 to 60 as most attractive and 19-year-olds as least attractive. Both gay and heterosexual men found younger partners to be more sexually appealing than did the women. Gay men rated younger partners as more sexually appealing than did the heterosexual men. Conversely, lesbians rated older partners as more sexually appealing than did the heterosexual women.

In another study of gay and bisexual men in three Ontario cities, Barry Adam (2000a) of Windsor University found that there was widespread acknowledgment of the ideal of youthfulness in the gay community. In particular, men who preferred men older than themselves noted that they often faced ridicule as a result. Nevertheless, the study showed considerable diversity in the age preferences of gay and bisexual men.

Who Is Right for You? Research shows that people tend to pair off with others who are similar in physical characteristics and personality traits.

Female jealousy of younger women is another thread that spans cultures. Sexual competition, according to Margaret Mead, generally involves

> the struggle between stronger older men and weaker younger men or between more attractive younger women and more entrenched older ones. (Mead, 1967, p. 198)

The evolutionary view of gender differences in preferences for mates is largely speculative and not fully consistent with the evidence. Despite gender differences, both men and women report that they place greater weight on personal characteristics than on physical features in judging prospective mates (Buss, 1994). Many women, like men, do prefer physically appealing partners (Bixler, 1989). Women also tend to marry men similar to themselves in physical attractiveness as well as socioeconomic standing. Note also that older men are more likely than younger men to die from natural causes. From the standpoint of reproductive advantages, women would thus achieve greater success by marrying fit, younger males who are likely to survive during the child-rearing years than by marrying older, higher-status males. Moreover, similar cultural influences, rather than inherited dispositions, may explain commonalities across cultures in gender differences in mate preferences. For example, in societies in which women are economically dependent on men, a man's appeal may depend more on his financial resources than on his physical appeal.

The Matching Hypothesis: Who Is "Right" for You?

Do not despair if you are less than exquisite in appearance, along with most of us mere mortals. You may be saved from permanently blending in with the wallpaper by the effects of the **matching hypothesis**. This concept holds that people tend to develop romantic relationships with people who are similar to themselves in physical attractiveness rather than with the local Will Smith or Britney Spears look-alike.

Researchers have found that people who are dating steadily, engaged, or married tend to be matched in physical attractiveness (Kalick, 1988). Young married couples even tend to be matched in weight (Schafer & Keith, 1990). The central motive for seeking "matches" seems to be fear of rejection by more appealing people (Bernstein et al., 1983).

Matching hypothesis The concept that people tend to develop romantic relationships with people who are similar to themselves in attractiveness.

There are exceptions to the matching hypothesis. Now and then we find a beautiful woman married to a plain or homely man (or vice versa). How do we explain it? What, after all, would *she* see in *him*? According to one study (Bar-Tal & Saxe, 1976), people judging "mismatched" pairs may tend to ascribe wealth, intelligence, or success to the man. We seek an unseen factor that will balance the physical attractiveness of one partner. For some mismatched couples, similarities in attitudes and personalities may balance out differences in physical attractiveness.

MORE THAN BEAUTY Matching applies not only to physical appeal. Our sex and marital partners tend to be like us in race and ethnicity, age, level of education, and religion. According to the 1996 census, 95% of Canadians choose partners (married or common-law) of the same racial background as their own (Riedmann, Lamanna, & Nelson, 2003). Another reason is that we are drawn to people whose attitudes are similar to ours. People similar in background are more likely to be similar in their attitudes. Similarity in attitudes and tastes is a key contributor to attraction, friendships, and love relationships (Cappella & Palmer, 1990; Griffin & Sparks, 1990; Laumann et al., 1994).

Let us also note a gender difference. Evidence shows that women place greater weight than men on attitude similarity as a determinant of attraction to a stranger of the other gender, whereas men place more value on physical attractiveness (Feingold, 1991).

We also tend to *assume* that people we find attractive share our attitudes (Dawes, 1989; Marks et al., 1981). When sexual attraction is strong, perhaps we want to think that we can iron out all the kinks in the relationship. Although similarity may be important in determining initial attraction, compatibility appears to be a stronger predictor of maintaining an intimate relationship (Vinacke et al., 1988).

Has anyone told you that you are good-looking, brilliant, and emotionally mature to boot? That your taste is elegant? Ah, what superb judgment!

Reciprocity: If You Like Me, You Must Have Excellent Judgment

When we feel admired and complimented, we tend to return these feelings and behaviours. This is called **reciprocity**. Reciprocity is a potent determinant of attraction (Condon & Crano, 1988). We tend to be much more warm, helpful, and candid when we are with strangers who we believe like us (Clark et al., 1989; Curtis & Miller, 1986). We even tend to welcome positive comments from others when we know those remarks to be inaccurate (Swann et al., 1987).

Perhaps the power of reciprocity has enabled many couples to become happy with one another and reasonably well adjusted. By reciprocating positive words and actions, a person can perhaps stoke neutral or mild feelings into robust, affirmative feelings of attraction.

Reciprocity Mutual exchange.

A World of Diversity

"THE (ELECTRONIC) NEARNESS OF YOU"

Physical closeness, or proximity, has always been a factor in interpersonal attraction. People have always been drawn to the boy or girl next door (or next cave?). People tend to form romantic relationships with the people they meet in the neighbourhood, in school, in their religious community, or on the job.

In the age of electronics, proximity is paradoxical. You can find yourself corresponding with, and perhaps feeling attracted to, people who are as close as the monitor in front of your nose, yet thousands of miles away in the flesh.

When you meet somebody in person, you immediately observe what they look like, you hear their voice, and—according to some researchers—perhaps you get something like a sniff of their pheromones. But when you meet somebody in a chatroom or a computer-mediated multiuser dungeon, the cues that might spark interest are different. Mantovani (2001) notes that in the case of online relationships, the use of the written (keyboarded) language becomes more important; timing and the speed of writing and responding are crucial; and punctuation and those smi-

ley-faced emoticons can all make a difference. But frequency of contact in the virtual world, as in the real world, plays a role. (Levine, 2000; Mantovani, 2001). Visiting the same chatroom repeatedly allows mutual awareness to develop and suggests similarity in interests.

Deb Levine (2000) notes that people are more likely to disclose intimate information about themselves on the Internet, perhaps because the actual—or unknown—distance between the parties provides a sense of security. Similarly, other people are quicker to reciprocate expressions of interest. Levine notes that flirting and erotic activity on the Internet can be extremely exciting, but they can also build unrealistic expectations and dis-

qualify participants for relationships in the physical world. (Would you want to have a real-world relationship with someone who quickly enters sexual discussions online?)

Levine and Mantovani both warn that expressions of similarity are easy to feign on the net. Levine (2000) warns against becoming overly wrapped up in people who are reluctant to exchange sound files or pictures. And she adds that it makes sense to meet in the real world within a month or so to check out the accuracy of computer-mediated impressions—preferably in a safe, public place.

Attraction can lead to feelings of love. Let us now turn to that most fascinating topic.

"Surfing Blind?"
What "rules" of interpersonal attraction apply when people meet online? They cannot directly see or hear each other, so what cues do they rely on to determine whether there is a fit? What happens when one person wants to see, hear, or meet the other?

Columbia University's "Go Ask Alice"
Offers online advice about relationships in a question-and-answer format.
www.goaskalice. columbia.edu

Love

Romantic love is hardly unique to our culture. Researchers report finding evidence of romantic love in 147 of the 166 different cultures they studied in a recent cross-cultural comparison (Jankowiak & Fischer, 1992).

Our culture idealizes the concept of romantic love. Thus, we readily identify with the plight of the "star-crossed" lovers in *Romeo and Juliet* and *West Side Story*, who sacrificed themselves for love. We learn that "love makes the world go round" and that "love is everything." In Reginald Bibby's (2001) survey of Canadian teenagers, three-quarters viewed being loved as a very important goal. About one-half of adult Canadians report that they are very satisfied with the amount of love in their lives (*Maclean's*, 1998). Like other aspects of sexual and social behaviour among humans, the concept of love must be understood within a cultural context. Luckily (or miserably), we have such a context in Western culture.

The Greek Heritage

The concept of love can be traced back at least as far as the classical age of Greece. The Greeks distinguished four concepts related to the modern meanings of love: **storge**, **agape**, **philia**, and **eros**.

Eros is closest in meaning to our concept of passion. Eros was a character in Greek mythology (transformed in Roman mythology into Cupido, now called Cupid) who would shoot unsuspecting people with his love arrows, causing them to fall madly in love with the person who was nearest to them at the time. Erotic love embraces sudden passionate desire: "love at first sight" and "falling head over heels in love." Younger university students are more likely to believe in love at first sight and that "love conquers all" than older (and wiser?) university students (Knox et al., 1999). Passion can be so gripping that one is convinced one's life has been changed forever. This feeling of sudden transformation was captured by the Italian poet Dante Alighieri (1265–1321), who exclaimed upon first beholding his beloved Beatrice, "*Incipit vita nuova*," which can be translated as "My life begins anew." Romantic love can also be earthy and sexy. In fact, sexual arousal and desire may be the strongest component of passionate or romantic love. Romantic love begins with a powerful physical attraction or feelings of passion and is associated with strong physiological arousal.

Unlike the Greeks, we tend to use the word *love* to describe everything from feelings of affection toward another to romantic ardour to sexual intercourse ("making love"). Still, different types or styles of love are recognized in our own culture, as we shall see.

Romantic Love in Contemporary Western Culture

The experience of *romantic love*, as opposed to loving attachment or sexual arousal per se, occurs within a cultural context in which the concept is idealized. Western culture has a long tradition of idealizing the concept of romantic love, as represented, for instance, by romantic fairy tales that have been passed down through the generations. In fact, our exposure to the concept of romantic love may begin with hearing the fairy tales of Sleeping Beauty, Cinderella, and Snow White—along with their princes charming. Later, perhaps, the concept of romantic love blossoms with exposure to romantic novels, television and film scripts, and the heady tales of friends and relatives.

During adolescence, strong sexual arousal, along with an idealized image of the object of our desires, leads us to label our feelings as love. We may learn to speak of love rather than lust, because sexual desire in the absence of a committed relationship might be viewed as primitive or animalistic. Being "in love" ennobles attraction and sexual arousal, not only to society but also to oneself. Unlike lust, love can be discussed at the dinner table. If others think we are too young to experience "the real thing"—which presumably includes knowledge of and respect for the other person's personality traits—our feelings may be called "puppy love" or a "crush."

Western society maintains much of the double standard toward sexuality. Thus, women are more often expected to justify sexual experiences as involving someone they love. Young men usually need not attribute sexual urges to love, so men are more likely to deem love a "mushy" concept. The vast majority of people in Canada

Storge (STORE-gay)
Loving attachment and non-sexual affection; the type of emotion that binds parents to children.

Agape (AH-gah-pay)
Selfless love; a kind of love that is similar to generosity and charity.

Philia (FEEL-yuh)
Friendship love, which is based on liking and respect rather than sexual desire.

Eros The kind of love that is closest in meaning to the modern-day concept of passion.

Infatuation or "True Love"?
Infatuation is a state of intense absorption in another person.
It is characterized by sexual longing and general excitement.
Infatuation is often referred to as passion or a crush.
Infatuation is assumed to fade as relationships develop.

nonetheless believe that romantic love is a prerequisite to marriage. Romantic love is rated by Canadian young people as the most important reason for marriage (Compas, 1998).

When reciprocated, romantic love is usually a source of deep fulfillment and ecstasy. When love is unrequited, however, it can lead to emptiness, anxiety, or despair. Romantic love can thus teeter between states of ecstasy and misery (Hatfield, 1988). Perhaps no other feature of our lives can lift us up so high or plunge us so low as romantic love.

INFATUATION VERSUS "TRUE LOVE": WILL TIME TELL?

Perhaps you first noticed each other when your eyes met across a crowded room, like the star-crossed lovers in *West Side Story*. Or perhaps you met when you were both assigned to the same Bunsen burner in chemistry lab—less romantic, but closer to the flame. However it happened, the meeting triggered such an electric charge through your body that you could not get him (or her) out of your mind. Were you truly in love, however, or was it merely a passing fancy? Was it infatuation or "the real thing"—a "true," lasting, and mutual love? How do you tell them apart?

Perhaps you don't, at least not at first. **Infatuation** is a state of intense absorption in or focus on another person. It is usually accompanied by sexual desire, elation, and general physiological arousal or excitement. Some refer to infatuation as "passion." Others dub it a "crush." Both monikers suggest that it is a passing fancy. In infatuation, your heart may pound whenever the other person draws near or enters your fantasies.

For the first month or two, infatuation and the more enduring forms of romantic love are hard to differentiate. At first, both may be characterized by intense focusing or absorption. Infatuated people may become so absorbed that they cannot sleep, work, or carry out routine chores. Logic and reason are swept aside. Infatuated people hold idealized images of their love objects and overlook their faults. Caution may be cast to the winds. In some cases, couples in the throes of infatuation rush to get married, only to find, a few weeks or months later, that they are not well suited to each other

As time goes on, signs that distinguish infatuation from a lasting romantic love begin to emerge. The partners begin to view each other more realistically and are better able to determine whether the relationship should continue. Although the tendency to idealize one's lover is strongest at the outset of a relationship, we should note that a so-called "positive illusion" tends to persist in relationships (Martz et al., 1998). That is, we maintain some tendency to differentiate our partners from the average and also to differentiate the value of our relationships from the average.

Infatuation has been likened to a state of love (Sternberg, 1986) that is based on intense feelings of passion but not on the deeper feelings of attachment and caring that typify a more lasting mutual love. Although infatuation may be a passing fancy, it can be supplanted by the deeper feelings of attachment and caring that characterize more lasting love relationships.

Note, too, that infatuation is not a necessary first step on the path to a lasting mutual love. Some couples develop deep feelings of love without ever experiencing the fireworks of infatuation (Sternberg, 1986). And sometimes one partner is infatuated while the other manages to keep his or her head below the clouds.

Infatuation A state of intense absorption in or focus on another person, which is usually accompanied by sexual desire, elation, and general physiological arousal or excitement; passion.

Contemporary Models of Love: Dare Science Intrude?

Despite the importance of love, scientists have historically paid little attention to it. Some people believe that love cannot be analyzed scientifically. Love, they maintain, should be left to the poets, philosophers, and theologians. Yet researchers are now applying the scientific method to the study of love. They recognize that love is a complex concept, involving many areas of experience—emotional, cognitive, and motivational (Sternberg & Grajek, 1984). They have reinforced the Greek view that there are different kinds and styles of love. Let us consider some of the views of love that have emerged from modern theorists and researchers.

LOVE AS APPRAISAL OF AROUSAL   Social psychologists Ellen Berscheid and Elaine Hatfield (Berscheid & Walster, 1978; Walster & Walster, 1978) define **romantic love** in terms of a state of intense physiological arousal and the cognitive appraisal of that arousal as love. The physiological arousal may be experienced as a pounding heart, sweaty palms, and butterflies in the stomach when one is in the presence of, or thinks about, one's love interest. Cognitive appraisal of the arousal means attributing it to some cause, such as fear or love. The perception that one has fallen in love is thus derived from several simultaneous events: (1) a state of intense physiological arousal that is connected with an appropriate love object (that is, a person, not an event like a rock concert), (2) a cultural setting that idealizes romantic love, and (3) the attribution of the arousal to feelings of love toward the person.

STYLES OF LOVE   Some psychologists speak in terms of *styles* of love. Susan and Clyde Hendrick (2002) speak of love as a positive emotion that contributes to happiness, feelings of psychological well-being, and optimism about the future. The Hendricks (2003) developed a Love Attitude Scale that suggests the existence of six styles of love. The following is a list of these styles. Each one is exemplified by statements similar to those on the original scale. As you can see, the styles owe a debt to the Greeks:

1. *Romantic love (eros):* "My lover fits my ideal." "My lover and I were attracted to one another immediately."

2. *Game-playing love (ludus):* "I keep my lover up in the air about my commitment." "I get over love affairs pretty easily."

3. *Friendship (storge, philia):* "The best love grows out of an enduring friendship."

4. *Logical love (pragma):* "I consider a lover's potential in life before committing myself." "I consider whether my lover will be a good parent."

5. *Possessive, excited love (mania):* "I get so excited about my love that I cannot sleep." "When my lover ignores me, I get sick all over."

6. *Selfless love (agape):* "I would do anything I can to help my lover." "My lover's needs and wishes are more important than my own."

Most people who are "in love" experience a number of these styles, but the Hendricks (1986) found some interesting gender differences in styles of love. University men are significantly more likely to develop game-playing and romantic love styles. University women are more apt to develop friendly, logical, and possessive love styles.

STERNBERG'S TRIANGULAR THEORY OF LOVE   Psychologist Robert Sternberg (1986, 1988) offers a "triangular theory" of love that organizes the relationships among kinds of love discussed by many theorists, including passionate love, romantic love, and companionate love (Hatfield & Rapson, 2002; Hendrick & Hendrick, 2003). The three components of love are:

Romantic love A kind of love characterized by feelings of passion and intimacy.

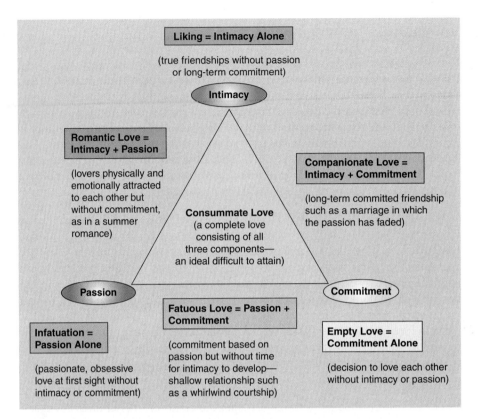

Figure 6.2 The Triangular Model of Love.

According to psychologist Robert Sternberg, love consists of three components, represented by the vertices of this triangle. Various kinds of love consist of different combinations of these components. Romantic love, for example, consists of passion and intimacy. Consummate love—the cultural ideal—consists of all three.

1. *Intimacy:* the experience of warmth toward another person that arises from feelings of closeness, bondedness, and connectedness to the other. Intimacy also involves the desire to give and receive emotional support and to share one's innermost thoughts with the other.

2. *Passion:* an intense romantic or sexual desire for another person, which is accompanied by physiological arousal.

3. *Commitment:* a component of love that involves *dedication* to maintaining the relationship through good times and bad.

According to Sternberg's model, love can be conceptualized in terms of a triangle in which each vertex represents one of these basic elements of love (see Figure 6.2). The way the components are balanced can be represented by the shape of the triangle. For example, a love in which all three components are equally balanced—as in consummate love—would be represented by an equilateral triangle, as in Figure 6.2.

Couples are apparently well matched if they possess corresponding levels of passion, intimacy, and commitment (Drigotas et al., 1999; Sternberg, 1988). Compatibility can be represented visually in terms of the congruence of the love triangles. Figure 6.3(a) shows a perfect match, in which the triangles are congruent. Figure 6.3(b) depicts a good match; the partners are similar in the three dimensions. Figure 6.3(c) shows a mismatch; major differences exist between the partners on all three components. Relationships may run aground when partners are mismatched. A relationship may fizzle, rather than sizzle, if one partner experiences more pas-

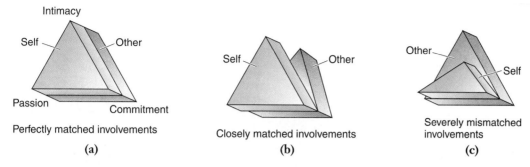

Figure 6.3 Compatibility and Incompatibility, According to the Triangular Model of Love.

Compatibility in terms of Sternberg's types of love can be represented as triangles. (a) A perfect match in which triangles are congruent. (b) A good match; the partners are similar on the three dimensions. (c) A mismatch. Major differences exist between the partners on all three components.

sion than the other, or if one wants a long-term relationship when the other's idea of commitment is to stay the whole night.

According to the Sternberg model, various combinations of the three elements of love characterize different types of love relationships (Sternberg, 1986, 1988) (see Figure 6.3). For example, *infatuation* (passionate love) is typified by strong sexual desire, but not by intimacy and commitment. The partners may each feel passionate love for the other, or such feelings may go unrequited.

Liking is a basis for friendship. It consists of feelings of closeness and emotional warmth without passion or commitment. Liking is not felt toward passing acquaintances. It is reserved for people to whom one feels close enough to share one's innermost feelings and thoughts. We sometimes develop these intimate relationships without making the commitment to maintaining a long-term relationship that typifies other types of love. Liking may develop into a passionate love, however, or into a more committed form of friendship called *companionate love* by many writers, including Sternberg (1988), Clyde and Susan Hendrick (2003), and Elaine Hatfield (Hatfield & Rapson, 2002).

Can lovers also be friends, or shall the twain never meet? There is no reason why people in love should not become good friends—perhaps even the best of friends. Sternberg's model recognizes that the intimacy we find in true friendships and the passion we find in love are blended in two forms of love: romantic love and consummate love. These types of love differ along the dimension of commitment, however.

Romantic love has both passion and intimacy but lacks commitment. Romantic love may burn brightly and then flicker out. Or it may develop into a more complete love, called *consummate love*, in which all three components flower. Desire is accompanied by a deeper intimacy and commitment. The flames of passion can be stoked across the years, even if they do not burn quite so brightly as they once did. Consummate love is most special, and it certainly is an ideal toward which many Westerners strive.

In *empty love*, by contrast, there is nothing *but* commitment. Neither the warm, emotional embrace of intimacy nor the flame of passion exists. With empty love, one's lover is a person whom one tolerates and remains with because of a sense of duty. People often remain in an empty-love relationship because of either personal prescription or social prescription (Cox et al., 1997). *Personal prescription* is based on the belief that one should persist in a relationship. *Social prescription* is based on the belief that one's friends or family members believe that it is right to persist in a relationship.

Applied Knowledge

UNDERSTANDING THE PHASES OF LOVE

Although romantic love may become transformed into companionate love, the process by which this transformation takes place remains vague (Shaver et al., 1988). Companionate love, however, need not be sexless or lacking in romance. Although passion may have ebbed, the giving and receiving of sexual pleasure can help strengthen bonds. Partners may feel that their sex lives have even become more deeply satisfying as they seek to please each other by practising what they have learned about each other's sexual needs and wants.

The balance among Sternberg's three aspects of love is likely to shift through the course of a relationship. A healthy dose of all three components—found in consummate love—typifies, for many of us, an ideal marriage. At the outset of marriage, passions may be strong but intimacy weak. Couples may only just be getting to know each other's innermost thoughts and feelings. Time alone does not cause intimacy and commitment to grow, however. Some couples are able to peer into each other's deeper selves and form meaningful commitments at relatively early stages in their relationships. Other long-married couples may remain distant or waver in their commitment. Some couples experience only a faint flickering of passion early in the relationship. Then it becomes quickly extinguished. For some, the flames of passion burn ever bright. Yet many married couples find that passion tends to fade while intimacy and commitment grow stronger.

Knowing about these components of love may help couples avoid pitfalls. Couples who recognize that passion exerts a strong pull early in a relationship may be less likely to rush into marriage. Couples who recognize that it is normal for passions to fade may avoid assuming that their love is at an end when it may simply be changing into a deeper, more intimate and committed form of love. This knowledge may also encourage couples to focus on finding ways of rekindling the embers of romance, rather than looking to escape at the first sign that the embers have cooled.

Sometimes a love relationship has both passion and commitment but lacks intimacy. Sternberg calls this *fatuous (foolish) love*. Fatuous love is associated with whirlwind courtships that burn brightly but briefly as the partners come to realize that they are not well matched. Intimacy can develop in such relationships, but couples who rush into marriage often find that the realities of marriage give the lie to their expectations:

> They expect a marriage made in heaven, but do not realize what they must do truly to maintain such a marriage. They base the relationship on passion and are disappointed when the passion starts to fade. They feel short-changed—they have gotten much less than they bargained for. The problem, of course, is that they bargained for too much of one thing [passion] and not enough of another [intimacy]. (Sternberg, 1988, p. 128)

In *companionate love*, finally, intimacy and commitment are strong, but passion is lacking. This form of love typifies long-term (so-called Platonic) friendships and those marriages in which passion has ebbed but a deep and abiding friendship remains (Hatfield & Rapson, 2002).

In this chapter, we have discussed interpersonal attraction—the force that initiates social contact. In the next chapter, we follow the development of social contacts into intimate relationships.

Summing Up

Attraction

A number of factors determine interpersonal attraction.

Physical Attractiveness: How Important Is Looking Good?

Physical attractiveness is a major determinant of sexual attraction. In our culture, slenderness is in style. Both genders consider smiling faces more attractive. Socially dominant men, but not dominant women, are usually found attractive. Women place greater emphasis on such traits as vocational status and earning potential, whereas men give more consideration to physical attractiveness. Some evolutionary psychologists believe that evolutionary forces favour such gender differences in preferred traits because these traits offer reproductive advantages.

The Matching Hypothesis: Who Is Right for You?

According to the matching hypothesis, people tend to develop romantic relationships with people who are similar to themselves in attractiveness.

Similarity in Attitudes: Do Opposites Attract?

Similarity in attitudes and tastes is a strong contributor to attraction, friendships, and love relationships.

Reciprocity: If You Like Me, You Must Have Excellent Judgment

Through reciprocation of positive words and actions, neutral or mild feelings may be stoked into feelings of attraction.

Love

In our culture, we are brought up to idealize the concept of romantic love.

The Greek Heritage

The Greeks had four concepts related to the modern meanings of love: storge, agape, philia, and eros.

Romantic Love in Contemporary Western Culture

Western culture has a long tradition of idealizing the concept of romantic love. Most people in Canada see romantic love as a prerequisite to marriage. Early in a relationship, infatuation and more enduring forms of romantic love may be indistinguishable.

Contemporary Models of Love: Dare Science Intrude?

Researchers are now applying the scientific method to the study of love.

Berscheid and Hatfield define romantic love in terms of intense physiological arousal and cognitive appraisal of that arousal as love.

Hendrick and Hendrick suggest that there are six styles of love among college students: romantic love, game-playing love, friendship, logical love, possessive love, and selfless love.

Sternberg suggests that there are three distinct components of love: intimacy, passion, and commitment. Various combinations of these components typify different kinds of love. Romantic love is characterized by the combination of passion and intimacy.

Test Yourself

Multiple-Choice Questions

1. **Research suggests that**
   a. smaller waist-to-hip ratios in women are generally considered more attractive
   b. heavier females are considered more attractive
   c. there are universal standards of attractiveness
   d. shorter males are considered more attractive

2. **University men on average think that their physique is?**
   a. too heavy to appeal to women
   b. not muscular enough to appeal to women
   c. close to ideal
   d. less attractive than that of their friends

3. **Female university students generally see themselves as**
   a. attractive enough to "get" most men
   b. smaller than they actually are
   c. much heavier than the ideal
   d. more attractive than their friends

4. **A number of studies have shown that**
   a. men are more attracted to socially dominant women
   b. women are more attracted to socially dominant men
   c. there are no gender differences in attraction
   d. social dominance is not important in attraction

5. **Research suggests that regardless of ethnicity, men find all of the following attractive in women except**
   a. large eyes
   b. wide-set eyes
   c. full lower lips
   d. heavy eyebrows

6. **In choosing a mate, women generally place greater emphasis than men on _____, while men place greater emphasis on _____.**

   a. earning potential, warmth, and dependability; youth and physical attractiveness
   b. physical strength; education and intelligence
   c. political and social attitudes; family background
   d. men and women have the same preferences

7. **The idea that people are more likely to look for romantic relationships with those who are similar to themselves is known as the**
   a. reciprocity theory
   b. matching hypothesis
   c. love profile
   d. intimacy theory

8. **The ancient Greeks distinguished between _____ varieties of love.**
   a. one
   b. two
   c. three
   d. four

9. **Sternberg's triangular theory of love includes intimacy, passion, and _____.**
   a. reciprocity
   b. sexuality
   c. commitment
   d. delight

10. **In the early stages of a relationship, love and _____ may be difficult to distinguish.**
    a. infatuation
    b. friendship
    c. empty love
    d. fatuous love

Critical Thinking Questions

1. Have you ever been in love? How could you distinguish between love and infatuation?

2. What traits or characteristics are most important to you when you think about a potential date? A marriage partner? Are they the same or different? Why?

3. Would you date someone of another religion or ethnic group? Why or why not? How do you think your friends and family would react?

4. Would you consider a relationship with someone you have only met online in a chat room? Why or why not? What would you be most concerned about?

Companion Website

Visit our Companion Website at www.pearsoned.ca/rathus, **where you can use the interactive Study Guide and link to additional resources on topics discussed in this text.**

Chapter 7
Relationships, Intimacy, and Communication

Will you, won't you, will you, won't you, will you join the dance?
—Lewis Carroll, *Alice in Wonderland*

No man is an island, entire of itself.
—John Donne

"One, two. One, two." A great opening line? In the film *Play It Again, Sam,* Woody Allen plays the role of Allan Felix, a social klutz who has just been divorced. Diane Keaton plays his platonic friend Linda. At a bar one evening with Linda and her husband, Allan Felix spots a young woman on the dance floor who is so attractive that he wishes *he* could have *her* children.

The thing to do, Linda prompts him, is to begin dancing, then dance over to her and "say something." With a bit more prodding, Linda convinces Allan to dance. It's so simple, she tells him. He need only keep time—"One, two, one, two."

"One, two," repeats Allan. Linda shoves him off toward his dream woman.

Hesitantly, Allan dances up to her. Working up courage, he says, "One, two. One, two, one, two." He is ignored and finds his way back to Linda.

"Allan, try something more meaningful," Linda implores.

Once more, Allan dances nervously back toward the woman of his dreams. He stammers, "Three, four, three, four."

"*Speak* to her, Allan," Linda insists.

He dances up to her again and tries, "You interested in dancing at all?"

"Get lost, creep," she replies.

Allan dances rapidly back toward Linda. "What'd she say?" Linda asks. "She'd rather not," he shrugs.

So much for "One, two, one, two," and, for that matter, "Three, four, three, four." Striking up a relationship requires some social skills, and the first few conversational steps can be big ones.

In this chapter we first define the stages that lead to intimacy in relationships. We define intimacy and see that not all relationships achieve this level of interrelatedness, even some supposedly deep and permanent relationships such as marriage. Moreover, we do not all have partners with whom we can develop intimate relationships; some of us remain alone and, perhaps, lonely. Finally, we discuss the ways in which communication contributes to relationships and sexual satisfaction, and we enumerate ways of enhancing communication skills.

The ABC(DE)'s of Romantic Relationships

Social exchange theory The view that the development of a relationship reflects the unfolding of social exchanges—that is, the rewards and costs of maintaining the relationship as opposed to those of ending it.

ABCDE model Levinger's view, which approaches romantic relationships in terms of five stages: Attraction, Building, Continuation, Deterioration, and Ending.

Romantic relationships, like people, undergo stages of development. According to **social-exchange theory**, this development reflects the unfolding of social exchanges, which involve the rewards and costs of maintaining the relationship, compared with the rewards and costs of dissolving it. During each stage, positive factors sway partners toward maintaining and enhancing their relationship. Negative factors incline them toward letting it deteriorate and end.

Numerous investigators have viewed the development of romantic relationships in terms of phases or stages (Berscheid & Reis, 1998; Dindia & Timmerman, 2003; Hendrick & Hendrick, 2000; Honeycutt & Cantrill, 2001; Levinger, 1980). From their work, we can build a five-stage **ABCDE model** of romantic relationships: (1) *A*ttraction, (2) *B*uilding, (3) *C*ontinuation, (4) *D*eterioration, and (5) termination, or *E*nding.

The A's—Attraction

Attraction occurs when two people become aware of each other and find one another appealing or enticing. We may find ourselves attracted to an enchanting person "across a crowded room," in a nearby office, or in a new class. We may meet others through blind dates, introductions by mutual friends, computer match-ups, or by "accident."

Being in a good mood apparently heightens feelings of attraction. George Levinger and his colleagues (Forgas et al., 1994) exposed 128 male and female moviegoers to either a happy or a sad film. Those who had been shown the happy film reported more positive feelings about their partners and their relationships. (Think twice about what you take your date to see!)

According to the Compas (1998) study, 33% of single Canadians usually meet dating partners through their friends (see Figure 7.1). Other common sources of dates are bars or dances (17%), social settings such as health clubs or volunteer organizations (15%), and school or work (12%). Few meet partners through their family (3%), in a religious setting (3%), or through personal ads or dating services (2%).

Today, there is increasing attention to dating on the Internet. In Canada there are numerous online sites promoting dating and sexual relationships for people of all sexual orientations and preferences. The most popular Canadian site is Lavalife.ca. However, the site's supremacy is being challenged by sites like Meet Me in Toronto (www.meetmeinto.com), which has become one of the largest online communities in Toronto. The site is popular among young party-going adults who want to meet someone living in their own community (Heath-Rawlings, 2004).

In a recent survey of gay and bisexual men in Ontario, 35% reported they had met a sexual partner online within the previous six months. However, by far the most common meeting place was the gay bar (Myers et al, 2004).

While men are more likely than women to go online to meet potential dating partners, women are more likely than men to sign up with introduction agencies. Susan Kates, the owner of Dinnerworks.ca, a company that organizes dinner parties for singles in Toronto, reports that 70% of her clients are women ("Two girls . . . ," 2004).

Research in Action

DATING ONLINE

Robert Brym from the University of Toronto and Rhonda Lenton of McMaster University have conducted a study of the online dating experiences of 7700 Canadians (Brym & Lenton, 2001). They found there were twice as many male as female online daters. About one-third of the respondents had not met anyone in person, almost one-half had met between one and five people, and the remainder had met more than five. The majority had talked on the phone and exchanged pictures before agreeing to meet. Most people said that they used online dating sites primarily to find dating partners and to establish a long-term relationship. However, more than twice as many men (53%) as women (20%) said that they dated online in order to find a sexual partner. Among online daters who had met dates in person, about two-thirds had had sex with at least one. Sixty percent had

formed at least one long-term friendship and about one-quarter said they had met someone they came to regard as a partner.

Brym and Lenton (2001) believe that online dating will become more popular in the future for the following reasons:

- The number of singles in the population is rapidly increasing.
- Increasing time pressures lead people to look for more efficient ways of meeting others for intimate relationships.
- Increasing mobility means that single people are finding it harder to meet others for dating.
- Concerns about sexual harassment make it more difficult to date someone at work.

Figure 7.1 How Canadians Meet Dating Partners.

According to the Compas (1998) study, the most common way that single Canadians meet dating partners is through friends. The next most common ways are in social settings such as bars or health clubs.

Source: Compas.

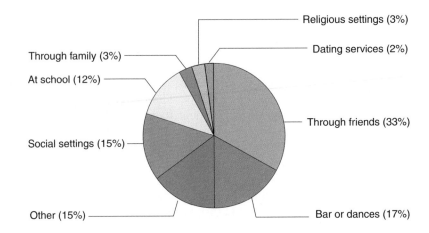

Religious settings (3%)
Dating services (2%)
Through family (3%)
At school (12%)
Through friends (33%)
Social settings (15%)
Other (15%)
Bar or dances (17%)

Canada Matchmaker
Provides information on Canadian singles who are looking for partners.

www.canadamatch maker.net

Gay Matches Canada
Meet single gay men or women.

www.gaymatches canada.com

The workplace does not seem to be as popular a meeting place for potential mates as used to be the case—probably because of concerns over possible sexual harassment. An online survey of 34 000 workers on the Monsters.ca career website found some interesting cultural differences in attitude. Europeans (65%) were the most accepting of office romances while Americans (30%) were the least accepting and Canadians (43%) were in the middle (Prashad, 2004).

Safety is one of people's main concerns about online dating. However, only 10% of those who went on a date with someone they met online reported that they had been frightened by the experience (Brym & Lenton, 2001).

How do you feel about the idea of meeting a potential dating partner on the Internet? Do you think more people will be meeting on the Internet in future?

For people who are uncomfortable about meeting online, there are many other options. In particular, there are numerous events focused on bringing singles together. In Toronto, one of the largest events for singles is the "Playing for Matches" fundraiser for a local hospital. This event, which attracts almost 2000 singles, has everyone complete a questionnaire ahead of time in an attempt to match up people with similar interests.

The B's—Building

Building a relationship follows initial attraction. Factors that motivate us to try to build relationships include similarity in the level of physical attractiveness, similarity in attitudes, and mutual liking and positive evaluations. Factors that may deter us from trying to build relationships include lack of physical appeal, dissimilarity in attitudes, and negative mutual evaluations.

NOT SO SMALL TALK: AN AUDITION FOR BUILDING A RELATIONSHIP In the early stages of building a relationship, we typically look for common ground in the form of overlapping attitudes and interests, and we check out our feelings of attraction. At this point, the determination of whether to strive

How Will She Get Rid of Him?
Perhaps she will give him a phony email address. Some women now use email as a method of avoiding seeing people they do not want to go out with. They may give out their actual email addresses but never respond, or they may give out seldom used or erroneous email addresses. It's like giving out the wrong phone number. (Bye bye.)

to develop the relationship is often made, at least in part, on the basis of **small talk**. Small talk allows an exchange of information but stresses breadth of topic coverage rather than in-depth discussion. Engaging in small talk may seem "phony," but premature self-disclosure of intimate information may repel the other person, as we shall see.

Small talk is a trial balloon for friendship. Successful small talk encourages a couple to venture beneath the surface. At a cocktail party, people may flit about from person to person, exchanging small talk, but now and then a couple finds common ground and pairs off.

Making Overtures.
A couple of singles try to make a connection at Playing with Matches, Canada's largest singles event.

THE "OPENING LINE": HOW DO YOU GET THINGS STARTED? One kind of small talk is the greeting, or opening line. We usually precede verbal greetings with eye contact and decide to begin talking if this eye contact is reciprocated. Avoidance of eye contact may mean that the person is shy, but it could also signify lack of interest. If you would like to progress from initial attraction to surface contact, try a smile and direct eye contact. If the eye contact is reciprocated, choose an opening line, or greeting. Because your opening line can be important, you may prefer to say something more meaningful than "one, two, one, two."

Here are some types of greetings, or opening lines:

Verbal salutes, such as "Good morning."

Personal inquiries, such as "How are you doing?"

Compliments, such as "I like your outfit."

References to your mutual surroundings, such as "What do you think of that painting?" or "This is a nice apartment house, isn't it?"

References to people or events outside the immediate setting, such as "How do you like this weather we've been having?" (Opening gambits about the weather may work best when accompanied by a self-deprecating grin to acknowledge how corny the remark might seem.)

References to the other person's behaviour, such as "I couldn't help noticing you were sitting alone," or "I see you out on this track every Saturday morning."

References to your own behaviour, or to yourself, such as "Hi, my name is Allan Felix" (feel free to use your own name, if you prefer).

The simple "Hi" or "Hello" is very useful. A friendly glance followed by a cheerful hello ought to give you some idea of whether the attraction is reciprocated. If the hello is returned with a friendly smile and inviting eye contact, follow it up with another greeting, such as a reference to your surroundings, the other person's behaviour, or your name.

EXCHANGING "NAME, RANK, AND SERIAL NUMBER" Early exchanges are likely to include name, occupation, marital status, and hometown. Each person seeks a sociological profile of the other to discover common ground that may provide a basis for pursuing the conversation. An unspoken rule seems to be at work: "If I provide you with some information about myself, you will reciprocate by

Small talk A superficial kind of conversation that allows exchange of information but stresses breadth of topic coverage rather than in-depth discussion.

Research in Action

SEXUALLY DIRECT APPROACHES IN SINGLES BARS

While most people follow traditional strategies for meeting potential partners, in some situations initial approaches are more explicitly sexual. In a survey of female students at the University of Guelph who went to singles bars, more than 80% reported that men had approached them using a sexually overt approach behaviour (Huber, 2005). About half of the women had themselves initiated such behaviours with someone they did not know. The specific behaviours were buttock touching over clothes, breast/chest touching over clothes, genital touching over clothes, grinding pelvis to pelvis, and grinding from behind. The grinding behaviours were the most commonly experienced, while breast and genital touching were the least experienced. About 90% said they would be bothered by breast and/or genital approaches, and about half said they would be bothered by buttock touching or grinding.

Sexually overt approaches are far less common in other contexts. Indeed, in most other contexts, these behaviours would be almost universally defined as sexual harassment or sexual assault. However, in the bar context only about one-quarter of the women defined buttock touching or grinding approaches as harassment while about three-quarters saw breast or genital touching as harassment.

giving me an equal amount of information about yourself. Or 'I'll tell you my home-town if you tell me yours'" (Knapp & Vangelista, 2000). If the other person is unresponsive, she or he may not be attracted to you, and you may wish to try someone else. But you may also be awkward in your approach or perhaps turn the other person off by disclosing too much about yourself at once.

SELF-DISCLOSURE: YOU TELL ME AND I'LL TELL YOU . . . CAREFULLY

Opening up, or **self-disclosure**, is central to building intimate relationships. But just what sort of information is safe to disclose upon first meeting someone? If you refuse to go beyond name, rank, and serial number, you may look uninterested or as though you are trying to keep things under wraps. If, on the other hand, you blurt out the fact that you have a terrible rash on your thigh, it's likely that you have disclosed too much too soon.

Research suggests that we should refrain from disclosing certain types of information too rapidly if we want to make a good impression. In one study, confederates of the experimenters (Wortman et al., 1976) engaged in 10-minute conversations with study participants. Some confederates were "early disclosers," who shared intimate information early. Others, "late disclosers," shared intimate information toward the end of the conversation only. In both cases, the information was identical. Study participants then rated the disclosers. Early disclosers were rated as less mature, less secure, less well adjusted, and less genuine than the late disclosers. Study participants also preferred to continue relationships with the late disclosers. We may say we value openness and honesty in our relationships, but it may be a social mistake to open up too soon.

On the other hand, rapid self-disclosure seems to be something of a new norm when people meet in cyberspace (Ben-Ze'ev, 2003). Cyberspace allows for relative anonymity and enables people to control what they want to reveal—to safeguard their privacy even as they increase their emotional closeness and openness. The very nature of privacy changes in cyberspace.

If the surface contact provided by small talk and initial self-disclosure has been mutually rewarding, partners in a relationship tend to develop deeper feelings of liking for each other (Collins & Miller, 1994). Self-disclosure may continue to build gradually through the course of a relationship as partners come to trust each other enough to share confidences and more intimate feelings.

Self-disclosure The revelation of personal—perhaps intimate—information.

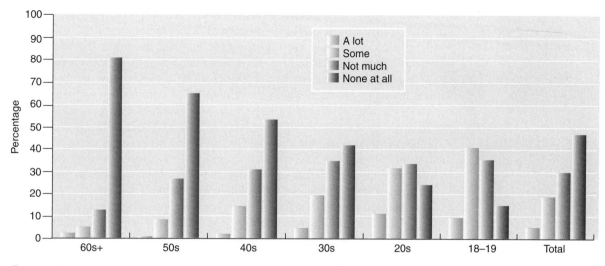

Figure 7.2 Disclosure of Sexual Details to Close Friend, by Age.

According to the Compas (1998) study, young Canadian adults are far more disclosing about their sexuality than those in their 60s.

Source: Compas (1998). Modern life survey of the Canadian adult population.

GENDER DIFFERENCES IN SELF-DISCLOSURE A woman complains to a friend: "He never opens up to me. It's like living with a stone wall." Women commonly declare that men are loath to express their feelings. Researchers find that masculine-typed individuals, whether male or female, tend to be less willing to disclose their feelings, perhaps in adherence to the traditional "strong and silent" masculine stereotype. A study by Susan Basow and Kimberly Rubenfeld (2003) found that feminine-typed individuals are more likely to be empathetic and to listen to other people's troubles than masculine-typed individuals, regardless of their anatomic sex.

However, the belief that women are open and men tight-lipped appears to be something of a myth. Overall, researchers find that women are only slightly more revealing about themselves than men (Dindia & Allen, 1992). When Canadians were asked in the Compas (1998) survey about how much detail they shared about their sexual life with their close friends, close to as many females (43%) as males (50%) said they did not share any information. Hardly any of the females (6%) or males (4%) said that they shared a lot of details. As shown in Figure 7.2, age was a much stronger predictor of disclosure than gender. Among those 18 or 19, 86% disclosed to their friends compared with only 16% of those age 60 and older.

Robin Milhausen and Michael Cho are hosts of the Canadian television series Sex, Toys and Chocolate. *Unlike most Canadians, the guests on this show are extremely open in disclosing their sexual preferences and behaviours.*

While sexual disclosure can be very rewarding as a means of strengthening relationships, it may also be costly to oneself and one's relationship. In revealing personal information, people are highly aware that the listener might evaluate it negatively and even use it to hurt the person. For example, in a much-publicized case, Canadian writer Evelyn Lau, a former lover of the novelist W. P. Kinsella, wrote a magazine article in which she discussed and critiqued his sexual performance. He sued her, claiming that she had violated his privacy (Canadian Press, 1999).

The media have become very bold in discussing the sex lives of public figures such as politicians and celebrities. For example, newspapers around the world openly printed explicit details of the affair between Monica Lewinsky and former U.S. President Bill Clinton: the thong bikini, the oral sex, the cigar.

In Canada, real people openly discuss their sex lives on programs such as *Sex with Sue*, *Sex, Toys and Chocolate*, and *Kink*. Even the more conservative CBC television show *Newsworld* has shown the documentary *Sex, Truth and Video*, which involved 30 women of various ages speaking openly and explicitly about their own sexuality. The openness of participants on these programs is in direct contrast to the reticence of most Canadians.

Apparent disclosure is not always honest. Some people select information carefully to manipulate others, and even invent the stories they "disclose." Researchers at Queen's University found that men with higher scores on a test of psychopathy were more likely to use deception both in sexual and nonsexual situations. These men were also more likely to have a history of unstable sexual relationships (Seto et al., 1997).

SEXUAL INITIATION Initiating sex is stereotypically considered to be the male's role. In a study of cohabiting and married individuals in New Brunswick (Byers & Heinlein, 1989), men initiated sex twice as often as did the women. As well, the men considered initiating sex but did not do so more often than did the women. Contrary to the stereotype that men are always available for sex, men refused initiations to have sex proportionally as often as did the women. Similarly, the women accepted sexual initiations as often as did the men.

Research in Action

SEXUAL DISCLOSURE AMONG UNIVERSITY STUDENTS

A New Brunswick study of students in dating relationships found that women disclosed slightly more information about both sexual and nonsexual issues than did men (Byers & Demmons, 1999). The students disclosed to their dating partners more about nonsexual than sexual issues and more about their sexual likes than their sexual dislikes. Those who were more disclosing about nonsexual issues were also more disclosing about sexual issues (although most did not fully reveal all their true sexual feelings). A key factor in the amount of disclosure was whether the partner was also disclosing. Those who were more open were more satisfied with their level of sexual communication, and ultimately with their sexual relationship.

In another New Brunswick study, the process by which sexual self-disclosure related to sexual satisfaction seemed to differ for men and women (MacNeil, 2004). For men, there was a direct relationship between sexual disclosure and sexual satisfaction. For women, disclosing about nonsexual issues seemed to be more important: Women who could freely disclose about other aspects of their relationship were more satisfied with their relationship in general, and this accounted for their greater sexual satisfaction. In other words, it seems that for women, relationship satisfaction is a key factor in sexual satisfaction.

In an earlier study, female students at the University of Guelph were asked how much they disclosed about eight sexual topics (Herold & Way, 1988). The least disclosed topics were masturbation and sexual thoughts. The women were divided about revealing their sexual past, with less than half believing that "a woman who truly loves her partner should be willing to tell him about all her previous sexual experience." When asked how comfortable they were discussing sexual topics, half of the women who had experienced intercourse said they were very comfortable compared with only a quarter of those who had not.

Like the New Brunswick study, a key factor influencing the amount of disclosure was the reciprocity effect, whereby disclosure increases when the other person also discloses. Thus, the strongest predictor of whether women were disclosing about their sexuality was the sexual comfort level of the target person. The next strongest predictor was whether the woman perceived that the target person had similar sexual attitudes.

Sexually experienced women who had high self-esteem were more disclosing than those with low self-esteem. People with high self-esteem feel less threatened by the possibility that others might judge their sexual behaviours. Those who felt guilty about their sexuality were less disclosing. People who feel guilty worry about the judgments of others, and might feel even more guilty if they reveal their sexual thoughts and experiences to others (Herold & Way, 1988).

In a follow-up study of dating individuals, O'Sullivan and Byers (1992) again found that men initiated sex more often than women. The invitations were mainly in the form of either nonverbal gestures or indirect verbal offers. Only in a minority of situations was a direct verbal request used.

What about situations where the woman wants to have sex but has a reluctant partner? How does she influence her partner to have sex? To answer this question, researchers at the University of Waterloo (Clements-Schreiber & Rempel, 1995) surveyed a community sample of married and single women. About half the women said they would directly ask their partner to have sex. The most common strategies, which more than 90% said they would use, included arranging an opportunity to be alone with him, paying a lot of attention to him, and touching him affectionately. The next most common strategies, indicated by 70% or more of the women involved, were kissing him passionately, setting a romantic mood with candlelight and music, dressing in a seductive way, rubbing his back and shoulders, and letting their hands wander around his body.

At the University of Guelph, students were asked how they ask for and give sexual consent (Humphreys, 2004). Only about one-third said that they explicitly asked for sex. The three most common nonverbal behaviours used by both genders were kissing the partner, moving closer, and touching him or her sexually. The most common ways in which two-thirds of both males and females indicated consent for sex were by not stopping their partner from kissing and sexual touching, kissing their partner, moving closer, and touching their partner sexually. About half said they gave consent by *not* saying no. About half the men and one-third of the women indicated giving consent by saying yes. The study clearly indicated that young people find directly asking for sex to be problematic, with two-thirds agreeing that verbally asking for sexual consent is awkward.

When asked how consent should be obtained, more than half (65% of females and 53% of males) preferred that one should ask first before engaging in any sexual activity. But a large minority (35% of females, 47% of males) preferred to assume consent and to continue with the sexual behaviour until their partner indicated otherwise. Interestingly, although sexual consent has been stressed in many campus educational programs, only about half of the students had discussed the topic with their friends.

A controversial policy developed by Antioch College in Ohio requires that verbal consent be obtained at every step of a sexual encounter. For example, if a woman wanted to kiss her partner, according to the policy, she would need to directly ask if she could kiss him. Later, if he wished to touch her breasts, he would need to ask directly if he could do so and she would have to say yes, verbally. When asked their opinion about this policy, students at the University of Guelph felt this type of consent procedure was not practical and would not be followed by the great majority of young people (Humphreys & Herold, 2003).

In a study of communication about such sexual health issues as HIV and pregnancy prevention at the University of Guelph (Cleary et al., 2002), female students typically reported that they did not discuss these issues prior to engaging in sexual intercourse for the first time with a new partner. Generally, the women reported feeling uncomfortable about initiating discussion about sexual health topics and sensed that their partner was uncomfortable as well. They feared offending their partner and possibly risking a negative reaction from him.

The C's—Continuation

Once a relationship has been established, the couple embarks upon the stage of continuation. Factors that encourage continuation include seeking ways to introduce variety and maintain interest (such as trying out new sexual practices and social activities), showing evidence of caring and positive evaluation (such as sending birthday and Valentine's Day cards), showing lack of jealousy, perceiving fairness in the relationship, and experiencing mutual feelings of general satisfaction.

Numerous studies find that men tend to be more reluctant than women to make commitments. David Popenoe, co-director of the National Marriage Project at Rutgers University in New Jersey, conducted a study with 60 unmarried heterosexual men and found that the commonness of cohabitation is one reason why they are reluctant to make a commitment. In cohabitation, sex—traditionally a key reason for men to marry—is readily available. Popenoe (cited in Hussain, 2002) notes that "In a sense, with cohabitation he gets a quasi-wife without having to commit."

In committed relationships, a delicate balance exists between individuality and mutuality. In healthy unions, a strong sense of togetherness does not eradicate individuality. Partners in such relationships remain free to be themselves. Neither seeks to dominate the other or to submerge himself or herself into the personality of the other. Each partner maintains individual interests, likes and dislikes, needs and goals.

Factors that can throw continuing relationships into a downward spiral include boredom, as in falling into a rut in leisure activities or sexual practices. Yet boredom does not always end relationships. Consider a study of 12 men who admitted to experiencing sexual boredom in long-term heterosexual relationships (Tunariu & Reavey, 2003). The men were not happy with sexual boredom, particularly in a culture in which men are viewed as highly sexual and romantic love is supposed to remain passionate. On the other hand, they viewed their boredom as a normal trade-off for so-called true love and long-term companionship.

Other factors that contribute to the discontinuation of a relationship include evidence of negative evaluation (such as bickering, and forgetting anniversaries and other important dates or pretending that they do not exist), lack of fairness in the relationship (such as one partner's always deciding how the couple will spend their free time), jealousy, and general dissatisfaction.

Keeping in Touch—Or at Least in Electronic Touch.
When today's couples must be separated, many of them keep in touch by means of tools like instant messages, videoconferencing software, Web phones, and wireless communications. Some couples train Webcams on each other's bedrooms, not necessarily for sexual purposes but to maintain a kind of intimacy.

Jealousy: Is the World a Real-Life *Temptation Island?*

Anthropologists find evidence of jealousy in all cultures, although it may vary in amount and intensity across and within cultures. It appears to be more common and intense among cultures with a stronger *machismo* tradition, in which men are expected to display their virility. It is also powerful in cultures in which men view a woman's infidelity as a threat to their honour.

The emotion of jealousy accounts in part for the popularity of the reality TV show *Temptation Island.* On this show, people in committed relationships are exposed to attractive others, and the audience is apparently intrigued by the question of how much temptation the contestant on the show can withstand. No doubt, members of the audience also speculate on how much temptation they themselves could withstand.

Sexual jealousy is aroused when we suspect that an intimate relationship is threatened by a rival. Lovers can become jealous when others show sexual interest in their partners or when their partners show an interest (even a casual or nonsexual interest) in another. Jealousy can lead to loss of feelings of affection, to feelings of insecurity and rejection, to anxiety and loss of self-esteem, and to mistrust of one's partner and potential rivals (Peretti & Pudowski, 1997). Jealousy is one of the most commonly mentioned reasons why relationships fail (Zusman & Knox, 1998).

Feelings of possessiveness, which are related to jealousy, can also subject a relationship to stress. In extreme cases, jealousy can cause depression or give rise to spouse abuse, suicide, or murder. But milder forms of jealousy are not necessarily destructive to a relationship. They may even serve the positive function of revealing how much one cares for one's partner.

What causes jealousy? Experience and personality variables play roles. People may become mistrustful of their partners because former partners had cheated. People with low self-esteem may experience sexual jealousy because they become overly dependent on their partners. They may fear that they will not be able to find another partner if their present partner leaves.

JEALOUSY AND EVOLUTIONARY THEORY Sex differences in jealousy appear to support evolutionary theory. Males seem to be more upset by sexual infidelity, females by emotional infidelity (Shackelford et al., 2002). That is, males are made more insecure and angry when their partners have sexual relations with someone else. Females are made more insecure and angry when their partners become emotionally attached to someone else. Why? Evolutionary theory hypothesizes that sexual jealousy was shaped by natural selection as a method of assuring males that their female partner's offspring is their own, and of assuring females that their male partners will continue to provide resources to facilitate child rearing (Buss, 2003; Harris, 2003).

Interestingly, the hypothesized gender difference in reactions to infidelity disappear when one's partner has an affair with someone of his or her own sex (Sagarin et al., 2003). Is it because the affair carries no threat of impregnation (a view that would be consistent with evolutionary theory)?

How Do People's Partners Feel When Their Lovers Are Tempted by Rivals Like Those Who Inhabit Temptation Island?
Does the opportunity to "spy on" another person's feelings of jealousy contribute to the popularity of reality TV shows like Temptation Island? *How do we explain feelings of jealousy? What does jealousy do to an intimate relationship?*

Or is it because the victim consoles himself or herself by thinking that he or she really isn't competing in the same arena with the intruder? Are both explanations and other explanations possible?

And then there are some studies that fail to support evolutionary theory (Harris, 2000; DeSteno et al., 2002). However, the validity of these studies has also been challenged. Evolutionary theory remains in the forefront of approaches to understanding jealousy and (possible) gender differences in jealousy.

A COGNITIVE PERSPECTIVE   In recent years, cognitive theory has gained importance in many areas of the behavioural sciences, and sexual jealousy is no exception. In two studies, Stacie Bauerle and her colleagues (2002) presented 156 college undergraduates and 128 members of the general population with various scenarios in which their partners were unfaithful. By and large, jealousy increased when the individuals attributed their partner's infidelity to *internal* causes, such as clear personal choice. When they attributed the infidelity to *external* causes, such as alcohol or social pressure, the individuals in the study reported feeling significantly less jealous. ("Don't blame me; it was the alcohol.")

The D's—Deterioration

Deterioration is the fourth stage of a relationship. It is not usually a stage that we seek, and it is certainly not an inevitability. Factors that can deter or slow deterioration include putting time and energy into the relationship, striving to cultivate the relationship, and showing patience—for example, giving the relationship a reasonable opportunity to improve. Factors that foster deterioration include failure to invest time and energy in the relationship, deciding to put an end to it, and simply permitting deterioration to proceed unchecked.

A relationship begins to deteriorate when one or both partners deem the relationship to be less enticing or rewarding than it has been. Couples who work toward maintaining and enhancing their relationships, however, may find that these become stronger and more meaningful.

The E's—Ending

Ending is the fifth and final stage of a relationship. Like deterioration, it is not necessarily desirable and need not be inevitable. Various factors can prevent a deteriorating relationship from ending. For example, people who continue to find some sources of satisfaction, who are committed to maintaining the relationship, or who believe that they will eventually be able to overcome their problems are more likely to invest what they must to prevent the collapse.

According to social-exchange theory, relationships draw to a close when negative forces hold sway—when the partners find little satisfaction in the affiliation, when the barriers to leaving the relationship are low (that is, the social, religious, and financial constraints are manageable), and especially when alternative partners are available (Black et al., 1991; Karney & Bradbury, 1995). Problems in communication and jealousy are among the most common reasons for ending a relationship (Zusman & Knox, 1998). The availability of alternatives decreases one's commitment to and investment in a relationship (Knox et al., 1997; Rusbult et al., 1998). This fact has been widely recognized throughout the ages, which is one reason why patriarchal cultures like to keep their women locked up as much as possible. It also underlies the sexist advice that one should keep one's wife pregnant in summer and barefoot in winter.

About six out of seven students at a large Southeastern U.S. university reported that they ended relationships by having frank discussions about them with their partners (Knox et al., 1998). Honesty helped them maintain friendly feelings once the romantic relationship had come to an end.

The swan song of a relationship—moving on—is not always a bad thing. When people are definitely incompatible, and when genuine attempts to preserve the relationship have faltered, ending the relationship can offer each partner a chance for happiness with someone else.

Intimacy

Intimacy involves feelings of emotional closeness and connectedness with another person and the desire to share each other's innermost thoughts and feelings. Intimate relationships are also characterized by attitudes of mutual trust, caring, and acceptance.

Sternberg's (1986) triangular theory of love (see Chapter 6) regards intimacy as a basic component of romantic love. But people can be intimate and *not* be in love, at least not in romantic love. Close friends and family members become emotionally intimate when they care deeply for each other and share their private feelings and experiences. It is not necessary for people to be *sexually* intimate to have an emotionally intimate relationship. Nor does sexual intimacy automatically produce emotional intimacy. People who are sexually involved may still fail to touch each other's lives in emotionally intimate ways. Even couples who fall in love may not be able to forge an intimate relationship because of unwillingness or inability to exchange innermost thoughts and feelings. Sometimes people are more emotionally intimate with friends than with spouses.

Let us now consider some of the factors that are involved in intimate relationships.

Knowing and Liking Yourself

Some social scientists suggest that an initial step toward intimacy with others is getting to know and like *yourself*. By coming to know and value yourself, you identify your innermost feelings and needs and develop the security to share them.

Trusting and Caring

Two of the most important ingredients of an intimate relationship are trust and caring. When trust exists in a relationship, partners feel secure that disclosing intimate feelings will not lead to ridicule, rejection, or other kinds of harm. Trust usually builds gradually, as partners learn whether or not it is safe to share confidences.

Trusting and Caring.
Trusting and caring are key ingredients of an intimate relationship. Trust gives partners the security they need to disclose intimate feelings. Caring is an emotional connection that allows intimacy to develop.

Research shows that people come to trust their partners when they see that their partners have made sincere investments in the relationship, such as making sacrifices to be with them (e.g., earning the disapproval of one's family, driving one's partner somewhere rather than studying) (Wieselquist et al., 1999). Commitment and trust in a relationship can be seen as developing according to a model of **mutual cyclical growth**. According to this model,

- Feelings that one needs one's partner promote a strong sense of commitment to and dependence on the relationship (Wieselquist et al., 1999).

- Commitment to the relationship encourages one to do things that are good for the relationship (to perform "pro-relationship acts").

- One's partner perceives the pro-relationship acts.

- Perception of the pro-relationship acts enhances the partner's trust in the other partner and in the relationship.

- Feelings of trust increase the willingness of the partners to increase their feelings that they need each other and the relationship.

Caring is an emotional bond that allows intimacy to develop. In caring relationships, partners seek to gratify each other's needs and interests. Caring also involves willingness to make sacrifices for the other person. Research shows that willingness to sacrifice is connected with strong commitment to the relationship, with a high level of satisfaction in the relationship, and, interestingly, with a lack of alternatives to the relationship (Van Lange et al., 1997). In other words, it may not be so easy to find another partner if one does not make the sacrifices required to remain in the relationship. Self-sacrifice can sometimes be self-serving!

Being Honest

Because intimacy involves the sharing of one's innermost thoughts and feelings, honesty is a core feature of intimacy. A person need not be an "open book" to develop and maintain intimacy, however. Some aspects of experience are better kept even from one's most intimate partners, for they may be too embarrassing or threatening to reveal (Finkenauer & Hazam, 2000). For example, we would not expect partners to disclose every passing sexual fantasy.

Intimate relationships thus usually involve balances in which some things are revealed and others are not. Total honesty could devastate a relationship (Finkenauer & Hazam, 2000). Many people cannot handle having intimate partners divulge the details of past sexual experiences. The recipient may wonder, "Why is Kimball telling me this? Am I as good a lover as _____? Is Kimball still in love with _____? What else did Kimball do with _____?" Discretion thus also buttresses intimate relationships. As Gordon and Snyder (1989) put it, "Honesty means *saying what you mean*, not revealing every detail" (p. 24). Nor is intimacy established by frank but brutal criticism, even if it is honest.

Mutual cyclical growth
The view that the need for one's partner promotes commitment; this commitment promotes acts that enhance the relationship; these acts build trust; and one's partner's commitment to the relationship increases.

Communicating

Good communication is another hallmark of an intimate relationship. Partners are able to share their most personal thoughts and feelings clearly and honestly. Communication is a two-way street. It embraces sending and receiving messages.

Almost all communication research has been done with heterosexuals. Researchers in Montreal wanted to determine if findings regarding communication processes were generalizable to the gay population (Julien et al., 2003). They found that communication behaviours were similar for heterosexual, gay male, and lesbian couples.

The good communicator is a skilled listener as well as a clear speaker (Tannen, 1990). We generally associate communication with *talk*, which involves the use of verbal messages to convey a thought or a feeling. However, much communication is nonverbal.

NONVERBAL COMMUNICATION: THE BODY SPEAKS Although the spoken word is a primary form of communication, we often express our feelings through nonverbal channels as well, such as by tone of voice, gestures, body posture, and facial expressions (Tannen, 1990). People may place more weight on how words are said than on their denotative meaning. People also accentuate the meaning of their words through gestures, raising or lowering their voices, or using a sterner or softer tone of voice.

Nonverbal communication is used not only to accentuate the spoken word but also to express feelings directly. We are sometimes better able to convey our feelings through body language than by the use of words.

All in all, there are many ways in which we communicate with others through verbal and nonverbal channels. Let us now look at ways in which partners can learn to communicate better with each other, especially about sex. Many couples, even couples who are able to share their deepest thoughts and feelings, may flounder at communicating their sexual needs and preferences. Couples who have lived together for decades may know each other's tastes in food, music, and movies about as well as they know their own but may still hesitate to share their sexual likes and dislikes (Harris & Johnson, 2000; Whitten, 2001). They may also be reluctant, for fear of opening wounds in the relationship, to exchange their feelings about other aspects of their relationship, including each other's habits, appearance, and gender-stereotypical attitudes.

Communication Skills for Enhancing Relationships and Sexual Relations

Marital counsellors and sex therapists might be as busy as the proverbial Maytag repairman if more couples communicated with each other about their sexual feelings. Unfortunately, when it comes to sex, the most overlooked four-letter word may be *talk*.

Many couples suffer for years because one or both partners are unwilling to speak up. Or problems arise when one partner misinterprets the other. One partner might interpret the other's groans or grimaces of pleasure as signs of pain and pull back during sex, leaving the other frustrated. Improved communication may be no panacea, but it helps. Clear communication can take the guesswork out of relationships, avert misunderstandings, relieve resentments and frustrations, and increase both sexual and general satisfaction with the relationship.

Common Difficulties in Sexual Communication

Why is it so difficult for couples to communicate about sex? Here are some possibilities:

ON "MAKING WHOOPIE"—IS SEX TALK VULGAR? Vulgarity, like beauty, is to some degree in the eye of the beholder. One couple's vulgarity may be another couple's pillow talk. Some people may maintain a Victorian belief that no talk about sex is fit for mixed company, even between intimate partners. Sex, that is, is something you may do, but not something to be talked about. Other couples may be willing in principle to talk about sex, but find the reality difficult because they lack an agreeable, common language.

Selfhelp Magazine's Features articles on relationship issues, such as effective communication and finding a partner.
www.shpm.com

How, for example, are they to refer to their genitals or to sexual activities? One partner may prefer to use coarse words to refer to them. (As the forbidden fruit is often the sweetest, some people feel sexually aroused when they or their partners "talk dirty.") The other might prefer more clinical terms. A partner who likes to use slang for the sex organs might be regarded by the other as vulgar or demeaning. One who uses clinical terms, such as *fellatio* or *coitus*, might be regarded as, well, clinical. Some couples compromise and try to use terms that are neither vulgar nor clinical. They might speak, for example, of "doing it" rather than "screwing" (and the like) at one extreme or of "engaging in sexual intercourse" at the other. (The title of the Eddie Cantor musical of the 1930s suggests that some people once spoke of "making whoopie.") Or they might speak of "kissing me down there" rather than of "eating me" or of practising fellatio or cunnilingus.

ON IRRATIONAL BELIEFS Many couples also harbour irrational beliefs about relationships and sex, such as the notion that people should somehow *know* what their partners want without having to ask. Men, in particular, seem burdened with the stereotype that they should have a natural expertise at sex. Women may feel it is "unladylike" to talk openly about their sexual needs and feelings. Both partners may hold the idealized romantic notion that "all you need is love" to achieve sexual happiness. But such knowledge does not arise from instinct or from love. It is learned—or it remains unknown.

A related irrational belief is that one's partner will read one's mind. We may erroneously assume that if our partners truly loved us, they would somehow know what types of sexual stimulation we desire. Unfortunately—or fortunately—others cannot read our minds. We must assume the responsibility for communicating our preferences.

Some people communicate more effectively than others, perhaps because they are more sensitive to others' needs or because their parents served as good models as communicators. But communication skills can be acquired at any time. Learning takes time and work, but the following guidelines should prove helpful if you want to enhance your communication skills. The skills can also improve communication in areas of intimacy other than the sexual.

Getting Started

How do you broach tough topics? Here are some ideas.

TALKING ABOUT TALKING You can start by talking about talking. You can inform your partner that it is difficult for you to talk about problems and conflicts: "You know, I've always found it awkward to find a way of bringing things up" or "You know, I think other people have an easier time than I do when it comes to talking about some things." You can allude to troublesome things that happened in the past when you attempted to resolve conflicts. This approach encourages your partner to invite you to proceed.

Broaching the subject of sex can be difficult. Even couples who gab endlessly about finances, children, and work may clam up about sex. Thus, it may be helpful first to agree to talk about talking about sex. You can admit that it is difficult to talk about sex. You can say that your sexual relationship is important to you and that you want to do everything you can to enhance it. Gently probe your partner's willingness to set aside time to talk about sex, preferably when you can dim the lights and avoid interruptions.

The "right time" may be when you are both relaxed, rested, and not pressed for time. The "right place" can be any place where you can enjoy privacy and talk undisturbed. Sex talk need not be limited to the bedroom. Couples may feel more comfortable talking about sex over dinner, when cuddling on the sofa, or when just relaxing together.

Active Listening.
Effective communication requires listening to the other person's view of things. You can listen actively by maintaining eye contact and modifying your facial expression to show that you understand your partner's feelings and ideas. You can ask helpful questions, such as "Did I disappoint you when I ...?"

REQUESTING PERMISSION TO BRING UP A TOPIC Another possibility is to request permission to raise an issue. You can say something like this: "There's something on my mind. Do you have a few minutes? Is now a good time to tell you about it?" Or you can say, "There's something that we need to talk about, but I'm not sure how to bring it up. Can you help me with it?"

GIVING YOUR PARTNER PERMISSION TO SAY SOMETHING THAT MIGHT BE UPSETTING TO YOU You can tell your partner that it is okay to point out ways in which you can become a more effective lover. For example, you can say, "I know that you don't want to hurt my feelings, but I wonder if I'm doing anything that you'd rather I didn't do?"

Listening to the Other Side

Skilled listening involves such skills as active listening, paraphrasing, the use of reinforcement, and valuing your partner even when the two of you disagree.

LISTENING ACTIVELY To listen actively rather than passively, first adopt the attitude that you may actually learn something—or perceive things from another vantage point—by listening. Second, recognize that even though the other person is doing the talking, you shouldn't just sit there. In other words, it is not helpful to stare off into space while your partner is talking, or to offer a begrudging "mm-hmm" now and then to be polite. Instead, you can listen actively by maintaining eye contact and modifying your facial expression to show that you understand his or her feelings and ideas (Cole & Cole, 1999). For example, nod your head when appropriate.

Listening actively also involves asking helpful questions, such as "Would you please give me an example?"

An active listener does not simply hear what the other person is saying, but also focuses attentively on the speaker's words and gestures to grasp the full meaning. Nonverbal cues may reveal more about the speaker's inner feelings than the spoken word. Good listeners do not interrupt, change the topic, or walk away when their partners are speaking.

PARAPHRASING Paraphrasing shows that you understand what your partner is trying to say. In paraphrasing, you recast or restate the speaker's words to confirm that you have understood correctly. For example, suppose your partner says, "You hardly ever say anything when we're making love. I don't want you to scream or make obligatory grunts or do something silly, but sometimes I wonder if I'm trying to make love to a brick wall." You can paraphrase this comment by saying something like: "So it's sort of hard to know if I'm really enjoying it."

REINFORCING THE OTHER PERSON'S WILLINGNESS TO COMMUNICATE Even when you disagree with what your partner is saying, you can maintain good relations and keep channels of communication open by saying something like "I really appreciate your taking the time to try to work this out with me" or "I hope you'll think it's okay if I don't see things entirely in the same way, but I'm glad that we had a chance to talk about it."

SHOWING THAT YOU VALUE YOUR PARTNER, EVEN WHEN THE TWO OF YOU DISAGREE When you disagree with your partner, do so in a way that shows that you still value your partner as a person. In other words, say something like "I love you very much, but it annoys me when you . . . " rather than "You're really contemptible for . . ." By so doing, you encourage your partner to disclose sensitive material without risk of attack or of losing your love or support.

Applied Knowledge

COMMUNICATING SEXUAL NEEDS

Learning About Your Partner's Needs

Listening is basic to learning about another person's needs, but sometimes it helps to go a few steps further.

Asking Questions to Draw the Other Person Out
You can ask open-ended questions that allow for a broader exploration of issues, such as these:

- "What do you like best about the way we make love?"
- "Do you think that I do things to bug you?"
- "Does it bother you that I go to bed later than you do?"
- "Does anything disappoint you about our relationship?"
- "Do you think that I do things that are inconsiderate when you're studying for a test?"

Closed-ended questions that call for a limited range of responses tend to be most useful when you're looking for a simple yes-or-no type of response. ("Would you rather make love with the stereo off?")

Using Self-Disclosure Self-disclosure is essential to developing intimacy. You can also use self-disclosure to learn more about your partner's needs, because communicating your own feelings and ideas invites reciprocation. For example, you might say, "There are times when I feel that I disappoint you when we make love. Should I be doing something differently?"

Granting Permission for the Other Person to Say Something That Might Upset You You can ask your partner to level with you about an irksome issue. You can say that you recognize that it may be awkward to discuss it but that you will try your best to listen conscientiously and not get too disturbed. You can also limit communication to one such difficult issue per conversation. If the entire emotional dam were to burst, the job of mopping up could be overwhelming.

Providing Information

There are many skilful ways of communicating information, including "accentuating the positive" and using verbal and nonverbal cues. When you want to get something across, remember that it is irrational to expect that your partner can read your mind. He or she can tell when you're wearing a grumpy face, but your expression does not provide much information about your specific feelings. When your partner asks, "What would you like me to do?" responding with "Well, I think you can figure out what I want" or "Just do whatever you think is best" is not very helpful. Only you know what pleases you. Your partner is not a mind reader.

Accentuating the Positive Let your partner know when he or she is doing something right! Speak up or find another way to express your appreciation. Accentuating the positive is rewarding and also informs your partner about what pleases you. In other words, don't just wait around until your partner does something wrong and then seize the opportunity to complain!

Using Verbal Cues Sexual activity provides an excellent opportunity for direct communication. You can say something like "Oh, that's great" or "Don't stop." Or you can ask for feedback, as in "How does this feel?" Feedback provides direct guidance about what is pleasing. Partners can also make specific requests and suggestions.

Using Nonverbal Cues Sexual communication also occurs without words. Couples learn to interpret each other's facial expressions as signs of pleasure, anxiety, boredom, even disgust. Our body language also communicates our likes and dislikes. Our partners may lean toward us or away from us when we touch them, or they may relax or tense up; in any case, they speak volumes in silence.

The following exercises may help couples use nonverbal cues to communicate their sexual likes and dislikes. Similar exercises are used by sex therapists to help couples with sexual dysfunctions.

1. *Taking turns petting.* Taking turns petting can help partners learn what turns each other on. Each partner takes turns caressing the other, stopping frequently enough to receive feedback by asking questions like "How does that feel?" The recipient is responsible for giving feedback, which can be expressed either verbally ("Yes, that's it—yes, just like that" or "No, a little lighter than that") or nonverbally, such as by making certain appreciative or disapproving sounds. Verbal feedback is usually more direct and less prone to misinterpretation. The knowledge gained through this exercise can be incorporated into the couple's regular pattern of lovemaking.

2. *Directing your partner's hand.* Gently guiding your partner's hand—to show your partner where and how you like to be touched—is a most direct way of communicating sexual preferences. While taking turns petting, and during other acts of lovemaking, one partner can gently guide the other's fingers and hands through the most satisfying strokes and caresses. Women might show their partner how to caress the breasts or clitoral shaft in this

manner. Men might cup their partner's hands to show them how to stroke the penile shaft or caress the testes.

3. *Signalling.* Couples can use agreed-upon nonverbal cues to signal sexual pleasure. For example, one partner may rub the other in a certain way, or tap the other, to sig-

nal that something is being done right. The recipient of the signal takes mental notes and incorporates the pleasurable stimulation into the couple's lovemaking. This is a sort of "hit or miss" technique, but even near misses can be rewarding.

Making Sexual Requests

A basic part of improving relationships or lovemaking is asking partners to change their behaviour—to do something differently or to stop doing something that hurts or is no longer gratifying. As shown in Table 7.1, almost half of Canadians (46%) report that they are "very comfortable" in asking a sexual partner to try something new or different in their sexual relationship, with only 17% saying that they are not comfortable (Compas, 1998). Those aged 50 and over were the least comfortable about this. Table 7.2 shows some interesting regional differences, with people in Quebec being the most likely to say they are "very comfortable" requesting something new sexually and those in the Prairies the least likely.

TABLE 7.1
How Comfortable Canadians Are with Asking a Partner to Try Something New in Their Sexual Relationship

	Males	Females	Total
Very	45.2%	46.5%	45.8%
Somewhat	39.8	34.5	37.2
Not really	10.2	11.5	10.8
Not at all	4.8	7.5	6.1

Source: Compas (1998). Modern life survey of the Canadian adult population.

TABLE 7.2
Regional Differences in Comfort Asking a Partner to Try Something New

	Region					
	Atlantic	Quebec	Ontario	Prairies	B.C.	Total
Very	44.6%	58.5%	41.2%	36.9%	46.4%	45.8%
Somewhat	37.5	28.8	40.5	42.9	36.8	37.2
Not really	12.5	6.8<	10.9	15.0	10.0	10.8
Not at all	5.4	5.9	7.4	5.1	6.8	6.1

Source: Compas (1998). Modern life survey of the Canadian adult population.

Summing Up

The ABC(DE)'s of Romantic Relationships

Levinger proposes an ABCDE model of romantic relationships. The letters refer to five stages: attraction, building, continuation, deterioration, and ending.

The A's—Attraction

The major promoter of attraction is propinquity.

The B's—Building

Similarity in the level of physical attractiveness, similarity in attitudes, and liking motivate us to build relationships.

The C's—Continuation

Factors such as variety, caring, positive evaluations, lack of jealousy, perceived fairness in the relationship, and mutual feelings of satisfaction encourage us to continue relationships.

The D's—Deterioration

The factors that foster deterioration include failure to invest time and energy in the relationship, deciding to put an end to it, and simply permitting deterioration to proceed unchecked.

The E's—Ending

Relationships tend to end when the partners find little satisfaction in the affiliation, when alternative partners are available, when couples are not committed to preserving the relationship, and when they expect it to falter.

Intimacy

Intimacy involves feelings of emotional closeness with another person and the desire to share each other's innermost thoughts and feelings.

Knowing and Liking Yourself

An initial step toward intimacy with others is getting to know and like yourself so that you can identify your innermost feelings and develop the security to share them.

Trusting and Caring

Intimate relationships require trust, caring, and tenderness.

Being Honest

Honesty is a core feature of intimacy.

Communicating

Communication is a two-way street. It embraces sending *and* receiving messages. We often express feelings through nonverbal channels such as tone of voice, gestures, body posture, and facial expressions.

Communication Skills for Enhancing Relationships and Sexual Relations

Common Difficulties in Sexual Communication

Couples may find it difficult to talk about sex because of the lack of an agreeable common language. Many couples also harbour irrational beliefs about relationships and sex.

Getting Started

Ways of getting started in communicating include talking about talking, requesting permission to raise an issue, and granting one's partner permission to say things that might be upsetting.

Listening to the Other Side

Skilled listening involves elements such as active listening, paraphrasing, the use of reinforcement, and valuing your partner even when you disagree.

Making Requests

A basic part of improving relationships or lovemaking is asking partners to change their behaviour.

Test Yourself

Multiple-Choice Questions

1. **The most common way that single Canadians meet dating partners is**
   a. through friends
   b. in bars or clubs
   c. at school
   d. on the Internet

2. **Research has shown that**
   a. women are much more likely to disclose their feelings than men
   b. men are much more likely to disclose their feelings than women
   c. there are few gender-based differences in self-disclosure
   d. older people are much more likely to disclose their feelings than younger people

3. **All of the following encourage the continuation of relationships except**
   a. maintaining interest
   b. evidence of caring
   c. mutual satisfaction
   d. jealousy

4. **All of the following can cause jealousy except**
   a. having a former partner cheat on you
   b. a lack of self-confidence
   c. a fear of not being able to find another partner
   d. a high level of independence

5. **Recent research has shown that men are more upset by _____ infidelity and women by _____infidelity.**
   a. sexual/emotional
   b. emotional/sexual
   c. sexual/sexual
   d. emotional/emotional

6. **Social exchange theory suggests that relationships may end when**
   a. barriers to leaving the relationship are high
   b. the couple stops having sex
   c. alternative partners are available
   d. family pressures are too strong

7. **Which of the following statements is true about emotional intimacy?**
   a. It is necessary to be sexually intimate in order to have emotional intimacy.
   b. It is necessary to be emotionally intimate in order to have sexual intimacy.
   c. Some people may share greater emotional intimacy with friends than with partners.
   d. Emotional intimacy between friends is seen as wrong in Canada.

8. **Which of the following is *not* one of the irrational beliefs about communication that are described in the text?**
   a. Men should have a natural expertise at sex.
   b. People should know what their partners want without having to ask.
   c. Good communication can enhance all aspects of a relationship
   d. It is "unladylike" for women to talk about their sexual needs and feelings.

9. **Which of the following is <u>not</u> one of the suggestions described in the text to learn about your partner's needs?**
   a. using self disclosure
   b. asking open-ended questions
   c. giving permission for the other person to say something that might upset you
   d. criticizing your partner's performance in bed

10. **The most successful intimate relationships are characterized by**
    a. total honesty about past sexual experiences
    b. secrecy about past sexual experiences
    c. totally honest criticism
    d. discretion in revealing details of past relationships

Critical Thinking Questions

1. Have you ever signed up with an online dating service? How did the experience turn out? Would you do it again? If you haven't, would you? Why or why not?

2. Have you ever had a partner who was extremely jealous? What was the most difficult part of the relationship? How did you deal with the jealousy?

3. Have you ever met someone online and then met face to face? Was this a successful experience? Did your impressions of this person change after you met face to face?

4. Have you ever sat next to someone on a bus or a plane and disclosed to them details of your life that you would not share with a friend? How did you feel about this afterwards? Why do many people find it easy to talk like this to total strangers?

5. Have you ever been in a relationship that had problems in communication? How did this affect the relationship?

Companion
Website

Visit our Companion Website at www.pearsoned.ca/rathus, **where you can use the interactive Study Guide and link to additional resources on topics discussed in this text.**

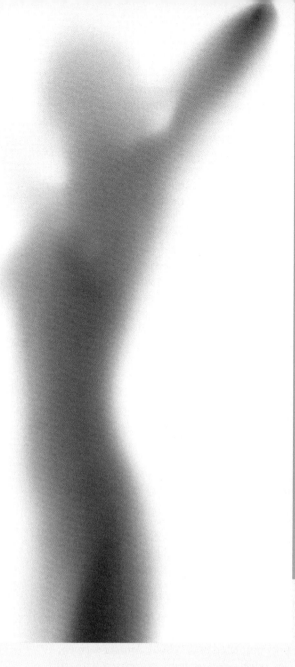

Chapter 8
Sexual Techniques and Behaviour Patterns

This is the chapter that describes sexual techniques and statistical breakdowns of "who does what with whom." There is great variety in human sexual expression. Some of us practise few, if any, of the techniques in this chapter. Some of us practise most or all of them. Some of us practise some of them some of the time. Our knowledge of the prevalence of these techniques comes from sex surveys. Of course, surveys are plagued by problems such as nonrepresentative sampling, social desirability, and volunteer bias. Therefore, we must be cautious in generalizing on the basis of their results. Surveys provide our best "guesstimate" of the prevalence of sexual behaviours. They do not provide precise figures.

Readers of this textbook are as varied in their sexual values, preferences, and attitudes as is society in general. Some of the techniques discussed may thus strike some readers as indecent. Our aim is to provide information about the diversity of sexual expression. We are not seeking consensus on what is acceptable. Nor do we pass judgments or encourage readers to expand their sexual repertoires.

The human body is sensitive to many forms of sexual stimulation. Yet we reiterate the theme that biology is not destiny: A biological capacity does not impose a behavioural requirement. Cultural expectations, personal values, and individual experience—not only our biological capacities—determine our sexual behaviour. What is right for you is right for you, but not necessarily for your neighbour.

We begin by reviewing the techniques that people practise by themselves to derive sexual pleasure: masturbation and sexual fantasy. We then consider techniques that involve a partner.

Solitary Sexual Behaviour

Various forms of sexual expression do not require a partner or are not generally practised in the presence of a partner. Masturbation, which involves direct stimulation of the genitals, is one of the principal forms of one-person sexual expression. Other forms of individual sexual experience, such as thinking about sex and sexual fantasy, may or may not be accompanied by genital stimulation.

According to the national survey conducted by Compas polling, Canadian men report thinking about sex much more often than women do—a gender difference found across all age and educational levels (Fischtein & Herold, 2002). About half of men (46%) but only 11% of women think about sex several times a day. Those who are younger and who are university educated think about sex more often than those who are older and who have not completed high school. Among women, 49% of those in their 20s think about sex once a day or more compared with 10% of women in their 60s. Ninety percent of men in their 20s have sexual thoughts at least once a day compared with 35% of men in their 60s.

Use of Fantasy

People may use sexual fantasies when they are alone or to heighten sexual excitement with a partner (Eggers, 2000; Leitenberg & Henning, 1995). Some couples find it sexually arousing to share fantasies or to enact them with their partners. Sexual fantasies may be experienced without sexual behaviour, as in erotic dreams or daydreams. Masturbators often require some form of cognitive stimulation, such as indulging in a favourite fantasy or reading or viewing erotica, to increase their arousal to the point of orgasm.

How common are sexual fantasies? At an Ontario university, 97% of the female students reported having experienced sexual fantasies (Pelletier & Herold, 1988). Of those who had masturbated, 87% fantasized during masturbation, with 57% always fantasizing during masturbation. Of those with intercourse experience, 73% had fantasized during intercourse, but only 10% usually or always fantasized during intercourse. Most had also fantasized in nonsexual situations (84%). Interestingly,

TABLE 8.1
Sexual Fantasies of University Females

Fantasy	Situation During Which Fantasy Occurred			
	Masturbation	**Coitus**	**Nonsexual**	**Total**
Sex with boyfriend	54%	49%	69%	90%
Undressed by male	46	39	54	79
Previous sexual experience	44	31	58	78
Intercourse in exotic place	33	43	55	72
Undressing a male	26	28	54	71
Cunnilingus	48	46	41	66
Intercourse with male friend	31	14	47	60
Forced sex with male	30	26	31	51
Fellatio	21	28	34	49
Intercourse with male stranger	24	9	34	46
Intercourse with famous person	19	6	34	38
Doing striptease	15	10	26	37
Male masturbating	32	12	19	33
Sex with many men	26	11	17	29
Sex with objects	25	9	13	23
Sex with other watching	20	11	6	21
Female masturbating	18	4	7	18
Sex with female	15	4	9	18
Forced sex with more than one male	15	9	9	18
Anal sex	9	12	9	17
Group sex with males and females	10	3	9	16
Sex with relative	3	0	12	14
Sex with animal	8	3	4	9
Sadomasochistic sex	1	4	4	7

Note: The percentages in the Masturbation and Coitus columns are based on those who had experienced the fantasies while engaged in those behaviours. The percentage in the Total column represents those who had experienced that fantasy in one or more of the situations.

Source: L. A. Pelletier & E. S. Herold (1988). The relationship of age, sex guilt and sexual experience with female sexual fantasies. Journal of Sex Research, 24, 250–256.

the women experienced a greater number of different types of fantasies in nonsexual situations than in sexual ones. This suggests that in sexual situations, women focus on those fantasies they find to be the most arousing. Table 8.1 presents a complete breakdown of this data.

That the most common fantasy was about one's boyfriend is not consistent with studies of married women (Davidson & Hoffman, 1986), who reported commonly fantasizing about other men rather than their husband. It appears that when women become involved in long-term relationships, the object of their fantasy switches to that of other men.

In the Ontario study of female students, one-half of the women had forced-sex fantasies (Pelletier and Herold, 1988). It is important to note that this does *not* mean that they want in reality to be sexually assaulted. In the fantasy situation, the women are the ones who are actually in control.

About one-quarter of the women had sexual fantasies once a day or more often and about one-half fantasized a few times a week. When asked why they fantasized, three-quarters said it was a pleasant way to pass the time. About one-half said they fantasized to become aroused, and 30% to help achieve orgasm. Interestingly, 30% used fantasy to help them fall asleep.

One stereotype about fantasies holds that people who are sexually deprived fantasize the most about sex. In fact, Pelletier and Herold found that the women with the most sexual experience and who had most sexual partners fantasized about sex more often and had a greater number of more explicit sexual fantasies. For example, those with oral sex experience fantasized more about oral sex than women who had not experienced oral sex. Those women who felt guilty about sex fantasized less.

Among university students in British Columbia, males had more fantasies than females (Meston et al., 1996). Males in particular fantasized more than females about having many partners and about engaging in oral and anal sex.

Sexual fantasies can be experienced as either positive or negative, or both. In a study of students at the University of New Brunswick, positive types of feelings were experienced more often than negative ones (Renaud & Byers, 1999). More positive feelings were experienced for fantasies involving a loved one and more negative feelings were experienced for fantasies involving casual sex. Having intercourse with a loved one was the most common fantasy of both genders. Men were more likely than women to have fantasies of anonymous sex and sex with multiple partners.

Evolutionary theorists conjecture that women are relatively more likely to fantasize about the images of familiar lovers because female reproductive success in ancestral times was more likely to depend on an emotionally close, protective relationship with a reliable partner (Symons, 1995). Women can bear and rear relatively few offspring. Thus, they would have a relatively greater genetic investment than men in each reproductive opportunity.

Whether or not the wellspring of sexual fantasy themes lies in our genetic heritage, we should not confuse sexual fantasies with behaviour. Fantasies are imaginary. Most people do not intend to act out their fantasies. They use them as a means of inducing or enhancing sexual pleasure (Reinisch, 1990).

As already mentioned, fantasizing about forcing someone into sexual activity, or about being victimized, does not mean that one wants these events to occur (Leitenberg & Henning, 1995; Reinisch, 1990). Women who imagine themselves being sexually coerced remain in control of their fantasies. Real assault victims are not. Nor is it unusual for heterosexual people to have episodic fantasies about sexual activity with people of their own gender, or for gay males or lesbians to fantasize about sexual activity with people of the other gender. In neither case does the person necessarily intend to act out the fantasy.

Why do people fantasize when they masturbate? Masturbation fantasies serve several functions. For one, they increase or facilitate sexual arousal. Sex therapists encourage clients to use sexual fantasies to enhance sexual arousal (e.g., Heiman & LoPiccolo, 1987). Sexual fantasies are highly arousing, in part because fantasizers can command the imagined sexual encounter. They may imagine that people who will not give them the time of day find them irresistible and are willing to fulfill their sexual desires. Or fantasizers may picture improbable or impossible arousing situations, such as sexual activity on a commercial airliner or while skydiving. Some masturbation fantasies may be arousing because they permit us to deviate from traditional gender roles. Women might fantasize about taking an aggressive role or forcing someone into sexual activity. Men, by contrast, may imagine being overtaken by a horde of sexually aggressive women. Other fantasies involve sexual transgressions or "forbidden" behaviours, such as exposing oneself, doing a striptease before strangers, engaging in sexual activity with strangers, or sadomasochistic sex (S&M).

Masturbation fantasies can also allow people to rehearse sexual encounters. We may envision the unfolding of an intended sexual encounter, from greeting a date at the door, through dinner and a movie, and finally to the bedroom. We can mentally rehearse what we would say and do as a way of preparing for the date. Finally, masturbation fantasies may fill in the missing love object when we are alone or our partners are away.

Masturbation

Some older dictionaries define masturbation as "self-abuse." This definition provides clues to historical cultural attitudes toward the practice. **Masturbation** may be practised by manual stimulation of the genitals, perhaps with the aid of artificial stimulation, such as a vibrator. It may employ an object, such as a pillow or a **dildo**, that touches the genitals. Even before we conceive of sexual experiences with others, we may learn early in childhood that touching our genitals can produce pleasure.

Within the Judeo-Christian tradition, masturbation has been strongly condemned as sinful (Allen, 2000). Early Judeo-Christian attitudes toward masturbation reflected the censure that greeted nonprocreative sexual acts.

Until very recently, the history of cultural attitudes toward masturbation in Western society has been one of almost continual condemnation of the practice on moral and religious grounds—and even on medical grounds. Masturbation was thought to be physically and mentally harmful, as well as degrading. The eighteenth-century physicians S. A. D. Tissot and Benjamin Rush believed that masturbation caused tuberculosis, "nervous diseases," poor eyesight, memory loss, and epilepsy.

Many clergy and medical authorities of the nineteenth century were persuaded that certain foods had a stimulating effect on the sex organs. One of the more influential writers was the superintendent of the Battle Creek Sanatorium in Michigan, Dr. J. H. Kellogg (1852–1943), better known to you as the creator of the modern breakfast cereal. Kellogg identified 39 signs of masturbation, including acne, paleness, heart palpitations, rounded shoulders, weak backs, and convulsions. Kellogg believed that sexual desires could be controlled by sticking to a diet of simple foods, especially grains, including the corn flakes that have since borne his name. (We wonder how Kellogg would react to the energizing, sugar-coated cereals that bear his name now.)

Many nineteenth-century physicians also advised parents to take measures to prevent their children from masturbating. Kellogg suggested that parents bandage or cage their children's genitals or tie their hands. Some of the contraptions devised to prevent masturbation were barbarous (see Figure 8.1).

Despite this history, there is no scientific evidence that masturbation is harmful, save for rare injuries to the genitals from rough stimulation. Sex therapists have even found that masturbation has therapeutic benefits. It has emerged as a treatment for women who have difficulty reaching orgasm.

Masturbation Sexual self-stimulation.

Dildo A penis-shaped object used in sexual activity.

 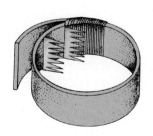

Figure 8.1 Devices Designed to Curb Masturbation.

Because of widespread beliefs that masturbation was harmful, various contraptions were introduced in the nineteenth century to prevent the practice in children. Some of the devices were barbarous.

Of course, people who consider masturbation wrong, harmful, or sinful may experience anxiety or guilt if they masturbate or wish to masturbate. These negative emotions are linked to their attitudes toward masturbation, not to masturbation per se (Michael et al., 1994).

Until recently, masturbation was considered such a taboo topic that it was avoided by the mass media. Now Hollywood is openly presenting masturbation, as seen in such hit films as *American Pie, There's Something About Mary,* and *American Beauty.* On the television series *Seinfeld,* one of the most memorable episodes involved the lead characters in a competition to see who could go the longest time without masturbating. In Canada, the producers of the Discovery Channel series *The Sex Files* presented an entire show on masturbation during prime-time television viewing. The program included a sequence involving a group of women learning how to reach orgasm with a vibrator.

Another indication of masturbation's coming of age is that May has been declared Masturbation Month. This first began at the Good Vibrations sex shop in San Francisco in 1995 with the objective of promoting the benefits of masturbation. Many sex shops across North America have joined this annual promotion. In May 2005, Toronto's Come As You Are held a Masturbate-A-Thon for which people solicited pledges for sex-oriented charities, with donations based on the number of minutes the volunteer masturbated.

Surveys indicate that most people masturbate at some time, including many married people. The incidence of masturbation is generally greater among men than women. However, there are women who masturbate frequently and men who rarely if ever do so (Michael et al., 1994).

A survey of university students in British Columbia found that nearly twice as many men (80%) as women (48%) reported some experience with masturbation (Meston, Trapnell, & Gorzalka, 1996). Of those students who had masturbated, men did so more often than did the women. Among female students surveyed at an Ontario university, 69% had masturbated (Pelletier & Herold, 1988). (Only students in senior-level classes [mean age of 21.5] were surveyed, which may account for why these percentages are higher than those of the B.C. study. As age increases, so does the proportion of people who masturbate.) About one-third of the students felt guilty about masturbation.

At another Ontario university, more men (84%) than women (62%) had first masturbated before the age of 16 (Rye, 2001). More than 90% of the students had fantasized during masturbation, with 27% of the women and 7% of the men using mechanical aids such as a vibrator. While 92% of the women and 75% of the men reported having had an orgasm in more than half of their masturbation experiences, more women (17%) than men (6%) said they had more than one orgasm in more than half of these experiences (Rye, 2001).

Research in Action

ONLINE MASTURBATION

In a survey of university students, University of Victoria researcher Sylvain Boies (2002) found that many had engaged in masturbation while online at the computer (72% of males and 21% of females). Among those who had actually viewed sexually explicit material online, 83% of the men and 55% of the women had masturbated while online. Those who approved of these materials were more likely to masturbate online than those who disapproved. Not surprisingly, 80% of those who found online sexually explicit material to be arousing had masturbated while online compared with only 25% of those who said that this material was not arousing.

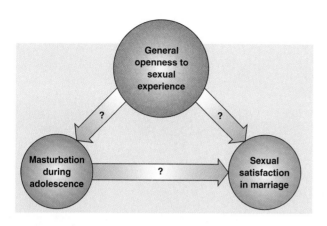

Figure 8.2 What Are the Connections Between Masturbation During Adolescence and Sexual Satisfaction in Marriage?

There is a positive correlation between masturbation during adolescence and sexual satisfaction in marriage. What hypotheses can we make about the causal connections? Does experience with masturbation teach people about their sexual needs so that they are more likely to obtain adequate sexual stimulation in marriage? Are people who masturbate early generally more open to exploring their sexuality and learning about the types of stimulation that arouse them? Such attitudes might also increase the likelihood that people would seek the coital stimulation they need to achieve sexual gratification in marriage.

Most surveys of masturbation have sampled university students. One exception is David McKenzie's (2005) study of Anglican and United Church clergy in British Columbia. Eighty-five percent of the male and female clergy reported that they masturbated.

Despite the sexual revolution, women may still find masturbation less pleasurable or acceptable than men do (Leitenberg et al., 1993). Women may still be subject to traditional socialization pressures that teach that sexual activity for pleasure's sake is more of a taboo for women than for men. Then, too, women are more likely to pursue sexual activity within the context of a relationship.

Education would appear to be a liberating influence on masturbation. For both genders, people with more education reported more frequent masturbation. Perhaps better-educated people are less likely to believe the old horror stories about masturbation or to be subject to traditional social restrictions. Conservative religious beliefs appear to constrain masturbation.

There appears to be a link between attitudes toward masturbation and orgasmic potential. A study of women revealed more negative attitudes toward masturbation among a group of 21- to 40-year-olds who had never achieved orgasm than among a comparison group of women who had (Kelly et al., 1990). Adolescent masturbation probably also sets the stage for marital sexual satisfaction by yielding information about the types of stimulation people need to obtain sexual gratification.

In our efforts to correct misinformation about masturbation, we do not wish to leave the impression that there is anything wrong with people who choose *not* to masturbate. Nor do we wish to imply that people *should* masturbate. Rather, we believe that it is up to the individual to decide for themselves.

MASTURBATION TECHNIQUES USED BY MALES

Sex is like bridge—if you don't have a good partner, you'd better have a good hand.

—Contemporary bathroom graffiti

Although masturbation techniques vary widely, most men report that they masturbate by manual manipulation of the penis (see Figure 8.3). Typically, they take one or two minutes to reach orgasm (Hite, 1981). Men tend to grip the penile shaft with one hand, jerking it up and down in a milking motion. Some men move the whole hand up and down the penis, while others use just two fingers, generally the thumb and index finger. Men usually shift from a gentler rubbing action during the flaccid

Figure 8.3 Male Masturbation.

Masturbation techniques vary widely, but most men report that they masturbate by manual manipulation of the penis. They tend to grip the penile shaft with one hand and jerk it up and down in a milking motion.

or semi-erect state of arousal to a more vigorous milking motion once full erection takes place. Men are also likely to stroke the glans and frenulum lightly at the outset, but their grip tightens and their motions speed up as orgasm nears. At orgasm, the penile shaft may be gripped tightly, but the glans has become sensitive, and contact with it is usually avoided. (Likewise, women usually avoid stimulating the clitoris directly during orgasm because of increased sensitivity.)

Some men use soapsuds (which may become irritating) as a lubricant for masturbation during baths or showers. Other lubricants, such as petroleum jelly or K-Y jelly, may also be used to reduce friction and to simulate the moist conditions of coitus.

A few men prefer to masturbate by rubbing the penis and testicles against clothing or bedding. A very few men rub their genitals against inflatable dolls sold in sex shops. These dolls may come with artificial mouths or vaginas that can be filled with warm water to mimic the sensations of coitus. Artificial vaginas are also for sale.

Some men strap vibrators to the backs of their hands. Electrical vibrators save labour but do not simulate the type of up-and-down motions of the penis that men favour. Hence, they are not used very often. Most men rely heavily on fantasy or erotic photos or videos but do not use sex-shop devices.

MASTURBATION TECHNIQUES USED BY FEMALES Techniques of female masturbation also vary widely. In fact, Masters and Johnson reported never observing two women masturbate in precisely the same way. Even when the general technique was similar, women varied in the tempo and style of their self-caresses. But some general trends have been noted. Most women masturbate by massaging the mons, labia minora, and clitoral region with circular or back-and-forth motions (Hite, 1976). They may also straddle the clitoris with their fingers, stroking the shaft rather than the glans (see Figure 8.4).

The glans may be lightly touched early during arousal, but because of its exquisite sensitivity, it is rarely stroked for any length of time during masturbation. Women typically achieve clitoral stimulation by rubbing or stroking the clitoral shaft or pulling or tugging on the vaginal lips. Some women also massage other sensitive areas, such as their breasts or nipples, with their free hand. Many women, like men, fantasize during masturbation (Leitenberg & Henning, 1995).

Sex shops sell dildos, which women can use to rub their vulvas or to insert vaginally. Penis-shaped vibrators may be used in a similar fashion. Many women masturbate during baths, some by spraying their genitals with water-massage

Figure 8.4 Female Masturbation.

Techniques of female masturbation vary so widely that Masters and Johnson reported never observing two women masturbating in precisely the same way. Most women, however, masturbate by massaging the mons, labia minora, and clitoral region, either with circular or back-and-forth motions.

showerheads. In the nearby World of Diversity feature, Canadian writer Buffy Childerhose discusses some myths about vibrators and notes that they have become more mainstream and acceptable to women across Canada.

Handheld electrical vibrators (see Figure 8.5) provide a constant massaging action against the genitals that can be erotic. Women who use vibrators often experiment with different models to find one with the shape and intensity of vibration that suits them.

Figure 8.5 Electric Vibrators.

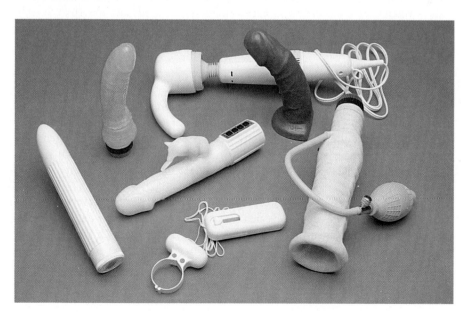

A World of Diversity

TOYS IN BABELAND

When the power died in Helen C.'s Montreal apartment during the ice storm of 1998, it wasn't the frigid winds of a Quebec winter that made her blood run cold. No, the thought that sent shivers down her spine was this: her vibrator was a plug-in.

No longer the preserve of sleazy boutiques, sex toys have finally gone mainstream. From coyly named "personal massagers" to the explicitly dubbed Clit Lane, our toys have come a long way, baby. And so have we. Before buying a vibrator, Helen rarely climaxed, with or without a partner. "My orgasms were very timid; I didn't understand what the fuss was about." After hearing a friend wax poetic about a vibrator, she finally took matters into her own hands. "I felt like I'd learned a new language instantly,"

Helen says, recalling her orgasm, "I finally understood what everyone was talking about."

Even today, some women think sex toys are only for perverts, which is like saying that pleasure is only for perverts. Guilt about sexual pleasure lies at the root of many women's misconceptions about "jilling off."

No More Plain Brown Wrappers

Back in the days of disco, the only places to get sex toys were dingy stores run by men who were eager to be your toy, not just sell you one. Today's sex shops are more user-friendly, and mail order and the Web allow for discreet home shopping. The luxury of anonymous buying has tempted so many women that babes in toyland are now a marketing target.

Another trend is women's boutiques. With their roots in home sex-toy parties of the '70s, female-oriented sex stores are taking "petting the bunny" into the 21st century.

There are a handful of women's sexuality stores that have Canada buzzing. Halifax is home to Venus Envy, Toronto boasts both Good for Her and Come as You Are and Vancouver is the site of Womyns' Ware (home of the aforementioned Clit Lane). These stores offer high-quality products and much more.

"Our mandate is much broader than retail," explains Womyns' Ware co-owner Janna Sylvest. "It's about recognizing women's sexuality as something sacred and powerful."

Source: Buffy Childerhose (1999, March). From "Toys in Babeland," Chatelaine, *pp. 94, 97.*

Sexual Behaviour with Others

Partners' feelings for one another, and the quality of their relationships, may be stronger determinants of their sexual arousal and response than the techniques that they employ. Partners are most likely to experience mutually enjoyable sexual interactions when they are sensitive to each other's sexual needs and incorporate techniques with which they are both comfortable. As with other aspects of sharing relationships, communication is the most important "sexual" technique.

Foreplay

Various forms of noncoital sex, such as cuddling, kissing, petting, and oral–genital contact, are used as **foreplay**. The pattern and duration of foreplay vary widely within and across cultures. Broude and Greene (1976) found that prolonged foreplay was the norm in about half of the societies in their cross-cultural sample. Foreplay was minimal in 1 out of 10 societies and virtually absent in about one-third of them.

Frequently, there is a gender difference in the amount of foreplay desired. A survey of U.S. college students revealed that women wanted longer periods of foreplay (and "afterplay") than men did (Denny et al., 1984). Because women usually require a longer period of stimulation during sex with a partner to reach orgasm, increasing the duration of foreplay may increase female coital responsiveness.

Kissing, genital touching, and oral–genital contact may also be experienced as ends in themselves, not as preludes to coitus. Yet some people object to petting for

Foreplay Physical interactions that are sexually stimulating and set the stage for intercourse.

Research in Action

DURATION OF FOREPLAY

In a recent study of heterosexual couples, Andrea Miller and Sandra Byers (2004) of the University of New Brunswick found that the men and women were similar in their desired duration of foreplay. However, the women underestimated both their partner's and the average male's desired duration.

Perhaps women are influenced by societal stereotypes that men are mainly interested in intercourse. Interestingly, the men were accurate in estimating how much time their partner, and the average woman, wanted to spend in foreplay. However, like the women, the men underestimated how much time the average man would like to spend.

petting's sake, equating it with masturbation as a form of sexual activity without a "product." Many people behave as though all sexual contact had to lead to coitus, perhaps because of the importance that our culture places on it.

Kissing

Kissing is almost universal in our culture, but it occurs less often among the world's cultures than manual or oral stimulation of the genitals (Frayser, 1985). Couples may kiss for its own enjoyment or as a prelude to intercourse, in which case it is a part of foreplay. In *simple kissing*, the partners keep their mouths closed. Simple kissing may develop into caresses of the lips with the tongue or into nibbling of the lower lip. In what Kinsey called *deep kissing*, which is also called French kissing or soul kissing, the partners part their lips and insert their tongues into each other's mouths. Some prefer the lips parted slightly. Others open their mouths widely.

Kissing is not limited to the partner's mouth. Among male university students in British Columbia, 77% of the non-Asians had kissed a female's breasts, compared with 61% of Asians. Among the women, 83% of the non-Asians had had their breasts kissed by a male, compared with 55% of the Asian women (Meston et al., 1996). Women usually prefer several minutes of body contact and gentle caresses before they want their partner to kiss their breasts or suck or lick their nipples. Women also usually do not prefer a hard sucking action unless they are highly aroused. Many women are reluctant to tell their partners that sucking hurts, because they do not want to interfere with their partner's pleasure.

Other parts of the body are also often kissed, including the hands and feet, the neck and earlobes, the insides of the thighs, and the genitals themselves.

Touching

Touching or caressing erogenous zones with the hands or other parts of the body can be highly arousing. Even simple hand-holding can be sexually stimulating for couples who are sexually attracted to one another. The hands are very rich in nerve endings.

Touching is a common form of foreplay. Both men and women generally prefer manual or oral stimulation of the genitals as a prelude to intercourse. Women generally prefer that direct caressing of the genitals be focused around the clitoris but not directly on the extremely sensitive clitoral glans. Men sometimes assume (often mistakenly) that their partners want them to insert their finger or fingers into the vagina as a form of foreplay. But not all women enjoy this form of stimulation.

Some women go along with it because it's what their partners want or something they *think* their partners want. Ironically, men may do it because they assume that their *partners* want it. When in doubt, it would not hurt to ask. If you are not

Applied Knowledge

TECHNIQUES OF MANUAL STIMULATION OF THE GENITALS

Here again, variability in technique is the rule, so partners need to communicate their preferences. The man's partner may use two hands to stimulate his genitals. One may be used to fondle the scrotum, by gently squeezing the skin between the fingers (taking care not to apply pressure to the testes themselves). The other hand may circle the coronal ridge and engage in gentle stroking of the penis, followed by more vigorous up-and-down movements as the man becomes more aroused.

The penis may also be gently rolled back and forth between the palms as though one were making a ball of clay into a sausage, increasing pressure as arousal progresses. Note that men who are highly aroused or who have just had an orgasm may find direct stimulation of the penile glans uncomfortable.

The woman may prefer that her partner approach genital stimulation gradually, following stimulation of other body parts. Genital stimulation may begin with light, stroking motions of the inner thighs and move on to the vaginal lips (labia) and the clitoral area. Women may enjoy pressure against the mons pubis from the heel of the hand, or they may like tactile stimulation of the labia, which are sensitive to stroking motions. Clitoral stimulation can focus on the clitoral shaft or the region surrounding the shaft, rather than on the clitoris itself, because of the extreme sensitivity of the clitoral glans to touch.

Moreover, the clitoris should not be stroked if it is dry, lest it become irritated. Because it produces no lubrication of its own, a finger may enter the outer portion of the vagina to apply some vaginal lubrication to the clitoral region.

Some, but not all, women enjoy having a finger inserted into the vagina, which can stroke the vaginal walls or simulate thrusting of the penis. Vaginal insertion is usually preferred, if at all, only after the woman has become highly aroused. Many women desire that their partners discontinue stroking motions while they are experiencing orgasm, but others want stimulation to continue. Men and women may physically guide their partners' hands or otherwise indicate what types of strokes they find most pleasurable.

If a finger is to be inserted into the vagina, it should be clean. Fingernails should be well trimmed. Inserting into

sure what to say, you can always blame us: "Listen, I read this thing in my human sexuality text, and I was wondering . . ." Among students at an Ontario university, more than 90% reported that they had experienced having their genitals manually stimulated by their partner (Rye, 2001).

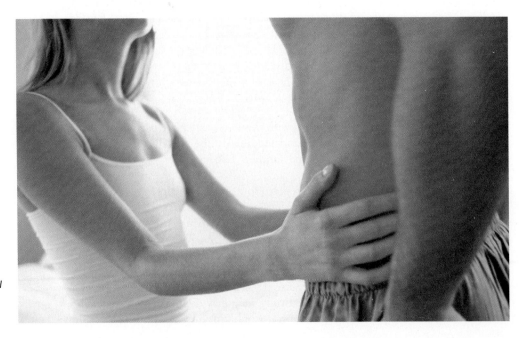

How Touching?
Touching is a common form of foreplay. Most people like manual or oral stimulation of the genital organs as a prelude to sexual intercourse.

the vagina fingers that have been in the anus is dangerous. The fingers may transfer microbes from the woman's digestive tract, where they do no harm, to the woman's reproductive tract, where they can cause serious infections.

Across Canada some sex educators (mainly those associated with sex toy stores) offer practical courses for adults on enhancing sexual pleasure, including techniques of manual and/or oral stimulation of the genitals. Good for Her (www.goodforher.com) in Toronto also offers courses on kissing, stripping for your love, and anal sex. Some individuals engage in the sexual practice called "fisting." Fisting is the insertion of the fist or hand into the vagina or the rectum. Fisting is more common among male–male than among male–female couples, and it carries the risk of infection or injury to the rectum or anus. A survey of 75 gay men in Australia found that fisting was usually done with gloves, although fingering was not (Richters et al., 2003).

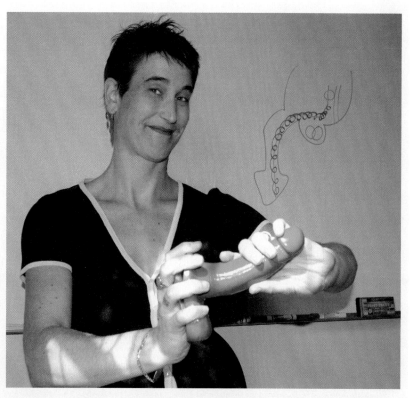

Carlyle Jansen at Good for Her in Toronto gives a course called The Art and Joy of a Hand Job. She uses a dildo to illustrate manual sex techniques.

Masters and Johnson (1979) noted gender differences with respect to preferences in foreplay. Men typically prefer direct stroking of their genitals by their partner early in lovemaking. Women, however, tend to prefer that their partners caress their genitals after a period of general body contact that includes holding, hugging, and non-genital massage. This is not a hard and fast (or slow) rule, but it concurs with other observations that men tend to be more genitally oriented than women. Women are more likely to view sex within a broader framework of affection and love.

Stimulation of the Breasts

Men are more likely to stimulate women's breasts than to enjoy having their own breasts fondled, even though the breasts (and especially the nipples) are erotically sensitive in both sexes. Most, but not all, women enjoy stimulation of the breasts. Some women are capable of achieving orgasm from stimulation of the breasts alone.

The hands and the mouth can be used to stimulate the breasts and the nipples. The desired type and intensity of stimulation of the breasts varies from person to person, so partners need to communicate their preferences.

Gay men apparently make more use of stimulation of their partner's nipples than heterosexual women do. Gay male couples tend to engage in sexual activities such as kissing, hugging, petting, mutual masturbation, fellatio, and anal intercourse. Masters and Johnson's (1979) laboratory observations of sexual relations between gay males showed that gay males spent a good deal of time caressing their partners' bodies before approaching the genitals (Figure 8.6). After hugging and kissing, 31 of 42 gay male couples observed by Masters and Johnson used oral or manual nipple stimulation.

Although some heterosexual men enjoy having their breasts and nipples stimulated by their partners, many—perhaps most—do not. Many men are unaware that

Figure 8.6 Gay Males Hugging.

Masters and Johnson's observations suggest that gay males are likely to spend more time than heterosexual males in hugging their partners. Gay males are also more likely than heterosexual males to want their nipples to be caressed.

Figure 8.7 Lesbians Holding One Another.

This position enables lesbians to hug one another and to reach one another's genitals. If they draw a bit closer, they can rub against one another's genitals.

their breasts are erotically sensitive. Others may feel uncomfortable receiving a form of stimulation that they have learned to associate with the stereotypical feminine sexual role.

Sexual techniques practiced by lesbians vary. Lesbian couples report kissing, manual and oral breast stimulation, and manual and oral stimulation of the genitals. Manual genital stimulation is a common and frequent sexual activity among lesbian couples. Most lesbian couples also engage in genital apposition. That is, they position themselves so as to rub their genitals together rhythmically. Like gay males, lesbians spend a good deal of time holding, kissing, and caressing each other's bodies before they approach the breasts and genitals (Figure 8.7). By contrast, heterosexual males tend to move quickly to stimulate their partners' breasts or start directly with genital stimulation (Masters & Johnson, 1979).

Like heterosexual women, lesbians are less genitally oriented and less fixated on orgasm than are men. Lesbians generally begin stimulating their partners with more general genital stimulation rather than direct clitoral stimulation, whereas heterosexual males often begin by stimulating the clitoris (Masters & Johnson, 1979). Traditionally, most lesbian couples did not engage in deep penetration of the vagina with fingers. Rather, they used more shallow vaginal penetration, focusing stimulation on the vaginal lips and entrance. However, in recent times, lesbians are being encouraged to be more adventurous and to engage in deep penetration, sometimes with the use of dildoes.

Oral–Genital Stimulation

Oral stimulation of the male genitals is called **fellatio**. Fellatio is referred to by slang terms such as *blow job, sucking, sucking off,* or *giving head.* Oral stimulation of the female genitals is called **cunnilingus**, which is referred to by slang expressions such as *eating* (a woman) or *going down* on her.

The popularity of oral–genital stimulation has increased dramatically since Kinsey's day, especially among young married couples. Kinsey and his colleagues (1948, 1953) found that at least 60% of married, college-educated couples had experienced oral–genital contact. Such experiences were reported by only about 20% of couples who had only a high school education and by 10% of couples who had only a grade school education.

The Compas poll has been the only national survey of Canadians to date to ask about oral sex. Although almost all the participants in that survey responded to these questions, they had the highest refusal rates, with three times as many women (15%) as men (5%) refusing to answer the question (Fischtein & Herold, 2002). The majority of both men (89%) and women (78%) reported having experienced giving and/or receiving oral sex, a gender difference that may be at least partially accounted for by the women's higher refusal rate. Interestingly, the proportion who had received oral sex was almost the same as for those who gave it.

Research with gay and bisexual men in Ontario found that almost all of the men surveyed had engaged in oral sex in the previous three months (Myers et al., 2004). Of those who engaged in insertive oral sex with a regular partner, about 80% did not use a condom. Similarly, most heterosexual couples do not use condoms when having oral sex.

The age differences in oral sex experience among Canadians reveal a much greater acceptance of oral sex among the younger age groups (see Table 8.2). The most notable differences are those between people in their 60s and in their 50s. One explanation is that those who are in their 50s experienced their adolescence at the time of the sexual revolution, when many changes in sexual behaviours were occurring. Changes in the acceptance of oral sex behaviours were so dramatic that they have been referred to as the second stage in the sexual revolution, with the first stage having focused on changes in rates of premarital intercourse (Herold, 1984).

Canadians who have not completed high school are the least likely to have experienced oral sex. This is especially true for women, with half of those who have not completed high school saying that they have not experienced oral sex (Fischtein & Herold, 2002). The data on oral sex as well as other sexual practices suggests that those with less education are less experimental and perhaps more concerned about the "normality" of these practices.

Fellatio Oral stimulation of the male genitals.

Cunnilingus Oral stimulation of the female genitals.

TABLE 8.2
Oral Sex Experience Among Canadians, by Age

Age Cohort	Males	Females
60s	54%	28.8%
50s	85.9	77.8
40s	91.1	81.1
30s	93.5	90
20s	97.9	92.4

Source: D. S. Fischtein & E. S. Herold (2002, June). Gender differences in sexual attitudes and behaviours among Canadian adults: A national survey. Poster session presented at the annual meeting of the International Academy of Sex Research, Hamburg, Germany. Based on the Compas poll.

Other trends can be seen by looking at a study of female university students in Ontario. One-half of the women surveyed had brought their partners to orgasm through oral sex and about half had had an orgasm while receiving oral sex (Herold & Way, 1983). Among those who had not experienced coitus, one-third had engaged in oral sex. Among those who had experienced coitus, 87% had experienced cunnilingus and 87% had performed fellatio. Four-fifths of those who had not performed oral sex said they would feel guilty if they did, whereas only one-fifth of those who had performed oral sex said they felt guilty about it. About 10% experienced oral sex three or more times a week and about one-quarter experienced it one to two times a week.

In a more recent study at the University of Guelph, Tanya Hill (2005) found that 89% of female students had engaged in oral sex with their most recent partner. About one-half reported they engaged in oral sex most of the time when having sexual relations with their partner.

Like touching, oral–genital stimulation can be used as a prelude to intercourse or as a sexual end in itself. If orgasm is reached through oral–genital stimulation, a woman may be concerned about tasting or swallowing a man's ejaculate. There is no scientific evidence that swallowing semen is harmful to one's health, unless the man is infected with a sexually transmitted disease in which semen can act as a conduit of infections (Reinisch, 1990). Note that oral–genital contact with the genitals of an infected partner, even without contact with semen, may transmit harmful organisms. Couples are thus advised to practise "safer sex" techniques unless they know that they and their partners are free of sexually transmitted diseases (Reinisch, 1990).

Applied Knowledge

ORAL SEX TECHNIQUES

Techniques of Fellatio

Although the word *fellatio* is derived from a Latin root that means "to suck," a sucking action is generally not highly arousing. The up-and-down movements of the penis in the partner's mouth, and the licking of the penis, are generally the most stimulating. Gentle licking of the scrotum may also be highly arousing.

The mouth is stimulating to the penis because it contains warm, moist mucous membranes, as does the vagina. Muscles of the mouth and jaw can create varied pressure and movements. Erection may be stimulated by gently pulling the penis with the mouth (being careful never to touch the penis with the teeth) and simultaneously providing manual stimulation, as described earlier.

Higher levels of sexual arousal or orgasm can be promoted by moving the penis in and out of the mouth, simulating the motion of the penis in the vagina during intercourse. The speed of the motions can be varied, and manual stimulation near the base of the penis (firmly encircling the lower portion of the penis or providing pressure behind the scrotum) can also be stimulating.

Some people may gag during fellatio, a reflex that is triggered by pressure of the penis against the back of the tongue or against the throat. Gagging may be avoided if the man's partner grasps the shaft of the penis with one hand and controls the depth of penetration. Gagging is less likely to occur if the partner performing fellatio is on top, rather than below, and if there is verbal communication about how deep the man should penetrate. Gagging may also be overcome by allowing gradually deeper penetration of the penis over successive occasions while keeping the throat muscles relaxed.

Techniques of Cunnilingus

Women can be highly aroused by their partner's tongue because it is soft, warm, and well lubricated. In contrast to a finger, the tongue can almost never be used too harshly. A woman may thus be more receptive to direct clitoral contact by a tongue. Cunnilingus provides such intense stimulation that many women find it to be the best means for achieving orgasm. Some women cannot reach orgasm in any other way (Hite, 1976).

In performing cunnilingus, the partner may begin by kissing and licking the woman's abdomen and inner thighs, gradually nearing the vulva. Gentle tugging at or sucking of the labia minora can be stimulating, but the partner should take care not to bite. Many women enjoy licking of the clitoral region, and others desire sucking of the clitoris itself. The tongue may also be inserted into the vagina, where it may imitate the thrusts of intercourse.

"69"

The term *sixty-nine,* or *soixante-neuf* in French, describes simultaneous oral–genital stimulation (see Figure 8.8). The numerals 6 and 9 are used because they resemble two partners who are upside-down and facing each other.

The "69" position has the psychologically positive feature of allowing couples to experience simultaneous stimulation, but it can be awkward if two people are not similar in size. Some couples avoid "69" because it deprives each partner of the opportunity to focus fully on receiving or providing sexual pleasure. The "69" technique may be practised side by side or with one partner on top of the other. But here again there are no strict rules, and couples often alternate positions.

Figure 8.8 Simultaneous Oral–Genital Contact.

The "69" position allows partners to engage in simultaneous oral–genital stimulation.

Despite the popularity of oral sex among couples today, those who desire to abstain from it have no reason to consider themselves abnormal.

People offer various reasons for abstaining from oral sex. Although natural body odours may be arousing to some people, others are disturbed by the genital odours to which oral sex exposes them. Some people object on grounds of cleanliness. They view the genitals as "dirty" because of their proximity to the urinary and anal openings. Concerns about offensive odours or cleanliness may be relieved by thoroughly washing the genitals beforehand.

Some women prefer not to taste or swallow semen because they find the ejaculate "dirty," sinful, or repulsive. Others are put off by the taste or texture. Semen has a salty taste and a texture similar to that of an egg white. If couples are to engage in unprotected oral sex, open discussion of feelings can enhance pleasure and diminish anxiety. For example, the man can be encouraged to warn his partner or remove his penis from her mouth when he is nearing ejaculation.

Let us dispel a couple of myths about semen. For one thing, it is impossible to become pregnant by swallowing semen. For another, semen is not fattening. The average amount of semen expelled in the ejaculate contains only about 5 calories. On the other hand, it is not our intention to encourage swallowing of semen. The aesthetics of swallowing semen have little or nothing to do with concerns about pregnancy or weight. They involve the preferences of the individual.

Some of the objections expressed by people who are reluctant to engage in oral sex may be overcome. Others, such as beliefs that oral–genital contact is offensive or repulsive, are more deeply rooted. Shyness and embarrassment may also deter a person from engaging in oral sex.

Sexual Intercourse: Positions and Techniques

Sexual intercourse, or *coitus* (from the Latin *coire*, which means "to go together"), is sexual activity in which the penis is inserted into the vagina. Intercourse may take place in many different positions. Each position, however, must allow the genitals to be aligned so that the penis is contained by the vagina. In addition to varying positions, couples vary the depth and rate of thrusting (in-and-out motions) and the sources of additional sexual stimulation.

Though the number of possible coital positions is virtually endless, we will focus on four of the most commonly used positions: the male-superior (man-on-top) position, the female-superior (woman-on-top) position, the lateral-entry (side-entry) position, and the rear-entry position. Although it does not technically fit the definition of sexual intercourse, we shall also discuss anal intercourse, a sexual technique used by both male–female and male–male couples.

Couples can use a variety of sexual positions and techniques to spice up their sex lives. Many couples like to try having sex in different types of locations, such as the outdoors. Some desire to have sex on an airplane, commonly referred to as joining the "Mile High Club." Love Air, a small airline company in Pemberton, British Columbia, offers couples the opportunity to have sex in private aboard a Cessna 206. There is a bed at the back of the plane and a curtain separates them from the pilot (Yearwood-Lee, 2002).

THE MALE-SUPERIOR (MAN-ON-TOP) POSITION   The male-superior position (this "superiority" simply reflects the couple's body positions, but it has sometimes been taken as a symbol of male domination) has also been called the **missionary position**. In this position the partners face each other. The man lies above the woman, perhaps supporting himself on his hands and knees rather than resting his full weight on his partner (see Figure 8.9). Even so, it is easier for the man to move than for the woman, which suggests that he is responsible for directing their activity.

Many sex therapists suggest that it is preferable for the woman to guide the penis into the vagina, rather than having the man do so. The idea is that the woman can feel the location of the vaginal opening and determine the proper angle of entry. To accomplish this, the woman must feel comfortable "taking charge" of the couple's lovemaking. With the breaking down of the traditional stereotype of the female as passive, women are feeling more comfortable taking this role. The male-superior position has the advantage of permitting the couple to face one another so that kissing is easier. The woman may run her hands along her partner's body, stroking his buttocks and perhaps cupping a hand beneath his scrotum to increase stimulation as he reaches orgasm.

But the male-superior position makes it difficult for the man to caress his partner while simultaneously supporting himself with his hands. Therefore, the position may not be favoured by women who enjoy having their partners provide manual clitoral stimulation during coitus.

Missionary position The coital position in which the man is on top. Also termed the *male-superior position*.

Figure 8.9 The Male-Superior Coital Position.

In this position the couple face each other. The man lies above the woman, perhaps supporting himself on his hands and knees rather than allowing his full weight to press against his
partner. The position is also (somewhat disparagingly) referred to as the missionary position.
(Primitive peoples have supposedly reported that this position never occurred to them until
Western visitors described it.)

THE FEMALE-SUPERIOR (WOMAN-ON-TOP) POSITION In the female-
superior position, the couple face each other with the woman on top. The woman
straddles the male from above, controlling the angle of penile entry and the depth
of thrusting (see Figure 8.10). Some women maintain a sitting position; others lie
on top of their partners. Many women vary their position.

In the female-superior position, the woman is psychologically—and to some
degree physically—in charge. She can move as rapidly or as slowly as she wishes
with little effort, adjusting her body to vary the angle and depth of penetration. The
woman can, in effect, guarantee that she receives adequate clitoral stimulation,
either by the penis or manually by his hand or her own. This position thus facilitates orgasm in the woman.

THE LATERAL-ENTRY (SIDE-ENTRY) POSITION In the lateral-entry position,
the man and woman lie side by side, facing each other (see Figure 8.11). This position has the advantages of allowing each partner relatively free movement and easy
access to the other. The man and woman may kiss freely, and they can stroke each
other's bodies with a free arm. The position is not physically taxing, because both
partners are resting easily on the bedding. Thus it is an excellent position for prolonged coitus, for older couples, and when couples are somewhat fatigued. The lateral position is useful during pregnancy (at least until the final stages, when the
distension of the woman's abdomen may make lateral entry difficult).

THE REAR-ENTRY POSITION In the rear-entry position, the man faces the
woman's rear. In one variation (see Figure 8.12), the woman supports herself on her
hands and knees while the man supports himself on his knees, entering her from

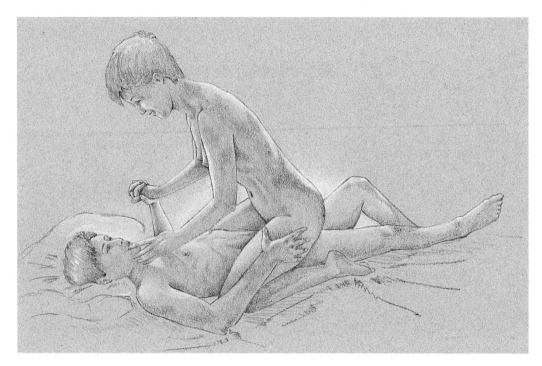

Figure 8.10 The Female-Superior Coital Position.

The woman straddles the male from above, controlling the angle of penile entry and the depth of thrusting. The female-superior position puts the woman psychologically and physically in charge. The woman can ensure that she receives adequate clitoral stimulation from the penis or the hand. This position also tends to be less stimulating for the male and may thus help him to control ejaculation.

behind. In another, the couple lies alongside one another and the woman lifts one leg, draping it backward over her partner's thigh. The latter position is particularly useful during the later stages of pregnancy.

Figure 8.11 The Lateral-Entry Coital Position.

In this position, the couple face each other side by side. Each partner has relatively free movement and easy access to the other. Because both partners rest easily on the bedding, it is an excellent position for prolonged coitus and for coitus when couples are fatigued.

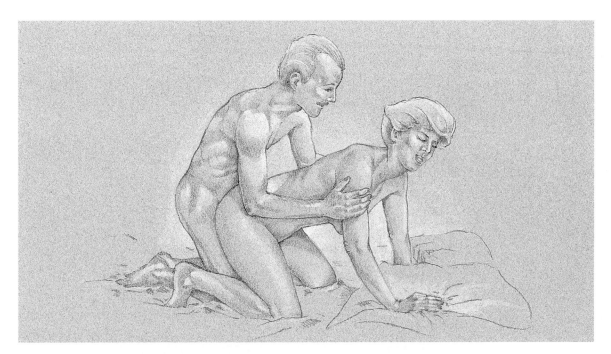

Figure 8.12 The Rear-Entry Coital Position.

The rear-entry position is highly erotic for men who enjoy viewing and pressing their abdomens against their partners' buttocks. However, some couples feel uncomfortable about the position because of its association with animal mating patterns. The position is also impersonal in that the partners do not face each other. Moreover, some couples dislike the feeling that the man is psychologically in charge because he can see his partner but she cannot readily see him.

The rear-entry position may be highly stimulating for both partners. Men may enjoy viewing and pressing their abdomens against their partner's buttocks. The man can reach around or underneath to provide additional stimulation of the clitoris or breasts, and she may reach behind (if she is on her hands and knees) to stroke or grasp her partner's testicles.

Some couples may feel uncomfortable about using the position because of its association with animal mating patterns. The position is also impersonal in the sense that the partners do not face each other, which may create a sense of emotional distance.

In a study among students at a university in British Columbia, the two most popular positions were the male superior and the female superior and the least popular was lateral entry (Meston et al., 196). Table 8.3 provides a breakdown of how Asian and non-Asian students responded.

USE OF FANTASY DURING COITUS As with masturbation, mental excursions into fantasy during coitus may be used to enhance sexual arousal and response (Davidson & Hoffman, 1986). In a sense, coital fantasies allow couples to inject sexual variety and even offbeat sexual escapades into their sexual activity without being unfaithful. Fantasies have historically been viewed as evil, however. People believed that fantasies, like dreams, were placed in the mind by agents of the devil. Despite this tradition, researchers find that most married people have engaged in coital fantasies (Davidson & Hoffman, 1986). Nor does there appear to be any connection between sexual dissatisfaction with one's relationship and the use of coital fantasies (Davidson & Hoffman, 1986). Thus, coital fantasies are not a form of compensation for an unrewarding sexual relationship.

The Sex Coach at iVillage Offers advice about sexual techniques and sexual satisfaction. **www.ivillage.com/ relationships**

TABLE 8.3
Intercourse Positions Used by Asian and Non-Asian Students in British Columbia

Position	Male		Female	
	Non-Asian	Asian	Non-Asian	Asian
Male above	63%	35%	69%	36%
Female above	58	34	66	33
From rear	45	27	60	22
Sitting	41	28	57	28
Side by side	36	19	50	19

Note: The sample included both those who had experienced sexual intercourse and those who had not. If this analysis had included only the former group, the percentages for each sexual position would have been higher.

Source: Adapted from C. M. Meston, P. D. Trapnell, & B. B. Gorzalka (1996). Ethnic and gender differences in sexuality: Variations in sexual behavior between Asian and Non-Asian university students. Archives of Sexual Behavior, 25, 33–72.

Lest you think that coital fantasies arise only out of sexual monotony in marriage, consider that many if not most unmarried people also fantasize during sexual relations. In one study of sexually experienced, single undergraduates, Sue (1979) found that virtually the same percentages of men (58.6%) and women (59.4%) reported "sometimes" or "almost always" fantasizing during coitus.

Studies of coital fantasies by Hariton and Singer (1974) and Sue (1979), among others, find that sexual fantasies during intercourse are common among couples with close relationships and are a means of facilitating sexual arousal. By facilitating sexual arousal, coital fantasies may help strengthen the intimate bond between the partners. Evidence does not show coital fantasies to be a sign of a troubled relationship.

Partners are often reluctant to share their coital fantasies, or even to admit having them. This is especially true when the fantasy is about someone other than the partner. The fantasizer might fear being accused of harbouring extramarital desires. Or the fantasizer might fear that the partner will interpret fantasies as a sign of rejection: "What's the matter, don't I turn you on any more?" Any perceived merits of self-disclosure are best weighed against one's partner's potential reactions to coital fantasies.

ANAL INTERCOURSE Anal intercourse can be practised by male–female couples and male–male couples. It involves insertion of the penis into the rectum.

The rectum is richly endowed with nerve endings and is thus highly sensitive to sexual stimulation. Anal intercourse is also referred to as "Greek culture," or lovemaking in the "Greek style," because of bisexuality in ancient Greece among males. Both women and men may reach orgasm through receiving the penis in the rectum.

In anal intercourse, the penetrating male usually situates himself behind his partner. (He can also lie above or below his partner in a face-to-face position.) The receiving partner can supplement anal stimulation with manual stimulation of the clitoral region or penis to reach orgasm. Because the rectum produces no natural lubrication, people engaging in anal intercourse are advised to use an artificial lubricant, such as K-Y jelly.

Women often report wanting their partner's fingers in the anus at the height of passion or at the moment of orgasm. A finger in the rectum during orgasm can heighten sexual sensation because the anal sphincters contract during orgasm. Although some men also want a finger in the anus, many resist because they associate anal penetration with the female role or with male–male sexual activity. However, the desire to be entered by one's partner is not necessarily connected with sexual orientation. A gay male or lesbian sexual orientation refers to the eroticization of members of one's own gender, not to the desire to penetrate or be penetrated.

> **Anilingus** Oral stimulation of the anus.

Many couples are repulsed by the idea of anal intercourse. They view it as unnatural, immoral, or risky. Yet others find anal sex to be an enjoyable sexual variation, though perhaps not a regular feature of their sexual diet.

The NHSLS (National Health and Social Life Survey of Americans) found that 1 man in 4 (26%) and 1 woman in 5 (20%) reported having engaged in anal sex at some time during their lives (Laumann et al., 1994). Yet only about 1 person in 10 (10% of the men and 9% of the women) had engaged in anal sex during the past year. As with oral sex, there was a higher incidence of anal sex among more highly educated people in the NHSLS survey. For example, about 30% of the male college graduates had engaged in anal sex, as compared with 23% of male high school graduates. About 29% of the women with advanced college degrees had engaged in anal sex, as compared with about 17% of the women who had graduated only from high school (Laumann et al., 1994). Education appears to be a liberating experience in sexual experimentation.

Not all gay males enjoy or practise anal intercourse. Of those who do, most alternate between being the inserter and being the insertee. Interviews with 51 gay men suggest that playing the inserter role in anal intercourse is sometimes associated with fantasies of domination, and the insertee role with fantasies of submission (Kippax & Smith, 2001). But some gays who practised anal intercourse denied that sex had anything to do with power and with a dimension of activity–passivity; they felt that sex was about sharing.

Some couples kiss or lick the anus in their foreplay. This practice is called **anilingus**. In the Ontario survey of gay and bisexual men, about one-half had engaged in anilingus within the previous three months (Myers et al., 2004). Oral–anal sex carries a serious health risk, however, because micro-organisms that cause intestinal diseases and various sexually transmitted diseases can be spread through oral–anal contact.

Research in Action

INCIDENCE OF ANAL INTERCOURSE

In a study of university students in British Columbia, 19% of the non-Asian females reported engaging in anal intercourse compared with 3% of the Asian females. Five percent of the non-Asian men and 6% of the Asian men engaged in anal intercourse (Meston et al., 1996). More of the students had engaged in caressing of the anal area. About half (45%) of the non-Asian women reported having their anal area caressed compared with 28% of the non-Asian men. About one-fifth of the Asian men and women had experienced caressing of the anal area.

At the University of Waterloo, more students had engaged in anal intercourse without a condom (15%) than with a condom (9%) (Rye, 2001). Among female students at the University of Guelph, 13% had engaged in anal intercourse with their most recent partner. However, of those who had engaged in anal sex, most said that they rarely did this (Hill, 2005).

Anal intercourse is more common among gay males than among heterosexual couples. In a study of almost 5000 gay males from across Canada, 62% had engaged in anal intercourse in the previous three months (Myers et al., 1996). In a more recent study of gay and bisexual men in Ontario having sex with a regular partner within the previous three months, 40% reported engaging in insertive anal sex without a condom while 44% had engaged in insertive anal sex with a condom (Myers et al., 2004).

Research in Action

FEELINGS ABOUT SEXUAL BEHAVIOURS

The fact that people engage in certain behaviours does not necessarily mean they have positive feelings about those behaviours. University of McGill researchers Eric Ochs and Yitzchak Binik (1999) surveyed 70 couples about their ex-

perience with 68 sexual behaviours, including how comfortable they felt about each of them. Women rated themselves as more comfortable than did the men on the least sexually explicit behaviours (cuddling, hugging, and dancing). The men were more comfortable than the women with fellatio, anal intercourse, woman-on-top intercourse, and vaginal rear-entry intercourse.

Many couples today hesitate to engage in anal intercourse because of the fear of AIDS and other sexually transmitted infections (STIs). The AIDS virus and other micro-organisms that cause STIs, such as gonorrhea, syphilis, and hepatitis, can be spread by anal intercourse, because small tears in the rectal tissues may allow the microbes to enter the recipient's blood system. Women also run a greater risk of contracting HIV, the virus that causes AIDS, from anal intercourse than from vaginal intercourse—just as receptive anal intercourse in gay men carries a high risk of infection (Voeller, 1991). However, partners who are both infection-free are at no risk of contracting STIs through any sexual act.

In this chapter, we have observed many of the variations in human sexual expression. No other species shows such diversity in sexual behaviour.

Summing Up

Solitary Sexual Behaviour

Use of Fantasy

Sexual fantasies are often incorporated during masturbation or during sex with another person to heighten sexual response. Sexual fantasies range from the realistic to genuine flights of fancy. Many people fantasize about sexual activities that they would not actually engage in.

Masturbation

Masturbation may be practised by means of manual stimulation of the genitals, perhaps with the aid of an electric vibrator or an object that provides tactile stimulation. Within the Judeo-Christian tradition, masturbation has been condemned as sinful. Until recent years, masturbation was thought to be physically and mentally harmful, yet contemporary scholars see masturbation as harmless. Surveys indicate that most people have masturbated at some point in their lives.

Sexual Behaviour with Others

Foreplay

The pattern and duration of foreplay vary widely within and across cultures. Women usually desire longer periods of foreplay than men do.

Kissing

Couples kiss for its own enjoyment or as a prelude to intercourse.

Touching

Touching or caressing erogenous zones with the hands or other parts of the body can be highly arousing. Men typically prefer direct stroking of their genitals by their partner early in lovemaking. Women, however, tend to prefer that their partners caress their genitals after a period of general body contact.

Stimulation of the Breasts

Most, but not all, women enjoy stimulation of the breasts. The hands and the mouth can be used to stimulate the breasts.

Oral–Genital Stimulation

The popularity of oral–genital stimulation has increased dramatically since Kinsey's day. It is especially popular among young people and people with university educations.

Sexual Intercourse: Positions and Techniques

Four of the most commonly used coital positions are the male-superior position, the female-superior position, the lateral-entry position, and the rear-entry position.

Anal Sex

Most gay males and a significant minority of heterosexuals engage in anal sex.

Test Yourself

Multiple-Choice Questions

1. **Women who have fantasies about being sexually coerced**
   a. have been sexually abused as children
   b. believe that men should be sexually dominant
   c. have sadomasochistic tendencies
   d. remain in control, unlike women who are sexually assaulted

2. **The most common sexual fantasy reported by both men and women is**
   a. having intercourse with a colleague or classmate
   b. having intercourse with a loved one
   c. having a same-sex sexual encounter
   d. having sex with more than one person

3. **Masturbation is more common among**
   a. less-educated men
   b. men than women
   c. younger adults than older adults
   d. women than men

4. **The finding that men find masturbation more pleasurable than women is most likely due to**
   a. differences in socialization between men and women
   b. ethnocentricity
   c. the greater variety of sexual behaviours available to men
   d. women's lack of visual acuity

5. **Most men report that they masturbate by**
   a. using electric devices such as vibrators
   b. manual stimulation of the penis
   c. using sex dolls or artificial vaginas
   d. rubbing the penis against a pillow

6. **Masters and Johnson reported that**
   a. most women masturbate by constant stroking of the clitoris
   b. all women touch their breasts during masturbation
   c. no two women were observed masturbating in exactly the same way
   d. there was an absence of fantasy during masturbation in women

7. **The varieties of physical contact that occur before sexual intercourse are collectively called**
   a. prologue
   b. foreplay
   c. othercourse
   d. afterplay

8. **According to the text, most women prefer _____ as a prelude to intercourse**
   a. inserting fingers into the anus
   b. hard sucking on the breasts
   c. inserting fingers into the vagina
   d. caressing the area around the clitoris

9. **Which statement is true about breast stimulation?**
   a. Most men's breasts are not erotically sensitive.
   b. Some women are able to reach orgasm from breast stimulation alone.
   c. Men are more likely to touch their own breasts than their partners'.
   d. Women prefer manual stimulation of the breasts to manual stimulation of the clitoris.

10. **Oral sex is more common among**
    a. people in lower paying jobs
    b. couples living together
    c. dating couples
    d. people with more education

Critical Thinking Questions

1. Have you ever wondered if your sexual fantasies are "normal"?

2. While you were growing up, did you receive negative messages about masturbation from your parents? From your friends? Has this affected how you view this behaviour?

3. How do you feel about masturbating to online sexual images? If you do so, would you tell your best friend? Your girlfriend or boyfriend? Why or why not?

4. Were you ever punished severely for masturbating as a child? Do you think that this has affected your behaviour as an adult? Explain.

Companion Website

Visit our Companion Website at www.pearsoned.ca/rathus, where you can use the interactive Study Guide and link to additional resources on topics discussed in this text.

Chapter 9
Sexual
Orientation

Sexual Orientation

Sexual orientation refers to one's erotic attractions toward, and interests in developing romantic relationships with, members of one's own or the other gender (American Psychological Association, 1998b). A **heterosexual orientation** refers to an erotic attraction to, and preference for developing romantic relationships with, members of the other gender. (Many gay people refer to heterosexual people as being *straight*, or as *straights*.) Note that we say *other gender*, not *opposite gender*. Social critics tell us that many problems that arise between men and women are based on the idea that they are polar opposites (Bem, 1993). Research and common sense suggest that men and women are more alike in personality and behaviour than they are different.

A **homosexual orientation** refers to an erotic attraction to, and interest in forming romantic relationships with, members of one's own gender. The term *homosexuality* denotes sexual interest in members of one's own gender and applies to both men and women. Homosexual men are often referred to as **gay males**. Homosexual women are also called **lesbians** or *gay women*. Gay males and lesbians are also referred to collectively as gays or gay people. The term **bisexuality** refers to an orientation in which one is sexually attracted to, and interested in forming romantic relationships with, both males and females.

Coming to Terms with Terms

Now that we have defined the term *homosexuality*, let us note that we will use it only sparingly. Many gay people object to the term *homosexual* because they feel that it draws too much attention to sexual behaviour. Moreover, the term bears a social stigma. Many gays would prefer terms such as *gay male* or *lesbian sexual orientation*, if a term must be used to set them apart. We therefore use the terms *gay male* and *lesbian* instead of *homosexual* when we refer to sexual orientation. As noted by the

Sexual orientation The direction of one's sexual interests—toward members of the same gender, members of the other gender, or both.

Heterosexual orientation Erotic attraction to, and preference for developing romantic relationships with, members of the other gender.

Homosexual orientation Erotic attraction to, and preference for developing romantic relationships with, members of one's own gender. (From the Greek *homos*, which means "same," not the Latin *homo*, which means "man.")

Gay males Males who are erotically attracted to, and desire to form romantic relationships with, other males.

Lesbians Females who are erotically attracted to, and desire to form romantic relationships with, other females. (After *Lesbos*, the Greek island on which, legend has it, female–female sexual activity was idealized.)

Bisexuality Erotic attraction to, and interest in developing romantic relationships with, males and females.

Are These Women "Homosexuals," or "Lesbians," or Do They Have a "Lesbian Sexual Orientation"?
What terms shall we use to discuss sexual orientation? Many gay people object to the term homosexual because it focuses on sexual behaviour rather than on relationships. Moreover, the term bears a social stigma. Therefore, they prefer terms such as gay male or lesbian sexual orientation, if terms must set them apart.

American Psychological Association's (1991) Committee on Lesbian and Gay Concerns, the word *homosexual* has also been historically associated with concepts of deviance and mental illness. It perpetuates negative stereotypes of gay people. Also, the term is often used to refer to men only. It thus renders lesbians invisible.

Holly Devor (2002)—now Aaron Devor—argues that transgendered people (discussed in Chapter 5) should also be included under the topic of sexual orientation. Devor reasons that, since transgendered people have been the most visible minority among people engaged in same-sex practices, they face many of the same issues and concerns as do gay, lesbian, and bisexual people. Yet transgendered people lack the legal protection granted to gay males and lesbians. It should be noted, however, that some within the transgendered community identify themselves as "trans," and view their issues as related to gender, not to sexual orientation.

Currently, most organizations that represent gay males and lesbians also include transgender people, although this was not true in the past. As a sign of inclusivity, many organizations have adopted the label LGBTQ (lesbian, gay, bisexual, transgender, and queer). The formerly derogatory term *queer* has been reclaimed in Canada by several gay, lesbian, and bisexual organizations as a means of encompassing such previously excluded groups as transgender people (Devor, 2002).

Then, too, the word *homosexual* is ambiguous in meaning—that is, does it refer to sexual behaviour or sexual orientation? In this book, your authors speak of male–female sexual behaviour (not *heterosexual* behaviour), male–male sexual behaviour, and female–female sexual behaviour. Researchers often use the terms MSM (men having sex with men) and WSW (women having sex with women).

Heterosexuals tend to focus almost exclusively on sexual aspects of male–male and female–female relationships. But the love relationships of gay people, like those of heterosexual people, often involve more than sex. In a study of Ontario men, Barry Adam (2000b) at the University of Windsor found that for gay men the concept of "gay" centred on the possibility for emotional involvement and relationships rather than on sexual behaviour. These attachments, like male–female attachments, provide a framework for love and intimacy. Although sex and love are common features of relationships, neither is a *necessary* prerequisite for a relationship. Sexual orientations are not defined by sexual activity per se but rather by the *direction* of one's romantic interests and erotic attractions.

Sexual Orientation and Gender Identity

Because gay people are attracted to members of their own gender, some people assume that they would prefer to be members of the other gender. Like heterosexual people, however, gay people have a gender identity that is consistent with their anatomic gender. Unlike transsexuals, gay people do not see themselves as desiring to be the other gender.

Determining Sexual Orientation

Determining a person's sexual orientation might seem to be a clear-cut task. Some people are exclusively gay and limit their sexual activities to partners of their own gender. Others are strictly heterosexual and limit their sexual activities to partners of the other gender. Many people fall somewhere in between, however. Where might we draw the line between a gay male and lesbian sexual orientation, on the one hand, and a heterosexual orientation, on the other? Where do we draw the line between these orientations and bisexuality?

It is possible—indeed not unusual—for people to have had some sexual experiences with people of their own gender yet define themselves as heterosexual. In one study, among those reporting sexual experiences with both men and women in

Canadian Psychology Association, Section on Sexual Orientation and Gender Identity Issues (SOGII)
www.cpa.ca/sogii

adulthood, more than two out of three perceived themselves to be heterosexual rather than bisexual (Lever et al., 1992). For many of these men, sexual experiences with other men were limited to a brief period of their lives and did not alter their sexual orientations. Lacking heterosexual outlets, prison inmates may have sexual experiences with people of their own gender while they maintain their heterosexual identities. Such inmates would form sexual relationships with people of the other gender if they were available, and they return to male–female sexual behaviour upon release from prison. Physical affection also helps some prisoners, male and female, cope with loneliness and isolation. Males who engage in prostitution with male clients may separate their sexual orientation from their "trade." Many fantasize about a female when permitting a client to fellate them. The behaviour is male–male. The person's sexual *orientation* may be heterosexual.

Gay males and lesbians, too, may engage in male–female sexual activity while maintaining a gay sexual orientation. In the Ontario Men's Survey of gay and bisexual men, 83% of respondents identified themselves as gay, yet 61% reported having ever had sex with a woman (Myers et al., 2004). Some gay males and lesbians marry members of the other gender but continue to harbour unfulfilled desires for members of their own gender. Then, too, some people are bisexual but may not have acted upon their attraction to members of their own gender.

Sexual orientation is not necessarily expressed in sexual behaviour. Many people come to perceive themselves as gay or heterosexual long before they ever engage in sex with members of their own gender. Some people, gay and heterosexual alike, adopt a celibate lifestyle for religious or ascetic reasons and abstain from sexual relationships. Some remain celibate not by choice but because of lack of partners.

People's erotic interests and fantasies may also shift over time. Gay males and lesbians may experience sporadic **heteroerotic** interests. Heterosexual people may have occasional **homoerotic** interests. Women's sexual orientations are apparently somewhat more flexible or plastic than men's, with women being somewhat more dependent on social experience (Bailey, 2003a; Diamond, 2000, 2002, 2003a). A classic survey of homosexuals found that about 50% of lesbians reported that they are sometimes attracted to men (Bell & Weinberg, 1978). Lisa M. Diamond (2003b) conducted a survey of lesbian and bisexual women that involved three interviews over a five-year period. She found that more than 25% of the women relinquished their lesbian or bisexual orientation as time went on. Half of these relabelled themselves as heterosexual, and the other half renounced any effort at self-labelling. (Note that the majority of lesbian and bisexual women [75%] did not change their sexual orientation.) Some people also over time shift their sexual orientation label from heterosexual to gay, lesbian, or bisexual.

Some heterosexual people report fantasies about sexual activity with people of their own sex (see Chapter 8). In their classic study of homosexuals, Masters and Johnson (1979) found that many gay people reported having fantasies about sexual activity with people of the other sex.

Attraction to people of the other gender and attraction to people of one's own gender may thus not be mutually exclusive. People may have various degrees of sexual interest in, and sexual experience with, people of either gender. Kinsey and his colleagues recognized that the boundaries between gay male and lesbian sexual orientations, on the one hand, and a heterosexual orientation, on the other, are sometimes blurry. They thus proposed thinking in terms of a continuum of sexual orientation rather than two poles.

THE KINSEY CONTINUUM Kinsey and his colleagues (1948, 1953) conceived a seven-point "heterosexual–homosexual continuum" (see Figure 9.1). People are located on the continuum according to their patterns of sexual attraction and behaviour. People in category 0 are considered exclusively heterosexual. People in category 6 are considered exclusively gay.

Heteroerotic Of an erotic nature and involving members of the other gender.

Homoerotic Of an erotic nature and involving members of one's own gender.

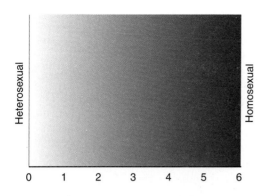

Figure 9.1 The Kinsey Continuum.

Kinsey and his colleagues conceived of a 7-point heterosexual–homosexual continuum that classifies people according to their same-sex behaviour and the magnitude of their attraction to members of their own gender. People in category 0, who accounted for most of Kinsey's study participants, were considered exclusively heterosexual. People in category 6 were considered exclusively homosexual.

What percentage of the population, then, is gay? The percentages depend on the standards one uses. Kinsey and his colleagues reported that about 4% of men and 1% to 3% of women in their samples were exclusively gay (6 on their scale). A larger percentage of people were considered predominantly gay (scale points 4 or 5) or predominantly heterosexual (1 or 2 on the scale). Some were classified as equally gay and heterosexual in orientation and could be labelled bisexual (scale point 3). Most people were classified as exclusively heterosexual (scale point 0). Thirty-seven percent of the men and 13% of the women told interviewers that they had reached orgasm through sexual activity with someone of their own gender at some time after puberty. Fifty percent of the men who remained single until age 35 reported they had reached orgasm through sexual activity with other males.

Many people in Kinsey's day were startled by these figures. They meant that sexual activity with people of one's own gender, especially among males, was more widespread than had been believed. But Kinsey's figures for male–male sexual activity may have been exaggerated. For instance, his finding that 37% of males had reached orgasm through sexual activity with other males was based on a sample that included a high proportion of former prisoners. Findings may also have been distorted by the researchers' efforts to recruit known gay people into their samples. Once these sources of possible bias are corrected, the incidence of male–male sexual activity drops from 37% to about 25%. Because Kinsey's sample was not drawn at random, however, we cannot say whether it represented the general population.

Statistics concerning *past* sexual activity with a member of one's own gender can be misleading. They may represent a single episode or a brief period of adolescent experimentation. Half of the men who reported male–male sexual activity in Kinsey's sample limited it to the ages of 12 to 14. Another third had had male–male sexual experience by the age of 18, but not again.

Kinsey's research also showed that sexual behaviour patterns can change, sometimes dramatically so (Sanders et al., 1990). Sexual experiences or feelings involving people of one's own gender are common, especially in adolescence, and do not mean that one will engage in sexual activity exclusively with people of one's own gender in adulthood (Bullough, 1990).

What did Kinsey find with respect to more enduring patterns of male–male and female–female sexual activity? Estimates based on an analysis of Kinsey's data (Gebhard, 1977) suggest that 13% of the men and 7% of the women, or 10% for both genders combined, were either predominantly or exclusively interested in, and sexually active with, people of their own gender for at least three years between the ages of 16 and 55.

CURRENT ESTIMATES OF SEXUAL ORIENTATION The controversy over how many people are gay continues. Current estimates generally find lower percentages of gay people in the population than Kinsey did. Considering data drawn from studies conducted in the United States, Asia, and Pacific island countries, Milton Diamond (1993) estimates that only about 5% of men and 2% to 3% of women across different cultures have engaged in sexual activity with someone of their own gender on at least one occasion since adolescence.

The approach that is used to measure sexual orientation strongly influences the results. In a study of men who have sex in parks in Ottawa, Huber and Kleinplatz (2002) found that 80% identified themselves as gay, 17% as bisexual, and only 3% as heterosexual. Similar results were found when they surveyed men in bathhouses. And in a large Canadian study of gay and bisexual men, 81% described themselves as gay and about 15% said they were bisexual, with the rest saying they were heterosexual or other (Myers, Godin, et al., 1993). However, in terms of actual experience with men or women, less than half (44%) had had sex only with men in their lifetime, 13% had had sex with both men and women in the past year, and 41% said they were currently gay but had had sex with women in the past.

The 1998 Compas survey asked Canadians, "In general, whom are you most attracted to?" As shown in Table 9.1, about 8% of males and 10% of females said they were attracted to the same sex. However, less than 2% of the men said they were attracted only to men and less than 1% of the women said they were attracted only to women.

In the Canada Youth and AIDS Survey (Boyce, 2003), students were asked to indicate their sexual orientation, as indicated by their physical attraction to members of the same gender, the other gender, or both genders. Girls were more likely to admit to a same-sex attraction. In Grade 11, more males (1.5%) and females (3%) indicated being physically attracted to both sexes than to their own sex exclusively (0.9% of males and 1.7% of females).

In a 2004 survey of Canadians aged 13 to 29 (designed by Kris Wells of the University of Alberta), 3.5% of respondents identified themselves as GLBT (gay, lesbian, bisexual, or transgendered) (Youthography Ping Survey, 2004). Slightly more males than females identified themselves this way.

In 2003 Statistics Canada for the first time included a question on sexual orientation as part of its Canadian Community Health Survey. Among the 135 000 respondents aged 18 to 59, 1.0% reported that they were gay or lesbian and 0.7% said they were bisexual. Twice as many men (1.3%) as women (0.7%) reported they were homosexual. However, more women (0.9%) than men (0.6%) reported they were bisexual (Statistics Canada, 2004).

Another approach to determining sexual orientation involves measuring physiological responses to sexual stimuli. Researchers in Quebec have devised a method of measuring sexual preference in virtual reality (Renaud et al., 2002). This involves measuring a respondent's computer interaction with an image of a naked woman as a measure of his or her sexual preference.

Surveys reveal the percentages only of people *willing to admit* to certain behaviours or sexual orientations (Cronin, 1993; Isay, 1993). "We can't count people who simply don't want to be counted" (Cronin, 1993). Surveys may omit gay people who

TABLE 9.1
Sexual Attraction Preferences of Canadian Men and Women

	Males	Females
Only men	1.6%	90.1%
Mostly men	0.5	6.7
Both men and women	1.9	2.2
Mostly women	4.5	0.1
Only women	91.4	0.8

Source: Based on analysis of Compas (1998) Modern life survey of the Canadian population.

hesitate to proclaim their sexual orientation because of social stigma or repression of their sexual feelings.

CHALLENGES TO THE KINSEY CONTINUUM Although the Kinsey continuum has been widely adopted by sex researchers, it is not universally accepted. Kinsey believed that exclusive heterosexual and gay sexual orientations lie at opposite poles of one continuum. Therefore, the more heterosexual a person is, the less gay that person is, and vice versa (Sanders et al., 1990).

Viewing gay and heterosexual orientations as opposite poles of one continuum is akin to the traditional view of masculinity and femininity as polar opposites, such that the more masculine one is, the less feminine, and vice versa. Viewing men and women as opposites has led to misunderstandings, and even hostility, between the genders (Bem, 1993). But we may also regard masculinity and femininity as independent personality dimensions. Similarly, the view of gay people and heterosexuals as opposites has also led to misunderstandings and hostility. Yet these sexual orientations may also be separate dimensions, rather than polar opposites.

Psychologist Michael Storms (1980) suggests that gay and heterosexual orientations are independent dimensions. Thus, one can be high or low on both dimensions simultaneously. Storms (1980) suggests that there are separate dimensions of responsiveness to male–female stimulation (heteroeroticism) and sexual stimulation that involves someone of the same gender (homoeroticism), as shown in Figure 9.2. According to this model, bisexuals are high in both dimensions, whereas people who are low in both are essentially asexual. According to Kinsey, bisexual individuals would be *less* responsive to stimulation by people of the other gender than heterosexual people are, but *more* responsive than heterosexuals to stimulation by people of their own gender. According to the two-dimensional model, however, bisexual people may be just as responsive to stimulation by people of the other gender as heterosexual people are, and just as responsive to stimulation by people of their own gender as gay people are.

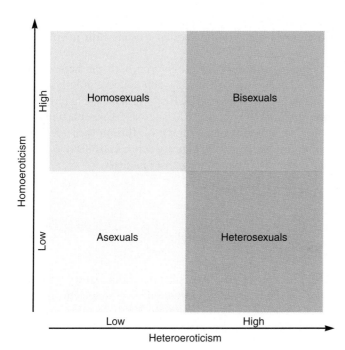

Figure 9.2 Heterosexuality and Homosexuality as Separate Dimensions.

According to this model, homosexuality and heterosexuality are independent dimensions. One can thus be high or low on both dimensions at the same time. Most people are high in one dimension. Bisexuals are high in both dimensions. People who are low in both are considered asexual.

FANTASY AS THE MEASURE Kinsey argued that the content of erotic fantasies is an excellent gauge of sexual orientation. To test this formulation, Storms (1980) investigated the erotic fantasies of heterosexual, gay, and bisexual people. He found that heterosexual students reported significantly more fantasies about the other gender than about their own gender. Gay students reported more frequent fantasies about their own gender. Bisexuals, as predicted, reported a high level of both kinds of fantasies. Gay students were also more likely to have fantasies about the other gender than heterosexual students were to have fantasies about their own gender.

Bisexuality

Bisexual people are attracted to both males and females. Many have a somewhat stronger attraction to one gender than to the other, yet they remain bisexual (Weinberg et al., 1994). Kinsey and his colleagues considered people rated as 3's to be bisexual (see Figure 9.1).

About 1% of the people (0.8% of the men and 0.9% of the women) surveyed in the American NHSLS study (Laumann et al., 1994) reported having a bisexual *identity*. About 4% said they were sexually attracted to both women and men. However, the Canadian studies discussed in the previous section reported higher percentages for bisexual experience and attraction (Compas, 1998; Myers et al., 1993).

Bisexual people are sometimes said to "swing both ways," or to be "A/C-D/C" (as in alternating current and direct current). Some gay people (and some heterosexual people) believe that claims to bisexuality are a "cop-out" that people use to deny being gay. Perhaps they fear leaving their spouses or dread coming out (declaring their gay male or lesbian sexual orientation publicly). Others view bisexuality as a form of sexual experimentation with people of one's own gender by people who are mostly heterosexual. But many avowed bisexual people disagree. They report that they can maintain erotic interests in, and romantic relationships with, members of both genders. Some authors (e.g., Weinrich & Klein, 2002) insist that bisexuality is an authentic sexual orientation and not just a cover for a gay male or lesbian sexual orientation.

Some bisexual people follow lifestyles that permit them to satisfy their dual inclinations. Others feel pressured by heterosexual and gay people alike to commit themselves one way or the other (Garber, 1995; Weinberg et al., 1994). Some gay people also mask their sexual orientation by adopting a bisexual lifestyle. That is, they get married but also enter into clandestine sexual liaisons with members of their own gender.

Bisexuals encounter prejudice and discrimination from both the heterosexual and homosexual communities. Surveys of more than 600 college undergraduates confirm that biphobia, or dislike of bisexuals, can be found in both the heterosexual and homosexual populations (Mulick & Wright, 2002). To assist bisexuals in dealing with these issues, groups such as Bisexual Women of Toronto provide counselling and support. One of their objectives is to educate community service groups about the effects of prejudice and discrimination against bisexuals.

Perspectives on Gay Male and Lesbian Sexual Orientations

Gay male and lesbian sexual orientations have existed throughout history. Attitudes toward them have varied widely. They have been tolerated in some societies, openly encouraged in others, but condemned in most (Bullough, 1990). In this section we review historical and other perspectives on gay male and lesbian sexual orientations.

Historical Perspectives

Some ancient societies such as the Greeks were openly accepting of male–male sexual behaviour (see Chapter 1). Many famous people throughout history, such as Alexander the Great, have been gay. Yet most cultures have held negative attitudes toward homosexuality.

In Western culture, few sexual practices have met with such widespread censure as sexual activities with members of one's own gender. Jews and Christians have traditionally referred to male–male sexual activity as the sin of Sodom. Hence the origins of the term *sodomy*, which generally denotes anal intercourse (and sometimes oral–genital contact). According to the Book of Genesis, the city of Sodom was destroyed by God. Yet it is unclear what behaviour incurred God's wrath. Pope Gregory III was not ambiguous, however, in his eighth-century account of the city's obliteration as a punishment for sexual activity with members of one's own gender.

Despite the history of opposition to gay male and lesbian sexual orientations, some churches today are performing marriages of gay couples—or at least "blessing" these relationships. The Metropolitan Community Church has many gay male and lesbian parishioners in Canada. The first Canadian church to perform formal marriage ceremonies for same-sex couples was the Metropolitan Church in Toronto. In 2002, Anglican Church leaders of the Diocese of New Westminster, British Columbia, voted in favour of blessing same-sex unions. It was the first diocese of the Anglican Church in Canada to take this step. Since then an increasing number of churches have performed same-sex marriages.

Many Canadian churches allow for the ordination of gay male and lesbian clergy, providing they remain celibate. Some churches, however, such as the Unitarian and the United Church of Canada, do accept clergy who are involved in same-sex relationships. Yet some of the more conservative churches and religious groups, such as Focus on the Family, continue to oppose equal rights, including same-sex marriages, for anyone whose sexual orientation is not heterosexual.

Cross-Cultural Perspectives

Male–male sexual behaviour has been practised in many preliterate societies. In their review of the literature on 76 preliterate societies, Ford and Beach (1951) found that in 49 societies (64%), male–male sexual interactions were viewed as normal and deemed socially acceptable for some members of the group. The other 27 societies (36%) had sanctions against male–male sexual behaviour. Nevertheless, male–male sexual activity persisted.

Sexual activities between males are sometimes limited to rites that mark the young male's initiation into manhood. In some preliterate societies, semen is believed to boost strength and virility. Older males thus transmit semen to younger males through oral or anal sexual activities. Among the Sambian people of New Guinea, a tribe of warlike headhunters, 9- to 12-year-old males leave their parents' households and live in a "clubhouse" with other prepubertal and adolescent males. There they undergo sexual rites of passage. To acquire the fierce manhood of the headhunter, they perform fellatio on older males and drink "men's milk" (semen) (Bailey, 2003b). The ingestion of semen is believed to give rise to puberty. Following puberty, adolescents are fellated by younger males (Baldwin & Baldwin, 1989). By the age of 19, however, young men are expected to take brides and enter exclusively male–female sexual relationships.

These practices of Sambian culture might seem to suggest that the sexual orientations of males are fluid and malleable. The practices involve *behaviour*, however, not *sexual orientation*. Male–male sexual behaviour among Sambians takes place within a cultural context that bears little resemblance to consensual male–male sexual activity in Western society. The prepubertal Sambian male does not *seek* sexual liaisons with other males. He is removed from his home and thrust into male–male sexual encounters by older males (Baldwin & Baldwin, 1989).

Little is known about female–female sexual activity in non-Western cultures. Evidence of female–female sexual behaviour was found by Ford and Beach in only 17 of the 76 societies they studied. Perhaps female sexual behaviour in general, not just sexual activity with other females, was more likely to be repressed. Of course, it is also possible that women are less likely than men to develop sexual interests in, or romantic relationships with, members of their own gender. Whatever the reasons, this cross-cultural evidence is consistent with data from our own culture. Here, too, males are more likely than females to develop sexual interests in, or romantic relationships with, members of their own gender (Laumann et al., 1994).

Cross-Species Perspectives

Many of us have observed animals engaging in sexual behaviours that resemble male–male or female–female contacts among humans, such as mounting others of their own sex. But what do these behaviours signify?

A male baboon may present his rear and allow himself to be mounted by another male. This behaviour may resemble anal intercourse among gay men. But is the behaviour sexually motivated? Mounting behaviour among male baboons may represent a type of dominance ritual in which lower-ranking males adopt a submissive (feminine) posture to ward off attack from dominant males (Nadler, 1990). (Some male–male acts among people also involve themes of dominance, as in the case of a dominant male prisoner forcing a less dominant one to submit to anal intercourse.) In other cases, male baboons may be seeking favours or protection from more dominant males (Nadler, 1990). Among juvenile animals, male–male

A World of Diversity

ETHNICITY AND SEXUAL ORIENTATION: A MATTER OF BELONGING

Because of societal prejudices, it is difficult for many young people to come to terms with an emerging lesbian or gay male sexual orientation. You might assume that people who have been subjected to prejudice and discrimination—members of ethnic minority groups—would be more tolerant than others of people with a lesbian or gay male sexual orientation. However, such an assumption might not be warranted.

By and large, a lesbian or gay male sexual orientation is rejected by many ethnic minority groups in Canada. For example, about 80% of First Nations

people in Ontario believe that homosexuality is wrong (Myers et al., 1993). The Ethnocultural Communities Facing AIDS study sponsored by Health Canada found that both the Chinese and South Asian communities strongly disapprove of same-sex relationships, which they view as abnormal. Because they fear bringing shame to their families, lesbians and gay males in those communities feel pressured to keep their sexual orientations a secret or to move to communities where they can live openly without sanction.

In her study of gay male Vietnamese immigrants in Toronto, Cynthia Vo (2001), a graduate student at the University of Guelph, found that only a small minority of the gay men chose to come out to their parents. Many felt their parents would no longer be

proud of them. They were worried about bringing shame to the family and causing their parents to lose face in the community.

If any generalization is possible, it may be that lesbians and gay men find more of a sense of belonging in the gay community than in their ethnic communities. Yet members of some minority groups may feel that their issues are not addressed by mainstream gay male and lesbian organizations. Among Vietnamese gay men in Toronto, for example, some stated that they felt more discrimination from the white gay community than they did from Canadian society at large (Vo, 2001). As a result, gay Asians have formed their own groups, including Gay Asians of the Vancouver Area and the Bubble Tea Lounge community in Toronto.

behaviours may also be a form of play. Females may also attempt to mount other females, but here too, the motives may not be the same as those of humans.

Paul Vasey of the University of Lethbridge has done considerable research on sexual preference and orientation in female Japanese macaques. Vasey (2002) has found that these females routinely engage in sexual behaviours with both males and females. Often female Japanese macaques will choose to have sex with other females even if willing male partners are available. On the basis of his observations, Vasey surmises that female same-sex behaviour in Japanese macaques is a form of sexual behaviour and exemplifies a bisexual orientation.

Attitudes Toward Sexual Orientation in Contemporary Society

Historically speaking, negative attitudes toward gay people have pervaded our society. Today, however, there is far greater acceptance in Canadian society of equal rights for gay people. According to University of Manitoba professor Bob Altemeyer (2001), a major factor in this acceptance has been increased contact with persons known to be gay, brought about by the fact that gays and lesbians have been increasingly open about revealing their sexual orientation. Similarly, in a survey of civic leaders in Hamilton, McMaster professor Rhoda Howard-Hassmann (2001) found that learning a relative, neighbour, co-worker, or client was gay not only made people more accepting of gays but humanized gays in their mind.

Approximately three-quarters of both teenagers and adults feel that homosexuals should be entitled to the same rights as other Canadians. Older adults, however, are less accepting of equal rights than younger Canadians (Bibby, 2001). Slightly more than half of Canadians approve of homosexual relationships (adults 60% and teenagers 54%). And, compared with when they were teenagers, more than half of Canadian adults report that they have become more approving of homosexuality, with fewer than 10% having become less approving. Women tend to be somewhat more approving of homosexuality than men are (Bibby, 2001).

Despite opposition by a vociferous minority, most Canadians accept same-sex marriage. In a 2003 national survey conducted by the Centre for Research and Information on Canada, 61% of Canadian adults approved of same-sex marriage (Hurst, 2003). In a separate national survey of Canadian young people, only a minority (23%) disapproved of same-sex marriage and even fewer (15%) said they would never vote for a gay or lesbian political candidate (Youthography Ping Survey, 2004).

B. J. Rye (2002) of St. Jerome's College at the University of Waterloo found that, among university students, a majority (69%) believed that homosexual couples would be desirable candidates to adopt children; a higher percentage (91%) felt this way about heterosexual couples, however. A Léger Marketing survey in 2001 found that 53% of Canadians believe that same-sex couples should have the right to adopt children (Canadian Press, 2001).

HOMOPHOBIA **Homophobia** takes many forms, including

- Use of derogatory names (such as *queer*, *faggot*, and *dyke*).
- Telling disparaging "queer jokes."
- Barring gay people from housing, employment, or social opportunities.
- Taunting (verbal abuse).
- **Gay bashing** (physical abuse).

Although homophobia is more common among heterosexuals, gay people can also be homophobic.

Homophobia A cluster of negative attitudes and feelings toward gay people, including intolerance, hatred, and fear.

Gay bashing Violence against homosexuals.

One of the root words from which *homophobia* is derived means "fear." Although some psychologists link homophobia to fear of a gay male or lesbian sexual orientation within oneself, homophobic attitudes may also be embedded within a cluster of stereotypical gender-role attitudes toward family life (Cotten-Huston & Waite, 2000). These attitudes support male dominance and the belief that it is natural and appropriate for women to sacrifice for their husbands and children (Cotten-Huston & Waite, 2000; Marsiglio, 1993b). People who have a strong stake in maintaining stereotypical gender roles may feel more readily threatened by the existence of the gay male or lesbian sexual orientation, because gay people appear to confuse or reverse these roles. Men have more of a stake in maintaining the tradition of male dominance, so perhaps it is not surprising that college men are more intolerant of gay males than college women are (Schellenberg et al., 1999).

Homophobic attitudes are more common among males who identify with a traditional male gender role and those who hold a fundamentalist religious orientation (Cotten-Huston & Waite, 2000; Marsiglio, 1993b). Similarly, researchers find that university students who hold a conservative political orientation tend to be more accepting of negative attitudes toward gay people than are liberal students (Cotten-Huston & Waite, 2000). Other university samples find male students to be more homophobic than women (Kunkel & Temple, 1992; Schellenberg et al., 1999). In addition, business and science students at a Canadian university were found to be more intolerant of gay people than students in the arts and social sciences (Schellenberg et al., 1999).

Generally speaking, heterosexual men are less tolerant of gay people than are heterosexual women (Kerns & Fine, 1994; Seltzer, 1992; Whitley & Kite, 1995). Perhaps some heterosexual men are threatened by the possibility of discovering male–male sexual impulses within themselves (Freiberg, 1995). In an outcome consistent with this view, Kite (1992) found that heterosexual males tend to hold more negative attitudes toward gay men than toward lesbians. At least some homophobic men may have homoerotic impulses of which they are unaware. Denial of these impulses may be connected with their fear and disapproval of gay males.

GAY BASHING Although strides toward social acceptance of gay people have been made, gay bashing still occurs throughout society, including on university campuses. In a survey of GLBT people on 14 U.S. campuses, about 30% reported experiencing harassment because of their sexual orientation in the previous 12 months. A large percentage (77%) of 121 lesbian and gay male undergraduate students in one survey at Pennsylvania State University reported that they had been verbally insulted. Nearly one in three (31%) reported being chased or followed (D'Augelli, 1992). Nearly 20% said they had been physically assaulted. In a survey of Canadian youth aged 15 to 19, 24% reported having seen an act of violence or verbal abuse directed at a GLBT person by someone from their own age group (Youthography Ping Survey, 2004).

Douglas Victor Janoff, in his book *Pink Blood: Homophobic Violence in Canada* (2005), has thoroughly documented cases of gay bashing occurring in Canada since 1990. According to Janoff, hundreds of gay, lesbian, bisexual, and transgendered people have been assaulted or murdered in Canada in recent years. Yet for the most part these incidents have not been documented in Canadian criminology textbooks or other academic publications.

One of the most widely publicized cases of gay bashing in Canada took place in 2001, when 41-year-old Aaron Webster was murdered in Vancouver's Stanley Park by four attackers who hit him in the throat with a baseball bat or pool cue. In 2005, two women in Montreal kissed each other while waiting for a street light to change; a man was so incensed that he hit both of them.

SEXUAL ORIENTATION AND CANADIAN LAW Considerable progress has been made in Canada by gay and lesbian rights organizations in their fight for equality. The first major breakthrough came in 1969 when Prime Minister Pierre Trudeau obtained passage in Parliament of an amendment to the Criminal Code that decriminalized same-sex behaviour between consenting adults. Since then other major pieces of legislation have benefited gay males and lesbians:

- In 1995 the federal government passed the Hate Crimes Act, which imposes harsh penalties on those who assault members of minority groups such as gay males and lesbians.

- In 1996 Parliament added the words "sexual orientation" as a prohibited ground of discrimination in the Canadian Human Rights Act.

- In 2003 the House of Commons extended hate-crimes protection to gay males and lesbians.

- In 2005 the House of Commons and the Senate passed legislation to extend civil marriage rights to same-sex couples. (However, in the lead-up to the January 2006 election, Stephen Harper's Conservatives suggested that they would reopen the issue of same-sex marriage.)

The national lobby group Equality for Gays and Lesbians Everywhere (EGALE) is at the forefront in fighting for equality through the legal system. Other significant advances for gay rights have come from court rulings under the Charter of Rights and Freedoms and the Canadian Human Rights Act:

- In 1992, the Supreme Court of Canada ruled that the Canadian Armed Forces cannot discriminate against gay males and lesbians and must allow them the right to join the military.

- In 1998, the Supreme Court of Canada ordered the Alberta government to include protection for gay males and lesbians under Alberta human rights legislation.

- In 1999, the Supreme Court of Canada ruled that the Province of Ontario's definition of spouse violated the Charter of Rights because it applied only to heterosexuals and not to gay males and lesbians.

- In 2002, when Marc Hall, a gay student in Toronto, was refused the right by the Catholic school board to take his partner to the high school prom, he went to court to appeal the board's decision. The Ontario Supreme Court judge ruled that Hall could go to the prom because the school board had violated his constitutional right to equality. (This case is discussed further in Chapter 12.)

- In 2002, the Ontario Supreme Court ruled that because the legal definition of marriage is discriminatory it should be changed to include same-sex couples. (This is discussed further in Chapter 12.)

- In 2004 the Supreme Court of Canada ruled that Parliament has the authority to redefine marriage to include same-sex couples.

GAY ACTIVISM During the past generation, gay people have organized effective political action to fight discrimination. In a comprehensive analysis of the history of same-sex relationships and of the gay rights movement in Canada, Gary Kinsman (1996) of Laurentian University argues that, by challenging heterosexuality as the societal norm and affirming their right to sexual self-determination, gay males and lesbians are also helping other groups achieve greater sexual freedom.

The AIDS epidemic has had a profound effect on the political agenda of gay-rights organizations. Most Canadian cities have AIDS organizations, with the largest being the AIDS committee of Toronto. These organizations combat the AIDS epidemic on several fronts:

Svend Robinson, former MP. Svend Robinson was the first member of Canada's Parliament to openly acknowledge that he was gay.

Outing The revelation of the identities of gay people by other gay people. The method is intended to combat discrimination against gay people by forcing individuals out of the closet and into the fray.

Butch A lesbian who assumes a traditional masculine gender role.

Femme A lesbian who assumes a traditional feminine gender role.

1. They lobby for increased funding for AIDS research and treatment.
2. They educate the gay and wider communities on the dangers of high-risk sexual behaviour.
3. They encourage gay men and others to adopt safer sex practices, including the use of condoms.
4. They protect the civil rights of people with AIDS and carriers of HIV (the virus that causes AIDS) with respect to employment, housing, and medical and dental treatment.
5. They provide counselling and support services for people with HIV/AIDS.

Some gay-rights organizations work within the mainstream political process. Others, such as the militant Act-Up organization, have taken a more strident and confrontational stance to secure more funding for AIDS research and treatment. Some militant gay groups use the method of **outing** to combat discrimination. In this method, gay people unmask other gay people without their consent, forcing them "out of the closet." Many gay people protest this practice vehemently, terming it a "gay witch hunt."

STEREOTYPES AND SEXUAL BEHAVIOUR Among heterosexual people, sexual aggressiveness is linked to the masculine gender role. Sexual passivity is linked to the feminine role. Some heterosexual people assume (often erroneously) that in gay male and lesbian relationships, one partner consistently assumes the masculine role in sexual relations, and the other the feminine role.

Many gay couples, however, vary the active and passive roles. Among gay male couples, for example, roles in anal intercourse (*inserter* versus *insertee*) and in fellatio often alternate. Contrary to popular assumptions, sexual behaviour between lesbians seldom reflects distinct **butch–femme** gender roles. Most lesbians report both providing and receiving oral–genital stimulation. Typically, partners alternate roles or simultaneously perform and receive oral stimulation. Many gay people claim that the labels *masculine* and *feminine* represent only "the straight community's" efforts to pigeonhole them in terms that "straights" can understand.

A World of Diversity

LESBIAN AND GAY MALE ACTIVISM IN TORONTO

According to the 2001 census, 6685 same-sex couples lived in Toronto (Statistics Canada, 2002a), the city with the largest lesbian and gay male community in Canada. In 1981, a large-scale police raid on Toronto bathhouses resulted in the arrest of 300 men, making it the second largest mass arrest in Canada. The police raid shocked the lesbian and gay community, and thousands of gay men and lesbians gathered in downtown Toronto in the

first major Canadian gay rights protest. Like the Stonewall riots in 1969, when the gay community in New York protested against police raids on the Stonewall gay bar, the protest was a major turning point for the development of gay rights activism in Canada.

The first Lesbian and Gay Pride Day was held in Toronto in 1981. In the early years of Gay Pride celebrations, many politicians did not want to be seen as supporting these events. In the mid-1980s, for example, Toronto mayor Art Eggleton refused to publicly recognize Gay Pride celebrations by not proclaiming Pride Week. By the later 1980s

and the 1990s, however, Gay Pride celebrations, especially the parade, became increasingly accepted by the public and by politicians, and in 1991 Mayor Eggleton officially proclaimed Pride Week for the first time. The events celebrating Gay Pride Day have grown enormously over the years; several hundred thousand people now attend the Toronto parade. In fact, the parade has become so mainstream that by 1998 politicians such as Toronto mayor Mel Lastman took part in it. In 2005, for the first time the Toronto police chief rode in the parade. Many large corporations sponsor the parade, and the Web site for Tourism Toronto features a link to gay activities in the city. Today a number of Canadian cities hold Gay Pride parades, including smaller cities such as Windsor and Fredericton.

But despite the many gains in human rights, the struggle continues. In 2000, for example, the lesbian community in Toronto was angered when the Toronto police raided an all-female bathhouse event entitled the "Pussy Palace." In the ensuing court case, the judge condemned the manner in which the raid had been carried out by male police officers and dismissed the charges against the two women who held the liquor licence for the event. The mayor of Edmonton, Bill Smith, had for several years refused to proclaim Gay Pride Week. However, when the Alberta Human Rights Commission ruled against his stand in 2003, Smith relented. More recently, the mayor of London, Ontario, refused to proclaim Gay Pride Week and avoided the

Mayor Caves In, Proclaims Gay Pride Week in Edmonton.
Edmonton resident Matalus kisses a mask of Edmonton mayor Bill Smith, who for seven years refused to proclaim Gay Pride Week. In 2002, Smith changed his stand in response to a ruling by the Alberta Human Rights Commission.

human rights battle by stating that London would have no more theme weeks of any kind.

What Determines Sexual Orientation?

What causes a person to be gay or straight? Some people believe that gays are "born that way"; others (generally heterosexuals) believe that gays voluntarily choose to be gay. In recent years, researchers have focused considerable attention on the determinants of sexual orientation.

Biological Perspectives

Is sexual orientation an *inborn* trait that is transmitted genetically, like eye colour or height? Does it reflect hormonal influences? Biological perspectives focus on the possible roles of evolution, genetics, and hormonal influences in shaping sexual orientation.

THE EVOLUTIONARY PERSPECTIVE It might seem ironic that evolutionary theorists have endeavoured to explain gay male and lesbian sexual orientations. After all, gay males and lesbians are not motivated to engage in sexual activity with members of the other gender. How, then, can these sexual orientations confer any evolutionary advantage?

To answer this question, we must look to the group or the species rather than the individual. Kirkpatrick (2000) suggests that male–male and female–female sexual behaviours derive from individual selection for reciprocal *altruism*. That is, strong male–male and female–female alliances have advantages for *group* survival in that they bind group members together emotionally. This hypothesis remains speculative.

GENETICS AND SEXUAL ORIENTATION Considerable evidence exists that gay male and lesbian sexual orientations run in families (Bailey et al., 1999; Dawood et al., 2000; Kendler, Thornton, et al., 2000). In one study, for example, 22% of the brothers of a sample of 51 predominantly gay men were either gay or bisexual themselves. This is nearly four times the proportion expected in the general population (Pillard & Weinrich, 1986). Although such evidence is consistent with a genetic explanation, families also share a common environment.

Twin studies also shed light on the possible role of heredity (Bailey 2003b, Kendler et al., 2000). **Monozygotic (MZ) twins**, or identical twins, develop from a single fertilized ovum and share 100% of their heredity. **Dizygotic (DZ) twins**, or fraternal twins, develop from two fertilized ova. Like other brothers and sisters, DZ twins share only 50% of their heredity. Thus, if a gay male or lesbian sexual orientation were transmitted genetically, it should be found about twice as often among identical twins of gay people as among fraternal twins. Because MZ and DZ twins who are reared together share similar environmental influences, differences in the degree of **concordance** for a given trait between the types of twin pairs are further indicative of genetic origins.

Several studies have looked at gay men with twin brothers (Kendler et al., 2000). In one of the most carefully conducted twin studies, about 52% of identical (MZ) twin pairs were found to be "concordant" (in agreement) for a gay male sexual orientation, compared with 22% of fraternal (DZ) twins and only 11% of adoptive brothers (Bailey, 2003a). Bear in mind that MZ twins are more likely than DZ twins to be dressed alike and treated alike. Thus, their greater concordance for a gay sexual orientation may at least in part reflect environmental factors (Kendler et al., 2000).

Researchers have found evidence linking a region on the X sex chromosome to a gay male sexual orientation (Bailey et al., 1999). One group of researchers (Hamer et al., 1993) found that gay males were more likely than the general population to have gay male relatives on their mothers' side of the family. Yet they did not have a greater than expected number of gay male relatives on the paternal side of the family. This pattern of inheritance is consistent with genetic traits, such as hemophilia, that are linked to the X sex chromosome, which men receive from their mothers.

The researchers then examined the X sex chromosome in 40 pairs of gay male, non-twin brothers. In 33 of the pairs, the brothers had identical DNA markers on the end tip of the X chromosome. For brothers overall in the general population, about half would be expected to have inherited this chromosomal structure. It is suspected, therefore, that this chromosomal region may hold a gene that predisposes men to a gay male sexual orientation.

The researchers cautioned that they had not found a particular gene linked to sexual orientation, just a general location where the gene may be found. Nor do scientists know how such a gene or combination of genes might account for sexual orientation. Perhaps a particular gene governs the development of proteins that sculpt parts of the brain in ways that favour the development of a gay male sexual orientation. On the other hand, a number of the gay brothers (7 of the 40 pairs) did *not* share the chromosomal marker.

PRENATAL INFLUENCES AND SEXUAL ORIENTATION Sex hormones strongly influence the mating behaviour of other species (Crews, 1994). Researchers have thus looked into the possible role of hormonal factors in determining sexual orientation in humans.

Testosterone is essential to male sexual differentiation. Thus, levels of testosterone and its by-products in the blood and urine have been studied as possible influences on sexual orientation. Research has failed to connect sexual orientation in either gender with differences in the levels of either male or female sex hormones in adulthood (Friedman & Downey, 1994). In adulthood, testosterone appears to have **activating effects**. That is, it affects the intensity of sexual desire, but not the preference for partners of the same or the other gender (Whalen et al., 1990).

Monozygotic (MZ) twins
Twins who develop from the same fertilized ovum; identical twins.

Dizygotic (DZ) twins
Twins who develop from different fertilized ova; fraternal twins.

Concordance Agreement.

Activating effects Those effects of sex hormones that influence the level of the sex drive, but not sexual orientation.

What of the possible *prenatal* effects of sex hormones? Pregnant rats in experiments were given anti-androgen drugs that block the effects of testosterone. When the drugs were given during critical periods in which the fetuses' brains were becoming sexually differentiated, male offspring were likely to show feminine mating patterns as adults (Ellis & Ames, 1987). The adult males became receptive to mounting attempts by other males and failed to mount females.

Do prenatal sex hormones play a similar role in determining sexual orientation in people? There is suggestive evidence. For example, Meyer-Bahlburg and his colleagues (1995) interviewed groups of women exposed prenatally to DES, a synthetic estrogen. They found that these women were more likely to be rated as lesbian or bisexual than women who were not exposed to DES. Sari van Anders and Elizabeth Hampson (2005) at the University of Western Ontario found that women who were not strictly heterosexual had superior spatial ability relative to heterosexual women. They suggest that the relationship between increased spatial abilities and heteroflexible sexual orientation may be affected by high levels of androgens prior to birth.

Research in Action

BIRTH ORDER AND SEXUAL ORIENTATION

Ray Blanchard and colleagues at the Centre for Addiction and Mental Health–Clarke Institute in Toronto have conducted several studies analyzing the relationship of birth order to sexual orientation. In Blanchard et al. (2002), they built upon their previous findings that the odds of a man being gay increase in proportion to the number of his older brothers. They concluded that a gay male with three or more older brothers can attribute most of the origin of his sexual orientation to that effect. They also concluded that femininity in male children tends to be predictive of homosexuality. (However, not all gay men were feminine boys.) In their 2002 study they analyzed a sample of feminine boys, who they assumed on the basis of previous research were likely to be gay, and confirmed that those who had two or more older brothers weighed less at birth than heterosexual males who had older brothers. Blanchard et al. concluded that prenatal factors increase the odds of homosexuality in later-born males. In explaining this finding, the researchers hypothesized that the process is immunologic—that anti-male antibodies are produced by the mothers in response to immunization by male fetuses—and that this could decrease the birth weight of later male fetuses as well as increase the odds of their becoming gay. In effect, this process influences aspects of sexual differentiation in the brain of the fetus.

In more recent research, Blanchard (2004) analyzed data from a total of 10 143 respondents and again found that homosexuality in males was predicted by a higher number of older brothers, but not by numbers of older or younger sisters or younger brothers. This relationship between older brothers and sexual orientation has not been found among females. Similarly, Anthony Bogaert (2005) at Brock University reported that fraternal birth order is more influential than sibling sex ratio in affecting men's sexual orientation. Blanchard and Bogaert (2004) estimate that about 1 in 4 gay men can attribute their sexual orientation to this fraternal birth order effect.

Further support for prenatal influences is also indicated by researchers at the Toronto Centre for Addiction and Mental Health who have studied the association of handedness and sexual orientation. In a review of the literature on this relationship, Lalumiere et al. (2000) concluded that "non-right-handedness" is related to homosexual orientation in both males and females. The researchers hypothesized that disruptive events causing instability in the neurodevelopmental stage can modify sexual differentiation of the brain through either hormonal or immunological mechanisms.

We emphasize that while the above findings suggest that certain factors are predictive of homosexuality, their predictive power is relatively low. Most fourth- and fifth-born sons and most left-handed males are not homosexual. The statistical relationship between birth order and homosexuality does not necessarily establish a firm biological connection. Learning theorists might, for example, argue that later-born males are often treated differently because they have older brothers, and this may account for the increased probability of their becoming gay.

THE STRUCTURE OF THE BRAIN Evidence suggests that there may be structural differences between the brains of heterosexual and gay men. In 1991, Simon Levay, a neurobiologist at the Salk Institute in La Jolla, California, performed autopsies on the brains of 35 AIDS victims—19 gay men and 16 presumably heterosexual men. He found that a segment of the hypothalamus—specifically, the *third interstitial nucleus of the anterior hypothalamus*—in the brains of the gay men was less than half the size of that same segment in the heterosexual men. The same brain segment was larger in the brain tissues of heterosexual men than in brain tissues obtained from a comparison group of 6 presumably heterosexual women. No significant differences in size were found between the brain tissues of the gay men and the women, however.

LeVay's findings are intriguing but preliminary. We do not know, for example, whether the structural differences he found are innate. Nor do the findings prove that biology is destiny. As Richard Nakamura, a scientist with the National Institute of Mental Health, commented, "This [LeVay's findings] shouldn't be taken to mean that you're automatically [gay] if you have a structure of one size versus a structure of another size" (Angier, 1991).

The belief that sexual orientation is innate, or inborn, has many adherents in both the scientific and general communities. Support for the possible influences of prenatal hormonal factors in "sculpting" the brain in a masculine or feminine direction is based largely on animal studies, however. Direct evidence with people is lacking. We must also be careful in generalizing results from species other than our own.

We also need to be aware that biological factors operate in social context. Thus it is possible that the relationship between biological factors and homosexuality could be affected by social conditions.

Social-Psychological Perspectives

Do family relationships play a role in the origins of sexual orientation? What are the effects of childhood sexual experiences? Psychoanalytic theory and learning theory provide two of the major social-psychological approaches to understanding the origins of sexual orientation.

PSYCHOANALYTIC VIEWS Sigmund Freud, the originator of psychoanalytic theory, believed that children enter the world open to all forms of sexual stimulation. However, through proper resolution of the Oedipus complex, a boy will forsake his incestuous desires for his mother and come to identify with his father. As a result, his erotic attraction to his mother will eventually be transferred onto more appropriate *female* partners. A girl, through proper resolution of her Electra complex, will identify with her mother and seek erotic stimulation from men when she becomes sexually mature.

In Freud's view, a gay male or lesbian sexual orientation results from failure to resolve the Oedipus complex successfully by identifying with the parent of the same gender. In men, faulty resolution of the Oedipus complex is most likely to result from the so-called classic pattern of an emotionally "close-binding" mother and a "detached-hostile" father. A boy reared in such a family may come to identify with his mother and even to "transform himself into her" (Freud, 1922/1959, p. 40). He may thus become effeminate and develop sexual interests in men.

Freud believed that the mechanism of unresolved **castration anxiety** plays a role in a gay male sexual orientation. By the time the Oedipus complex takes effect,

Castration anxiety In psychoanalytic theory, a man's fear that his genitals will be removed. Castration anxiety is an element of the Oedipus complex and is implicated in the directionality of erotic interests.

the boy will have learned from self-stimulation that he can obtain sexual pleasure from his penis. In his youthful fantasies, he associates this pleasure with mental images of his mother. Similarly, he is likely to have learned that females do not possess a penis. The psychoanalyst theorizes that somewhere along the line, the boy may also have been warned that his penis will be removed if he plays with himself. From all this, the boy may surmise that females—including his mother—once had penises but that they were removed.

During the throes of the Oedipus complex, the boy unconsciously comes to fear that his father, his rival in love for the mother, will retaliate by removing the organ that the boy has come to associate with sexual pleasure. His fear causes him to repress his sexual desire for his mother and to identify with the potential aggressor—his father. The boy thus overcomes his castration anxiety and is headed along the path of adult heterosexuality.

If the Oedipus complex is not successfully resolved, castration anxiety may persist. When sexually mature, the man will not be able to tolerate sex with women. Their lack of a penis will arouse unconscious castration anxiety within him. The supposed Electra complex in little girls follows a somewhat different course. Freud believed that little girls become envious of boys' penises because they lack their own. This concept of **penis envy** was one of Freud's most controversial beliefs. In Freud's view, jealousy leads little girls to resent their mothers, whom they blame for their anatomic "deficiency," and to turn from their mothers to their fathers as sexual objects. They now desire to possess the father, because the father's penis provides what they lack. But incestuous desires bring the girl into competition with her mother. Motivated by fear that her mother will withdraw her love if these desires persist, the girl normally represses them and identifies with her mother. She then develops traditional feminine interests and eventually seeks erotic stimulation from men. She supplants her childhood desire for a penis with a desire to marry a man and bear children. The baby, emitted from between her legs, serves as the ultimate penis substitute.

A nagging problem in assessing the validity of Freudian theory is that many of its concepts, such as castration anxiety and penis envy, are believed to operate at an unconscious level. As such, they lie beyond the scope of scientific observation and measurement.

More recent evidence has brought the issue of familial closeness between gay men and their parents into sharper perspective. Richard Pillard and his colleagues (Pillard & Weinrich, 1986; Pillard, 1990) found that gay males described themselves as more distant from their fathers during childhood than did either heterosexual controls or the gay men's own heterosexual brothers. The gay men in their sample also reported greater closeness to their mothers. Still, the father's psychological distance from the son may have reflected the son's alienation from him, not the reverse. That is, the son may have been so attached to his mother, or so uninterested in traditional masculine activities, that he rebuffed paternal attempts to engage him in conventional father–son activities.

LEARNING THEORIES Learning theorists agree with Freud that early experiences play an important role in the development of sexual orientation. They focus, however, on the role of reinforcement of early patterns of sexual behaviour rather than on the resolution of unconscious conflicts. People generally repeat pleasurable activities and discontinue painful ones. Thus, people may learn to engage in sexual activity with people of their own gender if childhood sexual experimentation with them is connected with sexual pleasure.

Penis envy In psychoanalytic theory, the girl's wish to have a penis.

If sexual motivation is high, as it tends to be during adolescence, and the only outlets are with others of one's own gender, adolescents may experiment sexually with them. If these encounters are pleasurable, and heterosexual experiences are unpleasant, a firmer gay male or lesbian sexual orientation may develop (Gagnon & Simon, 1973). Conversely, pain, anxiety, or social disapproval may be connected with early contacts with people of one's own gender. In such cases, the child may learn to inhibit feelings of attraction to people of her or his own gender and develop a firmer heterosexual orientation.

Although learning may play a role in the development of a gay male or lesbian sexual orientation, learning theorists have not identified specific learning experiences that would lead to these orientations. Moreover, most adolescent encounters with people of the same gender, even if they are pleasurable, do not lead to an adult gay male or lesbian sexual orientation. Many heterosexual people have had adolescent encounters with members of their own gender without affecting their adult orientations. This is true even of people whose early sexual interactions with the other gender were fumbling and frustrating. Moreover, the overwhelming majority of gay males and lesbians were aware of sexual interest in people of their own gender *before* they had sexual encounters with them, pleasurable or otherwise (Bell et al., 1981; Savin-Williams & Diamond, 2000).

GENDER NONCONFORMITY   On average, gay males tend to be somewhat feminine and lesbians to be somewhat masculine, but there is a good deal of variation within each group (Bailey et al., 1997; Dawood et al., 2000). Thus it seems that stereotypes of the effeminate gay male and the masculine lesbian are exaggerated. Gender nonconformity is rooted in childhood; gay males and lesbians are more likely than heterosexuals to report childhood behaviour stereotypical of the other gender (Bailey & Zucker, 1995; Friedman & Downey, 1994). Many gay males and lesbians recall acting and feeling "different" from their childhood peers. Many gay males report that they avoided participating in competitive sports as children and that they were more fearful of physical injury, and were more likely to avoid getting into fights, than heterosexual males (Dawood et al., 2000). Some gay males recall feeling different as early as age three or four (Isay, 1990). Feelings of differentness were often related to behaviour stereotypical of the other gender.

Gay males are also more likely to recall feeling more sensitive than their peers during childhood (Isay, 1990). They cried more easily. Their feelings were more readily hurt. They had more artistic interests. They had fewer male buddies but more female playmates. As well, gay males are more likely than their heterosexual counterparts to have preferred "girls' toys." They preferred playing with girls to playing with trucks or guns or engaging in rough-and-tumble play (Dawood et al., 2000). Their preferences often led to their being called "sissies." Gay men also recall more cross-dressing during childhood. They preferred the company of older women to that of older men and engaged in childhood sex play with other boys rather than with girls.

According to University of British Columbia researchers, this childhood gender nonconformity found in many gay males often leads to social rejection by parents and peers (Landolt et al., 2004). This rejection is a major factor in the difficulty many gay males have in accepting their sexual orientation.

There is also evidence of masculine-typed behaviour among lesbians as children (Bailey & Zucker, 1995). Lesbians are more likely than heterosexual women to perceive themselves as having been "tomboys." They were more likely to prefer rough-and-tumble games to playing with dolls and enjoyed wearing boy's clothing rather than "cutesy" dresses.

An important study by Devendra Singh and colleagues (1999) relates gender nonconformity in lesbians to the butch–femme dimension and biological factors.

The investigators compared self-identified butch and femme lesbians on various personality, behavioural, and biological measures. They found that butch lesbians were significantly more likely than femme lesbians to recall gender-atypical behavioural preferences in childhood. Butch lesbians also had higher waist-to-hip ratios and higher testosterone levels in their saliva, both of which are more typical of males. The Singh group suggests that their findings support the validity of the butch–femme distinction and that the distinction may be caused by differences in exposure to prenatal androgens (male sex hormones).

The Singh findings are especially important in suggesting that while some lesbians were tomboys, others clearly were not. Similarly, while some gay men were effeminate in childhood, many others were not. While the research points to certain trends in childhood as related to homosexuality, we need to be cautious about overgeneralizing these trends.

How might extreme childhood effeminacy lead to a gay male sexual orientation? Green (1987) speculates that the social detachment of these boys from male peers and role models (especially fathers) creates strong, unfulfilled cravings for male affection. This craving then leads them to seek males as partners in sex and love relationships in adolescence and adulthood.

Of course, there is another possibility, as suggested in research by J. Michael Bailey and his colleagues (Bailey et al., 2000; Dawood et al., 2000): Gender nonconformity appears to be somewhat heritable. Moreover, if a tendency toward homosexuality is inherited, gender nonconformity could well be that tendency.

What can we conclude about the origins of homosexuality? All in all, the origins of a gay male or lesbian sexual orientation remain mysterious and complex—just as mysterious as the origins of heterosexuality. In reviewing theories and research, we are left with the impression that sexual orientation is unlikely to have a single cause. Sexual orientation appears to spring from multiple origins, including biological and psychosocial factors (Strickland, 1995). Genetic and biochemical factors (such as hormone levels) may affect the prenatal organization of the brain (Money, 1994). These factors may predispose people to a certain sexual orientation. But it may be that early socialization experiences are also necessary to give rise to a gay male, lesbian, heterosexual, or bisexual sexual orientation. The precise influences and interactions of these factors have so far eluded researchers. The reasons that some people are homosexual remain no clearer than the reasons that most people are heterosexual.

Coming Out: Coming to Terms with Being Gay

Gay men and lesbians usually speak of the process of accepting their sexual orientation as "coming out" or as "coming out of the closet." Coming out is a two-pronged process: coming out to oneself (recognizing one's gay male or lesbian sexual orientation) and coming out to others (declaring one's orientation to the world). Coming out can create a sense of pride in one's sexual orientation and foster the ability to form emotionally and sexually satisfying relationships with gay male or lesbian partners.

Coming Out to Oneself

According to Ritch Savin-Williams and Lisa Diamond (2000), the development of sexual identity in gay males and lesbians involves four steps or features: attraction to members of the same sex, self-labelling as gay or lesbian, sexual contact with members of the same sex, and disclosure of one's sexual orientation to other people. The researchers by and large found a 10-year gap between initial attraction to members of one's own sex, which tended to occur at about the age of 8 or 9, and disclosure of one's orientation to other people, which usually occurred at about age 18. In keeping with sex differences noted in Chapter 5, females were more likely to focus on the emotional or romantic aspects of their budding feelings. Males were more likely to focus on the sexual aspects. Males—who are generally more open than females to sexual experimentation—were likely to become involved in sexual activity with other males before they labelled themselves as gay. Females, on the other hand, were more likely to label themselves as lesbians before pursuing relationships with other females.

Two researchers in human sexuality note that

Sexual orientation emerges strongly during early adolescence. Youths with emerging identities that are gay, lesbian, or bisexual, living in generally hostile climates, face particular dilemmas. They are well aware that in many secondary schools the words "fag" and "dyke" are terms of denigration and that anyone who is openly gay, lesbian, or bisexual is open to social exclusion and psychological and physical persecution. Some of their families too will express negative feelings about people who are gay, lesbian, or bisexual; youths in such families may be victimized if they disclose that they are not heterosexual. (Bagley & D'Augelli, 2000)

For some people, coming to recognize and accept a gay male or lesbian sexual orientation involves gradually stripping away layers of denial. For others it may be a sudden awakening. Alberta professors Kevin Alderson and Ronna Jevne (2003) have explored the psychic conflict that is involved in the coming out process and have conceptualized this as a struggle between catalysts that push gay males to acknowledge their sexual orientation and hindrances that block the acceptance of their identity. They identify the major catalyst as developing an increased awareness of being gay and gay culture and the major hindrance as fear and condemnation of homosexuals. Alderson and Jevne believe that a person will self-identify as gay only when the catalysts overpower the hindrances.

Applied Knowledge

SUPPORT PROGRAMS FOR LESBIANS AND GAY MALES

Some cities offer support and counselling for gay males and lesbians through programs such as the Sexual Orientation and Youth Project of Central Toronto Youth Services. Telephone hotline services also provide information to gay, lesbian, and bisexual youth. Ontario researcher Margaret Schneider (1991) found that the supportive contact with other lesbians and gay youth provided by these kinds of services is an important factor in helping young people to accept

their sexual orientation. For those who struggle with the process of coming out, the Internet provides valuable information and access to resources, such as discussed in the nearby World of Diversity feature.

Some school boards have included discussion of sexual orientation in their school curricula. In 1992, the Toronto Board of Education approved the first Canadian high school curriculum guide on the topics of homosexuality and homophobia (Barrett et al., 1997). Since then many school boards and teachers associations in Canada have adopted policies and programs designed to reduce homophobia and

make schools a safer and more accepting place for gay and lesbian youth. Education faculty and students at the University of Alberta have played a major role in initiating these policies and programs. In particular, they have encouraged the development of gay–straight student alliances.

The Toronto School Board has developed a Triangle program for lesbian, gay, bisexual, and transgender (LGBT) students. This innovative program offers Canada's only classroom for LGBT students.

Alderson (2003) is highly critical of fixed-stage models of gay identity acquisition, such as those proposed by Savin-Williams and Diamond (2000), which assume that all people coming out go through a series of well-defined stages. He charges that they fail to take into account environmental influences. As shown in the World of Diversity box, individuals may follow different paths.

A World of Diversity

HIS CROSS TO BEAR

Jon Dobbin used to have a speech prepared for his two sons about homosexuality.

He never delivered it.

For most of their lives, the boys were brought up with the teachings of a strict, fundamentalist church near Chatham.

They did not watch television, nor did they go to movies very often. Their perception of the outside world was shaped entirely in the church.

And when it came to homosexuality, the congregation's views were clear. So Dobbin, who served as a church elder,

Jon Dobbin, 44. Once married with children, Dobbin is divorced after accepting that he is gay.

prepared a sermon for his children that was long on Biblical references and decidedly short on tolerance.

"I would have told my sons that the Bible calls it an abomination," he said. "I would have told them that in the Old Testament it was punished by death. That's how much it was disapproved of. I would have told them it is no less wrong now than it was then. I would have told them it's unnatural."

But the subject didn't come up until years later, when his sons reached their teens. They were 13 and 17 years of age when Dobbin sat them down in his bedroom six years ago to tell them he was getting a divorce from their mother.

He also told them that he was gay.

"There was shock, but there was mostly silence," Dobbin said. "They just stared at me in disbelief. I told them—and at that point I was still afraid to use the word gay— that I was a homosexual. I wanted my sons to know why I was divorcing. I didn't want to make up stuff or say vague things like 'I need space' or 'I need some time for myself.' I needed to tell them the truth."

Dobbin said that his Christian faith began evaporating years ear-

lier as he struggled with his identity. While he didn't have a religious upbringing, he was drawn to Christian fundamentalism while in his teens. The church offered a semblance of family and strict structure that he thought he needed.

He married at the age of 19, knowing full well that he was gay but hoping family life would set him straight.

"Being married and having a family, I thought that was a life that would be most fulfilling," he said.

"In my late 30s, I didn't like who I was. I hated myself. I had to face up to who I was and I had to live openly as who I was: a gay man."

After moving to Guelph two years ago, Dobbin co-founded a support group for gay fathers with similar stories. Simply dubbed the Fathers Group, it consists of roughly 20 gay men from Guelph, Waterloo Region and Hamilton. They hold weekly meetings in the city.

Most of the men in the Fathers Group were involved in heterosexual relationships and had children before coming out as gay men, Dobbin said.

"Their stories are all very different," he said. "But one similarity is that the men were often in marriages or long-term relationships with women and after a lot of internal struggle came to accept that they are gay or bisexual. When that comes out, the marriage would often dissolve."

Source: Eric Volmers, Guelph Mercury, *August 6, 2005, pp. 1, 2. Reprinted with permission of* Guelph Mercury.

Applied Knowledge

COUNSELLING GAY MALES AND LESBIANS

Karine Blais and colleagues (2004) at the University of Montreal have outlined some key issues relating to sexual orientation that therapists need to be knowledgeable about. These include

- homophobia
- HIV
- the lack of conjugal role models
- the "coming out" process

However, it is also important for therapists to recognize that gay and lesbian couples face many of the issues faced by heterosexual couples. The

Toronto Centre for Addictions and Mental Health has prepared a handbook, *Asking the Right Questions*, to guide therapists who counsel gay and lesbian clients.

Alderson (2003) has developed an ecological model of gay male identity that incorporates both external (social and environmental) and internal psychological influences that lead to a gay self-definition. In his model, cognitive dissonance about being gay plays a key role in the movement toward identity development. Alderson believes that his ecological model provides clinicians with a useful framework for counselling gay males and in particular helping those who are questioning their sexual identities.

In a survey of 14 Canadian universities, Alderson (2004) also found that graduate students in clinical psychology and counselling received little training on issues facing lesbians, gays, and bisexuals. Graduates of these programs feel that they are not prepared to work with sexual minority clients.

Recognition of a gay sexual orientation may be only the first step in a lifelong process of sexual identity formation. Acceptance of being gay becomes part of one's self-definition (Isay, 1990). The term *gay identity*, or *homosexual identity*, refers to the subjective sense of being gay.

A World of Diversity

WEB OFFERS SAFE HAVEN FOR THOSE WHO AREN'T OUT

The Internet can bring the world into the home for some. For others, it can help them reach out into the community.

That's especially true if you're gay, lesbian, bisexual, transgendered, or even confused about what label you

wish others to put on you.

"The Internet can provide in minutes the information and personal contacts it would have taken months or years to find offline," says Margaret Robinson, a theology student at the University of Toronto and co-chair for the Toronto Dyke March, which is part of Pride Toronto. "For people who, for whatever reason, are not yet out, the Internet provides anonymity. That can

make it easier for some people to express feelings they aren't yet fully comfortable verbalizing in person. Also, the Internet allows you to find resources and groups that are specifically bisexual, which is important for people first coming out."

Source: Peter Krivel, The Toronto Star, *June 18, 2001.*

Coming Out to Others

There are different patterns of coming out to others. Coming out occasionally means making an open declaration to the world. Some individuals inform only one or a few select people. Others may tell friends but not family members

Many gay men and lesbians remain reluctant to declare their sexual orientation, even to friends and family. Disclosure is fraught with the risk of loss of jobs, friendships, and social standing (Bagley & D'Augelli, 2000). Gay men and lesbians often anticipate that family members will have negative reactions, including denial, anger, and rejection (Bagley & D'Augelli, 2000). Family members and loved ones may refuse to hear or may be unwilling to accept reality, as Martha Barron Barrett notes in her book *Invisible Lives*, which chronicles the lives of a sample of lesbians in the United States.

> Parents, children, neighbors, and friends of lesbians deny, or compartmentalize, or struggle with their knowledge in the same way the women themselves do. "My parents know I've lived with my partner for six years. She goes home with me. We sleep in the same bed there. The word *lesbian* has never been mentioned. I told my mother and she said, 'Well, now that's over with. We don't need to mention it again.' She never has, and that was ten years ago. I don't know if she ever told my father." (Barrett, 1990, p. 52)

Some families are more accepting. They may in fact have had suspicions and prepared themselves for such news. Then, too, many families are initially rejecting but often eventually come to at least grudging acceptance that a family member is gay.

Dave Vervoort (1999), a University of Guelph graduate student, conducted an online survey of gay fathers, almost all of whom lived in Canada or the U.S. Most of the fathers had their children living with them or had joint custody. In coming out to their children about their sexual orientation, the fathers reported that the response was generally more positive than anticipated. Only about 10% of the children were clearly upset about the disclosure. Older children were more negative. However, over time even many of these children became more positive in their acceptance of their father's gay status.

Another University of Guelph graduate student, Daniel Mahoney (1994), interviewed parents who belong to the support group Parents, Friends and Family of Lesbians and Gays (PFLAG) to discover how they reacted when they found out their children were gay or lesbian. All the parents reported that their initial reactions were highly emotional, involving "shock, denial, guilt and shame." Each felt that he or she now had to deal with the new identity of being a parent of a lesbian or gay child. However, all the parents in the study felt that it was essential to accept their son's or daughter's sexual orientation, since they feared that otherwise they might lose their child. Acceptance was a way of expressing their unconditional love. Of course, some parents are not as accepting as those included in Mahoney's study.

Adjustment of Gay Males and Lesbians

Until 1973, gay male and lesbian sexual orientations were in and of themselves considered to be mental illnesses by the American Psychiatric Association and were listed as such in their diagnostic manual. But in that year, the members of the association voted to drop a gay male or lesbian sexual orientation from its list of mental disorders, although a diagnostic category remains for people with persistent and marked distress about their sexual orientation (American Psychiatric Association, 2000).

Carefully controlled studies have found that gay males and lesbians are more likely than heterosexuals to experience feelings of anxiety and depression and that they are more prone to suicide (Bagley & D'Augelli, 2000; Savin-Williams, 2001).

Parents and Friends of Lesbians and Gays (Canada) Promotes the health and well-being of gay, lesbian, bisexual, and transgendered persons and their families and friends through support and education.

www.pflag.ca

University of Calgary researchers found that gay and bisexual males were 14 times as likely to consider suicide as heterosexual males (Bagley & Tremblay, 1997). Gay males, moreover, are more likely to have eating disorders (anorexia nervosa and bulimia nervosa) than heterosexual males (Ferguson et al., 1999).

A key reason for adjustment problems among gays and lesbians is the stress of societal oppression and rejection. For some, adjustment is related to conflict over their sexual orientation (Simonsen et al., 2000). Yet it is important to acknowledge that many gay males and lesbians are well adjusted. Those who accept their sexual orientation and, in particular, those who are openly gay are more likely to be well adjusted.

Sexual Orientation and Family

In recent years there has been considerable analysis and debate surrounding gay and lesbian marriage and parenting. Certainly, the changes in Canadian law that allowed gay marriages to take place have accelerated discussion of these topics.

In 2001 the Canadian census obtained data for the first time about same-sex couples. There were 34 200 same-sex couples counted, representing 0.5% of all couples (Statistics Canada, 2002). Eighty-five percent of the male and 75% of the female couples live in the larger urban areas of Canada. About 15% of female same-sex couples have children living with them, compared with 3% of male couples. The 2006 census will, for the first time, include same-sex marriages.

There have been two Canadian studies of married lesbian and gay male couples (Alderson, 2004; MacIntosh & Reissing, 2004). The couples surveyed reported the following benefits of being married:

- social sanction; greater acceptance and normalization of their relationship by friends and family
- feeling equal to heterosexuals with regard to making decisions for an ill partner, caring for children, and receiving benefits related to inheritance and insurance
- feeling closer to their partner and more secure about their relationship
- decrease in feelings of internalized homophobia
- more openness to the idea of having children in their relationship

It should be noted that not everyone in the gay community supports same-sex marriage. Those who are opposed tend to criticize marriage as a patriarchal heterosexual institution. However, the married same-sex couples do not share this view and argue that the legalization of marriage offers the freedom of choice. These married couples also oppose the proposal of the Conservative Party of Canada to offer civil unions instead of marriage, believing that civil unions are not equal to marriage (MacIntosh & Reissing, 2004).

There has been relatively little research on lesbian and gay couples and families. Deborah Foster (2004), a doctoral student at the University of Alberta, has provided a comprehensive analysis of the research on lesbian families. She notes that most lesbian families were formed as a result of the birth mother having had children in a heterosexual relationship, leaving that relationship and then living in a lesbian relationship. Foster concludes that children raised in lesbian families are just as well adjusted, if not more so, than those raised in heterosexual families. Similar findings have been reported for children raised by gay male parents (Vervoort, 1999).

Patterns of Sexual Activity Among Gay Males and Lesbians

Heterosexual people are often confused about the sexual practices of gay couples. They may wonder, "Just what do they do?" Generally speaking, gay couples express

The Foundation for Equal Families
Offers up-to-date developments on issues relating to gay and lesbian unions in Canada.

www.ffef.ca

themselves sexually through as wide a range of activities as do heterosexual couples, with the exception of vaginal intercourse. But there are shades of difference between gay and heterosexual couples in sexual techniques.

Sexual Techniques

In an Ontario survey of Canadian gay and bisexual men, more than half of the men reported having sex in the previous three months with at least one regular partner (someone the respondent had sex with more than once); also, more than half had engaged in sex in the previous three months with at least one casual partner (someone he had sex with only once) (Myers et al., 2004). The most common sexual activities reported for the previous three months were deep tongue kissing, oral sex without a condom, and mutual masturbation. Table 9.2 lists the types of behaviours experienced by the respondents. The types of sexual behaviours experienced were fairly similar for both regular and casual partners, with the exception of anal sex without a condom, which was experienced twice as often with a regular partner than with a casual partner. Forty-four percent said they had never engaged in receptive anal intercourse without a condom.

Risks of infection and of injury to the rectum or anus are associated with another sexual practice called *fisting*: the insertion of the fist or hand into the rectum, usually after the bowels have been evacuated with an enema.

Sexual techniques practised by lesbians vary. Lesbian couples engage in kissing, manual and oral breast stimulation, and manual and oral stimulation of the genitals (Kinsey et al., 1953). Most lesbian couples also engage in genital apposition. That is, they position themselves in such a way as to rub their genitals together rhythmically.

Differences in Sexual Relationships Between Gay Males and Lesbians

Researchers have consistently found that gay males are more likely than lesbians to engage in casual sex with many partners. Lesbians more often confine their sexual activity to a committed, affectionate relationship (Peplau & Cochran, 1990). These

Table 9.2 Sexual Behaviours of Gay and Bisexual Men in Ontario in Past Three Months

	With Regular Male Partner (%)	With Casual Male Partner (%)
Mutual masturbation	81	78
Oral sex—no condom (I)	86	80
Deep tongue kissing	86	78
Oral sex—no condom (R)	80	73
Anal sex with condom (I)	44	47
Oral–anal	53	40
Anal sex—no condom (I)	41	21
Anal sex with condom (R)	36	35
Anal sex—no condom (R)	34	6

Note: I = Insertive, R = Receptive

Source: T. Myers & D. Allman, 2004. Ontario Men's Survey. Ottawa: Canadian Public Health Association.

differences parallel those found for heterosexuals. As discussed in Chapter 5, heterosexual men are more likely than heterosexual women to report engaging in casual sex and to report having sex with more partners.

University of Guelph graduate student Melanie Beres conducted an Internet study of men who have sex with men (MSM) and women who have sex with women (WSW). The study participants were located mainly through university Web sites, and most lived in Canada and the United States. Beres et al. (2004) found that the number of partners was much higher for the men, with 32% of the MSM having had 22 or more partners, compared with only 2% of the WSW. And 80% of the WSW reported 6 or fewer partners, compared with only 31% of the MSM. In the survey of gay and bisexual men in Ontario (Myers et al., 2004), only 24% reported having had sex with just one partner the previous year, while 10% had sex with 30 or more partners.

In the same survey, respondents were asked where they had looked for sex with men during the previous year (Myers et al., 2004). By far the most common place was a gay bar (60%) and the second most common places included the Internet (35%) and bathhouses (31%). In a separate Ontario study of bathhouse culture (Haubrich et al., 2004), gay men were asked their reasons for going to a bathhouse. Most stated that the predominant reason was for sexual release in an environment that they considered personally safe. They did not expect to develop a relationship with someone they met there.

In an earlier Canadian survey, 57% said they attended gay bars at least once a week while only 7% said they went to bathhouses that often (Myers et al., 1993). In the study by Beres (2002), three-quarters of both MSM and WSW in Canada and the U.S. met partners through friends. The MSM (65%) were also more likely than the WSW (29%) to use the Internet to find partners.

Despite the advent of AIDS, some gay men, like some heterosexual people, continue high-risk behaviour. For example, they engage in unprotected anal intercourse and sexual activity with multiple partners. The earlier Canadian survey of gay and bisexual men found that, of the men who had engaged in anal intercourse during the previous three months, 23% had not used a condom each time (Myers et al., 1993). Since the early 1990s, it seems that the level of sexual risk-taking has increased. In the Ontario study (Myers et al., 2004), 40% of the men who had engaged in anal sex in the previous three months had not used a condom each time. The increases were especially notable in Toronto. When asked why they hadn't used a condom the last time they had unprotected anal intercourse, half of the men said they were having sex with a regular partner. About one-quarter said they were HIV-negative, the sex was too exciting to put on a condom, or putting on a condom makes them lose their erection. About one-fifth were practising the withdrawal method of removing the penis prior to ejaculation.

A study of gay men in Ontario (Calzavara et al., 2003) found that half were not putting on condoms when engaging in anal sex until they were about to ejaculate. These men are at risk of HIV infection because the HIV virus can be present in pre-ejaculatory fluid. In fact, the study found that those men who delayed putting on the condom until just before they ejaculated were six times as likely to become infected with the HIV virus as those who put them on early (Calzavara et al., 2003). These findings clearly demonstrate the importance of applying a condom prior to anal penetration.

In a study of older gay males in Toronto, some of the men felt that when they had sex with a younger man they would not insist that he use a condom (Murray & Adam, 2001). Because the older men perceived themselves as less desirable, they felt they had to go along with whatever the younger man desired. As well, many older men find that wearing a condom makes it more difficult to get and keep an erection.

Three-fourths of the respondents in the Ontario survey had been tested for the HIV antibody. The Ontario study was the first major survey conducted in the gay community to determine the rate of HIV infection based on obtaining a biological specimen. Among the 77% of men who provided a saliva specimen, 6% tested HIV-positive. Men from Toronto and those with less education were the most likely to test positive. Of those who tested HIV-positive, about one-quarter either did not know their HIV status or chose not to disclose it in this study (Myers et al., 2004).

Gay Lifestyles

One of the mistakes that laypeople (and some researchers) make is to treat gay people as though they were all the same. Variations in sexual expression exist within and across sexual orientations. Descriptions of gay and heterosexual lifestyles must consider individual differences.

Gay men and lesbians in larger urban centres can usually look to gay communal structures to provide services and support. These include gay-rights organizations and gay-oriented newspapers, magazines, bookstores, housing cooperatives, medical services, and other support services (Gagnon, 1990). The gay community provides a sense of acceptance and belonging that gay people do not typically find in society at large.

Not all gay people, however, feel that they are a part of the "gay community" or participate in gay rights organizations. For many, their sexual orientation is a part of their identity but not a dominant theme that governs their social and political activities. Homosexuals, like heterosexuals, have many different styles of life. Things are no simpler in the gay world than in the straight world.

The Advocate
This magazine for gay males and lesbians contains up-to-date news, profiles of notable people (gay and straight), reviews of media events, and articles about the adjustment of gay males and lesbians.
www.advocate.com

Sexual Orientation and Relationships.
Gay people, like heterosexuals, have a variety of types of relationship. Some go from partner to partner. Others form stable relationships. Some avoid sexual intimacy and committed relationships altogether. As Alexandre Dumas said, "All generalizations are dangerous. Even this one."

Summing Up

Sexual Orientation

Coming to Terms with Terms

Sexual orientation describes the directionality of one's sexual and romantic interests—toward members of the same gender, members of the other gender, or both. Gay male and lesbian sexual orientations denote sexual and romantic interest in members of one's own gender.

Sexual Orientation and Gender Identity

Gay males and lesbians have a gender identity that is consistent with their chromosomal and anatomic sex.

Determining Sexual Orientation

Kinsey and his colleagues found evidence of degrees of homosexuality and heterosexuality, with bisexuality representing a midpoint between the two. However, some recent theorists suggest that heterosexuality and homosexuality may be separate dimensions rather than polar opposites.

Bisexuality

Bisexual people are attracted to both males and females. Many have a somewhat stronger attraction to one gender than to the other, yet they remain bisexual.

Perspectives on Gay Male and Lesbian Sexual Orientations

Historical Perspectives

Throughout much of Western history, gay people have been deemed sinful and criminal.

Cross-Cultural Perspectives

Male–male sexual behaviour is practised by at least some members of many preliterate societies.

Cross-Species Perspectives

Many animals engage in behaviours that resemble male–male and female–female contacts among humans, but we must be cautious in ascribing motives to animals.

Attitudes Toward Sexual Orientation in Contemporary Society

Attitudes toward gay people have shifted, though homophobia persists. The majority of Canadians now approve of same-sex relationships. During the past generation, gay males and lesbians have organized effective political groups to fight discrimination and win legal rights, such as the right to marry.

What Determines Sexual Orientation?

Biological Perspectives

Evidence of a genetic contribution to sexual orientation is accumulating. Research has failed to connect sexual orientation with differences in current (adult) levels of sex hormones. Prenatal sex hormones may, however, play a role in determining sexual orientation in humans.

Social-Psychological Perspectives

Psychoanalytic theory connects sexual orientation with unconscious castration anxiety and improper resolution of the Oedipus complex. Learning theorists focus on the role of reinforcement of early patterns of sexual behaviour. Although only a few gay people fit the stereotypes of "swishy" men and "butch" women, research finds that as children, homosexuals report a greater incidence of behaviour stereotypical of the other gender than do heterosexual reference groups.

Coming Out: Coming to Terms with Being Gay

Coming out is a two-pronged process: coming out to oneself and coming out to others.

Coming Out to Oneself

Recognizing and accepting one's gay sexual orientation may occur as a gradual process or as a sudden awakening.

Coming Out to Others

Many gay males and lesbians fear rejection if they disclose their sexual orientation. Some families struggle with the knowledge; others are more accepting.

Adjustment of Gay Males and Lesbians

Evidence has failed to show that gay males, lesbians, and bisexuals are more emotionally unstable or more subject to psychiatric disorders than heterosexual people are.

Sexual Orientation and Family

Children raised by same-sex couples appear to be as well-adjusted as those raised by heterosexual couples.

Patterns of Sexual Activity Among Gay Males and Lesbians

Gay people generally express themselves sexually through as wide a range of activities as heterosexual people do, with the exception of vaginal intercourse.

Differences in Sexual Relationships Between Gay Males and Lesbians

Gay males are more likely than lesbians to engage in casual sex with many partners. Lesbians more often confine sexual activity to a committed, affectionate relationship.

Gay Lifestyles

Gay people do not adopt a single, stereotypical lifestyle.

Test Yourself

Multiple-Choice Questions

1. Sexual orientation is
   a. completely genetically determined
   b. fixed and unchanging
   c. an excellent predictor of sexual behaviour
   d. not necessarily a good predictor of sexual behaviour

2. Gay people
   a. always wish they were the other gender
   b. have a gender identity consistent with their anatomical gender
   c. often wish they were the other gender
   d. always behave like the other gender in childhood

3. According to Statistics Canada, more men than women report that they are _____ and more women than men report that they are

   _____.
   a. bisexual; homosexual
   b. homosexual; bisexual
   c. homosexual; asexual
   d. asexual; homosexual

4. Psychologist Michael Storms suggests that
   a. heterosexuality and homosexuality are at opposite ends of a continuum of sexual orientation
   b. asexuality is a completely separate dimension
   c. homosexuality and heterosexuality are separate and independent dimensions
   d. bisexual individuals are at the midpoint of the continuum between heterosexuality and homosexuality

5. In preliterate societies, sexual activity between males may be limited to men who are
   a. uneducated
   b. being initiated into manhood
   c. outcasts
   d. unable to find an appropriate bride

6. A 2003 poll of adult Canadians found that _____ favoured same-sex marriages.
   a. 21%
   b. 41%
   c. 61%
   d. 81%

7. Which of the following most accurately explains how a learning theorist would explain a homosexual orientation?
   a. A young child has a pleasurable same-sex experience.
   b. A child is exposed to gay and lesbian issues in a sexuality class at school.
   c. A young adult goes to a gay pride parade and experiments with a gay lifestyle.
   d. A young teenager reads about homosexuality, which then influences him to become gay himself.

8. Strongly held negative attitudes toward homosexuality are referred to as
   a. homeopathy
   b. homophilia
   c. homophobia
   d. homoerotic

9. Traditional Western religions are most likely to condemn homosexuality as "unnatural" because
   a. homosexuality is closely associated with Eastern religions
   b. homosexuality does not lead directly to procreation
   c. homosexuals seduce children
   d. homosexual couples corrupt heterosexual couples

10. Research on lesbian mothers and their children suggests that
    a. all the female children studied grew up to become lesbians themselves
    b. the children were at least as well adjusted as children raised in heterosexual families
    c. all the male children studied grew up to become gay men
    d. the children's gender identity was adversely affected

Critical Thinking Questions

1. What messages did you receive about homosexuality from your parents? Were they positive or negative? Did you receive different messages from your friends?

2. Why do you think men tend to be more homophobic than women?

3. People who believe that sexual orientation is biological tend to be more tolerant of homosexuality than those who do not. How would you explain this?

4. If you are a gay male or a lesbian, have you come out to your family? Your friends? If so, how did you find the experience? If not, why not?

5. If you are heterosexual, has a close friend or family member ever come out to you that they were gay or lesbian? What was your initial reaction? Why do you think you reacted this way?

Companion
Website

Visit our Companion Website at www.pearsoned.ca/rathus, **where you can use the interactive Study Guide and link to additional resources on topics discussed in this text.**

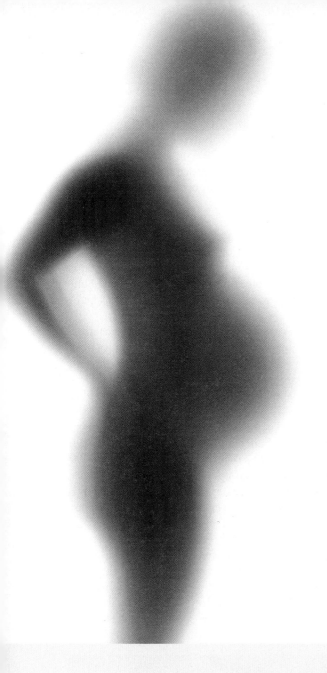

Chapter 10
Conception, Pregnancy, and Childbirth

Figure 10.1 Human Sperm Swarming Around an Ovum in a Fallopian Tube.

Fertilization normally occurs in a fallopian tube, not in the uterus.

Zona pellucida A gelatinous layer that surrounds an ovum. (From roots that mean "zone that light can shine through.")

Hyaluronidase An enzyme that briefly thins the zona pellucida, enabling one sperm to penetrate. (From roots that mean "substance that breaks down a glasslike fluid.")

When Elaine used her ovulation-timing kit the previous morning, it showed that she was about to ovulate. So later that night, Elaine and Dennis had made love, hoping that Elaine would conceive. Dennis ejaculated hundreds of millions of sperm within Elaine's vagina. Only a few thousand survived the journey through the cervix and uterus to the fallopian tube that contained the ovum, released just hours earlier. Of these, a few hundred remained to bombard the ovum. One succeeded in penetrating the ovum's covering, resulting in conception.

Conception

Conception is the union of a sperm cell and an ovum. On the one hand, conception is the beginning of a new human life. On the other hand, conception is the end of a fantastic voyage, in which a viable ovum—one of only several hundred that will mature and ripen during a woman's lifetime—unites with one of several hundred *million* sperm produced by a man in the average ejaculate.

Ova carry X sex chromosomes. Sperm carry either X or Y sex chromosomes. Girls are conceived from the union of an ovum and an X-bearing sperm, boys from the union of an ovum and a Y-bearing sperm. The 200 to 400 million sperm in an average ejaculate may seem excessive, given that only one can fertilize an egg. Only 1 in 1000 will ever arrive in the vicinity of an ovum, however. Millions deposited in the vagina simply flow out of the woman's body because of gravity, unless she remains prone for quite some time. Normal vaginal acidity kills many more. Many surviving sperm swim (against the current of fluid coming from the cervix) through the os and into the uterus. Surviving sperm may reach the fallopian tubes 60 to 90 minutes after ejaculation. About half the sperm end up in the wrong tube—that is, the one that does not contain the egg. Perhaps some 2000 sperm find their way into the right tube. Fewer still manage to swim the final 5 centimetres (2 inches) against the currents generated by the cilia that line the tube.

Fertilization normally occurs in a fallopian tube. (Figure 10.1 shows sperm swarming around an egg in a fallopian tube.) Ova contain chromosomes, proteins, fats, and nutritious fluid and are surrounded by a gelatinous layer called the **zona pellucida**. This layer must be penetrated if fertilization is to occur. Sperm that have completed their journey secrete the enzyme **hyaluronidase**, which briefly thins the zona pellucida, enabling one sperm to penetrate. Once a sperm has entered, the

Research in Action

BIRTH TRENDS

For several years there has been a decline in the Canadian birth rate and an increase in the age at which women have their first baby. In 2002, the birth rate dropped to 10.5 live births for every 1000 Canadians—the lowest figure since birth rates were first recorded in 1921.

In 2003, Statistics Canada estimated that Canadian women would have an average of 1.53 children. In 2003 the lowest birth rate was in Newfoundland and Labrador and the highest was in Nunavut and the Northwest Territories (Statistics Canada, 2005b).

Nationally in 2003, 48% of births were to women aged 30 and older—a dramatic change from 1983, when 24.6% of

births were to women aged 30 and older. Among women having their first baby, the average age was 28 years in 2003 (Statistics Canada, 2005b).

Why is the birth rate declining? Why are women giving birth later in life? There are a number of reasons:

- Women are marrying later.
- More women are completing higher education.
- Women are entering the workforce later.
- Changing values emphasize individual happiness and career achievement rather than having children.
- Material possessions are more socially valued at the same time as the cost of raising children rises.

zona pellucida thickens, locking other sperm out. The corresponding chromosomes in the sperm and ovum line up opposite each other. Conception occurs as the chromosomes from the sperm and ovum combine to form 23 new pairs, which carry a unique set of genetic instructions.

Applied Knowledge

OPTIMIZING THE CHANCES OF CONCEPTION

Some couples may wish to optimize their chances of conceiving during a particular month so that birth occurs at a desired time. Others may have difficulty conceiving and wish to maximize their chances for a few months before consulting a fertility specialist. Some fairly simple procedures can dramatically increase the chances of conceiving for couples without serious fertility problems.

The ovum can be fertilized for about 4 to 20 hours after ovulation

(Wilcox et al., 2000). Sperm are most active within 48 hours after ejaculation. So one way of optimizing the chances of conception is to engage in coitus within a few hours of ovulation. There are a number of ways to predict ovulation.

Using the Basal Body Temperature Chart Few women have perfectly regular cycles, so they can only guess when they are ovulating (Wilcox et al., 2000). A basal body temperature (BBT) chart (Figure 10.2) may help provide a more reliable estimate.

As shown in the figure, body temperature is fairly even before ovulation,

and early-morning body temperature is generally below 37°C (98.6°F). But just before ovulation, basal temperature dips slightly. Then, on the day after ovulation, temperature tends to rise by about 0.2 to 0.4°C (0.4 to 0.8°F) and to remain higher until menstruation. In using the BBT method, a woman attempts to detect these temperature changes by tracking her temperature just after awakening each morning but before rising from bed. Thermometers that provide finely graded readings, such as electronic digital thermometers, are best suited for determining these minor changes. The couple record the woman's temperature and

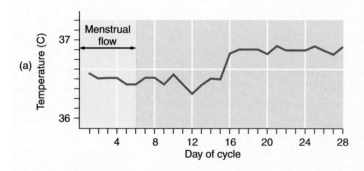

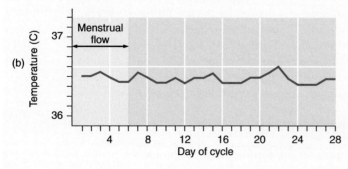

Figure 10.2 A Basal Body Temperature (BBT) Chart.

Because most women have somewhat irregular menstrual cycles, they may not be able to predict ovulation perfectly. The basal body temperature (BBT) chart helps them to do so. Body temperature is fairly even before ovulation but dips slightly just before ovulation. On the day following ovulation, temperature rises about 0.2 to 0.4°C (0.4 to 0.8°F) above the level before ovulation. Part (a) represents a cycle in which a sustained elevation in temperature occurred following ovulation on day 15. Part (b) shows no substantial temperature rise, which is indicative of an absence of ovulation in this cycle.

Source: Adapted from R. C. Kolodny, W. H. Masters, and V. E. Johnson. Textbook of Sexual Medicine.

the day of the cycle (as well as the day of the month) and indicate whether they have engaged in coitus. With regular charting for six months, the woman may learn to predict the day of ovulation more accurately—assuming that her cycles are fairly regular.

Opinion is divided as to whether it is better for couples to have coitus every 24 hours or every 36 to 48 hours for the several-day period during which ovulation is expected. More frequent coitus around the time of ovulation gives more chances for conception. Less frequent coitus (that is, every 36 to 48 hours) leads to a higher sperm count during each ejaculation. Most fertility specialists recommend that couples seeking to conceive a baby have intercourse once every day or two during the week in which the woman expects to ovulate. However, men with lower than normal sperm counts may be advised to wait 48 hours between ejaculations.

Analyzing Urine or Saliva for Luteinizing Hormone Over-the-counter kits are more accurate than the BBT method and predict ovulation by analyzing the woman's urine or saliva for the surge in luteinizing hormone (LH) that precedes ovulation by about 12 to 24 hours.

Tracking Vaginal Mucus Women can track the thickness of their vaginal mucus during the phases of the menstrual cycle by rolling it between their fingers and noting changes in texture. The mucus is thick, white, and cloudy during most phases of the cycle. It becomes thin, slippery, and clear for a few days preceding ovulation. A day or so after ovulation, the mucus again thickens and becomes opaque.

Additional Considerations Coitus in the male-superior position allows sperm to be deposited deeper in the vagina and minimizes leakage of sperm out of the vagina due to gravity. Women

may improve their chances of conceiving by lying on their backs and drawing their knees close to their breasts after ejaculation. This position, perhaps aided by the use of a pillow beneath the buttocks, may prevent sperm from dripping out quickly and elevate the pool of semen in relation to the cervix. It thus makes gravity work for, rather than against, conception. Women may also lie as still as possible for about 30 to 60 minutes after ejaculation to help sperm move toward the cervical opening.

Women with severely retroverted, or "tipped," uteruses may profit from supporting themselves on their elbows and knees and having their partners enter them from behind. Again, this position helps prevent semen from dripping out of the vagina.

The man should penetrate the woman as deeply as possible just before ejaculation, hold still during ejaculation, and then withdraw slowly in a straight line to avoid dispersing the pool of semen.

Infertility and Alternative Ways of Becoming Parents

For couples who want children, few problems are more frustrating than the inability to conceive. Physicians often recommend that couples try to conceive on their own for six months before seeking medical assistance. The term **infertility** is usually not applied until the failure to conceive has persisted for more than a year. The nearby World of Diversity box offers a personal perspective on the frustrations and disappointments experienced by one couple as they cope with infertility.

Because the likelihood of infertility increases with age, the current somewhat elevated incidence of infertility is partially the result of a rise in couples who postpone childbearing until their 30s and 40s (Sheehy, 1995). All in all, about 15% of couples in North America have fertility problems (Howards, 1995). However, about half of them eventually succeed in conceiving a child (Jones & Toner, 1993). Many treatment options are available, ranging from drugs to stimulate ovulation to newer reproductive technologies, such as in vitro fertilization.

Male Fertility Problems

Although most concerns about fertility have traditionally centred on women, the problem lies with the man in about 30% of cases (Howards, 1995). In about 20% of cases, problems are found in both partners (Hatcher et al., 1998; Howards, 1995).

Infertility Inability to conceive a child.

A World of Diversity

MY FATHERHOOD DREAMS

The Joys of Fatherhood.
Some people long for nothing more than to hold their own child.

I always figured I'd be a father by the time I was 30. I know I'd be a good one, too. Growing up, I always preferred to hang out with the kids—regardless if it was my younger cousin or a squad of neighbourhood children. I still do, actually. (OK, probably because I'm still a bit of a kid myself.) But I'm two years past that 30-year mark now and not a dad—though certainly not by choice. It turns out my wife Tammy and I are victims of some cruel trick of nature, because despite wanting nothing greater out of life than children to raise, there's been no drug, technique or sage advice that has brought us any closer to our goal.

Well, so far, at least. We still hold out hope, but we get more anxious with every month that ticks by. I've discovered that being unable to conceive a child is the most depressing thing a couple can face.

We started trying soon after we were married in 1999. A year later, after switching to boxer shorts, trying new techniques and (at least pretending) to "just let things happen," we spoke to our family doctor, who referred us to another doctor who referred us to another doctor. In some ways, it would be easier if they found something that medically disqualified us from having kids. Then, we could just get on with adoption rather than go through more frustration. But no: we're part of that 20 per cent of couples whose infertility is unexplained.

We started with a prescription for a drug called Clomiphene. It tricks the brain into thinking the ovaries are slacking off. After a year, we moved to Gonal-F, which I would inject into the tissue around Tammy's stomach. (That was fun: a spot of blood popped up once and I nearly passed out.) Gonal-F is supposed to stimulate egg production and carried a 25-per-cent chance of multiple pregnancies. We joked that we would publish a request for names for our 16 children.

But no luck. It's always the same: the anticipation builds up during the final two weeks of the cycle, and we're carefully pessimistic—if it doesn't work again, we won't have too far to fall. Like most couples, we handle disappointment differently. My wife needs comfort, attention and talk; I withdraw, stave off bouts of blinding fury, and want desperately to *fix it*.

But even with our troubles, I never question our resolve to have kids, mostly because of our niece, Madeline. When my little brother walked out of the hospital room with her, he wore a smile radiating with wonder. She's almost three now, beautiful and very smart. Every once in a while she'll spend the day with us and run circles through the house while we play "scare me": kitchen, dining room, living room . . . *BOO!* Kitchen, dining room, living room . . . *BOO!* She has this way of all of a sudden saying or doing something that fills us with this alien flush of happiness that I'm sure fathers experience all the time. Just little things like, one afternoon, we were eating Jello and I was doing something to make her laugh. In the midst of an infectious giggle she sputtered, *"Uuuncle Miiiike."* That's all it takes. Another time, while I was absorbed in a World Series game, Maddie suddenly appeared at my chair and handed me a huge birthday card marked with bright crayons. My control was exemplary: I fought off a flash of red heat to my face and gave her a big hug.

My worst fear is of finding myself old and grey one day with no memory of holding my child for the first time, of watching game-winning home runs, meeting first boyfriends, crying at weddings. Will I consider my life unfulfilled, maybe even wasted? What fond memories will I have to look back on? My dedicated years of work, the oak entertainment centre I built, the time I barbequed that steak perfectly? Just not the same thing.

I kissed my wife good night about an hour and a half after celebrating the arrival of the New Year. We talked about our hopes for 2003. She admitted she almost started crying at about five minutes to midnight, when the thought struck her that, a year from now, nothing may have changed. We hugged each other and promised—once again—that we'd try and think about it in a positive way. I turned out the light and lay beside her, and thought, for the millionth time, how much I want to be a dad.

Source: Michael Snider, Maclean's, *February 10, 2003, p. 52. Reprinted with permission of* Maclean's.

Fertility problems in the male reflect abnormalities such as:

1. Low sperm count
2. Irregularly shaped sperm—for example, malformed heads or tails
3. Low sperm **motility**
4. Chronic diseases such as diabetes, as well as infections such as sexually transmitted infections
5. Injury to the testes
6. An **autoimmune response**, in which antibodies produced by the man deactivate his own sperm
7. A pituitary imbalance and/or thyroid disease

Problems in producing normal, abundant sperm may be caused by genetic factors, advanced age, hormonal problems, diabetes, injuries to the testes, varicose veins in the scrotum, drugs (alcohol, narcotics, marijuana, and/or tobacco), antihypertensive medications, environmental toxins, excess heat, and emotional stress.

Low sperm count (or the absence of sperm) is the most common problem. Sperm counts of 40 million to 150 million sperm per millilitre of semen are considered normal. A count of fewer than 20 million is generally regarded as low. Sperm production may be low among men with undescended testes that were not surgically corrected before puberty. Frequent ejaculation can reduce sperm counts. Sperm production may also be impaired in men whose testicles are consistently 1 or 2 degrees above the typical scrotal temperature of 34 to 35°C (94 to 95°F) (Leary, 1990). Frequent hot baths and tight-fitting underwear can also reduce sperm production, at least temporarily. Some men may encounter fertility problems from prolonged athletic activity or use of electric blankets. In such cases the problem can be readily corrected. Male runners with fertility problems are often counselled to take time off to increase their sperm counts.

Sometimes the sperm count is adequate, but prostate, hormonal, or other factors deprive sperm of motility or deform them. Motility can also be hampered by scar tissue from infections. Scarring may prevent sperm from passing through parts of the male reproductive system, such as the vas deferens.

Sperm counts have been increased by surgical repair of the varicose veins in the scrotum. Microsurgery can also open blocked passageways that prevent the outflow of sperm (Schroeder-Printzen et al., 2000). Researchers are also investigating the effects on sperm production of special cooling undergarments.

ARTIFICIAL INSEMINATION The sperm of men with low sperm counts can be collected and quick-frozen. The sperm from multiple ejaculations can then be injected into a woman's uterus at the time of ovulation. This is one kind of **artificial insemination**. The sperm of a man with low sperm motility can also be injected into his partner's uterus, so that the sperm begin their journey closer to the fallopian tubes. Sperm from a donor can be used to artificially inseminate a woman whose partner is completely infertile or has an extremely low sperm count. The child then bears the genes of one of the parents, the mother. A donor can be chosen who resembles the man in physical traits and ethnic background.

A variation of artificial insemination has been used with some men with very low (or zero!) sperm counts in the semen, immature sperm, or immotile sperm. Immature sperm can be removed from a testicle by a thin needle and then directly injected into an egg in a laboratory dish (Brody, 1995b). The method has even been successful with a few men who have only tailless spermatids in the testes.

In 2002, the Canadian health minister introduced legislation that would require the creation of a databank on sperm donors (Minister of Health, 2002). Offspring of the donors would be allowed to obtain medical information regarding the donor, although the identity of the donor would be revealed only with his consent.

Motility Self-propulsion. A measure of the viability of sperm cells.

Autoimmune response The production of antibodies that attack naturally occurring substances that are (incorrectly) recognized as being foreign or harmful.

Artificial insemination The introduction of sperm into the reproductive tract through means other than sexual intercourse.

Female Fertility Problems

The major causes of infertility in women are:

1. Irregular ovulation, including failure to ovulate
2. Obstructions or malfunctions of the reproductive tract, which are often caused by infections or diseases involving the reproductive tract
3. Endometriosis
4. Declining hormone levels of estrogen and progesterone that occur with aging and may prevent the ovum from becoming fertilized or remaining implanted in the uterus

From 10% to 15% of female infertility problems stem from failure to ovulate. Many factors can play a role in failure to ovulate, including hormonal irregularities, malnutrition, genetic factors, stress, and chronic disease. Failure to ovulate may occur in response to low levels of body fat, as in the cases of athletes and women with eating disorders (Frisch, 1997).

Ovulation may often be induced by the use of fertility drugs such as *clomiphene* (Clomid). Clomiphene stimulates the pituitary gland to secrete FSH and LH, which in turn stimulate maturation of ova. Clomiphene leads to conception in the majority of cases of infertility that are due *solely* to irregular or absent ovulation (Reinisch, 1990). But because infertility can have multiple causes, only about half of women who use clomiphene become pregnant. Another infertility drug, Pergonal, contains a high concentration of FSH, which directly stimulates maturation of ovarian follicles. Like clomiphene, Pergonal has high success rates with women whose infertility is due to lack of ovulation. Clomiphene and Pergonal have been linked to multiple births, including quadruplets and even quintuplets (Gleicher et al., 2000). University of McGill researchers found that 41% of patients at an infertility clinic actually preferred to have multiple births so that they could have an "instant" family (Child, Henderson, & Tan, 2004). This desire was especially strong among couples who had no children and had been infertile for a long time.

Local infections that scar the fallopian tubes and other organs impede the passage of sperm or ova. Such infections include pelvic inflammatory disease—an inflammation of the woman's internal reproductive tract that can be caused by various infectious agents, such as the bacteria responsible for gonorrhea and chlamydia (see Chapter 14).

In **endometriosis**, cells break away from the uterine lining (the endometrium) and become implanted and grow elsewhere. When they develop on the surface of the ovaries or fallopian tubes, they may block the passage of ova or impair conception. About one case in six of female sterility is believed to be due to endometriosis. Hormone treatments and surgery sometimes reduce the blockage to the point where the woman can conceive. A physician may suspect endometriosis during a pelvic exam, but it is diagnosed with certainty by **laparoscopy**. A long, narrow tube is inserted through an incision in the navel, permitting the physician to inspect the organs in the pelvic cavity visually. The incision is practically undetectable.

Several methods help many couples with problems such as blocked fallopian tubes bear children.

IN VITRO FERTILIZATION When Louise Brown was born in England in 1978 after being conceived by **in vitro fertilization** (IVF), the event made headlines around the world. Louise was dubbed the world's first "test-tube baby." Conception actually took place in a laboratory dish (not a test tube), and the embryo was implanted in the mother's uterus, where it developed to term. Before in vitro fertilization, fertility drugs stimulate ripening of ova. Ripe ova are then surgically removed from an ovary and placed in a laboratory dish along with the father's

Endometriosis An abnormal condition in which endometrial tissue is sloughed off into the abdominal cavity rather than out of the body during menstruation. The condition is characterized by abdominal pain and may cause infertility.

Laparoscopy A medical procedure in which a long, narrow tube (laparoscope) is inserted through an incision in the navel, permitting the visual inspection of organs in the pelvic cavity. (From the Greek *lapara*, which means "flank.")

In vitro fertilization A method of conception in which mature ova are surgically removed from an ovary and placed in a laboratory dish along with sperm.

Infertility Awareness Association of Canada
www.iaac.ca

Gay Adoption.
Robert Gibson and Thomas Jones of Brampton, Ontario, adopted two half-brothers with the help of the Children's Aid Society of Toronto. They are among a growing number of gay couples in Canada who are applying to adopt.

sperm. Fertilized ova are then injected into the mother's uterus to become implanted in the uterine wall.

GIFT In **gamete intrafallopian transfer (GIFT)**, sperm and ova are inserted together into a fallopian tube for fertilization. Conception occurs in a fallopian tube rather than in a laboratory dish.

ZIFT **Zygote intrafallopian transfer (ZIFT)** involves a combination of IVF and GIFT. Sperm and ova are combined in a laboratory dish. After fertilization, the zygote is placed in the mother's fallopian tube to begin its journey to the uterus for implantation. ZIFT has an advantage over GIFT in that the fertility specialists can ascertain that fertilization has occurred before insertion is performed.

Gamete intrafallopian transfer (GIFT) A method of conception in which sperm and ova are inserted into a fallopian tube to encourage conception.

Zygote intrafallopian transfer (ZIFT) A method of conception in which an ovum is fertilized in a laboratory dish and then placed in a fallopian tube.

Donor IVF A variation of in vitro fertilization in which the ovum is taken from one woman, fertilized, and then injected into the uterus or fallopian tube of another woman.

Embryonic transfer A method of conception in which a woman volunteer is artificially inseminated by the male partner of the intended mother, after which the embryo is removed from the volunteer and inserted within the uterus of the intended mother.

Surrogate mother A woman who is impregnated with the sperm of a prospective father via artificial insemination, carries the embryo and fetus to term, and then gives the child to the prospective parents.

DONOR IVF "I tell her mommy was having trouble with, I call them ovums, not eggs," says a 50-year-old female therapist in Los Angeles (cited in Stolberg, 1998a). "I say that I needed these to have a baby, and there was this wonderful woman and she was willing to give me some, and that was how she helped us. I want to be honest that we got pregnant in a special way."

That special way is termed **donor IVF**, which is a variation of the IVF procedure in which the ovum is taken from another woman, fertilized, and then injected into the uterus or fallopian tube of the intended mother. The procedure is used when the intended mother does not produce ova. The number of births brought about by this method has been mushrooming in recent years (Stolberg, 1998a).

EMBRYONIC TRANSFER A similar method for women who do not produce ova of their own is **embryonic transfer**. In this method, a woman volunteer is artificially inseminated by the male partner of the infertile woman. Five days later the embryo is removed from the volunteer and inserted within the uterus of the mother-to-be, where it is hoped that it will become implanted.

Success with in vitro fertilization drops from nearly 30% in women in their mid-20s to 10% to 15% in women in their late 30s (Toner et al., 1991).

SURROGATE MOTHERHOOD A **surrogate mother** is artificially inseminated by the husband of the infertile woman and carries the baby to term.

ADOPTION Adoption is yet another way for people to obtain children. Despite the occasional conflicts in which adoptive parents are pitted against biological parents who change their minds about giving their children up for adoption, most adoptions result in the formation of loving new families.

In Canada, adolescent mothers are the most common providers of babies for adoption (Daly & Sobol, 1994). However, because most young women who experience unwanted pregnancies today either keep the baby or have an abortion, there are far fewer Canadian babies available for adoption. The three most common reasons why adolescent mothers give their babies up for adoption are that they are too young to parent, they lack the financial resources to parent, and parenting interferes with educational and career goals. And since public agencies have more children who are older and with special needs, and consequently harder to place, many couples turn to private agencies, which tend to have mostly healthy babies. Couples are also increasingly adopting babies from other countries.

Daly and Sobol (1994) found that the major restriction on adoption placement was sexual orientation, with only about 4% of agencies stating that they would place a child with a same-sex couple without any reservations. In the 1990s, however, court rulings and provincial legislation that provided greater equality for same-sex couples paved the road for an increase in same-sex adoptions. In 1995, for example, an Ontario lesbian went to court seeking the right to adopt her partner's child. The judge ruled that the Ontario adoption law defining a spouse as a person of the opposite sex was unconstitutional, and that the woman should be able to adopt (Gower and Philp, 2002a). In 1996, British Columbia became the first province to pass legislation granting same-sex couples the same rights to adopt as those of heterosexual couples. Since then, most other provinces have passed similar legislation. Consequently, Canada has become a world leader in facilitating adoptions for gays and lesbians. However, this does not mean that same-sex couples are not still facing prejudice by adoption agencies.

Canadian Legislation Governing Reproductive Technologies

In 2004, the Canadian Parliament passed legislation to regulate reproductive technologies. This legislation came 12 years after the first commission on reproductive technologies was established, a fact that highlights just how contentious are the issues relating to these technologies. The main provisions of the Act Respecting Assisted Human Reproduction include:

- Banning the cloning of humans
- Banning the selection of a baby's sex for non-medical purposes
- Making it illegal to pay women to be surrogate mothers
- Making it illegal to pay for sperm donations

After the Act was passed, there were fewer sperm donations in Canada and infertility clinics had to import sperm from the United States. The United States allows for payment to sperm donors and to surrogate mothers.

Can You Select the Gender of Your Child? Would You Want to Do So?
There are various approaches to selecting the gender of one's children, some of which are more reliable than others. If you could choose, would you prefer to have girls or boys? Do you believe that it is ethical to select the gender of your children? Why or why not?

One of the most controversial provisions was the permitting of research using stem cells from embryos left over from infertility treatment. Leaders of the pro-life movement are critical of the legislation, arguing that the use of embryos in this way diminishes the value of human life. Proponents of the research argue that stem cells can play a vital role in helping to provide cures for such diseases as cancer, diabetes, and Parkinson's disease.

Pregnancy

Women react to becoming pregnant in different ways. For those who are psychologically and economically prepared, pregnancy may be greeted with joyous celebration. Some women feel that pregnancy helps fulfill their sense of womanhood:

> Being pregnant meant I was a woman. I was enthralled with my belly growing. I went out right away and got maternity clothes.
>
> It gave me a sense that I was actually a woman. I had never felt sexy before . . . I felt very voluptuous. (Boston Women's Health Book Collective, 1992; Copyright © 1984, 1992 by The Boston Women's Health Book Collective. Reprinted with permission.)

On the other hand, an unwanted pregnancy may evoke feelings of fear and hopelessness, as occurs with many teenagers.

In this section we examine biological and psychological aspects of pregnancy: signs of pregnancy, prenatal development, complications, effects of drugs and sex, and the psychological experiences of pregnant women and fathers.

Early Signs of Pregnancy

For many women the first sign of pregnancy is missing a period. But some women have irregular menstrual cycles or miss a period because of stress. Missing a period is thus not a fully reliable indicator. Some women also experience cyclic bleeding or spotting during pregnancy, although the blood flow is usually lighter than normal. If a woman's basal body temperature remains high for about three weeks after ovulation, there is reason to suspect pregnancy even if she spots two weeks after ovulation.

Pregnancy Tests

You may have heard your parents say that they learned your mother was pregnant by means of the "rabbit test," in which a sample of the mother's urine was injected into a laboratory animal. This procedure, which was once commonly used to confirm pregnancy, relied on the fact that women produce **human chorionic gonadotropin** (HCG) shortly after conception. HCG causes rabbits, mice, or rats to ovulate.

Today, pregnancy can be confirmed in minutes by tests that directly detect HCG in the urine as early as the third week of pregnancy. A blood test—the *beta subunit HCG radioimmunoassay* (RIA)—can detect HCG in the woman's blood as early as the eighth day of pregnancy, about five days preceding her expected period.

Over-the-counter home pregnancy tests are also available. They too test the woman's urine for HCG and are intended to be used as early as one day after a missed period. Laboratory-based tests are considered 98% or 99% accurate. Home-based tests performed by lay people are somewhat less accurate. Women are advised to consult their physicians if they suspect that they are pregnant or wish to confirm a home pregnancy test result.

About a month after a woman misses her period, a health professional may be able to confirm pregnancy by pelvic exam. Women who are pregnant usually show

Human chorionic gonadotropin A hormone produced by women shortly after conception, which stimulates the corpus luteum to continue to produce progesterone. The presence of HCG in a woman's urine indicates that she is pregnant.

Hegar's sign. Hegar's sign is softness of a section of the uterus between the uterine body and the cervix, which may be palpated (felt) by the woman's physician by placing a hand on the abdomen and two fingers in the vagina.

Early Effects of Pregnancy

Just a few days after conception, a woman may note tenderness of the breasts. Hormonal stimulation of the mammary glands may make the breasts more sensitive and cause sensations of tingling and fullness.

The term **morning sickness** refers to the nausea, food aversions, and vomiting that many women experience during pregnancy. Women carrying more than one child usually experience more nausea. Although called morning sickness, nausea and vomiting during pregnancy can occur any time during the day or night and is not a "sickness" at all, but rather a perfectly normal part of pregnancy (Flaxman & Sherman, 2000).

In some cases, morning sickness is so severe that the woman cannot eat regularly and must be hospitalized to ensure that she and the fetus receive adequate nutrition. In milder cases, having small amounts of food in the stomach throughout the day is helpful. Many women find that eating a few crackers at bedtime and before getting out of bed in the morning is effective. Other women profit from medication. Morning sickness usually—but not always—subsides by about the twelfth week of pregnancy.

Pregnant women may experience greater-than-normal fatigue during the early weeks, sleeping longer and falling asleep more readily than usual. Frequent urination, which may also be experienced, is caused by pressure from the swelling uterus on the bladder.

Miscarriage (Spontaneous Abortion)

Miscarriages have many causes, including chromosomal defects in the fetus and abnormalities of the placenta and uterus. Miscarriage is more prevalent among older mothers (Stein & Susser, 2000). About three in four miscarriages occur in the first 16 weeks of pregnancy, and the great majority of these occur in the first 7 weeks. Some miscarriages occur so early that the woman is not aware she was pregnant.

After a miscarriage, a couple may feel a deep sense of loss and undergo a period of mourning. Emotional support from friends and family often helps the couple cope with the loss. In most cases, women who miscarry can carry subsequent pregnancies to term.

Sex During Pregnancy

Most health professionals concur that coitus is safe throughout the course of pregnancy until the start of labour, provided that the pregnancy is developing normally and the woman has no history of miscarriages. Women who experience bleeding or cramps during pregnancy may be advised by their obstetricians not to engage in coitus.

There is often an initial decline in sexual interest among pregnant women during the first trimester. There is increased interest during the second trimester and another decline in interest during the third. Many women show declines in sexual interest and activity during the first trimester because of fatigue, nausea, or misguided concerns that coitus will harm the embryo or fetus. Also during the first trimester, vasocongestion may cause tenderness of the breasts, discouraging

Hegar's sign Softness of a section of the uterus between the uterine body and the cervix, which indicates that a woman is pregnant.

Morning sickness Symptoms of pregnancy, including nausea, aversions to specific foods, and vomiting.

Miscarriage A spontaneous abortion.

fondling and sucking. One study found that 90% of 570 women were engaging in coitus at five months into their pregnancies (Byrd et al., 1998). Researchers in Israel reported a gradual decline in sexual interest and frequency of intercourse and orgasm during pregnancy among a sample of 219 women. The greatest decline occurred during the third trimester (Hart et al., 1991). Pain during intercourse is also commonly reported, especially in the third trimester.

As the woman's abdominal region swells, the popular male-superior position becomes unwieldy. The female-superior, lateral-entry, and rear-entry positions are common alternatives. Manual and oral sex can continue as usual.

Some women are concerned that the uterine contractions of orgasm may dislodge an embryo. Such concerns are usually unfounded, unless the woman has a history of miscarriage or is currently at risk of miscarriage. Women and their partners are advised to consult their obstetricians for the latest information.

Psychological Changes During Pregnancy

A woman's psychological response to pregnancy reflects her desire to be pregnant, her physical changes, and her attitudes toward these changes. Women with the financial, social, and psychological resources to meet the needs of pregnancy and child rearing may welcome pregnancy. Some describe it as the most wondrous experience of their lives. Other women may question their ability to handle their pregnancies and childbirth. Or they may fear that pregnancy will interfere with their careers or their mates' feelings about them. In general, women who want to have a baby and choose to become pregnant are better adjusted during their pregnancies. The first trimester may be difficult for women who are ambivalent about pregnancy. At that stage symptoms like morning sickness are most pronounced, and women must come to terms with being pregnant. The second trimester is generally less tempestuous. Morning sickness and other symptoms have largely vanished. It is not yet difficult to move about, and the woman need not yet face the delivery. Women first note fetal movement during the second trimester, and for many the experience is stirring:

> I was lying on my stomach and felt—something, like someone lightly touching my deep insides. Then I just sat very still and . . . felt the hugeness of having something living growing in me. Then I said, No, it's not possible, it's too early yet, and then I started to cry . . . That one moment was my first body awareness of another living thing inside me. (Boston Women's Health Book Collective, 1992; Copyright © 1984, 1992 by The Boston Women's Health Book Collective. Reprinted with permission.)

During the third trimester it is normal, especially for first-time mothers, to worry about the mechanics of delivery and whether the child will be normal. The woman becomes increasingly heavy and literally "bent out of shape." It may become difficult to get up from a chair or out of bed. She must sit farther from the steering wheel when driving. Muscle tension from supporting the extra weight in her abdomen may cause backaches. She may feel impatient in the days and weeks just before delivery.

Men, like women, respond to pregnancy according to the degree to which they want the child. Many men are proud and look forward to the child with great anticipation. In such cases, pregnancy may bring parents closer together. But fathers who are financially or emotionally unprepared may consider the pregnancy a "trap." Now and then an expectant father experiences some signs of pregnancy, including morning sickness and vomiting. This reaction is termed a **sympathetic pregnancy.**

Sympathetic pregnancy
The experiencing of a number of signs of pregnancy by the father.

Prenatal Development

We can date pregnancy from the onset of the last menstrual cycle before conception, which makes the normal gestation period 280 days. We can also date pregnancy from the date at which fertilization was assumed to have taken place, which normally corresponds to two weeks after the beginning of the woman's last menstrual cycle. In this case, the normal gestation period is 266 days.

Once pregnancy has been confirmed, the delivery date may be calculated by *Nagele's rule:*

■ Jot down the date of the first day of the last menstrual period.

■ Add seven days.

■ Subtract three months.

■ Add one year.

Few babies are born exactly when they are due, but the great majority are delivered during a 10-day period that spans the date.

Shortly after conception, the single cell that results from the union of sperm and egg begins to multiply—becoming two cells, then four, then eight, and so on. During the weeks and months that follow, tissues, structures, and organs begin to form, and the fetus gradually takes on the shape of a human being. By the time the fetus is born, it consists of hundreds of billions of cells—more cells than there are stars in the Milky Way galaxy. Prenatal development can be divided into three periods: the *germinal stage*, which corresponds to about the first two weeks, the *embryonic stage*, which coincides with the first two months, and the *fetal stage*. We also commonly speak of prenatal development in terms of three trimesters of three months each.

The Germinal Stage

Within 36 hours after conception, the zygote divides into two cells. It then divides repeatedly, becoming 32 cells within another 36 hours as it continues its journey to the uterus. It takes the zygote perhaps three or four days to reach the uterus. This mass of dividing cells then wanders about the uterus for perhaps another three or four days before it begins to become implanted in the uterine wall. Implantation takes about another week. This period from conception to implantation is termed the **germinal stage** or the **period of the ovum** (see Figure 10.3).

Several days into the germinal stage, the cell mass takes the form of a fluid-filled ball of cells, which is called a **blastocyst**. Already some cell differentiation has begun. Cells begin to separate into groups that will eventually become different structures. Within a thickened mass of cells that is called the **embryonic disk**, two distinct inner layers of cells are beginning to form. These cells will become the embryo and eventually the fetus. The outer part of the blastocyst, called the **trophoblast**, consists of several membranes from which the amniotic sac, placenta, and umbilical cord eventually develop.

Implantation may be accompanied by some bleeding, which results from the usual rupturing of some small blood vessels that line the uterus. Bleeding can also be a sign of a miscarriage—although most women who experience implantation bleeding do not miscarry but go on to have normal pregnancies and deliver healthy babies.

The Embryonic Stage

The period from implantation to about the eighth week of development is called the **embryonic stage**. The major organ systems of the body begin to differentiate during this stage.

Germinal stage The period of prenatal development before implantation in the uterus.

Period of the ovum Germinal stage.

Blastocyst A stage of embryonic development within the germinal stage of prenatal development, at which the embryo is a sphere of cells surrounding a cavity of fluid.

Embryonic disk The plate-like inner part of the blastocyst, which differentiates into the ectoderm, mesoderm, and endoderm of the embryo.

Trophoblast The outer part of the blastocyst, from which the amniotic sac, placenta, and umbilical cord develop.

Embryonic stage The stage of prenatal development that lasts from implantation through the eighth week and is characterized by the differentiation of the major organ systems.

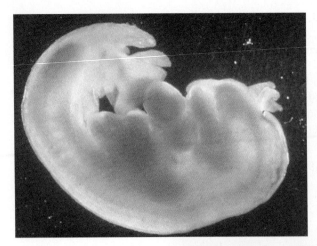
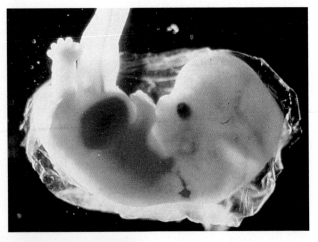
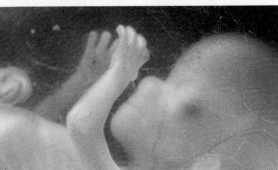

Prenatal Development.
Developmental changes are most
rapid and dramatic during prenatal
development. Within a few months,
a human embryo and then fetus
advances from weighing a gram to
several kilograms, and from one cell
to billions of cells.

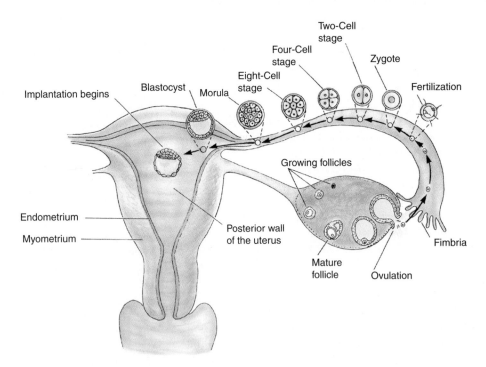

Figure 10.3 The Ovarian Cycle, Conception, and the Early Days of the Germinal Stage.

The zygote first divides about 36 hours after conception. Continuing division creates the hollow sphere of cells termed the blastocyst. The blastocyst normally becomes implanted in the wall of the uterus.

Development of the embryo follows two trends, **cephalocaudal** and **proximodistal**. Growth of the head (the cephalic region) takes precedence over the growth of the lower parts of the body. You can also think of the body as containing a central axis that coincides with the spinal cord. The growth of the organ systems that lie close to this axis (that is, *proximal* to the axis) takes precedence over the growth of those that lie farther away toward the extremities (that is, *distal* to the axis). Relatively early maturation of the brain and organ systems that lie near the central axis allows these organs to facilitate further development of the embryo and fetus.

As the embryonic stage unfolds, the nervous system, sensory organs, hair, nails, and teeth and the outer layer of skin begin to develop from the outer layer of cells, or **ectoderm**, of the embryonic disk. By about three weeks after conception, two ridges appear in the embryo and fold together to form the **neural tube**. This tube develops into the nervous system. The inner layer of the embryonic disk is called the **endoderm**. From this layer develop the respiratory and digestive systems and organs such as the liver and the pancreas. A short time later in the embryonic stage, the middle layer of cells, or **mesoderm**, differentiates and develops into the reproductive, excretory, and circulatory systems, as well as the skeleton, the muscles, and the inner layer of the skin.

During the third week of development, the head and blood vessels begin to form. By the fourth week, a primitive heart begins to beat and pump blood in an embryo that measures but $\frac{1}{2}$ centimetre (a fifth of an inch) in length. The heart will normally continue to beat without rest for every minute of every day for the better part of a century. By the end of the first month of development, we can see the beginnings of the arms and legs—"arm buds" and "leg buds." The mouth, eyes, ears, and nose begin to take shape. The brain and other parts of the nervous system begin to develop.

The arms and legs develop in accordance with the proximodistal principle. First the upper arms and legs develop. Then the forearms and lower legs. Then the hands and feet form, followed by webbed fingers and toes by about six to eight weeks into development. The webbing is gone by the end of the second month. By this time the head has become rounded, and the limbs have elongated and separated. Facial features are visible. During the second month, nervous impulses also begin to travel through the developing nervous system.

THE AMNIOTIC SAC The embryo—and later the fetus—develop within a protective environment in the mother's uterus called the **amniotic sac**, which is surrounded by a clear membrane. The embryo and fetus are suspended within the sac in **amniotic fluid**. The amniotic fluid acts like a shock absorber. It cushions the embryo from damage that might result from the mother's movements.

THE PLACENTA Nutrients and waste products are exchanged between mother and embryo (or fetus) through a mass of tissue called the **placenta**. The placenta is unique in origin. It develops from material supplied by both mother and embryo. The fetus is connected to the placenta by the **umbilical cord**. The mother is connected to the placenta by the system of blood vessels in the uterine wall. The umbilical cord develops about five weeks after conception and reaches 50 centimetres (20 inches) in length. It contains two arteries through which maternal nutrients reach the embryo. A vein transports waste products back to the mother. The circulatory systems of mother and embryo do not mix.

The placenta is also an endocrine gland. It secretes hormones that preserve the pregnancy, stimulate the uterine contractions that induce childbirth, and help prepare the breasts for breast-feeding. The placenta itself secretes increasing amounts of estrogen and progesterone. Ultimately, the placenta passes from the woman's body after delivery. For this reason it is also called the afterbirth.

Cephalocaudal From the head downward. (From Latin roots that mean "head" and "tail.")

Proximodistal From the central axis of the body outward. (From Latin roots that mean "near" and "far.")

Ectoderm The outermost cell layer of the newly formed embryo, from which the skin and nervous system develop.

Neural tube A hollow area in the blastocyst from which the nervous system will develop.

Endoderm The inner layer of the newly formed embryo, from which the lungs and digestive system develop.

Mesoderm The central layer of the embryo, from which the bones and muscles develop.

Amniotic sac The sac containing the fetus.

Amniotic fluid Fluid within the amniotic sac that suspends and protects the fetus.

Placenta An organ connected to the fetus by the umbilical cord. The placenta serves as a relay station between mother and fetus, allowing the exchange of nutrients and wastes.

Umbilical cord A tube that connects the fetus to the placenta.

The Fetal Stage

The fetal stage begins by the ninth week and continues until birth. By about the ninth or tenth week, the fetus begins to respond to the outside world by turning in the direction of external stimulation. By the end of the first trimester, the major organ systems, the fingers and toes, and the external genitals have been formed. The gender of the fetus can be determined visually. The eyes have become clearly distinguishable.

During the second trimester the fetus increases dramatically in size, and its organ systems continue to mature. The brain now contributes to the regulation of basic body functions.

Usually by the middle of the fourth month the mother can feel the first fetal movements. By the end of the second trimester, the fetus moves its limbs so vigorously that the mother may complain of being kicked—often at 4:00 A.M. It opens and shuts its eyes, sucks its thumb, alternates between periods of wakefulness and sleep, and perceives lights and sounds.

Near the end of the second trimester the fetus approaches the **age of viability**. Still, only a minority of babies born at the end of the second trimester who weigh under a kilogram will survive—even with intense medical efforts.

During the third trimester, the organ systems continue to mature and enlarge. The heart and lungs become increasingly capable of maintaining independent life. Typically, during the seventh month the fetus turns upside down in the uterus so that it will be head first, or in a **cephalic presentation**, for delivery. But some fetuses do not turn during this month. If such a fetus is born prematurely, it can have either a **breech presentation** (bottom first) or a shoulder-first presentation, which can complicate problems of prematurity.

During the final months of pregnancy, the mother may become concerned that the fetus seems to be less active than before. Most of the time, the change in activity level is normal. The fetus has merely grown so large that it is cramped, and its movements are restricted.

Environmental Influences on Prenatal Development

We focus in this next section on the environmental factors that affect prenatal development. These include the mother's diet, maternal diseases and disorders, and the mother's use of drugs.

THE MOTHER'S DIET Malnutrition in the mother can adversely affect fetal development. Pregnant women who are adequately nourished are more likely to deliver babies of average or above-average size. Their infants are also less likely to develop colds and serious respiratory disorders. However, maternal *obesity* is linked with a higher risk of stillbirth (Cnattingius et al., 1998).

A woman can expect to gain at least 9 kilograms during pregnancy because of the growth of the placenta, amniotic fluid, and the fetus itself. Slender women may gain 14 kilograms.

MATERNAL DISEASES AND DISORDERS Environmental influences or agents that can harm the embryo or fetus are called **teratogens**. These include drugs taken by the mother, such as alcohol and even Aspirin, as well as substances produced by the mother's body, such as Rh-positive antibodies. Other teratogens include the metals lead and mercury, radiation, and disease-causing organisms such as viruses and bacteria. Although many disease-causing organisms cannot pass through the placenta to infect the embryo or fetus, some extremely small organisms, such as those that cause syphilis, measles, mumps, and chicken pox, can.

Age of viability The age at which a fetus can sustain independent life.

Cephalic presentation Emergence of the baby head first from the womb.

Breech presentation Emergence of the baby feet first from the womb.

Teratogens Environmental influences or agents that can damage an embryo or fetus. (From the Greek *teras*, which means "monster.")

CRITICAL PERIODS OF VULNERABILITY The times at which exposure to particular teratogens can cause the greatest harm are termed **critical periods of vulnerability**. Critical periods correspond to the times at which the structures most affected by the teratogens are developing (see Figure 10.4). The heart, for example, develops rapidly from the third to the fifth week after conception. It may be most vulnerable to certain teratogens at this time. The arms and legs, which develop later, are most vulnerable from the fourth through the eighth week of development. Because the major organ systems differentiate during the embryonic stage, the embryo is most vulnerable to the effects of teratogens during this stage (Koren et al., 1998). Let us now consider some of the most damaging effects of specific maternal diseases and disorders.

RUBELLA (GERMAN MEASLES) **Rubella** is a viral infection. Women who contract rubella during the first month or two of pregnancy, when rapid differentiation of major organ systems is taking place, may bear children who are deaf or who develop mental retardation, heart disease, or cataracts.

Most Canadian women have either had rubella as children, or have been vaccinated against it. Women who do not know whether they are immune to rubella may be tested. If they are not immune, they can be vaccinated *before pregnancy*. Inoculation during pregnancy is considered risky because the vaccine causes a mild case of the disease in the mother, and this can affect the embryo or fetus. Increased awareness of the dangers of rubella during pregnancy, and of the preventive effects of inoculation, has led to a dramatic decline in the number of children born in Canada with defects caused by rubella.

> **Critical period of vulnerability** A period of time during which an embryo or fetus is vulnerable to the effects of a teratogen.
>
> **Rubella** A viral infection that can cause mental retardation and heart disease in an embryo. Also called *German measles*.

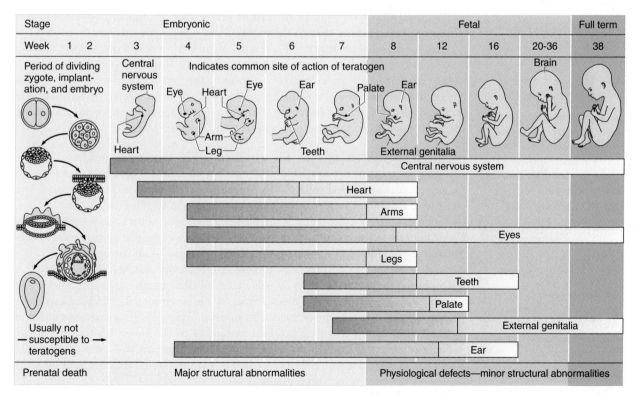

Figure 10.4 Critical Periods in Prenatal Development.

The developing embryo is most vulnerable to teratogens when the organ systems are taking shape. The periods of greatest vulnerability of organ systems are shown in grey. Periods of lesser vulnerability are shown in yellow.

SYPHILIS Maternal **syphilis** may cause miscarriage or **stillbirth**, or it may be passed along to the child in the form of congenital syphilis. Congenital syphilis can impair the vision and hearing, damage the liver, or deform the bones and teeth.

Routine blood tests early in pregnancy can diagnose syphilis and other problems. Because the bacteria that cause syphilis do not readily cross the placental membrane during the first months of pregnancy, the fetus will probably not contract syphilis if an infected mother is treated successfully with antibiotics before the fourth month of pregnancy.

ACQUIRED IMMUNODEFICIENCY SYNDROME (AIDS) **Acquired immunodeficiency syndrome (AIDS)** is caused by the *human immunodeficiency virus* (HIV). HIV is blood-borne and is sometimes transmitted through the placenta to infect the fetus. The rupturing of blood vessels in mother and baby during childbirth provides another opportunity for transmission of HIV. *However, the majority of babies born to mothers who are infected with HIV do not become infected themselves.* Using antiviral medication can also minimize the probability of transmission (see Chapter 14). HIV can also be transmitted to children by breast-feeding.

TOXEMIA **Toxemia**, a life-threatening condition characterized by high blood pressure, may afflict women late in the second trimester of pregnancy or early in the third. If left untreated, it can lead to maternal or fetal death. Babies born to women with toxemia are often undersized or premature.

Toxemia appears to be linked to malnutrition. Ironically, undernourished women may gain weight rapidly through fluid retention, but their swollen appearance may discourage them from eating. Pregnant women who gain weight rapidly but have not increased their food intake should consult their obstetricians.

ECTOPIC PREGNANCY In an **ectopic pregnancy**, the fertilized ovum implants itself somewhere other than in the uterus. Most ectopic pregnancies occur in a fallopian tube ("tubal pregnancies") when the ovum is prevented from moving into the uterus because of obstructions caused by infections. If ectopic pregnancies do not abort spontaneously, they must be removed by surgery or use of medicines such as methotrexate, because the fetus cannot develop to term. Delay in removal may cause hemorrhaging and the death of the mother. A woman with a tubal pregnancy will not menstruate but may notice spotty bleeding and abdominal pain.

RH INCOMPATIBILITY In **Rh incompatibility**, antibodies produced by the mother are transmitted to a fetus or newborn infant. *Rh* is a blood protein found in some people's red blood cells. Rh incompatibility occurs when a woman who does not have this blood factor, and is thus *Rh-negative*, is carrying an *Rh-positive* fetus, which can happen if the father is Rh-positive. However, it becomes a problem only in a minority of the resulting pregnancies. In such cases the mother's antibodies attack the red blood cells of the fetus, which can cause brain damage or death.

Because mother and fetus have separate circulatory systems, it is unlikely that Rh-positive fetal red blood cells will enter the Rh-negative mother's body. The probability of an exchange of blood increases during childbirth, however, especially when the placenta becomes detached from the uterine wall. If an exchange of blood occurs, the mother will then produce antibodies to the baby's Rh-positive blood. The mother's antibodies may enter the fetal bloodstream and cause a condition called *fetal erythroblastosis*, which can result in anemia, mental deficiency, or even the death of the fetus or newborn infant.

Fortunately, blood-typing of pregnant women significantly decreases the threat of uncontrolled erythroblastosis. If an Rh-negative mother is injected with the vaccine Rhogam within 72 hours after delivery of an Rh-positive baby, she will not develop the dangerous antibodies and thus will not pass them on to the fetus in a subsequent pregnancy. A fetus or newborn child at risk for erythroblastosis may also

Syphilis A sexually transmitted disease caused by a bacterial infection.

Stillbirth The birth of a dead fetus.

Acquired immunodeficiency syndrome (AIDS) A sexually transmitted infection that destroys white blood cells in the immune system, leaving the body vulnerable to various "opportunistic" infections.

Toxemia A life-threatening condition that is characterized by high blood pressure.

Ectopic pregnancy A pregnancy in which the fertilized ovum becomes implanted somewhere other than in the uterus.

Rh incompatibility A condition in which antibodies produced by a pregnant woman are transmitted to the fetus and may cause brain damage or death.

receive a preventive blood transfusion to remove the mother's Rh-positive antibodies from its blood.

MEDICATIONS TAKEN BY THE MOTHER (AND THE FATHER) Some widely used drugs, including nonprescription drugs, are linked with birth abnormalities (Koren et al., 1998).

Paternal use of certain drugs also may endanger the fetus. One question is whether drugs alter the genetic material in the father's sperm.

Several antibiotics may harm a fetus, especially if they are taken during certain periods of fetal development. Tetracycline may yellow the teeth and deform the bones (Koren et al., 1998). Other antibiotics have been implicated in deafness and jaundice.

The tranquillizers Librium and Valium cross the placental membrane and may cause birth defects such as harelip. Sedatives, such as the barbiturate *phenobarbital*, are suspected of decreasing testosterone production and causing reproductive problems in the sons of women who use them during pregnancy.

Acne drugs such as Accutane can cause physical and mental handicaps in the children of women who use them during pregnancy. Antihistamines, used commonly for allergies, may deform the fetus.

If you are pregnant or suspect that you are, it is advisable to consult your obstetrician before taking any and all drugs, not just prescription drugs. Your obstetrician can usually direct you to a safe and effective substitute for a drug that could harm a fetus.

HORMONES The hormones progestin and DES (short for *diethylstilbestrol*), a powerful estrogen, have sometimes been used to help women at risk of miscarriage maintain their pregnancies. When taken at about the time that sex organs differentiate, progestin, which is similar in composition to male sex hormones, can masculinize the external sex organs of embryos with female (XX) sex chromosomal structures. Progestin taken during the first trimester has also been linked to increased levels of aggressive behaviour during childhood.

VITAMINS Many pregnant women are prescribed daily doses of multivitamins to maintain their own health and to promote the development of a healthy pregnancy. "Too much of a good thing," however, may be hazardous. High doses of vitamins such as A, B_6, D, and K have been linked to birth defects. Vitamin A excesses have been linked to cleft palate and eye damage, and excesses of vitamin D to mental retardation.

STREET DRUGS Maternal use (and sometimes paternal use) of illegal drugs can also place the fetus at risk. Narcotics such as heroin and methadone can readily pass from mother to fetus through the placental membrane. Narcotics are addictive. Fetuses of mothers who use them regularly during their pregnancies can become addicted in utero. At birth, such babies may undergo withdrawal and show muscle tension and agitation. Women who use narcotics are advised to notify their obstetricians so that measures can be taken to aid the infants before and after delivery.

ALCOHOL Mothers who drink heavily during pregnancy expose the fetus to greater risk of birth defects, infant mortality, sensory and motor problems, and mental retardation (Barr et al., 1990; Coles, 1994). Nearly 40% of children whose mothers drank heavily during pregnancy develop **fetal alcohol syndrome** (FAS). FAS is a cluster of symptoms typified by developmental lags and characteristic facial features, such as an underdeveloped upper jaw, flattened nose, and widely spaced eyes. Infants with FAS are often smaller than average and have smaller-than-average brains. They may be mentally retarded, lack coordination, and have deformed limbs and heart problems. A milder version is fetal alcohol effects (FAE). People

Fetal alcohol syndrome A cluster of symptoms caused by maternal drinking, in which the child shows developmental lags and characteristic facial features such as an underdeveloped upper jaw, flattened nose, and widely spaced eyes.

with fetal alcohol effects show no facial deformation or mental retardation, but often have poor impulse control.

Although research suggests that light drinking is unlikely to harm the fetus in most cases (Jacobson & Jacobson, 1994), FAS has been found even among the children of mothers who drank only 60 millilitres (2 ounces) of alcohol a day during the first trimester (Astley et al., 1992).

A high proportion of children in Canada who are in foster homes waiting to be adopted have FAS. For example, it is estimated that about half of the permanent wards of the Winnipeg Child and Family Services have FAS (Gower & Philp, 2002b). Yet, few adoptive parents are aware of FAS or that their adopted children are at high risk of having been damaged in the womb by alcohol.

Health officials have initiated various information campaigns to alert women about the risks of drinking alcohol before and during pregnancy. In the Algoma district of Ontario, for example, information about alcohol and pregnancy was provided through grocery stores in the form of milk-bag cutters and non-alcoholic recipe books (Howson, 1998).

CIGARETTE SMOKING Cigarette smoke contains chemicals, such as carbon monoxide and the stimulant nicotine, that are transmitted to the fetus. It also lessens the amount of oxygen received by the fetus (Gruslin et al., 2000). Maternal smoking increases the risk of spontaneous abortion and complications during pregnancy such as premature rupturing of the amniotic sac, stillbirth, premature birth, low birth weight, and early infant mortality (English & Eskenazi, 1992; Floyd et al., 1993; USDHHS, 1992). The health risks generally increase with the amount smoked.

Maternal smoking may also impair intellectual development. In one study, women who smoked during pregnancy were 50% more likely than women who did not to have children whose intelligence test scores placed them in the mentally retarded range (that is, beneath an IQ score of 70) when the children were 10 years old (Drews et al., 1996).

Low birth weight is the most common risk factor for infant disease and mortality (USDHHS, 1992). Maternal smoking during pregnancy more than doubles

Don't Do It!
Smoking cigarettes and pregnancy do not mix. Maternal smoking has been shown to increase the risk of spontaneous abortion and of complications during pregnancy. It is connected with premature rupturing of the amniotic sac, stillbirth, premature birth, low birth weight, early infant mortality, and even delayed intellectual development.

the risk of low birth weight (Mayer et al., 1990). The combination of smoking and drinking alcohol places the child at greater risk of low birth weight than either practice alone (Day & Richardson, 1994). As many as one in four cases of low birth weight could be prevented if mothers-to-be stopped smoking during pregnancy (USDHHS, 1990). The earlier the pregnant smoker quits, the better for the baby (and for herself!). Simply cutting down on smoking during pregnancy may not offer much protection in preventing low birth weight, however (USDHHS, 1990).

Maternal smoking affects the fetal heart rate (Graca et al., 1991) and increases the risk of sudden infant death syndrome (SIDS) (Feng, 1993; Haglund & Cnattingius, 1990; Malloy et al., 1992; Schoendorf & Kiely, 1992; Zhang & Fried, 1992). Maternal smoking has also been linked to reduced lung function in newborns (Hanrahan et al., 1992) and to asthma in childhood (Martinez et al., 1992).

Evidence also points to reduced attention spans, hyperactivity, and lower IQ and achievement test scores in children exposed to maternal smoking during and after pregnancy (Barr et al., 1990).

Smoking by the father (or other household members) may be dangerous to a fetus because secondary smoke (smoke exhaled by the smoker or emitted from the tip of a lit cigarette) may be absorbed by the mother and passed along to the fetus. Passive exposure to second-hand smoke during infancy is also linked to increased risk of SIDS (Schoendorf & Kiely, 1992).

The majority of women in Canada of reproductive age drink alcohol, at least occasionally. More than one in four smoke cigarettes. Many of them do not suspend drug use until they learn that they are pregnant. Unfortunately, this knowledge may not be obtained until a woman is weeks into the pregnancy. Damage to the fetus may thus have already occurred. Many women are unwilling or unable to change their drug use habits even after learning they are pregnant. Among women who smoke, only one in five quits smoking when she becomes pregnant (Floyd et al., 1993).

Research in Action

REDUCING HEALTH RISK FACTORS FOR PREGNANT TEENS

The rates of teen pregnancy and low birth weights in Northern Ontario are higher than for the rest of the province. These concerns led health units in the districts of Sudbury, Manitoulin, and Algoma to conduct a three-year teen prenatal study (PHERO, 1999) involving 397 pregnant teens aged 14 to 19 years old.

Before they knew they were pregnant, 90% of these teens smoked, 90% drank alcohol, and about two-thirds used illicit drugs. During the period of the study, alcohol and drug use was reduced dramatically to 8% and 5%, respectively. However, it was more difficult to reduce smoking, with 60% continuing to smoke. Those who continued to smoke, drink alcohol, and take drugs were less likely than those who stopped to believe that these practices were harmful to the baby. As well, barriers to quitting included the addictive

nature of tobacco, the use of cigarettes as a means of dealing with stress, and the fact that people around them smoked. About four-fifths of the teenagers studied reported that they tried to improve their eating habits, with about half taking prenatal vitamins. The main barrier to improved nutrition was the lack of sufficient money to pay for proper food.

Those who continued with risky health practices had more problematic births:

- Those who smoked during pregnancy were more than twice as likely as nonsmokers to have low-birth-weight and/or premature babies.
- Those who drank during pregnancy were more than twice as likely as nondrinkers to have low-birth-weight babies.
- Those who had inadequate nutrition were more than twice as likely as those who ate well to have low-birth-weight babies.

■ Drug users were more than three times as likely as non-users to have premature babies.

This study of high-risk teenage mothers shows that, when given proper health education along with supportive counselling, the majority of teen mothers do make significant changes in their alcohol consumption, drug use, and nutritional habits. Most really do want to do "what is best for the baby." Unfortunately, the addictive nature of tobacco makes it more difficult to quit smoking, and in this area greater efforts need to be made.

OTHER AGENTS X-rays increase the risk of malformed organs in the fetus, especially within a month and a half after conception. (Ultrasound has not been shown to harm the embryo or fetus.)

Chromosomal and Genetic Abnormalities

Not all of us have the normal complement of chromosomes. Some of us have genes that threaten our health or our existence (see Table 10.1 for a summary).

AVERTING CHROMOSOMAL AND GENETIC ABNORMALITIES On the basis of information about a couple's medical background and family history of genetic defects, genetic counsellors help couples assess the risks of passing along genetic defects to their children. Some couples who face a high risk of passing along genetic defects to their children decide to adopt. Other couples decide to have an abortion if the fetus is determined to have certain abnormalities. Various medical procedures are used to detect the presence of these disorders in the fetus.

Parental blood tests can suggest the presence of problems such as sickle-cell anemia, Tay–Sachs disease, and neural tube defects. Still other tests examine fetal

TABLE 10.1
Some Chromosomal and Genetic Abnormalities

Health Problem	About ...
Cystic fibrosis	A genetic disease in which the pancreas and lungs become clogged with mucus, which impairs the processes of respiration and digestion.
Down syndrome	A condition characterized by a 3rd chromosome on the 21st pair. The child with Down syndrome has a characteristic fold of skin over the eye and mental retardation. The risk of having a child with the syndrome increases as parents increase in age.
Hemophilia	A sex-linked disorder in which blood does not clot properly.
Huntington's chorea	A fatal neurological disorder whose onset occurs in middle adulthood.
Neural tube defects	Disorders of the brain or spine, such as *anencephaly*, in which part of the brain is missing, and *spina bifida*, in which part of the spine is exposed or missing. Anencephaly is fatal shortly after birth, but some spina bifida victims survive for a number of years, though with severe handicaps.
Phenylketonuria	A disorder in which children cannot metabolize phenylalanine, which builds up in the form of phenylpyruvic acid and causes mental retardation. The disorder can be diagnosed at birth and controlled by diet.
Retina blastoma	A form of blindness caused by a dominant gene.
Sickle-cell anemia	A blood disorder that mostly afflicts people of African descent, in which deformed blood cells obstruct small blood vessels, decreasing their capacity to carry oxygen and heightening the risk of occasionally fatal infections.
Tay–Sachs disease	A fatal neurological disorder that primarily afflicts Jews of European origin.

DNA and can indicate the presence of Huntington's chorea, cystic fibrosis, and other disorders. Blood tests also now allow detection of Down syndrome during the first trimester (Haddow et al., 1998).

Childbirth

Early in the ninth month of pregnancy, the fetus's head settles in the pelvis. This shift is called "dropping" or "lightening." The woman may actually feel lighter because of lessened pressure on the diaphragm. About a day or so before the beginning of labour, the woman may notice blood in her vaginal secretions because fetal pressure on the pelvis may rupture superficial blood vessels in the birth canal. Tissue that had plugged the cervix, possibly preventing entry of infectious agents from the vagina, becomes dislodged. There is a resultant discharge of bloody mucus. At about this time, 1 woman in 10 also has a rush of warm "water" from the vagina. The "water" is amniotic fluid, and it means that the amniotic sac has burst. Labour usually begins within a day after rupture of the amniotic sac. For most women the amniotic sac does not burst until the end of the first stage of childbirth. Other signs of impending labour include indigestion, diarrhea, abdominal cramps, and an ache in the small of the back. Labour begins with the onset of regular uterine contractions.

The first uterine contractions are relatively painless and are called **Braxton–Hicks contractions**, or false labour contractions. They are "false" because they do not widen the cervix or advance the baby through the birth canal. They tend to increase in frequency but are less regular than labour contractions. Real labour contractions, by contrast, become more intense when the woman moves around or walks.

The initiation of labour may involve the secretion of hormones by the fetal adrenal and pituitary glands that stimulate the placenta and the mother's uterus to secrete **prostaglandins**. Prostaglandins stimulate the uterine musculature to contract. It would make sense for the fetus to have a mechanism for signalling the mother that it is mature enough to sustain independent life. The mechanisms that initiate and maintain labour are not fully understood, however. Later in labour the pituitary gland releases **oxytocin**, a hormone that stimulates contractions strong enough to expel the baby.

The Stages of Childbirth

Childbirth begins with the onset of labour and has three stages.

THE FIRST STAGE In the first stage, uterine contractions **efface** and **dilate** the cervix to about 10 centimetres (4 inches) in diameter, so that the baby may pass. Stretching of the cervix causes most of the pain of childbirth. A woman may experience little or no pain if her cervix dilates easily and quickly. The first stage may last from a couple of hours to more than a day. Twelve to 24 hours of labour is considered about average for a first pregnancy. In later pregnancies labour takes about half this time.

The initial contractions are usually mild and spaced widely, at intervals of 10 to 20 minutes. They may last 20 to 40 seconds. As time passes, contractions become more frequent, long, strong, and regular.

Transition is the process that occurs when the cervix becomes almost fully dilated and the baby's head begins to move into the vagina, or birth canal. Contractions usually come quickly during transition. Transition usually lasts about 30 minutes or less and is often accompanied by feelings of nausea, chills, and intense pain.

Braxton–Hicks contractions So-called false labour contractions that are relatively painless.

Prostaglandins Uterine hormones that stimulate uterine contractions..

Oxytocin A pituitary hormone that stimulates uterine contractions.

Efface To become thin.

Dilate To open or widen.

Transition The process during which the cervix becomes almost fully dilated and the head of the fetus begins to move into the birth canal.

Episiotomy A surgical incision in the perineum that widens the birth canal, preventing random tearing during childbirth.

Perineum The area between the vulva and the anus.

THE SECOND STAGE The second stage of childbirth follows transition and begins when the cervix has become fully dilated and the baby begins to move into the vagina and first appears at the opening of the birth canal. The second stage is shorter than the first stage. It lasts from a few minutes to a few hours and ends with the birth of the baby.

Each contraction of the second stage propels the baby farther along the birth canal (vagina). When the baby's head becomes visible at the vaginal opening, it is said to have *crowned*. The baby typically emerges fully a few minutes after crowning.

An **episiotomy** may be performed on the mother when the baby's head has crowned. The purpose is to prevent the random tearing of the **perineum** that can occur if it becomes extremely effaced. Episiotomies are controversial, however (Roberts, 2000). The incision can cause infection and pain and can create discomfort and itching as it heals. In some cases the discomfort interferes with coitus for months. Physicians generally agree that an episiotomy should be performed if the baby's shoulders are too wide to emerge without causing tearing or if the baby's heartbeat drops for an extended period of time (Eason & Feldman, 2000).

In Canada the number of episiotomies is decreasing. In 1991, episiotomies were performed in almost half of vaginal births. By 2001, this occurred in only about one-quarter of vaginal births. Rates have also fallen in the United States and other countries (Canadian Institute for Health Information, 2004).

With or without an episiotomy, the baby's passageway to the external world is a tight fit. As a result, the baby may look as though it has been through a prizefight. Its head may be elongated, its nose flattened, and its ears bent. Although parents may be concerned about whether the baby's features will assume a more typical shape, they nearly always do.

THE THIRD STAGE The third, or placental, stage of childbirth may last from a few minutes to an hour or more. During this stage, the placenta is expelled. Detachment of the placenta from the uterine wall may cause some bleeding. The uterus begins the process of contracting to a smaller size. The attending physician sews up the episiotomy or any tears in the perineum.

IN THE NEW WORLD As the baby's head emerges, mucus is cleared from its mouth by means of suction aspiration to prevent the breathing passageway from being obstructed. Aspiration is often repeated once the baby is fully delivered. (Newly delivered babies are no longer routinely held upside down to help expel mucus. Nor is the baby slapped on the buttocks to stimulate breathing, as in old films.)

Once the baby is breathing adequately, the umbilical cord is clamped and severed about 7.5 centimetres (3 inches) from the baby's body. The stump of the umbilical cord dries and falls off in its own time, usually in 7 to 10 days.

While the mother is in the third stage of labour, the nurse may perform procedures on the baby, such as placing drops of silver nitrate or an antibiotic ointment into the eyes. This procedure is required to prevent bacterial infections in the newborn's eyes.

Coming into the World.
Childbirth progresses through three stages. In the first stage, uterine contractions efface and dilate the cervix so that the baby can pass through. The second stage lasts from a few minutes to a few hours and ends with the birth of the baby. During the third stage, the placenta is expelled.

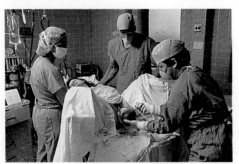

Methods of Childbirth

Until the twentieth century, childbirth was usually an event that happened at home and involved the mother, a midwife, family, and friends. These days women in Canada typically give birth in hospitals attended by obstetricians who use surgical instruments and anaesthetics to protect mothers and children from infection, complications, and pain. Medical procedures save lives but also make childbearing more impersonal. Social critics argue that these procedures have medicalized a natural process, usurping control over women's bodies and, through the use of drugs, denying many women the experience of giving birth.

ANAESTHETIZED CHILDBIRTH During the past two centuries, science and medicine have led to the expectation that women should experience minimal discomfort during childbirth. Today some anaesthesia is used to minimize or eliminate pain in most Canadian deliveries.

Anaesthetic drugs, as well as tranquillizers and narcotics, decrease the strength of uterine contractions during delivery. They may thus delay the process of cervical dilation and prolong labour. They also reduce the woman's ability to push the baby through the birth canal. And because they cross the placental membrane, they also lower the newborn's overall responsiveness. However, there is little evidence that medicated childbirth has serious, long-term consequences for children.

NATURAL CHILDBIRTH Partly as a reaction against the use of anaesthetics, English obstetrician Grantly Dick-Read endorsed **natural childbirth** in his 1944 book *Childbirth Without Fear.* Dick-Read argued that women's labour pains were heightened by their fear of the unknown and resultant muscle tensions. Many of Dick-Read's contributions came to be regarded as accepted practice in modern childbirth procedures, such as the emphasis on informing women about the biological aspects of reproduction and childbirth, the encouragement of physical fitness, and the teaching of relaxation and breathing exercises.

PREPARED CHILDBIRTH: THE LAMAZE METHOD The French obstetrician Fernand Lamaze visited the Soviet Union in 1951 and found that many Russian women bore babies without anaesthetics and without reporting a great deal of pain. Lamaze returned to Western Europe with some of the techniques the women used; they are now termed the **Lamaze method**, or *prepared childbirth.* Lamaze (1981) argued that women can learn to conserve energy during childbirth and reduce the pain of uterine contractions by associating the contractions with other responses, such as thinking of pleasant mental images such as beach scenes, or engaging in breathing and relaxation exercises.

A pregnant woman typically attends Lamaze classes with a "coach"—usually the father—who will aid her in the delivery room by timing contractions, offering emotional support, and coaching her in the breathing and relaxation exercises. The woman and her partner also receive more general information about childbirth. The father is integrated into the process, and many couples report that their marriages are strengthened as a result.

The Lamaze method is flexible about the use of anaesthetics. Many women report some pain during delivery and obtain anaesthetics. However, the Lamaze method appears to help women gain a greater sense of control over the delivery process.

CAESAREAN SECTION In a **caesarean section**, the baby is delivered through surgery rather than naturally through the vagina. In a caesarean section (C-section for short) the woman is anaesthetized, and incisions are made in the abdomen and uterus so that the surgeon can remove the baby. The incisions are then sewn up and the mother can begin walking, often on the same day, although generally with some discomfort for a while. Although most C-sections are without complications, some cause urinary tract infections, inflammation of the wall of the uterus, blood clots, or hemorrhaging.

C-sections are most likely to be advised when normal delivery is difficult or threatening to the health of the mother or child. Vaginal deliveries can become difficult if the baby is large, the mother's pelvis is small or misshapen, or the mother is tired, weakened, or aging (Roberts, 2000). Herpes and HIV infections in the birth canal can be bypassed by C-section. C-sections are also likely to be performed if the

Natural childbirth A method of childbirth in which women use no anaesthesia but are given other strategies for coping with discomfort and are educated about childbirth.

Lamaze method A childbirth method in which women learn about childbirth, learn to relax and to breathe in patterns that conserve energy and lessen pain, and have a coach (usually the father) present at childbirth. Also termed *prepared childbirth.*

Caesarean section A method of childbirth in which the fetus is delivered through a surgical incision in the abdomen.

baby presents for delivery in the breech position (feet downward) or the **transverse position** (lying crosswise) or if the baby is in distress.

Use of the C-section has mushroomed. In Canada, in 2001, C-section rates reached an all-time high of 22.5% on in-hospital deliveries. More Canadian women are having C-sections the first time they give birth and fewer are delivering vaginally after having a previous C-section birth. (Canadian Institute for Health Information, 2004). In 2004, the Society of Obstetricians and Gynecologists of Canada recommended that pregnant women should be allowed to choose to have a C-section even if there are no medical reasons for it, providing women are informed ahead of time of the risks and benefits.

Much of the increase in the rate of C-sections reflects advances in medical technology (such as use of fetal monitors that allow doctors to detect fetal distress), fear of malpractice suits, financial incentives for hospitals and physicians, and, simply, current medical practice patterns (DiMatteo et al., 1996).

Consumer advocates advise pregnant women who would prefer to deliver vaginally to ask about the rates of C-sections when they are choosing a physician and a hospital ("After years of decline," 2000). Women can try to choose obstetricians who have lower rates or who are open to a second opinion for elective surgery.

Birth Problems

Most deliveries are uncomplicated, or "unremarkable" in the medical sense— although childbirth is the most remarkable experience of many parents' lives. Problems can and do occur, however. Some of the most common birth problems are anoxia and the birth of preterm and low-birth-weight babies.

ANOXIA Prenatal **anoxia** can cause various problems in the neonate and can affect later development. It leads to complications such as brain damage and mental retardation. Prolonged anoxia during delivery can also result in cerebral palsy and possibly death.

The baby is supplied with oxygen through the umbilical cord. Passage through the birth canal squeezes the umbilical cord. Temporary squeezing, like holding one's breath for a moment, is unlikely to cause problems. (In fact, slight oxygen deprivation at birth is not unusual because the transition from receiving oxygen through the umbilical cord to independent breathing may not happen immediately after the baby emerges.) Fetal monitoring can help detect significant anoxia early, before damage occurs. A C-section can be performed if the fetus appears to be in distress.

Transverse position A crosswise birth position.

Anoxia Oxygen deprivation.

Applied Knowledge

CHILDBIRTH ADVICE IS JUST KEYSTROKES AWAY

You're pregnant and it's midnight. You've just felt a couple of abdominal twinges and you're a little worried. You know your obstetrician's probably asleep and since you still have a couple

of weeks to go before the baby's due, you don't want to rush to the emergency room. Right now, some good, solid medical information would be ever so reassuring.

If you've got an Internet connection, help could be just a few keystrokes away. These days, the Web is teeming with birth-related sites. The Net-savvy

mother-to-be can research labor issues, find a childbirth class, chat with other expectant women, and shop for everything from pregnancy vitamins to maternity fitness wear.

Of course, as with everything that appears on the Web, there's a certain amount of drivel and misinformation. So MSNBC has rounded up some experts to help you find the best places to dock your surfboard.

For trustworthy medical advice, you should probably stick to sites that are affiliated with either an academic institution or an established professional organization, suggests Dr. David Toub, director of quality improvement at Keystone Mercy Health Plan and a member of the department of obstetrics and gynecology at the Pennsylvania Hospital in Philadelphia.

Another option is to seek sites that have input from recognized experts, such as **Obgyn.net**. This site also contains chats and forums that focus on such subjects as pregnancy, birth, and breast-feeding.

Another good site for conversation about pregnancy and baby-rearing is **iVillage.com.**

Source: From Linda Carroll (2000). "Childbirth Advice Keystrokes Away: How to Find the Best Web Sites." MSNBC online. Reprinted by permission of MSNBC Interactive News.

PRETERM AND LOW-BIRTH-WEIGHT CHILDREN A neonate is considered to be premature, or **preterm**, if it is born before 37 weeks of gestation. The normal period of gestation is 40 weeks. Prematurity is generally linked with low birth weight, because the fetus normally makes dramatic gains in weight during the last weeks of pregnancy.

Regardless of the length of its gestation period, a newborn baby is considered to have a low birth weight if it weighs less than about 2 kilograms (5 pounds). Preterm and low-birth-weight babies face a heightened risk of infant mortality from causes ranging from asphyxia and infections to sudden infant death syndrome (SIDS) (Berger, 2000; Kramer et al., 2000). Neurological and developmental problems are also common among preterm infants, especially those born at or prior to 25 weeks of gestation (Wood et al., 2000).

Preterm infants usually remain in the hospital for a time. There they can be monitored and placed in incubators that provide a temperature-controlled environment and offer some protection from infection. If necessary, they may also receive oxygen. Although remarkable advances are being made in our ability to help preterm babies survive, the likelihood of developmental disabilities continues to increase dramatically for babies who are born at 25 weeks of gestation or earlier (Cole, 2000).

Preterm Born before 37 weeks of gestation.

Postpartum Following birth.

Postpartum depression Persistent and severe mood changes during the postpartum period, involving feelings of despair and apathy and characterized by changes in appetite and sleep, low self-esteem, and difficulty concentrating.

The Postpartum Period

The weeks after delivery are called the **postpartum** period. The first few days postpartum are frequently happy ones. The long wait is over, as are the discomforts of childbirth. However, a sizable number of women experience feelings of depression in the days and sometimes weeks and months after childbirth.

Maternal Depression

Many new mothers experience mood changes after childbirth. During the days or weeks following the delivery of their babies, as many as 80% of new mothers (Morris, 2000) experience periods of sadness, tearfulness, and irritability that are commonly called the "postpartum blues," the "maternity blues," or the "baby blues." This downswing in mood typically occurs around the third day after delivery (Samuels & Samuels, 1986). The baby blues usually last less than a week and are generally believed to be a normal response to hormonal and psychological changes that attend childbirth (Morris, 2000).

Some mothers experience more persistent and severe mood changes, called **postpartum depression** (PPD) (Morris, 2000). PPD may last a year or even longer. PPD can involve extreme sadness or despair, apathy, changes in appetite and sleep patterns, low self-esteem, and difficulty concentrating.

The Canadian Health Network Provides links to resources and information on topics related to healthy pregnancy, breast-feeding, infertility, etc.

www.canadian-health-network.ca

The La Leche League
Provides information, support, and encouragement to women who want to breast-feed.

www.lalecheleague. org

Like the "maternity blues," PPD may reflect a combination of physiological and psychological factors. Hormonal changes may play a role in PPD, but women with PPD are more likely than those with the maternity blues to have been susceptible to depression before and during their pregnancies (O'Hara et al., 1984). Psychosocial factors such as stress, a troubled marriage, or the need to adjust to an unwanted or sick baby may all increase a woman's susceptibility to PPD (Gitlin & Pasnau, 1989; O'Hara et al., 1984, 1991). First-time mothers, single mothers, and mothers who lack social support from their partners or family members face the greatest risk of PPD (Gitlin & Pasnau, 1989).

Lesbian mothers are also at risk for maternal depression. University of Toronto researcher Lori Ross in reviewing the research literature concluded that lesbian mothers may experience more stress because of less support from their own parents and because of societal prejudices. On the other hand, there are also factors reducing stress and the likelihood of postpartum depression. For example, lesbian pregnancies are more likely to be planned, and there is more of an equal division of labour in child-care among lesbian couples (Ross, 2005).

New fathers may also have bouts of depression. New mothers are not the only ones who must adjust to the responsibilities of parenthood. Fathers too may feel overwhelmed or unable to cope.

Breast-feeding

Breast-feeding reduces the baby's general risk of infections by transmitting the mother's antibodies to the baby. Breast-feeding also reduces the incidence of allergies in babies, particularly in allergy-prone infants (Barisic, 1998). On the other hand, HIV (the AIDS virus) can be transmitted to infants via breast milk. According to UN estimates, one-third of the infants with HIV around the world were infected via breast milk (Meier, 1997). Moreover, when undernourished mothers in developing countries breast-feed their babies, the babies too can become malnourished (Crossette, 2000).

Research in Action

BREAST-FEEDING VERSUS BOTTLE-FEEDING

In 2003 the Canadian Community Health Survey of women who had given birth in the previous five years found that 85% of Canadian mothers breast-feed their newborns. This represents a marked increase from the mid-1960s, when only about 25% of Canadian women breast-fed. Canadian public health guidelines call for exclusive breast-feeding for at least the first six months. However, only 17% of Canadian women breast-feed that long (Miller & McLean, 2005).

As shown in Table 10.2, breast-feeding rates are lower in the Atlantic provinces and Quebec than in the rest of Canada.

Researchers at McMaster University (Callen & Pinelli, 2004) conducted a comparative literature review of breast-feeding patterns in Canada, the United States, Europe, and Australia. Rates and duration of breast-feeding of infants were higher in Europe and Australia than in Canada and the United States. Across all four countries, breast-feeding incidence and duration were highest among women who were older, were married, were better educated, and had higher incomes.

In the 2003 Canadian Community Health Survey, immigrants were more likely to breast-feed than Canadian-born women, and women in urban areas were more likely to breast -eed than women in rural areas.

The most common reason Canadian mothers give for breast-feeding is that it is better for the baby. When asked why they did not breast-feed, common answers were:

- there was not enough breast milk
- the baby weaned himself or herself
- the mother returned to work or school
- it was inconvenient or tiring (Statistics Canada, 2005)

Reactions to breast-feeding vary. Many women enjoy the emotional intimacy of breast-feeding. Some find it physically enjoyable. Others find it unpleasant and a nuisance. Some appreciate the convenience of having nothing to buy, stir, warm, refrigerate, and cart along. Others are embarrassed at uncovering their breasts in public or find it constraining to have the baby with them most of the time. Some choose to share feeding chores with the father, who is equally equipped to prepare and hold a bottle, but not, of course, to breast-feed (although he can give a baby expressed milk in a bottle when the mother is not available).

Most Canadians are supportive of breast-feeding. However, in a study of longer-term breast-feeding, Brock University researcher Lynn Rempel (2004) found that mothers who were breast-feeding at nine months perceived that approval for breast-feeding declined as the baby got older.

Table 10.2
Percentage of Canadian Women Who Breast-Feed at Birth and at 6 Months

Province	At Birth	At 6 Months
Newfoundland and Labrador	63	9
Prince Edward Island	77	12
Nova Scotia	76	14
New Brunswick	64	8
Quebec	76	10
Ontario	87	18
Manitoba	89	18
Saskatchewan	86	18
Alberta	90	22
British Columbia	93	28

Source: Statistics Canada, Canadian Community Health Survey, 2003.

DOES BREAST-FEEDING AFFECT SEXUAL BEHAVIOUR? In an analysis of the research literature, researchers at the University of British Columbia found that women who breast-feed are more likely than those who bottle-feed to experience decreased sexual desire, decreased frequency of sexual intercourse, and painful intercourse because of lack of vaginal lubrication (LaMarre et al., 2003).

LaMarre et al. (2003) conclude that breast-feeding decreases both androgen levels, leading to decreased sexual desire, and estrogen levels, leading to vaginal dryness. Also, breast-feeding mothers are more fatigued from having to get up at night to breast-feed their child. However, differences in sexuality between breast-feeders and bottle-feeders diminish considerably after 12 months.

The hormones prolactin and oxytocin are involved in breast-feeding. **Prolactin** stimulates production of milk, or **lactation**, two to three days after delivery. Oxytocin causes the breasts to eject milk and is secreted in response to suckling. When an infant is weaned, secretion of prolactin and oxytocin is discontinued, and lactation comes to an end.

Uterine contractions that occur during breast-feeding help return the uterus to its typical size, leading the belly to flatten more quickly. Because of the expenditure of energy, breast-feeding may also help women lose the extra weight of pregnancy more quickly. Breast-feeding also delays resumption of normal menstrual cycles. Breast-feeding is not a perfectly reliable birth-control method, however.

Prolactin A pituitary hormone that stimulates production of milk. (From roots that mean "for milk.")

Lactation Production of milk by the mammary glands.

Applied Knowledge

WHERE TO GET HELP BREAST-FEEDING

During pregnancy, women tend to romanticize breast-feeding, assuming that this natural function will be pleasant and trouble-free. But many women encounter problems, ranging from local irritation to difficulty maintaining the flow of milk. As noted by lactation con-sultant Corky Harvey (2000), breast-feeding can be painful, inconvenient, and stressful, especially at first.

Harvey suggests that women who are having problems breast-feeding call the hospital where they delivered and ask whether it has a lactation consultant or can refer them to one. Or call your pediatrician or obstetrician or a friend or relative who has successfully breast-fed.

The Internet can also be helpful: Try **www. breastfeeding.org**, **www.breastfeeding.com**, **www. lalecheleague.org**, or **www.ILCA.org**, the site for the International Lactation Consultants Association.

Should a woman breast-feed her baby? The issue has become highly politicized (Law, 2000). Much of the vast literature on breast-feeding has little to do with the advantages of breast milk or formula, but with occupational and domestic arrangements, day care, mother–infant bonding, and the politics of domestic decision making. Although breast-feeding has benefits for both mother and infant, each woman must weigh these benefits against the difficulties breast-feeding may pose for her.

Resumption of Ovulation and Menstruation

For close to a month after delivery, women experience a reddish vaginal discharge called **lochia**. A non-nursing mother does not resume actual menstrual periods until two to three months postpartum. The first few cycles are likely to be irregular. Many women incorrectly assume that they will resume menstruating after childbirth by first having a menstrual period and then ovulating two weeks later. In most cases the opposite is true. Ovulation precedes the first menstrual period after childbirth. Thus a woman may become pregnant before the menstrual phase of her first postpartum cycle. Some women, but not all, who suffered premenstrual syndrome before their pregnancies find that their periods give them less discomfort after the birth of their children.

Resumption of Sexual Activity

The resumption of coitus depends on a couple's level of sexual interest, the healing of episiotomies or other injuries, fatigue, the recommendations of obstetricians, and, of course, tradition. Obstetricians usually advise a six-week waiting period for safety and comfort. One study of 570 women found that they actually resumed sexual intercourse an average of seven weeks after childbirth (Byrd et al., 1998).

Women typically prefer to delay coitus until it becomes physically comfortable, generally when the episiotomy or other lacerations have healed and the lochia has ended. This may take several weeks. Women who breast-feed may also find that they have less vaginal lubrication, and the dryness can cause discomfort during coitus. K-Y jelly or other lubricants may help in such cases. Couples may enjoy other forms of sexual activity earlier; as soon as both partners are interested and comfortable.

The return of sexual interest and resumption of sexual activity may take longer for some couples than for others. Sexual interest depends more on psychological

Lochia A reddish vaginal discharge that may persist for a month after delivery. (From the Greek *lochios*, which means "of childbirth.")

than on physical factors. Many couples encounter declining sexual interest and activity in the first year following childbirth, generally because child care can sap energy and limit free time. Generally speaking, couples whose sexual relationships were satisfying before the baby arrived tend to show greater sexual interest and to resume sexual activity earlier than those who had less satisfying relationships beforehand. (No surprise.)

Summing Up

Conception: Against All Odds

Conception is the union of a sperm cell and an ovum. Fertilization normally occurs in a fallopian tube.

Optimizing the Chances of Conception

Optimizing the chances of conception means engaging in coitus at the time of ovulation. Ovulation can be predicted by calculating the woman's basal body temperature, analyzing the woman's urine for luteinizing hormone, or tracking the thickness of vaginal mucus.

Infertility and Alternative Ways of Becoming Parents

Male Fertility Problems

Fertility problems in the male include low sperm count, irregularly shaped sperm, low sperm motility, certain chronic or infectious diseases, trauma to the testes, an autoimmune response to sperm, and pituitary imbalances and/or thyroid disease.

Female Fertility Problems

The major causes of infertility in women include irregular ovulation, obstructions or malfunctions of the reproductive tract, endometriosis, and the decline of hormone levels with age. Failure to ovulate may often be overcome by fertility drugs. Methods for overcoming other female fertility problems include in vitro fertilization, GIFT, ZIFT, donor IVF, embryonic transfer, and surrogate motherhood.

Canadian Legislation Governing Reproductive Technology

The Act Respecting Human Reproduction includes a controversial provision that would allow research using stem cells from embryos left over from infertility treatment.

Pregnancy

Early Signs of Pregnancy

Early signs include a missed period, presence of HCG in the blood or urine, and Hegar's sign.

Pregnancy Tests

Pregnancy tests detect the presence of human chorionic gonadotropin (HCG) in the woman's urine or blood.

Early Effects of Pregnancy

Early effects include tenderness in the breasts and morning sickness.

Miscarriage (Spontaneous Abortion)

Miscarriages have many causes, including chromosomal defects in the fetus and abnormalities of the placenta and uterus.

Sex During Pregnancy

Most health professionals concur that in most cases, coitus is safe until the start of labour.

Psychological Changes During Pregnancy

A woman's psychological response to pregnancy reflects her desire to be pregnant, her physical changes, and her attitudes toward these changes. Men, like women, respond to pregnancy according to the degree to which they want the child.

Prenatal Development

The Germinal Stage

The germinal stage is the period from conception to implantation.

The Embryonic Stage

The embryonic stage begins with implantation, extends to about the eighth week of development, and is characterized by differentiation of the major organ systems.

The Fetal Stage

The fetal stage begins by the ninth week, continues until the birth of the baby, and is characterized by continued maturation of the fetus's organ systems and dramatic increases in size.

Environmental Influences on Prenatal Development

Environmental factors that affect prenatal development include the mother's diet, maternal diseases and disorders, and drugs. Maternal malnutrition has been linked to low birth weight and infant mortality. Exposure to particular teratogens causes the greatest harm during critical periods of vulnerability.

Chromosomal and Genetic Abnormalities

Chromosomal and genetic abnormalities can lead to cystic fibrosis, Down syndrome, hemophilia, Huntington's chorea, neural tube defects, phenylketonuria, retina blastoma, sickle-cell anemia, and Tay–Sachs disease. Parental blood tests, amniocentesis, and ultrasound allow parents to learn whether the fetus has, or is at risk for, many such disorders.

Childbirth

The Stages of Childbirth

In the first stage, uterine contractions efface and dilate the cervix so that the baby may pass through. The first stage may last from a couple of hours to more than a day. The second stage lasts from a few minutes to a few hours and ends with the birth of the baby. During the third stage, the placenta is expelled.

Methods of Childbirth

Contemporary methods for facilitating childbirth include anaesthetized childbirth, natural childbirth, the Lamaze method, and caesarean section.

Birth Problems

Prenatal anoxia can cause brain damage and mental retardation in the child. Preterm and low-birth-weight babies have a heightened risk of infant mortality.

The Postpartum Period

Maternal Depression

Many new mothers experience transient mood changes after childbirth. Women with postpartum depression experience lingering depression following childbirth.

Breast-Feeding

Breast-feeding is associated with fewer infections and allergic reactions in the baby than bottle-feeding. Long-term studies, however, show few differences between children whose parents used one or the other feeding method.

Resumption of Ovulation and Menstruation

The first few menstrual cycles following childbirth are likely to be irregular.

Resumption of Sexual Activity

Obstetricians usually advise waiting about six weeks after childbirth before resuming coitus. Couples need not wait this long to enjoy other forms of sexual activity.

Test Yourself

Multiple-Choice Questions

1. According to Statistics Canada, in 2003, nearly half of all babies born in Canada were born to mothers over _____ years of age.
   a. 20
   b. 25
   c. 30
   d. 40

2. _____ may carry either X or Y chromosomes.
   a. Sperm
   b. Ova
   c. Gametes
   d. Blastocysts

3. The most common cause of fertility problems in males is/are _____.
   a. sexually transmitted infections
   b. injury to the testes
   c. low sperm count
   d. old age

4. All of the following can cause infertility in females except
   a. failure to ovulate
   b. sexually transmitted infections
   c. declining levels of estrogen
   d. use of illicit drugs

5. **Which of the following statements is true?**
a. Surrogate motherhood is becoming more common in Canada.
b. Surrogate motherhood contracts must specify the amount of financial support that will be provided.
c. Surrogate motherhood is legal if both parties agree to it.
d. It is illegal to pay a woman to be a surrogate mother.

6. **The first stage of prenatal development is the**

    _____.

a. embryonic
b. placental
c. fetal
d. germinal

7. **Most ectopic pregnancies occur in the**

    _____.

a. ovary
b. cervix
c. fallopian tube
d. uterus

8. **Which stage of childbirth ends with the birth of the baby?**
a. the first stage
b. the second stage
c. the third stage
d. the fourth stage

9. **Approximately _____ percent of women experience some sadness, irritability, or low mood following the birth of a baby.**
a. 25
b. 40
c. 65
d. 80

10. **Which statement about postpartum depression (PPD) is false?**
a. Women who lack social support are more likely to suffer from PPD.
b. PPD can involve feelings of extreme sadness and apathy.
c. PPD may be caused by a combination of physiological and psychological factors.
d. Women with PPD are always a danger to their babies.

Critical Thinking Questions

1. Today's reproductive technologies make it possible for infertile couples to have children, for women to have babies after menopause, and for women to become mothers to their own grandchildren using eggs donated by their daughters. It might even be possible for parents to choose to have a child of a particular genetic makeup in order to provide bone marrow or other tissue to save another of their children. However, the development of these technologies has leapfrogged ahead of society's efforts to grapple with their ethical, moral, and legal implications. Where should the line be drawn in determining how far medical science should go in these matters?

2. A good friend of yours is pregnant. You notice that she is still drinking alcohol and smoking cigarettes. Would you confront her about these behaviours? Why or why not?

3. You read a news report that doctors can determine whether a fetus is likely to be heterosexual or homosexual. Should parents have the right to choose the sexual orientation of their children, even to the extent of aborting a "gay" or "lesbian" fetus (or, perhaps for a gay couple, a "heterosexual" fetus)? Why or why not?

Companion Website

Visit our Companion Website at www.pearsoned.ca/rathus, **where you can use the interactive Study Guide and link to additional resources on topics discussed in this text.**

Chapter 11
Contraception and Abortion

Historical Perspectives on Contraception

People have been devising means of contraception since they became aware of the relationship between coitus and conception. Greek and Roman women placed absorbent materials within the vagina to absorb semen. The use of sheaths or coverings for the penis has a long history. Sheaths worn over the penis as decorative covers can be traced to ancient Egypt (1350 B.C.). Sheaths of linen were first described in European writings in 1564 by the Italian anatomist Fallopius (from whom the name of the fallopian tube is derived). Linen sheaths were used, without success, as a barrier against syphilis. The term **condom** was not used to describe penile sheaths until the eighteenth century. At that time, sheaths made of animal intestines became popular as a means of preventing sexually transmitted infections and unwanted pregnancies.

Condoms made of rubber (hence the slang "rubbers") were introduced shortly after Charles Goodyear invented vulcanization of rubber in 1843. Many other forms of contraception were also used widely in the nineteenth century, including withdrawal, vaginal sponges, and douching. Examples of many of these historical contraceptives are displayed in the History of Contraception Museum at Janssen-Ortho, Inc., in Toronto. Percy Skuy, who was president of Ortho-McNeil, began the museum in 1965.

Sheep Caecum

History of Contraception Museum.
This museum was established in Toronto by the pharmaceutical firm Janssen-Ortho, Inc. One of the artifacts on display is the caecum (intestinal pouch) of a sheep, which was used by early Egyptian males as a form of condom.

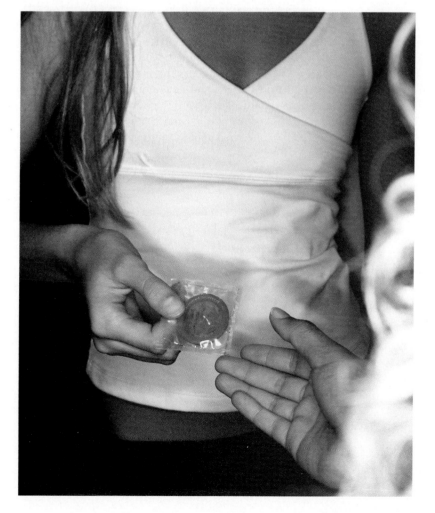

The Condom.
Condoms were once considered a man's domain. Today many women are insisting on their use, and often it is the woman who buys and carries them.

Condom A sheath made of animal membrane or latex that covers the penis during coitus and serves as a barrier to sperm following ejaculation.

Research in Action

CONTRACEPTIVE USE IN CANADA

In 2002, Bill Fisher of the University of Western Ontario, along with Richard Boroditsky of the University of Manitoba and Brian Morris at the University of Toronto, conducted their fourth national survey on the contraceptive attitudes and behaviours of Canadian women aged 15 to 44 (Fisher et al., 2004a, 2004b). In total, 1582 responses were received for a response rate of 47%, down from 70% in the 1984 Canadian Fertility Study.

Almost all of the women were familiar with oral contraceptives (96%) and condoms (93%). Only around one-half were familiar with other methods such as sterilization (62%), withdrawal (59%), the morning-after pill (57%), and intrauterine devices (50%). Oral contraceptives were by far the preferred method, with 63% favouring them and 31% currently using them. In second place were condoms and sterilization. Thirty-eight percent had a very favourable opinion of con-

doms and 21% were currently using them, while 39% had a very positive view of male sterilization and 15% said their male partner had been sterilized. Nine percent of the respondents reported they did not use contraception.

In analyzing contraceptive trends since 1993, Fisher et al. concluded:

- Canadian women consistently rate oral contraceptives highly and continue to use them more than any other contraceptive.
- Approval ratings for condoms have risen slightly, while actual condom use has declined.
- Female sterilization and IUDs have fallen out of favour.
- Women frequently switch their methods of contraception.
- Younger women are more likely to use oral contraceptives and condoms, while older women are more likely to use sterilization.

Relatively few studies of contraceptive use have focused on immigrant groups in Canada. One exception is a study of ethnic Chinese women in Vancouver who wanted to have an abortion (Wiebe et al., 2002). There was a clear difference between the Chinese women born in Canada and new immigrants. The Chinese immigrant women had more negative attitudes toward the birth control pill. In particular, single female immigrants linked using oral contraceptives with promiscuity and "bad women." Some were also concerned about weight gain and infertility.

A World of Diversity

HISTORY OF BIRTH CONTROL IN CANADA

Birth control was legal in Canada until the nineteenth century, when laws were introduced forbidding the use of birth control and abortion. It was even illegal to provide information about birth control. Because contraceptives were associated with loose morals and prostitution, it was considered unacceptable for doctors to discuss birth control with their patients.

The movement to legalize contraception in Canada began in the 1920s with female activists in Vancouver, who formed the Canadian Birth Control League. In the following years, several women's groups from across Canada also began to lobby politicians to change the law that prohibited the use of birth control. A few men also joined the cause.

Despite protests by some physicians, Mary Hawkins established the first Canadian birth control clinic in

Hamilton, Ontario, in the early 1930s. In 1937, clinics were also set up in Windsor and Kitchener. A prominent supporter of birth control education at that time was A. R. Kaufman, a wealthy Kitchener businessman who hired women to deliver birth control information door to door.

The first major legal challenge to the law forbidding the dissemination of birth control information came with the arrest of Dorothea Palmer (an employee of Kaufman) for promoting birth control in the poorer districts of the Ottawa region. Her arrest sparked protests and support by birth control activists, including Kaufman, who helped to win her acquittal in court. This victory helped to legitimize birth control education and spurred the birth control movement to make greater efforts in the struggle to legalize all birth control activities.

By the 1960s, the use of contraceptives (particularly the birth control pill) had become so widespread that most Canadians did not realize that contraceptives were still illegal. The 1960 arrest of Harold Fine, a Toronto pharmacist, for selling condoms enraged many Canadians. As a result, in 1961 Barbara and George Cadbury established the Planned Parenthood Association of Toronto with the objective of amending the Criminal Code.

And in 1965 another leader in the birth control movement, Dr. Marion Powell, opened the first city-funded public health clinic (focused on family planning) in Scarborough, Ontario.

In 1963 the General Council of the Canadian Medical Association supported an amendment to the Criminal Code to decriminalize contraception. That year the first bill was submitted in Parliament calling for the removal of birth control from the Criminal Code. However, it was not until 1969, under the leadership of Prime Minister Pierre Trudeau, that contraception became legal and abortion was allowed under restricted conditions.

Since 1988, the provision of contraceptive advice and services by physicians has been considered an essential part of their role. In 2002, for example, the Ontario College of Physicians and

Surgeons charged a Barrie physician who refused to prescribe the birth control pill to unmarried women with professional misconduct. The physician, a born-again Christian, believed that prescribing the pill would promote fornication.

The use of **artificial contraception** continues to be opposed by many groups, including the Roman Catholic Church. Yet many individual Catholics, including many priests, hold liberal attitudes toward contraception.

Sources: The Planned Parenthood Federation of Canada (1999), A History of Birth Control in Canada; Kimberly E. Liu and William A. Fisher (2002), "Canadian Physician's Role in Contraception from the 19th Century to Now," Journal of Obstetrics and Gynaecology Canada, 24(3), 239–44.

Methods of Contraception

There are many methods of contraception, including oral contraceptives (the pill), intrauterine devices (IUDs), diaphragms, spermicides, condoms, withdrawal (coitus interruptus), and timing of ovulation (rhythm). There are also other less used methods and some devices under development.

Oral Contraceptives ("the Pill")

An **oral contraceptive** is commonly referred to as a birth-control pill or simply "the pill." However, there are many kinds of birth-control pills that vary in the type and dosages of hormones they contain. Birth-control pills fall into two major categories: combination pills and minipills.

Combination pills contain a combination of synthetic forms of the hormones estrogen and progesterone (progestin). Most combination pills provide a steady dose of synthetic estrogen and progesterone. Other combination pills, called *multiphasic* pills, vary the dosage of these hormones across the menstrual cycle to reduce the overall dosages to which the woman is exposed and possible side effects. The **minipill** contains synthetic progesterone (progestin) only.

Available only by prescription, oral contraceptives (OCs) are currently used by 31% of women in Canada (Fisher et al., 2003). The great majority of Canadian women (83%) use the pill at some time, and, on average, women begin using the pill at age 17. Thirty-four percent of women begin taking the pill before initiating intercourse and 15% start pill use and having intercourse at the same time.

The study respondents generally overestimated negative side effects and underestimated positive effects. Many women were not aware that the pill can make periods lighter and reduce the risk of certain cancers (Fisher et al., 2003).

HOW THEY WORK   Women cannot conceive when they are already pregnant because their bodies suppress maturation of egg follicles and ovulation. The combination pill fools the brain into acting as though the woman is already pregnant, so

The Canadian Federation for Sexual Health Formerly the Planned Parenthood Federation of Canada, this organization is dedicated to promoting sexual and reproductive health.
www.cfsh.ca

Artificial contraception A method of contraception that applies a human-made device.

Oral contraceptive A contraceptive, consisting of sex hormones, which is taken by mouth.

Combination pill A birth-control pill that contains synthetic estrogen and progesterone.

Minipill A birth-control pill that contains synthetic progesterone but no estrogen.

that no additional ova mature or are released. If ovulation does not take place, a woman cannot become pregnant.

In a normal menstrual cycle, low levels of estrogen during and just after the menstrual phase stimulate the pituitary gland to secrete FSH, which in turn stimulates the maturation of ovarian follicles. The estrogen in the combination pill inhibits FSH production, so follicles do not mature. The progesterone (progestin) inhibits the pituitary's secretion of LH, which would otherwise lead to ovulation. The woman continues to have menstrual periods, but there is no unfertilized ovum to be sloughed off in the menstrual flow.

The combination pill is taken for 21 days of the typical 28-day cycle. Then, for seven days, the woman takes either no pill at all or an inert placebo pill to maintain the habit of taking a pill a day. The sudden drop in hormone levels causes the endometrium to disintegrate and menstruation to follow three or four days after the last pill has been taken. Then the cycle is repeated.

The progestin in the combination pill also increases the thickness and acidity of the cervical mucus. The mucus thus becomes a more resistant barrier to sperm and inhibits development of the endometrium. Therefore, even if an egg were somehow to mature and become fertilized in a fallopian tube, sperm would not be likely to survive the passage through the cervix. Even if sperm were somehow to succeed in fertilizing an egg, the failure of the endometrium to develop would mean that the fertilized ovum could not become implanted in the uterus. Progestin may also impede the progress of ova through the fallopian tubes and make it more difficult for sperm to penetrate ova.

The minipill contains progestin but no estrogen. Minipills are taken daily through the menstrual cycle, even during menstruation. They act in two ways. They thicken the cervical mucus to impede the passage of sperm through the cervix, and they render the inner lining of the uterus less receptive to a fertilized egg. Thus, even if the woman does conceive, the fertilized egg will pass from the body rather than becoming implanted in the uterine wall. It contains no estrogen, so the mini pill does not usually prevent ovulation. The combination pill, by contrast, works directly to prevent ovulation.

EFFECTIVENESS OF BIRTH-CONTROL PILLS The failure rate of the birth-control pill associated with perfect use is very low: 0.5% or less, depending on the type of pill (see Table 11.1). The failure rate increases to 3% in typical use. Failures can occur when women forget to take the pill for two days or more, when they do not use backup methods when they first go on the pill, and when they switch from one brand to another.

Half of Canadian women believe that it is easy to forget to take the pill every day. Sixty-two percent of current OC users report they had missed at least one pill during the previous six months (Fisher et al., 2003).

In 2004 the World Health Organization (WHO) issued new guidelines regarding missed pills. First, a woman who misses taking a pill should take one as soon as possible and then continue taking one each day. However, a woman who misses three or more combination pills in a row should use condoms or abstain from sexual intercourse until she has taken pills for seven days in a row. With the lowest-dose pills, a woman should take extra precautions after missing two (Info Reports, 2005).

REVERSIBILITY The use of oral contraceptives may temporarily reduce fertility after they are discontinued but is not associated with permanent infertility (Mishell, 1989). Nine of ten women begin ovulating regularly within three months of suspending use (Reinisch, 1990). However, women who frequently start and stop usage may later incur fertility problems (Reinisch, 1990). When a woman appears not to be ovulating after going off the pill, a drug like clomiphene is often used to induce ovulation.

ADVANTAGES AND DISADVANTAGES The great advantage of oral contraception is that when used properly, it is nearly 100% effective. Unlike many other forms of contraception, such as the condom or diaphragm, its use does not interfere with sexual spontaneity or diminish sexual sensations. The sex act need not be interrupted, as it would be by use of a condom.

Birth-control pills may also have some *healthful* side effects. They appear to reduce the risk of pelvic inflammatory disease (PID), benign ovarian cysts, and fibrocystic (benign) breast growths (Gilbert, 1996). The pill regularizes menstrual cycles and reduces menstrual cramping and premenstrual discomfort. The pill may also be helpful in the treatment of iron-deficiency anemia and facial acne. The combination pill reduces the risks of ovarian and endometrial cancer, even for a number of years after the woman has stopped taking it (Gnagy et al., 2000; Hatcher & Guillebaud, 1998; Narod et al., 1998). The pill's protective effects against invasive ovarian cancer increase with the length of use (Gnagy et al., 2000).

The pill does have some disadvantages. It confers no protection against STIs. Canadian women who use the pill are more likely to report a history of STIs than are condom users. Typically, women stop using condoms when they begin using the pill (Fisher et al., 2003). Moreover, it may reduce the effectiveness of antibiotics used to treat STIs. Going on the pill requires medical consultation, so a woman must plan to begin using the pill at least several weeks before becoming sexually active or before discontinuing the use of other contraceptives.

The main drawbacks of birth-control pills are potential side effects and possible health risks. Although a good deal of research suggests that the pill is safe for healthy women, in 2000 the American College of Obstetricians and Gynecologists released a bulletin suggesting caution in women with various pre-existing medical conditions. These include hypertension, diabetes, migraine headaches, fibrocystic breast tissue, uterine fibroids, and elevated cholesterol level (Voelker, 2000).

The estrogen in combination pills may produce side effects such as nausea and vomiting, fluid retention (feeling bloated), weight gain, increased vaginal discharge, headaches, tenderness in the breasts, and dizziness. Many of these are temporary. When they persist, women may be switched from one pill to another, perhaps to one with lower doses of hormones. Pregnant women produce high estrogen levels in the corpus luteum and placenta. The combination pill artificially raises levels of estrogen, so it is not surprising that some women who use it have side effects that mimic the early signs of pregnancy, such as weight gain or nausea ("morning sickness"). Weight gain can result from estrogen (through fluid retention) or progestin (through increased appetite and development of muscle). Oral contraceptives may also increase blood pressure in some women, but clinically significant elevations are rare in women who use the low-dose pills available today (Hatcher, 2001). Still, it is wise for women who use the pill to have their blood pressure checked regularly. Women who encounter problems with high blood pressure from taking the pill are usually advised to switch to another form of contraception.

Many women experience hormone withdrawal symptoms during periods when they do not take the pill (Sulak et al., 2000). These include headaches, pelvic pain, bloating, and breast tenderness.

Many women have avoided using the pill because of the risk of blood clots. The lower dosages of estrogen found in most types of birth-control pills today are associated with much lower risk of blood clots than was the case in the 1960s and 1970s, when higher dosages were used (Gilbert, 1996). Still, women who are at increased risk for blood clotting, such as women with a history of circulatory problems or stroke, are typically advised not to use the pill.

Women who are considering using the pill need to weigh the benefits and risks with their health-care providers. For the great majority of young, healthy women in their 20s and early 30s, the pill is unlikely to cause blood clots or other cardiovascular problems (Hatcher & Guillebaud, 1998). Although research has found the pill to be safe for most women who do not smoke and are younger than 35, pill users may have a slightly higher chance than nonusers of developing blood clots in the veins and lungs, stroke, and heart attack (Rako, 2003).

Some women should not be on the pill at all (Calderone & Johnson, 1989; Hatcher, 2001; Reinisch, 1990). These include women who have had circulatory problems or blood clots and those who have suffered a heart attack or stroke or have a history of coronary disease, breast or uterine cancer, undiagnosed genital bleeding, liver tumours, or sickle-cell anemia (because of associated blood-clotting problems). Because of their increased risk of cardiovascular problems, caution should be exercised when the combination pill is used with women over 35 years of age who smoke (Hatcher, 2001). Nursing mothers should also avoid using the pill; the hormones may be passed to the baby in the mother's milk.

The pill may also have psychological effects. Some users report depression or irritability. Switching brands or altering doses may help. Evidence is lacking concerning the effects of lower-estrogen pills on sexual desire.

Progestin fosters male secondary sex characteristics, so women who take the minipill may develop acne, facial hair, thinning of scalp hair, reduction in breast size, vaginal dryness, and missed or shorter periods. Irregular bleeding, or so-called breakthrough bleeding, between menstrual periods is a common side effect of the minipill. Irregular bleeding should be brought to the attention of a health professional. Because they can produce vaginal dryness, minipills can hinder vaginal lubrication during intercourse, decreasing sexual sensations and rendering sex painful.

Results from several large-scale studies show no overall increase in the rates of breast cancer among pill users (Hatcher, 2001). The evidence linking use of the pill to increased risk of cervical cancer is mixed, with some studies showing such a link and others showing none (Hatcher, 2001).

Women considering the pill are advised to have a thorough medical evaluation to rule out pre-existing conditions that might make its use unsafe. Women who begin to use the pill, regardless of their age or risk status, should pay attention to changes in their physical condition, have regular checkups, and promptly report any physical complaints or unusual symptoms to their physicians.

EMERGENCY CONTRACEPTION (EC) Emergency contraception (the so-called morning-after pill) is taken after sexual intercourse. The most recommended EC pill is levonorgestrel, also know as Plan B. It is not generally considered an abortion pill because it cannot end an established pregnancy. Rather, Plan B prevents ovulation by preventing the joining of sperm and egg and by preventing a fertilized egg from attaching to the uterine wall.

EC should be taken as soon as possible after unprotected intercourse. It is most effective when taken within 72 hours. More recent research suggests it may still be effective even if taken within 120 hours. The World Health Organization recommends a single 1.5 mg pill of levonorgestrel (Info Reports, 2005). The other option is two 0.75 doses of levonorgestrel. An alternative EC is the Yuzpe regimen, which consists of two doses of combined estrogen-levonorgestrel with the second dose taken 12 hours after the first.

Slightly less than half of Canadian women report being familiar with the morning-after pill (Fisher et al., 2003). In 2005, Health Canada allowed pharmacists to provide Plan B without a prescription. Previously, Plan B had been available without a doctor's prescription only in British Columbia, Quebec, and Ontario. In British Columbia, more than half of the women who obtained the morning-after pill from a pharmacist did so on evenings or weekends (PPFC, 2002). However, because Plan B is no longer a prescription drug in Canada, it is not covered under drug benefit plans. The medication costs about $25.

In contrast, the Food and Drug Administration in the United States refused to make a decision on allowing Plan B without prescription. This action was contrary

Research in Action

USE OF EMERGENCY CONTRACEPTION

In British Columbia a study was done of EC use both before and after the treatment was provided without a prescription (Soon et al., 2005). The key findings were:

- EC use was highest among women aged 20–24 years; the second-highest users were 15–19-year-olds.
- More than half of users (56%) obtained EC within 24 hours of having unprotected intercourse, and almost all (98%) within 72 hours.

- Very few women used EC on a regular basis, with only 2.5% receiving EC three or more times a year and 1.1% obtaining EC for future use.
- More than half of women receiving EC (56%) reported using a method of birth control that had failed.
- The provision of EC without a doctor's prescription significantly increased the use of EC.

The researchers concluded that the provision of EC without a prescription will be an important factor in reducing unwanted pregnancies and abortions in Canada.

to the advice of its own scientific advisors, clearly indicating that the U.S. agency was responding to political pressure from conservative politicians. The anti-abortion movement in the United States had intensely lobbied President Bush not to allow over-the-counter sales of EC because they believed that this would encourage more teenagers to engage in sex (Associated Press, 2005).

EC pills have a higher hormone content than most birth-control pills. For this reason, nausea is a common side effect, occurring in perhaps 70% of users. Nausea is usually mild and passes within a day or two after treatment, but it can be treated with antinausea medication (Hatcher, 2001). Because of the strength of the dosage, the EC pill is not recommended as a regular form of birth control.

Intrauterine Devices (IUDs)

Intrauterine devices (IUDs) are small objects of various shapes that are inserted into the uterus. IUDs have been used by humans since Greek times. Today, they are inserted into the uterus by a physician or nurse practitioner and are usually left in place for a year or more. Fine plastic threads or strings hang down from the IUD into the vagina, so that the woman can check to be sure it is still in place.

IUDs are used by more than 80 million women around the world (Hatcher, 2001). IUDs are used by only 1% of sexually active women of child-bearing age in Canada (Fisher et al., 2003).

IUDs achieved their greatest popularity in Canada in the 1960s and 1970s. A sharp drop-off in their use during the 1980s occurred after a popular model, the Dalkon Shield, was linked to a high incidence of pelvic infections and tubal infertility (Hatcher, 2001).

The only IUD currently available in Canada, the Nova-T, is a T-shaped copper-based device (see Figure 11.1). The Nova-T can be left in place for seven years (Montreal Health Press, 1999), unless the woman is allergic to copper (Hatcher et al., 1994).

HOW THEY WORK We do not know exactly how IUDs work. A foreign body, such as the IUD, apparently irritates the uterine lining. This irritation gives rise to mild inflammation and to the production of antibodies that may be toxic to sperm or to fertilized ova and/or may prevent fertilized eggs from becoming implanted.

> **Intrauterine device** A small object that is inserted into the uterus and left in place to prevent conception. Abbreviated IUD.

Figure 11.1 Nova-T.

Nova-T is the only IUD available in Canada. A T-shaped copper-based device, it can be left in place for seven years, unless the woman is allergic to copper.

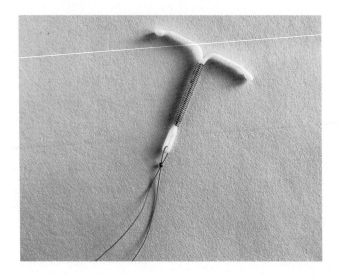

EFFECTIVENESS The failure rate associated with typical use of IUDs is about 2% or less (see Table 11.1). Most failures occur within three months of insertion, often because the device shifts position or is expelled.

The IUD may irritate the muscular layer of the uterine wall, causing contractions that expel it through the vagina. The device is most likely to be expelled during menstruation, so users are advised to check their sanitary napkins or tampons before discarding them. Women who use IUDs are advised to check the string several times a month to ensure that the IUD is in place. Spontaneous expulsions occur in 2% to 10% of users within the first year of use (Stewart, 1998).

REVERSIBILITY IUDs may be removed readily by professionals. About 9 out of 10 former IUD users who wish to do so become pregnant within a year (Hatcher, 2001).

ADVANTAGES AND DISADVANTAGES The IUD has three major advantages: (1) it is highly effective; (2) it does not diminish sexual spontaneity or sexual sensations; and (3) once it is in place, the woman need not do anything more to prevent pregnancy (other than check that it remains in place). The small risk of failure is reduced in effect to zero if the couple also use an additional form of birth control, such as the diaphragm or condom.

If IUDs are so effective and relatively "maintenance free," why are they not more popular? One reason is that insertion can be painful. Another reason is side effects. The most common side effects are excessive menstrual cramping, irregular bleeding (spotting) between periods, and heavier-than-usual menstrual bleeding (Hatcher, 2001). These generally occur shortly following insertion and are among the primary reasons why women ask to have the device removed. A more serious concern is the possible risk of pelvic inflammatory disease (PID), a serious disease that can become life-threatening if left untreated (Stewart, 1998). Women who use the IUD may have an increased risk of PID (Cates, 1998).

PID can produce scar tissue that blocks the fallopian tubes, causing infertility. Women with pelvic infections should not use an IUD (Stewart, 1998). Women who have risk factors for PID may also wish to consider the advisability of an IUD. Risk factors include a recent episode of gonorrhea or chlamydia, recurrent episodes of these STIs, sexual contact with multiple partners, and sexual contact with a partner who has had multiple sexual partners.

Another risk in using an IUD is that the device may perforate (tear) the uterine or cervical walls, which can cause bleeding, pain, and adhesions and become life-threatening. Perforations are usually caused by improper insertion and occur in perhaps 1 case in 1000 (Reinisch, 1990). IUD users are also at greater risk for ectopic pregnancies, both during and after usage, and for miscarriage. Ectopic pregnancies occur in about 5% of women who become pregnant while using an IUD (Hatcher, 2001).

The Diaphragm

The **diaphragm** is a shallow cup or dome made of thin latex rubber (see Figure 11.2). The rim is a flexible metal ring covered with rubber. Diaphragms come in different sizes to allow a precise fit.

Diaphragms are available by prescription and must be fitted to the contour of the vagina by a health professional. Several sizes and types of diaphragms may be tried during a fitting. Women practise insertion in a health professional's office so that they can be guided as needed.

HOW IT WORKS The diaphragm is inserted and removed by the woman, much like a tampon. It is akin to a condom in that it forms a barrier against sperm when placed snugly over the cervical opening. Yet it is unreliable when used alone. Thus, the diaphragm should be used in conjunction with a spermicidal cream or jelly. The diaphragm's main function is to keep the spermicide in place.

HOW IT IS USED The diaphragm should be inserted no more than two hours before coitus, because the spermicides that are used may begin to lose effectiveness beyond this time. Some health professionals, however, suggest that the diaphragm may be inserted up to six hours preceding intercourse. (It seems reasonable to err on the side of caution and assume that there is a two-hour time limit.) The woman or her partner places a tablespoonful of spermicidal cream or jelly on the inside of

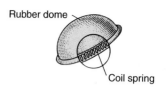
Rubber dome
Coil spring

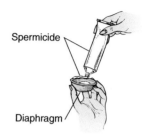
Spermicide
Diaphragm

Figure 11.2 A Diaphragm.

The diaphragm is a shallow cup or dome made of latex. Diaphragms must be fitted to the contour of the vagina by a health professional. The diaphragm forms a barrier to sperm but should be used in conjunction with a spermicidal cream or jelly.

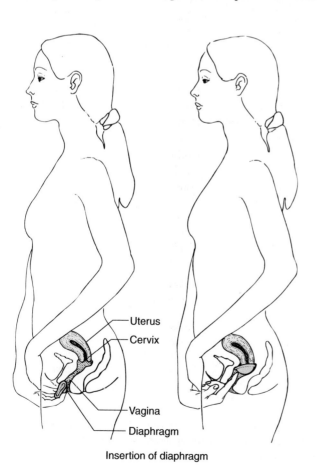
Uterus
Cervix
Vagina
Diaphragm
Insertion of diaphragm

Figure 11.3 Inserting and Checking the Diaphragm.

Women are instructed in the insertion of the diaphragm by a health professional. In practice, a woman and her partner may find inserting it together an erotic experience.

Diaphragm A shallow rubber cup or dome, fitted to the contour of a woman's vagina, that is coated with a spermicide and inserted prior to coitus to prevent conception.

the cup and spreads it inside the rim. (Cream spread outside the rim might cause the diaphragm to slip.) The woman opens the inner lips of the vagina with one hand and folds the diaphragm with the other by squeezing the ring. She inserts the diaphragm against the cervix, with the inner side facing upward (see Figure 11.3). Her partner can help insert the diaphragm, but the woman is advised to check its placement. Some women prefer a plastic insertion device, but most find it easier to insert the diaphragm without it. The diaphragm should be left in place *at least six hours* after intercourse to allow the spermicide to kill any remaining sperm in the vagina (Hatcher, 2001). To guard against toxic shock syndrome (TSS), it should not be left in place longer than 24 hours.

After use, the diaphragm should be washed with mild soap and warm water and stored in a dry, cool place. When cared for properly, a diaphragm can last about two years. Women may need to be refitted after pregnancy or a change in weight of 5 kilograms (10 pounds) or more.

EFFECTIVENESS If it is used consistently and correctly, the failure rate of the diaphragm is estimated to be 6% during the first year of use (see Table 11.1). In typical use, however, the failure rate is believed to be three times as high—18%. Some women become pregnant because they do not use the diaphragm during every coital experience. Others may insert it too early or not leave it in long enough. The diaphragm may not fit well, or it may slip—especially if the couple is acrobatic. Effectiveness is also seriously compromised when the diaphragm is not used along with a correctly applied spermicide.

ADVANTAGES AND DISADVANTAGES The major advantage of the diaphragm is that when used correctly, it is a safe and effective means of birth control and does not alter the woman's hormone production or reproductive cycle. The diaphragm can be used as needed, whereas the pill must be used daily and the IUD remains in place whether or not the woman engages in coitus. Another advantage is the virtual absence of side effects. The few women who are allergic to the rubber in the diaphragm can switch to a plastic model.

The major disadvantage is the high pregnancy rate associated with typical use. Nearly 1 in 5 typical users (18%) of the diaphragm combined with spermicidal cream or jelly becomes pregnant during the first year of use (Hatcher, 2001). Another disadvantage is the need to insert the diaphragm prior to intercourse, which the couple may find disruptive. The woman's partner may find the taste of the spermicides used in conjunction with the diaphragm to be unpleasant during

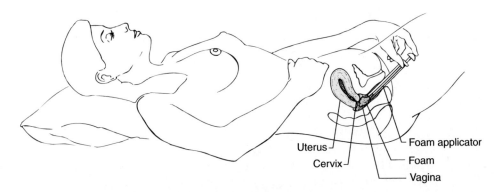

Uterus — Foam applicator
Cervix — Foam
— Vagina

Figure 11.4 Applying Spermicidal Foam.

Spermicidal jellies and creams come in tubes with plastic applicators. Spermicidal foam comes in a pressurized can and is applied with a plastic applicator in much the same way as spermicidal jellies and creams.

oral sex. About 1 woman or man in 20 may develop allergies to the particular spermicide that is used, which can lead to irritation of the genitals. This problem may also be alleviated by switching to another brand.

Spermicides

Spermicides are agents that kill sperm. They come in different forms, including jellies and creams, suppositories, aerosol foam, and a contraceptive film. Spermicides should be left in place in the vagina (no douching) for *at least 6 to 8 hours* after coitus (Cates & Raymond, 1998).

HOW THEY ARE USED   Spermicidal jellies, creams, foam, and suppositories should be used no more than 60 minutes preceding coitus to provide maximum effectiveness (Cates & Raymond, 1998). Spermicidal jellies and creams come in tubes with plastic applicators that introduce the spermicide into the vagina (see Figure 11.4). Spermicidal foam is a fluffy white cream with the consistency of shaving cream. It is contained in a pressurized can and is introduced with a plastic applicator in much the same way as spermicidal jellies and creams.

Vaginal suppositories are inserted into the upper vagina, near the cervix, where they release spermicide as they dissolve. Unlike spermicidal jellies, creams, and foam, which become effective immediately when applied, suppositories must be inserted no less than 10 to 15 minutes before coitus so that they have sufficient time to dissolve (Cates & Raymond, 1998).

Spermicidal film consists of thin, 5-centimetre (2-inch) square sheets saturated with spermicide. When placed in the vagina, they dissolve into a gel and release the spermicide. The spermicidal film should be inserted at least five minutes before intercourse to allow time for it to melt and for the spermicide to be dispersed. It remains effective for upwards of one hour. Some users find that it tends to adhere to the fingertips, which makes it difficult to insert correctly.

HOW THEY WORK   Spermicides coat the cervical opening, blocking the passage of sperm and killing sperm by chemical action.

EFFECTIVENESS   In typical use, the first-year failure rate of spermicides used alone is 21 pregnancies per year per 100 users (Cates & Raymond, 1998). When used correctly and consistently, the failure rate is estimated to drop to about 6 pregnancies per 100 users in the first year. All forms of spermicide are more effective when they are combined with other forms of contraception, such as the condom.

ADVANTAGES AND DISADVANTAGES   The major advantages of spermicides are that they do not alter the woman's natural biological processes and are applied only as needed. Unlike a diaphragm, they do not require a doctor's prescription or a fitting.

The major disadvantage is the high failure rate among typical users. Foam often fails when the can is not shaken enough, when too little is used, when it is not applied deeply enough within the vagina near the cervix, or when it is used after coitus has begun.

Spermicides occasionally cause vaginal or penile irritation. Some partners find the taste of spermicides unpleasant. (Couples can engage in oral sex before applying spermicides.) Spermicides may pose a danger to an embryo, so women who suspect they are pregnant are advised to suspend use until they find out for certain.

It was once thought that spermicides that contain nonoxynol-9 might provide some protection against STIs such as HIV/AIDS, genital herpes, trichomoniasis ("trich"), syphilis, and chlamydia (Reinisch, 1990). Yet a controlled experiment in Africa did not find that nonoxynol-9 afforded any protection against disease-causing agents (Roddy et al., 1998). In fact, some research suggests that nonoxynol-9

Figure 11.5 Condoms.

Some condoms are plain-tipped, whereas others have nipples or reservoirs that catch semen and may help prevent the condom from bursting during ejaculation. Latex condoms form effective barriers to the tiny AIDS virus.

Prophylactic An agent that protects against disease.

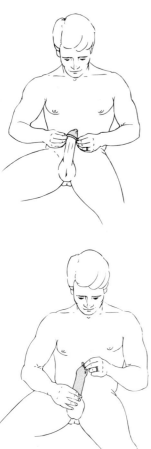

Figure 11.6 Applying a Condom.

First the rolled-up condom is placed on the head of the penis, and then it is rolled down the shaft of the penis.

If a condom without a reservoir tip is used, a 1-centimetre (half-inch) space should be left at the tip for the ejaculate to accumulate.

may actually increase the risk of HIV infection by causing lesions and ulcerations to the mucous membranes of the genitals (Cherniak, 1999).

Male Condoms.

Condoms are also called "rubbers," "safes," **prophylactics** (because latex condoms protect against HIV and other STIs), and "skins" (referring to those that are made from lamb intestines). They are less effective than the pill or IUD, may disrupt sexual spontaneity, and can decrease coital sensations because they prevent the penis from actually touching the vaginal wall.

Most Canadian women (76%) have used a condom at least once, and 21% indicate that the condom is their current method of contraception (Fisher et al., 2003). Among those who report using only condoms, 70% indicated using condoms every time they have intercourse.

Typically Canadian women use condoms when first beginning a sexual relationship with a new partner and then switch to OCs. The most common reasons given for discontinuing condom use are that the woman has only one partner (47%), or that she knows and trusts her partner (46%). Other reasons are decreased sexual sensation for the partner (19%) or for the woman (14%). Only 4% of women say they stopped using a condom because their partner refused to use them; however, 14% say it would be difficult to get their partner to use condoms.

Typically, discussions about condoms and sexual pleasure focus on male sexual pleasure. However, among Canadian women who have used condoms, about as many say that condoms make sex less enjoyable for women (30%) as for men (33%) (Fisher et al., 2003).

Some condoms are made of latex rubber. Thinner, more expensive condoms ("skins") are made from the intestinal membranes of lambs. The latter allow greater sexual sensation but do not protect so well against STIs. Only latex condoms are effective against the tiny AIDS virus. Some condoms have plain ends. Others have nipples or reservoirs (see Figure 11.5) that catch semen and may help prevent the condom from bursting during ejaculation.

HOW THEY WORK A condom is a cylindrical sheath that serves as a barrier, preventing the passage of sperm and disease-carrying micro-organisms from the man to his partner. It also helps prevent infected vaginal fluids (and micro-organisms) from entering the man's urethral opening or penetrating through small cracks in the skin of the penis.

HOW THEY ARE USED The condom is rolled onto the penis once erection is achieved and before contact between the penis and the vagina (see Figure 11.6). If the condom is *not* used until moments before the point of ejaculation, sperm-carrying fluid from the Cowper's glands or from preorgasmic spasms may already have passed into the vagina. Nor does the condom afford protection against STIs if it is fitted after penetration. In a study of condom users at Indiana University, 43%

of the males reported that sometimes they did not put the condom on until after they started having intercourse and 15% sometimes removed the condom before they had finished intercourse (Crosby et al., 2002).

Between 1% and 2% of condoms break or fall off during intercourse or when the penis is being withdrawn afterward (Warner & Hatcher, 1998). Condoms also sometimes slip down the shaft of the penis without falling off.

Applied Knowledge

USING A CONDOM EFFECTIVELY

To use a condom most effectively and to help prevent it from either breaking or falling off, a couple should observe the following guidelines:

- Use a condom each and every time you have intercourse. Inexperienced users should also practise putting on a condom before they have occasion to use one with a partner.
- Handle the condom carefully, making sure not to damage it with your fingernails, teeth, or sharp objects.
- Place the condom on the erect penis before it touches the vulva.
- Uncircumcised men should pull back the foreskin before putting on the condom.
- If you use a spermicide, put some inside the tip of the condom before placing the condom on the penis. You may also wish to use additional spermicide applied by an applicator inside the vagina to provide extra protection, especially in the event that the condom breaks.
- Do not pull the condom tightly against the tip of the penis.
- For a condom without a reservoir tip, leave a small empty space—about a centimetre (half an inch)—at the end of the condom to hold semen, yet do not

allow any air to be trapped at the tip. Some condoms come equipped with a reservoir (nipple) tip that will hold semen.
- Unroll the condom all the way to the base of the penis.
- Ensure that adequate vaginal lubrication during intercourse is present, using lubricants if necessary. But use only water-based lubricants such as contraceptive jelly or K-Y jelly. Never use an oil-based lubricant that can weaken the latex material, such as petroleum jelly (Vaseline), cold cream, baby oil or lotion, mineral oil, massage oil, vegetable oil, Crisco, hand or body lotions, and most skin creams. Do not use saliva as a lubricant because it may contain infectious organisms, such as viruses.
- If the condom breaks during intercourse, withdraw the penis immediately, put on a new condom, and use more spermicide.
- After ejaculation, carefully withdraw the penis while it is still erect.
- Hold the rim of the condom firmly against the base of the penis as the penis is withdrawn, to prevent the condom from slipping off.
- Remove the condom carefully from the penis, making sure that semen doesn't leak out.
- Wrap the used condom in a tissue, and discard it in the garbage.

(Condoms can be hard to flush down the toilet.) Wash your hands thoroughly with soap and water.

Because condoms can be eroded by exposure to body heat or other sources of heat, they should not be kept for any length of time in a pocket or the glove compartment of a car. Nor should a condom be used more than once. Here are some other things you should *never* do with a condom:

- Never test a condom by inflating it or stretching it.
- Never use a condom after its expiration date.
- Never use damaged condoms. Condoms that are sticky, gummy, discoloured, brittle, or show other signs of deterioration should be considered damaged.
- Never use a condom if the sealed packet containing the condom is damaged, cracked, or brittle; the condom itself may be damaged or defective.
- Do not open the sealed packet until you are ready to use the condom. A condom contained in a packet that has been opened can become dry and brittle within a few hours, causing it to tear more easily. The box that contains the condom packets, however, may be opened at any time.
- Never use the same condom twice. Use a new condom if you switch the site of intercourse,

such as from the vagina to the anus or from the anus to the mouth, during a single sexual act.

■   If you want to carry a condom with you, place it in a loose jacket pocket or purse, not in your pants pocket or in a wallet held in your pants pocket, where it might be exposed to body heat.

EFFECTIVENESS In typical use, the failure rate of the male condom is estimated at 12% (see Table 11.1). That is, 12 women out of 100 whose partners rely on condoms alone for contraception can expect to become pregnant during the first year of use. This rate drops dramatically if the condom is used correctly and combined with the use of a spermicide (Warner & Hatcher, 1998). The effectiveness of a condom and spermicide combined, when used correctly and consistently, rivals that of the birth-control pill.

ADVANTAGES AND DISADVANTAGES Condoms have the advantage of being readily available. They can be purchased without prescription.

One disadvantage of the condom is that it may render sex less spontaneous. The couple must interrupt lovemaking to apply the condom. Condoms may also lessen sexual sensations. Some men experience erectile difficulties when using a condom. In a study of university males, one-fifth lost their erection before the condom was put on and one-fifth lost their erection after the condom was on and intercourse had begun (Crosby et al., 2002). Some males take Viagra as a means of overcoming this problem. Condoms also sometimes slip off or tear, allowing sperm to leak through.

On the other hand, condoms are almost entirely free of side effects. They offer protection against STIs that is unparalleled among contraceptive devices. Both partners can share putting on the condom, which makes it an erotic part of their lovemaking, not an intrusion. The use of textured or ultrathin condoms may increase sensitivity, especially for the male. Sex in the age of AIDS has given condoms a new respectability, even a certain trendiness. Note, for example, the "designer colours" and styles on display at your local pharmacy. Advertisers now also target women in their ads, suggesting that women, like men, can come prepared with condoms.

It is tempting to claim that the condom has a perfect safety record and no side effects. Let us settle for "close to perfect." Some people have allergic reactions to the spermicides with which some lubricated condoms are coated or that the woman may apply. In such cases the couple may need to use a condom without a spermicidal lubricant or stop using supplemental spermicides. Some people are allergic to latex.

Interestingly, although health educators emphasize the importance of using condoms in preventing STI/HIV infection, many people who use condoms do so for pregnancy prevention. In a sample of men and women from Ottawa, more than two-thirds said that the most important reason they used condoms was to prevent pregnancy (Edgley, 2002). And in the Canadian contraceptive study, only 10% of the women who had switched to using condoms from another method of birth control did so to protect against STIs or HIV (Fisher et al., 1999).

There are many factors that might influence the decision to use condoms. Concerns about partner reaction when initiating condom use is discussed in the nearby Research in Action feature.

Research in Action

ATTITUDES TOWARD SUGGESTING A CONDOM

One of the stereotypes about condom use is that people are reluctant to suggest using a condom for fear of offending their partner. In a study of Ontario university students, Davidson-Harden et al. (2000) surveyed attitudes toward people who initiate condom use within the context of exclusive dating relationships. Both men and women rated individuals of either gender who initiated condom use more favourably than unfavourably. The researchers concluded that it has become less socially acceptable to engage in sexual intercourse without using a condom.

In an Ontario study of patrons of singles bars, Herold and Mewhinney (1993) asked about attitudes and intentions toward condom use with someone the person had just met. Almost all the men (96%) and women (98%) said they would have no objection if their partner suggested using a

condom, and only about a quarter of the respondents said they would be uncomfortable suggesting condom use to a new partner. Women were more likely than men to say they would insist on condom use. Eighty-five percent of the women and 57% of the men said they would insist on condom use even if the partner didn't agree, and fewer women (12%) than men (22%) said they would have intercourse if the partner refused to use a condom.

These results suggest that, faced with the prospect of using a condom with a partner one has just met, men are more influenced by the partner's attitudes than are women, perhaps because women worry more than men about getting infected with an STI or the AIDS virus (Herold & Mewhinney, 1993). And given that half of the women and three-quarters of the men said they might be less likely to use a condom in the heat of passion, factors other than partner reluctance, especially the level of arousal, might be more important in explaining the nonuse of a condom.

Withdrawal (Coitus Interruptus)

In *coitus interruptus* (withdrawal), the man removes his penis from the vagina before ejaculating. Withdrawal has a first-year failure rate among typical users of about 20% (Kowal, 1998). There are several reasons for these failures. The man may not withdraw in time. Even if the penis is withdrawn just before ejaculation, some ejaculate may still fall on the vaginal lips, and sperm may find their way to the fallopian tubes. Active sperm may also be present in the *pre*-ejaculatory secretions of fluid from the Cowper's glands, a discharge of which the man is usually unaware and cannot control. Despite the risks of using withdrawal as a method of birth control, 6% of Canadian women report using this method (Fisher et al., 2003).

Fertility Awareness Methods (Rhythm Methods)

Fertility awareness methods, or *rhythm* methods, rely on awareness of the fertile segments of the woman's menstrual cycle. Terms such as *natural birth control* and *natural family planning* also refer to these methods. The essence of such methods is that coitus is avoided on days when conception is most likely. Fertility awareness methods are used by about 2% of sexually active Canadian women aged 15 to 44. While 40% of Canadian women are aware of these methods, only 7% have very favourable opinions of them and only 2% report using them (Fisher et al., 2003).

Because the rhythm method does not employ artificial devices, it is acceptable to the Roman Catholic Church. Fertility awareness methods (FAM) are typically taught by Catholic organizations.

In a survey of married couples who had received instruction about FAM at a Catholic hospital in Ontario (Daly & Herold, 1985), more than half the respondents were Catholic and two-thirds had completed college or university. Interestingly, only a few (17%) cited religious reasons for learning about FAM, with most reporting that it was a safe and healthy alternative to other methods. And although traditional Church teachings about this method emphasize total abstinence from sex during the fertile period, 61% of the couples defined abstinence in a liberal way, as allowing for orgasm through non-intercourse means. Another 17% said that abstinence could include genital contact but not to orgasm. At the time of the study, 42% of the sample were using FAM, 32% had discontinued use, and 25% were using the method to determine the fertile period, at which time they used a barrier device such as a condom. This latter behaviour is also contrary to traditional teachings about FAM. Those continuing to use FAM differed from the other two groups in two main respects: they would be less likely to be upset by having an unplanned pregnancy and were more likely to believe that FAM was extremely effective.

HOW THEY WORK A number of rhythm methods are used to predict the likelihood of conception. They are the mirror images of the methods that couples use to increase their chances of conceiving (see Chapter 10). Methods for enhancing the chances of conception seek to predict the time of ovulation so that the couple can arrange to have sperm present in the woman's reproductive tract at about that time. As methods of *birth control*, rhythm methods seek to predict ovulation so that the couple can *abstain* from coitus when the woman is fertile.

THE CALENDAR METHOD The **calendar method** assumes that ovulation occurs 14 days prior to menstruation. The couple abstains from intercourse during the period that begins three days prior to day 13 (because sperm are unlikely to survive for more than 72 hours in the female reproductive tract) and ends two days after day 15 (because an unfertilized ovum is unlikely to remain receptive to fertilization for longer than 48 hours). The period of abstention thus covers days 10 to 17 of the woman's cycle (Wilcox et al., 2000).

When a woman has regular 28-day cycles, predicting the period of abstention is relatively straightforward. Women with irregular cycles are generally advised to chart their cycles for 10 to 12 months to determine their shortest and longest cycles. The first day of menstruation counts as day 1 of the cycle. The last day of the cycle is the day preceding the onset of menstruation.

Most women who follow the calendar method need to abstain from coitus for at least 10 days during the middle of each cycle. Moreover, the calendar method cannot ensure that the woman's longest or shortest menstrual cycles will occur during the 10- to 12-month period of baseline tracking. Some women, too, have such irregular cycles that the range of "unsafe" days cannot be predicted reliably even if baseline tracking is extended.

THE BASAL BODY TEMPERATURE (BBT) METHOD In the **basal body temperature (BBT) method**, the woman tracks her body temperature upon awakening each morning to detect the small changes that occur directly before and after ovulation. A woman's basal body temperature sometimes dips slightly just before ovulation and then tends to rise between 0.2 and 0.4°C (0.4 and 0.8°F) just before, during, and after ovulation. It remains elevated until the onset of menstruation. (The rise in temperature is caused by the increased production of progesterone by the corpus luteum during the luteal phase of the cycle.) Thermometers that provide finely graded readings, such as electronic thermometers, are best suited for determining minor changes. A major problem with the BBT method is that it does not indicate the several *unsafe* preovulatory days during which sperm deposited in the vagina may remain viable. Rather, the BBT method indicates when a woman *has* ovulated. Thus many women use the calendar method to predict the number of "safe" days prior to ovulation and the BBT method to determine the number of "unsafe" days after. A woman would avoid coitus during the "unsafe" preovulatory period (as determined by the calendar method) and then for three days when her temperature rises and remains elevated. A drawback of the BBT method is that

Calendar method A fertility awareness (rhythm) method of contraception that relies on prediction of ovulation by tracking menstrual cycles, typically for a 10- to 12-month period, and assuming that ovulation occurs 14 days before menstruation.

Basal body temperature (BBT) method A fertility awareness method of contraception that relies on prediction of ovulation by tracking the woman's temperature during the course of the menstrual cycle.

changes in body temperature may also result from factors unrelated to ovulation, such as infections, sleeplessness, and stress. This is why some women triple-check themselves by also tracking their cervical mucus.

THE CERVICAL MUCUS (OVULATION) METHOD   The **ovulation method** tracks changes in the **viscosity** of the cervical mucus. Following menstruation, the vagina feels rather dry. There is also little or no discharge from the cervix. These dry days are relatively safe. Then a mucus discharge appears in the vagina that is first thick, sticky, and white or cloudy in colour. Coitus (or unprotected coitus) should be avoided at the first sign of any mucus. As the cycle progresses, the mucus discharge thins and clears, becoming slippery or stringy, like raw egg white. These are the **peak days**. This mucus discharge, called the *ovulatory mucus*, may be accompanied by a feeling of vaginal lubrication or wetness. Ovulation takes place about a day after the last peak day (about four days after this ovulatory mucus first appears). Then the mucus becomes cloudy and tacky once more. Intercourse may resume four days following the last peak day.

One problem with the mucus method is that some women have difficulty detecting changes in the mucus discharge. Such changes may also result from infections, certain medications, or contraceptive creams, jellies, or foam. Sexual arousal may also induce changes in viscosity.

OVULATION-PREDICTION KITS   Predicting ovulation is more accurate with an ovulation-prediction kit. These kits enable women to test their urine daily for the presence of luteinizing hormone (LH). LH levels surge about 12 to 24 hours prior to ovulation. Ovulation-prediction kits are more accurate than the BBT method. Some couples use the kits to enhance their chances of conceiving a child by engaging in coitus when ovulation appears imminent. Others use them as a means of birth control to find out when to avoid coitus. When used correctly, ovulation-predicting kits are highly accurate.

Ovulation kits are expensive and require that the woman's urine be tested each morning. Nor do they reveal the full range of the unsafe *pre*ovulatory period during which sperm may remain viable in the vagina. A couple might thus choose to use the kits to determine the unsafe period following ovulation and use the calendar method to determine the unsafe period preceding ovulation.

EFFECTIVENESS   The estimated first-year failure rate in typical use is 20%, which is high but no higher than that for the use of contraceptive devices such as the cervical cap or the female condom (see Table 11.1). Still, perhaps one in five typical users will become pregnant during the first year of use. (You may have heard the joke: "What do you call people who use the rhythm method? Parents!") Fewer failures occur when these methods are applied conscientiously, when a combination of rhythm methods is used, and when the woman's cycles are quite regular. Restricting coitus to the postovulatory period can reduce the pregnancy rate to 1% (Jennings et al., 1998). The trick is to determine when ovulation occurs. The pregnancy rate can be reduced to practically zero if rhythm methods are used with other forms of birth control, such as the condom or diaphragm.

ADVANTAGES AND DISADVANTAGES   Because they are a natural form of birth control, rhythm methods appeal to many people who, for religious or other reasons, prefer not to use artificial means. No devices or chemicals are used, so there are no side effects. Nor do they cause any loss of sensation, as condoms do. Nor is there disruption of lovemaking, as with condoms, diaphragms, or foam, although lovemaking could be said to be quite "disrupted" during the period of abstention. Rhythm methods are inexpensive, except for ovulation-prediction kits. Both partners may share the responsibility for rhythm methods. The man, for example, can take his partner's temperature or assist with the charting. All rhythm methods are fully reversible.

Ovulation method A fertility awareness method of contraception that relies on prediction of ovulation by tracking the viscosity of the cervical mucus.

Viscosity Stickiness, consistency.

Peak days The days during the menstrual cycle when a woman is most likely to be fertile.

A disadvantage is the fact that the reliability of rhythm methods is low. Rhythm methods may be unsuitable for women with irregular cycles. Women with irregular cycles who ovulate as early as a week after their menstrual flows can become pregnant even if they engage in unprotected intercourse only when they are menstruating, because some sperm remaining in a woman's reproductive tract may survive for up to eight days and fertilize an ovum that is released at that time. Moreover, the rhythm method requires abstaining from coitus for several days, or perhaps weeks, each month. Rhythm methods also require that records of the menstrual cycle be kept for many months prior to implementation. Unlike diaphragms, condoms, or spermicides, rhythm methods cannot be used at a moment's notice. Finally, rhythm methods do not offer any protection against STIs.

Sterilization

Many people decide to be sterilized when they plan to have no children or no more children. With the exception of abstinence, sterilization is the most effective form of contraception. Yet the prospect of **sterilization** arouses strong feelings because a person is transformed all at once, and presumably permanently, from someone who might be capable of bearing children to someone who cannot. This transformation often involves a profound change in self-concept. These feelings are especially strong in men and women who link fertility to their sense of masculinity or femininity.

Sterilization is the most widely used form of birth control among Canadian married couples aged 35 to 44. Among Canadian women in this group 32% report that their male partner has been sterilized while 14% report that they themselves have been sterilized (Fisher et al., 2003). Married women in Canada are more likely to rely on a permanent method of contraception (tubal sterilization or vasectomy) than are single women.

MALE STERILIZATION   The male sterilization procedure used today is the **vasectomy**.

A vasectomy is usually carried out in a doctor's office, under local anaesthesia, in 15 to 20 minutes. Small incisions are made in the scrotum. Each vas is cut, a small segment is removed, and the ends are tied off or cauterized (to prevent them from growing back together) (see Figure 11.7). Now sperm can no longer reach the urethra. Instead, they are harmlessly reabsorbed by the body.

The man can usually resume sexual relations within a few days. Because some sperm may be present in his reproductive tract for a few weeks, however, he is best advised to use an additional contraceptive method until his ejaculate shows a zero sperm count. Some health professionals recommend that the man have a follow-up sperm count a year after his vasectomy to ensure that the cut ends of the vas deferens have not grown together.

According to guidelines established by the World Health Organization in 2004, men are advised to wait three months after a vasectomy before relying on it for contraception. This advice is based on an analysis of several studies which found that for the great majority of men, vasectomies are completely effective after three months (Info Reports, 2005).

Vasectomy does not diminish sex drive or result in any change in sexual arousal, erectile or ejaculatory ability, or sensations of ejaculation. Male sex hormones and sperm are still produced by the testes. Without a passageway to the urethra, however, sperm are no longer expelled with the ejaculate. Sperm account for only about 1% of the ejaculate, so the volume of the ejaculate is not noticeably different.

Though there are no confirmed long-term health risks of vasectomy (Reinisch, 1990), two studies of more than 73 000 men who had undergone vasectomies raise concerns that the procedure may not be as risk-free as people generally believe. The studies showed that men who had had vasectomies more than 20 years earlier faced

Sterilization Surgical procedures that render people incapable of reproduction without affecting sexual activity.

Vasectomy The surgical method of male sterilization in which sperm are prevented from reaching the urethra by cutting each vas deferens and tying it back or cauterizing it.

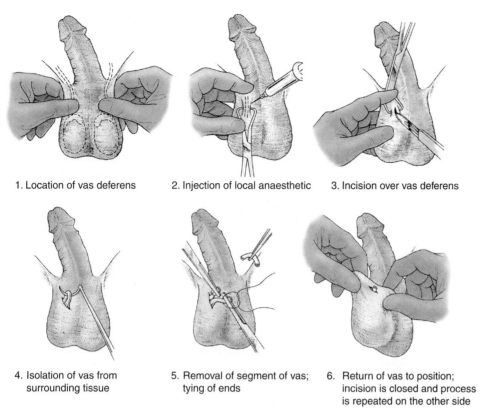

1. Location of vas deferens   2. Injection of local anaesthetic   3. Incision over vas deferens

4. Isolation of vas from surrounding tissue   5. Removal of segment of vas; tying of ends   6. Return of vas to position; incision is closed and process is repeated on the other side

Figure 11.7 Vasectomy.

The male sterilization procedure is usually carried out in a doctor's office, using local anaesthesia. Small incisions are made in the scrotum. Each vas deferens is cut, and the ends are tied off or cauterized to prevent sperm from reaching the urethra. Sperm are harmlessly reabsorbed by the body after the operation.

a slightly increased risk of prostate cancer (Altman, 1993; Giovannucci et al., 1993a, 1993b). The studies found a correlation between vasectomies and the risk of prostate cancer but did not establish a causal connection. It is possible that factors other than the vasectomy itself explain the greater risk faced by vasectomized men. The results also conflict with earlier studies showing either no link between vasectomies and the risk of prostate cancer or even a *lower* risk among vasectomized men. Health professionals recommend that men with vasectomies have annual screenings for prostate cancer.

The vasectomy is nearly 100% effective. Fewer than two pregnancies occur during the first year among 1000 couples in which the man has undergone a vasectomy (see Table 11.1). The few failures stem from sperm remaining in the male's genital tract shortly after the operation or from the growing together of the segments of a vas deferens.

Minor complications are reported in 4% or 5% of cases. They typically involve temporary local inflammation or swelling after the operation. Ice packs and anti-inflammatory drugs, such as Aspirin, may help reduce swelling and discomfort. More serious but rarer medical complications include infection of the epididymis (Reinisch, 1990).

Reversibility is simple in concept but not in practice. Thus, vasectomies should be considered permanent. In an operation to reverse a vasectomy, called a **vasovasotomy**, the ends of the vas deferens are sewn together, and in a few days they grow together. Estimates of success at reversal, as measured by subsequent pregnancies, range from 16% to 79% (Hatcher, 2001). Some vasectomized men develop anti-

Vasovasotomy The surgical method of reversing vasectomy in which the cut or cauterized ends of the vas deferens are sewn together.

Tubal sterilization The most common method of female sterilization, in which the fallopian tubes are surgically blocked to prevent the meeting of sperm and ova. Also called *tubal ligation.*

Minilaparotomy A kind of tubal sterilization in which a small incision is made in the abdomen to provide access to the fallopian tubes.

Laparoscopy Tubal sterilization by means of a *laparoscope,* which is inserted through a small incision just below the navel and used to cauterize, cut, or clamp the fallopian tubes. Sometimes referred to as "belly-button surgery."

Culpotomy A kind of tubal sterilization in which the fallopian tubes are approached through an incision in the back wall of the vagina.

Hysterectomy Surgical removal of the uterus. (*Not* appropriate as a method of sterilization.)

bodies that attack their own sperm. The production of antibodies does not appear to endanger the man's health (Hatcher, 2001), but it may contribute to infertility following reconnection.

FEMALE STERILIZATION While the male sterilization rate is increasing, the rate of female sterilization in Canada is decreasing (Fisher et al. 2002).

Tubal sterilization, also called *tubal ligation*, is the most common method of female sterilization. Tubal sterilization prevents ova and sperm from passing through the fallopian tubes. The two main surgical procedures for tubal sterilization are *minilaparotomy* and *laparoscopy*. In a **minilaparotomy**, a small incision is made in the abdomen, just above the pubic hairline, to provide access to the fallopian tubes. Each tube is cut and either tied back or clamped with a clip. In a **laparoscopy** (see Figure 11.8), sometimes called "belly-button surgery," the fallopian tubes are approached through a small incision in the abdomen just below the navel. The surgeon uses a narrow, lighted viewing instrument called a *laparoscope* to locate the tubes. A small section of each of the tubes is cauterized, cut, or clamped. The woman usually returns to her daily routine in a few days and can resume coitus when it becomes comfortable. In an alternative sterilization procedure, a **culpotomy**, the fallopian tubes are approached through an incision in the back wall of the vagina.

None of these methods disrupts sex drive or sexual response. The menstrual cycle is undisturbed. The unfertilized egg is simply reabsorbed by the body, rather than being sloughed off in the menstrual flow.

A **hysterectomy** also results in sterility. A hysterectomy is a major operation that is commonly performed because of cancer or other diseases of the reproductive tract; it is inappropriate as a method of sterilization. Hysterectomy carries the risks of major surgery, and when the ovaries are removed along with the uterus, it induces a "surgical menopause" because the woman no longer produces female sex hormones.

Female sterilization is highly effective in preventing pregnancy, although slightly less effective than male sterilization. Overall, about 1 woman in 200 (0.4%) is likely to become pregnant in the first year following a tubal sterilization (Hatcher,

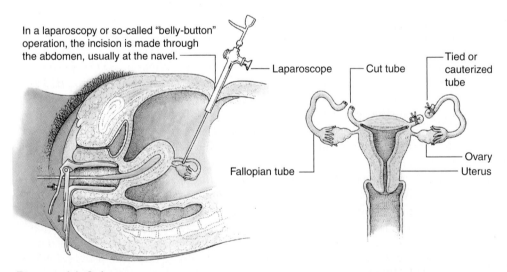

In a laparoscopy or so-called "belly-button" operation, the incision is made through the abdomen, usually at the navel. — Laparoscope — Cut tube — Tied or cauterized tube

Fallopian tube — — Ovary — Uterus

Figure 11.8 Laparoscopy.

In this method of female sterilization, the surgeon approaches the fallopian tubes through a small incision in the abdomen just below the navel. A narrow instrument called a *laparoscope* is inserted through the incision, and a small section of each fallopian tube is cauterized, cut, or clamped to prevent ova from joining with sperm.

2001); this is most likely to result from a failed surgical procedure or a pregnancy undetected at the time of the procedure. Like vasectomy, tubal ligation should be considered irreversible. Reversals are successful, as measured by subsequent pregnancies, in 43% to 88% of cases (Hatcher, 2001). Reversal is, however, difficult and costly.

The most common complications are abdominal infections, excessive bleeding, inadvertent punctures of nearby organs, and scarring.

ADVANTAGES AND DISADVANTAGES OF STERILIZATION The major advantages of sterilization are effectiveness and permanence. Sterilization is nearly 100% effective. Following surgery, the couple need not do anything more to prevent conception. The permanence is also its major drawback, however. People sometimes change their minds about wanting to have children.

Sterilization procedures create varying risks of complications following surgery, and women generally incur greater risks than men. Another disadvantage of sterilization is that it affords no protection against STIs. People who are sterilized may still wish to use condoms and spermicides for protection against STIs.

Other Methods of Contraception

NORPLANT Norplant, like the pill, relies on female sex hormones to suppress fertility. But rather than the woman taking a pill once a day, tubes implanted in her body release a small, steady dose of progestin into her bloodstream, providing continuous contraceptive protection for as long as five years (Hatcher, 1998). The progestin in the Norplant system suppresses ovulation and thickens the cervical mucus so that sperm cannot pass. The contraceptive effect occurs within 24 hours of insertion. After five years the spent tubes are replaced. An alternative implant, Norplant-2, consists of two hormone-releasing tubes that provide at least three years of protection.

Norplant is reported to have an extremely low failure rate of less than 1%. A key advantage of Norplant is its convenience. The hormone is dispensed automatically. The woman need not remember to take a pill each day, insert a device before coitus, or check that an IUD is in place. The most commonly reported side effect is abnormal menstrual bleeding (Hatcher, 2001).

DEPO-PROVERA Depo-Provera (medroxyprogesterone acetate) became available in Canada in 1997. It is a long-acting, synthetic form of progesterone that works as a contraceptive by inhibiting ovulation. The progesterone signals the pituitary gland in the brain to stop producing hormones that would lead to the release of mature ova by the ovaries. Administered by injection once every three months, Depo-Provera is an effective form of contraception, with reported failure rates of less than 1 pregnancy per 100 women during the first year of use (Hatcher, 2001). A World Health Organization study of 12 000 women found no links between the drug and the risk of ovarian or cervical cancer (Walt, 1993). Yet the drug may produce such side effects as weight gain, menstrual irregularity, and spotting between periods (Hatcher, 2001). Use of Depo-Provera has also been linked to osteoporosis, a condition involving bone loss that can cause bones to become brittle and fracture easily.

THE CERVICAL CAP The cervical cap is a dome-shaped rubber cup. It comes in different sizes and must be fitted by a health professional. It is smaller than the diaphragm, however—about the size of a thimble—and is meant to fit snugly over the cervical opening.

Like the diaphragm, the cap is intended to be used with a spermicide applied inside it (Hatcher, 2001). When inserting it, the woman (or her partner) fills the cap about a third full of spermicide. Then, squeezing the edges together, the woman inserts the cap high in the vagina, so that it presses firmly against the cervix. It should be left in place for at least eight hours after intercourse. The cap provides continuous protection for upwards of 48 hours without the need for additional spermicide. To reduce the risk of toxic shock syndrome, the cap should not be left in place longer than 48 hours.

The failure rate in typical use is estimated to be high, ranging from 18% in women who have not borne children to 36% in women who have (Hatcher, 2001).

Some women find the cap uncomfortable. The cap can also become dislodged during sexual activity or lose its fit as the cervix changes over the menstrual cycle. Side effects include urinary tract infections and allergic reactions or sensitivities to the rubber or spermicide. Other disadvantages include the expense and inconvenience of being fitted by a health professional. Moreover, some women are shaped so that the cap does not remain in place. For these reasons, and because they may be hard to obtain, cervical caps are not very popular.

THE FEMALE CONDOM The female condom consists of a polyurethane (plastic) sheath that is used to line the vagina during intercourse. It is held in place at each end by a flexible plastic ring. The female condom provides a secure but flexible shield that barricades against sperm but allows the penis to move freely within the vagina during coitus. It can be inserted as much as eight hours before intercourse but should be removed immediately afterward (Hatcher, 2001). A new one must be used for each act of intercourse.

Like the male condom, the female condom may offer some protection against STIs. Dr. Mary E. Guinan (1992) of the Centers for Disease Control points out that women can use the female condom if their partners refuse to wear a male condom. Cynthia Pearson (1992) of the National Women's Health Network notes that the female condom "for the first time [gives] women control over exposure to sexually transmitted disease, including AIDS."

The female condom (brand name: Reality) carries a warning label that it appears to be less effective than the male latex condom in preventing pregnancies and transmission of STIs. During test trials, the pregnancy rate was estimated to range between 21% and 26%, but it is estimated to be as low as 5% among cautious users (Hatcher, 2001). Evidence concerning the effectiveness of the female condom in providing protection against STIs is scarce (Centers for Disease Control, 1993).

Many women complain that the female condom is bulky and difficult to insert (Stewart, 1992). Still, it is the first barrier method of contraception that women control themselves and that is effective against STIs. Naming the device Reality suggests that it may be used most widely by women faced with the reality of male partners who refuse to use condoms themselves or who fail to use them consistently or properly. The female condom costs several times as much as the male condom.

Fisher and his colleagues (2004) found that only 34% of Canadian women had heard of the female condom, and only 6% had a very favourable opinion of it. The Toronto Public Health Department developed an educational program to promote the female condom with a group of women who were at high risk for STIs and unwanted pregnancy. The two key factors affecting whether the women used the female condom were whether they liked using it and whether they felt comfortable inserting it. Cost presented another obstacle, with most of the women saying they would not continue using the condom if they had to pay its full retail price (Hardwick, 2002).

THE SKIN PATCH One new hormonal method is a skin patch that is worn three weeks each month and can be readily replaced by the woman. The Ortho Evra patch was introduced by Ortho-McNeil Pharmaceuticals in 2002. The skin patch is a convenient means of receiving a continuous dose of hormones without having to remember to take a pill.

THE VAGINAL RING The vaginal ring delivers hormones through the skin. It can be worn in the vagina for three months before replacement. Shaped like a diaphragm, the ring contains either a combination of estrogen and progestin or progestin only.

> **Douche** To rinse or wash the vaginal canal by inserting a liquid and allowing it to drain out.

THE CONTRACEPTIVE SPONGE The contraceptive sponge is a soft, disposable device. Unlike the diaphragm, the sponge does not need to be fitted. Like the diaphragm, it provides a barrier that holds a spermicide, but the spermicide is built in. The sponge can also be inserted into the vagina several hours before coitus and has the additional advantage of absorbing sperm. It is odourless and tasteless, and users found it less drippy than the diaphragm. On the negative side, about 1 user in 20 (male and female) is mildly irritated by the spermicide. There is also a remote chance of toxic shock syndrome (TSS): 1 case arose for every 4 *million* days of use.

DOUCHING Many couples believe that if a woman **douches** shortly after coitus, she will not become pregnant. Women who douche for contraceptive purposes often use syringes to flush the vagina with water or a spermicidal agent. The water is intended to wash sperm out, the spermicides to kill them. Douching is ineffective, however, because large numbers of sperm move beyond the range of the douche seconds after ejaculation. Douching, at best, has a failure rate among typical users of 40% (Reinisch, 1990), too high to be considered reliable.

Regular douching may also alter the natural chemistry of the vagina, increasing the risk of vaginal infection. In short, douching is a "nonmethod" of contraception.

Applied Knowledge

SELECTING A METHOD OF CONTRACEPTION

If you believe that you and your partner should use contraception, how will you determine which method is right for you? There is no simple answer. What is right for your friends may be wrong for you. You and your partner will make your own selections, but there are some issues you may want to consider:

1. *Convenience.* Is the method convenient? The convenience of a method depends on a number of

factors. Does it require a device that must be purchased in advance? If so, can it be purchased over the counter as needed, or are a consultation with a doctor and a prescription required? Will the method work at a moment's notice, or, as with the birth-control pill, will it require time to reach maximum effectiveness? Some couples feel that few things dampen ardour and spontaneity more quickly than the need to pay attention to a contraceptive device in the heat of passion. Use of contraceptives like the condom and the diaphragm need not interrupt sexual activity, however. Both partners can share in applying the device. Some couples find that this becomes an erotic aspect of their lovemaking.

2. *Moral acceptability.* A method that is morally acceptable to one person may be objectionable to another.

3. *Cost.* Methods vary in cost. Prescribed methods, such as pills, may be covered by a drug plan. Other methods, such as rhythm methods, are essentially free.

4. *Sharing responsibility.* Most forms of birth control place the burden of responsibility largely, if not entirely, on the woman. The woman must consult with her doctor to obtain birth-control pills or other prescription devices such as diaphragms, cervical caps, Norplant, and IUDs. The woman must take birth-control pills reliably or check to see that her IUD remains in place.

Some couples prefer methods that allow for greater sharing of responsibility, such as alternating use of the condom and diaphragm. A man can also share the responsibility for the birth-control pill by accompanying his partner on her medical visits, sharing the expense, and helping her remember to take her pill.

5. *Safety.* How safe is the method? What are the side effects? What health risks are associated with its use? Can your partner's health or comfort be affected by its use?

6. *Reversibility.* Reversibility refers to the effects of a birth-control technique or device. In most cases the effects of birth-control methods can be fully reversed by discontinuing their use. In other cases reversibility may not occur immediately, as with oral contraceptives. One form of contraception, sterilization, should be considered irreversible, although many attempts at reversal have been successful.

7. *Protection against sexually transmitted infections (STIs).* Birth-control methods vary in the degree of protection they afford against STIs such as gonorrhea, chlamydia, and AIDS.

8. *Effectiveness.* Techniques and devices vary widely in their effectiveness in actual use. The failure rate for a particular method refers to the percentage of women who become pregnant when using the method for a given period of time, such as during the first year of use. Most contraceptive methods are not used correctly all or even much of the time. Thus it is instructive to compare the failure rate among people who use a particular method or device *perfectly* (consistently and correctly) with the failure rate among *typical* users. Failure rates among typical users are often considerably higher because of incorrect, unreliable, or inconsistent use. Table 11.1 shows the failure rates, continuation rates, reversibility, and degree of protection against STIs associated with various contraceptive methods.

The Search Goes On

Even now, in the third millennium, the ideal contraceptive does not yet seem to be within our grasp. However, it does appear that we will be making new advances in mechanical- and chemical-barrier methods, systems for delivering hormones, intrauterine devices (IUDs), and systemic methods for men (such as a male pill).

One "male pill" under development includes testosterone and another hormone called progestogen (Cohen, 1998). This pill is 95% effective in reducing the sperm counts to levels at which impregnation is highly unlikely, and it may be available within a few years. In a University of Edinburgh study, about two out of three men said that they would use such a pill if it were safe and effective (Cohen, 1998). Yet a survey of college men in the United States found that only one in five expressed willingness to take a male pill (Laird, 1994). The men believed that taking a male pill would be more of a bother than having one's partner take a female pill and more "contrary to nature"!

It seems that many women, too, are not comfortable with the idea of a male pill. Sixty-three percent of young Canadian women (aged 18–24) in a 2004 Ipsos-Reid poll said that they would not trust a man to take a pill every day. Three-quarters said they are more responsible about birth control than are men.

Developed by the Society of Obstetricians and Gynaecologists of Canada, this site provides reliable information on contraception.

www.sexualityandu.ca

TABLE 11.1
Approximate Failure Rates of Various Methods of Birth Control (in percentage of women using the method who become pregnant within the first year of use)

Method	% of Women Experiencing an Accidental Pregnancy within the First Year of Use		% of Women Continuing Use at 1 Year[3]	Reversibility	Protection Against Sexually Transmitted Infections (STIs)
	Typical Use[1]	Perfect Use[2]			
Chance[4]	85	85		yes (unless fertility has been impaired by exposure to an STI)	no
Spermicides[5]	26	6	43	yes	no
Periodic Abstinence	20		67	yes	no
Calendar		9			
Ovulation Method		3			
Sympto-Thermal[6]		2			
Post-Ovulation		1			
Withdrawal	19	4		yes	no
Cervical Cap[7]					
Parous Women[8]	40	30	45	yes	some
Nulliparous Women[9]	20	9	58	yes	some
Diaphragm[7]	20	6	58	yes	some
Condom Alone					
Female (Reality)	21	5	56	yes	yes
Male	14	3	63	yes	yes
Pill	3		72	yes	no, but may reduce the risk of PID[10]
Progestin Only		0.5			
Combined		0.1			
IUD					
Nova-T[11]	—	—	—	yes, except if fertility is impaired	no, and may increase the risk of PID
Depo-Provera	0.3	0.3	70	yes	no
Norplant (6 capsules)	0.05	0.05	85	yes	no
Female Sterilization	0.5	0.5	100	questionable	no
Male Sterilization	0.15	0.10	100	questionable	no

[1]Among typical couples who initiate use of a method (not necessarily for the first time), the percentage who experience an accidental pregnancy during the first year if they do not stop use for any other reason.

[2]Among couples who initiate a method (not necessarily for the first time) and who use it perfectly (both consistently and correctly), the percentage who experience an accidental pregnancy during the first year if they do not stop use for any other reason.

[3]Among couples attempting to avoid pregnancy, the percentage who continue to use a method for one year.

[4]The percentages failing in columns (2) and (3) are based on data from populations where contraception is not used and from women who cease using contraception in order to become pregnant. Among such populations, about 89% become pregnant within one year. This estimate was lowered slightly (to 85%) to represent the percentage who would become pregnant within one year among women now relying on reversible methods of contraception if they abandoned contraception altogether.

5Foams, creams, gels, vaginal suppositories, and vaginal film.

[6]Cervical mucus (ovulation) method supplemented by calendar in the pre-ovulatory and basal body temperature in the post-ovulatory period.

[7]With spermicidal cream or jelly.

[8]Women who have borne children.

[9]Women who have not borne children.

[10]Pelvic inflammatory disease.

[11]The source documents provided data for brands of IUDs available in the U.S. but not in Canada. Failure rates for all brands listed were 2% or less; the Nova-T presumably has a similarly low failure rate.

Sources: For failure rates and percentages of women discontinuing use, adapted from Hatcher (2001) and Hatcher et al. (1994). Information on reversibility and protection against STIs added.

Induced abortion The purposeful termination of a pregnancy before the embryo or fetus is capable of sustaining independent life. (From the Latin *abortio*, which means "that which is miscarried.")

Canadian Abortion Rights Action League
Canada's pro-choice volunteer organization works to ensure that all women have total reproductive freedom to exercise the right to safe, accessible abortion.

www.caral.ca

The National Right to Life Committee
Contains the organization's views on when human life begins, the negative aspects of abortion, and so on.

www.nrlc.org

The search for the perfect contraceptive continues. It is difficult to say precisely what that contraceptive will look like, but it will be safe and effective, and it will not interfere at all with sexual spontaneity or sexual pleasure.

Abortion

An **induced abortion** (in contrast to a *spontaneous abortion*, or miscarriage) is the purposeful termination of a pregnancy. Perhaps more than any other contemporary social issue, induced abortion (hereafter referred to simply as abortion) has divided neighbours and family members into opposing camps.

Abortion is rarely used as a primary means of birth control. It usually comes into play when other methods have failed. The many reasons why women have abortions include psychological factors as well as external circumstances. Abortion is often motivated by a desire to reduce the risk of physical, economic, psychological, and social disadvantages that the woman perceives for herself and her present and future children should she take the pregnancy to term (Russo et al., 1992).

Moral concerns about abortion often turn on the question of when human life begins. However, the question of when *human* life begins is a matter of definition that is apparently unanswerable by science.

Historical and Legal Perspectives on Abortion

Societal attitudes toward abortion have varied across cultures and times in history. Abortion was permitted in ancient Greece and Rome. The Bible does not specifically prohibit abortion (Sagan & Dryan, 1990). For much of its history, the Roman Catholic Church held to Thomas Aquinas's belief that ensoulment of the fetus did not occur for at least 40 days after conception. In 1869, Pope Pius IX declared that human life begins at conception. Thus an abortion at any stage of pregnancy became murder in the eyes of the Church and grounds for excommunication.

A World of Diversity

ABORTION IN CANADA

Abortion was illegal in Canada until 1969, when Parliament amended the Criminal Code so that abortion could be performed under limited circumstances. Abortions could be performed only in accredited hospitals with the approval of a Therapeutic Abortion Committee. It had to be shown that the abortion was justified, in that continuation of the pregnancy would endanger the woman's life or health. Only a minority of physicians were willing to perform abortions, and not all

Choosing Sides.
Retired Toronto priest Ted Colleton confronts pro-choice advocates during an anti-abortion protest by World Youth Day participants outside the Scott Clinic.

Dr. Henry Morgentaler. Dr. Henry Morgentaler has fought numerous court battles to secure Canadian women greater access to abortions. He established private abortion clinics in a number of provinces so that women could have access to adequate medical services. His life has been threatened on many occasions, and in 1992 his Toronto clinic was set on fire.

provinces were willing to provide access to abortions. The struggle continued between pro-life groups, which sought greater restrictions on abortions, and the pro-choice movement, which sought to make abortions available to any Canadian woman who wanted one.

The right-to-life (pro-life) movement asserts that human life begins at conception and thus views abortion as the murder of an unborn child (Sagan & Dryan, 1990). Some in the pro-life movement brook no exception to their opposition to abortion. Others would permit abortion to save the mother's life or when a pregnancy results from rape or incest. The pro-choice movement contends that abortion is a matter of personal choice and that the government has no right to interfere with a woman's right to terminate a pregnancy. Pro-choice advocates argue that women are free to control what happens within their bodies, including pregnancies.

Both groups have heavily lobbied politicians to support their cause. Some pro-life groups use such tactics as picketing hospitals and clinics where abortions are performed as well as the homes of physicians who perform abortions. Three Canadian physicians

have been shot in their homes by anti-abortion extremists. The harassing tactics used by some of these groups have led provinces such as Ontario and British Columbia to restrict picketing outside abortion clinics.

Dr. Henry Morgentaler, the leader of the pro-choice movement in Canada, challenged the law by establishing private abortion clinics. Dr. Morgentaler has won several legal challenges against provincial governments that wanted to close his clinics (although in 1974 he was imprisoned for 10 months by the Quebec government after the Quebec Court of Appeal overturned a jury's acquittal). Juries refused to convict Morgentaler because they believed he was providing an important medical service for women. He was also supported by such pro-choice groups as the Canadian Abortion Rights Action League (CARAL). In her book *Morgentaler: A Difficult Hero,* Catherine Dunphy (1996) provides a detailed account of Dr. Morgentaler's personal struggle to improve women's access to abortion services.

The Supreme Court of Canada overturned the abortion law in 1988, stating that it violated the Charter of Rights and Freedoms, and there has

been no federal law restricting abortion since then. And in 1989, after a Quebec man went to court in an attempt to prevent his former girlfriend from having an abortion, an important precedent was set when the Supreme Court of Canada ruled that he could not stop the abortion because the law does not recognize a father's right to do so.

Despite these legal decisions, today only a minority of hospitals perform abortions and these are located only in urban areas. In 2003 CARAL found that only 18% of general hospitals in Canada provided abortion services. Quebec had the highest percentage (35%) of its hospitals providing abortions while Ontario had the second highest (23%). Prince Edward Island and Nunavut did not offer any abortion services, and some provinces, such as New Brunswick, restricted women's access to abortions at public hospitals and have not been willing to fund private abortion clinics (CARAL, 2003). In 2005, Federal Health Minister Ujal Dosanjh threatened to reduce health funding to New Brunswick for refusing to cover the costs of abortions performed at a private clinic in Fredericton.

In 2002, 105 154 abortions were performed in Canada (Statistics Canada, 2005c). The abortion rate is highest among women in their 20s, who account for 52% of all women who obtained an abortion in 2002. In the Canadian Contraceptive Study (Fisher et al., 1999), 28% of women reported having an unplanned pregnancy. Of these, 13% ended in miscarriage, 35% in abortion, 56% of babies were kept, and 3% were placed for adoption. Abortion was twice as likely among single women (50%) as married women (28%).

Attitudes Toward Legalized Abortion

Although Canadians are divided in their opinions on abortion, most accept abortion under certain circumstances. Reginald Bibby (2001) of the University of Lethbridge found that most Canadian adults (90%) and teenagers (84%) believe that abortion

Vacuum aspiration
Removal of the uterine contents via suction. An abortion method used early in pregnancy. (From the Latin *aspirare,* which means "to breathe upon.")

should be legal when rape is involved, but fewer (adults 43%, teenagers 55%) believe it should be legal for any reason.

Many people in the pro-choice movement argue that if abortions were to be made illegal again, thousands of women, especially poor women, would die or suffer serious physical consequences from botched or nonsterile abortions. People in the pro-life movement counter that alternatives to abortion, such as adoption, are available to pregnant women. Pro-choice advocates argue that the debate about abortion should be framed not only by notions of the mother's right to privacy but also by the issue of the quality of life of an unwanted child. They argue that minority and physically or mentally disabled children are often hard to place for adoption. These children often spend their childhood being shuffled from one foster home to another. Pro-life advocates counter that killing a fetus eliminates any potential that it might have, despite hardships, of living a fruitful and meaningful life.

Methods of Abortion

Regardless of the moral, legal, and political issues that surround abortion, many abortion methods are in use today.

VACUUM ASPIRATION **Vacuum aspiration,** or suction curettage, is the safest and most common method of abortion in Canada. It is relatively painless and inexpensive. It can be done with little or no anaesthesia in a medical office or clinic, but only during the first trimester. Later, thinning of the uterine walls increases the risks of perforation and bleeding.

In the procedure, the cervix is usually dilated first by insertion of progressively larger curved metal rods, or "dilators," or by insertion, hours earlier, of a stick of seaweed called *Laminaria digitata. Laminaria* expands as it absorbs cervical moisture, providing a gentler means of opening the os. Then an angled tube connected to an aspirator (suction machine) is inserted through the cervix into the uterus. The uterine contents are then evacuated (emptied) by suction (see Figure 11.9). Possible complications include perforation of the uterus, infection, cervical lacerations, and hemorrhaging, but these are rare.

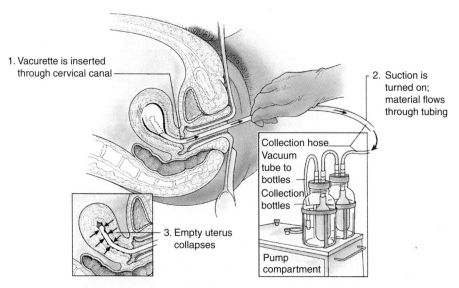

1. Vacurette is inserted through cervical canal

2. Suction is turned on; material flows through tubing

Collection hose
Vacuum tube to bottles
Collection bottles

3. Empty uterus collapses

Pump compartment

Figure 11.9 Vacuum Aspiration.

This is the safest and most common method of abortion, but it can be performed only during the first trimester. An angled tube is inserted through the cervix into the uterus, and the uterine contents are then evacuated (emptied) by suction.

DILATION AND CURETTAGE (D&C) The **D&C** was once the customary method of performing abortions. It now accounts for only a small number of abortions. It is usually performed 8 to 20 weeks following the last menstrual period (LMP). Once the cervix has been dilated, the uterine contents are scraped from the uterine lining with a blunt scraping tool.

D&Cs are carried out in a hospital, usually under general anaesthesia. The scraping increases the chances of hemorrhaging, infection, and perforation. Because of these risks, D&Cs have largely been replaced by the vacuum aspiration method. D&Cs are still used to treat various gynecological problems, however, such as abnormally heavy menstrual bleeding.

DILATION AND EVACUATION (D& E) The **D&E** is used most commonly during the second trimester, when vacuum aspiration alone would be too risky. The D&E combines suction and the D&C. First the cervix is dilated. The cervix must also be dilated more fully than with vacuum aspiration to allow for passage of the larger fetus. Then a suction tube is inserted to remove some of the contents of the uterus. But suction alone cannot safely remove all uterine contents, so the remaining contents are removed with forceps. A blunt scraper may also be used to scrape the uterine wall to make sure that the lining has been removed fully. Like the D&C, the D&E is usually performed in a hospital under general anaesthesia. Most women recover quickly and relatively painlessly. In rare instances, however, complications arise. These include excessive bleeding, infection, and perforation of the uterine lining (Thompson, 1993).

INDUCING LABOUR BY INTRA-AMNIOTIC INFUSION Second-trimester abortions are sometimes performed by chemically inducing premature labour and delivery. The procedure, which must be performed in a hospital, is called instillation, or **intra-amniotic infusion**. It is usually performed when fetal development has progressed beyond the point at which other methods are deemed safe. A saline (salt) solution or a solution of prostaglandins (hormones that stimulate uterine contractions during labour) is injected into the amniotic sac. Prostaglandins may also be administered by vaginal suppository. Uterine contractions (labour) begin within a few hours after infusion. The fetus and placenta are expelled from the uterus within the next 24 to 48 hours.

Intra-amniotic infusion accounts for only a small number of abortions. Medical complications, risks, and costs are greater with this procedure than with other methods of abortion. Overly rapid labour can tear the cervix, but previous dilation of the cervix with *Laminaria digitata* (described earlier) lessens the risk. Perforation, infection, and hemorrhaging are rare when prostaglandins are used, but about half the recipients experience nausea and vomiting, diarrhea, or headaches. Saline infusion can cause shock and even death if the solution is carelessly introduced into the bloodstream.

HYSTEROTOMY The **hysterotomy** is, in effect, a caesarean section. Incisions are made in the abdomen and uterus, and the fetus and uterine contents are removed. Hysterotomy may be performed during the late second trimester, between the 16th and 24th weeks after the last menstrual period. It is performed very rarely, usually only when intra-amniotic infusion is not advised. A hysterotomy is major surgery that must be carried out under general anaesthesia in a hospital. Hysterotomy involves risks of complications from the anaesthesia and the surgery itself.

ABORTION DRUGS RU-486 (mifepristone) was approved in France in the late 1980s. It has not yet been approved for use in Canada, although it is available in several European countries and the United States. The chemical mifepristone induces early abortion by blocking the effects of progesterone. Progesterone is the hormone that stimulates proliferation of the endometrium, allowing implantation of the fertilized ovum and, subsequently, development of the placenta.

D&C Abbreviation for *dilation and curettage*, an operation in which the cervix is dilated and the uterine contents are then gently scraped away.

D&E Abbreviation for dilation and evacuation, an abortion method in which the cervix is dilated prior to vacuum aspiration and uterine contents are removed with forceps.

Intra-amniotic infusion An abortion method in which a substance is injected into the amniotic sac to induce premature labour. Also called *instillation*.

Hysterotomy An abortion method in which the fetus is removed by caesarean section.

RU-486 can be used only within 49 days of the beginning of the woman's last menstrual period ("FDA approves," 2000). The typical course is for the woman to take three mifepristone pills. Two days later, she is given a second oral drug, misoprostol, that causes uterine contractions to expel the embryo. There is also usually a follow-up visit within two weeks to make sure that the abortion is complete and the woman is well.

The pill was developed in France, and increasing numbers of women around the world are opting for early abortion without surgery (Davis, 2000). Nearly half of French women who seek abortion prefer RU-486 to surgical methods, including vacuum aspiration (Christin-Maitre et al., 2000).

Supporters of RU-486 argue that it offers a safe, noninvasive substitute for more costly and unpleasant abortion procedures (Christin-Maitre et al., 2000). Moreover, use of RU-486 means that a woman need not run a gauntlet of demonstrators to visit an abortion clinic or hospital. Supporters also note that RU-486 may reduce the numbers of women who die each year of complications from self-induced abortions. Such women are usually too poor to avail themselves of legally sanctioned abortion facilities, or they live in Third World countries that lack adequate medical services.

RU-486's introduction in Canada is being delayed largely because of opposition by pro-life groups. Opponents argue that RU-486 makes abortions more accessible and difficult to regulate. Pro-life groups consider abortion to be murder, whether it is induced by surgery or by a pill.

Psychological Consequences of Abortion

The woman who faces an unwanted pregnancy may experience a range of negative emotions, including fear, anger directed inward ("How could I let this happen?"), guilt ("What would my parents think if they knew I was having an abortion?"), and ambivalence ("Will I regret it if I have an abortion? Will I regret it more if I don't?")

Women's reactions depend on various factors, including the support they receive from others (or the lack thereof) and the strength of their relationships with their partners. Women with greater support from their male partners or parents tend to show a more positive emotional reaction following an abortion (Armsworth, 1991). Generally speaking, the sooner the abortion occurs, the less stressful it is. Women who have a difficult time reaching an abortion decision, who blame the pregnancy on their character, who have lower coping ability, and who have less social support experience more distress following abortion (Major & Cozzarelli, 1992).

Consider one survey of several hundred women reported in *Archives of General Psychiatry* (Major et al., 2000) who showed up at one of three sites for a first-trimester abortion. More than 1000 women were approached at random as they arrived at the clinic, and 882 (85%) agreed to be followed for two years so that their responses could be assessed at various times. Of these 882, 442 were actually followed for the two years. As shown in Figure 11.10, the majority (72%) said they were satisfied with their decision to have the abortion. A majority said they would make the same decision if they had it to do over (69%) and that they had experienced more benefit than harm from having the abortion (72%). Moreover, four out of five women (80%) were *not* depressed.

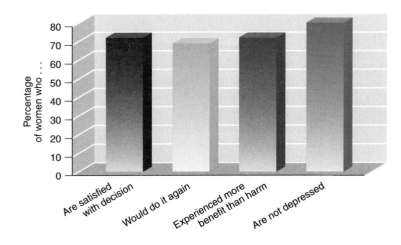

Figure 11.10 Women's Psychological Adjustment Two Years After Having Had an Abortion.

Of several hundred respondents to an *Archives of General Psychiatry* survey, 72% of those who had had an abortion reported being satisfied with their decision two years after the fact. How do you interpret the finding? Do you focus on the finding that the great majority of women are satisfied with their choice or on the finding that significant numbers of women (28%) are not?

Source: Data from B. Major, C. Cozzarelli, M. L. Cooper, J. Zwbek, C. Richards, et al. (2000). "Psychological Responses of Women after First-Trimester Abortion." *Archives of General Psychiatry, 57,* 777–784.

Summing Up

Birth-control methods include contraception and induced abortion.

Historical Perspectives on Contraception

Attempts at contraception are ancient. However, the provision of contraceptive information and services was illegal in Canada until 1969.

Methods of Contraception

Oral Contraceptives ("the Pill")

Birth-control pills include combination pills and mini pills. Combination pills contain estrogen and progestin and fool the brain into acting as though the woman is already pregnant, so that no additional ova mature or are released. Minipills contain progestin, thicken the cervical mucus to impede the passage of sperm through the cervix, and render the inner lining of the uterus less receptive to a fertilized egg. Oral contraception is nearly 100% effective. The main drawbacks are side effects and potential health risks. "Morning-after" pills prevent implantation of a fertilized ovum in the uterus.

Intrauterine Devices (IUDs)

The IUD apparently irritates the uterine lining, causing inflammation and the production of antibodies that may be toxic to sperm or fertilized ova and/or may prevent fertilized eggs from becoming implanted. The IUD is highly effective, but there are possible troublesome side effects and the potential for serious health complications.

The Diaphragm

The diaphragm covers the cervix and should be used with a spermicidal cream or jelly. It must be fitted by a health professional.

Spermicides

Spermicides block the passage of sperm and kill sperm. Their failure rate is high.

Male Condoms

Latex condoms afford protection against STIs. Condoms are the only contraceptive device worn by men and the only readily reversible method of contraception that is available to men.

Withdrawal (Coitus Interruptus)

Withdrawal requires no special equipment but has a high failure rate.

Fertility Awareness Methods (Rhythm Methods)

Rhythm methods rely on awareness of the fertile segments of the woman's menstrual cycle. Rhythm methods include the calendar method, the basal body temperature method, and the cervical mucus method. Their failure rate is high in typical use.

Sterilization

Sterilization methods should be considered permanent, although they can be reversed in many cases. The vasectomy is usually carried out under local anaesthesia in 15 to 20 minutes. Female sterilization methods prevent ova and sperm from passing through the fallopian tubes.

Other Methods of Contraception

Less commonly used methods include methods of delivering hormones such as Norplant (implanted tubes), Depo-Provera (injections), the skin patch, and the vaginal ring; barrier/spermicide methods such as the cervical cap, the female condom, and the contraceptive sponge; and douching, which is a "non-method."

The Search Goes On

A male pill is under development.

Abortion

Moral concerns about abortion often turn on the question of when human life begins—a question of definition.

Historical and Legal Perspectives on Abortion

Societal attitudes toward abortion have varied across cultures and times in history. In 1969, the Canadian Parliament modified the Criminal Code to allow abortions to be performed under specific conditions. In 1988, the Supreme Court of Canada ruled that the abortion law restricted the rights of women, and women were thus allowed the right to abortion without restriction. In reality, however, abortion services are limited in many parts of Canada.

Attitudes Toward Legalized Abortion

Most Canadians approve of abortion under certain circumstances. The pro-choice movement argues that women have a right to determine what happens in their own bodies; the pro-life movement argues that the fetus is a human being with rights of its own.

Methods of Abortion

Abortion methods in use today include vacuum aspiration, D&C, D&E, induction of labour by intra-amniotic infusion, hysterotomy, and drugs.

Psychological Consequences of Abortion

Women may experience distress after an abortion, but most are satisfied with their decision to have one.

Test Yourself

Multiple-Choice Questions

1. Over the course of a lifetime, more Canadian women use _____ than any other method of contraception.
   a. intrauterine devices
   b. sterilization
   c. oral contraceptives
   d. diaphragms

2. Which statement about birth control pills is true?
   a. They fool the brain into thinking the woman is already pregnant.
   b. If used correctly, they are 100% effective.
   c. They ensure ovulation on day 21 of the woman's menstrual cycle.
   d. They offer excellent protection against sexually transmitted infections.

3. Recent research suggests that Canadian women _____ the disadvantages and _____ the advantages of oral contraceptives.
   a. underestimate/overestimate
   b. overestimate/underestimate
   c. overestimate/overestimate
   d. underestimate/underestimate

4. All of the following are potential side effects of birth control pills except
   a. nausea and vomiting
   b. low blood pressure
   c. fluid retention
   d. weight gain

5. Emergency contraception (morning-after pills)
   a. is illegal in Canada
   b. is available without a prescription
   c. contain higher levels of testosterone than the pills available in Europe
   d. is available only to victims of sexual assault

6. Which of the following statements about intrauterine devices is true?
   a. The percentage of Canadian women using IUDs has decreased since 1980.
   b. An IUD containing progestin is available in Canada.
   c. Approximately 10% of Canadian women currently use this method of birth control.
   d. IUDs offer significant protection against sexually transmitted infections.

7. What percentage of Canadian women say that they have used a condom at least once?
   a. 41%
   b. 51%
   c. 76%
   d. 91%

8. Among married couples aged 35–44,
   _____ is/are the most
   commonly used form of contraception.
   a. diaphragms
   b. oral contraceptives
   c. condoms
   d. sterilization

9. There has been no federal law restricting abortions
   in Canada since the Supreme Court ruling in
   a. 1965
   b. 1977
   c. 1988
   d. 2004

10. The safest and most common method of abortion is
    a. dilation and evacuation (D&E).
    b. intra-amniotic infusion
    c. dilation and curettage (D&C)
    d. vacuum aspiration

Critical Thinking Questions

1. Have you ever discussed the use of birth control with a partner or potential partner? If not, why not? If you
   have, did you find it difficult to talk about? Why or why not?

2. If you are female, have you ever been faced with an unintended pregnancy? If so, what did you do about it?
   What factors influenced your decision? Were your friends supportive of your choice? Your partner? Your
   family?

3. If you are male, has a sexual partner of yours ever been faced with an unintended pregnancy? If so, what was
   done about it? Were you part of the decision making process? Why or why not?

4. A friend of yours who you know does not want a child tells you that she is sexually active but not using any
   birth control. Would you discuss this behaviour with her? Why or why not?

Visit our Companion Website at www.pearsoned.ca/rathus,
where you can use the interactive Study Guide and link to
additional resources on topics discussed in this text.

Chapter 12
Sexuality Across the Life Cycle

A World of Diversity

CROSS-CULTURAL PERSPECTIVES ON CHILDHOOD SEXUALITY

Although we are born with the capacity for sexual response, our expression of sexuality largely reflects the culture in which we are reared. Cultures vary in their attitudes and practices concerning human sexuality, especially childhood and adolescent sexuality. Some may be characterized as sexually permissive, others as sexually restrictive. Broude and Greene (1976) analyzed attitudes toward, and frequency of, premarital sex among 114 of the world's societies. Most societies (55%) either disapproved of or disallowed premarital sex among females. Despite societal prohibitions, premarital sex among females was common or universal in two-thirds of the societies sampled. Female premarital sex was uncommon or absent in the other

third. Premarital sex among males was even more common.

Sexually Permissive Societies

Ford and Beach (1951) noted that when masturbation was permitted in a society, children progressed from occasional genital touching to more purposeful masturbation by about 6 to 8 years of age. Sexually permissive cultures also allow sexual expression among peers. Among the Seniang people of Oceania, boys and girls publicly simulated coitus without fear of reproach by adults (Ford & Beach, 1951). Among the Trobrianders of the South Pacific, girls were usually initiated into sexual intercourse by 6 or 8 years of age, boys by age 10 or 12.

Societies that permit sex play among children also tend to encourage open discussion of sex and to allow children to observe sexual behaviour among adults. Among the Trukese of

the South Pacific, children learned about sex by observing and asking adults.

Sexually Restrictive Societies

Ford and Beach (1951) found that only a minority of preliterate societies were sexually restrictive. The Apinaye people of South America warned their children not to masturbate and thrashed them if they were suspected of doing so. Sexually restrictive societies discourage masturbation and sex play among children. Children who disobey are punished. Such societies also tend not to talk about sex. Parents try to keep their children ignorant about reproduction. Premarital sex and watching adults engage in sex are also restricted.

Many societies hold to a sexual double standard by which boys are allowed greater sexual freedom than girls.

In this chapter we discuss sexuality across the life cycle. Within children's personal and social experiences lie the seeds of later sexual competence and self-esteem—or the seeds of incompetence, guilt, and shame. While people experience changes in their sexuality throughout their lives, most continue to enjoy sexual relations well into old age.

Given concerns over issues such as teen pregnancy and sexually transmitted infections, much research has been conducted in Canada on adolescent sexuality. Accordingly, in this chapter we will present a wealth of Canadian data on young people, including statistics from major national surveys. However, with the exception of the 1998 Compas survey and some data from Statistics Canada, we have less national information on adult sexuality in general and we especially lack Canadian data on aging and sexuality.

Hardly any research has been conducted on childhood sexuality, with the exception of child sexual abuse. As a result, we know far more about childhood sexual abuse in Canada than we do about normal childhood sexual development.

Infancy (Birth to Two Years): The Search for the Origins of Human Sexuality

Fetuses not only have erections; they also suck their fingers. The sucking reflex allows babies to gain nourishment, which is necessary for survival. But, as Sigmund

Freud hypothesized, infants also seem to reap sensual pleasure from sucking fingers, pacifiers, nipples, or whatever else fits into the mouth. This is not surprising, given the sensitivity of the mouth's mucous lining.

Stimulation of the genitals in infancy may also produce sensations of pleasure. Parents who touch their infants' genitals while changing or washing them may discover the infants smiling or becoming excited. Infants discover the pleasure of self-stimulation (masturbation) for themselves when they gain the capacity to manipulate their genitals with their hands.

Boys are often born with erections. Most have erections during the first few weeks. Signs of sexual arousal in infant girls, such as vaginal lubrication, are less readily detected. Yet evidence of lubrication and genital swelling has been reported (Martinson, 1976).

Do not, however, interpret children's responses according to adult concepts of sexuality. Lubrication and erection are reflexes, not necessarily signals of "interest" in sex. Infants have the biological capacity for these reflexes, but we cannot say what, if anything, the reflexes mean to them.

At least some infants seem capable of sexual responses that closely resemble orgasm. Kinsey and his colleagues (1953) noted that baby boys show behaviours that resemble adult orgasm by as early as five months, baby girls as early as four months. Orgasmic responses in boys are similar to those in men—but without ejaculation. Ejaculation occurs only after puberty.

Masturbation is typical for infants and young children and tends to start between 6 and 12 months. At early ages, children usually masturbate by rubbing the genitals against a soft object, such as a towel, bedding, or a doll. As the child matures and becomes capable of more coordinated hand movements, direct manual stimulation of the genitals is often preferred.

Masturbation to orgasm is rare until the second year, however (Reinisch, 1990). Some children begin masturbating to orgasm later. Some never do.

Children in North America typically do not engage in genital play with others until about the age of two. Then, as an expression of their curiosity about their environment and other people, they may investigate other children's genitals or hug, cuddle, kiss, or climb on top of them.

Early Childhood (Three to Eight Years)

In early childhood, children have an interest in sexual anatomy and sexual behaviour. Children often show each other their bodies. The unwritten rule seems to be "I'll show you mine if you'll show me yours."

Because of the difficulties in conducting research with children, statistics concerning the incidence of masturbation in children are inconclusive. Parents may not wish to respond to questions about the sexual conduct of their children. Or if they do, they may have a tendency to present their children as little "gentlemen" and "ladies" and perhaps underreport their sexual activity. Their biases may also lead them not to perceive their children's genital touching as masturbation. Many parents will not even permit their adolescents, let alone younger children, to be interviewed about their sexual behaviour (Fisher & Hall, 1988). When we are asked to look back as adults, our memories may be less than accurate.

Three- and four-year-olds commonly express affection through kissing. Curiosity about the genitals may occur by this stage. Sex games like "show" and "playing doctor" may begin earlier, but they become common between the ages of 6 and 10 (Reinisch, 1990). Much of this sexual activity takes place in same-gender groups, although mixed-gender sex games are not uncommon. Children may show their genitals to each other, touch each other's genitals, or masturbate together.

Children's knowledge of sex varies widely. Ronald and Juliette Goldman (1982) interviewed 813 children in Sweden, Australia, Canada, the United States, and Great Britain. They found that among five-year-olds, Swedish children had more accurate knowledge of genital differences and the proper names for genitals than did the children from the other countries. Children in Sweden were also less embarrassed discussing these issues than were the others. The Goldmans attributed these differences to the fact that Sweden has mandatory sex education programs beginning in kindergarten.

Preadolescence (Nine to Thirteen Years)

During preadolescence children typically form relationships with a close "best friend" that enable them to share secrets and confidences. The friends are usually peers of the same gender. Preadolescents also tend to socialize with larger networks of friends in gender-segregated groups. At this stage boys are likely to think that girls are "dorks." To girls at this stage, "dork" is too nice an epithet to apply to most boys.

Preadolescents grow increasingly preoccupied with, and self-conscious about, their bodies. Their peers pressure preadolescents to conform to dress codes, standards of "correct" slang, and group standards concerning sex and drugs. Peer disapproval can be an intense punishment.

Sexual urges are experienced by many preadolescents but may not emerge until adolescence. Sigmund Freud had theorized that sexual impulses are hidden ("latent") during preadolescence, but many preadolescents are quite active sexually.

Preadolescent sex play often involves mutual display of the genitals, with or without touching. Such sexual experiences are quite common and do not appear to impair future sexual adjustment (Leitenberg et al., 1989).

Although preadolescents tend to socialize in same-gender groups, interest in the other gender among heterosexuals tends to increase gradually as they approach puberty. Group dating and mixed-gender parties often provide preadolescents with their first exposure to heterosexual activities. Couples may not begin to pair off until early or middle adolescence.

Much preadolescent sexual behaviour among members of the same gender is simply exploration. Some incidents reflect lack of availability of partners of the opposite gender. As with younger children, experiences with children of the same gender during preadolescence may be more common than heterosexual experiences (Leitenberg et al., 1989). These activities are usually limited to touching of each other's genitals or mutual masturbation. Because preadolescents generally socialize within their gender, it is not surprising that their sexual explorations are also often within their gender. Most same-gender sexual experiences involve single episodes or short-lived relationships and are not signs of a budding gay orientation.

At What Age Does Curiosity About Sex Develop?
Children are naturally inquisitive about sexual anatomy and sexual behaviour. Much curiosity is triggered when they become aware that males and females differ in anatomy.

Applied Knowledge

HOW SHOULD PARENTS REACT TO CHILDREN WHO MASTURBATE?

Few parents today believe that children who masturbate set the stage for phys-

ical and mental maladies. Still, some parents react with concern, disgust, or shock when their children masturbate.

Parents who are unaware that masturbation is commonplace among children may erroneously assume that

children who masturbate are oversexed or aberrant. The parent may pull a child's hands away and scold her or him. Some may even slap the child's hand. Once the child is capable of understanding speech, the parent may say things like "Don't touch down there! That's a bad thing to do. Stop doing that." Threats and punishments may be used. Or parents may fail to acknowledge the behaviour openly but move the hands away from the genitals or pick up the child whenever he or she is discovered masturbating.

Sex educators Mary Calderone and Eric Johnson (1989) argue that punishment will not stop children from masturbating. It may cause them to become secretive and guilty about it, however. Sex guilt tends to persist and may impede sexual pleasure in marriage. June Reinisch (1990), director of the Kinsey Institute, notes that

> Parents who scowl, scold, or punish in response to a child's exploring his or her genitals may be

teaching the child that this kind of pleasure is wrong and that the *child* is "bad" for engaging in this kind of behavior. This message may hinder the ability to give and receive erotic pleasure as an adult and ultimately interfere with the ability to establish a loving and intimate relationship. (p. 248)

Calderone, Johnson, and Reinisch concur, however, that children need to learn that masturbation in public is not acceptable in our culture. Calderone and Johnson suggest that the child who masturbates in front of others can be told something like this:

> I'm glad you've found your body feels good, but when you want to touch your body that way, it's

more private to be in your room by yourself. (p. 138)

Reinisch adds that parents are important shapers of their children's sexuality and, more broadly, of their self-esteem. Acknowledging the child's sexuality, rather than rejecting and discouraging it, can strengthen children's self-esteem, build a positive body image, and encourage competence and assertiveness.

Not all authorities—and certainly not all parents—endorse such views. Some object to masturbation on religious or moral grounds. Others feel uncomfortable or conflicted about masturbation themselves. Parents must decide for themselves how best to react when they discover their children masturbating..

Puberty The stage of development during which reproduction first becomes possible. Puberty begins with the appearance of *secondary sex characteristics* and ends when the long bones make no further gains in length. (From the Latin *puber,* which means "of ripe age.")

Secondary sex characteristics Physical characteristics that differentiate males and females and that usually appear at puberty but are not directly involved in reproduction, such as the bodily distribution of hair and fat, the development of muscle mass, and deepening of the voice.

Primary sex characteristics Physical characteristics that differentiate males and females and are directly involved in reproduction, such as the sex organs.

Menarche (men-AR-kee) The onset of menstruation; first menstruation. (From Greek roots that mean "month" [*men*] and "beginning" [*arche*].)

Adolescence

Adolescence is bounded by the advent of puberty at the earlier end and the capacity to take on adult responsibilities at the later end. In our society adolescents are "neither fish nor fowl," as the saying goes—neither children nor adults. Adolescents may be able to reproduce and are often taller than their parents, but they may not be allowed to get driver's licences or attend R-rated films. They are prevented from working long hours and must usually stay in school until age 16. They cannot marry until they reach the "age of consent." The message is clear: Adults see adolescents as impulsive and as needing to be restricted for "their own good." Given these restrictions, a sex drive that is heightened by surges of sex hormones, and media inundation with sexual themes, it is not surprising that many adolescents are in conflict with their families about going around with certain friends, about sex, and about using the family car.

Puberty

Puberty begins with the appearance of **secondary sex characteristics** and ends when the long bones make no further gains in length (see Table 12.1). The appearance of strands of pubic hair is often the first visible sign of puberty. Puberty also involves changes in **primary sex characteristics**. Once puberty begins, most major changes occur within three years in girls and within four years in boys (Etaugh & Rathus, 1995).

Toward the end of puberty, reproduction becomes possible. The two principal markers of reproductive potential are **menarche** in the girl and the first ejaculation in the boy. But these events do not generally herald immediate fertility.

Girls experience menarche between the ages of 10 and 18. In the 1890s, Canadian girls typically reached menarche by about 14.8 years. Since then, the age of menarche has declined sharply, probably as a result of improved nutrition and health care. The average age of menarche in Canada is now between 12 and 13 (Wyshuk & Frisch, as cited by Maticka-Tyndale, 2001).

The **critical fat hypothesis** suggests that girls must reach a certain body weight (perhaps 47–50 kilograms, or 103 to 109 pounds) to trigger pubertal changes such as menarche, and children today tend to achieve larger body sizes sooner. According to this hypothesis, body fat plays a crucial role because fat cells secrete leptin, a chemical that then signals the body to secrete a cascade of hormones that increases the levels of estrogen in the body. It is known that menarche comes later to girls who have a lower percentage of body fat, such as athletes (Frisch, 1997).

PUBERTAL CHANGES IN THE FEMALE First menstruation, or menarche, is the most obvious sign of puberty in girls. Yet other, less obvious changes have already set the stage for menstruation. Between 8 and 14 years of age, release of FSH by the pituitary gland causes the ovaries to begin to secrete estrogen. Estrogen has several major effects on pubertal development. For one, it stimulates the growth of breast tissue ("breast buds"), perhaps as early as age eight or nine. The breasts usually begin to enlarge during the tenth year.

Estrogen also promotes the growth of the uterus, thickening of the vaginal lining, and the growth of fatty and supporting tissue in the hips and buttocks. This tissue and the widening of the pelvis cause the hips to become rounded and permit childbearing. But growth of fatty deposits and connective tissue varies considerably. Some women may have pronounced breasts; others may have relatively large hips.

Small amounts of androgens produced by the female's adrenal glands, along with estrogen, stimulate development of pubic and underarm hair, beginning at about age 11. Excessive androgen production can darken or thicken facial hair.

Estrogen causes the labia to grow during puberty, but androgens cause the clitoris to develop. Estrogen stimulates growth of the vagina and uterus. Estrogen typically slows down the female growth spurt some years before that of the male. Estrogen production becomes cyclical in puberty and regulates the menstrual cycle. Following menarche, a girl's early menstrual cycles are typically **anovulatory**— without ovulation. Girls cannot become pregnant until ovulation occurs, and ovulation may lag behind menarche by as much as two years. And ovulation may not be reliable at first, so a girl may be relatively infertile. Some teenagers, however, are highly fertile soon after menarche (Reinisch, 1990).

PUBERTAL CHANGES IN THE MALE At puberty the hypothalamus signals the pituitary to increase production of FSH and LH. These releasing hormones stimulate the testes to increase their output of testosterone. Testosterone prompts growth

Critical fat hypothesis
The view that girls must reach a certain body weight to trigger pubertal changes such as menarche.

Anovulatory Without ovulation.

Scarleteen
A sex education Web site for teenagers.
www.scarleteen.com

Adolescence.
Adolescence begins with puberty. Adolescents in our society are "neither fish nor fowl"—neither children nor adults. They may be capable of reproduction and be larger than their parents, but they may not be allowed to get driver's licences or attend R-rated films. Many adults see adolescents as impulsive—as needing to be controlled "for their own good." However, adolescents have a sex drive that is heightened by surges of sex hormones, and they are flooded with sexual themes in the media. Therefore it is not surprising that many of them are in conflict with their families about issues of autonomy and sexual behaviour.

Nocturnal emission
Involuntary ejaculation of seminal fluid while asleep. Also referred to as a "wet dream," although the individual need not be dreaming about sex, or dreaming at all, at the time.

of the male genitals: the testes, scrotum, and penis. It fosters differentiation of male secondary sex characteristics: the growth of facial, body, and pubic hair and the deepening of the voice. Testicle growth, in turn, accelerates testosterone production and pubertal changes. The testes continue to grow, and the scrotal sac becomes larger and hangs loosely from the body. The penis widens and lengthens, and pubic hair appears.

By age 13 or 14, erections become frequent. Indeed, many junior high school boys dread being caught between classes with erections or being asked to stand before the class. Under the influence of testosterone, the prostate and seminal vesicles—the organs that produce semen—increase in size, and semen production begins. Boys typically experience their first ejaculation by age 13 or 14, most often through masturbation. There is much variation, however. First ejaculations may occur as early as age eight or not until the early 20s (Reinisch, 1990). Mature sperm are not usually found in the ejaculate until about a year after the first ejaculation, at age 14 on the average (Kulin et al., 1989). But sperm may be present in the first ejaculate (Reinisch, 1990), so pubertal boys should not assume that they have an infertile "grace period" following their first ejaculation. About a year after their first ejaculation, boys may begin to experience **nocturnal emissions**, which are also

TABLE 12.1
Stages in Pubertal Development

In Females

Beginning sometime between ages 8 and 11	Pituitary hormones stimulate ovaries to increase production of estrogen. Internal reproductive organs begin to grow.
Beginning sometime between ages 9 and 15	First the areola (the darker area around the nipple) and then the breasts increase in size and become more rounded. Pubic hair becomes darker and coarser. Growth in height continues. Body fat continues to round body contours. A normal vaginal discharge becomes noticeable. Sweat and oil glands increase in activity, and acne may appear. Internal and external reproductive organs and genitals grow, making the vagina longer and the labia more pronounced.
Beginning sometime between ages 10 and 16	Areola and nipples grow, often forming a second mound sticking out from the rounded breast mound. Pubic hair begins to grow in a triangular shape and to cover the centre of the mons. Underarm hair appears. Menarche occurs. Internal reproductive organs continue to develop. Ovaries may begin to release mature eggs capable of being fertilized. Growth in height slows.
Beginning sometime between ages 12 and 19	Breasts near adult size and shape. Pubic hair fully covers the mons and spreads to the top of the thighs. The voice may deepen slightly (but not as much as in males). Menstrual cycles gradually become more regular. Some further changes in body shape may occur into the young woman's early 20s.

This table is a general guideline. Changes may appear sooner or later than shown and do not always appear in the indicated sequence.

called wet dreams because of the belief that nocturnal emissions accompany erotic dreams—which need not be so.

Underarm hair appears at about age 15. Facial hair is at first a fuzz on the upper lip. A beard does not appear for another two or three years. Only half of boys shave (of necessity) by age 17. The beard and chest hair continue to develop past the age of 20. At age 14 or 15, the voice deepens because of the growth of the **larynx** and the lengthening of the vocal cords. Development is gradual, and the voices of adolescent boys sometimes crack embarrassingly.

Boys and girls undergo general growth spurts during puberty. Girls usually shoot up before boys. Individuals differ, however, and some boys spurt sooner than some girls.

Increases in muscle mass produce increases in weight. The shoulders and the circumference of the chest widen. At the age of 18 or so, men stop growing taller because estrogen prevents the long bones from making further gains in length (Smith et al., 1994). Males normally produce some estrogen in the adrenal glands and testes. Nearly one in two boys experiences temporary enlargement of the breasts, or **gynecomastia**, during puberty; this also is caused by estrogen.

Larynx A structure of muscle and cartilage that lies at the upper end of the trachea and contains the vocal cords; the voice box.

Gynecomastia Overdevelopment of a male's breasts. (From Greek roots that mean "woman" [*gyne*] and "breast" [*mastos*].)

In Males

Beginning sometime between ages 9 and 15	The testicles begin to grow. The skin of the scrotum becomes redder and coarser. A few straight pubic hairs appear at the base of the penis. Muscle mass develops, and the boy begins to grow taller. The areola grows larger and darker.
Beginning sometime between ages 11 and 16	The penis begins to grow longer. The testicles and scrotum continue to grow. Pubic hair becomes coarser and more curled and spreads to cover the area between the legs. The body gains in height. The shoulders broaden. The hips narrow. The larynx enlarges, resulting in a deepening of the voice. Sparse facial and underarm hair appears.
Beginning sometime between ages 11 and 17	The penis begins to increase in circumference as well as in length (though more slowly). The testicles continue to increase in size. The texture of the pubic hair is more like an adult's. Growth of facial and underarm hair increases. Shaving may begin. First ejaculation occurs. In nearly half of all boys, gynecomastia (breast enlargement) occurs, which then decreases in a year or two. Increased skin oils may produce acne.
Beginning sometime between ages 14 and 18	The body nears final adult height, and the genitals achieve adult shape and size, with pubic hair spreading to the thighs and slightly upward toward the belly. Chest hair appears. Facial hair reaches full growth. Shaving becomes more frequent. For some young men, further increases in height, body hair, and muscle growth and strength continue into their early 20s.

With all these dramatic physical changes occurring so quickly, it is no surprise that body image can be of great concern to both male and female adolescents. Adolescent girls are typically more concerned about body image issues than are boys. Among Canadian teenagers, more girls (45%) than boys (21%) report that they are troubled a lot by their weight, although almost as many boys (45%) as girls report that they are troubled a lot by their looks (Bibby, 2001).

Masturbation

Masturbation is a major sexual outlet during adolescence. Yet many Canadian teens, especially girls, have negative attitudes toward masturbation. In the 2002 Canadian schools study, only 32% of Grade 11 girls compared with 63% of boys approved of masturbation (Boyce et al., 2003).

Male–Female Sexual Behaviour

Young people today start dating and "going steady" earlier than in past generations. These changes have implications for teenage pregnancy. Teens who date earlier (by age 14) are more likely to engage in coitus during high school (Miller et al., 1986). Teens who initiate sexual intercourse earlier are also less likely to use contraception and more likely to incur an unwanted pregnancy. If the young woman decides to keep her baby, she is also more likely to have to leave school and scuttle educational and vocational plans. Early dating does not always lead to early coitus, however. Nor does early coitus always lead to unwanted pregnancies. Still, some young women find their options in adulthood restricted by a chain of events that began in early adolescence.

DATING In his study of 3500 Canadian youth aged 15 to 19, Reginald Bibby (2001), a sociologist at the University of Lethbridge in Alberta and one of Canada's foremost experts on adolescents, found that dating is an important part of the lives of most adolescents. Two-thirds reported that they derive high levels of enjoyment from it, with one-third saying that not having a girlfriend or boyfriend bothered them a lot. Twenty-five percent of the girls and 17% of the boys reported that they had conflicts with their parents over dating, suggesting that Canadian parents are more concerned about the dating of their daughters than of their sons.

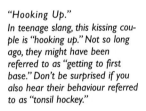

"Hooking Up."
In teenage slang, this kissing couple is "hooking up." Not so long ago, they might have been referred to as "getting to first base." Don't be surprised if you also hear their behaviour referred to as "tonsil hockey."

Twice as many boys (53%) as girls (27%) reported they weren't dating anyone (Bibby, 2001), probably owing to the fact that many adolescent girls date older males. The norms in adolescent culture are not supportive of having more than one dating partner at the same time, and only 6% of boys and 12% of girls report dating several people. About one-quarter of adolescents report that they are seriously involved in a dating relationship with one person. It should be noted that, although researchers use the concept of dating for the sake of consistency, young people today are more likely to use terms such as *seeing each other* instead of dating and *going together* instead of steady dating (Larson, Golts, & Munro, 2000).

In recent years there have been major changes in dating norms. For example, in the past it was expected that it was up to the boy to ask a girl for a date. However, in the 2002 Canadian schools survey, more than 90% of boys and girls agreed that it is acceptable for a girl to ask someone out on a date (Boyce et al., 2003).

As shown in Table 12.2, Canadian adolescents generally agree that as the level of dating increases, the acceptability of more intimate sexual behaviours also increases (Bibby, 2001). Almost all agree that kissing is acceptable after a few dates and more than two-thirds agree that it is acceptable on the first date. More than 80% feel that petting is acceptable after a few dates (or earlier). There are major gender differences in the acceptability of sexual intercourse, with far more males (68%) than females (36%) saying that it is okay to have sex after a few dates. These differing standards can lead to sexual conflict and tension between dating partners.

PETTING Many adolescents use petting to express affection, satisfy their curiosities, heighten their sexual arousal, and reach orgasm while avoiding pregnancy and maintaining virginity.

In the 2002 Canadian school survey, students were asked if they had engaged in touching above the waist and below the waist. Two-thirds of the Grade 9 students and four-fifths of the Grade 11 students had engaged in touching above the waist. Among the Grade 7 students, 46% of boys reported this behaviour, compared with 34% of girls (Boyce et al., 2003).

Fewer of the students had engaged in touching below the waist, with about half of the Grade 9s reporting this behaviour, compared with three-fourths of the

TABLE 12.2
Percentage of Canadian Adolescents Aged 15 to 19 Who Consider Various Sexual Behaviours Acceptable on Dates

Kissing	Males	Females
First date	78%	68%
After a few dates	21	30
Not acceptable after a few dates	1	2
Petting		
First date	43	22
After a few dates	50	63
Not acceptable after a few dates	7	15
Intercourse		
First date	18	4
After a few dates	50	32
Not acceptable after a few dates	32	64

Source: Adapted from R. Bibby (2001). Canada's Teens: Today, Yesterday, and Tomorrow. Toronto: Stoddart.

Grade 11s. Among the Grade 7 students, more boys (33%) reported experiencing this behaviour than girls (23%).

ORAL SEX The incidence of premarital oral sex has increased twofold to threefold since Kinsey's time. More Canadian youth experience oral sex than have sexual intercourse. About one-third of Canadian students in Grade 9 and one-half in Grade 11 report having experienced oral sex (Boyce et al., 2003).

In the past few years there have been several newspaper articles on the topic of teenage girls performing oral sex on boys. One of the most publicized stories occurred in Charlottetown, Prince Edward Island, where two boys aged 17 and 18 were convicted of having sexual contact with two girls under the age of 14 (which is the legal age of consent in Canada). The girls testified that they voluntarily performed oral sex on the boys and that they had no other physical contact such as kissing or sexual touching. One girl who was 12 at the time of the incident said that performing oral sex was not a "big deal" (Armstrong, 2003).

In an earlier study of Ontario female university students, 61% had performed oral sex on a male and 68% had received oral sex stimulation from a male (Herold & Way, 1983). One-half of the women had brought their partners to orgasm through oral sex and one-half had themselves had an orgasm while receiving oral sex. Among those who had not experienced coitus, one-third had engaged in oral sex.

SEXUAL INTERCOURSE In the 2002 survey of Canadian students, 23% of Grade 9 boys and 19% of Grade 9 girls said they had engaged in vaginal intercourse. Among Grade 11 students, more girls (46%) than boys (40%) had experienced intercourse. The proportion of students who experienced intercourse was lower overall in 2002 than in 1989; however, it was higher among the Grade 11 girls (Boyce et al., 2003).

Data on sexual intercourse were also obtained by Statistics Canada in the 2003 Canadian Community Health Survey. Here Statistics Canada separately analyzed data from a sample of 18 084 Canadians between the ages of 15 and 24 (Rotermann, 2005). The percentages of youth reporting that they had experienced intercourse are shown in Table 12.3. The highest percentage of sexually experienced youth were in the provinces of Quebec and Newfoundland and Labrador, with the next highest in New Brunswick.

In another striking change, young women today experience their first intercourse at a very similar age to that of young men. Among 18- and 19-year-olds, 51.5% of the women and 51% of the men had their first intercourse before the age of 18 (Maticka-Tyndale et al., 2001).

Yet most parents do not believe that their children have had intercourse. In a national survey sponsored by *Maclean's* magazine in 2002, parents of 13- to 18-year-olds were asked if their teens had experienced sex. Only 23% of parents in Quebec and hardly any parents outside of Quebec (4%) said they had (Dreidger, 2002).

TABLE 12.3
Percentage of Canadian Youth Who Have Experienced Sexual Intercourse

Age Category	Experienced Intercourse
15–17	28%
18–19	65
20–24	80

Source: Data from M. Rotermann (2005). Sex, Condoms and STDs Among Young People. *Health Reports, 16*, Statistics Canada Catalogue 82-9003.

ATTITUDES TO PREMARITAL INTERCOURSE The most significant changes in sexual attitudes in Canada occurred in the late 1960s and early 1970s. Prior to that time societal attitudes were firmly opposed to premarital sex (Herold, 1984). In the early 1960s, for example, Canadian writer Pierre Berton wrote an article for *Maclean's* magazine in which he said that if his daughter were to have premarital sex, he preferred that she did it at home in bed rather than in the back seat of a car. *Maclean's* received so many complaints about his views that he was fired from the magazine. In the mid-1960s, however, many young people began to assertively question the legitimacy of allowing traditional institutions to establish and control societal norms.

In a more recent study of sexual attitudes, only 17% of Canadians said that sex before marriage was wrong. However, a majority (75%) believed that sex before the age of 16 was wrong (Weidmer, Treas, & Newcomb, 1998). And in a 2002 survey sponsored by *Maclean's*, parents were asked what they thought was the appropriate age for teens to have sex outside of marriage. Only 5% of parents in Quebec and less than 1% of parents in the rest of Canada approved of sex before the age of 16 (Dreidger, 2002).

Many adolescents perceive their parents as disapproving of their having sex. In a Saskatchewan survey of high school students, about three-quarters of those who had not had intercourse and about half of those who had felt that their parents would disapprove (Hampton et al., 2001).

Canadian youth are more accepting of premarital sex than are older people. In 1995, 90% of 18- to 34-year-olds approved of premarital sex compared with 60% of those aged 55 and older (Bibby, 2001). A large majority of adolescents (82%) approve of premarital sex if the two people love each other, and over half (58%) approve if the two people like each other (Bibby, 2001).

Although societal attitudes have become more accepting of premarital sex, parents tend to be more conservative when it comes to their own children. The 2002 *Maclean's*-sponsored national survey asked "Should your teens be allowed to spend the night together in your home with their sex partner?" Most parents responded that this was unacceptable, with 41% of Quebec parents and only 14% of parents outside of Quebec approving (Dreidger, 2002).

FACTORS RELATED TO AGE OF FIRST SEXUAL INTERCOURSE Various social factors are predictive of intercourse at a young age. According to the 2001 National Longitudinal Survey of Children and Youth, Canadian adolescents who begin having sex at younger ages tend to also begin smoking by the age of 12 or 13, indicating that they do not conform to societal norms in general. Drinking alcohol at age 12 or 13 was associated with early age of intercourse for girls but not for boys. There was a striking gender difference in the role of self-esteem. Girls with a weak self-concept were more likely to have early intercourse, whereas boys with a *strong* self-concept were more likely to engage in intercourse. Physical characteristics also played a stronger role with girls: Girls who reached puberty at a young age and who were not overweight were more likely to have early intercourse (Statistics Canada, 2005d). In the 2002 Canadian schools survey, poor school attachment and poor relationships with parents were also predictive of early sexual intercourse (Boyce et al., 2003).

Among high school girls in Nova Scotia, Donald Langille (2002) of Dalhousie University found that the strongest predictors of having sexual intercourse at a young age were:

- not living with both parents
- father's low level of education
- infrequent church attendance

ADAMANT VIRGINS, POTENTIAL NONVIRGINS, AND NONVIRGINS

When studying factors related to sexual experience, most researchers categorize their sample into those who are and those who are not sexually experienced. However, in order to better understand the interaction of attitudes and behaviour, Herold and Goodwin (1981) differentiated students according to three categories: adamant virgins, potential nonvirgins, and nonvirgins. Adamant virgins believe that they should not have sex until marriage. They tend to be very religious, and have friends who are opposed to premarital sex. Potential nonvirgins have not experienced coitus but do not believe they should wait until marriage to have sexual intercourse. They are similar to the nonvirgins in accepting the idea of premarital sex; however, they are less likely to have sexually experienced friends and less likely to be in a love relationship. When asked why they have not had intercourse, they are likely to say that they have not met the right person or that they are not yet ready for sex (Herold & Goodwin, 1981).

These beliefs are reflected in a national survey of Canadian adolescents who were asked if sex before marriage is acceptable when the two people love each other (Bibby, 2001). Almost all of those who attended religious services less than weekly felt that it was (91%), compared with fewer than half of those who attended on a weekly basis (49%). However, the sexual attitudes and behaviour of most Canadian youth are not influenced by religion. Although about three-quarters say they identify with a particular religious group, only 22% attend religious services at least once a week (Bibby, 2001).

In the 2002 Canadian schools survey, only 11% of girls and 5% of boys in Grade 9 gave wanting to be a virgin until marriage as a reason for not having sexual intercourse. Only 3% of boys and 4% of girls gave religious beliefs as a reason for not having sex. The most common reasons for not having intercourse were not being ready, not having had the opportunity, and not having met the right person (Boyce et al., 2003).

Research in Action

THE FIRST TIME

For most Canadian young people, having sexual intercourse for the first time is one of the most significant events in their lives. The event also is of interest to society in general because of concerns about unwanted pregnancy, sexually transmitted infections, and sexual coercion. For many religious and ethnic groups, having sexual intercourse outside of the marital bond is seen as a serious violation of cultural norms and family honour. Consequently, first intercourse for most young people is an important decision.

Because of the double standard, first intercourse has traditionally been seen as the woman giving a gift to the man. Thus it has been seen as having more negative consequences for the woman.

Given changing attitudes regarding sex, do males and females still experience their first intercourse differently? University of Alberta researchers Lily Tsui and Elena Nicoladis (2004), in surveying university students, found that while there were some differences in the physical response of the genders, there were similarities in social-psychological aspects.

The two main gender differences concerned pain and orgasm. About half of the women but only 5% of the men reported experiencing pain at first intercourse. Most men (76%) experienced orgasm at first intercourse compared with only 12% of women. Not surprisingly, then, more men (62%) than women (35%) reported being physically satisfied after first intercourse.

In terms of emotional context, more women (63%) than men (43%) believed they were in love when they first had intercourse. However, about half of both genders said they were emotionally satisfied after first intercourse, and almost all said that they had sex again with the same partner and stayed together as a couple or became a couple after. They were also similar in reporting no regrets over first intercourse (males 76%, females 72%) and in rating the experience positively (males 72%, females 62%).

That most women rated their first intercourse experience positively is interesting, considering that half of them experienced pain and few had an orgasm. This suggests that many women do not focus only on physical sensations. Often women as well as men report satisfaction that in "doing it" they have achieved a major step toward adulthood.

SEXUAL FREQUENCY AND NUMBER OF SEXUAL PARTNERS Having experienced sexual intercourse does not mean that one is currently having sexual relations. In fact, only a minority of Canadian adolescents are having sexual relations on a frequent basis, with 25% reporting that they have sex at least once a week (Bibby, 2001). As well, it should be noted that studies such as Bibby's have a methodological weakness in that they refer to *sex* rather than *sexual intercourse*. Bibby cautions that while most teens use the word *sex* to refer to sexual intercourse, not all of them do.

Typically, males report having more sexual partners than do females. Twenty-one percent of adolescent males in Bibby's 2001 Canadian survey report having two or more partners during the current year, compared with 13% of females (Bibby, 2001). In the 2002 Canadian schools survey, about one-half of the Grade 11 students reported having only one sexual partner (males 43%, females 54%). Only a small minority of boys (15%) and girls (9%) reported six or more partners (Boyce et al., 2003). The number of partners was lower than reported in the 1989 school survey.

Age of first intercourse is a significant predictor of number of partners, with those beginning sexual intercourse at younger ages having more partners (Rotermann, 2005). Having more than one partner does not necessarily mean, however, that one is engaging in casual relations. The pattern for most youth is serial monogamy, whereby a person has sex within the context of a committed love relationship; when that relationship ends then he or she has sex in another committed relationship.

MOTIVES FOR INTERCOURSE Having sexual intercourse is motivated by a number of factors. In the 2002 Canadian school survey, the most common reason given for having sexual intercourse was "love for the person," with more girls than boys giving this reason. The second most common reason was "curiosity/experimentation" (Boyce et al., 2003).

This quote from a 19-year-old Ontario university student typifies the motivations of many young women:

> Sexual intercourse was for me mainly an expression of the love I felt for my partner whom I wanted to satisfy. Also, in a more minor way it satisfied an intense curiosity I had about sexual intercourse. (Herold, 1984, p. 19)

YOUNG PEOPLE AND CASUAL SEX Generally, males are more in favour of casual sex than are females. In the 2002 Canadian schools survey, twice as many Grade 11 boys (66%) approved of casual sex as did girls (32%) (Boyce et al., 2003). A study of high school students in Vancouver, British Columbia, and Amherst, Nova Scotia, found that girls were judged more negatively for engaging in casual sex than were boys. However, those girls who displayed greater self-confidence and whose parents were from higher social classes were less likely to be judged negatively (Shoveller et al., 2004).

The AIDS epidemic and concern over sexual health risk-taking behaviours have led to an increasing number of studies on casual sex. Rates of casual sex are difficult to determine, however, because there are so many differing definitions. Some researchers have focused on the time between first meeting someone and having sex with them (Herold & Mewhinney, 1993), while others have considered the lack of emotional involvement with the partner (Townsend, 1995).

In a study of 230 Ontario female university students, four different measures of casual sex were used (Weaver & Herold, 2000). The results showed how choosing a particular indicator has a strong impact on determining the percentage of people who are considered to be engaging in casual sex. Only 13% of the female students reported they had engaged in sexual intercourse with someone they had met the same day or night, but three times as many (36%) reported they had had sexual intercourse with someone they were not in a committed relationship with. The rates of casual sex jumped substantially when noncoital sexual experiences were measured. One-half had engaged in hand–genital and/or oral sex with someone they had met that day and three-quarters had experienced these behaviours with someone they were not in a committed relationship with. Most reported having only one or two casual sex partners, however.

More of the women in the Ontario study who had experienced any of the casual sex behaviours thought casual sex was enjoyable (76%) than those who had not (57%). When asked what aspects of casual sex were appealing, one-third said there was nothing appealing. Sexual pleasure was by far the most common reason given for having casual sex. Other reasons were to live it up, to fulfill sexual fantasies, the novelty of new partners, to improve sexual technique, doing the forbidden, heightened self-esteem, feeling good about one's body, and the thrill of attracting new partners.

When asked which factors might prevent them from engaging in casual sex, more than 90% of the women surveyed responded that they were concerned about AIDS, STIs, and pregnancy. The next major concerns related to morality, guilt, loose reputation, and fear of being physically harmed. Those who had not experienced casual sex were far more concerned about the moral issue than those who had.

Most studies of casual sex have used university samples. However, in one study, 169 people at singles bars were surveyed to see if they would have higher rates of casual sex than samples of university students (Herold & Mewhinney, 1993). Indeed, more of the females (49%) reported engaging in sexual intercourse the same day they met someone than in the above study of university females (13%) (Weaver & Herold, 2000).

The singles bar study revealed significant gender differences. More males than females reported casual sex experience, and the males were more likely to anticipate ahead of time that they might engage in casual sex. They enjoyed casual sex more, and felt less guilt about having casual sex. The women were more concerned with the risks, with 52% of the females compared with 7% of the males saying that they were worried about being physically harmed when alone with someone they had just met. The women were also more concerned about AIDS and STIs (Herold & Mewhinney, 1993).

A World of Diversity

SEX ON SPRING BREAK

Every winter thousands of Canadian college and university students travel to Florida and other destinations in search of fun and relaxation. Researchers Eleanor Maticka-Tyndale, Edward Herold, and Dawn Mewhinney have done extensive research on students going on spring break in Florida. Since relatively few studies have looked

at how particular contexts can reduce people's inhibitions, a major goal of the research was to determine how the situational context of spring break may influence sexual attitudes and behaviour. (Nonetheless, those who went away on spring break were not representative of students in general; they were more sexually experienced and drank more alcohol at home than those who did not go on spring break.)

In a preliminary study of university students' perceptions of spring-break norms, two-thirds agreed that students on spring break are more likely to have casual sex than they are while at school (Mewhinney, Herold, & Maticka-Tyndale, 1995). In a second study, which involved 151 students who were on their way to spring break and 681 who completed questionnaires during or after spring break, five main themes emerged (Maticka-Tyndale & Herold, 1997):

- travelling with a group of friends
- perpetual party atmosphere
- high alcohol consumption
- sexually suggestive contests and displays
- perception that casual sex is common

It was accepted that people would engage in types of behaviour, such as wet T-shirt contests, that they might not engage in at home, and that most did not expect to form long-lasting relationships with the opposite sex (Maticka-Tyndale & Herold, 1997).

Many more men (55%) than women (11%) went on spring break with the intention of engaging in casual sex. However, there was no actual difference in the percentage of men (15%) and women (13%) who actually engaged in sexual intercourse while on spring break with someone they had not known previously. Of those who did not have sexual intercourse, about half engaged in sexual "fooling around" with someone new. The fact that more men than women were interested in having casual sex meant that it was far easier for women to meet potential partners (Maticka-Tyndale, Herold, & Mewhinney, 1998).

Contraceptive Use

In the 2002 Canadian schools survey, between 5% and 10% of students did not use any method of contraception at last sexual intercourse. Almost a third of Grade 11 students who are sexually active use both the birth control pill and condoms. More girls (20%) than boys (11%) report using only birth control pills, while more boys (42%) than girls (28%) report using condoms only (Boyce et al., 2003).

As adolescents get older and form longer-term relationships, they switch from using the condom to using the pill. Researchers at Okanagan University College in British Columbia found that young people in monogamous relationships do not use condoms because they love and trust their partner to be faithful (Netting & Burnett, 2004). The most common reason Canadian teens give for not using condoms are that they did not expect to have sex, they are using another method of birth control, and they had too much alcohol or drugs (Boyce et al., 2003).

In the 2003 Canadian Community Health Survey, young people between the ages of 20 and 24 were the least likely to be using condoms, with 44% saying they did not use a condom at last intercourse. Also, those who began having intercourse at younger ages were less likely to use a condom currently. As well, those who had had only one sex partner in the previous year were less likely to use a condom (Rotermann, 2005).

Male–Male and Female–Female Sexual Behaviour

About 5% of the adolescents in the Coles and Stokes (1985) national survey in the Unites States reported sexual experiences with people of their own gender. More than nine out of ten experiences among adolescents of the same gender are between peers. Seduction of adolescents by gay male and lesbian adults is relatively rare. Most adolescent sexual encounters with people of the same gender are transitory. They most often include mutual masturbation, fondling, and genital display.

Many gay males and lesbians, of course, develop a firm sense of being gay during adolescence. Coming to terms with adolescence is often a difficult struggle, but it is frequently more intense for gay people (Baker, 1990) (see Chapter 9). Adolescents can be particularly cruel in their stigmatization, referring to gay peers as "homos," "queers," "faggots," and so on. Many adolescent gays therefore feel isolated and lonely and decide to cloak their sexual orientation. Many do not express their sexual orientation at all until after their high school years.

Adding to the strain of developing a gay identity in a largely hostile society is the threat of AIDS, which is all the more pressing a threat to young gay males because of the toll that AIDS has taken on the gay male community (Baker, 1990).

A World of Diversity

GAY PROM DATE

They danced the night away.

Marc Hall, the shy, blue-coiffed 17-year-old Oshawa student who wouldn't take no for an answer when told he couldn't take his boyfriend to his high-school prom, won a major court victory for Catholic students yesterday.

In a comprehensive and clear decision granting Hall's request for an injunction, Mr. Justice Robert MacKinnon of the Superior Court of Justice said a ban on same-sex dates at the prom was a clear violation of Hall's constitutional rights, and ordered the Durham Catholic School Board to allow Hall and Jean-Paul Dumond, 21, to attend the dance.

School board chair Mary Ann Martin said while the board was "extremely disappointed" with the ruling, Hall and his date would be allowed to attend the prom "if they wish."

While Hall's legal team said the ruling would set a precedent for gay and lesbian rights in the education system, Martin disagreed, saying the ruling applied only to the prom.

The board would continue to apply the teachings of the Roman Catholic Church to school-sponsored activities, she said.

Both the board and Hall's lawyers say they are ready to continue with a full trial on the issue and take it all the way to the Supreme Court of Canada if necessary.

But for Hall and his date, last night was a time to celebrate as they rode in a long black stretch limousine to the prom.

Hall, in a white tuxedo and blue tie, said he "was very happy and so excited that we won." When he first heard the news from his lawyer at his home in Oshawa, he said, "I was jumping up and down and everybody was shouting.

"I feel at ease now knowing that we are free of discrimination," said the Grade 12 student at Monsignor John Pereyma Catholic High School.

In addition to allowing Hall to take his date of choice to the prom, MacKinnon's ruling made some significant statements about the Catholic Church's stand on homosexuality, gay rights in schools and Catholic schools' rights under the British North America Act of 1867.

But school board lawyer Peter Lauwers called the ruling "bad law," say-

Gay Date at School Prom.
Marc Hall, 17, heads to his Toronto school prom with Jean-Paul Dumond, 21. Coming to terms with adolescence is often a difficult struggle, but it is frequently more intense for gay people.

ing the judge made "too broad" a decision based on a single case.

Source: Stan Josey (2002, May 11). From "Gay Prom Battle Ends with a Waltz." The Toronto Star.

Teenage Pregnancy

In Canada in 2001 there were 541 pregnancies to teenage females under the age of 15 and 37 081 pregnancies to those 15 to 19 years old. The rate of pregnancies among Canadian teenagers has dropped dramatically by about a third since 1974. As well, the proportion of Canadian pregnancies accounted for by teenage girls dropped from 14% in 1974 to 8% in 2001 (Statistics Canada, 2004b).

About half of teenage pregnancies end in an abortion (Maticka-Tyndale et al., 2001). Of those teenagers who go to term, about four-fifths choose to keep their babies. Teenage births are highest in the Canadian territories, with the Prairie provinces having the next highest rate. This could be attributed to the higher Aboriginal populations in these areas, since the pregnancy rate for this group is about four times higher than for non-Aboriginal populations (Maticka-Tyndale et al., 2001).

The rates of teen pregnancy in Canada are about the same as in Great Britain but about double the rates in France and Sweden. Of the Western countries, the United States has the highest rate of teen pregnancy (almost twice the Canadian rate). However, as in Canada, the rate of teen pregnancy has been dropping in the United States. Some researchers attribute the higher U.S. teen pregnancy rate mainly to the fact that American teens are less likely to use hormonal contraception than teens in the other countries (Darroch, Frost, & Singh, 2001).

The consequences of unplanned teenage pregnancies can devastate young mothers, their children, and society at large. Even young people themselves perceive teenage parenthood to be disastrous (Moore & Stief, 1992). Teenage mothers are more likely to live in poverty and to receive welfare than their peers (Grogger & Bronars, 1993). Poverty, joblessness, and lack of hope for the future are recurrent themes in adolescent pregnancy (Desmond, 1994). In the United States, half of teenage mothers quit school and go on public assistance (Kantrowitz, 1990a). Few receive consistent emotional or financial help from the fathers, who generally cannot support themselves, much less a family. Working teenage mothers earn just half as much as those who give birth in their 20s (CDC, 2000e).

Barely able to cope with one baby, many young mothers who give birth at age 15 or 16 have at least one more baby by the time they are 20. Among teenage girls who become pregnant, nearly one in five will become pregnant again within a year. More than 3 in 10 will have a repeat pregnancy within two years. Undereducated, unskilled, and overburdened, these young mothers face a constant uphill struggle.

The children of teenage mothers are at greater risk of physical, emotional, and intellectual problems in their preschool years, owing to poor nutrition and health care, family instability, and inadequate parenting (Furstenberg et al., 1989; Hechtman, 1989). They are more aggressive and impulsive as preschoolers than are children of older mothers (Furstenberg et al., 1989). They do more poorly in school. They are also more likely to suffer maternal abuse or neglect (Felsman et al., 1987; Kinard & Reinherz, 1987).

Researchers in Nova Scotia have determined that a number of community and familial factors such as single-parent families, lower levels of education, and low levels of church attendance increase the possibility of teenage pregnancy occurring. Higher rates of teen pregnancy also occur in communities with higher proportions of First Nations and Black people (Langille, Flowerdew, & Andreou, 2004).

Impaired family relationships, problems in school, emotional problems, misunderstandings about reproduction or contraception, and lack of contraception also play roles (Hechtman, 1989). Some adolescent girls believe that a baby will elicit a commitment from their partners or fill an emotional void. Some become pregnant as a way of rebelling against their parents. Some poor teenagers view early childbearing as the best of the severely limited options they perceive for their futures. But the largest number become pregnant because of misunderstandings about reproduction and contraception or miscalculations about the odds of conception. Even many teens who are relatively well informed about contraception fail to use it consistently (Hechtman, 1989).

More attention has been focused on teenage mothers, but young fathers bear an equal responsibility for teenage pregnancies. A U.S. survey based on a nationally representative sample of 1880 young men aged 15 through 19 showed that socioeconomically disadvantaged young men in particular appeared to view paternity as a source of self-esteem and were consequently more likely than more affluent young men to say that fathering a child would make them feel like a real man and that they would be pleased—or at least not as upset—with an unplanned pregnancy (Marsiglio, 1993a). Thus, poor young men were less likely to have used an effective contraceptive method during their most recent sexual experience.

Adulthood

Canadians entering adulthood today face a wider range of sexual choices and lifestyles than did earlier generations. The sexual revolution loosened traditional constraints on sexual choices, especially for women. Couples experiment with lifestyles that would have been unthinkable in earlier generations. An increasing number of young people choose to remain single as a way of life, not merely as a way station preceding the arrival of Mr. or Ms. Right.

In this section, we discuss diverse forms of adult sexuality in Canada today, including singlehood, marriage, and alternative lifestyles such as cohabitation, open marriage, and group marriage. Let us begin as people begin—with singlehood.

Singlehood

Recent years have seen a sharp increase in the numbers of single young people in our society. "Singlehood," not marriage, is now the most common lifestyle among people in their early 20s. Though marriages may be made in heaven, many Canadians are saying heaven can wait. About one-quarter of Canadians aged 15 and over are single (never married). Of those between 20 and 24, 90% of men and 77% of women are single; for those between 25 and 29 the proportion drops to 57% of men and 39% of women (Statistics Canada, 1996). Several factors contribute to the increased proportion of singles. For one thing, more people are postponing marriage to pursue educational and career goals. Many young people are deciding to "live together" (cohabit), at least for a while, rather than get married.

As you can see in Figure 12.1, people are getting married later. According to the 2001 census, the typical man in Canada today gets married for the first time at 30.2, compared with 25 in 1960. The typical woman gets married today at 28.2, compared with 22 in 1960 (Statistics Canada, 2003a). In 2001 the rate of marriage dropped to the lowest level ever recorded in Canada.

Many young adults in Canada live in the parental home, especially males. Two-thirds of men aged 20 to 24 live with their parents compared with about half the women of that age (Statistics Canada, 2002). Many young adults live with their parents when they are going to university or when they are trying to find a job. And, because of the high cost of rental housing, many cannot afford to rent their own apartment.

Less social stigma is attached to remaining single today. Women over the age of 30 are no longer likely to be described as "spinsters" (Edwards, 2000). But although single people are less likely today to be perceived as socially inadequate or as failures, some unmarried people still encounter stereotypes. Men who have never married may be suspected of being gay. Single women may feel that men perceive

Figure 12.1 Average Age of First Marriage in Canada.

The age at first marriage has substantially increased in Canada, partly because many adults live together before getting married.

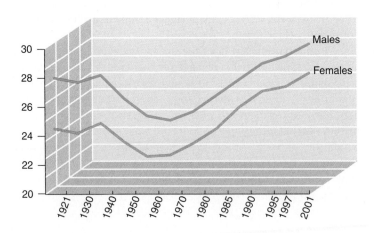

them as "loose." Many single people do not choose to be single. Some remain single because they have not yet found Mr. or Ms. Right. However, many young people see singlehood as an alternative, open-ended way of life, not just a temporary stage that precedes marriage. Now that career options for women have expanded, they are not as financially dependent on men as were their mothers and grandmothers. A number of career women, like young career-oriented men, choose to remain single (at least for a time) to focus on their careers.

In the 2001 General Social Survey on family and marital history, Canadian singles were asked if they expected to marry. Statistics Canada (2005e) focused their analysis on "mature singles" who do not expect to marry. Mature singles were older than the average age at which Canadians first marry (28 for women, 30 for men) but younger than 55. Mature singles who did not expect to marry placed less importance on love and being part of a couple and /or being married. Among the mature singles, francophones in Quebec were far less likely to expect they would get married than anglophones outside of Quebec. Also, those who had less education, earned less income, and were single parents had the lowest expectations of ever getting married (Statistics Canada, 2005e).

Singlehood is not without its problems. Many single people are lonely. Some singles express concern about their lack of a steady, meaningful social relationship. Others, usually women, worry about their physical safety. Some people living alone find it difficult to satisfy their needs for intimacy, companionship, sex, and emotional support. Despite these concerns, most singles are well adjusted and content. Singles who have a greater number of friends and a supportive social network tend to be more satisfied with their lifestyles.

The 1998 Compas survey asked single Canadians to indicate from a list of words which one best reflects their feelings about being single. The responses indicate a range of both positive and negative feelings. The most common response (31%) was "freedom" (see Table 12.4).

Singles.
There is no single "singles scene." Although some singles meet in singles bars, many meet in more casual settings, such as the neighbourhood laundromat. Some singles advertise online or in newspapers or magazines.

TABLE 12.4
Canadians' Feelings About Being Single

	Males	Females	Total
Exciting	6.2%	8.5%	7.3%
Fun	15.4	14.3	14.9
Confusing	14.7	14.3	14.5
Lonely	17.5	12.4	15.1
Dangerous	3.8	7.0	5.3
Frustrating	9.6	9.7	9.6
Freedom	29.8	32.6	31.1
None of the above	3.1	2.1	2.6

Note: Respondents could list up to three words. This table reports only the first word chosen.

Source: Compas (1998). Modern life survey of the Canadian population.

A World of Diversity

CANADIAN FEMALE TOURISTS AND BEACH BOYS IN THE DOMINICAN REPUBLIC

In recent years, some researchers have begun to study how social context can affect sexual behaviour. One such context is that of vacation travel, which is often associated with "sun, sand, and sex." Typically, people on vacation are in a party mood, drink more alcohol, and are open to meeting new people.

A Canadian study analyzed how the social context of the vacation structured the interpersonal dynamics that occurred in the Dominican Republic between Canadian female tourists and local men who were commonly known as "beach boys" (referred to locally as "sanky panky") (Herold, Garcia, & Demoya, 2001). While the female tourists had more economic power, the men were more knowledgeable about how to use the local cultural context to their advantage to obtain wanted resources from the women. The crossing of traditional racial boundaries added another layer of complexity.

The female tourists in the study often met beach boys—men who work as tour guides, waiters, or bartenders, or in beach or sports equipment rental, or lottery tickets or condominium timeshares sales—since their jobs provided the men a legitimate excuse for approaching female tourists and made it easy to initiate social contact. The beach boys were usually younger, ranging in age from 17 to 25, and in good physical shape.

For some beach boys, particularly the younger ones, the sexual conquest of tourists was a major objective. However, the main reason given by the professional beach boys for their involvement with female tourists was economic. Their material goals ranged from free meals and entertainment, driving a current-model rental car, and buying new clothes or jewellery, to buying a motorcycle or starting a small business, trips to Canada and other countries, or being sponsored through marriage to live and work there.

Most first-time female tourists did not anticipate becoming involved with a local male. (Interestingly, more francophone tourists from Quebec than anglophone tourists from Ontario anticipated that they would.) Of those who did become involved, most viewed their relationship as romantic rather than sexual (first-time romantic tourists). A minority of first-time tourists did anticipate involvement, however, and focused on the sexual aspects (first-time sex tourists). Generally, these women had heard about the experiences of other women who had been to the Dominican Republic, and in particular about the sexual prowess of the local men. Of those women who had been to the Dominican Republic before and had had a romantic relationship with a local man, many returned because they wished to maintain this love relationship (romantic returnees). A minority of the women returned with the objective of maximizing their sexual pleasure. Most of these women sought to have sex with one partner with whom they wished to spend most of their time (romantic sex tourists), while some preferred to have casual sex with a number of partners (adventurer sex tourists).

Which female tourists were pursued by the beach boys depended on the men's motivations. Those who sought only sexual conquest preferred young, attractive, preferably blonde women—women who were unlikely to provide money. (Having a relationship with this kind of woman also enhanced a beach boy's reputation among his peers.) But for the majority of beach boys who were primarily interested in making money, the main target groups were women past the age of 40 or younger, overweight women. In selecting these women, the beach boys were conscious of playing on female vulnerability. Many of these women may not have been used to having males pay romantic attention to

---

Three-quarters of both men and women said that women were more choosy in selecting a dating partner (Compas, 1998), yet almost equal percentages of women (80%) and men (76%) found it difficult to find a good dating partner (Compas, 1998). Adding to the challenge, 42% of single Canadians (and more women than men) were not comfortable asking for a date (see Table 12.5).

People are also uncertain about what dating guidelines they should follow. Fein and Schneider's 1990s book *The Rules* advised women that they needed to follow more traditional guidelines if they wanted to get a desirable man to marry them. When Canadian singles were asked their opinions about these rules, most disagreed with those such as "She should always let the man ask her on date" (68% disagreed) and "She should not accept any invitation for a Saturday date received after the pre-

What Are the Dynamics of This Relationship? Many Canadian female tourists in the Dominican Republic and on other islands in the Caribbean develop sexual and/or romantic relationships with local men, often referred to as "beach boys."

them; this may have been a new experience or one they had not had in a long time. According to the beach boys, these vulnerable women fell in love more readily and were usually more open about their financial situation, and thus likely to provide more money than other women. The men who chose overweight women believed that, since Canadian males prefer thin women, the overweight women had had few sexual partners and thus were less likely to pass on a sexually transmitted infection. The men also reported that overweight or older women were less embarrassed to be seen with them.

The men aimed to provide a total relationship involving a diversity of experiences, including sightseeing, going dancing, and going to restaurants. If a relationship developed, most preferred to be with the same woman during the entire time she was on her vacation. (Of course, beach boys were more likely to receive a monetary or gift reward if they remained with one woman.) The beach boys usually took their dates to places where they were well known so that the women would quickly notice they were popular, thus adding to their appeal.

The beach boys continually attempted to refine their seduction skills. They often compared their different techniques of seduction with other beach boys and provided one another with specific examples. The younger beach boys looked up to the older ones for words of wisdom about the seduction process.

The men commented that tourists who were sexual adventurers differed significantly from other women, including Dominican women, in their sexual practices and expectations. These women were uninhibited, and were more likely to take the initiative in sexual advances and to suggest a diversity of sexual activities. They typically urged the man to be more sexually assertive, and were more responsive during sex.

One beach boy cited this example of being in a hotel room with a woman: "She was screaming so loudly at orgasm that the hotel watchman knocked on the door, believing that I was hurting her."

Most of the beach boys said they didn't like using condoms because it reduced their sexual pleasure, and further reasoned that overweight women were unlikely to have an STI since they had not had much sexual experience. (The men also believed that if a woman was overweight she was in a healthy condition and not infected with an STI.) Indeed, because they felt confident they could judge by a woman's appearance alone whether she had AIDS or an STI, many believed it was not necessary for them to use a condom. Most of the female tourists insisted that the man wear a condom, however. A condom was typically used when the couple first had intercourse, but was discontinued after a few times. Only about a third of the beach boys reported that they used a condom every time they had sexual intercourse with a tourist. Some of the men commented on the frequent breakage of condoms, which may be attributed to their lack of knowledge of how to properly use them.

Inherent in the results of this study is the issue of exploitation. Do you think the female tourists used their wealthier status to exploit the beach boys? Do you think the men used tactics of manipulation to exploit the female tourists? Or was neither group exploited?

TABLE 12.5
How Comfortable Are Canadians in Asking for a Date?

	Males	Females	Total
Very	25.3%	16.4%	21.2%
Somewhat	40.3	32.4	36.6
Not really	26.6	24.0	25.4
Not at all	7.8	27.2	16.8

Source: Compas (1998). Modern life survey of the Canadian population.

Elizabeth Abbott.
Elizabeth Abbott, the dean of women at University of Toronto's Trinity College, is author of A History of Celibacy (1999). In her book Abbott reflects that she may remain celibate for the rest of her life.

vious Wednesday" (85% disagreed). However, 66% agreed with the rule "She should not be sexually available for at least a few weeks after the first date" (Compas, 1998). This last rule was most strongly endorsed in the Maritimes and least endorsed in Quebec.

There is no one "singles scene." Single people differ in their sexual interests and lifestyles. Many achieve emotional and psychological security through a network of intimate relationships with friends. Most are sexually active and practise **serial monogamy**. Other singles have a primary sexual relationship with one steady partner but occasional brief flings. A few, even in this age of AIDS, are "swinging singles." That is, they pursue casual sexual encounters, or "one-night stands." Seventeen percent of Canadians report that they have had sex with a stranger (*Maclean's*/CTV poll, 1994).

Although the stereotype of the "swinging single" is pervasive, 50% of Canadian singles are not even dating (Compas, 1998). Here there are some interesting gender and age differences. Among people in their 20s almost twice as many men (46%) as women (27%) are not dating, whereas among singles in their 50s, more women (79%) than men (64%) are not dating. Single men are more open to the idea of the "swinging singles" than are women. When asked if they would have sexual intercourse with an attractive person they just met (if that person was free of infection) 55% of Canadian men but only 8% of Canadian women said that they would (Compas, 1998).

Some singles remain celibate, either by choice or for lack of opportunity. People choose **celibacy** for a number of reasons. Nuns and priests do so for religious reasons. Others believe that celibacy allows them to focus their energies and attention on work or to commit themselves to an important cause. They see celibacy as a temporary accommodation to other pursuits. Others remain celibate because they view sex outside of marriage as immoral. Still others remain celibate because they find the prospects of sexual activity aversive or unalluring, or for fear of contracting STIs.

In her book *A History of Celibacy*, Elizabeth Abbott (1999), the dean of women at Trinity College, University of Toronto, discusses her own reasons for becoming celibate after her divorce. She emphasizes that her decision was based on personal growth rather than on moralistic reasons. In particular, she finds that celibacy makes her life less stressful and allows her greater freedom: "Much as I once reveled in sexual indulgence, I realized that at this stage of my life, I value even more the independence and serenity chaste solitude brings me" (Abbott, 1999, p. 9).

Cohabitation

Social scientists believe that **cohabitation** has become accepted within the social mainstream. Among Canadians, 84% approve of cohabitation (Bibby, 2001). We seldom hear cohabitation referred to as "living in sin" or "shacking up," as we once did. People today are more likely to refer to cohabitation with value-free expressions such as "living together."

There are considerable differences among Canadians of various ethnic backgrounds in the acceptability of cohabitation. Acceptance is higher among those of British origin than among South Europeans. The Chinese are less accepting, and the Indo-Canadian community is the least accepting (Michell, 2001).

COHABITATION TRENDS IN CANADA Since the 1970s, the proportion of Canadians who are not married but who live together as a couple has significantly increased. In 2001, about 1.2 million couples were cohabiting (Statistics Canada,

Serial monogamy A pattern of becoming involved in one exclusive relationship after another, as opposed to engaging in multiple sexual relationships at the same time.

Celibacy Complete sexual abstinence. (Sometimes used to describe the state of being unmarried, especially in the case of people who take vows to remain single.)

Cohabitation Living together as though married but without legal sanction.

2002). The legal term for this is common-law union. The proportion of Canadians living in common-law relationships is about double that of the United States.

Based on findings from the 2001 census, Statistics Canada (2002f) estimated that 53% of Canadians who are between the ages of 20 and 29 will experience their first living-together arrangement as a common-law relationship. These types of relationships are especially popular in Quebec, which has the highest proportion of couples beginning their first union as a common-law one. About 30% of all couples in Quebec live in a common-law relationship, one of the highest rates in the world. These relationships are less likely to lead to marriage. Among Quebec women in their 30s who started living in a common-law relationship, only one-third had married their partner at the time of the 2001 census, compared with 59% of women in the rest of Canada (Statistics Canada, 2002f).

Most Canadians living common-law do marry, however. About two-fifths of those in their 30s first live in a common-law relationship and about 80% of them will eventually marry someone. Children are common in cohabiting households, as nearly half of cohabiting couples have children in the household (Statistics Canada, 2002f).

REASONS FOR COHABITATION Why do people cohabit? Cohabitation, like marriage, is an alternative to the loneliness that can accompany living alone. Romantic partners may have deep feelings for each other but not be ready to get married. Some couples prefer cohabitation because it provides a consistent relationship without the legal entanglements of marriage (Steinhauer, 1995).

Many cohabitors feel less commitment to their relationships than married people do (Nock, 1995). Ruth, an 84-year-old woman, has been living with her partner, age 85, for four years. "I'm a free spirit," she says. "I need my space. Sometimes we think of marriage, but then I think that I don't want to be tied down" (cited in Steinhauer, 1995, p. C7).

Economic factors come into play as well. Emotionally committed couples may decide to cohabit because of the economic advantages of sharing household expenses. Some older people live together rather than marry because of resistance from adult children (Yorburg, 1995). Some children fear that a parent will be victimized by a needy senior citizen. Others may not want their inheritances to come into question.

COHABITATION FIRST AND MARRIAGE LATER: BENEFIT OR RISK? Cohabiting couples may believe that cohabitation will strengthen their eventual marriage by helping them iron out the kinks in their relationship. Yet cohabitors who later marry also run a serious risk of getting divorced. In Canada, married people who live together prior to their marriage are twice as likely to separate as those who did not first live together (Statistics Canada, 2002). Among those in their 30s who live together prior to marriage, 63% separate, compared with 30% of those who do not first live together. Why might cohabiting couples run a greater risk of divorce than couples who did not cohabit prior to marriage? Do not assume that cohabitation somehow causes divorce. We must be cautious about drawing causal conclusions from correlational data. Note that none of the couples in these studies were *randomly assigned* to cohabitation or noncohabitation. Therefore, *selection factors*—the factors that lead some couples to cohabit and others not to cohabit—may explain the results (see Figure 12.2). Cohabitors tend to be more committed to personal independence than noncohabitors (Bumpass, 1995). They also tend to be less traditional and less religious. All in all, people who cohabit prior to marriage tend to be less committed to the values and interests traditionally associated with the institution of marriage. The attitudes of cohabitors, and not cohabitation itself, may thus account for their higher rates of marital dissolution.

Figure 12.2 Does Cohabitation Prior to Marriage Increase the Risk of Eventual Divorce?

There is a correlational relationship between cohabitation prior to marriage and the risk of divorce later on. Does cohabitation increase the risk of divorce, or do other factors—such as a commitment to personal independence—contribute both to the likelihood of cohabitation and to eventual divorce?

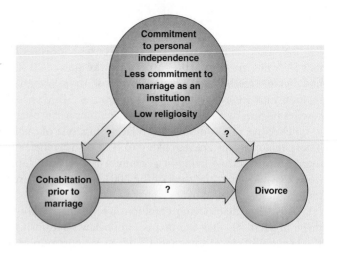

Marriage

Marriage is found in all human societies. Most people in every known society—sometimes nearly all—get married at least once. Marriage is our most common lifestyle. Statistics Canada (2005e) estimates that three-quarters of Canadians who are in their 30s will marry at some point in their lives. Most people see marriage as permanent.

Traditionally, societies have defined marriage as applying only to heterosexual couples. This definition was challenged by same-sex couples in Canada, who argued that not allowing same-sex marriage restricted their freedom. In July 2002, the Ontario Superior Court ruled that the traditional definition of marriage was discriminatory to lesbians and gays and ordered governments to redefine the term *marriage* to include recognition of same-sex couples. In this landmark decision, the judges argued that prohibiting same-sex couples from marrying was a violation of the Canadian Charter of Rights and Freedoms. In 2005 the Canadian Parliament passed legislation allowing same-sex couples to marry. (Same-sex marriages are also discussed in Chapters 1 and 9.)

WHY DO PEOPLE MARRY? Marriage meets personal and cultural needs. It legitimizes sexual relations and provides a legal sanction for deeply committed relationships. It permits the maintenance of a home life and provides an institution in which

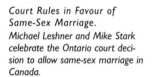

Court Rules in Favour of Same-Sex Marriage.
Michael Leshner and Mike Stark celebrate the Ontario court decision to allow same-sex marriage in Canada.

children can be supported and socialized into adopting the norms of the family and the culture at large. Marriage restricts sexual relations so that a man can be assured—or at least can assume—that his wife's children are his. Marriage also permits the orderly transmission of wealth from one family to another and from one generation to another. As late as the seventeenth and eighteenth centuries, most European marriages were arranged by the parents, generally on the basis of how the marriage would benefit the families.

Notions such as romantic love, equality, and the very radical concept that men as well as women would do well to aspire to the ideal of faithfulness are recent additions to the structure of marriage in Western society. Not until the nineteenth century did the notion of love as a basis for marriage become widespread in Western culture.

When Canadians were asked why people should get married, almost all (95%) said for love (Compas, 1998). The next common reasons were for companionship (83%) and to have children (82%). Two-thirds cited having a regular and safe sex partner. In addition, three-quarters of Canadians believe sex is a necessary part of a happy marriage (*Maclean's*/CTV Poll, 1994).

TYPES OF MARRIAGE There are two major types of marriage: monogamy and polygamy. In **monogamy**, a husband and wife are wed only to each other. But let us not confuse monogamy, which is a form of matrimony, with sexual exclusivity. People who are monogamously wedded often do have extramarital affairs, as we shall see, but they are considered to be married to only one person at a time. In **polygamy**, a person has more than one spouse and is permitted sexual access to each of them.

In Bountiful, British Columbia, a religious group openly practises polygamy. The group is a breakaway sect of the Mormon Church. Girls as young as 15 or 16 are commonly forced to marry much older men who already have wives. The British Columbia government has been reluctant to charge community members with violating Canada's anti-polygamy law, however, because the Canadian Charter of Rights protects religious freedom (Canadian Press, 2005b).

Polygyny is by far the most prevalent form of polygamy among the world's preliterate societies (Frayser, 1985). **Polyandry** is practised only rarely. In polygynous societies, men are permitted to have multiple wives if they can support them; more rarely, a man will have one wife and one or more concubines. Economic factors and the availability of prospective mates usually limit the opportunities for men to wed more than one woman at a time, however. In many cases, only wealthy men can afford to support multiple wives and the children of these unions. In addition, few if any societies have enough women to allow most men to have two or more wives (Harris & Johnson, 2000; Whitten, 2001). For these reasons, even in societies that prefer polygyny, fewer than half of the men at any given time actually have multiple mates (Ford & Beach, 1951).

WHOM WE MARRY Most preliterate societies regulate the selection of spouses in some way. The universal incest taboo proscribes matings between close relatives. Societal rules and customs also determine which people are desirable mates and which are not.

In Western cultures, mate selection is presumably free. Parents today seldom arrange marriages, although they may still encourage their child to date that wonderful son or daughter of the solid churchgoing couple who live down the street. However, among recent immigrants to Canada from the Middle East and East Asia, arranged marriages are relatively common.

Because we make choices, we tend to marry people who attract us. These people are usually similar to us in physical attractiveness and attitudes, and even in minute details. We are more often than not similar to our mates in characteristics such as height, weight, personality traits, and intelligence (Buss, 1994;

The Vanier Institute of the Family
Contains educational material and research on Canadian families.
www.vifamily.ca

Monogamy Marriage to one person.

Polygamy Simultaneous marriage to more than one person.

Polygyny A form of marriage in which a man is married to more than one woman at the same time.

Polyandry A form of marriage in which a woman is married to more than one man at the same time.

Arranged Marriage in Canada. A number of ethnic groups in Canada still engage in the practice of arranged marriages. Often they have arranged marriages with partners from their country of origin.

Lesnik-Oberstein & Cohen, 1984; Schafer & Keith, 1990). The people we marry also seem likely to meet our material, sexual, and psychological needs.

The concept of "like marrying like" is termed **homogamy**. We usually marry people of the same racial/ethnic background, educational level, and religion. However, with the increased cultural diversity in Canada, the number of people who choose a partner outside of their racial or ethnic group is increasing. In 2001 there were 452 000 individuals who formed mixed couples—a 35% increase from 1991. Mixed unions comprise 3.2% of all couples in Canada. In the 20–29 age group the proportions of mixed unions were 13% in Vancouver, 11% in Toronto, and 6% in Montreal. Japanese Canadians are the most likely to choose a partner from outside of their ethnic group, and South Asians are the least likely (Statistics Canada, 2004c).

Marriages between individuals who are alike may stand a better chance of survival, because the partners are more likely to share their values and attitudes (Michael et al., 1994).

We also tend to follow *age homogamy* (Michael et al., 1994). Age homogamy—the selection of a partner who falls in one's own age range—may reflect the tendency to marry early in adulthood. Persons who marry late or who remarry tend not to select partners so close in age. Bridegrooms tend to be two to five years older than their wives, on the average, in European, North American, and South American countries (Buss, 1994).

When it comes to picking a mate, men tend to be the romantics, women the pragmatists. Men are more likely to believe that each person has one true love whom they are destined to find (Peplau & Gordon, 1985). Men are more likely to believe in love at first sight. Women, on the other hand, are more likely to value financial security as much as passion. Women are also less likely to believe that love conquers all—especially economic problems. When Canadians were asked "Who is more choosy in selecting a marriage partner?" both men and women (57%) were more likely to say that women are (Compas, 1998). Considerably fewer believed that men are more choosy (28%) or that the genders are equally choosy (15%). In her study of male–female relationships in Canada and the United States, Dennis (1992) concludes that women have raised their expectations so high that many will never meet their ideal man and thus will have to decide whether to lower their standards or to remain single.

Homogamy The practice of marrying someone who is similar to oneself in social background and standing. (From Greek roots that mean "same" [*homos*] and "marriage" [*gamos*].)

Marital Sexuality

Patterns of marital sexuality vary across cultures, yet anthropologists have noted some common threads (Harris & Johnson, 2000; Whitten, 2001). Privacy for sexual relations is valued in nearly all cultures. Most cultures also place restrictions on coitus during menstruation, during at least some stages of pregnancy, and for a time after childbirth.

THE SEXUAL REVOLUTION HITS HOME We usually think of the sexual revolution in terms of the changes in sexual behaviours and attitudes that occurred among young, unmarried people. Indeed, most Canadians accept the idea that spouses will have had premarital sex with another person. Only 18% believe that "the ideal marriage partner should never have had any previous sexual partners" (Compas, 1998), with three-quarters agreeing that "the ideal marriage partner has had some but not too many partners."

The sexual revolution, however, also ushered in profound changes in marital sexuality. Compared with Kinsey's "pre-revolution" samples from the late 1930s and 1940s, married couples today engage in coitus more frequently, with greater variety, and for longer durations. And they report higher levels of sexual satisfaction, especially in comparison with those who are single. The sexual revolution also helped dislodge traditional male dominance in sexual behaviour. In essence, male dominance is the view that sexual pleasure is meant for men but not women and that it is the duty of women to satisfy their husbands' sexual needs and serve as passive "receptacles."

Marital foreplay has become more varied since Kinsey's day. Couples in more recent surveys report using a wider variety of foreplay techniques, including oral stimulation of the breasts and oral–genital contact (Blumstein & Schwartz, 1983; Hunt, 1974).

How frequently do married couples engage in coitus? Canadian data (Compas, 1998) do not allow a direct comparison with the Kinsey figures. As shown in Table 12.6, however, Canadian adults most commonly report having sex once or twice a week. These figures are somewhat in keeping with Kinsey's. People who are married or in common-law relationships have sex more often than singles, and those who are in common-law relationships have sex more often than those who are married. These data certainly call into the question the image of the "swinging single."

Studies consistently find that the frequency of sexual relations declines with age (Call et al., 1995; Compas, 1998; Laumann et al., 1994). Regardless of a couple's age, sexual frequency also appears to decline with years of marriage (Blumstein & Schwartz, 1990).

TABLE 12.6
Frequency of Sexual Intercourse During Previous Four Weeks by Relationship Status

Frequency	Single	Married	Common-law	Total
Did not have sex	47.5%	11.3%	8.1%	25.3%
Less than once a week	12.5	15.0	12.9	13.8
Once or twice a week	21.9	52.9	41.1	39.3
Three to four times a week	14.4	17.8	29.0	17.7
Five or more times a week	3.7	3.0	8.9	3.9

Note: Single includes never married, divorced, and widowed.

Source: Compas (1998). Modern life survey of the Canadian population.

In coitus, as in foreplay, the marital bed since Kinsey's day has become a stage on which the players act more varied roles. Today's couples use greater variety in coital positions.

Kinsey's study participants mainly limited coitus to the male-superior position. As many as 70% of Kinsey's males used the male-superior position exclusively (Kinsey et al., 1948). Perhaps three couples in ten used the female-superior position frequently. One in four or five used the lateral-entry position frequently, and about one in ten had used the rear-entry position. Younger and more highly educated men showed greater variety, however. In a more recent study among Montreal couples, the male-superior and female-superior were the two most popular positions (Ochs & Binik, 1999).

An often overlooked but important difference between Kinsey's and current samples involves the length of intercourse. In Kinsey's time it was widely believed that the "virile" man ejaculated rapidly during intercourse. Kinsey estimated that most men reached orgasm within two minutes after penetration, many within 10 or 20 seconds. Kinsey recognized that women usually took longer to reach orgasm through coitus; some clinicians were already asserting that a man's ejaculation was "premature" unless he delayed it until "the female [was] ready to reach orgasm" (1948, p. 580).

Even today's less highly educated couples appear to be more sophisticated than Kinsey's in their recognition of the need for sexual variety and in their focus on exchanging sexual pleasure rather than reaching orgasm rapidly (Michael et al., 1994). Canadians report that their sexual encounters last 39 minutes on average (*Maclean's*/CTV Poll, 1994). In a study of 77 cohabiting or married individuals in New Brunswick (Byers & Heinlein, 1989), sexual episodes were reported to last about half an hour on average (ranging from five minutes to two hours). Intercourse itself on average lasted about a quarter of an hour (ranging from two minutes to 1.25 hours).

SEXUAL SATISFACTION Researchers at the University of New Brunswick found that perceptions of rewards and costs are related to feelings of sexual satisfaction (Lawrence & Byers, 1995). (Rewards include the amount of fun experienced during sex, pleasurable physical sensations from touching and caressing, and feeling comfortable with one's partner. Costs include too-infrequent sexual activity and poor sexual communication with one's partner.) People who believe they are getting many sexual rewards and low sexual costs are likely to have a high level of sexual satisfaction. This is especially true when the rewards are greater and the costs lower than originally expected.

Other researchers have found that wives who talk openly to their husbands about their sexual feelings and needs report higher levels of sexual satisfaction (Banmen & Vogel, 1985; Tavris & Sadd, 1977). Among both men and women in New Brunswick who were in long-term relationships, sexual satisfaction was higher for those who could tell their partners about their sexual likes and dislikes (MacNeil & Byers, 1997). Interestingly, satisfaction was also higher for those who could openly communicate about nonsexual topics.

Couples who are in more committed relationships report higher levels of sexual satisfaction than those who are in noncommitted relationships. When asked how satisfied they are with their sex lives, two-thirds of Canadians who are married or in common-law relationships say they are very satisfied, compared with 44% of those who are single (Compas, 1998) (see Figure 12.3).

SEXUAL CONFLICT Couples can experience conflict over any number of sexual issues. In a study of couples in New Brunswick, one-quarter of the men were concerned that "I like to do things my partner does not" and one-third of the women were concerned that my "partner chooses inconvenient times for sex" (MacNeil &

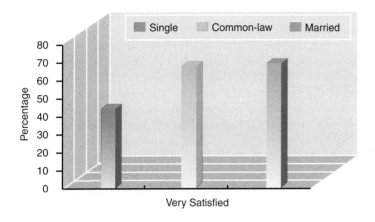

Figure 12.3 Relationship Status and Level of Sexual Satisfaction.

According to the Compas study (1998), married Canadians experience higher levels of satisfaction than those who are single (including divorced and widowed) or living common-law. Those who were married also reported the highest sexual frequency. Do these results mean that married people are more satisfied, or are they just more likely to report that they are satisfied?

Source: Compas (1998).

Byers, 1997). More than one-third of Canadians have conflicts over sex at least once a month, with those in common-law relationships having conflicts more often than married couples (Compas, 1998) (see Table 12.7).

B. J. Rye (2001) at the University of Waterloo found that 21% of students were often having serious and frequent disagreement about the occurrence of sex. Almost three times as many males (45%) as females (15%) were concerned that their partner's sexual desire was lower than what the respondent would like.

Extramarital Sex

Why do people engage in extramarital sex? What does it mean? What are its effects on a marriage?

Some people engage in extramarital sex for variety (Lamanna & Riedmann, 1997). Some have affairs to break the routine of a confining marriage. Others enter affairs for reasons similar to the nonsexual reasons why adolescents often have sex: as a way of expressing hostility toward a spouse or retaliating for injustice. Husbands and wives who engage in affairs often report that they are not satisfied with or fulfilled by their marital relationships. Curiosity and desire for personal growth are often more prominent motives than marital dissatisfaction. Middle-aged people may have affairs to boost their self-esteem or to prove that they are still attractive.

Many times the sexual motive is less pressing than the desire for emotional closeness. Some women say they are seeking someone they can talk to or communicate with (Lamanna & Riedmann, 1997). There is a notable gender difference here. According to Janis Abrahms Spring (1997), author of *After the Affair* (a self-

TABLE 12.7
Frequency of Conflicts Canadians Experience with Their Partner over Sex

	Males		Females	
	Common-law	Married	Common-law	Married
Often	1.4%	1.4%	3.6%	2.5%
Several times a month	4.2	3.5	8.9	7.8
Once or twice a month	39.4	30.1	35.7	28.6
Never	54.9	65.1	51.8	61.2

Source: Compas (1998). Modern life survey of the Canadian population.

help book designed to help people save their marriages after an affair), men may be seeking sex in affairs. Seventy-seven percent of women who have had affairs, compared with 43% of the men, cite love as their justification (Townsend, 1995). Men who have had affairs are more likely than women to cite a need for sexual excitement as a justification—75% versus 55% (Glass & Wright, 1992).

These data support the view, expressed repeatedly throughout this text, that women are less accepting of sex without emotional involvement (Townsend, 1995). Men are more likely than women to "separate sex and love; women appear to believe that love and sex go together and that falling in love justifies sexual involvement" (Glass & Wright, 1992, p. 361). Men (whether single, married, or cohabiting) are also generally more approving of extramarital affairs than women are (Glass & Wright, 1992). But note that these are all *group* differences. Many individual men are interested primarily in the extramarital relationship rather than the sex per se. Similarly, many women are out for the sex and not the relationship.

PATTERNS OF EXTRAMARITAL SEX Let us begin with a few definitions. **Extramarital sex** (an "affair") is usually conducted without the spouse's knowledge or approval. Secret affairs are referred to as **conventional adultery**, infidelity, or simply "cheating." Conventional adultery runs the gamut from the "one-night stand" to the affair that persists for years. (Bill Clinton's affair with Gennifer Flowers was alleged to have continued for a dozen years.) In **consensual adultery**, extramarital relationships are conducted openly—that is, with the knowledge and consent of the partner. In what is called **swinging**, **comarital sex**, or mate swapping, the partner participates.

How many people "cheat" on their spouses? Viewers of TV talk shows may get the impression that everyone cheats, but surveys paint a different picture. In U.S. surveys conducted between 1988 and 1996 by the respected National Opinion Research Center, about one husband in four or five, and one wife in eight, admitted to marital infidelity (Alterman, 1997; "Cheating," 1993). Similarly, more than 90% of the married women and 75% of the married men in the NHSLS study reported remaining loyal to their spouses (Laumann et al., 1994).

In a 1994 poll by *Maclean's*, fewer Canadians admitted to having an extramarital affair (men 14%, women 7%) than has been reported in American surveys. The rates for extramarital sex are higher in Quebec than for any other province. Similar rates were found in a 2005 Compas poll, in which 10% of married Canadians said that an extramarital affair had occurred in their marriage. Of course, what we do not know is whether Canadians are less likely to have affairs than Americans or whether they are less willing to admit it.

In the 2005 Compas survey about half of respondents believed that in Canadian society being faithful is not as important as it once was. One reflection of this belief might be the popularity of the Toronto-based Web site (**www.ashleymadison.com**) for attached people who want to have sexual flings. The Ashley Madison agency claims that more than half a million people have signed up as members since the site was launched in 2002.

ATTITUDES TOWARD EXTRAMARITAL SEX The sexual revolution does not seem to have changed attitudes toward extramarital sex. Most married couples embrace the value of monogamy as the cornerstone of their marital relationship (Blumstein & Schwartz, 1990). As shown in Table 12.8, almost all Canadians in married or common-law relationships say that they would be bothered if their partner had sexual intercourse with someone else. However, about one-half of Canadians are accepting of their partner having a "very close but nonsexual relationship" with someone of the opposite sex (Compas, 1998).

Extramarital sex Sexual relations between a married person and someone other than his or her spouse.

Conventional adultery Extramarital sex that is kept hidden from one's spouse.

Consensual adultery Extramarital sex that is engaged in openly with the knowledge and consent of one's spouse.

Swinging A form of consensual adultery in which both spouses share extramarital sexual experiences. Also referred to as *mate swapping*.

Comarital sex Swinging; mate swapping.

TABLE 12.8
Percentage of Canadians Who Would Be Bothered if Their Partner Had Sexual Intercourse with Someone Else

	Males		Females	
	Common-law	**Married**	**Common-law**	**Married**
Very	93.0	89.6	100.0	92.4
Somewhat	4.2	8.7	0.0	6.1
Not really	2.8	0.7	0.0	0.6
Not at all	0.0	0.0	0.0	0.9

Source: Compas (1998). Modern life survey of the Canadian population.

In a 2005 Compas survey, Canadians were asked if an act of unfaithfulness by their partner would mean the end of their relationship. Less than half (41%) said it definitely would and 27% said it probably would.

EFFECTS OF EXTRAMARITAL SEX The discovery of infidelity can evoke a range of emotional responses. The spouse may be filled with anger, jealousy, even shame. Feelings of inadequacy and doubts about one's attractiveness and desirability may surface. Infidelity may be seen by the betrayed spouse as a serious breach of trust and intimacy. Marriages that are not terminated in the wake of the disclosure may survive in a damaged condition (Charny & Parnass, 1995).

The harm an affair does to a marriage may reflect the meaning of the affair to the individual and his or her spouse. Deborah Lamberti, director of a counselling and psychotherapy centre in New York City, points again to women's traditional intertwining of sex with relationships and argues that "Men don't view sex with another person as a reason to leave a primary relationship" (1997, pp. 131–132). Women may recognize this and be able to tell themselves that their husbands are sleeping with someone else just for physical reasons. But women are more concerned about remaining monogamous. Therefore, if a woman is sleeping with another man, she may already have a foot out the door, so to speak. Alterman (1997) also notes that a wife's affair may be an unforgivable blow to the husband's ego or

A Web Site for Flings.
The Ashley Madison Web site attracts many people who are in relationships but who want to have flings. The site claims that more than half a million people have subscribed to it. This claim suggests that more Canadians might be having affairs than are willing to admit it to researchers.

*Moonlight Magic, a Swingers'
Club Web site in Calgary.
There are many swingers' groups
across Canada.*

pride. A woman may be more likely to see the transgression as a threat to the structure of her life.

If a person has an affair because the marriage is deeply troubled, the affair may be one more factor that speeds its dissolution. The effects on the marriage may depend on the nature of the affair. It may be easier to understand that a spouse has fallen prey to an isolated, unplanned encounter than to accept an extended affair (Charny & Parnass, 1995). In some cases the discovery of infidelity stimulates the couple to work to improve their relationship. If the extramarital activity continues, however, it may undermine the couple's efforts to restore their relationship.

SWINGING Swinging—also called "mate swapping" or comarital sex—is a form of consensual adultery in which both partners openly share sexual experiences with other people. Most swingers seek to avoid emotional entanglements with their swinging partners, but they may fail to separate their emotions from their sexual activity. Emotional intimacy between swinging partners can be even more threatening to the swingers' primary relationships than sexual intimacy.

Swingers tend to be of European descent, to be fairly affluent and well-educated and to have only nominal religious affiliations (Jenks, 1985). Solid statistics on the prevalence of swinging are lacking. However, in recent years there seems to be an increase in the number of swingers, and swingers' clubs are flourishing across Canada and the United States. The North American Swing Club Association states that there are more than 3 million participants in North America (Porter, 2003).

Until recently, Canadians who engaged in swinging or ran swingers' clubs could be charged with various offences under the Criminal Code, usually with having sex in a public place (public indecency) or with running a common bawdy house (a place used for prostitution or for acts of indecency). However, in 2005 the Supreme Court of Canada ruled that swinging was not illegal. The case, which involved the owners of two Montreal swingers' clubs, turned on the concept of indecency. The Court declared that sexual activity of consensual swingers was not harmful to Canadian society, and was therefore not indecent. The Supreme Court's verdict is highly significant because it used the criteria of harm to society, rather than community standards of morality, as a test for indecent behaviour.

Alternative Lifestyles

Marriages are generally based on the expectation of sexual exclusivity. However, alternative or nontraditional lifestyles, such as open marriages and group marriages, permit intimate relationships with people outside the marriage. Such alternative lifestyles attracted a flurry of attention during the heyday of the sexual revolution in the 1970s, but even then, they were more often talked about than practised (Harris & Johnson, 2000; Whitten, 2001).

A term that is commonly used today in referring to different forms of non-monogamy is polyamory. **Polyamory** is a general concept that covers the various forms of extramarital relationships. It refers to open relationships that allow for consensual sexual and/or emotional interactions with more than one partner.

OPEN MARRIAGE **Open marriage** is based on the view that people's needs for intimacy are unlikely to be gratified through one relationship. Proponents argue that the core marriage can be enhanced if the partners have the opportunity to develop emotionally intimate relationships with others (O'Neill & O'Neill, 1972).

The prevalence of open marriages, like that of swinging, remains unknown. Nor are there much data on which to base conclusions about the success of open marriages. Rubin and Adams (1986) found no differences in longevity between sexually open and sexually exclusive marriages over a five-year period.

GROUP MARRIAGE **Group marriage** also attracted some adherents during the sexual revolution of the 1960s and 1970s. In a group marriage, three or more people share an intimate relationship, although they are not legally married. Each member feels committed or married to at least two others. The major motive for group marriage is extension of intimacy beyond one spouse in order to increase personal fulfillment (Constantine & Constantine, 1973). Members of eight out of nine group marriages surveyed by the Constantines also admitted interest in a variety of sexual partners, however.

Group marriages differ from swinging in that participants share their innermost thoughts and feelings and expect their bonds to be permanent. Group marriages, therefore, are not perceived merely as vehicles for legitimizing mate swapping. Adherents expect children to profit by observing several adult role models and by escaping the "smothering" possessiveness of exclusive parent–child relationships.

Although they provide sexual variety, group marriages require adjustment to at least two other people—not just one. Moreover, legal and social problems can arise with respect to issues such as paternity and inheritance. Managing money may also be stressful, with arguments arising over joint accounts and who can spend how much for what. Sexual jealousies often arise as well. Given these problems, it is not surprising that group marriages are rare and have a high failure rate.

Group marriages are not unique to our culture. Although the practice has arisen rarely, other cultures have developed analogous marital customs (Werner & Cohen, 1990). Among the Chukchee people of Siberia, for example, group marriages sometimes involved as many as 10 couples. The men in such marriages, who considered themselves "companions-in-wives," had sexual rights to each wife.

The ideal of the traditional marriage remains strong in our culture. Men are somewhat more likely than women to participate or express an interest in lifestyles that permit greater sexual freedom and, perhaps, entail less personal responsibility (Knox, 1988). But even most of those who have tried alternative lifestyles such as cohabitation, open marriage, or group marriage enter into traditional marriages at some time.

The Polyamory Society
This nonprofit organization promotes and supports the interests of individuals of multipartner relationships and families.

www.polyamorysociety. org

Polyamory Any form of open relationship that allows for consensual sexual and/or emotional interactions with more than one partner.

Open marriage A marriage characterized by the personal privacy of the spouses and the agreed-upon liberty of each spouse to form intimate relationships, which may include sexually intimate relationships, with people other than the spouse.

Group marriage A social arrangement in which three or more people share an intimate relationship. Group marriages are illegal in Canada.

All in all, most adults still seem to feel about marriage the way Winston Churchill felt about democracy: It's flawed, laden with problems, and frustrating—but preferable to the alternatives.

Divorce

> My wife and I were considering a divorce, but after pricing lawyers we decided to buy a new car instead.
>
> —Henny Youngman

More than one-third of Canadians divorce within 30 years of marriage (Statistics Canada, 2005f). The divorce rate in 2003 was about three times as high as in 1968. The peak was reached in 1987 in response to changes in the Divorce Act in 1985, which made it easier to obtain a divorce. There has also been a significant increase in the number of people experiencing their second divorce. In 2003, 16.2% of divorces involved men who had been previously divorced, compared with only 5.4% in 1973 (Statistics Canada, 2005). Interestingly, divorces are most likely to occur after three to four years of marriage. Quebec has the highest rate of divorce and Newfoundland and Labrador has the lowest (Statistics Canada, 2005).

The first same-sex divorce happened in 2004. Two lesbians in Ontario divorced after five days of marriage (Tyler, 2004). In 2005, a Vancouver judge granted a divorce to a woman on the basis that her husband had engaged in adultery with another man. The judge decided that she had the authority to change the legal definition of adultery, which had been limited to people of the opposite sex (Canadian Press, August 31, 2005).

With the increasing acceptance of cohabitation, more and more divorced people choose to live common-law instead of remarrying (Statistics Canada, 2005f). However, the rate of breakups in common-law relationships is much greater than for married couples.

The greater number of divorces has resulted in a large increase in the number of stepfamilies. In 2001, there were about 500 000 stepfamilies in Canada, an increase of 17% from 1995 (Statistics Canada, 2005f).

Canada's no-fault divorce laws allow a divorce to be granted without a finding of marital misconduct. The increased economic independence of women has also contributed to the rising divorce rate. More women today have the economic means of breaking away from a troubled marriage. Today, more people consider marriage an alterable condition than in prior generations.

People today hold higher expectations of marriage than did their parents or grandparents. They expect marriage to be personally fulfilling as well as to function as an institution for rearing children. Many demand the right to be happy in marriage. The most common reasons given for a divorce today are problems in communication and a lack of understanding. When it is the woman who seeks to end a marriage today, her reasons often include a husband's criticism, defensiveness, contempt, and stonewalling—not lack of support (Carrère et al., 2000; Gottman et al., 1998).

THE COST OF DIVORCE Divorce often causes financial and emotional problems. When a household splits, the resources often cannot maintain the earlier standard of living for each partner. Financially speaking, divorce hits women harder than men. In the first year following divorce, women's income declines by 50% while men's decreases by 25% (Finnie, 1993). Women who have not pursued a career may have to struggle to compete with younger, more experienced workers. Divorced mothers often face the combined stress of being solely responsible for rearing their children and needing to increase their income to make ends meet. Divorced fathers may find it difficult to pay alimony and child support while attempting to establish a new lifestyle.

Divorce can also prompt feelings of failure as a spouse and parent, loneliness and uncertainty about the future, and depression. Married people appear to be better able to cope with the stresses and strains of life, perhaps because they can rely on each other for emotional support. Divorced and separated people have the highest rates of physical and mental illness in the population, and divorced people have higher rates of suicide than married people (Carrère et al., 2000; Gottman et al., 1998). On the other hand, divorce can be a time of personal growth and renewal. It can provide an opportunity for people to take stock of themselves and establish a new, more rewarding life.

Children are often the biggest losers when parents get a divorce (Ellis, 2000). On the other hand, chronic marital conflict or fighting is also connected with serious psychological distress in children and adolescents (Ellis, 2000; Erel & Burman, 1995; Harold et al., 1997). Boys have more trouble adjusting to conflict or divorce and may exhibit conduct problems at school and increased anxiety and dependence (Grych & Fincham, 1993; Holden & Ritchie, 1991).

Wallerstein and Blakeslee (1989) reported that about four out of ten children in their case studies showed problems such as anxiety, academic underachievement, decreased self-worth, and anger ten years after the divorce. A "sleeper effect" was also described. Apparently well-adjusted children of divorce developed problems in early adulthood, especially difficulties trusting that their partners in intimate relationships would make lasting commitments. Researchers attribute children's problems after divorce not only to the divorce itself but also to a subsequent decline in the quality of parenting. Children's adjustment is enhanced when parents maintain their parenting responsibilities and set aside their differences long enough to agree on child-rearing practices (Wallerstein & Blakeslee, 1989). Children of divorce also benefit when divorced parents encourage each other to continue to play important roles in their children's lives and avoid saying negative things about each other in their children's presence.

Remarriages are even more likely than first marriages to end in divorce (Lown & Dolan, 1988). One reason is the selection factor. That is, among people who get married, divorced people are a subgroup who are relatively less inclined than others to persist in a troubled marriage. Many divorced people who remarry are also encumbered with alimony and child-support payments that strain their new marriages. Many bring children from their earlier marriages to their new ones.

What of the long-term consequences of divorce? In one study, only one person in five reported, five years after the fact, that divorce had been a mistake (Wallerstein & Kelly, 1980). Most felt that the divorce had enhanced their lives. Most, however, also reported that they had underestimated the emotional pain they would endure.

The Later Years

Which is the fastest-growing segment of the population? People aged 65 and above. More than 4 million people in Canada are senior citizens, and their number is growing fast. This "greying" of the population may have a profound effect on our views of older people, especially concerning their sexuality. Many people in our culture see sexual activity as appropriate only for the young (Reiss, 1988). This belief falls within a constellation of unfounded cultural myths about older people, which includes the notions that older people are sexless, that older people with sexual urges are abnormal, and that older males with sexual interests are "dirty old men."

Researchers find that sexual daydreaming, sex drive, and sexual activity tend to decline with age, whereas negative sexual attitudes tend to increase (Purifoy et al., 1992). In the 1998 Compas survey of Canadians, only 20% of men over the age of 60 said they thought about sex several times a day, compared with 65% of men in their 20s (see Chapter 8). Among women over 60, only 3% thought about sex several times a day compared with 15% of women in their 20s. One-third of women in their 60s said they never thought about sex compared with only 3% of women in their 20s.

You're Never Too Old!
A common sexual myth in Canada is that the elderly, especially women, are not interested in sex. Sonia McMahon, 69, stakes out first place in a lineup of hundreds awaiting the arrival of Toronto fire-fighters for their 2002 charity calendar signing in the men's underwear department of the Bay. Obviously no one told Sonia that she's too old to be interested in sexually attractive men.

Single Seniors
This online dating service is geared to 50-plus seniors.

www.singleseniors.net

The Compas survey also found that people over 50 were *less* likely than younger people to do the following:

- feel comfortable asking their sexual partner to try something new
- share any information about their sex lives with their friends
- have conflicts with their partner over sex
- engage in oral sex
- use condoms

Yet research does not support the belief that older people inevitably lose their sexuality as they age. For example, since Viagra was introduced into Canada in 1999, millions of these pills have been sold, many to older men.

Stephen Katz and Barbara Marshall (2003) from Trent University in Ontario analyzed the role of Viagra in changing our perceptions of sexual functioning in older men. Katz and Marshall state that declining sexual function in older men used to be seen as a normal part of the aging process—a process that men were encouraged to accept as inevitable.

Sexuality in Late Adulthood. Are older people sexually active? If they are, are they abnormal or deviant? Although young people often find it difficult to imagine older people engaging in sexual activity, it is normal to retain sexual interest and activity for a lifetime.

Today, our society is encouraged by marketers to believe that many of the limitations of aging can be overcome. Erectile dysfunction is no longer seen as a natural accompaniment to aging but rather a sexual problem that most men can remedy—simply by taking a pill. Indeed, advertising for Viagra suggests that any older man can be just as sexually functional as a 20-year-old.

However, people who are exposed to cultural views that sex among older people is deviant may renounce sex as they age. Those who remain sexually active may be bothered by guilt (Reiss, 1988). A key question is to what extent the research findings on age differences are a result of cohort effects rather than aging. In other words, are older people today more conservative about sex because they grew up in a more conservative time period or are they more conservative simply because as people age, they adopt more conservative values?

Sexual activity among older people, as among other groups, is influenced not only by physical structures and changes but also by psychological well-being, feelings of intimacy, and cultural expectations.

Physical Changes

Although many older people retain the capacity to respond sexually, physical changes do occur as the years pass (see Table 12.9). If we are aware of them, we will not view them as abnormal or find ourselves unprepared to cope with them. Many potential problems can be averted by adjusting our expectations or making some changes to accommodate the aging process.

CHANGES IN THE FEMALE Many of the physical changes in women stem from decline in the production of estrogen around the time of menopause. The vaginal walls lose much elasticity and the thick, corrugated texture of the childbearing years. They grow paler and thinner. Thus coitus may become irritating. The thinning of the walls may also exert greater pressure on the bladder and urethra during coitus, leading in some cases to urinary urgency and burning urination that may persist for days.

The vagina also shrinks in size. The labia majora lose much of their fatty deposits and become thin. The introitus becomes relatively constricted, and penile entry may become somewhat difficult. This "problem," however, has a positive aspect: Increased friction between the penis and vaginal walls may heighten sexual sensations. The uterus decreases in size after menopause and no longer becomes so congested during sexual arousal. Following menopause, women also produce less vaginal lubrication, and the lubrication that is produced may take minutes, rather than seconds, to appear. Lack of adequate lubrication is also a major reason for painful coitus.

Many of these changes may be slowed or reversed through estrogen-replacement therapy (see Chapter 3) or topical application of estrogen-containing cream. Natural lubrication may also be increased through more elaborate foreplay. The need for more foreplay may encourage the man to become a more considerate lover. (Older men too are likely to need more time to become aroused.) An artificial lubricant can also ease problems posed by difficult entry or painful thrusting.

Women's breasts show smaller increases in size with sexual arousal as they age, but the nipples still become erect. Because the muscle tone of the urethra and anal sphincters decreases, the spasms of orgasm become less powerful and fewer in number. Thus orgasms may feel less intense. The uterine contractions that occur dur-

TABLE 12.9
Changes in Sexual Arousal Often Associated with Aging

Changes in the Female	Changes in the Male
Reduced myotonia (muscle tension)	Longer time to erection and orgasm
Reduced vaginal lubrication	Need for more direct stimulation for erection and orgasm
Reduced elasticity of the vaginal walls	Less semen emitted during ejaculation
Smaller increases in breast size during sexual arousal	Erections may be less firm
Reduced intensity of muscle spasms at orgasm	Testicles may not elevate as high into the scrotum
	Less intense orgasmic contractions
	Lessened feeling of a need to ejaculate during sex
	Longer refractory period

Source: Copyright © 1990 by The Kinsey Institute for Research in Sex, Gender, and Reproduction. From **The Kinsey Institute New Report on Sex.** *Reprinted with permission from St. Martin's Press, New York.*

ing orgasm become discouragingly painful for some postmenopausal women. Despite these changes, women can retain their ability to achieve orgasm well into their advanced years. The subjective experience of orgasm also remains highly satisfying, despite the lessened intensity of muscular contractions.

CHANGES IN THE MALE Age-related changes tend to occur more gradually in men than in women and are not clearly connected with any one biological event, as they are with menopause in the woman. Male adolescents may achieve erection in a matter of seconds through sexual fantasy alone. After about age 50, men take progressively longer to achieve erection. Erections become less firm, perhaps because of lowered testosterone production. Older men may require minutes of direct stimulation of the penis to achieve an erection. Couples can adjust to these changes by extending the length and variety of foreplay.

Most men remain capable of erection throughout their lives. Erectile dysfunction is not inevitable with aging. Men generally require more time to reach orgasm as they age, however, which may also reflect lowered testosterone production. In the eyes of their sex partners, however, delayed ejaculation may make them better lovers.

The testes often decrease slightly in size and produce less testosterone with age. Testosterone production usually declines gradually from about age 40 to age 60 and then begins to level off. However, the decline is not inevitable and may be related to the man's general health. Sperm production tends to decline as the seminiferous tubules degenerate, but viable sperm may be produced quite late in life. Men in their 70s, 80s, and even 90s have fathered children.

Nocturnal erections tend to diminish in intensity, duration, and frequency as men age, but they do not normally disappear in healthy men (Reinisch, 1990; Schiavi et al., 1990). The refractory period tends to lengthen with age. An adolescent may require only a few minutes to regain erection and ejaculate again after a first orgasm, whereas a man in his 30s may require half an hour. Past age 50, the refractory period may increase to several hours.

Older men produce less ejaculate, and it may seep rather than shoot out. Though the contractions of orgasm still begin at 0.8-second intervals, they become weaker and fewer. Still, the number and strength of spasms do not translate precisely into subjective pleasure. An older male may enjoy orgasm as thoroughly as he did at a younger age. Attitudes and expectations can be as important as the contractions themselves.

An 82-year-old man commented as follows on his changing sexual abilities:

> I come maybe once in every three sexual encounters these days with my wife. My erection comes and goes, and it's not a big concern to us. I get as much pleasure from touching and thrusting as I do from an ejaculation. When I was younger it was inconceivable to me that I might enjoy sex without an orgasm, but I can see now that in those days I missed out on some pleasure by making orgasm such a focus. (Gordon & Snyder, 1989, p. 153)

In sum, most physical changes do not bring a man's or a woman's sex life to a grinding halt. People's attitudes, sexual histories, and partners are usually more important factors in sexual behaviour and enjoyment.

Patterns of Sexual Activity

Despite the decline in certain physical functions, older people can continue to lead a vibrant, fulfilling sex life. In fact, years of sexual experience may more than compensate for any diminution of physical responsiveness (Hodson & Skeen, 1994).

Unfortunately, people who overreact to expected changes in sexual response may conclude that their sex lives are over and give up on sexual activity or even on expressing any physical affection (Dunn, 1998).

Research in Action

EFFECTS OF AGING ON GAY MALES AND LESBIANS

Only limited research has been carried out on the effects of aging on gay males. James Murray of the AIDS Committee of Toronto and Barry Adam of the University of Windsor (2001) conducted interviews in Toronto with gay and bisexual men aged 40 and over to find out some of their concerns about aging in the context of HIV. A common concern was that, because the gay community values youth and attractiveness, older men are at a disadvantage in finding sexual partners. Consequently, older gay men often see themselves as "invisible" and rejected by younger men. Clearly, several of the men believed they were no longer seen as desirable and consequently felt unwelcome in gay social gatherings. Feelings of isolation and loneliness were common themes, especially for those who had lost their partner and close friends to AIDS.

Positive aspects of aging were also expressed, however. For some, the attainment of an intimate relationship out-weighed diminished sexual prowess. And because the sex drive was now less urgent, some men felt that they could be in greater control of their sexuality. Finally, those who were most involved in gay community organizations felt that the social connections they established there would be a source of support as they aged (Murray & Adam, 2001).

Montreal researchers have found that older lesbians as well as gay males experience feeling of exclusion within gay and lesbian organizations because of age discrimination (Brotman et al., 2003). In addition, the older age groups feel doubly discriminated against in their interactions with health agencies in the broader society, because of both their sexual orientation and their age. Many from the older generation have not been open in society about their sexual orientation and experience considerable fear when dealing with health and social agencies. Not surprisingly, most agencies do not know how to respond to the unique needs of older lesbians and gay males. This is especially true in settings such as nursing homes where workers may be homophobic (Brotman et al., 2003).

A study of 100 older men in England found that the key factor in whether they continued to engage in sexual activity was the availability of a partner, not physical condition (Jones et al., 1994). Sex therapist Helen Singer Kaplan (1990) concluded,

A World of Diversity

SEXUAL INTERCOURSE AMONG OLDER CANADIANS

In the 1996/97 National Population Health Survey (NPHS), 81% of women aged 55–59 reported having sexual intercourse in the previous 12 months (Fraser et al., 2005). In the 1998 Compas survey of Canadians, 65% of men and 39% of women over the age of 60 reported that they were having sexual intercourse. Among this group, 74% of men and 39% of women were having sex at least once a week. These gender differences can be explained by the fact that, because women outlive men, more older women than men do not have a sexual partner, and thus have less opportunity to have sex. Among Canadians 65 years of age and older, 61% of the men live with a spouse or partner compared with only 35% of the women (Statistics Canada, 2002h).

Several factors play a role in declining sexual activity, including physical problems, boredom, and cultural attitudes toward sex among the aging. Among Canadians 50 years and over, four-fifths report that general health problems negatively affect their sex life (Compas, 1998). In the 1996/97 NPHS, sexual intercourse was more frequent among midlife women who were physically active, in excellent health, and had more education (Fraser et al., 2005).

In a Canadian study of 215 married people who were middle-aged and older (51 to 81 years of age), those aged 65 or above showed lower coital frequency than younger respondents (Libman, 1989). Coital frequency, however, is not synonymous with sexual satisfaction. No sizable differences emerged in the level of sexual satisfaction between older and younger groups.

Because sex is among the last pleasure-giving biological processes to deteriorate, it is potentially an enduring source of gratification at a time when these are becoming fewer and fewer, and a link to the joys of youth. These are important ingredients in the [older] person's emotional well-being. (pp. 185, 204)

Despite general trends, sexuality among older people is variable (Knox, 1988). Some become disgusted by sex; others simply lose interest. In contrast, many older people engage in intercourse, oral sex, and masturbation at least as often as when they were younger. A six-year longitudinal study of older married couples found that one in five actually increased their coital frequency over time (Palmore, 1981).

The frequency of masturbation also generally declines with age for both men and women, although an increase may occur following a marital separation, a divorce, or the death of a spouse (Hegeler & Mortensen, 1977). Still, continued masturbation was reported by nearly half (46%) among a sample of people aged 60 to 91 (Starr & Weiner, 1981). This is a high level of acceptance among people who were reared during a time when masturbation was generally viewed as harmful (Kammeyer, 1990).

Couples may accommodate to the physical changes of aging by broadening their sexual repertoire to include more diverse forms of stimulation. Many respondents to a *Consumer Reports* survey reported using oral–genital stimulation, sexual fantasy, sexually explicit materials, anal stimulation, vibrators, and other sexual techniques to offset problems in achieving lubrication or erection (Brecher, 1984). Sexual satisfaction may be derived from manual or oral stimulation, cuddling, caressing, and tenderness, as well as from intercourse to orgasm.

The availability of a sexually interested and supportive partner may be the most important determinant of continued sexual activity. Many women discontinue sexual activity because of the death of their husbands.

Summing Up

Infancy (Birth to Two Years): A Search for the Origins of Human Sexuality

Fetuses have been found to have erections and to suck their fingers. Stimulation of the genitals in infancy may produce sensations of pleasure. Pelvic thrusting has been observed in humans as early as eight months of age. Masturbation may begin as early as 6 to 12 months. Some infants seem capable of sexual responses that closely resemble orgasm. Self-stimulation for pleasure (masturbation) typically occurs among children as young as 6 to 12 months of age. Canadian children typically do not engage in genital play with others until about the age of two.

Early Childhood (Three to Eight Years)

Masturbation

Statistics concerning the incidence of masturbation at ages three to eight are inconclusive. In early childhood,

children show curiosity about the genitals and may play "doctor." Same-gender sexual play may be more common than heterosexual play and does not presage adult sexual orientation.

Preadolescence (Nine to Thirteen Years)

Preadolescents tend to socialize with best friends and with large groups and to become self-conscious about their bodies.

Masturbation is apparently the primary means of achieving orgasm during preadolescence for both genders.

Preadolescent sex play often involves mutual display of the genitals, with or without touching. Group dating and mixed-gender parties often provide preadolescents with their first exposure to heterosexual activities. Much preadolescent same-gender sexual behaviour involves sexual exploration and is short-lived.

Adolescence

Adolescence is bounded by the advent of puberty at the earlier end and by the capacity to take on adult responsibilities at the later. The conflicts and distress experienced by many adolescents apparently reflect the cultural expectations to which they are exposed.

Puberty

Pubertal changes are ushered in by sex hormones. Puberty begins with the appearance of secondary sex characteristics and ends when the long bones make no further gains in length. Once puberty begins, most major changes in primary sex characteristics occur within three years in girls and within four years in boys.

Masturbation

Masturbation is a major sexual outlet during adolescence.

Male–Female Sexual Behaviour

Adolescents today date and "go steady" earlier than in past generations. Many adolescents use petting as a way of achieving sexual gratification without becoming pregnant or ending one's virginity. The incidence of premarital intercourse, especially for females, has increased dramatically since Kinsey's day.

Contraceptive Use

Sexually active teenagers use contraception inconsistently, if at all.

Male–Male and Female–Female Sexual Behaviour

Most adolescent same-gender sexual encounters are transitory. Coming to terms with adolescence is often more intense for gay males and lesbians, largely because gay male and lesbian sexual orientations are stigmatized in our society.

Teenage Pregnancy

Rates of teenage pregnancy have declined. Teenage pregnancy can be devastating for both mother and child.

Early and Middle Adulthood

Singlehood

Recent years have seen a sharp increase in the numbers of single young people in our society. Reasons include increased permissiveness toward premarital sex and, particularly for women, the desire to become established in a career. No one lifestyle characterizes single people.

Cohabitation

Some couples prefer cohabitation because it provides a consistent intimate relationship without the legal and economic entanglements of marriage.

Cohabitors who later marry may run a greater risk of divorce than noncohabitors, perhaps because cohabitors are a more liberal group.

Marriage

Marriage is found in all human societies and is our most common lifestyle. Throughout Western history, marriages have legitimized sexual relations, sanctioned the permanence of a deeply committed relationship, provided for the orderly transmission of wealth, and established a setting for child rearing. In Western society today, romantic love is seen as an essential aspect of marriage.

People in Canada tend to marry within their geographical area and social class. They tend to marry people similar to themselves in physical attractiveness, people whose attitudes are similar to their own, and people who seem likely to meet their material, sexual, and psychological needs.

Marital Sexuality

Until the sexual revolution, Western culture could be characterized as sexually restrictive, even in its attitudes toward marital sex. Married couples today engage in coitus more frequently and for longer durations of time than in Kinsey's day. They report higher levels of sexual satisfaction and engage in a greater variety of sexual activities.

Extramarital Sex

In most cases, extramarital relationships are conducted without the spouse's knowledge or approval. People may have affairs for sexual variety, to punish their spouses, to achieve emotional closeness, or to prove that they are attractive. Extramarital sex continues to be viewed negatively by the majority of married people in our society.

Alternative Lifestyles

Polyamory includes arrangements such as open marriages and group marriages that permit intimate relationships with people outside the marriage.

Divorce

About one-third of the marriages in Canada end in divorce. Reasons include relaxed restrictions on divorce, greater financial independence among women, and wider acceptance of the idea that marriages should be happy. Divorce is often associated with financial and emotional problems, both for the couple and for their children.

The Later Years

There are a number of unfounded cultural myths about sexuality among older people, including the stereotypes that older people are sexless and that older people with sexual urges are abnormal.

Physical Changes

Physical changes as the years pass can impair sexual

activity. Many potential problems can be averted by altering expectations and making changes to accommodate the aging process.

Patterns of Sexual Activity

Sexual activity tends to decline with age, but continued sexual activity can boost self-esteem and be an important source of gratification.

Test Yourself

Multiple-Choice Questions

1. Masturbation in children tends to start between

   _____.

   a. 6 and 12 months
   b. 18 and 24 months
   c. 30 and 36 months
   d. five and six years

2. Sex games like "show me yours" and "playing doctor" become more common between the ages of

   a. 2 and 3
   b. 5 and 8
   c. 6 and 10
   d. 12 and older

3. Same-gender sexual play in childhood
   a. is a sign that the child will grow up gay or lesbian
   d. is much more common in boys than in girls
   c. is much more common in girls than in boys
   d. does not predict adult sexual orientation

4. Which of the following is not one of the effects of estrogen during puberty?
   a. thickening of the vaginal lining
   b. enlargement of the labia
   c. the growth of the vagina and uterus
   d. the development of the clitoris

5. Most adolescent males experience their first ejaculation through
   a. sexual intercourse
   b. nocturnal emissions
   c. masturbation
   d. oral sex

6. Half of Canadian adolescents have their first experience of sexual intercourse by the age of
   a. 14
   b. 16
   c. 18
   d. 20

7. Which of the following does the chapter *not* give as one of the reasons why teenage girls have babies?
   a. They feel that the baby will fill an emotional void in their lives.
   b. They get pregnant as a way to rebel against their parents.
   c. They miscalculate the odds of conception.
   d. They get pregnant to collect social benefits.

8. The average age of marriage is _____ for men and _____ for women.
   a. 28; 30
   b. 30; 28
   c. 25; 22
   d. 22; 25

9. About _____ of individuals who first cohabit will eventually get married.
   a. 50%
   b. 70%
   c. 80%
   d. 90%

10. Canadian divorce rates increased sharply in the late 1980s due to
    a. the sexual revolution
    b. an increase in the number of people having extra-marital affairs
    c. a relaxation of legal restrictions
    d. the feminist movement

Critical Thinking Questions

1. Would you characterize your own background as sexually permissive or restrictive? Why?

2. If you have not had a consensual sexual experience with another person, under what circumstances do you think this will take place? Are you waiting for the right person, for love, or for marriage?

3. If you have had a consensual sexual experience with another person, recall the first time it happened. What were your reasons? How old were you? How did you find the experience?

4. Would you consider cohabiting with someone? Why or why not? What would your parents think about it? Your grandparents?

5. Have you ever had a partner who "cheated" on you? How did you handle it? What effect did this have on the relationship?

Visit our Companion Website at www.pearsoned.ca/rathus, where you can use the interactive Study Guide and link to additional resources on topics discussed in this text.

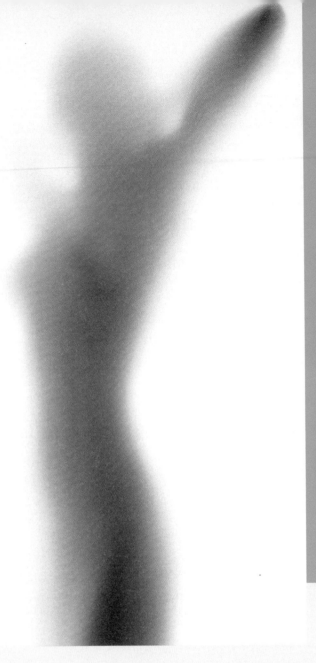

Chapter 13
Sexual Dysfunctions

Sexual dysfunctions are recurring difficulties in becoming sexually aroused or reaching orgasm. Many of us are troubled by sexual problems from time to time. Men occasionally have difficulty achieving an erection or ejaculate more rapidly than they would like. Most women occasionally have difficulty achieving orgasm or becoming sufficiently lubricated. People are not considered to have a sexual dysfunction, however, unless the problem is persistent and causes distress.

Although there are different types of sexual dysfunctions, they share some features. People with sexual dysfunctions may avoid sexual opportunities for fear of failure. They may anticipate that sex will result in frustration or physical pain rather than pleasure and gratification. Because of the emphasis that our culture places on sexual competence, people with sexual dysfunctions may feel inadequate or incompetent, feelings that diminish their self-esteem. They may experience guilt, shame, frustration, depression, and anxiety.

Many people with sexual dysfunctions find it difficult to talk about them, even with their spouses or helping professionals. A woman who cannot reach orgasm with her husband may fake orgasms rather than "make a fuss." A man may find it difficult to admit erectile problems to his physician during a physical. Many physicians are also uncomfortable talking about sexual matters and may never inquire about sexual problems.

> **Sexual dysfunctions**
> Persistent or recurrent difficulties in becoming sexually aroused or reaching orgasm.

Research in Action

SEXUAL PROBLEMS IN CANADA

Because many people are reluctant to admit to sexual problems, we do not have precise figures on their frequencies. The best current information we have in Canada is based on the Canadian Contraceptive Survey (Fisher et al., 2004b). The survey asked women if they had experienced five possible types of sexual difficulties: low sexual desire, painful intercourse, lack of orgasm during intercourse, partner's erectile difficulties, and partner's premature ejaculation. About half of the women had experienced at least one of these problems. More married women reported sexual difficulties than did single women.

The most common problem reported by Canadian women (43%) was diminished sexual desire. Married women (57%) were twice as likely to report low desire as unmarried women (26%). The second most common problem was difficulty with orgasm, with 24% of women saying that they do not usually have an orgasm during intercourse. Fifteen percent reported that they have problems with painful intercourse. The percentages of Canadian women reporting these sexual problems is similar to those reported by American women (Laumann et al., 1994).

In the Fisher et al. (2003) Contraceptive Survey, very few women reported that their partners have problems with either ejaculating too soon (7%) or maintaining an erection (6%). However, in another national survey of Canadians, 11.7% of women reported that their partners had experienced erectile dysfunction in the previous six months, with 10.4% of men reporting this dysfunction (Auld & Brock, 2002). These percentages are similar to those found in a national U.S. survey, in which 10% of men said that they had problems maintaining an erection during intercourse and 29% that they ejaculated too soon (Laumann et al., 1994). In the Canadian study, the rate of erectile dysfunction was determined by combining those who said they had experienced erectile dysfunction in the previous six months with those who had a low score measuring erectile dysfunction on the Sexual Health Inventory for Men (SHIM). Using these combined scores, Auld and Brock concluded that 27% of Canadian men experience erectile dysfunction. Obviously, the reported rate of this dysfunction is strongly influenced by the measures used.

The Compas survey (1998) asked Canadians to indicate which factors have a negative impact on their sex life. As shown in Table 13.1, the two most common factors were being too tired and being too busy. (These are obviously a reflection of the hectic lives that many Canadians lead.) More women (41%) than men (26%) reported that their own lack of desire has a negative impact. Similarly, 42% of the men and only 18% of the women said that their partner's lack of desire had a negative impact on their sex life.

Married people (75%) were more likely than singles (51%) to report that being tired, or their partner's being too tired, has a negative effect on their sex life. As well, more of those who are married (41%) than single (21%) said that having children in the household has a similar negative effect (Compas, 1998).

To what extent do people find their sexual problems to be frustrating? Tanya Hill (2005) conducted an online survey of 236 University of Guelph females (aged 17–24). Traditionally, it was believed that women did not get sexually frustrated because of the stereotype that sexual pleasure was not important to women. Contrary to this belief, three-quarters of the female students said that they felt sexually frustrated at least some of the time and 9% said they often felt frustrated.

The most frustrating situations for the women were

- not experiencing an orgasm during intercourse
- partner not being affectionate
- partner being unavailable
- partner refusing to have sex

Despite the prevalence of sexual problems, many people are reluctant to seek professional advice. Only a third of Canadian women reported that they have asked their doctor about sexual issues (Fisher et al., 2003). In another study of women at an Ontario clinic, only 16% of those who had experienced sexual problems had discussed these with a doctor (Fisher et al., 2000).

TABLE 13.1
Factors Having a Negative Impact on the Sex Lives of Canadians

	Men	Women
Too tired	63%	67%
Too busy	56	49
Relationship problems	38	35
Your lack of desire	26	41
Children in the house	31	35
Health problems	24	33
Partner's lack of desire	42	18
Lack of partner	33	22
Money or job problems	24	21
Your partner's appearance	12	8
Your partner's feelings about your appearance	11	9

Source: Compas (1998). Modern life survey of the Canadian population.

Types of Sexual Dysfunctions

Sexual desire disorders
Sexual dysfunctions in which people have persistent or recurrent lack of sexual desire or aversion to sexual contact.

Sexual arousal disorders
Sexual dysfunctions in which people persistently or recurrently fail to become adequately sexually aroused to engage in or sustain sexual intercourse.

The most widely used system of classification of sexual dysfunctions is based on the American Psychiatric Association's *Diagnostic and Statistical Manual of Mental Disorders* (the DSM) of 2000. The DSM, which is now in its fourth edition, groups sexual dysfunctions into four categories:

1. **Sexual desire disorders**. These involve dysfunctions in sexual desire, interest, or drive, in which the person experiences a lack of sexual desire or an aversion to genital sexual contact.

2. **Sexual arousal disorders**. Sexual arousal is principally characterized by erection in the male and by vaginal lubrication and swelling of the external genitalia in the female. In men, sexual arousal disorders involve recurrent difficulty in achieving or sustaining erections sufficient to engage successfully in sexual

intercourse. In women, they typically involve failure to become sufficiently lubricated.

3. **Orgasmic disorders**. Men or women may encounter difficulties achieving orgasm or may reach orgasm more rapidly than they would like. Women are more likely to encounter difficulties reaching orgasm; men are more likely to experience overly rapid orgasm (premature ejaculation). But some men have trouble reaching orgasm during coitus, and a few women complain of overly rapid orgasms.

4. **Sexual pain disorders**. Both men and women may suffer from **dyspareunia** (painful intercourse). Women may experience **vaginismus**, which prevents penetration by the penis or renders penetration painful.

Sexual dysfunctions may also be classified as either lifelong or acquired. *Lifelong* dysfunctions have existed throughout the person's lifetime. *Acquired* dysfunctions develop following a period of normal functioning. They also may be classified as generalized or situational. *Generalized* dysfunctions affect a person's general sexual functioning. *Situational* dysfunctions affect sexual functioning only in some sexual situations (such as during coitus but not during masturbation) or occur with some partners but not with others. Consider, for example, a man who has never been able to get or maintain an erection during sexual relations with a partner but can do so during masturbation. His dysfunction would be classified as lifelong and situational.

Sexual Desire Disorders

Sexual desire disorders involve lack of sexual desire or interest and/or aversion to genital sexual activity. People with little or no sexual interest or desire are said to have *hypoactive sexual desire disorder*. The problem is more common among women than men. Nevertheless, the belief that men are always eager and willing to engage in sexual activity is no more than a myth.

Lack of sexual desire does not imply that a person is unable to get an erection, lubricate adequately, or reach orgasm. Some people with low sexual desire do have such problems. Others can become sexually aroused and reach orgasm when stimulated adequately. Many enjoy sexual activity, even if they are unlikely to initiate it. Many appreciate the affection and closeness of physical intimacy but have no interest in genital stimulation.

Hypoactive sexual desire is one of the most commonly diagnosed sexual dysfunctions (Letourneau & O'Donohue, 1993). Yet there is no clear consensus among clinicians and researchers concerning the definition of low sexual desire. How much sexual interest or desire is "normal"? There is no standard level of sexual desire, and lack of desire is usually considered a problem when couples recognize that their level of sexual interest has gotten so low that little remains. Sometimes the lack of desire is limited to one partner. When one member of a couple is more interested in sex than the other, sex therapists often recommend that couples try to reach a compromise. They also attempt to uncover and resolve problems in the relationship that may dampen the sexual ardour of one or both partners.

A debate is under way about when to consider lack of sexual desire among women a dysfunction (Basson, 2002; Bean, 2002). The literature on gender differences strongly suggests that women, in general, are less interested in sex than men are (Peplau, 2003). This is not to suggest that there is anything wrong with women who experience strong, regular sexual urges. On the other hand, some researchers note that the definition of lack of desire as a dysfunction, as applied to women, attempts to impose on women a male model of what is normal (Bean, 2002). Keep in mind that lack of desire usually does not come to the health practitioner's attention unless one partner is more desirous of sex than the other. That is usually the situation in which the less-interested partner is exposed to the possibility of being labelled with a dysfunction.

Orgasmic disorders Sexual dysfunctions in which people persistently or recurrently have difficulty reaching orgasm despite attaining a level of sexual stimulation that would normally result in orgasm, or reach orgasm more rapidly than they would like.

Sexual pain disorder Sexual dysfunctions in which people persistently or recurrently experience pain during coitus.

Dyspareunia A sexual dysfunction characterized by persistent or recurrent pain during sexual intercourse. (From roots that mean "badly paired.")

Vaginismus A sexual dysfunction characterized by involuntary contraction of the muscles surrounding the vaginal barrel, preventing penile penetration or rendering penetration painful.

Biological and psychosocial factors—hormonal deficiencies, depression, dissatisfaction with one's relationship, and so on—contribute to lack of desire (Frohlich & Meston, 2002). Among the medical conditions that diminish sexual desire are testosterone deficiencies, thyroid overactivity or underactivity, and temporal lobe epilepsy. Sexual desire is stoked by testosterone, which is produced by men in the testes and by both men and women in the adrenal glands (Tuiten et al., 2000). Women may experience less sexual desire when their adrenal glands are surgically removed. Low sexual interest, along with erectile difficulties, are also common among men with hypogonadism, which is treated with testosterone (Lue, 2000).

Researchers find men with hypoactive sexual desire disorder to be older than women with the disorder (Ghizzani, 2003; Morley & van den Berg, 2000). A gradual decline in sexual desire, among men, may be explained in part by the reduction in testosterone levels that occurs in middle and later life (Morley & van den Berg, 2000; Perry et al., 2001). But women's sexual desire may also decline with age because of physical and psychological changes, as we will see (Kingsberg, 2002). Abrupt changes in sexual desire are more often explained by psychological and interpersonal factors such as depression, stress, and problems in the relationship (Bancroft et al., 2003; Frohlich & Meston, 2002; Graham, 2003).

Psychological problems can contribute to low sexual desire (Bancroft et al., 2003; Ghizzani, 2003). Anxiety is the most commonly reported factor. Anxiety may dampen sexual desire, including performance anxiety (anxiety over being evaluated negatively), anxiety involving fears of pleasure or loss of control, and deeper sources of anxiety related to fears of injury. Depression is a common cause of lack of desire (Frohlich & Meston, 2002). A history of sexual assault has also been linked to low sexual desire.

Some medications, including those used to control anxiety or hypertension, may also reduce desire. Changing medications or doses may restore the person's previous level of desire.

SEXUAL AVERSION DISORDER People with low sexual desire may have little or no interest in sex, but they are not repelled by genital contact. Some people, however, find sex disgusting or aversive and avoid genital contact.

Some researchers consider sexual aversion to be a *sexual phobia* or *sexual panic state* with intense, irrational fears of sexual contact and a pressing desire to avoid sexual situations (Kaplan, 1987). A history of erectile problems can cause sexual aversion in men. A history of sexual trauma, such as rape or childhood sexual abuse or incest, often figures prominently in cases of sexual aversion, especially in women.

Sexual Arousal Disorders

When we are sexually stimulated, our bodies normally respond with **vasocongestion**, which produces erection in the male and vaginal lubrication in the female. People with sexual arousal disorders, however, do not have or sustain the lubrication or erection necessary to facilitate sexual activity. Or they lack the subjective feelings of sexual pleasure or excitement that normally accompany sexual arousal (American Psychiatric Association, 2000).

Problems of sexual arousal have sometimes been labelled *impotence* in the male and *frigidity* in the female. But these terms are pejorative, so many professionals prefer to use less threatening, more descriptive labels.

MALE ERECTILE DISORDER Sexual arousal disorder in the male is called **male erectile disorder** or *erectile dysfunction*. It is characterized by persistent difficulty in getting or maintaining an erection sufficient to allow the completion of sexual activity. In most cases the failure is limited to sexual activity with partners, or with some partners and not others. It can thus be classified as *situational*. In rare cases the dysfunction is found during any sexual activity, including masturbation. In such cases,

Vasocongestion
Engorgement of blood vessels with blood, which swells the genitals and breasts during sexual arousal.

Male erectile disorder
Persistent difficulty getting or maintaining an erection sufficient to allow the man to engage in or complete sexual intercourse. Also termed *erectile dysfunction*.

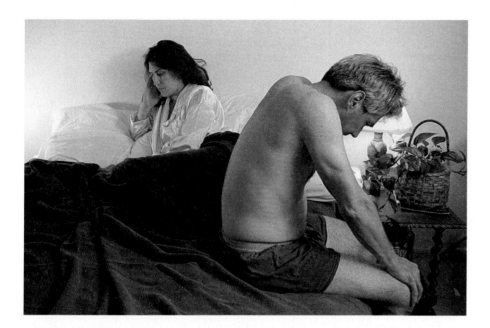

it is considered *generalized*. Some men with erectile disorder are unable to attain an erection with their partners. Others can achieve erection but not sustain it (or recover it) long enough for penetration and ejaculation.

The incidence of erectile disorder increases with age and is believed to affect as many as one man in two between the ages of 40 and 70—at least intermittently (Feldman et al., 1994). Occasional problems in getting or maintaining an erection are quite common. Fatigue, alcohol, anxiety over impressing a new partner, and other factors may account for a transient episode. Even an isolated occurrence, however, can lead to a persistent problem if the man fears recurrence. The more anxious and concerned the man becomes about his sexual ability, the more likely he is to suffer **performance anxiety**. This anxiety can contribute to repeated failure, and a vicious circle of anxiety and failure may develop.

A man with erectile problems may try to "will" an erection, which can compound the problem. Each failure may further demoralize and defeat him. He may ruminate about his sexual inadequacy, setting the stage for yet more anxiety. His partner may try to comfort and support him by saying things like "It can happen to anyone," "Don't worry about it," or "It will get better in time." But attempts at reassurance may be to no avail. As one client put it,

> I always felt inferior, like I was on probation, having to prove myself. I felt like I was up against the wall. You can't imagine how embarrassing this [erectile failure] was. It's like you walk out [naked] in front of an audience that you think is a nudist convention and it turns out to be a tuxedo convention.

—The Authors' Files

The vicious circle of anxiety and erectile failure may be interrupted if the man recognizes that occasional problems are normal and does not overreact. However, the emphasis in our culture on men's sexual prowess may spur them to view occasional failures as catastrophes rather than transient disappointments. Viewing occasional problems as an inconvenience, rather than a tragedy, may help avert the development of persistent erectile difficulties.

Performance anxiety is a prominent cause of erectile disorder. So are other psychological factors such as depression, lack of self-esteem, and problems in the relationship. Biological factors can also play a causal role, as we shall see.

The Canadian Erectile Difficulties Resource Centre
www.edhelp.ca

Performance anxiety
Anxiety concerning one's ability to perform behaviours, especially behaviours that may be evaluated by other people.

FEMALE SEXUAL AROUSAL DISORDER Women may encounter persistent difficulties becoming sexually excited or sufficiently lubricated in response to sexual stimulation. In some cases these difficulties are lifelong. In others they develop after a period of normal functioning. In some cases difficulties are pervasive and occur during both masturbation and sex with a partner. More often they occur in specific situations. For example, they occur with some partners and not with others, or during coitus but not during oral–genital sex or masturbation.

According to Vancouver therapist Rosemary Basson (2004), most women with arousal disorder experience little or no subjective arousal or sexual excitement. These women can be categorized into two groups. In the first are women who experience no subjective arousal and do not feel any genital response (Combined Arousal Disorder). In the second group are women who are aware of their genitals physically responding to stimulation yet feel no subjective arousal (Subjective Arousal Disorder).

There is also a minority of women who can become aroused by many different kinds of stimuli but do not find stimulation of their genitals to be arousing (Genital Arousal Disorder). Women with this disorder can still have a high interest in sex and become subjectively aroused providing there is non-genital stimulation (Basson, 2004).

Female sexual arousal disorder, like its male counterpart, may have physical causes. A thorough evaluation by a medical specialist (a urologist in the case of a male, a gynecologist in the case of a female) is recommended. Any neurological, vascular, or hormonal problem that interferes with the lubrication or swelling response of the vagina to sexual stimulation may contribute to female sexual arousal disorder. For example, diabetes mellitus may lead to diminished sexual excitement in women because of the degeneration of the nerves servicing the clitoris and the blood vessel (vascular) damage it causes. Reduced estrogen production can also result in vaginal dryness.

Female sexual arousal disorder more commonly has psychological causes, however. In some cases, women harbour deep-seated anger and resentment toward their partners. They thus find it difficult to turn off these feelings when they go to bed. In other cases, sexual trauma is implicated. Survivors of sexual abuse often find it difficult to respond sexually to their partners. Childhood sexual abuse is especially prevalent in cases of female sexual arousal disorder (Bean, 2002).

Feelings of helplessness, anger, or guilt—or even flashbacks of the abuse—may surface when the woman begins sexual activity, undermining her ability to become aroused. Other psychosocial causes include anxiety or guilt about sex and ineffective stimulation by the partner (Bean, 2002).

Orgasmic Disorders

Three disorders can impair the orgasm phase of the sexual response cycle: (1) male orgasmic disorder, (2) female orgasmic disorder, and (3) premature ejaculation.

In female or male orgasmic disorder, the woman or man is persistently delayed in reaching orgasm or does not reach orgasm at all, despite achieving sexual stimulation that would normally be of sufficient intensity to result in orgasm. The problem is more common among women than men. In some cases, a person can reach orgasm without difficulty while engaging in sexual relations with one partner, but not with another.

MALE ORGASMIC DISORDER Male orgasmic disorder has also been termed *delayed ejaculation*, *retarded ejaculation*, and *ejaculatory incompetence*. The problem may be lifelong or acquired, generalized or situational. There are very few cases of men who have never ejaculated. In most cases the disorder is limited to coitus. The man may be capable of ejaculating during masturbation or oral sex but may find it difficult, if not impossible—despite high levels of sexual excitement—to ejaculate during intercourse. There is a myth that men with male orgasmic disorder and their female partners enjoy this condition, because it enables them to "go on forever" (Dekker, 1993). Actually, the experience is frustrating for both partners.

Male orgasmic disorder may be caused by physical problems, such as multiple sclerosis or neurological damage, that interfere with neural control of ejaculation. It may also be a side effect of certain drugs. Various psychological factors may also play a role, including performance anxiety, sexual guilt, and hostility toward one's partner. Masters and Johnson (1970) found that men with this problem frequently have strict religious backgrounds that may leave a residue of unresolved guilt about sex, which inhibits ejaculation. Emotional factors such as fear of pregnancy and anger toward one's partner can also play a role.

FEMALE ORGASMIC DISORDER Women with female orgasmic disorder are unable to reach orgasm or have difficulty reaching orgasm following what would usually be an adequate amount of sexual stimulation. Women with this disorder cannot have an orgasm even if they are highly aroused (Basson, 2004). Women who have never reached orgasm through any means are sometimes labelled **anorgasmic** or *preorgasmic.*

Some couples expect that both partners should reach orgasm during intercourse. But this is not the way it works for many women. A woman who reaches orgasm through masturbation or oral sex may not necessarily reach orgasm dependably during coitus with her partner (Stock, 1993). Penile thrusting during coitus may not provide sufficient clitoral stimulation to facilitate orgasm. University of Waterloo researcher B. J. Rye (2001) found that 93% of university women sometimes or usually need direct clitoral stimulation during intercourse in order to have an orgasm. Only 46% of the women surveyed have an orgasm during at least half of their intercourse experiences, and 49% say that it often takes them a long time to have an orgasm. Not reaching orgasm during intercourse is not considered orgasmic disorder if the woman reaches orgasm through other activities with a partner.

PREMATURE EJACULATION Men with **premature ejaculation** ejaculate too rapidly to permit their partners or themselves to enjoy sexual relations fully. The degree of prematurity varies. Some men ejaculate during foreplay, even at the sight of their partner disrobing. But most ejaculate either just before or immediately after penetration or following a few coital thrusts.

Guy Grenier and Sandra Byers (2001) of the University of New Brunswick have studied the ejaculatory behaviour of a community sample of men. In this study the term rapid ejaculation (RE) was used instead of PE. The men report that intercourse typically lasts about eight minutes before they ejaculate. They also report that ejaculation happens quicker than they desire in about a third of their acts of sexual intercourse. The men attempt to delay the timing of their ejaculation during about half of their intercourse experiences.

The percentage of men experiencing RE varies widely (between 4% and 61%) depending on what criteria are used (Grenier & Byers, 2001). Twenty-three percent of the men in the study identified themselves as having a problem with premature ejaculation. These men ejaculate sooner than other men, perceive less control over the timing of ejaculation, and are more concerned over ejaculating sooner than desired.

Just what constitutes *prematurity?* Some definitions focus on a particular time period during which a man should be able to control ejaculation. Is ejaculation within 30 seconds of intromission premature? Within one minute? Ten minutes? There is no clear cutoff. Some scholars argue that the focus should be on whether the couple is satisfied with the duration of coitus rather than on a specific time period.

Anorgasmic Never having reached orgasm. (Literally, "without orgasm.")

Premature ejaculation A sexual dysfunction in which ejaculation occurs with minimal sexual stimulation and before the man desires it.

In another study of 52 New Brunswick couples, Byers & Grenier (2003) compared the men's and women's reports of the man's ejaculatory behaviour. There was only moderate agreement between the men and women. The women tended to underestimate how seriously the male partner viewed RE. However, both the men and women reported lower sexual satisfaction in response to the man's problem with RE (Byers & Grenier).

Helen Singer Kaplan (1974) suggested that the label *premature* should be applied to cases in which men persistently or recurrently lack voluntary control over their ejaculations. This may sound like a contradiction in terms, given that ejaculation is a reflex, and reflexes need not involve thought or conscious control. Kaplan means that a man may control his ejaculation by learning to regulate the amount of sexual stimulation he experiences so that it remains below the threshold at which the ejaculation reflex is triggered.

Sexual Pain Disorders

For most of us, coitus is a source of pleasure. For some of us, however, coitus gives rise to pain and discomfort.

DYSPAREUNIA Traditionally, dyspareunia was defined as painful coitus. However, it also includes those women who have persistent pain with attempted vaginal intercourse (Basson, 2004). Some therapists and researchers believe a more accurate terms is "vulvodynia" (Pukall et al., 2003).

Dyspareunia is one of the most common sexual dysfunctions and is also a common complaint of women seeking gynecological services (Quevillon, 1993). The location of the pain can vary. For example, it can be at the entrance to the vagina, in the vagina, or in the pelvic region (Pukall et al., 2003). Painful intercourse is less common in men and is generally associated with genital infections that cause burning or painful ejaculation.

Pain is a sign that something is wrong—physically or psychologically. Dyspareunia may result from physical causes, emotional factors, or an interaction of the two (Meana & Binik, 1994). The most common cause of coital pain in women is inadequate lubrication. In such a case, additional foreplay or artificial lubrication may help. Vaginal infections and sexually transmitted infections (STIs) may also produce coital pain. Allergic reactions to spermicides, even the latex material in condoms, can give rise to coital pain or irritation. Pain during deep thrusting may be caused by endometriosis or pelvic inflammatory disease (PID), by other diseases or structural disorders of the reproductive organs (Reid & Lininger, 1993), or by penile contact with the cervix.

Psychological factors such as unresolved guilt or anxiety about sex or the lingering effects of sexual trauma may also be involved. These factors may inhibit lubrication and cause involuntary contractions of the vaginal musculature, making penetration painful or uncomfortable.

Researchers in Montreal (Binik et al., 2002) have extensively studied dyspareunia in women and evaluated various treatment strategies. They found that women with dyspareunia had lower tolerance for pain, not only in the vaginal area but also on the upper arm, suggesting that a generalized hypersensitivity may contribute to this problem in some women (Pukall et al., 2002).

Based on these findings, Binik (2005) argues that dyspareunia should be categorized as a pain disorder rather than a sexual dysfunction as defined by the American Psychiatric Association (DSM-IV) and should be assessed and treated like other pain disorders. Binik's recommendations have caused considerable controversy. Kenneth Zucker, editor of *Archives of Sexual Behavior,* asked 18 experts to comment on them in the February 2005 edition of the journal. There was only limited support for Binik's proposals.

Binik (2005) believes that every case of dyspareunia has both physiological and psychological components. Interestingly, they found that women who believe their pain is due to psychosocial factors report higher levels of pain and more sexual problems than women who believe their pain is due to physical causes. Because of the complexity (both physical and psychological) surrounding the problem of dyspareunia, Binik et al. believe that multidisciplinary teams should be established to deal with it. They note that for many women the pain arising from dyspareunia cannot be totally eliminated, and that these women need to be taught coping strategies for managing the pain.

VAGINISMUS Vaginismus involves an involuntary contraction of the pelvic muscles that surround the outer third of the vaginal barrel. Avoidance of penetration seems to be the key factor differentiating vaginismus from dyspareunia (Bergeron & Lord, 2003). Vaginismus occurs reflexively during attempts at vaginal penetration, making entry by the penis painful or impossible. These reflexive contractions are accompanied by a deep-seated fear of penetration (Beck, 1993). Some women with vaginismus are unable to tolerate penetration by any object, including a finger, a tampon, or a physician's speculum. The prevalence of vaginismus is unknown.

The woman with vaginismus usually is not aware that she is contracting her vaginal muscles. Women with vaginismus often have histories of sexual trauma, sexual assault, or botched abortions that resulted in vaginal injuries. They may desire sexual relations. They may be capable of becoming sexually aroused and achieving orgasm. However, fear of penetration triggers an involuntary spasm of the vaginal musculature at the point of penile insertion. Vaginismus can also be a cause or an effect of dyspareunia. Women who experience painful coitus may develop a fear of penetration. Fear then leads to the development of involuntary vaginal contractions. Women with vaginismus may experience pain during coital attempts if the couple tries to force penetration. Vaginismus and dyspareunia may also give rise to, or result from, erectile disorder in men (Speckens et al., 1995). Feelings of failure and anxiety come to overwhelm both partners.

Some researchers in Montreal (Reissing et al., 2004) are critical of the lack of rigorous research on vaginismus. They disagree that vaginismus is easily diagnosed and easily treated. Instead they propose that cases diagnosed as vaginismus should be reconceptualized as either an aversion to vaginal penetration or as a genital pain disorder. These distinctions are important in suggesting different courses of treatment.

Origins of Sexual Dysfunctions

Sexual dysfunctions can result from many different causes. Many cases involve a combination of organic and psychological factors.

Organic Causes

Physical factors, such as fatigue and lowered testosterone levels, can dampen sexual desire and reduce responsiveness. Fatigue may lead to male erectile disorder and male orgasmic disorder, and to female orgasmic disorder and inadequate lubrication. But these will be isolated incidents unless the person attaches too much meaning to them and becomes concerned about future performance. Painful coitus, however, often reflects organic factors such as underlying infections. Orgasmic functioning in both men and women can be affected by various medical conditions, including coronary heart disease, diabetes mellitus, multiple sclerosis, and spinal cord injuries; by complications from certain surgical procedures (such as removal of the prostate in men); by endocrinological (hormone) problems; and by the use of some medicines, such as drugs used to treat hypertension and psychiatric disorders.

A World of Diversity

INIS BEAG AND MANGAIA—WORLDS APART

Let us invite you on a journey back in time and to two islands that are a world apart—sexually as well as geographically. The sexual attitudes and practices present at the time that researchers investigated these societies will shed some light on the role of cultural values in determining what is sexually normal and what is sexually dysfunctional.

Our first stop is the island of Inis Beag, which lies off the misty coast of Ireland. When anthropologist John Messenger (1971) visited Inis Beag in the 1950s and 1960s, he found that the residents of this Irish community did not believe that it is normal for women to experience orgasm. Messenger reported that any woman who found pleasure in sex—especially the intense waves of pleasure that can accompany orgasm—was viewed as deviant. Premarital sex was all but unknown on Inis Beag. Prior to marriage, men and women socialized apart. Marriage came relatively late—usually in the middle 30s for men and the middle 20s for women. Mothers taught their daughters that they would have to submit to their husbands' animal cravings in order to obey God's injunction to "be fruitful and multiply." The women

Polynesia.
Cultural expectations affect our judgments about what kinds of sexual behaviour are functional and what kinds are dysfunctional. Some Polynesian cultures are sexually permissive. They encourage children to explore their sexuality. Men may be expected to bring their partners to orgasm several times before ejaculating. In such cultures, should men who ejaculate before their partners have multiple orgasms be diagnosed with premature ejaculation? (Paul Gauguin, And the gold of their bodies. Photo: B. Hatala. Musée d'Orsay, Paris, France. Courtesy of Réunion des Musées Nationaux/Art Resource, NY.)

of Inis Beag did not need to be overly concerned about frequent sexual intercourse, however, because the men of the island believed that sexual activity would drain their strength. Because of taboos against nudity, married couples engaged in intercourse with their underclothes on. Intercourse took place in the dark—literally as well as figuratively.

Our next stop is Mangaia. Mangaia is a Polynesian pearl of an island. Marshall (1971) observed that from an early age, Mangaian boys and girls were encouraged to get in touch with their own sexuality through sexual play and masturbation. At about the age of 13, Mangaian boys were initiated into manhood by adults who instructed them in sexual techniques. Mangaian males were taught the merit of bringing their female partners to multiple orgasms before ejaculating. Boys practised their

new techniques with girlfriends on secluded beaches or beneath the listing fronds of palms. They sometimes visited girlfriends in the evening in the huts where they slept with their families.

Girls, too, learned techniques of coitus from their elders. Typically they were initiated by an experienced male relative. Mangaians looked on virginity with disdain, because virgins do not know how to provide sexual pleasure. Thus the older relative made his contribution to the family by initiating the girl.

All in all, the sharp contrasts between Inis Beag and Mangaia illustrate how concepts of normality are embedded within a cultural context. Behaviour that is judged to be normal in one culture may be regarded as abnormal in another. How might our own cultural expectations influence our judgments about sexual dysfunction?

Generally speaking, Edward Laumann and his colleagues (1999) found that poor health can contribute to all kinds of sexual dysfunctions in men, but mostly to sexual pain in women.

It was once believed that the great majority of cases of erectile disorder had psychological causes (Masters & Johnson, 1970). It is now known that organic factors are involved in as many as 80% of cases (Brody, 1998b). But psychological factors such as anger and depression may prolong or worsen the problem even when there are organic factors (Feldman et al., 1994).

Organic causes of erectile disorder affect the flow of blood to and through the penis—a problem that becomes more common as men age—or damage the nerves involved in erection (Goldstein, 1998, 2000). Erectile problems can arise when clogged or narrow arteries leading to the penis deprive the penis of oxygen (Lipshultz, 1996). For example, erectile disorder is common among men with diabetes mellitus, a disease that can damage blood vessels and nerves. Eric Rimm (2000) of the Harvard School of Public Health studied 2000 men and found that erectile dysfunction was connected with a large waist, physical inactivity, and drinking too much alcohol (or not having any alcohol!). The condition common to these men may be high cholesterol levels. Cholesterol can impede the flow of blood to the penis just as it impedes the flow of blood to the heart.

Examination of the Massachusetts Male Aging Study database reveals that men who exercise regularly seem to ward off erectile dysfunction (Derby, 2000). Men who burned 200 calories or more a day in physical activity—an amount that can be achieved by briskly walking three kilometres—cut their risk of erectile dysfunction about in half. Again, exercise seems to work by preventing the clogging of arteries, thereby keeping them clear for the flow of blood into the penis.

Nerve damage resulting from prostate surgery may impair erectile response. Erectile disorder may also result from multiple sclerosis (MS), a disease in which nerve cells lose the protective coatings that facilitate transmission of neural messages. MS has also been implicated in male orgasmic disorder. Chronic kidney disease, hypertension, cancer, emphysema, and coronary heart disease can all impair erectile response. So can endocrine disorders that impair testosterone production (Ralph & McNicholas, 2000).

Women also develop vascular or nervous disorders that impair genital blood flow, decreasing lubrication and sexual excitement, rendering intercourse painful, and reducing their ability to reach orgasm. As with men, these problems become more likely as women age.

People with sexual dysfunctions are generally advised to undergo a physical examination to determine whether their problems are biologically based. Men with erectile disorder may be evaluated in a sleep centre to determine whether they attain erections while asleep. Healthy men usually have erections during rapid-eye-movement (REM) sleep, which occurs every 90 to 100 minutes. Men with organically based erectile disorder often do not have nocturnal erections. However, this technique, which is called nocturnal penile **tumescence** (NPT), may yield misleading results (Meisler & Carey, 1990).

Prescription drugs and illicit drugs account for many cases of erectile disorder. Antidepressant medication and antipsychotic drugs may impair erectile functioning and cause orgasmic disorders (Ashton et al., 2000; Michelson et al., 2000). Tranquillizers such as Valium and Xanax may cause orgasmic disorder in either gender. Antihypertensive drugs can lead to erectile failure (Ralph & McNicholas, 2000). Switching to antihypertensive drugs that do not impair sexual response or adjusting the dose may help. Other drugs that can lead to erectile disorder include adrenergic blockers, diuretics, cholesterol-lowering drugs ("statins"), anticonvulsants, anti-Parkinson drugs, and dyspepsia and ulcer-healing drugs (Ralph & McNicholas, 2000). Central nervous system depressants such as alcohol, heroin, and morphine can reduce sexual desire and impair sexual arousal (Segraves & Segraves, 1993).

Psychosocial Causes

Psychosocial factors connected with sexual dysfunctions include—but are not necessarily limited to—cultural influences, economic problems, psychosexual trauma, marital dissatisfaction, psychological conflict, lack of sexual skills, irrational beliefs, and performance anxiety (Laumann et al., 1999).

Tumescence Swelling; erection. (From the Latin *tumere*, which means "to swell." *Tumour* has the same root.)

CULTURAL INFLUENCES Children reared in sexually repressive cultural or home environments may learn to respond to sex with feelings of anxiety and shame rather than sexual arousal and pleasure. People whose parents instilled in them a sense of guilt about touching their genitals may find it difficult to accept their sex organs as sources of pleasure.

In most cultures, sexual pleasure has traditionally been a male preserve. Young women may be reared to believe that sex is a duty to be performed for their husbands, not a source of personal pleasure. Although the traditional double standard may have diminished in Canada in recent years, girls may still be exposed to relatively repressive attitudes. Women are more likely than men in our culture to be taught to repress their sexual desires and even to fear their sexuality. Self-control and vigilance—not sexual awareness and acceptance—become identified as feminine virtues. Women reared with such attitudes may be less likely to learn about their sexual potential or express their erotic preferences to their partners.

Women who are exposed to negative attitudes about sex during childhood and adolescence find it difficult to suddenly view sex as a source of pleasure and satisfaction once they are married. The result of a lifetime of learning to turn themselves off sexually may lead to difficulties experiencing the full expression of sexual arousal and enjoyment when an acceptable opportunity arises (Bean, 2002).

PSYCHOSEXUAL TRAUMA Women and men who were sexually victimized in childhood are more likely to experience difficulty in becoming sexually aroused (Laumann et al., 1999). Learning theorists focus on the role of conditioned anxiety in explaining sexual dysfunctions. Sexual stimuli come to elicit anxiety when they have been paired with physically or psychologically painful experiences, such as sexual assault, incest, or sexual molestation. Conditioned anxiety can stifle sexual arousal. Researchers in Hamilton, Ontario, found that women who experience painful intercourse are more likely to have negative memories of their first sexual experience and a history of treatment of phobias (Lamont et al., 2001).

A World of Diversity

AN ODD COUPLE: KORO AND DHAT SYNDROMES

Koro Syndrome

Koro syndrome is found primarily in China and some other East Asian countries. People with Koro syndrome fear that their genitals are shrinking and retracting into the body, a condition that they believe will be fatal. Koro syndrome has been identified mainly in young men, although some cases have also been reported in women. People with Koro syndrome show signs of acute anxiety, including profuse sweating, breathlessness, and heart palpitations. Men with the disorder have been known to use mechanical devices, such as chopsticks, to try to prevent the penis from retracting into the body.

Reassurance by a health professional that fears that the genitals will retract into the body are unfounded often put an end to Koro episodes. In any event, Koro episodes tend to pass with time.

Dhat Syndrome

Dhat syndrome is found among young South Asian males and involves excessive fears over the loss of seminal fluid during nocturnal emissions (Akhtar, 1988). Some men with Dhat syndrome also believe (incorrectly) that semen mixes with urine and is excreted by urinating.

There is a widespread belief within Indian culture (and other Asian cultures) that the loss of semen is harmful because it depletes the body of physical and mental energy (Chadda & Ahuja, 1990). Therefore, men with Dhat syndrome may visit physician after physician to find help in preventing nocturnal emissions or the imagined loss of semen mixed with urine.

SEXUAL ORIENTATION Some gay males and lesbians test their sexual orientation by developing heterosexual relationships, even marrying and rearing children with partners of the other gender. Others may wish to maintain the appearance of heterosexuality to avoid the social stigma that society attaches to a gay sexual identity. In such cases, problems in arousal or performance with heterosexual partners can be due to a lack of heteroerotic interests (Laumann et al., 1999). A lack of heterosexual response is not a problem for people who are committed to a gay lifestyle, however. Sexual dysfunctions may also occur in gay relationships, as they do in heterosexual relationships.

A Vicious Circle? Marital Conflict and Sexual Desire. Marital conflicts may dampen sexual interest. Lack of sexual interest may then further increase marital strain and dissatisfaction.

INEFFECTIVE SEXUAL TECHNIQUES In some marriages, couples practise a narrow range of sexual techniques because they have fallen into a certain routine or because one partner controls the timing and sequence of sexual techniques. The woman who remains unknowledgeable about the erotic importance of her clitoris may be unlikely to seek direct clitoral stimulation. The man who responds to a temporary erectile failure by trying to force an erection may be unintentionally setting himself up for repeated failure. The couple who fail to communicate their sexual preferences or to experiment with altering their sexual techniques may find themselves losing interest. Brevity of foreplay and coitus may contribute to female orgasmic disorder.

EMOTIONAL FACTORS Orgasm involves a sudden loss of voluntary control. Fear of losing control, or "letting go," may block sexual arousal. Other emotional factors, especially depression, are often implicated in sexual dysfunctions (Ralph & McNicholas, 2000). Vancouver therapist Rosemary Basson (1995) reports that many women experiencing lifelong vaginismus have a high incidence of nonsexual stress in their lives.

PROBLEMS IN THE RELATIONSHIP Problems in the relationship are important and often pivotal factors in sexual dysfunctions (Catalan et al., 1990; Fish et al., 1994; Leiblum & Rosen, 1991). Basson (2002) believes that lack of emotional intimacy often plays a key role in women's low sexual desire because it weakens the motivation to engage in sex. Problems in a relationship are not so easily left at the bedroom door. Couples usually find that their sexual relationships are no better than the other facets of their relationships. Couples who harbour resentment toward one another may make sex their arena of combat. They may fail to become aroused by their partners or "withhold" orgasm to make their partners feel guilty or inadequate. Problems in communication may also play a role. Troubled relationships are usually characterized by poor communication.

LACK OF SEXUAL SKILLS Sexual competency involves the acquisition of sexual knowledge and skills and is based largely on learning. We generally learn through trial and error, and by talking and reading about sex, what makes us and others feel good. Some people may not develop sexual competency because of a lack of opportunity to acquire knowledge and experience—even within marriage. People with sexual dysfunctions may have been reared in families in which discussions of sexuality were off limits and early sexual experimentation was harshly punished.

IRRATIONAL BELIEFS Psychologist Albert Ellis (1977) points out that irrational beliefs and attitudes may contribute to sexual dysfunctions. Negative feelings such as anxiety and fear, Ellis submits, do not stem directly from the events we experience, but rather from our interpretations of these events. If a person encounters a certain event, like an erectile or orgasmic disorder, on a given day and then *believes* that the event is awful or catastrophic, he or she will exaggerate feelings of disappointment and set the stage for future problems.

PERFORMANCE ANXIETY Anxiety—especially performance anxiety—plays an important role in the development of sexual dysfunctions. Performance anxiety occurs when a person becomes overly concerned with how well he or she performs a certain act or task. Performance anxiety may place a dysfunctional individual in a role as spectator rather than performer. Rather than focusing on erotic sensations and allowing involuntary responses such as erection, lubrication, and orgasm to occur naturally, he or she focuses on self-doubts and fears and thinks, "Will I be able to do it this time? Will this be another failure?"

Performance anxiety can set the stage for a vicious circle in which a sexual failure increases anxiety. Anxiety then leads to repeated failure, and so on. Sex therapists emphasize the need to break this cycle by removing the need to perform.

Treatment of Sexual Dysfunctions

When Kinsey conducted his surveys in the 1930s and 1940s, there was no effective treatment for sexual dysfunctions. At the time, the predominant model of therapy for sexual dysfunctions was long-term psychoanalysis.

Since that time, behavioural models of short-term treatment, collectively called **sex therapy**, have emerged. These models aim to modify the dysfunctional behaviour as directly as possible. Sex therapists also recognize the roles of childhood conflicts, self-defeating attitudes, and the quality of the partners' relationship. Therefore, they draw upon various forms of therapy as needed (LoPiccolo, 1994; Rosen et al., 1994).

Although the particular approaches vary, sex therapies aim to

1. change self-defeating beliefs and attitudes
2. teach sexual skills
3. enhance sexual knowledge
4. improve sexual communication
5. reduce performance anxiety

Sex therapy usually involves both partners, although individual therapy is preferred in some cases. Therapists find that granting people "permission" to experiment sexually or discuss negative attitudes about sex helps many people overcome sexual problems without the need for more intensive therapy. Some therapists encourage their clients to view educational sex videos as an enhancement to the therapy program. Ottawa therapist Peggy Kleinplatz (1997) believes that these videos can help couples to communicate more effectively about their sexual desires and problems.

Today biological treatments have also been emerging for various sexual dysfunctions. Since 1998, most public attention has been focused on Viagra, a drug that is helpful in most cases of erectile dysfunction. But biological treatments are also emerging for premature ejaculation, female orgasmic dysfunction, and lack of sexual desire.

An important issue in therapy is gender. Many therapists have adopted feminist perspectives in their practice in order to challenge sexist ways of thinking. Calgary therapists Mary Valentich and James Gripton (1992) have broadened this approach to encompass a gender-sensitive practice. This involves analyzing gender issues facing both women and men and critiquing how traditional gender roles restrict the

Sex therapy A collective term for short-term behavioural models for treatment of sexual dysfunctions.

sexual fulfillment of both genders. Such analysis encourages people to find their own ways of expressing love and sex so that they don't have to follow the traditional gender scripts.

In the next section we will explore both psychological and behavioural approaches to the treatment of sexual dysfunctions. Let us begin with the ground-breaking work of Masters and Johnson.

The Masters-and-Johnson Approach

Masters and Johnson pioneered the use of direct behavioural approaches to treating sexual dysfunctions (Masters & Johnson, 1970). A female–male therapy team focuses on the couple as the unit of treatment during a two-week residential program. Masters and Johnson consider the couple, not the individual, dysfunctional. A couple may describe the husband's erectile disorder as the problem, but this problem is likely to have led to problems in the couple by the time they seek therapy. Similarly, a man whose wife has an orgasmic disorder is likely to be anxious about his ability to provide effective sexual stimulation.

Anxieties and resentments are aired, but the focus of treatment is behavioural change. Couples perform daily sexual homework assignments, such as **sensate focus exercises**, in the privacy of their own rooms.

Sensate focus sessions are carried out in the nude. Partners take turns giving and receiving stimulation in nongenital areas of the body. Without touching the breasts or genitals, the giver massages or fondles the receiving partner in order to provide pleasure under relaxing and nondemanding conditions. Because genital activity is restricted, there is no pressure to "perform." The giving partner is freed to engage in trial-and-error learning about the receiving partner's sensate preferences. The receiving partner is freed to enjoy the experience without feeling rushed to reciprocate or obliged to perform by becoming sexually aroused. The receiving partner's only responsibility is to direct the giving partner as needed. In addition to these general sensate focus exercises, Masters and Johnson used specific assignments designed to help couples overcome particular sexual dysfunctions.

Masters and Johnson were pioneers in the development of sex therapy. Yet many sex therapists have departed from the Masters-and-Johnson format. Some therapists work individually with preorgasmic women rather than the couple. Group treatment programs have also been used successfully in treating female orgasmic disorder (Killmann et al., 1987).

The Helen Singer Kaplan Approach

Kaplan (1974) called her approach *psychosexual therapy*. Psychosexual therapy combines behavioural and psychoanalytic methods. Kaplan believed that sexual dysfunctions have both *immediate* causes and *remote* causes (underlying intrapsychic conflicts that date from childhood). Kaplan began therapy with the behavioural approach. She focused on improving the couple's communication, eliminating performance anxiety, and fostering sexual skills and knowledge. She used a brief form of insight-oriented therapy when it appeared that remote causes impeded response to the behavioural program. In so doing, she hoped to bring to awareness unconscious conflicts that are believed to have stifled the person's sexual desires or responsiveness.

Let us now consider some of the specific techniques that sex therapists have introduced in treating several of the major types of sexual dysfunctions.

Sexual Desire Disorders

Some sex therapists help kindle the sexual appetites of people with hypoactive sexual desire by prescribing self-stimulation exercises combined with erotic fantasies

Sensate focus exercises
Exercises in which sex partners take turns giving and receiving pleasurable stimulation in nongenital areas of the body.

(LoPiccolo & Friedman, 1988). Sex therapists may also assist dysfunctional couples by prescribing sensate focus exercises, enhancing communication, and expanding the couple's repertoire of sexual skills. Sex therapists recognize that hypoactive sexual desire is often a complex problem that requires more intensive treatment than problems of the arousal or orgasm phases (Leiblum & Rosen, 1988). Helen Singer Kaplan (1987) argues that insight-oriented approaches are especially helpful in the treatment of hypoactive sexual desire and sexual aversion to uncover and resolve deep-seated psychological conflicts.

Some cases of hypoactive sexual desire in men involve hormonal deficiencies, especially deficiencies in testosterone. But testosterone replacement therapy works with only about half of men who have low testosterone levels (Rakic et al., 1997). Among women, as among men, lack of sexual desire can be connected with low levels of androgens, and testosterone shows promise in heightening desire (Tuiten et al., 2000).

When lack of desire is connected with depression, sexual interests may rebound when the depression lifts. Treatment in such cases may involve psychotherapy or chemotherapy, not sex therapy per se. When problems in the relationship are involved, marital or couples therapy may be indicated to improve the relationship. Once interpersonal problems are ironed out, sexual interest may return.

Treatment of sexual aversion disorder may involve a multifaceted approach, including biological treatments, such as the use of medications to reduce anxiety, and psychological treatments designed to help the individual overcome the underlying sexual phobia. Couples therapy may be used in cases in which sexual aversions arise from problems in relationships (Gold & Gold, 1993). Sensate focus exercises may be used to lessen generalized anxiety about sexual contact. But fears of specific aspects of the sexual act may need to be overcome through behavioural exercises in which the client learns to manage the stimuli that evoke fears of sexual contact:

> Bridget, 26, and Bryan, 30, had been married for four years but had never consummated their relationship because Bridget would panic whenever Bryan attempted coitus with her. Although she enjoyed foreplay and was capable of achieving orgasm with clitoral stimulation, her fears of sexual contact were triggered by Bryan's attempts at vaginal penetration. The therapist employed a program of gradual exposure to the feared stimuli to allow Bridget the opportunity to overcome her fears in small, graduated steps. First she was instructed to view her genitals in a mirror when she was alone—this in order to violate her long-standing prohibition against looking at and enjoying her body. This exercise initially made her feel anxious, but with repeated exposure she became comfortable performing it and then progressed to touching her genitals directly. When she became comfortable with this step, and reported experiencing pleasurable erotic sensations, she was instructed to insert a finger into the vagina. She encountered intense anxiety at this step and required daily practice for two weeks before she could tolerate inserting her finger into her vagina without discomfort. Her husband was then brought into the treatment process. The couple was instructed to have Bridget insert her own finger in her vagina while Bryan watched. When she was comfortable with this exercise, she then guided his finger into her vagina. Later he placed one and then two fingers into her vagina, while she controlled the depth, speed, and duration of penetration. When she felt ready, they proceeded to attempt penile penetration in the female-superior position, which allowed her to maintain control over penetration. Over time, Bridget became more comfortable with penetration to the point where the couple developed a normal sexual relationship. (Adapted from Kaplan, 1987, pp. 102–103)

Sexual Arousal Disorders

Men with chronic erectile disorder may believe that they have "forgotten" how to have an erection. Erection, however, is an involuntary reflex, not a skill.

In sex therapy, women who have trouble becoming lubricated and men with erectile problems learn that they need not "do" anything to become sexually aroused. As long as their problems are psychologically and not organically based, they need only receive sexual stimulation under relaxed circumstances so that anxiety does not inhibit their natural reflexes.

In order to reduce performance anxiety, the partners engage in nondemanding sexual contacts—contacts that do not demand lubrication or erection. They may start with nongenital sensate focus exercises in the style of Masters and Johnson. After a couple of sessions, sensate focus extends to the genitals. The position shown in Figure 13.1 allows the woman easy access to her partner's genitals. She repeatedly "teases" him to erection and allows the erection to subside. Thus she avoids creating performance anxiety that could lead to loss of erection. By repeatedly regaining his erection, the man loses the fear that loss of erection means it will not return. He learns also to focus on erotic sensations for their own sake. He experiences no demand to perform, because the couple is instructed to refrain from coitus.

Are They Fit for Sex?
Research now clearly shows that one's general health is an important factor in sexual functioning. In fact, males who maintain a healthful lifestyle are much less likely to develop erectile problems as they age.

Figure 13.1 The Training Position Recommended by Masters and Johnson for Treatment of Erectile Disorder and Premature Ejaculation.

By lying in front of her partner, who has his legs spread, the woman has ready access to his genitals. In one part of a program designed to overcome erectile disorder, she repeatedly "teases" him to erection and allows the erection to subside. Thus she avoids creating performance anxiety that could lead to loss of erection. Through repeated regaining of erection, the man loses his fear that loss of erection means it will not return.

Even when the dysfunctional partner can reliably become sexually excited (denoted by erection in the male and lubrication in the female), the couple does not immediately attempt coitus; this might rekindle performance anxiety. Rather, the couple engages in a series of nondemanding, pleasurable sexual activities, which eventually culminate in coitus.

In Masters and Johnson's approach, the couple begin coitus after about 10 days of treatment. The woman teases the man to erection while she is sitting above him, straddling his thighs. When he is erect, *she* inserts the penis (to avoid fumbling attempts at entry) and moves slowly back and forth in a *nondemanding way*. Neither attempts to reach orgasm. If erection is lost, teasing and coitus are repeated. Once the couple become confident that erection can be retained—or reinstated if lost—they may increase coital thrusting gradually to reach orgasm.

BIOLOGICAL APPROACHES TO TREATMENT OF ERECTILE DISORDER

The world's attention has recently been focused on biological approaches to treating erectile disorder. Biological or biomedical approaches are helpful in treating erectile disorder, especially when organic factors are involved. Treatments include surgery, medication, and vacuum pumps.

Surgery Two main types of surgery are used in treating erectile disorder: vascular surgery and the installation of penile implants. *Vascular surgery* can help in cases in which the blood vessels that supply the penis are blocked or in which structural defects in the penis restrict blood flow (Cowley & Rogers, 1997). An arterial bypass operation reroutes vessels around the blockage.

A *penile implant* may be used when other treatments fail. Implants are either malleable (semirigid) or inflatable. The semirigid implant is made of rods of silicone rubber that remain in a *permanent* semirigid position. It is rigid enough for intercourse but permits the penis to hang reasonably close to the body at other times. The inflatable type requires more extensive surgery. Cylinders are implanted in the penis. A fluid reservoir is placed near the bladder, and a tiny pump is inserted in the scrotum. To attain erection, the man squeezes the pump, releasing fluid into the cylinders. When the erection is no longer needed, a release valve returns the fluid to the reservoir, deflating the penis. The inflatable implant more closely duplicates the normal processes of tumescence and detumescence. Implant surgery is irreversible (Padma-Nathan et al., 1997) and thus not the first choice of treatment.

Medication There are several ways in which medication can be used to help men with erectile problems. For example, *hormone (testosterone) treatments* help restore the sex drive and erectile ability in many men with abnormally low levels of testosterone (Lue, 2000; Rakic et al., 1997). There is no evidence that hormone therapy helps men who already have normal hormone levels.

The muscle relaxants *alprostadil* (brand names Caverject and Edex) and *phentolamine* (Invicorp) can be injected into the corpus cavernosum of the penis. These chemicals relax the muscles that surround the small blood vessels in the penis. The vessels dilate and allow blood to flow into the penis more freely. In the case of alprostadil, erections last for an hour or more and occur whether or not there is sexual stimulation. A physician teaches the man how to inject himself. Phentolamine is used along with the protein VIP, and erection occurs only when sexual stimulation is applied.

Injections are most effective for men with problems in the transmission of nerve signals that regulate erection (Altman, 1995). They are less effective for men with vascular problems that restrict the flow of blood into the penis.

Injections may have side effects, including pain from the injection itself and prolonged, painful erections (*priapism*) (Ralph & McNicholas, 2000). Many men find the idea of penile injections distasteful (the "wince factor") and refuse them. "Putting a needle in your penis is not everybody's idea of foreplay," notes Dr. John Seely (Kolata, 2000).

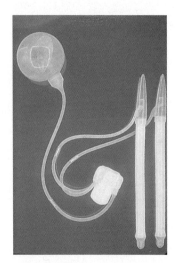

A Penile Implant.

Penile implants provide erection when the man's cardiovascular system does not do the job. This implant consists of cylinders that are implanted in the penis. A fluid reservoir (top left) is placed near the bladder. A pump (lower middle) is typically inserted in the scrotum. Squeezing the pump forces fluid into the cylinders, inflating the penis. Tripping a release valve later returns the fluid to the reservoir, deflating the penis.

Alprostadil is also available as a suppository in gel form (brand name MUSE), which is inserted into the tip of the penis by an applicator.

Other medications are taken orally. For example, the oral form of sildenafil is sold as Viagra, and the oral form of vardenafil is sold as Levitra. The oral form of tadalafil (Cialis) becomes effective in about half an hour and lasts up to 36 hours. Users in France dubbed it "the weekend pill." The drug apomorphine (Uprima) heightens brain levels of dopamine, a neurotransmitter involved in erection, and is available in the United Kingdom and advertised online (do not use it without consulting your physician). Researchers became aware of the potential benefits of dopamine-enhancing drugs through research with Parkinson's disease. Parkinson's is apparently caused by the death of dopamine-producing cells and is connected with loss of motor coordination and erectile dysfunction. L-dopa and other drugs that are used to treat Parkinson's raise dopamine levels and frequently have the "side effect" of erection (Kolata, 2000).

Viagra was hailed as a miracle drug when it hit the market in early 1998. It sold faster than any new drug had ever sold. The stock of Pfizer Company, which produces Viagra, shot up after the appearance of the drug. A study published in the *New England Journal of Medicine* tested the effects of Viagra on more than 800 men with erectile dysfunction due both to psychological causes and to a number of organic causes (Goldstein et al., 1998). In one phase of the study, 69% of attempts to engage in intercourse were successful for men taking Viagra, compared to 22% for men taking a placebo. A Canadian study (Carrier et al., 2005) found that Viagra was still effective after three years.

Erection Wars?
In an effort to reassure men with erectile dysfunction who fear that it may be unmanly to use Viagra, Levitra, or Cialis, marketers are recruiting athletic superstars like NASCAR driver Mark Martin to endorse their products.

Oral medications (pills) are the most popular biological treatment of erectile problems. They are helpful with most men and avoid the "wince factor." Viagra, Levitra, and Cialis have side effects, though, such as migraine headaches and flushing. The migraines are not surprising, because they are related to increased blood flow, and these drugs are not precise enough to direct blood only to the genitals. Soon after Viagra was approved by the FDA, there were scattered reports of men with cardiovascular problems experiencing heart attacks. A carefully conducted study of the effects of Viagra on 14 older men with at least one severely constricted coronary artery suggests that Viagra by itself has no adverse effects on the blood supply to the heart (Hermann et al., 2000). It would appear that men who are using a class of medicines known as nitrates to help them manage cardiovascular disease run a greater risk from Viagra.

In a study by Bill Fisher of the University of Western Ontario and colleagues (2005), many women whose partners had erectile dysfunction reported that they also experienced diminished sexual desire, arousal, orgasm, and sexual satisfaction. A significant proportion of women whose partners used an erection drug experienced increased sexual desire, arousal, and orgasm.

Vacuum Pumps   A *vacuum constriction device* (VCD) helps men achieve erections through vacuum pressure. The device (brand name ErecAid) consists of a cylinder that is connected to a hand-operated vacuum pump. It creates a vacuum when it is held over the limp penis. The vacuum induces erection by increasing the flow of blood into the penis. Rubber bands that are then applied around the base of the penis can maintain the erection for as long as 30 minutes.

Applied Knowledge

THINKING CRITICALLY ABOUT BUYING VIAGRA AND OTHER DRUGS ONLINE

Viagra is a prescription drug. Many men who might otherwise use Viagra are reluctant to discuss erectile dysfunction with their physicians. The anonymity of doing things on the Net is a lure—you don't have to admit your personal worries to your doctor face to face. Some men, unfortunately, do not even have a regular physician. What to do?

Many have discovered that by searching *Viagra* on the Net, they can find many Web sites where they can "consult" with online physicians, obtain a prescription, and order the drug for home delivery. Easy! A few questions and a fee, and they've got it. But is it

wise? Perhaps, perhaps not.

Prescriptions are needed for various drugs because physicians are better equipped than most laypeople to diagnose an individual's health problems, understand the chemical nature and side effects of the drugs available for treatment, and predict how the drugs will affect the individual patient. The physicians are also usually prepared to deal with the unexpected effects of the drugs, and there can be many.

So ask yourself what kind of physician will prescribe drugs online, without personally knowing the patient. Is it possible that some of them would have difficulty establishing private practices or getting jobs in hospitals? If you have a question about the drug once you use it, will you be able to get back to the prescriber easily for an answer, or

will you wind up making an embarrassed call to your own physician—or a trip to the emergency room?

While surfing the Net, you will also come across sites that claim to have "natural" preparations (including a variety of herbs) that are as effective as Viagra, but without the side effects and without the need to get a prescription. Use some critical thinking: Are you convinced of the effectiveness and safety of these preparations? Because they are foods (sort of) rather than drugs, they escape the scrutiny of government regulators. That is, the government is not watching over them. Be warned.

In sum, even if it is convenient to buy a drug online, you are well advised to get your prescription face to face—from a doctor you know and trust.

Should You Buy Viagra Online?
Many Web sites enable men to consult with physicians and order Viagra online. Is it wise to purchase Viagra—or any other prescription drug—online? Prescriptions are needed for drugs when the person's diagnosis is in question and when the drugs have side effects. Physicians are better equipped than most laypeople to diagnose health problems, understand the chemical composition and effects of drugs, and predict how drugs will affect the individual.

Research in Action

SEX THERAPY ON THE INTERNET

Eric Ochs and Yitzchak Binik of McGill University (2000) developed a computer program called Sexpert that provides online sexual counselling for couples. The Sexpert program asks couples detailed questions about their sexual behaviours, including initiation, foreplay, intercourse positions, and afterplay, and nonsexual aspects of their relationship. This interactive program gives couples feedback about their responses and provides information about related aspects of sexual functioning.

In their evaluative studies of Sexpert, Ochs and Binik found that although participants' initial reactions to the idea were negative, couples who used the program reported positive changes in foreplay activities and improved communication about sex. These couples rated the program more highly than sex education books or videos, but less highly than a therapist.

Many people who have sexual problems like the anonymity of using a computer program. However, more research is needed to determine how effective online therapy might be. It may prove to be most effective if used along with the traditional face-to-face therapy rather than as a substitute.

However, side effects such as pain and black-and-blue marks are common. The rubber bands prevent normal ejaculation, so semen remains trapped in the urethra until the bands are released. The quality of the erections produced by the device is also inferior to spontaneous erections (Spark, 1991).

FEMALE SEXUAL AROUSAL DISORDER Psychological treatments for female sexual arousal disorder parallel those for orgasmic disorder and are discussed in the following pages. Here let us briefly note that they involve sex education (labelling the parts, discussing their functions, and explaining how to arouse them), searching out and coping with possible cognitive interference (such as negative sexual attitudes), creating nondemanding situations in which sexual arousal may occur, and—when appropriate—working on problems in the relationship.

Yet many cases of female sexual arousal disorder reflect impaired blood flow to the genitals, just as in erectile disorder. Female sexual arousal involves vaginal lubrication, which permits sexual intercourse without a great deal of pain-causing friction. Lubrication is made possible by vasocongestion—the flow of blood into the genitals. Lack of lubrication can reflect the physical effects of aging, menopause, or surgically induced menopause.

Sometimes all that is necessary to deal with lack of lubrication is an artificial lubricant such as K-Y Jelly. But lessened blood flow to the genitals can also sap sexual pleasure and, as a consequence, lessen a woman's desire for sex.

Just as biological treatments for erectile disorder are mushrooming, so are biological treatments for female sexual arousal disorder. For example, drugs identical or similar to those used for men are being investigated for use with women.

In a study with 35 women, Berman (2000) found they reported greater vaginal lubrication and stronger orgasms after using Viagra. However, in a large survey of estrogen-deficient women, Basson and her colleagues (2002) found that Viagra was not effective in increasing sexual desire. Likewise, in a separate laboratory study of 35 postmenopausal women, British Columbia researchers Rosemary Basson and Lori Brotto (2003) found that in general, Viagra did not help those with sexual arousal and orgasm problems. However, improvement was seen among a subgroup who did not have vaginal engorgement during sexual arousal. More research needs to be done to determine the effect of drugs such as Viagra on women's sexual functioning.

Figure 13.2

A Clitoral Device That Stimulates Genital Vasocongestion in Women by Creating (Gentle) Suction Over the Clitoris.

Three medical scientists from Queen's University (Dr. Alvaro Morales, Dr. Jerome Heaton, and Dr. Michael Adams) have recently developed Uprima, a drug that treats erectile dysfunction, but which they believe will be of equal benefit to women (Steed, 2002). Early clinical trials in Europe suggest that Uprima has a positive effect on women's sexual arousal and response. The drug, which is dissolved under the tongue and is effective within 10 minutes, "stimulates receptors in the hypothalamus, a section of the brain that's critical in triggering sexual response in women and men" (Steed, p. H6).

There is even a device—Eros—that is a parallel to the vacuum pump used by some men with erectile disorder. It is a clitoral device that was approved by the U.S. Food and Drug Administration in 2000 and is available in the United States by prescription. The clitoris swells during sexual arousal because of vasocongestion, and vasocongestion increases clitoral sexual sensations, thus moving somewhat in step with sexual interest and lubrication. The device creates "gentle" suction over the clitoris, increasing vasocongestion and sexual sensations (Leland, 2000; see Figure 13.2).

Canadian sex therapists Peggy Kleinplatz (2003) and Rosemary Basson (2000) have been very vocal in their opposition to what they view as the "medicalization of female sexuality." Indeed, it is important to note that there are often other factors involved in cases of sexual dysfunction, such as intimacy and relationship issues, and that if these are not addressed the sexual problem will likely persist.

Orgasmic Disorders

Women who have never experienced orgasm often harbour negative sexual attitudes that cause anxiety and inhibit sexual response. Treatment in such cases may first address these attitudes.

Masters and Johnson use a couples-oriented approach in treating anorgasmic women. They begin with sensate focus exercises. Then, during genital massage and later during coitus, the woman guides her partner in the caresses and movements that she finds sexually exciting. Taking charge helps free the woman from the traditional stereotype of the passive, subordinate female role.

Masters and Johnson recommend a training position (see Figure 13.3) that gives the man access to his partner's breasts and genitals. She can guide his hands to show him the types of stimulation she enjoys. The genital play is *nondemanding*. The goal is to learn to provide and enjoy effective sexual stimulation, not to reach orgasm. The clitoris is not stimulated early, because doing so may produce a high level of stimulation before the woman is prepared.

After a number of occasions of genital play, the couple has coitus in the female-superior position (see Figure 13.4). This position allows the woman freedom of movement and control over her genital sensations. She is told to regard the penis as her "toy." The couple engage in several sessions of deliberately slow thrusting to sensitize the woman to sensations produced by the penis and break the common counterproductive pattern of desperate, rapid thrusting.

Orgasm cannot be willed or forced. When a woman receives effective stimulation, feels free to focus on erotic sensations, and feels that nothing is being demanded of her, she will generally reach orgasm. Once the woman is able to attain orgasm in the female-superior position, the couple may extend their sexual repertoire to other positions.

Masters and Johnson prefer working with the couple in cases of anorgasmia, but other sex therapists prefer to begin working with the woman individually through masturbation (Barbach, 1975; Heiman & LoPiccolo, 1987). This approach assumes that the woman accepts masturbation as a therapy tool.

Our focus has been on sexual techniques, but it is worth noting that a combination of approaches that focus on sexual techniques and underlying interpersonal

Figure 13.3 The Training Position for Nondemanding Stimulation of the Female Genitals.

This position gives the man access to his partner's breasts and genitals. She can guide his hands to show him what types of stimulation she enjoys.

Figure 13.4 Coitus in the Female-Superior Position.

In treatment of female orgasmic disorder, the couple undertake coitus in the female-superior position after a number of occasions of genital play. This position allows the woman freedom of movement and control over her genital sensations. She is told to regard the penis as her "toy." The couple engage in several sessions of deliberately slow thrusting to sensitize the woman to sensations produced by the penis and to break the common counterproductive pattern of desperate, rapid thrusting.

Applied Knowledge

MASTURBATION PROGRAMS FOR WOMEN IN SEX THERAPY

Masturbation provides women with opportunities to learn about their own bodies at their own pace. It frees them of the need to rely on a partner or to please a partner. The sexual pleasure they experience helps counter lingering sexual anxieties. Although there is some variation among therapists, the following elements are commonly found in directed masturbation programs:

1. *Education.* The woman and her sex partner (if she has one) are educated about female sexuality.

2. *Self-exploration.* Self-exploration is encouraged as a way of increasing the woman's sense of body awareness. She may hold a mirror between her legs to locate her sexual anatomic features. Kegel exercises may be prescribed to help tone and strengthen the pubococcygeus (PC) muscle that surrounds the vagina and to increase her awareness of genital sensations and her sense of control.

3. *Self-massage.* Once the woman feels comfortable about exploring her body, she creates a relaxing setting for self-massage. She chooses a time and place where she is free from distractions. She begins to explore the sensitivity of her body to touch, discovering and then repeating the caresses that she finds pleasurable. At first, self-massage is not concentrated on the genitals. It encompasses other sensitive parts of the body. She

may incorporate stimulation of the nipples and breasts and then direct genital stimulation, focusing on the clitoral area and experimenting with hand movements. Nonalcohol-based oils and lotions may be used to enhance the sensuous quality of the massage and to provide lubrication for the external genitalia. Kegel exercises may also be performed during self-stimulation to increase awareness of vaginal sensations and increase muscle tension. Some women use their dominant hand to stimulate their breasts while the other hand massages the genitals. No two women approach masturbation in quite the same way. In order to prevent performance anxiety, the woman does not attempt to reach orgasm during the first few occasions.

4. *Giving oneself permission.* The woman may be advised to practise assertive thoughts to dispel lingering guilt and anxiety about masturbation. For example, she might repeat to herself, "This is my body. I have a right to learn about my body and receive pleasure from it."

5. *Use of fantasy.* Arousal is heightened through the use of sexual images, fantasies, and fantasy aids, such as erotic written or visual materials.

6. *Allowing, not forcing, orgasm.* It may take weeks of masturbation to reach orgasm, especially for women who have never experienced orgasm. By focusing on her erotic sensations and fantasies, but not demanding orgasm, the

woman lowers performance anxiety and creates the stimulating conditions needed to reach orgasm.

7. *Use of a vibrator.* A vibrator may be recommended to provide more intense stimulation, especially for women who find that manual stimulation is insufficient.

8. *Involvement of the partner.* Once the woman is capable of regularly achieving orgasm through masturbation, the focus may shift to the woman's sexual relationship with her partner. Nondemanding sensate focus exercises may be followed by nondemanding coitus. The female-superior position is often used. It enables the woman to control the depth, angle, and rate of thrusting. She thus ensures that she receives the kinds of stimulation she needs to reach orgasm.

Kaplan (1974) suggests a bridge manoeuvre to assist couples who are interested in making the transition from a combination of manual and coital stimulation to coital stimulation alone as a means for reaching orgasm. Manual stimulation during coitus is used until the woman senses that she is about to reach orgasm. Manual stimulation is then stopped and the woman thrusts with her pelvis to provide the stimulation necessary to reach orgasm. Over time the manual clitoral stimulation is discontinued earlier and earlier. Although some couples may prefer this "hands-off" approach to inducing orgasm, Kaplan points out that there is nothing wrong with combining manual stimulation and penile thrusting.

problems may be more effective than focusing on sexual techniques alone, at least for couples whose relationships are troubled (Killmann et al., 1987; LoPiccolo & Stock, 1986).

MALE ORGASMIC DISORDER Treatment of male orgasmic disorder generally focuses on increasing sexual stimulation and reducing performance anxiety (LoPiccolo & Stock, 1986). Masters and Johnson instruct the couple to practise sensate focus exercises for several days, during which the man makes no attempt to ejaculate. The couple is then instructed to bring the man to orgasm in any way they can, usually by the woman's stroking his penis. Once the husband can ejaculate in the woman's presence, she brings him to the point at which he is about to ejaculate. Then, in the female-superior position, she inserts the penis and thrusts vigorously to bring him to orgasm. If he loses the feeling that he is about to ejaculate, the process is repeated. Even if ejaculation occurs at the point of penetration, it often helps break the pattern of inability to ejaculate within the vagina.

PREMATURE EJACULATION

Psychological Approaches to Treatment of Premature Ejaculation   In the Masters-and-Johnson approach, sensate focus exercises are followed by practice in the training position shown in Figure 13.1. The woman teases her partner to erection and uses the **squeeze technique** when he indicates that he is about to ejaculate. She squeezes the tip of the penis, which temporarily prevents ejaculation. This process is repeated three or four times in a 15- to 20-minute session before the man purposely ejaculates.

In the squeeze technique (which should be used only following personal instruction from a sex therapist), the woman holds the penis between the thumb and first two fingers of the same hand. The thumb presses against the frenulum. The fingers straddle the coronal ridge on the other side of the penis. Squeezing the thumb and forefingers together fairly hard for about 20 seconds (or until the man's urge to ejaculate passes) prevents ejaculation. The erect penis can withstand fairly strong pressure without discomfort, but erection may be partially lost.

After two or three days of these sessions, Masters and Johnson have the couple begin coitus in the female-superior position because it creates less pressure to ejaculate. The woman inserts the penis. At first she contains it without thrusting, allowing the man to get used to intravaginal sensations. If he signals that he is about to ejaculate, she lifts off and squeezes the penis. After some repetitions, she begins slowly to move backward and forward, lifting off and squeezing as needed. The man learns gradually to tolerate higher levels of sexual stimulation without ejaculating.

The alternating "stop-start" method for treating premature ejaculation was introduced by urologist James Semans (1956). The method can be applied to manual stimulation or coitus. For example, the woman can manually stimulate her partner until he is about to ejaculate. He then signals her to suspend sexual stimulation and allows his arousal to subside before stimulation is resumed. This process enables the man to recognize the cues that precede his point of ejaculatory inevitability, or "point of no return," and to tolerate longer periods of sexual stimulation. When the stop-start technique is applied to coitus, the couple begin with simple vaginal containment with no pelvic thrusting, preferably in the female-superior position. The man withdraws if he feels he is about to ejaculate. As the man's sense of control increases, thrusting can begin, along with variations in coital positions. The couple again stop when the man signals that he is approaching ejaculatory inevitability.

> **Squeeze technique** A method for treating premature ejaculation whereby the tip of the penis is squeezed to prevent ejaculation temporarily.

Gay men also face problems with premature ejaculation when engaging in anal sex. Their partners could use either the squeeze technique or the stop-start method.

Biological Approaches to Treatment of Premature Ejaculation In pilot studies, serotonin transporter inhibitors ("antidepressant" drugs generally used for psychological problems) have been helpful in treating premature ejaculation. One of the more promising PE drugs is called dapoxetine. Half of the men using this drug report that it helps significantly in controlling the timing of ejaculation and in improving sexual satisfaction (Pryor, 2005). It remains to be seen whether medications continue to show positive effects.

Sexual Pain Disorders

DYSPAREUNIA Dyspareunia, or painful intercourse, generally calls for medical intervention to identify and treat any underlying physical problems, such as urinary tract genital infections, that might give rise to pain (Laumann et al., 1999). When dyspareunia is caused by vaginismus, treatment through the behavioural approach described below may eliminate pain.

VAGINISMUS Vaginismus is generally treated with behavioural exercises in which plastic vaginal dilators of increasing size are inserted to help relax the vaginal musculature. A gynecologist may first demonstrate insertion of the narrowest dilator. Later the woman herself practises insertion of wider dilators at home. The woman increases the size of the dilator as she becomes capable of tolerating insertion and containment (for 10 or 15 minutes) without discomfort or pain. The woman herself—not her partner or therapist—controls the pace of treatment (LoPiccolo & Stock, 1986). The woman's or her partner's fingers (first the littlest finger, then two fingers, and so on) may be used in place of the plastic dilators, with the woman controlling the speed and depth of penetration. When the woman is able to tolerate dilators (or fingers) equivalent in thickness to the penis, the couple may attempt coitus. Still, the woman should control insertion. Circumstances should be relaxed and nondemanding. The idea is to avoid resensitizing her to fears of penetration. Because vaginismus often occurs among women with a history of sexual trauma, such as rape or incest, treatment for the psychological effects of these experiences may also be in order (LoPiccolo & Stock, 1986).

Evaluation of Sex Therapy

Masters and Johnson (1970) reported an overall success rate of about 80% in treating sexual dysfunctions in their two-week intensive program. Some dysfunctions proved more difficult to treat than others.

Other researchers have reported more modest levels of success in treating erectile disorder (Barlow, 1986). Nevertheless, long-term follow-up evaluations support the general effectiveness of sex therapy for erectile disorder (Everaerd, 1993). Yet problems do recur in some cases and are not always easily overcome (Everaerd, 1993). With the addition of biological treatments to the arsenal, the great majority of erectile problems can be successfully treated in one way or another (Lue, 2000).

We lack controlled studies of treatments of male orgasmic disorder (Dekker, 1993). Other than the original Masters-and-Johnson studies, results have been generally disappointing, with most people showing only modest improvement, if any (Dekker, 1993). New techniques in treating low sexual desire are also needed because the available techniques are often inadequate.

Sex therapy approaches to treating vaginismus and premature ejaculation have produced consistent levels of success (Beck, 1993; O'Donohue et al., 1993). Reported success in treating vaginismus has ranged as high as 80% (Hawton & Catalan, 1990) to 100% in Masters and Johnson's (1970) original research.

Treatment of premature ejaculation has resulted in success rates above 90% for the squeeze technique and the stop-start technique, but there are few data on the long-term results (LoPiccolo & Stock, 1986).

LoPiccolo and Stock (1986) found that 95% of a sample of 150 previously anorgasmic women were able to achieve orgasm through a directed-masturbation program. About 85% of these women were able to reach orgasm through manual stimulation by their partners. Only about 40%, however, were able to achieve orgasm during coitus.

Research in Action

EFFECTIVENESS OF TREATMENT PROGRAMS FOR DYSPAREUNIA

A team of researchers from Canada and the U.S. led by Sophie Bergeron and Yitzchak Binik of McGill University (Bergeron et al., 2001) have conducted controlled studies of the effectiveness of three types of treatment programs for dyspareunia resulting from vulvar vestibulitis (a sharp, burning pain experienced when direct pressure is applied just inside the vaginal opening). The three approaches were cognitive-behavioural therapy, biofeedback, and surgery involving the excision of the vestibular area. While each of the treatments resulted in pain reduction, the surgery had the highest success rate. The three treatment approaches were equally successful in improving psychological adjustment and sexual functioning. (However, the researchers note that some of the women who were assigned to the surgical treatment refused to go ahead with that intervention.) The findings indicate that both psychological and surgical interventions can be useful in the treatment of dyspareunia.

A World of Diversity

ALTERNATIVE APPROACHES TO SEX THERAPY

Ottawa sex therapist Peggy Kleinplatz (2003) has developed an innovative alternative approach to sex therapy. She argues that most sex therapy is too focused on treating symptoms and solving problems. Instead, therapists should focus on personal growth, which includes enhancing sexual relationships and erotic potential. Kleinplatz is especially concerned about the focus on pills and devices. The medical model emphasizes performance measures such as frequency and firmness of erections and ignores the quality of interactions (e.g., satisfaction, intimacy).

Kleinplatz believes that many therapists are personally uncomfortable with promoting eroticism, and attempt only to enable couples to engage in the mechanics of sexual intercourse rather than helping them maximize sexual pleasure (Kleinplatz, 2001). This mechanical approach results in sexual boredom for many couples, who come to rely on specific routines for achieving orgasm and then are afraid to risk trying new, and possibly more fulfilling, approaches.

According to Kleinplatz (2003), many couples want to excite their partners and establish a deep, sensual connection that will bring more intense sexual ecstasy. Eroticism, in Kleinplatz's view, is the key to maintaining sexual desire. The erotic encounter should focus on pleasure for its own sake rather than the tension release of orgasm (Kleinplatz, 1992).

Kleinplatz presents a more thorough discussion of the field of sex therapy in her 2001 book, *New Directions in Sex Therapy: Innovations and Alternatives.*

Many couples who believe it is important for the woman to reach orgasm during coitus are able to accomplish this end by combining direct clitoral stimulation with coital stimulation (LoPiccolo & Stock, 1986).

Many people who experience sexual dysfunctions do not seek professional help, largely because of feelings of embarrassment. In a survey of Canadian men, only about one-quarter of those who were experiencing erectile difficulties had discussed this with a physician (Auld & Brock, 2002). Twenty-nine percent of those who had talked to a physician about their problem were dissatisfied with the outcome, mainly because their physician had not taken the problem seriously or else was not properly informed about sexual dysfunctions. Only 48% of the men said that they experienced an improvement in their sexual functioning after consulting with their physician.

This is not surprising, as most helping professionals are not adequately trained to provide sex therapy. A survey of clinical psychologists in Ottawa (Di Giulio & Reissing, 2004) found that most had limited sex therapy training and only 22% said they were very comfortable dealing with sexual issues with their clients. Only 14% said they frequently asked clients about their sexual health concerns.

In a survey of Canadian clinical psychology graduate students, fewer than a third felt they had received adequate education about human sexuality topics, with the exception of sexual orientation issues and dealing with victims of sexual violence (Miller & Byers, 2005). However, there is hope for improvements in future training. Almost all of the students (86%) said they would like more sexuality education and 97% believed that it was important for psychology students to receive sexuality education.

Applied Knowledge

HOW DO YOU FIND A QUALIFIED SEX THERAPIST?

Many people do not know where to go for help if they have a sexual problem. How would you locate a sex therapist if you had a sexual dysfunction? Since the provinces do not regulate use of the term *sex therapist*, it is essential to determine that a sex therapist is a member of a recognized profession (such as psychology, social work, medicine, or marriage and family counselling) and has had training and supervision in sex therapy. (Specialized clinics focusing on men's sexual dysfunctions have been established in Ontario and British Columbia, for example.) Professionals are usually licensed or certified by their provinces. (All provinces require licensing of psy-

chologists and physicians, but some provinces do not license social workers or marriage counsellors.) Only physicians are permitted to bill their provincial health plans for providing sex therapy services.

If you are uncertain how to locate a qualified sex therapist in your area, try your university or college psychology department, health department, or counselling centre; a medical or psychological association; a marriage and family therapy association; a family physician; or your instructor.

Relatively few people in Canada have been trained as specialists in sex therapy. The only Canadian organization that certifies sex therapists is the Board of Examiners in Sex Therapy and Counselling in Ontario (BESTCO), comprising professionals from diverse backgrounds with clinical expertise in human sexual concerns.

Some Canadian therapists are also certified by American-based organizations such as the American Association of Sex Educators, Counselors, and Therapists (AASECT) and the Society for Sex Therapy and Research (SSTAR).

Ethical professionals are not annoyed or embarrassed if you ask them (1) what their profession is, (2) where they earned their advanced degree, and (3) whether they are licensed or certified, or if you inquire about (4) their fees, (5) their plans for treatment, and (6) their training in human sexuality and sex therapy. These questions are important because there is such a wide diversity in the professional background and training of sex therapists. Accordingly, the type of treatments and services that are available vary enormously (Kleinplatz, 2003). If the therapist hems and haws, asks why you are asking such questions, or fails to provide a direct answer, beware.

Professionals are also prohibited, by the ethical principles of their professions, from engaging in unethical practices, such as sexual relations with their clients. The nature of therapy creates an unequal power relationship between the therapist and the client. The therapist is perceived as an expert whose suggestions are likely to carry great authority. Clients may thus be vulnerable to exploitation by therapists who misuse their therapeutic authority. Let's be absolutely clear here: There is no therapeutic justification for a therapist to engage in sexual activity with a client. Any therapist who makes a sexual overture toward a client, or tries to persuade a client to engage in sexual relations, is acting unethically.

Summing Up

Types of Sexual Dysfunctions

Sexual dysfunctions are difficulties in becoming sexually aroused or reaching orgasm.

Sexual Desire Disorders

These disorders involve dysfunctions in sexual desire, interest, or drive, in which the person experiences a lack of sexual desire or an aversion to genital sexual contact.

Sexual Arousal Disorders

In men, sexual arousal disorders involve recurrent difficulty in getting or sustaining an erection sufficient to engage successfully in sexual intercourse. In women, they typically involve failure to become sufficiently lubricated.

Orgasmic Disorders

Women are more likely to encounter difficulties reaching orgasm. Men are more likely to have premature ejaculation.

Sexual Pain Disorders

These disorders include dyspareunia and vaginismus.

Origins of Sexual Dysfunctions

Many sexual dysfunctions involve the interaction of organic and psychological factors.

Organic Causes

Fatigue may lead to erectile disorder in men and to orgasmic disorder and dyspareunia in women. Dyspareunia often reflects vaginal infections and STIs. Organic factors are believed to be involved in the majority of cases of erectile disorder. Medications and other drugs may also impair sexual functioning.

Psychosocial Causes

Psychosocial factors that are connected with sexual dysfunctions include cultural influences, psychosexual trauma, a gay sexual orientation, marital dissatisfaction, psychological conflict, lack of sexual skills, irrational beliefs, and performance anxiety. Children reared in sexually repressive cultural or home environments may learn to respond to sex with feelings of anxiety and shame rather than sexual arousal and pleasure. Many people do not acquire sexual competencies because they have had no opportunity to acquire knowledge and experience, even within marriage. Irrational beliefs and attitudes such as excessive needs for approval and perfectionism may also contribute to sexual problems. Performance anxiety may place a dysfunctional individual in a spectator rather than performer role.

Treatment of Sexual Dysfunctions

Sex therapy aims to modify dysfunctional behaviour directly by changing self-defeating beliefs and attitudes, fostering sexual skills and knowledge, enhancing sexual communication, and suggesting behavioural exercises to enhance sexual stimulation while reducing performance anxiety.

The Masters-and-Johnson Approach

Masters and Johnson pioneered the direct, behavioural approach to treating sexual dysfunctions. A male-and-female therapy team is employed during an in-residence program that focuses on the couple as the unit of treatment. Sensate focus exercises are used to enable the partners to give each other pleasure in a nondemanding situation.

The Helen Singer Kaplan Approach

Kaplan's *psychosexual therapy* combines behavioural and psychoanalytic methods.

Sexual Desire Disorders

Some sex therapists help kindle the sexual appetites of people with inhibited sexual desire by prescribing self-stimulation exercises combined with erotic fantasies.

Sexual Arousal Disorders

Men and women with impaired sexual arousal receive sexual stimulation from their partners under relaxed circumstances so that anxiety does not inhibit their natural reflexes. Biological treatments such as the drug Viagra are also used with male erectile disorder.

Orgasmic Disorders

Masters and Johnson use a couples-oriented approach in treating anorgasmic women. Other sex therapists prefer a program of directed masturbation to enable women to learn about their own bodies at their own pace and free them of the need to rely on a partner or please a partner.

Premature ejaculation is usually treated with the squeeze technique or the stop-start method. Biological treatment methods for female orgasmic disorder and premature ejaculation are under development.

Sexual Pain Disorders

Dyspareunia, or painful intercourse, is generally treated with medical intervention. Vaginismus is generally treated with plastic vaginal dilators of increasing size.

Evaluation of Sex Therapy

The success of sex therapy has varied with the type of sexual dysfunction treated.

Test Yourself

Multiple-Choice Questions

1. The most commonly reported sexual problem for women, according to the 2003 Canadian Contraceptive Study, was
   a. partner ejaculating too soon
   b. painful intercourse
   c. low sexual desire
   d. lack of orgasm

2. In a 2005 survey women reported all of the following situations to be frustrating except
   a. partner not being affectionate
   b. not achieving orgasm
   c. partner refusing to have sex
   d. too many partners available

3. _____ involve a lack of sexual interest or an aversion to sexual activity.
   a. Sexual arousal disorders
   b. Sexual pain disorders
   c. Sexual desire disorders
   d. Sexual orgasm disorders

4. Low levels of sexual desire in women are often due to
   a. estrogen imbalance
   b. vaginal dryness
   c. psychological issues
   d. lack of a partner

5. _____ is a common cause of erectile difficulties.
   a. Orgasm anxiety
   b. Ejaculatory incompetence
   c. Performance anxiety
   d. Hyposensitivity of the penis

6. An involuntary contraction of the muscles that makes penetration painful or impossible is known as
   a. dyspareunia
   b. vaginismus
   c. phimosis
   d. anorgasmia

7. There is evidence that organic factors are involved in as many as _____ of cases of erectile dysfunction
   a. 20%
   b. 40%
   c. 60%
   d. 80%

8. Which of the following is not one of the psychosocial factors associated with sexual dysfunctions?
   a. dissatisfaction with the relationship
   b. lack of sexual skills
   c. anxiety due to previous negative experience
   d. side effects of prescription drugs

9. A behavioural approach to treating sex disorders might include all of the following except
   a. adjusting hormone balance to improve sexual functioning
   b. changing self-defeating beliefs and attitudes
   c. enhancing sexual knowledge
   d. improving communication skills

10. Treatment for _____ and _____ has produced high success rates.
    a. sexual arousal disorders; sexual desire disorders
    b. dyspareunia; erectile disorders
    d. vaginismus; premature ejaculation
    d. ejaculatory incompetence; low sexual desire

Critical Thinking Questions

1. Have you ever experienced a sexual problem? How did you react in this situation? How did your partner react? Could you talk about it? Why do you think you reacted the way you did?

2. Why do you think so many people find it difficult to admit that they have had a sexual dysfunction? Do you think it is more difficult for men or women to talk about their sexual problems? Why?

3. Would you buy drugs like Viagra over the Internet? Why or why not?

Visit our Companion Website at www.pearsoned.ca/rathus, where you can use the interactive Study Guide and link to additional resources on topics discussed in this text.

Chapter 14
Sexually Transmitted Infections

It seems you can't pick up a newspaper or turn on the TV without hearing about AIDS. AIDS is indeed a scary thing, a very scary thing. But although it is the most deadly of the **sexually transmitted infections** (STIs), others pose much wider threats (Stolberg, 1998b).

University students have become reasonably well informed about AIDS. However, many are unaware that chlamydia can go undetected for years. Moreover, if it is left untreated, it can cause pelvic inflammation and infertility. Many—perhaps most—students are ignorant about HPV, which is linked to cervical cancer (Josefsson et al., 2000). STIs are transmitted through sexual means, such as vaginal or anal intercourse or oral sex. They were formerly called *sexually transmitted diseases* (STDs) and before that *venereal diseases* (VDs)—after Venus, the Roman goddess of love.

Some STIs can be spread (and often are) through non-sexual contact as well. For example, AIDS and viral hepatitis may be spread by sharing contaminated needles. And yes, a few STIs (such as "crabs") may be picked up from bedding or other objects, such as moist towels, that harbour the organisms that cause these STIs.

Who Is at Risk?
Evidence suggests that many young people are sexually active. Thus it is important that they be aware of the risks involved and take responsibility for their sexual health.

An Epidemic

STIs are rampant. The World Health Organization estimates that at least 333 million people around the world are stricken with curable STIs each year (WHO, 1995). The United States is believed to have the highest rate of infection by STIs in the industrialized world ("CDC tackles surge," 1998).

Some people have STIs and do not realize it. Ignorance is not bliss, however. Some STIs may not produce noticeable symptoms, but they can be harmful if left untreated. STIs can also be painful and, in the cases of AIDS and advanced syphilis, lethal. Overall, STIs are believed to account for 15% to 30% of cases of infertility among women. In addition to their biological effects, STIs exact an emotional toll and strain relationships to the breaking point.

Canadian youth are especially vulnerable to STIs. Among Canadians, the highest rates for STIs and the largest increases in their transmission are occurring among those between the ages of 15 and 24 (Health Canada, 2001). And according to the Canadian Contraception Study (Fisher & Boroditsky, 2000), 17% of Canadian women aged 18 to 24 have been diagnosed with an STI. Among these women, the most common infections are chlamydia and HPV (genital warts). Rates of STI infection are also relatively high among men who have sex with men. In the 2002 Ontario survey of gay and bisexual men, 24% reported that they had ever had an STI (Myers et al., 2004).

Why the surge in the incidence of STIs? One reason is that many Canadians do not worry about becoming infected. In the 2002 Canada Youth and AIDS Survey, only 45% of youth said they were worried about catching HIV/AIDS—fewer than in 1989 (Boyse et al., 2003). Montreal researchers Rupert Klein and Barbel Knauper (2003) found that some young people purposely avoid thinking about STIs and consequently are less likely to discuss safer sex with a partner and less likely to use condoms.

Another reason is that many Canadians fail to use latex condoms consistently, if at all (Fisher et al., 2004a, 2004b). Overall, the percentage of Canadian women currently using condoms declined from 25% in 1995 to 18% in 2002 (Fisher et al., 2003b). Some people do not use condoms because the woman is on the pill. Although birth-control pills are reliable methods of contraception, they do not pre-

Sexually transmitted infections (STIs)
Infections that are communicated through sexual contact. (Some, such as HIV/AIDS, can also be transmitted in other ways.)

vent the spread of STIs. In the Canadian Contraceptive Study, women using oral contraceptives were more likely to report having had an STI than women who were using condoms (Fisher et al., 2004a, 2004b)

Other risk factors include early sexual involvement and sex with multiple partners. Drug use is also associated with an increased risk of STIs. People who abuse drugs are more likely than others to engage in risky sexual practices (Lowry et al., 1994; Rotheram-Borus et al., 1994). Moreover, certain forms of drug use, such as needle sharing, can directly transmit infectious organisms like HIV.

Rates of unprotected sex have also been increasing among gay and bisexual men. In the 2002 Ontario Men's survey (Myers et al., 2004) 40% of the men reported engaging in unprotected anal sex the previous year, compared with 20% of men in the 1991 Canadian survey (Myers, Godin, et al., 1993).

Bacterial Infections

Without the one-celled micro-organisms we call **bacteria**, there would be no wine. Bacteria are essential to fermentation. They also play vital roles in our digestive system. Unfortunately, bacteria also cause many diseases, including the common STIs chlamydia, gonorrhea, and syphilis. Statistics on these STIs are provided by the Public Health Agency of Canada.

Chlamydia

Chlamydia, a bacterial STI, is the most common STI in Canada. Rates of chlamydia declined from 1992 to 1997, but have increased since then. There were 29 951 reported cases of chlamydia in the first six months of 2004, with more than twice as many women as men contracting the disease (Public Health Agency of Canada, 2005a). The infection rates are far higher in the Yukon and the Northwest Territories than for the rest of Canada, reflecting the higher incidence among First Nations people. Young people between the ages of 15 and 24 account for about two-thirds of reported cases of chlamydia in Canada (Public Health Agency of Canada, 2005). Girls are more vulnerable than boys, as shown in Figure 14.1.

Rates of infection are extremely high among Canadian youth living on the street. In fact, chlamydia rates are nine times greater among street youth than among youth in general (Shields et al., 2004).

The highest rates are among First Nations youth (Shields et al., 2004). According to the 2003 Canadian Community Health Survey, First Nations youth

Bacteria Plural of *bacterium*, a class of one-celled micro-organisms that have no chlorophyll and can give rise to many illnesses. (From the Greek *baktron*, which means "stick," referring to the fact that many bacteria are rod-shaped.)

Figure 14.1 Rates of Chlamydia Infections in Canada Among Those Aged 15–19.

Rates of chlamydia infection in Canada are much higher for 15- to 19-year-old girls than for boys in the same age group.

Source: Data from Division of Sexual Health Promotion and STD Prevention and Control, Bureau of HIV/AIDS, STD and TB, STD Data Tables, Appendix 1.1 [on-line].
Available: **http://www.hc-sc.gc.ca/ pphb-dgspsp/std-mts/ stddata1201/ tab11-1_html**

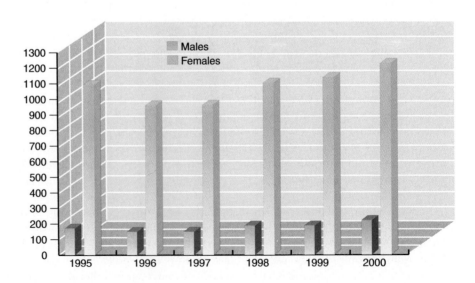

are two-and-a-half times as likely to have an STI as Canadian youth in general (Rotermann, 2005).

Chlamydia infections are caused by the *Chlamydia trachomatis* bacterium, a parasitic organism that can survive only within cells. This bacterium can cause several different types of infection, including *nongonococcal urethritis (NGU)* in men and women, *epididymitis* (infection of the epididymis) in men, and *cervicitis* (infection of the cervix), *endometritis* (infection of the endometrium), and pelvic inflammatory disease (PID) in women (Hatcher, 2001).

TRANSMISSION *Chlamydia trachomatis* is usually transmitted through sexual intercourse—vaginal or anal. *Chlamydia trachomatis* may also cause an eye infection if a person touches his or her eyes after handling the genitals of an infected partner. Oral sex with an infected partner can infect the throat. Newborns can acquire potentially serious chlamydia eye infections as they pass through the cervix of an infected mother during birth. Even newborns delivered by caesarean section may be infected if the amniotic sac breaks before delivery (Wingood & DiClemente, 2002).

SYMPTOMS Chlamydia infections usually produce symptoms that are similar to, but milder than, those of gonorrhea. In men, *chlamydia trachomatis* can lead to nongonococcal urethritis (NGU). *Urethritis* is an inflammation of the urethra. NGU refers to forms of urethritis that are not caused by the gonococcal bacterium. (NGU is generally diagnosed only in men. In women, an inflammation of the urethra caused by *chlamydia trachomatis* is called a chlamydia infection or simply chlamydia.) NGU was formerly called nonspecific urethritis, or NSU. Many organisms can cause NGU. *Chlamydia trachomatis* accounts for about half of the cases among men (Hatcher, 2001).

NGU in men may give rise to a thin, whitish discharge from the penis and some burning or other pain during urination. These contrast with the yellow-green discharge and more intense pain produced by gonorrhea. There may be soreness in the scrotum and feelings of heaviness in the testes. NGU is about two to three times as prevalent among American men as gonorrhea (Hatcher, 2001). Men 20 to 24 years of age are most at risk of contracting gonorrhea and NGU, presumably because of their high levels of sexual activity (Montano et al., 2001).

In women, chlamydial infections usually give rise to infections of the urethra or cervix. Women, like men, may experience burning when they urinate, genital irritation, and a mild (vaginal) discharge. Women are also likely to have pelvic pain and irregular menstrual cycles. The cervix may look swollen and inflamed.

Yet as many as 25% of men and 70% of women infected with chlamydia show no symptoms (Hatcher, 2001). For this reason, chlamydia has been dubbed "the silent disease." People without symptoms may go untreated and unknowingly pass along their infections to their partners. In women, an untreated chlamydial infection can spread throughout the reproductive system, leading to pelvic inflammatory disease (PID) and to scarring of the fallopian tubes, resulting in infertility (Garland et al., 1990; Hodgson et al., 1990). Women with a history of exposure to *Chlamydia trachomatis* also stand twice as much chance as others of incurring an ectopic (tubal) pregnancy (Sherman et al., 1990).

Untreated chlamydial infections can also damage the internal reproductive organs of men. About 50% of cases of epididymitis are caused by chlamydial infections (Hatcher, 2001). Yet only about 1% or 2% of men with untreated NGU caused by *Chlamydia trachomatis* go on to develop epididymitis. The long-term effects of untreated chlamydial infections in men remain undetermined.

A Silent Disease.
There are many thousands of new cases of chlamydia in Canada each year, and many—perhaps most—of them go undiagnosed and untreated. Because so many cases are symptom-free, infected individuals may unknowingly pass the infection to others and develop various health problems that could have been treated early.

Chlamydial infections frequently occur together with other STIs, most often gonorrhea. Nearly half of all cases of gonorrhea involve coexisting chlamydial infections (Hatcher, 2001).

DIAGNOSIS AND TREATMENT The Abbott Testpack permits physicians to verify a diagnosis of chlamydia in women. The test analyzes a cervical smear (like a Pap smear) and identifies 75% to 80% of infected cases. In men, a swab is inserted through the penile opening, and the extracted fluid is analyzed to detect the presence of *Chlamydia trachomatis*.

Antibiotics other than penicillin are highly effective in eradicating chlamydia infections. (Penicillin, effective in treating gonorrhea, is ineffective against *Chlamydia trachomatis*.) Treatment of sex partners is considered critical regardless of whether the partner shows symptoms, to prevent the infection from bouncing back and forth (Hatcher, 2001). Because of the risks that untreated chlamydial infections pose, especially to women, and the high rate of symptom-free infections, many physicians screen young women for chlamydia during regular checkups.

Gonorrhea

Gonorrhea An STI caused by the *Neisseria gonorrhoeae* bacterium and characterized by a discharge and burning urination. Left untreated, gonorrhea can give rise to pelvic inflammatory disease (PID) and infertility. (From the Greek *gonos*, which means "seed," and *rheein*, which means "to flow," referring to the fact that in ancient times, the penile discharge characteristic of the illness was erroneously interpreted as a loss of seminal fluid.)

Pharyngeal gonorrhea A gonorrheal infection of the pharynx (the cavity leading from the mouth and nasal passages to the larynx and esophagus) that is characterized by a sore throat.

Ophthalmia neonatorum A gonorrheal infection of the eyes of newborn children, who contract the disease by passing through an infected birth canal. (From the Greek *ophthalmos*, which means "eye.")

Gonorrhea—also known as "the clap" or "the drip"—was once the most widespread STI in Canada, but it has since been replaced by chlamydia. The rate of infection declined substantially from the mid-1980s through to 1997, apparently because of safer sexual practices. However, the rate increased again in the late 1990s, possibly because of the advances in the treatment of HIV/AIDS. As HIV/AIDS becomes less frightening, people may engage in more spontaneous sexual behaviour and increase the rate of STIs (CDC, 2000b). Since 1997, reported cases have been increasing more rapidly among men than among women (Hansen et al., 2003). In the first six months of 2004, 4013 new cases of gonorrhea were reported in Canada. Most new cases are contracted by males between the ages of 20 and 29 and by females between the ages of 15 and 24. This gender difference can be explained by the fact that females generally have sexual partners who are older than themselves (Health Canada, 2002).

TRANSMISSION Gonococcal bacteria require a warm, moist environment like that found along the mucous membranes of the urinary tract in both genders and the cervix in women. Outside the body, they die in about a minute. There is no evidence that gonorrhea can be picked up from public toilet seats or by touching dry objects. In rare cases, gonorrhea is contracted by contact with a moist, warm towel or sheet used immediately beforehand by an infected person. Gonorrhea is nearly always transmitted by unprotected vaginal, oral, or anal sexual activity, or from mother to newborn during delivery.

A person who performs fellatio on an infected man may develop **pharyngeal gonorrhea**, which produces a throat infection. Mouth-to-mouth kissing and cunnilingus are less likely to spread gonorrhea. The eyes provide a good environment for the bacterium. Thus a person whose hands come into contact with infected genitals and who inadvertently touches his or her eyes afterward may infect them. A baby may contract gonorrhea of the eyes (**ophthalmia neonatorum**) when passing through the birth canal of an infected mother. This disorder may cause blindness, but it has become rare because the eyes of newborns are treated routinely with silver nitrate or penicillin ointment; these compounds are toxic to gonococcal bacteria.

TABLE 14.1
Causes, Modes of Transmission, Symptoms, Diagnosis, and Treatment of Major
Sexually Transmitted Infections (STIs)

STI and Pathogen	Modes of Transmission	Symptoms	Diagnosis	Treatment
		Bacterial Diseases		
Gonorrhea ("clap," "drip"): gonococcus bacterium (*Neisseria gonorrhoeae*)	Transmitted by vaginal, oral, or anal sexual activity, or from mother to newborn during delivery	In men, yellowish, thick penile discharge, burning urination In women, increased vaginal discharge, burning urination, irregular menstrual bleeding (most women show no early symptoms)	Clinical inspection, culture of sample discharge	Antibiotics: ceftriaxone, ciprofloaxacin, cefixime, ofloxacin
Syphilis: *Treponema pallidum*	Transmitted by vaginal, oral, or anal sexual activity, or by touching an infectious chancre	In primary stage, a hard, round, painless chancre or sore appears at site of infection within 2 to 4 weeks. May progress through secondary, latent, and tertiary stages, if left untreated	Primary-stage syphilis is diagnosed by clinical examination and by examination of fluid from a chancre in a dark-field test. Secondary-stage syphilis is diagnosed by blood test (the VDRL)	Penicillin; or doxycycline, tetracycline, or erythromycin for nonpregnant penicillin-allergic patients
Chlamydia and nongonococcal urethritis (NGU): *Chlamydia trachomatis* bacterium; NGU in men may also be caused by *Ureaplasma urealyticum* bacterium and other pathogens	Transmitted by vaginal, oral, or anal sexual activity; to the eye by touching one's eyes after touching the genitals of an infected partner, or to newborns passing through the birth canal of an infected mother	In women, frequent and painful urination, lower abdominal pain and inflammation, and vaginal discharge (but most women are symptom-free) In men, symptoms are similar to, but milder than, those of gonorrhea—burning or painful urination, slight penile discharge (most men are also symptom-free) Sore throat may indicate infection from oral–genital contact	The Abbott Testpack analyzes a cervical smear in women; in men, an extract of fluid from the penis is analyzed	Antibiotics: azithromycin, doxycycline, ofloxacin, amoxicillin
		Vaginal Infections		
Bacterial vaginosis: *Gardnerella vaginalis* bacterium and others	Can arise by overgrowth of organisms in vagina, allergic reactions, etc.; also transmitted by sexual contact	In women, thin, foul-smelling vaginal discharge, irritation of genitals, and mild pain during urination In men, inflammation of penile foreskin and glans, urethritis, and cystitis Both sexes may be symptom-free	Culture and examination of bacterium	Metronidazole, clindamycin

(continues)

TABLE 14.1 (continued)
Causes, Modes of Transmission, Symptoms, Diagnosis, and Treatment of Major
Sexually Transmitted Infections (STIs)

STI and Pathogen	Modes of Transmission	Symptoms	Diagnosis	Treatment
Vaginal Infections (continued)				
Candidiasis (monilia-sis, thrush, "yeast infec-tion"): *Candida albicans*—a yeastlike fungus	Can arise by over-growth of fungus in vagina; may also be transmitted by sexual contact or by sharing a washcloth with an infected person	In women, vulval itching; white, cheesy, foul-smelling discharge; sore-ness or swelling of vaginal and vulval tissues In men, itching and burning on urination, or a reddening of the penis	Diagnosis usually made on basis of symptoms	Single-dose oral flucona-zole, or suppositories of miconazole, clotrima-zole, or butaconazole; modification of use of other medicines and chemical agents; keeping infected area dry
Trichomoniasis ("trich"): *Trichomonas vaginalis*, a protozoan (one-celled animal)	Almost always trans-mitted sexually	In women, foamy, yel-lowish, odorous vaginal discharge; itching or burning sensation in vulva. Many women are symptom-free Men are usually symp-tom-free, but mild ure-thritis is possible	Microscopic examina-tion of a smear of vagi-nal secretions, or of culture of the sample (latter method pre-ferred)	Metronidazole
Viral Diseases				
Oral herpes: *Herpes simplex virus-type 1 (HSV-1)*	Touching, kissing, sexual contact with sores or blisters; sharing cups, towels, toilet seats	Cold sores or fever blisters on the lips, mouth, or throat; her-petic sores on the geni-tals	Usually clinical inspec-tion	Over-the-counter lip balms, cold-sore med-ications; check with your physician, however
Genital herpes: *Herpes simplex virus-type 2 (HSV-2)*	Almost always by means of vaginal, oral, or anal sexual activity; most contagious during active outbreaks of the disease	Painful, reddish bumps around the genitals, thighs, or buttocks; in women, may also be in the vagina or on the cervix. Bumps become blisters or sores that fill with pus and break, shedding viral particles. Other possible symp-toms: burning urination, fever, aches and pains, swollen glands; in women, vaginal dis-charge	Clinical inspection of sores; culture and examination of fluid drawn from the base of a genital sore	There is no cure, but the antiviral drugs acy-clovir, famciclovir, and valacyclovir may pro-vide relief and prompt healing over; people with herpes often profit from counselling and group support as well
Viral hepatitis: hepa-titis A, B, C, and D type viruses	Sexual contact, espe-cially involving the anus (especially hepatitis A); contact with infected fecal matter; transfusion of contaminated blood (especially hepatitis B and C)	Ranges from being symptom-free to mild flulike symptoms and more severe symptoms, including fever, abdomi-nal pain, vomiting, and "jaundiced" (yellowish) skin and eyes	Examination of blood for hepatitis antibodies; liver biopsy	Treatment usually involves bed rest, intake of fluids, and, sometimes, antibiotics to ward off bacterial infections that might take hold because of lowered resistance. Alpha interferon is sometimes used in treating hepatitis C

(continues)

TABLE 14.1   (continued)
Causes, Modes of Transmission, Symptoms, Diagnosis, and Treatment of Major Sexually Transmitted Infections (STIs)

STI and Pathogen	Modes of Transmission	Symptoms	Diagnosis	Treatment
Viral Diseases (continued)				
Acquired immuno-deficiency syndrome (AIDS): *Human immunodeficiency virus (HIV)*	HIV is transmitted by sexual contact; by infusion with contaminated blood; from mother to fetus during pregnancy, or through childbirth or breast-feeding	Infected people may initially have no symptoms or develop mild flulike symptoms, which may then disappear for many years prior to the development of "full-blown" AIDS. The symptoms of full-blown AIDS include fever, weight loss, fatigue, diarrhea, and opportunistic infections such as rare forms of cancer (Kaposi's sarcoma) and pneumonia (PCP)	Blood, saliva, or urine tests detect HIV antibodies. More expensive tests confirm the presence of the virus (HIV) itself. The diagnosis of HIV/AIDS is usually made on the basis of antibodies, a low count of CD4 cells, and/or the presence of indicator diseases	There is no cure for HIV infection or AIDS. Treatment ("HAART") is a "cocktail" of antiviral drugs including a protease inhibitor and nucleoside analogues such as Zidovudine. New drugs such as fusion inhibitors are also joining the arsenal
Genital warts (venereal warts): *Human papilloma virus (HPV)*	Transmission is by sexual and other forms of contact, such as with infected towels or clothing	Appearance of painless warts, often resembling cauliflowers, on the penis, foreskin, scrotum, or internal urethra in men; or on the vulva, labia, wall of the vagina, or cervix in women. May occur around the anus and in the rectum of both genders	Clinical inspection	Methods include cryotherapy (freezing), podophyllin, trichloroacetic acid (TCA) or bichloroacetic acid (BCA), burning, and surgical removal
Ectoparasitic Infestations				
Pediculosis ("crabs"): *Phthirus pubis (pubic lice)*	Transmission is by sexual contact, or by contact with an infested towel, sheet, or toilet seat	Intense itching in pubic area and other hairy regions to which lice can attach	Clinical examination	Lindane (brand name: Kwellada)—a prescription shampoo; nonprescription medications containing pyrethrins or piperonal butoxide (brand names: R&C; Nix)
Scabies: *Sarcoptes scabiei*	Transmission is by sexual contact, or by contact with infested clothing or bed linen, towels, and other fabrics	Intense itching; reddish lines on skin where mites have burrowed in; welts and pus-filled blisters in affected areas	Clinical inspection	Lindane (Kwellada)

Source: Adapted from Rathus, S.A. (2005). Psychology: Concepts and connections, 9th ed. Belmont, CA: Wadsworth.

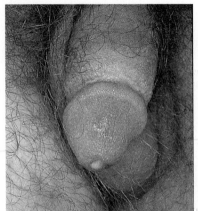

Figure 14.2 Gonorrheal Discharge.

Gonorrhea in the male often causes a thick, yellowish, pus-like discharge from the penis.

A gonorrheal infection may be spread from the penis to the partner's rectum during anal intercourse. A cervical gonorrheal infection can be spread to the rectum if an infected woman and her partner follow vaginal intercourse with anal intercourse. Gonorrhea is less likely to be spread by vaginal discharge than by penile discharge.

Gonorrhea is highly contagious. Women stand nearly a 50% chance of contracting gonorrhea after one exposure. Men have a 25% risk of infection (Hatcher, 2001). The risks to women are apparently greater because women retain infected semen in the vagina. The risk of infection increases with repeated exposure.

SYMPTOMS Most men experience symptoms within two to five days after infection. Symptoms include a penile discharge that is clear at first (Figure 14.1). Within a day it turns yellow to yellow-green, thickens, and becomes pus-like. The urethra becomes inflamed, and urination is accompanied by a burning sensation. About 30–40% of males have swelling and tenderness in the lymph glands of the groin. Inflammation and other symptoms may become chronic if left untreated.

The initial symptoms of gonorrhea usually abate within a few weeks without treatment, leading people to think of gonorrhea as being no worse than a bad cold. However, the gonococcus bacterium usually continues to damage the body even though the early symptoms fade.

The primary site of infection in women is the cervix, where gonorrhea causes **cervicitis**. Cervicitis may cause a yellowish to yellow-green pus-like discharge that irritates the vulva. If the infection spreads to the urethra, women may also note burning urination. *However, about 80% of the women who contract gonorrhea have no symptoms during the early stages of the infection.* Because many infected women do not seek treatment until symptoms develop, they may unknowingly infect another sex partner.

When gonorrhea is not treated early, it may spread through the urogenital systems in both genders and strike the internal reproductive organs. In men, it can lead to **epididymitis**, which can cause fertility problems. Swelling and feelings of tenderness or pain in the scrotum are the principal symptoms of epididymitis. Fever may also be present. Occasionally the kidneys are affected.

In women, the bacterium can spread through the cervix to the uterus, fallopian tubes, ovaries, and other parts of the abdominal cavity, causing **pelvic inflammatory disease** (PID). Symptoms of PID include cramps, abdominal pain and tenderness, cervical tenderness and discharge, irregular menstrual cycles, coital pain, fever, nausea, and vomiting. PID may also occur without symptoms. Whether or not there are symptoms, PID can cause scarring that blocks the fallopian tubes, leading to infertility. PID is a serious illness that requires aggressive treatment with antibiotics. Surgery may be needed to remove infected tissue. Unfortunately, many women become aware of a gonococcal infection only when they develop PID. These consequences are all the more unfortunate because gonorrhea, when diagnosed and treated early, clears up rapidly in over 90% of cases.

Cervicitis Inflammation of the cervix.

Epididymitis Inflammation of the epididymis.

DIAGNOSIS AND TREATMENT Diagnosis of gonorrhea involves clinical inspection of the genitals by a physician (a family practitioner, urologist, or gynecologist) and the culturing and examination of a sample of genital discharge.

Antibiotics are the standard treatment for gonorrhea. Penicillin was once the favoured antibiotic, but the rise of penicillin-resistant strains of *Neisseria gonorrhoeae* has required that alternative antibiotics be used (Hatcher, 2001). Because gonorrhea and chlamydia often occur together, people who are infected with gonorrhea are usually also treated for chlamydia through the use of another antibiotic (Hatcher, 2001). Sex partners of people with gonorrhea should also be examined.

Syphilis

In 1905 the German scientist Fritz Schaudinn isolated the bacterium that causes **syphilis**. It is *Treponema pallidum* (*T. pallidum*, for short). The name is derived from Greek and Latin roots that mean a "faintly coloured (pallid) turning thread"—a good description of the corkscrew-like shape of the microscopic organism. Because of the spiral shape, *T. pallidum* is also called a *spirochete*, from Greek roots that mean "spiral" and "hair."

The incidence of syphilis decreased in Canada with the introduction of penicillin in the 1940s. In recent years the rate of syphilis has been increasing, especially among males. In the first six months of 2004, 598 cases had been reported. This represents a 900% increase since 1997 (Public Health Agency of Canada, 2005b). However, compared with gonorrhea and chlamydia, the number of cases of syphilis is relatively small. According to the British Columbia Centre for Disease Control (2002), British Columbia has experienced the largest outbreak of syphilis in North America. About half the reported cases have been among sex trade workers and their clients in Vancouver's downtown East Side, which has a high rate of drug use. The remaining cases have involved gay men, heterosexuals who do not use condoms consistently, street youth, and sexually active injection-drug users. Several cases have also been contracted by travellers to Asia and Central America. Although syphilis is less widespread than it has been, its effects can be extremely harmful. They can include heart disease, blindness, gross confusion, and death.

TRANSMISSION Syphilis, like gonorrhea, is most often transmitted by vaginal or anal intercourse or by oral–genital or oral–anal contact with an infected person. The spirochete is usually transmitted when open lesions on an infected person come into contact with the mucous membranes or skin abrasions of the partner's body during sexual activity. The chance of contracting syphilis from one sexual contact with an infected partner is estimated at one in three (Wingood & DiClemente, 2002).

Syphilis may also be contracted by touching an infectious **chancre**, but not by using the same toilet seat as an infected person.

Pregnant women may transmit syphilis to their fetuses, because the spirochete can cross the placental membrane. Miscarriage, stillbirth, or **congenital syphilis**

Pelvic inflammatory disease Inflammation of the pelvic region—possibly including the cervix, uterus, fallopian tubes, abdominal cavity, and ovaries—that can be caused by organisms such as *Neisseria gonorrhoeae*. Its symptoms are abdominal pain, tenderness, nausea, fever, and irregular menstrual cycles. The condition may lead to infertility.

Syphilis An STI that is caused by the *Treponema pallidum* bacterium and may progress through several stages of development— often from a chancre to a skin rash to damage to the cardiovascular or central nervous system. (From the Greek *siphlos*, which means "maimed" or "crippled.")

Chancre A sore or ulcer.

Congenital syphilis A syphilis infection that is present at birth.

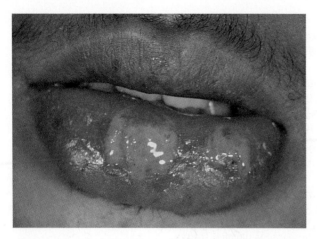

Figure 14.3 Syphilis Chancre.

The first stage, or primary stage, of a syphilis infection is marked by the appearance of a painless sore, or chancre, at the site of the infection.

VDRL The test named after the Venereal Disease Research Laboratory of the U.S. Public Health Service that checks for the presence of antibodies to *Treponema pallidum* in the blood.

Antibodies Specialized proteins produced by the white blood cells of the immune system in response to disease organisms and other toxic substances. Antibodies recognize and attack the invading organisms or substances.

may result. Congenital syphilis may impair vision and hearing or deform bones and teeth. Blood tests are administered routinely during pregnancy to diagnose syphilis in the mother so that congenital problems in the baby may be averted. The fetus will probably not be harmed if an infected mother is treated before the fourth month of pregnancy.

SYMPTOMS AND COURSE OF ILLNESS Syphilis develops through several stages. In the first stage, or *primary stage*, of syphilis, a painless chancre (a hard, round, ulcer-like lesion with raised edges) appears at the site of infection two to four weeks after contact. When women are infected, the chancre usually forms on the vaginal walls or the cervix. It may also form on the external genitalia, most often on the labia. When men are infected, the chancre usually forms on the penile glans. It may also form on the scrotum or penile shaft. If the mode of transmission is oral sex, the chancre may appear on the lips or tongue (see Figure 14.3). If the infection is spread by anal sex, the rectum may be the site of the chancre. The chancre disappears within a few weeks, but if the infection remains untreated, syphilis will continue to work within the body.

The *secondary stage* begins a few weeks to a few months later. A skin rash develops, consisting of painless, reddish, raised bumps that darken after a while and burst, oozing a discharge. Other symptoms include sores in the mouth, painful swelling of joints, a sore throat, headaches, and fever. A person with syphilis may thus wrongly assume that he or she has the flu.

These symptoms also disappear. Syphilis then enters the *latent stage* and may lie dormant for 1 to 40 years. But spirochetes continue to multiply and burrow into the circulatory system, central nervous system (brain and spinal cord), and bones. The person may no longer be contagious to sex partners after several years in the latent stage, but a pregnant woman may transmit the infection to her newborn at any time.

In many cases the disease eventually progresses to the late stage, or *tertiary stage*. A large ulcer may form on the skin, muscle tissue, digestive organs, lungs, liver, or other organs. This destructive ulcer can often be successfully treated, but still more serious damage can occur as the infection attacks the central nervous system or the cardiovascular system (the heart and the major blood vessels). Either outcome can be fatal. The primary and secondary symptoms of syphilis inevitably disappear. Infected people may thus be tempted to believe that they are no longer at risk and fail to see a doctor. This is unfortunate, because failure to eradicate the infection through proper treatment may eventually lead to dire consequences.

DIAGNOSIS AND TREATMENT Primary-stage syphilis is diagnosed by clinical examination. If a chancre is found, fluid drawn from it can be examined under a microscope. The spirochetes are usually quite visible. Blood tests are not definitive until the secondary stage begins. The most frequently used blood test is the **VDRL**. The VDRL tests for the presence of **antibodies** to *Treponema pallidum* in the blood.

Penicillin is the treatment of choice for syphilis, although for people allergic to penicillin, doxycycline and some other antibiotics can be used (Hatcher, 2001). Sex partners of persons infected with syphilis should also be evaluated by a physician.

Other Bacterial Infections

Several other types of bacterial STIs occur less commonly in Canada and the United States. These include chancroid, shigellosis, granuloma inguinale, and lymphogranuloma venereum.

CHANCROID **Chancroid**, or "soft chancre," is caused by the bacterium *Hemophilus ducreyi*. It is more commonly found in the tropics and eastern nations than in western countries. The chancroid sore consists of a cluster of small bumps or pimples on the genitals, the perineum (the area of skin that lies between the genitals and the anus), or the anus itself. These lesions usually appear within seven days of infection. Within a few days the lesion ruptures, producing an open sore or ulcer. Several ulcers may merge with other ulcers, forming giant ulcers (Ronald & Albritton, 1990). There is usually an accompanying swelling of a nearby lymph node. In contrast to the syphilis chancre, the chancroid ulcer has a soft rim (hence its name) and is painful in men. Women frequently do not experience any pain and may be unaware of being infected (Ronald & Albritton, 1990). The bacterium is typically transmitted through sexual or bodily contact with the lesion or its discharge. Diagnosis is usually confirmed by culturing the bacterium, which is found in pus from the sore, and examining it under a microscope. Antibiotics are usually effective in treating the disease (Hatcher, 2001).

SHIGELLOSIS **Shigellosis** is caused by the *Shigella* bacterium and is characterized by fever and severe abdominal symptoms, including diarrhea and inflammation of the large intestine. Shigellosis can result from food poisoning, but it is also often contracted by oral contact with infected fecal material, which may stem from oral–anal sex. Shigellosis often resolves itself, but people with the disease may become severely dehydrated from the diarrhea. Severe cases are usually treated with antibiotics.

GRANULOMA INGUINALE Rare in Canada and the United States, **granuloma inguinale**, like chancroid, is more common in tropical regions. It is caused by the bacterium *Calymmatobacterium granulomatous* and is not as contagious as many other STIs. Primary symptoms are painless red bumps or sores in the groin area that ulcerate and spread. Like chancroid, it is usually spread by intimate bodily or sexual contact with a lesion or its discharge. Diagnosis is confirmed by microscopic examination of tissue at the rim of the sore. Antibiotics are effective in treating this disorder (Hatcher, 2001). If left untreated, however, the disease may lead to the development of fistulas (holes) in the rectum or bladder, destruction of the tissues or organs that underlie the infection, or scarring of skin tissue that results in **elephantiasis**, the condition that afflicted the so-called elephant man in the nineteenth century.

LYMPHOGRANULOMA VENEREUM (LGV) **Lymphogranuloma venereum** (LGV) is another tropical STI that occurs only rarely in Canada. In August 2005, the Public Health Agency of Canada announced that 33 cases of LGV had been reported among men having sex with men. Most of the infected men also had co-infections with other STIs, HIV, and Hepatitis C.

LGV is caused by several strains of the *Chlamydia trachomatis* bacterium. LGV usually enters the body through the penis, vulva, or cervix, where a small, painless sore may form. The sore may go unnoticed, but a nearby lymph gland in the groin swells and grows tender. Other symptoms mimic those of flu: chills, fever, and headache. Backache (especially in women) and arthritic complaints (painful joints) may also occur. If LGV is untreated, complications such as growths and fistulas in the genitals and elephantiasis of the legs and genitals may occur. Diagnosis is made by skin tests and blood tests. Antibiotics are the usual treatment (Hatcher, 2001).

Vaginal Infections

Vaginitis is any kind of vaginal infection or inflammation. Women with vaginitis may encounter genital irritation or itching and burning during urination, but the most common symptom is an odorous discharge.

Chancroid An STI caused by the *Hemophilus ducreyi* bacterium. Also called *soft chancre*.

Shigellosis An STI caused by the *Shigella* bacterium.

Granuloma inguinale A tropical STI caused by the *Calymmatobacterium granulomatous* bacterium.

Elephantiasis A disease characterized by enlargement of parts of the body, especially the legs and genitals, and by hardening and ulceration of the surrounding skin. (From the Greek *elephas*, which means "elephant," referring to the resemblance of the affected skin areas to elephant hide.)

Lymphogranuloma venereum A tropical STI caused by the *Chlamydia trachomatis* bacterium.

Vaginitis Any type of vaginal infection or inflammation.

Most cases of vaginitis are caused by organisms that reside in the vagina or by sexually transmitted organisms. Organisms that reside in the vagina may overgrow and cause symptoms when the environmental balance of the vagina is upset by factors such as birth-control pills, antibiotics, dietary changes, excessive douching, or nylon underwear or pantyhose. (See Chapter 3 for suggestions on reducing the risk of vaginitis.) Still other cases are caused by sensitivities or allergic reactions to various chemicals.

The great majority of vaginal infections (Wingood & DiClemente, 2002) involve bacterial vaginosis (BV), candidiasis (commonly called a "yeast" infection), or trichomoniasis ("trich"). Bacterial vaginosis is the most common form of vaginitis, followed by candidiasis, then by trichomoniasis, but some cases involve combinations of the three.

The microbes that cause vaginal infections in women can also infect the man's urethral tract. A "vaginal infection" can be passed back and forth between sex partners (Wingood & DiClemente, 2002).

Bacterial Vaginosis

Bacterial vaginosis (BV, formerly called *nonspecific vaginitis*) is most often caused by overgrowth of the bacterium *Gardnerella vaginalis* (Wingood & DiClemente, 2002). The bacterium is transmitted primarily through sexual contact. The most characteristic symptom in women is a thin, foul-smelling vaginal discharge, but infected women often have no symptoms. Diagnosis requires culturing the bacterium in the laboratory (Wingood & DiClemente, 2002). Besides causing troublesome symptoms in some cases, BV may increase the risk of various gynecological problems, including infections of the reproductive tract (Hillier & Holmes, 1990). Oral treatments are recommended and are effective in about 90% of cases (Wingood & DiClemente, 2002). Topical treatments are also effective. Recurrences are common, however.

Questions remain about whether the male partner should also be treated. The bacterium can usually be found in the male urethra but does not generally cause symptoms (Wingood & DiClemente, 2002).

A common misperception is that there is no risk of STIs being transmitted between female sex partners. However, there is a high prevalence of BV among lesbian women. One study of lesbian and bisexual women found that even though one-half of those between the ages of 18 and 22 had a history of BV, they perceived little risk of STI infection from female partners (Marazzo, 2005). The women took no precautions with their partners to prevent STIs. In particular, they did not wash their hands before sexual activity, did not use rubber gloves for vaginal or oral penetration, and shared sex toys without washing them or using them with condoms.

Candidiasis

Also known as *moniliasis, thrush*, or (most commonly) a yeast infection, **candidiasis** is caused by a yeast-like fungus, *Candida albicans*. Candidiasis commonly produces soreness, inflammation, and intense (sometimes maddening!) itching around the vulva that is accompanied by a thick, white, curd-like vaginal discharge (see Figure 14.4). Yeast generally produces no symptoms when the vaginal environment is normal. Yeast infections can also occur in the mouth in both men and women and in the penis in men.

Infections most often arise from changes in the vaginal environment that allow the fungus to overgrow. Factors such as the use of antibiotics, birth-control pills, or intrauterine devices (IUDs), pregnancy, and diabetes may alter the vaginal balance, allowing the fungus that causes yeast infections to grow to infectious levels (Wingood & DiClemente, 2002). Wearing nylon underwear and tight, restrictive, poorly ventilated clothing may also set the stage for a yeast infection.

Bacterial vaginosis
A form of vaginitis usually caused by the *Gardnerella vaginalis* bacterium.

Candidiasis A form of vaginitis caused by a yeast-like fungus, *Candida albicans*.

Diet may play a role in recurrent yeast infections. Reducing one's intake of substances that produce excessive excretion of urinary sugars (such as dairy products, sugar, and artificial sweeteners) apparently reduces the frequency of recurrent yeast infections. The daily ingestion of half a litre (one pint) of yogurt containing active bacterial (*Lactobacillus acidophilus*) cultures helped reduce the rate of recurrent infections in one sample of women (Hilton et al., 1992).

Candidiasis can be passed back and forth between sex partners through vaginal intercourse. It can also be passed back and forth between the mouth and the genitals through oral–genital contact and can infect the anus through anal intercourse. However, most infections in women are believed to be caused by an overgrowth of "yeast" normally found in the vagina, not by sexual transmission. Still, it is advisable to evaluate both partners simultaneously. Whereas most men with *Candida* have no symptoms, some may develop NGU or a genital thrush that is accompanied by itching and burning during urination or reddening of the penis. Candidiasis may also be transmitted by nonsexual means, such as between women who share a washcloth.

In Canada, about 75% of women will have at least one episode of candidiasis during their lifetime. It is one of the most common medical problems faced by Canadian women, and accounts for more than 1 million visits to physician offices per year (Public Health Agency of Canada, 2005c). About 50% of women have recurrent infections. Recommended treatment is vaginal suppositories or creams (Hatcher, 2001; Wingood & DiClemente, 2002). Many of these treatments are sold over the counter. We recommend that women with vaginal complaints consult their physician before taking any of these medications, to ensure that they receive the proper diagnosis and treatment.

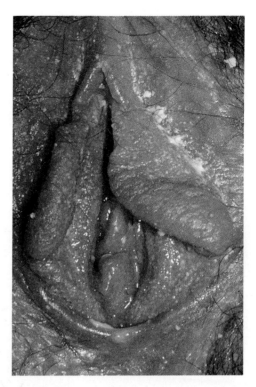

**Figure 14.4
Candidiasis.**

A "yeast infection" is caused by the *Candida albicans* fungus and causes soreness, inflammation, and itching around the vulva that is accompanied by a thick, white vaginal discharge.

Trichomoniasis

Trichomoniasis ("trich") is caused by *Trichomonas vaginalis*. *Trichomonas vaginalis* is a one-celled parasite. Trichomoniasis is the most common parasitic STI (Wingood & DiClemente, 2002). Symptoms in women include burning or itching in the vulva, mild pain during urination or coitus, and an odorous, foamy, whitish to yellowish-green discharge. Lower abdominal pain is reported by 5% to 12% of infected women (Rein & Muller, 1990). Many women notice that symptoms appear or worsen during, or just after, their menstrual periods. Trichomoniasis facilitates the transmission of HIV (Wingood & DiClemente, 2002) and is also linked to the development of tubal adhesions that can result in infertility (Grodstein et al., 1993). As with many other STIs, about half of infected women have no symptoms (Wingood & DiClemente, 2002).

Unlike candidiasis, trichomoniasis is nearly always sexually transmitted. Because the parasite can survive for several hours on moist surfaces outside the body, trich can be communicated from contact with infected semen or vaginal discharges on towels, washcloths, and bedclothes. This parasite is one of the few disease agents that can be picked up from a toilet seat, but it would have to directly touch the penis or vulva (Wingood & DiClemente, 2002).

Trichomonas vaginalis can cause NGU in the male, which can be symptom-free or can cause a slight penile discharge that is usually noticeable prior to first urination in the morning. There may be tingling, itching, and other irritating sensations in the urethral tract. Yet most infected men are symptom-free. Therefore, they can unwittingly transfer the organism to their sex partners. Perhaps three or four in ten male partners of infected women are found to harbour *Trichomonas vaginalis* them-

Trichomoniasis A form of vaginitis caused by the protozoan *Trichomonas vaginalis*.

selves (Wingood & DiClemente, 2002). Diagnosis is frequently made by microscopic examination of a smear of a woman's vaginal fluids in a physician's office. Diagnosis based on examination of cultures grown from the vaginal smear is considered more reliable, however.

Except during the first three months of pregnancy, trichomoniasis is usually treated in both partners, whether or not they report symptoms. When both partners are treated simultaneously, the success rate approaches 100% (Hatcher, 2001; Wingood & DiClemente, 2002).

Viral Infections

Viruses are tiny particles of DNA surrounded by a protein coating. They are incapable of reproducing on their own. When they invade a body cell, however, they can direct the cell's own reproductive machinery to spin off new viral particles that spread to other cells, causing infection. In this section we discuss several viral STIs: HIV/AIDS, herpes, viral hepatitis, and genital warts.

HIV/AIDS

AIDS is the acronym for **acquired immunodeficiency syndrome**. AIDS is a fatal syndrome that is caused by the **human immunodeficiency virus (HIV)**. HIV attacks and disables the immune system, the body's natural line of defence, stripping it of its ability to fend off disease-causing organisms.

PREVALENCE OF HIV According to the Public Health Agency of Canada, from 1985 (when HIV testing began) through December 2004, 57 674 people were diagnosed with HIV in Canada. The number of reported HIV-positive tests decreased from 1995 to 2000 but increased by 20% from 2111 in 2000 to 2259 in 2004. The proportion of positive HIV tests among women increased from less than 10% in 1995 to over one-quarter of the cases. Among women the largest increase is among those 15 to 29 years of age. In 2004, 42.4% of new HIV cases in the 15–29 age group were among women. The proportion of HIV infections acquired through heterosexual contact is increasing and now accounts for a third of all positive HIV tests. A significant proportion of the heterosexual HIV infections originated in countries having high HIV prevalence rates, such as those in Africa (Public Health Agency of Canada, 2005). Although the proportion of heterosexually acquired HIV infections is increasing, higher prevalence rates are found among men who have sex with men and injection drug users

PREVALENCE OF AIDS By the end of 2005 there were 19 828 reported cases of AIDS in Canada (Public Health Agency of Canada, 2005).

In 2004 women accounted for 20% of the total number of reported AIDS cases, a significant increase from 10.7% in the period from 1985 to 1995. The most dramatic increase has occurred among women in the 15- to 29-year-old age group, with 45% of AIDS-related infections in that age group now occurring among women. In 2004 men who have sex with men accounted for about a third of AIDS cases. This is a major decrease, in that prior to 1994, this group accounted for three-quarters of all AIDS cases.

Disproportionately high numbers of Canadians who are First Nations or Black are living with HIV/AIDS. Prior to 1992, First Nations people accounted for 1.3% of AIDS cases; this increased to 15% in 2004. Black Canadians accounted for 8% of AIDS cases prior to 1992, and 15.5% in 2004 (Public Agency of Canada, 2005).

THE IMMUNE SYSTEM AND AIDS AIDS is caused by a virus that attacks the body's **immune system**—the body's natural line of defence against disease-causing organisms. The immune system combats disease in a number of ways. It produces white blood cells that envelop and kill **pathogens** such as bacteria, viruses, and fungi; worn-out body cells; and cancer cells. White blood cells are referred to as **leukocytes**. Leukocytes engage in microscopic warfare. They undertake search-and-destroy missions. They identify and eradicate foreign agents and debilitated cells.

Leukocytes recognize foreign agents by their surface fragments. The surface fragments are termed **antigens** because the body reacts to their presence by developing specialized proteins, or **antibodies**. Antibodies attach themselves to the foreign bodies, inactivate them, and mark them for destruction. (Infection by HIV may be determined by examining the blood or saliva for the presence of antibodies to the virus.)

Rather than mark pathogens for destruction or war against them, special "memory lymphocytes" are held in reserve. Memory lymphocytes can remain in the bloodstream for years, and they form the basis for a quick immune response to an invader the second time around.

Another function of the immune system is to promote **inflammation**. When you suffer an injury, blood vessels in the region initially contract to check bleeding. Then they dilate. Dilation expands blood flow to the injured region, causing the redness and warmth that identify inflammation. The elevated blood supply also brings in an army of leukocytes to combat invading microscopic life forms, such as bacteria, that might otherwise use the local injury to establish a beachhead into the body.

EFFECTS OF HIV ON THE IMMUNE SYSTEM Spikes (technically known as "gpl20" spikes) on the surface of HIV allow it to bind to sites on cells in the immune system (Sodroski et al., 1998). Like other viruses, HIV uses the cells it invades to spin off copies of itself. HIV uses the enzyme *reverse transcriptase* to cause the genes in the cells it attacks to make proteins that the virus needs in order to reproduce.

HIV directly attacks the immune system by invading and destroying a type of lymphocyte called the CD4 cell or helper T-cell (see Figure 14.5). The CD4 cell is the quarterback of the immune system. CD4 cells "recognize" invading pathogens and signal B-lymphocytes or B-cells—another kind of white blood cell—to produce antibodies that inactivate pathogens and mark them for annihilation. CD4 cells also signal another class of T-cells, called killer T-cells, to destroy infected cells. By attacking and destroying helper T-cells, HIV disables the very cells on which the body relies to fight off this and other diseases. As HIV cripples the body's defences, the individual is exposed to infections that would not otherwise take hold. Cancer cells might also proliferate. Although the CD4 cells appear to be its main target, HIV also attacks other types of white blood cells.

The blood normally contains about 1000 CD4 cells per cubic millimetre. The numbers of CD4 cells may remain at about this level for years following HIV infection. Many people show no symptoms and appear healthy while CD4 cells remain at this level. Then, for reasons that are not clearly understood, the levels of CD4 cells begin to drop off, although symptoms may not appear for a decade or more. As the numbers of CD4 cells decline, symptoms generally increase, and people fall prey to diseases that their weakened immune systems are unable to fight off. People become most vulnerable to opportunistic infections when the level of CD4 cells falls below 200 per cubic millimetre. Researchers in Vancouver have discovered that treatment for symptoms of AIDS can be started later than previously thought with no difference in health outcomes (Hogg et al., 2001). Specifically, patients can wait till their CD4 cell count drops to 300 instead of 500.

PROGRESSION OF HIV/AIDS HIV follows a complex course once it enters the body. Shortly after infection, the person may experience mild flu-like symptoms—fatigue, fever, headaches and muscle pain, lack of appetite, nausea, swollen glands,

Pathogen An agent, especially a micro-organism, that can cause a disease. (From the Greek *pathos*, which means "suffering" or "disease," and *genic*, which means "forming" or "coming into being.")

Leukocytes White blood cells that are essential to the body's defences against infection. (From the Greek *leukos*, which means "white" and *kytos*, which means "a hollow" and is used in combination with other word forms to mean "cell.")

Antigen A protein, toxin, or other substance to which the body reacts by producing antibodies. (Combined word formed from *antibody generator*.)

Antibodies Specialized proteins that develop in the body in response to antigens and that inactivate foreign bodies.

Inflammation Redness and warmth that develop at the site of an injury, reflecting the dilation of blood vessels that permits the expanded flow of leukocytes to the region.

A World of Diversity

THE NEW FACE OF HIV/AIDS

Kaitlin Morrison lost her virginity at 13 and, she says, it was "downhill from there." At 14, she left her parents' home in Port McNeill, B.C., on the northeast coast of Vancouver Island. She was a "party girl" and a "real rebel," she says, heavy into drugs (never needles, though). Now 23, Morrison recalls how narcotics like cocaine and ecstasy could blunt her judgment, so the sex wasn't always safe. After fleeing an abusive relationship in Calgary, at 19 she returned to Vancouver Island, settling in Port Hardy. She was HIV-free: she'd had herself tested. Then she met "a nice, clean-cut guy" with a good job. They had casual sex. He didn't always wear a condom. "Three days after my 20th birthday," recalls Morrison, "I was diagnosed."

As Ottawa works to develop a new strategy against AIDS, far too many Canadians still think HIV is the bane of gay men and injection-drug users. But the reality is much different, says Barbara Clow, executive director of the Atlantic Centre of Excellence for Women's Health in Halifax. Awareness programs from the early 1990s have actually decreased infection rates among gays and addicts. In contrast, HIV spread by heterosexual contact has risen sharply in Canada.

Despite the warnings, too many teenagers continue to have sex without condoms. Meantime, young women like Morrison have all too quietly become the new face of this deadly disease. Today, she works for AIDS Vancouver Island, running a needle-exchange program and sharing her experiences with teens. She is stunned by how many kids still think HIV/AIDS can be cured. "It makes me sick," says Morrison. "A lack of knowledge is exactly what's going to feed this epidemic." That, and ignoring the fact that young heterosexual women are increasingly at risk.

The New Face of AIDS.
HIV infection rates are increasing among young Canadian women. Kaitlin Morrison was diagnosed with HIV just after turning 20.

Source: Danylo Hawaleshka, Maclean's, May 30, 2005, p. 41. Reprinted with permission of Maclean's.

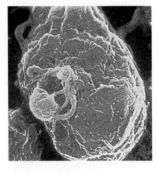

Figure 14.5 HIV (the AIDS Virus) Attacks a White Blood Cell.

HIV progressively weakens the immune system, leaving the body vulnerable to infections and diseases that would otherwise be fended off.

and possibly a rash. Such symptoms usually disappear within a few weeks. The infected person may dismiss them as a passing case of flu. People who enter this symptom-free or carrier state generally look and act well and do not realize that they are infectious. Thus they can unwittingly pass the virus along to others.

Most people who are infected with HIV remain symptom-free for years. Some enter a symptomatic state (previously labelled *AIDS-related complex*, or ARC) that is typically marked by symptoms such as chronically swollen lymph nodes and intermittent weight loss, fever, fatigue, and diarrhea. This symptomatic state does not constitute full-blown AIDS, but it shows that HIV is undermining the integrity of the immune system.

The beginnings of full-blown AIDS are often marked by such symptoms as swollen lymph nodes, fatigue, fever, night sweats, diarrhea, and weight loss that cannot be attributed to dieting or exercise.

AIDS is connected with the appearance of diseases such as pneumocystis carinii pneumonia (PCP), Kaposi's sarcoma (a form of cancer), toxoplasmosis of the brain (an infection of parasites), and *Herpes simplex* with chronic ulcers. These diseases are termed **opportunistic diseases** because they are not likely to emerge unless a disabled immune system provides the opportunity.

About 10% of people with AIDS have a wasting syndrome. Wasting, the unintentional loss of more than 10% of a person's body weight, is connected with AIDS, some other infections, and cancer (Grunfeld, 1995). It appears that people with

AIDS who waste away do so because they take in less energy, not because they burn more calories (Macallan et al., 1995).

As AIDS progresses, the individual grows thinner and more fatigued. He or she becomes unable to perform ordinary life functions and falls prey to opportunistic infections. If left untreated, AIDS nearly always results in death within a few years.

Could This Couple Be Transmitting HIV?
HIV is a blood-borne virus that is transmitted via various bodily fluids, including blood, semen, and vaginal fluids. However, HIV has not been found to occur in infectious quantities in saliva.

TRANSMISSION HIV can be transmitted by certain contaminated bodily fluids: blood, semen, vaginal secretions, and breast milk. The first three of these may enter the body through vaginal, anal, or oral–genital intercourse with an infected partner. An African study that followed seropositive mothers and their babies for two years found that the probability of transmission of HIV via breast milk was about 16.2% (one in six) (Nduati et al., 2000). Other avenues of infection include sharing a hypodermic needle with an infected person (as do many people who inject drugs), transfusion with contaminated blood, transplants of organs and tissues that have been infected with HIV, artificial insemination with infected semen, or being stuck by a needle used previously on an infected person. HIV may enter the body through tiny cuts or sores in the mucosal lining of the vagina, the rectum, and even the mouth. These cuts or sores can be so tiny that you are not aware of them.

Transmission of HIV through kissing—even prolonged kissing or "French" kissing—is considered unlikely. When a person injects drugs, a small amount of his or her blood remains inside the needle and syringe. If the person is HIV-infected, the virus may be found in the blood remaining in the needle or syringe. Others who use the needle inject the infected blood into their bloodstream. HIV can also be spread by sharing needles used for other purposes, such as injecting steroids, ear piercing, or tattooing.

HIV can also be transmitted from mother to fetus during pregnancy or from mother to child through childbirth or breast-feeding (Mofenson, 2000; Wood et al., 2000). Transmission is most likely to occur during childbirth. In 2004, 163 infants in Canada were born to HIV-positive mothers. However, only 2% of those infants became HIV infected, as 96% of the mothers received antiviral therapy (Public Health Agency of Canada, 2005).

Male-to-female transmission through vaginal intercourse is about twice as likely as female-to-male transmission (CDC, 2000a), partly because more of the virus is found in the ejaculate than in vaginal secretions. A man's ejaculate may also remain for many days in the vagina, providing greater opportunity for infection to occur. Male–female or male–male anal intercourse is especially risky, particularly to the recipient, because it often tears or abrades rectal tissue, facilitating entry of the virus into the bloodstream (Caceres & van-Griensven, 1994).

Worldwide, male–female sexual intercourse accounts for the majority of cases of HIV/AIDS. In Canada, many cases of male–female transmission occur within the community of people who inject drugs and their sex partners.

In the early years of the AIDS epidemic, HIV spread rapidly among hemophiliacs who had unknowingly been transfused with contaminated blood. But blood supplies are now routinely screened for HIV. Medical authorities now consider the risk of HIV transmission through transfusion of screened blood to be negligible if not entirely absent (Klein, H. G., 2000).

Factors That Affect the Risk of Sexual Transmission Some people seem more likely than others to communicate HIV, and others seem to be especially vulnerable to HIV infection. Why, for instance, are some people infected by one sexual contact with an infected partner, whereas others are not infected during months or years of unprotected sex? Several factors appear to affect the risk of HIV infection and the development of AIDS:

■   The probability of sexual transmission rises with the number of sexual contacts with an infected partner.

Opportunistic diseases Diseases that take hold only when the immune system is weakened and unable to fend them off. Kaposi's sarcoma and pneumocystis carinii pneumonia (PCP) are examples of opportunistic diseases found in people with AIDS.

Welcome to Condom Country. Condom ads based on the ruggedly masculine Marlboro country tobacco ads are used by the AIDS Committee of Toronto during Pride Week to encourage gay men to use condoms.

- The probability of transmission is also affected by the type of sexual activity. Anal intercourse, for example, provides a convenient port of entry for HIV because it often tears or abrades the rectal lining. In a Toronto study of men who had sex with men who had AIDS, those men who engaged in either insertive or receptive anal intercourse were more likely to be HIV-positive themselves (Coates et al., 1988). Those men who engaged in activities that could damage the lining of the rectum, such as rectal douching, receptive fisting, and placing of objects in the anus, were also at greater risk of HIV infection.

- The amount of virus in semen also affects the probability of infection. The quantity of HIV in the semen peaks shortly after initial infection and when full-blown AIDS develops.

- STIs such as genital warts, gonorrhea, trichomoniasis, and chlamydia inflame the genital region, which heightens the risk of sexual transmission of other STIs (Stolberg, 1998b). STIs that produce genital ulcers, such as syphilis and genital herpes, may heighten vulnerability to HIV infection by allowing the virus to enter the circulatory system through the ulcers.

- Circumcision lowers the risk of infection.

- Genetic factors may also be at work. About 1% of people of Western European descent have inherited a gene that prevents HIV from entering cells in the immune system from both parents and are apparently immune to HIV infection. Perhaps 20% of individuals of Western European descent have inherited the gene from one parent; HIV disease appears to progress more slowly in these people. Some prostitutes in Thailand and Africa, where HIV infection has been running rampant, also appear to be immune to HIV infection (Royce et al., 1997).

DIAGNOSIS OF HIV/AIDS In a Toronto study of 40 HIV-positive women from a diversity of socioeconomic backgrounds, 61% did not have an HIV test until after they had developed symptoms, or someone with whom they were intimate, or their child, tested positive for HIV or became ill (Jackson et al., 1997). Almost all (90%) did not perceive themselves to be at risk of HIV until they found out they were HIV-positive. Almost half indicated that they had not received any counselling about their HIV status.

The most widely used test for HIV infection is the enzyme-linked immunosorbent assay (ELISA), which may take several days to yield results. ELISA does not directly detect HIV in the blood. Instead, it reveals HIV antibodies. People may show an antibody response to HIV long before they develop symptoms of infection. A positive (**seropositive**) test result means that antibodies were found and usually indicates that the person is infected with HIV. A negative (**seronegative**) outcome means that antibodies to HIV were not detected.

ELISA can be performed on samples of blood, saliva, or urine. A group of Ontario researchers have demonstrated that the saliva test is almost as accurate as the blood test (Major et al., 1991). A saliva test is less expensive and might encourage people who avoid blood tests to be tested. Although HIV antibodies can be detected in saliva, HIV itself is not found in measurable quantities. This is why kissing is not considered an avenue of transmission of HIV. The saliva is absorbed by a cotton pad on a stick that is placed between the lower gum and the cheek. The saliva in the cotton, like blood, undergoes ELISA in a laboratory.

Seropositive Having a pathogen or antibodies to that pathogen in the bloodstream.

Seronegative Lacking a pathogen or antibodies to that pathogen in the bloodstream.

TREATMENT OF HIV/AIDS For many years, researchers were frustrated by failure in the effort to develop effective vaccines and treatments for HIV/AIDS. There is still no safe, effective vaccine, but recent developments in drug therapy have raised hopes in the area of treatment.

The ideal vaccine against AIDS would be safe and inexpensive and would confer lifetime protection against all strains of the disease with a single dose. Such a vaccine may take some time to develop; but researchers are becoming more hopeful.

Today many drugs are used to combat HIV/AIDS. They offer a good deal of hope for people with HIV/AIDS, including pregnant women who are infected with HIV. Zidovudine (previously referred to as AZT) has been the most widely used HIV/AIDS drug. Zidovudine is one of a number of so-called nucleoside analogues that inhibit replication (reproduction) of HIV by targeting the enzyme called reverse transcriptase. Other nucleoside analogues are ddI, ddC, d4T, and 3TC. Zidovudine in many cases delays the progression of the infection and increases the blood count of CD4 cells. HIV-infected pregnant women who use zidovudine reduce the rate of HIV infection in their newborns by two-thirds (Connor et al., 1994). Zidovudine helps prevent transmission during childbirth by decreasing the amount of the virus in the mother's bloodstream (Meyer, 1998). Only 8% of the babies born to the zidovudine-treated women became infected with HIV, as compared with 25% of babies whose mothers were untreated. Zidovudine is generally used for 26 weeks prior to childbirth. However, using zidovudine for even the final few weeks cuts the transmission rate of HIV from mother to child by half (Meyer, 1998).

The results of the European Mode of Delivery Collaboration Trial on the efficacy of elective C-section versus vaginal delivery show that C-section further decreases the risk of maternal transmission of HIV to the baby (Ricci et al., 2000). The study enlisted about 400 seropositive mothers. All mothers received zidovudine during pregnancy. Half of the mothers were assigned at random to deliver vaginally, half by C-section. The HIV infection rate was 10.6% for babies delivered vaginally (not too different from the 8% reported by Meyer, 1998) and 1.7% for babies delivered by C-section. Thus the combination of zidovudine during pregnancy and delivery by C-section cuts the chance that a seropositive mother will transmit HIV to her baby to about 1 in 50.

A new generation of drugs that block the replication of HIV, called *protease inhibitors*, are more effective treatments for HIV/AIDS. Protease inhibitors block reproduction of HIV particles by targeting the protease enzyme. A combination, or "cocktail," of antiviral drugs including zidovudine, another nucleoside analogue, and a protease inhibitor has become the standard treatment of HIV/AIDS (Gallant, 2000). This combination—referred to as **HAART** (for "highly active antiretroviral therapy")—decreases the likelihood that HIV will develop resistance to treatment. It has reduced HIV below detectable levels in many infected people (Lederman & Valdez, 2000). It has created hope that AIDS will become increasingly manageable—a chronic health problem as opposed to a terminal illness. HAART is expensive, however, and many people who could benefit from it cannot afford it.

HAART has worked many wonders to date in reducing the death rate from AIDS (Flexner, 1998; Lederman & Valdez, 2000). Yet even when HIV has been reduced to "undetectable levels" by ordinary means, scientists have been able to use methods of close scrutiny to locate it in "resting" (nonreplicating) CD4 cells (Lederman & Valdez, 2000). Therefore, HAART does not appear to be a cure. The encouraging news is that after using HAART, some HIV-infected people can go on drug "vacations" without their HIV levels bouncing back. Perhaps HAART gave their immune systems the opportunity to learn to manage HIV.

Promising results are also reported in treating the opportunistic infections, such as PCP (Bozzette et al., 1995) and fungal infections (Powderly et al., 1995), that take hold in people with weakened immune systems (Clumeck, 1995).

HAART (pronounced *HEART*) The acronym for "highly active antiretroviral therapy," which refers to the combination, or "cocktail," of drugs used to treat HIV/AIDS: a protease inhibitor in combination with a couple of other antiretroviral agents.

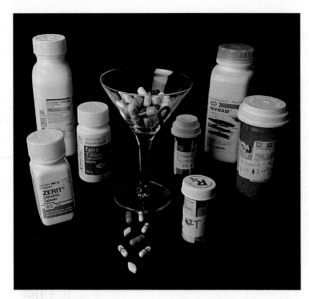

HAART.

HAART is the acronym for "highly active antiretroviral therapy." It refers to a combination, or "cocktail," of antiviral drugs—including zidovudine, another nucleoside analogue, and a protease inhibitor —that has become the standard treatment of HIV/AIDS. The combination of drugs decreases the likelihood that HIV will develop resistance to drug therapy. HAART has reduced HIV in blood to below-detectable levels in many infected individuals. However, it is expensive, there are side effects, and it does not work for everyone.

In sum, we finally have some good news about HIV/AIDS. Many people who had believed that they were doomed have been given a new lease on life. Only a few years ago, infection with HIV was considered a death sentence. Almost everyone who was infected with HIV eventually developed symptoms, grew progressively weaker and sicker, and died. But HAART and better treatment of opportunistic diseases have made dramatic inroads into the death rate from AIDS in Canada.

In Windsor, Ontario, researchers have studied how the newer HAART therapies for HIV have affected the lives of 31 men and 4 women who are HIV-positive (Adams et al., 2001). While many reported substantial improvement in their health as a consequence of the therapies, some emphasized that their condition was "tolerable." Those who had been recently diagnosed as experiencing symptoms related to HIV were all responding well. Many felt that they could lead more normal lives. Most reported that sexual desire decreased significantly at the time of HIV diagnosis but that sexual desire and activity returned over time. Severity of illness rather than relationship status was the strongest predictor of sexual activity. Most of those who did not have any physical symptoms were sexually active, whereas those who had the most severe physical symptoms were not. However, some avoided sexual activity because they did not want to put a partner at risk. For those who did not feel comfortable disclosing their HIV status to others, the Internet provided a source of information and friendship. Several were involved in HIV/AIDS support groups.

PREVENTION What can we do to curb the spread of HIV/AIDS? Given that we lack both vaccine and cure, prevention is our best hope. Our discussion of prevention will focus on sexual transmission, but other efforts have been made to prevent transmission of HIV from mother to child, through the injection of drugs with shared needles, and through blood transfusions. For example, HIV-infected women are advised to avoid breast-feeding. Zidovudine and other measures, such as C-section, decrease the probability of transmission through childbirth (Ricci et al., 2000). At its 2002 annual meeting, the Canadian Medical Association recommended that all pregnant women in Canada should be screened for the HIV virus in order to prevent transmission of the virus to their babies. The screening of potential blood donors has rendered the probability of transmission via blood transfusion almost negligible. Reducing the risk of infection through unsafe sexual contact has been less successful, however.

Most prevention efforts focus on education. Sexually active people have been advised to alter their sexual behaviour by practising abstinence, by limiting their sexual experiences to a lifelong monogamous relationship, or by practising "safe sex"—which, as we shall see, could more accurately be dubbed "safer sex."

The advent of HIV/AIDS presents the medical, mental health, and educational communities with an unprecedented challenge: to develop programs to contain its spread and to treat people with HIV/AIDS compassionately. Although HIV/AIDS is frightening, it is preventable. For the latest information on HIV/AIDS, call the Toronto AIDS hotline: 1-800-267-6600. The call is free and anonymous. We expand our discussion of prevention of HIV/AIDS in the section entitled "Prevention of STIs" later in this chapter.

A World of Diversity

GENDER IS A CRUCIAL ISSUE IN THE FIGHT AGAINST HIV/AIDS

Gender inequality is a fundamental driving force of the AIDS epidemic, a fact that we must address in responding to the epidemic, according to Peter Piot (2000), executive director of the Joint United Nations Program on HIV/AIDS (UNAIDS).

Today, women's increased vulnerability to HIV is becoming better understood. Women's economic dependence on men makes them less able to protect themselves, and social norms limit their access to information about sexual matters. At the same time, greater social acceptance of high-risk male sexual behaviour can expose both men and their partners to infection.

"Slowing down the spread of HIV means important changes are needed in relationships between men and women," said Dr. Piot. "Men have a crucial role to play in bringing about this kind of radical change."

That change in men's behaviour can influence the course of the AIDS epidemic was the theme of the year 2000 World AIDS Campaign to involve men more fully in preventing the spread of HIV, the virus that causes AIDS.

"We must stop seeing men as some kind of problem and begin seeing them as part of the solution," said Dr. Piot. "Working with men to change their behaviour and attitudes has tremendous potential to slow down the epidemic. It will also improve the lives of men themselves, not to mention those of their families."

Source: Adapted from UNAIDS Press Release (2000, June 5). "Gender Is Crucial Issue in Fight Against AIDS, Says Head of UNAIDS." New York. Reproduced by kind permission of the Joint United Nations Programme on HIV/AIDS (UNAIDS).

Speaking Up.
In Canada, more men than women have HIV/AIDS. However, biological and social factors make women and girls more vulnerable to HIV/AIDS than men, especially in adolescence and youth. Women around the world are more likely to be infected than men, and the numbers of infected women in Canada may be "catching up" with those of men. Violence—or the threat of violence—against women increases their vulnerability to HIV/AIDS and reduces their ability to protect themselves against infection.

Herpes

Once you get herpes, it's yours for life. After the initial attack, it remains an unwelcome guest in your body forever. It finds a cozy place to lie low until it stirs up trouble again. It causes recurrent outbreaks that often happen at the worst times, such as around final exams. This is not just bad luck. Stress can depress the functioning of the immune system and heighten the likelihood of outbreaks.

Not only are you stuck with the virus; you can also pass it along to sex partners for the rest of your life. Flare-ups may continue to recur, sometimes with annoying frequency. On the other hand, some people have no recurrences. Still others have mild, brief recurrences that become less frequent over time.

Different types of herpes are caused by variants of the *Herpes simplex* virus. The most common type, ***Herpes simplex* virus type 1** (HSV-1), causes oral herpes. Oral herpes is characterized by cold sores or fever blisters on the lips or mouth. It can also be transferred to the genitals by the hands or by oral–genital contact (Mertz et al., 1992). **Genital herpes** is caused by a related but distinct virus, the ***Herpes simplex* virus type 2** (HSV-2). This virus produces painful, shallow sores and blisters on the genitals. HSV-2 can also be transferred to the mouth through oral–genital contact. Both types of herpes can be transmitted sexually.

> ***Herpes simplex* virus type 1** The virus that causes oral herpes, which is characterized by cold sores or fever blisters on the lips or mouth. Abbreviated *HSV-1*.
>
> **Genital herpes** An STI caused by the *Herpes simplex* virus type 2 and characterized by painful, shallow sores and blisters on the genitals.
>
> ***Herpes simplex* virus type 2** The virus that causes genital herpes. Abbreviated *HSV-2*.

Physicians are not required to report cases of herpes to public health officials, so there are no precise statistics on its prevalence.

TRANSMISSION Herpes can be transmitted through oral, anal, or vaginal sexual activity with an infected person (Martin et al., 1998; Mertz et al., 1992; Wald et al., 1995). The herpes viruses can also survive for several hours on toilet seats or other objects, where they can be picked up by direct contact. Oral herpes is easily contracted by drinking from the same cup as an infected person, by kissing, and even by sharing towels. But genital herpes is generally spread by coitus or by oral or anal sex.

Many people do not realize that they are infected, and so they can unknowingly transmit the virus through sexual contact. And many of the people who do know they are infected don't realize that they can pass along the virus even when they have no noticeable outbreak (Mertz et al., 1992; Wald et al., 1995). Although genital herpes is most contagious during active flare-ups, it can also be transmitted when an infected partner has no symptoms (genital sores or feelings of burning or itching in the genitals). Any intimate contact with an infected person carries some risk of transmission of the virus, even if the infected person never has another outbreak. People may also be infected with the virus and have *no* outbreaks, and yet pass the virus along to others.

Herpes can also be spread from one part of the body to another by touching the infected area and then touching another body part. One potentially serious result is a herpes infection of the eye: **ocular herpes**. Thorough washing with soap and water after touching an infected area may reduce the risk of spreading the infection to other parts of the body. Still, it is best to avoid touching the infected area altogether, especially if there are active sores.

Women with genital herpes are more likely than the general population to have miscarriages. Passage through the birth canal of an infected mother can infect babies with genital herpes, damaging or killing them (Whitley et al., 1991). Obstetricians thus often perform caesarean sections if the mother has active lesions or **prodromal symptoms** at the time of delivery (Osborne & Adelson, 1990). Herpes can also place women at greater risk of genital cancers, such as cervical cancer. (All women, not just women with herpes, are advised to have regular pelvic examinations, including Pap tests for early detection of cervical cancer.)

SYMPTOMS Genital lesions or sores appear about six to eight days after infection with genital herpes. At first they appear as reddish, painful bumps, or papules, along the penis or vulva (see Figure 14.6). They may also appear on the thighs or buttocks, in the vagina, or on the cervix. These papules turn into groups of small blisters that are filled with fluid containing infectious viral particles. The blisters are attacked by the body's immune system (white blood cells). They fill with pus, burst, and become extremely painful, shallow sores or ulcers surrounded by a red ring. People are especially infectious during such outbreaks, because the ulcers shed millions of viral particles. Other symptoms may include headaches and muscle aches, swollen lymph glands, fever, burning urination, and a vaginal discharge. The blisters crust over and heal in one to three weeks. Internal sores in the vagina or on the cervix may take 10 days longer than external (labial) sores to heal. Physicians thus advise infected women to avoid unprotected intercourse for at least 10 days after the healing of external sores.

Although the symptoms disappear, the disease does not. The virus remains in the body permanently, burrowing into nerve cells in the base of the spine, where it may lie dormant for years or for a lifetime. The infected person is least contagious during this dormant stage. For reasons that remain unclear, the virus becomes reactivated and gives rise to recurrences in most cases.

Ocular herpes A herpes infection of the eye, usually caused by touching an infected area of the body and then touching the eye.

Prodromal symptoms Warning symptoms that signal the onset or flare-up of a disease. (From the Greek *prodromos*, which means "forerunner.")

Recurrences may be related to infections (such as a cold), stress, fatigue, depression, exposure to the sun, and hormonal changes such as those that occur during pregnancy or menstruation. Recurrences tend to occur within 3 to 12 months of the initial episode and to affect the same part of the body.

The symptoms of oral herpes include sores or blisters on the lips, the inside of the mouth, the tongue, or the throat. Fever and feelings of sickness may occur. The gums may swell and redden. The sores heal over in about two weeks, and the virus retreats into nerve cells at the base of the neck, where it lies dormant between flare-ups.

DIAGNOSIS AND TREATMENT
Genital herpes is first diagnosed by clinical inspection of herpetic sores or ulcers in the mouth or on the genitals. A sample of fluid may be taken from the base of a genital sore and cultured in the laboratory to detect the growth of the virus.

Viruses, unlike the bacteria that cause gonorrhea or syphilis, do not respond to antibiotics. Antiviral drugs can relieve pain, speed healing, and reduce the duration of viral shedding (Hatcher, 2001). Oral administration of antiviral drugs may reduce the severity of the initial episode and, if taken regularly, the frequency and duration of recurrent outbreaks (Hatcher, 2001). On the other hand, users may develop tolerance to these drugs, necessitating larger doses to maintain effectiveness (Drew, 2000).

Warm baths, loosely fitting clothing, Aspirin, and cold, wet compresses may relieve pain during flare-ups. People with herpes are advised to maintain regular sleeping habits and to learn to manage stress.

COPING WITH GENITAL HERPES The psychological problems connected with herpes can be more distressing than the physical effects of the illness. The prospects of a lifetime of recurrences and concerns about infecting one's sex partners exacerbate the emotional impact of herpes.

Most people with herpes learn to cope. Some are helped by support groups that share ways of living with the disease. A caring and trusting partner is important.

The attitudes of people with herpes also play a role in their success in adjusting to it. People who view herpes as a manageable illness or problem, not as a medical disaster or a character deficit, seem to find it easier to cope.

Viral Hepatitis

Hepatitis is an inflammation of the liver that may be caused by such factors as chronic alcoholism and exposure to toxic materials. Viral hepatitis comprises several different types of hepatitis caused by related, but distinct, viruses. The major types are *hepatitis A* (formerly called infectious hepatitis), *hepatitis B* (formerly called serum hepatitis), *hepatitis C* (formerly called hepatitis non-A, non-B), and *hepatitis D*.

Most people with acute hepatitis have no symptoms. When symptoms do appear, they often include **jaundice**, feelings of weakness and nausea, loss of appetite, abdominal discomfort, whitish bowel movements, and brownish or tea-

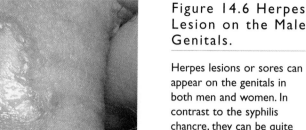

Figure 14.6 Herpes Lesion on the Male Genitals.

Herpes lesions or sores can appear on the genitals in both men and women. In contrast to the syphilis chancre, they can be quite painful. Herpes is most likely to be transmitted during outbreaks of the disease (when the sores are present, that is), but it can be transmitted at other times as well. Stress increases the likelihood of outbreaks. Antiviral drugs tend to decrease the frequency, duration, and discomfort of outbreaks.

Hepatitis An inflammation of the liver. (From the Greek *hepar*, which means "liver.")

Jaundice A yellowish discoloration of the skin and the whites of the eyes. (From the Old French *jaune*, which meaans "yellow.")

Genital warts An STI that is caused by the human papilloma virus and takes the form of warts that appear around the genitals and anus.

coloured urine. The symptoms of hepatitis B tend to be more severe and long-lasting than those of hepatitis A or C. In about 10% of cases, hepatitis B leads to chronic liver disease. Hepatitis C tends to have milder symptoms but often leads to chronic liver disease such as cirrhosis or cancer of the liver. Hepatitis D—also called *delta hepatitis* or type D hepatitis—occurs only in the presence of hepatitis B. Hepatitis D, which has symptoms similar to those of hepatitis B, can produce severe liver damage and often leads to death.

The hepatitis A virus is transmitted through contact with infected fecal matter found in contaminated food or water, and by oral contact with fecal matter, such as through oral–anal sexual activity (licking or mouthing the partner's anus). (It is largely because of the risk of hepatitis A that restaurant employees are required to wash their hands after using the toilet.) Ingesting uncooked infested shellfish is also a frequent means of transmission of hepatitis A (Lemon & Newbold, 1990).

Hepatitis B can be transmitted sexually through anal, vaginal, or oral intercourse with an infected partner; through transfusion with contaminated blood supplies; by the sharing of contaminated needles or syringes; and by contact with contaminated saliva, menstrual blood, nasal mucus, or semen (Lemon & Newbold, 1990). Sharing razors, toothbrushes, or other personal articles with an infected person can also transmit hepatitis B. Hepatitis C and hepatitis D can be transmitted sexually or through contact with contaminated blood. A person can transmit the viruses that cause hepatitis even if he or she is unaware of having any symptoms of the disease.

In Canada, infection rates for hepatitis A and B declined significantly during the 1990s. However, rates of hepatitis C have increased, and of the hepatitis viruses, it has by far the highest rate of infection (Health Canada, 2001).

Hepatitis is usually diagnosed by testing blood samples for the presence of hepatitis antigens and antibodies. There is no cure for viral hepatitis. Bed rest and fluids are usually recommended until the acute stage of the infection subsides, generally in a few weeks. Full recovery may take months. A vaccine provides protection against hepatitis B and also against hepatitis D, because hepatitis D can occur only if hepatitis B is present (Hatcher, 2001). Hepatitis B vaccine is routinely given to young adolescents or to both infants and young adolescents in most provinces and territories.

Genital Warts

The *human papilloma virus* (HPV) causes **genital warts** (formerly termed *venereal warts*). HPV, with signs of infection found in nearly half of the adult women in some countries, is the world's most common sexually transmitted infection (Ho et al., 1998). The prevalence of HPV in diverse groupings of Canadian women ranges from 20 to 33% (Public Health Agency of Canada, 2001). Although the warts may appear in visible areas of the skin, in perhaps 7 out of 10 cases they appear in areas that cannot be seen, such as on the cervix in women or in the urethra in men (Wingood & DiClemente, 2002). They occur most commonly among people 20 to 24 years old (Wingood & DiClemente, 2002). Within a few months following infection, the warts are usually found in the genital and anal regions. Women are more susceptible to HPV infection because cells in the cervix divide swiftly, facilitating the multiplication of HPV (Blakeslee, 1992).

Genital warts are similar to common plantar warts—itchy bumps that vary in size and shape. Genital warts are hard and yellow-grey when they form on dry skin. They take on pink, soft, cauliflower shapes in moist areas such as the lower vagina (see Figure 14.7). In men they appear on the penis, foreskin, and scrotum and in the urethra. They appear on the vulva, along the vaginal wall, and on the cervix in women. They can also occur outside the genital area—for example, in the mouth; on the lips, eyelids, or nipples; around the anus; or in the rectum.

Figure 14.8 Genital Warts.

Genital warts are caused by the human papilloma virus (HPV) and may have a cauliflower-like appearance. Many—perhaps most—cases occur where they can go visually undetected. HPV is implicated in cervical cancer, and women should be checked regularly for genital warts and other possibly "silent" STIs.

Genital warts may not cause any symptoms, but those that form on the urethra can cause bleeding or painful discharges. HPV has been implicated in cancers of the genital organs, particularly cervical cancer and penile cancer (Koutsky et al., 1992). Ninety percent of cases of cervical cancer are linked to certain strains of HPV (Cannistra & Niloff, 1996; Reaney, 1998).

HPV can be transmitted sexually through skin-to-skin contact during vaginal, anal, and oral sex. It can also be transmitted by other forms of contact, such as touching infected towels or clothing. The incubation period may vary from a few weeks to a couple of years.

Freezing the wart (*cryotherapy*) with liquid nitrogen is a preferred treatment. One alternative treatment involves painting or coating the warts over several days with a solution, gel, or cream (Hatcher, 2001). Unfortunately, although the warts themselves may be removed, treatment does not rid the body of the virus (Hatcher, 2001). There may thus be recurrences. The warts can also be treated by a doctor with electrodes (burning) or surgery (by laser or surgical removal).

Researchers are attempting to develop a vaccine for HPV, an effort based on the discovery of molecules that inform the immune system that the virus is present (Reaney, 1998). One of the leading researchers in developing a vaccine is Alex Ferenczy at McGill University. Ferenczy believes that vaccines used to prevent HPV will significantly decrease the incidence of cervical cancer (Branswell, 2005).

For the time being, however, prevention means using latex condoms, which help reduce the risk of contracting HPV. They do not eliminate the risk entirely, because the virus can be transmitted from areas of the skin not protected by condoms, such as the scrotum. People with active warts should probably avoid sexual contact until the warts are removed and the area heals completely.

> **Ectoparasites** Parasites that live on the outside of the host's body—in contrast to *endoparasites*, which live within the body. (From the Greek *ektos*, which means "outside.")
>
> **Pediculosis** A parasitic infestation by pubic lice (*Pthirus pubis*) that causes itching.

Ectoparasitic Infestations

Ectoparasites, as opposed to *endoparasites*, live on the outer surfaces of animals (*ecto* means "outer"). *Trichomonas vaginalis*, which causes trichomoniasis, is an endoparasite (*endo* means "inner"). Ectoparasites are larger than the agents that cause other STIs. In this section we consider two types of STIs caused by ectoparasites: pediculosis and scabies.

Pediculosis

Pediculosis is the name given to an infestation of a parasite whose proper Latin name, *Pthirus pubis* (pubic lice), sounds rather too dignified for these bothersome (dare we say ugly?) creatures that are better known as crabs. Pubic lice are commonly called crabs because, under the microscope, they are somewhat similar in appearance to crabs (see Figure 14.8). They belong to a family of insects called biting lice. Another member of the family, the human head louse, is an annoying insect that clings to hair on the scalp and often spreads among schoolchildren.

In the adult stage, pubic lice are large enough to be seen with the naked eye. They are spread sexually but can also be transmitted via contact with an infested towel, sheet, or—yes—toilet seat. They can survive for only about 24 hours without a human host, but they may deposit eggs that can take up to seven days to hatch in bedding or towels (Wingood & DiClemente, 2002). Therefore, all bedding, towels, and clothes that have been used by an infested person must be either dry-cleaned or washed in hot water and dried on the hot cycle to ensure that they are safe. Fingers may also transmit the lice from the genitals to other hair-covered parts of the body, including the scalp and armpits. Sexual contact should be avoided until the infestation is eradicated.

Figure 14.8 Pubic Lice.

Pediculosis is an infestation by pubic lice (*Pthirus pubis*). Pubic lice are commonly called "crabs" because of their appearance under a microscope.

Itching, ranging from the mildly irritating to the intolerable, is the most prominent symptom of a pubic lice infestation. The itching is caused by the "crabs" attaching themselves to the pubic hair and piercing the skin to feed on the blood of their hosts. (Yecch!) The life span of these insects is only about a month, but they are prolific egg-layers and may spawn several generations before they die. An infestation can be treated effectively with a non-prescription medication. A careful re-examination of the body is necessary after four to seven days of treatment to ensure that all lice and eggs were killed (Wingood & DiClemente, 2002).

Scabies

Scabies (short for *Sarcoptes scabiei*) is a parasitic infestation caused by a tiny mite that may be transmitted through sexual contact or contact with infested clothing, bed linen, towels, and other fabrics. The mites attach themselves to the base of pubic hair and burrow into the skin, where they lay eggs and subsist for the duration of their 30-day life span. Like pubic lice, scabies are often found in the genital region and cause itching and discomfort. They are also responsible for reddish lines (created by burrowing) and for sores, welts, or blisters on the skin. Unlike lice, they are too tiny to be seen by the naked eye. Diagnosis is made by detecting the mite or its by-products via microscopic examination of scrapings from suspicious-looking areas of skin (Levine, 1991). Scabies are most often found on the hands and wrists, but they may also appear on the genitals, buttocks, armpits, and feet (Wingood & DiClemente, 2002). They do not appear above the neck—thankfully!

Scabies, like pubic lice, may be treated effectively with 1% lindane (Kwellada). The entire body from the neck down must be coated with a thin layer of the medication, which should not be washed off for eight hours. But lindane should not be used by women who are pregnant or lactating. To avoid reinfection, sex partners and others in close bodily contact with infected individuals should also be treated. Clothing and bed linen that the infected person has used must be washed and dried on the hot cycle or dry-cleaned. As with "crabs," sexual contact should be avoided until the infestation is eliminated.

Prevention of STIs
Knowledge of STIs and AIDS

A first step in prevention is knowledge. Yet many Canadians lack up-to-date knowledge about STIs and HIV/AIDS. The Canadian Youth, Sexual Health and HIV/AIDS Study asked students a number of questions about these topics (Boyce et al., 2003). One of the disappointing findings was that in 2002 the adolescents were less knowledgeable in some areas than were youth in the 1989 study. For example, fewer students in Grade 7 were knowledgeable about the risks of HIV transmission from sharing drug needles, sex without condoms, and multiple partners. Also, fewer adolescents in 2002 knew that it was incorrect to assume HIV/AIDS can be cured if treated early. Whereas almost all of the Grade 7 students in 1989 (89%) knew that blood tests can detect HIV, only 59% knew this in 2002.

On the other hand, knowledge had increased about other STIs. As an example, more of the 2002 adolescents knew that chlamydia can lead to serious complications. However, there are some important facts that many youth of today are not aware of. For example, more than 40% of Grade 11 students do not know that a person can get genital herpes from having oral sex or that many people with STIs do not show any signs or symptoms (Boyce et al., 2003).

Scabies A parasitic infestation caused by a tiny mite (*Sarcoptes scabiei*) that causes itching.

Sources of Help

Many different strategies are being used to inform the public about STI/AIDS. All provinces and territories have STI/AIDS telephone information lines that offer anonymous counselling and information about a wide range of sexual health issues. In 2000 the most common questions among the 25 280 calls to the Toronto line related to unprotected sex or condom failure. The type of sexual contact most asked about was vaginal intercourse, and more questions were asked about STIs than about birth control. On the subject of HIV testing, the callers' main concerns were pretest counselling; testing options, including anonymous testing; and incubation/seroconversion time frames (Public Health and Epidemiology Report Ontario, 2002).

PROVINCIAL TOLL-FREE HOTLINES FOR INFORMATION ABOUT AIDS AND OTHER STIs These hotlines provide information about AIDS and other STIs, as well as referral sources. You needn't give your name or identify yourself to obtain information.

British Columbia: 1-800-661-4337

Alberta: 1-800-772-2437

Saskatchewan: 1-800-667-6876

Manitoba: 1-800-782-2437

Ontario: 1-800-668-2437

Quebec: 1-866 -521-7432

Newfoundland: 1-800-563-1575

New Brunswick: 1-800-561-4009

Nova Scotia: 1-800-566-2437

PEI: 1-800-314-2437

Northwest Territories: 1-800-661-0844

Nunavut: 1-800-661-0795

Yukon: 1-800-661-0507

Reasons for Engaging in Risky Sexual Behaviour

Despite widespread awareness of STIs, many people still engage in risky sexual practices, which increases the chances of their becoming infected.

Researchers have identified several factors that underlie risky sexual behaviour among young people:

1. *Perceived low risk of infection.* One of the major stumbling blocks in promoting safer-sex practices is that many young heterosexuals perceive a low risk of contracting HIV (Nadeau et al., 1993; Oswalt & Matsen, 1993). People who perceive themselves as being at low risk are less likely to alter their behaviour.

   Given the relatively low rate of known infections among heterosexuals who do not inject drugs, many heterosexuals may perceive risky sexual practices to be a reasonable gamble (Pinkerton & Abramson, 1992). Heterosexuals who have never had a friend or relative with HIV/AIDS may dismiss it as a problem that affects other types of people. Even gay men may operate under the "I'm not the type" fallacy and underestimate their personal risks. In the 2002 survey of gay and bisexual men in Ontario, half of the men who had never had an HIV test said this was because they were at low risk of infection (Myers et al., 2004).

2. *Negative attitudes toward condom use.* Many factors discourage condom use. Some people feel embarrassed to buy them. For others, the risk of being

infected with HIV seems to fly out of their minds whenever the opportunity for sex arises. Some claim that interrupting the sexual act to apply a condom dampens romantic ardour. Some people just regard them as too much of a fuss. Many men say that condoms deprive them of sexual pleasure. Unless such obstacles to using condoms are overcome, efforts to stem the tide of HIV infection may be thwarted.

Reasons for not using condoms can be complex. In an Ontario study, high-risk gay and bisexual men gave the following reasons:

- loss of erection
- urgency of passion overcoming fears of infection
- stress and depression overcoming rational prevention
- low self-esteem, leading to indifference about consequences
- relying on intuition to determine that a partner is HIV-negative
- developing a trusting relationship with a partner (Adam et al., 2005)

A common trend among Canadians is to use a condom at the beginning of a relationship and then to stop using it as the relationship continues. As people become more committed to a relationship, they become more trusting of their partner and are less willing to consider the possibility that he or she may have an STI (Maticka-Tyndale, 1997). It has also been found that the more in love a woman is with her partner, the more strongly she comes to believe that she is not at risk for getting an STI from him (Knauper et al., 2002).

Rupert Klein and Barbel Knauper (2002) of McGill University found that female university students believe that the use of condoms signifies a lack of commitment and trust in the relationship. To counter this trend, some providers of sexual health services, such as Calgary Health Services, encourage women who are going on the pill to also use condoms (Wong-Reiger et al., 1996). Interestingly, among both female and male sex-trade workers, condoms are less likely to be used with relationship partners than with clients (Allman, 1999).

3. *Myth of personal invulnerability.* Some people believe that they are somehow immune to AIDS and other diseases. Even students who are generally well informed about STIs may think of themselves as personally immune. A third-year university student explained to an interviewer why she did not insist that her partners use a condom: "I have an attitude—it may be wrong—that any guy I would sleep with would not have AIDS" (Johnson, 1990, p. A18). The adventurous spirit that we often associate with youth may confer on young people a dangerous sense of immortality and a greater willingness to take risks (CDC, 2000d; King, 2000). Perceptions of personal invulnerability help to explain why AIDS education does not always translate into behavioural change.

Research in Action

THE INFORMATION–MOTIVATION–BEHAVIOURAL SKILLS MODEL

Simply providing information about AIDS is not enough to decrease the incidence of HIV infection. For the last several years Bill Fisher of the University of Western Ontario has conducted research into factors affecting the use of safer-sex practices among various groups, including high school and university students, inner-city minority youth, and gay males. Fisher and his colleagues developed a theoretical model (the Information–Motivation–Behavioural Skills Model) to explain what determines behaviours to prevent STIs (Fisher & Fisher, 1992). The model has also been used to explain contraceptive use.

According to this model, people need to be informed not only about causes of STI/AIDS but also about effective means of prevention, including instruction on how to use condoms correctly. The model encourages the development of positive attitudes toward the use of condoms and strong social support for their use. Developing communication skills helps people become more assertive in insisting on condom use, especially with a reluctant partner. Behavioural skills also include gaining experience in going to a pharmacy or sexual health clinic to overcome any embarrassment in obtaining condoms.

Fisher has incorporated the basic principles of this model in the Web site **www.sexualityandu.ca**. Researchers at the University of New Brunswick have demonstrated that students who were taught safer-sex communication skills and how to eroticize condoms used condoms more than those who were provided only with information (Ploem & Byers, 1997).

Applied Knowledge

PREVENTING STIs

Prevention is the best way to control the spread of STIs, especially those for which there is no cure or vaccine. There are many things that you can do to lower your risk of contracting STIs.

Consider Abstinence or Monogamy

The only fully effective strategies to prevent the sexual transmission of STIs are abstinence and maintaining a monogamous sexual relationship with an uninfected partner.

Be Knowledgeable About the Risks

Many of us try to put the dangers of STIs out of our minds—especially in moments of passion. In a U.S. national study of 18- to 26-year-olds, two-thirds of those who were infected with chlamydia or gonorrhea did not perceive themselves as being at risk for infection (Ford, 2004). Make a pact with yourself to refuse to play the dangerous game of pretending that the dangers of STIs do not exist or that you are somehow immune.

Remain Sober and Drug Free

Alcohol and other drugs increase the likelihood of engaging in risky sexual behaviour. In a study of men who had sex with a man who was HIV-positive, researchers at the University of Toronto found that safer-sex practices were least likely when the men were drinking or doing drugs (Calzavara et al., 1992). In Toronto, some gay and bisexual men using crystal meth reported that it reduced sexual inhibitions and intensified the sexual experience (Myers et al., 2004b). North American AIDS organizations are concerned that the search for heightened sexual pleasure through the use of crystal meth is contributing to an increase in HIV infections. In 2005 the AIDS Committee of Toronto warned that taking crystal meth increases sexual risk-taking among gay and bisexual men.

Inspect Yourself and Your Partner

Inspect yourself and your partner for any discharge, bumps, rashes, warts, blisters, chancres, sores, lice, or foul odours. Do not expect to find telltale signs of an HIV infection, but remember that infected people often have other STIs. Check out any unusual feature with a physician before you engage in sexual activity.

Use Latex Condoms

Latex condoms are effective in blocking nearly all sexually transmissible organisms. Improper or inconsistent use is a common reason for failure. Yet even when used properly, condoms cannot block disease-causing organisms that are transmitted externally, such as those that cause herpes, genital warts, and ectoparasitic infestations.

Use Barrier Devices When Practising Oral Sex (Fellatio or Cunnilingus)

If you decide to practise oral sex, use a condom before practising fellatio and a dental dam (a square piece of latex rubber used by dentists during oral surgery) to cover the vagina before engaging in cunnilingus.

Avoid High-Risk Sexual Behaviours

Avoid unprotected vaginal or anal intercourse (intercourse without the use of a latex condom). Unprotected anal intercourse is one of the riskiest practices. Other behaviours that carry risk include unprotected oral–genital activity, insertion of a hand or fist ("fisting") into someone's rectum or vagina, or any activity in which you or your partner would come into contact with the other's blood, semen, or vaginal secretions. Oral–anal sex, or anilingus (sometimes called rimming), should be avoided because of the potential of transmitting microbes between the mouth and the anus.

Wash the Genitals Before and After Sex

Washing the genitals before and after sex removes a quantity of potentially harmful agents. Do not, however, deceive yourself into believing that washing your genitals is an effective substitute for safer sex.

Have Regular Medical Checkups

Many people are symptomless carriers of STIs, especially of chlamydial infections. Medical checkups enable them to learn about and receive treatment for disorders that might otherwise go unnoticed. Many physicians advise routine testing of asymptomatic young women for chlamydial infections to prevent the hidden damage that can occur when the infection goes untreated.

Engage in Noncoital Sexual Activities

Other forms of sexual expression, such as hugging, massage, caressing, mutual masturbation, and rubbing bodies together without vaginal, anal, or oral contact, are low-risk ways of finding sexual pleasure, so long as neither semen nor vaginal fluids come into contact with mucous membranes or breaks in the skin. Many sexologists refer to such activities as **outercourse** to distinguish them from sexual intercourse. Sharing sexual fantasies can be very titillating, as can taking a bath or shower together. Vibrators, dildos, and other "sex toys" may also be erotically stimulating and carry a low risk of infection if they are washed thoroughly with soap and water before use and between uses by two people.

Limit the Number of Partners

Having sex with multiple partners—especially "one-night stands"—increases your risk of sexual contact with an infected person.

Do Not Assume That You Can Always Determine Your Partner's Sexual History

People are not always truthful about their sexual past. Many people who are infected with the HIV virus do not disclose this to their partners. In the 2002 Ontario study of gay and bisexual men, 45% of those with HIV infection said that in the previous three months they did not disclose this to casual sex partners and another 30% said they sometimes disclosed their status. Unfortunately, we do not have comparable data regarding disclosure among HIV-positive heterosexuals. However, cases brought before the courts indicate there are many HIV-infected heterosexuals who do not disclose their status to sexual partners.

In Kitchener, Ontario, a man pleaded guilty to charges of aggravated assault for infecting four women with the HIV virus. Even though he knew that he was HIV-positive, he had unprotected sex with the women and did not tell them he was infected (Wood, 2002). More recently in Toronto, a man, originally from Trinidad, was charged with aggravated assault and endangering life after his wife died of AIDS-related illnesses, because he had not told her that he was HIV-positive. After the man's arrest, five other women complained to police that he had had sexual contact with them but did not disclose this HIV status (Powell & Chung, 2005). Almost all of the non-disclosure cases have involved HIV-positive men. However, in 2005, an HIV-positive female soldier from Camp Borden, Ontario, was charged with assault after she engaged in unprotected sex with a male soldier without informing him that she had HIV (Verma, 2005).

Positive Love
A dating site for people with STIs.
www.positivelove.com

Outercourse Forms of sexual expression, such as massage, hugging, caressing, mutual masturbation, and rubbing bodies together, that do not involve the exchange of body fluids. (Contrast with *intercourse*.)

Research in Action

ATTITUDES TOWARD PEOPLE WITH STIs/AIDS

Having an STI or AIDS seems to carry more stigma than having any other kind of disease. Heterosexuals appear to worry more about this than gay males. In a Windsor study of HIV-positive persons who were taking combination therapies, the heterosexuals were much more secretive about their HIV status because they perceived they would receive little support from others (Adams et al., 2001). Gay males, on the other hand, felt accepted by their friends and social networks. Adams and colleagues attribute this difference to the perception among heterosexuals that HIV is not a part of their community. However, whether gay or straight, almost all the participants worried that disclosure in the workplace could lead to discrimination and job loss.

Respondents to a survey of university students in New Brunswick had more negative attitudes toward a man who had an STI or AIDS than to a man who had cancer (Fish & Rye, 1991). The male students had more negative attitudes than the females.

In the Canada Youth and AIDS study, most youth displayed accepting attitudes toward people with HIV/AIDS. Also, they were more accepting than were youth in 1989. Fewer than 10% of Grade 11 students said that they could not be a friend of someone who has HIV/AIDS. Only about 5% felt that people who have HIV/AIDS get what they deserve. However, about 40% believed that people who have HIV/AIDS should not be allowed to serve the public. Students in Grade 7 had less accepting attitudes than students in Grades 9 and 11 (Boyce et al., 2003).

It is important to reduce this kind of prejudice. One way to do so is to include people living with AIDS in classroom presentations so that students can interact with them (Fish & Rye, 1991).

Summing Up

An Epidemic
Although public attention has been riveted on AIDS for a decade, other STIs, such as chlamydia and genital warts, pose wider threats.

Bacterial Infections
Bacteria are one-celled micro-organisms that cause many illnesses.

Chlamydia
Chlamydia or chlamydial infections are caused by the *Chlamydia trachomatous* bacterium. The symptoms of chlamydial infections resemble those of gonorrhea but tend to be milder. Chlamydial infections also respond to antibiotics.

Gonorrhea
Gonorrhea is caused by the gonococcus bacterium. For men, symptoms include a penile discharge and burning urination. Most women are asymptomatic. If left untreated, gonorrhea can attack the internal reproductive organs and lead to PID in women. Gonorrhea is treated with antibiotics.

Syphilis
Syphilis is caused by the *Treponema pallidum* bacterium. Syphilis undergoes several stages of development. Although it can lie dormant for many years, it may be lethal. Syphilis is treated with antibiotics.

Other Bacterial Infections
Bacterial STIs that occur less commonly in Canada include chancroid, shigellosis, granuloma inguinale, and lymphogranuloma venereum.

Vaginal Infections
Vaginitis is usually characterized by a foul-smelling discharge, genital irritation, and burning during urination. Most cases involve bacterial vaginosis, candidiasis, or trichomoniasis.

Bacterial Vaginosis
Bacterial vaginosis is usually caused by the *Gardnerella vaginalis* bacterium.

Candidiasis
Candidiasis is caused by a yeast-like fungus, *Candida albicans*. Infections usually arise from changes in the vaginal environment that allow the fungus to overgrow.

Trichomoniasis

"Trich" is caused by a protozoan called *Trichomonas vaginalis*.

Viral Infections

Viruses are particles of DNA that reproduce by invading a body cell and directing the cell's own reproductive machinery to spin off new viral particles.

HIV/AIDS

AIDS is caused by HIV, which attacks the body's immune system. As HIV disables the body's natural defences, the person becomes vulnerable to opportunistic diseases—such as serious infections and cancers—that are normally held in check. HIV is a blood-borne virus that is also found in semen, vaginal secretions, and breast milk. Common avenues of transmission include sexual intercourse, transfusion with contaminated blood, sharing a hypodermic needle with an infected person, childbirth, and breast-feeding. HIV infection is usually diagnosed through blood, saliva, and urine tests that detect HIV antibodies. There is no cure for AIDS, and an effective, safe vaccine has not yet been developed. The most effective form of treatment as this book goes to press is HAART, which includes a protease inhibitor along with other antiviral agents.

Herpes

Oral herpes is caused by the *Herpes simplex* virus type 1 (HSV-1). Genital herpes is caused by the *Herpes simplex* virus type 2 (HSV-2), which produces painful, shallow sores and blisters on the genitals. A vaccine helps prevent women from contracting genital herpes but is ineffective with men. Antiviral drugs can relieve pain and speed healing during flare-ups.

Viral Hepatitis

There are several types of hepatitis caused by different hepatitis viruses. Most cases of hepatitis are transmitted sexually or by contact with contaminated blood or fecal matter.

Genital Warts

Genital warts are caused by the human papilloma virus (HPV). HPV has been linked to cancers of the genital tract. Freezing the wart is a preferred treatment for removal of the wart, but the virus remains in the body afterward.

Ectoparasitic Infestations

Pediculosis

Pediculosis ("crabs") is caused by pubic lice (*Pthirus pubis*). Pubic lice attach themselves to pubic hair and feed on the blood of their hosts, which often causes itching. Infestations can be treated with the prescription medication lindane or with nonprescription medications that contain pyrethrins or piperonal butoxide.

Scabies

Scabies (*Sarcoptes scabiei*) is a parasitic infestation with a tiny mite that causes itching. Scabies, like pubic lice, is treated with lindane.

Prevention of STIs

Knowledge of STIs and AIDS

Many Canadian youth have gaps in their knowledge of AIDS and other STIs.

Sources of Help

All provinces and territories have information lines that offer anonymous information and counselling.

Reasons for Engaging in Risky Sexual Behaviour

People are more likely to engage in risky behaviour if they believe they are at low risk of infection, have negative attitudes toward condoms, and feel personally invulnerable.

Test Yourself

Multiple-Choice Questions

1. Many Canadian university students are unaware of the HPV virus which causes

   _____.

   a. genital herpes
   b. hepatitis B
   c. genital warts
   d. molluscum contagiosum

2. As many as _____ of men and _____ of women with chlamydia have no symptoms.

   a. 15%; 25%
   b. 75%; 50%
   c. 35%; 10%
   d. 25%; 70%

3. Untreated gonorrhea can lead to
_____ in men.
a. premature ejaculation
b. epididymitis *(circled)*
c. pelvic inflammatory disease
d. cervicitis

4. _____ and
_____ often occur
together.
a. Chlamydia and gonorrhea *(circled)*
b. Herpes and HPV
c. Syphilis and shigellosis
d. Trichomonas and scabies

5. About _____ of women will experience
at least one yeast infection during their lifetime.
a. 15% *(circled)*
b. 50%
c. 75%
d. 90%

6. HIV directly attacks the immune system by destroying _____.
a. pathogenic cells
b. CD4 cells *(circled)*
c. red blood cells
d. platelets

7. All of the following have been shown to transmit
HIV infection except
a. artificial insemination with infected semen
b. kissing *(circled)*
c. breast-feeding
d. unprotected sexual intercourse

8. The current standard of treatment for HIV/AIDS,
known as _____, consists
of a mixture of antiretroviral drugs and protease
inhibitors.
a. ELISA
b. AIDSBS
c. HAART *(circled)*
d. LSMFT

9. Which of the following is a cure for genital herpes?
a. freezing the herpes lesions with liquid nitrogen
b. applying acyclovir ointment three times a day
c. penicillin or other antibiotics for two weeks
d. there is no cure for genital herpes *(circled)*

10. Which of the following is not considered to be an
effective prevention strategy for reducing your risk
of STIs?
a. avoiding the use of alcohol or other drugs
b. using birth control pills effectively *(circled)*
c. avoiding high-risk sexual behaviours
d. using latex condoms for all forms of genital sexual
activity

Critical Thinking Questions

1. How would you bring up the topic of sexually transmitted infections with a new sexual partner? What might
stop you from bringing up the subject?

2. Would you tell a potential sex partner about any STIs that you have, or about any risky sexual behaviour you
have engaged in? Why or why not?

3. How would you feel if you found out that your spouse or sexual partner had infected you with an STI?
What effect do you think this would have on the relationship?

4. Should the Canadian government sponsor needle exchange programs in order to reduce the transmission of
HIV/AIDS? Why or why not?

5. You and some friends are sitting around over a beer or two. One of your friends is certain that he or she
could tell what sort of person would have an STI, and would never have sex with "someone like that." How
could you respond to this statement?

Companion
Website

Visit our Companion Website at www.pearsoned.ca/rathus,
where you can use the interactive Study Guide and link to
additional resources on topics discussed in this text.

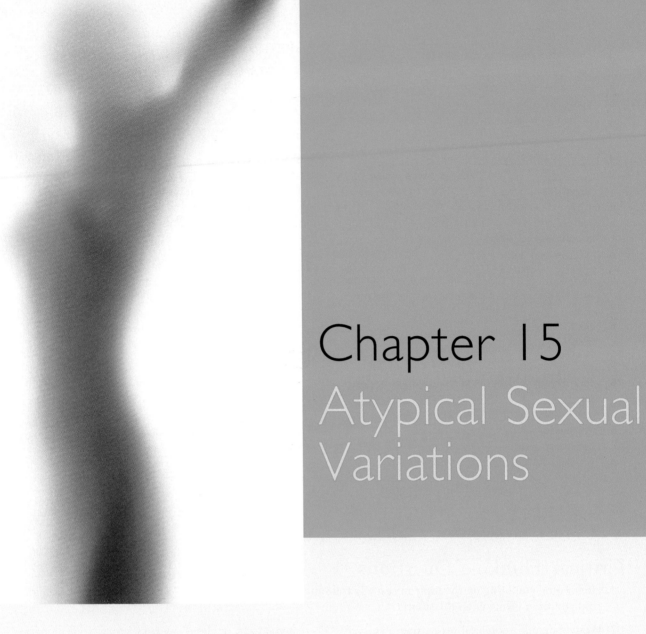

Chapter 15
Atypical Sexual Variations

People often wonder about their own sexuality. A common concern is, "Am I normal?" To answer this question we need to be aware of the criteria used to define normality. In this chapter we analyze the concept of normality and discuss a number of sexual behaviours that are viewed as deviating from the norm. First, let us consider how we define *normality*.

Normal Versus Deviant Sexual Behaviour

One common approach to defining normality is based on a statistical norm. From this perspective, rare or unusual sexual behaviours are considered abnormal or deviant. The statistical approach may seem value-free, because the yardstick of normality is based on the frequency of behaviour, not on any judgment of its social acceptability. By this standard, engaging in coitus while standing, or more than seven times a week, might be considered deviant. However, the choice of behaviours we subject to statistical comparison is not divorced from our underlying values. *Statistical* infrequency, then, is not a sufficient criterion for classifying behaviour as abnormal or deviant. We must also consider whether the sexual practice deviates from a *social* norm.

What is considered normal in one culture or at a particular time may be considered abnormal in other cultures and at other times. A gay male or lesbian sexual orientation was considered abnormal throughout most of Western history and was labelled a mental disorder by the American Psychiatric Association. But in 1973, the "disorder" of gay male or lesbian sexual orientation was dropped from the association's official diagnostic manual.

In our own culture, sexual practices such as oral sex and masturbation were once considered deviant or abnormal. Today, however, they are practised so widely that few people would label them deviant. Concepts of "normalcy" and "deviance," then, reflect the mores and customs of a particular culture at a given time.

Another way to determine sexual deviance is to classify sexual practices as deviant when they involve the persistent preference for nongenital sexual outlets (Seligman & Hardenburg, 2000). If a man prefers fondling a woman's panties to engaging in sexual relations with her, or prefers to masturbate against her foot rather than engage in coitus, his behaviour is likely to be labelled deviant.

Because of the confusing array of meanings of the terms *deviant* and *abnormal*, we prefer to speak about unusual patterns of sexual arousal or behaviour as "atypical variations" in sexual behaviour rather than as "sexual deviations." Atypical patterns of sexual arousal or behaviour that become problematic in the eyes of the individual or of society are labelled *paraphilias* by the American Psychiatric Association in their catalogue of sexual disorders (DSM-IV-TR, 2000). Clinicians consider paraphilias to be mental disorders. But milder forms of these behaviours may be practised by many people and fall within the normal spectrum of human sexuality. According to Ottawa psychiatrist Paul Fedoroff, a major factor in delineating paraphilic disorders is that they "involve sex without the possibility of a consensual, mutually reciprocal relationship" (Fedoroff, 2003, p. 336).

Research in Action

FEMALE PARAPHILICS

Many people believe that women do not engage in paraphilic activities, partly because so little research has been conducted in this area. One of the relatively few studies on female paraphilics was conducted by Paul Fedoroff, an Ottawa psychiatrist and one of Canada's leading experts on paraphilias, along with colleagues Alicia Fishell and Beverly Fedoroff. The study was based on 14 women who were referred to clinics in Canada, the United States, or Great Britain. Each of the women typically had more than one paraphilic disorder, the most common of which were pedophilia, sexual sadism, and exhibitionism. Only 3 of the 14 women reported having experienced past sexual victimization.

In one of the cases, a heterosexual woman was self-referred because of a tendency to exhibit:

> She described a ritual of undressing herself and masturbating with the lights on in front of her apartment window, approximately 5 times a month. While she was aroused by the idea of being seen by male strangers, she denied any wish to engage in sex with anyone who saw her. Unless she was involved in "really bizarre situations" she had primary anorgasmia even when masturbating.
>
> At one point she began driving her truck through unfamiliar neighbourhoods with pet food in an attempt to befriend cats and dogs which she would "abduct." She would coax the cats to lick her genitals by placing honey on her vaginal area. She would perform oral sex on male dogs who she "abducted" in a similar manner. She also described sexual fantasies about having sex with boys and girls between the ages of 8 and 10. On one occasion she had "punished" an 8-year-old boy she was baby-sitting by squeezing his penis and "physically smacked him around." She was sexually aroused by

this activity and would often masturbate while recalling this episode.

> Three years prior to assessment, she had become involved in a unique form of prostitution in which she would flag down taxis from her truck and then proceed to talk the taxi driver into paying to have sex with her. She did the same thing with men she met on "phone sex lines." She did this for about a year and then stopped because she said, "It wasn't me." She had been engaged but found she could not have sex with her male partner unless she acted out her paraphilic interests (activities that caused him to leave her). (p. 133)

Fedoroff et al. offer these comments on the case:

> This woman's presentation is typical of many self-referred men who are not facing charges in that there are multiple, highly idiosyncratic and obligatory sex "rituals" described. She was "obsessed" with sex, devoting the majority of her waking days to fulfilling her sexual desires. However, she also described high levels of sex guilt (a finding also characteristic of male sex offenders). Although she found these activities highly sexually arousing, they were at the same time highly aversive to her, particularly "because she was a Christian." This case is also instructive because her partner (in this case, a male) was not supportive of her paraphilic activities. This woman found it impossible to forgo her paraphilic activities, even though she knew it spelled the end of the most important romantic relationship she had ever established. (p. 133)

Source: Adapted from J. P. Fedoroff, A. Fishell, & B. Fedoroff (1999). "A Case Series of Women Evaluated for Paraphilic Disorders." The Canadian Journal of Human Sexuality, 8, 127–140.

Paraphilia A diagnostic category used by the American Psychiatric Association to describe atypical patterns of sexual arousal or behaviour that become problematic in the eyes of the individual or society, such as fetishism and exhibitionism. The urges are recurrent and either are acted on or are distressing to the individual. (From Greek roots that mean "to the side of" [*para-*] and "loving" [*philos*].)

The Paraphilias

Paraphilias involve sexual arousal in response to unusual stimuli such as children or other nonconsenting persons (including unsuspecting people whom one watches or to whom one exposes one's genitals), nonhuman objects (such as shoes, leather, rubber, or undergarments), or pain or humiliation (Seligman & Hardenburg, 2000). The psychiatric diagnosis of paraphilia requires that the person has acted on the urges in socially unacceptable ways or is distinctly distressed by them.

People with paraphilias usually feel that their urges are insistent, demanding, or compulsory (Seligman & Hardenburg, 2000). They may describe themselves as overcome by these urges now and then. People with paraphilias tend to experience their urges as beyond their control, just as drug addicts and compulsive gamblers see themselves as helpless to avert irresistible urges. For these reasons, theorists have speculated that paraphilias may represent a type of sexual compulsion or an addiction.

Paraphilias vary in severity. In some cases the person can function sexually in the absence of the unusual stimuli and seldom if ever acts on his or her deviant urges. In other cases the person resorts to paraphilic behaviour only in times of stress. In more extreme forms, the person repeatedly engages in paraphilic behaviour and may become preoccupied with thoughts and fantasies about these experiences. In such cases the person may not be able to become sexually aroused without either fantasizing about the paraphilic stimulus or having it present. For some people, paraphilic behaviour is the only means of attaining sexual gratification.

The person with a paraphilia typically replays the paraphilic act in sexual fantasies to stimulate arousal during masturbation or sexual relations. It is as though he or she is mentally replaying a videotape of the paraphilic scene. The scene grows stale after a while, however. According to sex researcher John Money, "The tape wears out and he has to perform another paraphilic act, in effect, to create a new movie" (quoted in Brody, 1990, p. C12).

Some paraphilias are generally harmless and victimless, such as *fetishism* and cross-dressing to achieve sexual arousal (*transvestic fetishism*). Indeed, because behaviours such as cross-dressing do not harm others, some experts, such as Charles Moser, a physician in San Francisco, and Peggy Kleinplatz, a psychologist in Ottawa, believe that they should not be categorized as sexual disorders (Moser & Kleinplatz, 2002). Michael Seto and Howard Barbaree of the Centre for Addiction and Mental Health in Toronto further argue that sexual preferences for particular types of people or activities are strongly influenced by cultural values (Seto & Barbaree, 2000). Until a few years ago, for example, homosexuality was considered to be a pathology.

Because of these concerns, Charles Moser (2001) has proposed that the concept of Sexual Interest Disorder (SID) should be used in place of paraphilia. Here Moser calls for eliminating the naming of specific interests because he argues that a behaviour by itself is not an indication of pathology. Rather the key issue is whether that behaviour is causing distress or dysfunction for the individual.

Moser also argues that therapists should not always work toward eliminating a particular sexual interest but should offer clients the option of learning how to express the interest in a healthier manner. However, Moser does not propose that all sexual interests should be acceptable.

Some paraphilic behaviours, such as exposing oneself in public or enticing children into sexual relations, do have victims and may cause severe physical or psychological harm. They are also against the law. Sexual sadism, in which sexual arousal is connected to hurting or humiliating another person, can be very harmful when it is forced upon a nonconsenting person. Some brutal rapes involve sexual sadism.

Except in the case of sexual masochism, paraphilias are believed to occur mostly among men (Seligman & Hardenburg, 2000). (See the nearby Research in Action feature for a Canadian study on female paraphilics.) Because people are generally unwilling to talk about them, the prevalence of paraphilias in the general population remains unknown. Much of what we have learned about paraphilias derives from the reported experiences of people who have been apprehended for performing illegal acts (such as exposing themselves in public) and the few who have voluntarily sought help. The characteristics of people who have not been identified or studied remain virtually unknown.

In this chapter we discuss all the major types of paraphilia except *pedophilia*. In pedophilia, children become the objects of sexual arousal. Pedophilia often takes the form of sexual coercion of children, as in incest or sexual molestation. It is discussed in Chapter 16, as a form of sexual coercion.

Fetishism.
Whiplash (**www.whiplash.ca**) *is a Canadian fetish magazine. In fetishism, inanimate objects such as leather shoes or boots, or parts of the body such as feet, elicit sexual arousal. Many fetishists cannot achieve sexual arousal without having contact with the desired objects or fantasizing about them. Women's undergarments and objects made of rubber, leather, silk, or fur are common fetishistic objects.*

Fetishism A paraphilia in which an inanimate object such as an article of clothing or items made of rubber, leather, or silk elicit sexual arousal.

Partialism A paraphilia related to fetishism in which sexual arousal is exaggeratedly associated with a particular body part, such as feet, breasts, or buttocks.

Transvestism A paraphilia in which a person repeatedly cross-dresses to achieve sexual arousal or gratification or is troubled by persistent, recurring urges to cross-dress. (From the Latin root *trans-*, which means "cross," and *vestis*, which means "garment.") Also known as *transvestic fetishism.*

Fetishism

In **fetishism**, an inanimate object elicits sexual arousal. Articles of clothing (for example, women's panties, bras, lingerie, stockings, gloves, shoes, or boots) and materials made of rubber, leather, silk, or fur are among the more common fetishistic objects. Leather boots and high-heeled shoes are especially popular.

The fetishist may act on the urges to engage in fetishistic behaviour, such as masturbating by stroking an object or while fantasizing about it, or he may be distressed about such urges or fantasies but not act on them. In a related paraphilia, **partialism**, people are excessively aroused by a particular body part, such as the feet, breasts, or buttocks.

Most fetishes and partialisms are harmless. Fetishistic practices are nearly always private and involve masturbation or are incorporated into coitus with a willing partner. Only rarely have fetishists coerced others into paraphilic activities. Yet some partialists have touched parts of women's bodies in public. And some fetishists have committed burglaries to acquire the fetishistic objects. In Calgary, a man was charged with stealing women's panties during real estate tours of houses that were for sale and then placing obscene phone calls to the occupants of the houses ("Man accused," 2002).

Transvestism

Transvestism may be viewed as a type of fetish. Whereas other fetishists become sexually aroused by handling the fetishistic object while they masturbate, transvestites become excited by wearing articles of clothing—the fetishistic objects—of the other gender. Most are married and are otherwise masculine in behaviour and dress.

Transvestism may overlap with transsexualism, but it is not quite the same. First let us note that some transvestites and some transsexuals appear to be motivated by autogynephilia—a condition in which the individual is sexually stimulated by fantasies that their own bodies are female (Bailey, 2003). But there are differences between transvestites and transsexuals. Transvestites are usually adequately gratified by cross-dressing and masturbating or engaging in sexual activity with others while cross-dressing. They may also find it highly gratifying to masturbate while fantasizing about episodes of cross-dressing. But many transvestites have masculine gender identities and do not seek to change their anatomic sex. Yet some male transvestites are gay or show some aspects of a feminine gender identity. Transsexuals usually cross-dress because they are uncomfortable with the attire associated with their anatomic sex and truly wish to be members of the other sex. For this reason, as noted in Chapter 5, transsexuals may seek sex reassignment.

The origins of transvestism remain obscure. Family relationships appear to play a role, however. Transvestites are more likely than other people to be oldest children or only children (Schott, 1995). They also report closer relationships with their mothers than with their fathers (Schott, 1995). Some transvestites report a history of "petticoat punishment" during childhood. That is, they were humiliated by being dressed in girl's attire. Some authorities have speculated that the adult transvestite might be attempting psychologically to convert humiliation into mastery by

achieving an erection and engaging in sexual activity despite being attired in female clothing (Geer et al., 1984). Transvestism can also be looked at as an attempt by males to escape the narrow confines of the masculine role (Bullough, 1991).

Transvestic behaviours may range from wearing a single female garment when alone to sporting dresses, wigs, makeup, and feminine mannerisms at a transvestite club. Some transvestites become sexually aroused by masquerading as women and attracting the interest of unsuspecting males. They sometimes entice these men or string them along until they find some excuse to back out before their anatomic sex is revealed. The great majority of transvestites do not engage in antisocial or illegal behaviour. Most practise their sexual predilection in private and would be horrified or embarrassed to be discovered by associates while dressed in female attire.

Although some transvestites persuade their female partners to permit them to wear feminine attire during their sexual activities, most keep their transvestic urges and activities to themselves. A survey of 504 transvestite men showed that most had kept their transvestism a secret from their wives-to-be, hoping not to be bothered by their urge to cross-dress once they were married (Weinberg & Bullough, 1986, 1988). The urges continued into their marriages, however, and the wives eventually discovered their husbands' secrets. The wives interviewed tended to react with confusion, surprise, or shock upon discovering their husbands' cross-dressing (Bullough & Weinberg, 1989). Most tried to be understanding at first. Some assisted their husbands in their cross-dressing, such as by helping them apply makeup. Yet the longer the women were married, the more negative their attitudes tended to become toward their husbands' cross-dressing. Over time, wives generally learned to be tolerant, though not supportive, of their husbands' cross-dressing. Kathleen Cairns, a Calgary therapist, found that wives of cross-dressers required several sessions with a therapist to deal with the fear, betrayal, and grief they experienced upon learning of their husband's behaviour (Cairns, 1997). She also found that wives were far more concerned than the husbands about their children finding out about the cross-dressing.

Exhibitionism

Exhibitionism ("flashing") entails persistent, powerful urges and sexual fantasies involving exposing one's genitals to unsuspecting strangers for the purpose of

Exhibitionism A paraphilia characterized by persistent, powerful urges and sexual fantasies that involve exposing one's genitals to unsuspecting strangers for the purpose of achieving sexual arousal or gratification.

achieving sexual arousal or gratification. The urges are either acted on or are disturbing to the individual. Exhibitionists are mostly males.

What we know of exhibitionists, as with most other people with paraphilias, is almost entirely derived from studies of men who have been apprehended or have been treated by mental health professionals. Such knowledge may yield a biased picture of exhibitionists. Although about one in three arrests for sexual offences involves exhibitionism, relatively few reported incidents result in apprehension and conviction (Cox, 1988). Studies in England, Guatemala, the United States, and Hong Kong show that fewer than 20% of occurrences are reported to the police (Cox, 1988). The characteristics of most perpetrators may thus differ from those of people who have been available for study.

Exhibitionism usually begins before age 18 (American Psychiatric Association, 2000). The urge to exhibit oneself, if not the actual act, usually begins in early adolescence, generally between the ages of 13 and 16 (Freund et al., 1988). The frequency of exhibitionism declines markedly after the age of 40 (American Psychiatric Association, 2000). The typical exhibitionist does not attempt further sexual contact with the victim. An Ontario study of exhibitionists who were repeat offenders found that 12% were also convicted of other sexual offences and 17% were convicted of violent crimes (Rabinowitz et al., 2002).

The police may sometimes trivialize exhibitionism as a "nuisance crime," but the psychological consequences can be serious for victims, especially young children. Victims may feel violated and may be bothered by recurrent images or nightmares. They may also develop fears of venturing out on their own.

Some evidence suggests that exhibitionists may be attempting to assert their masculinity by evoking a response from their victims. A number of exhibitionists have reported that they hoped the women would enjoy the experience and be impressed with the size of their penis (Langevin et al., 1979).

Other studies show exhibitionists to be shy, dependent, passive, lacking in sexual and social skills, and even inhibited (Dwyer, 1988). Exhibitionists who are socially shy or inadequate may be using exhibitionism as a substitute for the intimate relationships they cannot develop.

The preferred victims are typically girls or young women (Freund & Blanchard, 1986). The typical exhibitionist drives up to, or walks in front of, a stranger and exposes his penis. In one sample of 130 exhibitionists, about 50% reported that they always or nearly always had erections when they exposed themselves (Langevin et al., 1979). After his victim has registered fear, disgust, confusion, or surprise, an exhibitionist typically covers himself and flees. He usually masturbates, either while exposing himself or shortly afterward while thinking about the act and the victim's response (American Psychiatric Association, 2000; Blair & Lanyon, 1981). Some exhibitionists ejaculate during the act. Most of the 238 exhibitionists in an Ontario study reported masturbating to orgasm while exposing themselves or afterward while fantasizing about it (Freund et al., 1988).

Exhibitionism can take a diversity of forms. After the Gwen Jacobs case (in which the Ontario Court of Appeal ruled that it was legal for women to go topless; see Chapter 1), some women purposely bared their breasts in an exhibitionistic manner. In Windsor, Ontario, two young women from Michigan approached police officers and asked if it was legal to go topless in Canada. When the officers said it was, the women raised their tops, exposing their breasts (Canadian Press, 1997). It has now become commonplace at certain public events (such as at the Rolling Stones Toronto SARS concert) for women to expose their breasts. Also, at various university campuses across Canada and the United States, young women have bared their breasts in public for the *Girls Gone Wild* Web site. The Internet has greatly facilitated a new variation of exhibitionism in which ordinary people can post pictures of themselves either masturbating or having sex with a partner. Some Canadian adult Web sites have pictures of women exhibiting themselves in public places.

One of the most widely publicized incidents occurred at a rowdy hockey game between 11-year-olds in a Toronto suburb. One of the hockey moms taunted parents of the opposing team by lifting her blouse above her chest and shaking her bra-covered breasts from side to side (Vincent, 2004).

Sometimes a couple will engage in public exhibitionism. At a Toronto Blue Jays game, for example, a man and woman had sex by the window of their hotel room, which directly faced the playing field, and thousands of fans got to watch more than the baseball game. And at the Elora Gorge in Ontario, a man in a car motioned for a 14-year-old boy to approach the car, whereupon the boy saw a woman performing oral sex on the driver. The man and woman were fined for committing an indecent act (Tracey, 2000).

Definitions of exhibitionism also bring into focus the boundaries between normal and abnormal behaviour. Are exotic dancers (stripteasers) or nude sunbathers exhibitionists? After all, aren't they also exposing themselves to strangers? But exotic dancers—male or female—remove their clothes to sexually excite or entertain an audience that is paying to watch them. Their motive is (usually) to earn a living. Sunbathers in their "birthday suits" may also seek to sexually arouse others, not themselves. Of course, they may also be seeking an all-over tan or trying to avoid feeling encumbered by clothing. In any case, stripteasers and sunbathers do not expose themselves to unsuspecting others, and hence these behaviours are not regarded as exhibitionistic.

It is also normal to become sexually excited while stripping before one's sex partner. In fact, stripping has become mainstream, as indicated by the thousands of women from across Canada who have taken "Stripping for Your Lover" workshops taught by former stripper Mary Taylor. Such stripping is done to excite a willing partner, not to surprise or shock a stranger.

Obscene Telephone Calling

Like exhibitionists, obscene phone callers (nearly all of whom are male) seek to become sexually aroused by shocking their victims. Whereas an exhibitionist exposes his genitals to produce the desired response, the obscene phone caller exposes himself verbally by uttering obscenities and sexual provocations to a nonconsenting person. Because of such similarities, obscene telephone calling is sometimes considered a subtype of exhibitionism. The American Psychiatric Association (2000) labels this type of paraphilia **telephone scatologia** (lewdness).

There are many patterns of obscene phone calling (Matek, 1988). Some callers limit themselves to obscenities. Others make sexual overtures. Some just breathe heavily into the receiver. Others describe their masturbatory activity to their victims. Some profess to have previously met the victim at a social gathering or through a mutual acquaintance. Some even present themselves as "taking a sex survey" and ask a series of personally revealing questions.

The typical obscene phone caller is a socially inadequate heterosexual male who has had difficulty forming intimate relationships with women. The relative safety and anonymity of the telephone may shield him from the risk of rejection. A reaction of shock or fright from his victims may fill him with feelings of power and control that are lacking in his life, especially in his relationships with women.

Obscene phone calls are illegal, but it has been difficult for authorities to track down perpetrators (Matek, 1988). Call tracing can help police track obscene or offending phone callers. Call tracing works in different ways in different locales. *Caller ID*, which reveals the caller's telephone number, is available in many places. Though this service may deter some obscene callers, others may use public phones instead of their home phones. Callers may also be able to block the display of their telephone numbers electronically. Check with your local telephone company if you are interested in these services.

Telephone scatologia
A paraphilia characterized by the making of obscene telephone calls. (From the Greek *skatos*, which means "excrement.")

Applied Knowledge

RESPONDING TO EXHIBITIONISTS AND OBSCENE PHONE CALLERS

How to Respond to an Exhibitionist

It is understandable that an unsuspecting woman who is exposed to an exhibitionist may react with shock, surprise, or fear. Unfortunately, her display of shock or fear may reinforce the flasher's tendencies to expose himself. She may fear that the flasher, who has already broken at least one social code, is likely to assault her physically as well. Fortunately, most exhibitionists do not seek actual sexual contact with their victims and run away before they can be apprehended by the police or passersby.

When possible, showing no reaction or simply continuing on one's way may be the best response. If women do desire to respond to the flasher, they might calmly say something like "You really need professional help. You should see a professional to help you with this problem." All should promptly report the incident to police, so that authorities can apprehend the offender.

How to Respond to an Obscene Phone Caller

What should a woman do if she receives an obscene phone call? Advice generally parallels that given to women who are victimized by exhibitionists. Above all, women are advised to remain calm and not to reveal shock or fright, because such reactions tend to reinforce the caller and increase the probability of repeat calls. Women may be best advised to say nothing at all and gently hang up the receiver. A woman might alternatively offer a brief response that alludes to the caller's problems before hanging up. She might say in a calm but strong voice, "It's unfortunate that you have this problem. I think you should seek professional help." If she should receive repeated calls, the woman might request an unlisted number or contact the police about tracing the calls. Many women list themselves only by their initials in the phone directory so as to disguise their gender. But this practice is so widespread that obscene callers may assume that people listed by initials are women living alone.

Voyeurism

Voyeurism involves strong, repetitive urges to observe unsuspecting strangers who are naked, disrobing, or engaged in sexual relations (American Psychiatric Association, 2000). The voyeur becomes sexually aroused by the act of watching and typically does not seek sexual relations with the observed person. In Toronto, Kurt Freund and colleagues found that 12% of university males and 23% of a sample of community males had masturbated while watching a female who was unaware of their presence (Freund et al., 1997).

The voyeur may masturbate while peeping or afterward while replaying the incident in his imagination or engaging in voyeuristic fantasies. The voyeur may fantasize about making love to the observed person but have no intention of actually doing so.

Are people voyeurs if they become sexually aroused by the sight of their lovers undressing? What about people who enjoy watching pornographic films or stripteasers? No, no, and no. The people being observed are not unsuspecting strangers. The lover knows that his or her partner is watching. Porn actors and strippers know that others will be viewing them. They would not be performing if they did not expect or have an audience.

It is perfectly normal for men and women to be sexually stimulated by the sight of other people who are nude, undressing, or engaged in sexual relations. Voyeurism is characterized by urges to spy on *unsuspecting* strangers.

Although most voyeurs are nonviolent, some commit violent crimes such as assault and rape (Langevin, 2003). Voyeurs who break into and enter homes or buildings, or who tap at windows to gain the attention of victims, are among the more dangerous.

Voyeurism A paraphilia characterized by strong, repetitive urges and related sexual fantasies of observing unsuspecting strangers who are naked, disrobing, or engaged in sexual relations. (From the French *voir*, which means "to see.")

A World of Diversity

IT SEEMS LIKE VOYEURS ARE EVERYWHERE

Traditionally, the voyeur has been categorized as a "peeping Tom" who looks through windows hoping to see a woman undressing. In recent years, voyeurs have been caught in many other kinds of situations. The development of small video cameras and lenses has made voyeurism easier. Consider the following examples:

■ In Toronto, a man secretly video-taped women using a washroom in a rooming house.

■ In Winnipeg, a restaurant owner installed a camera just above the toilet in the women's washroom.

■ In Edmonton, a landlord using a camera hooked up to his computer spied on a female tenant living in the basement apartment.

■ In Peterborough, a man hid in the tank of a female outhouse where he was covered in excrement so that he could watch women urinating and defecating.

■ In Toronto, a man attached the lens of a video camera to his shoe and used this to film under women's skirts in shopping malls and other public locations. He posted these video shots for sale on the Internet at an "Up-Skirt" Web site.

■ In Toronto, a medical technician used a video camera hidden in a medical laboratory's change room to film women undressing.

■ In Peterborough, a man used a two-way mirror in a Kentucky Fried Chicken outlet to spy on women who were changing into their work uniforms.

■ In Toronto, a man secretly video-taped his sexual behaviour with a teacher's aide and blackmailed her into paying him money so that he would not show the tape to her parents and her employer.

In 2005, Parliament passed legislation that makes it a crime to secretly observe or record a person in situations where privacy is expected. This includes situations where someone is nude or engaging in sexual activity. But it also includes situations where a person is fully clothed and someone observes or records them for sexual purposes. Shortly after the legislation was passed, a Toronto man was charged after he was seen at a grocery store crouching down next to young girls and pointing a camera phone under their skirts while their parents were shopping (Powell, 2005).

Because of concerns over the misuse of camera phones many fitness centres and other organizations have banned them, especially in change rooms.

Shooting Private Parts in Public Places.
In places like malls, police are beginning to catch people who are trying to shoot private parts in public places. They aim compact camcorders up women's skirts in crowded stores and shopping malls, parks, and fairs. Sometimes they post the pictures on the Internet. Often the pictures wind up for sale on sex sites.

Sexual Masochism

Although pleasure and pain may seem like polar opposites, some people experience sexual pleasure through having pain or humiliation inflicted on them by their sex partners. People who associate the receipt of pain or humiliation with sexual arousal are called **sexual masochists**. A sexual masochist either acts on or is distressed by persistent urges and sexual fantasies involving the desire to be bound, flogged, humiliated, or made to suffer in some way by a sexual partner so as to achieve sex-

Sexual masochism A paraphilia characterized by the desire or need for pain or humiliation to enhance sexual arousal so that gratification may be attained. (From the name of Leopold von Sacher-Masoch.)

ual excitement. In extreme cases, the person is incapable of becoming sexually aroused unless pain or humiliation is incorporated into the sexual act.

Sexual masochism is the only paraphilia that is found among women with some frequency (American Psychiatric Association, 2000). Even sexual masochism, however, is much more prevalent among men than women. Male masochists may outnumber females by a margin of 20 to 1 (American Psychiatric Association, 2000).

The word *masochism* is derived from the name of the Austrian storyteller Leopold von Sacher-Masoch (1835–1895). He wrote tales of men who derived sexual satisfaction from having a female partner inflict pain on them, typically by flagellation (beating or whipping).

Sexual masochists may derive pleasure from various types of punishing experiences, including being restrained (a practice known as **bondage**), blindfolded (sensory bondage), spanked, whipped, or made to perform humiliating acts, such as walking around on all fours and licking the boots or shoes of the sex partner or being subjected to vulgar insults. Some masochists have their partners humiliate them by urinating or defecating on them. Some masochists prefer a particular source of pain. Others seek an assortment. But we should not think that sexual masochists enjoy other types of pain that are not connected with their sexual practices. Sexual masochists are no more likely than anyone else to derive pleasure from the pain they experience when they accidentally stub their toes or touch a hot appliance. Pain has erotic value only within a sexual context. It must be part of an elaborate sexual ritual.

Sexual masochists and **sexual sadists** often form sexual relationships to meet each other's needs. Some sexual masochists enlist the services of prostitutes or obtain the cooperation of their regular sexual partners to enact their masochistic fantasies.

While it may seem contradictory for pain to become connected with sexual pleasure, the association of sexual arousal with mildly painful stimuli is actually quite common. The eroticization of mild forms of pain (love bites, hair pulls, minor scratches) may fall within the normal range of sexual variation. Pain from these sources increases overall bodily arousal, which may enhance sexual excitement. Some of us become sexually excited when our partners "talk dirty" to us or call us vulgar names. When the urge for pain for purposes of sexual arousal becomes so persistent or strong that it overshadows other sources of sexual stimulation, or when the masochistic experience causes physical or psychological harm, many would say that the boundary between normality and abnormality has been breached.

Baumeister (1988a) proposes that independent and responsible selfhood becomes burdensome or stressful at times. Sexual masochism provides a temporary reprieve from the responsibilities of independent selfhood. It is a blunting of one's ordinary level of self-awareness that is achieved by "focusing on immediate sensations (both painful and pleasant) and on being a sexual object" (Baumeister, 1988a, p. 54).

Sexual masochism can range from relatively benign to potentially lethal practices, such as **hypoxyphilia**. Hypoxyphiliacs put plastic bags over their heads, nooses around their necks, or pressure on their chests to deprive themselves of oxygen temporarily and enhance their sexual arousal. They usually fantasize that they are being strangled by a lover. They try to discontinue oxygen deprivation before they lose consciousness, but some miscalculations result in death by suffocation or strangulation (Blanchard & Hucker, 1991).

Sexual Sadism

Sadism is named after the infamous Marquis de Sade (1774–1814), a Frenchman who wrote tales of becoming sexually aroused by inflicting pain or humiliation on others. The virtuous Justine, the heroine of his novel of the same name, endures

Bondage Ritual restraint, as by shackles, as practised by many sexual masochists.

Sexual sadists People who become sexually aroused by inflicting pain or humiliation on others.

Hypoxyphilia A practice in which a person seeks to enhance sexual arousal, usually during masturbation, by becoming deprived of oxygen. (From the Greek root meaning "under" [*hypo-*].)

Sexual sadism A paraphilia characterized by the desire or need to inflict pain or humiliation on others to enhance sexual arousal so that gratification is attained. (From the name of the Marquis de Sade.)

terrible suffering at the hands of fiendish men. She is at one time bound and spread-eagled so that bloodhounds can savage her. She then seeks refuge with a surgeon who tries to dismember her. Later she falls into the clutches of a sabrewielding mass murderer, but Nature saves her with a timely thunderbolt.

Sexual sadism is characterized by persistent, powerful urges and sexual fantasies involving the inflicting of pain and suffering on others to achieve sexual excitement or gratification. The urges are acted on or are disturbing enough to cause personal distress. Some sexual sadists cannot become sexually aroused unless they make their sex partners suffer. Others can become sexually excited without such acts.

Some sadists hurt or humiliate willing partners, such as prostitutes or sexual masochists. Others—a small minority—stalk and attack nonconsenting victims.

Geoffrey Rush as the Marquis de Sade in the Film Quills. Sexual sadism is a fascinating topic in literature and among social and behavioural scientists.

SADOMASOCHISM **Sadomasochism (S&M)** is *mutually gratifying sexual interactions* between *consenting partners*. Occasional S&M is quite common among the general population. Couples may incorporate light forms of S&M in their lovemaking now and then, such as mild dominance and submission games or gentle physical restraint. It is also not uncommon for lovers to scratch or bite their partners to heighten their mutual arousal during coitus. They generally do not inflict severe pain or damage, however.

Twenty-two percent of the men and 12% of the women surveyed by Kinsey and his colleagues (1953) reported at least some sexual response to sadomasochistic stories. Although some milder forms of sadomasochism may fall within the boundaries of normal sexual variation, sadomasochism becomes pathological when such fantasies are acted on in ways that become destructive, dangerous, or distressing to oneself or others. How would you categorize the following example?

> A 25-year-old female graduate student described a range of masochistic experiences. She reported feelings of sexual excitement during arguments with her husband when he would scream at her or hit her in a rage. She would sometimes taunt him to make love to her in a brutal fashion, as though she were being raped. She found the brutality and sense of being punished to be sexually stimulating. She had also begun having sex with strange men and enjoyed being physically punished by them during sex more than any other type of sexual stimulus. Being beaten or whipped produced the most intense sexual experiences she had ever had. Although she recognized the dangers posed by her sexual behavior, and felt somewhat ashamed about it, she was not sure that she wanted treatment for "it" because of the pleasure that it provided her. (Adapted from DSM, 2000, pp. 87–88)

In one subculture, sadomasochism is the preferred or even the exclusive form of sexual gratification. People in this subculture seek one another out through mutual contacts, S&M social organizations, or personal ads in S&M magazines. The S&M subculture has spawned magazines and clubs catering to people who describe themselves as "into S&M," as well as sex shops that sell sadomasochistic paraphernalia. These include leather restraints and leather face masks that resemble the ancient masks of executioners.

Participants in sadomasochism often engage in highly elaborate rituals involving dominance and submission. Rituals are staged as though they were scenes in a play (Weinberg et al., 1984). In the "master and slave" game, the sadist leads the

Sadomasochism A mutually gratifying sexual interaction between consenting sex partners in which sexual arousal is associated with the infliction and receipt of pain or humiliation. Commonly known as *S&M*.

masochist around by a leash. The masochist performs degrading or menial acts. In bondage and discipline (B&D), the dominant partner restrains the submissive partner and flagellates (spanks or whips) or sexually stimulates the submissive partner. The erotic appeal of bondage seems to be connected with controlling or being controlled.

Various types of stimulation may be used to administer pain during S&M encounters, but pain is not always employed. When it is, it is usually mild or moderate. Psychological pain, or humiliation, is perhaps as common as physical pain. Pain may also be used symbolically, as in the case of a sadist who uses a harmless, soft rubber paddle to spank the masochist. Thus, the erotic appeal of pain for some S&M participants may derive from the ritual of control rather than from the pain itself (Weinberg, 1987).

Extreme forms of pain, such as torture and severe beatings, are rarely reported by sadomasochists (Breslow et al., 1985). Masochists may seek pain, but they usually avoid serious injury and dangerous partners (Baumeister, 1988b).

S&M participants may be heterosexual, gay, or bisexual (Breslow et al., 1986). They may assume either the masochistic or the sadistic role, or they may alternate roles depending on the sexual script. People who seek sexual excitement by enacting both sadistic and masochistic roles are known as *sadomasochists*. In heterosexual relationships the partners may reverse traditional gender roles. The man may assume the submissive or masochistic role, and the woman may take the dominant or sadistic role (Reinisch, 1990).

A survey of S&M participants drawn from ads in S&M magazines found that about three out of four were male (Breslow et al., 1985). Most were married. Women respondents engaged in S&M more often and had more partners than men. (Apparently, a greater number of men than women seek partners for S&M.)

The causes of sexual masochism and sadism, as of other paraphilias, are unclear. Humans may possess a physiological capacity to experience heightened sexual arousal from the receipt or infliction of pain (which may explain the prevalence of love bites). Mild pain may heighten physiological arousal in both aggressor and victim, adding to the effects of sexual stimulation.

Pain may also have more direct biological links to pleasure. Natural chemicals called *endorphins*, similar to opiates, are released in the brain in response to pain and produce feelings of euphoria and general well-being. Perhaps, then, pleasure is derived from pain because of the release or augmentation of endorphins (Weinberg, 1987).

Frotteurism

Frotteurism A paraphilia characterized by recurrent, powerful sexual urges and related fantasies that involve rubbing against or touching a nonconsenting person. (From the French *frotter,* which means "to rub.")

Toucherism A practice related to frotteurism and characterized by the persistent urge to fondle nonconsenting strangers.

Frotteurism (also known as "mashing") is rubbing against or touching a nonconsenting person. As with other paraphilias, a diagnosis of frotteurism requires either acting on these urges or being distressed by them. Mashing has been reported exclusively among males (American Psychiatric Association, 2000).

Most mashing takes place in crowded places, such as buses, subway cars, or elevators. The man finds the rubbing or the touching, not the coercive nature of the act, to be sexually stimulating. While rubbing against a woman, he may fantasize a consensual, affectionate sexual relationship with her. Typically, the man incorporates images of his mashing within his masturbation fantasies. Mashing also incorporates a related practice, **toucherism**: the fondling of nonconsenting strangers.

Mashing may be so fleeting and furtive that the woman may not realize what has happened (DSM, 2000). Mashers thus stand little chance of being caught.

Many mashers have difficulty forming relationships with women and are handicapped by fears of rejection. Mashing provides sexual contact in a relatively nonthreatening context.

Other Paraphilias

Let us consider some other, less common, paraphilias.

ZOOPHILIA A person with **zoophilia** experiences repeated, intense urges and related fantasies involving sexual contact with animals. As with other paraphilias, the urges may be acted on or cause personal distress. The term *bestiality* applies to actual sexual contact with an animal.

Although the prevalence of zoophilia in the general population is unknown, Kinsey and his colleagues (1948, 1953) found that about 8% of the men and 3% to 4% of the women interviewed admitted to sexual contacts with animals. Men more often had sexual contact with farm animals, such as calves and sheep. Women more often reported sexual contacts with household pets. Men were more likely to masturbate or copulate with the animals. Women more often reported general body contact. People of both genders reported encouraging the animals to lick their genitals. A few women reported that they had trained a dog to engage in coitus with them. Urban–rural differences also emerged. Rates of bestiality were higher among boys reared on farms. Compared with only a few city boys, 17% of farm boys had reached orgasm at some time through sexual contact with dogs, cows, and goats. These contacts were generally restricted to adolescence, when human outlets were not available. Still, adults sometimes engage in sexual contacts with animals.

In Canada it is a criminal offence to have sex with an animal. In 2003, a 28-year-old Toronto man was charged with cruelty to animals after he was seen having sex with a pregnant Jersey cow. He refused to dismount from the animal even after farm employees repeatedly screamed at him (Godfrey, 2003).

NECROPHILIA In **necrophilia**, a rare paraphilia, a person desires sex with corpses. Three types of necrophilia have been identified (Rosman & Resnick, 1989). In *regular necrophilia*, the person has sex with a deceased person. In *necrophilic homicide*, the person commits murder to obtain a corpse for sexual purposes. In *necrophilic fantasy*, the person fantasizes about sex with a corpse but does not actually carry out necrophilic acts. Necrophiles often obtain jobs that provide them with access to corpses, such as working in cemeteries, morgues, or funeral homes. The primary motivation for necrophilia appears to be the desire to possess sexually a completely unresisting and nonrejecting partner (Rosman & Resnick, 1989).

OTHER LESS COMMON PARAPHILIAS In **klismaphilia**, sexual arousal is derived from the use of enemas. Klismaphiles generally prefer the receiving role to the giving role. Klismaphiles may have derived sexual pleasure in childhood from the anal stimulation provided by parents giving them enemas.

In **coprophilia**, sexual arousal is connected with feces. The person may desire to be defecated on or to defecate on a sex partner. The association of feces with sexual arousal may also be a throwback to childhood.

In **urophilia**, sexual arousal is associated with urine. As with coprophilia, the person may desire to be urinated on or to urinate on a sexual partner. Also like coprophilia, urophilia may have childhood origins.

Theoretical Perspectives

The paraphilias are among the most fascinating and perplexing variations in sexual behaviour. Let us consider explanations that have been advanced from the major theoretical perspectives.

Zoophilia A paraphilia involving persistent or repeated sexual urges and related fantasies that involve sexual contact with animals.

Necrophilia A paraphilia characterized by desire for sexual activity with corpses. (From the Greek *nekros,* which means "dead body.")

Klismaphilia A paraphilia in which sexual arousal is derived from the use of enemas.

Coprophilia A paraphilia in which sexual arousal is attained in connection with feces. (From the Greek *copros,* which means "dung.")

Urophilia A paraphilia in which sexual arousal is associated with urine.

Biological Perspectives

Researchers are investigating whether there are biological factors in paraphilic behaviour. The biological perspective looks into factors such as the endocrine system (hormones) and the nervous system.

Because testosterone is linked to sex drive, researchers have focused on differences in testosterone levels between people with paraphilias and people without them. One study found evidence of some hormonal differences between a group of 16 male exhibitionists and controls (Lang et al., 1989). Although no differences in overall levels of testosterone were found, researchers reported that exhibitionists evidenced significantly elevated levels of the measure of testosterone believed to be most closely linked to sex drive. The implication would be that exhibitionists may have biologically elevated sex drives, although the results would not address why exhibitionists expose themselves to achieve, or in response to, sexual arousal.

Other studies appear to confirm that many paraphilics do have higher-than-normal sex drives (Haake et al., 2003; Kafka, 2003). A German study, for example, found that people with paraphilias had shorter refractory periods after orgasm by masturbation than most men and experienced a higher frequency of sexual fantasies and urges (Haake et al., 2003). Kafka (2003) refers to this heightened sex drive as *hypersexual desire*—the opposite of hypoactive sexual desire disorder (see Chapter 13). Bradford concurs and believes that paraphilics of this type could be considered to have *hyperactive sexual desire disorder.*

But these studies address the strength of the sex drive, not the direction it takes. A more recent study used the electroencephalograph (EEG) to investigate electrical responses in the brain among paraphilics and control subjects. They measured what is termed "evoked electrical potentials" to erotic stimuli in a sample of 62 right-handed men, half of whom were considered normal in terms of their sexual fantasies and behaviours (the control subjects), and half of whom had been diagnosed as paraphilic (fetishistic and sadomasochistic) (Waismann et al., 2003). The men were shown three sets of 57 slides each in random order— 57 paraphilic slides that portrayed fetishistic and sadomasochistic themes, 57 "normal" slides that depicted nude women, coitus, and oral sex, and 57 neutral slides of landscapes, street scenes, and the like. An electrical response labelled "P600" was determined to be the best indicator of sexual arousal in the men. It was found that the main site for evoking the P600 response to "normal" sexual stimuli was on the right side of the brain. The main site for paraphilic stimuli was the left, frontal part of the brain. Paraphilic men showed a significantly greater response than control subjects in the P600 response in the left, frontal part of the brain.

Another neurological study may offer some insight into masochism. A research team from Massachusetts General Hospital found that the same neural circuits in the brain are often activated either by painful or by pleasurable stimuli (Becerra et al., 2001). The researchers discovered that a painfully hot (115°F/46°C) stimulus to the hand activated areas of the brain believed to involve "reward" circuitry. The researchers had set out to find ways to help chronic pain patients, not to investigate sexual masochism, but their findings certainly have implications for masochism.

Psychologist J. Michael Bailey (2003a) believes that as time goes on, we will learn more about potential biological foundations of paraphilic behaviour. Better understanding of these atypical patterns of sexual behaviour may lead to the development of more effective treatments.

A World of Diversity

SEXUAL ADDICTION AND COMPULSIVITY

In Prince Edward Island, a politician resigned from the Liberal caucus of the legislature after admitting that he had billed more than $1000 in phone-sex charges to his legislature calling card. At a news conference, he said that he was addicted to phoning females on adult phone lines (Canadian Press, 1995a). That is, he had lost control over his sexual behaviour. What is a sexual addiction? What is sexual compulsivity?

What Is a Sexual Addiction?

A person with a sexual addiction

- Uses sexual behaviour as a means of reducing anxiety
- Lacks control over his or her sexual impulses
- Typically experiences minimal satisfaction from sexual contacts

- Feels bad about his or her sexual contacts but engages in the behaviour repeatedly
- Engages in illicit sexual behaviour that endangers his or her own well-being and the well-being of his or her family
- Cannot resist sexual opportunities
- Continues sexual contacts that are nonintimate, dangerous, or undesirable

Characteristics of addiction include *tolerance* and *withdrawal symptoms*. As with other addictions, the sexually addicted person may experience tolerance—that is, may seek increasingly illicit sexual contacts or experiences. When the sexual activity is discontinued, the person may also experience withdrawal symptoms, such as anxiety and preoccupation with the craved activity.

What Is Sexual Compulsivity?

Sexual compulsivity is an obsessive-compulsive disorder. In an obsessive-

compulsive disorder, an individual cannot eradicate certain thoughts or ideas from his or her mind and has extreme difficulty controlling his or her behaviour. For example, some people have "checking" compulsions in which they check and recheck whether they have locked every door and window before they can leave home. (And then they may check some more and remain uneasy about the possibility of error.) Sexual compulsivity is manifested by means of sexual activity and may involve a specific paraphilia. Like sexual addiction, a sexual compulsion becomes the centre of the person's life. As such, it may interfere with personal relationships, work, and health. There may also be legal consequences.

Sources: American Psychiatric Association, 2000; **www.mastersandjohnson.com,** *2000.*

Research in Action

"CYBERSEX ADDICTION"—A NEW PSYCHOLOGICAL DISORDER?

Sex is the hottest topic among adult users of the Internet. Studies show that fully a third of all visits are directed to sexually oriented Web sites, chat rooms, and news groups.

For most people these forays into cybersex are relatively harmless recreational pursuits, but experts in the field say that the affordability, accessibility, and anonymity of the Internet are fuelling a brand-new psychological disorder—cybersex addiction—that appears to be spreading with astonishing rapidity and bringing turmoil to the lives of those affected.

Writing in the journal *Sexual Addiction and Compulsivity* (**www.tandfdc.com/jnls/sac.htm**), psychologist Al Cooper of Stanford University and his colleagues (2000) report that many of the men and women who now spend dozens of hours each week seeking sexual stimulation from their computers deny that they have a problem and refuse to seek help until their marriages and/or their jobs are in serious jeopardy.

Those most strongly hooked on Internet sex are likely to spend hours each day masturbating to pornographic images or having "mutual" online sex with someone contacted through a chat room. Occasionally, they progress to off-line affairs with sex partners they meet online.

Cooper and his colleagues (1999, 2000) conducted the largest and most detailed survey of online sex. The survey, conducted online among 9265 men and women who admitted surfing the Net for sexually oriented sites, indicated that at least 1% were seriously hooked on online sex.

According to Dr. Cooper, who works at the San Jose Marital and Sexuality Center in Santa Clara, California, cybersex compulsives are just like drug addicts. They "use the Internet as an important part of their sexual acting out, much like a drug addict who has a 'drug of choice,'" and often with serious harm to their home lives and livelihood. Especially vulnerable to becoming hooked on Internet sex, he wrote, are "those users whose sexuality may have been suppressed and limited all their lives [who] suddenly find an infinite supply of sexual opportunities" on the Internet.

The sexual stimulation and release obtained through cybersex also contribute to the pursuit of the activity, Dr. Schwartz said. "Intense orgasms from the minimal investment of a few keystrokes are powerfully reinforcing," he noted, adding that "Cybersex affords easy, inexpensive access to a myriad of ritualized encounters with idealized partners."

Cybersex compulsives can become so involved with their online activities that they ignore their partners and children and risk their jobs. In Dr. Cooper's survey, 20% of the men and 12% of the women reported they had used computers at work for some sexual pursuits. Many companies now monitor employees' online activities, and repeated visits to sexually oriented sites have cost people their jobs.

And some people, including two physicians, have landed in federal prison for two years because they downloaded

Do People Become Addicted to Cybersex?
According to Dr. Mark Schwartz of the Masters and Johnson Institute, for some people "sex on the Net is like heroin. It grabs them and takes over their lives." Some people spend hours each day masturbating to pornographic images they find online or engaging in "mutual" online sex with someone they contact through a chat room. Is becoming hooked on cybersex a safe kind of "addiction"? What do you think?

child pornography when authorities were watching, Dr. Schwartz said.

Still, most who pursue cybersex consider it harmless and safe to do so. Although social and safety concerns and fear of discovery may prevent someone from visiting an adult bookstore or prostitute, there are no such constraints when pornography and sexual partners can be called up at any time of the day or night on a computer screen in one's home or office.

Source: From J. E. Brody (2000, May 16). "Cybersex Gives Birth to a Psychological Disorder." The New York Times, p. F7. Copyright © 2000 by The New York Times Co. Adapted by permission.

Psychoanalytic Perspectives

Classical psychoanalytic theory suggests that paraphilias are psychological defences, usually against unresolved castration anxiety dating back to the Oedipus complex (Horne, 2003). To the transvestic man, the sight of a woman's vagina threatens to arouse castration anxiety. It reminds him that women do not have penises and that he might suffer the same fate.

The paraphilias have provided a fertile ground for psychoanalytic theories. However, only clinical case studies support the role of such unconscious processes as unresolved castration anxiety. The basic shortcoming of psychoanalytic theory is that many of its key concepts involve unconscious mechanisms that cannot be directly observed or measured. Thus, psychoanalytic theories remain interesting but speculative hypotheses about the origins of these unusual sexual behaviour patterns.

Learning Perspectives

Learning theorists believe that fetishes and other paraphilias are learned behaviours that are acquired through experience. An object may acquire sexually arousing

Sex Addicts Anonymous (SAA)
www.sexaa.org

properties through association with sexual arousal or orgasm. According to the conditioning model, a boy who catches a glimpse of his mother's stockings hanging on the towel rack while he is masturbating may go on to develop a fetish for stockings (Breslow, 1989). Orgasm in the presence of the object would reinforce the erotic connection, especially if the experience occurs repeatedly.

Along these lines, Breslow (1989) proposed a learning theory explanation that describes the development of paraphilias in terms of the gradual acquisition of sexual arousal to an unusual object or activity through its incorporation in masturbatory fantasies. A transvestite, for example, may have achieved an erection while trying on his mother's panties in childhood. The paraphilic object or activity is then incorporated within masturbatory fantasies and is reinforced by orgasm. The paraphilic object or activity is then repeatedly used as a masturbatory aid, further strengthening the erotic bond.

Friedrich and Gerber (1994) studied five adolescent boys who practised hypoxyphilia and found extensive early histories of choking in combination with physical or sexual abuse. The combination seems to have encouraged each of the boys to associate choking with sexual arousal.

Learning explanations of sexual masochism focus on the pairing of sexual excitement with punishment. For example, a child may be punished when discovered masturbating. Or a boy may reflexively experience an erection if his penis accidentally rubs against the parent's body as he is being spanked. With repeated encounters like these, pain and pleasure may become linked in the person's sexual arousal system.

Modelling or observational learning may also play a role in the development of some cases. Parents, for example, may inadvertently model exhibitionistic behaviour to young sons, which can lead the sons to eroticize the act of exposing themselves. Young people may also read books or magazines or view films or TV programs with paraphilic content. Media may give them the idea of trying paraphilic behaviour, and they may find it exciting, especially if acts such as exhibitionism or voyeurism provide a rush of adrenaline.

Sociological Perspectives

Most people indulge paraphilias privately. Sexual masochists and sadists require a partner, however, except for the few masochists who practise only autoerotic forms of masochism and the few sadists who stalk nonconsenting partners. Most sadomasochists also relate in one way or another to the sadomasochistic subculture. It is within the S&M subculture—the loosely connected network of S&M clubs, specialty shops, organizations, magazines, and so on—that S&M rituals are learned, sexual contacts made, sadomasochistic identities confirmed, and sexual paraphernalia acquired. But the S&M subculture exists in the context of the larger society, and the rituals it invents mirror the social and gender roles that exist in the larger society.

Martin Weinberg (1987) proposes a sociological model that focuses on the social context of sadomasochism. Noting that S&M rituals generally involve some form of dominance and submission, Weinberg attributes their erotic appeal to the opportunity to reverse the customary power relationships that exist between the genders and social classes in society at large. Within the confines of the carefully scripted S&M encounter, the meek can be powerful and the powerful meek (Geer et al., 1984). Those who customarily hold high-status positions that require them to be in control and responsible may be attracted by the opportunity to surrender control to another person. Dominance and submission games also offer opportunities to accentuate or reverse the gender stereotypes that identify masculinity with dominance and femininity with submissiveness.

Individual sadomasochistic interests may become institutionalized as an S&M subculture in societies (like ours) that have certain social characteristics:

(1) Dominance–submission relationships are embedded within the culture, and aggression is socially valued. (2) There is an unequal distribution of power between people from different gender or social class categories. (3) There are enough affluent people to enable them to participate in such leisure-time activities. (4) Imagination and creativity, important elements in the development of S&M scripts and fantasies, are socially valued and encouraged (Weinberg, 1987).

An Integrated Perspective: The "Lovemap"

Like other sexual patterns, the paraphilias may have multiple biological, psychological, and sociocultural origins (Seligman & Hardenburg, 2000). Our understanding of them may thus be best approached from a theoretical framework that incorporates multiple perspectives, as found in the work of John Money and his colleagues (1989).

John Money (2000) traces the origins of paraphilias to childhood. He believes that childhood experiences etch a pattern in the brain, called a **lovemap**, that determines what types of stimuli and activities become sexually arousing to the individual. In the case of paraphilias, these lovemaps become distorted, or "vandalized," by early traumatic experiences, such as incest, overbearing antisexual upbringing, and physical abuse or neglect.

Research suggests that voyeurs and exhibitionists often were the victims of childhood sexual abuse (Lee et al., 2002). Not all children exposed to such influences develop paraphilic compulsions, however. For reasons that remain unknown, some children exposed to such influences appear to be more vulnerable than others to developing distorted lovemaps. A genetic predisposition, hormonal factors, brain abnormalities, or a combination of these and other factors may play a role in determining one's vulnerability to vandalized lovemaps (Brody, 1990a).

Treatment of the Paraphilias

The treatment of these atypical patterns of sexual behaviour raises a number of issues. First, people with paraphilias usually do not want or seek treatment, at least not voluntarily. They are generally seen by mental health workers only when they come into conflict with the law or at the urging of their family members or sexual partners who have discovered them performing the paraphilic behaviour or found evidence of their paraphilic interests. They often deny that they are offenders, even after they are apprehended and convicted.

Paraphilic behaviour is a source of pleasure, so many people are not motivated to give it up. The individual typically perceives his problems as stemming from society's intolerance, not from feelings of guilt or shame.

Second, helping professionals may encounter ethical problems when they are asked to contribute to a judicial process by trying to persuade a sex offender that he (virtually all are male) *ought* to change his behaviour. Helping professionals traditionally help clients clarify or meet their own goals; it is not their role to impose societal goals on the individual. Many helping professionals believe that the criminal justice system, not they, ought to enforce social standards.

The third issue is a treatment problem. Therapists realize that they are generally less successful with resistant or recalcitrant clients. Unless the motivation to change is present, therapeutic efforts are often wasted.

The fourth problem is the issue of perceived responsibility. Sex offenders almost invariably claim that they are unable to control their urges and impulses. Such claims of uncontrollability are often self-serving and may lead others to treat offenders with greater sympathy and understanding. Most therapies, however, are based on the belief that whatever causes may have led to the problem behaviour, and however difficult it may be to resist these unusual sexual urges, accepting personal responsibility for one's actions is a prelude to change. Thus, if therapy is to be con-

Lovemap A representation in the brain of the idealized lover and of idealized erotic activity with the lover.

structive, it is necessary to break through the client's personal mythology that he is powerless to control his behaviour.

Despite these issues, many offenders are referred for treatment by the courts. A few seek therapy themselves because they have come to see how their behaviour harms themselves or others. Let us consider some of the ways in which therapists treat people with these atypical sexual behaviour patterns.

Psychotherapy

Psychoanalysis focuses on resolving the unconscious conflicts that are believed to originate in childhood and to give rise in adulthood to pathological problems such as paraphilias. The aim of therapy is to help bring unconscious conflicts, principally Oedipal conflicts, into conscious awareness so that they can be worked through in light of the individual's adult personality.

Psychoanalytic therapy for the paraphilias has not been subjected to experimental analysis. We thus do not know whether successes are due to the psychoanalytic treatment itself or to other factors, such as spontaneous improvement or a client's willingness to change.

Cognitive-Behaviour Therapy

Whereas traditional psychoanalysis tends to entail a lengthy process of exploration of the childhood origins of problem behaviours, **cognitive-behaviour therapy** is briefer and focuses directly on changing behaviour. Cognitive-behaviour therapy has spawned a number of techniques to help eliminate paraphilic behaviours and strengthen appropriate sexual behaviours. These techniques include systematic desensitization, aversion therapy, social skills training, covert sensitization, and orgasmic reconditioning, to name a few.

Systematic desensitization attempts to break the link between the sexual stimulus (such as a fetishistic stimulus) and the inappropriate response (sexual arousal). The client is first taught to relax selected muscle groups in the body.

Muscle relaxation is then paired repeatedly with each of a series of progressively more arousing paraphilic images or fantasies. Relaxation comes to replace sexual arousal in response to each of these stimuli, even the most provocative.

In **aversion therapy**, the undesirable sexual behaviour (for example, masturbation to fetishistic fantasies) is paired repeatedly with an aversive stimulus (such as a harmless but painful electric shock or a nausea-inducing chemical) in the hope that the client will develop a conditioned aversion to the paraphilic behaviour.

Covert sensitization is a variation of aversion therapy in which paraphilic fantasies are paired with an aversive stimulus in imagination. In a broad-scale application, 38 **pedophiles** and 62 exhibitionists, more than half of whom were court-referred, were treated by pairing imagined aversive images or odours with fantasies of the problem behaviour (Maletzky, 1980). Clients were instructed to fantasize pedophiliac or exhibitionistic scenes. Then,

> At a point when sexual pleasure is aroused, aversive images are presented. Examples might include a pedophiliac fellating a child, but discovering a festering sore on the boy's penis, an exhibitionist exposing to a woman but suddenly being discovered by his wife or the police, or a pedophiliac laying a young boy down in a field, only to lie next to him in a pile of dog feces. (Maletzky, 1980, p. 308)

Maletzky used this treatment weekly for six months and then followed it with booster sessions every three months over a three-year period. The procedure resulted in at least a 75% reduction in the deviant activities and fantasies for over 80% of the study participants, at follow-up periods of up to 36 months.

Cognitive-behaviour therapy The systematic application of the principles of learning to help people modify problem behaviour.

Systematic desensitization A method for terminating the connection between a stimulus (such as a fetishistic object) and an inappropriate response (such as sexual arousal to the paraphilic stimulus). Muscle relaxation is practised in connection with each stimulus in a series of increasingly arousing stimuli, so that the person learns to remain relaxed (and not sexually aroused) in their presence.

Aversion therapy A method for terminating undesirable sexual behaviour in which the behaviour is repeatedly paired with an aversive stimulus such as electric shock so that a conditioned aversion develops.

Covert sensitization A form of aversion therapy in which thoughts of engaging in undesirable behaviour are paired repeatedly with imagined aversive stimuli.

Pedophiles Persons with pedophilia, a paraphilia involving sexual interest in children.

Is Her Behaviour Appropriate or Inappropriate?
Most theorists suggest that early learning experiences contribute to the development of paraphilias. Is this woman's interaction with her young child of the sort that can lead to sexual problems as the child matures?

Social skills training focuses on helping the individual improve his ability to relate to the other gender. The therapist might first model a desired behaviour, such as how to ask a woman out on a date or how to handle a rejection. The client might then role-play the behaviour, with the therapist playing the part of the woman. Following the role-play enactment, the therapist would provide feedback and additional guidance and modelling to help the client improve his skills. This process would be repeated until the client mastered the skill.

Orgasmic reconditioning aims to increase sexual arousal to socially appropriate sexual stimuli by pairing culturally appropriate imagery with orgasmic pleasure. The person is instructed to become sexually aroused by masturbating to paraphilic images or fantasies. But as he approaches the point of orgasm, he switches to appropriate imagery and focuses on it during orgasm. These images and fantasies eventually acquire the capacity to elicit sexual arousal. Orgasmic reconditioning is often combined with other techniques, such as social skills training, so that more desirable social behaviours can be strengthened as well (Adams et al., 1981).

Although behaviour therapy techniques tend to have higher reported success rates than most other methods, they too are limited by reliance on uncontrolled case studies. Without appropriate controls, we cannot isolate the effective elements of therapy or determine that the results were not due merely to the passage of time or other factors unrelated to the treatment. It is possible that clients who are highly motivated to change may succeed in doing so with *any* systematic approach.

Medical Approaches

There is no medical "cure" for the paraphilias. Yet some progress has recently been reported in using antidepressants such as Prozac (fluoxetine hydrochloride) in treating exhibitionism, voyeurism, and fetishism (Roesler & Witztum, 2000). Why Prozac? In addition to treating depression, Prozac has been helpful in treating obsessive-compulsive disorder, a type of emotional disorder involving recurrent obsessions (intrusive ideas) and/or compulsions (urges to repeat a certain behaviour or thought). Researchers speculate that paraphilias may be linked to obsessive-compulsive disorder (Kruesi et al., 1992). People with paraphilias often experience intrusive, repetitive thoughts or images of the paraphilic object or stimulus, such as mental images of young children. Many also report feeling compelled to carry out the paraphilic acts repeatedly. Paraphilias may belong to what researchers have dubbed an obsessive-compulsive spectrum of behaviours (Kruesi et al., 1992).

People who experience such intense urges that they are at risk of committing sexual offences may be helped by **anti-androgen drugs**, which reduce the level of testosterone in the bloodstream (Roesler & Witztum, 2000). Testosterone is closely linked to sex drive and interest. *Medroxyprogesterone acetate* (MPA) (trade name: Depo-Provera), which is administered in weekly injections, is the anti-androgen that has been used most extensively in the treatment of sex offenders. In men, anti-androgens reduce testosterone to a level that is typical of a prepubertal boy (Bradford, 2001). They consequently reduce sexual desire and the frequency of erections and ejaculations (Bradford, 2001).

Depo-Provera suppresses the sexual appetite in men. It can lower the intensity of sex drive and erotic fantasies and urges so that the man may feel less compelled to act on them (Roesler & Witztum, 2000). The use of anti-androgens is sometimes incorrectly referred to as *chemical castration*. Surgical castration—the surgical removal of the testes—has sometimes been performed on convicted rapists and violent sex offenders (Roesler & Witztum, 2000). Unlike surgical castration, the effects of anti-androgens can be reversed when the treatment is terminated.

Social skills training
Behaviour therapy methods that rely on a therapist's coaching and practice to build social skills.

Orgasmic reconditioning
A method for strengthening the connection between sexual arousal and appropriate sexual stimuli (such as fantasies about an adult of the other gender) by repeatedly pairing the desired stimuli with orgasm.

Anti-androgen drug
A chemical substance that reduces the sex drive by lowering the level of testosterone in the bloodstream.

Evidence suggests that anti-androgens help some people when they are used in conjunction with psychological treatment (Roesler & Witztum, 2000). However, according to Ottawa psychiatrist Paul Fedoroff (1995), the value of anti-androgens has been limited by high refusal and dropout rates. Questions also remain concerning side effects.

Ottawa psychiatrist John Bradford has conducted extensive research into the use of pharmacological approaches in treating sexual deviation. In one study, Bradford and others (1995) used the SSRI (selective serotonin reuptake inhibitor) sertraline with pedophiles. The drug reduced all the deviant sexual behaviours but did not decrease normal sexual arousal to consenting sex with adults.

Bradford (2000) has suggested a six-level schema for treatment based on the severity of the deviation. The first level involves the use of cognitive-behavioural treatment, which is provided in all treatment programs. The second level involves treating mild paraphilia, beginning with SSRIs such as Prozac, which is used in treating depression. If the SSRIs are not effective within four to six weeks, a small dose of an anti-androgen would be added in level 3. For moderate and some severe cases, anti-androgen or hormonal treatments would be given in level 4. In more severe cases (level 5), these treatments would be given through injections. For the most serious cases, and especially for those determined to be catastrophic (level 6), the therapist would seek to completely reduce androgens and the sex drive through high dosages of anti-androgens or a luteinizing-hormone-releasing hormone (LHRH).

At all levels of treatment, the goal is to suppress deviant fantasies, urges, and behaviours. Treatment at levels 4 and 5 aims for a strong reduction in sex drive, and at level 6 for the elimination or near-elimination of the sex drive (Bradford, 2000). The broader objective of these treatments is to reduce the possibility of recidivism and further victimization.

Although we have amassed a great deal of research on atypical variations in sexual behaviour, our understanding of them and our treatment approaches to them remain largely in their infancy.

Summing Up

Normal Versus Deviant Sexual Behaviour

What is considered normal in one culture or at a particular time may be considered abnormal in other cultures or at other times. Atypical patterns of sexual arousal or behaviour that become problematic in the eyes of the individual or society are labelled *paraphilias*.

The Paraphilias

Paraphilias involve sexual arousal in response to unusual stimuli such as children or other nonconsenting persons, certain objects, or pain or humiliation. The psychiatric diagnosis of paraphilia requires that the person has acted on these persistent urges in socially unacceptable ways or is distinctly distressed by them. Except in the case of sexual masochism, paraphilias are believed to occur almost exclusively among men.

Fetishism

In fetishism, an inanimate object comes to elicit sexual arousal. In partialism, people are inordinately aroused by a particular body part, such as the feet.

Transvestism

Whereas other fetishists become sexually aroused by handling the fetishistic object while they masturbate, transvestites become excited by wearing articles of clothing—the fetishistic objects—of the other gender.

Exhibitionism

An exhibitionist experiences the compulsion to expose himself to strangers. The typical exhibitionist does not attempt further sexual contact with the victim and so does not usually pose a physical threat.

Obscene Telephone Calling

The obscene phone caller is motivated to become sexually aroused by shocking his victim. Such callers typically masturbate during the phone call or shortly afterward.

Voyeurism

Voyeurs become sexually aroused by watching and do not seek sexual relations with the target. The voyeur may masturbate while peeping or afterward while engaging in voyeuristic fantasies. Like exhibitionists, voyeurs tend to harbour feelings of inadequacy and poor self-esteem and to lack social and sexual skills.

Sexual Masochism

Sexual masochists associate the receipt of pain or humiliation with sexual arousal. Sexual masochists and sexual sadists sometimes form liaisons to meet each other's needs.

Sexual Sadism

Sexual sadism is characterized by persistent, powerful urges and sexual fantasies involving the inflicting of pain and suffering on others to achieve sexual excitement or gratification. Sadomasochists enjoy playing both sadistic and masochistic roles.

Frotteurism

Most frotteuristic acts—rubbing against nonconsenting persons, also known as mashing—take place in crowded places, such as buses, subway cars, or elevators.

Other Paraphilias

Zoophiles desire to have sexual contact with animals. Necrophiles desire to have sexual contact with dead bodies.

Theoretical Perspectives

Biological Perspectives

The links between paraphilias and biological factors have yet to be fully explored.

Psychoanalytic Perspectives

Classical psychoanalytic theory suggests that paraphilias in males are psychological defences against castration anxiety.

Learning Perspectives

Some learning theorists have argued that unusual stimuli may acquire sexually arousing properties through association with sexual arousal or orgasm. Another possibility is that unusual stimuli gradually acquire sexually arousing properties by being incorporated into masturbatory fantasies.

Sociological Perspectives

According to Weinberg's sociological model, the erotic appeal of S&M rituals may result from the opportunity to reverse the customary power relationships that exist between the gender and social classes in society at large.

An Integrated Perspective: The "Lovemap"

Money suggests that childhood experiences etch a pattern in the brain—a lovemap—that determines the types of stimuli and activities that become sexually arousing. In the case of paraphilias, these lovemaps become distorted by early traumatic experiences.

Treatment of the Paraphilias

People with paraphilias may be motivated to seek help because of fears of exposure, criminal prosecution, or humiliation, but they seldom desire to surrender their sexual preferences.

Psychotherapy

Psychoanalysis aims to bring unconscious Oedipal conflicts into awareness so that they can be worked through in adulthood.

Cognitive-Behaviour Therapy

Cognitive-behaviour therapy attempts to eliminate paraphilic behaviours through techniques such as systematic desensitization, aversion therapy, social skills training, covert sensitization, and orgasmic reconditioning.

Biochemical Approaches

The antidepressant Prozac has shown some promise in treating paraphilias. By reducing sex drives, anti-androgen drugs can help people who have difficulty combatting paraphilic urges. They may be most helpful when used in conjunction with psychological treatment.

Test Yourself

Multiple-Choice Questions

1. Sexual behaviours may be considered deviant as a result of the imposition of

   a. social norms
   b. research norms
   c. physical needs
   d. psychological needs

2. One of the major difficulties in discussing atypical sexual behaviours is
   a. finding volunteers for research studies
   b. establishing what constitutes "normal" sexual behaviour
   c. determining underlying thoughts and emotions
   d. helping people who feel guilty or ashamed

3. Except for _____, paraphilias are found almost exclusively in men.
   a. partialism
   b. sexual masochism
   c. transvestism
   d. phone sex

4. A man who is troubled by his desire to dress in women's clothing for the purposes of sexual gratification is labelled a _____.
   a. transsexual
   b. partialist
   c. frotteur
   d. transvestite

5. Which of the following statements is false?
   a. Transvestites are more likely to be older or only children than younger children.
   b. Transvestites are more likely to have closer relationships with their mothers than with their fathers.
   c. Transvestites are more likely to have a gay or lesbian sibling.
   d. Transvestites are more likely to have been forced to wear girls' clothes as a punishment.

6. Approximately what percentage of exhibitionists have been convicted of violent crimes?
   a. 7
   b. 17
   c. 27
   d. 37

7. Stripteasers and sunbathers at nude beaches
   a. are not regarded as exhibitionists
   b. engage in a form of mild exhibitionism
   c. are referred to as "flashers"
   d. are referred to as "normal exhibitionists"

8. _____ involves mutually gratifying sexual interactions between consenting partners.
   a. Voyeurism
   b. Frotteurism
   c. Exhibitionism
   d. Sadomasochism

9. Research on the relationship between testosterone levels and paraphilias has shown that
   a. most paraphilics have increased levels of testosterone
   b. most paraphilics have decreased levels of testosterone
   c. most paraphilics have testosterone levels within normal limits
   d. most paraphilics use anabolic steroids

10. A brain pattern of the ideal lover and ideal erotic activities is known as a _____.
   a. sexual script
   b. lovemap
   c. gender stereotype
   d. fantasy

Critical Thinking Questions

1. How do you decide if a sexual behaviour is "normal"? Where do you draw the line for others? For yourself?

2. When is it okay to cross dress? For a costume party? As part of a role in a play? At a viewing of *The Rocky Horror Picture Show*? In class? As you answered these questions, were you thinking of men or women?

3. Criminal behaviours such as flashing are sometimes referred to as "nuisance" offences, implying that they are basically harmless. Do you agree or disagree? If you have ever experienced one of these offences, do you think your experience affected your answer?

4. Can you think of any explanations for the finding that nearly all people with paraphilias are male?

Visit our Companion Website at www.pearsoned.ca/rathus, **where you can use the interactive Study Guide and link to additional resources on topics discussed in this text.**

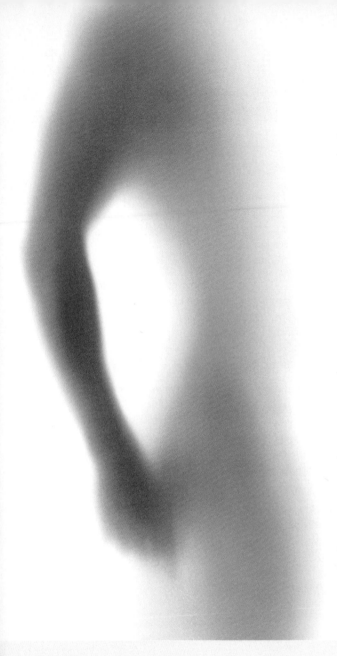

Chapter 16
Sexual Coercion

In recent years there has been a flood of publicity about high-profile sexual assault cases involving celebrities (Michael Jackson), sport stars (Kobe Bryant), politicians, and members of the military.

This chapter is about sexual coercion. As well as actual force or threat, sexual coercion includes *any* sexual activity between an adult and a child. Even when children cooperate, sexual relations with children are considered coercive because children are below the legal age of consent. In this chapter we also look at diverse forms of sexual pressure and sexual harassment.

Sexual Assault

Until 1983 the word *rape* was used in the Canadian Criminal Code to describe forced sexual intercourse. (The American justice system still uses the word, although the definition varies from state to state.) **Sexual assault** has replaced *rape* as the term used in the Canadian legal system. There are three levels of sexual assault. Level 1 encompasses any nonconsensual bodily contact for a sexual purpose, including touching, kissing, and oral, vaginal, and anal sex. Bodily contact can involve any part of the accused's body or an object. Level 2 is sexual assault with a weapon, in which the weapon is used to threaten or injure the victim. Level 3 is aggravated sexual assault, in which the victim is maimed or disfigured or has her or his life endangered. The central issue in determining whether an assault has occurred is whether consent was freely given. The person has to be capable of giving consent; therefore, a person who is drunk, under the influence of drugs, unconscious, fearful, or under age is not considered able to give consent.

Underlining changes to the Criminal Code was the feminist perspective that sexual assault is an act of power and dominance rather than of sex. The Canadian law regarding sexual assault is gender neutral, in that it recognizes that sexual assault can be committed by women against men as well as by someone of the same gender. The law also acknowledges that sexual assault can be committed by one's spouse.

It is important to note that consent for one type of sexual behaviour does not mean consent for other behaviours. In Guelph, Ontario, a man received a jail sentence because he engaged in anal sex despite his partner's objections. After having sexual relations together for some months, the man asked the woman about having anal sex; she did not want to try it, however. A week later, during a sexual interaction that had included vaginal intercourse, he penetrated the woman anally despite her resistance. The woman later went to the police, and the man was charged with sexual assault ("Sexual assault plea," 1994). In another case, a Toronto man received a jail sentence after he removed his condom during sexual intercourse. The victim had consented to having intercourse only if the man was wearing a condom, but he continued having sex with her nonetheless (Oakes, 1994). More recently, an orderly visited the maternity ward in a Toronto hospital and told female patients that he was a lactation consultant (there were in fact no male lactation consultants at the hospital). Because he was wearing the appropriate hospital gown, the patients assumed he was there to show them how to breast-feed properly. He was later charged with sexual assault after one of the patients asked a nurse if the lactation consultant would be returning ("House arrest," 2002).

In Canada, people who are infected with the HIV virus can be charged with sexual assault if they do not disclose their HIV status to their partners before engaging in sexual behaviour with them. Across Canada there have been several such convictions (discussed in Chapter 14).

Incidence of Sexual Assault

According to Statistics Canada (2003b), in 2002 there were 27 100 sexual offences reported to the police. Level 1 offences accounted for 88% of these and the more

Sexual assault
Nonconsensual bodily contact for a sexual purpose.

serious assault levels 2 and 3 accounted for 2%, with other sexual offences (mainly against children) accounting for 10%. Once reported, sexual offences are less likely than other violent offences to result in charges. However, once convicted, sexual offenders in adult court are more likely to be imprisoned than other violent offenders (Statistics Canada, 2003).

The number of reported sexual assaults decreased by 36% from 1993 to 2002 (the decrease occurred every year, except for a 1% increase from 2000 to 2001). Rates of sexual assault vary considerably across the country, with the lowest rate per 100 000 population in Quebec (50) and the highest rates in Canada's North (Yukon 254, Northwest Territories 360, and Nunavut 788). Among cities, the highest rates are in St. John's and Saskatoon. Youth between the ages of 12 and 17 account for 17% of sexual assaults. Among adults, males are the offender in 98% of sexual assaults. The rate of offending is highest among males between the ages of 25 and 44 and lowest for males aged 55 and older (Statistics Canada, 2002g).

What proportion of women are sexually assaulted? Social surveys on sexual assault experiences produce varying findings, depending on what questions are asked and what groups are sampled:

■ In 1993, Statistics Canada surveyed a national sample of 13 300 Canadian women. The survey asked if, since the age of 16, the women had experienced unwanted sexual touching or force or attempted force aimed at engaging them in any sexual activity. Thirty-nine percent of the women reported having experienced one or both of these situations (Roberts, 1994).

■ In a survey of women attending gynecology clinics in London, Ontario, 23% reported that they had been verbally or physically coerced into having sexual contact against their will (Fisher et al., 2000).

A World of Diversity

NOT ALL SEX OFFENDERS ARE MEN

Not too long ago it used to be believed that women did not commit sexual assaults. However, in recent years there have been numerous media stories of sexual assaults committed by women:

■ In Hamilton, Ontario, a teenage girl sought revenge against another girl who she said had stolen her boyfriend. She forced the other girl to take off her clothes and left her naked in an underground parking garage ("Girl lied," 2001).

■ In St. Catharine's, Ontario, a 42-year-old woman pleaded guilty to assault after she undid her son's pants and forcefully grabbed his genitals in front of his friends ("Mother guilty," 1999).

■ In Uxbridge, Ontario, two female employees (aged 41, 29) at a young-offender facility were charged with sexually assaulting male inmates ("Jail workers," 2002).

■ In Guelph, Ontario, a 31-year-old woman admitted in court that she had sex with her son's 13-year-old friend (Tracey, 2001).

■ In Kitchener, Ontario, a 35-year-old woman pleaded guilty to having sexual intercourse with her two teenage sons on two separate occasions (Wood, 2004).

■ In Saskatoon, a 13-year-old girl pleaded guilty to forcing an older teenage girl to work as a street prostitute (Canadian Press, 2001a).

■ In Vernon, British Columbia, a 24-year-old woman who pretended she was a man in order to have sex with young women was convicted of sexually assaulting five girls between the ages of 12 and 17 (Canadian Press, 1995b).

■ In Kamloops, British Columbia, a 32-year-old mother was convicted of sexual exploitation for having sex with her 16-year-old female foster child. The woman and the teenager began living together as a couple in a love relationship (Bailey, I., 2000).

Sometimes, sexual assault by a woman involves aiding or abetting men who are attacking another woman. In such cases, a woman may be used to lure another woman to a reasonably safe place for the assault, or the woman may hold the other woman down while she is assaulted.

It remains true, however, that the vast majority of sexual assaults are committed by men.

- Twelve percent of female students surveyed at an Ontario university reported having been forced to have sex by physical threats, and 8% said they had been forced to have sex because of verbal threats (Rye, 2001).

- In the Ethnocultural Communities Facing AIDS study of Canadian immigrants from diverse regions of the world, 39% of women and 19% of men from English-speaking Caribbean countries reported that they had been coerced or forced to have sex against their will, compared with 8% of women and 1% of men from the Latin American communities (Maticka-Tyndale et al., 1995). (This study is described in more detail in Chapter 1.)

Although people of all ages, races, and social classes are sexually assaulted, children and younger women are more likely to be assaulted. In 2003, in Canada, 61% of victims of sexual offences reported to police were children and youth under the age of 18 (Statistics Canada, 2005). Among this age group, 80% of sexual assault victims are female. A study of street youth in Toronto found that young women who are homeless are at even greater risk of being sexually assaulted (Gaetz, 2004).

Most sexual assaults go unreported; according to the 1993 Statistics Canada survey, only 6% of women who experienced sexual assault had reported it to the police. The belief that the incident was too minor to report, the expectation that the police would not be able to do anything, and the desire to protect their privacy were the main reasons the women gave for not reporting (Roberts, 1994). On the other hand, there are also some cases in which an alleged assault did not take place. One of the most publicized examples of this occurred when a councillor in Alberta disappeared for three days and was found in Las Vegas. She initially claimed she had been kidnapped and sexually assaulted. However, she later retracted her story (Canadian Press, 2003a). It is important to put cases of false reporting in perspective. Such cases are vastly outnumbered by assaults that go unreported.

In Canada there is a rising incidence of drug-facilitated sexual assaults. A study based in British Columbia concluded that in 2002, 27% of sexual assaults involved drugs such as GHB and Rohypnol (McGregor et al., 2004). These drugs are typically mixed in with drinks served to the victim. They are odourless and tasteless and result in loosened inhibitions and amnesia for up to 12 hours. Often the victims have little or no memory of what occurred after ingesting the drug and thus are less likely to report the incident.

In Toronto, a man visiting a couple put a drug into a drink and served it to them. He then sexually assaulted both the man and the woman. In court the two victims reported that for brief moments they observed the accused sexually assaulting one or both of them, but because of the drug's effect, they could not act to stop the assaults. The accused was found guilty of sexual assault and of administering a noxious substance (Small, 2004).

Types of Sexual Assault

One of the central myths in our culture is that most sexual assaults are perpetrated by strangers lurking in dark alleyways or by intruders who climb through open windows in the middle of the night. In fact, most women are assaulted by men they know—and often by men they have come to trust (Roberts, 1994).

STRANGER SEXUAL ASSAULT **Stranger assault** refers to a sexual assault that is committed by an assailant (or assailants) not previously known to the person attacked. In 2002 only 20% of reported sexual assaults in Canada were committed by a stranger (Statistics Canada, 2003b). The stranger often selects targets who seem vulnerable— women who live alone, who are older or retarded, who are walking down deserted streets, or who are asleep or intoxicated. After choosing a target, the assailant may search for a safe time and place to commit the crime, such as a deserted, run-down part of town, a darkened street, or a second-floor apartment without window bars or locks.

Stranger sexual assault Sexual assault that is committed by an assailant previously unknown to the person who is assaulted.

ACQUAINTANCE SEXUAL ASSAULT   Canadians are more likely to be assaulted by people they know than by strangers. In Canada in 2002, 51% of victims of sexual offences were sexually assaulted by a friend or acquaintance, while 28% were victimized by a family member (Statistics Canada, 2003b). **Acquaintance assaults** are much less likely than assaults by strangers to be reported to the police (Schafran, 1995), in part because victims may not perceive coercion by acquaintances as an assault.

DATE SEXUAL ASSAULT One of the most common forms of acquaintance sexual assault occurs within the dating context. Men who sexually assault a dating partner may believe that acceptance of a date indicates willingness to engage in coitus. Other men assume that women who frequent places like singles bars are expressing tacit agreement to have sex with men who show interest in them. Some assailants believe that a woman who resists advances is just "protesting too much" so that she will not appear "easy." They interpret resistance as coyness, in other words; as a ploy in the cat-and-mouse game that to them typifies the "battle of the sexes." They may believe that when a woman says no, she means maybe, and when she says maybe, she means yes. They may thus not see themselves as committing sexual assault—but of course they are.

It is important, however, to acknowledge that most people will not force a non-consenting person to have sex. For example, in a study of New Brunswick university students, Byers and Lewis (1988) found that most males accepted a dating partner's refusal to have sex.

The issue of consent lies at the heart of whether a sexual act is an assault. Unlike cases of stranger assault, date sexual assault occurs within a context in which sexual relations could occur voluntarily. Thus, the issue of consent can become murky. The defendant may concede that sexual intercourse took place but claim that it was consensual. Judges and juries face the task of discerning shadings in the meaning of "consent." Lawyers on both sides vie to persuade them to see things their way.

Sexual assault charges in a dating situation often come down to his word against hers. Her word often becomes less persuasive in the eyes of the jury if it was clear that she had consented to mutual activities beforehand, such as sharing dinner, attending the movies together, accompanying him to his home, sharing a drink alone, and perhaps kissing or petting. Let us state in no uncertain terms, however, that it does not matter whether the woman wore a "sexy" outfit, was "on the pill," or shared a passionate kiss or embrace with the man. If the encounter ended with the woman's being forcibly violated, then it is a sexual assault. When a woman says no, a man must take no for an answer.

The problem of date sexual assault has been subjected to closer public scrutiny in recent years. "Take Back the Night" marches have become a common form of student protest on university campuses against the sexual misconduct of men. Many universities have mandated date sexual assault seminars and workshops.

GANGS AND SEXUAL ASSAULT Exercise of power appears to be the major motive behind gang assaults, although some attackers may also be expressing anger against women. Gang members often believe that once women engage in coitus, they are "whores." Thus, each offending gang member may become more aggressive as he takes his turn.

The Koss college survey (Koss et al., 1987) showed that sexual assaults involving a group of assailants tend to be more vicious than individual assaults (Gidycz & Koss, 1990). Relatively few survivors of gang assaults reported the attack to police or sought support from a crisis centre.

SEXUAL ASSAULT AGAINST MALES According to 1997 data from police forces in six provinces, 18% of sexual offence victims are men; however, males comprise

Acquaintance sexual assault Sexual assault by an acquaintance of the person who is assaulted.

31% of victims under the age of 12 (Statistics Canada, 1997). In a study of university students in New Brunswick, about one-fifth of the men reported that in the previous year they had been coerced into having sex (O'Sullivan et al., 1998).

This finding runs contrary to the stereotype that men are willing to have sex all the time. Many women believe this stereotype, as demonstrated in a study of women living in the Kitchener/Waterloo area of Ontario (Clements-Schreiber & Rempel, 1995). Eighty-five percent of the women believed that it is easy for a woman to sexually arouse a man if she wants to, and 68% believed that men enjoy getting sexual advances from women even when they don't respond positively. According to the researchers, it is beliefs such as these that might make women think that male refusals should not be taken seriously.

Sarrel and Masters (1992) reported 11 cases of men who were sexually assaulted by women, including one case of a 37-year-old man who was coerced into sexual intercourse by two women who accosted him at gunpoint. In another case, a 27-year-old man fell asleep in his hotel room with a woman he had just met in a bar and then awakened to find that he was bound to his bed, gagged, and blindfolded. He was then forced into sexual intercourse with four different women, who threatened him with castration if he did not perform satisfactorily.

Although not considered sexual assault, some women use sexual enticement as a means of robbing a man. In Guelph, Ontario, after a man went to the apartment of a woman he had met, she began performing oral sex on him and stole money from his wallet in the process (Tracey, 1999). In Toronto, a woman arranged dates with men after putting personal ads in newspapers. She would find a reason to persuade the man to use an automatic teller machine, note his PIN number, and later steal his wallet ("Woman faces," 2000). In Winnipeg, a man met a woman through a chat line and agreed to go to her house for a "sexual fantasy." When he arrived, two men stole his wallet and forced him to give them his PIN number ("Chat-line romance," 2000). In Brampton, Ontario, a 34-year-old man arranged to meet a woman he chatted with online. When he arrived, he was met by two men who robbed him at knife point, threatened to shoot him, and held him captive for 14 hours (Appleby, 2005). There may well be many other cases that are not reported because adult males would typically be embarrassed about being in these situations. What is most interesting about these examples of male victimization is that there are no education programs warning adult males about being cautious on the Internet.

Despite the examples given, most sexual assaults against men are committed by other men. While they often occur in prison settings, some occur outside prison walls. In recent years the media have been full of stories about men in positions of authority, such as teachers and priests, assaulting boys.

There have been few studies of sexual assault on gay and bisexual men. Researchers in Vancouver (Ratner et al., 2003) asked 358 gay and bisexual men aged 19 to 35 if they had ever been forced into unwanted sex. Fourteen percent reported having been coerced or forced into sex before the age of 14. Half of the reported incidents involved forced receptive anal intercourse. Men who had been sexually coerced had lower self-esteem and higher rates of depression. They were more likely to abuse alcohol and to have attempted suicide.

Males can also be assaulted in college sports hazing rituals. A rookie football player withdrew from McGill University after his teammates forced him to go down on all fours and prodded him anally with a broom handle. Other rookies were coerced into simulating oral sex on one another in their boxer shorts (Peritz, 2005).

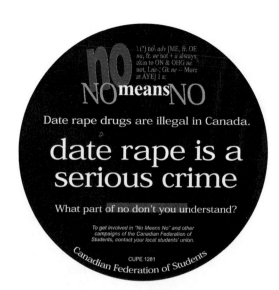

Combatting Sexual Assault on Campus.

Many Canadian universities and colleges have instituted awareness programs to combat the problem of date sexual assault and other sexual assaults on campus.

Male survivors tend to suffer greater physical injury than female survivors (Kaufman et al., 1980). Males are more often attacked by multiple assailants, are held captive longer, and are more often reluctant to report the assault (Gerrol & Resick, 1988; Groth & Burgess, 1980; Myers, 1989). After all, victimization does not fit the male stereotype of capacity for self-defence. Men are expected to be not only strong but also silent. However, male survivors may suffer traumatic effects similar to those suffered by female survivors (Calhoun & Atkeson, 1991). Additionally, boys assaulted by men may become confused about their sexual orientation.

MARITAL SEXUAL ASSAULT Although there are many countries where it is not against the law for a husband to sexually assault his wife, in Canada it is clearly illegal. Motives for marital sexual assault vary. A husband may be unwilling to accept a rebuff because he believes that he is entitled to sexual access to his wife any time he desires it. He may believe it is his wife's duty to satisfy his sexual needs even when she is uninterested. Some men use sex to dominate their wives. Others degrade their wives through sex, especially after arguments. Sexual coercion often occurs within a pattern of marital violence, battering, and physical intimidation (Finkelhor & Yllo, 1982; Russell, 1982).

Social Attitudes and Myths That Encourage Sexual Assault

Many people believe a number of myths about sexual assault, such as "Women say no when they mean yes," "All women like a man who is pushy and forceful," and "The way women dress, they are just asking to be assaulted." Yet another myth is that deep down, women want to be assaulted (Osman, 2003).

Sexual assault myths create a social climate that legitimizes sexual assault. Though both men and women may subscribe to sexual assault myths, researchers at the University of British Columbia found that male students show greater acceptance of these myths than do female students (Kennedy & Gorzalka, 2002). There are also ethnic differences, with Asian students being more likely to accept these myths. However, the longer the Asian students have been in Canada, the less likely they are to accept these myths. Men also cling more stubbornly to myths about date sexual assault, even after taking date sexual assault education classes designed to challenge these views (Lenihan et al., 1992). Such myths do not occur in a social vacuum. They are related to other social attitudes, including gender-role stereotyping, perception of sex as adversarial, and acceptance of violence in relationships.

Many observers contend that our society encourages sexual assault by socializing males into socially and sexually dominant roles. Males are often reinforced from childhood for aggressive and competitive behaviour.

Research with university students supports the connection between stereotypical masculine identification and tendencies to sexual assault. In New Brunswick, researchers compared students who believed in strictly traditional gender roles with students who held less rigid attitudes. Men who engaged in coercive sex were found to be more likely to hold more traditional views of women's roles and more likely to hold coercion-supportive beliefs (Byers & Eno, 1991). Men with traditional views were more likely to ignore a partner's saying that she does not want to have sex. The "traditionalists" express a greater likelihood of committing sexual assault, are more accepting of violence against women, are more likely to blame sexual assault survivors, and are more aroused by depictions of sexual assault (Raichle & Lambert, 2000).

Young men may come to view dates not as chances to get to know their partners but as opportunities for sexual conquest, in which the object is to overcome their partners' resistance. Sexual behaviour and sports in our culture are linked through common idioms. A young man may be taunted by his friends after a date with a woman with such questions as "Did you score?" or, more bluntly, "Did you get in?"

Some researchers, such as Queen's University psychologist Vernon Quinsey, hypothesize that evolutionary psychology can account for the role of male sexual competitiveness in sexual assault. According to this perspective, since the main constraint on male reproductive success is the limited number of potential mating partners, males are obliged to compete with each other for mating opportunities. In order to increase their opportunities, some men will engage in sexual coercion (Quinsey, 2002). For example, Lalumiere and Quinsey (1996) found that men with extensive casual-sex experience have higher rates of sexual coercion than other men.

Characteristics of Sexually Coercive Men

Although sexual aggressiveness may be woven into our social fabric, not all men are equally vulnerable to such cultural influences. Canadian researchers are playing a leading role in determining factors that predict which men are more likely to be sexually coercive.

Some sexually coercive men feel socially inadequate and report that they cannot find willing partners. Some lack social skills and avoid social interactions with women (Overholser & Beck, 1986). Some are basically antisocial and have long histories of violent behaviour (Knight et al., 1991). Several Canadian studies have identified particular characteristics of sexually coercive men. Both sensation seeking and an early history of behavioural problems are strongly related to sexual coercion (Harris et al., 2003; Lalumiere & Quinsey, 1996). Sexually coercive men were found to have high levels of hostility, poor sexual adjustment, and serious problems with alcohol (Firestone et al., 1998). Men with these characteristics tend to act on their impulses regardless of the cost to the person they attack. Some were sexually victimized or physically assaulted as children (Groth, 1978; Sack & Mason, 1980). As adults, they may be identifying with the aggressor role in interpersonal relationships. The use of alcohol may also dampen self-restraint and spur sexual aggressiveness. In an Ontario population survey, adults who reported experiencing parental sexual abuse were more than twice as likely to have had parents who had

What Motivates Sexual Assailants?
Sure, sexual assault has a good deal to do with sex—but is it sex for the sake of sex or is sex used as a weapon? Research suggests that many sexual assailants use sex to express anger toward women, power over women, or sadistic impulses. In fact, some men do not become sexually aroused unless they hurt or humiliate women. Make no mistake about it: Sexual assault is a crime of violence and should be treated as such.

substance abuse problems (Walsh et al., 2003). In another Ontario study, sexual offenders had significantly greater problems with alcohol abuse than other violent offenders (Looman et al., 2004). The researchers speculated that something about the combination of alcohol abuse and problems with intimacy contributes specifically to sexual offending.

In a sample of men from a Canadian city, beliefs in sexual-assault myths and hostility were *not* predictive of male coercive behaviour (Senn et al., 2000). The fact that this is one of the few studies on sexual coercion that has attempted to randomly sample men from the community may account for findings that differ in some ways from those of other studies. The study did find that men who were sexually coercive were more likely to have experienced childhood abuse, had more sexual partners during adolescence, and lacked the ability to express their emotions (Senn et al., 2000). In another study of male sexual aggressors, University of Montreal researchers reported that male adult sexual aggressors were more likely to have experienced childhood sexual abuse, pornography during childhood/adolescence, and deviant sexual fantasies during childhood/adolescence (Beauregard et al., 2004).

For some sexually coercive men, violence and sexual arousal become enmeshed. Thus, they seek to combine sex and violence to enhance their sexual arousal (Quinsey et al., 1984). Some studies find that sexually coercive men are more sexually aroused (as measured by the size of erections) by verbal descriptions, films, or audiotapes that portray themes of sexual assault than are other people (Lalumiere et al., 2003). Other researchers, however, have failed to find deviant patterns of arousal in sexually coercive men (Hall, 1989). These researchers find that, as a group, sexually coercive men, like most other people, are more aroused by stimuli depicting mutually consenting sexual activity than by sexual assault stimuli.

According to some Canadian psychologists (Harris et al., 1999), these discrepant findings may be explained by the fact that some sexual offenders deliberately modify their arousal levels in these studies so as to appear like non-sex offenders. To improve the accuracy of arousal testing, Harris et al. found that requiring study participants to complete a semantic tracking task that involves pushing two different buttons in response to sexual touching and sexual violence words was better able to differentiate sexual offenders from nonoffenders than using only phallometric measures of erections.

Motives in Sexual Assault

Although sexual arousal is an obvious and important element in sexual assault (Barbaree & Marshall, 1991), some researchers argue that anger and power are the basic motivations for sexual assault (Gebhard et al., 1965; Groth & Birnbaum, 1979). Other researchers believe that sexual motivation plays a key role in at least some sexual assaults (Baumeister et al., 2002).

Adjustment of Sexual Assault Survivors

Many women who are sexually assaulted fear for their lives during the attack. Whether or not weapons or threats are used, the experience of being dominated by an unpredictable and threatening assailant is terrifying. The woman does not know whether she will survive and may feel helpless to do anything about it. Afterward, many survivors enter a **crisis.**

Crisis A highly stressful situation that can involve shock, loss of self-esteem, and lessened capacity for making decisions.

Many survivors are extremely distraught in the days and weeks following the sexual assault (Koss et al., 2003). They have trouble sleeping and cry frequently. They tend to report eating problems, cystitis, headaches, irritability, mood changes, anxiety and depression, and menstrual irregularity. They may become withdrawn, sullen, and mistrustful (McArthur, 1990). Some survivors experience feelings of guilt and shame (McArthur, 1990). Emotional distress tends to peak in severity by about three weeks following the assault and generally remains high for about a month before beginning to abate (Koss et al., 2003). About one survivor in four encounters emotional problems that linger beyond a year (Calhoun & Atkeson, 1991).

Sexual assault survivors may also suffer physical injuries and may contract sexually transmitted infections, even AIDS, as a result of a sexual assault. They may also be at risk for long-term health complications. Survivors may encounter problems at work, such as trouble relating to co-workers or bosses or difficulty concentrating. Work adjustment, however, usually returns to normal within a year (Calhoun & Atkeson, 1991). Relationships with spouses or partners may also be impaired. Disturbances in sexual functioning are common and may last for years—or even a lifetime. Survivors often report a lack of sexual desire, fear of sex, and difficulty becoming sexually aroused (Koss et al., 2003).

SEXUAL ASSAULT AND PSYCHOLOGICAL DISORDERS Sexual assault survivors are at higher-than-average risk of developing anxiety disorders and depression, and of abusing alcohol and other substances. Researchers at Carleton University found that university women who had experienced sexual coercion in their dating relationships were more likely to have lower levels of self-esteem and sexual self-esteem. They were also more likely to experience depression (Offman & Matheson, 2004). Survivors may experience **post-traumatic stress disorder** (PTSD) (Koss et al., 2003), a disorder brought on by exposure to a traumatic event; for example, it is often seen in soldiers who have been in combat (American Psychiatric Association, 2000). People with PTSD may have flashbacks to the traumatic experience, disturbing dreams, emotional numbing, and nervousness. PTSD may persist for years. The person may also develop fears of situations connected with the traumatic event. For example, a woman who was sexually assaulted on an elevator may develop a fear of riding in elevators by herself. Researchers also report that women who blame themselves for the sexual assault tend to suffer more severe depression and adjustment problems, including sexual problems (Koss et al., 2002).

IF YOU ARE SEXUALLY ASSAULTED . . . Elizabeth Powell (1996) offers the following suggestions to those who are sexually assaulted:

1   Don't change anything about your body—don't wash, don't even comb your hair. Leave your clothes as they are. Otherwise you could destroy evidence.

2.   Strongly consider reporting the incident to police. You may prevent another woman from being assaulted, and you will be taking charge, starting on the path from victim to survivor.

3.   Ask a relative or friend to take you to a hospital if you can't get an ambulance or a police car. If you call the hospital, tell them why you're requesting an ambulance, in case they are able to send someone trained to deal with sexual assault cases.

4.   Seek help in an assertive way. Seek medical help. Injuries you are unaware of may be detected. Insist that a written or photographic record be made to document your condition. If you decide to file charges, the prosecutor may need this evidence to obtain a conviction.

5.   Question health professionals. Ask about your biological risks. Ask what treatments are available. Ask for whatever will help make you comfortable. Call the shots. Demand confidentiality if that's what you want. Refuse what you don't want.

You may also wish to call a sexual assault hotline or sexual assault crisis centre for advice, if one is available in your area. A sexual assault crisis volunteer may be available to accompany you to the hospital and help see you through the medical evaluation and police investigation if you report the attack.

Post-traumatic stress disorder A type of stress reaction brought on by a traumatic event and characterized by flashbacks of the experience in the form of disturbing dreams or intrusive recollections, a sense of emotional numbing or restricted range of feelings, and heightened body arousal. Abbreviated *PTSD*.

Canadian Association of Sexual Assault Centres
Lists sexual assault crisis centres and transition houses.

www.casac.ca

Treatment of Sexual Assault Survivors

Treatment of sexual assault survivors typically involves a two-stage process of helping the victim through the crisis after the attack and then helping to foster long-term adjustment. Crisis intervention typically provides the survivor with support and information to help her express her feelings and develop strategies for coping with the trauma.

It is especially important for family and friends to be supportive by assuring the victim that they believe her account and that they will support whatever decisions she makes about reporting the assault and seeking professional help. This will help her regain feelings of empowerment.

Psychotherapy, involving group or individual approaches, can help the survivor cope with the emotional consequences of sexual assault, avoid self-blame, improve self-esteem, validate the welter of feelings surrounding the experience, and establish or maintain loving relationships. Therapists also recognize the importance of helping the sexual assault survivor mobilize social support. In major cities and many towns, concerned men and women have formed sexual assault crisis centres and hotlines, peer counselling groups, and referral agencies geared to assessing and meeting survivors' needs after the assault. Some counsellors are specially trained to mediate between survivors of sexual assault and their loved ones—husbands, lovers, and so forth. These counsellors help people to discuss and work through the often complex emotional legacy of sexual assault. Phone numbers for these services can be obtained from crisis centres, women's shelters, hospital emergency departments, the police department, or the telephone directory.

Preventing Sexual Assault

Eliminating sexual assault altogether would probably require massive changes in cultural attitudes and socialization processes. However, educational intervention on a smaller scale may reduce its incidence. Many colleges and universities offer educational programs about date sexual assault.

A World of Diversity

BLAMING THE VICTIM TO AN EXTREME

This is a story about women that begins with a man. His name is Ghazi al Marine. He had been married just three months—the happiest months of his life, he told us—when a killer came to their home and shot his wife.

"She was lying in that corner," he says, pointing. "The blood was everywhere."

That night, police arrested her brother. Apparently, he murdered his sister to preserve his family's honor—an honor that was stained when she was raped three years ago. From the time

she was raped until her marriage, she had lived in a prison. Not because she had done anything wrong but because, like dozens of other women, she needed to be protected from her family.

The reputation of a family in certain countries rests on the reputation of its women. All it takes for violence to be justified is for a woman to be seen with a man she is not related to, for her to reject an unwanted suitor, or even [for her] to be the victim of a sexual crime.

In Jordan, more than 30 women a year are killed in the name of "honor," which means one-third of the nation's murders. In Pakistan, human rights

organizations say, thousands of women and girls are stabbed, shot, maimed or burned each year.

In Bangladesh, a typical punishment is sulfuric acid thrown in the woman's face. "Why did they do this to us?" asks Bina Akhtar in a *20/20* interview. "We didn't harm anyone." "It's the male feeling that they are responsible and authorized to control women's lives and bodies," says Asthma Khadar, a Jordanian human rights lawyer.

Source: Reprinted with permission from Sheila MacVicar (2000, June 5). "Crimes in the Name of Honor." **www.abcnews.com**.

Taking Back the Night. Whose fault is it if a woman is sexually assaulted when she goes out alone at night? Many women—and men who care about women—have marched to demonstrate their disgust with the men who might assault them if they were out walking by them- selves and with a society that too often blames the victim for what happens to her.

Until the basic cultural attitudes that support sexual assault change, however, "sexual assault prevention" means that women must take a number of precautions. Why should women be advised to take measures to avoid sexual assault? Is not the very listing of such measures a subtle way of blaming the woman if she should fall prey to an attacker? No! To provide the information is not to blame the person who is attacked. The offender is *always* responsible for the assault. But taking certain pre- cautions, such as those discussed in the nearby Applied Knowledge feature, may lower a woman's risk of being assaulted.

Applied Knowledge

SEXUAL ASSAULT PREVENTION

The New Our Bodies, Ourselves (Boston Women's Health Book Collective, 1992; Copyright © 1984, 1992 by The Boston Women's Health Book Collective. Reprinted with permission) lists several suggestions that may help prevent sexual assault:

- Establish a set of signals with other women in the building or neighborhood.
- List yourself in the phone direc- tory and on the mailbox by your first initials only.

- Use dead-bolt locks.
- Keep doorways and entries well lit.
- Keep your keys handy when approaching the car or the front door.
- Avoid deserted areas.
- Do not allow strange men into your house or apartment without first checking their credentials.
- Check out the back seat of your car before entering.
- Don't give rides to hitchhikers (including women hitchhikers).

Powell (1996) adds the following suggestions for avoiding date sexual assault:

- Communicate your sexual limits to your date. Tell your partner how far you would like to go so that he will know what the limits are. For example, if your partner starts fondling you in ways that make you uncomfortable, you might say, "I'd prefer if you didn't touch me there. I really like you, but I prefer not getting so intimate at this point in our relationship."
- Meet new dates in public places, and avoid driving with a stranger or a group of people you've met. When meeting a new date, drive in your own car and meet your date at a public place. Don't drive

with strangers or offer rides to strangers or groups of people. In some cases of date sexual assault, the group disappears just prior to the assault.

■ State your refusal definitively. Be firm in refusing a sexual overture. Look your partner straight in the eye. The more definite you are, the less likely that your partner will misinterpret your wishes.

■ Become aware of your fears. Take notice of any fears of displeasing your partner that might stifle your assertiveness. If your partner is truly respectful of you, you need not fear an angry or demeaning response. But if your partner is not respectful, it is best to become aware of it and end the relationship right there.

■ Pay attention to your "vibes." Trust your gut-level feelings. Many victims of acquaintance sexual assault said afterward that they had had a strange feeling about the man but failed to pay attention to it.

■ Be especially cautious if you are in a new environment, be it a college or a foreign country. You may be especially vulnerable to exploitation when you are becoming acquainted with a new environment, different people, and different customs.

■ If you have broken off a relationship with someone you don't really like or feel good about, don't let him into your place. Many so-called date sexual assaults are committed by ex-lovers and ex-boyfriends.

Confronting an Attacker: Should You Fight, Flee, or Plead?

What if you are accosted by a sexual assailant? Should you try to fight him off, flee, or try to plead with him to stop? Some women have thwarted attacks by pleading or crying. Yet research has shown that less forceful forms of resistance, such as pleading, begging, or reasoning, can be dangerous strategies. They may not fend off the attack and may heighten the probability of injury (Bart & O'Brien, 1985). Screaming may be particularly effective in warding off some attacks (Byers & Lewis, 1988). Running away is sometimes an effective strategy for avoiding a sexual assault (Bart & O'Brien, 1985), but running may not be effective if the woman is outnumbered by a group of assailants (Gidycz & Koss, 1990). No single strategy is likely to be helpful in all sexual assault cases.

Self-defence training may help women become better prepared to fend off an assailant. Yet physical resistance may spur some assailants to become more aggressive (Powell, 1996). Thompson (1991) suggests that effective self-defence is built upon the use of multiple strategies, ranging from attempts to avoid potential sexual assault situations (such as by installing home security systems or walking only in well-lit areas), to acquiescence when active resistance would seem too risky, to the use of more active verbal or physical forms of resistance in some low-risk situations.

Coercive Verbal Pressure Tactics

Verbal sexual coercion is persistent verbal pressure or the use of seduction "lines" to manipulate a person into sexual activity. Verbal coercion is difficult to define precisely. People use a wide spectrum of persuasion ranging from coaxing to outright bullying and threats; in the middle of the spectrum is a grey area that might be considered coercive by some but not by others. Verbal coercion is used far more often than physical coercion. In a study involving students from more than 40 universities and community colleges across Canada, DeKeseredy and Kelly (1993) found that since beginning university, 32% of the women had given in to sex play (not involving intercourse) because they were overwhelmed by a man's continual arguments and pressure. Twenty percent said they had given in to sexual intercourse because of this kind of verbal pressure. Among a community sample of men from an Ontario city, 23% reported that they had used arguments and verbal pressure to try to get a woman to engage in sex play, and 9% said they had used this kind of pressure to have sexual intercourse (Senn et al., 2000).

Researchers in Toronto studied young adults who were involved in street life to find out what strategies were used to coerce a dating partner into having sex (Strike et al., 2001). The sample included heterosexual, gay, lesbian, and bisexual people. Almost all the men and women had experienced being pressured to have sex, and 62% of the men and 42% of the women admitted pressuring a date to have sex. The tactics used to get sex included

■ *Using alcohol and drugs to loosen a partner's reluctance to have sex.* Some of those who had been coerced said they used alcohol or drugs to loosen their own inhibitions.

■ *Using obligations, expectations, and guilt.* Some coerced their partner by threatening to end the relationship or to get sex elsewhere. Another strategy involved saying how much they were looking forward to having sex. Some would make their partner feel that they were obliged to have sex, and would try to make them feel guilty for not having it. A commonly held belief was that if one's partner paid for date-related expenses such as dinner and drinks, one was obliged to have sex.

■ *Exploiting emotional and economic vulnerability.* People with low self-esteem may be told that they are worthless and should consider themselves lucky to be in their current relationship. Some of the men and women admitted that they manipulated a person who had little or no economic resources by providing food, housing, or money in return for sex. A more extreme example of this exploitation occurred when a man provided a woman with shelter and demanded that she provide sex not only to him but to his friends as well.

A number of the participants in the study admitted that they had developed a sophisticated set of strategies to obtain sex, strategies that included knowing when and how to use them. While some would continue to pressure a reluctant partner, others stopped trying to get sex when the partner was adamant in refusing it. Those who had been coerced to have sex often resigned themselves to simply getting it over with so that their partner would stop bothering them (Strike et al., 2001).

With a community-based sample of men living in Windsor, Ontario, Senn and colleagues (2000) found that the most common strategy used to coerce a reluctant partner into having sex involved continual arguments and verbal pressure. The second most common strategy involved providing the woman with alcohol or drugs.

A common sexual stereotype is that women never have to use pressure tactics to engage in sex with a male partner. Researchers at the University of Guelph found that some young women used a diversity of sexual pressure tactics to get a reluctant male partner to engage in sex (Parr-LeFeuve & Desmarais, 2005).

Verbal coercion also occurs in same-sex relationships. In a study of these relationships in Canada and the United States, Melanie Beres (2002) found that 23% of women involved in lesbian relationships have experienced sexual coercion from another woman. The rates for men are somewhat higher, with 35% having experienced sexual coercion from another man.

Sexual Abuse of Children

Many view sexual abuse of children as among the most heinous of crimes. Canadians are shocked and horrified when they find out about children being sexually abused. One of the most publicized cases was the sexual abuse of boys by priests at the Mount Cashel orphanage in Newfoundland. Eleven priests were convicted for those offences and the Newfoundland government paid $11 million to 40 abuse victims. Children who are sexually assaulted often suffer social and emotional

The Mount Cashel Scandal. One of the most publicized child sex-abuse cases in Canada involved Catholic priests at the Mount Cashel orphanage in Newfoundland.

problems that impair their development and persist into adulthood, affecting their self-esteem and their ability to form intimate relationships.

No one knows how many children are sexually abused. *Sexual Offences Against Children and Youth*, the 1984 Badgley Report commissioned by the Canadian Parliament, estimated that 9% of boys and 22% of girls were sexually assaulted before the age of 18. In 2003 there were just over 9000 reported sexual assaults against children and youth aged 17 and under (Statistics Canada, 2005g). Eighty percent of the victims were female and two-thirds of these females were between 11 and 17 years old. In a sample of men from an Ontario city, 8% reported having been sexually abused in childhood (Senn et al., 2000). Whatever its actual prevalence, sexual abuse of children cuts across all racial, ethnic, and economic boundaries (Alter-Reid et al., 1986).

What Is Sexual Abuse of Children?

Sexual abuse of children ranges from exhibitionism, kissing, fondling, and sexual touching to oral sex and anal intercourse and, with girls, vaginal intercourse. Sexual contact between an adult and a child is abusive, even if the child is willing, because children are legally incapable of consenting to sexual activity. (Acts such as touching children's sexual organs while changing or bathing them, sleeping with children, or appearing nude before them are not usually considered sexual contact; they are open to interpretation but are often innocent [Haugaard, 2000).]

Voluntary sexual activity *between children* of similar ages is not sexual abuse. Children often engage in consensual sex play with peers or siblings, as in "playing doctor" or in mutual masturbation. Although such experiences may be recalled in adulthood with feelings of shame or guilt, they are not typically harmful. When the experience involves coercion, or when one child is significantly older or in a position of power over the younger child, the sexual contact may be considered sexual abuse.

In Canada it is against the law for an adult or teenager to engage in any type of sexual activity, ranging from kissing to intercourse, with a child under the age of 14 (except for sexual activity between a child who is at least 12 years old and someone less than two years older).

In Prince Edward Island, a 19-year-old male with a promising baseball career was sentenced to 45 days in jail after he admitted that he had received oral sex from two girls aged 12 and 13. The man claimed that he believed the girls were older than 14 and that they were the ones who had initiated contact and offered to perform oral sex (Canadian Press, 2003b). This story resulted in media articles suggesting that "rainbow parties" in which young teenage girls take turns performing oral sex on several males are commonplace. However, the extent to which such behaviour actually occurs is unknown. According to the Canada Youth and AIDS Survey, 28% of Grade 9 girls and 32% of Grade 9 boys have experienced oral sex at least once (Boyse et al., 2003).

In 2005, the Conservative Party of Canada proposed that the legal age of consent should be raised from 14 to 16 to protect adolescents in that age group from adult sexual exploitation. However, Justice Minister Irwin Cotler agued against raising the age of consent because of the possibility that many teenagers who engage in consensual sex with other teenagers might be faced with criminal charges (Schmitz, 2005).

In 1985 Parliament amended the Criminal Code and made it an offence for a person in a position of trust or authority to have any sexual contact, consensual or not, with a person under 18. Interestingly, there has been more controversy about this law when the accused has been a female, probably because of traditional stereotypes that young males who are involved sexually with an older female are "lucky" rather than being exploited. In Sechelt, British Columbia, a 29-year-old female high school teacher was convicted of exploiting a minor after she had consensual sexual relations with one of her high school students, who was 17 years old. The male high school student publicly opposed the conviction because he said that he was the one who pursued and seduced the teacher. He claimed that he was not a victim, and even his mother approved of the relationship (Dreidger, 2003). In recent years there have been more than a dozen cases across Canada of female teachers charged with having sexual relationships with male students.

To provide greater protection to youth aged 14 to 18, in 2002 legislation created a new category of sexual exploitation—adults who, because of their age and/or position of authority, are able to coerce young people into having sex. An addition to the Criminal Code also makes it illegal for adults to use the Internet to lure a person whom they believe is under the age of 18 for the purpose of committing sexual assault, or to entice a child believed to be under the age of 14 into sexual relations. The first person charged under this law was a 33-year-old Toronto man who arranged a meeting with an 11-year-old girl he met on the Internet. He was also charged with sexual assault after he spent the night with the girl in a hotel room. The man was convicted of Internet luring, abduction of a person under age 16, and sexual interference (Levy, 2004). In Barrie, Ontario, a 14-year-old boy was charged with Internet luring of two girls who were under the age of 14. He met the girls on an Internet chat program and is believed to be the youngest person ever charged with this offence (Love, 2004).

To combat Internet luring, police have laid traps by posing as children in chatrooms. In 2005 a Toronto detective posed as a 12-year-old girl on the Yahoo chatroom "Teen Oh Canada Chat." A man entered the chatroom and engaged in casual conversation with the "girl." After a few months, they arranged to meet to have sex. At this meeting, the police arrested a 36-year-old pastor (Naili & Josey, 2005).

Patterns of Abuse

Children from stable, middle-class families appear to be generally at lower risk of encountering sexual abuse than children from poorer, less cohesive families (Edwards et al., 2003). In most cases, children who are sexually abused are not accosted by the proverbial stranger lurking in the schoolyard. According to Canadian police reports in 2003, half of all victims under the age of six were sexually assaulted by a family member and only 4% were assaulted by a stranger. Among victims aged 14 to 17, 20% were assaulted by a family member and another 20% were assaulted by a stranger (Statistics Canada, 2005). In many cases, the molesters are people who are close to them: relatives, step-relatives, family friends, and neighbours (Edwards et al., 2003). Estimates of the percentage of sexually molested children who are abused by family members have ranged from 10% to 50% of cases (Waterman & Lusk, 1986).

Parents who discover that their child has been abused by a family member are often reluctant to notify authorities. The decision to report the abuse to the police depends largely on the relationship between the abuser and the person who discovers the abuse (Finkelhor, 1984).

Typically, the child initially trusts the abuser. Physical force is seldom needed to gain compliance, largely because of the child's helplessness, gullibility, and submission to adult authority. Whereas most sexually abused children are abused only once, those who are abused by family members are more likely to suffer repeated acts of abuse (Briere & Runtz, 1987).

Genital fondling is the most common type of abuse (Knudsen, 1991). In one sample of women who had been molested in childhood, most of the contacts involved genital fondling (38% of cases) or exhibitionism (20% of cases). Intercourse occurred in only 4% of cases (Knudsen, 1991). Repeated abuse by a family member, however, commonly follows a pattern that begins with affectionate fondling during the preschool years, and progresses to oral sex or mutual masturbation during the early school years and then to sexual penetration (vaginal or anal intercourse) during preadolescence or adolescence (Waterman & Lusk, 1986).

Abused children rarely report the abuse, often because of fear of retaliation from the abuser or because they believe they will be blamed for it. Adults may suspect abuse if a child shows sudden personality changes or develops fears, problems in school, or difficulty eating or sleeping. A pediatrician may discover physical signs of abuse during a medical exam.

TYPES OF ABUSERS Researchers find that the overwhelming majority of people who sexually abuse children (both boys and girls) are males (Thomlison et al., 1991). Although most child abusers are adults, some are adolescents. Male adolescent sex offenders are more likely than other adolescents to have been molested themselves as boys (Becker et al., 1989; Muster, 1992). Some adolescent sex offenders may be imitating their own victimization.

Although the great majority of sexual abusers are male, the number of female sexual abusers may be greater than has been generally believed (Banning, 1989). Many female sexual abusers may go undetected because society accords women a much freer range of physical contact with children than it does men. A study of a sample of Canadian police officers and psychiatrists found that among these groups there was a culture of denial of women as potential sexual aggressors (Denov, 2001).

CHILD SEX TOURISM Some Canadians travel to developing countries to have sex with children, partly because there is less chance of being prosecuted in those countries. In 1997 the Canadian government changed the Criminal Code so that Canadians who sexually abuse children while out of the country could be prosecuted. In 2002 prosecution was made easier by an amendment that no longer required the agreement of the country where the offence occurred. In 2005 the first conviction was obtained under this legislation. A B.C. man was convicted of having sex with children under the age of 14 in Cambodia (Girard, 2005).

Pedophilia

Pedophilia A type of paraphilia that is defined by sexual attraction to unusual stimuli: children. (From the Greek *paidos*, which means "child," not the Latin *pedis*, which means "foot.")

Pedophilia is a paraphilia in which an adult finds children to be the preferred and sometimes exclusive objects of sexual desire The prevalence of **pedophilia** in the general population is unknown (Ames & Houston, 1990). Although pedophiles are sometimes called child molesters, not all child molesters are pedophiles. Pedophilia involves persistent or recurrent sexual attraction to children. Some molesters, however, may seek sexual contacts with children only when they are under unusual stress or lack other sexual outlets. Thus they do not meet the clinical definition of pedophilia.

Pedophiles are almost exclusively male, although some isolated cases of female pedophiles have been reported (Cooper et al., 1990). Some pedophiles are sexually attracted only to children; others are sexually attracted to adults as well. Some pedophiles limit their sexual interest in children to incestuous relationships with family members; others abuse children to whom they are unrelated. Some pedophiles limit their sexual interest in children to looking at them or undressing them; others fondle them or masturbate in their presence. Some manipulate or coerce children into oral, anal, or vaginal intercourse.

Children tend not to be worldly wise. They can often be taken in by pedophiles who tell them that they want to "show them something," "teach them something," or "do something with them that they will like." Some pedophiles seek to gain the child's affection, and, later, to discourage the child from disclosing the sexual activity by showering the child with attention and gifts. Others threaten the child or the child's family to prevent disclosure.

Research suggests that sexual attraction to children may be more common than is generally believed (Briere & Runtz, 1989). Fortunately, most people with such erotic interests never act on them.

Pedophilia may have complex and varied origins. Some pedophiles who are lacking in social skills may turn to children after failing to establish gratifying relationships with adult women (Overholser & Beck, 1986). Research generally supports the stereotype of the pedophile as weak, passive, and shy—a socially inept, isolated man who feels threatened by mature relationships (Ames & Houston, 1990).

Pedophiles who engage in incestuous relationships with their own children present a somewhat different picture. They tend to fall on one or the other end of the dominance spectrum. Some are very dominant, others very passive. Few are found between these extremes (Ames & Houston, 1990).

Some pedophiles were sexually abused as children and may be attempting to establish feelings of mastery by reversing the situation (De Young, 1982). Cycles of abuse may be perpetuated from generation to generation if children who are sexually abused become victimizers or partners of victimizers as adults.

Ray Blanchard and colleagues at the Centre for Addiction and Mental Health in Toronto are exploring how disturbances in early neurodevelopment are related to pedophilia. They find that pedophiles are more likely to have experienced serious head injuries before the age of six and that these injuries are associated with lower levels of intelligence and memory loss. Also, pedophilia is somewhat related to being left-handed, which may be attributed to altered fetal development (Blanchard et al., 2002; Cantor et al., 2004).

A group of Ontario researchers has also found that men who have older brothers are more prone to sexually coercing both children and adults (Lalumiere et al., 1998). Also, males with older brothers are more likely to choose male victims.

Incest

Incest involves people who are related by blood, or *consanguineous*. The law may also proscribe coitus between, say, a stepfather and stepdaughter. Although a few societies have permitted incestuous pairings among royalty, all known cultures have some sort of incest taboo.

Let us further consider the two most common incest patterns, father–daughter incest and brother–sister incest.

Incest Marriage or sexual relations between people who are so closely related (by "blood") that sexual relations are prohibited and punishable by law. (From the Latin *in-*, which means "not," and *castus*, which means "chaste.")

So There Really Was a Monster in Her Bedroom.

Not all monsters are make-believe. Some, like the perpetrators of incest, are members of the family.

FATHER–DAUGHTER INCEST Most of our knowledge of incestuous relationships concerns father–daughter incest. Why? Most identified cases involve fathers who were eventually incarcerated.

Father–daughter incest often begins with affectionate cuddling or embraces and then progresses to teasing sexual play, lengthy caresses, hugs, kisses, and genital contact, even penetration. In some cases genital contact occurs more abruptly, usually when the father has been drinking or arguing with his wife. Force is not typically used to gain compliance, but daughters are sometimes physically overcome and injured by their fathers.

BROTHER–SISTER INCEST Brother–sister incest, not parent–child incest, is the most common type of incest (Waterman & Lusk, 1986). Brother–sister incest is also believed to be greatly underreported, possibly because it tends to be transient and is apparently less harmful than parent–child incest. Finkelhor (1990) found that 21% of the college men in his sample, and 39% of the college women, reported incestuous relationships with a sibling of the other gender. Only 4% reported an incestuous relationship with their fathers. Incest between siblings of the same gender is rare (Waterman & Lusk, 1986).

In sibling incest, the brother usually initiates sexual activity and assumes the dominant role. Some brothers and sisters may view their sexual activity as natural and not know that it is taboo (Knox, 1988).

Evidence on the effects of incest between brothers and sisters is mixed. In a study of university undergraduates, those who reported childhood incest with siblings did not reveal greater evidence of sexual adjustment problems than other undergraduates (Greenwald & Leitenberg, 1989). Sibling incest is most likely to be harmful when it is recurrent or forced or when parental response is harsh (Knox, 1988; Laviola, 1989).

MOTHER–SON INCEST Mother–son incest occurs far less frequently than father–daughter incest. However, it may also be that boys who are sexually abused by their mothers are less likely to report it. Nevertheless, these cases do occur.

In an unusual case in Cambridge, Ontario, a mother and son had three children. The son was 16 years old when he fathered the first child with his mother. In an attempt to cover up the incestuous relationship, the son fabricated identity documents. Both mother and son were found guilty of incest (Wood, 2005).

FAMILY FACTORS IN INCEST Incest frequently occurs within the context of general family disruption; there may also be spouse abuse, a dysfunctional marriage, or alcoholic or physically abusive parents. Stressful events in the father's life, such as the loss of a job or problems at work, often precede the initiation of incest (Waterman, 1986).

Fathers who abuse older daughters tend to be domineering and authoritarian with their families (Waterman, 1986). Fathers who abuse younger, preschool daughters are more likely to be passive, dependent, and low in self-esteem.

Marriages in incestuous families tend to be characterized by an uneven power relationship between the spouses. The abusive father is usually dominant. Another thread that frequently runs through incestuous families is a troubled sexual relationship between the spouses. The wife often rejects the husband sexually (Waterman, 1986).

Gebhard and his colleagues (1965) found that many fathers who committed incest with their daughters were religiously devout, fundamentalist, and moralistic. Perhaps such men, when sexually frustrated, are less likely to seek extramarital and extrafamilial sexual outlets or to turn to masturbation as a sexual release. In many cases, the father is under stress but does not find adequate emotional and sexual support from his wife (Gagnon, 1977). He turns to a daughter as a wife surrogate, often when he has been drinking alcohol (Gebhard et al., 1965). The daughter may become, in her father's fantasies, the "woman of the house." This fantasy may become his justification for continuing the incestuous relationship. In some incestuous families, a role reversal occurs. The abused daughter assumes many of the mother's responsibilities for managing the household and caring for the younger children (Waterman, 1986).

Incestuous abuse is often repeated from generation to generation. One study found that in 154 cases of children who were sexually abused within the family, more than a third of the male offenders and about half of the mothers had been either abused themselves or exposed to abuse as children (Faller, 1989).

Sociocultural factors, such as poverty, overcrowded living conditions, and social or geographical isolation, may contribute to incest in some families (Waterman, 1986). Sibling incest may be encouraged by the crowded living conditions and open sexuality that occur among some economically disadvantaged families (Waterman, 1986).

Applied Knowledge

NEW METHODS OF GETTING TO THE TRUTH IN CASES OF CHILD ABUSE

As social scientists continue to conduct research, what are the brightest prospects for determining the truth in cases of child abuse? The American Academy of Child and Adolescent Psychiatry (1998) points out that no particular pattern of behaviour in children proves that they have been abused. The best hope for unearthing childhood sexual abuse might simply be more careful interviewing. Because children are suggestible, it is important not to ask leading questions that may result in false accusations. Guidelines for interviews that avoid suggesting abuse include the following (Goldberg, 1998):

How Do We Get at the Truth in Cases of Sexual Abuse of Children?
Serious doubts have been raised about the use of anatomically correct dolls and about interviewing children. Children are quite likely to report remembering events suggested by the examiner, whether or not those events happened.

■ Interview the children in an open-ended way rather than describing specific events and asking whether they occurred. *Don't* say, "Did he touch your vagina?" (a leading question). Rather, say, "Tell me everything that happened in John's apartment."

■ Use interviewers who are unbiased—who have no preconceived ideas about whether abuse occurred or who might have been guilty of it.

■ Keep the number of questions and the number of interviews to a minimum. Not only are interviews taxing to children, but exposure to many questions or interviews begins to plant suggestions in their minds.

■ Do not ask children to imagine sexual acts, because they may then become confused about what is real and what is fantasy.

■ Do not pressure children to respond, especially by bribing them or threatening them. Aside from the obvious inappropriateness of such courses of action, they may pressure children to invent abuses that did not occur.

Effects of Sexual Abuse of Children

The effects of sexual abuse are varied, and there is no single identifiable syndrome that emerges from sexual abuse (Saywitz et al., 2000). Children who are sexually abused may suffer from a litany of short- and long-term psychological complaints, including anger, depression, anxiety, eating disorders, inappropriate sexual behaviour, aggressive behaviour, self-destructive behaviour, sexual promiscuity, drug abuse, suicide attempts, post-traumatic stress disorder, low self-esteem, sexual dysfunction, mistrust of others, and feelings of detachment (Meston & Heiman, 2000; Saywitz et al., 2000). Sexual abuse may also have physical effects such as genital injuries and may cause stress-related problems such as stomachaches and headaches.

Abused children commonly "act out." Younger children have tantrums or display aggressive or antisocial behaviour. Older children turn to substance abuse (Kendler et al., 2000). Some abused children become withdrawn and retreat into fantasy or refuse to leave the house. Regressive behaviours, such as thumb sucking, fear of the dark, and fear of strangers, are also common among sexually abused children. On the heels of the assault and in the ensuing years, many survivors of childhood sexual abuse—like many sexual assault survivors—show signs of post-traumatic stress disorder. They suffer flashbacks, nightmares, numbing of emotions, and feelings of estrangement from others (Finkelhor, 1990).

The sexual development of abused children may also be adversely affected. For example, the survivor may become prematurely sexually active or promiscuous in adolescence and adulthood (Kendler et al., 2000; Tharinger, 1990). Researchers find that adolescent girls who are sexually abused tend to engage in consensual coitus at earlier ages than nonabused peers (Wyatt, 1988).

The long-term consequences of sexual abuse in childhood tend to be greater for children who were abused by their fathers or stepfathers, who experienced penetration, who were forced, and who suffered more prolonged and severe abuse (Cheasty, 1998; Wyatt & Newcomb, 1990). Children who suffer incest often feel a deep sense of betrayal by the offender and, perhaps, by other family members—especially their mothers, whom they perceive as failing to protect them (Finkelhor, 1988). Incest survivors may feel powerless to control their bodies or their lives.

Late adolescence and early adulthood seem to pose especially difficult periods for survivors of childhood sexual abuse. Studies of women in these age groups reveal more psychological and social problems in abused women (Jackson et al., 1990; Kendler et al., 2000). Effects of childhood sexual abuse are often long-lasting.

Applied Knowledge

PREVENTING SEXUAL ABUSE OF CHILDREN

Many of us were taught by our parents never to accept a ride or an offer of candy from a stranger. However, many instances of sexual abuse are perpetrated by familiar adults—often a family member or friend (Zielbauer, 2000). Prevention programs help children understand what sexual abuse is and how they can avoid it. In addition to learning to avoid strangers, children need to recognize the differences between acceptable touching, such as an affectionate embrace or pat on the head, and unacceptable or "bad" touching. Even children of elementary school age can learn the distinction between "good touching" and "bad touching" (Tully, 1992). Good school-based programs are generally helpful in preparing children to handle an actual encounter with a potential molester (Goleman, 1993). Children who receive comprehensive training are more likely to use strategies such as running away, yelling, or saying no when they are threatened by an abuser. They are also more likely to report such incidents to adults.

Researchers recognize that children can easily be intimidated or overpowered by adults or older children.

Children may be unable to say no in a sexually abusive situation, even though they want to and know it is the right thing to do (Waterman et al., 1986). Although children may not always be able to prevent abuse, they can be encouraged to tell someone about it. Most prevention programs emphasize teaching children messages such as "It's not your fault," "Never keep a bad or scary secret," and "Always tell your parents about this, especially if someone says you shouldn't tell them" (Waterman et al., 1986).

Children also need to be alerted to the types of threats they might receive for disclosing the abuse. They are more likely to resist threats if they are reassured that they will be believed if they disclose the abuse, that their parents will continue to love them, and that they and their families will be protected from the molester.

School-based prevention programs focus on protecting the child. In Canada, teachers and helping professionals are required to report suspected abuse to authorities. Tighter controls and better screening are needed to monitor the hiring of daycare employees. Administrators and teachers in preschool and daycare facilities also need to be educated to recognize the signs of sexual abuse and to report suspected cases (Waterman et al., 1986). Treatment programs to help people who are sexually attracted to children *before* they commit abusive acts would also be of use.

Treatment of Survivors of Sexual Abuse

Psychotherapy in adulthood often becomes the first opportunity for survivors to confront residual feelings of pain, anger, and misplaced guilt (Ratican, 1992). Group or individual therapy can help improve survivors' self-esteem and their ability to develop intimate relationships. Most therapists recommend a multicomponent treatment approach, which may involve individual therapy for the child, mother, and father; group therapy for the adolescent or even preadolescent survivor; art therapy or play therapy for the younger child (e.g., using drawings or puppets to express feelings); marital counselling for the parents; and family therapy for the entire family (de Luca et al., 1992).

Treatment of Sexual Assailants and Child Molesters

What does *treatment* mean? When a helping professional treats someone, the goal is usually to help that individual. When we speak of treating a sex offender, the goal is just as likely—or more likely—to be to help society by eliminating the problem behaviour. The results of prison-based treatment programs have been mixed at best. Consider a Canadian study of 54 sexual assailants who participated in a treatment program. Following release from prison, 28% were later convicted of a sexual offence and 43% were convicted of a violent offence (Rice et al., 1990). Treatment also failed to curb recidivism among a sample of 136 child molesters (Rice et al., 1991).

A group of Canadian and American researchers has conducted an extensive review of the effectiveness of psychological treatment programs for sex offenders. They found that treatment programs conducted prior to 1980 had little effect. However, current treatments to prevent sex offenders from repeating their offences (see below) have shown some effect in reducing rates of recidivism (Hanson et al., 2002).

Ottawa researchers have found that rates of recidivism are lower among incest offenders who have not committed any other type of sexual offence. In an Ontario study, 26% of men who had committed a non-incestuous assault committed another sexual assault after their release from prison (Firestone et al., 1998). However, of a sample of men who had committed incest but no other kind of sexual offence, only a small percentage (6.4%) committed sexual offences 12 years after being released from prison (Firestone et al., 1999).

In a comprehensive analysis of treatment programs for adult sexual offenders, researchers in Ontario arrived at a number of conclusions about the programs' likelihood of success (Rice et al., 2001). Treatments that are insight-oriented and focused on building the offenders' self-esteem have not been successful, nor have programs focused only on punishing the offender. Successful programs, on the other hand, are likely to include the following elements:

- skills-based training that emphasizes problem-solving
- modelling of positive societal behaviours
- non-punitive orientation
- modifying antecedents to criminal behaviour, such as alcohol abuse
- supervised community living experiences that teach relevant everyday living and working skills (Rice et al., 2001)

Some Canadian communities such as Victoria, Winnipeg, and Kitchener, Ontario, have volunteer groups known as Circles of Support and Accountability (COSA), which have the twin goals of community protection and offender rehabilitation. These trained volunteer groups help integrate sexual offenders into the community and help them avoid reoffending by assisting them to meet their intimacy and relationship needs. This process assumes that in order to protect the community, offenders do not need to be isolated from the community (Petrunik, 2003). An evaluation project in Ontario found that involvement in a COSA can reduce further sexual offending by more than 60% (Wilson, 2005).

In the past, some programs have used extreme measures such as surgical castration to lower the offender's sex drive. Surgical castration raises ethical concerns because of its invasive character and irreversibility. Anti-androgen drugs such as Depo-Provera chemically reduce testosterone levels and the level of sex drive (Roesler & Witztum, 2000), but are reversible (Roesler & Witztum, 2000). Such treatment is less successful with men whose motivations for sexual assault relate to power and anger against women.

In 2004 the Canadian federal government, in response to pressure from community groups, some provincial governments, and police forces, established a national sex offender registry. Convicted sex offenders must register within 15 days of being released from prison and must reregister annually and within two weeks of moving. Police agencies from across Canada have access to this database, which they believe will help them in investigating cases of sexual assault. However, some legal experts have argued that the registry violates the human rights of the offender, who can never have his name removed from the list even after having lived as a model citizen for many years. As well, no other category of offender is required to register with the police after being released from prison. What is your opinion of this issue?

Sexual Harassment

In the film *Disclosure*, Demi Moore plays a supervisor who uses her power over an employee to harass him into sexual activity. What *is* **sexual harassment**? The term can be difficult to define (Lewin, 1998). For example, U.S. President Bill Clinton was accused of "groping" a resistant White House volunteer and of placing her hand on his penis. Such behaviour would clearly constitute sexual harassment. But Clinton also engaged in fellatio with a young White House intern, Monica Lewinsky. Although Lewinsky participated voluntarily, some critics suggest that Clinton's power over the intern caused their interaction to constitute sexual harassment.

Any behaviour that is sexual and unwanted by the target person is considered to be sexual harassment (Aggarwal, 1992) and is forbidden by both federal and provincial human rights legislation. Examples of sexual harassment range from

> **Sexual harassment**
> Deliberate or repeated unsolicited verbal comments, gestures, or physical contact of a sexual nature that the recipient does not welcome.

unwelcome sexual jokes, overtures, suggestive comments, and sexual innuendos to outright sexual assault. Both men and women can commit, and be subjected to, sexual harassment.

Evidence shows that people subjected to sexual harassment do suffer from it. In a survey of Canadian women in the workforce, among those who had been sexually harassed, 30% reported that their job was affected and 14% reported personal difficulties resulting from the harassment (Crocker & Kalemba, 1999). Some find harassment on the job so unbearable that they resign.

Sexual harassment may have more to do with the abuse of power than with sexual desire (Goleman, 1991; Tedeschi & Felson, 1994). Relatively few cases of sexual harassment involve outright requests for sexual favours. The harasser is usually in a dominant position and abuses that position by exploiting the victim's vulnerability. Sexual harassment may also occur between patients and doctors and between therapists and clients. Therapists may use their power and influence to pressure clients into sexual relations. In Canada, professional organizations for teachers, doctors, and therapists have strict ethical guidelines that forbid sexual contact between doctors and patients, therapists and clients, and teachers and students.

Sexual Harassment in the Workplace

Harassers in the workplace can be employers, supervisors, co-workers, or clients of a company. If a worker asks a co-worker for a date and is refused, it is not sexual harassment. If the co-worker persists with unwelcome advances and does not take no for an answer, however, the behaviour crosses the line and becomes harassment.

Perhaps the most severe form of sexual harassment, short of an outright assault, involves an employer or supervisor who demands sexual favours as a condition of employment or advancement. In Canada, Human Rights Commissions have expanded the definition of sexual harassment in the workplace to include any behaviour of a sexual nature that interferes with an individual's work performance or creates a hostile, intimidating, or offensive work environment. Canadian legislation also recognizes sexual harassment as a form of sex discrimination.

Some companies and organizations have gone a step further, banning their employees from having any sexual contact with other employees, even if it is consensual. A Canadian Armed Forces ban on all forms of sexual activity (including flirting and holding hands) at an overseas peacekeeping base led to a 2001 court challenge. The military judge upheld the ban, arguing that sexual activity "could lead to feelings of jealousy, even violence, feelings of favouritism and disrupting the feelings of cohesion and morale" (Weber, 2001, p. A3).

In a widely publicized 2005 case, the City of Toronto suspended a female senior manager and her (married) male second-in-command, who admitted they had had an affair. Concerns were raised that the assistant's rapid promotion—from temporary employee to a senior position in only 10 months—resulted from favouritism on the part of his boss, who was also his lover.

Employers can be held responsible not only for their own actions, but also for sexual harassment by their employees when they either knew or *should have known* that harassment was taking place and failed to eliminate it promptly (McKinney & Maroules, 1991). To protect themselves, many companies and universities have developed programs to educate workers about sexual harassment, established mechanisms for dealing with complaints, and imposed sanctions against harassers.

Relatively few people who encounter sexual harassment in the workplace file formal complaints or seek legal remedies. Among Canadian women, the most common responses to sexual harassment are to either confront the harasser (38%) or to ignore the incident (20%). Relatively few (5%) report it. One percent have quit their jobs because of the harassment. Like people subjected to other forms of sexual coercion, those experiencing sexual harassment often do not report the offence for fear that they will not be believed or will be subjected to retaliation. Some fear they will be branded as "troublemakers" or that they will lose their jobs (Goleman, 1991).

Researchers at the University of British Columbia found that male students were more tolerant of behaviours indicative of sexual harassment than were female students. As well, Asian students were more tolerant of these behaviours than were non-Asian students. However, the longer the Asian students had been in Canada, the less accepting they were of these behaviours. This trend indicates that over time, Asians tend to become acculturated to the views of other Canadians regarding sexual harassment (Kennedy & Gorzalka, 2002).

How common is sexual harassment in the workplace? In a national survey of about 2000 Canadian working women, 56% reported experiencing sexual harassment in the previous year and 77% said that they had experienced sexual harassment in their lifetime (Crocker & Kalemba, 1999). The three most common types of incidents were staring, jokes, and remarks about women or about the respondents themselves. The least common incidents were use of physical force, threats, and bribery.

Another Canadian survey (Compas, 1998) asked respondents how they felt the new rules against sexual harassment had affected gender relations in the workplace. Canadians were clearly divided in their opinions. A third of the respondents believed that the new rules had not changed gender relations; another third believed they had improved relations; and the final third believed that the rules had worsened relations (although they were opposed to sexual harassment, they felt that some rules, for example, those forbidding co-workers from dating each other, had become too strict).

Research in Action

GENDER AND PERCEPTIONS OF SEXUAL HARASSMENT

Often the genders differ in their perceptions of sexual harassment. University of Windsor researchers Pek Ne Knoo and Charlene Senn (2004) asked students to rate the offensiveness of 10 types of email message. Emails containing sexual content were rated as more offensive by women than by men. In particular, women found a sexual proposition from a stranger extremely offensive; the men found it enjoyable.

Robin Milhausen (2000) of the University of Guelph surveyed 413 young adults at university and in the community about workplace behaviour and perceptions. The majority of both men and women believed that men have to be more careful than women in the workplace about making sexual jokes, sexual comments, and comments about the physical appearance of a co-worker, and about making any kind of sexual contact with a co-worker. For example, 80% of the men and 68% of the women said that men have to be more careful than women about making sexual comments. Only a minority (15% of men and 29% of women) felt that both genders have to be careful, while hardly any (4% of men and 2% of women) said that women have to be more careful.

Sexual Harassment on Campus

Kathleen Cairns and Doyle Hatt (1995) of the University of Calgary found that, among graduate students at a large Canadian university, 9% of the women and 2% of the men had experienced sexual harassment. The most common form involved sexist remarks and sexual comments, with very few experiencing sexual coercion. The female students were harassed mainly by male professors and instructors, but also by other students. Male graduate students reported being harassed mainly by female students. Researchers at the Ontario Institute for Studies in Education surveyed psychologists in Ontario about their experiences of sexual harassment while they were in graduate school (Schneider et al, 2002). The reported incidence of harassment was much higher than that found by Cairns and Hatt, most likely because the Ontario researchers measured a wider scope of harassment experiences. Sixty percent of the psychologists reported that by far the most common type of harassment was that of professors telling suggestive jokes or stories. Similar to the Calgary study, very few reported having experienced sexual coercion from their professors.

Harassers are typically (but not always) male. Most students who encounter sexual harassment do not report the incident. If they do, it is usually to a confidante and not a person in authority.

Most forms of harassment involve unequal power relationships between the harasser and the person harassed. *Peer harassment* involves people who are equal in power, as in the cases of repeated sexual taunts from fellow employees, students, or colleagues. In some cases, the harasser may even have less formal power than the person harassed. For example, both female and male professors have been sexually harassed by students.

University faculty associations in Canada support policies on sexual harassment. However, faculty associations are also concerned that these policies may in some instances limit academic freedom, and especially the ability to have an open discussion of controversial topics. For example, consider the case of an Ontario university law professor. In teaching his students about the arguments for and against an anti-pornography law, he asked them to adopt a perspective that was contrary to their own. Some of the students, upset at having to argue against their own beliefs, complained to the university's sexual harassment officer. The official warned the instructor that if he repeated the class exercise it could lead to a sexual harassment investigation (Fekete, 1994). What is your opinion of this case? Do you think the professor should not have asked students to take part in this classroom exercise? Or do you think that asking students to adopt a contrary perspective can be an effective way of helping them to better understand points of view that differ from their own and should therefore be considered a legitimate approach to teaching?

Canadian universities have established educational programs designed to prevent sexual harassment. At the University of Calgary, May Valentich and Shirley Voyana Wilson established a brief educational session designed to teach undergraduate engineering students about the sexual and gender-related situations they might encounter in a workplace setting. In their evaluations, 91% of the students rated the session as useful (Valentich & Wilson, 1995).

Sexual Harassment in the Schools

Playful sexual antics are common during adolescence. However, unwelcome sexual advances and lewd comments go beyond playfulness and have become a concern to many of Canada's teens.

A research team from York University consisting of Loren McMaster, Jennifer Connolly, and Debra Pepler, along with Wendy McCraig of Queen's University, conducted a study of peer-to-peer sexual harassment among 1213 youths from Grades 6 to 8 in a large Canadian city (McMaster et al., 2002). The study defined sexual harassment as unwanted sexual attention, and asked students if they had perpetrated or experienced any of 10 types of sexual harassment. Boys were significantly more likely to report perpetration (36%) than were girls (21%), but both genders were about equally likely to report victimization (boys 42%, girls 38%). For both boys and girls, the three behaviours most commonly experienced were homophobic name calling; sexual comments, jokes, and looks; and being flashed or mooned. The boys perpetrated more same-sex harassment while the girls perpetrated more cross-sex harassment. The most common form of same-sex harassment among boys was homophobic name calling.

The researchers found that those students who were at a more advanced stage of pubertal development both perpetrated and experienced sexual harassment more than did other students. McMaster et al. (2002) concluded that for some youth, harassment is a phase of development, but for others it is part of a developmental pattern that includes other forms of aggression such as bullying and is a predictor of aggression in future dating relationships.

Higher levels of harassment were found in a study of 565 older adolescents in the provinces of British Columbia and New Brunswick (Dahinten, 2003). The picture that emerges from this poll of teenagers in Grades 9 through 11 indicates that sexual taunts and advances have become part of an unwelcome ritual for many students, especially girls, as they try to make their way through the hallways and stairwells of high schools. Almost all of the students reported experiencing at least one form of sexual harassment during the preceding two months, with about two-thirds of the girls and half of the boys experiencing five or more forms of harassment. The most common forms of harassment for two-thirds of the girls were being the target of sexual comments or whistles, sexual gestures, or stares and derogatory comments about females.

However, most of the behaviours were not labelled as sexual harassment by the students. Of those who had experienced at least one of the 19 items measuring sexual harassment, only 35% of the girls and 14% of the boys replied yes to the general item asking if they had been sexually harassed. This discrepancy in the labelling of behaviours clearly illustrates how the type of measurement one chooses can influence the incidence of harassment that is reported in the research literature. It also raises an important question: Is it legitimate for researchers to categorize behaviours as harassment when the people experiencing them do not consider them harassment? What do you think?

Girls were more likely than boys to report that they were upset when experiencing the sexual harassment behaviours. For boys the most upsetting experiences were "being the target of sexual rumours or graffiti" and "being followed or pestered for a date." Among girls, the most upsetting experiences were "being forced to do something other than kissing or hugging" and "being the target of sexual rumours." Most of the students responded passively to the harassment, and hardly any complained to a teacher or more formally made a complaint through the school system (Dahinten, 2003).

Today, there is considerable concern in Canadian high schools about Web sites that spread sexual rumours about students. The most typical rumours are about boys being gay and girls being promiscuous. These Web sites can be extremely nasty and hateful, and can demoralize the students who are discussed on them. An even more hurtful form of harassment is posting sexual pictures on a Web site without the person's consent, as discussed in the box below.

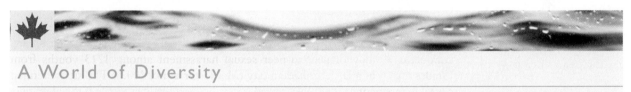

A World of Diversity

NUDE PHOTOS MAKE WEB CALAMITY FOR GIRL

A 16-year-old Toronto girl is struggling with a cyber nightmare after sexually explicit photos taken by a vengeful ex-boyfriend were posted on the Internet. Although child-pornography charges have been laid, police can't get the anonymous webmaster to remove the photos.

The pictures appeared in February, shortly after the girl told police that her former boyfriend had extorted money from her in a matter unrelated to the photos.

He decided to exact his revenge by posting five nude photos of her on the Internet. What's more, he constructed the web page to make it seem as though she had placed them there herself.

The accused, who is 16 and can't be identified, wrote a short entry impersonating her.

Detective Constable Chris Purchas of the Toronto Police sex crimes unit said the entry makes the girl appear to be "acting in a promiscuous manner, inviting other people to address her sexually."

It was the teenager's friends who first told her that she had been exposed for all the world to see. It has been two months since she found out. She feels humiliated and has missed several weeks of school, Det. Constable Purchas said.

The photos, which were taken with the girl's consent, are still up on the Web, and are starting to appear on other sites.

"What's happening is people are going on the Internet and copying them and reposting them on other websites, making other allegations slandering her character and so forth," he said. "These pictures can never be retrieved."

Det. Constable Purchas said that despite their best efforts the police

can't even get the original posting down. The website, which is a general-interest, youth-oriented site with thousands of hits each day, is overseen by a U.S.-based company whose main purpose is to block authorities from uncovering the true operators of websites.

"The Internet provider is not being very co-operative and they're ignoring our requests to have the pictures removed," he said.

The website has a lot of traffic from Canadian customers, he said, mostly between the ages of 14 and 30, and there is no other pornographic material on the site. It's mainly frequented for discussion boards, he said.

The ex-boyfriend has been charged with possessing and distributing child pornography and with impersonation with intent. Police hope a vigorous prosecution will prevent this type of offence from becoming a new trend.

"That's our fear," Det. Constable Purchas said. "We're trying to send a message in the hope that we won't see more of this."

He said although it's still a relatively rare kind of offence, everyone should be aware that with the advent of the Internet racy photos could end up anywhere.

"Be careful what you give to your boyfriends because the potential (for harm) is most certainly there," he said. "Twenty years ago, if a boyfriend had an off-colour picture of a girlfriend and things didn't go well, the most he could

do is photocopy it and put it on a bus shed or put it up around the school. Now he has a worldwide forum at his fingertips."

The relationship went sour in October of 2004, about a year after the pair started dating. The girl was 15 when the photos were taken and she knew that her ex-boyfriend still had them when they broke up.

The police say that before they broke up the boy was angry because she had given another male friend an

expensive gift. He is alleged to have threatened to hurt her unless she gave him cash. Shortly after he was charged in connection with those allegations, the nude pictures appeared on the Web.

SOURCE: Reprinted with permission from Joe Friesen (2005, April 22) "Nude Photos Make Web Calamity for Girl," The Globe and Mail.

Applied Knowledge

HOW TO RESIST SEXUAL HARASSMENT

What would you do if you were sexually harassed by an employer or a professor? How would you handle it? Would you try to ignore it and hope that it would stop? What actions might you take? We offer some suggestions, adapted from Powell (1996), that may be helpful. Recognize, however, that responsibility for sexual harassment always lies squarely with the perpetrator and with the organization that permits sexual harassment to take place, not with the person subjected to the harassment.

1. *Convey a professional attitude.* Harassment may be stopped cold by responding to the harasser with a businesslike, professional attitude.

2. *Discourage harassing behaviour, and encourage appropriate behaviour.* Harassment may also be stopped cold by shaping the harasser's

behaviour. Your reactions to the harasser may encourage businesslike behaviour and discourage flirtatious or suggestive behaviour. If a harassing professor suggests that you come back after school to review your term paper so that the two of you will be undisturbed, set limits assertively. Tell the professor that you'd feel more comfortable discussing the paper during regular office hours. Remain task-oriented. Stick to business. The harasser should quickly get the message that you insist on maintaining a strictly professional relationship. If the harasser persists, however, do not blame yourself. You are responsible only for your own actions. When the harasser persists, a more direct response may be appropriate: "Professor Jones, I'd like to keep our relationship on a purely professional basis, okay?"

3. *Avoid being alone with the harasser.* If you are being harassed by your

professor but need some advice about preparing your term paper, approach him or her after class when other students are milling about, not privately during office hours. Or bring a friend to wait outside the office while you consult the professor.

4. *Maintain a record.* Keep a record of all incidents of harassment to use as documentation in the event that you decide to lodge an official complaint. The record should include the following: (1) where the incident took place; (2) the date and time; (3) what happened, including the exact words that were used, if you can recall them; (4) how you felt; and (5) the names of witnesses.

5. *Talk with the harasser.* It may be uncomfortable to address the issue directly with a harasser, but doing so puts the offender on notice that you are aware of the harassment and want it to stop. It

may be helpful to frame your approach in terms of a description of the specific offending actions (e.g., "When we were alone in the office, you repeatedly attempted to touch me or brush up against me"); your feelings about the offending behaviour ("It made me feel like my privacy was being violated"); and what you would like the offender to do ("So I'd like you to agree never to attempt to touch me again, okay?"). Having a talk with the harasser may stop the harassment. If the harasser denies the accusations, it may be necessary to take further action.

6. *Write a letter to the harasser.* Set down on paper a record of the offending behaviour, and put the harasser on notice that the harassment must stop. Your letter might (1) describe what happened ("Several times you have made sexist comments about my body"); (2) describe how you feel ("It made me feel like a sexual object when you talked to me that way"); and (3) describe what you would like the harasser to do ("I want you to stop making sexist comments to me").

7. *Seek support.* Support from people you trust can help you through the often trying process of resisting sexual harassment. Talking with others enables you to express your feelings and receive emotional support, encouragement, and advice. In addition, it may strengthen your case if you have the opportunity to identify and talk with other people who have been harassed by the offender.

8. *File a complaint.* Companies and organizations are required by law to respond reasonably to complaints of sexual harassment. In large organizations, a designated official (a human rights officer) is usually charged with handling such complaints. Set up an appointment with this official to discuss your experiences. The major government agencies that handle charges of sexual harassment are the Provincial Human Rights Offices (look under the government section of your phone book for the telephone number of the nearest office).

9. *Seek legal remedies.* Sexual harassment is illegal and actionable. If you are considering legal action, consult a lawyer familiar with this area of law.

In closing, we repeat: The question is not what persons who suffer sexual assault, incest, and sexual harassment will do to redress the harm that has been done to them. The question is what all of us will do to reshape our society so that sex can no longer be used as an instrument of power, coercion, and violence.

Summing Up

Sexual Assault

Although sexual motivation plays a role in many sexual assaults, the use of sex to express aggression, anger, and power is more fundamental to our understanding of sexual assault. The definition of sexual assault involves more than just sexual intercourse.

Types of Sexual Assault

Types of sexual assaults include stranger sexual assault, acquaintance sexual assault, date sexual assault, and marital sexual assault. Women are more likely to be sexually assaulted by men they know than by strangers. Assaults against males are most often committed by males. Husbands who sexually assault their wives can now be prosecuted under the Canadian sexual assault laws.

Social Attitudes and Myths That Encourage Sexual Assault

Social attitudes such as gender-role stereotyping, seeing sex as adversarial, and acceptance of violence in interpersonal relationships all help create a climate that encourages sexual assault.

Characteristics of Sexually Coercive Men

Some sexually coercive men feel socially inadequate, lack social skills, and avoid social interactions with women. Some are basically antisocial and have long histories of violent behaviour. Canadian studies have also identified an early history of behavioural problems, sensation seeking, high levels of hostility, poor sexual adjustment, serious problems with alcohol, and sexual victimization or physical assault as children.

Adjustment of Sexual Assault Survivors

Sexual assault survivors often experience post-traumatic stress disorder (PTSD).

Treatment of Sexual Assault Survivors

Treatment of sexual assault survivors typically involves helping them through the crisis period following the attack and then helping to foster long-term adjustment.

Preventing Sexual Assault

Sexual assault prevention involves educating society at large and familiarizing women with a number of precautions that they can take. Whether or not women take precautions to prevent sexual assault, however, the assailant is always the one responsible for the assault.

Coercive Pressure Tactics

Verbal sexual coercion involves the use of verbal pressure or seduction lines to manipulate a person into having sexual relations.

Sexual Abuse of Children

Like sexual assault, sexual abuse of children is greatly underreported.

What Is Sexual Abuse of Children?

Any form of sexual contact between an adult and a child is abusive, even if force or physical threat is not used, because children are legally incapable of consenting to sexual activity with adults.

Patterns of Abuse

Sexual abuse of children, like sexual assault and other forms of sexual coercion, cuts across all socioeconomic classes. In most cases, the molesters are close to the children they abuse—relatives, step-relatives, family friends, and neighbours. Genital fondling is the most common type of abuse.

Pedophilia

Pedophilia is a type of paraphilia in which adults are sexually attracted to children. Pedophiles are almost exclusively male.

Incest

Incest is marriage or sexual relations between people who are so closely related that sex is prohibited and punished by virtue of the kinship tie. Father–daughter incest is more likely to be reported and prosecuted, but brother–sister incest is the most common type of incest. Incest frequently occurs within the context of general family disruption.

Effects of Sexual Abuse of Children

Children who are sexually abused often suffer social and emotional problems that impair their development and persist into adulthood, affecting their self-esteem and their formation of intimate relationships.

Treatment of Survivors of Sexual Abuse

Psychotherapy may help adult survivors of sexual abuse improve their self-esteem and ability to develop intimate relationships.

Treatment of Sexual Assailants and Child Molesters

The effectiveness of prison-based rehabilitation programs and anti-androgen drugs in curbing repeat offences requires further empirical support.

Sexual Harassment

Sexual Harassment in the Workplace

The definition of sexual harassment in the workplace has been expanded to include any behaviour of a sexual nature that interferes with an individual's work performance or creates a hostile, intimidating, or offensive work environment.

Sexual Harassment on Campus

Most incidents of sexual harassment on campus are in the form of sexist comments. Female students report they are more likely to be harassed by instructors while male students report they are more likely to be harassed by other students. Professors may also be harassed by students.

Sexual Harassment in the Schools

Sexual harassment at school has become an unwelcome ritual that many junior and senior high school students are forced to endure.

Test Yourself

Multiple-Choice Questions

1. Sexual assault involving a weapon would be categorized as _____ under the Criminal Code of Canada
   a. level 1
   b. level 2
   c. level 3
   d. level 4

2. What percentage of sexual assaults are committed by strangers?
   a. 20
   b. 30
   c. 40
   d. 50

3. Approximately what percentage of victims of sexual assault are males?
   a. 8
   b. 13
   c. 18
   d. 23

4. Men who believe strongly in stereotypical gender roles are likely to do all of the following except
   a. condone violence toward women
   b. blame sexual assault survivors for what happened to them
   c. ignore a partner's saying that she does not want to have sex
   d. play violent video games

5. All of the following are suggestions about what to do if you are sexually assaulted except
   a. Do not wash, change your clothes, or comb your hair.
   b. Seek medical help and make sure that any injuries are documented.
   c. Think about reporting the assault to the police.
   d. Do not talk to anyone about the assault.

6. Treatment for sexual assault survivors is usually a two-stage process. The first stage involves helping the person through the immediate crisis. The second involves
   a. remembering exactly what happened on the day of the assault
   b. learning to forgive the offender
   c. fostering long-term adjustment
   d. telling friends and family about the assault

7. Less forceful forms of resistance, such as pleading or reasoning with the offender,
   a. are the most effective ways to prevent sexual assault
   b. will reduce the risk of injury
   c. may actually increase the risk of injury
   d. work better for male victims

8. The most common type of child sexual abuse is_____.
   a. genital fondling
   b. vaginal intercourse
   c. oral sex
   d. kissing

9. The most common type of incest is
   _____
   a. father–daughter
   b. stepfather–stepdaughter
   c. brother–sister
   d. mother–son

10. When it comes to assessing behaviours as sexually harassing,
    a. men perceive more behaviours as offensive than women
    b. men and women have similar perceptions of behaviours
    c. women perceive more behaviours as offensive than men
    d. women perceive all sexual behaviour in the workplace as offensive

Critical Thinking Questions

1. Have you ever tried to convince someone to have sexual intercourse with you even after they said no? What eventually happened? How do you feel about it? How would you feel if the other person was your sister?

2. Has anyone ever tried to convince you to have sexual intercourse even when you didn't want to? What happened? How do you feel about it? How do you feel about the other person? About yourself?

3. A woman goes to a bar, has a few too many drinks, dances suggestively with several men, and goes home with one of them. If she later reports that she has been sexually assaulted, do you think she is to blame? If she had been assaulted on the street waiting for a bus at the same time of night, would she be less to blame? Why or why not?

4. Have you ever been sexually harassed by a professor, employer, co-worker, or fellow student? Did you report it? What was the outcome? Are you satisfied with the outcome? If this happened again, what, if anything, would you do differently?

Visit our Companion Website at www.pearsoned.ca/rathus, where you can use the interactive Study Guide and link to additional resources on topics discussed in this text.

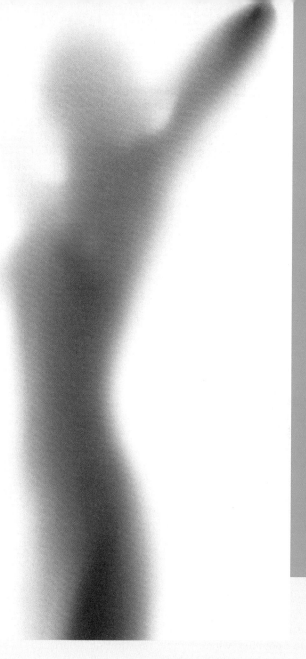

Chapter 17
Commercial Sex

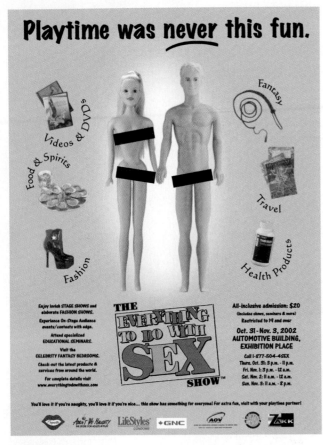

The Everything to Do with Sex Show.

This trade show attracts many thousands of visitors to Toronto. The exhibitors sell all kinds of erotic products, including toys and sex videos. The business of sex is obviously booming in Canada!

A few years ago, England's floppy-haired actor Hugh Grant was caught with a prostitute in a BMW on Hollywood's Sunset Boulevard. Why? His girlfriend was supermodel Elizabeth Hurley, who at the time was promoting the perfume called "Pleasures." Grant exemplified good looks, charm, innocence, and success. Still, he sought the sexual services of a woman for hire.

The World of Commercial Sex: A Disneyland for Adults

Sex as commerce runs the gamut from adult movie theatres and bookshops to strip shows, sex toy shops, erotic hotels and motels, escort/outcall services, "massage parlours," "900" telephone services, cyber-sex (e.g., sex over the Internet), and the use of sex appeal in advertisements for a wide range of products (Weitzer, 1999). The "world of commercial sex is a kind of X-rated amusement park—Disneyland for Adults" (Edgley, 1989, p. 372). The types of sexual commerce seem unlimited. For example, in Cambridge, Ontario, a restaurant owner, in order to increase his business, hired waitresses two days a week who wore lingerie in order to attract customers (Greeno, 2002). In Toronto, the annual Everything to Do with Sex Show has hundreds of exhibitors selling all kinds of products and services related to sex. Many thousands of people attend this event.

Prostitution

Prostitution is often called "the world's oldest profession"—for good reason. It can be traced at least to ancient Mesopotamia, where temple prostitution flourished. Prostitution also flourished in medieval Europe and during the sexually repressive Victorian period in the nineteenth century. Then, as now, the major motive for becoming a prostitute was economic. Many poor women were drawn to prostitution as a means of survival. In Victorian England, prostitution was widely regarded as a necessary outlet for men to satisfy their sexual appetites. It was widely held that women would not enjoy sex. Therefore, it was commonly believed that it was better for a man to visit a prostitute than to "soil" his wife with his carnal passions.

Prostitution and the Law in Canada

Canadian laws governing prostitution are confusing—while prostitution itself is legal, almost all the activities involved with it are illegal. The Criminal Code prohibits a number of activities related to prostitution, including (1) transporting or directing, or offering to transport or direct, another person to a common bawdy house, (2) keeping, being an inmate of, being found without lawful excuse in, or allowing a place to be used for the purpose of a common bawdy house, and (3) procuring and living off the avails of prostitution. In other words, it is against the law to engage in activities that facilitate prostitution, or to be in a house of prostitution.

Prostitution The sale of sexual activity for money or goods of value, such as drugs. (From the Latin *prostituere*, which means "to cause to stand in front of." The implication is that one is offering one's body for sale.)

Some Canadian cities, such as Edmonton, Vancouver, Calgary, Winnipeg, and Windsor, have attempted to regulate prostitution by licensing escorts and escort agencies. These cities require that owners of escort agencies and the escorts themselves register with the local police and pay a licensing fee. They are also required to keep records of clients' names and addresses. However, obtaining a city license is no guarantee that these escort services will not face prosecution for engaging in prostitution-related activities.

University of Windsor researchers Eleanor Maticka-Tyndale, Jacqueline Lewis, and Megan Street (2005) have analyzed the process of licensing escorts in Windsor. When escorts and agencies were first given licences, there was a feeling that they would be treated as other legitimate businesses. The city bylaws purposely did not mention the word *sex* in their descriptions of the escort business. However, after obtaining their licences, the escorts felt that the police were treating them as undesirable businesses. They felt victimized when the police used entrapment techniques, such as encouraging the escort to negotiate a fee for sexual service and then charging them for engaging in illegal activities.

In 1983 the Canadian justice minister appointed a special committee (the Fraser Commission) to study pornography and prostitution and to make recommendations to Parliament. Although the committee recommended that prostitution offences be removed from the Criminal Code, the federal government instead brought in more restrictive legislation with the aim of decreasing street prostitution.

In order to make it easier for police forces to prosecute prostitutes as well as their clients, the Criminal Code was changed so that it became illegal to communicate with or stop a person in a public place (including a motor vehicle) to obtain the sexual services of a prostitute. The new legislation was soon challenged as being inconsistent with the Canadian Charter of Rights and Freedoms. In 1990, the Supreme Court ruled that the freedom of expression as granted by the Charter could be limited because street solicitation caused too great a social nuisance. Nonetheless, while the new legislation did facilitate the prosecution of both prostitutes and clients, it did not in fact decrease street prostitution (Gemme, 1993).

The police and politicians have been particularly concerned about teenage prostitution. Accordingly, Parliament significantly increased penalties for clients who attempt to obtain the sexual services of a person under the age of 18. And in 1999 Alberta passed the Protection of Children Involved in Prostitution Act, which allows police or social workers to apprehend child prostitutes under the age of 18 and keep them in safe houses for up to 72 hours.

Police in Canada often use the strategy of entrapment to obtain convictions against prostitutes and their clients. Plain-clothes male officers pretend they are clients wanting sex—for example, by obtaining topless body rubs at massage studios—in order to determine whether sex is being sold on the premises. Similarly, female police officers will act as "decoys" by standing in a location frequented by street prostitutes. When a man approaches and suggests having sex for money, he is immediately arrested and charged with communicating for the purposes of prostitution.

Police are less likely to entrap those who engage in homosexual prostitution (Gemme, 1993), possibly because male police officers are reluctant to act as decoys for potential male clients. However, the gay and lesbian communities face the possibility of arrest for other kinds of activities. For example, while investigating "Sperm Attack Mondays," where male dancers at a gay strip club would ejaculate on stage, Toronto police laid bawdy-house charges against 11 dancers and 4 customers. Although these were later dropped, the club and its owners were still charged. The police also raided a Toronto gay pornography bar and laid public-indecency charges against men who were engaged in consensual sex in cubicles (Woods, 2000).

In recent years politicians and police forces have targeted the customers of prostitutes. For example, in 2005 the provincial government in Manitoba introduced legislation to suspend the driver's licence of a man convicted of soliciting a prostitute.

Some Canadian cities have established "john schools" for men who have no previous criminal record but who are charged with communicating for the purposes of prostitution. In return for attending the day-long school, charges against the clients are erased from the official court record. Typically, the men listen to presentations from street prostitutes about the negative effect that prostitution has had on them. They also receive lectures on sexually transmitted infections, and, in some instances, community representatives talk about the impact of street prostitution on their communities. The men are expected to provide a donation to help support the program (Fischer et al., 2002).

University of Calgary researcher Erin Van Brunschot (2003) found that the john schools mainly targeted men from lower socioeconomic levels who cannot afford the higher-priced services offered in massage parlours or by escorts. Van Brunschot criticizes the programs' focus on morality and shame and one-sided, negative view of prostitution. For example, prostitute groups advocating the legalization of their profession are not invited to take part in the program. These groups are concerned that the john schools program reduces the income of sex workers who voluntarily choose to work in that profession. The program also does not take into account the fact that there are many Canadians who believe that prostitution should be legalized.

Attempts over the years to legalize prostitution in Canada have all been resisted by government leaders. Because of concern over the deaths of more than 50 prostitutes in Vancouver, in 2005 the youth wing of the federal Liberal Party proposed a resolution to delete section 213 of the Canadian Criminal Code which forbids communication for the purposes of prostitution. The resolution was defeated at the Liberal Policy Convention, and instead the Liberal Party called for review of Canada's prostitution laws. Prime Minister Paul Martin was strongly opposed to the idea of legalizing prostitution (O'Neil, 2005). Because prostitution remains a topic of controversy, few politicians are willing to be seen as in favour of legalizing it.

Canadian Attitudes Toward Prostitution

The majority of Canadians are in favour of legalizing prostitution. According to the 1998 Compas poll, two-thirds of respondents support legalizing prostitution if it is

Amsterdam's Red-Light District. Prostitution is legal in Amsterdam's red-light district. Tourists wend their way through the narrow streets by the canals, doing "window shopping." Prim grandmothers sometimes join the audiences at the live sex shows. District landmarks include the Erotic Museum and the Casa Rosso. Along with the nearby Rembrandts, Rubens, and van Goghs, the district is so thoroughly ingrained in Amsterdam's culture that the police have issued a guide to enjoying the district—safely.

A World of Diversity

FROM RUSSIA, WITH ... SEX?

From Russia, with Love is the title of the James Bond novel by Ian Fleming, of course. But a new chapter is being written in the annals of prostitution, and it could very easily be titled *From Russia, with Sex*. Russia and its Slavic neighbours Ukraine and Belarus have largely replaced Thailand and the Philippines as the centre of the world-wide business that traffics in women. Economic problems in the former Soviet Union have opened a profitable market to the criminal gangs that have risen since the fall of communism (Smale, 2000). Russian crime gangs

based in Moscow arrange for security, connections with brothel owners in various countries, and false documents.

Irina is from Ukraine, 21, and self-confident. Like many other Ukrainian women, she wound up in Israel. She had answered a newspaper ad and crossed the Mediterranean on a tour boat for Haifa, intending to make her fortune dancing in the nude on table-tops. For her, Israel was a new world, filled with hope, until she was driven to a brothel and her boss burned her passport while she watched.

"I own you," he said (Specter, 1998). "You are my property, and you will work until you earn your way out. Don't try to leave. You have no papers

and you don't speak Hebrew. You will be arrested and deported. Then we will get you and bring you back."

Irina and others like her begin their hellish journeys seeking a better life. The average salary today in Ukraine is $30 a month, and young women are lured by local ads for lucrative jobs in foreign countries.

The women who are seeking their fortunes usually do not understand what is happening to them until it is too late. Once they reach their destination, their passports are confiscated, their cash is taken, and they become sexual slaves.

regulated by health authorities. Church attendance is one of the strongest predictors of attitudes toward prostitution, with twice as many of those who attend once a week or more (52%) believing that prostitution should be kept completely against the law, compared with 26% of those who do not attend church once a week or more. Interestingly, people in their 20s or younger are also less accepting of prostitution (Compas, 1998), perhaps because they tend to be more idealistic about relationships. However, most Canadians still personally disapprove of prostitution, with 88% feeling that it is unacceptable to pay for sex (*Maclean's*, 1998).

Types of Female Prostitutes

Female prostitutes—commonly called hookers, whores, working girls, or escorts—are usually classified according to the settings in which they work. The major types of prostitutes today are streetwalkers; brothel or "house" prostitutes, many of whom work in massage parlours; and "escorts" or call girls (many prostitutes today have their customers "let their fingers do the walking through the Yellow Pages").

It is important to note that there are jobs other than prostitution, such as phone sex and stripping, that involve sex for money. The more inclusive term *sex-trade worker* is used to take into account these other occupations. Many sex-trade workers engage in that work only on a part-time and/or temporary basis. For example, in her study of female strippers, Jacqueline Lewis of the University of Windsor (1998) distinguished between career and short-term-goal-oriented dancers. The latter group included several university students:

And I looked at the salaries these people were making and it was, you know, a thousand dollars a night, some nights, and it was really, really substantially helping with their tuition. And these were people working on Master's degrees and Doctorates and all kinds of things and I thought, "Wow, if they can do this, hey, maybe I can." (Lewis, 1998, p. 59)

Streetwalkers Prostitutes who solicit customers on the streets.

Pimps Men who serve as agents for prostitutes and live off their earnings. (From the Middle French *pimper*, which means "to dress smartly.")

Lewis (1998) notes that, until the 1960s, stripping was typically part of a burlesque show. Total nudity was not allowed; the dancers stayed on stage and touching them was prohibited. Since then stripping has undergone significant changes in Canada: Today there is complete nudity, and table and lap dances often allow for some physical and sexual contact between dancers and their customers.

STREETWALKERS Part of the mystery about Hugh Grant was why he would resort to the services of any prostitute. Another part of it was why he would seek out a **streetwalker**.

Although most prostitutes are streetwalkers, streetwalkers occupy the bottom rung in the hierarchy of prostitutes. They earn the lowest incomes and are usually the least desirable. They also incur the greatest risk of abuse by customers and **pimps**. A study of street prostitutes in western Canada found that many experienced violence not only from clients and pimps but also from other streetwalkers, intimate partners, and police (Nixon et al., 2002).

Streetwalkers operate in the open. They are thus more likely than other prostitutes to draw attention to themselves and risk arrest (Shaver, 2005). To avoid arrest, streetwalkers may be indirect about their services. They may ask passersby if they are interested in a "good time" or some "fun" rather than offering sex per se.

There is the stereotype of the prostitute as a sexually unresponsive woman who feigns sexual arousal with johns while she keeps one eye glued to the clock. Most street prostitutes in a Philadelphia sample, however, reported that some forms of sex with customers were "very satisfying" (Savitz & Rosen, 1988). More than 60% of the prostitutes reported achieving orgasm with customers at least occasionally. Most prostitutes also reported that they had enjoyable sexual relationships in their private lives and were regularly orgasmic.

In most locales, penalties for prostitution involve small fines or short jail terms. Many police departments, besieged by drug peddling and violent crimes, consider prostitution a "minor" or "nuisance" crime (Carvajal, 1995). Many prostitutes find the criminal justice system a revolving door. They pay the fine. They spend a night or two in jail. They return to the streets.

Some streetwalkers support a pimp, especially those who are younger and who have less than high school education (Shaver, 2005). A pimp acts as lover–father–companion–master. He provides streetwalkers with protection, bail, and sometimes room and board, in exchange for a high percentage of their earnings, often more than 90%. Prostitutes are often physically abused by their pimps, who may use threats and beatings as a means of control (Williamson & Cluse-Tolar, 2002).

Streetwalkers who work hotels and conventions generally hold a higher status than those who work the streets or bars. Clients are typically conventioneers or businessmen travelling away from home. The hotel prostitute must be skilled in conveying subtle messages to potential clients without attracting the attention of hotel management or security. They usually provide sexual services in the client's hotel room. Some hotel managers will tolerate known prostitutes (usually for a payoff under the table), so long as the woman conducts herself discreetly.

BROTHEL PROSTITUTION Many brothel prostitutes occupy a middle position in the hierarchy of prostitutes, between streetwalkers on one side and call girls on the other

A Streetwalker.

Some prostitutes—called streetwalkers—ply their trade by walking the streets and hawking their wares to pedestrians and those who drive by. Others, who may be connected with "massage" or "escort" services, let their customers' fingers do the walking through the Yellow Pages. Still others advertise online.

(Edgley, 1989). They work in a brothel, or—more commonly today—in a massage parlour.

The life of the brothel (or "house") prostitute is usually neither as lucrative as that of the call girl nor as degrading as that of the streetwalker. Some prostitutes who work in massage parlours or for escort services may not consider themselves "real prostitutes" because they do not walk the streets and because they work for businesses that present a legitimate front (Edgley, 1989).

THE MASSAGE PARLOUR Many massage parlours are legitimate establishments that provide massage—and only massage—to customers. Masseuses and masseurs are licensed by provincial governments, and laws prohibit them from offering sexual services. Many localities require that the masseuse or masseur keep certain parts of her or his body clothed and not touch the client's genitals.

Many massage parlours serve as fronts for prostitution, however. In these establishments, clients typically pay fees for a standard massage and then tip the workers for sexual extras.

To avoid massage parlour regulations, some owners have obtained licences claiming they are holistic health centres or aromatherapy centres. In May 2005 the *Toronto Star* ran front-page exposés of the "holistic health centre" industry, with headlines such as "What can Toronto do about sex dens?" At one of the holistic centres the reporters visited, the manager outlined the additional options available beyond the $40 entrance fee: $20 for a topless massage, $40 for a nude massage, and $60 for a body slide (the nude masseuse slides herself over the naked body of the client). Many places also offer a nude reverse in which clients can massage the naked masseuse (Cribb & Brazao, 2005). The articles created a furor at City Hall, and Toronto City Council instructed its licensing staff and police to clamp down on agencies that were not legitimate health centres.

Massage parlour workers generally offer to perform manual stimulation of the penis ("a local" or a "rub and tug"). Most do not offer oral sex or coitus ("full service"), mistakenly believing this will protect them from prosecution.

ESCORT SERVICES If Hugh Grant had hired an "escort," we would probably never have learned of it. Conventioneers and businessmen are more likely to turn to the listings for "massage" and "escort services" in the telephone directory or under the personal ads in local newspapers than to seek hotel prostitutes. Services that provide "outcall" send masseuses (or masseurs) or escorts to the hotel room.

Escort services are typically (but not always) fronts for prostitution. Escort services are found in every major Canadian city and present themselves as legitimate businesses providing escorts for men. Indeed, one will find female companionship for corporate functions and for unattached men travelling away from home under "escort services." Many escort services provide only prostitution, however, and clients of other escort services sometimes negotiate sexual services after formal escort duties are completed—or in their stead.

Prostitutes who work for escort services often come from middle-class backgrounds and are well educated—the better to hold their own in social conversation. Escort services may establish arrangements with legitimate companies to provide "escorts" for visiting customers or potential clients.

CALL GIRLS **Call girls** occupy the highest rungs on the social ladder of female prostitution. Many of them overlap with escorts. Call girls tend to be the most attractive and well-educated prostitutes and tend to charge more for their services. Many come from middle-class backgrounds (Edgley, 1989). Unlike other types of prostitutes, call girls usually work on their own. Thus they need not split their income with a pimp, escort service, or massage parlour. Consequently, they can afford a luxurious lifestyle when business is good, living in expensive neighbourhoods and wearing stylish clothes, and they can be more selective about the customers they will accept.

Call girls Prostitutes who arrange for their sexual contacts by telephone. *Call* refers both to telephone calls and to being "on call."

Call girls may escort their clients to dinner and social functions, providing not only sex but also charming and gracious conversation (Edgley, 1989).They give clients the feeling that they are important and attractive. They may simulate sexual pleasure and create the illusion that time does not matter. It does, of course. To the call girl, as to other entrepreneurs, time is money.

Call girls may receive clients in their apartments ("incalls") or make "outcalls" to clients' homes and hotels. Some call girls trade or sell "black books" that list clients and their sexual preferences. To protect themselves from police and abusive clients, call girls may insist on seeing a client's business card or learning his home telephone number before personal contact is made. They may investigate whether the customer is in fact the person he purports to be.

Characteristics of Female Prostitutes

No single factor explains women's entry into prostitution. Yet poverty and sexual and/or physical abuse figure prominently in the backgrounds of many prostitutes. They often come from conflict-ridden or single-parent homes in poor urban areas or rural farming communities.

Researchers also find a high level of psychological disturbance among prostitutes. Melissa Farley and her colleagues (1998) interviewed nearly 500 prostitutes from the United States, Europe, Africa, and Asia and found that nearly two-thirds of them could be diagnosed with **post-traumatic stress disorder** (PTSD). Ninety percent said that they wanted to get out of "the life."

Poverty accounts for the entry of young women into prostitution in many countries. In some Third World nations, such as Thailand, many rural, impoverished parents in effect sell daughters to recruiters who place them in brothels in cities (Erlanger, 1991; Goldberg, 1995). Many of the women send home whatever money they can and also work hard to try to pay off the procurers and break free of their financial bonds.

In Canada and the United States, many initiates into street prostitution are teenage runaways. While some come from middle-class or affluent homes, others are reared in poverty. Family discord and dysfunction frequently set the stage for their entry into street life and prostitution (Dalla, 2003). Many teenage runaways perceive life on the street—despite its dangers—to be the only possible escape from family strife and conflict, or from the physical, emotional, or sexual abuse they suffer at home. Teenage runaways with marginal skills and limited means of support may find few alternatives to prostitution. It is not long before the teenage runaway is approached by a pimp or a john. A study of 149 teenage runaways in Toronto found that 67% of the boys and 82% of the girls who had been away from home for more than a year had been offered money to engage in sexual activity with an adult (Hartman et al., 1987).

In a study of street prostitutes in Montreal, Robert Gemme (1998) of the University of Quebec found that 44% had been sexually abused and 33% had been sexually assaulted prior to becoming involved in the sex trade.

Not all sexually abused children become prostitutes, of course. In one sample of predominantly female 16- to 18-year-olds who had been sexually abused, 12% became involved in prostitution (Seng, 1989). A more recent study of female street youth in Montreal found that those who became involved in prostitution were no more likely to have experienced childhood sexual abuse than those who did not become prostitutes (Weber et al., 2004).

Abused children who run away from home are much more likely to become involved in prostitution than those who do not (Seng, 1989). Runaways are also more likely to become drug and alcohol abusers. In the Montreal study (Weber et al., 2004), females who were heavy drug users were more likely to become involved in street prostitution.

Post-traumatic stress disorder A type of stress reaction brought on by a traumatic event and characterized by flashbacks of the experience in the form of disturbing dreams or intrusive recollections, a sense of emotional numbing or restricted range of feelings, and heightened body arousal. Abbreviated *PTSD*.

Interestingly, in the Montreal study, having a female sex partner was one of the strongest predictors of female street youths becoming prostitutes. This was especially true if the female sex partner was also involved in prostitution (Weber et al., 2004). More research is needed to determine the role that having a female sex partner may play in initiating young street females into prostitution.

It should be noted that the great majority of studies on prostitutes have focused on street prostitutes, and that these findings may not reflect the characteristics of other categories of prostitutes, such as call girls. Frances Shaver (2002) of Concordia University in Montreal has conducted several field studies of prostitutes in Canada, and believes that much of the material on prostitutes overstates the disadvantaged backgrounds of the sex workers. As noted above, for example, some university students may engage in some form of sex work such as stripping because the pay is better than for many other kinds of jobs (Lewis, 1999). Shaver (1996a) argues that researchers who study prostitutes from a deviance perspective typically ignore the fact that some prostitutes voluntarily choose to enter this business and do not feel that they are victims. According to Shaver, they feel they have a lot of control over their work in that "the prostitute sets the price, chooses the client and has the last say as to when, how and even if sex takes place" (p. 219). Shaver believes that many of the problems associated with prostitution would diminish if it were recognized as a legitimate work profession.

Customers of Female Prostitutes

Hugh Grant was a "john" or a "trick." That is how many prostitutes refer to their customers. Men who use female prostitutes come from all walks of life and represent all socioeconomic and racial groups.

A Vancouver survey of 500 men arrested for soliciting prostitutes found that the johns were in many respects similar to other Canadian men (Kennedy et al., 2003). They ranged in age from 18 to 92, with an average age of 38. More than half were married or in a serious relationship. Their level of income, education, and ethnic background were similar to the Vancouver population. On average the men had used the services of prostitutes 19 times. Seventy percent reported that no one close to them knew they visited prostitutes. They did not differ from a comparison group of university men in sexual attitudes, sex drive, and belief in rape myths (Kennedy et al., 2003).

TYPES OF CUSTOMER Most patrons are "occasional johns." Examples include travelling salesmen or military personnel who are stopping over in town without their regular sex partners. Men are more interested than women in sexual novelty or variety (Barash & Lipton, 2001; Klusmann, 2002; Schmitt, 2003), and variety may provide a major motive for occasional johns.

"Habitual johns" use prostitutes as their major or exclusive sexual outlet. Some habitual johns have never established an intimate sexual relationship. Some wealthy men who wish to avoid intimate relationships habitually patronize call girls.

"Compulsive johns" feel driven to prostitutes to meet some psychological or sexual need. They may repeatedly resolve to stop using prostitutes but feel unable to control their compulsions. Some compulsive johns engage in acts of fetishism or transvestism with prostitutes but would not inform their wives or girlfriends of their variant interests. Some men who are compulsive users of prostitutes suffer from a **whore–Madonna complex**. They see women as either sinners or saints. They can permit themselves to enjoy sex only with prostitutes or would ask only prostitutes to engage in acts such as fellatio. They see marital coitus as a duty or an obligation.

MOTIVES FOR USING PROSTITUTES Though the reasons for using prostitutes vary, researchers have identified six of the most common (Edgley, 1989; Gagnon, 1977):

Whore–Madonna complex A rigid stereotyping of women as either sinners or saints.

1. *Sex without negotiation.* Prostitution may be attractive to men who do not want to spend the time, effort, and money involved in dating and getting to know someone simply to obtain sex. As Edgley comments, the customer "gives [the prostitute] money for sex, she gives sex in return. The entire matter is simple, direct, and sure" (p. 393). Hugh Grant might have wanted to have sex, and his girlfriend was a continent and an ocean away. The streetwalker was willing to supply sex in the absence of a relationship.

2. *Sex without commitment.* Prostitutes require no commitment from the man other than payment for services rendered. The prostitute will not call him at home or expect to be called in return.

3. *Sex for eroticism and variety.* Many prostitutes offer "something extra" in the way of novel or kinky sex—for example, oral sex, use of costumes (such as leather attire), and S&M rituals (such as bondage and discipline or spanking). Men may desire such activity but be unable to obtain it with their regular partners. They may even be afraid to mention the idea. Prostitutes may also be attractive to men who seek variety or novelty in sex partners.

4. *Prostitution as sociability.* In the nineteenth and early twentieth centuries, the brothel served not only as a place to obtain sex but also as a kind of "stopping off" place between home and work—referred to by some writers as a "third place" (Oldenburg & Brissett, 1980). The local tavern and pool hall are nonsexual "third places." At times, sex was secondary to the companionship and amiable conversation that men would find in brothels, especially in the days of the "bawdy houses" of the pioneer West.

5. *Sex away from home.* The greatest contemporary use of prostitution occurs among men who are away from home, such as businessmen at conventions and sports fans at out-of-town sporting events.

6. *Problematical sex.* People who have physical disabilities or disfiguring conditions sometimes seek the services of prostitutes because of difficulty attracting other partners or because of fears of rejection. Some lonely men who lack sex partners may seek prostitutes as substitutes.

Male Prostitution

Male prostitution includes both male–male and male–female activities. Male prostitutes who service female clients—gigolos—are rare. Gigolos' clients are typically older, wealthy, unattached women. Gigolos may serve as escorts or as surrogate sons for the women, and they may or may not offer sexual services. Many gigolos are struggling actors or models.

The overwhelming majority of male prostitutes service gay men. Men who engage in male prostitution are called **hustlers**. Their patrons are typically called **scores**. Hustlers average 17 to 18 years of age and become initiated into prostitution at an average age of 14 (Coleman, 1989). They typically have less than Grade 11 educations and few, if any, marketable skills. The majority come from working-class and lower-class backgrounds. Many male prostitutes, like many female prostitutes, come from families troubled by conflict, alcoholism, and/or physical or sexual abuse (Minichiello et al., 2001).

Hustlers may be gay, bisexual, or heterosexual in orientation. In a large-scale Australian study, half of the male prostitutes surveyed described themselves as being gay (Minichiello et al., 2001). About one-third (31%) said they were bisexual, and 5.5% considered themselves "straight."

The major motive for entering male prostitution, as for female prostitution, is money. In one study, 69% of male prostitutes cited money as their principal motive (Zhou et al., 2002). Running away from home typically serves as an entry point for male as well as female prostitution.

Hustlers Men who engage in prostitution with male customers.

Scores Customers of hustlers.

A World of Diversity

SCHOOLGIRLS AS SEX TOYS

A disturbing new national pastime has taken root in Japan: a male obsession with schoolgirls dressed in uniforms.

In Tokyo there are now several hundred "image clubs," where Japanese men pay $150 an hour to act out their fantasies with make-believe schoolgirls in make-believe classrooms, locker rooms, or commuter trains. A customer may, for example, act the part of a teacher who walks into a classroom and tears the clothes off a schoolgirl. Or he may choose to fondle a schoolgirl on a crowded commuter train.

The clubs are but one part of a growing national obsession—and a growing national market—that the Japanese call "Loli-con," after Lolita. Hiroyuki Fukuda edits one Japanese magazine called *Anatomical Illustrations of Junior High School Girls* and another called *V-Club*, featuring pictures of naked elementary school girls. And a number of schoolgirls earn extra money as prostitutes.

Why? First because it's legal for men in Tokyo to have sex with children who are older than 12. And second, says Masao Miyamoto, a male psychiatrist, because many Japanese men feel threatened by the growing sophistication of older women. So they turn to schoolgirls.

Source: Reprinted from "Schoolgirls as Sex Toys." (1997, April 6). The New York Times, p. E2.

Japanese Schoolgirls.
Sad to say, many Japanese men are obsessed with schoolgirls dressed in uniforms such as these. In Tokyo, it is legal for men to have sex with children who are older than 12. Many men are willing to pay for the privilege.

Heterosexual hustlers may try to detach themselves psychologically from male clients by refusing to kiss or hug them or to perform fellatio. Gagnon (1977) writes, "As long as the [client's] head is below the [hustler's] belly button and contact is on the penis, it is the other person who is [gay]" (p. 264). To become aroused, heterosexual hustlers may fantasize about women while the "score" is fellating them. Many heterosexual male prostitutes maintain heterosexual relationships in their private lives while "turning tricks" with men to earn money.

Frances Shaver (1996a) has done comparisons of male and female street prostitutes in Montreal. Half of the women were working for a pimp, but none of the men were. As well, more of the women indicated that sex work was their only source of income. The women serviced twice as many (28.5) clients per week as the men (14.5). However, the men typically spent about twice as long with each client (40 minutes versus 20) and were more likely to include nongenital touching as well as kissing in their services. Finally, the women were much more likely to experience sexual and physical assault as well as robbery. That female prostitutes face greater danger than males is also reflected in murder statistics; between the years 1991 and 1995, for example, of the 63 reported murders of sex workers in Canada, 60 were women (Allman, 1999).

Coleman (1989) identifies several types of male prostitutes:

- *Kept boys* have relationships with older, economically secure men who keep them in an affluent lifestyle. The older male, or "sugar daddy," often assumes a parental role.

- *Call boys*, like call girls, may work on their own or through an agency or escort service.

- *Punks* are prison inmates who are used sexually by other inmates and rewarded with protection or goods such as cigarettes and drugs.

- *Drag prostitutes* are transvestites or presurgical male-to-female transsexuals who impersonate female prostitutes and have sex with men who are frequently unaware of their gender. Some drag prostitutes limit themselves to fellatio on their customers to conceal their gender. Others take the passive role in anal sex (Boles & Elifson, 1994).

- *Brothel prostitutes* are rarer than their female counterparts. Fewer houses of male prostitution exist.

- *Bar hustlers and street hustlers*, like their female counterparts, have the lowest status and ply their trade in gay bars or on streets frequented by gay passersby. Street hustlers are the most common and typically the youngest subtype. They are also the most visible and consequently the ones most likely to draw the attention of the police.

Male prostitutes typically have shorter careers than their female counterparts (Price, 1989). By and large, male prostitution is an adolescent enterprise. The younger the hustler, the higher the fee he can command and the more tricks he can turn. By the time he reaches his mid-20s, he may be forced to engage in sexual activities he might have rejected when younger or to seek clients in sleazier places.

Why do men purchase the services of male prostitutes? In a British Columbia study, clients of male sex workers generally fell into one of three categories: men who kept their desire to have sex with other men hidden from others; men who wanted to have sex with younger men; and men who could not attract regular male sex partners (Allman, 1999).

HIV/AIDS and Prostitution

Concern about the spread of sexually transmitted infections via prostitution is nothing new. In the 1960s two of three prostitutes surveyed by Gebhard (1969) had contracted gonorrhea or syphilis. Though prostitutes are still exposed to a heightened risk of contracting or spreading these and other sexually transmitted infections, such as chlamydia, today the risk of AIDS poses a more deadly threat. The risk of HIV transmission has been linked to both male and female prostitution (Zhou et al., 2002).

An Alberta study of male sex workers found that two-thirds always used a condom with clients (Romanowski et al., 1994). In Montreal, about a third of both male and female prostitutes reported that they had had an STI within the previous two years (Shaver, 1996b). All the women said they always used condoms with clients when engaging in vaginal or anal sex, and 97% always used a condom with oral sex. Among the male prostitutes, 90% reported using a condom with clients during anal sex but only 50% used a condom with oral sex. (Condoms were used far less often with men who were not clients.) A more recent study of Montreal male street youth involved in sex work had similar findings, with many not using condoms, especially when having oral sex (Haley et al., 2004).

A particular risk factor for HIV infection is unprotected anal intercourse. Among female street youth in Montreal, those who engaged in prostitution were twice as likely to have experienced anal intercourse as those who did not engage in prostitution. Many did not consistently use condoms when having anal intercourse (Weber et al., 2002).

Sex with prostitutes is the most important factor in the male–female transmission of HIV in Africa, where the infection is spread predominantly via male–female sexual intercourse. In Canada and the United States, some prostitutes and their clients and other sex partners inject drugs and share contaminated needles. A Canadian study found that sex workers who inject drugs are less likely to use condoms and more likely to be infected with the HIV virus (Allman, 1999). HIV may be spread by unprotected sex from prostitutes to customers and then to the customers' wives or lovers. One American study found that the rate of HIV infection was 50% for gay male prostitutes, 36.5% for bisexual male prostitutes, and 18.5% for heterosexual male prostitutes (Boles & Elifson, 1994). Customers of such men may thus be exposing their wives and girlfriends to HIV.

Sexually Explicit Material

The production and distribution of sexually explicit material (SEM)—traditionally defined as pornography—is a boom industry (Lane, 2000). Sexually explicit movies have moved from sleazy adult theatres to living rooms in the form of videocassette and DVD rentals and sales. Nobody knows how many people bring sexually explicit photos, videos, and even live sex from foreign nations into their homes via the Internet every day. However, an estimated 30 000 to 60 000 sex-oriented Web sites are currently in use (Lane, 2000).

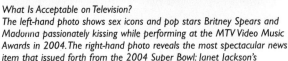

What Is Acceptable on Television?
The left-hand photo shows sex icons and pop stars Britney Spears and Madonna passionately kissing while performing at the MTV Video Music Awards in 2004. The right-hand photo reveals the most spectacular news item that issued forth from the 2004 Super Bowl: Janet Jackson's "wardrobe malfunction." Although other performers had gyrated incessantly, grabbed their crotches, and rapped about rape and mayhem, it was Janet Jackson's breast and a nipple adornment that kept cable "news" show talking heads Sean Hannity and Joe Scarborough frothing at the mouth for weeks. Nobody objected to Justin Timberlake's role-play of attacking Jackson during the song, with lyrics asserting that he was going to have her naked. Message: Violence is fine. Sex? Keep it (literally) hidden.

What Is Pornographic?

Pornography Written, visual, or audiotaped material that is sexually explicit and produced for purposes of eliciting or enhancing sexual arousal. (From Greek roots that mean "to write about prostitutes.") Today, pornography has a negative connotation and is typically associated with SEM that is violent and/or degrading.

Prurient Tending to excite lust; lewd. (From the Latin *prurire*, which means "to itch" in the sense of "to long for.")

Webster's Deluxe Unabridged Dictionary defines **pornography** as "writing, pictures, etc., intended to arouse sexual desire." The inclusion of the word *intended* places the determination of what is pornographic in the mind of the person composing the work. Applying this definition makes it all but impossible to determine what is pornographic. If a filmmaker admits that he or she wanted to arouse the audience sexually, we may judge the work to be pornographic even if no naked bodies or explicit sex scenes are shown. On the other hand, explicit representations of people engaged in sexual activity would not be pornographic if the work was intended as an artistic expression rather than created for its **prurient** value. Many works that were once prohibited in Canada because of explicit sexual content, such as the novels *Tropic of Cancer* by Henry Miller, *Lady Chatterley's Lover* by D. H. Lawrence, and *Ulysses* by James Joyce, are now generally considered literary works rather than excursions into pornography. Even Mark Twain's *Huckleberry Finn*, John Steinbeck's *The Grapes of Wrath*, and Ernest Hemingway's *For Whom the Bell Tolls* have been banned in some places because local citizens found them offensive, obscene, or morally objectionable.

Some people oppose pornography on moral grounds. Some feminists oppose pornography because it portrays women in degrading and dehumanizing roles, as sex objects who are subservient to men's wishes, as sexually insatiable nymphomaniacs, or as sexual masochists who enjoy being raped and violated. Moreover, some feminists hold that depictions of women in sexually subordinate roles may encourage men to treat them as sex objects and increase the potential for rape (Itzin, 2002). In Canada and the United States, feminist efforts to censor pornography were particularly powerful in the 1980s. These censorship efforts continue today, as seen in both nearby World of Diversity boxes.

A World of Diversity

SHOULD THIS PHOTO BE CENSORED?

In the spring of 2005 a group of feminists in Guelph, Ontario, were disturbed when *Echo* magazine placed a close-up picture of a woman diving into a pool on the cover of its *Hot Summer Guide* issue. *Echo* is a Guelph publication that advertises local events and happenings.

The woman diving into the pool is Melanie Gillis, the wife of the publisher of the magazine, who took the picture. Gillis is a Guelph photographer who specializes in maternity and family photography. She also does nude photography.

The feminist group upset by the photo removed several copies of the

Should This Photo Be Censored?
Some feminists in Guelph destroyed copies of Echo *magazine for publishing this cover photo. They claimed it objectified women. Do you think they were right to have removed and destroyed copies of the magazine?*

magazine from downtown display boxes and destroyed them. They also removed the cover from several other copies. One of the women left a phone message at the office of *Echo* explaining that the photo objectified women and thereby contributed to misogyny. They found the photo to be "horribly offensive" and "disgusting" (Gillis, 2005). Following the incident, a number of *Echo* readers wrote letters to the editor deploring the censorship actions. *Echo* then invited Guelph feminist Nicole Freeman to express her views. Freeman (2005) said the photo shocked and angered her because

- It is an example of business exploiting women by using women's bodies to sell products.
- This display of a woman's body is dehumanizing and objectifying and contributes to sexism and misogyny (hatred of women).
- The photo is focused on sexualized body parts which invites the viewer to be a voyeur.

- Men in reacting to this kind of image are more likely to act violently toward women.
- The photo reinforces male dominance and patriarchy.

In responding to these criticisms, Gillis (2005) sought the advice of Dr. Judy Taylor, professor of Sociology and Women's Studies at the University of Toronto. Professor Taylor stated that she found the photo to be harmless and not particularly sexual, and that she was not offended by it.

Gillis also included in her article these two letters to the editor, as they reflected her own feelings toward the censorship actions of the feminist group:

It looks more like you oppressed *Echo*. Not only did you oppress *Echo* but you oppressed everyone in downtown Guelph who relies on the publication for info on coming events and local news.

Ever heard of having fun! I hate you feminist types who assume

that every pretty woman out there who doesn't trash men all the time is dumb, and allowing herself to be objectified....You do not have the right to censor what other people read....People like you are anti-feminist because you remove choice and ridicule women for choosing a path that you would not have taken.

What do you think about the reasons given for censoring the photo? Do you feel the actions of the feminist group were justified?

This story of censorship is not an isolated one. Almost every day in Canada people are making decisions about what is or is not appropriate for us to see or read.

Source: Nicole Freeman (2005, June 16). "Blatant Objectification: Echo's Hot Summer Issue Crossed the Line." Echo, pp. 10–11. Melanie Gillis. (2005, June 16). "It's My Ass." p. 11.

There is definitely a subjective element in the definition of pornography. An erotic statue that sexually arouses viewers may not be considered pornographic if the sculptor's intent was artistic. A grainy photograph of a naked body that was intended to excite sexually may be pornographic. One alternative definition finds material pornographic when it is judged to be offensive by others. This definition, too, relies on subjective judgment—in this case, that of the person exposed to the material. In other words, one person's pornography is another person's work of art. In Guelph, Ontario, a fountain with a statue of a mother, father, and two children raised objections by some fundamentalist Christian groups who claimed that the statue was pornographic because the people it depicted were naked.

Legislative bodies usually write laws about **obscenity** rather than pornography. Even the Supreme Court of Canada has had a difficult time defining obscenity and determining where, if anywhere, laws against obscenity run afoul of the guarantee of the Canadian Charter of Rights and Freedoms.

Let us first define SEM as written, visual, or audiotaped material that is graphic and produced for purposes of eliciting or enhancing sexual arousal. This has been the traditional definition of pornography. In the 1980s feminist groups began to differentiate two types of SEM: pornography and erotica. Pornography was defined as SEM that involved violence and/or degradation against women Erotica was defined as SEM that did not involve violence or degradation against women. **Erotica** may be as sexually explicit as pornography is.

SEM is often classified as either hard-core or soft-core. Hard-core SEM includes graphic and sexually explicit depictions of sex organs and sexual acts. Soft-core material, as represented by R-rated films and *Playboy* photo spreads, features more stylized nude photos and suggested (or simulated) rather than explicit sexual acts.

Obscenity That which offends people's feelings or goes beyond prevailing standards of decency or modesty. (From the Latin *caenum*, which means "filth.")

A World of Diversity

HOW DO WE DECIDE IF AN AD IS TOO SEXY?

This ad of two young women dressing a snowman with clothes taken from a shivering man was rejected by the Toronto Transit Commission (TTC) for being of questionable taste (Powell, 2002). The TTC was concerned that the public would be upset by the ad's sexual connotations, in that one of the women had her hand on the pant zipper of the snowman, indicating that she was beginning to undress him. In its defence, the company that designed the ad claimed that the woman was in fact playfully pulling up the zipper—and that the snowman was not a real

Snowman Jean Machine Ad.
This holiday poster was considered too sexy to be displayed in Toronto subways.

person. The TTC did accept a toned-down version of the ad, which showed the girl in front gesturing at the snowman's chest rather than zipping or unzipping his pants.

Do you think the ad is too sexy for public consumption? What values inform your decision?

SEM and the Law in Canada

Laws against obscenity provide the legal framework for outlawing the dissemination of pornography. Because the definition of obscenity relies on offending people or running afoul of community standards, that which is deemed obscene may vary from person to person and from culture to culture. The word *obscene* extends beyond sexual matters. One could judge TV violence or beer commercials obscene because they are personally offensive or are offensive to women, even if such depictions do not meet legal criteria for obscenity. Would you define the snowman ad shown in the World of Diversity box as obscene?

The Supreme Court of Canada has been strongly influenced by the feminist argument that pornography is exploitative of and degrading to women. For example, the Women's Legal Education and Action Fund argues that pornography causes violence against women, a view that was used by the Supreme Court to uphold the right of censorship in the Regina v. Butler case. This 1992 case concerned the police raid of a Winnipeg store that sold sexually explicit videos. In his appeal to the Supreme Court, Donald Butler, the owner of the store, argued that according to the Charter of Rights and Freedoms he had a right to freedom of expression.

In upholding the constitutionality of the federal obscenity law, the Supreme Court argued that for a work to be considered "obscene" there must be "undue" exploitation of sex. A "community standard of tolerance" test must be applied in order to determine whether undue exploitation had occurred. The courts must consider whether a community would accept or tolerate others being exposed to these materials, taking into consideration the possibility of harm that may result from such exposure. A key factor is whether the exploitation of sex is seen to be degrading or dehumanizing to society in general and in particular to women.

In the Butler case the Supreme Court devised three categories for obscenity. The first category involves material that mixes sex with violence and/or includes children. The second category includes material that involves sex and degradation and is seen as thus encouraging violence or harm to women. Materials falling into either of these categories are deemed to be obscene. The third category involves SEM that is considered to be nonviolent and not degrading to women and does not involve children. Materials falling into the third category are not categorized as involving the undue exploitation of sex and are therefore considered to be acceptable in Canadian society.

All materials such as books and videos that come into Canada can be confiscated by Customs Canada if they are deemed as violating Canada's obscenity laws. Canada Customs also plays a major role in controlling the availability of SEM in Canada. Prior to December 2000, customs officers could seize materials and prohibit them from arriving at their intended destination without having to offer any justification for their decision. (The onus was on those whose materials were seized to prove in court that they were not obscene.) This happened several times to gay and lesbian bookstores. One of these stores, Little Sisters in Vancouver, went to court to challenge these censorship practices. As a result, in 2000 the Supreme Court accused Canada Customs of being especially prejudiced toward gay and lesbian erotic materials, and ruled that it must defend its actions in court. The court did, however, accept the right of customs officials to seize gay and lesbian erotic materials deemed to be obscene (MacCharles, 2000).

Civil libertarians were strongly opposed to legal changes resulting from the Butler decision, feeling that the new interpretations were too restrictive. They were also concerned about the potential subjectivity involved in trying to determine which materials were degrading. However, in some respects the new interpretation of obscenity allowed for greater permissiveness in legalizing previously banned explicit materials.

The Supreme Court decision had a monumental effect on changing the guidelines used by provincial censorship boards. In Canada, censorship and/or classification of films is the responsibility of the provinces. Until the 1992 Butler decision, some provincial censorship boards, particularly in the province of Ontario, banned any scenes of hard-core or penetrative sex. The Ontario censor board revised its guidelines after 1992, which resulted in the legitimizing of sexually explicit films and videos and an increase in the number of adult video stores. Nevertheless, the board continued to censor more material than did other provinces. For example, in 2001 Ontario banned the film *Fat Girl* because it contains scenes of teenage nudity and sexual activity; the film was shown in British Columbia and Quebec without any cuts having to be made (Pevere, 2001).

Until 2005, all films that were either rented on video or shown in theatres had to be approved by the film review board. According to Robert Warren, chair of the Ontario Film Review Board, more than half the films and videos submitted for review were adult sex movies. In 2000, more than 2000 such films and videos were approved by the board, and 1.25 million copies of sex videos were provided with Ontario Film Review Board stickers indicating that they had been approved. Stores selling obscene films or videos not approved by the film review board could be fined up to $100 000 (Brooks, 2001).

In 2004 an Ontario court judge ruled that the Ontario requirement that all films be approved before they could be shown in the province violated freedom of expression under the Canadian Charter of Rights. Thus the Ontario Film Review Board's power of censorship was ruled as being unconstitutional. The court case resulted from a charge against a gay and lesbian bookstore, the Glad Day Bookshop in Toronto. The store was charged for distributing the sexually explicit video *Descent* without having the video approved by the review board.

In response to the court ruling, the Ontario government declared that the film review board would no longer censor films but would classify them with PG, G ,and R ratings. Note that while the provincial government in Ontario no longer censors films, video stores can still be charged by police for selling materials that are defined as obscene under the Criminal Code (Benzie, 2004).

In the 1990s, cable television companies in Canada started offering pay-per-view adult movies, which have become a highly profitable aspect of the cable television business. Canadian satellite companies have also begun to offer adult channels. In the winter of 2001, however, CBC TV presented a documentary about two adult channels that showed sexually explicit scenes involving domination, bondage, and spanking. The negative publicity surrounding the showing of this documentary led the owners of the satellite company to immediately remove the two channels from their offerings.

Many Canadian employers have policies that forbid the viewing of SEM in the workplace. Some use filtering software to prevent employees from visiting certain Web sites and screen email messages for offensive content. Some employees have lost their jobs because they looked at SEM on the Internet while at work. In 2003 six employees at the Catholic Children's Aid in Toronto were fired after it was discovered that they had been exchanging SEM in their office emails. Contrary to the stereotype that only males engage in this behaviour, four of the six fired employees were women (Brennan, 2004).

Child pornography complicates matters further. People who do not find depictions, however explicit, of consensual sexual activity between adults to be obscene may regard child pornography as obscene. Canada's first Criminal Code law specifically directed toward child pornography was enacted in 1993. It made it illegal to sell child pornography, as well as to possess anything depicting people under the age of 18 as engaging in real or simulated sexual behaviour. It also forbids visual representations that are intended for sexual purposes of the sex organs of people under the age of 18 and written materials and pictures that advocate having sex with an underage person. The law does allow for exemption from prosecution if the material has artistic merit or an educational, scientific, or medical purpose.

One of the most controversial legal decisions regarding pornography occurred in 1999, when a British Columbia Supreme Court judge ruled that the Criminal Code section prohibiting simple possession of child pornographic materials violated a Vancouver man's right to freedom of expression in that his stories about young boys had artistic merit. Many members of Parliament were so incensed by the ruling that they wanted the government to override the Constitution so as to ensure that the child pornography law would be upheld.

In 2001 the Supreme Court of Canada did uphold the law; however, it allowed for minor exceptions. These include private materials, such as drawings or personal journals, that are intended only for the eyes of the person who created them. Another exemption allows for SEM created by children or adolescents, such as a photograph of themselves, which is meant to be kept in strict privacy and only for personal use.

Legislation passed in 2005 narrowed the defence allowed individuals accused of possessing child pornography. The accused must prove that they were using the material for a legitimate purpose related to the administration of justice, science, medicine, education, or art and that this purpose does not pose an undue risk of harm to children.

The definition of child pornography was broadened to include audio formats and written material that describes prohibited sexual activity with children created for a sexual purpose. As well, the maximum penalty for possessing child pornography was increased from 6 to 18 months. The legislation also prohibited advertising child pornography.

To avoid police detection, some people who access child pornography use their laptop computer to tap into someone else's wireless network. In one of the first legal cases involving this situation, Toronto police arrested a man who was in front of a house in his car downloading images of a girl involved in a sex act with an adult. The man was charged with possession of child pornography and theft of communications (Millar, 2003).

The practice of using a laptop to get into someone else's wireless network without their permission is called "war driving." Many people do not turn on the security features for their wireless network, which makes them vulnerable to war drivers who can access the computer and its files and do whatever they want online—including accessing sexually explicit Web sites (Miller, 2003).

Attitudes Toward and Use of SEM

Most of us have been exposed to SEM, whether in the form of a novel, an article in *Playboy* or *Playgirl* (purchased, no doubt, for its literary value), or an explicit film. People in Canada and the United States are typically introduced to SEM by their high school years, often by peers (Bryant & Brown, 1989). Females are more likely to have been exposed to SEM by their boyfriends than the reverse (Bryant & Brown, 1989).

Canadians are increasingly using the Internet to view SEM. Among university students in British Columbia, 42% had viewed sexually explicit materials while online (males 75%, females 27%) and about half had begun viewing them before the age of 17 (Boies, 2002). Those who viewed SEM found it sexually arousing (82%) and learned new sexual techniques from it (63%), while 40% had masturbated while online. Yet 57% were disturbed by what they saw. There were notable gender differences in response, especially with regard to masturbating while online (males 70%, females 22%). Nine percent of both men and women had entered sexually focused chat lines, and 8% had met sexual partners online. Finding online SEM sexually arousing was one of the best predictors of online SEM experience, especially for masturbating while online (Boies, 2002).

A more recent survey of students at the University of Guelph found higher rates of exposure to online SEM (Byers, 2005). Almost all of the men (95%) and half of the women (53%) had accessed nude pictures, and three-quarters of the men and half of the women had accessed sexually explicit movies while online. The men spent more time per week viewing and sending SEM than did the women (2.8 vs. 0.2 hours). Yet, about the same proportion of women (64%) as men (60%) had ever sent sexually explicit emails. Another major gender difference was that 69% of the men but only 18% of the women had saved SEM to their computer (Byers, 2005).

Of the total sample, 92% said they were heterosexual, 5% were bisexual, 2% of the men were gay, and 1% of the women were lesbian. Far more men had accessed lesbian SEM (73%) than gay male SEM (18%). Most of the women had not accessed either of these kinds of SEM. Interestingly, more of the women (27%) had accessed lesbian SEM than gay male material (12%).

In responding to a 1992 Gallup poll, 55% of Canadians said that adults should be allowed to buy or rent videos containing explicit scenes of sexual intercourse, 37% disagreed, and 7% gave no opinion (Barrett et al., 1997). People living in Quebec were the most approving, while those in Atlantic Canada were the least. Men were more approving than women, and younger adults were more approving than older adults.

Men, Women, and SEM

Researchers have found that both men and women are physiologically sexually aroused by sexually explicit pictures, movies, and audiotaped passages (Goleman, 1995). That is, both men and women respond to sexually explicit stimuli with vasocongestion of the genitals and myotonia (muscle tension). However, in women there is a significant difference between physiological response and subjective feelings of arousal. Despite what is happening within their bodies, women tend to rate romantic scenes as more sexually arousing than sexually explicit scenes (Laan & Heiman, 1994). Women, remember, are less accepting than men of sex without emotional involvement (Peplau, 2003). Most women want sex to be related to an emotional connection. It is romance that encourages most women to follow the lead of genital arousal, when they do so. Even in the choice of erotic materials, women are much more likely than men to want the element of romance to be included (Hardy, 2001).

In practice, visual SEM (sexually explicit pictures or films) is largely a male preserve (Boies, 2002; Goodson et al., 2001). Most erotic visual materials are produced by men for men. Anthony Bogaert (2001) at Brock University found that the most popular type of films preferred by men were those that portrayed women as having insatiable sexual desires. Women may find SEM a "turn-off" or disgusting, especially when it portrays women in unflattering roles—as "whorish" and subservient to the desires of men.

From the evolutionary perspective, could a basic evolutionary process be at work? Did ancestral men who were more sexually aroused by the sight of a passing female have reproductive advantages over their less arousable peers? Women, by contrast, have fewer mating opportunities and must make the most of any reproductive opportunity by selecting the best possible mate and provider. To be sexually aroused by the sight of male genitalia might encourage random matings, which would undermine women's reproductive success.

Are women really not interested in viewing SEM? To determine the validity of this commonly held belief, the Canadian author of this text and graduate student Kelli-an Lawrence (1988) surveyed women attending a fitness centre in Guelph, Ontario. Two-thirds had read at least one erotic novel within the previous year, whereas only about one-third had viewed a sexually explicit video. The women almost always acquired erotic novels themselves and read them alone. Sex videos, however, were primarily provided by a partner and viewed with him.

Among those who had seen sexually explicit videos, one-half reported that they would feel sexually aroused watching a sex video with their partner or spouse, whereas only one-quarter felt they would be sexually aroused viewing a sex video with female friends or in a mixed group. Not surprisingly, women who had not seen an explicit video had significantly more negative feelings toward them than women who had.

More favourable attitudes toward the use of SEM were found among women who had more liberal sexual attitudes and greater sexual experience, and who were less likely to define themselves as feminists. Those who attended religious services more often had more negative attitudes toward SEM.

A more recent study of women in Sweden found that almost all (85%) had been exposed to SEM (Rogala & Tydén, 2003). Sixty-five percent of those who had viewed these materials believed that their viewing had positive effects, such as making them feel sexy or encouraging them to try new things. Twenty-seven percent reacted negatively; for example, some felt that their partner would want to make them perform sexual behaviours they did not want to be involved in.

In her book *The Princess at the Window*, Canadian feminist Donna Laframboise (1996) disputes the notion that women are not interested in SEM. Rather, she argues that women are more likely to prefer written rather than visual pornography. Laframboise uses illustrations from a number of recent erotic romance novels to demonstrate how these novels have become more explicit and daring in recent years. According to Laframboise, "These books are about female desire as a powerful force in its own right, as something that has the ability to overcome fear and shatter social convention" (p. 261).

There has been a virtual explosion in the number of erotic titles written by women for women, both in bookstores and on the Internet. Toronto marriage and sex therapist Joan Marsman believes this is a positive trend: "There has been lots of love scenes and romance in literature, but for women to claim the erotic, I think it's very healthy. It's part of building fantasy and heightening arousal" (Black, 1999).

It also appears that more Canadian women are comfortable posing in SEM such as topless or nude photographs. Both the Canadian Women's Nordic Ski Team and the Canadian Women's Rugby Team had some of their members pose in nude or semi-nude calendar photos to raise funds for their sports team. As well, women of varying ages from across Canada have posed topless in the annual Breast of Canada calendar, a fundraiser for breast cancer prevention.

Breast of Canada Calendar

www.breastofcanada. com

WOMEN'S RESPONSE TO SEM WHEN WATCHING WITH A PARTNER OR FRIEND

Responses to SEM have usually been measured in laboratory situations, where viewers are usually alone, in pairs, or in groups of strangers. Charlene Senn of the University of Windsor and Serge Desmarais of the University of Guelph (2005) conducted a study to determine if women's responses would be affected by having them watch SEM with either a same-sex friend or a male partner. The participants were randomly assigned to watch one of three types of SEM (violent, sexist, and consensual erotica). They were also randomly assigned to bring either a same-sex friend or a male dating/sexual partner to the lab. The participants and companions rated 50 slides and were given 10 minutes to discuss the images and their reactions with their companion.

The violent images were rated the most negatively, the sexist ones were rated less negatively, and the consensual erotic images were viewed least negatively. Male partners evaluated the three types of SEM more positively than did the female friends. The sexist images were the only type that were rated negatively by the women and positively by the men. Not surprisingly, in their discussions the female participants had less agreement about the slides with male partners than with female friends. Nevertheless, about three-quarters of the participants and their companions said the other person was in agreement with their views.

The mood state of the participants and companions was determined before viewing the images, after viewing the images, and after the discussion. Among the female participants, the mood state was the most negative before seeing the slides, probably because of anxiety over not knowing what they were about to see. The mood state became less negative after seeing the consensual erotic images, and even less negative after discussing them. However, participants who saw the violent SEM retained a highly negative mood after discussing them. The mood state of those who discussed the sexist SEM was somewhat improved but still highly negative.

Source: Senn, C., & Desmarais, S. (2004). The impact of interaction with a partner or friend on the exposure effects of pornography and erotica. Violence and Victims, 19(6), 19–32.

Also on the rise is boudoir photography, in which women have themselves photographed in sexually provocative poses, for their own enjoyment or as gifts for boyfriends and husbands. Photographer Mark Laurie in Calgary has taken pictures of more than 4000 women over the past 25 years, ranging from seductive poses to completely nude ones (Mark, 2003).

Finally, many Canadian couples of all sexual orientations use modern technology such as digital cameras to produce homemade SEM for their own private consumption. This involves taking nude photographs and videos of their partner or of both of them having sex together.

SEM and Sexual Coercion

Is SEM a harmless diversion or an inducement to commit sexual violence or other antisocial acts? Let us consider sources of evidence in examining this highly charged issue, beginning with the findings of a 1985 Canadian government commission.

THE FRASER COMMISSION REPORT In the 1980s, the Canadian government appointed a special committee to study the issues of prostitution and pornography and to make policy recommendations based on the outcome of its findings. This committee's report became known as the Fraser Commission Report (1985). Despite hearing from numerous individuals and groups that pornography is harmful to society, the Fraser Commission concluded that the available evidence did not support the belief that pornography leads to such antisocial behaviour as violent crime, sexual abuse of children, and the disintegration of communities and society.

SEM AND SEX OFFENDERS Another approach to examining the role of SEM in crimes of sexual violence involves comparing the experiences of sex offenders and

Boudoir Photography.
As shown in this photo by Melanie Gillis, many Canadian women are having seductive pictures of themselves taken by professional photographers as gifts for their boyfriend or husband.

nonoffenders with sexually explicit materials. In a review of the research literature, Marshall (1989) found little or no difference in the level of exposure to SEM between incarcerated sex offenders and comparison groups of felons who were incarcerated for nonsexual crimes.

Yet evidence also shows that as many as one in three sexual assailants and child molesters uses SEM to become sexually aroused immediately before and during the commission of their crimes. These findings suggest that SEM may stimulate sexually deviant urges in certain subgroups of men who are predisposed to commit crimes of sexual violence (Marshall, 1989). In a more recent Ontario study, 17% of sex offenders reported they used SEM while committing sexual offences. This involved either showing the victims SEM or taking pictures of the victims (Langevin & Curnoe, 2004).

VIOLENT SEM Laboratory-based studies have shown that men exposed to violent SEM are more likely to become aggressive against females and to show less sensitivity toward women who have been sexually assaulted. In one study, men showed more aggression toward female confederates after watching a sexual assault scene if the victim was shown as enjoying the assault or becoming aroused (Donnerstein & Berkowitz, 1981). These findings suggest that such depictions may legitimize violence against women in the viewer's mind, reinforcing the cultural myth that women need to be dominated and are sexually aroused by an overpowering male.

Yet research suggests that it is the violence in violent SEM, not its sexual explicitness, that hardens men's attitudes toward sexual assault survivors. In one study (Donnerstein & Linz, 1987), university men were exposed to films consisting of violent SEM, of nonviolent SEM (a couple having consensual intercourse), or of violence that was not sexually explicit. The violent films both showed a woman being tied up and slapped at gunpoint, but the non-sexually explicit version contained no nudity or explicit sexual activity. The men had first been either angered or treated in a neutral manner by a female confederate of the experimenter. The results showed that both violent sexually explicit films and violent non-sexually explicit films produced greater acceptance of rape myths than nonviolent SEM, greater reported willingness to force a woman into sexual activity, and greater reported likelihood of engaging in sexual assault (if the man also knew that he could get away with it). These effects occurred regardless of whether or not the man was angered by the woman.

On the basis of a review of the research literature, Linz (1989) concluded that short-term and prolonged exposure to sexual violence, whether sexually explicit or not, lessens sensitivity toward survivors of sexual assault and increases acceptance of the use of force in sexual encounters.

Research on the effects of SEM should be interpreted with caution, however. Most of it has employed university students, whose behaviour may or may not be typical of people in general or of people with propensities toward sexual violence. Another issue is that most studies in this area are laboratory-based experiments that involve simulated aggression or judgments of sympathy toward hypothetical women who have been portrayed as sexual assault victims. None measured actual violence against women outside the lab. We still lack evidence that normal men have been, or would be, spurred to sexually assault women because of exposure to violent SEM or other media depictions of violence.

NONVIOLENT SEM Nonviolent SEM may not contain scenes of sexual violence, but it typically portrays women as sexually promiscuous, insatiable, and subservient. Might such portrayals of women reinforce traditional stereotypes of women as sex objects? Might they lead viewers to condone sexual assault by suggesting that women are essentially promiscuous? Might the depiction of women as readily sexually accessible inspire men to refuse to "take no for an answer" on dates?

Zillmann and Bryant (1984) exposed male and female study participants to six sessions of SEM over six consecutive weeks. Participants were exposed, during each weekly session, to a massive dose of SEM consisting of six nonviolent sexually explicit films ("Swedish Erotica"), or to an intermediate dose consisting of three sexually explicit and three neutral films, or to a no-dose control consisting of six nonsexual films. When later tested in a purportedly independent study, both males and females who received extended exposure to SEM, especially those who received the massive dose, gave more lenient punishments to a sexual assailant who was depicted in a newspaper article. Moreover, males became more callous in their attitudes toward women.

Not all researchers, however, find exposure to nonviolent SEM to increase callousness toward women. Some report finding that nonviolent SEM did not reduce the sensitivity of men (Linz et al., 1988) and women (Krafka, 1985) to female victims of sexual assault. Others report that nonviolent SEM did not increase men's aggression toward women in laboratory studies (Malamuth & Ceniti, 1986). Michael Seto, Alexandra Maric, and Howard Barbaree (2001) from the Centre for Addiction and Mental Health in Toronto conducted an extensive review of the research and concluded that there is little empirical support for the idea that SEM causes sexual aggression. Rather, they believe that men who are predisposed to sexual aggression are more likely to choose to view violent SEM and thus are most likely to show the strongest effects. Men who are not predisposed to sexual violence are unlikely to show any effect.

William Fisher, a psychology professor at the University of Western Ontario, has conducted several experimental studies to measure the effects of SEM. In one study, Barak and Fisher (1997) explored the effects of computer-based interactive erotic stimulation on men's attitudes and behaviours toward women. University men who were exposed to computer-based erotic stimuli showed significant increases in sexual arousal but did not show negative changes of attitude or behaviour toward women in comparison with a control condition. Specifically, exposure to interactive erotic stimulation did not result in aggressive behaviour toward women, nor did it affect men's attitudes toward women's rights and roles in society. As well, this exposure did not change men's perceptions of sexual assault myths.

Given the inconsistencies in the research findings and the limited amount of research on nonviolent SEM, Linz (1989) concludes that

> The data, *overall*, do not support the contention that exposure to nonviolent SEM has significant adverse effects on attitudes toward rape as a crime or more general evaluations of rape victims. (p. 74)

Yet another concern is the possible effect of nonviolent SEM on the viewer's sexual values. Nonviolent SEM typically features impromptu sexual encounters between new acquaintances. Might repeated exposure to such material alter viewers' attitudes toward traditional sexual values? Zillmann (1989) reports intriguing evidence that repeated exposure to this type of nonviolent SEM loosens traditional sexual and family values. When compared with people who viewed nonsexual films, men and women who were exposed to weekly, hour-long sessions involving scenes of explicit sexual encounters between new acquaintances over a six-week period showed attitudinal changes including greater acceptance of premarital and extramarital sex and of simultaneous sexual relationships with multiple partners.

Prolonged exposure to such SEM may also foster dissatisfaction with the physical appearance and sexual performance of one's intimate partners (Zillmann, 1989).

Another concern is that SEM does not offer realistic presentations of how most people function sexually. While many people in real life experience sexual problems, the people portrayed in the sexual media never have sexual problems. The actors are always able to have sex any time and any place for hours at a time. Penises are always erect, vaginas are continuously lubricated, and the women have an insatiable desire for sex, as well as orgasms that occur with little effort. Most of the actors do not use condoms and sexually transmitted infections are never discussed.

In sum, research on the effects of nonviolent SEM is so far inconclusive. The effects of nonviolent SEM may be more closely connected with whether women are presented in a dehumanizing manner than with sexual explicitness per se. No research has yet linked sexual explicitness itself with undesirable effects.

A group of researchers from Ireland and universities in western Canada (Morrison et al., 2004) are critical of most previous research for being narrowly focused on using a harm-based approach to studying the effects of SEM. They are also concerned that almost all of the research has surveyed only men and viewed women as victims.

Morrison and colleagues (2004) argue that researchers have generally ignored the fact that an increasing amount of sexually explicit material is being produced by women for women and couples, which indicates that many women are willing consumers of these materials.

To gain a broader perspective, these researchers surveyed 382 females and 202 males attending a university in western Canada. Among both genders, those who had higher sexual self-esteem and lower levels of sexual anxiety had a higher level of exposure to SEM on television or DVDs. Females who had more recent experience with vaginal and anal intercourse were also more likely to have seen SEM. Safer sex practices were not related to the degree of SEM exposure. Based on these findings, the researchers concluded that exposure to SEM is not related to many of the types of harm that are often discussed in the literature.

Summing Up

The World of Commercial Sex: A Disneyland for Adults

Commercial sex runs the gamut from "adult" movie theatres and bookshops to strip shows, sex toy shops, brothels, escort services, massage parlours, and "900" telephone services.

Prostitution

Prostitution can be traced back at least to Mesopotamia;

it flourished in medieval Europe and during the Victorian period. Then, as now, many poor women were drawn to prostitution as a means of survival.

Prostitution and the Law in Canada

The laws governing prostitution (the exchange of sex for money) in Canada are confusing because while prostitution itself is legal, almost all the activities that involve prostitution are illegal.

Canadian Attitudes Toward Prostitution

The majority of Canadians support legalizing prostitution, although most disapprove of it personally.

Types of Female Prostitutes

The major types of female prostitutes are streetwalkers, brothel prostitutes (many of whom work in massage parlours), escort services, and call girls. Streetwalkers often support, and are abused by, pimps.

Characteristics of Female Prostitutes

No single factor explains entry into female prostitution, but poverty and sexual and/or physical abuse figure prominently in the backgrounds of many prostitutes. Teenage runaways with marginal skills and limited means of support may find few alternatives to prostitution.

Customers of Female Prostitutes

Those who patronize prostitutes are often referred to as "johns" or "tricks." Most patrons are "occasional johns" with regular sex partners. Some people use prostitutes habitually or compulsively, however.

Male Prostitution

Most male prostitutes are "hustlers" who service male clients. Hustlers typically begin selling sex in their teens and may be gay or heterosexual in orientation.

HIV/AIDS and Prostitution

Prostitutes are at greater risk of contracting HIV infection because they have sexual relations with many partners, sometimes without protection. HIV may be spread by unprotected sex from prostitutes to customers, then to the customers' wives or lovers.

Sexually Explicit Material

What Is Pornographic?

Pornography is "writing, pictures, etc., intended to arouse sexual desire." The judgment of what is pornographic or obscene varies from person to person and from culture to culture.

SEM and the Law in Canada

The feminist movement has had a strong influence on federal laws governing SEM in Canada.

Attitudes Toward and Use of SEM

Canadians are typically introduced to SEM by their high school years. Accessing SEM on the Internet is increasingly common.

Men, Women, and SEM

Although both genders can become physiologically aroused by erotic materials, men are relatively more interested in sexually explicit pictures and films.

SEM and Sexual Coercion

Some researchers argue that it is the violence in violent SEM, and not sexual explicitness per se, that promotes violence against women. The effects of nonviolent SEM on normal populations remain unclear.

Test Yourself

Multiple-Choice Questions

1. Which of the following statements is true?
   a. Prostitution is illegal everywhere in Canada.
   b. Prostitution is known as the world's newest profession.
   c. In Quebec, prostitution is legal in licensed houses.
   d. Prostitution itself has never been illegal in Canada.

2. Among prostitutes, _____ have the lowest status and earn the lowest wages.
   a. streetwalkers
   b. brothel workers
   c. call girls
   d. massage parlour workers

3. Among prostitutes, _____ have the highest status and earn the highest wages.
   a. streetwalkers
   b. brothel workers
   c. call girls
   d. massage parlour workers

4. All of the following are important factors in the backgrounds of many young prostitutes except
   a. poverty
   b. sexual addiction
   c. physical abuse
   d. sexual abuse

5. Which of the following is not one of the common motives for using prostitutes?
   a. sex for eroticism and variety
   b. sex without commitment
   c. sex away from home
   d. sex to test one's sexual orientation

6. Men who engage in prostitution with male customers are commonly known as
   a. pimps
   b. gigolos
   c. hustlers
   d. johns

7. A photograph or video would be considered hard-core SEM if it contains
   a. hints or suggestions of sexual acts
   b. explicit depictions of sexual acts
   c. stylized nude photos
   d. nonconsensual sexual behaviour

8. Which of the following statements is true?
   a. Both men and women experience similar physical responses to sexually explicit materials.
   b. Women are more physically aroused by sexually explicit materials than men.
   c. Men are more physically aroused by sexually explicit materials than women.
   d. Alcohol is a major factor in determining physical responses to sexually explicit materials.

9. Most of the research on the effects of exposure to sexually explicit materials has focused on
   a. homosexual sexual behaviour
   b. sex with children
   c. consensual sexual behaviour
   d. sex and violence

10. Which of the following statements is true?
    a. Research has shown that exposure to sexually explicit material causes men to commit violent sexual crimes.
    b. There are a number of serious methodological and conceptual limitations to current research on the effects of exposure to sexually explicit materials.
    c. Research has shown that exposure to nonviolent sexually explicit materials results in significantly more negative effects.
    d. Research has shown that viewing sexually explicit materials can seriously harm a relationship.

Critical Thinking Questions

1. Should all aspects of prostitution be legal in Canada? Why or why not?

2. Take a look at one of your favourite magazines. Do you see advertisers using sex to sell their products? If these images were shown just as pictures, rather than as ads, would you see them as art or pornography? Explain your answer.

3. Have you ever watched sexually explicit material with a sex partner? Do you think this has helped or hurt your relationship?

4. You are having a late-night discussion about sexually explicit materials over a few beers with some friends. One of them says that since most sex offenders drank milk as children, we should ban milk along with the sexually explicit materials. How would you respond to this comment?

Companion
Website

Visit our Companion Website at www.pearsoned.ca/rathus, where you can use the interactive Study Guide and link to additional resources on topics discussed in this text.

Epilogue

Sex Education and Making Responsible Decisions

Making choices is deeply intertwined with our sexual experience. Although sex is a natural function, the ways in which we express our sexuality are matters of personal choice. We choose how, where, and with whom to become sexually involved. We may face a wide array of sexual decisions: Whom should I date? When should my partner and I become sexually intimate? Should I initiate sexual relations or wait for my partner to approach me? Should my partner and I practise contraception? If so, which method? Should I use a condom to protect against sexually transmitted infections (or insist that my partner does)? Should I be tested for HIV? Should I insist that my partner be tested for HIV before we engage in sexual relations?

In this epilogue we discuss the role of sex education in providing information to guide responsible decision-making.

Sources of Information About Sex

Today, we can learn about sex from many different sources. In the 2003 Canada Youth and AIDS Survey, students were asked for their main sources of information about sex and birth control (Boyce et al., 2003). About 45% of Grade 9 students said that school was their main source of information. More girls than boys listed friends and mother as their main sources of sex information, whereas more boys than girls said the school and the Internet were. Only 5% said medical professionals were their main source and hardly any (less than 2%) said that fathers were.

Many people believe that parents should have the main responsibility for providing sex education. In the Canada Youth and AIDS Survey, about a quarter of the boys said they could talk openly about sex with their father or mother, while 37% of girls said they could talk to their mother and far fewer (12%) said they could talk to their father (Boyce et al., 2003). Yet about two-thirds of high school students in a New Brunswick survey rated the sex education they received from parents as good to excellent. However, about one-half did not want their parents to talk to them more about sexuality (Byers et al., 2003).

Beginning in the 1960s, popular magazines became more open about sexuality, realizing that their readers were interested in finding out more about sex. These changes were particularly dramatic from the early 1960s to the early 1970s. A content analysis of popular magazines read by Canadian women in that time period showed a shift toward greater explicitness and more liberal views regarding sexuality (Herold & Foster, 1975).

The popular media are especially important for providing information about topics that are not covered in school programs, such as sexual techniques and pleasure. A study of women at an Ontario university found that women's magazines were a common source of sexuality information (Bielay & Herold, 1995). The most frequently read magazine (by 79%) was *Cosmopolitan*. (Students with more liberal sexual attitudes read the magazine more often than did students having more conservative values.) The women reported that, out of the 34 sexuality topics included in the survey, *Cosmopolitan* was their major magazine source of information for 25.

Although *Cosmopolitan* has an emphasis on sexual content, it is not considered a "sex" magazine but rather a "women's" magazine. This distinction is important in providing greater legitimacy both for the women who read it and the stores that sell it (Bielay & Herold, 1995).

Alternative forms of educating youth about sex have become popular today. The Facts of Life Line, for example, is a phone line sponsored by Planned Parenthood British Columbia that provides confidential information and counselling about all aspects of sexuality.

Several Web sites have also been developed by health, education, and social agencies to provide sex information. One of the most comprehensive is **www.sexualityandu.ca**, sponsored by the Society of Obstetricians and Gynaecologists of Canada. Developed by William Fisher at the University of Western Ontario, the site is based on Fisher's Information-Motivation-Behavioural Skills theoretical model (IMB), which emphasizes the motivation and behavioural skills required by individuals to act in a sexually healthy manner. In addition to providing information specifically for adolescents, the site has modules for adults, parents, and health-care providers. A similar innovative Web site has been developed by Alberta teachers and health professionals at **www.teachingsexualhealth.ca**. Teachers can browse and download lesson plans for teaching sex education by grade level and by topic.

Formal Sources of Sexuality Education

Because education in Canada is the responsibility of the provinces and the territories, the quality of sex education varies tremendously both across provinces and within them. And rather than being taught as a separate subject, sex education is usually included in health courses, often with a focus on its biological/reproductive aspects.

During the 1970s teenage pregnancy was a major concern in Canada, a fact that encouraged many school boards to incorporate sex education topics, particularly contraception, into the curriculum. Until that time contraception had not been taught in the schools, primarily because contraceptives were illegal until 1969. The spread of HIV in the 1980s further encouraged the teaching of sex education, especially the teaching about condoms.

Over the years, some religiously based groups have opposed sex education in Canadian schools and have pressured school boards to adopt programs that teach only sexual abstinence and that avoid subjects such as contraception and homosexuality. For the most part, however, these groups have not been influential in Canada. However, in the United States, conservative religious groups have had a strong voice in influencing President George W. Bush to spend hundreds of millions of dollars on abstinence-only sex education programs. These programs are not permitted to discuss the benefits of contraception. In contrast, the Canadian federal government does not support abstinence-only programs.

Most Canadians support sex education in the schools, including contraceptive methods (Maticka-Tyndale et al., 2001). In a study of 4200 parents in New Brunswick, 94% agreed that sexual health education should be provided by schools. Most of the parents supported the teaching of a broad range of topics, including homosexuality, masturbation, and sexual pleasure (Weaver et al., 2002).

Most Canadian provinces require that sex education be taught as a component of health education at least at the Grade 9 level. In 2005, the Quebec government no longer mandated sex education.

Unfortunately, sex education is not seen as a major priority in most Canadian school systems and the time allocated for instruction on sexual health is minimal. Thus many students are disappointed with the quality of sex education they receive. In a survey of New Brunswick high school students, only 13% rated their sexual health education as very good or excellent (Byers et al., 2003). Moreover, Canadian

Sue Johanson.
The most popular sex educator in Canada presents down-to-earth information in a humorous manner to youth and to adults. Johanson has given sex education talks in every part of Canada to a wide diversity of audiences.

students in 2002 were found to be less knowledgeable about STI and HIV transmission than were students in 1989 (Boyce et al., 2003).

A major criticism of school-based sex education programs is that they focus on harm. In an interview study, young adults in British Columbia and Nova Scotia expressed dissatisfaction with their sex education for neglecting the emotional and potentially positive aspects of sex. They stated that these programs were concerned only with providing information about pregnancy and STI prevention (Shoveller et al., 2004).

Many sex education programs do not address the needs of gay, lesbian, and bisexual youth. University of Alberta researchers Andre Grace and Kristopher Wells (2001) have analyzed many of the difficulties faced by these youth, such as feelings of isolation, fear of humiliation, and lack of social support. Nevertheless, in recent years several initiatives have been made to make schools more inclusive. For example, the Toronto District School Board established a Triangle program for lesbian, gay, bisexual, and transgendered (LGBT) youth.

Teachers' organizations across Canada have adopted policies that are supportive of LGBT youth. The Alberta Teachers' Association has been in the forefront in fighting discrimination based on sexual orientation. Under the leadership of the University of Alberta teaching faculty, guides have been developed for creating safe, caring, and inclusive schools and developing gay–straight alliances.

SEXUAL VALUES While Canadians want sex education in the schools, they differ about what values should be taught. Among 130 Ontario mothers of school-aged children, for example, 91% believed that the schools should teach sex education and 70% agreed that schools should teach contraceptive methods. Asked whether an important objective of sex education was to discourage premarital sex, however, 45% disagreed, 36% agreed, and 19% were undecided. The strongest predictor of attitudes to sex education was the mothers' attitudes to premarital sex. Those who were opposed to premarital sex were the least supportive of sex education and wanted the schools to teach conservative values (Marsman & Herold, 1986).

Alex McKay, in his 1998 book *Sexual Ideology and Schooling*, gives an insightful analysis of the battle over values. He discusses a range of sexual values along a continuum from restrictive to permissive and clearly shows how a particular sexual ideology can influence the objectives and content of sexuality education. McKay argues that students should be informed about the differing values perspectives so that they are better prepared to decide which sexual ideology they should choose for themselves.

CANADIAN GUIDELINES FOR SEXUAL HEALTH EDUCATION To facilitate the development of comprehensive education programs for healthy sexuality, Health Canada sponsored the Canadian Guidelines for Sexual Health Education. These guidelines, developed by experts in sexual health under the coordination of the Sex Information and Education Council of Canada (SIECCAN), not only focus on the prevention of sexual problems such as HIV/AIDS, but also promote sexual health enhancement, for example by promoting positive self-image and non-exploitative sexual satisfaction. These guidelines clearly illustrate how Canadian attitudes differ from American attitudes.

One of the guiding principles of the Canadian Guidelines is that effective sexual health education should be available to everyone, from young children to senior adults. Moreover, promoting healthy sexuality is not simply a matter of providing information, but also involves the development of motivations, insight, and skills so that people can establish and maintain sexual health. To encourage sexually active adolescents to use condoms, the guidelines maintain that schools should not only provide instructions on how to use a condom, but also explain why they are a good idea, help students to communicate about them, and consider ways to make them

The Alberta Teachers' Association Provides resources for building awareness of sexual orientation and gender identity issues. Click on Diversity, Equity and Human Rights under Issues in Education.
www.teachers.ab.ca

**Sex Information
and Education
Council of Canada
(SIECCAN)**

www.sieccan.org

more accessible. (Some Canadian schools, for example, have health clinics providing contraceptives; others have condom dispensers in the washrooms.)

The Canadian Guidelines can be viewed at the Web site of the Sex Information and Education Council of Canada (SIECCAN). The SIECCAN site also provides information on many of the commonly asked questions about sex education programs, such as "Are abstinence-only programs an appropriate form of school-based sexual health education?"

SEX EDUCATION CURRICULUM AND RESOURCES A wide variety of sex education programs and resources have been developed across Canada. In Ontario, Skills for Healthy Relationships is a sexual health curriculum for Grade 9 students developed by the Social Program Evaluation Group at Queen's University. This curriculum provides a practical example of the Canadian Guidelines and follows many of its principles. When the program was evaluated in a two-year follow-up with 6750 students from four provinces, the results showed that students who took the curriculum were less likely to have experienced first intercourse in the two years after the program than students who did not. However, they did not differ from students who had not taken the program with respect to condom use. Within both groups, 41% reported that they always used condoms (Maticka-Tyndale, 2001).

In Nova Scotia, the Office of Health Promotion consulted with 500 youth in developing a sex education book, *Sex—A Healthy Sexuality Resource*. The young people were asked what they "wanted to know, needed to know or wish they had been told" in order to make decisions about healthy sexuality. Consultations were also held with parents, teachers, and experts in sexual health. The book is colourful and presents practical information, such as how to avoid getting STIs and how to talk to one's parents about sex. The book can be viewed online at **www.gov.ns.ca/ohp**.

TRAINING OF SEXUAL HEALTH PROFESSIONALS A major limit to the effectiveness of sex education programs is the lack of training for teachers. Many teachers and therapists have not received adequate training in sexuality. For example, two-thirds of New Brunswick elementary and middle school teachers report that they have not received training to teach sex education (Cohen et al., 2004). Although many Canadian universities offer undergraduate courses in human sexuality, a surprising number have no sexuality courses. Few offer graduate programs.

The Université du Québec à Montréal offers both undergraduate and graduate degree programs (in French) in human sexuality. St. Jerome's University at the University of Waterloo offers an undergraduate program in Sexuality, Marriage, and Family Studies, directed by Dr. B. J. Rye. While other Canadian universities offer graduate courses and/or research specialization opportunities in sexuality, they do not offer degrees in human sexuality. Some training is provided through workshops dealing with specific issues such as sexual abuse. The largest annual conference on human sexuality in Canada is offered by the University of Guelph, where it was initiated by professor Ed Herold (Canadian author of this textbook).

Choices, Information, and Decision-Making

We have presented you with information that can help you make responsible sexual decisions. Information alone, however, is not enough to make decisions. Many issues raise moral concerns, such as premarital and extramarital sex, contraception, and abortion. No single value system defines us all. Each of us has a unique set of moral values—as a Canadian, as a member of one of Canada's hundreds of subcultures, as an individual. Indeed, the world of diversity in which we live is a mosaic of different moral codes and cultural traditions and beliefs. Gathering information and weighing the scientific evidence will alert you to what is possible in the contemporary world, but only you can determine which of your options are compatible with your own moral values.

Making decisions involves choosing among various courses of action. The act of not making a formal decision may itself represent a tacit decision. For example, we may vacillate about whether to use a particular form of birth control but continue to engage in unprotected sex. Is this because we have not made a decision or because we have decided that whatever will be will be?

Gathering information helps us to predict the outcomes of the decisions we make. This textbook provides you with a broad database concerning scientific developments and ways of relating to other people—including people who come from other cultures. By talking to people who have had similar questions or have wrestled with similar conflicts, you can also learn which decisions worked for them, which did not, and, perhaps, why. Or you may be able to learn what happens when people do not make decisions but simply hope for the best. You can also talk to your parents and friends, religious counsellors, course instructors, psychologists, and other helping professionals. Regarding which contraceptive method to use, you may wish to discuss the information in this book with a physician, nurse, or other health counsellor.

We have come a long way together, and we wish you well. Perhaps we have helped you to phrase some very important questions and to find some answers. We also hope that we have encouraged you to try to understand other people's sexual beliefs and values in light of their cultural backgrounds. Understanding is an essential milestone on the pathway to respect, and respect is vital to resolving conflicts and establishing healthy relationships.

Answer Key

Chapter 1	Chapter 2	Chapter 3	Chapter 4	Chapter 5	Chapter 6
1. b	1. b	1. c	1. c	1. c	1. a
2. b	2. c	2. b	2. c	2. b	2. c
3. c	3. d	3. b	3. c	3. d	3. c
4. d	4. a	4. c	4. b	4. a	4. b
5. a	5. c	5. d	5. b	5. d	5. d
6. a	6. b	6. a	6. d	6. a	6. a
7. d	7. b	7. c	7. c	7. b	7. b
8. a	8. d	8. d	8. a	8. c	8. d
9. b	9.)	9. c	9. c	9. b	9. c
10. a	10. c	10. a	10. d	10. b	10. a

Chapter 7	Chapter 8	Chapter 9	Chapter 10	Chapter 11	Chapter 12
1. a	1. d	1. d	1. c	1. c	1. a
2. c	2. b	2. b	2. a	2. a	2. c
3. d	3. b	3. b	3. c	3. b	3. d
4. d	4. a	4. c	4. d	4. b	4. d
5. a	5. b	5. b	5. d	5. b	5. c
6. c	6. c	6. c	6. d	6. a	6. c
7. c	7. b	7. a	7. c	7. c	7. d
8. c	8. d	8. c	8. b	8. d	8. b
9. d	9. b	9. b	9. d	9. d	9. c
10. d	10. d	10. b	10. d	10. d	10. c

Chapter 13	Chapter 14	Chapter 15	Chapter 16	Chapter 17
1. c	1. c	1. a	1. b	1. d
2. d	2. d	2. b	2. a	2. a
3. c	3. b	3. b	3. c	3. c
4. c	4. a	4. d	4. d	4. b
5. c	5. c	5. c	5. d	5. d
6. b	6. b	6. b	6. c	6. c
7. d	7. b	7. a	7. c	7. b
8. d	8. c	8. d	8. a	8. a
9. a	9. d	9. c	9. ᵃc	9. d
10. c	10. b	10. b	10. c	10. b

References

Abbott, E. (1999). *A history of celibacy*. New York: Harper Collins.

Abramowitz, S. (1986). Psychosocial outcomes of sex reassignment surgery. *Journal of Consulting and Clinical Psychology, 54*, 183–189.

Ackerman, D. (1990). *A natural history of the senses*. New York: Random House.

Adachi, M., et al. (2000). Androgen-insensitivity syndrome as a possible coactivator disease. *The New England Journal of Medicine* online, *343*(12).

Adam, B. D. (2000a). Age preferences among gay and bisexual men. *GLQ, 6*(3), 413–414.

Adam, B. D. (2000b). Love and sex in constructing identity among men who have sex with men. *International Journal of Sexuality and Gender Studies, 5*(5), 325–339.

Adam, B. D., Husbands, W., Murray, J., & Maxwell, J. (2005). AIDS optimism, condom fatigue, or self-esteem? Explaining unsafe sex among gay and bisexual men. *The Journal of Sex Research, 42*(3), 238–248.

Adam, B. D., Maticka-Tyndale, E., & Cohen, J. J. (2001). *Living with combination therapies*.

Adams, H. E., et al. (1981). Behavior therapy with sexual deviations. In S. M. Turner, K. S. Calhoun, & H. E. Adams (eds.), *Handbook of clinical behavior therapy* (pp. 318–346). New York: Wiley.

Adams, M. (2003). *Fire and ice: The United States, Canada and the myth of converging values*. Toronto: Penguin.

After years of decline, Caesareans on the rise again. (2000, August 29). *The Associated Press* online.

Aggarwal, A. P. (1992). *Sexual harassment: A guide for understanding and prevention*. Toronto: Butterworth Canada Ltd.

Ah Shene, D. (2003). Crystal Meth. *Developments, 23*(2). Alberta Alcohol and Drug Abuse Commission. [on-line]. Available: **http://corp.aadac.com/services/developments_newsletter/dev_news_vol23_issue2.asp**

Ahmed, R. A. (1991). Women in Egypt and the Sudan. In L. L. Adler (ed.), *Women in cross-cultural perspective* (pp. 107–134). New York: Praeger.

Akhtar, S. (1988). Four culture-bound psychiatric syndromes in India. *The International Journal of Social Psychiatry, 34*, 70–74.

Alderson, K. G. (2003). The ecological model of gay male identity. *Canadian Journal of Human Sexuality, 12*, 75–85.

Alderson, K. G., & Jevne, R. F. J. (2003). Yin and yang in mortal combat: The psychic conflict beneath the coming out process for gay males. *Guidance and Counselling, 18*, 128–141.

Alexander, C. J., Sipski, M. L., & Findley, T. W. (1993). Sexual activities, desire, and satisfaction in males pre- and post-spinal cord injury. *Archives of Sexual Behavior, 22*, 217–228.

Al-Krenawi, A., & Graham, J. R. (1999). The story of Bedouin-Arab women in a polygamous marriage. *Women's Studies International Forum, 22*, 497–509.

Allen, P. L. (2000). *The wages of sin: Sex and disease, past and present*. Chicago: University of Chicago Press.

Allman, D. (1999). *M is for mutual: A is for acts*. Ottawa: Health Canada.

Altemeyer, B. (2001). Changes in attitudes toward homosexuals. *Journal of Homosexuality, 42*(2), 63–75.

Alterman, E. (1997, November). Sex in the '90s. *Elle*, pp. 128–134.

Alter-Reid, K., et al. (1986). Sexual abuse of children: A review of the empirical findings. *Clinical Psychology Review, 6*, 249–266.

Altman, L. K. (1993a, February 21). New caution, and some reassurance, on vasectomy. *The New York Times*, Section 4, p. 2.

Altman, L. K. (1995, July 7). Drug for treating impotence is ready for sale, FDA says. *The New York Times*, p. A13.

Alzate, H. (1985). Vaginal eroticism: A replication study. *Archives of Sexual Behavior, 14*, 529–537.

Alzate, H., & Londono, M. L. (1984). Vaginal erotic sensitivity. *Journal of Sex and Marital Therapy, 10*, 49–56.

American Academy of Child and Adolescent Psychiatry. (1998). Cited in C. Goldberg (1998, September 8). Getting to the truth in child abuse cases: New methods. *The New York Times*, pp. F1, F5.

American Psychiatric Association. (2000). *Diagnostic and statistical manual of mental disorders*, 4th ed. Washington, DC: Author.

American Psychological Association, Committee on Gay and Lesbian Concerns. (1991). Avoiding heterosexual bias in language. *American Psychologist, 46*, 973–974.

American Psychological Association (1998, October 4). Answers to your questions about sexual orientation and homosexuality. APA Public Information Home Page: **www.apa.org**

Ames, M. A., & Houston, D. A. (1990). Legal, social, and biological definitions of pedophilia. *Archives of Sexual Behavior, 19*, 333–342.

Anderson, J. L., et al. (1992). Was the Duchess of Windsor right? A cross-cultural review of the socioecology of ideals of female body shape. *Ethology and Sociobiology, 13*, 197–227.

Angier, N. (1991, August 30). Zone of brain linked to men's sexual orientation. *The New York Times*, pp. A1, D18.

Angier, N. (1995, November 2). Study links brain to transsexuality. *The New York Times* online.

Appleby, T. (2005, March 23). Man's chat room friendship leads to abduction ordeal. *The Globe and Mail*.

Armstrong, K., Eisen, A., & Weber, B. (2000). Assessing the risk of breast cancer. *The New England Journal of Medicine* online, *342*(8).

Armstrong, N. (August 29, 2003). Oral sex 'no big deal,' 13-year-old testifies. *National Post*.

Armsworth, M. W. (1991). Psychological response to abortion. *Journal of Counseling and Development, 69*, 377–379.

Aronson, K. (2003). Alcohol: A recently identified risk factor for breast cancer. *Canadian Medical Association Journal, 168*(9), 1147–1148.

Asbell, B. (1995). *The pill: A biography of the drug that changed the world*. New York: Random House.

Ashton, A. K., et al. (2000). Antidepressant-induced sexual dysfunction and ginkgo biloba. *American Journal of Psychiatry, 157*, 836–837.

Associated Press (2005, September 1). FDA official quits over decision on contraception. *The Guelph Mercury*, p. A9.

Astley, S. J., et al. (1992). Analysis of facial shape in children gestationally exposed to marijuana, alcohol, and/or cocaine. *Pediatrics, 89*, 67–77.

Auld, R. B., & Brock, G. (2002). Sexuality and erectile dysfunction: Results of a national survey. *Journal of Sexual & Reproductive Medicine, 2*, 50–54.

Avery, R. (2002, February 22). MD refuses to prescribe pill, Viagra. *The Toronto Star*.

Bach, G. R., & Deutsch, R. M. (1970). *Pairing*. New York: Peter H. Wyden.

Bagley, C., & D'Augelli, A. R. (2000). Suicidal behaviour in gay, lesbian, and bisexual youth. *British Medical Journal, 320*, 1617–1618.

Bagley, C., & Tremblay, P. (1997). Suicidal behaviors in homosexual and bisexual males. *Crisis, 18*, 23–34.

Bailey, I. (2000, April 26). They are a couple and proud of it. *National Post*, pp. A1, A2.

Bailey, J. M. (2003a). Personal communication.

Bailey, J. M. (2003b). *The man who would be queen: The science of gender-bending and transsexualism*. Washington, DC: Joseph Henry Press.

Bailey, J. M., et al. (1999). A family history study of male sexual orientation using three independent samples. *Behavior Genetics, 29*(2), 79–86.

Bailey, J. M., Kim, P. Y., Hills, A., & Linsenmeier, J. A. W. (1997). Butch, femme, or straight acting? Partner preferences of gay men and lesbians. *Journal of*

Personality & Social Psychology, 73(5), 960–973.

Bailey, J. M., Kirk, K. M., Zhu, G., Dunne, M. P., & Martin, N. G. (2000). Do individual differences in sociosexuality represent genetic or environmentally contingent strategies? Evidence from the Australian twin registry. *Journal of Personality & Social Psychology, 78*(3), 537–545.

Bailey, J. M., & Zucker, K. J. (1995). Childhood sex-typed behavior and sexual orientation: A conceptual analysis and quantitative review. *Developmental Psychology, 31*, 43–55.

Bailey, R. C. (2000). A study in rural Uganda of heterosexual transmission of human immunodeficiency virus. *The New England Journal of Medicine* online, *343*(5).

Baker, J. N. (1990, Summer/Fall). Coming out. [Special issue]. *Newsweek*, pp. 60–61.

Baldwin, J. D., & Baldwin, J. I. (1989). The socialization of homosexuality and heterosexuality in a non-Western society. *Archives of Sexual Behavior, 18*, 13–29.

Bancroft, J. (1984). Hormones and human sexual behavior. *Journal of Sex and Marital Therapy, 10*, 3–21.

Bancroft, J. (1990). Commentary: Biological contributions to sexual orientation. In D. P. McWhirter, S. A. Sanders, & J. M. Reinisch (eds.), *Homosexuality/heterosexuality: Concepts of sexual orientation* (pp. 101–111). New York: Oxford University Press.

Bancroft, J., Loftus, J., & Long, J. S. (2003). Distress about sex: A national survey of women in heterosexual relationships. *Archives of Sexual Behavior, 32*(3), 193–208.

Banmen, J., & Vogel, N. (1985). The relationship between marital quality and interpersonal sexual communication. *Family Therapy, 12*, 45–58.

Banning, A. (1989). Mother-son incest: Confronting a prejudice. *Child Abuse and Neglect, 13*, 563–570.

Barak, A., & Fisher, W. A. (1997). Effects of interactive computer erotica on men's attitudes and behavior toward women: An experimental study. *Computers in Human Behavior, 13*, 353–369.

Barash, D. P., & Lipton, J. E. (2001). *The myth of monogamy*. New York: Freeman.

Barbach, L. G. (1975). *For yourself: The fulfillment of female sexuality*. New York: Doubleday.

Barbaree, H. E., & Marshall, W. L. (1991). The role of male sexual arousal in rape: Six models. *Journal of Consulting and Clinical Psychology, 59*, 621–630.

Barisic, S. (1998, February 18). Study: Breast milk is still best. The Associated Press online.

Barlow, D. H. (1986). Causes of sexual dysfunction: The role of anxiety and cognitive interference. *Journal of Consulting and Clinical Psychology, 54*, 140–148.

Barnard, N. D., Scialli, A. R., Hurlock, D., & Bertron, P. (2000). Diet and sex-hormone binding globulin, dysmenorrhea, and premenstrual symptoms. *Obstetrics & Gynecology, 95*, 245–250.

Barr, H. M., Streissguth, A. P., Darby, B. L., & Sampson, P. D. (1990). Prenatal exposure to alcohol, caffeine, tobacco, and aspirin. *Developmental Psychology, 26*, 339–348.

Barrett, M. B. (1990). *Invisible lives: The truth about millions of women-loving women.* New York: Harper & Row (Perennial Library).

Barrett, M., King, A., Levy, J., Maticka-Tyndale, E., & McKay, A. (1997). Canada. In R. Francoeur (ed.) *The Continuum complete international encyclopedia of sexuality* (pp. 221–343). New York: Continuum Publishing Company.

Bart, P. B., & O'Brien, P. B. (1985). *Stopping rape: Successful survival strategies.* Elmsford, NY: Pergamon Press.

Bar-Tal, D., & Saxe, L. (1976). Perceptions of similarly and dissimilarly physically attractive couples and individuals. *Journal of Personality and Social Psychology, 33*, 772–781.

Bartoshuk, L. M., & Beauchamp, G. K. (1994). Chemical senses. *Annual Review of Psychology, 45*, 419–449.

Basow, S. A., & Rubenfeld, K. (2003). "Troubles talk": Effects of gender and gender-typing. *Sex Roles, 48*(3–4), 183–187.

Basson, R. (1995). Pathophysiology of lifelong vaginismus. *Canadian Journal of Human Sexuality, 4*(3), 183–189.

Basson, R. (2001). Human sex-response cycles. *Journal of Sex and Marital Therapy, 27*, 33–43.

Basson, R. (2002). A model of women's sexual arousal. *Journal of Sex and Marital Therapy, 28*, 1–10.

Basson, R. (2004). Recent advances in women's sexual function and dysfunction. *Menopause, 11*(6 Pt 2), 714–725.

Basson, R., & Brotto, L. A. (2003). Sexual psychophysiology and effects of sildenafil citrate in oestrogenised women with acquired genital arousal disorder and impaired orgasm: A randomised controlled trial. *BJOG : An International Journal of Obstetrics and Gynaecology, 110*(11), 1014–1024.

Basson, R., McInnes, R., Smith, M. D., Hodgson, G., & Koppiker, N. (2002). Efficacy and safety of sildenafil citrate in women with sexual dysfunction associated with female sexual arousal disorder. *Journal of Women's Health & Gender-Based Medicine, 11*(4), 367–378.

Bauer, G. (2001, November). Boys must be boys. *Canadian Living*, pp. 186–192.

Bauerle, S. Y., Amirkhan J. H., & Hupka, R. B. (2002). An attribution theory analysis of romantic jealousy. *Motivation & Emotion, 26*(4), 297–319.

Baumeister, R. F. (1988a). Gender differences in masochistic scripts. *Journal of Sex Research, 25*, 478–499.

Baumeister, R. F. (1988b). Masochism as escape from self. *Journal of Sex Research, 25*, 28–59.

Baumeister, R. F. (2000). Gender differences in erotic plasticity: The female sex drive as socially flexible and responsive. *Psychological Bulletin, 126*, 347–374.

Baumeister, R. F., Catanese, K. R., & Wallace, H. M. (2002). Conquest by force: A narcissistic reactance theory of rape and sexual coercion. *Review of General Psychology, 6*(1), 92–135.

Bawden, J. (2002, January 19). Toppling TV taboos. *Starweek Magazine*, p. 6.

Bean, J. L. (2002). Expressions of female sexuality. *Journal of Sex & Marital Therapy, 28*(Suppl1), 29–38.

Beauregard, E., Lussier, P., & Proulx, J. (2004). An exploration of developmental factors related to deviant sexual preferences among adult rapists. *Sexual Abuse: A Journal of Research and Treatment, 16*(2), 151–161.

Becerra, L., Breiter, H. C., Wise, R., Gonzalez, R. G., & Borsook, D. (2001). Reward circuitry activation by noxious thermal stimuli. *Neuron, 32*(5), 927–946.

Beck, J. G. (1993). Vaginismus. In W. O'Donohue & J. H. Geer (eds.), *Handbook of sexual dysfunctions: Assessment and treatment* (pp. 381–397). Boston: Allyn & Bacon.

Becker, J. V., et al. (1989). Factors associated with erection in adolescent sex offenders. *Journal of Psychopathology and Behavioral Assessment, 11*, 353–362.

Belgrave, F. Z., van Oss Marian, B., & Chambers, D. B. (2000). Cultural, contextual, and intrapersonal predictors of risky sexual attitudes among urban African American girls in early adolescence. *Cultural Diversity and Ethnic Minority Psychology, 6*(3), 309–322.

Bell, A. P., & Weinberg, M. S. (1978). *Homosexualities: A study of diversity among men and women*. New York: Simon & Schuster.

Bell, A. P., Weinberg, M. S., & Hammersmith, S. K. (1981). *Sexual preference: Its development in men and women*. Bloomington, IN: University of Indiana Press.

Beller, M., & Gafni, N. (2000). Can item format (multiple choice vs. open-ended) account for gender differences in mathematics achievement? *Sex Roles, 42*(1–2), 1–21.

Bem, S. L. (1975). Sex role adaptability: One consequence of psychological androgyny. *Journal of Personality and Social Psychology, 31*, 634–643.

Bem, S. L. (1981). Gender schema theory: A cognitive account of sex typing. *Psychological Review, 88*, 354–364.

Bem, S. L. (1985). Androgyny and gender schema theory: A conceptual and empirical integration. In T. B. Sonderegger (ed.), *Nebraska symposium on motivation, 1984: Psychology and gender*. Lincoln: University of Nebraska Press.

Bem, S. L. (1993). *The lenses of gender*. New Haven, CT: Yale University Press.

Bem, S. L., Martyna, W., & Watson, C. (1976). Sex typing and androgyny: Further explorations of the expressive domain. *Journal of Personality and Social Psychology, 34*, 1016–1023.

Bentler, P. M. (1976). A typology of transsexualism: Gender identity theory and data. *Archives of Sexual Behavior, 5*, 567–584.

Ben-Ze'ev, A. (2003). Privacy, emotional closeness, and openness in cyberspace. *Computers in Human Behavior, 19*(4), 451–467.

Benzie, R. (2004, December 10). Film board cut out as censor. *The Toronto Star,* p. A4.

Beres, M. A. (2002*). Sexual consent behaviors in same sex relationships.* Unpublished master's thesis, University of Guelph.

Berger, L. (2000, June 25). A racial gap in infant deaths, and a search for reasons. *The New York Times,* p. WH13.

Bergeron, S., Binik, Y. M., Khalife, S., Pagidas, K., Glazer, H. I., Meana, M., & Amsel, R. (2001). A randomized comparison of group cognitive-behavioral therapy, surface electromyographic biofeedback, and vestibulectomy in the treatment of dyspareunia resulting from vulvar vestibulitis. *Pain, 91,* 297–306.

Bergeron, S., & Lord, M. (2003). The integration of pelvi-perineal re-education and cognitive-behavioural therapy in the multidisciplinary treatment of the sexual pain disorders. *Sexual & Relationship Therapy, 18*(2), 135–141.

Bernstein, W. M., et al. (1983). Causal ambiguity and heterosexual affiliation. *Journal of Experimental Social Psychology, 19,* 78–92.

Berscheid, E., & Walster, E. (1978). *Interpersonal attraction.* Reading, MA: Addison-Wesley.

Berscheid, E., & Reis, H. T. (1998). Attraction and close relationships. In D. T. Gilbert, S. T. Fiske, et al. (eds.), *The handbook of social psychology, Vol. 2* (4th ed.) (pp. 193–281). New York: McGraw-Hill.

Bibby, R. W. (2001). *Canada's teens: Today, yesterday and tomorrow.* Toronto: Stoddart.

Bielay, B., & Herold, E. S. (1995). Popular magazines as a source of sexuality information for university women. *Journal of Canadian Sexuality, 4,* 247–261.

Binik, Y. M., Reissing, E., Pukall, C., Flory, N., Payne, K. A., & Khalife, S. (2002). The female sexual pain disorders: Genital pain or sexual dysfunction? *Archives of Sexual Behavior, 31,* 425–429.

Bixler, R. H. (1989). Diversity: A historical/comparative perspective. *Behavioral and Brain Sciences, 12,* 15–16.

Bjorklund, D. F., & Kipp, K. (1996). Parental investment theory and gender differences in the evolution of inhibition mechanisms. *Psychological Bulletin, 120,* 163–188.

Black, D. (1999, July 10). Erotomania. *The Toronto Star.*

Black, D. (2004, May 11). A tragedy of misguided science. *The Toronto Star.*

Black, L. E., Eastwood, M. M., Sprenkle, D. H., & Smith, E. (1991). An exploratory analysis of the construct of leavers versus left as it relates to Levinger's social exchange theory of attractions, barriers, and alternative attractions. *Journal of Divorce & Remarriage, 15*(1–2), 127–139.

Blair, C. D., & Lanyon, R. I. (1981). Exhibitionism: A critical review of the etiology and treatment. *Psychological Bulletin, 89,* 439–443.

Blais, K., Collin-Vezina, D., Marcellin, K., & Picard, A. (2004). Current reality of homosexual couples: Clinical implications in the context of partnership counseling. *Canadian Psychology, 45*(2), 174–186.

Blakeslee, S. (1992, January 22). An epidemic of genital warts raises concern but not alarm. *The New York Times,* p. C12.

Blanchard, R. (1988). Nonhomosexual gender dysphoria. *Journal of Sex Research, 24,* 188–193.

Blanchard, R. (1989). The concept of autogynephilia and the typology of male gender dysphoria. *Journal of Nervous & Mental Disease, 177*(10), 616–623.

Blanchard, R. (2004). Quantitative and theoretical analyses of the relation between older brothers and homosexuality in men. *Journal of Theoretical Biology, 230,* 173–187.

Blanchard, R., & Bogaert, A. F. (2004). Proportion of homosexual men who owe their sexual orientation to fraternal birth order: An estimate based on two national probability samples. *American Journal of Human Biology, 16*(2), 151–157.

Blanchard, R., Christensen, B. K., Strong, S. M., Cantor, J. M., Kuban, M. E., Klassen, P., Dickey, R., & Blak, T. (2002). Retrospective self-reports of childhood accidents causing unconsciousness in phallometrically diagnosed pedophiles. *Archives of Sexual Behaviour, 31*(6), 511–526.

Blanchard, R., & Hucker, S. J. (1991). Age, transvestism, bondage, and concurrent paraphilic activities in 117 fatal cases of autoerotic asphyxia. *British Journal of Psychiatry, 159,* 371–377.

Blanchard, R., Steiner, B. W., & Clemmensen, L. H. (1985). Gender dysphoria, gender reorientation, and the clinical management of transsexualism. *Journal of Consulting and Clinical Psychology, 53,* 295–304.

Blanchard, R., Zucker, K. J., Cavacas, A., Allin, S., Bradley, S. J., & Schachter, D. C. (2002). Fraternal birth order and birth weight in probably prehomosexual feminine boys. *Hormones and Behavior, 41,* 321–327.

Blumstein, P., & Schwartz, P. (1983). *American couples: Money, work, sex.* New York: William Morrow.

Blumstein, P., & Schwartz, P. (1990). Intimate relationships and the creation of sexuality. In D. P. McWhirter, S. A. Sanders, & J. M. Reinisch (eds.), *Homosexuality/heterosexuality: Concepts of sexual orientation* (pp. 307–320). New York: Oxford University Press.

Bogaert, A. F. (1996). Volunteer bias in human sexuality research: Evidence for both sexuality and personality differences in males. *Archives of Sexual Behavior, 25*(2) 125–140.

Bogaert, A. F. (2001). Personality, individual differences, and preferences for sexual media. *Archives of Sexual Behavior, 30*(1), 29–53.

Bogaert, A. F. (2005). Sibling sex ratio and sexual orientation in men and women: New tests in two national probability samples. *Archives of Sexual Behavior, 34*(1), 111–116.

Boies, S. C. (2002). University students' uses of and reactions to online sexual information and entertainment: Links to online and offline sexual behavior. *Canadian Journal of Human Sexuality, 11*(2), 77–89.

Boles, J., & Elifson, K. W. (1994). Sexual identity and HIV: The male prostitute. *Journal of Sex Research, 31,* 39–46.

Boston Women's Health Book Collective. (1992). *The new our bodies, ourselves.* New York: Simon & Schuster.

Boyce, W., Doherty, M., Fortin, C., & Mackinnon. D. (2003). *Canadian youth, sexual health and HIV/AIDS study.* Toronto: Council of Ministers of Education.

Bozzette, S. A., et al. (1995). A randomized trial of three antipneumocystis agents in patients with advanced human immunodeficiency virus infection. *The New England Journal of Medicine, 332,* 693–699.

Bradford, J. M. W. (1998). Treatment of men with paraphilia. *The New England Journal of Medicine, 338,* 464–465.

Bradford, J. M. W. (2000). The treatment of sexual deviation using a pharmacological approach. *Journal of Sex Research, 37,* 248–257.

Bradford, J. M. W. (2001). The neurobiology, neuropharmacology, and pharmacological treatment of the paraphilias and compulsive sexual behaviour. *Canadian Journal of Psychiatry, 46*(1), 26–34.

Bradford, J. M. W., Greenberg, D., Gojer, J., Martindale, J. J., & Goldberg, M. (1995). Sertraline in the treatment of pedophilia: An open label study. *New Research Program Abstract SNR441;* American Psychiatric Association Meeting; (May 24) Miami, Florida.

Bradford, J. M. W., & Pawlak, A. (1993). Double-blind placebo crossover study of cyproterone acetate in the treatment of the paraphilias. *Archives of Sexual Behavior, 22*(5), 383–402.

Branswell, H. (May 5, 2005). Vaccines to prevent cervical cancer in a hot race to market. *The Globe and Mail.*

Brecher, E. M, and the Editors of Consumer Reports Books. (1984). *Love, sex, and aging.* Boston: Little, Brown.

Brennan, R. (2004, July 13). Ontario rehires 'smut' traders. *The Toronto Star.*

Breslow, N. (1989). Sources of confusion in the study and treatment of sadomasochism. *Journal of Social Behavior and Personality, 4,* 263–274.

Breslow, N., Evans, L., & Langley, J. (1985). On the prevalence and roles of females in the sadomasochistic subculture: Report on an empirical study. *Archives of Sexual Behavior, 14,* 303–317.

Breslow, N., Evans, L., & Langley, J. (1986). Comparisons among heterosexual, bisexual and homosexual male sadomasochists. *Journal of Homosexuality, 13,* 83–107.

Briere, J., & Runtz, M. (1987). Post sexual abuse trauma: Data and implications for clinical practice. *Journal of Interpersonal Violence, 2,* 367–379.

Briere, J., & Runtz, M. (1989). University males' sexual interest in children:

Predicting potential indices of "pedophilia" in a nonforensic sample. *Child Abuse and Neglect, 13*, 65–75.

British Columbia Centre for Disease Control (2002, March 11). Infectious syphilis: British Columbia. *Infectious diseases news brief, Division of disease surveillance*. BC Centre for Disease Control.

Broder, M. S., Kanouse, D. E., Mittman, B. S., & Bernstein, S. J. (2000). The appropriateness of recommendations for hysterectomy. *Obstetrics & Gynecology, 95*, 199–206.

Brody, J. E. (1990, January 23). Scientists trace aberrant sexuality. *The New York Times*, pp. C11, C12.

Brody, J. E. (1993, August 4). A new look at an old quest for sexual stimulants. *The New York Times*, p. C12.

Brody, J. E. (1995a, May 3). Breast scans may indeed help women under 50. *The New York Times*, p. C11.

Brody, J. E. (1995b, July 19). Revolution in treating infertile men turns hopelessness to parenthood. *The New York Times*, p. C8.

Brody, J. E. (1995c, August 30). Hormone replacement therapy for men: When does it help? *The New York Times*, p. C8.

Brody, J. E. (1998a, February 18). Studies confirm alcohol's link to breast cancer. *The New York Times* online.

Brody, J. E. (1998b). Sour note in the Viagra symphony. *The New York Times*, p. F7.

Bronner, E. (1998, February 1). "Just say maybe. No sexology, please. We're Americans." *The New York Times*, p. WK6.

Brooks, J. (2001, May 31). Film review delay at issue in video store trial. *The Toronto Star*.

Brotman, S., Ryan, B., & Cormier, R. (2003). The health and social service needs of gay and lesbian elders and their families in Canada. *The Gerontologist, 43*(2), 192–202.

Brotto, L. A., & Gorzalka, B. B. (2002). Genital and subjective sexual arousal in postmenopausal women: Influence of laboratory-induced hyperventilation. *Journal of Sex & Marital Therapy, 28*(Suppl1), 39–53.

Broude, G. J., & Greene, S. J. (1976). Cross-cultural codes on twenty sexual attitudes and practices. *Ethnology, 15*, 409–430.

Brown, M., Perry, A., Cheesman, A. D., & Pring, T. (2000). Pitch change in male-to-female transsexuals: Has phonosurgery a role to play? *International Journal of Language & Communication Disorders, 35*(1), 129–136.

Brown, N. R., & Sinclair, R. C. (1999). Estimating number of lifetime sexual partners: Men and women do it differently. *Journal of Sex Research, 36*(3), 292–297.

Brown, R. A. (1994). Romantic love and the spouse selection criteria of male and female Korean college students. *The Journal of Social Psychology, 134*(2), 183–189.

Bryant, H., & Brasher, P. (1995). Breast implants and breast cancer—Reanalysis of a linkage study. *The New England Journal of Medicine, 332*, 1535–1539.

Bryant, J., & Brown, D. (1989). Uses of pornography. In D. Zillmann & J. Bryant (eds.), *Pornography: Research advances and policy considerations* (pp. 25–55). Hillsdale, NJ: Lawrence Erlbaum Associates.

Brym, R., & Lenton, R. (2001). Love online: A report on digital dating in Canada. [on-line]. Available: **www.nelson.com/nelson/harcourt/sociology/newsociety3e/loveonline.pdf**

Bullough, V. (1990). The Kinsey Scale in historical perspective. In D. P. McWhirter, S. A. Sanders, & J. M. Reinisch (eds.), *Homosexuality/heterosexuality: Concepts of sexual orientation* (pp. 3–14). New York: Oxford University Press.

Bullough, V. L. (1991). Transvestism: A reexamination. *Journal of Psychology and Human Sexuality, 4*, 53–67.

Bullough, V. L., & Weinberg, T. S. (1989). Women married to transvestites: Problems and adjustments. *Journal of Psychology & Human Sexuality, 1*, 83–104.

Bumpass, L. (1995, July 6). Cited in J. Steinhauer. No marriage, no apologies. *The New York Times*, pp. C1, C7.

Buss, D. M. (1994). *The evolution of desire: Strategies of human mating*. New York: Basic Books.

Buss, D. M. (2003). The dangerous passion: Why jealousy is as necessary as love and sex. *Archives of Sexual Behavior, 32*(1), 79–80.

Buss, D. M., & Scmitt, D. P. (1993). Sexual strategies theory: An evolutionary perspective on human mating. *Psychological Review, 100*, 204–232.

Buunk, B. P., Dijkstra, P., Fetchenhauer, D., & Kenrick, D. T. (2002). Age and gender differences in mate selection criteria for various involvement levels. *Personal Relationships, 9*, 271–278.

Byers, E. S., & Demmons, S. (1999). Sexual satisfaction and sexual self-disclosure within dating relationships. *Journal of Sex Research, 36*, 180–189.

Byers, E. S., & Eno, R. (1991). Predicting men's sexual coercion and aggression from attitudes, dating history and sexual response. *Journal of Psychology and Human Sexuality, 4*, 55–69.

Byers, E. S., & Grenier, G. (2003). Premature or rapid ejaculation: Heterosexual couples' perceptions of men's ejaculatory behavior. *Archives of Sexual Behavior, 32*(3), 261–270.

Byers, E. S., & Heinlein, L. (1989). Predicting initiations and refusals of sexual activities in married and cohabiting heterosexual couples. *Journal of Sex Research, 26*, 210–231.

Byers, E. S., & Lewis, K. (1988). Dating couples' disagreements over the desired level of sexual intimacy. *Journal of Sex Research, 24*, 15–29.

Byers, E. S., Sears, H. A., Voyer, S. D., Thurlow, J. L., Cohen, J. N., & Weaver, A. D. (2003). An adolescent perspective on sexual health education at school and at home: I. High school students. *Canadian Journal of Human Sexuality, 12*(1), 1–17.

Byers, L. (2005). *Gendered use of and exposure to SEMI*. Paper presented at the 2005 Canadian Sociology Association Annual Meeting, London, ON.

Byrd, J., Hyde, J. S., DeLamater, J. D., & Plant, E. A. (1998). Sexuality during pregnancy and the year postpartum. *Journal of Family Practice, 47*(4), 305–308.

Caceres, C. F., & van-Griensven, G. J. P. (1994). Male homosexual transmission of HIV-1. *AIDS, 8*(8), 1051–1061.

Cairns, K. V. (1997). Counseling the partners of heterosexual male cross-dressers. *Canadian Journal of Human Sexuality, 6*, 297–306.

Cairns, K. V., & Hatt, D. G. (1995). Discrimination and sexual harassment in a graduate student sample. *Canadian Journal of Human Sexuality, 4*, 169–176.

Calderone, M. S., & Johnson, E. W. (1989). *Family book about sexuality*, rev. ed. New York: Harper & Row.

Calhoun, K. S., & Atkeson, B. M. (1991). *Treatment of rape victims: Facilitating social adjustment*. New York: Pergamon Press.

Call, V., Sprecher, S., & Schwartz, P. (1995). The incidence and frequency of marital sex in a national sample. *Journal of Marriage and the Family, 57*, 639–652.

Callen, J., & Pinelli, J. (2004). Incidence and duration of breastfeeding for term infants in Canada, United States, Europe, and Australia: Literature review. *Birth, 31*(4), 285–292.

Calzavara, L. M., Bullock, S. L., Myers, T., Marshall, V. W., & Cockerill, R. (1999). Sexual partnering and risk of HIV/STD among Aboriginals. *Canadian Journal of Public Health, 90*(3), 186–191.

Calzavara, L., Burchell, A. N., Remis, R. S., et al. (2003). Delayed application of condoms is a risk factor for human immunodeficiency virus infection among homosexual and bisexual men. *American Journal of Epidemiology, 157*(3), 210–217.

Calzavara, L. M., Coates, R., Raboud, J., Farewell, V., Read, S., Shepherd, F., Fanning, M., & MacFadden, D. (1992). Association between alcohol and drug use prior to sex and high risk sexual behavior in the Toronto sexual contact study cohort. *Canadian Journal of Infectious Diseases, 3*, 45A.

Canadian Abortion Rights Action League (2003). *Protecting abortion rights in Canada*. Ottawa.

Canadian Cancer Society (2002). **www.cancer.ca**

Canadian Cancer Society (2005). **www.cancer.ca**

Canadian Institute for Health Information. (2004). *Giving birth in Canada: A regional profile*.

Canadian Press (1995a, March 24). Sex calls topple MP. *The Guelph Mercury*.

Canadian Press (1995b, July 2). Woman posed as man for sex. *The Guelph Mercury*.

Canadian Press (1997, May 2). American girls flash Windsor cops. *The Guelph Mercury*.

Canadian Press (1999, March 10). Lau and Kinsella settle lawsuit, avoiding trial.

Canadian Press (2001, July 16). Massive support for gays, poll shows. *The Toronto Star*.

Canadian Press (2002, July 25). Net use still booming. Released by CNEWS Technews. [on-line]. Available: **http://cnews.canoe. ca/CNEWSTechNews0207/25_ internet-cp.html**

Canadian Press (2003a, May 21). Alberta alderwoman signs deal on U.S. charges. *The Guelph Mercury*, p. A9.

Canadian Press (2003b, December 23). Baseball hopeful gets jail for sex crimes against teens. *The Guelph Mercury*.

Canadian Press (2005a, August 31). Woman granted divorce for husband's affair with man. *The Guelph Mercury*.

Canadian Press (2005b). Polygamists in BC pose legal quandary. *The Toronto Star*.

Cannistra, S. A., & Niloff, J. M. (1996). Cancer of the uterine cervix. *The New England Journal of Medicine*, *334*, 1030–1038.

Cantor, J. M., Blanchard, R., Christensen, B. K., Dickey, R., Klassen, P. E., Beckstead, A. L. et al. (2004). Intelligence, memory, and handedness in pedophilia. *Neuropsychology*, *18*(1), 3–14.

Cappella, J. N., & Palmer, M. T. (1990). Attitude similarity, relational history, and attraction: The mediating effects of kinesic and vocal behaviors. *Communication Monographs*, *5*, 161–183.

Carani, C., et al. (1992). Effects of androgen treatment in impotent men with normal and low levels of free testosterone. *Archives of Sexual Behavior*, *19*, 223–234.

Carrère, S., Buehlman, K. T., Gottman, J. M., Coan, J. A., & Ruckstuhl, L. (2000). Predicting marital stability and divorce in newlywed couples. *Journal of Family Psychology*, *14*(1), 42–58.

Carrier, S., Morales, A., & Defoy, I. (2005) *Viagra long-term efficacy and quality of life: Results of Canadian long-term study*. Paper presented to World Congress of Sexology, Montreal.

Carvajal, D. (1995). Oldest profession's newest home. *The New York Times*, pp. L29, L32.

Catalan, J., Hawton, K., & Day, A. (1990). Couples referred to a sexual dysfunction clinic: Psychological and physical morbidity. *British Journal of Psychiatry*, *156*, 61–67.

Cates, W., Jr. (1998). Reproductive tract infections. In Hatcher, R. A., et al. (1998). *Contraceptive technology*, 17th rev. ed. (pp. 179–210). New York: Ardent Media.

Cates, W., Jr., & Raymond, E. G. (1998). Vaginal spermicides. In R. A. Hatcher, et al., *Contraceptive technology*, 17th rev. ed. (pp. 357–370). New York: Ardent Media.

Catlin, G. (2002). The health divide: How the sexes differ. *Health Reports*, *12*(3), 9–52.

CDC (See Centers for Disease Control; Centers for Disease Control and Prevention).

CDC tackles surge in sexual diseases. (1998, March 24). The Associated Press online.

Centers for Disease Control. (1993). Evaluation of surveillance for Chlamydia trachomatis infections in the United States, 1987 to 1991. *Mortality and Morbidity Weekly Report*, *41*, 945–950.

Centers for Disease Control and Prevention. (2000a). *HIV/AIDS surveillance report: U.S. HIV and AIDS cases reported through December 1999*, *11*(2).

Centers for Disease Control and Prevention. (2000b, June 23). Trends in gonorrhea rates—Selected states and United States, 1998. *Morbidity and Mortality Weekly Report*.

Centers for Disease Control and Prevention. (2000c, June 9). Youth risk behavior surveillance—United States, 1999. *Morbidity and Mortality Weekly Report*, *49*(SS05), 1–96.

Centers for Disease Control and Prevention. (2000d, June 9). Youth risk behavior surveillance—United States, 1999. *Morbidity and Mortality Weekly Report*, *49*(SS05), 1–96.

Chadda, R. K., & Ahuja, N. (1990). Dhat syndrome: A sex neurosis of the Indian subcontinent. *British Journal of Psychiatry*, *156*, 577–579.

Charny, I. W., & Parnass, S. (1995). The impact of extramarital relationships on the continuation of marriages. *Journal of Sex and Marital Therapy*, *21*, 100–115.

Chat-line romance a trap. (2000, February 4). *The Toronto Star*.

Cheasty, M. (1998, January 15). Cited in Sexually abused women prone to divorce as adults. Reuters News Agency online.

Cheating going out of style but sex is popular as ever. (1993, October 19). *Newsday*, p. 2.

Cherniak, D. (1999). *Birth control handbook, 30th anniversary edition*. Montreal: Montreal Health Press.

Child, T. J., Henderson, A. M., & Tan, S. L. (2004). The desire for multiple pregnancy in male and female infertility patients. *Human Reproduction*, *19*(3), 558–561.

Chiose, S. (2001). *Good girls do: Sex chronicles of a shameless generation*. Toronto: ECW Press.

Choi, P. Y. (1992). The psychological benefits of physical exercise: Implications for women and the menstrual cycle. [Special issue: The menstrual cycle]. *Journal of Reproductive and Infant Psychology*, *10*, 111–115.

Christin-Maitre, S., Bouchard, P., & Spitz, I. M. (2000). Drug therapy: Medical termination of pregnancy. *The New England Journal of Medicine* online, *342*(13).

Clark, M. S., Mills, J. R., & Corcoran, D. M. (1989). Keeping track of needs and inputs of friends and strangers. *Personality and Social Psychology Bulletin*, *15*, 533–542.

Cleary, J., Barhman, R., MacCormack, T. & Herold, E. (2002). Discussing sexual health with a partner: A qualitative study with young women. *Canadian Journal of Human Sexuality*, *11*(3–4), 117–132.

Clements-Schreiber, M. E., & Rempel, J. K. (1995). Women's acceptance of stereotypes about male sexuality: Correlations with strategies to influence reluctant partners. *Canadian Journal of Human Sexuality*, *4*(4), 223–236.

Clumeck, N. (1995). Primary prophylaxis against opportunistic infections in patients with AIDS. *The New England Journal of Medicine*, *332*, 739–740.

Cnattingius, S., Bergstrom, R., Lipworth, L., & Kramer, M. S. (1998). Prepregnancy weight and the risk of adverse pregnancy outcomes. *The New England Journal of Medicine*, *338*, 147–152.

Coates, R. A., Calzavara, L. M., Read, S. E., et al. (1988). Risk factors for HIV infection in male sexual contacts of men with AIDS or an AIDS-related condition. *American Journal of Epidemiology*, *128*(4), 729–739.

Coates, R. A., Soskolne, C. L., Calzavara, L., et al. (1986). The reliability of sexual histories in AIDS-related research: Evaluation of an interview administered questionnaire. *Canadian Journal of Public Health*, *77*, 343–348.

Cochran, W. G., Mosteller, F., & Tukey, J. W. (1953). Statistical problems of the Kinsey Report. *Journal of the American Statistical Association*, *48*, 673–716.

Cohen, A. B., & Tannenbaum, I. J. (2001). Lesbian and bisexual women's judgments of the attractiveness of different body types. *Journal of Sex Research*, *38*(3), 226–232.

Cohen, E. (1998, March 26). Study: "Male pill" proves 95% effective. CNN.

Cohen, J. N., Byers, E. S., Sears, H. A., & Weaver, A. D. (2004). Sexual health education: Attitudes, knowledge, and comfort of teachers in New Brunswick schools. *Canadian Journal of Human Sexuality*, *13*(1), 1–15.

Cohen, M. S. (2000). Preventing sexual transmission of HIV—New ideas from sub-Saharan Africa. *The New England Journal of Medicine*, *342*(13), 970–973.

Cohen-Kettenis, P. T., Owen, A., Kaijser, V. G., Bradley, S. J., & Zucker, K. J. (2003). Demographic characteristics, social competence, and behavior problems in children with gender identity disorder: A cross-national, cross-clinic comparative analysis. *Journal of Abnormal Child Psychology*, *31*(1), 41–53.

Cole, C. L., & Cole, A. L. (1999). Marriage enrichment and prevention really works: Interpersonal competence training to maintain and enhance relationships. *Family Relations: Interdisciplinary Journal of Applied Family Studies*, *48*(3), 273–275.

Cole, F. S. (2000). Extremely preterm birth—Defining the limits of hope. *The New England Journal of Medicine* online, *343*(6).

Cole, S. S. (1988). Women's sexuality, and disabilities. *Women and Therapy*, *7*, 277–294.

Coleman, E. (1989). The development of male prostitution activity among gay and bisexual adolescents [Special issue: Gay and lesbian youth]. *Journal of Homosexuality*, *17*, 131–149.

Coles, C. (1994). Critical periods for prenatal alcohol exposure: Evidence from animal and human studies. *Alcohol Health and Research World*, *18*(1), 22–29.

Coles, R., & Stokes, G. (1985). *Sex and the American teenager*. New York: Harper & Row.

Collaer, M. L., & Hines, M. (1995). Human behavioral sex differences: A role for gonadal hormones during early development? *Psychological Bulletin, 118,* 55–107.

Collins, N. L., & Miller, L. C. (1994). Self-disclosure and liking: A meta-analytic review. *Psychological Bulletin, 116,* 457–475.

Compas (1998). [Modern life survey of the Canadian adult population]. Unpublished raw data.

Condon, J. W., & Crano, W. D. (1988). Inferred evaluation and the relation between attitude similarity and interpersonal attraction. *Journal of Personality and Social Psychology, 54,* 789–797.

Connolly, J., Pepler, D., Craig, W., & Taradash, A. (2000). Dating experiences of bullies in early adolescence. *Child Maltreatment, 5*(4), 299–310.

Connor, E. M., et al. (1994). Reduction of maternal-infant transmission of human immunodeficiency virus type 1 with zidovudine treatment. *The New England Journal of Medicine, 331,* 1173–1180.

Constantine, L., & Constantine, J. (1973). *Group marriage.* New York: Macmillan.

Cooper, A., Delmonico, D. L., & Burg, R. (2000). Cybersex users, abusers, and compulsives: New findings and implications. *Sexual Addiction & Compulsivity, 7*(1–2), 5–29.

Cooper, A., Scherer, C. R., Boies, S. C., & Gordon, B. L. (1999). Sexuality on the Internet: From sexual exploration to pathological expression. *Professional Psychology: Research & Practice, 30*(2), 154–164.

Cooper, A. J., et al. (1990). A female sex offender with multiple paraphilias: A psychologic, physiologic (laboratory sexual arousal) and endocrine case study. *Canadian Journal of Psychiatry, 35,* 334–337.

Cotten-Huston, A. L., & Waite, B. M. (2000). Anti-homosexual attitudes in college students: Predictors and classroom interventions. *Journal of Homosexuality, 38*(3), 117–133.

Cowley, G., & Rogers, A. (1997, November 17). Rebuilding the male machine. *Newsweek,* pp. 66–67.

Cox, C. L., Wexler, M. O., Rusbult, C. E., & Gaines, S. O., Jr. (1997). Prescriptive support and commitment processes in close relationships. *Social Psychology Quarterly, 60*(1), 79–90.

Cox, D. J. (1988). Incidence and nature of male genital exposure behavior as reported by college women. *Journal of Sex Research, 24,* 227–234.

Craig, W. M., & Pepler, D. J. (1997). Observations of bullying and victimization in the school yard. *Canadian Journal of Social Psychology, 13,* 41–60.

Crews, D. (1994). Animal sexuality. *Scientific American, 270*(1), 108–114.

Cribb, R., & Brazao, D. (2005, May 10). What can Toronto do about sex dens? *The Toronto Star.*

Crocker, D., & Kalemba, V. (1999). The incidence and impact of women's experiences of sexual harassment in Canadian workplaces. *The Canadian Review of Sociology and Anthropology, 36*(4), 541–558.

Cronin, A. (1993, June 27). Two viewfinders, two views of gay America. *The New York Times,* Section 4, p. 10.

Crosby, R. A., Sanders, S. A., Yarber, W. L., Graham, C. A., & Dodge, B. (2002). Condom use errors and problems among college men. *Sexually Transmitted Diseases, 29,* 552–557.

Crossette, B. (1998, March 23). Mutilation seen as risk for the girls of immigrants. *The New York Times,* p. A3.

Crossette, B. (2000, August 29). Researchers raise fresh issues in breast-feeding debate. *The New York Times* online.

Crowe, L. C., & George, W. H. (1989). Alcohol and human sexuality: Review and integration. *Psychological Bulletin, 105,* 374–386.

Cummings, A. and Leschied, W. (eds.) (Fall 2002). *Violence in the lives of adolescent girls: Implications for educators and counsellors.* New York: Edwin Mellen Press.

Cunningham, G., Cordero, E., & Thornby, J. (1989). Testosterone replacement with transdermal therapeutic systems. *Journal of the American Medical Association, 261,* 2525–2531.

Cunningham, M. R., et al. (1995). "Their ideas of beauty are, on the whole, the same as ours": Consistency and variability in the cross-cultural perception of female physical attractiveness. *Journal of Personality and Social Psychology, 68*(2), 261–279.

Curtis, R. C., & Miller, K. (1986). Believing another likes or dislikes you: Behavior making the beliefs come true. *Journal Personality and Social Psychology, 51,* 284–290.

Cutler, W. B. (1999). Human sex-attractant hormones: Discovery, research, development, and application in sex therapy. *Psychiatric Annals, 29*(1), 54–59.

Cutler, W. B., Friedmann, E., & McCoy, N. L. (1998). Pheromonal influences on sociosexual behavior in men. *Archives of Sexual Behavior, 27*(1), 1–13.

Dabbs, J. M., Jr., & Morris, R. (1990). Testosterone, social class, and antisocial behavior in a sample of 4,462 men. *Psychological Science, 1,* 1–3.

Dahinten, V. S. (2003). Peer sexual harassment in adolescence: The function of gender. *The Canadian Journal of Nursing Research, 35*(2), 56–73.

Dalla, R. L. (2003). When the bough breaks... : Examining intergenerational parent–child relational patterns among street-level sex workers and their parents and children. *Applied Developmental Science, 7*(4), 216–228.

Daly, K. J., & Herold, E. S. (1985). Who uses natural family planning. *Canadian Journal of Public Health, 76,* 207–208.

Daly, K. J., & Sobol, M. P. (1994). Public and private adoption: A comparison of service and accessibility. *Family Relations, 43,* 86–93.

D'Amico, A. V., et al. (2000). Biochemical outcome following external beam radiation therapy with or without androgen suppression therapy for clinically localized prostate cancer. *Journal of the American Medical Association, 284,* 1280–1283.

Darling, C. A., Davidson, J. K., & Jennings, D. A. (1991). The female sexual response revisited: Understanding the multiorgasmic experience in women. *Archives of Sexual Behavior, 20,* 527–540.

Darroch, J. E., Frost, J. J., & Singh, S. (2001). *Teenage sexual and reproductive behavior in developed countries: Can more progress be made?* New York: Alan Guttmacher Institute.

D'Augelli, A. R. (1992). Lesbian and gay male undergraduates' experiences of harassment and fear on campus. *Journal of Interpersonal Violence, 7,* 383–395.

Davidson, J. K. (2004). *Fearless sex: A babe's guide to overcoming your romantic obsessions and getting the sex life you deserve.* 2nd ed. Gloucester, MA: Fair Winds Press.

Davidson, J. K., & Hoffman, L. E. (1986). Sexual fantasies and sexual satisfaction: An empirical analysis of erotic thought. *Journal of Sex Research, 22,* 184–205.

Davidson, K. J., Darling, C., & Conway-Welch, C. (1989). The role of the Grafenberg spot and female ejaculation in the female orgasmic response: An empirical analysis. *Journal of Sex and Marital Therapy, 15,* 10–119.

Davidson, N. E. (1995). Hormone-replacement therapy—Breast versus heart versus bone. *The New England Journal of Medicine, 332,* 1638–1639.

Davidson-Harden, J., Fisher, W. A., & Davidson, P. R. (2000). Attitudes toward people in exclusive dating relationships who initiate condom use. *Canadian Journal of Human Sexuality, 9,* 1–14.

Davis, A. (2000). Book review: A clinician's guide to medical and surgical abortion. *The New England Journal of Medicine* online, *343*(3).

Dawes, R. M. (1989). Statistical criteria for establishing a truly false consensus effect. *Journal of Experimental Social Psychology, 25,* 1–17.

Dawood, K., Pillard, R. C., Horvath, C., Revelle, W., & Bailey, J. M. (2000). Familial aspects of male homosexuality. *Archives of Sexual Behavior, 29*(2), 155–163.

Day, N. L., & Richardson, G. A. (1994). Comparative teratogenicity of alcohol and other drugs. *Alcohol Health and Research World, 18*(1), 42–48.

Deaux, K., & Lewis, L. L. (1983). Assessment of gender stereotypes: Methodology and components. *Psychological Documents, 13,* 25 (Ms. No. 2583).

Dekeseredy, W., & Kelly, K. (1993). The incidence and prevalence of woman abuse in Canadian university and college dating relationships. *Canadian Journal of Sociology, 18,* 137–159.

Dekker, J. (1993). Inhibited male orgasm. In W. O'Donohue & J. H. Geer (eds.), *Handbook of sexual dysfunctions: Assessment and treatment* (pp. 279–301). Boston: Allyn & Bacon.

Delmas, P. D., et al. (1997). Effects of raloxifene on bone mineral density, serum cholesterol concentrations, and uterine endometrium in postmenopausal women. *The New England Journal of Medicine, 337,* 1641–1648.

de Luca, R. V., et al. (1992). Group treatment for child sexual abuse. [Special Issue: Violence and its aftermath]. *Canadian Psychology, 33,* 168–179.

DeMont, J. (1999, December). Doing it and enjoying it. *Maclean's,* 44–46.

Dennerstein, L., Dudley, E. C., Hopper, J. L., Guthrie, J. R., & Burger, H. G. (2000). A prospective population-based study of menopausal symptoms. *Obstetrics & Gynecology, 96*(3), 351–358.

Dennis, W. (1992). *Hot and bothered: Men and women, sex and love in the nineties.* Toronto: Key Porter Books.

Denny, N., Field, J., & Quadagno, D. (1984). Sex differences in sexual needs and desires. *Archives of Sexual Behavior, 13,* 233–245.

Denov, M. S. (2001). A culture of denial: Exploring professional perspectives on female sex offending. *Canadian Journal of Criminology, 43*(3), 303–329.

den Tonkelaar, I., & Oddens, B. J. (2000). Determinants of long-term hormone replacement therapy and reasons for early discontinuation. *Obstetrics & Gynecology, 95*(4), 507–512.

de Raad, B., & Doddema-Winsemius, M. (1992). Factors in the assortment of human mates: Differential preferences in Germany and the Netherlands. *Personality and Individual Differences, 13,* 103–114.

Derby, C. A. (2000, October 2). Cited in "Study finds exercise reduces the risk of impotence." The Associated Press.

Desmond, A. M. (1994). Adolescent pregnancy in the United States: Not a minority issue. *Health Care for Women International, 15*(4), 325–331.

DeSteno, D., Bartlett, M. Y., Braverman, J., & Salovey, P. (2002). Sex differences in jealousy: Evolutionary mechanism or artifact of measurement? *Journal of Personality & Social Psychology, 83*(5), 1103–1116.

Devor, H. (1997*). FTM: Female-to-male transsexuals.* Bloomington, IN: Indiana University Press.

Devor, H. (2002). Who are "we"? Where sexual orientation meets gender identity. *Journal of Gay & Lesbian Psychotherapy, 6*(2), 5–21.

de Young, M. (1982). *The sexual victimization of children.* Jefferson, NC: McFarland & Company.

Diamond, L. M. (2000). Sexual identity, attractions, and behavior among young sexual-minority women over a 2-year period. *Developmental Psychology, 36*(2), 241–250.

Diamond, L. M. (2002). "Having a girlfriend without knowing it": Intimate friendships among adolescent sexual-minority women. *Journal of Lesbian Studies, 6*(1), 5–16.

Diamond, L. M. (2003a). What does sexual orientation orient? A biobehavioral model distinguishing romantic love and sexual desire. *Psychological Review, 110*(1), 173–192.

Diamond, L. M. (2003b). Was it a phase? Young women's relinquishment of lesbian/bisexual identities over a 5-year period. *Journal of Personality and Social Psychology, 84*(2), 352–364.

Diamond, M. (1993). Homosexuality and bisexuality in different populations. *Archives of Sexual Behavior, 22,* 291–310.

Diamond, M. (1996). Prenatal predisposition and the clinical management of some pediatric conditions. *Journal of Sex & Marital Therapy, 22*(3), 139–147.

Dick Read, G. (1944). *Childbirth without fear: The principles and practices of natural childbirth.* New York: Harper and Row.

Di Giulio, G., & Reissing, E. (2004). *Evaluation of clinical psychologists' provision of sexual health care needs.* Paper presented at Canadian Sex Research Forum Meeting, Fredericton.

DiMatteo, M. R., et al. (1996). Caesarean childbirth and psychosocial outcomes: A meta-analysis. *Health Psychology, 15,* 303–314.

Dindia, K., & Allen, M. (1992). Sex differences in self-disclosure: A meta-analysis. *Psychological Bulletin, 112,* 106–124.

Dindia, K., & Timmermann, L. (2003). Accomplishing romantic relationships. In J. O. Greene & B. R. Burleson (eds.), *Handbook of communication and social interaction skills* (pp. 685–721). Mahwah, NJ: Erlbaum.

Donnerstein, E., & Berkowitz, L. (1981). Victim reactions in aggressive erotic films as a factor in violence against women. *Journal of Personality and Social Psychology, 41,* 710–724.

Donnerstein, E. I., & Linz, D. G. (1987). *The question of pornography.* New York: The Free Press.

Dreidger, S. D. (2002, September 30). What parents don't know (or won't admit). *Maclean's,* 20–26.

Dreidger, S. (2003, May 19). The teacher's lesson. *Maclean's.*

Drew, W. L. (2000). Ganciclovir resistance: A matter of time and titre. *Lancet, 356,* 609–610.

Drews, C. D., et al. (1996, April). *Pediatrics.* Cited in "Smokers more likely to bear retarded babies, study says." (1996, April 10). *The New York Times,* p. B7.

Dreyfuss, I. A. (1998. February 8.) Exercise may cut breast cancer risk. Associated Press online.

Drigotas, S. M., Rusbult, C.E., & Verette, J. (1999). Level of commitment, mutuality of commitment, and couple well-being. *Personal Relationships, 6*(3), 389–409.

Drolet, M. (2002). *The "who, what, when and where" of gender pay differentials.* (Catalogue No. 71-584-MPE). Ottawa, ON: Minister of Industry.

Dunn, K., Cherkas, L., & Spector, T. (2005). Genetic influences on variation in female orgasmic function. *Biology Letters, 1,2.*

Dunn, M. E. (1998). Cited in Leary, W. E. (1998, September 29). Older people enjoy sex, survey says. *The New York Times,* p. F8.

Dunphy, C. (1996). *Morgentaler: A difficult hero.* Toronto: Random House.

Dwyer, M. (1988). Exhibitionism/voyeurism. *Journal of Social Work and Human Sexuality, 7,* 101–112.

Eason, E., & Feldman, P. (2000). Much ado about a little cut: Is episiotomy worthwhile? *Obstetrics & Gynecology, 95*(4), 616–618.

Eastell, R. (1998). Treatment of postmenopausal osteoporosis. *New England Journal of Medicine, 338,* 736–746.

Eckler, R. (2000, July 31). Why I'll never make it on to *Blind Date. National Post.*

Edgley, C. (1989). Commercial sex: Pornography, prostitution, and advertising. In K. McKinney & S. Sprecher (eds.), *Human sexuality: The societal and interpersonal context* (pp. 370–424). Norwood, NJ: Ablex.

Edgley, K. (2002). Condom use among heterosexual couples. Unpublished doctoral dissertation, University of Ottawa.

Edmonson, B. (1988). Disability and sexual adjustment. In V. B. Van Hasselt, P. S. Strain, & M. Hersen (eds.), *Handbook of developmental and physical disabilities* (pp. 91–106). New York: Pergamon Press.

Edwards, T. M. (2000, August 28). Single by choice. *Time Magazine* online, *156*(9).

Edwards, V. J., Holden, G. W., Felitti, V. J., & Anda, R. F. (2003). Relationship between multiple forms of childhood maltreatment and adult mental health in community respondents: Results from the Adverse Childhood Experiences study. *American Journal of Psychiatry, 160*(8), 1453–1460.

Eggers, D. (2000, May 7). Intimacies. *The New York Times Magazine,* pp. 76–77.

Ellis, A. (1962). *Reason and emotion in psychotherapy.* New York: Lyle Stuart.

Ellis, A. (1977). The basic clinical theory of rational-emotive therapy. In A. Ellis & R. Grieger (eds.), *Handbook of rational-emotive therapy.* New York: Springer.

Ellis, E. M. (2000). *Divorce wars: Interventions with families in conflict.* Washington, DC: American Psychological Association.

Ellis, L., & Ames, M. A. (1987). Neurohormonal functioning and sexual orientation: A theory of homosexuality-heterosexuality. *Psychological Bulletin, 101,* 233–258.

Emard, J. F., Drouin, G., Thouez, J. P., & Ghadirian, P. (2001). Vasectomy and prostate cancer in Quebec, Canada. *Health & Place, 7*(2), 131–139.

English, P. B., & Eskenazi, B. (1992). Reinterpreting the effects of maternal smoking on infant birthweight and perinatal mortality: A multivariate approach to birthweight standardization. *International Journal of Epidemiology, 21,* 1097–1105.

Erel, O., & Burman, B. (1995). Interrelatedness of marital relations and parent–child relations: A meta-analytic review. *Psychological Bulletin, 118,* 108–132.

Erlanger, S. (1991, July 14). A plague awaits. *The New York Times Magazine,* pp. 24ff.

Etaugh, C., & Rathus, S. A. (1995). *The world of children*. Ft. Worth, TX: Harcourt.

Evans, J. (2001). Men nurses and masculinities: Exploring gendered and sexual relations in nursing. Unpublished doctoral dissertation, Dalhousie University, Halifax.

Everaerd, W. (1993). Male erectile disorder. In W. O'Donohue & J. H. Geer (eds.), *Handbook of sexual dysfunctions: Assessment and treatment* (pp. 201–224). Boston: Allyn & Bacon.

Everitt, B. J. (1990). Sexual motivation: A neural and behavioural analysis of the mechanisms underlying appetitive and copulatory responses of male rats. *Neuroscience and Biobehavioral Reviews, 14*, 217–232.

Faller, K. C. (1989). Why sexual abuse? An exploration of the intergenerational hypothesis. *Child Abuse and Neglect, 13*, 543–548.

Fallon, A. E., & Rozin, P. (1985). Sex differences in perceptions of desirable body shape. *Journal of Abnormal Psychology, 94*, 102–105.

Farley, M., Baral, I., & Sezgin, U. (1998). Prostitution in five countries: Violence and post-traumatic stress disorder. *Feminism & Psychology, 8*(4), 405–426.

FDA approves abortion pill. (2000, September 28). Associated Press online.

Federman, D. D. (1994). Life without estrogen. *The New England Journal of Medicine, 331*, 1088–1089.

Federoff, J. P. (1995). Antiandrogens vs. serotonergic medications in the treatment of sex offenders: A preliminary compliance study. *Canadian Journal of Human Sexuality, 4*, 111–123.

Fedoroff, P. (2003). The Paraphilic World. In S. B. Levine, C. R. Risen, & S. E. Althof (eds.), *Handbook of clinical sexuality for mental health professionals* (pp. 333–355). New York: Brunner-Routledge.

Fedoroff, J. P., Fishell, A., & Fedoroff, B. (1999). A case series of women evaluated for baraphilic sexual disorders. *Canadian Journal of Human Sexuality, 8*, 127–140.

Feingold, A. (1991). Sex differences in the effects of similarity and physical attractiveness on opposite-sex attraction. *Basic and Applied Social Psychology, 12*, 357–367.

Feingold, A. (1994). Gender differences in personality: A meta-analysis. *Psychological Bulletin, 116*, 429–456.

Fekete, J. (1994*). Moral panic: Biopolitics rising*. Montreal: Robert Davies Publishing.

Feldman, H. A., Goldstein, I., Hatzichristou, D. G., Krane, R. J., McKinlay, J. B. (1994). Impotence and its medical and psychosocial correlates: Results of the Massachusetts Male Aging Study. *Journal of Urology, 151*(1), 54–61.

Felsman, D., Brannigan, G., & Yellin, P. (1987). Control theory in dealing with adolescent sexuality and pregnancy. *Journal of Sex Education and Therapy, 13*, 15–16.

Feng, T. (1993). Substance abuse in pregnancy. *Current Opinions in Obstetrics and Gynecology, 5*, 16–23.

Fergus, K. D., Gray, R. E., & Fitch, M. I. (2002). Sexual dysfunction and the preservation of manhood: Experiences of men with prostate cancer. *Journal of Health Psychology, 7*(3), 303–316.

Ferguson, D. M., Horwood, L. J., & Beautrais, A. L. (1999). Is sexual orientation related to mental health problems and suicidality in young people? *Archives of General Psychiatry, 56*(10), 876–880.

Fichner-Rathus, L. (2004). *Understanding art*. Belmont, CA: Wadsworth.

Finkelhor, D. (1984). *Child sexual abuse: Theory and research*. New York: The Free Press.

Finkelhor, D. (1988). The trauma of child sexual abuse: Two models. In G. E. Wyatt & J. G. Powell (eds.), *The lasting effects of child sexual abuse* (pp. 61–82). Newbury Park, CA: Sage.

Finkelhor, D. (1990). Early and long-term effects of child sexual abuse: An update. *Professional Psychology: Research and Practice, 21*, 325–330.

Finkelhor, D., & Yllo, K. (1982). Rape in marriage: A sociological view. In D. Finkelhor, R. J. Gelles, G. T. Hotaling, & M. A. Straus (eds.), *The dark side of families: Current family violence research* (pp. 119–130). Beverly Hills, CA: Sage.

Finkenauer, C., & Hazam, H. (2000). Disclosure and secrecy in marriage: Do both contribute to marital satisfaction? *Journal of Social & Personal Relationships, 17*(2), 245–263.

Finnie, R. (1993). Women, men and the economic consequences of divorce: Evidence from Canadian Longitudinal Data. *Canadian Review of Sociology and Anthropology, 30(2)*, 205–241.

Firestone, P., Bradford, J. M., McCoy, M., Greenberg, D. M., Amy, S., & Larose, M. R. (1998). Recidivism in convicted rapists. *Journal of the American Academy of Psychiatry and the Law, 26*, 185–200.

Firestone, P., Bradford, J. M., McCoy, M., Greenberg, D. M., Larose, M. R., Amy, S. (1999). Prediction of recidivism in incest offenders. *Journal of Interpersonal Violence, 14*, 511–531.

Fischer, B., Wortley, S., Webster, C., & Kirst, M. (2002). The socio-legal dynamics and implications of 'diversion': The case study of the Toronto 'john school' diversion programme for prostitution offenders. *Criminal Justice, 2*(4), 385–410.

Fischtein, D. S., & Herold, E. S. (2002, June). *Gender differences in sexual attitudes and behaviours among Canadian adults: A national survey*. Poster session presented at the annual meeting of the International Academy of Sex Research, Hamburg, Germany.

Fish, L. S., Busby, D., & Killian, K. (1994). Structural couple therapy in the treatment of inhibited sexual drive. *American Journal of Family Therapy, 22*(2), 113–125.

Fish, T. A., & Rye, B. J. (1991). Attitudes toward a homosexual or heterosexual person with AIDS. *Journal of Applied Social Psychology, 21*(8), 651–667.

Fisher, B. S., Daigle, L. E., Cullen, F. T., & Turner, M. G. (2003). Reporting sexual victimization to the police and others: Results from a national-level study of college women. *Criminal Justice & Behavior, 30*(1), 6–38.

Fisher, H. E. (2000). Brains do it: Lust, attraction and attachment. *Cerebrum, 2*, 23–42.

Fisher, J. D., & Fisher, W. A. (1992). Changing AIDS-risk behavior. *Psychological Bulletin, 111*, 455–474.

Fisher, T. D., & Hall, R. H. (1988). A scale for the comparison of the sexual attitudes of adolescents and their parents. *Journal of Sex Research, 24*, 90–100.

Fisher, W. A., & Boroditsky, R. (2000). Sexual activity, contraceptive choice and sexual and reproductive health indicators among single Canadian women aged 15–29: Additional findings from the Canadian contraception study. *Canadian Journal of Human Sexuality, 9*(2), 9–93.

Fisher, W. A., Boroditsky, R., & Bridges, M. L. (1999). The 1998 Canadian contraception study. *Canadian Journal of Human Sexuality, 8*(3), 161–220.

Fisher, W., Boroditsky, R., & Morris, B. (2004a). The 2002 Canadian contraception study: part 1. *Journal of Obstetrics and Gynaecology Canada, 26*(6), 580–590.

Fisher, W., Boroditsky, R., & Morris, B. (2004b). The 2002 Canadian contraception study: part 2. *Journal of Obstetrics and Gynaecology Canada, 26*(7), 646–656.

Fisher, W., et al. (2005). Association of PDE-5 inhibitor use in men with ED and sexual function of partners. Paper presented at the World Congress of Sexology, Montreal.

Fisher-Thompson, D. (1990). Adult sex typing of children's toys. *Sex Roles, 23*, 291–303.

Flaxman, S. M., & Sherman, P. W. (2000). Morning sickness: A mechanism for protecting mother and embryo. *The Quarterly Review of Biology, 5*(2), 113–148.

Flexner, C. (1998). Drug therapy: HIV-protease inhibitors. *The New England Journal of Medicine, 338*, 1281–1292.

Floyd, R. L., Rimer, B. K., Giovino, G. A., Mullen, P. D., & Sullivan, S. E. (1993). A review of smoking in pregnancy: Effects of pregnancy outcomes and cessation efforts. *Annual Review of Public Health, 14*, 379–411.

Ford, C. (2004). Perceived risk of chlamydial and gonococcal infection among sexually experienced young adults in the United States. *Perspectives on Sexual and Reproductive Health, 36*, 258–264.

Ford, C. S., & Beach, F. A. (1951). *Patterns of sexual behavior*. New York: Harper & Row.

Forgas, J. P., Levinger, G., & Moylan, S. J. (1994). Feeling good and feeling close: Affective influences on the perception of intimate relationships. *Personal Relationships, 1*(2), 165–184.

Fortier, C., & Julien, D. (2003). Conversion psychotherapies for homosexual and bisexual individuals: Ethical issues. *Canadian Psychology, 44*(4), 332–350.

Foster, D. (2005, in press). The formation and continuance of lesbian families in Canada. *Canadian Bulletin of Medical History*.

Franco, E. L., Schlecht, N. F., & Saslow, D. (2003). The epidemiology of cervical cancer. *Cancer Journal, 9*(5), 348–359.

Franzoi, S. L., & Herzog, M. E. (1987). Judging physical attractiveness: What body aspects do we use? *Personality and Social Psychology Bulletin, 13,* 19–33.

Frayser, S. (1985). *Varieties of sexual experience: An anthropological perspective on human sexuality.* New Haven, CT: Human Relations Area Files Press.

Freiberg, P. (1995). Psychologists examine attacks on homosexuals. *APA Monitor, 26*(6), 30–31.

Freud, S. (1922/1959). Analysis of a phobia in a 5-year-old boy. In A. & J. Strachey (ed. & trans.), *Collected papers,* Vol. 3. New York: Basic Books. (Original work published 1909.)

Freund, K., & Blanchard, R. (1986). The concept of courtship disorder. *Journal of Sex and Marital Therapy, 12,* 79–92.

Freund, K., Seto, M., & Kubian, M. (1997). Frotteurism and the theory of courtship disorder. In D. R. Laws & W. O'Donohue (eds.), *Sexual deviance: Theory, assessment, and treatment* (pp. 111–130). New York: Guilford.

Freund, K., Watson, R., & Rienzo, D. (1988). The value of self-reports in the study of voyeurism and exhibitionism. *Annals of Sex Research 1,* 243–262.

Friedman, R. C., & Downey, J. I. (1994). Homosexuality. *The New England Journal of Medicine, 331,* 923–930.

Friedrich, W. N., & Gerber, P. N. (1994). Autoerotic asphyxia: The development of a paraphilia. *Journal of the American Academy of Child and Adolescent Psychiatry, 33*(7), 970–974.

Friesen, J. (2005, April 22). Nude photos make Web calamity for girl. *The Globe and Mail.*

Frisch, R. (1997). Cited in Angier, N. (1997a). Chemical tied to fat control could help trigger puberty. *The New York Times,* C3.

Frohlich, P., & Meston, C. (2002). Sexual functioning and self-reported depressive symptoms among college women. *Journal of Sex Research, 39*(4), 321–325.

Furstenberg, F. F., Jr., Brooks-Gunn, J., Chase-Lansdale, L. (1989). Teenaged pregnancy and childbearing. *American Psychologist, 44,* 313–320.

Gaetz, S. (2004). Safe streets for whom? Homeless youth, social exclusion, and criminal victimization. *Canadian Journal of Criminology & Criminal Justice, 46*(4), 423–455.

Gagnon, J. H. (1977). *Human sexualities.* Glenview, IL: Scott, Foresman.

Gagnon, J. H. (1990). Gender preferences in erotic relations: The Kinsey scale and sexual scripts. In D. P. McWhirter, S. A. Sanders, & J. M. Reinisch (eds.), *Homosexuality/heterosexuality: Concepts of sexual orientation* (pp. 177–207). New York: Oxford University Press.

Gagnon, J. H., & Simon, W. (1973). *Sexual conduct: The social origins of human sexuality.* Chicago: Aldine.

Gallant, J. E. (2000). Strategies for long-term success in the treatment of HIV infection. *Journal of the American Medical Association, 283,* 1329–1334.

Garber, M. (1995). *Vice versa.* New York: Simon & Schuster.

Garland, S. M., Lees, M. I., & Skurrie, I. J. (1990). *Chlamydia trachomatis:* Role in tubal infertility. *Australian and New Zealand Journal of Obstetrics and Gynaecology, 30,* 83–86.

Gay, P. (1984). *The bourgeois experience: Victoria to Freud.* New York: Oxford University Press.

Gebhard, P. H. (1969). Misconceptions about female prostitutes. *Medical Aspects of Human Sexuality, 3,* 24–26.

Gebhard, P. H. (1976). The institute. In M. S. Weinberg (ed.), *Sex research: Studies from the Kinsey Institute.* New York: Oxford University Press.

Gebhard, P. H. (1977). *Memorandum on the incidence of homosexuals in the United States.* Bloomington, IN: Indiana University Institute for Sex Research.

Gebhard, P. H., et al. (1965). *Sex offenders: An analysis of types.* New York: Harper & Row.

Geer, J., Heiman, J., & Leitenberg, H. (1984). *Human sexuality.* Englewood Cliffs, NJ: Prentice-Hall.

Geiger, R. (1981). Neurophysiology of sexual response in spinal cord injury. In D. Bullard & S. Knight (eds.), *Sexuality and physical disability: Personal perspectives.* St. Louis: Mosby.

Gemme, R. (1993). Prostitution: A legal, criminological and sexological perspective. *The Canadian Journal of Human Sexuality, 4,* 227–238.

Gemme, R. (1998). Legal and sexological aspects of adult street prostitution: A case for sexual pluralism. In J. E. Elias, V. L. Bullough, V. Elias, & G. Brewer (eds.), *Prostitution: On whores, hustlers and johns.* New York: Prometheus Books. (pp. 474–487).

George, W. H., Stoner, S. A., Norris, J., Lopez, P. A., & Lehman, G. L. (2000). Alcohol expectancies and sexuality: A self-fulfilling prophecy analysis of dyadic perceptions and behavior. *Journal of Studies on Alcohol, 61*(1), 168–176.

Gerrol, R., & Resick, P. A. (1988, November). *Sex differences in social support and recovery from victimization.* Paper presented at the meeting of the Association for Advancement of Behavior Therapy, New York.

Ghizzani, A. (2003). Aging and male sexuality. *Archives of Sexual Behavior, 32*(3), 294–295.

Gibson, V. (2002). *Cougar: A Guide for Older Women Dating Younger Men.* Toronto: Key Porter.

Gidycz, C. A., & Koss, M. P. (1990). A comparison of group and individual sexual assault victims. *Psychology of Women Quarterly, 14,* 325–342.

Gijs, L., & Gooren, L. (1996). Hormonal and psychopharmacological interventions in the treatment of paraphilias: An update. *Journal of Sex Research, 33,* 273–290.

Gilbert, S. (1996, September 25). No long-term link is found between pill and breast cancer. *The New York Times,* p. C9.

Giles, G., Severi, G., English, D., et al. (2003). Sexual factors and prostate cancer. *British Journal of Urology, 92*(3), 211–216.

Gillis, J. S., & Avis, W. E. (1980). The male-taller norm in mate selection. *Personality and Social Psychology Bulletin, 6,* 396–401.

Giovannucci, E., et al. (1993a). A prospective cohort study of vasectomy and prostate cancer in U.S. men. *Journal of the American Medical Association, 269,* 873–877.

Giovannucci, E., et al. (1993b). A retrospective cohort study of vasectomy and prostate cancer in U.S. men. *Journal of the American Medical Association, 269,* 878–882.

Girard, D. (2005, June 2). First conviction in sex tourism case. *The Toronto Star.*

Girl lied about sex assault: Police. (2001, April 27). *The Toronto Star.*

Gitlin, M. J., & Pasnau, R. O. (1989). Psychiatric syndromes linked to reproductive function in women: A review of current knowledge. *American Journal of Psychiatry, 146,* 1413–1422.

Glass, S. P., & Wright, T. L. (1992). Justifications of extramarital relationships: The association between attitudes, behaviors, and gender. *Journal of Sex Research, 29,* 361–387.

Gleicher, N., Oleske, D. M., Tur-Kaspa, I., Vidali, A., & Karande, V. (2000). Reducing the risk of high-order multiple pregnancy after ovarian stimulation with gonadotropins. *The New England Journal of Medicine, 343*(1), 2–7.

Gnagy, S., Ming, E. E., Devesa, S. S., Hartge, P., & Whittemore, A. S. (2000). Declining ovarian cancer rates in U.S. women in relation to parity and oral contraceptive use. *Epidemiology, 11*(2), 102–105.

Godfrey, T. (December 19, 2003). Drifter arrested after cow assault. *The Toronto Sun.*

Gold, S. R., & Gold, R. G. (1993). Sexual aversions: A hidden disorder. In W. O'Donohue & J. H. Geer (eds.), *Handbook of sexual dysfunctions: Assessment and treatment* (pp. 83–102). Boston: Allyn & Bacon.

Goldberg, C. (1995, September 11). Sex slavery, Thailand to New York. *The New York Times,* pp. B1, B6.

Goldberg, C. (1998, September 8). Getting to the truth in child abuse cases: New methods. *The New York Times,* pp. F1, F5.

Goldman, R., & Goldman, J. (1982). *Children's sexual thinking: A comparative study of children aged five to fifteen years in Australia, North America, Britain, and Sweden.* London: Routledge & Kegan Paul.

Goldstein, I. (1998). Cited in Kolata, G. (1998, April 4). Impotence pill: Would it also help women? *The New York Times,* pp. A1, A6.

Goldstein, I. (2000). Cited in Norton, A. (2000, September 1). Exercise helps men avoid impotence. Reuters News Agency online.

Goldstein, I., et al. (1998). Oral sildenafil in the treatment of erectile dysfunction. *The New England Journal of Medicine, 338,* 1397–1404.

Goleman, D. (1988, October 18). Chemistry of sexual desire yields its elusive secrets. *The New York Times*, pp. C1, C15.

Goleman, D. (1991, October 22). Sexual harassment: It's about power, not lust. *The New York Times*, pp. C1, C12.

Goleman, D. (1993, October 6). Abuse-prevention efforts aid children. *The New York Times*, p. C13.

Goleman, D. (1995, June 14). Sex fantasy research said to neglect women. *The New York Times*, p. C14.

Goodson, P., McCormick, D., & Evans, A. (2001). Searching for sexually explicit materials on the Internet: An exploratory study of college students' behavior and attitudes. *Archives of Sexual Behavior, 30*(2), 101–118.

Gordon, S., & Snyder, C. W. (1989). *Personal issues in human sexuality: A guidebook for better sexual health*, 2nd ed. Boston: Allyn & Bacon.

Gottman, J. M., Coan, J., Carrère, S., & Swanson, C. (1998). Predicting marital happiness and stability from newlywed interactions. *Journal of Marriage and the Family, 60*, 5–22.

Gower, P., & Philp, M. (2002a, November 24). Two dads and a family. *The Toronto Star*, pp. A1, A16–17.

Gower, P., & Philp, M. (2002b, November 27). The curse of alcohol and pregnancy. *The Toronto Star*, pp. A1, A16–17.

Grabrick, D. M., et al. (2000). Risk of breast cancer with oral contraceptive use in women with a family history of breast cancer. *Journal of the American Medical Association, 284*(14), 1791–1798.

Graca, L. M., Cardoso, C. G., Clode, N., & Calhaz-Jorge, C. (1991). Acute effects of maternal cigarette smoking on fetal heart rate and fetal body movements felt by the mother. *Journal of Perinatal Medicine, 19*, 385–390.

Grace, A. P., & Wells, K. (2004). Engaging sex-and-gender differences: Educational and cultural change initiatives in Alberta. In J. McNinch & M. Cronin (eds.), *I could not speak my heart: Education and social justice for gay and lesbian youth* (pp. 289–307). Regina, SK: Canadian Plains Research Centre, University of Regina.

Graham, C. A. (2003). A new view of women's sexual problems. *Journal of Sex & Marital Therapy, 29*(4), 325–327.

Green, R. (1987). *The "sissy boy syndrome" and the development of homosexuality.* New Haven, CT: Yale University Press.

Greeno, C. (2002, February 5). Eatery banking and nearly-naked lunch. *The Guelph Mercury*, p. A5.

Greenwald, E., & Leitenberg, H. (1989). Long-term effects of sexual experiences with siblings and non-siblings during childhood. *Archives of Sexual Behavior, 18*, 389–399.

Grenier, G., & Byers, E. S. (2001). Operationalizing premature or rapid ejaculation. *Journal of Sex Research, 38*, 369–378.

Griffin, E., & Sparks, G. G. (1990). Friends forever: A longitudinal exploration of intimacy in same-sex friends and platonic

pairs. *Journal of Social and Personal Relationships, 7*, 29–46.

Grodstein, F., Goldman, M. G., & Cramer, D. W. (1993). Relation of tubal infertility to history of sexually transmitted diseases. *American Journal of Epidemiology, 137*, 577–584.

Grodstein, F., et al. (1996). Postmenopausal estrogen and progestin use and the risk of cardiovascular disease. *New England Journal of Medicine, 335*, 453–461.

Grodstein, F., et al. (1997). Postmenopausal hormonal therapy and mortality. *The New England Journal of Medicine, 336*, 1769–1775.

Grogger, J., & Bronars, S. (1993). The socioeconomic consequences of teenage childbearing: Findings from a natural experiment. *Family Planning Perspectives, 25*, 156–161.

Grön, G., Wunderlich, A. P., Spitzer, M., Tomczak, R., & Riepe, M. W. (2000). Brain activation during human navigation: Gender-different neural networks as substrate of performance. *Nature Neuroscience, 3*(4), 404–408.

Grosser, B. I., Monti-Bloch, L., Jennings-White, C., & Berliner, D. L. (2000). Behavioral and electrophysiological effects of androstadienone, a human pheromone. *Psychoneuroendocrinology, 25*(3), 289–300.

Groth, A. N. (1978). Patterns of sexual assault against children and adolescents. In A. W. Burgess, A. N. Groth, L. L. Holmstrom, & S. M. Sgroi (eds.), *Sexual assault of children and adolescents.* Toronto, Canada: Lexington Books.

Groth, A. N., & Birnbaum, H. J. (1979). *Men who rape: The psychology of the offender.* New York: Plenum Press.

Groth, A. N., & Burgess, A. W. (1980). Male rape: Offenders and victims. *American Journal of Psychiatry, 137*, 806–810.

Grunfeld, C. (1995). What causes wasting in AIDS? *The New England Journal of Medicine, 333*, 123–124.

Gruslin, A., et al. (2000). Maternal smoking and fetal erythropoietin levels. *Obstetrics & Gynecology, 95*(4), 561–564.

Grych, J. H., & Fincham, F. D. (1993). Children's appraisals of marital conflict. *Child Development, 64*, 215–230.

Guinan, M. E. (1992, February 1). Cited in W. E. Leary, U.S. panel backs approval of first condom for women. *The New York Times*, p. 7.

Gupta, M. (1994). Sexuality in the Indian subcontinent. *Sexual and Marital Therapy, 9*(1), 57–69.

Guzick, D. S., & Hoeger, K. (2000). Sex, hormones, and hysterectomies. *The New England Journal of Medicine* online, *343*(10).

Haake, P., et al. (2003). Acute neuroendocrine response to sexual stimulation in sexual offenders. *Canadian Journal of Psychiatry, 48*(4), 265–271.

Haddow, J. E., et al. (1998). Screening of maternal serum for fetal Down's syndrome in the first trimester. *The New England Journal of Medicine, 338*, 955–961.

Haglund, B., & Cnattingius, S. (1990). Cigarette smoking as a risk factor for sudden infant death syndrome: A population based study. *American Journal of Public Health, 80*, 29–32.

Halapy, E. E., Chiarelli, A. M., Klar, N., & Knight, J. (2004). Breast screening outcomes in women with and without a family history of breast and/or ovarian cancer. *Journal of Medical Screening, 11*(1), 32–38.

Haley, N., Roy, E., Leclerc, P., Boudreau, J. F., & Boivin, J. F. (2004). HIV risk profile of male street youth involved in survival sex. *Sexually Transmitted Infections, 80*(6) 526–530.

Hall, G. C. N. (1989). Sexual arousal and arousability in a sexual offender population. *Journal of Abnormal Psychology, 98*, 145–149.

Hallett, D. (2004, November 16). Boys take beating in '3Rs' testing. *The Guelph Tribune.*

Halperin D. T., & Bailey, R. C. (1999). Male circumcision and HIV infection: 10 years and counting. *Lancet, 354*, 1813–1815.

Halpern, D. F. (1997). Sex differences in intelligence: Implications for education. *American Psychologist, 52*, 1091–1102.

Halpern, D. F., & LaMay, M. L. (2000). The smarter sex: A critical review of sex differences in intelligence. *Educational Psychology Review, 12*(2), 229–246.

Hamer, D. H., et al. (1993, July 16). A linkage between DNA markers on the X chromosome and male sexual orientation. *Science, 261*, 321–327.

Hamilton, T. (2002, August 14). New breast cancer checks hailed. *The Toronto Star*, pp. A1, A19.

Hampton, M. R., Smith, P., Jeffery, B., & McWatters, B. (2001). Sexual experience, contraception and STI prevention among high school students: Results from a Canadian urban centre. *Canadian Journal of Human Sexuality, 10*(3–4), 111–126.

Hanrahan, J. P., et al. (1992). The effect of maternal smoking during pregnancy on early infant lung function. *American Review of Respiratory Disease, 145*, 1129–1135.

Hansen, L., Wong, T., & Perrin, M. (2003). Gonorrhoea resurgence in Canada. *International Journal of STD & AIDS, 14*(11), 727–731.

Hanson, R. K., Gordon, A., Harris, A. J. R., et al. (2002). First report of the collaborative outcome data project on the effectiveness of psychological treatment for sex offenders. *Sexual Abuse, 14*, 155–168.

Hardwick, D. (2002). Effectiveness of a female condom education and counseling intervention on women's consistency of condom use. Paper presented to the annual meeting of the Canadian Sex Research Forum, Toronto.

Hardy, S. (2001). More black lace: Women, eroticism and subjecthood. *Sexualities, 4*(4), 435–453.

Hariton, E. B., & Singer, J. L. (1974). Women's fantasies during sexual intercourse: Normative and theoretical implications. *Journal of Consulting and Clinical Psychology, 42*, 313–322.

Harold, G. T., Fincham, F. D., Osborne, L. N., & Conger, R. D. (1997). Mom and Dad are at it again: Adolescent perceptions of marital conflict and adolescent psychological distress. *Developmental Psychology, 33,* 333–350.

Harris, C. R. (2003). A review of sex differences in sexual jealousy, including self-report data, psychophysiological responses, interpersonal violence, and morbid jealousy. *Personality & Social Psychology Review, 7*(2), 102–128.

Harris, G. T., Rice, M., Chaplin, T., & Quinsey, V. (1999). Dissimulation in phallometric testing of rapists' sexual preferences. *Archives of Sexual Behavior, 28,* 223–232.

Harris, G. T., Rice, M. E., Quinsey, V. L., Lalumiere, M. L., Boer, D., & Lang, C. (2003). A multisite comparison of actuarial risk instruments for sex offenders. *Psychological Assessment, 15*(3), 413–425.

Harris, M., & Johnson, O. (2000). *Cultural anthropology,* 5th ed. Boston: Allyn & Bacon.

Hart, J., et al. (1991). Sexual behaviour in pregnancy: a study of 219 women. *Journal of Sex Education and Therapy, 17,* 86–90.

Hartman, C. R., Burgess, A. W., & McCormack, A. (1987). Pathways and cycles of runaways: A model for understanding repetitive runaway behavior. *Hospital and Community Psychiatry, 38,* 292–299.

Harvey, C. (2000, September 4). Where to go for help. *The Los Angeles Times* online.

Harvey, S. (1987). Female sexual behavior: Fluctuations during the menstrual cycle. *Journal of Psychosomatic Research, 31,* 101–110.

Hatcher, R. A. (1998). Depo-Provera, Norplant, and progestin-only pills (minipills). In Hatcher, R. A., et al., *Contraceptive technology,* 17th rev. ed. (pp. 467–510). New York: Ardent Media.

Hatcher, R. A. (2001). Contraceptive technologies. London: British Medical Association.

Hatcher, R. A., & Guillebaud, J. (1998). The pill: Combined oral contraceptives. In R. A. Hatcher et al., *Contraceptive technology,* 17th rev. ed. (pp. 405–466). New York: Ardent Media.

Hatcher, R. A., et al. (1998). *Contraceptive technology,* 17th rev. ed. New York: Ardent Media.

Hatfield, E. (1988). Passionate and companionate love. In R. J. Sternberg & M. L. Barnes (eds.), *The psychology of love* (pp. 191–217). New Haven, CT: Yale University Press.

Hatfield, E., & Rapson, R. L. (2002). Passionate love and sexual desire: Cultural and historical perspectives. In Vangelisti, A. L., Reis, H.T., et al. (eds.), *Stability and change in relationships. Advances in personal relationships* (pp. 306–324). New York: Cambridge University Press.

Hatfield, E., & Sprecher, S. (1986). Measuring passionate love in intimate relationships. *Journal of Adolescence, 9,* 383–410.

Haubrich, D. J., Myers, T., Calzavara, L., Ryder, K., & Medved, W. (2004). Gay and bisexual men's experiences of bathhouse culture and sex: 'Looking for love in all the wrong places.' *Culture, Health & Sexuality, 6*(1), 19–29.

Haugaard, J. J. (2000). The challenge of defining child sexual abuse. *American Psychologist, 55*(9), 1036–1039.

Hawton, K., & Catalan, J. (1990). Sex therapy for vaginismus: Characteristics of couples and treatment outcomes. *Sexual and Marital Therapy, 5,* 39–48.

Health Canada (2001). Sexually Transmitted Diseases Data Tables. Division of Sexual Health Promotion and STD Prevention and Control, Bureau of HIV/AIDS, STD & TB. Ottawa: Health Canada.

Health Canada (2002). Sexually Transmitted Diseases. Division of Sexual Health Promotion and STD Prevention and Control, Bureau of HIV/AIDS, STD & TB. Ottawa: Health Canada.

Heath-Rawlings, J. (2004). You can meet him in T.O. *Toronto Star,* April 13.

Hechtman, L. (1989). Teenage mothers and their children: Risks and problems: A review. *Canadian Journal of Psychiatry, 34,* 569–575.

Hegeler, S., & Mortensen, M. (1977). Sexual behavior in elderly Danish males. In R. Gemme & C. Wheeler (eds.), *Progress in sexology* (pp. 285–292). New York: Plenum Press.

Heiman, J. R., & LoPiccolo, J. (1987). *Becoming orgasmic,* 2nd ed. Englewood Cliffs, NJ: Prentice-Hall.

Hendrick, C., & Hendrick, S. (1986). A theory and method of love. *Journal of Personality and Social Psychology, 50,* 392–402.

Hendrick, C., & Hendrick, S. (eds.) (2000). *Close relationships: A sourcebook.* Thousand Oaks, CA: Sage.

Hendrick, C., & Hendrick, S. (2003). Romantic love: Measuring Cupid's arrow. In S. Lopez & C. R. Snyder (eds.), *Positive psychological assessment: A handbook of models and measures* (pp. 235–249). Washington, DC: American Psychological Association.

Hendrick, S., & Hendrick, C. (2002). Love. In S. Lopez & C. R. Snyder (eds.), *Handbook of positive psychology* (pp. 472–484). London, UK: Oxford University Press.

Herold, E. S. (1984). *Sexual behaviour of Canadian young people.* Markham, ON: Fitzhenry & Whiteside.

Herold, E. S., Corbesi, B., & Collins, J. (1994). Psychosocial aspects of female topless behavior on Australian beaches. *Journal of Sex Research, 31,* 133–142.

Herold, E. S., & Foster, M. E. (1975). Changing sexual references in mass circulation magazines. *The Family Coordinator,* 21–25.

Herold, E. S., Garcia, R., & DeMoya, T. (2001). Female tourists and beach boys: Romance or sex tourism? *Annals of Tourism Research, 28,* 978–997.

Herold, E. S., & Goodwin, M. S. (1981). Premarital sexual guilt and contraceptive attitudes and behavior. *Family Relations, 30,* 247–253.

Herold, E. S., & Mewhinney, D. K. (1993). Gender differences in casual sex and AIDS prevention: A survey of dating bars. *The Journal of Sex Research, 30,* 36–42.

Herold, E. S., & Way, L. (1983). Oral-genital sexual behavior in a sample of university females. *The Journal of Sex Research, 19,* 327–338.

Herold, E. S., & Way, L. (1988). Sexual self-disclosure among university women. *Journal of Sex Research, 24,* 1–14.

Herrmann, H. C., Chang, G., Klugherz, B. D., & Mahoney, P. D. (2000). Hemodynamic effects of sildenafil in men with severe coronary artery disease. *The New England Journal of Medicine, 342*(22), 1622–1626.

Herzog, L. (1989). Urinary tract infections and circumcision. *American Journal of Diseases of Children, 143,* 348–350.

Hill, T. (2005). *Female Sexual Frustration.* Unpublished M.A. thesis, University of Guelph.

Hillier, S., & Holmes, K. K. (1990). Bacterial vaginosis. In K. K. Holmes, P. Mardh, P. F. Sparling, & P. J. Wiesner (eds.), *Sexually transmitted diseases,* 2nd ed. (pp. 547–560). New York: McGraw-Hill.

Hilton, E., et al. (1992). Ingestion of yogurt containing *Lactobacillus acidophilus* as prophylaxis for candidal vaginitis. *Annals of Internal Medicine, 116,* 353–357.

Hite, S. (1976). *The Hite report.* New York: Macmillan.

Hite, S. (1981). *The Hite report on male sexuality.* New York: Knopf.

Ho, G. Y. F., et al. (1998, February 11). *The New England Journal of Medicine, 338.* Cited in Sexually active coeds at higher risk for. Reuters News Agency online.

Hock, Z. (1983). The G Spot. *Journal of Sex and Marital Therapy, 9,* 166–167.

Hodgson, R., et al. (1990). *Chlamydia trachomatis:* The prevalence, trend and importance in initial infertility management. *Australian and New Zealand Journal of Obstetrics and Gynaecology, 30,* 251–254.

Hodson, D. S., & Skeen, P. (1994). Sexuality and aging: The hammerlock of myths. *Journal of Applied Gerontology, 13*(3), 219–235.

Hogg, R. S., Yip, B., Chan, K. J., Wood, E., Craib, K. J., O'Shaughnessy, M. V., & Montaner, J. S. (2001). Rates of disease progression by baseline CD4 cell count and viral load after initiating triple-drug therapy. *Journal of the American Medical Association, 286*(20), 2568–2577.

Holden, G. W., & Ritchie, K. L. (1991). Linking extreme marital discord, child rearing, and child behavior problems. *Child Development, 62,* 311–327.

Honeycutt, J. M., & Cantrill, G. (2001). Cognition, communication, and romantic relationships. Mahwah, NJ: Erlbaum.

Horne, A. (2003). Oedipal aspirations and phallic fears: On fetishism in childhood and young adulthood. *Journal of Child Psychotherapy, 29*(1), 37–52.

House arrest in "lactation" case. (2002, October 12). *The Toronto Star,* p. A25.

Howard, J. A., Blumstein, P., & Schwartz, P. (1987). Social or evolutionary theories:

Some observations on preferences in mate selection. *Journal of Personality and Social Psychology, 53,* 194–200.

Howard-Hassmann, R. E. (2001). The gay cousin: Learning to accept gay rights. *Journal of Homosexuality, 42*(1), 127–149.

Howards, S. S. (1995). Current concepts: Treatment of male infertility. *The New England Journal of Medicine, 332,* 312–317.

Howson, T. (1998). Alcohol and pregnancy campaign. *Canadian Health Network.* [online]. Available: **www.opc.on.ca/beststart/ pract_prod/alc_reduction/alc_preg.html**

Huber, J. D. (2005). Sexually overt approaches in singles bars. MSc. Thesis University of Guelph.

Huber, J. D., & Kleinplatz, P. J. (2002). Sexual orientation identification of men who have sex with men in public settings in Canada. *Journal of Homosexuality, 42*(3), 1–20.

Hughes, I. A. (2000). A novel explanation for resistance to androgens. *The New England Journal of Medicine* online, *343*(12).

Humphreys, T. P. (2004). Understanding sexual consent: An empirical investigation of the normative script for young heterosexual adults. In M. Cowling & P. Reynolds (eds.), *Making sense of sexual consent.* Aldershot, UK: Ashgate.

Humphries, K. H., & Gill, S. (2003). Risks and benefits of hormone replacement therapy: the evidence speaks. *Canadian Medical Association Journal, 168*(8), 1001–1010.

Hunt, M. (1974). *Sexual behavior in the 1970's.* New York: Dell Books.

Hurst, L. (2003, August 17). A long trip to the altar. *The Toronto Star.*

Hussain, A. (2002, June 26). It's official! Men really are afraid of commitment. Reuters.

Hyde, J. S., Fennema, E., & Lamon, S. J. (1990). Gender differences in mathematics performance: A meta-analysis. *Psychological Bulletin, 107,* 139–155.

Hyde, J. S., & Plant, E. A. (1995). Magnitude of psychological gender differences: Another side to the story. *American Psychologist, 50,* 159–161.

Imperato-McGinley, J., et al. (1974). Steroid 5 reductase deficiency in man: An inherited form of male pseudohermaphroditism. *Science, 186,* 1213–1215.

Ince, J. (2003*). The politics of lust.* Vancouver: Pivotal Press.

Info reports (2005). *World health organization updates guidance on how to use contraceptives,* 4.

Isay, R. A. (1990). Psychoanalytic theory and the therapy of gay men. In D. P. McWhirter, S. A. Sanders, & J. M. Reinisch (eds.), *Homosexuality/heterosexuality: Concepts of sexual orientation* (pp. 283–303). New York: Oxford University Press.

Isay, R. A. (1993, April 23). Sex survey may say most about society's attitudes to gays. *The New York Times,* Section 4, p. 16 (letter).

Itzin, C. (2002). Pornography and the construction of misogyny. *Journal of Sexual Aggression, 8*(3), 4–42.

Jacklin, C. N, DiPietro, J. A., & Maccoby, E. E. (1984). Sex-typing behavior and sex-typing pressure in child-parent interaction. *Archives of Sexual Behavior, 13,* 413–425.

Jackson, J., et al. (1990). Young adult women who report childhood intrafamilial sexual abuse: Subsequent adjustment. *Archives of Sexual Behavior, 19,* 211–221.

Jackson, L. A., & Ervin, K. S. (1992). Height stereotypes of women and men: The liabilities of shortness for both sexes. *Journal of Social Psychology, 132,* 433–445.

Jackson, L. A., Millson, P., Calzavara, C., et al. (1997). HIV-positive women living in the metropolitan Toronto area: Their experiences and perceptions related to HIV testing. *Canadian Journal of Public Health, 88,* 18–22.

Jacob, S., & McClintock, M. K. (2000). Psychological state and mood effects of steroidal chemosignals in women and men. *Hormones and Behavior, 37*(1), 57–78.

Jacobson, J. L., & Jacobson, S. W. (1994). Prenatal alcohol exposure and neurobehavioral development: Where is the threshold? *Alcohol Health and Research World, 18*(1), 30–36.

Jail workers charged. (2002, May 24). *The Toronto Star.*

Jamison, P. L., & Gebhard, P. H. (1988). Penis size increase between flaccid and erect states: An analysis of the Kinsey data. *Journal of Sex Research, 24,* 177–183.

Jankowiak, W. R., & Fischer, E. F. (1992). A cross-cultural perspective on romantic love. *Ethnology, 31,* 149–155.

Jenish, D. (1994, January 3). Canada under the covers. *Maclean's,* 20–26.

Jenks, R. (1985). Swinging: A replication and test of a theory. *The Journal of Sex Research, 21,* 199–210.

Jennings, V. H., Lamprecht, V. M., & Kowal, D. (1998). Fertility awareness methods. In R. A. Hatcher et al. (1998). *Contraceptive technology,* 17th rev. ed. (pp. 309–324). New York: Ardent Media.

Johnson, B. D. (1999, March 8). Reinventing Alanis Morissette. *Maclean's,* pp. 46–51.

Johnson, D. (1990, March 8). AIDS clamor at colleges muffling older dangers. *The New York Times,* p. A18.

Jones, A., et al. (1994). Erectile disorder and the elderly: An analysis of the case for funding. *Sexual and Marital Therapy, 9*(1), 9–15.

Jones, H. W., & Toner, J. P. (1993). The infertile couple. *The New England Journal of Medicine, 329,* 1710–1715.

Josefsson, A. M., et al. (2000). Viral load of human papilloma virus 16 as a determinant for development of cervical carcinoma in situ: A nested case-control study. *The Lancet, 355,* 2189–2193.

Julien, D., Chartand, E., Simard, M-C., Bouthillier, D., & Begin, J. (2003).

Conflict, social support, and relationship quality: An observational study of heterosexual, gay male and lesbian couples' communication. *Journal of Family Psychology, 17*(3), 419–428.

Kafka, M. P. (2003). Sex offending and sexual appetite: The clinical and theoretical relevance of hypersexual desire. *International Journal of Offender Therapy & Comparative Criminology, 47*(4), 439–451.

Kalick, S. M. (1988). Physical attractiveness as a status cue. *Journal of Experimental Social Psychology, 24,* 469–489.

Kammeyer, K. C. W. (1990). *Marriage and family: A foundation for personal decisions,* 2nd ed. Boston: Allyn & Bacon, Inc.

Kantrowitz, B. (1990a, Summer/Fall special issue). High school homeroom. *Newsweek,* pp. 50–54.

Kaplan, H. S. (1974). *The new sex therapy: Active treatment of sexual dysfunctions.* New York: Brunner/Mazel.

Kaplan, H. S. (1979). *Disorders of sexual desire.* New York: Simon & Schuster.

Kaplan, H. S. (1987). *Sexual aversion, sexual phobias, and panic disorder.* New York: Brunner/Mazel.

Kaplan, H. S. (1990). Sex, intimacy, and the aging process. *Journal of the American Academy of Psychoanalysis, 18,* 185–205.

Karakiewicz, P. I., Tanguay, S., Kattan, M. W., Elhilali, M. M., & Aprikian, A. G. (2004). Erectile and urinary dysfunction after radical prostatectomy for prostate cancer in Quebec: A population-based study of 2415 men. *European Urology, 46*(2), 188–194.

Karama, S., Lecours, A., Leroux, J., et al. (2002). Areas of brain activation during viewing of erotic film excerpts. *Human Brain Mapping, 16,* 1–13.

Karney, B. R., & Bradbury, T. N. (1995). The longitudinal course of marital quality and stability: A review of theory, method, and research. *Psychological Bulletin, 118,* 3–34.

Kash, K. (1998). Cited in Zuger, A. (1998, January 6). Do breast self-exams save lives? Science still doesn't have answer. *The New York Times.*

Katz, S., & Marshall, B. (2003). New sex for old: Lifestyle, consumerism, and the ethics of aging well. *Journal of Aging Studies, 17*(1), 3–16.

Kaufman, A., et al. (1980). Male rape victims: Noninstitutionalized assault. *American Journal of Psychiatry, 137,* 221–223.

Kaufman, M., Silverberg, C., & Odette, F. (2003). *The Ultimate Guide to Sex and Disability.* San Francisco, CA: Cleis Press.

Kegel, A. H. (1952). Sexual functions of the pubococcygeus muscle. *Western Journal of Surgery, 60,* 521–524.

Kelly, M. P., Strassberg, D. S., & Kircher, J. R. (1990). Attitudinal and experiential correlates of anorgasmia. *Archives of Sexual Behavior, 19,* 165–177.

Kendler, K. S., et al. (2000). Childhood sexual abuse and adult psychiatric and substance use disorders in women: An epidemiological and co-twin control analysis. *Archives of General Psychiatry*, *57*(10), 953–959.

Kendler, K. S., Thornton, L. M., Gilman, S. E., & Kessler, R. C. (2000). Sexual orientation in a U.S. national sample of twin and nontwin sibling pairs. *American Journal of Psychiatry*, *157*, 1843–1846.

Kennedy, M. A., & Gorzalka, B. B. (2002). Asian and non-Asian attitudes toward rape, sexual harassment, and sexuality. *Sex Roles*, *46*(7-8), 227–238.

Kennedy, M. A., Gorzalka, B. B., & Yuille, J. C. (2003). *Prostitution myths held by consumers of the sex trade*. Paper presented at annual meeting of American Psychological Association, Toronto.

Kerns, J. G., & Fine, M. A. (1994). The relation between gender and negative attitudes toward gay men and lesbians: Do gender role attitudes mediate this relation? *Sex Roles*, *31*(5–6), 297–307.

Kettl, P., et al. (1991). Female sexuality after spinal cord injury. *Sexuality and Disability*, *9*, 287–295.

Keung, N. (1999, March 12). Is circumcision really necessary? *The Toronto Star*, pp. F1, F2.

Khalife, S., Binik, Y. M., Cohen, D. R., & Amsel, R. (2000). Evaluation of clitoral blood flow by color Doppler ultrasonography. *Journal of Sex and Marital Therapy, 26*, 187–189.

Killmann, P. R., et al. (1987). The treatment of secondary orgasmic dysfunction II. *Journal of Sex and Marital Therapy, 13*, 93–105.

Kimble, D. P. (1992). *Biological psychology*, 2nd ed. Fort Worth, TX: Harcourt.

Kimlika, T., Cross, H., & Tarnai, J. (1983). A comparison of androgynous, feminine, masculine, and undifferentiated women on self-esteem, body satisfaction, and sexual satisfaction. *Psychology of Women Quarterly*, *1*, 291–294.

Kinard, E., & Reinherz, H. (1987). School aptitude and achievement in children of adolescent mothers. *Journal of Youth and Adolescence*, *16*, 69–78.

King, A. J. C., Beazley, R. P., Warren, W. K., Hankins, C. A., Robertson, A. S., & Radford, J. L. (1989). Highlights from the Canada youth and AIDS study. *Journal of School Health 59*(4), 139–145.

King, R. (2000). Cited in Frazier, L. (2000, July 16). The new face of HIV is young, black. *The Washington Post*, p. C01.

Kingsberg, S. A. (2002). The impact of aging on sexual function in women and their partners. *Archives of Sexual Behavior, 31*(5), 431–437.

Kinsey, A. C., Pomeroy, W. B., & Martin, C. E. (1948). *Sexual behavior in the human male*. Philadelphia: W. B. Saunders.

Kinsey, A. C., Pomeroy, W. B., Martin, C. E., & Gebhard, P. H. (1953). *Sexual behavior in the human female*. Philadelphia: W. B. Saunders.

Kinsman, G. (1996). *The regulation of desire: Sexuality in Canada*. Montreal: Black Rose Books.

Kippax, S., & Smith, G. (2001). Anal intercourse and power in sex between men. *Sexualities, 4*(4), 413–434.

Kirkpatrick, R. C. (2000). The evolution of human homosexual behavior. *Current Anthropology, 41*(3), 385–413.

Kite, M. E. (1992). Individual differences in males' reactions to gay males and lesbians. *Journal of Applied Social Psychology, 22*, 1222–1239.

Kjerulff, K. H., et al. (2000). Effectiveness of hysterectomy. *Obstetrics & Gynecology, 95*, 319–326.

Klein, E. A. (2000). *Management of prostate cancer*. Totowa, NJ: Humana Press.

Klein, H. G. (2000). Will blood transfusion ever be safe enough? *Journal of the American Medical Association* online, *284*(2).

Klein, R., & Knauper, B. (2002). The role of suppression, inquiry, and mental representations of condoms in condom discontinuation. Paper presented at the annual meeting of the Canadian Sex Research Forum, Toronto.

Klein, R., & Knauper, B. (2003). The role of cognitive avoidance of STIs for discussing safer sex practices and for condom use consistency. *The Canadian Journal of Human Sexuality, 12*(3–4), 137–147.

Kleinplatz, P. J. (1992). The erotic experience and the intent to arouse. *Canadian Journal of Human Sexuality, 1*, 13–139.

Kleinplatz, P. J. (1997). "Educational" sex videos. What are they teaching? *Canadian Journal of Human Sexuality, 6*, 39–43.

Kleinplatz, P. J. (ed.) (2001). *New directions in sex therapy: Innovations and alternatives*. New York: Brunner-Routledge.

Kleinplatz, P. J. (2003). What's new in sex therapy? From stagnation to fragmentation. *Sexual & Relationship Therapy, 18*(1), 95–106.

Klepinger, D. H., et al. (1993). Perceptions of AIDS risk and severity and their association with risk-related behavior among U.S. men. *Family Planning Perspectives, 25*, 74–82.

Klusmann, D. (2002). Sexual motivation and the duration of partnership. *Archives of Sexual Behavior, 31*, 275–287.

Klüver, H., & Bucy, P. C. (1939). Preliminary analysis of functions of the temporal lobes in monkeys. *Archives of Neurology and Psychiatry, 42*, 979.

Knapp, M. L., & Vangelisti, A. L. (2000). *Interpersonal communication and human relationships*, 4th ed. Boston: Allyn & Bacon.

Knauper, B., Aydin, C., Atkinson, K., Guberman, C., & Kornik, R. (2002). Paper presented at the annual meeting of the Canadian Sex Research Forum, Toronto.

Knight, R. A., et al. (1991). *Antisocial personality disorder and Hare assessments of psychopathy among sexual offenders*. Manuscript in preparation.

Knight, S. E. (1989). Sexual concerns of the physically disabled. In B. W. Heller, L. M. Flohr, & L. S. Zegans (eds.), *Psychosocial interventions with physically disabled persons* (pp. 183–199). New Brunswick, NJ: Rutgers University Press.

Knox, D. (1988). *Choices in relationships*. St. Paul, MN: West.

Knox, D., Gibson, L., Zusman, M., & Gallmeier, C. (1997). Why college students end relationships. *College Student Journal, 31*(4), 449–452.

Knox, D., Schacht, C., & Zusman, M. E. (1999). Love relationships among college students. *College Student Journal, 31*(4), 445–448.

Knox, D., Zusman, M. E., & Nieves, W. (1998). Breaking away: How college students end love relationships. *College Student Journal, 32*(4), 482–484.

Knudsen, D. D. (1991). Child sexual coercion. In E. Grauerholz & M. A. Koralewski (eds.), *Sexual coercion: A sourcebook on its nature, causes, and prevention* (pp. 17–28). Lexington, MA: Lexington Books.

Knussman, R., Christiansen, K., & Couwenbergs, C. (1986). Relations between sex hormone levels and sexual behavior in men. *Archives of Sexual Behavior, 15*, 429–445.

Kockott, G., & Fahrner, E. (1987). Transsexuals who have not undergone surgery: A follow-up study. *Archives of Sexual Behavior, 16*, 511–522.

Kohlberg, L. (1966). A cognitive-developmental analysis of children's sex-role concepts and attitudes. In E. E. Maccoby (ed.), *The development of sex differences*. Stanford, CA: Stanford University Press.

Kolata, G. (1996, February 28). Study reports small risk, if any, from breast implants. *The New York Times*, p. A12.

Kolata, G. (2000, April 18). New name for impotence, and new drugs. *The New York Times*, pp. F6, F14.

Koo, M. M., Rohan, T. E., Jain, M., McLaughlin, J. R., & Corey, P. N. (2002). A cohort study of dietary fibre intake and menarche. *Public Health Nutrition, 5*(2), 353–360.

Koren, G., Pastuszak, A., & Ito, S. (1998). Drug therapy: Drugs in pregnancy. *The New England Journal of Medicine, 338*, 1128–1137.

Koss, M. P., Bailey, J. A., Yuan, N. P., Herrera, V. M., & Lichter, E. L. (2003). Depression and PTSD in survivors of male violence: Research and training initiatives to facilitate recovery. *Psychology of Women Quarterly, 27*(2), 130–142.

Koss, M. P., Figueredo, A. J., & Prince, R. J. (2002). Cognitive mediation of rape's mental, physical and social health impact: Tests of four models in cross-sectional data. *Journal of Consulting & Clinical Psychology, 70*(4), 926–941.

Koss, M. P., Gidycz, C. A., & Wisniewski, N. (1987). The scope of rape: Incidence and prevalence of sexual aggression and victimization in a national sample of higher education students. *Journal of Consulting and Clinical Psychology, 55*, 162–170.

Koutsky, L. A., et al. (1992). A cohort study of the risk of cervical intraepithelial neoplasia Grade 2 or 3 in relation to Papillomavirus infection. *The New England Journal of Medicine, 327*, 1272.

Kowal, D. (1998). Coitus interruptus (withdrawal). In Hatcher, R. A., et al. (1998). *Contraceptive technology*, 17th rev. ed. (pp. 303–308). New York: Ardent Media.

Krafka, C. L. (1985). *Sexually explicit, sexually violent, and violent media: Effects of multiple naturalistic exposures and debriefing on female viewers*. Unpublished doctoral dissertation, University of Wisconsin-Madison.

Kramer, M. S., et al. (2000). The contribution of mild and moderate preterm birth to infant mortality. *Journal of the American Medical Association, 284*, 843–849.

Kresin, D. (1993). Medical aspects of inhibited sexual desire disorder. In W. O'Donohue & J. H. Geer (eds.), *Handbook of sexual dysfunctions: Assessment and treatment* (pp. 15–52). Boston: Allyn & Bacon.

Kruesi, M. J. P., et al. (1992). Paraphilias: A double-blind cross-over comparison of clomipramine versus desipramine. *Archives of Sexual Behavior, 21*, 587–594.

Kuiper, B., & Cohen-Kettenis, P. (1988). Sex reassignment surgery: A study of 141 Dutch transsexuals. *Archives of Sexual Behavior, 17*, 439–457.

Kulin, H., et al. (1989). The onset of sperm production in pubertal boys. *American Journal of Diseases of Children, 143*, 190–193.

Kunkel, L. E., & Temple, L. L. (1992). Attitudes towards AIDS and homosexuals: Gender, marital status, and religion. *Journal of Applied Social Psychology, 22*, 1030–1040.

Laan, E., & Heiman, J. (1994). *Archives of Sexual Behavior*.

Ladas, A. K., Whipple, B., & Perry, J. D. (1982). *The G spot and other recent discoveries about human sexuality*. New York: Holt.

Laframboise, D. (1996). *The princess at the window: A new gender morality*. Toronto: Penguin Books.

Laird, J. (1994). A male pill? Gender discrepancies in contraceptive commitment. *Feminism and Psychology, 4*(3), 458–468.

Lalonde, R. N., Hynie, M., Pannu, M., & Tatla, S. (2004). The role of culture in interpersonal relationships: Do second generation South Asian Canadians want a traditional partner? *Journal of Cross-Cultural Psychology, 35*(5), 503–524.

Lalumiere, M. L., Blanchard, R., & Zucker, K. J. (2000). Sexual orientation and handedness in men and women: A meta-analysis. *Psychological Bulletin 126*(4), 575–592.

Lalumiere, M. L., Harris, G. T., Quinsey, V. L., & Rice, M. E. (1998). Sexual deviance and number of older brothers among sex offenders. *Sexual Abuse, 10*, 5–15.

Lalumiere, M. L., & Quinsey, V. L. (1996). Sexual deviance, antisociality, mating effort, and the use of sexually coercive behaviors. *Personality and Individual Differences, 21*, 33–48.

Lalumiere, M. L., Quinsey, V. L., Harris, G. T., Rice, M. E., & Trautrimas, C. (2003). Are rapists differently aroused by coercive sex in phallometric assessments?

Annals New York Academy of Sciences, 989, 211–224.

Lamanna, M. A., & Riedmann, A. (1997). *Marriages and families*, 6th ed. Belmont, CA: Wadsworth.

LaMarre, A. K., Paterson, L. Q., & Gorzalka, B. B. (2003). Breastfeeding and postpartum maternal sexual functioning: A review. *Canadian Journal of Human Sexuality, 12*(3–4), 151–168.

Lamaze, F. (1981). *Painless childbirth*. New York: Simon & Schuster.

Lamberti, D. (1997). Cited in Alterman, E. (1997, November). Sex in the '90s. *Elle*.

Lamont, J., Randazzo, J., Farad, M., Wilkins, A., & Daya, D. (2001). Psychosexual and social profiles of women with vulvodynia. *Journal of Sex & Marital Therapy, 27*, 551–555.

Landolt, M. A., Bartholomew, K., Saffrey, C., Oram, D., & Perlman, D. (2004). Gender nonconformity, childhood rejection, and adult attachment: A study of gay men. *Archives of Sexual Behavior, 33*(2), 117–128.

Lane, III, F. S. (2000). *Obscene profits: The entrepreneurs of pornography in the cyber age*. London: Routledge.

Lang, A. R. (1985). The social psychology of drinking and human sexuality. *Journal of Drug Issues, 15*, 273–289.

Lang, R. A., et al. (1989). An examination of sex hormones in genital exhibitionists. *Annals of Sex Research, 2*, 67–75.

Langevin, R. (2003). A study of the psychosexual characteristics of sex killers: Can we identify them before it is too late? *International Journal of Offender Therapy & Comparative Criminology, 47*(4), 366–382.

Langevin, R., et al. (1979). Experimental studies of the etiology of genital exhibitionism. *Archives of Sexual Behavior, 8*, 307–332.

Langevin, R., & Curnoe, S. (2004). The use of pornography during the commission of sexual offenses. *International Journal of Offender Therapy and Comparative Criminology, 48*(5), 572–586.

Langille, D. B. (2002). Factors associated with sexual intercourse before age 15 in Nova Scotia female adolescents. Paper presented at the annual meeting of the Canadian Sex Research Forum, Toronto.

Langille, D. B., Flowerdew, G., & Andreou, P. (2004). Teenage pregnancy in Nova Scotia communities: Associations with contextual factors. *Canadian Journal of Human Sexuality, 13*(2), 83–94.

Langlois, J. H., et al. (2000). Maxims or myths of beauty? A meta-analytic and theoretical review. *Psychological Bulletin, 126*(3), 390–423.

Larson, L. E., Goltz, J. W., & Munro, B. E. (2000). *Families in Canada: Social contexts, continuities and changes*. Scarborough, ON: Prentice Hall Allyn and Bacon.

Laumann, E. O., Gagnon, J. H., Michael, R. T., & Michaels, S. (1994). *The social organization of sexuality: Sexual practices in the United States*. Chicago: University of Chicago Press.

Laumann, E. O., Paik, A., & Rosen, R. C. (1999). Sexual dysfunction in the United

States: Prevalence and predictors. *Journal of the American Medical Association, 281*(6), 537–544.

Laviola, M. (1989). Effects of older brother–younger sister incest: A review of four cases. *Journal of Family Violence, 4*, 259–274.

Lavoisier, P., et al. (1995). Clitoral blood flow increases following vaginal pressure stimulation. *Archives of Sexual Behavior, 24*, 37–45.

Law, J. (2000). The politics of breastfeeding: Assessing risk, dividing labor. *Signs, 25*(2), 407–450.

Lawrence, K., & Byers, E. S. (1995). Sexual satisfaction in long-term heterosexual relationships: The interpersonal exchange model of sexual satisfaction. *Personal Relationships, 2*, 267–285.

Lawrence, K., & Herold, E. S. (1988). Women's attitudes toward and experience with sexually explicit materials. *Journal of Sex Research, 24*, 161–169.

Leary, W. E. (1990, September 13). New focus on sperm brings fertility successes. *The New York Times*, p. B11.

Lederman, M. M., & Valdez, H. (2000). Immune restoration with antiretroviral therapies: Implications for clinical management. *Journal of the American Medical Association, 284*, 223–228.

Lee, J. K. P., Jackson, H. J., Pattison, P., & Ward, T. (2002). Developmental risk factors for sexual offending. *Child Abuse & Neglect, 26*(1), 73–92.

Legato, M. J. (2000). Cited in "Study of children born without penises finds nature determines gender" (2000, May 12). The Associated Press online.

Leiblum, S. R., & Rosen, R. C. (eds.) (1988). *Sexual desire disorders*. New York: Guilford Press.

Leiblum, S. R., & Rosen, R. C. (1991). Couples therapy for erectile disorders: Conceptual and clinical considerations. [Special issue: The treatment of male erectile disorders]. *Journal of Sex and Marital Therapy, 17*, 147–159.

Leitenberg, H., Detzer, M. J., & Srebnik, D. (1993). Gender differences in masturbation and the relation of masturbation experience in preadolescence and/or early adolescence to sexual behavior and sexual adjustment in young adulthood. *Archives of Sexual Behavior, 22*, 87–98.

Leitenberg, H., Greenwald, E., & Tarran, M. J. (1989). The relation between sexual activity among children during preadolescence and/or early adolescence and sexual behavior and sexual adjustment in young adulthood. *Archives of Sexual Behavior, 18*, 299–313.

Leitenberg, H., & Henning, K. (1995). Sexual fantasy. *Psychological Bulletin, 117*, 469–496.

Leland, J. (2000, May 29). The science of women and sex. *Newsweek*, pp. 48–54.

Lemon, S. J., & Newbold, J. E. (1990). Viral hepatitis. In K. K. Holmes, P. Mardh, P. F. Sparling, & P. J. Wiesner (eds.), *Sexually transmitted diseases*, 2nd ed. (pp. 449–466). New York: McGraw-Hill.

Lenihan, G., Rawlins, M. E., Eberly, C. G., Buckley, B., & Masters, B. (1992). Gender differences in rape supportive attitudes before and after a date rape education intervention. *Journal of College Student Development, 33,* 331–338.

Lepischak, B. (2004). Building community for Toronto's lesbian, gay, bisexual, transsexual and transgender youth. *Journal of Gay & Lesbian Social Services: Issues in Practice, Policy & Research, 16*(3–4), 81–98.

Lesnik-Oberstein, M., & Cohen, L. (1984). Cognitive style, sensation seeking, and assortive mating. *Journal of Personality and Social Psychology, 46,* 57–66.

Letourneau, E., & O'Donohue, W. (1993). Sexual desire disorders. In W. O'Donohue & J. H. Geer (eds.), *Handbook of sexual dysfunctions: Assessment and treatment.* (pp. 53–81). Boston: Allyn & Bacon.

Lever, J., et al. (1992). Behavior patterns and sexual identity of bisexual males. *Journal of Sex Research, 29,* 141–167.

Levine, D. (2000). Virtual attraction: What rocks your boat. *CyberPsychology & Behavior 3*(4), 565–573.

Levine, G. I. (1991). Sexually transmitted parasitic diseases. *Primary Care: Clinics in Office Practice, 18,* 101–128.

Levinger, G. (1980). Toward the analysis of close relationships. *Journal of Experimental Social Psychology, 16,* 510–544.

Levy, H. (2004, November 25). Internet luring sentence sparks outrage. *Toronto Star.*

Levy, J. (1985). Right brain, left brain: Fact and fiction. *Psychology Today, 19*(5), 38–44.

Lewan, T. (1998, May 2). Not all women thrilled with Viagra. The Associated Press online.

Lewin, T. (1998, March 23). Debate centers on definition of harassment. *The New York Times,* pp. A1, A28.

Lewis, J. (1998). Learning to strip: The socialization experiences of exotic dancers. *The Canadian Journal of Human Sexuality, 7,* 51–66.

Libman, E. (1989). Sociocultural and cognitive factors in aging and sexual expression: Conceptual and research issues. *Canadian Psychology, 30,* 560–567.

Lichtenstein, P., et al. (2000). Environmental and heritable factors in the causation of cancer—Analyses of cohorts of twins from Sweden, Denmark, and Finland. *The New England Journal of Medicine, 343*(2), 78–85.

Lief, H. I., & Hubschman, L. (1993). Orgasm in the postoperative transsexual. *Archives of Sexual Behavior, 22,* 145–155.

Lindermalm, G., Korlin, D., & Uddenberg, N. (1986). Long-term follow-up of "sex change" in 134 male to female transsexuals. *Archives of Sexual Behavior, 15,* 187–210.

Linz, D. (1989). Exposure to sexually explicit materials and attitudes toward rape: A comparison of study results. *Journal of Sex Research, 26,* 50–84.

Linz, D., et al. (1988). The effects of long-term exposure to violent and sexually degrading depictions of women. *Journal of Personality and Social Psychology, 55,* 758–767.

Lipshultz, L. I. (1996). Injection therapy for erectile dysfunction. *The New England Journal of Medicine, 334,* 913–914.

Liu, K. E., & Fisher, W. A. (2002). Canadian physicians' role in contraception from the 19th century to now. *Journal of Obstetrics and Gynaecology Canada, 24,* 239–244.

Looman, J., Abracen, J., DiFazio, R., & Maillet, G. (2004). Alcohol and drug abuse among sexual and nonsexual offenders: Relationship to intimacy deficits and coping strategy. *Sexual Abuse: A Journal of Research and Treatment, 16*(3), 177–189.

LoPiccolo, J. (1994). The evolution of sex therapy. *Sexual and Marital Therapy, 9*(1), 5–7.

LoPiccolo, J., & Friedman, J. (1988). Broad-spectrum treatment of low sexual desire: Integration of cognitive, behavioral, and systemic therapy. In S. Leiblum & R. Rosen (eds.), *Sexual desire disorders.* New York: Guilford Press.

LoPiccolo, J., & Stock, W. E. (1986). Treatment of sexual dysfunction. *Journal of Consulting and Clinical Psychology, 54,* 158–167.

Lott, B. (1985). The potential enhancement of social/personality psychology through feminist research and vice versa. *American Psychologist, 40,* 155–164.

Love, N. (2004, March 20). Boy, 14, charged with luring girls over 'Net. *Toronto Star.*

Lown, J., & Dolan, E. (1988). Financial challenges in remarriage. *Lifestyles: Family and Economic Issues, 9,* 73–88.

Lowry, R., et al. (1994). Substance use and HIV-related sexual behaviors among U.S. high school students: Are they related? *American Journal of Public Health, 84*(7) 1116–1120.

Lue, T. F. (2000). Drug therapy: Erectile dysfunction. *The New England Journal of Medicine* online, *342*(24).

Lundstrom, B., Pauly, I., & Walinder, J. (1984). Outcome of sex reassignment surgery. *Acta Psychiatrica Scandinavica, 70,* 289–294.

Macallan, D. C., et al. (1995). Energy expenditure and wasting in human immunodeficiency virus infection. *The New England Journal of Medicine, 333,* 83–88.

MacCharles, T. (2000, December 16). Customs can stop gay erotica: Top court. *The Toronto Star,* p. A13.

Maccoby, E. E. (1990). Gender and relationships: A developmental account. *American Psychologist, 45,* 513–520.

MacDonald, T. K., MacDonald, G., Zanna, M. P., & Fong, G. T. (2000). Alcohol, sexual arousal, and intentions to use condoms in young men: Applying alcohol myopia theory to risky sexual behavior. *Health Psychology, 19,* 290–298.

MacIntosh, H., & Reissing, E. D. (under consideration). Legal same-sex marriage: The impact on the personal, social and relational lives of gay & lesbian couples. *Journal of Marital and Family Therapy.*

Mackie, M. (1991). *Gender relations in Canada: Further explorations.* Markham: Butterworths Canada Ltd.

Maclean's Magazine (1998, July 20). Findings from the GoldParlo Poll. *Maclean's,* 10.

MacNeil, S. (2004). It takes two: Modeling the role of sexual self-disclosure in sexual satisfaction. (Doctoral dissertation, **www.il.proquest.com/umi/**). *Dissertation Abstracts International: Section B: The Sciences & Engineering, 65* (1-B), 481. (UMI Dissertation Order Number AAINQ87631; Print).

MacNeil, S., & Byers, E. S. (1997). The relationships between sexual problems, communication and sexual satisfaction. *Canadian Journal of Human Sexuality, 6*(4), 277–283.

MacQueen, K. (2003). Boy vs. girl. *Maclean's.* May 26, 26–32.

Mah, K., & Binik, Y. (2002). Do all orgasms feel alike? Evaluating a two-dimensional model of the orgasm experience across gender and sexual context. *The Journal of Sex Research, 39,* 104–114.

Mahoney, D. (1994*). Staying connected: The coming out stories of parents with a lesbian daughter or gay son.* Unpublished Master's Thesis, University of Guelph.

Major, B., & Cozzarelli, C. (1992). Psychosocial predictors of adjustment to abortion. *Journal of Social Issues, 48,* 121–142.

Major, B., Cozzarelli, C., Cooper, M. L., Zubek, J., Richards, C., et al. (2000). Psychological responses of women after first-trimester abortion. *Archives of General Psychiatry, 57,* 777–784.

Major, C. J., Read, S. E., Coates, R. A., et al. (1991). Comparison of saliva and blood for human immunodeficiency virus prevalence testing. *Journal of Infectious Diseases, 163*(4), 699–702.

Malamuth, N. M., & Ceniti, J. (1986). Repeated exposure to violent and nonviolent pornography: Likelihood-of-raping ratings and laboratory aggression against women. *Aggressive Behavior, 12,* 129–137.

Maletzky, B. M. (1980). Self-referred vs. court-referred sexually deviant patients: Success with assisted covert sensitization. *Behavior Therapy, 11,* 306–314.

Malinowski, B. (1929). *The sexual life of savages in north-western Melanesia.* New York: Eugenics.

Malloy, M. H., Hoffman, H. J., Peterson, D. R. (1992). Sudden infant death syndrome and maternal smoking. *American Journal of Public Health, 82,* 1380–1382.

Man accused of stealing panties agrees to counselling. (2002, April 28). *National Post,* p. A6.

Mantovani, F. (2001). Cyber-attraction: The emergence of computer-mediated communication in the development of interpersonal relationships. In L. Anolli, R. Cieri, & G. Riva (eds.), *Say not to say: New perspectives on miscommunication* (pp. 236–252). Amsterdam, Holland: IOS Press.

Marchbanks, P. A., et al. (2000). Cigarette smoking and epithelial ovarian cancer by histological type. *Obstetrics & Gynecology, 95*, 255–260.

Marcus, D. K., & Miller, R. S. (2003). Sex differences in judgments of physical attractiveness: A social relations analysis. *Personality & Social Psychology Bulletin, (29)*3, 325–335.

Mark, M. (2003, October 1). Consenting adults: A look behind closed doors in Calgary. *The Calgary Sun.*

Marks, G., Miller, N., & Maruyama, G. (1981). Effect of targets' physical attractiveness on assumption of similarity. *Journal of Personality and Social Psychology, 41*, 198–206.

Marrazzo, J. M. (2005). Sexual practices, risk perception and knowledge of sexually transmitted disease risk among lesbian and bisexual women. *Perspectives on Sexual and Reproductive Health, 37*, 6–12.

Marshall, D. (1971). Sexual behavior on Mangaia. In D. Marshall & R. Suggs (eds.), *Human sexual behavior: Variations in the ethnographic spectrum* (pp. 103–162). New York: Basic Books.

Marshall, W. L. (1989). Pornography and sex offenders. In D. Zillmann & J. Bryant (eds.), *Pornography: Research advances and policy considerations* (pp. 185–214). Hillsdale, NJ: Lawrence Erlbaum Associates.

Marsiglio, W. (1993a). Adolescent males' orientation toward paternity and contraception. *Family Planning Perspectives, 25*, 22–31.

Marsiglio, W. (1993b). Attitudes toward homosexual activity and gays as friends: A national survey of heterosexual 15- to 19-year-old males. *Journal of Sex Research, 30*, 12–17.

Marsman, J. C., & Herold, E. S. (1986). Attitudes toward sex education and values in sex education. *Family Relations, 35*, 357–361.

Martin, C. L., & Halverson, C. F., Jr. (1981). A schematic processing model of sex typing and stereotyping in children. *Child Development, 54*, 1119–1134.

Martin, J. N., et al. (1998). Sexual transmission and the natural history of human herpes virus 8 infection. *The New England Journal of Medicine, 338*, 948–954.

Martinez, F. D., Cline, M., & Burrows, B. (1992). Increased incidence of asthma in children of smoking mothers. *Pediatrics, 89*, 21–26.

Martinson, F. M. (1976). Eroticism in infancy and childhood. *Journal of Sex Research, 2*, 251–262.

Martz, J. M., et al. (1998). Positive illusion in close relationships. *Personal Relationships, 5*(2), 159–181.

Marwick, C. (2000). Consensus panel considers osteoporosis. *Journal of the American Medical Association* online, *283*(16).

Masters, W. H., & Johnson, V. E. (1966). *Human sexual response.* Boston: Little, Brown.

Masters, W. H., & Johnson, V. E. (1979). *Homosexuality in perspective.* Boston: Little, Brown.

Masters, W. H., et al. (1989). *Human sexuality,* 4th ed. New York: HarperCollins.

Matek, O. (1988). Obscene phone callers. *Journal of Social Work and Human Sexuality, 7*, 113–130.

Maticka-Tyndale, E., (1997). Reducing the incidence of sexually transmitted disease through behavioral and social change. *Canadian Journal of Human Sexuality, 6*(2), 89–104.

Maticka-Tyndale, E. (2001). Sexual health and Canadian youth: How do we measure up? *Canadian Journal of Human Sexuality, 10*, 1–17.

Maticka-Tyndale, M., & Brooke, C. (2005). *Sexuality in Canada: Research.* Paper presented at the XVII World Congress of Sexology, Montreal.

Maticka-Tyndale, E., Godin, G., LeMay, G., Adrien, A., Manson-Singer, S., Willms, D., et al. (1996). Canadian ethnocultural communities facing AIDS: Overview and summary of survey results from phase III. *Canadian Journal of Public Health, 87*(supp. 1), S38–S43.

Maticka-Tyndale, E., & Herold, E. S. (1997). The scripting of sexual behaviour: Canadian university students on spring break in Florida. *The Canadian Journal of Human Sexuality, 6*, 317–328.

Maticka-Tyndale, E., Herold, E. S., & Mewhinney, D. K. (1998). Casual sex on spring break: Intentions and behaviors of Canadian students. *Journal of Sex Research, 35*, 254–264.

Maticka-Tyndale, E., Lewis, J., & Street, M. (2005). Making a place for escort work: A case study. *The Journal of Sex Research 42*(1), 46–53.

Maticka-Tyndale, E., McKay, A., & Barrett, M. (2001). *Teenage sexual and reproductive behavior in developed countries: Country report for Canada.* New York: Alan Guttmacher Institute.

Maticka-Tyndale, E., Shirpak, K., & Chinichian, M. (2005). *Sexual Health Education and Service Delivery within Islamic Tradition.* Presented at the Guelph Sexuality Conference, Guelph, ON.

Maybach, K. L., & Gold, S. R. (1994). Hyperfemininity and attraction to macho and non-macho men. *Journal of Sex Research, 31*(2), 91–98.

Mayer, J. P., Hawkins, B., & Todd, R. (1990). A randomized evaluation of smoking cessation interventions for pregnant women at a WIC [Women, Infants and Children] clinic. *American Journal of Public Health, 80*, 76–79.

McArthur, M. J. (1990). Reality therapy with rape victims. *Archives of Psychiatric Nursing, 4*, 360–365.

McGregor, M. J., Ericksen, J., Ronald, L. A., Janssen, P. A., Van Vliet, A., & Schulzer, M. (2004). Rising incidence of hospital-reported drug-facilitated sexual assault in a large urban community in Canada. *Canadian Journal of Public Health, 95*(6), 441–445.

McKay, A. (1998). *Sexual ideology and schooling.* London, ON: The Althouse Press.

McKenzie, D. (2003, July 5). Swinger predicts rise in sex clubs. *The Toronto Star.*

McKenzie, D. (2005). *The sex profiles of Anglican and United Church clergy in two regions of British Columbia.* Paper presented at the Society for the Scientific Study of Sexuality Western Region Meeting, San Francisco.

McKinney, K., & Maroules, N. (1991). Sexual harassment. In E. Grauerholz & M. A. Koralewski (eds.), *Sexual coercion: A sourcebook on its nature, causes, and prevention* (pp. 29–44). Lexington, MA: Lexington Books.

McMaster, L. E., Connolly, J., Pepler, D., & Craig, W. M. (2002). Peer to peer sexual harassment in early adolescence: A developmental perspective. *Development and Psycho-pathology, 14*, 91–105.

Mead, M. (1935). *Sex and temperament in three primitive societies.* New York: Dell.

Meana, M., & Binik, Y. M. (1994). Painful coitus: A review of female dyspareunia. *Journal of Nervous and Mental Disease, 182*(5), 264–272.

Meier, B. (1997, June 8). In war against AIDS, battle over baby formula reignites. *The New York Times*, pp. A1, A16.

Meisler, A. W., & Carey, M. P. (1990). A critical reevaluation of nocturnal penile tumescence monitoring in the diagnosis of erectile dysfunction. *Journal of Nervous and Mental Disease, 178*, 78–89.

Menon, V. (2002, May 14). Window undressing. *The Toronto Star*, p. B1.

Merrill, R. M., & Brawley, O. W. (2000). Prostate cancer incidence and mortality rates among White and Black men. *Epidemiology* online, *11*(2).

Mertz, G. J., et al. (1992). Risk factors for the sexual transmission of genital herpes. *Annals of Internal Medicine, 116*, 197–202.

Messenger, J. C. (1971). Sex and repression in an Irish folk community. In D. S. Marshall and R. C. Suggs (eds.), *Human sexual behavior: Variations in the ethnographic spectrum* (pp. 3–37). New York: Basic Books.

Meston, C. M., & Gorzalka, B. B. (1992). Psychoactive drugs and human sexual behavior: The role of serotonergic activity. *Journal of Psychoactive Drugs, 24*, 1–40.

Meston, C. M., & Gorzalka, B. B (1995). The effects of sympathetic activation on physiological and subjective sexual arousal in women. *Behavior Research and Therapy, 33*, 651–664.

Meston, C. M., & Heiman, J. R. (2000). Sexual abuse and sexual function: An examination of sexually relevant cognitive processes. *Journal of Consulting and Clinical Psychology, 68*(3), 399–406.

Meston, C. M., Heiman, J. R., Trapnell, P., & Paulhus, D. (1998). Socially desirable responding and sexuality self-reports. *The Journal of Sex Research, 35*, 148–157.

Meston, C. M., Trapnell, P. D., & Gorzalka, B. B. (1996). Ethnic and gender differences in sexuality: Variations in sexual behavior between Asian and non-Asian university students. *Archives of Sexual Behavior, 25*, 33–72.

Meston, C. M., Trapnell, P. D., & Gorzalka, B. B. (1998). Ethnic, gender and length-of-residency influences on sexual knowledge and attitudes. *The Journal of Sex Research, 35*(2), 176–188.

Mewhinney, D. K., Herold, E. S., & Maticka-Tyndale, E. (1995). Sexual scripts and risk-taking of Canadian university students on spring break in Daytona Beach, Florida. *Canadian Journal of Human Sexuality, 4,* 273–288.

Meyer, J. K., & Reter, D. J. (1979). Sex reassignment: Follow-up. *Archives of General Psychiatry, 36,* 1010–1015.

Meyer, T. (1998, February 18). AZT short treatment works. The Associated Press online.

Meyer-Bahlburg, H. F. L., et al. (1995). Prenatal estrogens and the development of homosexual orientation. *Developmental Psychology, 31*(1), 12–21.

Michael, R. T., Gagnon, J. H., Laumann, E. O., & Kolata, G. (1994). *Sex in America: A definitive survey.* Boston: Little, Brown.

Michelson, D., et al. (2000). Female sexual dysfunction associated with antidepressant administration: A randomized, placebo-controlled study of pharmacologic intervention. *American Journal of Psychiatry, 157,* 239–243.

Mikach, S. M., & Bailey, J. M. (1999). What distinguishes women with unusually high numbers of sex partners? *Evolution & Human Behavior, 20*(3), 141–150.

Milhausen, R. R. (2000). Double standard or reverse double standard: A comparative analysis of male and female perspectives. Unpublished masters thesis, University of Guelph.

Milhausen, R. R., & Herold, E. S. (1999). Does the sexual double standard still exist? Perceptions of university women. *Journal of Sex Research, 36*(4), 361–368.

Milhausen, R. R., & Herold, E. S. (2001). Reconceptualizing the sexual double standard. *Journal of Psychology and Human Sexuality, 13,* 63–83.

Millar, C. (2003, November 22). Web porn accessed from car. *The Toronto Star.*

Miller A. B., et al. (2000). Canadian national breast screening study—2: 13-year results of a randomized trial in women aged 50-59 years, *Journal of the National Cancer Institute, 92*(18): 1490–1499.

Miller, B. C., McCoy, J. K., & Olson, T. D. (1986). Dating age and stage as correlates of adolescent sexual attitudes and behavior. *Journal of Adolescent Research, 1,* 361–371.

Miller, S. A., & Byers, E. S. (2004). Actual and desired duration of foreplay and intercourse: Discordance and misperceptions within heterosexual couples. *Journal of Sex Research, 41*(3), 301–309.

Miller, S. A., & Byers, S. E. (2005) *The training of clinical psychologists in Canada: How prepared are students to deal with clients' sexual problems?* Paper presented at the World Congress of Sexology, Montreal.

Miller, W., and Maclean, H. (2005). Breastfeeding practices. Ottawa: Statistics Canada [Catalogue 82-003 Health Reports, Vol. 16, 2, March 2005.]

Minai, N. (1981). *Women in Islam: Tradition and transition in the Middle East.* London: John Murray.

Minichiello, V., et al. (2001). Male sex workers in three Australian cities: Socio-demographic and sex work characteristics. *Journal of Homosexuality, 42*(1), 29–51.

Minister of Health (2002, May 9). *House of Commons of Canada Bill C-56: An act respecting assisted human reproduction.* House of Commons of Canada, [49-50-51], 1st session, 37th Parliament.

Minnis, A. M., & Padim, N. S. (2005). Effectiveness of female controlled barrier methods in preventing sexually transmitted infections and HIV: Current evidence and future research directions. *Sexually Transmitted Infections, 81,* 193–200.

Mishell, D. R., Jr. (1989). Medical progress: Contraception. *The New England Journal of Medicine, 320,* 777–787.

Missailidis, K., & Gebre-Medhin, M. (2000). Female genital mutilation in eastern Ethiopia. *The Lancet, 356,* 137–138.

Mofenson, L. M. (2000). Perinatal exposure to zidovudine—Benefits and risks. *The New England Journal of Medicine* online, *343*(11).

Molloy, G. L., & Herold, E. S. (1985). Sexual counseling for the physically disabled: A comparison of health care professionals' attitudes and practices. *Canadian Family Physician, 31,* 2277–2285.

Money, J. (1994). The concept of gender identity disorder in childhood and adolescence after 39 years. *Journal of Sex and Marital Therapy, 20*(3), 163–177.

Money, J., & Ehrhardt, A. (1972). *Man and woman, boy and girl.* Baltimore, MD: The Johns Hopkins University Press.

Money, J., & Lamacz, M. (1989). *Vandalized lovemaps.* Buffalo, NY: Prometheus Books.

Money, J., Lehne, G., & Pierre-Jerome, F. (1984). Micropenis: Adult follow-up and comparison of size against new norms. *Journal of Sex and Marital Therapy, 10,* 105–116.

Montano, D., Kasprzyk, D., von Haeften, I., & Fishbein, M. (2001). Toward an understanding of condom use behaviours: A theoretical and methodological overview of Project SAFER. *Psychology, Health & Medicine, 6*(2), 139–150.

Montreal Health Press (1999). *Birth Control Handbook, 30th Anniversary Edition.* Montreal: Author.

Moore, K. A., & Stief, T. M. (1992). Changes in marriage and fertility behavior: Behavior versus attitudes of young adults. *Youth and Society, 22,* 362–386.

Morley, J. E., & van den Berg, L. (2000). *Endocrinology of aging.* Totowa, NJ: Humana Press.

Morris, L. B. (2000, June 25). For the partum blues, a question of whether to medicate. *The New York Times* online.

Morris, N., et al. (1987). Marital sex frequency and midcycle female testosterone. *Archives of Sexual Behavior, 7,* 157–173.

Morrison, G. G., Harriman, R., Morrison, M. A., Bearden, A., & Ellis, S. (2004). Correlates of exposure to sexually explicit material among Canadian post-secondary students. *The Canadian Journal of Human Sexuality, 13*(3–4), 143–157.

Mortola, J. F. (1998). Premenstrual syndrome—Pathophysiologic considerations. *The New England Journal of Medicine, 338,* 256–257.

Moser, C. (2001). Paraphilia: A critique of a confused concept. In P. Kleinplatz (ed.), *New directions in sex therapy: Innovations and alternatives* (pp. 91–108). New York: Brunner-Routledge.

Moser, C., & Kleinplatz, P. J. (2002, Spring). Transvestic fetishism: Psychopathology or iatrogenic artifact? *New Jersey Psychologist,* pp. 16–17.

Mother guilty of assault. (1999, February 18). *National Post.*

Muehlenhard, C. L. (2000). Categories and sexuality. *The Journal of Sex Research, 37*(2), 101–107.

Mulick, P. S., & Wright, L. W., Jr. (2002). Examining the existence of biphobia in the heterosexual and homosexual population. *Journal of Bisexuality, 2*(4), 45–64.

Murray, J., & Adam, B. (2001). Aging, sexuality and HIV issues among older gay men. *The Canadian Journal of Human Sexuality, 10,* 75–90.

Muster, N. J. (1992). Treating the adolescent victim-turned-offender. *Adolescence, 27,* 441–450.

Myers, M. F. (1989). Men sexually assaulted as adults and sexually abused as boys. *Archives of Sexual Behavior, 18,* 203–215.

Myers, T., Aguinaldo, J. P., Dakers, D., et al. (2004). How drug using men who have sex with men account for substance use during sexual behaviours: Questioning assumptions of HIV prevention and research. *Addiction Research and Theory, 12*(3), 213–229.

Myers, T., Allman, D., Calzavara, L., et al (2004). *Ontario men's survey.* Toronto: University of Toronto, HIV Social, Behavioural and Epidemiological Studies Unit.

Myers, T., Bullock, S. L., Calzavara, L. M., Cockerill, R., & Marshall, V. W. (1997). Differences in sexual risk-taking behaviour with state of inebriation in an Aboriginal population in Ontario, Canada. *Journal of Studies in Alcohol, 58,* 312–322.

Myers, T., Calzavara, L. M., Cockerill, R., Marshall, V. W., & Bullock, S. L. (1993). *The Ontario First Nations AIDS and healthy lifestyle survey.* Ottawa, ON: Canadian Public Health Association.

Myers, T., Godin, G., Calzavara, L., Lambert, J., & Locker, D. (1993). *The Canadian survey of gay and bisexual men and HIV infection: Men's survey.* Ottawa, ON: Canadian AIDS Society.

Myers, T., Godin, G., Lambert, J., Calzavara, L., & Locker, D. (1996). Sexual risk and HIV-testing behaviour by gay and bisexual men in Canada. *AIDS Care, 8*(3), 297–309.

Myers, T., Orr, K. W., Locker, D., & Jackson, E. A. (1993). Factors affecting gay and bisexual men's decisions and intentions to seek HIV testing. *American Journal of Public Health, 83,* 701–704.

Nadeau, R., et al. (1993). Knowledge and beliefs regarding STDs and condoms among students. *Canadian Journal of Public Health, 84,* 181–185.

Nadler, R. D. (1990). Homosexual behavior in nonhuman primates. In D. P. McWhirter, S. A. Sanders, & J. M. Reinisch (eds.), *Homosexuality/heterosexuality: Concepts of sexual orientation* (pp. 138–170). New York: Oxford University Press.

Naili, H., & Josey, S. (2005, August 11). Pastor faces sex charges. *The Toronto Star.*

Narod, S. A., et al. (1998). Oral contraceptives and the risk of hereditary ovarian cancer. *The New England Journal of Medicine 339,* 424–428.

National Cancer Institute. (2000). Available: **www.nci. nih.gov**

National Center for Biotechnology Information (NCBI). (2000, March 30). National Institutes of Health. Available: **www.ncbi.nlm.nih.gov/disease/SRY.htm**

Nduati, R., et al. (2000). Effect of breast-feeding and formula feeding on transmission of HIV-1. *Journal of the American Medical Association, 283,* 1167–1174.

Netting, N. S., & Burnett, M. L. (2004). Twenty years of student sexual behavior: Subcultural adaptations to a changing health environment. *Adolescence, 39*(153), 19–38.

Nevid, J. S. (1984). Sex differences in factors of romantic attraction. *Sex Roles, 11,* 401–411.

Nichols, M. (1999, February 22). Men's sexual health. *Maclean's,* pp. 30–31.

Nickel, J. C., Elhilali, M., Vallancien, G., & ALF-ONE Study Group. (2005). Benign prostatic hyperplasia (BPH) and prostatitis: Prevalence of painful ejaculation in men with clinical BPH. *BJU International, 95*(4), 571–574.

Nixon, K., Tutty, L., Downe, P., Gorkoff, K., & Ursel, J. (2002). The everyday occurrence: Violence in the lives of girls exploited through prostitution. *Violence Against Women. Special Violence Against Women and Girls in Prostitution, 8*(9), 1016–1043.

Nock, S. L. (1995). A comparison of marriages and cohabiting relationships. *Journal of Family Issues, 16*(1), 53–76.

Nosek, M. A., et al. (1994). Wellness models and sexuality among women with physical disabilities. *Journal of Applied Rehabilitation Counseling, 25*(1), 50–58.

Nour, N. W. (2000). Cited in Dreifus, C. (2000, July 11). A conversation with Dr. Nawal M. Nour: A life devoted to stopping the suffering of mutilation. *The New York Times* online.

Oakes, G. (1994, February 4). Lover who removed his condom jailed 45 days for sexual assault. *The Toronto Star.*

Ochs, R. (1994, January 11). Cervical cancer comeback. *New York Newsday,* pp. 55, 57.

Ochs, E. P., & Binik, Y. M. (1999). The use of couple data to determine reliability of self-reported sexual behavior. *Journal of Sex Research, 36*(4), 1–11.

Ochs, E. P., & Binik, Y. M. (2000). A sex-expert system on the Internet: Fact or fantasy. *Cyber Psychology & Behavior, 3,* 617–629.

O'Donohue, W., Letourneau, E., & Geer, J. H. (1993). Premature ejaculation. In W. O'Donohue & J. H. Geer (eds.), *Handbook of sexual dysfunctions: Assessment and treatment* (pp. 303–333). Boston: Allyn & Bacon.

Offman, A., & Kleinplatz, P. J. (2004). Does PMDD belong in the DSM? Challenging the medicalization of women's bodies. *Canadian Journal of Human Sexuality, 13*(1), 17–27.

Offman, A., & Matheson, K. (2004). The sexual self-perceptions of young women experiencing abuse in dating relationships. *Sex Roles, 51*(9–10), 551–560.

O'Hara, M. W., Neunaber, D. J., & Zekoski, E. M. (1984). Prospective study of postpartum depression: Prevalence, course, and predictive factors. *Journal of Abnormal Psychology, 93,* 158–171.

O'Hara, M. W., et al. (1991). Prospective study of postpartum blues: Biological and psychosocial factors. *Archives of General Psychiatry, 48,* 801–806.

Oldenburg, R., & Brissett, D. (1980, April). The essential hangout. *Psychology Today,* pp. 81–84.

O'Neil, P. (2005, March 7). Liberal convention rejects motion to legalize prostitution. *National Post.*

O'Neill, N., & O'Neill, G. (1972). *Open marriage.* New York: Evans.

Osborne, N. G., & Adelson, M. D. (1990). Herpes simplex and human papillomavirus genital infections: Controversy over obstetric management. *Clinical Obstetrics and Gynecology, 33,* 801–811.

Osman, S. L. (2003). Predicting men's rape perceptions based on the belief that "No" really means "Yes." *Journal of Applied Social Psychology, 33*(4), 683–692.

O'Sullivan, L. F., & Byers, E. S. (1992). College students' incorporation of initiator and restrictor roles in sexual dating interactions. *Journal of Sex Research, 29,* 435–446.

O'Sullivan, L. F., Byers, E. S., & Finkelman, L. (1998). A comparison of male and female college students' experiences of sexual coercion. *Psychology of Women Quarterly, 22,* 177–195.

Oswalt, R., & Matsen, K. (1993). Sex, AIDS, and the use of condoms: A survey of compliance in college students. *Psychological Reports, 72,* 764–766.

Overholser, J. C., & Beck, S. (1986). Multimethod assessment of rapists, child molesters, and three control groups on behavioral and psychological measures. *Journal of Consulting and Clinical Psychology, 54,* 682–687.

Padma-Nathan, H., et al. (1997). Treatment of men with erectile dysfunction with transurethral alprostadil. *The New England Journal of Medicine, 336,* 1–7.

Palace, E. M. (1995). Modification of dysfunctional patterns of sexual arousal through autonomic arousal and false physiological feedback. *Journal of Consulting and Clinical Psychology, 63,* 604–615.

Palmore, E. (1981). *Social patterns in normal aging: Findings from the Duke Longitudinal Study.* Durham, NC: Duke University Press.

Parr-LeFeuve, R., & Desmarais, S. (2005). Do young women use sexual pressure to initiate sex? Unpublished paper. University of Guelph, Dept. of Psychology.

Pauly, B., & Edgerton, M. (1986). The gender-identity movement. *Archives of Sexual Behavior, 15,* 315–329.

Pauly, I. B. (1974). Female transsexualism: Part 1. *Archives of Sexual Behavior, 3,* 487–508.

Pawlowski, B., & Koziel, S. (2002). The impact of traits offered in personal advertisements on response rates. *Evolution & Human Behavior 23*(2), 139–149.

Pearson, C. A. (1992, February 1). Cited in Leary, W. E. (1992). U.S. panel backs approval of first condom for women. *The New York Times,* p. 7.

Pek, N. K., & Senn, C. Y. (2004). Not wanted in the inbox! Evaluations of unsolicited and harassing e-mail. *Psychology of Women Quarterly, 28,* 204–214.

Pelletier, L. A., & Herold, E. S. (1988). The relationship of age, sex guilt and sexual experience with female sexual fantasies. *Journal of Sex Research, 24,* 250–256.

Peplau, L. A. (2003). Human sexuality: How do men and women differ? *Current Directions in Psychological Science, 12*(2), 37–40.

Peplau, L. A., & Cochran, S. D. (1990). A relationship perspective on homosexuality. In D. P. McWhirter, S. A. Sanders, & J. M. Reinisch (eds.), *Homosexuality/heterosexuality: Concepts of sexual orientation* (pp. 321–349). New York: Oxford University Press.

Peplau, L. A., & Gordon, S. L. (1985). Women and men in love: Sex differences in close heterosexual relationships. In V. O'Leary et al. (eds.), *Women, gender, and social psychology.* Hillsdale, NJ: Lawrence Erlbaum Associates.

Perduta-Fulginiti, P. S. (1992). Sexual functioning of women with complete spinal cord injury: Nursing implications. [Special issue: Nursing roles and perspectives]. *Sexuality and Disability, 10,* 103–118.

Peretti, P. O., & Pudowski, B. C. (1997). Influence of jealousy on male and female college daters. *Social Behavior & Personality, 25*(2), 155–160.

Peritz, I. (2005, September 23). Student leaves McGill over sports hazing ritual. *The Globe and Mail.*

Perrett, D. I. (1994). *Nature.* Cited in Brody, J. E. (1994, March 21). Notions of beauty transcend culture, new study suggests. *The New York Times,* p. A14.

Perry, A. (2003, February 21). Women seek more from the modern workplace. *The Toronto Star.*

Perry, D. G., & Bussey, K. (1979). The social learning theory of sex differences: Imitation is alive and well. *Journal of Personality and Social Psychology, 37,* 1699–1712.

Perry, J. D., & Whipple, B. (1981). Pelvic muscle strength of female ejaculation:

Evidence in support of a new theory of orgasm. *Journal of Sex Research, 17,* 22–39.

Perry, P. J., et al. (2001). Bioavailable testosterone as a correlate of cognition, psychological status, quality of life, and sexual function in aging males: Implications for testosterone replacement therapy. *Annals of Clinical Psychiatry, 13*(2), 75–80.

Petrunik, M. (2003). The hare and the tortoise: Dangerousness and sex offender policy in the United States and Canada. *Canadian Journal of Criminology & Criminal Justice, 45*(1), 43–72.

Pevere, G. (2001, November 24). See no evil. *The Toronto Star,* p. J1.

PHERO. (1999, November 26). The teen prenatal study of the Sudbury, Manitoulin and Algoma Districts. *Communique: Public Health Research, Education and Development Program,* 236–243.

Pillard, R. C. (1990). The Kinsey Scale: Is it familial? In D. P. McWhirter, S. A. Sanders, & J. M. Reinisch (eds.), *Homosexuality/heterosexuality: Concepts of sexual orientation* (pp. 88–100). New York: Oxford University Press.

Pillard, R. C., & Weinrich, J. D. (1986). Evidence of familial nature of male homosexuality. *Archives of Sexual Behavior, 43,* 808–812.

Pinkerton, S. D., & Abramson, P. R. (1992). Is risky sex rational? *Journal of Sex Research, 29,* 561–568.

Piot, P. Cited in UNAIDS Press Release (2000, June 5). Gender is crucial issue in fight against AIDS, says head of UNAIDS. New York.

Planned Parenthood Federation of Canada. (1999). A history of birth control in Canada. [Brochure].

Plant, E. A., Hyde, J. S., Keltner, D., & Devine, P. G. (2000). The gender stereotyping of emotions. *Psychology of Women Quarterly, 24*(1), 81–92.

Ploem, C., Byers, E. S. (1997). The effects of two AIDS risk-reduction interventions on heterosexual college women's AIDS-related knowledge, attitudes and condom use. *Journal of Psychology and Human Sexuality, 9,* 1–24.

Porter, C. (2003, July 18). The swing's their thing. *The Toronto Star.*

Potosky, A. L., et al. (2000). Health outcomes after prostatectomy or radiotherapy for prostate cancer: Results from the Prostate Cancer Outcomes Study. *Journal of the National Cancer Institute, 92,* 1582–1592.

Pound, N., Javed, M., Ruberto, C., Shaikh, M., & Del Vaille, A. P. (2002). Duration of sexual arousal predicts semen parameters for masturbatory ejaculates. *Physiology & Behavior, 76*(4), 685–689.

Powderly, W. G., et al. (1995). A randomized trial comparing fluconazole with clotrimazole troches for the prevention of fungal infections in patients with advanced human immunodeficiency virus infection. *The New England Journal of Medicine, 332,* 700–705.

Powell, B. (2002, November 27). Snowman ad gets frosty TTC reception. *The Toronto Star,* p. B1.

Powell, B. (2005, Sept. 21). The down side of camera cellphones. *The Toronto Star,* A4.

Powell, B., & Chung, E. (May 8, 2005). HIV case adds charges. *The Toronto Star.*

Powell, E. (1996). *Sex on your terms.* Boston: Allyn & Bacon.

PPFC (2002). Emergency contraception: Get the facts! [on-line]. Available: **www.ppfc.ca/faqs/access.htm**

Prashad, S. (2004). When cupid's arrow strikes at the office. *Toronto Star,* February 14, D14.

Preti, G., Cutler, W. B., et al. (1986). Human axillary secretions influence women's menstrual cycles: The role of donor extract of females. *Hormones and Behavior, 20,* 474–482.

Price, V. A. (1989). Characteristics and needs of Boston street youth: One agency's response [Special issue: Runaway, homeless, and shut-out children and youth in Canada, Europe, and the United States]. *Children and Youth Services Review, 11,* 75–90.

Prostrate Cancer in Ontario. (2003). *Public Health and Epidemiology Report, 14*(6), 81–83.

Pryor, J. (2005). *Efficacy and tolerability of dapoxetine in the treatment of premature ejaculation.* Presented to a meeting of the American Urological Association, San Antonio, Texas.

Public Health Agency of Canada. (2005a). *HIV and AIDS in Canada. Surveillance report to December 31, 2004.*

Public Health Agency of Canada. (2005b). Reported *cases and rates of notifiable STI from January 1 to June 30, 2004 and January 1 to June 30, 2003.*

Public Health Agency of Canada (2005c). Self-learning module, STD. Yeast vaginosis. Available: **www.phac-aspc.gc.ca/slm-maa/slides/other/pages/15.html**

Public Health & Epidemiology Report Ontario (2002, March/April). The Ontario Ministry of Health and Long-Term Care: AIDS and Sexual Health infoline 2000 Annual Report. *Public Health Branch, 13*(3), 39–41.

Pukall, C. F., Binik, Y. M., Khalife, S., Amsel, R., & Abbott, E. V. (2002). Vestibular tactile and pain thresholds in women with vulvar vestibulitis syndrome. *Pain, 96,* 163–175.

Pukall, C. F., Payne, K. A., Binik, Y. M., & Khalife, S. (2003). Pain measurement in vulvodynia. *Journal of Sex & Marital Therapy, 29*(s), 111–120.

Purifoy, F. E., Grodsky, A., & Giambra, L. M. (1992). The relationship of sexual daydreaming to sexual activity, sexual drive, and sexual attitudes for women across the life-span. *Archives of Sexual Behavior, 21,* 369–375.

Quevillon, R. P. (1993). Dyspareunia. In W. O'Donohue & J. H. Geer (eds.), *Handbook of sexual dysfunctions: Assessment and treatment* (pp. 367–380). Boston: Allyn & Bacon.

Quill, G. (2002, July 17). Edge 102 rapped for sexually explicit morning act. *The Toronto Star,* p. D3.

Quinsey, V. L. (2002). Evolutionary theory and animal behavior. *Legal and Criminological Psychology, 7,* 1–13.

Quinsey, V. L., Chaplin, T. C., & Upfold, D. (1984). Sexual arousal to nonsexual violence and sadomasochistic themes among rapists and non-sex-offenders. *Journal of Consulting and Clinical Psychology, 52,* 651–657.

Rabinowitz Greenberg, S. R., Firestone, P., Bradford, J. M., & Greenberg, D. M. (2002). Prediction of recidivism in exhibitionists: Psychological, phallometric, and offense factors. *Sexual Abuse: Journal of Research & Treatment, 14*(4), 329–347.

Radlove, S. (1983). Sexual response and gender roles. In E. R. Allgeier & N. B. McCormick (eds.), *Changing boundaries: Gender roles and sexual behavior.* Palo Alto, CA: Mayfield.

Raichle, K., & Lambert, A. J. (2000). The role of political ideology in mediating judgments of blame in rape victims and their assailants: A test of the just world, personal responsibility, and legitimization hypotheses. *Personality & Social Psychology Bulletin, 26*(7), 853–863.

Rakic, Z., Starcevic, V., Starcevic, V. P., & Marinkovic, J. (1997). Testosterone treatment in men with erectile disorder and low levels of total testosterone in serum. *Archives of Sexual Behavior, 26*(5), 495–504.

Rako, S. (2003). *No more periods? The risks of menstrual suppression and other cutting-edge issues about hormones and women's health.* New York: Crown.

Ralph, D., & McNicholas, T. (2000). UK management guidelines for erectile dysfunction. *British Medical Journal, 321,* 499–503.

Ramirez, A. (1990, August 12). The success of sweet smell. *The New York Times,* p. 10F.

Randall, H., & Byers, S. (2003). What is sex? Students' definitions of having sex, sexual partner, and unfaithful sexual behaviour. *The Canadian Journal of Human Sexuality, 12,* 87–96.

Rankin, S. R. (2003). *Campus climate for gay, lesbian, bisexual, and transgender people: A national perspective.* New York: The National Gay and Lesbian Task Force Policy Institute. Available: **www.ngltf.org**

Rathus, S. A. (2003). *Voyages: Childhood and Adolescence.* Belmont, CA: Wadsworth.

Ratican, K. L. (1992). Sexual abuse survivors: Identifying symptoms and special treatment considerations. *Journal of Counseling and Development, 71,* 33–38.

Ratner, P. A., Johnson, J. L., Shoveller, J. A., Chan, K., Martindale, S. L., Schilder, A. J., et al. (2003). Non-consensual sex experienced by men who have sex with men: Prevalence and association with mental health. *Patient Education and Counseling, 49*(1) 67–74.

Reaney, P. (1998, January 15). Discovery may lead to cervical cancer vaccine. Reuters News Agency online.

Reid, R., & Lininger, T. (1993). Sexual pain disorders in the female. In W. T. O'Donohue and J. H. Geer (eds.), *Handbook of sexual dysfunctions: Assessment and treatment.* Boston: Allyn and Bacon.

Rein, M. F., & Muller, M. (1990). *Trichomonas vaginalis* and trichomoniasis. In K. K. Holmes, P. Mardh, P. F. Sparling, & P. J. Wiesner (eds.), *Sexually transmitted diseases*, 2nd ed. (pp. 481–492). New York: McGraw-Hill.

Reinisch, J. M. (1990). *The Kinsey Institute new report on sex: What you must know to be sexually literate.* New York: St. Martin's Press.

Reiss, B. F. (1988, Spring/Summer). The long-lived person and sexuality. *Dynamic Psychotherapy, 6,* 79–86.

Reissing, E. K., Binik, Y. M., Khalife, S., Cohen, D., & Amsel, R. (2004). Vaginal spasm, pain, and behavior: An empirical investigation of the diagnosis of vaginismus. *Archives of Sexual Behavior, 33*(1), 5–17.

Rempel, L. A. (2004). Factors influencing the breastfeeding decisions of long-term breastfeeders. *Journal of Human Lactation: Official Journal of International Lactation Consultant Association, 20*(3), 306–318.

Rempel, J. K., & Baumgartner, B. (2003). The relationship between attitudes towards menstruation and sexual attitudes, desires, and behavior in women. *Archives of Sexual Behavior, 32*(2), 155–163.

Renaud, C. A., & Byers, E. S. (1999). Exploring the frequency, diversity and content of university students' positive and negative sexual cognitions. *Canadian Journal of Human Sexuality, 8,* 17–30.

Renaud, P., Rouleau, J. L., Granger, L., Barsetti, I., & Bouchard, S. (2002). Measuring sexual preferences in virtual reality: A pilot study. *Cyberpsychology and Behavior, 5*(1), 1–9.

Ricci, E., Parazzini, F., & Pardi, G. (2000). Caesarean section and antiretroviral treatment. *The Lancet, 355*(9202), 496–502.

Rice, M. E., Harris, G. T., & Quinsey, V. L. (1990). A follow-up of rapists assessed in a maximum-security psychiatric facility. *Journal of Interpersonal Violence, 5,* 435–448.

Rice, M. E., Quinsey, V. L., & Harris, G. T. (1991). Sexual recidivism among child molesters released from a maximum security psychiatric institution. *Journal of Consulting and Clinical Psychology, 59,* 381–386.

Richters, J., Hendry, O. L., & Kippax, S. (2003). When safe sex isn't safe. *Culture, Health & Sexuality, 5*(1), 37–52.

Rickwood, A. M. K., Kenny, S. E., & Donnell, S. C. (2000). Towards evidence based circumcision of English boys: Survey of trends in practice. *British Medical Journal, 321,* 792–793.

Riedmann, A., Lamanna, M., & Nelson, A. (2003). *Marriages and families,* 1st Canadian ed. Toronto: Thomson Canada.

Riggio, R. E., & Woll, S. B. (1984). The role of nonverbal cues and physical attractiveness in the selection of dating partners. *Journal of Social and Personal Relationships, 1,* 347–357.

Rimm, E. (2000). Lifestyle may play role in potential for impotence. Paper presented to the annual meeting of the American Urological Association, Atlanta.

Roberto, L. G. (1983). Issues in diagnosis and treatment of transsexualism. *Archives of Sexual Behavior, 12,* 445–473.

Roberts, J. M. (2000). Recent advances: Obstetrics. *British Medical Journal, 321*(7252), 33–35.

Roberts, J. V. (1994). Criminal justice processing of sexual assault cases. *Juristat Service Bulletin.* Canadian Centre for Justice Statistics, *14,* 1–19.

Roddy, R. E., et al. (1998). A controlled trial of Nonoxynol 9 film to reduce male-to-female transmission of sexually transmitted diseases. *The New England Journal of Medicine, 339,* 504–510.

Roehrich, L., & Kinder, B. N. (1991). Alcohol expectancies and male sexuality: Review and implications for sex therapy. *Journal of Sex & Marital Therapy, 17,* 45–54.

Roesler, A., & Witztum, E. (2000). Pharmacotherapy of paraphilias in the next millennium. *Behavioral Sciences & the Law, 18*(1), 43–56.

Rogala, C., & Tydén, T. (2003). Does pornography influence young women's sexual behavior? *Women's Health Issues, 13*(1), 39–43.

Romanowski, B., Campbell, P., Preiksaitis, J., & Fonseca, K. (1994). Human immunodeficiency virus seroprevalence and risk behaviors in patients attending sexually transmitted disease clinics in Alberta. *Sexually Transmitted Diseases,* September 1994, pp. 487–494, cited in Health Canada, HIV risk behaviours among Canadians: An inventory and synthesis, Division of HIV Epidemiology, Bureau of HIV/AIDS, STD and TB, LCDC, November 1998.

Ronald, A. R., & Albritton, W. (1990). Chancroid and *Haemophilus ducreyi.* In K. K. Holmes, P. Mardh, P. F. Sparling, & P. J. Wiesner (eds.), *Sexually transmitted diseases,* 2nd ed. (pp. 263–272). New York: McGraw-Hill.

Rose, P. G. (1996). Endometrial carcinoma. *The New England Journal of Medicine, 335,* 640–649.

Rosen, R. C., Leiblum, S. R., & Spector, I. P. (1994). Psychologically based treatment for male erectile disorder: A cognitive-interpersonal model. *Journal of Sex and Marital Therapy, 20*(2), 67–85.

Rosenthal, E. (1992, July 22). Her image of his ideal, in a faulty mirror. *The New York Times,* p. C12.

Rösler, A., & Witztum, E. (1998). Treatment of men with paraphilia with a long-acting analogue of gonadotropin releasing hormone. *The New England Journal of Medicine, 338,* 416–422.

Rosman, J. P., & Resnick, P. J. (1989). Sexual attraction to corpses: A psychiatric review of necrophilia. *Bulletin of the American Academy of Psychiatry and the Law, 17,* 153–163.

Ross, J. L., Roeltgen, D., Feuillan, P., Kushner, H., & Cutler, W. B. (2000). Use of estrogen in young girls with Turner syndrome: Effects on memory. *Neurology, 54*(1), 164–170.

Ross, L. E. (2005). Perinatal mental health in lesbian mothers: A review of potential risk and protective factors. *Women & Health, 41*(3).

Ross, L. E., & Steiner, M. (2003a). A biopsychosocial approach to premenstrual dysphoric disorder. *The Psychiatric Clinics of North America, 26*(3), 529–546.

Ross, L. E., & Steiner, M. (2003b). Therapeutic patents for the treatment of premenstrual syndrome and premenstrual dysphoric disorder: Historical perspectives and future directions. *Expert Opinions Therapy Patents, 13*(10), 1491–1499.

Ross, M., & Need, J. (1989). Effects of adequacy of gender reassignment surgery on psychological adjustment: A follow-up of fourteen male-to-female patients. *Archives of Sexual Behavior, 18,* 145–153.

Rotermann, M. (2005). Sex, condoms and STDs among young people. *Health Reports, 16,* Statistics Canada Catalogue 82-003.

Rotheram-Borus, M. J., Reid, H., & Rosario M. (1994). Factors mediating changes in sexual HIV risk behaviors among gay and bisexual male adolescents. *American Journal of Public Health, 84*(12), 1938–1946.

Royce, R. A., Seña, A., Cates, W., Jr., & Cohen, M. S. (1997). Sexual transmission of HIV. *The New England Journal of Medicine, 336,* 1072–1078.

Rozin, P., & Fallon, A. (1988). Body image, attitudes to weight, and misperceptions of figure preferences of the opposite sex: A comparison of men and women in two generations. *Journal of Abnormal Psychology, 97,* 342–345.

Rubin, A., & Adams, J. (1986). Outcomes of sexually open marriages. *Journal of Sex Research, 22,* 311–319.

Rusbult, C. E., Martz, J. M., & Agnew, C. R. (1998). The Investment Model Scale: Measuring commitment level, satisfaction level, quality of alternatives, and investment size. *Personal Relationships, 5*(4), 357–391.

Russell, D. (1982). *Rape in marriage.* New York: Macmillan.

Russo, N. F., Horn, J. D., & Schwartz, R. (1992). U.S. abortion in context: Selected characteristics and motivations of women seeking abortions. *Journal of Social Issues, 48,* 183–202.

Rye, B. J. (2001, June). Sex *differences in sexual attitudes and sexual behaviours of a sample of university students.* Poster session presented at the annual Guelph Sexuality Conference, Guelph, ON.

Rye, B. J. (2002). Attitudes toward gay and lesbian adoption. Paper presented at the Annual Meeting of the Society for the Scientific Study of Sexuality, Montreal.

Sack, W. H., & Mason, R. (1980). Child abuse and conviction of sexual crimes: A preliminary finding. *Law and Human Behavior, 4,* 211–215.

Sadalla, E. K., Kenrick, D. T., & Vershure, B. (1987). Dominance and heterosexual attraction. *Journal of Personality and Social Psychology, 52,* 730–738.

Sagan, C., & Dryan, A. (1990, April 22). The question of abortion: A search for answers. *Parade Magazine,* pp. 4–8.

Sagarin, B. J., Becker, D. V., Guadagno, R. E., Nicastle, D., & Millevoi, A. (2003). Sex differences (and similarities) in jealousy. The moderating influence of infidelity experience and sexual orientation of the infidelity. *Evolution & Human Behavior, 24*(1), 17–23.

Samuels, M., & Samuels, N. (1986). *The well pregnancy book*. New York: Simon & Schuster.

Sanchez-Guerrero, J., et al. (1995). Silicone breast implants and the risk of connective tissue diseases and symptoms. *The New England Journal of Medicine, 332*, 1666–1670.

Sanders, S. A., Reinisch, J. M., & McWhirter, D. P. (1990). Homosexuality/ heterosexuality: An overview. In D. P. McWhirter, S. A. Sanders, & J. M. Reinisch (eds.) *Homosexuality/heterosexuality: Concepts of sexual orientation* (pp. xix–xxvii). New York: Oxford University Press.

Sangrador, J. L., & Yela, C. (2000). "What is beautiful is loved": Physical attractiveness in love relationships in a representative sample. *Social Behavior & Personality, 28*(3), 207–218.

Sarrel, P., & Masters, W. (1982). Sexual molestation of men by women. *Archives of Sexual Behavior, 11*, 117–131.

Savin-Williams, R. C. (2001). Suicide attempts among sexual minority youths: Population and measurement issues. *Journal of Consulting and Clinical Psychology, 69*(6): 983–991.

Savin-Williams, R. C., & Diamond, L. M. (2000). Sexual identity trajectories among sexual-minority youths: Gender comparisons. *Archives of Sexual Behavior, 29*(6), 607–627.

Savitz, L., & Rosen, L. (1988). The sexuality of prostitutes: Sexual enjoyment reported by "streetwalkers." *Journal of Sex Research, 24*, 200–208.

Saywitz, K. J., Mannarino, A. P., Berliner, L., & Cohen, J. A. (2000). Treatment for sexually abused children and adolescents. *American Psychologist, 55*(9), 1040–1049.

Schafer, R. B., & Keith, P. M. (1990). Matching by weight in married couples: A life cycle perspective. *Journal of Social Psychology, 130*, 657–664.

Schafran, L. H. (1995, August 26). Rape is still underreported. *The New York Times*, p. A19.

Schellenberg, E. G., Hirt, J., & Sears, A. (1999). Attitudes toward homosexuals among students at a Canadian university. *Sex Roles, 40*(1–2), 139–152.

Schiavi, R. C., et al. (1990). Healthy aging and male sexual function. *American Journal of Psychiatry, 147*, 766–771.

Schmidt, S. (2002, April 13). Ridicule replaces violence. *National Post*, p. A5.

Schmitt, D. P. (2003). Universal sex differences in the desire for sexual variety: Tests from 52 nations, 6 continents, and 13 islands. *Journal of Personality and Social Psychology, 85*(1), 85–104.

Schmitt, D., Shackelford, T., Duntley, J., et al. (2002). Is there an early-30s peak in female sexual desire? Cross-sectional evidence from the United States and Canada. *The Canadian Journal of Human Sexuality, 11*, 1–18.

Schmitz, C. (2005, February 24). Age of consent bill could leave teens liable: Cotler. *National Post*.

Schneider, M., Baker, S., & Stermac, L. (2002). Sexual harassment experiences of psychologists and psychological associates during their graduate school training. *The Canadian Journal of Human Sexuality, 11*, 159–170.

Schoendorf, K. C., & Kiely, J. L. (1992). Relationship of sudden infant death syndrome to maternal smoking during and after pregnancy. *Pediatrics, 90*, 905–908.

Schoolgirls as sex toys. (1997, April 6). *The New York Times*, p. E2.

Schott, R. L. (1995). The childhood and family dynamics of transvestites. *Archives of Sexual Behavior, 24*, 309–327.

Schover, L. R., Fouladi, R. T., Warneke, C. L., Neese, L., Klein, E. A., Zippe, C., et al. (2004). Seeking help for erectile dysfunction after treatment for prostate cancer. *Archives of Sexual Behavior, 33*(5), 443–454.

Schroeder-Printzen, I., et al. (2000). Surgical therapy in infertile men with ejaculatory duct obstruction: Technique and outcome of a standardized surgical approach. *Human Reproduction, 15*, 1364–1368.

Seftel, A. D., Oates, R. D., & Krane, R. J. (1991). Disturbed sexual function in patients with spinal cord disease. *Neurologic Clinics, 9*, 757–778.

Segraves, R. T., & Segraves, K. B. (1993). Medical aspects of orgasm disorders. In W. O'Donohue & J. H. Geer (eds.), *Handbook of sexual dysfunctions: Assessment and treatment* (pp. 225–252). Boston: Allyn & Bacon.

Seligman, L., & Hardenburg, S. A. (2000). Assessment and treatment of paraphilias. *Journal of Counseling & Development, 78*(1), 107–113.

Seltzer, R. (1992). The social location of those holding antihomosexual attitudes. *Sex Roles, 26*, 391–398.

Selvin, B. W. (1993, June 1). Transsexuals are coming to terms with themselves and society. *New York Newsday*, pp. 55ff.

Semans, J. (1956). Premature ejaculation: A new approach. *Southern Medical Journal, 49*, 353–358.

Seng, M. J. (1989). Child sexual abuse and adolescent prostitution: A comparative analysis. *Adolescence, 24*, 665–675.

Senn, C. Y., & Desmarais, S. (2001). Are our recruitment practices for sex studies working across gender? The effect of topic and gender of recruiter on participation rates of university men and women. *Journal of Sex Research, 38*(2), 111–117.

Senn, C., & Desmarais, S. (2004). The impact of interaction with a partner or friend on the exposure effects of pornography and erotica. *Violence and Victims, 19*(6), 19–32.

Senn, C. Y., Desmarais, S., Verberg, N., & Wood, E. (2000). Predicting coercive sexual behavior across the lifespan in a random sample of Canadian men. *Journal of Social & Personal Relationships, 17*, 93–115.

Seto, M. C., & Barbaree, H. E. (2001). Paraphilias. In V. B. Van Hasseit & M. Hersen (eds.), *Aggression & violence: An introductory text* (pp. 198–213). New York: Allyn & Bacon.

Seto, M. C., Maric, A., & Barbaree, H. E. (2000). The role of pornography in the etiology of sexual aggression. *Aggression and Violent Behavior, 6*, 35–53.

Sexual assault plea shortens sentence. (1994, June 1). *The Guelph Mercury*.

Sexuality Education Resource Centre (2001). *Intergenerational communication— Training parents as resources in ethno-cultural communities project evaluation*. Winnipeg, MB: Paula Migliardi.

Shackelford, T. K, Buss, D. M., & Bennett, K. (2002). Forgiveness or breakup: Sex differences in responses to a partner's infidelity. *Cognition & Emotion, 16*(2), 299–307.

Shaver, F. M. (1996a). Prostitution: On the dark side of the service industry. In T. Fleming (ed.), *Post critical criminology* (pp. 42–45). Scarborough, ON: Prentice Hall.

Shaver, F. M. (1996b). The regulation of prostitution: Setting the morality trap. In B. Schissel & L. Mahood, *Social control in Canada* (pp. 204–226). Toronto: Oxford University Press.

Shaver, F. M. (2002, November). Prostitution portraits: A cautionary tale. Paper presented at the Annual Meeting of the Society for the Scientific Study of Sexuality, Montreal.

Shaver, F. M. (2005). Sex work research: Methodological and ethical challenges. *Journal of Interpersonal Violence, 20*(3), 296–319.

Shaver, P., Hazan, C., & Bradshaw, D. (1988). Love as attachment. In R. J. Sternberg & M. L. Barnes (eds.), *The psychology of love* (pp. 68–99). New Haven, CT: Yale University Press.

Sheehy, G. (1995). *New passages: Mapping your life across time*. New York: Random House.

Sheehy, G. (1998). *Understanding men's passages*. New York: Random House.

Sherman, K. J., et al. (1990). Sexually transmitted diseases and tubal pregnancy. *Sexually Transmitted Diseases, 17*, 115–121.

Sherwin, B. B., Gelfand, M. M., & Brender, W. (1985). Androgen enhances sexual motivation in females: A prospective, crossover study of sex steroid administration in the surgical menopause. *Psychosomatic Medicine, 47*, 339–351.

Shibley-Hyde, J., & Durik, A. M. (2000). Gender differences in erotic plasticity— Evolutionary or sociocultural forces? Comment on Baumeister (2000). *Psychological Bulletin, 126*, 375–379.

Shields, S. A., Wong, T., Mann, J., et al. (2004). Prevalence and correlates of chlamydia infection in Canadian street youth. *Journal of Adolescent Health, 34*(5), 384–390.

Shorter, E. (2005). *Written in the flesh: A history of desire*. Toronto: University of Toronto Press.

Shoveller, J. A., Johnson, J. L., Langille, D. B., & Mitchell, T. (2004). Socio-cultural influences on young people's sexual development. *Social Science & Medicine, 59*(3), 473–487.

Silverthorne, Z. A., & Quinsey, V. L. (2000). Sexual partner age preferences of homosexual and heterosexual men and women. *Archives of Sexual Behavior, 29,* 67–76.

Simonsen, G., Blazina, C., & Watkins, C. E., Jr. (2000). Gender role conflict and psychological well-being among gay men. *Journal of Counseling Psychology, 47*(1), 85–89.

Singer, J., & Singer, I. (1972). Types of female orgasm. *Journal of Sex Research, 8,* 255–267.

Singh, D., Vidaurri, M., Zambarano, R. J., & Dabbs, J. M. Jr. (1999). Lesbian erotic role identification: Behavioral, morphological, and hormonal correlates. *Journal of Personality and Social Psychology, 76*(6), 1035–1049.

Smale, A. (2000, June 11). After the fall, traffic in flesh, not dreams. *The New York Times* online.

Small, P. (2004, June 30). Used drug for sex assault. *The Toronto Star.*

Smith, E. P., et al. (1994). Estrogen resistance caused by a mutation in the estrogen-receptor gene in a man. *The New England Journal of Medicine, 331,* 1056–1061.

Smith, T. W. (1992). Discrepancies between men and women in reporting number of sexual partners: A summary from four countries. *Social Biology, 26,* 203–211.

Sodroski, J., et al. (1998). *Nature.* Cited in "Scientists uncover 'key' to AIDS virus." (1998, June 18). The Associated Press; CNN.

Sokoloff, H. (2003, April 4). Gender gap in math is down to a fraction. *National Post.*

Sommerfeld, J. (2000, April 18). Lifting the curse: Should monthly periods be optional? MSNBC online.

Soon, J. A., Levine, M., Osmond, B. L., Ensom, M. H. H., & Fielding, D. W. (2005). Effects of making emergency contraception available without a physician's prescription: A population-based study. *Canadian Medical Association Journal, 7,* 172.

Sourander, L. B. (1994). Geriatric aspects of estrogen effects and sexuality. *Gerontology, 40*(Suppl. 3), 14–17.

Spark, R. F. (1991). *Male sexual health: A couple's guide.* Mount Vernon, NY: Consumer Reports Books.

Speckens, A. E. M., et al. (1995). Psychosexual functioning of partners of men with presumed non-organic erectile dysfunction: Cause or consequence of the disorder? *Archives of Sexual Behavior, 24,* 157–172.

Specter, M. (1998, January 11). Traffickers' new cargo: Naive Slavic women. *The New York Times.*

Sprecher, S., Sullivan, Q., & Hatfield, E. (1994). Mate selection preferences: Gender differences examined in a national sample. *Journal of Personality and Social Psychology, 66*(6), 1074–1080.

Spring, J. A. (1997). Cited in Alterman, E. (1997, November). Sex in the '90s. *Elle,* p. 130.

Stanford, J. L., et al. (2000). Urinary and sexual function after radical prostatectomy for clinically localized prostate cancer: The Prostate Cancer Outcomes Study. *Journal of the American Medical Association, 283,* 354–360.

Starr, B. D., & Weiner, M. B. (1981). *The Starr-Weiner report on sex and sexuality in the mature years.* New York: Stein and Day.

Statistics Canada (1996). *The Daily, June 19, Canadian families: Diversity and change, 1995.* [on-line]. Available: **http://collection. nlc-bnc.ca/100/201/301/daily/ dailyh/1996/96-06/960619/d960619.htm**

Statistics Canada (1997). Sex offenders. *Juristat.* [Catalogue #8S-002XIE].

Statistics Canada (2002a). 2001 Census: A profile of the Canadian population: Where we live. [Catalogue #96F0030XIE01001 2001].

Statistics Canada (2002b). Crime statistics in Canada, 2001. *Juristat,* 22(b). [Catalogue. #85-002XIE].

Statistics Canada (2002c). *2001 Census: Age and sex counts for Canada, provinces and territories.* [Catalogue #96F0030XIE2001002].

Statistics Canada (2002d). 2001 Census: Families and household profile: Canada. [on-line]. Available: **www/2.Statcan.ca/ english/census01/products/analytic/ companion/fam/Canada.cfm**

Statistics Canada (2002e). *Family history.* [Catalogue No. 89-575-XIE].

Statistics Canada (2002f). *General social survey—Cycle 15: Changing conjugal life in Canada.* [Catalogue No. 89-576-XIE].

Statistics Canada (2002g). Crime statistics in Canada, 2001. *Juristat,* 22(b). [Catalogue. No. 85-002XIE].

Statistics Canada (2002h). *The Daily— Changing conjugal life in Canada.* [on-line] Available: **www.statcan.ca/DailyEnglish/ 020711/d020711a.htm**

Statistics Canada (2003a). *The Daily— Marriage statistics.* [on-line] Available: **www.statcan.ca/Daily/English/031120/ d031120c.htm**

Statistics Canada (2003b). *The Daily,* July 25, *Sexual offences.* [on-line]. Available: **www.statcan.ca/daily/English/050420/ d050420a.htm**

Statistics Canada (2004a). *The Daily,* June 15.

Statistics Canada (2004b), *Pregnancies.* [on-line]. Available: **www.statcan.ca/Daily/ English/041027/d041027d.htm**

Statistics Canada (2004c). *Spotlight: Mixed unions.* [on-line] Available: **www.statcan. ca/english/freepub/11-002-XIE/ 2004/06/17404/17404_04p.htm**

Statistics Canada. (2005a). *Study: Is postsecondary access more equitable in Canada or the United States?* [on-line]. Available: **www.statcan.ca/Daily/english/050315/ d050315c.htm**

Statistics Canada (2005b). *Births.* [on-line] Available: **www.statcan.ca/Daily/English/ 050712/d050712a.htm**

Statistics Canada (2005c). *Induced abortions.* [on-line]. Available: **www.statcan.ca/ Daily/English/050211/d050211a.htm**

Statistics Canada (2005d). *Early sexual intercourse, condom use and sexually transmitted diseases.* [on-line]. Available: **www.statcan.ca/Daily/English/050503/ d050503a.htm**

Statistics Canada (2005e). *Study: Mature singles who don't expect to marry.*

Statistics Canada (2005f). *The Daily— Divorce statistics.* [on-line] Available: **www.statcan.ca/Daily/English/050309/ d050309b.htm**

Statistics Canada (2005g). *The Daily,* April 20, *Children and youth as victims of violent crime.* [on-line]. Available: **www.statcan. ca/daily/English/050420/d050420a.htm**

Steed, J. (2002, December 6). A new Viagra for everyone? *The Toronto Star,* p. H1.

Ste ele, C. M., & Josephs, R. A. (1990). Alcohol myopia: Its prized and dangerous effects. *American Psychologist, 45,* 921–933.

Stein, D. J., Black, D. W., Shapira, N. A., & Spitzer, R. L. (2001). Hypersexual disorder and preoccupation with Internet pornography. *American Journal of Psychiatry, 158*(10), 1590–1594.

Stein, Z., & Susser, M. (2000). The risks of having children in later life. *British Medical Journal, 320*(7251), 1681–1682.

Steinhauer, J. (1995, July 6). No marriage, no apologies. *The New York Times,* pp. C1, C7.

Sternberg, R. J. (1986). A triangular theory of love. *Psychological Review, 93,* 119–135.

Sternberg, R. J. (1988). *The triangle of love: Intimacy, passion, commitment.* New York: Basic Books.

Sternberg, R. J., & Grajek, S. (1984). The nature of love. *Journal of Personality and Social Psychology, 47,* 312–329.

Stewart, F. H. (1992, February 1). Cited in Leary, W. E. (1992). U.S. panel backs approval of first condom for women. *The New York Times,* p. 7.

Stewart, G. K. (1998). Intrauterine devices (IUDs). In Hatcher, R. A., et al. (1998). *Contraceptive technology,* 17th rev. ed. (pp. 511–544). New York: Ardent Media.

Stock, W. E. (1993). Inhibited female orgasm. In W. O'Donohue & J. H. Geer (eds.), *Handbook of sexual dysfunctions: Assessment and treatment* (pp. 253–301). Boston: Allyn & Bacon.

Stolberg, S. G. (1998a, January 18). Quandary on donor eggs: What to tell the children. *The New York Times,* pp. 1, 20.

Stolberg, S. G. (1998b, March 9). U.S. awakes to epidemic of sexual diseases. *The New York Times,* pp. A1, A14.

Stoller, R. J. (1969). Parental influences in male transsexualism. In R. Green & J. Money (eds.), *Transsexualism and sex reassignment.* Baltimore: Johns Hopkins University Press.

Storms, M. D. (1980). Theories of sexual orientation. *Journal of Personality and Social Psychology, 38,* 783–792.

Strassberg, D. S., & Holty, S. (2003). An experimental study of women's Internet personal ads. *Archives of Sexual Behavior, 32*(3), 253–260.

Strickland, B. R. (1995). Research on sexual orientation and human development: A commentary. *Developmental Psychology, 31,* 137–140.

Strike, C., Myers, T., Calzavara, L., & Haubrich, D. (2001). Sexual coercion among young street involved adults: Perpetrators and victims' perspectives. *Violence and Victims, 16,* 537–551.

Sue, D. (1979). Erotic fantasies of college students during coitus. *Journal of Sex Research, 15,* 299–305.

Sulak, P. J., et al., (2000). Hormone withdrawal symptoms in oral contraceptive users. *Obstetrics & Gynecology, 95,* 261–266.

Swann, W. B., Jr., et al. (1987). Cognitive-affective crossfire: When self-consistency meets self-enhancement. *Journal of Personality and Social Psychology, 52,* 881–889.

Symons, D. (1995). Cited in Goleman, D. (1995, June 14). Sex fantasy research said to neglect women. *The New York Times,* p. C14.

Szasz, G., & Carpenter, C. (1989). Clinical observations in vibratory stimulation of the penis of men with spinal cord injury. *Archives of Sexual Behavior, 18,* 461–474.

Tannahill, R. (1980). *Sex in history.* Briarcliff Manor, NY: Stein and Day.

Tannen, D. (1990). *You just don't understand.* New York: Ballantine Books.

Tarone, R. E., Cho, K. C., & Brawley, O. W. (2000). Implications of stage-specific survival rates in assessing recent declines in prostate cancer mortality rates. *Epidemiology, 11*(2), 167–170.

Tavris, C., & Sadd, S. (1977). *The Redbook report on female sexuality.* New York: Delacorte.

Tedeschi, J. T., & Felson, R. B. (1994). *Violence, aggression, and coercive actions.* Washington, DC: American Psychological Association.

Teotonio, I. (2002, March 23). Steering girls away from violence. *The Toronto Star,* pp. L11, L17.

Tharinger, D. (1990). Impact of child sexual abuse on developing sexuality. *Professional Psychology: Research and Practice, 21,* 331–337.

Thomlison, B., et al. (1991, Fall). Characteristics of Canadian male and female child sexual abuse victims. [Special issue: Child sexual abuse]. *Journal of Child and Youth Care,* 65–76.

Thompson, D. S. (ed.) (1993) *Every woman's health: The complete guide to body and mind.* New York: Simon & Schuster.

Thompson, J. K., & Tantleff, S. (1992). Female and male ratings of upper torso: Actual, ideal, and stereotypical conceptions. *Journal of Social Behavior and Personality, 7,* 345–354.

Thompson, M. E. (1991). Self-defense against sexual coercion: Theory, research, and practice. In E. Grauerholz & M. A. Koralewski (eds.), *Sexual coercion: A sourcebook on its nature, causes, and prevention* (pp. 111–121). Lexington, MA: Lexington Books.

Tollison, C. D., & Adams, H. E. (1979). *Sexual disorders: Treatment, theory, and research.* New York: Gardner Press.

Toner, J. P., et al. (1991). Basal follicle-stimulating hormone level is a better predictor of in vitro fertilization performance than age. *Fertility and Sterility, 55,* 784–791.

Townsend, J. M. (1995). Sex without emotional involvement: An evolutionary interpretation of sex differences. *Archives of Sexual Behavior, 24,* 173–206.

Tracey, S. (1999, March 25). Woman gets bail on theft charge. *The Guelph Mercury.*

Tracey, S. (2000, February 29). Couple fined for exposing teen to sex episode in Gorge. *The Guelph Mercury,* p. A8.

Tracey, S. (2001, January 26). Woman admits to sex with boy. *The Guelph Mercury.*

Trieschmann, R. (1989). Psychosocial adjustment to spinal cord injury. In B. W. Heller, L. M. Flohr, & L. S. Zegans (eds.), *Psychosocial interventions with physically disabled persons* (pp. 117–136). New Brunswick, NJ: Rutgers University Press.

Tsui, L., & Nicoladis, E. (2004). Losing it: Similarities and differences in first intercourse experiences of men and women. *Canadian Journal of Human Sexuality, 13*(2), 95–106.

Tuiten, A., et al. (2000). Time course of effects of testosterone administration on sexual arousal in women. *Archives of General Psychiatry, 57,* 149–153.

Tunariu, A. D., & Reavey, R. (2003). Men in love: Living with sexual boredom. *Sexual and Relationship Therapy 13*(1), 63–94.

Tutty, L. M. (1992). The ability of elementary school children to learn child sexual abuse prevention concepts. *Child Abuse and Neglect, 16,* 369–384.

Tyler, T. (2004, September 14). Spouse ruling allows first gay divorce. *The Toronto Star.*

Udry, J. R., & Billy, J. O. G. (1987). Initiation of coitus in early adolescence. *American Sociological Review, 52,* 841–855.

Udry, J. R., Talbert, L., & Morris, N. M. (1986). Biosocial foundations for adolescent female sexuality. *Demography, 23*(2), 217–230.

Udry, J., et al. (1985). Serum androgenic hormones motivate sexual behavior in adolescent boys. *Fertility and Sterility, 43,* 90–94.

U.S. Department of Health and Human Services. (USDHHS). (1990). *The health benefits of smoking cessation: A report of the Surgeon General* (DHHS Publication No. CDC 90–8416). Rockville, MD: Public Health Service, Centers for Disease Control, Center for Chronic Disease Prevention and Health Promotion, Office on Smoking and Health.

U.S. Department of Health and Human Services. (USDHHS). (1992). Smoking and Health in the Americas. (DHHS Publications No. [CDC] 92-8419). Atlanta: Public Health Services, Centers for Diseases Control, National Center for Chronic Disease Prevention and Health Promotion, Office on Smoking and Health.

Valentich, M., & Gripton, J. (1992). Gender-sensitive practice in sexual problems. *Canadian Journal of Human Sexuality, 1,* 11–18.

Valentich, M., & Wilson, S. V. (1995). Teaching sexual and gender ethics to engineering students: A brief educational intervention. *Canadian Journal of Human Sexuality, 4*(4), 263–271.

van Anders, S. M. (2005). Testing the prenatal androgen hypothesis: Measuring digit ratios, sexual orientation, and spatial abilities in adults. *Hormones and Behavior, 47,* 92–98.

Van Brunschot, E. G. (2003). Community policing and "john schools." *The Canadian Review of Sociology and Anthropology, 40*(2), 215–232.

Van Lange, P. A. M., et al. (1997). Willingness to sacrifice in close relationships. *Journal of Personality & Social Psychology, 72*(6), 1373–1395.

Van Til, L., MacQuarrie, C., & Herbert, R. (2003). Understanding the barriers to cervical cancer screening among older women. *Qualitative Health Research, 13*(8), 1116–1131.

Vasey, P. L. (2002). Sexual partner preference in female Japanese macaques. *Archives of Sexual Behavior, 31*(1), 51–62.

Vazi, R., Best, D., Davis, S., & Kaiser, M. (1989). Evaluation of a testicular cancer curriculum for adolescents. *Journal of Pediatrics, 114,* 150–162.

Verma, S. (March 25, 2005). Woman charged in assault in HIV case on military base. *The Toronto Star.*

Vervoort, D. (1999*). Gay fathers coming out to their children: Reaching for integrity.* Unpublished master's thesis, University of Guelph.

Vinacke, W., et al. (1988). Similarity and complementarity in intimate couples. *Genetic, Social, and General Psychology Monographs, 114,* 51–76.

Vincent, D. (December 10, 2004). GTHL bans flashing mother. *The Toronto Star.*

Vo, C. (2001). *Vietnamese Immigrant Gay Men: Cultural and Personal Influences on Sexual Health.* Unpublished master's thesis, University of Guelph.

Voelker, R. (2000). Advisory on contraceptives. *Journal of the American Medical Association* online, *284*(8).

Voeller, B. (1991). AIDS and heterosexual anal intercourse. *Archives of Sexual Behavior, 20,* 233–276.

Von Krafft-Ebbing, R. (1978). *Psychopathia sexualis.* Philadelphia: F. A. Davis. (Original work published 1886.)

Voyer, D., Voyer, S., & Bryden, M. P. (1995). Magnitude of sex differences in spatial abilities: A meta-analysis and consideration of critical variables. *Psychological Bulletin, 117,* 250–270.

Waismann, R., Fenwick, P. B. C., Wilson, G. D., Hewett, T. D., & Lumsden, J. (2003). EEG responses to visual erotic stimuli in men with normal and paraphilic interests. *Archives of Sexual Behavior, 32*(2), 135–144.

Wald, A., et al. (1995). Virologic characteristics of subclinical and symptomatic genital herpes infections. *The New England Journal of Medicine, 333,* 770–775.

Walfish, S., & Mayerson, M. (1980). Sex role identity and attitudes toward sexuality. *Archives of Sexual Behavior, 9,* 199–204.

Wallerstein, J. S., & Blakeslee, S. (1989). *Second chances: Women and children a decade after divorce.* New York: Ticknor & Fields.

Wallerstein, J. S., & Kelly, J. B. (1980). *Surviving the breakup: How children and parents cope with divorce.* New York: Basic Books.

Walsh, C., MacMillan, H. L., & Jamieson, E. (2003). The relationship between parental substance abuse and child maltreatment: Findings from the Ontario health supplement. *Child Abuse & Neglect, 27*(12), 1409–1425.

Walsh, P. C. (1996). Treatment of benign prostatic hyperplasia. *The New England Journal of Medicine, 335,* 586–587.

Walster, E., & Walster, G. W. (1978). *A new look at love.* Reading, MA: Addison-Wesley.

Walt, V. (1993, July 26). Some second thoughts on depo. *New York Newsday,* p. 13.

Warner, D. L., & Hatcher, R. A. (1998). Male condoms. In Hatcher, R. A., et al., *Contraceptive technology,* 17th rev. ed. (pp. 325–356). New York: Ardent Media.

Wasson, J. H. (1998). Finasteride to prevent morbidity from benign prostate hyperplasia. *The New England Journal of Medicine, 338,* 612–613.

Waterman, J. (1986). Overview of treatment issues. In K. McFarlane et al. (eds.) *Sexual abuse of young children: Evaluation and treatment* (pp. 197–203). New York: Guilford.

Waterman, J., et al. (1986). Challenges for the future. In K. McFarlane et al. (eds.), *Sexual abuse of young children: Evaluation and treatment* (pp. 315–332). New York: Guilford.

Waterman, J., & Lusk, R. (1986). Scope of the problem. In K. MacFarlane et al. (eds.), *Sexual abuse of young children: Evaluation and treatment* (pp. 3–14). New York: Guilford.

Weaver, A. D., Byers, E. S., Sears, H. A., Cohen, J. N., & Randall, H. E. S. (2002). Sexual health education at school and at home: Attitudes and experiences of New Brunswick parents. *Canadian Journal of Human Sexuality, 11*(1), 19–31.

Weaver, S. J., & Herold, E. S (2000). Casual sex and women: Measurement and motivations issues. *Journal of Psychology and Human Sexuality, 12,* 23–41.

Weber, A. E., Boivin, J. F., Blais, L., Haley, N., & Roy, E. (2002). HIV risk profile and prostitution among female street youths. *Journal of Urban Health, 79*(4), 525–535.

Weber, A. E., Boivin, J. F., Blais, L., Haley, N., & Roy, E. (2004). Predictors of initiation into prostitution among female street youths. *Journal of Urban Health—Bulletin of New York Academy of Medicine, 81*(4), 584–595.

Weber, B. (2001, January 10). No sex please, we're in the army. *The Toronto Star,* p. A3.

Weidmer, E., Treas, J., & Newcomb, R. (1998). Attitudes toward nonmarital sex in twenty-four countries. *The Journal of Sex Research, 35,* 349–348.

Weinberg, M. S., Williams, C. J., & Moser, C. (1984). The social constituents of sadomasochism. *Social Problems, 31,* 379–389.

Weinberg, M. S., et al. (1994). *Dual attraction.* New York: Oxford University Press.

Weinberg, T. S. (1987). Sadomasochism in the United States: A review of recent sociological literature. *Journal of Sex Research, 23,* 50–69.

Weinberg, T. S., & Bullough, V. L. (1986). *Women married to transvestites: Problems and adjustments.* Paper presented at the annual meeting of the Society for the Study of Social Problems, New York.

Weinberg, T. S., & Bullough, V. L. (1988). Alienation, self-image, and the importance of support groups for the wives of transvestites. *Journal of Sex Research, 24,* 262–268.

Weinrich, J. D., & Klein, F. (2002). Bi-gay, bi-straight, and bi-bi: Three bisexual subgroups identified using cluster analysis of the Klein Sexual Orientation Grid. *Journal of Bisexuality 2*(4), 109–139.

Weiss, R. D., & Mirin, S. M. (1987). *Cocaine.* Washington, D.C.: American Psychiatric Press.

Weitzer, R. (1999). *Sex for sale: Prostitution, pornography, and the sex industry.* London: Routledge.

Werner, D., & Cohen, A. (1990). Instructor's edition. In C. R. Ember & M. Ember, *Anthropology,* 6th ed. (pp. I-1 to I-146). Englewood Cliffs, NJ: Prentice-Hall.

Whalen, R. E., Geary, D. C., & Johnson, F. (1990). Models of sexuality. In D. P. McWhirter, S. A. Sanders, & J. M. Reinisch (eds.), *Homosexuality/heterosexuality: Concepts of sexual orientation* (pp. 61–70). New York: Oxford University Press.

Whipple, B., & Komisaruk, B. R. (1988). Analgesia produced in women by genital self-stimulation. *Journal of Sex Research, 24,* 130–140.

Whitley, B. E., Jr. (1983). Sex role orientation and self-esteem: A critical meta-analysis. *Journal of Personality and Social Psychology, 44,* 765–788.

Whitley, B. E., Jr., & Kite, M. E. (1995). Sex differences in attitudes toward homosexuality. *Psychological Bulletin, 117,* 146–154.

Whitley, R., et al. (1991). Predictors of morbidity and mortality in infants with herpes simplex virus infections. *The New England Journal of Medicine, 324,* 450–454.

Whitten, P. (2001). *Anthropology: Contemporary perspectives,* 8th ed. Boston: Allyn & Bacon.

Wiebe, R., Sent, L., Fong, S., & Chan, J. (2002). Barriers to use of oral contraceptives in ethnic Chinese women presenting for abortion. *Contraception, 65*(2), 159–163.

Wieselquist, J., Rusbult, C. E., Foster, C. A., & Agnew, C. R. (1999). Commitment, pro-relationship behavior, and trust in close relationships. *Journal of Personality & Social Psychology, 77*(5), 942–966.

Wilcox, A. J., Dunson, D., & Baird, D. D. (2000). The timing of the "fertile window" in the menstrual cycle: Day-specific estimates from a prospective study. *British Medical Journal, 321,* 1259–1262.

Williams, D. E., & D'Alessandro, J. D. (1994). A comparison of three measures of androgyny and their relationship to psychological adjustment. *Journal of Social Behavior and Personality, 9*(3), 469–480.

Williams, J. E., & Best, D. L. (1994). Cross-cultural views of women and men. In W. J. Lonner & R. Malpass (eds.), *Psychology and culture.* Boston: Allyn & Bacon.

Williams, M. (1999, June 15). Study: Patch could restore sex drive. The Associated Press.

Williamson, C., & Cluse-Tolar, T. (2002). Pimp-controlled prostitution: Still an integral part of street life. *Violence Against Women, 8*(9), 1074–1092.

Wilson, R. J. (2005). *Circles of support and accountability: 10 years and counting.* Paper presented at World Congress of Sexology, Montreal.

Wingood, G. M., & DiClemente, R. J. (Eds.) (2002). *Handbook of women's sexual and reproductive health.* New York: Kluwer Academic/Plenum Publishers.

Wolman, T. (1985). Drug addiction. In M. Farber (ed.), *Human sexuality* (pp. 277–285). New York: MacMillan.

Woman faces 37 charges. (2000, February 25). *The Toronto Star.*

Wong-Reiger, D., LaBrie, M., Guyon, G., & Smith, L. (1996). *Evaluation of physician-based condom and pill education project.* International Conference on AIDS. Vancouver.

Wood, D. (2002, April 3). Man admits passing HIV to four women. *The Toronto Star,* p. A4.

Wood, D. (2004, October 3). Mother confesses to sex with sons. *The Toronto Star.*

Wood, D. (2005, August 18). Cambridge mother and son guilty of incest. *The Record.*

Wood, N. S., et al. (2000). Neurologic and developmental disability after extremely preterm birth. *The New England Journal of Medicine* online, *343*(6).

Woods, A. (2000, October 7). Lesbian bathhouse organizers charged. *The Toronto Star,* p. B1.

Workers cry foul over sex policy. (1996, December 19). *The Guelph Mercury,* p. A7.

Wortman, C. B., et al. (1976). Self-disclosure: An attributional perspective. *Journal of Personality and Social Psychology, 33,* 184–191.

Wyatt, G. E. (1988). The relationship between child sexual abuse and adolescent sexual functioning in Afro-American and white American women. *Annals of the New York Academy of Sciences, 528,* 111–122.

Wyatt, G. E., & Newcomb, M. (1990). Internal and external mediators of women's sexual abuse in childhood. *Journal of Consulting and Clinical Psychology, 58,* 758–767.

Wysocki, C. J., & Preti, G. (1998). Pheromonal influences. *Archives of Sexual Behavior, 27*(6), 627–629.

Yaffe, K., et al. (2000). Cognitive decline in women in relation to non-protein-bound oestradiol concentrations. *The Lancet, 356,* 708–712.

Yearwood-Lee, E. (2002, August 24). Love is in the air: Couples take easier, expensive route to joining mile-high club. *Canadian Press.* [on-line]. Available: **www. canoe.ca/TravelBC/milehigh_020819-cp.html**

Yorburg, B. (1995, July 9). Why couples choose to live together. *The New York Times,* p. 14.

Zaviacic, M., et al. (1988a). Concentrations of fructose in female ejaculate and urine: A comparative biochemical study. *Journal of Sex Research, 24,* 319–325.

Zaviacic, M., et al. (1988b). Female urethral expulsions evoked by local digital stimulation of the G-spot: Differences in the response patterns. *Journal of Sex Research, 24,* 311–318.

Zaviacic, M., & Whipple, B. (1993). Update on the female prostate and the phenomenon of female ejaculation. *Journal of Sex Research, 30,* 148–151.

Zhang, J., & Fried, D. B. (1992). Relationship of maternal smoking during pregnancy to placenta previa. *American Journal of Preventative Medicine, 8,* 278–282.

Zielbauer, P. (2000, May 22). Sex offender listings on Web set off debate. *The New York Times* online.

Zilbergeld, B. (1978). *Male Sexuality.* Boston: Little, Brown.

Zillmann, D. (1989). Effects of prolonged consumption of pornography. In D. Zillmann & J. Bryant (eds.), *Pornography: Research advances and policy considerations* (pp. 127–157). Hillsdale, NJ: Lawrence Erlbaum Associates.

Zillmann, D., & Bryant, J. (1984). Effects of massive exposure to pornography. In N. M. Malamuth & E. Donnerstein (eds.), *Pornography and sexual aggression* (pp. 115–138). New York: Academic Press.

Zucker, K. J. (2002). Intersexuality and gender identity differentiation. *Journal of Pediatric and Adolescent Gynecology, 15*(3), 3–13.

Zucker, K. J., Beaulieu, N., Bradley, S. J., Grimshaw, G. M., & Wilcox, A. (2001). Handedness in boys with gender identity disorder. *Journal of Child Psychology and Psychiatry, 42*(6), 767–776.

Zucker, K. J., Bradley, S. J., & Sanikhani, M. (1997). Sex differences in referral rates of children with gender identity disorder: Some hypotheses. *Journal of Abnormal Child Psychology, 25*(3), 217–227.

Zusman, M. E., & Knox, D. (1998). Relationship problems of casual and involved university students. *College Student Journal, 32*(4), 606–609.

Name Index

Subject Index

Photo Credits

Chapter 1: p. 6, Tannis Toohey/*Toronto Star*; p. 11, Ali Meyer/The Bridgeman Art Library, Ltd.; p. 14, © Bettmann/Corbis; p. 17, Kent Leireis/The Image Works; p. 21, David Austen/Stock Boston; p. 22, Elizabeth Crews/The Image Works; p. 25, CP Photo/St. Catharines *Standard*/Mike Conley. **Chapter 2:** p. 35 (both), Courtesy of Farrall Instruments; p. 38 © Hulton Getty; p. 39, *The Canadian Journal of Human Sexuality*, reprinted with permission from the Sex Information and Education Council of Canada; p. 49, © Royalty-Free/CORBIS. **Chapter 3:** p. 55 (all), © Susan Lerner 1999/Joel Gordon Photography 2004; p. 65, Catherine Leroy/SIPA Press; p. 70, Photo taken by Donna Harris; p. 67, www.melaniegillis.com; p. 68 (left), © Susan Lerner 1999/Joel Gordon Photography 2004; (middle) Custom Medical Stock Photo; (right) © Joel Gordon/Joel Gordon Photography 2004; p. 84 (left and right) © Joel Gordon/Joel Gordon Photography 2004; (middle) Custom Medical Stock Photo; p. 89, Cleo/PhotoEdit. **Chapter 4:** p. 104, Steve Russell/*Toronto Star*; p. 106, Luc Beziat/Stone/Getty Images; p. 107, © CAP Features/The Image Works; p. 109, Bruce Lee Smith/Liaison/Getty Images; p. 113, © M. K. Denny/PhotoEdit. **Chapter 5:** pp. 137 and 138, from John Money, *Sex Errors of the Body and Related Syndromes: A Guide for Counseling Children, Adolescents and Their Families*, 1994, pp. 37 and 46. Published by Paul H. Brookes Publishing Co., P. O. Box 10624, Baltimore, MD 21285–0624. Used with permission of the author; p. 139, CP PHOTO/*Winnipeg Free Press*/Files; p. 143, Pete Soos; p. 145 (top), CP Photo/J.P. Moczulski; p. 145 (bottom), Kevin Horan/Stone/Getty Images; p. 147, © Jose Luis Pelaez, Inc./CORBIS; p. 152, Tony Freeman/PhotoEdit; p. 155, © Royalty-Free/CORBIS; p. 159, Reuters News Picture Service/Photo by Tami Chappell. **Chapter 6:** p. 167 (top left), Adam Wolfitt/Woodfin Camp & Associates; (top middle) Reuters/Fred Prouser/Archive Photos; (top right) Claus Meyer/Black Star; (bottom left) Mitch Kezar/Black Star; (bottom right) Nicholas DeVore III/Photographers Aspen; p. 172 (left), Frank Siteman/Stock Boston; (right), Michael Newman/PhotoEdit; p. 174, David Young-Wolff/PhotoEdit; p. 176, Dana Edmunds/Taxi, Getty Images. **Chapter 7:** p. 186, Digital Vision/Getty Images; p. 187, Randy Quan/*Toronto Star*; p. 189, Courtesy of Discovery Health Channel; p. 192, David Young-Wolff/PhotoEdit; p. 193, Courtesy of Fox Broadcasting Co.; p. 195, Joel Gordon/© Joel Gordon Photography 2001; p. 198, Brown W. Cannon III/Stone/Getty Images. **Chapter 8:** p. 216, Photodisc Red/Getty Images; p. 217, www.melaniegillis.com. **Chapter 9:** p. 232, Joel Gordon/© Joel Gordon Photography 2001; p. 243, CP PHOTO/Tom Hanson, Courtesy of Svend Robinson; p. 245, CP PHOTO/*Edmonton Sun*–Perry Mah; p. 253, Nathan Denette, *Guelph Mercury*; p. 259, Chuck Nacke/Woodfin Camp & Associates. **Chapter 10:** p. 264, Francis Le Roy/Bio Cosmos/SPL/Science Source/Photo Researchers; p. 270, Patti Gower/Atkinson Foundation; p. 271, Anna Zuckerman/PhotoEdit; p. 276 (all), Petit Format/Nestle/Science Source/Photo Researchers; p. 282, Will Hart; p. 286, SIU/Science Source/Photo Researchers. **Chapter 11:** p. 297 (top), *History of Contraception* CD-ROM, Janssen-Ortho Inc.; (bottom), Dorling Kindersley; p. 304, Courtesy of Berlex Canada Inc.; p. 319, © Joel Gordon/Joel Gordon Photography 2004; p. 322, Colin McConnell/*Toronto Star*; p. 323, CP Photo/John Lehmann. **Chapter 12:** p. 333, Rick Smolen/Stock Boston; p. 335, David Harry Stewart/Stone/Getty Images; p. 338, Bob Torrez/Stone; p. 346, Tony Bock/*Toronto Star*; p. 349, Frank Herboldt/Stone/Getty Images; p. 351, Taxi/Ron Chapple; p. 352, © John Loper; p. 354, Tony Bock/*Toronto Star*; p. 356, CP PHOTO/*Toronto Sun*/Veronica Henri; p. 361, Courtesy The Ashley Madison Agency; p. 362, Courtesy of Moonlight Magic Private Social Club; p. 366 (top), Tannis Toohey/*Toronto Star*, (bottom), Laurence Monneret/Stone/Getty Images. **Chapter 13:** p. 379, © Michael Newman/PhotoEdit; p. 384, Paul Gauguin, *And the gold of their bodies*. Photo: B. Hatala, Musée d'Orsay, Paris, France. Courtesy of Réunion des Musées Nationaux/Art Resource/NY; p. 387, Robert A. Mitchell/Stone/Getty Images; p. 391, © Tom McCarthy/PhotoEdit; p. 392, G. Thomas Bishop/Custom Medical Stock Photo; p. 393, Johnny Crawford/The Image Works; p. 394, Courtesy of Pfizer Inc./COMA Media; p. 396, Courtesy of UroMetric Inc. **Chapter 14:** p. 407, Jim Corwin/Stone/Getty Images (This photograph is used for illustrative purposes only.); p. 408, Brian Palmer/Impact Visuals; p. 414, Courtesy of Dr. Nicholas J. Fiumara; p. 416, Custom Medical Stock Photo; p. 419, National Medical Slide/Custom Medical Stock Photo; p. 422, Christine van Reeuwyk; p. 423, Douglas Mason/Woodfin Camp & Associates; p. 424, Courtesy of AIDS Committee of Toronto; p. 426, Jana Birchum/Impact Visuals; p. 427, © F. Martinez/PhotoEdit; p. 429, Dr. John Wilson/Science Source/Photo Researchers; p. 430, BioPhoto Assoc./Science Source/Photo Researchers; p. 431, E. Gray/SPL/Science Source/Photo Researchers. **Chapter 15:** p. 444, Courtesy of *Whiplash*, Canada's Fetish Magazine; p. 445, Lee Snider/The Image Works; p. 449, Courtesy of Upskirtsniper.com; p. 451, David Apple/© Fox Searchlight/Photo Fest; p. 456, Bill Aron/PhotoEdit; p. 460, Bob Daemmrich/The Image Works. **Chapter 16:** p. 469, OPSEU "No Means No" coaster provided courtesy of Canadian Federation of Students; p. 417, Michael Nichols/Magnum Photos; p. 475, Carolina Kroon; p. 478, CP PHOTO/Andrew Vaughn; p. 482, Courtesy of La Porte County Child Abuse Prevention Council; p. 483, Charles Gupton/Stone; p. 487, John Coletti. **Chapter 17:** Advertisement provided by Freeland Marketing Inc., Producers of the Everything to Do with Sex Show™; p. 500, Todd Haimann/CORBIS; p. 502, Corbis Digital Stock; p. 507, Paul Chesley/Stone/Getty Images; p. 509 (left), AP Wide World Photos; (right), Pierre Ducharme/Reuters/CORBIS; p. 510, Sean Rosen; p. 512, The BrainStorm Group; p. 518, www.melaniegillis.com. **Epilogue:** p. 524, Courtesy of Sue Johanson.